General Electric Capital Corp. www.ge.com
General Motors Acceptance Corp. www.gmacfs.com
Government National Mortgage Association www.ginniemae.gov
Heritage Foundation www.heritage.org
Household International www.household.com
Institutional Investor www.institutionalinvestor.com
Insurance Information Institute www.iii.org
Insurance Service Office www.iso.com
International Monetary Fund (IMF) www.imf.org
Investment Company Institute www.ici.com
J.P. Morgan Chase www.jpmorganchase.com
KMV Corporation www.kmv.com
Loan Pricing Corporation www.loanpricing.com
Moody's www.moodys.com
Morningstar, Inc. www.morningstar.com
Mortgage Bankers Association www.mbaa.org
National Association of Insurance Commissioners (NAIC) www.naic.org
National Association of Securities Dealers www.nasd.com
National Credit Union Administration www.ncua.gov
New York Board of Trade www.nybot.com
New York Stock Exchange www.nyse.com
Office of the Comptroller of the Currency www.occ.treas.gov
Office of Thrift Supervision www.ots.treas.gov
Pension Benefit Guaranty Corporation www.pbgc.gov
Philadelphia Options Exchange www.phlx.com
RiskMetrics www.riskmetrics.com
Robert Morris Associates www.rmahq.com
Securities and Exchange Commission www.sec.gov
Securities Industry Association www.sia.com
Securities Investors Protection Corporation www.sipc.org
Standard and Poor's www.standardandpoors.com
State of New York Insurance Guarantee Fund www.ins.state.ny.us
Thomson Financial Securities Data Company www.tfibcm.com
U.S. Banker www.us-banker.com
U.S. Treasury www.ustreas.gov
Vanguard www.vanguard.com
The Wall Street Journal www.wsj.com
World Bank www.worldbank.org

PowerWeb: ETHICS IN FINANCE

Welcome to PowerWeb! This site has been designed to enhance your course—giving you access to readings, up-to-the-minute news, research links, and more!

To access PowerWeb:

1. Use a Web browser to go to http://register.dushkin.com.

2. Enter your unique access code in the space provided. You must enter the entire code as it appears in the box below when you register.

3. Your unique access code is in the box below.

4. After you have entered the "unique access code," click on the "Register" button to continue the registration process.

THIS UNIQUE ACCESS CODE WORKS FOR BOTH SITES.

na1529a3

Welcome to the EDUCATIONAL VERSION of Market Insight!

www.mhhe.com/edumarketinsight

Check out your textbook's website for details on how this special offer enhances the value of your purchase!

1. To get started, use your web browser to go to www.mhhe.com/edumarketinsight.

2. Enter your unique access code exactly as it appears in the box above.

3. You may be prompted to enter the unique access code for future use — *please keep this card.*

4. Your unique access code can be found in the box above.

ISBN 0-07-319549-9

Financial Institutions Management

A Risk Management Approach

The McGraw-Hill/Irwin Series in Finance, Insurance and Real Estate

Stephen A. Ross
Franco Modigliani Professor of Finance and Economics Sloan School of Management Massachusetts Institute of Technology Consulting Editor

FINANCIAL MANAGEMENT

Adair
Excel Applications for Corporate Finance
First Edition

Benninga and Sarig
Corporate Finance: A Valuation Approach

Block and Hirt
Foundations of Financial Management
Eleventh Edition

Brealey, Myers, and Allen
Principles of Corporate Finance
Eighth Edition

Brealey, Myers and Marcus
Fundamentals of Corporate Finance
Fourth Edition

Brooks
FinGame Online 4.0

Bruner
Case Studies in Finance: Managing for Corporate Value Creation
Fourth Edition

Chew
The New Corporate Finance: Where Theory Meets Practice
Third Edition

Chew and Gillan
Corporate Governance at the Crossroads: A Book of Readings
First Edition

DeMello
Cases in Finance
Second Edition

Grinblatt and Titman
Financial Markets and Corporate Strategy
Second Edition

Helfert
Techniques of Financial Analysis: A Guide to Value Creation
Eleventh Edition

Higgins
Analysis for Financial Management
Seventh Edition

Kester, Ruback, and Tufano
Case Problems in Finance
Twelfth Edition

Ross, Westerfield and Jaffe
Corporate Finance
Seventh Edition

Ross, Westerfield and Jordan
Essentials of Corporate Finance
Fourth Edition

Ross, Westerfield and Jordan
Fundamentals of Corporate Finance
Seventh Edition

Smith
The Modern Theory of Corporate Finance
Second Edition

White
Financial Analysis with an Electronic Calculator
Fifth Edition

INVESTMENTS

Bodie, Kane and Marcus
Essentials of Investments
Fifth Edition

Bodie, Kane and Marcus
Investments
Sixth Edition

Cohen, Zinbarg and Zeikel
Investment Analysis and Portfolio Management
Fifth Edition

Corrado and Jordan
Fundamentals of Investments: Valuation and Management
Third Edition

Farrell
Portfolio Management: Theory and Applications
Second Edition

Hirt and Block
Fundamentals of Investment Management
Eighth Edition

FINANCIAL INSTITUTIONS AND MARKETS

Cornett and Saunders
Fundamentals of Financial Institutions Management

Rose and Hudgins
Bank Management and Financial Services
Sixth Edition

Rose and Marquis
Money and Capital Markets: Financial Institutions and Instruments in a Global Marketplace
Ninth Edition

Santomero and Babbel
Financial Markets, Instruments, and Institutions
Second Edition

Saunders and Cornett
Financial Institutions Management: A Risk Management Approach
Fifth Edition

Saunders and Cornett
Financial Markets and Institutions: A Modern Perspective
Second Edition

INTERNATIONAL FINANCE

Beim and Calomiris
Emerging Financial Markets

Eun and Resnick
International Financial Management
Third Edition

Kuemmerle
Case Studies in International Entrepreneurship: Managing and Financing Ventures in the Global Economy
First Edition

Levich
International Financial Markets: Prices and Policies
Second Edition

REAL ESTATE

Brueggeman and Fisher
Real Estate Finance and Investments
Twelfth Edition

Corgel, Ling and Smith
Real Estate Perspectives: An Introduction to Real Estate
Fourth Edition

Ling and Archer
Real Estate Principles: A Value Approach
First Edition

FINANCIAL PLANNING AND INSURANCE

Allen, Melone, Rosenbloom and Mahoney
Pension Planning: Pension, Profit-Sharing, and Other Deferred Compensation Plans
Ninth Edition

Crawford
Life and Health Insurance Law
Eighth Edition (LOMA)

Harrington and Niehaus
Risk Management and Insurance
Second Edition

Hirsch
Casualty Claim Practice
Sixth Edition

Kapoor, Dlabay, and Hughes
Focus on Personal Finance: An Active Approach to Help You Develop Successful Financial Skills
First Edition

Kapoor, Dlabay and Hughes
Personal Finance
Seventh Edition

Williams, Smith and Young
Risk Management and Insurance
Eighth Edition

Financial Institutions Management

A Risk Management Approach   Fifth Edition

Anthony Saunders

John M. Schiff Professor of Finance
Salomon Center
Stern School of Business
New York University

Marcia Millon Cornett

Rehn Professor of Business
Southern Illinois University

McGraw-Hill Irwin

Boston   Burr Ridge, IL   Dubuque, IA   Madison, WI   New York   San Francisco   St. Louis
Bangkok   Bogotá   Caracas   Kuala Lumpur   Lisbon   London   Madrid   Mexico City
Milan   Montreal   New Delhi   Santiago   Seoul   Singapore   Sydney   Taipei   Toronto

McGraw-Hill
Irwin

FINANCIAL INSTITUTIONS MANAGEMENT: A RISK MANAGEMENT APPROACH

Published by McGraw-Hill/Irwin, a business unit of The McGraw-Hill Companies, Inc., 1221 Avenue of the Americas, New York, NY, 10020. Copyright © 2006, 2003, 2000, 1997, 1994 by The McGraw-Hill Companies, Inc. All rights reserved. No part of this publication may be reproduced or distributed in any form or by any means, or stored in a database or retrieval system, without the prior written consent of The McGraw-Hill Companies, Inc., including, but not limited to, in any network or other electronic storage or transmission, or broadcast for distance learning.

Some ancillaries, including electronic and print components, may not be available to customers outside the United States.

This book is printed on acid-free paper.

2 3 4 5 6 7 8 9 0 CCW/CCW 0 9 8 7 6 5

ISBN 0-07-295746-8

Publisher: *Stephen M. Patterson*
Editorial assistant: *Meghan Grosscup/Michelle Driscoll*
Executive marketing manager: *Rhonda Seelinger*
Senior media producer: *Anthony Sherman*
Project manager: *Kristin Puscas*
Production supervisor: *Gina Hangos*
Senior designer: *Mary E. Kazak*
Cover design: *Asylum Studios*
Supplement producer: *Joyce J. Chappetto*
Senior digital content specialist: *Brian Nacik*
Typeface: *10/12 Palatino*
Compositor: *Cenveo*
Printer: *Courier Westford*

Library of Congress Cataloging-in-Publication Data

Saunders, Anthony, 1949-
    Financial institutions management: a risk management approach / Anthony Saunders, Marcia Millon Cornett. -- 5th ed.
        p. cm. -- (The McGraw-Hill/Irwin series in finance, insurance, and real estate)
    Includes index.
    ISBN 0-07-295746-8 (alk. paper)
    1. Financial institutions--United States--Management. 2. Risk management–United States. 3. Financial services industry–United States--Management. I. Cornett, Marcia Millon II. Title. III. Series.
HG181.S33 2006
332.1′068--dc22   2004057815

www.mhhe.com

This book is dedicated to Pat, Nicholas, and Emily and to my mother, Evelyn.

Anthony Saunders

To the Millons and the Cornetts, especially Galen.

Marcia Millon Cornett

About the Authors

Anthony Saunders

Anthony Saunders is the John M. Schiff Professor of Finance and Chair of the Department of Finance at the Stern School of Business at New York University. Professor Saunders received his PhD from the London School of Economics and has taught both undergraduate- and graduate-level courses at NYU since 1978. Throughout his academic career, his teaching and research have specialized in financial institutions and international banking. He has served as a visiting professor all over the world, including INSEAD, the Stockholm School of Economics, and the University of Melbourne. He is currently on the Executive Committee of the Salomon Center for the Study of Financial Institutions, NYU.

Professor Saunders holds positions on the Board of Academic Consultants of the Federal Reserve Board of Governors as well as the Council of Research Advisors for the Federal National Mortgage Association. In addition, Dr. Saunders has acted as a visiting scholar at the Comptroller of the Currency and at the Federal Reserve Bank of Philadelphia. He also held a visiting position in the research department of the International Monetary Fund. He is an editor of the *Journal of Banking and Finance* and the *Journal of Financial Markets, Instruments and Institutions*, as well as the associate editor of eight other journals, including *Financial Management* and the *Journal of Money, Credit and Banking*. His research has been published in all the major money and banking and finance journals and in several books. In addition, he has authored or coauthored several professional books, the most recent of which is *Credit Risk Measurement: New Approaches to Value at Risk and Other Paradigms*, 2nd edition, John Wiley and Sons, New York, 2002.

Marcia Millon Cornett

Marcia Millon Cornett is the Rehn Professor of Business at Southern Illinois University at Carbondale. She received her BS degree in Economics from Knox College in Galesburg, Illinois, and her MBA and PhD degrees in Finance from Indiana University in Bloomington, Indiana. Dr. Cornett has written and published several articles in the areas of bank performance, bank regulation, and corporate finance. Articles authored by Dr. Cornett have appeared in such academic journals as the *Journal of Finance,* the *Journal of Money, Credit and Banking*, the *Journal of Financial Economics, Financial Management,* and the *Journal of Banking and Finance*. She served as an Associate Editor of *Financial Management* and is currently an Associate Editor for the *Journal of Banking and Finance, Journal of Financial Services Research, FMA Online,* the *Multinational Finance Journal* and the *Review of Financial Economics*. Dr. Cornett is currently a member of the Board of Directors, the Executive Committee, and the Finance Committee of the SIU Credit Union. Dr. Cornett has also taught at the University of Colorado, Boston College, and Southern Methodist University. She is a member of the Financial Management Association, the American Finance Association, and the Western Finance Association.

Preface

The financial services industry continues to undergo dramatic changes. Not only have the boundaries between traditional industry sectors, such as commercial banking and investment banking, broken down but competition is becoming increasingly global in nature. Many forces are contributing to this breakdown in interindustry and intercountry barriers, including financial innovation, technology, taxation, and regulation. It is in this context that this book is written. Although the traditional nature of each sector's product activity is analyzed, a greater emphasis is placed on *new* areas of activities such as asset securitization, off-balance-sheet banking, and international banking.

When the first edition of this text was released in 1994, it was the first to analyze modern financial institutions management from a risk perspective. Thus, the title, *Financial Institutions Management: A Modern Perspective*. At that time, traditional texts presented an overview of the industry sector by sector, concentrating on balance sheet presentations and overlooking management decision making and risk management. Over the last decade other texts have followed this change, such that a risk management approach to analyzing modern financial institutions is now well accepted. Thus, the revised title: *Financial Institutions Management: A Risk Management Approach.*

The fifth edition of this text takes the same innovative approach taken in the first four editions and focuses on managing return and risk in modern financial institutions (FIs). *Financial Institutions Management*'s central theme is that the risks faced by FI managers and the methods and markets through which these risks are managed are similar whether an institution is chartered as a commercial bank, a savings bank, an investment bank, or an insurance company.

As in any stockholder-owned corporation, the goal of FI managers should always be to maximize the value of the financial intermediary. However, pursuit of value maximization does not mean that risk management can be ignored.

Indeed, modern FIs are in the risk-management business. As we discuss in this book, in a world of perfect and frictionless capital markets, FIs would not exist and individuals would manage their own financial assets and portfolios. But since real-world financial markets are not perfect, FIs provide the positive function of bearing and managing risk on behalf of their customers through the pooling of risks and the sale of their services as risk specialists.

Intended Audience

Financial Institutions Management: A Risk Management Approach is aimed at upper-level undergraduate and MBA audiences. Occasionally there are more technical sections that are marked with a footnote. *These sections may be included or dropped from the chapter reading, depending on the rigor of the course, without harming the continuity of the chapters.*

Main Features

Throughout the text, special features have been integrated to encourage students' interaction with the text and to aid them in absorbing the material. Some of these features include:

- **Standard & Poor's Market Insight Questions,** which are included in the end-of-chapter questions and problems and which guide the student through this website to access data on specific financial institutions or industry sectors.
- **In-chapter Internet Exercises and references,** which guide the student to access the most recent data on the Web.
- **International material highlights,** which call out material relating to global issues.
- **In-chapter Examples,** which provide numerical demonstrations of the analytics described in various chapters.
- **Bold key terms and marginal glossary,** which highlight and define the main terms and concepts throughout the chapter.
- **Concept Questions,** which allow students to test themselves on the main concepts within each major chapter section.
- **Ethical Dilemmas, Industry Perspectives, and Technology in the News boxes,** which demonstrate the application of chapter material to real current events.

Organization

Since our focus is on return and risk and the sources of that return and risk, this book relates ways in which the managers of modern FIs can expand return with a managed level of risk to achieve the best, or most favorable, return-risk outcome for FI owners.

Chapter 1 introduces the special functions of FIs and takes an analytical look at how financial intermediation benefits today's economy. Chapters 2 to 6 provide an overview describing the key balance sheet and regulatory features of the major sectors of the U.S. financial services industry. We discuss depository institutions in Chapter 2, insurance institutions in Chapter 3, securities firms and investment banks in Chapter 4, mutual funds in Chapter 5, and finance companies in Chapter 6. In Chapter 7 we preview the risk measurement and management sections with an overview of the risks facing a modern FI. We divide the chapters on risk measurement and management into two sections: measuring risk and managing risk.

In Chapters 8 and 9 we start the risk-measurement section by investigating the net interest margin as a source of profitability and risk, with a focus on the effects of interest rate volatility and the mismatching of asset and liability durations on FI risk exposure. In Chapter 10 we analyze market risk, a risk that results when FIs actively trade bonds, equities, and foreign currencies.

In Chapter 11 we look at the measurement of credit risk on individual loans and bonds and how this risk adversely impacts an FI's profits through losses and provisions against the loan and debt security portfolio. In Chapter 12 we look at the risk of loan (asset) portfolios and the effects of loan concentrations on risk exposure. Modern FIs do more than generate returns and bear risk through traditional maturity mismatching and credit extensions. They also are increasingly engaging in off-balance-sheet activities to generate fee income (Chapter 13), making technological investments to reduce costs (Chapter 14), pursuing foreign exchange activities and overseas financial investments (Chapter 15), and engaging in sovereign lending and securities activities (Chapter 16). Each of these has implications for the size and variability of an FI's profits and/or revenues. In addition, as a by-product of the provision of their interest rate and credit intermediation services, FIs face liquidity risk. We analyze the special nature of this risk in Chapter 17.

In Chapter 18 we begin the risk-management section by looking at ways in which FIs can insulate themselves from liquidity risk. In Chapter 19 we look at the key role deposit insurance and other guaranty schemes play in reducing liquidity risk. At the core of FI risk insulation is the size and adequacy of the owners' capital or equity investment in the FI, which is the focus of Chapter 20. Chapters 21 to 23 analyze how and why product diversification and geographic diversification—both domestic and international—can improve an FI's return-risk performance and the impact of regulation on the diversification opportunity set. Chapters 24 through 28 review various new markets and instruments that have been innovated or engineered to allow FIs to better manage three important types of risk: interest rate risk, credit risk, and foreign exchange risk. These markets and instruments and their strategic use by FIs include futures and forwards (Chapter 24); options, caps, floors, and collars (Chapter 25); swaps (Chapter 26); loan sales (Chapter 27); and securitization (Chapter 28).

Changes in this Edition

Each chapter in this edition has been revised thoroughly to reflect the most up-to-date information available. End-of-chapter questions and problem material have also been revised to provide a more complete selection of testing material.

The following are some of the new features of this revision:

- In-chapter discussions of the many ethical controversies involving financial institutions (such as those involving commercial banks, investment banks, and mutual funds) have been added to most chapters.

- Ethical Dilemmas boxes have been added to many chapters which highlight specific news stories relating to the ethical controversies involving financial institutions in the early 2000s.

- The latest information pertaining to new capital adequacy rules (or Basel II) that are scheduled for implementation at the end of 2006 has been added to Chapter 20. The latest changes to deposit insurance premiums charged to financial institutions, insurance coverage for financial institutions customers, and the Federal Reserve's discount window lending programs are discussed in Chapter 19.

- Discussions of the impact of the Patriot Act and the Sarbanes-Oxley Act on financial institutions management are included in several chapters.

- The impact of the economic slowdown, the subsequent economic recovery in the United States and worldwide, and the impact of historically low interest rates on financial institutions are highlighted and discussed.

- The impact of the newest wave of bank mergers (domestic and international) is highlighted in Chapters 22 through 24.

- A discussion of the controversy surrounding the federal government's implicit backing of Fannie Mae and Freddie Mac and the impact the increased level of risk in these two agencies posed to the U.S. economy in the early 2000s is added to Chapter 28.

- Tables and figures in all chapters have been revised to include the most recently available data.
- Sections of the text that include a discussion of international issues and events are highlighted. These sections have been updated to contain the most recent issues pertaining to financial institutions worldwide.
- Appendices for Chapters 8, 11, 18, and 25 are available on the book's Web site at www.mhhe.com/saunders5e. The presence of an online appendix is specifically noted in the end-of-chapter material.
- Internet problems included in the end-of-chapter problems have been substantially enhanced. These problems now guide students through the Web site as they collect the requested data. Further, these problems now ask students to evaluate the data collected at the Web site.
- Internet Exercises have been added to the body of various chapters. These exercises guide the student to access the most recent data on the Web as it is discussed in the body of the chapter.
- S&P Market Insight problems have been added to the end-of-chapter problems. These problems require the use of the Educational Version of Market Insight, a Standard and Poor's Compustat® database. Over 600 companies (of which more than 100 are financial institutions) and key financial data pertaining to them are available as a problem-solving resource.
- Chapter Notation used in each chapter has been summarized and added to the book's Web site (located at www.mhhe.com/saunders5e). These have been summarized and are listed by chapter at the Web site.

We have retained and updated these features:

- The risk approach of *Financial Institutions Management* has been retained, keeping the first section of the text as an introduction and the last two sections as a risk measurement and risk management summary, respectively.
- We again present a detailed look at what is new in each of the different sectors of the financial institutions industry in the first six chapters of the text. We have highlighted the continued international coverage with a global issues icon throughout the text.
- The discussion of how the Financial Services Modernization Act of 1999 continues to affect financial institutions remains in several chapters.
- Chapter 14 includes material on electronic technology and the Internet's impact on financial services. Technological changes occurring over the last decade have changed the way financial institutions offer services to customers, both domestically and overseas. The effect of technology is also referenced in other chapters where relevant.
- Coverage of Credit Risk models (including newer models, such as KMV, CreditMetrics, and CreditRisk+) remains in the text.
- Coverage in the "Product Diversification" chapter and the "Geographic Diversification" chapter explores the increased inroads of banks into the insurance field, the move towards nationwide banking (in the United States), and the rapid growth of foreign banks and other intermediaries in the United States.
- A Web site has been expanded as a supplement to the text. The Web site, www.mhhe.com/saunders5e, will include information about the book and an Instructor's site containing the password protected Instructor's Manual and PowerPoint material.

- Numerous highlighted in-chapter Examples remain in the chapters.
- Technology in the News boxes on how technology and the Internet are affecting financial institutions as an industry have been updated.
- Internet references remain throughout each chapter as well as at the end of each chapter and Internet questions are found after the end-of-chapter questions.
- An extensive problem set can be found at the end of each chapter that allows students to practice a variety of skills using the same data or set of circumstances.

Ancillaries

To assist in course preparation, the following ancillaries are offered:

- New to this edition is the Saunders/Cornett *Financial Institutions Management* Web site: www.mhhe.com/saunders5e. This site will be accessible to both professors and students, having a username and password protecting the instructor's portion of the site. The site will include: About the Authors, Table of Contents, Internet Problems, URLs, PowerPoint, Instructor's Manual, Online Quizzes, and an Update Section.
- New to the fifth edition are online quizzes, available at www.mhhe.com/saunders5e, that provide students with chapter-specific interactive quizzing for self-evaluation.
- The *Instructor's Manual/Test Bank,* prepared by Ernie Swift, Georgia State University, is included on the Instructor's Resource CD and includes detailed chapter contents, additional examples for use in the classroom, PowerPoint teaching notes, complete solutions to end-of-chapter questions and problem material, and additional problems for test material.
- The PowerPoint Presentation System was created by Kenneth Stanton of the University of Baltimore and is included on the Instructor's Resource CD. It contains useful and graphically enhanced outlines, summaries, and exhibits from the text. The slides can be edited, printed, or arranged to fit the needs of your course.
- Brownstone, our computerized version of the test bank, allows the instructor to pick and choose the order and number of questions to include for each test, and is included on the Instructor's Resource CD.
- PowerWeb: Ethics in Finance offers current articles, curriculum-based materials, weekly updates with assessment, informative and timely world news, Web links, research tools, and interactive exercises, as well as providing instructors an easy way to integrate the Internet into a course. Free with the purchase of a new book, this feature can be found at www.dushkin.com/powerweb.
- As an interactive, online map, Finance around the World—an outstanding global financial resource that provides "live real-time links" for researching and exploring finance—allows you to access finance and business news and analysis from your favorite global region of interest.
- As an adopter of a McGraw-Hill text, you can easily provide a 15-week subscription to *The Wall Street Journal* in print and online for your students. For only $20, in addition to the price of the text, you can package a student subscription to *The Wall Street Journal* with your textbook. Experience with the *Journal* will give your students the tools to integrate the theories you teach in the classroom with real world examples. Please contact your McGraw-Hill/Irwin representative for ordering information.

Acknowledgments

Finally, we would like to thank the numerous colleagues who assisted with the first, second, third, and fourth editions of this book. Of great help were the book reviewers whose painstaking comments and advice guided the text through its first, second, and third revisions.

Michael H. Anderson
Suffolk University

M. E. Bond
University of Memphis

Yen Mow Chen
San Francisco State University

Jeffrey A. Clark
Florida State University

Robert A. Clark
Butler University

S. Steven Cole
University of North Texas

Paul Ellinger
University of Illinois

James H. Gilkeson
University of Central Florida

John H. Hand
Auburn University

Alan C. Hess
University of Washington—Seattle

Kevin Jacques
Georgetown University and Office of the Comptroller of the Currency

Julapa Jagtiani
Federal Reserve Bank of Chicago

Craig G. Johnson
California State University—Hayward

Nelson J. Lacey
University of Massachusetts at Amherst

Robert Lamy
Wake Forest University

Rick LeCompte
Wichita State University

Patricia C. Matthews
Mount Union College

Robert McLeod
University of Alabama

Rose M. Prasad
Central Michigan University

Tara Rice
Boston College

Don Sabbarese
Kennesaw State University

Daniel Singer
Towson University

Richard Stolz
California State University—Fullerton

James A. Verbrugge
University of Georgia

Sonya Williams-Stanton
University of Michigan—Ann Arbor

In addition, we gratefully acknowledge the contributions of the reviewers of the fourth edition:

Jack Aber
Boston University

Rita Biswas
SUNY—Albany

Douglas Cook
University of Mississippi

David Ely
San Diego State University

Elyas Elyasiani
Temple University

Yan He
San Francisco State University

Michael Toyne
Northeastern State University

Haluk Unal
University of Maryland

We very much appreciate the contributions of the book team at McGraw-Hill/Irwin: Steve Patterson, Publisher; Meghan Grosscup, Editorial Coordinator; Rhonda Seelinger, Executive Marketing Manager; Joyce Chapetto, Media Project Manager; Kristin Puscas, Project Manager; Gina Hangos, Production Supervisor; and Mary Kazak, Senior Designer. We are also grateful to our secretaries and assistants, Robyn Vanterpool, Ingrid Persaud, Anand Srinivasan, and Alex Fayman.

Anthony Saunders

Marcia Millon Cornett

Brief Contents

Contents

List of Industry Perspectives Boxes

List of Technology in the News Boxes

List of Ethical Dilemmas Boxes

Part One

Introduction

Chapter One

Why Are Financial Intermediaries Special?

INTRODUCTION

Over the last 70 years, the financial services industry has come full cycle. Originally, the banking industry operated as a full-service industry, performing directly or indirectly all financial services (commercial banking, investment banking, stock investing services, insurance providers, etc.). In the early 1930s, the economic and industrial collapse resulted in the separation of some of these activities. In the 1970s and 1980s, new, relatively unregulated financial services industries sprang up (mutual funds, brokerage funds, etc.) that separated financial services functions even further. As we enter the 21st century, regulatory barriers, technology, and financial innovation changes are such that a full set of financial services may again be offered by a single financial services firm. Not only are the boundaries between traditional industry sectors weakening, but competition is becoming global in nature as well. As the competitive environment changes, attention to profit and, more than ever, risk becomes increasingly important. The major themes of this book are the measurement and management of the risks of financial institutions. Financial institutions (e.g., banks, credit unions, insurance companies, and mutual funds), or FIs, perform the essential function of channeling funds from those with surplus funds (suppliers of funds) to those with shortages of funds (users of funds). In 2003, U.S. FIs held assets totaling over $16.59 trillion. In contrast, the U.S. motor vehicle and parts industry (e.g., General Motors and Ford Motor Corp.) held total assets of $0.90 trillion.

Although we might categorize or group FIs as life insurance companies, banks, finance companies, and so on, they face many common risks. Specifically, all FIs described in this chapter and Chapters 2 through 6 (1) hold some assets that are potentially subject to default or credit risk and (2) tend to mismatch the maturities of their balance sheet assets and liabilities to a greater or lesser extent and are thus exposed to interest rate risk. Moreover, all FIs are exposed to some degree of liability withdrawal or liquidity risk, depending on the type of claims they have sold to liability holders. In addition, most FIs are exposed to some type of underwriting risk, whether through the sale of securities or the issue of various types of credit guarantees on or off the balance sheet. Finally, all FIs are exposed to operating cost risks because the production of financial services requires the use of real

TABLE 1–1   Areas of Financial Intermediaries' Specialness in the Provision of Services

Information costs   The aggregation of funds in an FI provides greater incentive to collect information about customers (such as corporations) and to monitor their actions. The relatively large size of the FI allows this collection of information to be accomplished at a lower average cost (so-called economies of scale) than would be the case for individuals.

Liquidity and price risk   FIs provide financial claims to household savers with superior liquidity attributes and with lower price risk.

Transaction cost services   Similar to economies of scale in information production costs, an FI's size can result in economies of scale in transaction costs.

Maturity intermediation   FIs can better bear the risk of mismatching the maturities of their assets and liabilities.

Transmission of monetary supply   Depository institutions are the conduit through which monetary policy actions by the country's central bank (such as the Federal Reserve) impact the rest of the financial system and the economy.

Credit allocation   FIs are often viewed as the major, and sometimes only, source of financing for a particular sector of the economy, such as farming, small business, and residential real estate.

Intergenerational wealth transfers   FIs, especially life insurance companies and pension funds, provide savers with the ability to transfer wealth from one generation to the next.

Payment services   The efficiency with which depository institutions provide payment services such as check clearing directly benefits the economy.

Denomination intermediation   FIs, such as mutual funds, allow small investors to overcome constraints to buying assets imposed by large minimum denomination size.

resources and back-office support systems (labor and technology combined to provide services).

Because of these risks and the special role that FIs play in the financial system, FIs are singled out for special regulatory attention.[1] In this chapter, we first examine questions related to this specialness. In particular, what are the special functions that FIs—both depository institutions (banks, savings institutions, and credit unions) and nondepository institutions (insurance companies, securities firms, investment banks, finance companies, and mutual funds)—provide? These special functions are summarized in Table 1–1. How do these functions benefit the economy? Second, we investigate what makes some FIs more special than others. Third, we look at how unique and long-lived the special functions of FIs really are.

FINANCIAL INTERMEDIARIES' SPECIALNESS

To understand the important economic function of FIs, imagine a simple world in which FIs do not exist. In such a world, households generating excess savings by consuming less than they earn would have the basic choice: They could hold cash as an asset or invest in the securities issued by corporations. In general, corporations issue securities to finance their investments in real assets and cover the gap between their investment plans and their internally generated savings such as retained earnings.

As shown in Figure 1–1, in such a world, savings would flow from households to corporations; in return, financial claims (equity and debt securities) would flow from corporations to household savers.

---

[1] Some public utility suppliers, such as gas, electric, telephone, and water companies, are also singled out for regulation because of the special nature of their services and the costs imposed on society if they fail.

Funds are low

FIGURE 1–1

Flow of Funds in a World without FIs

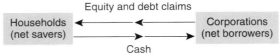

Equity and debt claims

Households (net savers) ← ← Corporations (net borrowers)

Cash

Monitoring FI

Lack of + risk

In an economy without FIs, the level of fund flows between household savers and the corporate sectors is likely to be quite low. There are several reasons for this. Once they have lent money to a firm by buying its financial claims, households need to monitor, or check, the actions of that firm. They must be sure that the firm's management neither absconds with nor wastes the funds on any projects with low or negative net present values. Such monitoring actions are extremely costly for any given household because they require considerable time and expense to collect sufficiently high-quality information relative to the size of the average household saver's investments. Given this, it is likely that each household would prefer to leave the monitoring to others; in the end, little or no monitoring would be done. The resulting lack of monitoring would reduce the attractiveness and increase the risk of investing in corporate debt and equity.

having cash on hand

The relatively long-term nature of corporate equity and debt, and the lack of a secondary market in which households can sell these securities, creates a second disincentive for household investors to hold the direct financial claims issued by corporations. Specifically, given the choice between holding cash and holding long-term securities, households may well choose to hold cash for **liquidity** reasons, especially if they plan to use savings to finance consumption expenditures in the near future.

liquidity

The ease of converting an asset into cash.

Finally, even if financial markets existed (without FIs to operate them) to provide liquidity services by allowing households to trade corporate debt and equity securities among themselves, investors also face a **price risk** on sale of securities, and the secondary market trading of securities involves various transaction costs. That is, the price at which household investors can sell securities on secondary markets such as the New York Stock Exchange may well differ from the price they initially paid for the securities.

price risk

The risk that the sale price of an asset will be lower than the purchase price of that asset.

3 reasons Household saver does not invest directly

Because of (1) monitoring costs, (2) liquidity costs, and (3) price risk, the average household saver may view direct investment in corporate securities as an unattractive proposition and prefer either not to save or to save in the form of cash.

Economy provides FI's to household savers

However, the economy has developed an alternative and indirect way to channel household savings to the corporate sector. This is to channel savings via FIs. Because of costs of monitoring, liquidity, and price risk, as well as for some other reasons, explained later, savers often prefer to hold the financial claims issued by FIs rather than those issued by corporations.

Consider Figure 1–2, which is a closer representation than Figure 1–1 of the world in which we live and the way funds flow in our economy. Notice how

FIGURE 1–2

Flow of Funds in a World with FIs

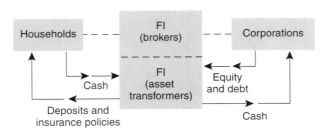

Households --- FI (brokers) --- Corporations

Cash

Deposits and insurance policies

FI (asset transformers)

Equity and debt

Cash

financial intermediaries or institutions are standing, or intermediating, between the household and corporate sectors.

These intermediaries fulfill two functions; any given FI might specialize in one or the other or might do both simultaneously. The first function is the brokerage function. When acting as a pure broker, an FI acts as an agent for the saver by providing information and transaction services. For example, full-service securities firms (e.g., Merrill Lynch) carry out investment research and make investment recommendations for their retail (or household) clients as well as conducting the purchase or sale of securities for commission or fees. Discount brokers (e.g., Charles Schwab) carry out the purchase or sale of securities at better prices and with greater efficiency than household savers could achieve by trading on their own. This efficiency results in reduced costs of trading, or **economies of scale** (see Chapter 21 for a detailed discussion). Independent insurance brokers identify the best types of insurance policies household savers can buy to fit their savings and retirement plans. In fulfilling a brokerage function, the FI plays an extremely important role by reducing transaction and information costs or imperfections between households and corporations. Thus, the FI encourages a higher rate of savings than would otherwise exist.[2]

The second function is the asset-transformation function. In acting as an **asset transformer,** the FI issues financial claims that are far more attractive to household savers than the claims directly issued by corporations. That is, for many households, the financial claims issued by FIs dominate those issued directly by corporations as a result of lower monitoring costs, lower liquidity costs, and lower price risk. In acting as asset transformers, FIs purchase the financial claims issued by corporations—equities, bonds, and other debt claims called **primary securities**—and finance these purchases by selling financial claims to household investors and other sectors in the form of deposits, insurance policies, and so on. The financial claims of FIs may be considered **secondary securities** because these assets are backed by the primary securities issued by commercial corporations that in turn invest in real assets. Specifically, FIs are independent market parties that create financial products whose value added to their clients is the transformation of financial risk.

Simplified balance sheets of a commercial firm and an FI are shown in Table 1–2. Note that in the real world, FIs hold a small proportion of their assets in the form of real assets such as bank branch buildings. These simplified balance sheets reflect a reasonably accurate characterization of the operational differences between commercial firms and FIs.

How can FIs purchase the direct or primary securities issued by corporations and profitably transform them into secondary securities more attractive to household savers? This question strikes at the very heart of what makes FIs special and important to the economy. The answer lies in the ability of FIs to better resolve the three costs facing a saver who chooses to invest directly in corporate securities.

economies of scale
The concept that the cost reduction in trading and other transaction services results from increased efficiency when FIs perform these services.

asset transformer
An FI issues financial claims that are more attractive to household savers than the claims directly issued by corporations.

primary securities
Securities issued by corporations and backed by the real assets of those corporations.

secondary securities
Securities issued by FIs and backed by primary securities.

---

[2] Most recently, with the introduction of new derivative securities markets for financial futures, options, and swaps, financial institutions that participate in the markets reduce transaction and information costs for firms and consumers wanting to hedge their risks. Thus, FIs encourage better risk management than otherwise would exist. See F. Allen and A. M. Santomero, "The Theory of Financial Intermediation," *Journal of Banking and Finance* 21 (1998), pp. 1461–85; B. Scholtens and D. van Wensveen," A Critique of the Theory of Financial Intermediation," *Journal of Banking and Finance* 24 (2000), pp. 1243–51; F. Allen, "Do Financial Institutions Matter?" *Journal of Finance* 56 (2001), pp. 1165–75; and F. Allen and A. M. Santomero, "What Do Financial Intermediaries Do?" *Journal of Banking and Finance* 25 (2001), pp. 271–94.

TABLE 1–2
Simplified Balance Sheets for a Commercial Firm and an FI

Commercial Firm		Financial Intermediary	
Assets	**Liabilities**	**Assets**	**Liabilities**
Real assets (plant, machinery)	Primary securities (debt, equity)	Primary securities (debt, equity)	Secondary securities (deposits and insurance policies)

Information Costs

One problem faced by an average saver directly investing in a commercial firm's financial claims is the high cost of information collection. Household savers must monitor the actions of firms in a timely and complete fashion after purchasing securities. Failure to monitor exposes investors to **agency costs,** that is, the risk that the firm's owners or managers will take actions with the saver's money contrary to the promises contained in the covenants of its securities contracts. Monitoring costs are part of overall agency costs. That is, agency costs arise whenever economic agents enter into contracts in a world of incomplete information and thus costly information collection. The more difficult and costly it is to collect information, the more likely it is that contracts will be broken. In this case the saver (the so-called principal) could be harmed by the actions taken by the borrowing firm (the so-called agent). One solution to this problem is for a large number of small savers to place their funds with a single FI. This FI groups these funds together and invests in the direct or primary financial claims issued by firms. This agglomeration of funds resolves a number of problems. First, the large FI now has a much greater incentive to collect information and monitor actions of the firm because it has far more at stake than does any small individual household. In a sense, small savers have appointed the FI as a **delegated monitor** to act on their behalf.[3] Not only does the FI have a greater incentive to collect information, the average cost of collecting information is lower. For example, the cost to a small investor of buying a $100 broker's report may seem inordinately high for a $10,000 investment. For an FI with $10 million under management, however, the cost seems trivial. Such economies of scale of information production and collection tend to enhance the advantages to savers of using FIs rather than directly investing themselves.

Second, associated with the greater incentive to monitor and the costs involved in failing to monitor appropriately, FIs may develop new secondary securities that enable them to monitor more effectively. Thus, a richer menu of contracts may improve the monitoring abilities of FIs. Perhaps the classic example of this is the bank loan. Bank loans are generally shorter-term debt contracts than bond contracts. This short-term nature allows the FI to exercise more monitoring power and control over the borrower. In particular, the information the FI generates regarding the firm is frequently updated as its loan renewal decisions are made. When bank loan contracts are sufficiently short term, the banker becomes almost like an insider to the firm regarding informational familiarity with its operations and financial conditions. Indeed, this more frequent monitoring often replaces the need for the

agency costs
Costs relating to the risk that the owners and managers of firms that receive savers' funds will take actions with those funds contrary to the best interests of the savers.

delegated monitor
An economic agent appointed to act on behalf of smaller agents in collecting information and/or investing funds on their behalf.

---

[3] For a theoretical modeling of the delegated monitor function, see D. W. Diamond, "Financial Intermediaries and Delegated Monitoring," *Review of Economic Studies* 51 (1984), pp. 393–414; and A. Winton, "Competition among Financial Intermediaries When Diversification Matters," *Journal of Financial Intermediation* 6 (1997), pp. 307–46.

relatively inflexible and hard-to-enforce covenants found in bond contracts.[4] Thus, by acting as a delegated monitor and producing better and more timely information, FIs reduce the degree of information imperfection and asymmetry between the ultimate suppliers and users of funds in the economy.

Liquidity and Price Risk

In addition to improving the flow and quality of information, FIs provide financial or secondary claims to household and other savers. Often, these claims have superior liquidity attributes compared with those of primary securities such as corporate equity and bonds. For example, banks and thrifts issue transaction account deposit contracts with a fixed principal value (and often a guaranteed interest rate) that can be withdrawn immediately on demand by household savers.[5] Money market mutual funds issue shares to household savers that allow those savers to enjoy almost fixed principal (depositlike) contracts while often earning interest rates higher than those on bank deposits. Even life insurance companies allow policyholders to borrow against their policies held with the company at very short notice. The real puzzle is how FIs such as depository institutions can offer highly liquid and low price-risk contracts to savers on the liability side of their balance sheets while investing in relatively illiquid and higher price-risk securities issued by corporations on the asset side. Furthermore, how can FIs be confident enough to guarantee that they can provide liquidity services to investors and savers when they themselves invest in risky asset portfolios? And why should savers and investors believe FIs' promises regarding the liquidity of their investments?

The answers to these questions lie in the ability of FIs to **diversify** away some but not all of their portfolio risks. The concept of diversification is familiar to all students of finance: Basically, as long as the returns on different investments are not perfectly *positively* correlated, by exploiting the benefits of size, FIs diversify away significant amounts of portfolio risk—especially the risk specific to the individual firm issuing any given security. Indeed, experiments in the United States and the United Kingdom have shown that equal investments in as few as 15 securities can bring significant diversification benefits to FIs and portfolio managers.[6] Further, as the number of securities in an FI's asset portfolio increases beyond 15 securities, portfolio risk falls, albeit at a diminishing rate. What is really going on here is that FIs exploit the law of large numbers in their investments, achieving a significant amount of diversification, whereas because of their small size, many household savers are constrained to holding relatively undiversified portfolios. This risk diversification allows an FI to predict more accurately its expected return on its asset portfolio. A domestically and globally diversified FI may be able to generate an

diversify
Reducing risk by holding a number of securities in a portfolio.

---

[4] For a further description and discussion of the special or unique nature of bank loans, see E. Fama, "What's Different about Banks?" *Journal of Monetary Economics* 15 (1985), pp. 29–39; C. James, "Some Evidence on the Uniqueness of Bank Loans," *Journal of Financial Economics* 19 (1987), pp. 217–35; M. T. Billett, M. J. Flannery, and J. A. Garfinkel, "The Effect of Lender Identity on a Borrowing Firm's Equity Return," *Journal of Finance* 50 (1995), pp. 699–718; W. A. Kracaw and M. Zenner, "The Wealth Effects of Bank Financing Announcements in Highly Leveraged Transactions," *Journal of Finance* 57 (1996), pp. 1931–46; and S. Dahiya, M. Puri, and A. Saunders, "Bank Borrowers and Loan Sales: New Evidence on the Uniqueness of Bank Loans," *Journal of Business* 76 (2003), pp. 563–82.

[5] Also, the largest commercial banks in the world make markets for swaps, allowing businesses to hedge various risks (such as interest rate risk and foreign exchange risk) on their balance sheets.

[6] For a review of such studies, see E. J. Elton and M. J. Gruber, *Modern Portfolio Theory and Investment Analysis,* 6th ed. (New York: John Wiley & Sons, 1998), chapter 2.

almost risk-free return on its assets. As a result, it can credibly fulfill its promise to households to supply highly liquid claims with little price or capital value risk. A good example of this is the ability of a bank to offer highly liquid demand deposits—with a fixed principal value—as liabilities, while at the same time investing in risky loans as assets. As long as an FI is sufficiently large to gain from diversification and monitoring, its financial claims are likely to be viewed as liquid and attractive to small savers compared with direct investments in the capital market.

Other Special Services

The preceding discussion has concentrated on three general or special services provided by FIs: reducing household savers' monitoring costs, increasing their liquidity, and reducing their price-risk exposure. Next, we discuss two other special services provided by FIs: reduced transaction costs and maturity intermediation.

Reduced Transaction Costs

Just as FIs provide potential economies of scale in information collection, they also provide potential economies of scale in transaction costs. For example, since May 1, 1975, fixed commissions for equity trades on the NYSE have been abolished. As a result, small retail buyers face higher commission charges or transaction costs than do large wholesale buyers. By grouping their assets in FIs that purchase assets in bulk—such as in mutual funds and pension funds—household savers can reduce the transaction costs of their asset purchases. In addition, bid–ask (buy–sell) spreads are normally lower for assets bought and sold in large quantities.

Maturity Intermediation

An additional dimension of FIs' ability to reduce risk by diversification is that they can better bear the risk of mismatching the maturities of their assets and liabilities than can small household savers. Thus, FIs offer maturity intermediation services to the rest of the economy. Specifically, through maturity mismatching, FIs can produce new types of contracts, such as long-term mortgage loans to households, while still raising funds with short-term liability contracts. Further, while such mismatches can subject an FI to interest rate risk (see Chapters 8 and 9), a large FI is better able to manage this risk through its superior access to markets and instruments for hedging such as loan sales and securitization (Chapters 27 and 28); futures (Chapter 24); swaps (Chapter 26); and options, caps, floors, and collars (Chapter 25).

Concept Questions

1. What are the three major risks to household savers from direct security purchases?
2. What are two major differences between brokers (such as security brokers) and depository institutions (such as commercial banks)?
3. What are primary securities and secondary securities?
4. What is the link between asset diversification and the liquidity of deposit contracts?

OTHER ASPECTS OF SPECIALNESS

The theory of the flow of funds points to three principal reasons for believing that FIs are special, along with two other associated reasons. In reality, academics, policymakers, and regulators identify other areas of specialness relating to certain specific functions of FIs or groups of FIs. We discuss these next.

The Transmission of Monetary Policy

[handwritten: Depository limits monetary policy]

The highly liquid nature of bank and thrift (depository institution) deposits has resulted in their acceptance by the public as the most widely used medium of exchange in the economy. Indeed, at the core of the three most commonly used definitions of the money supply—M1, M2, and M3[7]—lie depository institutions' deposit contracts. Because the liabilities of depository institutions are a significant component of the money supply that impacts the rate of inflation, they play a key role in the *transmission of monetary policy* from the central bank to the rest of the economy. That is, depository institutions are the conduit through which monetary policy actions impact the rest of the financial sector and the economy in general. Monetary policy actions include open market operations (the purchase and sale of securities in the U.S. Treasury securities market), setting the discount rate (the rate charged on "lender of last resort" borrowing from the Federal Reserve), and setting reserve requirements (the minimum amount of reserve assets depository institutions must hold to back deposits held as liabilities on their balance sheets).

Credit Allocation

[handwritten: Farming / Residential Real Estate Subsidies]

A further reason FIs are often viewed as special is that they are the major and sometimes the only source of finance for a particular sector of the economy pre-identified as being in special need of finance. Policymakers in the United States and a number of other countries, such as the United Kingdom, have identified *residential real estate* as needing special subsidies. This has enhanced the specialness of FIs that most commonly service the needs of that sector. In the United States, savings associations and savings banks have traditionally served the credit needs of the residential real estate sector.[8] In a similar fashion, farming is an especially important area of the economy in terms of the overall social welfare of the population. The U.S. government has even directly encouraged financial institutions to specialize in financing this area of activity through the creation of Federal Farm Credit Banks.

Intergenerational Wealth Transfers or Time Intermediation

[handwritten: generational wealth]

The ability of savers to transfer wealth between youth and old age and across generations is also of great importance to the social well-being of a country. Because of this, life insurance and pension funds (see Chapter 3) are often especially encouraged, via special taxation relief and other subsidy mechanisms, to service and accommodate those needs.

---

[7] M1: ($1,274.2 billion outstanding in July 2003) consists of (1) Currency outside the U.S. Treasury, Federal Reserve Banks, and the vaults of depository institutions. (2) Traveler's checks of nonbank issuers. (3) Demand deposits at all commercial banks other than those owed to depository institutions, the United States government, and foreign banks and official institutions, less cash items in the process of collection and Federal Reserve float. (4) Other checkable deposits (OCDs). M2: ($6,058.1 billion outstanding in July 2003) consists of M1 plus (1) Savings and small time deposits (time deposits in amounts of less than $100,000). (2) Other nondeposit obligations of depository institutions. M3: ($8,863.8 billion outstanding in July 2003) consists of M2 plus (1) Large time deposits (in amounts of $100,000 or more) issued by all depository institutions. (2) Other nondeposit obligations of depository institutions.

[8] E. Laderman and W. Passmore, "Is Mortgage Lending by Savings Associations Special?" Finance and Economics Discussion Series, Federal Reserve Board, 1998–02, find, however, that the elimination of specialized savings banks in the United States would not have a major effect on mortgage borrowers.

Payment Services

Depository institutions such as banks and thrifts (see Chapter 2) are special in that the efficiency with which they provide payment services directly benefits the economy. Two important payment services are check-clearing and wire transfer services. For example, on any given day, trillions of dollars worth of payments are effected through Fedwire and CHIPS, the two large wholesale payment wire networks in the United States (see Chapter 14). Any breakdowns in these systems probably would produce gridlock in the payment system with resulting harmful effects to the economy.

Denomination Intermediation

Both money market and debt-equity mutual funds are special because they provide services relating to denomination intermediation (see Chapter 5). Because they are sold in very large denominations, many assets are either out of reach of individual savers or would result in savers' holding highly undiversified asset portfolios. For example, the minimum size of a negotiable CD is $100,000 and commercial paper (short-term corporate debt) is often sold in minimum packages of $250,000 or more. Individually, a saver may be unable to purchase such instruments. However, by buying shares in a money market mutual fund along with other small investors, household savers overcome the constraints to buying assets imposed by large minimum denomination sizes. Such indirect access to these markets may allow small savers to generate higher returns on their portfolios as well.

SPECIALNESS AND REGULATION

In the preceding section, FIs were shown to be special because of the various services they provide to sectors of the economy. The general areas of FI specialness include:

- Information services.
- Liquidity services.
- Price-risk reduction services.
- Transaction cost services.
- Maturity intermediation services.

Areas of institution-specific specialness are as follows:

- Money supply transmission (banks).
- Credit allocation (thrifts, farm banks).
- Intergenerational transfers (pension funds, life insurance companies).
- Payment services (banks, thrifts).
- Denomination intermediation (mutual funds, pension funds).

Failure to provide these services or a breakdown in their efficient provision can be costly to both the ultimate sources (households) and users (firms) of savings. The **negative externalities**[9] affecting firms and households when something goes

negative externalities
Action by an economic agent imposing costs on other economic agents.

[9] A good example of a negative externality is the costs faced by small businesses in a one-bank town if the local bank fails. These businesses could find it difficult to get financing elsewhere, and their customers could be similarly disadvantaged. As a result, the failure of the bank may have a negative or contagious effect on the economic prospects of the whole community, resulting in lower sales, production, and employment.

wrong in the FI sector of the economy make a case for regulation. That is, FIs are regulated to protect against a disruption in the provision of the services discussed above and the costs this would impose on the economy and society at large. For example, bank failures may destroy household savings and at the same time restrict a firm's access to credit. Insurance company failures may leave households totally exposed in old age to catastrophic illnesses and sudden drops in income on retirement. Further, individual FI failures may create doubts in savers' minds regarding the stability and solvency of FIs in general and cause panics and even runs on sound institutions. In addition, racial, sexual, age, or other discrimination—such as mortgage **redlining**—may unfairly exclude some potential financial service consumers from the marketplace. This type of market failure needs to be corrected by regulation. Although regulation may be socially beneficial, it also imposes private costs, or a regulatory burden, on individual FI owners and managers. For example, regulations prohibit commercial banks from making loans to individual borrowers that exceed more than 10 percent of their equity capital even though the loans may have a positive net present value to the bank. Consequently, regulation is an attempt to enhance the social welfare benefits and mitigate the social costs of the provision of FI services. The private costs of regulation relative to its private benefits, for the producers of financial services, is called the **net regulatory burden.**[10]

Six types of regulation seek to enhance the net social welfare benefits of financial intermediaries' services: (1) safety and soundness regulation, (2) monetary policy regulation, (3) credit allocation regulation, (4) consumer protection regulation, (5) investor protection regulation, and (6) entry and chartering regulation. Regulations are imposed differentially on the various types of FIs. For example, depository institutions are the most heavily regulated of the FIs. Finance companies, on the other hand, are subject to much fewer regulations. Regulation can also be imposed at the federal or the state level and occasionally at the international level, as in the case of bank capital requirements (see Chapter 20).

Finally, some of these regulations are functional in nature, covering all FIs that carry out certain functions, such as payment services, while others are institution specific. Because of the historically segmented nature of the U.S. FI system, many regulations in that system are institution-specific, for example, consumer protection legislation imposed on bank credit allocation to local communities. However, these institution-specific regulations are increasingly being liberalized (see Chapter 21).

Safety and Soundness Regulation

To protect depositors and borrowers against the risk of FI failure due, for example, to a lack of diversification in asset portfolios, regulators have developed layers of protective mechanisms. These mechanisms are intended to ensure the safety and soundness of the FI and thus to maintain the credibility of the FI in the eyes of its borrowers and lenders. In the first layer of protection are requirements encouraging FIs to diversify their assets. Thus, banks are required not to make loans exceeding more than 10 percent of their own equity capital funds to any one company or borrower (see Chapter 11). A bank that has 6 percent of its assets funded by its own capital funds (and therefore 94 percent by deposits) can lend no more than 0.6 percent of its assets to any one party.

The second layer of protection concerns the minimum level of capital or equity funds that the owners of an FI need to contribute to the funding of its operations

redlining
The procedure by which a banker refuses to make loans to residents living inside given geographic boundaries.

net regulatory burden
The difference between the private costs of regulations and the private benefits for the producers of financial services.

---

[10] Other regulated firms, such as gas and electric utilities, also face a complex set of regulations imposing a net regulatory burden on their operations.

(see Chapter 20). For example, bank, thrift, and insurance regulators are concerned with the minimum ratio of capital to (risk) assets. The higher the proportion of capital contributed by owners, the greater the protection against insolvency risk to outside liability claimholders such as depositors and insurance policyholders. This is because losses on the asset portfolio due, for example, to the lack of diversification are legally borne by the equity holders first, and only after equity is totally wiped out by outside liability holders.[11] Consequently, by varying the required degree of equity capital, FI regulators can directly affect the degree of risk exposure faced by nonequity claimholders in FIs. (See Chapter 20 for more discussion on the role of capital in FIs.)

www.fdic.gov

www.sipc.org

The third layer of protection is the provision of guaranty funds such as the Bank Insurance Fund (BIF) for banks, the Savings Association Insurance Fund (SAIF) for savings associations,[12] the Security Investors Protection Corporation (SIPC) for securities firms, and the state guaranty funds established (with regulator encouragement) to meet insolvency losses to small claimholders in the life and property-casualty insurance industries (see Chapter 19). By protecting FI claimholders, when an FI collapses and owners' equity or net worth is wiped out, these funds create a demand for regulation of the insured institutions to protect the funds' resources (see Chapter 19 for more discussion). For example, the FDIC monitors and regulates participants in both BIF and SAIF.

The fourth layer of regulation is monitoring and surveillance itself. Regulators subject all FIs, whether banks, securities firms, or insurance companies, to varying degrees of monitoring and surveillance. This involves on-site examination as well as an FI's production of accounting statements and reports on a timely basis for off-site evaluation. Just as savers appoint FIs as delegated monitors to evaluate the behavior and actions of ultimate borrowers, society appoints regulators to monitor the behavior and performance of FIs.

Finally, note that regulation is not without costs for those regulated. For example, society's regulators may require FIs to have more equity capital than private owners believe is in their own best interests. Similarly, producing the information requested by regulators is costly for FIs because it involves the time of managers, lawyers, and accountants. Again, the socially optimal amount of information may differ from an FI's privately optimal amount.[13]

As noted earlier, the differences between the private benefits to an FI from being regulated—such as insurance fund guarantees—and the private costs it faces from adhering to regulation—such as examinations—is called the *net regulatory burden*. The higher the net regulatory burden on FIs, the more inefficiently they produce any given set of financial services from a private (FI) owner's perspective.

Monetary Policy Regulation

www.federalreserve.
gov

outside money
The part of the money supply directly produced by the government or central bank, such as notes and coin.

Another motivation for regulation concerns the special role banks play in the transmission of monetary policy from the Federal Reserve (the central bank) to the rest of the economy. The problem is that the central bank directly controls only the quantity of notes and coin in the economy—called **outside money**—whereas

---

[11] Thus, equity holders are junior claimants and debt holders are senior claimants to an FI's assets.

[12] The Federal Deposit Insurance Corporation (FDIC) manages both the bank (BIF) and savings association (SAIF) insurance funds.

[13] Also, a social cost rather than social benefit from regulation is the potential risk-increasing behavior (often called moral hazard) that results if deposit insurance and other guaranty funds provide coverage to FIs and their liability holders at less than the actuarially fair price (see Chapter 19 for further discussion).

inside money
The part of the money supply produced by the private banking system.

the bulk of the money supply consists of deposits—called **inside money.** In theory, a central bank can vary the quantity of cash or outside money and directly affect a bank's reserve position as well as the amount of loans and deposits it can create without formally regulating the bank's portfolio. In practice, regulators have chosen to impose formal controls.[14] In most countries, regulators commonly impose a minimum level of required cash reserves to be held against deposits (see Chapter 17). Some argue that imposing such reserve requirements makes the control of the money supply and its transmission more predictable. Such reserves also add to an FI's net regulatory burden if they are more than the institution believes are necessary for its own liquidity purposes. In general, whether banks or insurance companies, all FIs would choose to hold some cash reserves—even non-interest-bearing—to meet the liquidity and transaction needs of their customers directly. For well-managed FIs, however, this optimal level is normally low, especially if the central bank (or other regulatory body) does not pay interest on required reserves. As a result, FIs often view required reserves as similar to a tax and as a positive cost of undertaking intermediation.[15]

Credit Allocation Regulation

Credit allocation regulation supports the FI's lending to socially important sectors such as housing and farming. These regulations may require an FI to hold a minimum amount of assets in one particular sector of the economy or to set maximum interest rates, prices, or fees to subsidize certain sectors. Examples of asset restrictions include the qualified thrift lender (QTL) test, which requires thrifts to hold 65 percent of their assets in residential mortgage-related assets to retain a thrift charter, and insurance regulations, such as those in New York State that set maximums on the amount of foreign or international assets in which insurance companies can invest. Examples of interest rate restrictions are the usury laws set in many states on the maximum rates that can be charged on mortgages and/or consumer loans and regulations (now abolished) such as the Federal Reserve's Regulation Q maximums on time and savings deposit interest rates.

Such price and quantity restrictions may have justification on social welfare grounds—especially if society has a preference for strong (and subsidized) housing and farming sectors. However, they can also be harmful to FIs that have to bear the private costs of meeting many of these regulations. To the extent that the net private costs of such restrictions are positive, they add to the costs and reduce the efficiency with which FIs undertake intermediation.

Consumer Protection Regulation

Congress passed the Community Reinvestment Act (CRA) and the Home Mortgage Disclosure Act (HMDA) to prevent discrimination in lending. For example,

[14] In classic central banking theory, the quantity of bank deposits *(D)* is determined as the product of 1 over the banking system's required (or desired) ratio of cash reserves to deposits *(r)* times the quantity of bank reserves *(R)* outstanding, where *R* comprises notes and coin plus bank deposits held on reserve at the central bank. $D = (1/r) \times R$. Thus, by varying *R*, given a relatively stable reserve ratio *(r)*, the central bank can directly affect *D*, the quantity of deposits or inside money that, as just noted, is a large component of the money supply. Even if not required to do so by regulation, banks would still tend to hold some cash reserves as a liquidity precaution against the sudden withdrawal of deposits or the sudden arrival of new loan demand.

[15] In the United States, bank reserves held with the central bank (the Federal Reserve, or the Fed) are non-interest-bearing. In some other countries, interest is paid on bank reserves, thereby lowering the "regulatory tax" effect.

since 1975, the HMDA has assisted the public in determining whether banks and other mortgage-lending institutions are meeting the needs of their local communities. HMDA is especially concerned about discrimination on the basis of age, race, sex, or income. Since 1990, depository institutions have reported to their chief federal regulator on a standardized form the reasons credit was granted or denied. To get some idea of the information production cost of regulatory compliance in this area, consider that the Federal Financial Institutions Examination Council (FFIEC) processed information on as many as 31 million mortgage transactions from over 7,700 institutions in 2002. (The council is a federal supervisory body comprising the members of the Federal Reserve, the Federal Deposit Insurance Corporation, and the Office of the Comptroller of the Currency.)[16] Many analysts believe that community and consumer protection laws are imposing a considerable net regulatory burden on FIs without providing offsetting social benefits that enhance equal access to mortgage and lending markets. However, as deregulation proceeds and the trend toward consolidation and universal banking (see Chapter 2) continues, it is likely that such laws will be extended beyond banks to other financial service providers, such as insurance companies, that are not currently subject to CRA community lending requirements.

www.ffiec.gov
www.federalreserve.gov
www.fdic.gov
www.occ.treas.gov

Investor Protection Regulation

A considerable number of laws protect investors who use investment banks directly to purchase securities and/or indirectly to access securities markets through investing in mutual or pension funds. Various laws protect investors against abuses such as insider trading, lack of disclosure, outright malfeasance, and breach of fiduciary responsibilities (see Chapter 4). Important legislation affecting investment banks and mutual funds includes the Securities Acts of 1933 and 1934 and the Investment Company Act of 1940. As with consumer protection legislation, compliance with these acts can impose a net regulatory burden on FIs.[17]

Entry Regulation

The entry and activities of FIs are also regulated (e.g., new bank chartering regulations). Increasing or decreasing the cost of entry into a financial sector affects the profitability of firms already competing in that industry. Thus, the industries heavily protected against new entrants by high direct costs (e.g., through required equity or capital contributions) and high indirect costs (e.g., by restricting individuals who can establish FIs) of entry produce bigger profits for existing firms than those in which entry is relatively easy (see Chapters 22 and 23). In addition, regulations (such as the Financial Securities Modernization Act of 1999) define the scope of permitted activities under a given charter (see Chapter 21). The broader the set of financial service activities permitted under a given charter, the more valuable that charter is likely to be. Thus, barriers to entry and regulations pertaining to the

---

[16] The FFIEC also publishes aggregate statistics and analysis of CRA and HMDA data. The Federal Reserve and other regulators also rate bank compliance. For example, in 2003 the Federal Reserve judged 14.0 percent of the banks examined to be outstanding in CRA compliance, 86.0 percent as satisfactory, and 0.0 percent as needing to improve or as being in noncompliance.

[17] There have been a number of moves to extend these regulations to hedge funds, which have traditionally been outside SEC regulations and the securities acts as long as they have fewer than 100 "sophisticated" investors. It has been believed until recently that large sophisticated investors do not need such protections. However, recent scandals and failures relating to hedge funds and their investments—such as the failure of Long Term Capital Management in 1998 and its subsequent bailout—appear to be changing lawmakers' and regulators' perceptions.

scope of permitted activities affect the *charter value* of an FI and the size of its net regulatory burden.[18]

Concept Questions

1. Why should more regulation be imposed on FIs than on other types of private corporations?
2. Define the concept of net regulatory burden.
3. What six major types of regulation do FIs face?

THE CHANGING DYNAMICS OF SPECIALNESS

At any moment in time, each FI supplies a set of financial services (brokerage related, asset transformation related, or both) and is subject to a given net regulatory burden. As the demands for the special features of financial services change as a result of changing preferences and technology, one or more areas of the financial services industry become less profitable.[19] Similarly, changing regulations can increase or decrease the net regulatory burden faced in supplying financial services in any given area. These demand, cost, and regulatory pressures are reflected in changing market shares in different financial service areas as some contract and others expand. Clearly, an FI seeking to survive and prosper must be flexible enough to move to growing financial service areas and away from those that are contracting. If regulatory activity restrictions inhibit or reduce the flexibility with which FIs can alter their product mix, this will reduce their competitive ability and the efficiency with which financial services are delivered. That is, activity barriers within the financial services industry may reduce the ability to diversify and potentially add to the net regulatory burden faced by FIs.

Trends in the United States

In Table 1–3 we show the changing shares of total assets in the U.S. financial services industry from 1860 to 2003. A number of important trends are evident: Most apparent is the decline in the total share of depository institutions since the Second World War. Specifically, the share of commercial banks declined from 55.9 to 35.4 percent between 1948 and 2003, while the share of thrifts (savings banks, savings associations, and credit unions) fell from 12.3 to 10.2 percent over the same period. Similarly, life insurance companies also witnessed a secular decline in their share, from 24.3 to 17.4 percent. Thus, services provided by depository institutions (payment services, transaction costs services, information cost) have become relatively less significant as a portion of all services provided by FIs.

The most dramatically increasing trend is the rising share of investment companies, with investment companies (mutual funds and money market mutual funds) increasing their share from 1.3 to 18.2 percent between 1948 and 2003. Investment companies differ from banks and insurance companies in that they give savers cheaper access to the direct securities markets. They do so by exploiting the comparative advantages of size and diversification, with the transformation of financial claims, such as maturity transformation, a lesser concern. Thus, open-ended

---

[18] Indeed, the higher an FI's charter value, the lower the incentive it has to take risk. See, for example, A. Saunders and B. Wilson, "An Analysis of the Charter Value and Its Risk Constraining Incentives," *Journal of Financial Services Research* 19 (April/June 2001), pp. 185–96.

[19] See, for example, F. S. Mishkin and P. E. Strahan, "What Will Technology Do to Financial Structure?" NBER Working Paper, no. 6842, January 1999.

TABLE 1–3   Percentage Shares of Assets of Financial Institutions in the United States, 1860–2003

	1860	1880	1900	1912	1922	1929	1939	1948	1960	1970	1980	2000	2003*
Commercial banks	71.4%	60.6%	62.9%	64.5%	63.3%	53.7%	51.2%	55.9%	38.2%	37.9%	34.8%	35.6%	35.4%
Thrift institutions	17.8	22.8	18.2	14.8	13.9	14.0	13.6	12.3	19.7	20.4	21.4	10.0	10.2
Insurance companies	10.7	13.9	13.8	16.6	16.7	18.6	27.2	24.3	23.8	18.9	16.1	16.8	17.4
Investment companies	—	—	—	—	0.0	2.4	1.9	1.3	2.9	3.5	3.6	17.0	18.2
Pension funds	—	—	0.0	0.0	0.0	0.7	2.1	3.1	9.7	13.0	17.4	10.7	9.4
Finance companies	—	0.0	0.0	0.0	0.0	2.0	2.2	2.0	4.6	4.8	5.1	7.9	6.5
Securities brokers and dealers	0.0	0.0	3.8	3.0	5.3	8.1	1.5	1.0	1.1	1.2	1.1	1.5	2.3
Mortgage companies	0.0	2.7	1.3	1.2	0.8	0.6	0.3	0.1	†	†	0.4	0.3	0.2
Real estate investment trusts	—	—	—	—	—	—	—	—	0.0	0.3	0.1	0.2	0.4
Total (percent)	100.0%	100.0%	100.0%	100.0%	100.0%	100.0%	100.0%	100.0%	100.0%	100.0%	100.0%	100.0%	100.0%
Total (trillion dollars)	.001	.005	.016	.034	.075	.123	.129	.281	.596	1.328	4.025	14.75	16.59

*As of March 2003.
†Data not available.
Source: Randall Kroszner, "The Evolution of Universal Banking and Its Regulation in Twentieth Century America," Chapter 3 in Anthony Saunders and Ingo Walter, eds., *Universal Banking Financial System Design Reconsidered* (Burr Ridge, IL: Irwin, 1996); and Federal Reserve Board, "Flow of Fund Accounts," various issues. *www.federalreserve.gov*

mutual funds buy stocks and bonds directly in financial markets and issue savers shares whose value is linked in a direct pro rata fashion to the value of the mutual fund's asset portfolio. Similarly, money market mutual funds invest in short-term financial assets such as commercial paper, CDs, and Treasury bills and issue shares linked directly to the value of the underlying portfolio. To the extent that these funds efficiently diversify, they also offer price-risk protection and liquidity services.

The maturity and return characteristics of the financial claims issued by mutual funds closely reflect the maturities of the direct equity and debt securities portfolios in which they invest. In contrast, banks, thrifts, and insurance companies have lower correlations between their asset portfolio maturities and the promised maturity of their liabilities. Thus, banks may partially fund a 10-year commercial loan with demand deposits; a thrift may fund 30-year conventional mortgages with three-month time deposits.[20]

To the extent that the financial services market is efficient and these trends reflect the forces of demand and supply, they indicate a current trend: Savers increasingly prefer the denomination intermediation and information services provided by mutual funds. These FIs provide investments that closely mimic diversified

[20] The close links between the performance of their assets and liabilities have led to mutual funds and pension funds being called "transparent" intermediaries. By contrast, the lower correlation between the performance of the assets and liabilities of banks, thrifts, and insurance companies has led to their being called "opaque" intermediaries. See Steven A. Ross, "Institutional Markets, Financial Marketing, and Financial Innovation," *Journal of Finance*, July 1989, pp. 541–56.

Ethical **Dilemmas**

investments in the *direct* securities markets over the transformed financial claims offered by traditional FIs. This trend may also indicate that the net regulatory burden on traditional FIs—such as banks and insurance companies—is higher than that on investment companies. As a result, traditional FIs are unable to produce their services as cost efficiently as they could previously. As a result, it is increasingly important that FI managers deal with changing trends and reconsider how best to exploit any remaining competitive advantages to keep the net benefit of regulation positive for their FIs.

In addition to a secular decline in the use of services provided by depository institutions and insurance companies and an increase in the services provided by investment banks and mutual funds during the late 1900s, the early 2000s saw an overall weakening of public trust and confidence in the ethics followed by financial institutions. Specifically, tremendous publicity was generated concerning conflicts of interest in a number of financial institutions between analysts' research recommendations on stocks to buy or not buy and whether these firms played a role in underwriting the securities of the firms the analysts were recommending. As a result, several highly publicized securities violations resulted in criminal cases brought against securities law violators by state and federal prosecutors. In particular, the New York State attorney general forced Merrill Lynch to pay a $100 million penalty because of allegations that Merrill Lynch brokers gave investors overly optimistic reports about the stock of its investment banking clients. By year-end 2002, $1.4 billion of fines were assessed against financial institutions as a result of a broad investigation into whether securities firms misled small investors with faulty research and stock recommendations (see the Ethical Dilemmas box). Such

FIGURE 1–3
Equity Trading on the Internet

Source: Investment Company Institute, "Equity Ownership in America," 2002. *www.ici.org*

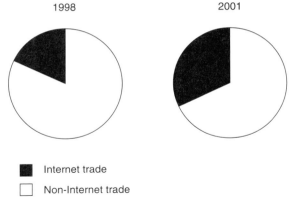

1998   2001

■ Internet trade
□ Non-Internet trade

allegations of securities law violations led to a loss in public trust and confidence in many sectors of the FI industry.

Future Trends

The growth of mutual funds coupled with the weakening of public trust and confidence (amid a multitude of regulatory investigations into the practices of investment advisors, brokers, and banks), and with investors' recent focus on direct investments in primary securities, may together signal the beginning of a secular trend away from intermediation as the most efficient mechanism for savers to channel funds to borrowers. While this trend may reflect changed investors' preferences toward risk and return, it may also reflect a decline in the relative costs of direct securities investment versus investment via FIs. This decline in costs has led to many FI products being "commoditized" and sold directly in financial markets; for example, many options initially offered over the counter by FIs eventually migrate to the public option markets as trading volume grows and trading terms become standardized. As Merton has noted, financial markets "tend to be efficient institutional alternatives to intermediaries when the products have standardized terms, can serve a large number of customers and are well-enough understood for transactors to be comfortable in assessing their prices . . . intermediaries are better suited for low volume products."[21]

Recent regulatory changes in the United States, such as the Financial Services Modernization Act of 1999, are also alleviating the net regulatory burden by allowing FIs to move across traditional product boundaries and lines (see Chapter 21). The result has been a number of mergers and acquisitions between commercial banks and investment banks, such as Citicorp's $83 billion merger with Travelers Group (which operated extensive insurance activities and owned Smith Barney and Salomon Brothers) and UBS's (the Swiss commercial bank) purchase of Paine Webber (the U.S. investment bank). At the same time, banking organizations (such as bank holding companies) are getting bigger via mergers (such as the mergers of J. P. Morgan Chase and Bank One) and other forms of consolidation. Larger size accommodates this expansion in service offerings while providing an enhanced potential to diversify risk and lower (average) costs (see Chapter 22).[22]

[21] R. Merton, "A Functional Perspective of Financial Intermediation," *Financial Management,* Summer 1995, p. 26.

[22] The number of banks in the United States dropped from 12,230 in 1990 to 7,833 in the second quarter of 2003, a decline of 36 percent. This decline is even more dramatic when it is realized that 1,785 new bank charters were granted in the 1990–2003 period.

TABLE 1–4
U.S. Private Placements (in billions of dollars)

	1990	1995	2000	2001	2002
144A placements	3.7	71.3	325.5	513.7	348.8
Total private placements	128.6	132.6	483.2	613.6	416.9

Source: *Investment Dealer's Digest*, various issues; and Thompson Financial Securities Data. *www.tfibcm.com*

As a result, bank profitability in the late 1990s and early 2000s has been considerably better than in the early 1990s—despite the effects of a recession, terrorist attacks on the World Trade Center and the Pentagon in September 2001, and numerous, highly publicized actions involving conflicts of interest including loans to companies like Enron (the second largest bankruptcy in U.S. history) (see Chapter 2).

Further, direct financial markets are also evolving fast; because of technological advances, the costs of direct access to financial markets by savers are ever falling and the relative benefits to the individual savers of investing through FIs are narrowing.

e-trading
Buying and selling shares on the Internet.

The ability to reduce transaction costs by **e-trading** on the Internet rather than using a traditional stockbroker and paying brokerage fees has reduced the need for FIs to perform these services. Figure 1–3 shows the increased use of the Internet to conduct equity trades over the period 1998 to 2001. In addition, a number of companies allow investors to buy their stock directly without using a broker. Among well-known companies that have instituted such stock purchase plans are Bell Atlantic, Bell/South, IBM, and Walt Disney. A final example is the private placement market, where securities are sold directly by corporations to investors without underwriters and with a minimum of public disclosure about the issuing firm. Privately placed bonds and equity have traditionally been the most illiquid of securities, with only the very largest FIs or institutional investors being able or willing to hold them in the

www.sec.gov

absence of a secondary market. In April 1990, the Securities and Exchange Commission amended Regulation 144A. This allowed large investors to begin trading these privately placed securities among themselves even though, in general, privately placed securities do not satisfy the stringent disclosure and informational requirements imposed by the SEC on approved publicly registered issues. While the SEC defined the large investors able to trade privately placed securities as those with assets of $100 million or more—which excludes all but the very wealthiest household savers—it is reasonable to ask how long this size restriction will stay in effect. As they get more sophisticated and the costs of information acquisition fall, smaller savers will increasingly demand access to the private placement market. In such a world, savers would have a choice between not only the secondary securities from FIs and the primary securities publicly offered by corporations but also publicly offered (registered) securities and privately offered (unregistered) securities.[23] Recent trends in the 144A Private Placement market are shown in Table 1–4.

Global Issues

In addition to these domestic trends, U.S. FIs must now compete not only with other domestic FIs but increasingly with foreign FIs that provide services (such as payment services and denomination intermediation) comparable to those of U.S. FIs. For example, Table 1–5 lists the 10 largest banks in the world, measured by total assets at the start of 2003. Notice that only 2 of the top 10 banks are U.S.

[23] Moreover, in 1999 the Internet gave small savers direct access to IPOs via a number of newly founded cyberspace underwriting firms. Until this technological advance, IPOs had been the preserve of mostly institutional buyers.

TABLE 1–5
The 10 Largest Banks in the World (in millions of dollars)

Source: *The Banker,* July 2003. *www.thebanker.com*

	Total Assets
1. Citigroup (United States)	$1,097,000
2. Mizuho Financial Group (Japan)	945,688
3. UBS (Switzerland)	825,000
4. Sumitomo Mitsui Financial (Japan)	802,674
5. Deutsche Bank (Germany)	794,984
6. Bank of Tokyo-Mitsubishi Tokyo Financial (Japan)	789,495
7. HSBC Holdings (United Kingdom)	746,335
8. J. P. Morgan Chase (United States)	745,156
9. BNP Paribas (France)	744,627
10. HypoVereinsbank (Germany)	724,540

banks. Table 1–6 lists foreign bank offices' assets and liabilities held in the United States from 1992 through June 2003. Total foreign bank assets over this period increased from $509.3 billion in 1992 to $806.3 billion in 1998 before falling back to $750.1 billion in 2003.

The world's six most active banks, based on the percent of their assets held outside their home countries, are listed in Table 1–7. These include the two big Swiss banks as well as one U.S. financial institution (American Express Bank). Interestingly, although in 2003 Japanese banks occupied 3 of the top 10 places of banks in the world in terms of asset size (see Table 1–5), they are absent from the list of banks with the most active international operations. Indeed, domestic problems, including a record number of bad loans (especially in real estate), and a recession, have induced Japanese banks to contract their foreign assets and international activities, as well as to merge. For example, the three-way merger between Industrial Bank of Japan, Fuji Bank, and Dai-Ichi Kangyo Bank in 2000 created the

TABLE 1–6
Foreign Bank Offices' Assets and Liabilities Held in the United States (in billions of dollars)

Source: Federal Reserve Board, "Flow of Fund Accounts," Statistical Releases, September 2003. *www.federalreserve.gov*

	1992	1994	1996	1998	2000	2003*
Financial Assets						
Total financial assets	$509.3	$589.7	$714.8	$806.3	$779.9	$750.1
Financial Liabilities						
Total financial liabilities	519.3	602.8	731.9	828.6	808.9	789.8

*As of June 2003.

TABLE 1–7
Top Global Banks

Source: *The Banker,* "Top 50 Global Banks," February 2003. *www.thebanker.com*

Banks	Home Country	Percentage of Overseas Business*
1. American Express Bank	United States	86.17%
2. UBS	Switzerland	84.41
3. Arab Banking Corporation	Bahrain	82.33
4. Credit Suisse Group	Switzerland	79.62
5. Standard Chartered	United Kingdom	69.64
6. Deutsche Bank	Germany	66.44

*Overseas business refers to the percentage of assets banks hold outside their home country.

world's largest banking group, Mizuho Financial Group, with assets of over $1,394 billion.[24] Mizuho fell to the number two spot, measured by asset size, in 2003.

Concept Questions

1. Is the share of bank and thrift assets growing as a proportion of total FI assets in the United States?
2. What are the fastest-growing FIs in the United States?
3. Define privately placed securities.
4. Describe the global challenges facing U.S. FIs in the early 2000s.

Internet Exercise

Go to the Web site of the Board of Governors of the Federal Reserve, and find the latest information available for foreign bank offices assets and liabilities held in the United States.

Go to the Board of Governors of the Federal Reserve Web site at **www.federalreserve.gov**. Click on "Economic Research and Data." Click on "Statistics: Releases and Historical Data." Under Quarterly, click on "Flow of Funds Accounts of the United States: Releases." Click on the most recent date. Click on "Level Tables." This will download a file on to your computer that will contain the most recent information in Table L.111.

Summary

This chapter described the various factors and forces impacting financial intermediaries and the specialness of the services they provide. These forces suggest that in the future, FIs that have historically relied on making profits by performing traditional special functions, such as asset transformation and the provision of liquidity services, will need to expand into selling financial services that interface with direct security market transactions, such as asset management, insurance, and underwriting services. This is not to say that specialized or niche FIs cannot survive but rather that only the most efficient FIs will prosper as the competitive value of a specialized FI charter declines.

The major theme of this book is the measurement and management of FI risks. In particular, although we might categorize or group FIs and label them life insurance companies, banks, finance companies, and so on, in fact, they face risks that are more common than different. Specifically, all the FIs described in this and the next five chapters (1) hold some assets that are potentially subject to default or credit risk and (2) tend to mismatch the maturities of their balance sheets to a greater or lesser extent and are thus exposed to interest rate risk. Moreover, all are exposed to some degree of saver withdrawal or liquidity risk depending on the type of claims sold to liability holders. And most are exposed to some type of underwriting risk, whether through the sale of securities or by issuing various types of credit guarantees on or off the balance sheet. Finally, all are exposed to operating cost risks because the production of financial services requires the use of real resources and back-office support systems.

In Chapters 7 through 28 of this textbook, we investigate the ways managers of FIs are measuring and managing this inventory of risks to produce the best return-risk trade-off for shareholders in an increasingly competitive and contestable market environment.

---

[24] It might also be noted that regulation is becoming more international as well—especially in Europe. See, for example, X. Vives, "Restructuring Regulation in the European Monetary Union," *Journal of Financial Services Research* 19 (February 2001), pp. 57–82.

Questions and Problems

1. What are five risks common to financial institutions?
2. Explain how economic transactions between household savers of funds and corporate users of funds would occur in a world without financial intermediaries.
3. Identify and explain three economic disincentives that probably would dampen the flow of funds between household savers of funds and corporate users of funds in an economic world without financial intermediaries.
4. Identify and explain the two functions in which FIs may specialize that would enable the smooth flow of funds from household savers to corporate users.
5. In what sense are the financial claims of FIs considered *secondary securities*, while the financial claims of commercial corporations are considered *primary securities?* How does the transformation process, or intermediation, reduce the risk, or economic disincentives, to savers?
6. Explain how financial institutions act as delegated monitors. What secondary benefits often accrue to the entire financial system because of this monitoring process?
7. What are five general areas of FI specialness that are caused by providing various services to sectors of the economy?
8. How do FIs solve the information and related *agency costs* when household savers invest directly in securities issued by corporations? What are agency costs?
9. What often is the benefit to the lenders, borrowers, and financial markets in general of the solution to the information problem provided by large financial institutions?
10. How do FIs alleviate the problem of liquidity risk faced by investors who wish to invest in the securities of corporations?
11. How do financial institutions help individual savers diversify their portfolio risks? Which type of financial institution is best able to achieve this goal?
12. How can financial institutions invest in high-risk assets with funding provided by low-risk liabilities from savers?
13. How can individual savers use financial institutions to reduce the transaction costs of investing in financial assets?
14. What is *maturity intermediation?* What are some of the ways the risks of maturity intermediation are managed by financial intermediaries?
15. What are five areas of institution-specific FI specialness, and which types of institutions are most likely to be the service providers?
16. How do depository institutions such as commercial banks assist in the implementation and transmission of monetary policy?
17. What is meant by credit allocation regulation? What social benefit is this type of regulation intended to provide?
18. Which intermediaries best fulfill the intergenerational wealth transfer function? What is this wealth transfer process?
19. What are two of the most important payment services provided by financial institutions? To what extent do these services efficiently provide benefits to the economy?
20. What is denomination intermediation? How do FIs assist in this process?
21. What is *negative externality?* In what ways do the existence of negative externalities justify the extra regulatory attention received by financial institutions?
22. If financial markets operated perfectly and costlessly, would there be a need for financial intermediaries?

23. What is mortgage redlining?
24. Why are FIs among the most regulated sectors in the world? When is the net regulatory burden positive?
25. What forms of protection and regulation do the regulators of FIs impose to ensure their safety and soundness?
26. In the transmission of monetary policy, what is the difference between *inside money* and *outside money?* How does the Federal Reserve Board try to control the amount of inside money? How can this regulatory position create a cost for depository financial institutions?
27. What are some examples of credit allocation regulation? How can this attempt to create social benefits create costs to a private institution?
28. What is the purpose of the Home Mortgage Disclosure Act? What are the social benefits desired from the legislation? How does the implementation of this legislation create a net regulatory burden on financial institutions?
29. What legislation has been passed specifically to protect investors who use investment banks directly or indirectly to purchase securities? Give some examples of the types of abuses for which protection is provided.
30. How do regulations regarding barriers to entry and the scope of permitted activities affect the *charter value* of financial institutions?
31. What reasons have been given for the growth of pension funds and investment companies at the expense of "traditional" banks and insurance companies?
32. What are some of the methods banking organizations have employed to reduce the net regulatory burden? What has been the effect on profitability?
33. What characteristics of financial products are necessary for financial markets to become efficient alternatives to financial intermediaries? Can you give some examples of the commoditization of products which were previously the sole property of financial institutions?
34. In what way has Regulation 144A of the Securities and Exchange Commission provided an incentive to the process of financial institution disintermediation?

Web Questions

35. Go to the Federal Reserve Board's Web site at **www.federalreserve.gov**. Find the latest figures for M1, M2, and M3 using the following steps. Click on "Economic Research and Data." Click on "Statistics: Releases and Historical Data." Click on "Money Stock Measures, *Releases*." Click on the most recent date. This downloads a file onto your computer that contains the relevant data. By what percentage have these measures of the money supply grown over the past year?
36. Go to the Federal Reserve Board's Web site at **www.federalreserve.gov**. Find the latest figures for financial assets outstanding at various types of financial institutions using the following steps. Click on "Economic Research and Data." Click on "Statistics: Releases and Historical Data." Click on "Flow of Funds Accounts of the United States, *Releases*." Click on the most recent date. Click on "Level tables." This downloads a file onto your computer that contains the relevant data. How has the percent of financial assets held by commercial banks changed since that listed in Table 1–3 for March 2003?

S&P Questions

37. Go to the Standard & Poor's Market Insight Web site at **www.mhhe.com/
    edumarketinsight**. Use the following steps to identify the Industry Description
    and Industry Constituents for the following industries: Diversified Banks,
    Investment Banking & Brokerage, Life & Health Insurance, and Property &
    Casualty Insurance. Click on "Educational Version of Market Insight." Enter
    your Site ID and click on "Login." Click on "Industry." From the Industry list,
    select (one at a time) "Banks," "Diversified Financial Services," "Life & Health
    Insurance," and "Property & Casualty." Click on "Go!" Click on "Industry
    Profile" and separately, "Industry Constituents."

38. Go to the Standard & Poor's Market Insight Web site at **www.mhhe.com/
    edumarketinsight**. Use the following steps to identify the Industry Financial
    Highlights for the following industries: Diversified Banks, Investment Bank-
    ing & Brokerage, Life & Health Insurance, and Property & Casualty Insurance.
    Click on "Educational Version of Market Insight." Enter your Site ID and click
    on "Login." Click on "Industry." From the Industry list, select (one at a time)
    "Banks," "Diversified Financial Services," "Life & Health Insurance," and
    "Property & Casualty." Click on any/all of the items listed under "Industry
    Financial Highlights."

Pertinent Web Sites

The Banker	www.thebanker.com
Board of Governors of the Federal Reserve	www.federalreserve.gov
Federal Deposit Insurance Corporation	www.fdic.gov
Federal Financial Institutions Examination Council	www.ffiec.gov
Investment Company Institute	www.ici.org
Office of the Comptroller of the Currency	www.occ.treas.gov
Securities and Exchange Commission	www.sec.gov
Securities Investors Protection Corporation	www.sipc.org
The Wall Street Journal	www.wsj.com
Thompson Financial Securities Data	www.tfibcm.com

Chapter Two

The Financial Services Industry: Depository Institutions

INTRODUCTION

The theme of this book is that the products sold and the risks faced by modern financial institutions are becoming increasingly similar, as are the techniques used to measure and manage those risks. To illustrate this, Tables 2–1A and 2–1B contrast the products sold by the financial services industry in 1950 with those sold in 2004. In this chapter we begin by describing three major FI groups—commercial banks, savings institutions, and credit unions—which are also called depository institutions because a significant proportion of their funds comes from customer deposits. In Chapters 3 through 6 other (nondepository) FIs will be described. We focus on four major characteristics of each group: (1) size, structure, and composition of the industry group, (2) balance sheets and recent trends, (3) regulation, and (4) industry performance. Figure 2–1 presents a very simplified product-based balance sheet for depository institutions. Notice that depository institutions offer products to their customers on both sides of their balance sheets (loans on the asset side and deposits on the liability side). This joint-product nature of the depository institution business creates special challenges for management as they deal with the many risks facing these institutions. These risks will be discussed later, in Chapters 8 through 28.

Table 2–2 lists the largest U.S. commercial banks and savings institutions in 2003. The ranking is by asset size and reflects the dramatic trend toward consolidation and mergers among financial service firms at the end of the 1990s. The largest bank is Citigroup, created from the merger of Citicorp and Travelers Insurance; the second-largest is J. P. Morgan Chase, created from the merger of J. P. Morgan and Chase Manhattan; and the third-largest is Bank of America, created by the merger of the old BankAmerica and NationsBank.[1] Note that Washington Mutual is the largest savings institution in the country—reflecting over 20 mergers and acquisitions by

---

[1] It should be noted that the acquisition of Bank One by J. P. Morgan Chase and that of FleetBoston Financial by Bank of America are currently pending (as of early 2004). The acquisition of these institutions by J. P. Morgan Chase and Bank of America will significantly increase the size of these institutions to over $1 trillion each.

TABLE 2–1A   Products Sold by the U.S. Financial Services Industry, 1950

Institution	Function							
	Payment Services	Savings Products	Fiduciary Services	Lending		Underwriting Issuance of		Insurance and Risk Management Products
				Business	Consumer	Equity	Debt	
Depository institutions	X	X	X	X	X			
Insurance companies		X		*				X
Finance companies				*	X			
Securities firms		X	X			X	X	
Pension funds		X						
Mutual funds		X						

*Minor involvement.

TABLE 2–1B   Products Sold by the U.S. Financial Services Industry, 2004

Institution	Function							
	Payment Services	Savings Products	Fiduciary Services	Lending		Underwriting Issuance of		Insurance and Risk Management Products
				Business	Consumer	Equity	Debt	
Depository institutions	X	X	X	X	X	X	X	X
Insurance companies	X	X	X	X	X	X	X	X
Finance companies	X	X	X	X	X	†	†	X
Securities firms	X	X	X	X	X	X	X	X
Pension funds		X	X	X				X
Mutual funds	X	X	X					X

†Selective involvement via affiliates

TABLE 2–2
Largest Depository Institutions, 2003 (banks and savings institutions ranked by total assets on December 31, 2003, in billions of dollars)

Source: Annual Reports, Spring 2004.

Company	Assets
Citigroup	$1,208.9
J. P. Morgan Chase*	770.9
Bank of America†	736.4
Wells Fargo	393.9
Wachovia	388.0
Bank One*	326.6
Washington Mutual	275.2
FleetBoston Financial†	200.2
U.S. Bancorp	188.8
Sun Trust Banks	181.0

*Merger pending as of January 2004.
†Merger pending as of October 2003.

FIGURE 2–1
A Simple Depository Institution Balance Sheet

Depository Institutions

Assets	Liabilities and Equity
Loans	Deposits
Other assets	Other liabilities and equity

the Seattle-based institution since 1990, including HF Ahmanson, then the nation's second-largest savings institution.

COMMERCIAL BANKS

commercial bank
A bank that accepts deposits and makes consumer, commercial, and real estate loans.

Commercial banks make up the largest group of depository institutions measured by asset size. They perform functions similar to those of savings institutions and credit unions; that is, they accept deposits (liabilities) and make loans (assets). However, they differ in their composition of assets and liabilities, which are much more varied. Commercial bank liabilities usually include several types of nondeposit sources of funds, while their loans are broader in range, including consumer, commercial, and real estate loans. Commercial banking activity is also regulated separately from the activities of savings institutions and credit unions. Within the banking industry the structure and composition of assets and liabilities also vary significantly across banks of different asset sizes. For example, as shown in Figure 2–2, small banks make proportionately fewer commercial and industrial (C&I) loans and more real estate loans than do big banks.

Size, Structure, and Composition of the Industry

At the beginning of 2004 the United States had 7,769 commercial banks. Even though this may seem a large number, in fact, the number of banks has been shrinking. For example, in 1985 there were 14,416 banks, and in 1989 there were 12,744. Figure 2–3 illustrates the number of bank mergers, bank failures, and new charters for the period 1980 through 2003. Notice that much of the change in the size, structure, and composition of this industry is the result of mergers and acquisitions. It was not until the 1980s and 1990s that regulators (such as the Federal Reserve or state banking authorities) allowed banks to merge with other banks across state lines (interstate mergers), and it has only been since 1994 that Congress has passed legislation (the Reigle-Neal Act) easing branching by banks across state lines. The result has been the announcements of the largest mergers and acquisitions ever, such as J. P. Morgan's acquisition of Chase Manhattan (for $33.6 billion) in September 2000, Norwest's acquisition of Wells Fargo (for $34.3 billion) in June 1998, Bank of America's acquisition of FleetBoston Financial (for $49.3 billion) in October 2003,

FIGURE 2–2
Breakdown of Loan Portfolios

Source: Federal Deposit Insurance Corporation, December 2003. *www.fdic.gov*

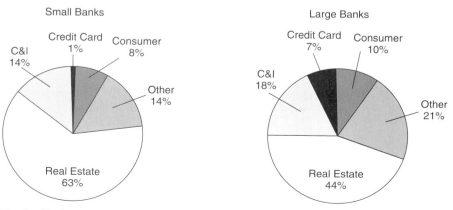

Note: Small banks are defined as banks with assets less than $1 billion. Large banks are defined as banks with assets of $1 billion or more.

FIGURE 2–3 Structural Changes in the Number of Commercial Banks, 1980–2003

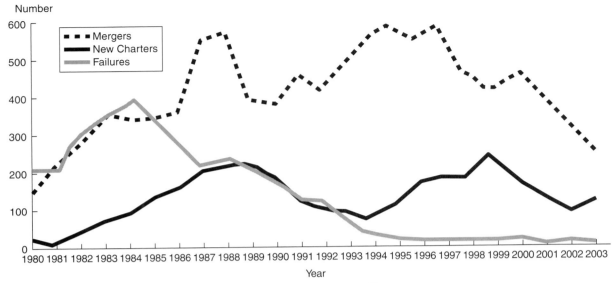

Source: Federal Deposit Insurance Corporation. *Quarterly Banking Profile*. Various issues. *www.fdic.gov*

TABLE 2–3 U.S. Bank Asset Concentration, 1984 versus 2003

	2003				1984			
	Number	Percent of Total	Assets*	Percent of Total	Number	Percent of Total	Assets*	Percent of Total
All FDIC-insured Commercial Banks	7,769		$7,602.5		14,483		$2,508.9	
1. Under $100 million	3,911	50.3%	200.7	2.6%	12,044	83.2%	404.2	16.1%
2. $100 million–$1 billion	3,434	44.2	910.0	12.0	2,161	14.9	513.9	20.5
3. $1 billion–$10 billion	341	4.4	947.3	12.5	254	1.7	725.9	28.9
4. $10 billion or more	83	1.1	5,544.5	72.9	24	0.2	864.8	34.5

*In billions of dollars.
Source: *FDIC Quarterly Banking Profile*, fourth quarter 1984 and 2003. *www.fdic.gov*

J. P. Morgan Chase's acquisition of Bank One (for $60.0 billion) in January 2004, and BankAmerica's acquisition of NationsBank (for $61.6 billion) in April 1998. Finally, it has only been since 1987 that banks have possessed (limited) powers to underwrite corporate securities. Full authority to enter the investment banking (and insurance) business was received only with the passage of the Financial Services Modernization Act in 1999. Thus, commercial banks may now merge with investment banks (and insurance companies). In subsequent chapters, we discuss the impact that changing regulations as well as technological advances have had on the drop in the number of commercial banks (e.g., technology changes [Chapter 14] regulatory changes [Chapters 21 and 22], and competition[2] [Chapter 22]).

A comparison of asset concentration by bank size (see Table 2–3) indicates that the consolidations in banking appear to have reduced the asset share of the smallest

[2] In particular, Chapter 22 provides a detailed discussion of the merger wave that swept the commercial banking industry in the 1990s and early 2000s.

community banks
Banks that specialize in retail or consumer banking.

banks (under $1 billion) from 36.6 percent in 1984 to 14.6 percent in 2003. These smaller or **community banks**—under $1 billion in asset size—tend to specialize in retail or consumer banking, such as providing residential mortgages and consumer loans and accessing the local deposit base. Clearly, this group of banks is decreasing in both number and importance.

The relative asset share of the largest banks (over $1 billion in assets), on the other hand, increased from 63.4 percent in 1984 to 85.4 percent in 2003. The majority of banks in the two largest size classes are often either **regional or superregional banks**. They engage in a more complete array of wholesale commercial banking activities, encompassing consumer and residential lending as well as commercial and industrial lending (C&I loans), both regionally and nationally. In addition, the big banks access markets for purchased funds—such as the interbank or **federal funds market**—to finance their lending and investment activities. However, some of the very biggest banks often have the separate title **money center banks**. Currently, five banking organizations constitute the money center bank group: Bank of New York, Deutsche Bank (through its U.S. acquisition of Bankers Trust), Citigroup, J. P. Morgan Chase, and HSBC Bank USA (formerly Republic NY Corporation).[3,4] This number has been declining because of the megamergers, discussed earlier.

regional or superregional banks
Banks that engage in a complete array of wholesale commercial banking activities.

federal funds market
An interbank market for short-term borrowing and lending of bank reserves.

money center banks
Banks that have a heavy reliance on nondeposit or borrowed sources of funds.

It is important to note that asset or lending size does not necessarily make a bank a money center bank. Thus, the new Bank of America Corporation, with $736 billion in assets in 2003 (the third-largest U.S. bank organization, created out of its merger with NationsBank), is not a money center bank, while Bank of New York (with only $96 billion in assets) is. What makes a bank a money center bank is partly location and partly its heavy reliance on nondeposit or borrowed sources of funds.[5] In fact, because of its extensive retail branch network,[6] Bank of America tends to be a net supplier of funds on the interbank market (federal funds market). By contrast, money center banks have few retail branches and rely almost entirely on wholesale and borrowed funds as sources of assets or liabilities. Money center banks are also major participants in foreign currency markets and are therefore subject to foreign exchange risk (see Chapter 15).

spread
The difference between lending and deposit rates.

The bigger banks tend to fund themselves in national markets and lend to larger corporations. This means that their **spreads** (i.e., the difference between lending and deposit rates) in the past (the mid-1990s) often were narrower than those of smaller regional banks, which were more sheltered from competition in highly localized markets. As a result, the largest banks' return on assets (ROA) was below that of smaller banks (see Table 2–4). However, as the barriers to interstate competition and expansion in banking have fallen in recent years and as large banks have focused more on off-balance-sheet activities to generate income (see below), the largest banks' ROAs as well as returns on equity (ROEs) have outperformed those of the smallest banks, especially those with assets under $100 million (see Table 2–4). Appendix 2A shows how a bank's ROE can be decomposed to examine

---

[3] Bank One's inclusion results from its acquisition of First Chicago in 1998. J. P. Morgan Chase and Bank One announced a merger in January 2004. Bankers Trust was purchased by Deutsche Bank (a German bank) in 1998. The Bankers Trust name, however, has been retained for U.S. operations. Republic NY Corporation was purchased by HSBC (a British bank) in 1999. Republic NY Bank has been retained for U.S. operations under the name HSBC Bank USA.

[4] These banking organizations are mostly holding companies that own and control the shares of a bank or banks.

[5] A money center bank normally is headquartered in New York or Chicago. These are the traditional national and regional centers for correspondent banking services offered to smaller community banks.

[6] In 2003 Bank of America had over 4,500 branches nationwide.

TABLE 2–4
ROA and ROE of
Banks by Size,
1990–2003

Source: Federal Deposit Insurance Corporation, March
2004. *www.fdic.gov*

Percentage Return on Assets (insured commercial banks by consolidated assets)

Year	All Banks	$0–$100 million	$100 million– $1 billion	$1 billion– $10 billion	$10 billion+
1990	0.49%	0.79%	0.78%	0.76%	0.38%
1995	1.17	1.18	1.25	1.28	1.10
1996	1.19	1.23	1.29	1.31	1.10
1997	1.24	1.25	1.39	1.30	1.18
1998	1.19	1.14	1.31	1.52	1.08
1999	1.31	1.01	1.34	1.48	1.28
2000	1.19	1.01	1.28	1.29	1.16
2001	1.16	0.91	1.20	1.31	1.13
2002	1.33	1.02	1.26	1.53	1.32
2003	1.40	0.94	1.27	1.46	1.42

Percentage Return on Equity (insured commercial banks by consolidated assets)

Year	All Banks	$0–$100 million	$100 million– $1 billion	$1 billion– $10 billion	$10 billion+
1990	7.64%	9.02%	9.95%	10.25%	6.68%
1995	14.68	11.37	13.48	15.04	15.60
1996	14.40	11.69	13.63	14.82	14.93
1997	14.71	11.57	14.50	14.30	15.32
1998	13.95	10.15	13.57	15.96	13.82
1999	15.34	9.07	14.24	16.02	15.97
2000	14.07	9.09	13.56	14.57	14.42
2001	13.10	8.07	12.24	13.77	13.43
2002	14.53	9.08	12.85	14.88	15.06
2003	15.31	8.19	12.80	14.00	16.37

the different underlying sources of profitability. This decomposition of ROE is often referred to as DuPont analysis.

The U.S. banking system is unique in that it consists of not only very big banks
but also a large number of relatively small community banks. This unique banking
structure is largely the result of a legal framework that until recently restricted
banks' abilities to diversify geographically. Over time, with regulatory change (see
below) and financial innovation, large banks have become complex organizations
engaged in a wide range of activities worldwide. These large banks provide a variety of services to their customers, but often rely on factual financial information,
computer models, and centralized decision making as the basis for conducting
business. Small banks focus more on relationship banking, often basing decisions
on personal knowledge of customers' creditworthiness and an understanding of
business conditions in the communities they serve. As discussed above, with increased merger activity over the last 20 years, the number of community banks
(while still large) has declined. Although community banks hold only a small
share of the nation's banking assets, they provide important financial services
(such as small-business lending) for which there are few, if any, substitutes. Thus,
community banks will likely continue to play an important role in the banking
industry even as technology and market conditions change.[7]

[7] See T. H. Hoenig, "The Role of Community Banks in the U.S. Economy," *Economic Review*, Federal
Reserve Bank of Kansas City, Second Quarter 2003, pp. 5–14.

FIGURE 2–4
Portfolio Shift: U.S. Commercial Banks' Financial Assets

Source: Federal Deposit Insurance Corporation, March 2004. *www.fdic.gov*

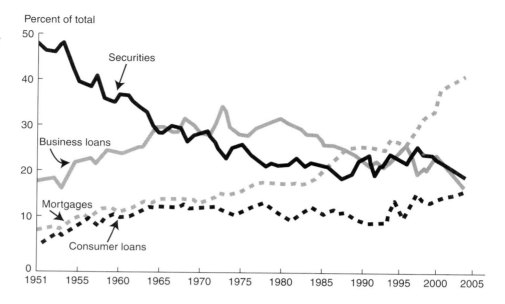

Balance Sheet and Recent Trends

Assets

Figure 2–4 shows the broad trends over the 1951–2003 period in the four principal earning asset areas of commercial banks: business loans (or C&I loans), securities, mortgages, and consumer loans. Although business loans were the major asset in bank balance sheets between 1965 and 1990, there has been a drop in their importance (as a proportion of the balance sheet) since 1990. This drop has been mirrored by an offsetting rise in holdings of securities and mortgages. These trends reflect a number of long-term and temporary influences. One important long-term influence has been the growth of the commercial paper market, which has become an alternative funding source for major corporations. Another has been the securitization of mortgages—the pooling and packaging of mortgage loans for sale in the form of bonds (see Chapter 28). A more temporary influence was the so-called credit crunch and decline in the demand for business loans as a result of the economic downturn and recession in 1989–92 and 2001–02.[8]

Look at the detailed balance sheet for all U.S. commercial banks as of December 31, 2003 (Table 2–5). Total loans amount to $4,351.7 billion, or 57.2 percent of total assets, and fall into four broad classes: business or C&I ($870.6 billion); commercial and residential real estate ($2,272.3 billion); individual, such as consumer loans for auto purchases and credit card debt ($770.5 billion); and all other loans, such as less developed country (LDC) loans ($375.8 billion). In the investment security portfolio of $1,789.3 billion, or 23.5 percent of total assets, U.S. government securities, such as Treasury bonds, constitute $1,005.8 billion, with other securities (in particular, municipal securities and investment-grade corporate bonds) making up the rest.[9]

[8] See David C. Wheelock, "Why No Business Loan Growth," *Monetary Trends,* Federal Reserve Bank of St. Louis, May 2004, p. 1.

[9] The footnotes to commercial bank balance sheets also distinguish between securities held by banks for trading purposes, normally for less than one year, and those held for longer-term investment purposes. The large money center banks are often active in the secondary market trading of government securities, reflecting their important role as primary dealers in government securities at the time of Treasury security auctions.

TABLE 2–5
Balance Sheet (all U.S. commercial banks) as of December 31, 2003 (in billions of dollars)

Source: Federal Deposit Insurance Corporation, December 31, 2003. *www.fdic.gov.*

Assets				
Loans and securities				$6,141.0
Investment securities			$1,789.3	
U.S. government securities		$1,005.8		
Other		783.5		
Total loans			4,351.7	
Interbank loans		142.5		
Loans excluding interbank		4,209.2		
Commercial and industrial	$870.6			
Real estate	2,272.3			
Revolving home equity	$284.5			
Other	1,987.8			
Individual		770.5		
All other		375.8		
Less: reserve for loan losses		80.0		
Total cash assets				387.6
Other assets				1,073.9
Total assets				7,602.5
Liabilities				
Total deposits				$5,028.9
Transaction accounts			$727.7	
Nontransaction accounts			4,301.2	
Large time deposits		$597.3		
Other		3,703.9		
Borrowings				1,643.3
Other liabilities				238.2
Total liabilities				6,910.4
Residual (assets less liabilities)				692.1

A major inference we can draw from this asset structure is that credit or default risk exposure is a major risk faced by modern commercial bank managers (see Chapters 11 and 12). Because commercial banks are highly leveraged and therefore hold little equity (see below) compared with total assets, even a relatively small number of loan defaults can wipe out the equity of a bank, leaving it insolvent.[10]

Liabilities

Commercial banks have two major sources of funds other than the equity provided by owners: deposits and borrowed or other liability funds. A major difference between banks and other firms is banks' high leverage. For example, banks had an average ratio of equity to assets of 9.10 percent in 2003; this implies that 90.90 percent of their assets were funded by debt, either deposits or borrowed funds.

Note in Table 2–5, the aggregate balance sheet of U.S. banks, that deposits amounted to $5,028.9 billion, or 66.1 percent of total liabilities and equity, and borrowings and other liabilities were $1,643.3 and $238.2 billion, respectively. Of the total stock of deposits, transaction accounts constituted 14.5 percent, or $727.7 billion.

---

[10] Losses such as those due to defaults are charged off against the equity (stockholders' stake) in a bank. Additions to the reserve for loan and lease losses account (and, in turn, the expense account "provisions for losses on loans and leases") to meet *expected* defaults reduce retained earnings and, thus, reduce equity of the bank. *Unexpected* defaults (e.g., due to a sudden major recession) are meant to be written off against the remainder of the bank's equity (e.g., its retained earnings and funds raised from share offerings).

transaction accounts
The sum of non-interest-bearing demand deposits and interest-bearing checking accounts.

NOW accounts
Interest-bearing checking accounts.

money market mutual funds
Specialized mutual funds that offers depositlike interest-bearing claims to savers.

negotiable CDs
Fixed-maturity interest-bearing deposits with face values over $100,000 that can be resold in the secondary market.

Transaction accounts are checkable deposits that bear no interest (demand deposits) or are interest bearing (most commonly called **NOW accounts**, or negotiable order of withdrawal accounts). Since their introduction in 1980, interest-bearing checking accounts—especially NOW accounts—have dominated the transaction accounts of banks. However, since limitations are imposed on the ability of corporations to hold such accounts and since there are minimum balance requirements for NOW accounts,[11] non-interest-bearing demand deposits are still held. The second major segment of deposits is retail or household savings and time deposits, normally individual account holdings of less than $100,000. Important components of bank retail savings accounts are small nontransaction accounts, which include passbook savings accounts and retail time deposits. Small nontransaction accounts constitute 73.6 percent of total deposits, or $3,703.9 billion. However, this disguises an important trend in the supply of these deposits to banks. Specifically, retail savings and time deposits have been falling in recent years, largely as a result of competition from **money market mutual funds**.[12] These funds pay a competitive rate of interest based on wholesale money market rates by pooling and investing funds (see Chapter 5) while requiring relatively small-denomination investments by mutual fund investors.

The third major source of deposit funds consists of large time deposits (over $100,000),[13] which amounted to $597.3 billion, or approximately 11.9 percent of the stock of deposits, in December 2003. These are primarily **negotiable certificates of deposit** (deposit claims with promised interest rates and fixed maturities of at least 14 days) that can be resold to outside investors in an organized secondary market. As such, they are usually distinguished from retail time deposits by their negotiability and secondary market liquidity.

Nondeposit liabilities comprise borrowings and other liabilities that together total 27.2 percent of all bank liabilities, or $1,881.5 billion. These categories include a broad array of instruments, such as purchases of federal funds (bank reserves) on the interbank market and repurchase agreements (temporary swaps of securities for federal funds) at the short end of the maturity spectrum to the issuance of notes and bonds at the longer end.[14]

Overall, the liability structure of bank balance sheets tends to reflect a shorter maturity structure than does the asset portfolio with relatively more liquid instruments such as deposits and interbank borrowings—used to fund less liquid assets such as loans. Thus, maturity mismatch or interest rate risk and liquidity risk are key exposure concerns for bank managers (see Chapters 8, 9, 17, and 18).

Equity

Commercial bank equity capital (9.10 percent of total liabilities and equity in 2003) consists mainly of common and preferred stock (listed at par value), surplus[15] or

[11] In the early 2000s, in an effort to attract new customers, many banks eliminated minimum balance requirements on NOW accounts. However, the many (and increased) fees on these accounts (such as overdraft charges) have more than offset the benefits of these new free checking features. See "Checking Is Free, But Bank Profits Are Hefty," *The New York Times,* November 12, 2002, p. C1.

[12] See U.S. General Accounting Office, "Mutual Funds: Impact on Bank Deposits and Credit Availability," GAO/GGD (September 1995).

[13] $100,000 is the cap for explicit coverage under bank deposit insurance. We discuss this in more detail in Chapter 19.

[14] These instruments are explained in greater detail in later chapters, especially Chapter 18.

[15] Surplus or additional paid-in capital shows the difference between the stock's par value and what the original stockholders paid when they bought the newly issued shares.

additional paid-in capital, and retained earnings. Regulators require banks to hold a minimum level of equity capital to act as a buffer against losses from their on- and off-balance-sheet activities (see Chapter 20). Because of the relatively low cost of deposit funding, banks tend to hold equity close to the minimum levels set by regulators. As we discuss in subsequent chapters, this impacts banks' exposures to risk and their ability to grow—both on and off the balance sheet—over time.

Internet Exercise	Go to the Federal Deposit Insurance Corporation Web site (**www.fdic.gov**) and find the latest balance sheet information available for commercial banks.
	Go to the Federal Deposit Insurance Corporation Web site at **www.fdic.gov**. Click on "Analysts." Click on "Statistics on Banking." Click on "Run Report." This will download a file onto your computer that will contain the most recent balance sheet information for commercial banks.

Off-Balance-Sheet Activities

The balance sheet itself does not reflect the total scope of bank activities. Banks conduct many fee-related activities off the balance sheet. Off-balance-sheet (OBS) activities are becoming increasingly important, in terms of their dollar value and the income they generate for banks—especially as the ability of banks to attract high-quality loan applicants and deposits becomes ever more difficult. OBS activities include issuing various types of guarantees (such as letters of credit), which often have a strong insurance underwriting element, and making future commitments to lend. Both services generate additional fee income for banks. Off-balance-sheet activities also involve engaging in derivative transactions—futures, forwards, options, and swaps.

off-balance-sheet asset
An item that moves onto the asset side of the balance sheet when a contingent event occurs.

Under current accounting standards, such activities are not shown on the current balance sheet. Rather, an item or activity is an **off-balance-sheet asset** if, when a contingent event occurs, the item or activity moves onto the asset side of the balance sheet or an income item is realized on the income statement. Conversely, an item or activity is an **off-balance-sheet liability** if, when a contingent event occurs, the item or activity moves onto the liability side of the balance sheet or an expense item is realized on the income statement.

off-balance-sheet liability
An item that moves onto the liability side of the balance sheet when a contingent event occurs.

By moving activities off the balance sheet, banks hope to earn additional fee income to complement declining margins or spreads on their traditional lending business. At the same time, they can avoid regulatory costs or "taxes" since reserve requirements and deposit insurance premiums are not levied on off-balance-sheet activities (see Chapter 13). Thus, banks have both earnings and regulatory "tax-avoidance" incentives to undertake activities off their balance sheets.

Off-balance-sheet activities, however, can involve risks that add to the overall insolvency exposure of an FI. Indeed, the failure of the U.K. investment bank Barings and the bankruptcy of Orange County in California in the 1990s have been linked to FIs' off-balance-sheet activities in derivatives. More recently, in 2001 Allied Irish Banks incurred a $750 million loss from foreign exchange derivative trades by a rogue trader, and in 2004 unauthorized trading of foreign currency options at National Australian Bank resulted in a loss of $485 million. However, off-balance-sheet activities and instruments have both risk-reducing as well as risk-increasing attributes, and, when used appropriately, they can reduce or hedge an FI's interest rate, credit, and foreign exchange risks.

We show the notional, or face, value of bank OBS activities, and their distribution and growth, for 1992 to 2003 in Table 2–6. Notice the relative growth in the notional

TABLE 2–6   Aggregate Volume of Off-Balance-Sheet Commitments and Contingencies by U.S. Commercial Banks, Annual Data as of December (in billions of dollars)

	1992	1996	2003	Distribution 2003
Commitments to lend	$1,272.0	$2,528.7	$5,398.9	6.9%
Future and forward contracts (exclude FX)				
On commodities and equities	26.3	101.6	104.9	0.1
On interest rates	1,738.1	3,201.2	7,209.8	9.3
Notional amount of credit derivatives	9.6	28.6	1,001.2	1.3
Standby contracts and other option contracts				
Option contracts on interest rates	1,012.7	3,156.2	12,539.5	16.1
Option contracts on foreign exchange	494.8	1,032.5	1,298.3	1.6
Option contracts on commodities	60.3	203.9	767.5	1.0
Commitments to buy FX (includes $U.S.), spot, and forward	3,015.5	5,000.8	4,351.1	5.6
Standby LCs and foreign office guarantees	162.5	211.0	348.9	0.5
(Amount of these items sold to others via participations)	(14.9)	(21.8)	(60.3)	
Commercial LCs	28.1	30.9	24.2	0.0
Participations in acceptances	1.0	2.4	0.5	0.0
Securities borrowed or lent	107.2	233.5	852.0	1.1
Other significant commitments and contingencies	8.7	14.0	53.3	0.0
Memoranda				
Notional value of all outstanding swaps	2,122.0	7,069.4	44,082.7	56.5
Outstanding principal balance of loans sold or swapped	10.7	11.4	2.5	0.0
Amount of recourse exposure on these mortgages	6.3	8.2	0.3	0.0
Total, including memoranda items	$10,200.3	$22,833.3	$78,035.6	100.0%
Total assets (on-balance-sheet items)	$3,476.4	$4,578.3	$7,602.5	

FX = foreign exchange; LC = letter of credit.
Sources: FDIC, *Statistics on Banking*, various issues. *www.fdic.gov*

dollar value of OBS activities in Table 2–6. By the end of 2003, the notional value of OBS bank activities was $78,035.6 billion compared with the $7,602.5 billion value of on-balance-sheet activities. It should be noted that the notional, or face, value of OBS activities does not accurately reflect the risk to the bank undertaking such activities. The potential for the bank to gain or lose is based on the possible change in the market value over the life of the contract rather than the notional, or face, value of the contract, normally less than 3 percent of the notional value of an OBS contract.[16]

The use of derivative contracts (futures and forwards, swaps, and options) accelerated during the 1992–2003 period and accounted for much of the growth in OBS activity. As we discuss in detail in Chapters 24 through 26, the significant growth in derivative securities activities by commercial banks has been a direct response to the increased interest rate risk, credit risk, and foreign exchange risk exposures they have faced, both domestically and internationally. In particular, these contracts offer banks a way to hedge these risks without having to make extensive changes on the balance sheet.[17]

Although the simple notional dollar value of OBS items overestimates their risk exposure amounts, the increase in these activities is still nothing short of

[16] For example, the market value of a swap (today) is the difference between the present value of the cash flows (expected) to be received minus the present value of cash flows expected to be paid (see Chapter 26).
[17] See, for example, "Derivatives Are a Boon to Lenders," *The Wall Street Journal*, November 14, 2002, p. C10.

phenomenal.[18] Indeed, this phenomenal increase has pushed regulators into imposing capital requirements on such activities and into explicitly recognizing an FI's solvency risk exposure from pursuing such activities. We describe these capital requirements in Chapter 20.

As noted in Table 2–6, major types of OBS activities for U.S. banks include the following:

- Loan commitments.
- Standby letters of credit and letters of credit.
- Derivative contracts: futures, forwards, swaps, and options.
- When-issued securities.
- Loans sold.

We discuss each of these and the risks they present in Chapter 13.

Other Fee-Generating Activities

Commercial banks engage in other fee-generating activities that cannot easily be identified from analyzing their on- and off-balance-sheet accounts. Two of these are trust services and correspondent banking.

Trust Services

The trust department of a commercial bank holds and manages assets for individuals or corporations. Only the largest banks have sufficient staff to offer trust services. Individual trusts represent about one-half of all trust assets managed by commercial banks. These trusts include estate assets and assets delegated to bank trust departments by less financially sophisticated investors. Pension fund assets are the second-largest group of assets managed by the trust departments of commercial banks. The banks manage the pension funds, act as trustees for any bonds held by the pension funds, and act as transfer and disbursement agents for the pension funds.

Correspondent Banking

Correspondent banking is the provision of banking services to other banks that do not have the staff resources to perform the service themselves. These services include check clearing and collection, foreign exchange trading, hedging services, and participation in large loan and security issuances. Correspondent banking services are generally sold as a package of services. Payment for the services is generally in the form of non-interest-bearing deposits held at the bank offering the correspondent services (see Chapter 13).

Regulation

The Regulators

Unlike countries that have one or sometimes two regulators, U.S. banks may be subject to the supervision and regulations of up to four separate regulators. The key regulators are the Federal Deposit Insurance Corporation (FDIC), the Office of the Comptroller of the Currency (OCC), the Federal Reserve System (FRS), and state bank regulators. Next, we look at the principal roles played by each regulator. Appendix 2B (located at the book's Web site, www.mhhe.com/saunders5e) lists in greater detail the regulators that oversee the various activities of depository institutions.

---

[18] This overestimation of risk exposure occurs because the risk exposure from a contingent claim (such as an option) is usually less than its face value (see Chapter 13).

FIGURE 2–5
Bank Regulators

Source: FDIC (internal figures), December 31, 2003.
www.fdic.gov

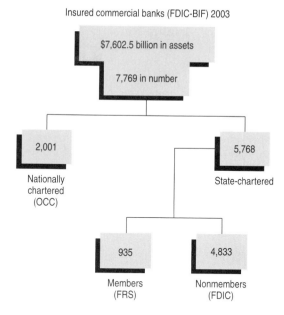

Insured commercial banks (FDIC-BIF) 2003

$7,602.5 billion in assets

7,769 in number

2,001
Nationally chartered (OCC)

5,768
State-chartered

935
Members (FRS)

4,833
Nonmembers (FDIC)

www.fdic.gov

The FDIC   Established in 1933, the Federal Deposit Insurance Corporation insures the deposits of member banks. In so doing, it levies insurance premiums on member banks, manages the deposit insurance fund, and carries out bank examinations. Further, when an insured bank is closed, the FDIC acts as the receiver and liquidator—although the closure decision itself is technically in the hands of the bank chartering or licensing agency, such as the OCC. Because of the problems in the thrift industry and the insolvency of the savings association insurance fund (FSLIC) in 1989, the FDIC now manages both the commercial bank insurance fund and the savings association insurance fund. The Bank Insurance Fund is called BIF, and the savings association fund is called SAIF (Savings Association Insurance Fund). The number of FDIC-BIF–insured banks and the division between nationally chartered and state chartered banks is shown in Figure 2–5.

www.occ.treas.gov

Office of the Comptroller of the Currency (OCC)   The OCC is the oldest bank regulatory agency; established in 1863, it is a subagency of the U.S. Treasury. Its primary function is to charter so-called national banks as well as to close them. In addition, the OCC examines national banks and has the power to approve or disapprove their merger applications. However, instead of seeking a national charter, banks can be chartered by any of 50 individual state bank regulatory agencies. The choice of being a nationally chartered or state chartered bank lies at the foundation of the **dual banking system** in the United States. While most large banks, such as Bank of America, choose national charters, this is not always the case. For example, Morgan Guaranty, the money center bank subsidiary of J. P. Morgan Chase, is chartered as a state bank under New York state law. In December 2003, 2,001 banks were *nationally* chartered and 5,768 were *state* chartered, with approximately 56 percent and 44 percent of total commercial bank assets, respectively.[19]

dual banking system
The coexistence of both nationally chartered and state-chartered banks in the United States.

[19] In early 2004 the regulation of banks by federal versus state regulators came under debate. In January 2004 the OCC proclaimed that it alone has the right to draft and enforce rules that govern not only nationally chartered bank holding companies, but also the more than 2,000 banks that operate as subsidiaries of these holding companies. The move outraged state regulators, who claimed the OCC was attempting to preempt states' authority and grab power. See "House Panel Attacks Regulator Battling the States over Banks," *The Wall Street Journal*, February 26, 2004, p. C5.

**www.federalreserve.
gov**

Federal Reserve System   Apart from being concerned with the conduct of monetary policy, as this country's central bank, the Federal Reserve also has regulatory power over some banks and, when relevant, their holding company parents. All the 2,001 nationally chartered banks in Figure 2–5 are automatically members of the Federal Reserve system; 935 state chartered banks also have chosen to become members. Since 1980, all banks have had to meet the same non-interest-bearing reserve requirements whether they are members of the Federal Reserve System (FRS) or not. The primary advantages of FRS membership are direct access to the federal funds wire transfer network for nationwide interbank borrowing and lending of reserves and to the discount window for lender of last resort borrowing of funds. Finally, many banks are often owned and controlled by parent **holding companies**; for example, Citigroup is the parent holding company of Citibank (a bank). Because the holding company's management can influence decisions taken by a bank subsidiary and thus influence its risk exposure, the Federal Reserve System regulates and examines bank holding companies as well as banks.

holding companies
Parent companies that own a controlling interest in subsidiary banks or other FIs.

Regulations

Commercial banks are among the most regulated firms in the U.S. economy. Because of the inherent special nature of banking and banking contracts (see Chapter 1), regulators have imposed numerous restrictions on their product and geographic activities. Table 2–7 lists the major laws from the McFadden Act of 1927 to the Financial Services Modernization Act of 1999 and briefly describes the key features of each act.

Even though we will go into greater detail about these regulations in later chapters (e.g., product diversification, Chapter 21; geographic diversification, Chapters 22 and 23), we now note the major objectives of each of these laws. The 1927 McFadden Act sought to restrict interstate bank branching, while the 1933 Glass-Steagall Act sought to separate commercial banking from investment banking by limiting the powers of commercial banks to engage in securities activities. Restrictions on the nonbank activities of commercial banks were strengthened by the Bank Holding Company Act of 1956 and its 1970 amendments, which limited the ability of a bank's parent holding company to engage in commercial, insurance, and other nonbank financial service activities. The 1978 International Banking Act extended federal regulation, such as the McFadden and Glass-Steagall Acts, to foreign branches and agencies in the United States for the first time, thereby seeking to level the competitive playing field between domestic and foreign banks. The 1980 DIDMCA and the 1982 DIA are mainly deregulation acts in that they eliminated interest ceilings on deposits and gave banks (and thrifts) new liability and asset powers.[20] As we discuss in the next section on thrifts, this deregulation is blamed in part for the thrift crisis that resulted in widespread failures and the insolvency of the FSLIC in 1989.

nonbank banks
Firms that undertake many of the activities of a commercial bank without meeting the legal definition of a bank.

The Competitive Equality in Banking Act (CEBA) of 1987 sought to impose controls over a growing number of **nonbank banks** that were established to get around interstate banking restrictions and restrictions on nonbank ownership of banks imposed under the 1927 McFadden and the 1956 Bank Holding Company Acts. In 1989 Congress responded to the problems of thrift banks and the collapse of the FSLIC with the passage of the FIRREA. In 1991 Congress enacted the FDICIA to deal with a large number of bank failures and the threatened insolvency of

---

[20] In particular, Regulation Q ceilings on bank deposit rates were phased out in stages between March 1980 and March 1986.

TABLE 2–7
Major Bank Laws,
Major Features

1927 The McFadden Act

1. Made branching of nationally chartered banks subject to the same branching regulations as state-chartered banks.
2. Liberalized national banks' securities underwriting activities, which previously had to be conducted through state-chartered affiliates.

1933 The Banking Acts of 1933

1. The Glass-Steagall Act generally prohibited commercial banks from underwriting securities with four exceptions:
   a. Municipal general obligation bonds.
   b. U.S. government bonds.
   c. Private placements.
   d. Real estate loans.
2. In addition, the acts established the FDIC to insure bank deposits.
3. The Glass-Steagall Act prohibited banks from paying interest on demand deposits.

1956 The Bank Holding Company Act

1. Restricted the banking and nonbanking acquisition activities of multibank holding companies.
2. Empowered the Federal Reserve to regulate multibank holding companies by:
   a. Determining permissible activities.
   b. Exercising supervisory authority.
   c. Exercising chartering authority.
   d. Conducting bank examinations.

1970 Amendments to the Bank Holding Company Act of 1956

1. Extended the BHC Act of 1956 to one-bank holding companies.
2. Restricted permissible BHC activities to those "closely related to banking."

1978 International Banking Act

1. Regulated foreign bank branches and agencies in the United States.
2. Subjected foreign banks to the McFadden and Glass-Steagall Acts.
3. Gave foreign banks access to Fedwire, the discount window, and deposit insurance.

1980 Depository Institutions Deregulation and Monetary Control Act (DIDMCA)

1. Set a six-year phaseout for Regulation Q interest rate ceilings on small time and savings deposits.
2. Authorized NOW accounts nationwide.
3. Introduced uniform reserve requirements for state-chartered and nationally chartered banks.
4. Increased the ceiling on deposit insurance coverage from $40,000 to $100,000.
5. Allowed federally chartered thrifts to make consumer and commercial loans (subject to size restrictions).

1982 Garn–St. Germain Depository Institutions Act (DIA)

1. Introduced money market deposit accounts (MMDAs) and super NOW accounts as interest rate–bearing savings accounts with limited check-writing features.
2. Allowed federally chartered thrifts more extensive lending powers and demand deposit–taking powers.
3. Allowed sound commercial banks to acquire failed savings institutions.
4. Reaffirmed limitations on bank powers to underwrite and distribute insurance.

1987 Competitive Equality in Banking Act (CEBA)

1. Redefined the definition of a *bank* to limit the growth of nonbank banks.
2. Sought to recapitalize the Federal Savings and Loan Insurance Corporation (FSLIC).

(continued)

TABLE 2–7
(continued)

1989 Financial Institutions Reform Recovery and Enforcement Act (FIRREA)

1. Limited savings banks' investments in nonresidential real estate, required divestiture of junk bond holdings (by 1994), and imposed a restrictive asset test for qualifications as a savings institution (the qualified thrift lender [QTL] test).
2. Equalized the capital requirements of thrifts and banks.
3. Replaced the FSLIC with the FDIC-SAIF.
4. Replaced the Federal Home Loan Bank Board as the charterer of federal savings and loans with the Office of Thrift Supervision (OTS), an agency of the Treasury.
5. Created the Resolution Trust Corporation (RTC) to resolve failed and failing savings institutions.

1991 Federal Deposit Insurance Corporation Improvement Act (FDICIA)

1. Introduced prompt corrective action (PCA), requiring mandatory interventions by regulators whenever a bank's capital falls.
2. Introduced risk-based deposit insurance premiums beginning in 1993.
3. Limited the use of too-big-to-fail bailouts by federal regulators for large banks.
4. Extended federal regulation over foreign bank branches and agencies in the Foreign Bank Supervision and Enhancement Act (FBSEA).

1994 Riegle-Neal Interstate Banking and Branching Efficiency Act

1. Permitted bank holding companies to acquire banks in other states, starting September 1995.
2. Invalidated the laws of states that allowed interstate banking only on a regional or reciprocal basis.
3. Beginning in June 1997, bank holding companies were permitted to convert out-of-state subsidiary banks into branches of a single interstate bank.
4. Newly chartered branches also permitted interstate if allowed by state law.

1999 Financial Services Modernization Act

1. Eliminated restrictions on banks, insurance companies, and securities firms entering into each others' areas of business. Allowed for the creation of a financial services holding company.
2. Provided for state regulation of insurance.
3. Streamlined bank holding company supervision, with the Federal Reserve as the umbrella holding company supervisor.
4. Prohibited FDIC assistance to affiliates and subsidiaries of banks and savings institutions.
5. Provided for national treatment of foreign banks engaging in activities authorized under the act.

---

financial services holding company
A financial institution that engages in banking activities and securities underwriting or any other financial activity.

the FDIC, the insurance fund for commercial banks. Both the FIRREA and FDICIA sought to pull back from some of the deregulatory elements of the 1980 DIDMCA and the 1982 DIA. In 1994 the Riegle-Neal Act rolled back many of the restrictions on interstate banking imposed by the 1927 McFadden and the 1956 Bank Holding Company Acts. In particular, since June 1997 bank holding companies have been permitted to convert their bank subsidiaries in various states into branches, thus making nationwide branching possible for the first time in 70 years. In 1999 the Financial Services Modernization Act repealed Glass-Steagall barriers between commercial banks and investment banks. The act allowed for the creation of a **financial services holding company** that could engage in banking activities *and* securities underwriting. This act also allows FI customers to opt out of any private information sharing an FI may want to pursue. Thus, FI

TABLE 2–8   Selected Indicators for U.S. Commercial Banks, 1989 through 2003

	2003	2002	2001	2000	1999	1997	1995	1993	1989
Number of institutions	7,769	7,887	8,079	8,315	8,580	9,143	9,940	10,958	12,709
Return on assets (%)	1.40	1.33	1.15	1.19	1.31	1.24	1.17	1.22	0.49
Return on equity (%)	15.31	14.49	13.09	14.07	15.31	14.71	14.68	15.67	7.71
Provision for loan losses to total assets (%)	0.47	0.71	0.67	0.47	0.38	0.39	0.29	0.45	0.94
Net charge-offs to loans (%)	0.89	1.12	0.95	0.64	0.61	0.64	0.49	0.85	1.16
Asset growth rate (%)	7.42	8.01	4.91	8.79	5.37	9.54	7.53	5.72	5.38
Net operating income growth (%)	14.92	20.49	−1.89	2.02	20.42	12.48	7.48	35.36	−38.70
Number of failed/assisted institutions	3	10	3	6	7	1	6	42	206

Source: FDIC, *Quarterly Banking Profile*, various issues; and *Historical Statistics*, 1989. *www.fdic.gov*

customers have some control over who will see and have access to their private information.[21]

Industry Performance

Table 2–8 presents selected performance ratios for the commercial banking industry for various years from 1989 through 2003. With the economic expansion in the U.S. economy and falling interest rates throughout most of the 1990s, U.S. commercial banks flourished for most of that period. In 1999 commercial bank earnings were a record $71.6 billion. More than two-thirds of all U.S. banks reported a return on assets (ROA) of 1 percent or higher, and the average ROA for all banks was 1.31 percent, up from 1.19 percent for the year 1998.[22] This, despite continued financial problems (or sovereign risk, see Chapter 16) in Southeast Asia, Russia, and South America. With the economic downturn in the early 2000s, however, bank performance deteriorated slightly. For example, commercial banks' string of eight consecutive years of record earnings ended in 2000 as their net income fell to $71.2 billion. Banks' provision for loan losses (or credit risk) rose to $9.5 billion in the fourth quarter of 2000, an increase of $3.4 billion (54.7 percent) from the level of a year earlier. This was the largest quarterly loss provision since the fourth quarter of 1991. Finally, the average ROA was 1.19 in 2000, down from 1.31 percent in 1999.

[21] While not specific to commercial banks, after the terrorist attacks on September 11, 2001, the U.S. Congress passed the USA Patriot Act of 2001. The act consists of a number of specific amendments to existing criminal laws designed to streamline early detection and investigation of suspected terrorist activity conducted through banks. Specifically, banks must define their methods for profiling new individual and corporate customers who are opening accounts, as well as for maintaining data on them. Further, the Sarbanes-Oxley Act of 2002 requires public companies to make sure their boards' audit committees have at least one individual who is familiar with generally accepted accounting principles (GAAP) and has experience with internal auditing controls, preparing or auditing financial statements of "generally comparable issuers," and applying GAAP guidelines for estimates, accruals, and reserves. Small banks—especially those in rural markets—might find it difficult and expensive to comply with these laws.

[22] ROA is calculated as net income divided by the book value of total assets. It reflects the earnings per dollar of assets for the bank. ROE is calculated as net income divided by common equity of the bank and measures the return to the bank's common stockholders.

High More interest income
Low Loan Loss provisions
High profitability

This downturn was short-lived, however. In 2001, net income of $74.3 billion easily surpassed the old record of $71.6 billion, and net income rose further, to $106.3 billion, in 2003. Moreover, in 2003, both ROA and ROE reached all-time highs of 1.40 percent and 15.34 percent, respectively. The two main sources of earnings strength in 2003 were higher noninterest income (up $18.9 billion, 10.3 percent) and lower loan loss provisions (down $14.2 billion, or 27.6 percent). The greatest improvement in profitability occurred at large institutions, whose earnings had been depressed in the early 2000s by credit losses on loans to corporate borrowers and by weakness in market-sensitive noninterest revenue. Only 5.7 percent of all institutions were unprofitable in 2003, the lowest proportion since 1997.

Several explanations have been offered for the strong performance of commercial banks during the early 2000s. First, the Federal Reserve cut interest rates 13 times during this period. Lower interest rates made debt cheaper to service and kept many households and small firms borrowing. Second, lower interest rates made home purchasing more affordable. Thus, the housing market boomed throughout the period. Third, the development of new financial instruments, such as credit derivatives and mortgage-backed securities, helped banks shift credit risk from their balance sheets to financial markets and other FIs such as insurance companies. Finally, improved information technology has helped banks manage their risk better. Nevertheless, the question still remains, what will happen to this industry if and when interest rates rise? If historical patterns hold, bank stocks should be highly vulnerable to rising interest rates. For example, mortgage originations, which totaled $3.3 trillion in 2003, are expected to fall to $1.6 trillion in 2004.

The performance of the late 1990s and early 2000s is quite an improvement from the recessionary and high interest rate conditions in which the industry operated in the late 1980s. As reported in Table 2–8, the average ROA and return on equity (ROE) for commercial banks in 2003 were 1.40 percent and 15.31 percent, respectively, compared with 1989 when the ROA and ROE averaged 0.49 percent and 7.71 percent, respectively. **Provision for loan losses** (bank management's expectations of losses on the current loan portfolio) to assets ratio and **net charge-offs** (actual losses on loans and leases) to loans ratio averaged 0.47 percent and 0.89 percent, respectively, in 2003, versus 0.94 percent and 1.16 percent, respectively, in 1989. **Net operating income** (income before taxes and extraordinary items) grew at an annualized rate of 14.92 percent in 2003 versus a *drop* of 38.70 percent in 1989. Finally, note that in 2003 only three U.S. commercial banks failed versus 206 failures in 1989. In response to such massive losses and failures in the industry, several regulations were proposed and enacted to prevent such occurrences from happening again. (We discuss the major changes in regulation and their impact in Chapters 21 and 22.) As a result of these changes and the strong U.S. economy, in the last 15 years or so the commercial banking industry essentially has gone from the brink of failure to a period of unprecedented profit and stability.

Nevertheless, as mentioned in Chapter 1, the early 2000s saw a weakening in public trust and confidence in the ethics followed by financial institutions. A number of commercial banks continue to deal with ethics-related issues. For example, in March 2004 Bank of America and FleetBoston Financial agreed to pay a combined $675 million to settle civil fraud charges relating to improper mutual fund trading. In July 2003 J. P. Morgan Chase and Citigroup settled with the New York District Attorney over allegations that the banks wrongly helped Enron hide its debt prior to the energy company's filing for Chapter 11 bankruptcy in December 2001. Related to the issue of ethics are conflicts of interest. A 2003 survey by the

provision for loan losses
Bank management's recognition of expected bad loans for the period.

net charge-offs
Actual losses on loans and leases.

net operating income
Income before taxes and extraordinary items.

Ethical **Dilemmas**

BANKS RAISE PRESSURE TO GET LOANS

Despite complaints from competitors and a number of recent regulatory investigations, pressure from banks to link lending to the purchase of investment banking and other services has increased at U.S. companies over the past year, according to a new survey of corporate finance officers. A study by the Association for Financial Professionals . . . shows that 56 percent of respondents from large companies said "the pressure to award additional business has increased over the last year." . . . Wall Street investment banks have long complained that commercial banks use loans as a lever to snare investment banking, underwriting, and other services from corporate borrowers. In response, the commercial banks claim that lending by itself isn't a sufficiently profitable business and that to make loans worthwhile, they have to wrap in other more lucrative services. They add that in many cases, companies demand that lending and other services be packaged together to ensure that the companies have greater access to credit. "Banks often require that other products and services be packaged along with credit—that's not news because it's done every day and it's perfectly permissible," said Beth Climo, executive director of the securities affiliate of the American Bankers Association. "It's very beneficial for customers and for the banks." However, the so-called tying of such services is illegal in some circumstances.

Source: *The Wall Street Journal*, March 19, 2003, p. C5, by Paul Beckett. Reprinted by permission of The Wall Street Journal. © 2003 Dow Jones & Company, Inc. All Rights Reserved Worldwide. *www.wsj.com*

Association for Financial Professionals found that management at 56 percent of companies with more than $1 billion in revenues believed that a commercial bank had refused to lend funds or changed the terms on which it was willing to lend because the company did not agree to do other business with the bank (see the Ethical Dilemmas box). Indeed, the National Association of Securities Dealers announced an investigation into this practice in which loans to companies are made only if the borrowers agree to give the lender lucrative fee-generating investment banking business. Most recently, in April 2004 Riggs National Bank, which provides banking services to most of Washington's foreign embassies and to American consulates worldwide, was swept up in controversy over allegations that some of its deposit accounts involved terrorist financing and money laundering. The investigation began as federal officials tried to track funds used by the September 11 hijackers. As the investigation wore on, banking regulators became increasingly alarmed by Riggs's practices. In July 2003 and again in July 2004, regulators publicly rebuked Riggs for failing to comply with anti–money laundering standards.[23] One congressional report stated that Riggs "turned a blind eye" to evidence of massive corruption involving U.S. oil companies and an African autocrat.

Also certain to affect the future performance of commercial banks (as well as savings institutions and credit unions) is the extent to which banks adopt the newest technology (see Chapter 14), including the extent to which industry participants embrace the Internet and online banking. Early entrants into Internet banking have

[23] See "Quality Eludes Bank of America," *The Wall Street Journal*, March 16, 2004, p. C1; "J. P. Morgan, Citigroup Will Pay $305 Million to Settle Enron Case," *The Wall Street Journal*, July 29, 2003, p. A1; "NASD Examines Issue of 'Tying' of Bank Loans," *The Wall Street Journal*, September 20, 2002, p. A3; "Executives See Rise in 'Tying' Loans to Other Fees," *The Wall Street Journal*, June 9, 2004, p. A1; "A Washington Bank, a Global Mess," *The New York Times*, April 11, 2004, p. 3-1; and "Riggs Bank Draws Harsh Criticism," *The Wall Street Journal*, July 15, 2004, p. A3.

been banks that have introduced new technology in markets with demographic and economic characteristics that help ensure customer acceptance, such as urban banks with a strong retail orientation that have tailored their Internet offerings to their retail customers. These early entrants have generally developed their Internet-related products to gain access to noncore, less traditional sources of funds. Appendix 2C (located at the book's Web site, **www.mhhe.com/saunders5e**) provides a short summary of technology-based wholesale and retail services provided by banks and other FIs. The performance of banks that have invested in Internet banking as a complement to their existing services has been similar to the performance of those without Internet banking, despite relatively high initial technology-related expenses. In particular, the banks with Internet banking services generally have higher noninterest income (which offsets any increased technology expenses). Further, the risk of banks offering Internet-related banking products appears to be similar to the risk of those banks without Internet banking.[24]

In addition to the development of Internet banking as a complement to the traditional services offered by commercial banks, a new segment of the industry has arisen that consists of Internet-only banks. That is, these banks have no "brick and mortar" facilities, or are banks without "walls." In these banks, all business is conducted over the Internet. However, Internet-only banks have yet to capture more than a small fraction of the banking market.

Concept Questions

1. What are the major assets held by commercial banks?
2. What are the major sources of funding for commercial banks?
3. Describe the responsibilities of the three federal regulatory agencies in the United States.
4. What are the major regulations that have affected the operations of U.S. commercial banks?
5. What has the trend in ROA and ROE been in the commercial banking industry over the last decade?

SAVINGS INSTITUTIONS

Savings institutions were first created in the early 1800s in response to commercial banks' concentration on serving the needs of business (commercial) enterprises rather than the needs of individuals requiring borrowed funds to purchase homes. Thus, the first savings institutions pooled individual savings and invested them mainly in mortgages and other securities. Today's savings institutions, however, generally perform services similar to those of commercial banks.

savings associations
Depository institutions that specialize in residential mortgages mostly backed by short-term deposits and other funds.

Savings institutions comprise two different groups of FIs: **savings associations** (SAs) and savings banks (SBs). They usually are grouped together because they not only provide important mortgage and/or lending services to households but also are important recipients of household savings. Historically, savings associations have concentrated more on residential mortgages, while savings banks have been operated as relatively diversified savings associations that have a large concentration of residential mortgage assets but hold commercial loans, corporate bonds, and corporate stock as well. In the next sections, we review these two groups.

[24] See R. J. Sullivan, "How Has the Adoption of Internet Banking Affected Performance and Risk in Banks?" *Financial Industry Perspectives*, Federal Reserve Bank of Kansas City, December 2000, pp. 1–16.

Savings Associations (SAs)

Size, Structure, and Composition of the Industry

Savings associations were historically referred to as savings and loans (S&Ls) associations. However, in the 1980s, federally chartered savings banks appeared in the United States. The term *savings association* has replaced "S&L association" to capture the resulting change in the structure of the industry. [25] These institutions have the same regulators as traditional savings and loans.

The savings association industry prospered throughout most of the 20th century. These specialized institutions made long-term residential mortgages backed by short-term savings deposits. At the end of the 1970s, slightly fewer than 4,000 savings associations had assets of approximately $0.6 trillion. Over the period October 1979 to October 1982, however, the Federal Reserve radically changed its monetary policy strategy by targeting bank reserves rather than interest rates in an attempt to lower the underlying rate of inflation (see Chapter 8 for more details). The Fed's restrictive monetary policy action led to a sudden and dramatic surge in interest rates, with rates on T-bills rising as high as 16 percent. This increase in short-term rates and the cost of funds had two effects. First, savings associations faced negative interest spreads or **net interest margins** (i.e., interest income minus interest expense divided by earning assets) in funding much of their fixed-rate long-term residential mortgage portfolios over this period. Second, they had to pay more competitive interest rates on savings deposits to prevent **disintermediation** and the reinvestment of those funds in money market mutual fund accounts. Their ability to do this was constrained by the Federal Reserve's **Regulation Q ceilings**, which limited the rates savings associations could pay on traditional passbook savings account and retail time deposits.[26]

In part to overcome the effects of rising rates and disintermediation on the savings association industry, Congress passed two acts, the DIDMCA and the DIA (see Table 2–7); these acts expanded the deposit-taking and asset-investment powers of savings associations. On the liability side, savings associations were allowed to offer NOW accounts and more market rate–sensitive liabilities, such as money market deposit accounts, to limit disintermediation and compete for funds. On the asset side, they were allowed to offer floating or adjustable rate mortgages and to a limited extent, expand into consumer and commercial lending. In addition, many state-chartered thrifts—especially in California, Texas, and Florida—received wider investment powers that included real estate development loans often made through special-purpose subsidiaries.

For many savings associations, the new powers created safer and more diversified institutions. For a small but significant group whose earnings and shareholders' capital were being eroded in traditional lines of business, this created an opportunity to take more risks in an attempt to return to profitability. However, in the mid-1980s, real estate and land prices in Texas and the Southwest collapsed. This was followed by economic downturns in the Northeast and Western states of the United States. Many borrowers with mortgage loans issued by savings associations in these areas defaulted. In other words, the credit or lending risks incurred

---

net interest margin
Interest income minus interest expense divided by earning assets.

disintermediation
Withdrawal of deposits from savings associations and other depository institutions and their reinvestment elsewhere.

Regulation Q ceiling
An interest ceiling imposed on small savings and time deposits at banks and thrifts until 1986.

---

[25] In 1978, the Federal Home Loan Bank Board (FHLBB), at the time the main regulator of savings associations, began chartering federal savings banks insured by the Federal Savings and Loan Insurance Corporation (FSLIC). In 1982, the FHLBB allowed S&Ls to convert to federal savings banks with bank (rather than S&L) names. As more and more S&Ls converted to savings banks, the title associated with this sector of the thrift industry was revised to reflect this change.

[26] These Regulation Q ceilings were usually set at rates of $5\frac{1}{4}$ or $5\frac{1}{2}$ percent.

FIGURE 2–6   Structural Changes in the Number of Savings Institutions, 1984–2003

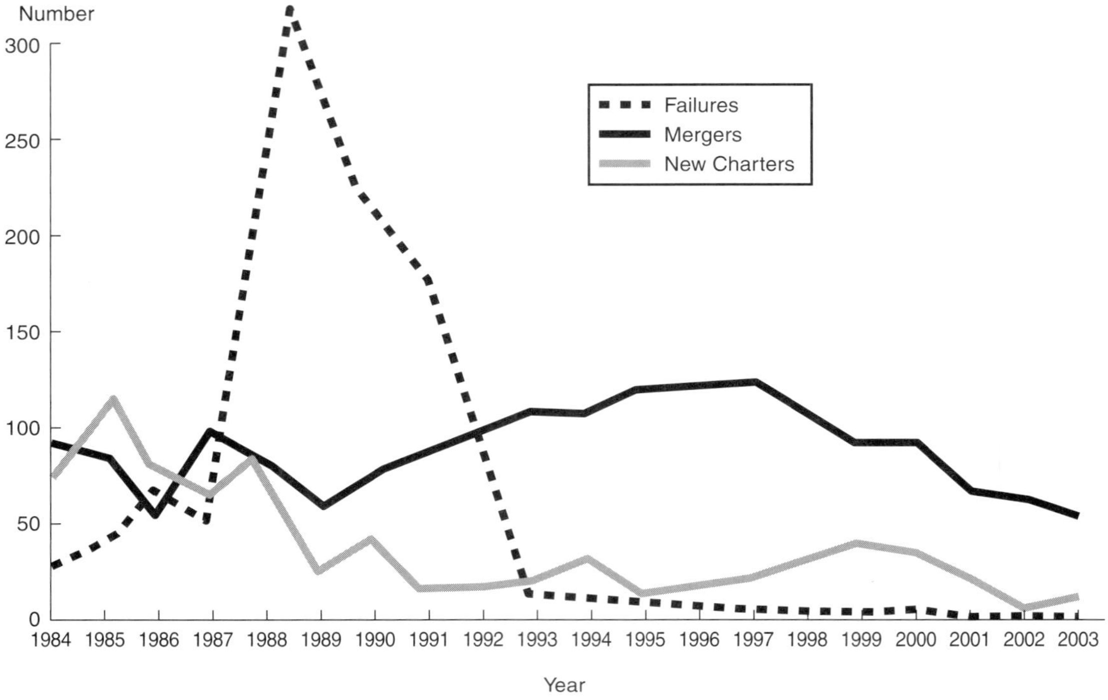

Source: Federal Deposit Insurance Corporation, *Quarterly Banking Profile,* various years. *www.fdic.gov*

regulator forbearance
A policy of not closing economically insolvent FIs, but allowing them to continue in operation.

savings institutions
Savings associations and savings banks combined.

by savings associations in these areas often failed to pay off. This risk-taking, or moral hazard, behavior was accentuated by the policies of the savings association insurer, the FSLIC. It chose not to close capital-depleted, economically insolvent savings associations (a policy of **regulator forbearance**) and to maintain deposit insurance premium assessments independent of the risk of the savings institution (see Chapter 19).[27] As a result, there was an increasing number of failures in the 1982–89 period aligned with rapid asset growth of the industry. Thus, while savings associations decreased in number from 4,000 in 1980 to 2,600 in 1989, or by 35 percent, their assets actually doubled from $600 billion to $1.2 trillion over that period. Figure 2–6 shows the number of failures, mergers, and new charters of **savings institutions** (savings associations and savings banks combined) from 1984 through 2003. Notice the large number of failures from 1987 through 1992 and the decline in the number of new charters.

The large number of savings institution failures, especially in 1988 and 1989, depleted the resources of the FSLIC to such an extent that by 1989 it was massively insolvent. The resulting legislation—the FIRREA of 1989—abolished the FSLIC and created a new insurance fund (SAIF) under the management of the FDIC. In addition, the act created the Resolution Trust Corporation (RTC) to close the most insolvent savings associations.[28] Further, the FIRREA strengthened the capital

[27] We discuss moral hazard behavior and the empirical evidence regarding such behavior in more detail in Chapter 19.

[28] At the time of its dissolution in 1995, the RTC had resolved or closed more than 700 savings institutions.

QTL test
Qualified thrift lender test that sets a floor on the mortgage-related assets held by thrifts (currently 65 percent).

requirements of savings associations and constrained their non-mortgage-related asset-holding powers under a newly imposed qualified thrift lender, or **QTL, test**. In 1991, Congress enacted the FDICIA. FDICIA introduced risk-based deposit insurance premiums (starting in 1993) in an attempt to limit excess risk taking by savings associations and banks. It also introduced a prompt corrective action (PCA) policy, such that regulators could close thrifts and banks faster (see Chapter 20). In particular, if a savings association's ratio of its equity capital to its assets fell below 2 percent, it had to be closed down or recapitalized within three months.

As a result of the closing of weak savings associations and the strengthening of capital requirements, the industry shrunk significantly, both in numbers and in asset size, in the 1990s. Thus, savings associations decreased in number from 2,600 in 1989 to 1,074 in 2003 (by 59 percent), and assets shrank from $1.2 trillion to $1,074 billion (by 11 percent) over that same period.[29]

Balance Sheet and Recent Trends

Even in its new shrunken state, concerns have been raised about the future viability of the savings association industry in traditional mortgage lending areas. This is partly due to intense competition for mortgages from other financial institutions, such as commercial banks and specialized mortgage bankers.[30] It is also due to the securitization of mortgages into mortgage-backed security pools by government-sponsored enterprises, which we discuss further in Chapter 28.[31] In addition, long-term mortgage lending exposes an FI to significant credit, interest rate, and liquidity risks.

Table 2–9, column (2), shows the balance sheet of SAIF-insured savings associations in 2003. On this balance sheet, mortgages and mortgage-backed securities (securitized pools of mortgages) account for 73.17 percent of total assets. This compares with 29.89 percent in commercial banks. As noted earlier, the FDICIA uses the qualified thrift lender (QTL) test to establish a minimum holding of 65 percent in mortgage-related assets for savings associations. Reflecting the enhanced lending powers established under the 1980 DIDMCA and the 1982 DIA, commercial loans and consumer loans amounted to 3.64 and 5.46 percent of assets, respectively. Finally, savings associations are required to hold cash and investment securities for liquidity risk purposes and to meet regulator-imposed reserve requirements. In December 2003, cash and U.S. Treasury securities holdings amounted to 3.04 percent of total assets, compared with 18.33 percent at commercial banks.

On the liability side of the balance sheet, small time and savings deposits are still the predominant source of funds, with total deposits accounting for 62.84 percent of total liabilities and net worth. The second most important source of funds consists of borrowings from the Federal Home Loan Banks (FHLBs), of which there are 12; these banks in turn are owned by the savings associations themselves. Because of their size and government-sponsored status, FHLBs have access to wholesale money markets and the capital market for notes and bonds and can relend the funds borrowed on these markets to savings associations at a small markup over wholesale cost. Other borrowed funds include repurchase

---

[29] Total assets for savings associations were as low as $864 billion in 2000, a drop of 28 percent from 1989.

[30] See, for example, W. R. Keeton and A. D. McKibben, "Changes in the Depository Industry in Tenth District States," Kansas City, *Economic Review,* Third Quarter 1997, pp. 55–76.

[31] The major enterprises are GNMA, FNMA, and FHLMC.

TABLE 2–9   Assets and Liabilities of Savings Banks and Savings Associations, December 31, 2003

	(1) BIF-Insured Savings Banks		(2) SAIF-Insured Savings Associations	
	($ millions)	(Percent)	($ millions)	(Percent)
Cash and due from	$ 8,598	1.82%	$ 30,238	3.02%
U.S. Treasury securities	2,679	0.57	149	0.02
Mortgage loans	274,571	57.98	596,184	59.57
MBS (includes CMOs, POs, IOs)	70,241	14.83	136,148	13.60
Bonds, notes, debentures, and other securities	44,197	9.33	71,285	7.12
Corporate stock	4,577	0.97	6,159	0.62
Commercial loans	15,305	3.23	36,399	3.64
Consumer loans	23,246	4.91	54,613	5.46
Other loans and financing leases	3,291	0.69	2,106	0.21
Less: allowance for loan losses and unearned income	(3,036)	(0.64)	(5,523)	(0.55)
Other assets	29,882	6.31	72,979	7.29
Total assets	$473,551	100.00%	$1,000,737	100.00%
Total deposits	$296,608	62.64%	$628,815	62.84%
Borrowings and mortgages warehousing	92,325	19.50	204,333	20.42
Federal funds and repurchase agreements	32,531	6.87	58,864	5.88
Other liabilities	6,415	1.35	15,652	1.56
Total liabilities	427,879	90.36	907,664	90.70
Net worth*	45,672	9.64	93,073	9.30
Total liabilities and net worth	$473,551	100.00%	$1,000,737	100.00%
Number of institutions		339		1,074

*Includes limited life preferred stock for BIF-insured state-chartered savings banks and redeemable preferred stock and minority interest for SAIF-insured institutions and BIF-insured FSBs.
Source: FDIC, December 2003. *www.fdic.gov*

agreements and direct federal fund borrowings. Finally, net worth, the book value of the equity holders' capital contribution, amounted to 9.30 percent of total assets in 2003. This compares with 9.10 percent at commercial banks.

Regulation

The two main regulators of savings associations are the Office of Thrift Supervision (OTS) and the FDIC-SAIF Fund.

www.ots.treas.gov

The Office of Thrift Supervision   Established in 1989 under the FIRREA, this office charters and examines all federal savings associations. Further, when savings associations are held by parent holding companies, it supervises the holding companies as well. State-chartered savings associations are regulated by state agencies rather than by the Office of Thrift Supervision.

www.fdic.gov

The FDIC-SAIF Fund   Also established in 1989 under the FIRREA and in the wake of the FSLIC insolvency, the FDIC oversees and manages the Savings Association Insurance Fund (SAIF). In 1996, as part of a plan to recapitalize the SAIF, commercial banks were required to pay for part of the burden. In return, Congress promised to eventually merge bank and thrift charters (and hence insurance funds) into one. This will require thrifts to operate under the same regulatory structure that applies to commercial banks.

Concept Questions

1. Are savings associations likely to be more or less exposed to interest rate risk than are banks? Explain your answer.
2. How do adjustable rate mortgages help savings associations?
3. Why should savings associations with little or no equity capital seek to take more risk than well-capitalized savings associations?
4. Why could it be argued that the QTL test makes savings associations more rather than less risky?

Savings Banks

Size, Structure, and Composition of the Industry

mutual organizations
Savings banks in which the depositors are also the legal owners of the bank.

Traditionally, savings banks were established as **mutual organizations** (in which the depositors are also legally the owners of the bank) in states that permitted such organizations. These states are largely confined to the East Coast—for example, New York, New Jersey, and the New England states. As a result, savings banks (unlike savings associations) were not as affected by the oil-based economic shocks that impacted Texas and the Southwest in the 1980s. Nevertheless, the crash in New England real estate values in 1990–91 presented equally troubling problems for this group. Indeed, many of the failures of savings institutions in the early 1990s (see Figure 2–6) were savings banks rather than savings associations. In addition, in recent years, many of these institutions—similar to savings associations—have switched from mutual to stock charters. Further, some (fewer than 20) have switched to federal charters. As a result, like savings associations, savings banks have decreased in both size and number. In December 2003, 339 savings banks had $474 billion in assets; their deposits are insured by the FDIC under the BIF. FDIC insurance under BIF is just one characteristic that distinguishes savings banks from savings associations, whose deposits are insured under the FDIC-SAIF.

Balance Sheet and Recent Trends

savings banks
Mostly mutually owned savings institutions that specialize in residential mortgages funded by deposits.

Notice the major similarities and differences between savings associations and **savings banks** in Table 2–9, which shows their respective assets and liabilities in December 2003. Savings banks [column (1) of Table 2–9] have a heavy concentration of 72.81 percent in mortgage loans and mortgage-backed securities (MBSs), but this is less than the savings associations' 73.17 percent in these assets. Over the years, savings banks have been allowed to diversify more into corporate bonds and stocks; their holdings are 10.30 percent compared with 7.74 percent for savings associations. On the liability and equity side, the ratio of the book value of net worth to total liabilities and net worth for savings banks stood at 9.64 percent (compared with 9.30 percent for savings associations) in 2003.

Regulation

Savings banks may be regulated at both the federal and state levels.

www.ots.treas.gov

The Office of Thrift Supervision   The Office of Thrift Supervision charters and examines all *federal* savings banks.

The FDIC-BIF   Savings banks are insured under the FDIC's BIF and are thus subject to supervision and examination by the FDIC.

www.fdic.gov

Other Regulators   State-chartered savings banks (the vast majority) are regulated by state agencies. Savings banks that adopt federal charters are subject to the regulations of the OTS (the same as savings associations).

TABLE 2–10   Selected Indicators for U.S. Savings Institutions, 1989 through 2003

	2003	2002	2001	2000	1999	1997	1995	1993	1989
Number of institutions	1,413	1,467	1,535	1,589	1,642	1,780	2,030	2,262	3,086
Return on assets (%)	1.28	1.16	1.07	0.92	1.00	0.93	0.77	0.71	−0.39
Return on equity (%)	13.66	12.37	12.33	11.14	11.73	10.84	9.40	9.32	−8.06
Noncurrent assets plus other real estate owned to assets (%)	0.62	0.69	0.65	0.56	0.58	0.95	1.20	2.10	2.78
Asset growth rate (%)	8.49	3.20	8.17	6.41	5.60	−0.21	1.70	−2.85	−11.14
Net operating income growth (%)	23.07	5.61	6.64	3.55	16.70	20.07	13.81	21.16	−58.95
Number of failed institutions	0	1	1	1	1	0	2	8	331

Source: FDIC, *Quarterly Banking Profile*, various issues, and *Historical Statistics*, 1989. *www.fdic.gov*

Concept Questions

1. List four characteristics that differentiate savings banks from savings associations.
2. How are savings banks regulated?

Recent Performance of Savings Associations and Savings Banks

Like commercial banks, savings institutions (savings associations and savings banks) experienced record profits in the mid- to late-1990s as interest rates (and thus the cost of funds to savings institutions) remained low and the U.S. economy expanded. The result was an increase in the spread between interest income and interest expense for savings institutions and consequently an increase in their net income. In 1999, savings institutions reported $10.7 billion in net income and an annualized ROA of 1.00 percent (this compares with an ROA of 1.31 percent over the same period for commercial banks). Only the $10.8 billion of net income reported in 1998 exceeded these results. Asset quality improvements were widespread during 1999, providing the most favorable net operating income that the industry had ever reported. However, as in the commercial banking industry, the downturn in the U.S. economy also resulted in a decline in savings institutions' profitability in 2000. Specifically, their ROA and ROE ratios fell slightly in 2000 to 0.92 percent and 11.14 percent, respectively, from their 1999 levels. Again, as with commercial banks, despite an economic recession, this downturn was short-lived. Both ROA and ROE increased to record levels each year from 2001 through 2003. The industry's net interest margins rose: The cost of funding earning assets declined by 2.70 percent while the yield on earning assets declined by only 2.35 percent. However, net charge-offs in 2003 were almost twice those in 2000. Table 2–10 presents several performance ratios for the industry for various years from 1989 through 2003.

Also like commercial banks, savings institutions experienced substantial consolidation in the 1990s. For example, the 1998 acquisition of H. F. Ahmanson & Co. by Washington Mutual Inc. for almost $10 billion was the fourth-largest bank–thrift merger completed in 1998.[32] Washington Mutual was the third-largest savings institutions in the United States early in 1997, while Ahmanson was the largest savings institution. In 1997, Washington Mutual bought Great Western, to

[32] Behind Travelers Group–Citigroup ($74 billion), NationsBank–BankAmerica ($67 billion), and BankOne–First Chicago NBD ($30 billion).

TABLE 2–11 U.S. Savings Institution Asset Concentration, 1992 versus 2003

	2003				1992			
	Number	Percent of Total	Assets*	Percent of Total	Number	Percent of Total	Assets*	Percent of Total
All FDIC-insured								
savings institutions	1,413		$1,474.3		2,391		$1,035.2	
1. Under $100 million	479	33.9%	24.9	1.7%	1,109	46.4%	55,946	5.4%
2. $100 million—$1 billion	777	55.0	250.6	17.0	1,093	45.7	315,246	30.5
3. $1 billion–$10 billion	110	7.8	217.6	14.8	181	7.6	479,526	46.3
4. $10 billion or more	47	3.3	981.2	66.5	8	0.3	184,476	17.8

Source: *FDIC Quarterly Banking Profile*, Fourth Quarter 1992 and Fourth Quarter 2003. *www.fdic.gov*
*In billions of dollars.

become the largest thrift in the country. Then, in March 1998, Washington Mutual bought Ahmanson to combine the two largest U.S. thrifts. Table 2–11 shows the industry consolidation in number and asset size over the period 1992–2003. Notice that over this period, the biggest savings institutions (over $10 billion in assets) grew in number from 8 to 47 and their control of industry assets grew from 17.8 percent to 66.5 percent.

Concept Questions

1. Describe the recent performance of savings institutions.
2. Describe the ways that profit trends for savings institutions have been similar to those of commercial banks in the 1990s and early 2000s.

CREDIT UNIONS

credit unions
Nonprofit depository institutions, owned by members with a common bond, specializing in small consumer loans.

Credit unions (CUs) are nonprofit depository institutions mutually organized and owned by their members (depositors). Credit unions (CUs) were first established in the United States in the early 1900s as self-help organizations intended to alleviate widespread poverty. The first credit unions were organized in the Northeast, initially in Massachusetts. Members paid an entrance fee and invested funds to purchase at least one deposit share in the CU. Members were expected to deposit their savings in the CU, and these funds were lent only to other members.

This limit in the customer base of CUs continues today as, unlike commercial banks and savings institutions, CUs are prohibited from serving the general public. Rather, in organizing a credit union, members are required to have a common bond of occupation (e.g., police CUs) or association (e.g., university-affiliated CUs), or to cover a well-defined neighborhood, community, or rural district. CUs may, however, have multiple groups with more than one type of membership.

The primary objective of credit unions is to satisfy the depository and lending needs of their members. CU member deposits (shares) are used to provide loans to other members in need of funds. Any earnings from these loans are used to pay higher rates on member deposits, charge lower rates on member loans, or attract new members to the CU. Because credit unions do not issue common stock, the members are legally the owners of a CU. Also, because credit unions are nonprofit organizations, their net income is not taxed and they are not subject to the local investment requirements established under the 1977 Community Reinvestment Act. This tax-exempt status allows CUs to offer higher rates on deposits, and charge

FIGURE 2–7
Credit Union versus
Bank Interest Rates

Source: Federal Reserve;
and National Credit Union
Administration, April 2004.
www.federalreserve.gov
www.ncua.gov

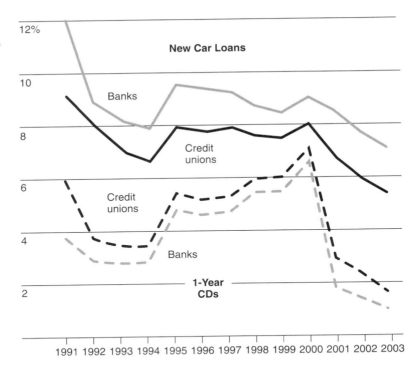

lower rates on some types of loans, than do banks and savings institutions. This is shown in Figure 2–7 for the period 1991–2003.

Size, Structure, and Composition of the Industry and Recent Trends

Credit unions are the most numerous of the institutions that make up the depository institutions segment of the FI industry, totaling 9,529 in 2003. Moreover, they were less affected by the crisis that impacted commercial banks and savings institutions in the 1980s[33] because traditionally, more than 40 percent of their assets have been in the form of small consumer loans, often for amounts less than $10,000. In addition, CUs tend to hold large amounts of government securities (20.1 percent of their assets in 2003) and relatively small amounts of residential mortgages. Their lending activities are funded by savings deposits contributed by over 80 million members who share some common thread or bond of association, usually geographic or occupational in nature.

To attract and keep customers, CUs have had to expand their services to compete with those of commercial banks and savings institutions. For example, CUs now offer products and services ranging from mortgages and auto loans (their traditional services) to credit lines and automated teller machines. Some credit unions now offer business and commercial loans to their employer groups. For example, in the late 1990s, AWANE (Automotive Wholesalers Association of New England)

---

[33] Credit unions have been covered by federal deposit insurance guarantees since 1971 (under the National Credit Union Share Insurance Fund). The depositor coverage cap of $100,000 is the same as that which currently exists for both commercial banks and savings institutions.

Credit Union's[34] business loans represented 13.6 percent of its lending and the CU participated actively in the Small Business Administration loan programs, which enabled it to sell a portion of those loans. In addition, commercial real estate lending accounted for 29.5 percent of AWANE's total lending. Because of their tax-exempt status, CUs can charge lower rates on these loans, providing CUs with a cost advantage over banks and savings institutions that is very attractive to customers.

As CUs have expanded in number, size, and services, bankers have claimed that CUs are unfairly competing with small banks that have historically been the major lenders in small towns. For example, the American Bankers Association has stated that the tax exemption for CUs gives them the equivalent of a $1 billion per year subsidy. The Credit Union National Association's (CUNA) response is that any cost to taxpayers from CUs' tax-exempt status is more than made up in benefits to members and therefore the social good they create. CUNA estimates that the benefits of CU membership can range from $200 to $500 a year per member or, with over 80 million members, a total benefit of $14 billion to $35 billion per year.

www.aba.com

In 1997 the banking industry filed two lawsuits in its push to narrow the widening membership rules governing credit unions that followed a 1982 legal interpretation of the original 1934 Federal Credit Union Act's definition of what constitutes a "group having a common bond of occupation or association." The first lawsuit (filed by four North Carolina banks and the American Bankers Association) challenged the ability of an occupation-based credit union (the AT&T Family Credit Union based in North Carolina) to accept members from companies unrelated to the firm that originally sponsored the CU. In the second lawsuit, the American Bankers Association asked the courts to bar the federal government from letting occupation-based credit unions convert to community-based charters. Bankers argued in both lawsuits that such actions, broadening the membership of credit unions under other than occupation-based guidelines, would further exploit an unfair advantage allowed by the credit unions' tax-exempt status. In February 1998 the Supreme Court sided with banks, stating that credit unions could no longer accept members who did not share the common bond of membership. In April 1998, however, the U.S. House of Representatives overwhelmingly passed a bill that allowed all existing members to keep their credit union accounts. The bill was passed by the Senate in July 1998 and signed into law by the president in August 1998. This legislation allowed CUs not only to keep their existing members but also to accept new groups of members—including small businesses and low-income communities—that were not considered part of the "common bond" of membership by the Supreme Court ruling.

Balance Sheets

Table 2–12 shows the assets and liabilities for credit unions in December 31, 2003. In that year 9,529 credit unions had assets of $617.3 billion. This compares with $155 billion in assets in 1987, for a growth rate of almost 300 percent over the period 1987–2003. Individually, credit unions tend to be very small, with an average size of $64.8 million in 2003 compared with $978.6 million for banks. The total

---

[34] AWANE is a trade association of companies that serve the automotive aftermarket through sales of auto parts and other items. It is the association of member companies and firms related to the automotive business, as well as their owners and employees, whom the AWANE Credit Union serves through its common bond.

TABLE 2–12
Assets and
Liabilities of Credit
Unions, December
31, 2003

Source: *Federal Reserve
Bulletin*, December 2003.
www.federalreserve.gov

	Billions of Dollars	Percent
Assets		
Checkable deposits and currency	$ 41.5	6.7%
Time and savings deposits	26.4	4.3
Federal funds and security RPs	1.6	0.3
Open market paper	1.6	0.3
U.S. government securities	124.4	20.1
Treasury	8.9	1.4
Agency	115.5	18.7
Home mortgages	181.1	29.3
Consumer credit	209.7	34.0
Credit market instruments	586.3	95.0
Mutual fund shares	4.1	0.7
Miscellaneous assets	26.9	4.3
Total assets	$617.3	100.0%
Liabilities and Equity		
Checkable	$ 67.4	10.9%
Small time and savings	424.0	68.7
Large time	53.6	8.7
Shares and deposits	545.0	88.3
Other loans and advances	9.1	1.5
Miscellaneous liabilities	6.3	1.0
Total liabilities	560.4	90.8
Total ownership shares	56.9	9.2

assets of all credit unions are approximately half the size of those of the largest U.S. banking organization, Citigroup.[35]

Given their emphasis on retail or consumer lending, discussed above, 34.0 percent of CU assets are in the form of small consumer loans and another 29.3 percent are in the form of home mortgages. Together, these member loans constitute 63.3 percent of total assets. Because of the common bond requirement on credit union customers, relatively few business or commercial loans are issued by CUs.

Credit unions also invest heavily in investment securities (25.0 percent of total assets in 2003). Further, 80.9 percent of the investment portfolios of CUs are in U.S. government Treasury securities or federal agency securities, while investments in other FIs (such as deposits of banks) totaled 17.2 percent of CUs' investment portfolios. Their investment portfolio composition, along with their cash holdings (6.7 percent of total assets), allow credit unions ample liquidity to meet their daily cash needs—such as share (deposit) withdrawals. Some CUs have also increased their off-balance-sheet activities. Specifically, unused loan commitments, including credit card limits and home equity lines of credit, totaled over $94 billion in 2003.

Credit union funding comes mainly from member deposits (88.3 percent of total funding in 2003). Figure 2–8 presents the distribution of these deposits in 2003.

---

[35] Whereas in the United States credit unions account for a relatively small proportion of the financial services industry, in many less developed countries they play an important role in mobilizing savings at the rural level. One very important credit union–type FI, first developed in Bangladesh and extended to other LDCs, has been the Grameen Bank. See, for example, H. K. Hassan and L. Renteria-Guerrero, "The Experience of the Grameen Bank of Bangladesh in Community Development," *International Journal of Social Economics* 24, no. 12 (1997), pp. 1488–1523.

FIGURE 2–8
Composition of
Credit Union
Deposits, 2003

Source: National Credit
Union Association, *Year-end
Statistics*, 2003. *www.ncua.gov*

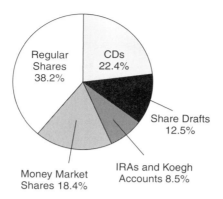

Regular share draft transaction accounts (similar to NOW accounts at other depository institutions) accounted for 38.2 percent of all CU deposits, followed by certificates of deposit (22.4 percent of deposits) and share accounts—similar to passbook savings accounts at other depository institutions, but so named to designate the deposit holders' ownership status—(12.5 percent of deposits). Credit unions tend to hold higher levels of equity than other depository institutions. Since CUs are not stockholder owned, this equity is basically the accumulation of past profits from CU activities that are "owned" collectively by member depositors. As will be discussed in Chapters 7 and 20, this equity protects a CU against losses on its loan portfolio as well as against other financial and operating risks. In December 2003, CUs' capital-to-assets ratio was 9.22 percent compared with 9.64 percent for savings associations, 9.30 percent for savings banks, and 9.10 percent for commercial banks.

Regulation

Like savings banks and savings associations, credit unions can be federally or state chartered. As of 2003, 61.5 percent of the 9,529 CUs were federally chartered and subject to National Credit Union Administration (NCUA) regulation, accounting for 55.7 percent of the total credit union membership and 54.9 percent of total assets. In addition, through its insurance fund (the National Credit Union Share Insurance Fund, or NCUSIF), the NCUA provides deposit insurance guarantees of up to $100,000 for insured credit unions. Currently, the NCUSIF covers 98 percent of all credit union deposits.

www.ncua.gov
www.cuna.org

Industry Performance

Like other depository institutions, the credit union industry has grown in asset size in the 1990s and early 2000s. Asset growth from 1999 to 2003 was more than 10 percent annually. In addition, CU membership increased from 75.4 million to over 81.8 million over the 1999–2003 period. Asset growth was especially pronounced among the largest CUs (with assets of over $500 million) as their assets increased by over 20 percent annually from 1999 through 2003. Figure 2–9 shows the trend in ROA for CUs from 1993 through 2003. The decrease in ROA over the period is mostly attributed to earnings decreases at the smaller CUs. For example, the largest credit unions experienced an ROA of 1.24 percent in 2003, while for the smallest CUs (with assets of less than $2 million) the ROA was 0.30. ROA for the whole industry was 0.98 percent. Smaller CUs generally have a smaller customer base

FIGURE 2–9
Return on Assets for Credit Unions, 1993 through 2003

Source: National Credit Union Association, *Year-end Statistics*, 2003. *www.ncua.gov*

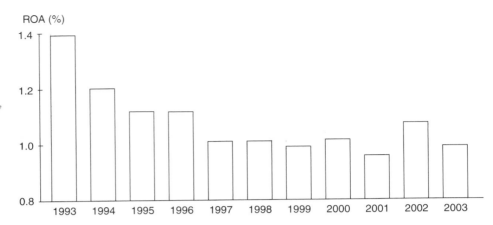

with which to issue quality loans and have higher overhead expenses per dollar of assets. Thus, their ROAs have been hurt.

Given the mutual-ownership status of this industry, however, growth in ROA (or profits) is not necessarily the primary goal of CUs. Rather, as long as capital or equity levels are sufficient to protect a CU against unexpected losses on its credit portfolio as well as other financial and operational risks, this not-for-profit industry has a primary goal of serving the deposit and lending needs of its members. This contrasts with the emphasis placed on profitability by stockholder-owned commercial banks and savings institutions.

Concept Questions

1. How do credit unions differ from commercial banks and savings institutions?
2. Why have credit unions prospered in recent years compared with savings associations and savings banks?
3. What is the major asset held by credit unions?
4. Why do commercial banks and savings institutions claim that credit unions have an unfair advantage in providing bank services?

GLOBAL ISSUES: JAPAN, CHINA, AND GERMANY

While U.S. depository institution performance deteriorated only slightly in the early 2000s, not all countries fared as well. In April 2001, the Japanese government announced plans for a government-backed purchase of ¥11,000 billion ($90 billion) of shares of Japanese banks as part of an increasingly frantic drive to avert a banking crisis, recover from a 16-year low in the levels of Japanese stock markets, and stem the country's economic decline. This was the third major attempt to bail out the banking system since 1998. Previous attempts had been unsuccessful. For example, in March 2001, Fitch Investors Service (a major international rating agency) put 19 of the biggest Japanese banks on its credit watch list. The purchase of bank shares was intended to offset losses from writing off bad loans (estimated to be as high as ¥32,000 billion ($260 billion) in bank portfolios. Foreign financial institutions were also solicited in attempts to prevent a complete financial collapse in Japan. For instance, in October 2003, Goldman Sachs set up an investment fund to buy as much as ¥1 trillion ($9.1 billion) in nonperforming loans from the Sumitomo Mitsui Banking Corporation. Earlier, in January 2003, Goldman agreed to buy ¥150.3 billion ($1.4 billion) of preferred shares from Sumitomo. Merrill Lynch and Deutsche Bank also bought troubled assets from Japanese banks. These efforts, along with a strengthening Japanese economy, appear to have averted a disaster. By the end of 2003, Japanese banks posted their largest earnings in years. Specifically, as of September 2003, Japan's eight biggest banking groups all reported positive six-month net profits.[36]

In China, however, the banking industry deteriorated in the early 2000s. China's four state-run banks had about $120 billion in nonperforming loans, accounting for about 21 percent of total loans. Private economists put the percentage of nonperforming loans closer to 50 percent of total loans. Looking to clean up its troubled banking sector, the China Banking Regulatory Commission unveiled a comprehensive plan to overhaul the country's banking system, one that included a shift by China from restricting overseas competition to allowing it. The plan gives foreign banks greater scope to operate. Measures include raising the ceiling on foreign ownership in Chinese financial institutions from 15 percent to 20 percent for a single investor, expanding the number of cities where foreign branches can do some local currency business, and easing capital requirements for branches.

Also experiencing trouble in the early 2000s were Germany's largest banks, which were experiencing their worst downturn since World War II. German banks' problems were due to mounting bad loans (the result of low growth and high unemployment in Germany for nearly a decade) which resulted in plummeting profits and share prices. Further, smaller local banks increasingly competed for loan business, contributing to a crisis for the country's biggest banks. Backed by government guarantees on their own borrowing, small banks enjoyed high credit ratings and low cost of funds. This resulted in a tradition of low lending rates that left these banks with 67 percent of the small business loan market and 39 percent of all checking accounts. Without a robust stream of loan income, the large German banks were heavily reliant on trading and fee income from securities business. But that income dried up with the fall in the stock market.

Summary

This chapter provided an overview of the major activities of commercial banks, savings institutions, and credit unions. It also described the agencies that regulate these depository institutions. The Federal Reserve System, the FDIC, the OTS, and the Office of the Comptroller of the Currency, in conjunction with state regulators, are the agencies that oversee the activities of these institutions. Each of these institutions relies heavily on deposits to fund its activities, although borrowed funds are becoming increasingly important for the largest institutions. Historically, commercial banks have concentrated on commercial or business lending and on investing in securities, while savings institutions have concentrated on mortgage lending and credit unions have concentrated on consumer lending. These differences are being eroded as a result of competitive forces, regulation, and changing financial and business technology. Specifically, in the late 1990s and early 2000s, the largest group of assets in commercial bank portfolios were mortgage related, and the largest banking organization, Citigroup, was created out of a merger with an insurance company (Travelers) that owned a major securities firm (Salomon Brothers).

[36] See "Respite for Japanese Banks," *The Wall Street Journal*, November 26, 2003. p. C12; and "Japan's Banks Post Profits," *The Wall Street Journal*, May 25, 2004, p. C14.

Questions and Problems

1. What are the differences between community banks, regional banks, and money center banks? Contrast the business activities, location, and markets of each of these bank groups.

2. Use the data in Table 2–4 for the banks in the two asset size groups (a) $100 million–$1 billion and (b) over $10 billion to answer the following questions.

   a. Why have the ratios for ROA and ROE tended to increase for both groups over the 1990–2003 period? Identify and discuss the primary variables that affect ROA and ROE as they relate to these two size groups.

   b. Why is ROA for the smaller banks generally larger than ROA for the large banks?

   c. Why is the ratio for ROE consistently larger for the large bank group?

   d. Using the information on ROE decomposition in Appendix 2A, calculate the ratio of equity to total assets for each of the two bank groups for the period 1990–2003. Why has there been such dramatic change in the values over this time period, and why is there a difference in the size of the ratio for the two groups?

3. What factors have caused the decrease in loan volume relative to other assets on the balance sheets of commercial banks? How has each of these factors been related to the change and development of the financial services industry during the 1990s and early 2000s? What strategic changes have banks implemented to deal with changes in the financial services environment?

4. What are the major uses of funds for commercial banks in the United States? What are the primary risks to a bank caused by each use of funds? Which of the risks is most critical to the continuing operation of a bank?

5. What are the major sources of funds for commercial banks in the United States? How is the landscape for these funds changing and why?

6. What are the three major segments of deposit funding? How are these segments changing over time? Why? What strategic impact do these changes have on the profitable operation of a bank?

7. How does the liability maturity structure of a bank's balance sheet compare with the maturity structure of the asset portfolio? What risks are created or intensified by these differences?

8. The following balance sheet accounts have been taken from the annual report for a U.S. bank. Arrange the accounts in balance sheet order and determine the value of total assets. Based on the balance sheet structure, would you classify this bank as a community bank, regional bank, or money center bank?

Premises	$ 1,078	Net loans	$29,981
Savings deposits	3,292	Short-term borrowing	2,080
Cash	2,660	Other liabilities	778
NOW accounts	12,816	Equity	3,272
Long-term debt	1,191	Investment securities	5,334
Other assets	1,633	Demand deposits	5,939
Intangible assets	758	Certificates of deposit (under $100,000)	$ 9,853
Other time deposits	$ 2,333	Federal funds sold	$ 110

9. What types of activities are normally classified as off-balance-sheet (OBS) activities?

   a. How does an OBS activity move onto the balance sheet as an asset or liability?

   b. What are the benefits of OBS activities to a bank?

   c. What are the risks of OBS activities to a bank?

10. Use the data in Table 2–6 to answer the following questions.

   a. What was the average annual growth rate in OBS total commitments over the period 1992–2003?

   b. What categories of contingencies have had the highest annual growth rates?

   c. What factors are credited for the significant growth in derivative securities activities by banks?

11. For each of the following banking organizations, identify which regulatory agencies (OCC, FRB, FDIC, or state banking commission) may have some regulatory supervision responsibility:

   a. State-chartered, nonmember non–holding company bank.

   b. State-chartered, nonmember holding company bank.

   c. State-chartered member bank.

   d. Nationally chartered non–holding company bank.

   e. Nationally chartered holding company bank.

12. What factors normally are given credit for the revitalization of the banking industry during the 1990s? How is Internet banking expected to provide benefits in the future?

13. What factors are given credit for the strong performance of commercial banks in the early 2000s?

14. What are the main features of the Riegle-Neal Interstate Banking and Branching Efficiency Act of 1994? What major impact on commercial banking activity is expected from this legislation?

15. What happened in 1979 to cause the failure of many savings associations during the early 1980s? What was the effect of this change on the operating statements of savings associations?

16. How did two pieces of regulatory legislation—the DIDMCA in 1980 and the DIA in 1982—change the operating profitability of savings associations in the early 1980s? What impact did these pieces of legislation ultimately have on the risk posture of the savings association industry? How did the FSLIC react to this change in operating performance and risk?

17. How do the asset and liability structures of a savings association compare with the asset and liability structures of a commercial bank? How do these structural differences affect the risks and operating performance of savings association? What is the QTL test?

18. How do savings banks differ from savings associations? Differentiate in terms of risk, operating performance, balance sheet structure, and regulatory responsibility.

19. How did the Financial Institutions Reform, Recovery, and Enforcement Act (FIRREA) of 1989 and the Federal Deposit Insurance Corporation Improvement Act of 1991 reverse some of the key features of earlier legislation?

20. What is the "common bond" membership qualification under which credit unions have been formed and operated? How does this qualification affect the operational objective of a credit union?

21. What are the operating advantages of credit unions that have caused concern among commercial bankers? What has been the response of the Credit Union National Association to the banks' criticism?

22. How does the asset structure of credit unions compare with the asset structure of commercial banks and savings institutions and credit unions? Refer to Tables 2–5, 2–9, and 2–12 to formulate your answer.

23. Compare and contrast the performance of the U.S. depository institution industry with those of Japan, China, and Germany.

Web Questions

24. Go to the FDIC Web site at **www.fdic.gov** and find the most recent breakdown of U.S. bank asset concentrations using the following steps. Click on "Analysts." From there click On "FDIC Quality Banking Profile" and then click on "Quarterly Banking Profile." Click on "Commercial Bank Section." Then click on "TABLE III-A. Full Year 20XX, FDIC-Insured Commercial Banks." This will bring the files up on your computer that contain the relevant data. How have the number and dollar value of assets held by commercial banks changed since 2003?

25. Go to the Federal Reserve Board's Web site at **www.federalreserve.gov** and find the most recent balance sheet information for the credit union industry using the following steps. Click on "Economic Research and Data." Click on "Statistics: Releases and Historical Data." Click on "Flow of Funds Accounts of the United States, *Releases*." Click on the most recent date. Click on "Level tables." Using information in this file (in Table L 115) update Table 2–12. How have the assets and liabilities of credit unions changed since December 2003?

26. Go to the National Credit Union Association Web site at **www.ncua.gov** to collect the most recent information on number of credit unions, assets of credit unions, and membership in credit unions using the following steps. Under "Resources," click on "Reports, Plans, and Statistics." Click on "Credit Union Statistics." Click on the most recent statistical data. This will download a file on to your computer that will contain the necessary data. How have these data changed since 2003?

S&P Questions

STANDARD
&POOR'S

27. Go to the Standard & Poor's Market Insight Web site at **www.mhhe.com/edumarketinsight**. Identify the industry description and industry constituents for banks using the following steps. Click on "Educational Version of Market Insight." Enter your Site ID and click on "Login." Click on "Industry." From the Industry list, select "Banks." Click on "Go!" Click on "Industry Profile" and separately, "Industry Constituents."

STANDARD
&POOR'S

28. Go to the Standard & Poor's Market Insight Web site at **www.mhhe.com/edumarketinsight**. Look up the industry financial highlights for banks as posted by S&P using the following steps. Click on "Educational Version of Market Insight." Enter your Site ID and click on "Login." Click on "Industry." From the Industry list, select "Banks." Click on "Go!" Click on any/all of the items listed under "Industry Financial Highlights."

STANDARD
&POOR'S

29. Go to the Standard & Poor's Market Insight Web site at **www.mhhe.com/edumarketinsight**. Find the most recent balance sheets for Bank of America (BAC) and MBNA (KRB) using the following steps. Click on "Educational Version of Market Insight." Enter your Site ID and click on "Login." Click on

"Company." Enter "BAC" in the "Ticker:" box and click on "Go!" Click on "FS Ann. Balance Sheet." This will download the Balance Sheet for Bank of America which contains the balances for Loans, Total Assets, and Stockholders Equity. Repeat the process by entering "KRB" in the "Ticker:" box to get information on MBNA. Compare the ratios of loans to total assets and of stockholders' equity to total assets from these balance sheets with that for the banking industry, as listed in Table 2–5.

STANDARD &POOR'S

30. Go to the Standard & Poor's Market Insight Web site at **www.mhhe.com/ edumarketinsight**. Find the most recent balance sheets for Washington Mutual (WM) and Golden West Financial (GDW) using the following steps. Click on "Educational Version of Market Insight." Enter your Site ID and click on "Login." Click on "Company." Enter "WM" in the "Ticker:" box and click on "Go!" Click on "FS Ann. Balance Sheet." This will download the Balance Sheet for Washington Mutual which contains the balances for Loans, Total Assets, and Stockholders Equity. Repeat the process by entering "GDW" in the "Ticker:" box to get information on Golden West Financial. Compare the ratios of loans to total assets and of stockholders' equity to total assets from these balance sheets with that for the savings association industry, as listed in Table 2–9.

Pertinent Web Sites

American Banks Association	**www.aba.com**
Board of Governors of the Federal Reserve	**www.federalreserve.gov**
Credit Union National Association	**www.cuna.org**
Federal Deposit Insurance Corporation	**www.fdic.gov**
National Credit Union Administration	**www.ncua.gov**
Office of the Comptroller of the Currency	**www.occ.treas.gov**
Office of Thrift Supervision	**www.ots.treas.gov**
The Wall Street Journal	**www.wsj.com**

www.mhhe.com/saunders5e

Appendix 2A

Financial Statement Analysis Using a Return on Equity (ROE) Framework

Between 1992 and 2000 the commercial banking industry experienced a period of record profits. This was quite a change from the late 1980s and early 1990s, when banks were failing in record numbers. Despite record profits, many FIs have areas of weakness and inefficiency that need to be addressed. One way of identifying weaknesses and problem areas is through an analysis of financial statements. In particular, an analysis of selected accounting ratios—ratio analysis—allows FI managers to evaluate the current performance of an FI, the change in an FI's performance over

FIGURE 2A–1
**Breakdown of ROE
into Various
Financial Ratios**

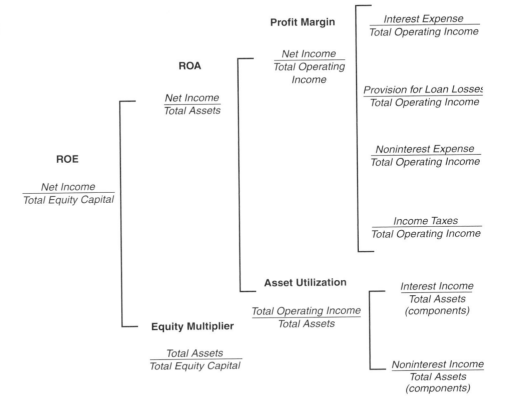

TABLE 2A–1
Role of ROE, ROA,
EM, PM, and AU in
Analyzing an FI's
Performance

Return on Equity (ROE): measures overall profitability of the FI per dollar of equity.
Return on Assets (ROA): measures profit generated relative to the FI's assets.
Equity Multiplier (EM): measures the extent to which assets of the FI are funded with equity relative to debt.
Profit Margin (PM): measures the ability to pay expenses and generate net income from interest and noninterest income.
Asset Utilization (AU): measures the amount of interest and noninterest income generated per dollar of total assets.

time (*time series analysis* of ratios over a period of time), and the performance of an FI relative to competitor FIs (*cross-sectional analysis* of ratios across a group of FIs).

Figure 2A–1 provides a summary of the breakdown of the return on equity (ROE) framework. This framework is similar to the DuPont analysis frequently used by managers of nonfinancial institutions. The ROE framework starts with a frequently used measure of profitability—return on equity (ROE)—and then decomposes ROE to identify strengths and weaknesses in an FI's performance.[1] Such a decomposition provides a convenient and systematic method for identifying

[1]Many large banks also use a risk-adjusted return on capital (RAROC) measure to evaluate the impact of credit risk on bank performance. ROE does not consider the bank's risk in lending as does RAROC. RAROC is described in Chapter 11.

the strengths and weaknesses of an FI's performance. Identification of strengths and weaknesses and the reasons for them provide a useful tool for FI managers as they look for ways to improve performance. Table 2A–1 summarizes the role of ROE and the first two levels (from Figure 2A–1) of its decomposition in analyzing an FI's performance.

These ratios are related as follows (see Figure 2A–1):

$$ROE = ROA \times EM$$
$$ROA = PM \times AU$$

In turn, the PM and AU ratios can also be broken down and shown to depend on key financial ratios (see Figure 2A–1).

Appendix 2B

Depository Institutions and Their Regulators

View Appendix 2B at the Web site for this textbook (**www.mhhe.com/saunders5e**).

Appendix 2C

Technology in Commercial Banking

View Appendix 2C at the Web site for this textbook (**www.mhhe.com/saunders5e**).

Chapter **Three**

The Financial Services Industry: Insurance Companies

INTRODUCTION

The primary function of insurance companies is to protect individuals and corporations (policyholders) from adverse events. By accepting premiums, insurance companies promise policyholders compensation if certain specified events occur. These policies represent financial liabilities to the insurance company. With the premiums collected, insurance companies invest in financial securities such as corporate bonds and stocks. The industry is classified into two major groups: life and property–casualty. Life insurance provides protection against the possibility of untimely death, illnesses, and retirement. Property insurance protects against personal injury and liability such as accidents, theft, and fire. However, as will become clear, insurance companies also sell a variety of investment products in a similar fashion to other financial service firms, such as mutual funds (Chapter 5) and depository institutions (Chapter 2).

As in Chapter 2, where we discussed banks and thrifts, in this chapter we describe the main features of life insurance and property–casualty insurance companies by concentrating on (1) the size, structure, and composition of the industry in which they operate, (2) balance sheets and recent trends, and (3) regulations for each. We also look at global competition and trends in this industry.

LIFE INSURANCE COMPANIES

Size, Structure, and Composition of the Industry

In the early 2000s, the United States had approximately 1,500 life insurance companies compared with over 2,300 in 1988. The aggregate assets of life insurance companies were $3.4 trillion at the beginning of 2003 compared with $1.12 trillion in 1988. The four largest life insurance companies, in terms of total assets (listed in Table 3–1) wrote 19 percent of the industry's $2.9 trillion new life insurance premium business in 2002. Interestingly, many of these insurance policies are sold through commercial banks. For example, in 2002 Nationwide sold $38.1 million in life insurance policies through banks, a 28 percent increase over 2001. In 2002

TABLE 3–1
Biggest Life Insurers

Source: *Best's Review*, July 2003; and author's research. *www.ambest.com*

Rank	Insurance Company	Form of Ownership	Assets in Billions
1	Metropolitan Life	Stock	$245.0
2	American International Group	Stock	233.7
3	Prudential of America	Stock	205.7
4	Aegon USA Inc.	Mutual	144.5
5	Teachers Insurance and Annuity	Stock	144.5
6	Hartford Life	Stock	136.8
7	ING Group	Stock	125.8
8	New York Life	Mutual	121.9
9	Northwestern Mutual	Mutual	102.9
10	Nationwide	Stock	87.4

bank sales of all types of insurance contracts increased by 26 percent overall, to $69.5 billion. This is up from $27.7 billion in 1997.

Although not to the extent seen in the banking industry, the life insurance industry has seen some major mergers in recent years (e.g., SunAmerica and AIG and Prudential and Cigna) as competition within the industry and from other FIs has increased. In addition, many of the largest insurance companies, such as Metropolitan and Prudential, have converted to stockholder-controlled companies. In so doing, they gain access to the equity markets in order to realize additional capital for future business expansions and to compete with the rapidly consolidating banking industry. Since a mutual company is owned by its policyholders, the existing capital and reserves (equal to accumulated past profits) have to be distributed to the insurer's policyholders. Table 3–1 lists the form of ownership for the top 10 life insurers in the United States, while Figure 3–1 illustrates the difference between a mutual insurer and a stock insurance company.

Life insurance allows individuals and their beneficiaries to protect against losses in income through premature death or retirement. By pooling risks, life insurance transfers income-related uncertainties from the insured individual to a group. While life insurance may be the core activity area, modern life insurance companies also sell annuity contracts, manage pension plans, and provide accident and health insurance (Figure 3–2 shows the distribution of premiums written for the various lines of insurance in 2002). We discuss these different activity lines in the following sections.

FIGURE 3–1
Mutual versus Stock Insurance Companies

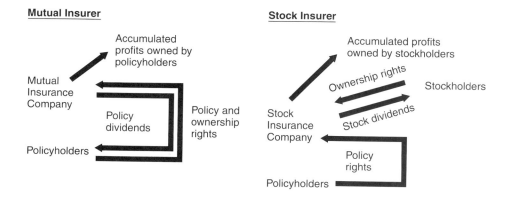

FIGURE 3–2
Distribution of
Premiums Written
on Various Life
Insurance Lines

Source: *Best's Review*,
September 2003.
www.ambest.com

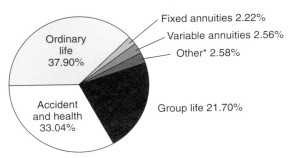

*Includes credit life and industrial life.

One problem that naturally faces life insurance companies (as well as property–casualty insurers) is the so-called adverse selection problem. Adverse selection is a problem in that customers who apply for insurance policies are more likely to be those most in need of insurance (i.e., someone with chronic health problems is more likely to purchase a life insurance policy than someone in perfect health). Thus, in calculating the probability of having to pay out on an insurance contract and, in turn, determining the insurance premium to charge, insurance companies' use of health (and other) statistics representing the overall population may not be appropriate (since the insurance company's pool of customers is more prone to health problems than the overall population). Insurance companies deal with the adverse selection problem by establishing different pools of the population based on health and related characteristics (such as income). By altering the pool used to determine the probability of losses to a particular customer's health characteristics, the insurance company can more accurately determine the probability of having to pay out on a policy and can adjust the insurance premium accordingly.

As the various types of insurance policies and services offered are described below, notice that some policies (such as universal life policies and annuities) provide not only insurance features but also savings components. For example, universal life policy payouts are a function of the interest earned on the investment of the policyholder's premiums.

Life Insurance

The four basic classes or lines of life insurance are distinguished by the manner in which they are sold or marketed to purchasers. These classes are (1) ordinary life, (2) group life, (3) industrial life, and (4) credit life. Among the life insurance policies in force in the United States, ordinary life accounted for approximately 69 percent, group life for less than 30 percent, and industrial life and credit life together for less than 1 percent of the over $26 trillion contract value in force at the beginning of 2003.

Ordinary Life   Ordinary life insurance involves policies marketed on an individual basis, usually in units of $1,000, on which policyholders make periodic premium payments. Despite the enormous variety of contractual forms, there are essentially five basic contractual types. The first three are traditional forms of ordinary life insurance, and the last two are newer contracts that originated in the 1970s and 1980s as a result of increased competition for savings from other segments of the financial services industry. The three traditional contractual forms are term life, whole life, and endowment life. The two newer forms are variable life and universal life. The key features of each of these contractual forms are as follows:

- *Term life.* A term life policy is the closest to pure life insurance, with no savings element attached. Essentially, the individual receives a payout contingent on death during the coverage period. The term of coverage can vary from as little as 1 year to 40 years or more.

- *Whole life.* A whole life policy protects the individual over an entire lifetime. In return for periodic or level premiums, the individual's beneficiaries receive the face value of the life insurance contract on death. Thus, there is certainty that if the policyholder continues to make premium payments, the insurance company will make a payment—unlike term insurance. As a result, whole life has a savings element as well as a pure insurance element.

- *Endowment life.* An endowment life policy combines a pure (term) insurance element with a savings element. It guarantees a payout to the beneficiaries of the policy if death occurs during some endowment period (e.g., prior to reaching retirement age). An insured person who lives to the endowment date receives the face amount of the policy.

- *Variable life.* Unlike traditional policies that promise to pay the insured the fixed or face amount of a policy if a contingency arises, variable life insurance invests fixed premium payments in mutual funds of stocks, bonds, and money market instruments. Usually, policyholders can choose mutual fund investments to reflect their risk preferences. Thus, variable life provides an alternative way to build savings compared with the more traditional policies such as whole life because the value of the policy increases or decreases with the asset returns of the mutual fund in which the premiums are invested.

- *Universal life and variable universal life.* Universal life allows both the premium amounts and the maturity of the life contract to be changed by the insured, unlike traditional policies that maintain premiums at a given level over a fixed contract period. In addition, for some contracts, insurers invest premiums in money, equity, or bond mutual funds—as in variable life insurance—so that the savings or investment component of the contract reflects market returns. In this case, the policy is called variable universal life.

Group Life Insurance   Group life insurance covers a large number of insured persons under a single policy. Usually issued to corporate employers, these policies may be either contributory (where both the employer and employee cover a share of the employee's cost of the insurance) or noncontributory (where the employee does not contribute to the cost of the insurance) for the employees. Cost economies represent the principal advantage of group life over ordinary life policies. Cost economies result from mass administration of plans, lower costs for evaluating individuals through medical screening and other rating systems, and reduced selling and commission costs.

Industrial Life   Industrial life insurance currently represents a very small area of coverage. Industrial life usually involves weekly payments directly collected by representatives of the companies. To a large extent, the growth of group life insurance has led to the demise of industrial life as a major activity class.

Credit Life   Credit life insurance is sold to protect lenders against a borrower's death prior to the repayment of a debt contract such as a mortgage or car loan. Usually, the face amount of the insurance policy reflects the outstanding principal and interest on the loan.

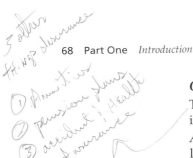

Other Life Insurer Activities

Three other major activities of life insurance companies involve the sale of annuities, private pension plans, and accident and health insurance.

Annuities   Annuities represent the reverse of life insurance activities. Whereas life insurance involves different contractual methods of *building up* a fund, annuities involve different methods of *liquidating* a fund, such as paying out a fund's proceeds. As with life insurance contracts, many different types of annuity contracts have been developed. Specifically, they can be sold to an individual or a group and on a fixed or a variable basis by being linked to the return on some underlying investment portfolio. Individuals can purchase annuities with a single payment or with payments spread over a number of years. The annuity builds up a fund whose returns are tax deferred; that is, they are not subject to capital gains taxes on their investments. Payments may be structured to start immediately, or they can be deferred (at which time taxes are paid based on the income tax rate of the annuity receiver). These payments may cease on death or continue to be paid to beneficiaries for a number of years after death. Annuity sales in 2002 topped $223 billion ($119 billion of which were variable annuities), compared with $26 billion in 1996.[1] Growth has been large despite the 1997 reduction in the capital gains tax rate from 28 percent to 20 percent.

The year 2004 saw the first action against an insurance company involving alleged unethical practices. In a sweeping investigation of variable annuity sales, federal and state regulators prepared a case against Conseco, asserting that the insurer provided advantages to big investors that could increase profits but hurt small investors. Until recently, many variable annuities permitted almost unlimited movement of money among asset pools in which annuity funds were invested. Regulators assert that in the early 2000s, companies had increasingly imposed limits on asset pool movements by smaller investors (annuity holders). Regulators were also investigating a number of other insurance companies and brokerage companies for similar practices.

Private Pension Funds   Insurance companies offer many alternative pension plans to private employers in an effort to attract this business from other financial service companies, such as commercial banks and security firms. Some of their innovative pension plans are based on guaranteed investment contracts (GICs). This means the insurer guarantees not only the rate of interest credited to a pension plan over a given period—for example, five years—but also the annuity rates on beneficiaries' contracts. Other plans include immediate participation and separate account plans that follow more aggressive investment strategies than traditional life insurance, such as investing premiums in special-purpose equity mutual funds. In the early 2000s, life insurance companies were managing over $1.4 trillion in pension fund assets, equal to approximately 30 percent of all private pension plans.

Accident and Health Insurance   While life insurance protects against mortality risk, accident and health insurance protect against morbidity, or ill health, risk. Over $1.54 trillion in premiums were written by life and health companies in the accident–health area in the early 2000s. The major activity line is group insurance, providing health insurance coverage to corporate employees. Life insurance companies write more than 50 percent of all health insurance premiums. However, the growth in health maintenance organizations (HMOs) (nonregulated providers of

[1] As discussed in Chapter 21, life insurers are facing increasingly intense competition from banks in the annuity product market.

TABLE 3–2 Distribution of Assets of U.S. Life Insurance Companies

Year	Total Assets (millions)	Government Securities	Corporate Securities		Mortgages	Policy Loans	Miscellaneous U.S. Assets
			Bonds	Stocks			
1917	$ 5,941	9.6%	33.2%	1.4%	34.0%	13.6%	5.2%
1920	7,320	18.4	26.7	1.0	33.4	11.7	6.5
1930	18,880	8.0	26.0	2.8	40.2	14.9	5.2
1940	30,802	27.5	28.1	2.0	19.4	10.0	6.3
1950	64,020	25.2	36.3	3.3	25.1	3.8	4.1
1960	119,576	9.9	39.1	4.2	34.9	4.4	4.4
1970	207,254	5.3	35.3	7.4	35.9	7.8	5.3
1980	479,210	6.9	37.5	9.9	27.4	8.6	6.6
1990	1,408,208	15.0	41.4	9.1	19.2	4.4	7.8
1995	2,131,900	18.6	41.4	17.4	9.9	4.5	6.3
2000	3,133,900	9.3	39.1	31.5	7.5	3.2	9.4
2001	3,224,600	9.5	41.6	27.9	7.6	3.2	10.2
2002	3,335,000	12.3	43.4	23.6	7.5	3.1	10.1
2003	3,823,400	11.7	41.8	27.8	6.8	2.7	9.2

Note: Beginning with 1962, these data include the assets of separate accounts.
Source: American Council of Life Insurance, *Life Insurance Fact Book*, 1994; *Best's Review*, October 1996; and *Federal Reserve Bulletin*, various issues.
www.federalreserve.gov

health insurance) in the late 1990s has cut into this line of business. For example, a 1998 survey of 11 major life insurance companies, conducted by A. M. Best,[2] reported that from 1996 to 1997 the number of enrollees in life insurance company–sponsored health insurance plans dropped by more than 8 percent and more than 25 percent of the companies' existing policies were dropped. Overall, premiums dropped nearly 7 percent. In contrast, HMO enrollment increased more than 7 percent from 1996 to 1997.[3] Other coverages include credit health plans by which individuals have their debt repayments insured against unexpected health contingencies and various types of renewable, nonrenewable, and guaranteed health and accident plans for individuals. In many respects, the loss exposures faced by insurers in accident and health lines are more similar to those faced under property–casualty insurance than to those faced under traditional life insurance (see section below on property–casualty insurance).

Balance Sheet and Recent Trends

Assets

Because of the long-term nature of their liabilities (as a result of the long-term nature of life insurance policyholders' claims) and the need to generate competitive returns on the savings elements of life insurance products, life insurance companies concentrate their asset investments at the longer end of the maturity spectrum (e.g., bonds, equities, and government securities). Look at Table 3–2, where we show the distribution of life insurance companies' assets.

[2] A. M. Best is a leading source of information on the insurance industry. The company provides quantitative and qualitative data on the performance of individual insurance companies as well as the industry as a whole.

[3] A. M. Best's *Supplemental Rating Questionnaire*, 1998.

policy loans
Loans made by an insurance company to its policyholders using their policies as collateral.

As you can see, in 2003, 11.7 percent of assets were invested in government securities, 69.6 percent in corporate bonds and stocks, and 6.8 percent in mortgages, with other loans—including **policy loans** (loans made to policyholders using their policies as collateral)—making up the balance. While commercial banks are the major issuers of new mortgages (sometimes keeping the mortgages on their books and sometimes selling them to secondary market investors), insurance companies hold mortgages as investment securities. That is, they purchase many mortgages in the secondary markets (see Chapters 27 and 28). The major trends have been a long-term increase in the proportion of bonds and equities[4] and a decline in the proportion of mortgages in the balance sheet (see below). Thus, insurance company managers must be able to measure and manage the credit risk, interest rate risk, and other risks associated with these securities.

Liabilities

policy reserves
A liability item for insurers that reflects their expected payment commitment on existing policy contracts.

surrender value of a policy
The cash value of a policy received from the insurer if a policyholder surrenders the policy before maturity. The cash surrender value is normally only a portion of the contract's face value.

separate account
Annuity programs sponsored by life insurance companies in which the payoff on the policy is linked to the assets in which policy premiums are invested.

The aggregate balance sheet for the life insurance industry at the beginning of 2003 is shown in Table 3–3. Looking at the liability side of the balance sheet, we see that $1.692 trillion, or 50.2 percent, of total liabilities and capital are net **policy reserves** (the expected payment commitment on existing policy contracts). These reserves are based on actuarial assumptions regarding the insurers' expected future liability commitments to pay out on present contracts, including death benefits, matured endowments (lump sum or otherwise), and the cash **surrender values of policies** (the cash value paid to the policyholder if the policy is surrendered before it matures). Even though the actuarial assumptions underlying policy reserves are normally very conservative, unexpected fluctuations in future required payouts can occur; thus, underwriting life insurance is risky. For example, mortality rates—and life insurance payouts—might unexpectedly increase above those defined by historically based mortality tables as a result of a catastrophic epidemic illness such as AIDS. To meet unexpected future losses, the life insurer holds a capital and surplus reserve fund with which to meet such losses (and reduce insolvency risk). The capital and surplus reserves of life insurers in 2003 were $195 billion, or 5.8 percent of total assets.[5] **Separate account** business represented 28.5 percent of total assets in 2003. A separate account is a fund established and held separately from the insurance company's other assets. These funds may be invested without regard to the usual diversification restrictions; that is, they may be invested in all stocks, all bonds, and so forth. The payoff on the life insurance policy thus depends on the return on the funds in the separate account. Another important life insurer liability, GICs (7.6 percent of total assets), are short- and medium-term debt instruments sold by insurance companies to fund their pension plan business (see deposit-type contracts in Table 3–3).

Regulation

McCarran-Ferguson Act of 1945
Legislation confirming the primacy of state over federal regulation of insurance companies.

The most important legislation affecting the regulation of life insurance companies is the **McCarran-Ferguson Act of 1945**, which confirms the primacy of state over federal regulation of insurance companies. Thus, unlike the depository institutions we discussed in Chapter 2, which can be chartered either at the federal or the state

---

[4] The bull market of the 1980s and 1990s probably constitutes a major reason for the large percentage of assets invested in equities.

[5] An additional line of defense against unexpected underwriting losses is the insurer's investment income from its asset portfolio plus any new premium income flows.

TABLE 3–3
Life Insurance
Industry Balance
Sheet, 2003
(in millions of
dollars)

Source: Reprinted with
permission from *Best's
Aggregates & Averages*,
Life-Health, 2003, p. 2.
www.ambest.com

Assets			Percent of Total Assets
Bonds		$1,703,154	50.6%
Preferred stock		24,091	0.7
Common stock		55,334	1.6
Mortgage loans		242,927	7.2
Real estate		21,687	0.6
Policy loans		104,292	3.1
Cash and short-term investments		83,441	2.5
Other invested assets		67,292	2.0
Life and annuity premium due		14,421	0.4
Accident and health premium due		5,581	0.2
Accrued investment income		28,218	0.8
Separate account assets		958,408	28.5
Other assets		59,857	1.8
Total assets		$3,368,703	100.0%
Liabilities and Capital/Surplus			
Net policy reserves		$1,691,905	50.2%
Deposit-type contracts		256,279	7.6
Policy claims		34,415	1.0
Dividend reserve		17,956	0.5
Interest maintenance reserve		10,178	0.3
Commissions, taxes, expenses		24,898	0.7
Asset valuation reserve		22,788	0.7
Other liabilities		159,962	4.8
Separate account business		955,759	28.4
Total capital and surplus		194,563	5.8
Capital	3,857		0.1
Treasury stock	(318)		0.0
Paid-in and contributed surplus	82,418		2.4
Surplus notes	16,836		0.5
Unassigned surplus	73,578		2.2
Other surplus	2,952		0.1
Other reserves	15,240		0.5
Total liabilities and capital/surplus		$3,368,703	100.0%

www.naic.org

level, chartering of life insurers is done entirely at the state level. In addition to chartering, state insurance commissions supervise and examine insurance companies by using a coordinated examination system developed by the National Association of Insurance Commissioners (NAIC). An example of state insurance regulatory actions is the 1997 case of Prudential Insurance Company. Prudential's policyholders filed and settled (for $410 million) a class-action lawsuit claiming that Prudential's sales representatives defrauded customers by talking them into using the built-up cash value of older life insurance coverages to buy new, costlier policies. An 18-month deceptive sales practices investigation was undertaken by a task force of state insurance regulators from 45 states. The report resulting from this investigation was instrumental in determining the legal settlement.[6]

[6] See, for example, "Prudential's Policy Sales Off by 27% in the U.S.," *New York Times*, Business Day, March 4, 1998, p. D1.

In early 2004 the prospect of the federal government's gaining a role in the regulation of the insurance industry gained momentum. The chairman of the House Committee on Financial Services spelled out plans for 2004 legislation that would create a council of federal and state officials to oversee insurance (life as well as property–casualty) nationally, with a presidential appointee as its head. The legislation would force states to adopt uniform standards and permit the market to determine insurance prices rather than have them determined by state regulators, as is generally the case. For several years state regulators have been trying to simplify and speed their procedures on rates, conditions of coverage, and approval of new insurance products. But progress has been slow. The results have been complaints that cumbersome and costly state regulation was failing to meet the needs of both insurance companies and their customers. Many of the nation's biggest insurers have been campaigning for a dual system, which would create a federal regulator but also permit companies to choose whether to be regulated at the federal level or the state level. The proposal has met resistance from the states, consumer groups, and some members of Congress.[7]

insurance guarantee funds
Funds consisting of required contributions from within-state insurance companies to compensate insurance company policyholders if there is a failure.

www.ins.state.ny.us

Other than supervision and examination, states promote life **insurance guarantee funds.** Unlike banks and thrifts, life insurers have no access to a federal guarantee fund. These state guarantee funds differ in a number of important ways from deposit insurance. First, although these programs are sponsored by state insurance regulators, they are actually run and administered by the (private) insurance companies themselves.

Second, unlike SAIF or BIF, in which the FDIC has established a permanent reserve fund by requiring banks to pay annual premiums in excess of payouts to resolve failures (see Chapter 19), no such permanent guarantee fund exists for the insurance industry—with the sole exception of the P&C and life guarantee funds in the state of New York. This means that contributions are paid into the guarantee fund by surviving firms in a state only after an insurance company has actually failed.

Third, the size of the required contributions that surviving insurers make to protect policyholders in failed insurance companies differs widely from state to state. In those states that have guarantee funds, each surviving insurer is normally levied a pro rata amount, according to the size of its statewide premium income. This amount either helps pay off small policyholders after the assets of the failed insurer have been liquidated or acts as a cash injection to make the acquisition of a failed insurer attractive. The definition of small policyholders varies among states in the range of holding policies from $100,000 to $500,000.

Finally, because no permanent fund exists and the annual pro rata payments to meet payouts to failed insurer policyholders are often legally capped, a delay usually occurs before small policyholders receive the cash surrender values of their policies or other payment obligations from the guarantee fund. This contrasts with deposit insurance, which normally provides insured depositors immediate coverage of their claims up to $100,000.

As discussed in Chapter 21, a piece of legislation that will have a major impact on state regulation of the insurance (both life insurance and property–casualty insurance) industry in the future is the Financial Services Modernization Act of 1999. This legislation allows insurance companies and depository institutions (as

---

[7] See "New Momentum for Letting U.S. Help Regulate Nation's Insurers," *New York Times*, March 18, 2004, p. B8.

TABLE 3–4
Major Insurers That
Have Applied for
Savings Bank
Charters, January 1,
1997–August 29,
2003*

Source: U.S. Department of
the Treasury, Office of Thrift
Supervision, April 2004.
www.ots.ustreas.gov

Applicant	Bank Entity
Allstate Insurance Co.	Allstate Federal Savings Bank
American Financial Group Inc.	Great American Savings Bank
American International Group Inc.	AIG FSB
AmerUs Group	AmerUs Home Equity Bank F.A.
CNA Financial Corp.	CNA Trust Corp.
Conseco Inc.	Conseco Bank FSB
First American Financial Corp.	First American Trust FSB
Guardian Life Insurance Co.	Guardian Trust Co. FSB
Hartford Group	The Hartford Bank
Massachusetts Mutual Life Insurance Co.	The MassMutual Trust Co.
Metropolitan Life Insurance Co.	Metlife Bank & Trust Co. FSB
MONY Group Inc.	Advest Bank & Trust Co.
Nationwide Insurance	Nationwide Trust Co. FSB
New York Life Insurance Co.	New York Life Trust Co. FSB
Northwestern Mutual Life Insurance Co.	Northwestern Mutual Trust Co.
Phoenix Home Life Mutual Insurance Co.	New London Trust FSB
Principal Life Insurance Co.	Principal Bank
State Farm Mutual Auto Insurance Co.	State Farm Bank FSB
Teachers Insurance & Annuity Association	TIAA-CREF Trust Co. FSB
United Services Automobile Association	USAA Federal Savings Bank

*Based on companies in the 2002 Fortune 500 that filed applications with the Office of Thrift Supervision between January 1997 and September 2003.

well as investment banks) to engage in each other's businesses. Table 3–4 lists insurers that applied for a savings bank charter from January 1997 through August 2003.

Concept Questions

1. What is the difference between a life insurance contract and an annuity contract?
2. Describe the different forms of ordinary life insurance.
3. Why do life insurance companies invest in long-term assets?
4. What is the major source of life insurance underwriting risk?
5. Who are the main regulators of the life insurance industry?
6. Why is traditional life insurance in decline?

PROPERTY–CASUALTY INSURANCE

Size, Structure, and Composition of the Industry

Currently, some 3,200 companies sell property–casualty (PC) insurance, with approximately half of these firms writing PC business in all or most of the United States. The U.S. PC insurance industry is quite concentrated. Collectively, the top 10 firms have a 45 percent share of the overall PC market measured by premiums written, and the top 200 firms made up over 95 percent of the industry premiums written.[8] In 2002, the top firm (State Farm) wrote 11.3 percent of all PC insurance premiums, while the second-ranked insurer (Allstate) wrote 6.2 percent (i.e., a joint total of 17.5 percent of premiums written). In contrast, in 1985, these top two firms wrote 14.5 percent of the total industry insurance premiums. Thus, the industry

[8]*Best's Review*, August 2003, p. 78. **www.ambest.com**

TABLE 3–5
Two-Firm Insurance Seller Premium Concentrations for 18 Property–Casualty Lines, 1986–2002

Source: Reprinted with permission from *Best's Review,* August 1987 and August 2003.
www.ambest.com

	Two-Firm (Seller) Concentration Ratio	
	1986	**2002**
Fire	13.5%	21.8%
Allied lines	11.6	21.4
Multiple peril crop	9.8	35.7
Homeowners multiple peril	27.9	33.9
Commercial multiple peril	14.1	15.8
Ocean marine	20.0	23.2
Inland marine	15.7	16.5
Medical malpractice	24.4	17.9
Workers' compensation	16.8	21.5
Other liability	18.4	28.7
Aircraft	23.0	31.8
Private passenger auto liability	29.9	29.7
Commercial auto liability	11.9	12.4
Private passenger auto physical damage	29.3	30.3
Commercial auto physical damage	7.6	13.0
Fidelity	34.5	32.0
Surety	13.5	26.5
Boiler and machinery	40.0	41.8
Earthquake	29.2	35.3
Total	13.9	17.5

leaders appear to be increasing their domination of this financial service sector. As with banks, much of this consolidation is coming through mergers and acquisitions. For example, in late 2003 St. Paul Companies acquired Travelers Property Casualty Corporation in a $16.4 billion stock swap to create St. Paul Travelers. The acquisition moved the combined companies into the number three position (based on total assets) among all PC insurers.

Table 3–5 shows the average two-firm concentration ratios for 19 property–casualty lines over the 1986–2002 period. In 1986, these concentration ratios varied from a low of 7.6 percent in commercial auto physical damage to a high of 40 percent in boiler and machinery. In 2002, concentration ratios ranged from 12.4 percent in commercial auto physical damage to 41.8 percent in boiler and machinery. The total assets of the PC industry in 2003 were $1,043 billion, or approximately 30 percent of the life insurance industry's assets.

Property–Casualty Insurance

Property insurance involves insurance coverages related to the loss of real and personal property. Casualty—or, perhaps more accurately, liability—insurance concerns protection against legal liability exposures. However, the distinctions between the two broad areas of property and liability insurance are increasingly becoming blurred. This is due to the tendency of PC insurers to offer multiple activity line coverages combining features of property and liability insurance into single policy packages, for example, homeowners multiple peril insurance. Below, we describe the key features of the main PC lines. Note, however, that some PC activity lines are marketed as different products to both individuals and commercial firms (e.g., auto insurance) while other lines are marketed to one specific group (e.g., boiler and machinery insurance targeted at commercial purchasers). To understand

TABLE 3–6
Property and
Casualty Insurance
Industry
Underwriting by
Lines, 2002

Source: Reprinted with
permission from *Best's
Review,* August 2003, p. 78.
www.ambest.com

	Premiums Written*	Losses Incurred†
Fire	$ 8,312,072	30.0
Allied lines	6,037,636	44.7
Multiple peril (MP) crop	2,897,450	129.8
Farm owners MP	1,944,422	67.1
Homeowners MP	42,651,032	66.2
Commercial MP—nonliability	17,695,153	56.3
Commercial MP—liability	11,530,517	55.2
Mortgage guaranty	3,871,104	33.2
Ocean marine	2,347,536	59.0
Inland marine	10,144,937	45.1
Financial guaranty	2,645,745	5.5
Medical malpractice	8,928,252	95.1
Earthquake	1,697,700	28.5
Group accident and health (A&H)	9,187,282	77.6
Other A&H	3,689,817	65.0
Workers' compensation	43,124,735	79.8
Other liability	39,781,754	91.8
Products liability	3,067,009	204.6
Private passenger auto liability	83,203,032	72.4
Commercial auto liability	19,826,750	70.9
Private passenger auto physical damage (PD)	60,550,519	61.6
Commercial auto PD	7,251,460	54.1
Aircraft	2,318,967	62.4
Fidelity	1,007,691	59.9
Surety	3,626,152	65.0
Federal flood	1,524,838	24.4
Federal employees health	2,231,754	91.6
Burglary and theft	111,757	17.2
Boiler and machinery	1,139,498	25.5
Credit	683,476	47.8
Other lines	3,770,540	69.0
Totals	$406,737,588	69.7

*In thousands of dollars.
†To premiums earned.

**net premiums
written**
The entire amount of
premiums on insur-
ance contracts
written.

the importance of each line in terms of premium income and losses incurred, look at Table 3–6. The following data show the changing composition in **net premiums written** (NPW) (the entire amount of premiums on insurance contracts written) for major PC lines over the 1960–2002 period. Important PC lines include the following:

- *Fire insurance and allied lines.* Protects against the perils of fire, lightning, and re-moval of property damaged in a fire (3.5 percent of all premiums written in 2002; 16.6 percent in 1960).

- *Homeowners multiple peril (MP) insurance.* Protects against multiple perils of damage to a personal dwelling and personal property as well as providing lia-bility coverage against the financial consequences of legal liability due to injury done to others. Thus, it combines features of both property and liability insur-ance (10.5 percent of all premiums written in 2002; 5.2 percent in 1960).

- *Commercial multiple peril insurance.* Protects commercial firms against perils; sim-ilar to homeowners multiple peril insurance (7.2 percent of all premiums writ-ten in 2002; 0.4 percent in 1960).

- *Automobile liability and physical damage (PD) insurance.* Provides protection against (1) losses resulting from legal liability due to the ownership or use of the vehicle (auto liability) and (2) theft of or damage to vehicles (auto physical damage) (42.0 percent of all premiums written in 2002; 43.0 percent in 1960).
- *Liability insurance (other than auto).* Provides either individuals or commercial firms with protection against non-automobile-related legal liability. For commercial firms, this includes protection against liabilities relating to their business operations (other than personal injury to employees covered by workers' compensation insurance) and product liability hazards (22.7 percent of all premiums written in 2002; 6.6 percent in 1960).

Balance Sheet and Recent Trends

The Balance Sheet and Underwriting Risk

The balance sheet of PC firms at the beginning of 2003 is shown in Table 3–7. Similar to life insurance companies, PC insurers invest the majority of their assets in long-term securities, thus subjecting them to credit and interest rate risks. Bonds ($570.3 billion), preferred stock ($9.6 billion), and common stock ($101.5 billion) constituted 65.3 percent of total assets in 2003. PC insurers hold mainly long-term securities for two reasons. First, PC insurers, like life insurers, hold long-term assets to match the maturity of their longer-term contractual liabilities. Second, PC insurers, unlike life insurers, have more uncertain payouts on their insurance contracts (i.e., they incur greater levels of liquidity risk). Thus, their asset structure includes many assets with relatively fixed returns that can be liquidated easily and at low cost. Looking at their liabilities, we can see that major components are the loss reserves set aside to meet expected losses ($345.2 billion) from *underwriting* the PC lines just described and the loss adjustment expense ($67.3 billion) item, which relates to expected administrative and related costs of adjusting (settling) these claims. The two items combined constitute 39.6 percent of total liabilities and capital. **Unearned premiums** (a reserve set-aside that contains the portion of a premium that has been paid before insurance coverage has been provided) are also a major liability, representing 15.2 percent of total liabilities and capital.

unearned premiums
Reserve set-aside that contains the portion of a premium that has been paid before insurance coverage has been provided.

To understand how and why a loss reserve on the liability side of the balance sheet is established, we need to understand the risks of underwriting PC insurance. In particular, PC underwriting risk results when the premiums generated on a given insurance line are insufficient to cover (1) the claims (losses) incurred insuring against the peril and (2) the administrative expenses of providing that insurance (legal expenses, commissions, taxes, etc.) after taking into account (3) the investment income generated between the time premiums are received and the time claims are paid. Thus, underwriting risk may result from (1) unexpected increases in loss rates, (2) unexpected increases in expenses, and/or (3) unexpected decreases in investment yields or returns. Next, we look more carefully at each of these three areas of PC underwriting risk.

Loss Risk   The key feature of claims loss exposure is the actuarial *predictability* of losses relative to premiums earned. This predictability depends on a number of characteristics or features of the perils insured, specifically:

- *Property versus liability.* In general, the maximum levels of losses are more predictable for property lines than for liability lines. For example, the monetary value of the loss of, or damage to, an auto is relatively easy to calculate, while the upper limit to the losses an insurer might be exposed to in a product liability line—for example, asbestos damage to workers' health under other liability insurance—may be difficult, if not impossible, to estimate.

TABLE 3–7 Balance Sheet for the Property–Casualty Industry, 2003 (in millions of dollars)

Assets			Percent of Total Assets
Unaffiliated investments		$ 790,272	75.8%
Bonds	570,299		54.7%
Preferred stocks	9,574		0.9
Common stocks	101,484		9.7
Mortgage loans	1,961		0.2
Real estate investments	1,394		0.1
Cash and short-term investments	72,413		7.0
Other invested assets	33,147		3.2
Investments in affiliates		50,498	4.8
Real estate, office		8,344	0.8
Premium balances		98,603	9.4
Amounts-deductible and service-only plans		1,882	0.2
Reinsurance funds		9,563	0.9
Reinsurance recoverable		24,412	2.3
Federal income taxes recoverable		19,463	1.9
Guaranty funds receivable		769	0.1
Electronic data processing equipment		1,786	0.2
Accrued interest		8,158	0.8
Foreign exchange rate adjustments		44	0.0
Receivables from affiliates		13,478	1.3
Association accounts		1,870	0.2
Receivable uninsured accident and health plans		91	0.0
Future investment income on loss reserves		125	0.0
Other assets		13,577	1.3
Total assets		$1,042,935	100.0%
Liabilities and Capital/Surplus			
Losses		$ 345,191	33.1%
Loss adjustment expenses		67,273	6.5
Reinsurance payable on paid losses		8,070	0.8
Commissions, taxes, expenses		25,644	2.5
Federal income taxes		9,305	0.9
Borrowed money		2,177	0.2
Unearned premiums		158,645	15.2
Dividends to stockholders		155	0.0
Dividends to policyholders		1,048	0.1
Ceded reinsurance premiums payable		24,848	2.4
Reinsurance funds		31,481	3.0
Loss portfolio transfer (assumed)		13,422	1.3
Loss portfolio transfer (ceded)		(12,423)	−1.2
Amounts retained for others		5,718	0.5
Remittances not allowed		1,383	0.1
Foreign exchange rate adjustments		702	0.1
Drafts outstanding		4,235	0.4
Payable to affiliates		9,251	0.9
Payable for securities		10,724	1.0
Amounts held for uninsured accident and health plans		2	0.0
Capital notes		88	0.0
Discount on loss reserve		(451)	−0.0
Other liabilities		26,431	2.5
Conditional reserves		19,111	1.8
Policyholders' surplus		290,905	27.9

(continued)

TABLE 3–7   *(continued)*

Assets		Percent of Total Assets
Capital paid up	$ 4,934	0.5
Guaranty funds	262	0.0
Surplus notes	8,050	0.8
Assigned funds	127,790	12.2
Unassigned funds	149,869	14.4
Total liabilities and capital/surplus	$1,042,935	100.0%

Source: Reprinted with permission from *A.M. Best's Aggregates and Averages,* property–casualty, 2003, p. 1. *www.ambest.com*

frequency of loss
The probability that a loss will occur.

severity of loss
The size of the loss.

- *Severity versus frequency.* In general, loss rates are more predictable on low-severity, high-frequency lines than they are on high-severity, low-frequency lines. For example, losses in fire, auto, and homeowners peril lines tend to involve events expected to occur with a high frequency and to be independently distributed across any pool of the insured. Furthermore, the dollar loss on each event in the insured pool tends to be relatively small. Applying the law of large numbers, insurers can estimate the expected loss potential of such lines—the **frequency of loss** times the size of the loss (**severity of loss**)—within quite small probability bounds. Other lines, such as earthquake, hurricane, and financial guaranty insurance, tend to insure very low-probability (frequency) events. Here the probabilities are not always stationary, the individual risks in the insured pool are not independent, and the severity of the loss could be enormous. This means that estimating expected loss rates (frequency times severity) is extremely difficult in these coverage areas. For example, even with the new federal terrorism insurance program introduced in 2002, coverage for high-profile buildings in big cities, as well as other properties considered potential targets, remains expensive. Under the 2002 federal program, the government is responsible for 90 percent of insurance industry losses that arise from any future terrorist incidents that exceed a minimum amount. The government's losses are capped at $100 billion per year. Each insurer has a maximum amount it would pay before federal aid kicks in. In 2003, the amount was 7 percent of each company's commercial property–casualty premiums, rising to 15 percent in 2005. The result is that in some cases, the cost of terrorism insurance has been reduced significantly since the new law took effect. But those buildings viewed as target risks will continue to have much higher premiums than properties outside of major cities. This higher uncertainty of losses forces PC firms to invest in more short-term assets and hold a larger percentage of capital and reserves than life insurance firms hold.[9]

[9] An alternative to managing risk on a PC insurer's balance sheet is to purchase reinsurance from a reinsurance company. Reinsurance is essentially insurance for insurance companies. It is a way for primary insurance companies to protect against unforeseen or extraordinary losses. Depending on the contract, reinsurance can enable the insurer to improve its capital position, expand its business, limit losses, and stabilize cash flows, among other things. In addition, the reinsurer, drawing information from many primary insurers, will usually have a far larger pool of data for assessing risks. Reinsurance takes a variety of forms. It may represent a layer of risk, such as losses within certain limits, say, $5 million to $10 million, that will be paid by the reinsurer to the primary insurance company for which a premium is paid, or a sharing of both losses and profits for certain types of business. Reinsurance is an international business. About 75 percent of the reinsurance business that comes from U.S. insurance companies is written by non-U.S. reinsurers such as Munich Re. Some investment banks are now setting up reinsurers as part of a move to develop

long-tail loss
A claim that is made some time after a policy was written.

- *Long tail versus short tail.* Some liability lines suffer from a long-tail risk exposure phenomenon that makes the estimation of expected losses difficult. This **long-tail loss** arises in policies in which the insured event occurs during a coverage period but a claim is not filed or reported until many years later. The delay in filing of a claim is in accordance with the terms of the insurance contract and often occurs because the detrimental consequences of the event are not known for a period of time after the event actually occurs. Losses incurred but not reported have caused insurers significant problems in lines such as medical malpractice and other liability insurance where product damage suits (e.g., the Dalkon shield case and asbestos cases) have mushroomed many years after the event occurred and the coverage period expired.[10] For example, in 2002 Halliburton, a major U.S. corporation, agreed to pay $4 billion in cash and stock, and to seek bankruptcy protection for a subsidiary to settle more than 300,000 asbestos claims. To resolve its growing asbestos liability, Halliburton considered a novel step that put one of its biggest subsidiaries into bankruptcy courts, while allowing Halliburton to hold on to the rest of its businesses. Questions still remain about how much insurance companies will be required to reimburse Halliburton for the cost of asbestos case settlements and when. The company had only $1.6 billion of expected insurance on its books for asbestos claims. If Halliburton is successful in putting just one of its subsidiaries (and not the entire firm) into bankruptcy, it could set a precedent for many companies, such as Honeywell International and Dow Chemical, which were also trying to contain their asbestos risk in subsidiaries.

- *Product inflation versus social inflation.* Loss rates on all PC property policies are adversely affected by unexpected increases in inflation. Such increases were triggered, for example, by the oil price shocks of 1973, 1978, and potentially, 2003–04. However, in addition to a systematic unexpected inflation risk in each line, there may be line-specific inflation risks. The inflation risk of property lines is likely to reflect the approximate underlying inflation risk of the economy. Liability lines may be subject to social inflation, as reflected in juries' willingness to award punitive and other liability damages at rates far above the underlying rate of inflation. Such social inflation has been particularly prevalent in commercial liability and medical malpractice insurance and has been directly attributed by some analysts to faults in the U.S. civil litigation system.

loss ratio
Ratio that measures pure losses incurred to premiums earned.

premiums earned
Premiums received and earned on insurance contracts because time has passed with no claim being filed.

The **loss ratio** measures the actual losses incurred on a line. It measures the ratio of losses incurred to **premiums earned** (premiums received and earned on insurance contracts because time has passed with no claim being filed). Thus, a loss ratio less than 100 means that premiums earned were sufficient to cover losses incurred on that line. Aggregate loss ratios for the period 1951–2003 are shown in

---

alternative risk financing deals such as catastrophe bonds. Insurers and reinsurers also typically issue catastrophe bonds. The bonds pay high interest rates and diversify an investor's portfolio because natural disasters occur randomly and are not associated with (independent of) economic factors. Depending on how the bond is structured, if losses reach the threshold specified in the bond-offering, the investor may lose all or part of the principal or interest. For example, a deep-discount or zero-coupon catastrophe bond would pay $100(1 - \alpha)$ on maturity, where α is the loss rate due to the catastrophe. Thus, Munich Re issued a $250 million catastrophe bond in 2001 where α (the loss rate) reflected losses incurred on all reinsurer policies over a 24-hour period should an event (such as a flood or hurricane) occur and losses exceed a certain threshold. The required yield on these bonds reflected the risk-free rate plus a premium reflecting investors' expectations regarding the probability of the event's occurring.

[10] In some product liability cases, such as those involving asbestos, the nature of the risk being covered was not fully understood at the time many of the policies were written.

TABLE 3–8
Industry
Underwriting
Ratios

Source: *Best's Review,*
various issues.
www.ambest.com

Year	Loss Ratio*	Expense Ratio†	Combined Ratio	Dividends to Policyholders‡	Combined Ratio after Dividends
1951	60.3	34.0	94.3	2.6	96.9
1960	63.8	32.2	96.0	2.2	98.1
1965	70.3	30.4	100.7	1.9	102.6
1970	70.8	27.6	98.4	1.7	100.1
1975	79.3	27.3	106.6	1.3	107.9
1980	74.9	26.5	101.4	1.7	103.1
1985	88.7	25.9	114.6	1.6	116.3
1990	82.3	26.0	108.3	1.2	109.6
1995	78.8	26.2	105.0	1.4	106.4
1997	72.8	27.1	99.9	1.7	101.6
2000	81.4	27.8	109.2	1.3	110.5
2001	88.4	26.9	115.3	0.7	116.0
2002	81.1	25.6	106.7	0.5	107.2
2003	74.7	24.9	99.6	0.5	100.1

*Losses and adjustment expenses incurred to premiums earned.
†Expenses incurred (before federal income taxes) to premiums written.
‡Dividends to policyholders to premiums earned.

Table 3–8. Notice the steady increase in industry loss ratios over the period, increasing from the 60 percent range in the 1950s to the 70 and 80 percent range in the 1980s and 1990s. For example, in 2002, the aggregate loss ratio on all PC lines was 88.4. This includes, however, loss adjustment expenses (LAE)—see below—as well as (pure) losses. The (pure) loss ratio, net of LAE, in 2002 was 69.7 (see Table 3–6).

Expense Risk   The two major sources of expense risk to PC insurers are (1) loss adjustment expenses (LAE) and (2) commissions and other expenses. Loss adjustment expenses relate to the costs surrounding the loss settlement process; for example, many PC insurers employ adjusters who determine the liability of the insurer and the size of the adjustment or settlement to be made. The other major area of expense occurs in the commission costs paid to insurance brokers and sales agents and other expenses related to the acquisition of business. As mentioned above, the loss ratio reported in Table 3–8 includes LAE. The expense ratio reported in Table 3–8 reflects commissions and other (non-LAE) expenses for PC insurers over the 1951–2003 period. In contrast to the increasing trend in the loss ratio, the expense ratio generally decreased over the period shown. Expense can account for significant portions of the overall costs of operations. In 2003, for example, expenses—other than LAE—amounted to 24.9 percent of premiums written. Clearly, sharp rises in insurance broker commissions and other operating costs can rapidly render an insurance line unprofitable. Indeed, one of the reasons for the secular decline in the expense ratio has been the switch in the way PC insurance has been distributed. Specifically, rather than relying on independent brokers to sell policies (the American agency method of distribution), large insurance companies are increasingly selling insurance to the public directly through their own brokers (the direct writer method of distribution). A number of researchers[11] have

[11] See, for example, N. D. Chidambaran, T. A. Pugel, and A. Saunders, "An Investigation of the Performance of the U.S. Property–Casualty Insurance Industry," *Journal of Risk and Insurance* 64 (June 1997), pp. 371–82; and J. D. Cummins and J. Van Derhei, "A Note on the Relative Efficiency of Property-Liability Insurance Distribution Systems," *Bell Journal of Economics* (Autumn 1979), pp. 709–19.

found that the costs of the American agency distribution system are much higher than those of the direct writer distribution system.

A common measure of the overall underwriting profitability of a line, which includes both loss and expense experience, is the **combined ratio.** Technically, the combined ratio is equal to the loss ratio plus the ratios of LAE to premiums earned, commissions and other acquisition costs and general expense costs to premiums written, plus any dividends paid to policyholders as a proportion of premiums earned. The combined ratio after dividends adds any dividends paid to policyholders as a proportion of premiums earned to the combined ratio. If the combined ratio is less than 100, premiums alone are sufficient to cover both losses and expenses related to the line.

If premiums are insufficient and the combined ratio exceeds 100, the PC insurer must rely on investment income earned on premiums for overall profitability. For example, in 2001 the combined ratio before dividend payments was 116.0, indicating that premiums alone were insufficient to cover the costs of both losses and expenses related to writing PC insurance. Table 3–8 presents the combined ratio and its components for the PC industry for the years 1951–2003. We see that the trend over this period is toward decreased profitability. The industry's premiums generally covered losses and expenses until the 1980s. Since then premiums have been unable to cover losses and expenses (i.e., combined ratios have generally been greater than 100).

Investment Yield/Return Risk   As discussed above, when the combined ratio is more than 100, overall profitability can be ensured only by a sufficient investment return on premiums earned. That is, PC firms invest premiums in assets between the time they are received and the time they are paid out to meet claims. For example, in 2002 net investment income to premiums earned (or the PC insurers' investment yield) was 10.5 percent. As a result, the overall average profitability (or **operating ratio**) of PC insurers was 96.7. It was equal to the combined ratio after dividends (107.2) minus the investment yield (10.5). Since the operating ratio was less than 100, PC insurers were profitable in 2002. However, lower net returns on investments (e.g., 5 percent rather than 10.5 percent) would have meant that underwriting PC insurance was marginally unprofitable (i.e., the operating ratio of insurers in this case would have been 102.2). Thus, the effect of interest rates and default rates on PC insurers' investments is crucial to PC insurers' overall profitability. That is, measuring and managing credit and interest rate risk are key concerns of PC managers.

Consider the following example. Suppose an insurance company's projected loss ratio is 79.8 percent, its expense ratio is 27.9 percent, and it pays 2 percent of its premiums earned to policyholders as dividends. The combined ratio (after dividends) for this insurance company is equal to:

$$\text{Loss ratio} + \text{Expense ratio} + \text{Dividend ratio} = \text{Combined ratio after dividends}$$
$$79.8 \quad + \quad 27.9 \quad + \quad 2.0 \quad = \quad 109.7$$

Thus, expected losses on all PC lines, expenses, and dividends exceeded premiums earned by 9.7 percent.

If the company's investment portfolio, however, yielded 12 percent, the operating ratio and overall profitability of the PC insurer would be:

$$\text{Operating ratio} = \text{Combined ratio after dividends} - \text{Investment yield}$$
$$= \quad 109.7 \quad - \quad 12.0$$
$$= \quad 97.7 \text{ percent}$$

combined ratio
Ratio that measures the overall underwriting profitability of a line; it is equal to the loss ratio plus the ratios of loss adjustment expenses to premiums earned and commission and other acquisition costs to premiums written plus any dividends paid to policyholders as a proportion of premiums earned.

operating ratio
A measure of the overall profitability of a PC insurer; it equals the combined ratio minus the investment yield.

and

$$\text{Overall profitability} = 100 - \text{Operating ratio}$$
$$= 100 - 97.7$$
$$= 2.3 \text{ percent}$$

As can be seen, the high investment returns (12 percent) make the PC insurer profitable overall.

Given the importance of investment returns to PC insurers' profitability, we can see from the balance sheet in Table 3–7 that bonds—both Treasury and corporate—dominated the asset portfolios of PC insurers. Bonds constituted 54.7 percent of total assets and 72.2 percent of financial assets (so-called unaffiliated investments) in 2003.

Finally, if losses, expenses, and other costs are higher and investment yields are lower than expected so that operating losses are incurred, PC insurers carry a significant amount of surplus reserves (policyholder surplus) to reduce the risk of insolvency. In 2003, the ratio of policyholder surplus to assets was 27.9 percent.

Recent Trends

While catastrophes should be random, the period 1987–2004 was characterized by a number of catastrophes of historically high severity, as shown in Figure 3–3. As a result, the period 1987–2004 was not very profitable for the PC industry. In particular, the combined ratio (the measure of loss plus expense risk) increased from 104.6 in 1987 to 115.7 in 1992. (Remember that a combined ratio higher than 100 is bad in that it means that losses, expenses, and dividends totaled *more* than premiums earned.) The major reason for this rise was a succession of catastrophes from Hurricane Hugo in 1989, the San Francisco earthquake in 1991, the Oakland fires of 1991, and the almost $20 billion in losses incurred in Florida as a result of Hurricane Andrew in 1991. In the terminology of PC insurers, the industry was in the trough of an **underwriting cycle,** or underwriting conditions were hard. These cycles are characterized by periods of rising premiums leading to increased profitability. Following a period of solid but not spectacular rates of returns, the industry enters a down phase in which premiums soften as the supply of insurance products increases. Most analysts agree that a cycle that affects all lines simultaneously is unlikely. However, variations in premiums and profitability among individual lines and sectors will continue. As an example of how bad things can be in this industry, after 20 years of profits, Lloyd's of London (arguably one of the world's most well-known and respected insurers) posted a £510 million loss in 1991.[12]

In 1993 the industry showed signs of improvement, with the combined ratio falling to 106.9. However, in 1994 that ratio rose again to 108.4, partly as a result of the Northridge earthquake with estimated losses of $7 billion to $10 billion. The industry ratio fell back down to 101.6 in 1997. However, major losses associated with El Niño (e.g., Hurricane Georges and Midwest storms) drove the combined ratio back up to 105.6 in 1998. The combined ratio increased even further to 107.9 in 1999 and 110.5 in 2000. Part of these increases is attributable to an increase in amounts paid on asbestos claims. In 1999, $3.4 billion was paid out on these claims, the largest payouts ever. The Insurance Services Office, Inc., estimates that the combined ratio for 1999, 107.9, would have been one percentage point lower without these claims.

underwriting cycle
The tendency of profits in the PC industry to follow a cyclical pattern.

www.iso.com

---

[12] As explained by Lloyd's management, the loss was a result of four years of unprecedented disaster claims. As a result of their losses, a group of Lloyd's investors sued the company for negligence in their business operations (some of these cases were still working their way through the legal system in the late 1990s).

FIGURE 3–3 U.S. Catastrophes, 1949–2003

Catastrophe	Year	Amount ($ millions)
Terrorist attacks on WTC and Pentagon	2001	$40,000
Florida Hurricanes	2004	25,000
Hurricane Andrew	1992	19,900
Northridge earthquake	1994	7,200
Hurricane Hugo	1989	4,939
Midwest tornadoes	2003	3,100
Hurricane Georges	1998	2,900
Hurricane Betsy	1965	2,346
Hurricane Opal	1995	2,100
Blizzard of 1996	1996	2,000
Hurricane Iniki	1992	1,646
Blizzard of 1993	1993	1,625
Hurricane Floyd	1999	1,600
Hurricane Fran	1995	1,600

Catastrophe	Year	Amount ($ millions)
Hurricane Frederic	1979	$1,575
Wind, hail, tornadoes	1974	1,395
Minnesota storms	1998	1,300
Freeze	1983	1,280
Oakland fire	1991	1,273
Hurricane Cecelia	1970	1,169
Wind	1950	1,136
California earthquake	1989	1,130
Midwest drought	2000	1,100
Texas hailstorm	1995	1,100
Midwest storms	1998	1,000
Hurricane Isabel	2003	1,000
Hurricane Alicia	1983	983
L.A. riots	1992	797

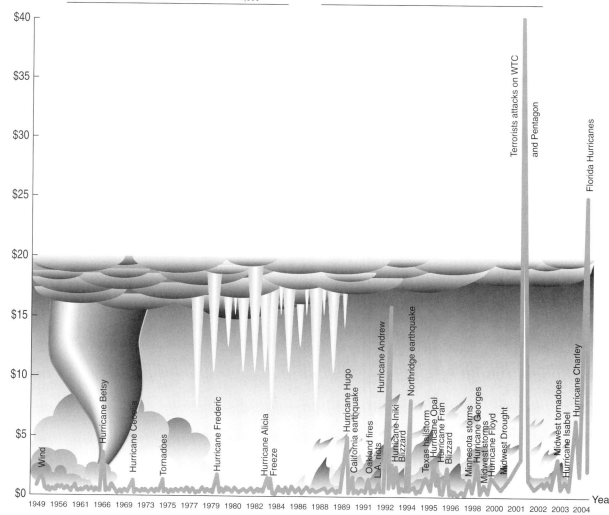

Source: Richard L. Sandor, Centre Financial Products, 1949–1994; author's research, 1995–2004.

Also affecting the profitability of the insurance industry (both life and health and PC) has been the introduction of technology and insurance services offered on the Internet. In 2000, insurers spent more than $12 billion on technological investments, equal to about 4 percent of premiums written and 16 percent of their controllable expenses. The investment in technology was intended to both manage customer relations and reduce operating costs (by some estimates as much as 70 percent).

The year 2001 saw yet another blow to the insurance industry and the world with the terrorist attacks on the World Trade Center and the Pentagon. Early estimates of the costs of these attacks to insurance companies were as high as $40 billion. It was estimated that only 10 percent of the September 11 losses were reported in 2001, and yet the losses attributed to the terrorist attacks added an estimated 4 percentage points to the combined ratio after dividends of 116.0. Because of the tremendous impact these attacks had on the health of the U.S. insurance industry, the Bush administration proposed that the U.S. government pay the majority of the losses of the insurance industry due to the attacks. The proposal capped insurers' 2002 liabilities at $12 billion, 2003 liabilities at $23 billion, and 2004 liabilities at $36 billion. Despite this bailout of the industry, many insurers did not survive and those that did were forced to increase premiums significantly.[13]

The traditional reaction to losses or poor profit results has been the exit from the industry—through failure or acquisition—of less profitable firms and a rapid increase in premiums among the remaining firms. Historically, this has resulted in a fall in the combined ratio as premiums rise and an improvement occurs in the operating ratio and PC industry profitability. In the late 1990s and early 2000s, the PC industry was in a phase of firm exit and consolidation consistent with the initial upward phase of the profitability cycle.

After several tumultuous years, 2003 saw profitability in the PC industry improve. The combined ratio after dividends was 100.1, down sharply from 107.2 in 2002, and much better than most analysts and industry experts expected. The 2003 results were the best since 1979, when the combined ratio was 100.6. Despite the decrease in the combined ratio to 100.1, it is important to note that in the 2000s, a combined ratio of 100 is not what it was 25 years ago. The industry's combined ratio of 100.6 in 1979 resulted in a 15.5 percent ROE for the industry, in large part because of much higher interest rates at that time relative to today. In 2003, the industry saw a 9.4 percent ROE. Insurers would have needed a combined ratio of 94.3 to produce a 15 percent ROE given the prevailing market interest rates and tax conditions. Note that the average yield on 10-year Treasury securities in 1979 was 9.43 percent, compared with only 4.01 percent in 2003. Finally, 2004 saw an increase in losses for the PC industry as Florida and the East coast were hit with several major hurricanes including Hurricanes Charley Frances with total loses of $25 billion.

Regulation

www.naic.org

As with life insurance companies, PC insurers are chartered by states and regulated by state commissions. In addition, state guaranty funds provide some protection to policyholders if an insurance company fails. The National Association of Insurance Commissioners (NAIC) also provides various services to state regulatory commissions. These services include a standardized examination system called IRIS (Insurance Regulatory Information System) to identify insurers with loss, combined, and other ratios outside the normal ranges.

---

[13] See also "The Risk That Nobody Wants," *The Economist*, November 17, 2001, pp. 66–68.

An additional burden that PC insurers face in some activity lines—especially auto insurance and workers' compensation insurance—is rate regulation. That is, given the public utility nature of some insurance lines, state commissioners set ceilings on premiums and premium increases, usually based on specific cost of capital and line risk exposure formulas for the insurance suppliers. This had led some insurers to leave states such as New Jersey, Florida, and California, which have the most restrictive regulations.[14]

More recently, as was the case with other sectors of the FI industry, PC insurance companies came under scrutiny for alleged inconsistencies in fees paid to brokers and consultants for arranging certain policies (see the Ethical Dilemmas box). The inconsistencies became public when the New York Attorney General's Office sent subpoenas to several PC insurance brokers instructing them to save all relevant documents.[15]

Concept Questions

1. Why do PC insurers hold more capital and reserves than do life insurers?
2. Why are life insurers' assets, on average, longer in maturity than those of PC insurers?
3. Describe the main lines of insurance offered by PC insurers.
4. What are the components of the combined ratio?
5. How does the operating ratio differ from the combined ratio?
6. Why does the combined ratio tend to behave cyclically?

GLOBAL ISSUES

Like the other sectors of the financial institutions industry, the insurance sector is becoming increasingly global. Table 3–9 lists the top 10 countries in terms of total premiums written in 2003 (in U.S. dollars) and their percentage share of the world market. Panel A lists the data for life insurers, while panel B lists the data for PC insurers. Table 3–10 lists the top 10 insurance companies worldwide by total revenues. While North America, Japan, and Western Europe dominate the global market, all regions are engaged in the insurance business and many insurers are engaged internationally.

Globalization has certainly affected the U.S. insurance market. In the early 2000s, insurers headquartered outside the United States accounted for over 10 percent of all premiums written in the United States. Because of lax regulations, such as lower capital regulations, many insurance companies have set up offices in the Cayman Islands and the Bahamas. Indeed, it has been estimated that 44 percent of the insurance companies selling life insurance in the Caribbean are from outside the region. The pressure of the global economy, the inability of local insurers to serve all domestic customers, and the domestic demand for better economic performance have caused governments around the world to introduce and accelerate insurance market reform. This includes improving insurance and insurance supervision by formulating common principles and practices across nations. One consequence of these changes is that there have been a number of mergers of insurance companies across country borders, such as the Dutch ING Group's 2000 acquisition of the U.S. Aetna for $7.75 billion.

---

[14] J. A. Fields, C. Ghosh, and L. S. Klein, "From Competition to Regulation: The Six-Year Battle to Regulate California's Insurance Markets," Working Paper, University of Connecticut, March 1996.

[15] See also "Insurance Fees Are Scrutinized," *The Wall Street Journal*, May 17, 2004, p. C1.

TABLE 3–9
The World's Top Countries in Terms of Insurance Premiums Written

Source: Swiss Re, sigma No 3/2004.

Rank	Country	Premiums Written (in billions of US$)	Share of World Market
Panel A: Life Insurers			
1	United States	$480.9	28.8%
2	Japan	381.3	22.8
3	United Kingdom	154.8	9.3
4	France	105.4	6.3
5	Germany	76.7	4.6
6	Italy	71.7	4.3
7	South Korea	42.0	2.5
8	China	32.4	1.9
9	Netherlands	25.4	1.5
10	Switzerland	24.7	1.5
Panel B: Property–Casualty Insurers			
1	United States	$574.6	45.3%
2	Japan	97.5	7.7
3	Germany	94.1	7.4
4	United Kingdom	91.9	7.2
5	France	58.2	4.6
6	Italy	40.1	3.2
7	Canada	36.3	2.9
8	Spain	27.0	2.1
9	Netherlands	24.9	2.0
10	Australia	18.0	1.4

TABLE 3–10
World's Largest Insurance Companies by Total Revenues

Source: Insurance Information Institute Web site, 2004. *www.iii.org*

Rank	Company	Revenues (in millions of US$)	Home Country
Panel A: Life Insurers			
1	ING Group	$88,102	Netherlands
2	AXA Group	62,051	France
3	Nippon Life Insurance	61,175	Japan
4	Assicurazioni Generali	55,105	Italy
5	Aviva	53,723	United Kingdom
6	Dai-Ichi Mutual Life	46,445	Japan
7	Sumitomo Life Insurance	42,220	Japan
8	Prudential	39,410	United Kingdom
9	MetLife	33,967	United States
10	Aegon	26,803	Netherlands
Panel B: Property–Casualty Insurers			
1	Allianz	$74,178	Germany
2	American International Group	44,637	United States
3	Munich Re Group	41,974	Germany
4	State Farm Insurance	40,656	United States
5	Berkshire Hathaway	39,962	United States
6	Zurich Financial Services	38,400	Switzerland
7	Allstate	26,959	United States
8	Millea Holdings	26,018	Japan
9	Swiss Reinsurance	24,028	Switzerland
10	Royal and Sun Alliance	20,953	United Kingdom

Ethical Dilemmas

SPITZER STUDIES NEW CONFLICTS ON INSURANCE

Insurance companies routinely pay fees to brokers and consultants who advise employers on where to buy policies for workers, a little-noticed potential conflict that appears to fall within the scope of New York Attorney General Eliot Spitzer's investigation of the industry. Since Mr. Spitzer's inquiry became public last month, most attention has focused on insurance companies paying brokers and consultants for arranging certain property-and-casualty insurance policies, not employee life-insurance and health benefit plans. At issue is whether these fees compromise the independence of the brokers and consultants, who are supposed to provide unbiased advice to their corporate clients on where to get the best insurance deal. The fees typically reward brokers and consultants for bringing volume business to a carrier. . . .

Critics say these fees can compromise a broker's independence, particularly when they aren't fully disclosed. As agents of the insurance buyer, brokers and consultants are supposed to represent a client's best interests: undisclosed payment directly from an insurance carrier could provide reasons to place business with a particular carrier at variance with the client's best interest. . . . Undisclosed fees from arranging employee benefits mean workers themselves could be the ultimate loser, the critics say. That is because many group-benefit programs let employees buy additional coverage with their own money. Additional payments from an insurer to consultants and brokers would likely be built into the premium structures that these employees must pay.

There are concerns for employers as well: Under federal law, they have a fiduciary responsibility to their employees for the benefits they provide. "If there are silent deals out there or secret deals, those have a direct impact to employees' costs," said Terry Havens, managing partner of Havensure, a Cincinnati employee-benefits consulting firm. . . ."That's real damage to real people," Mr. Havens said. But many employers may not be aware of the payments, current and former consultants say. "Most of the time it's not disclosed. . . ." A former consultant who now manages a corporation's employee benefits from in-house explained that such payments may not show up in the typical disclosures to employers because they don't stem from any single client, but rather from the total business that a consultant places with the insurer. . . .

Source: *The Wall Street Journal*, May 5, 2004, p. C1, by Theo Francis. Reprinted by permission of The Wall Street Journal. © 2004 Dow Jones & Company, Inc. All Rights Reserved Worldwide. *www.wsj.com*

As with commercial banks, Japanese non–life insurance companies suffered severe losses in the early 2000s. Six of the nine major non–life insurance groups that announced earnings (for the April through December 2003 period) saw their net premiums drop relative to the prior year. The main factor in the decline was the sluggish performance of automobile insurance, which accounts for roughly half the revenue for these firms. The total net premiums of the nine groups declined 0.5 percent on the year to ¥4.9 trillion (US$46.4 billion). Life insurers did not fare much better. In 2004, many Japanese life insurers took steps to boost reserves and repair their capital bases after two very difficult years. The sector is expected to continue facing problems due to asset deflation, low interest rates, and a shrinking market for life insurance products.

Summary

This chapter examined the activities and regulation of insurance companies. The first part of the chapter described the various classes of life insurance and recent trends. The second part covered property–casualty companies. The various lines that make up property–casualty insurance are becoming increasingly blurred as multiple activity line coverages are offered. Both life and property–casualty insurance companies are regulated at the state rather than the federal level. In addition, both are coming under threat from other financial service firms that offer similar or competitive products.

Questions and Problems

1. What is the primary function of an insurance company? How does this function compare with the primary function of a depository institution?

2. What is the adverse selection problem? How does adverse selection affect the profitable management of an insurance company?

3. What are the similarities and differences among the four basic lines of life insurance products?

4. Explain how annuity activities represent the reverse of life insurance activities.

5. Explain how life insurance and annuity products can be used to create a steady stream of cash disbursements and payments to avoid paying or receiving a single lump-sum cash amount.

6. a. Calculate the annual cash flows of a $1 million, 20-year fixed-payment annuity earning a guaranteed 10 percent per annum if payments are to begin at the end of the current year.

   b. Calculate the annual cash flows of a $1 million, 20-year fixed-payment annuity earning a guaranteed 10 percent per annum if payments are to begin at the end of year 5.

   c. What is the amount of the annuity purchase required if you wish to receive a fixed payment of $200,000 for 20 years? Assume that the annuity will earn 10 percent per annum.

7. You deposit $10,000 annually into a life insurance fund for the next 10 years, after which time you plan to retire.

   a. If the deposits are made at the beginning of the year and earn an interest rate of 8 percent, what will be the amount of retirement funds at the end of year 10?

   b. Instead of a lump sum, you wish to receive annuities for the next 20 years (years 11 through 30). What is the constant annual payment you expect to receive at the beginning of each year if you assume an interest rate of 8 percent during the distribution period?

   c. Repeat parts (a) and (b) above assuming earning rates of 7 percent and 9 percent during the deposit period and earning rates of 7 percent and 9 percent during the distribution period. During which period does the change in the earning rate have the greatest impact?

8. a. Suppose a 65-year-old person wants to purchase an annuity from an insurance company that would pay $20,000 per year until the end of that person's life. The insurance company expects this person to live for 15 more years and would be willing to pay 6 percent on the annuity. How much should the insurance company ask this person to pay for the annuity?

   b. A second 65-year-old person wants the same $20,000 annuity, but this person is much healthier and is expected to live for 20 years. If the same 6 percent interest rate applies, how much should this healthier person be charged for the annuity?

   c. In each case, what is the difference in the purchase price of the annuity if the distribution payments are made at the beginning of the year?

9. Contrast the balance sheet of a life insurance company with the balance sheet of a commercial bank and with that of a savings association. Explain the

balance sheet differences in terms of the differences in the primary functions of the three organizations.

10. Using the data in Table 3–2, how has the composition of assets of U.S. life insurance companies changed over time?

11. How do life insurance companies earn a profit?

12. How would the balance sheet of a life insurance company change if it offered to run a private pension fund for another company?

13. How does the regulation of insurance companies differ from the regulation of depository institutions? What are the major pieces of life insurance regulatory legislation?

14. How do state guarantee funds for life insurance companies compare with deposit insurance for commercial banks and thrifts?

15. What are the two major activity lines of property–casualty insurance firms?

16. How have the product lines of property–casualty insurance companies changed over time?

17. Contrast the balance sheet of a property–casualty insurance company with the balance sheet of a commercial bank. Explain the balance sheet differences in terms of the differences in the primary functions of the two organizations.

18. What are the three sources of underwriting risk in the property–casualty insurance industry?

19. How do unexpected increases in inflation affect property–casualty insurers?

20. Identify the four characteristics or features of the perils insured against by property–casualty insurance. Rank the features in terms of actuarial predictability and total loss potential.

21. Insurance companies will charge a higher premium for which of the insurance lines listed below? Why?

    a. Low-severity, high-frequency lines versus high-severity, low-frequency lines.

    b. Long-tail lines versus short-tail lines.

22. What does the loss ratio measure? What has been the long-term trend of the loss ratio? Why?

23. What does the expense ratio measure? Identify and explain the two major sources of expense risk to a property–casualty insurer. Why has the long-term trend in this ratio been decreasing?

24. How is the combined ratio defined? What does it measure?

25. What is the investment yield on premiums earned? Why has this ratio become so important to property–casualty insurers?

26. Use the data in Table 3–8. Since 1980, what has been the necessary investment yield for the industry to enable the operating ratio to be less than 100 in each year? How is this requirement related to the interest rate risk and credit risk faced by a property–casualty insurer?

27. An insurance company's projected loss ratio is 77.5 percent, and its loss adjustment expense ratio is 12.9 percent. The company estimates that commission payments and dividends to policyholders will be 16 percent. What must be the minimum yield on investments to achieve a positive operating ratio?

28. a. What is the combined ratio for a property insurer who has a simple loss ratio of 73 percent, a loss adjustment expense of 12.5 percent, and a ratio of commissions and other acquisition expenses of 18 percent?

    b. What is the combined ratio adjusted for investment yield if the company earns an investment yield of 8 percent?

29. An insurance company collected $3.6 million in premiums and disbursed $1.96 million in losses. Loss adjustment expenses amounted to 6.6 percent, and dividends paid to policyholders totaled 1.2 percent. The total income generated from the company's investments was $170,000 after all expenses were paid. What is the net profitability in dollars?

Web Questions

30. Go to the FDIC Web site at **www.federalreserve.gov** and find the most recent distribution of life insurance industry assets for Table 3–2. Click on "Statistics: Releases and Historical Data." Click on "Flow of Fund Accounts of the United States," "*Releases.*" Click on the most recent date. Click on "*Level tables.*" This will bring the file (Table L.117) onto your computer that contains the relevant data. How have the values of government securities, corporate securities, mortgages, and policy loans changed since 2003?

31. Go to the Insurance Information Institute's Web site at **www.iii.org** and use the following steps to find the most recent data on the largest life insurance companies by total revenue. Click on the "Facts and Statistics." Click on "Financial Services." Click on "Life Insurance." This will bring the file onto your computer that contains the relevant data. What are total revenues and assets of the top 10 life insurance companies?

S&P Questions

STANDARD &POOR'S

32. Go to the Standard & Poor's Market Insight Web site at **www.mhhe.com/ edumarketinsight** and identify the industry description and industry constituents for life and health insurance and property–casualty insurance using the following steps. Click on "Educational Version of Market Insight." Enter your Site ID and click on "Login." Click on "Industry." From the Industry list, select "Life & Health Insurance." Click on "Go!" Click on "GICS Sub-Industry Profile" and separately, "GICS Sub-Industry Constituents." Repeat these steps selecting Property & Casualty from the Industry List.

STANDARD &POOR'S

33. Go to the Standard & Poor's Market Insight Web site at **www.mhhe.com/ edumarketinsight** and look up the industry financial highlights as posted by S&P for the life and health insurance and property–casualty insurance industries using the following steps. Click on "Educational Version of Market Insight." Enter your Site ID and click on "Login." Click on "Industry." From the Industry list, select "Life & Health Insurance." Click on "Go!" Click on any/all of the items listed under "GICS Sub-Industry Financial Highlights." Repeat these steps selecting Property & Casualty from the Industry List.

STANDARD &POOR'S

34. Go to the Standard & Poor's Market Insight Web site at **www.mhhe.com/ edumarketinsight** and find the most recent balance sheets for MetLife (MET) and American International Group (AIG) using the following steps. Click on "Educational Version of Market Insight." Enter your Site ID and click on "Login." Click on "Company." Enter "MET" in the "Ticker:" box

and click on "Go!" Click on "Excel Analytics." Click on "FS Ann. Balance Sheet." This will download the balance sheet for MetLife which contains the balances for Fixed Income Securities, Equity Securities, Total Assets, and Mortgage Loans. Repeat the process by entering "AIG" in the "Ticker:" box to get information on American International Group. Compare the ratios of bonds (fixed-income securities) to total assets, preferred stock and common stock (equity securities) to total assets, and mortgage loans to total assets from these balance sheets with those for the life insurance industry, as listed in Table 3–3.

STANDARD
&POOR'S

35. Go to the Standard & Poor's Market Insight Web site at **www.mhhe.com/ edumarketinsight** and find the most recent balance sheets for Allstate Corporation (ALL) and Cigna (CI) using the following steps. Click on "Educational Version of Market Insight." Enter your Site ID and click on "Login." Click on "Company." Enter "ALL" in the "Ticker:" box and click on "Go!" Click on "Excel Analytics." Click on "FS Ann. Balance Sheet." This will download the balance sheet for Allstate which contains the balances for Total Equity and Total Assets. Repeat the process by entering "CI" in the "Ticker:" box to get information on Cigna. Compare the equity ratio for these companies from their balance sheets with that for the property–casualty insurance industry, as listed in Table 3–7.

Pertinent Web Sites

A. M. Best	www.ambest.com
Board of Governors of the Federal Reserve	www.federalreserve.gov
Insurance Information Institute	www.iii.org
Insurance Services Offices, Inc.	www.iso.com
National Association of Insurance Commissioners	www.naic.org
Office of Thrift Supervision	www.ots.treas.gov
State of New York Insurance Guaranty Fund	www.ins.state.ny.us
The Wall Street Journal	www.wsj.com

Chapter **Four**

The Financial Services Industry: Securities Firms and Investment Banks

INTRODUCTION

Investment banking involves the raising of debt and equity securities for corporations or governments. This includes the origination, underwriting, and placement of securities in money and capital markets for corporate or government issuers. Securities services involve assistance in the trading of securities in the secondary markets (brokerage services and/or market making). Together these services are performed by the securities firms and investment banking industry. The largest companies in this industry perform both sets of services (i.e., underwriting and brokerage services). These full-line firms (e.g., Merrill Lynch) are generally called investment banks. Many other firms concentrate their services in one area only (either securities trading or securities underwriting). That is, some firms in the industry specialize in the purchase, sale, and brokerage of existing securities (the retail side of the business) and are called securities firms, while other firms specialize in originating, underwriting, and distributing issues of new securities (the commercial side of the business) and are called investment banks.

Investment banking also includes corporate finance activities such as advising on mergers and acquisitions (M&As), as well as advising on the restructuring of existing corporations. Figure 4–1 reports merger activity for the period 1990–2003. Total dollar volume (measured by transaction value) of domestic M&As increased from less than $200 billion in 1990 to $1.83 trillion in 2000 (reflecting 10,864 deals). The investment bank Goldman Sachs was involved in over $807 billion worth of these mergers in 2000, followed by Credit Suisse First Boston with $611 billion and Morgan Stanley with $578 billion. This merger wave was not restricted to the United States. For example, in 2000 there were over 36,700 merger and acquisition deals globally, valued at over $3.49 trillion, with Goldman Sachs advising on 420 transactions with a market value of $1.28 trillion. However, reflecting the downturn in the U.S. economy, M&A transactions fell 53 percent in 2001 to $819 billion on only 7,525 deals (the first time since 1995 there were fewer than 10,000 deals). Similarly, worldwide M&As fell to $1.74 trillion in 2001. Domestic M&A activity

FIGURE 4–1

Attracting Partners

Source: Thomson Financial
Securities Data, 2004.
www.tfibcm.com

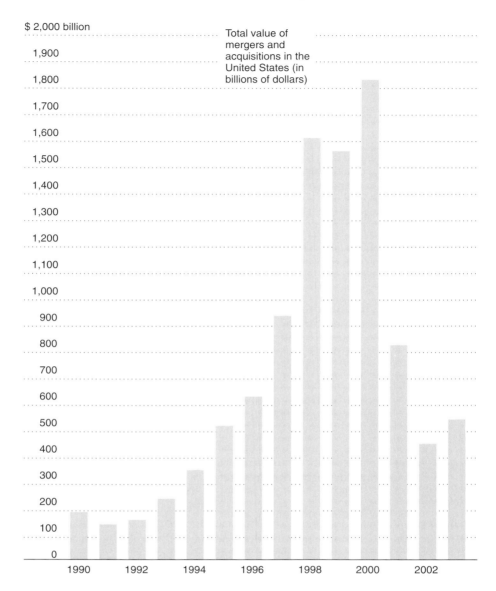

bottomed out at $458 billion in 2002 (while worldwide activity fell to $1.2 trillion) before recovering (along with the economy) to $525 billion in the United States (and $1.3 trillion worldwide) in 2003. M&A activity in the first quarter of 2004 then soared to $228 billion in the United States and to over $535 billion worldwide. Interestingly, M&As involving financial institutions led the way with deals including J. P. Morgan Chase's acquisition of Bank One for $60.0 billion and Bank of America's acquisition of FleetBoston Financial for $49 billion.

In this chapter we present an overview of (1) the size, structure, and composition of the industry, (2) the balance sheet and recent trends, and (3) the regulation of the industry. After studying the chapter, the reader should have a basic understanding of the services provided by securities firms and investment banks, as well as the major trends in the industry.

SIZE, STRUCTURE, AND COMPOSITION OF THE INDUSTRY

Because of the emphasis on securities trading and underwriting, the size of the industry is usually measured by the equity capital of the firms participating in the industry. Securities trading and underwriting is a financial service that requires no investment in assets or liability funding (such as the issuance of loans funded through deposits or payments on insurance contracts funded through insurance premiums). Rather, securities trading and underwriting is a profit-generating activity that does not require FIs to actually hold or invest in the securities they trade or issue for their customers, except for very short periods either as part of their trading inventory or during the underwriting period for new issues. Accordingly, asset value is not traditionally a measure of the size of a firm in this industry. Instead, the equity or capital of the FI is used as the most common benchmark of relative size. Equity capital in this industry amounted to $149.5 billion at the end of 2003, supporting total assets of $3.98 trillion.

Beginning in 1980 and extending up to the stock market crash of October 19, 1987, the number of firms in the industry expanded dramatically from 5,248 to 9,515. The aftermath of the crash saw a major shakeout, with the number of firms declining to 6,549 by 2003, a decline of 31 percent since 1987. Concentration of business among the largest firms over this period has increased dramatically. The largest investment bank in 1987, Salomon Brothers, held capital of $3.21 billion. By 2003 the largest investment bank, Morgan Stanley, held capital of $24.8 billion. Some of the significant growth in size has come through M&As among the top-ranked firms. Table 4–1 lists major U.S. securities industry M&A transactions, many of which involve repeated ownership changes of the same company. Notice from this table that most of the major mergers occurred in 1997 through 2000. Notice too how many recent mergers and acquisitions have been interindustry mergers (i.e., insurance companies and investment banks). Recent regulatory changes such as the Financial Services Modernization Act of 1999 (discussed in Chapter 2 and described in more detail in Chapter 21) are a primary cause for such mergers.

The firms in the industry can be divided along a number of dimensions. First are the largest firms, the so-called national full-line firms, which service both retail customers (especially in acting as **broker–dealers,** thus assisting in the trading of existing securities) and corporate customers (such as **underwriting,** thus assisting in the issue of new securities). The major (ranked by capital) national full-line firms are Merrill Lynch and Morgan Stanley. In 1997 Morgan Stanley, ranked sixth in size of capital, and Dean Witter Discover, ranked fifth in capital size, merged to create one of the largest investment banks in the world. Second are the national full-line firms that specialize more in corporate finance and are highly active in trading securities. Examples are Goldman Sachs and Salomon Brothers/Smith Barney, the investment banking arm of Citigroup (created from the merger of Travelers and Citicorp in 1998). Third, the rest of the industry comprises:

1. Specialized investment bank subsidiaries of commercial bank holding companies (such as J. P. Morgan Chase).[1]

broker–dealers
Assist in the trading of existing securities.

underwriting
Assisting in the issue of new securities.

[1] These so-called Section 20 subsidiaries are discussed in more detail in Chapter 21. Since 1987 bank holding companies have been allowed to establish special investment bank subsidiaries (Section 20 subsidiaries) that can underwrite corporate debt and equity on the same terms as investment banks (since 1999). Section 20 subsidiaries are rapidly being phased out as banking organizations became full-service universal banks by establishing financial service holding companies under the 1999 Financial Services Modernization Act.

TABLE 4–1
Major U.S.
Securities Industry
Merger and
Acquisition
Transactions

Source: Thomson Financial
Securities Data; *The Wall
Street Journal,* and author's
figures.

Rank	Deal	Price in billions of dollars	Year
1	Citicorp merges with Travelers (which owns Smith Barney and Salomon).	$83.0	1998
2	Bank of America acquires FleetBoston.*	49.3	2003
3	J. P. Morgan acquires Bank One.*	60.0	2004
4	Chase acquires J. P. Morgan.*	35.0	2000
5	UBS acquires Paine Webber Group.	12.0	2000
6	Credit Suisse First Boston acquires Donaldson Lufkin Jenrette.	11.5	2000
7	Dean Witter merges with Morgan Stanley.†	10.2	1997
8	Deutsche Bank acquires Bankers Trust*	10.1	1998
9	Travelers acquires Salomon Inc.	9.0	1997
10	Goldman Sachs acquires Spear, Leeds & Kellogg.	6.5	2000
11	Sears spins off Dean Witter, Discover.	5.0	1993
12	Bankers Trust acquires Alex Brown.	2.1	1997
13	Mellon Bank acquires Dreyfus.	1.8	1993
14	American Express spins off Lehman Bros. Holdings.	1.6	1994
15	Fleet Financial acquires Quick and Reilly.	1.6	1997
16	Chase acquires Hambrecht & Quist.	1.3	1998
17	Primerica acquires Shearson.	1.2	1993
18	NationsBank acquires Montgomery Securities.	1.2	1997
19	First Union acquires Everen Capital.	1.2	1999
20	Credit Suisse acquires First Boston.	1.1	1988

*These organizations own section 20 securities subsidiaries and/or are established financial service holding companies under the 1999 Financial Services Modernization Act.
†Value of Dean Witter, Discover shares to be exchanged for Morgan Stanley stock, based on closing price of $40.625 on February 5, 1997.

discount brokers
Stockbrokers that
conduct trades for
customers but do
not offer investment
advice.

2. Specialized **discount brokers** that effect trades for customers on- or offline without offering investment advice or tips (such as Charles Schwab).[2]

3. Regional securities firms that are often subdivided into large, medium, and small categories and concentrate on servicing customers in a particular region, such as New York or California (such as Deutsche Bank Alex Brown, Inc.).

4. Specialized electronic trading securities firms (such as E*trade) that provide a platform for customers to trade without the use of a broker. Rather, trades are enacted on a computer via the Internet.

5. Venture capital firms that pool money from individual investors and other FIs (e.g., hedge funds, pension funds, and insurance companies) to fund relatively small and new businesses (e.g., in biotechnology).[3]

Securities firms and investment banks engage in as many as seven key activity areas.[4] Note that while each activity is available to a firm's customers independently, many of these activities can be and are conducted simultaneously, such as

---

[2] Discount brokers usually charge lower commissions than do full-service brokers such as Merrill Lynch.

[3] Venture capital firms generally play an active management role in the firms in which they invest, often including a seat on the board of directors, and hold significant equity stakes. This differentiates them from traditional banking and securities firms.

[4] See Ernest Bloch, *Inside Investment Banking,* 2d ed. (Chicago: Irwin, 1989), for a similar list.

TABLE 4–2
Top Underwriters of Global Debt and Equity

Source: Reprinted with permission of Thomson Financial Securities Data, 2004. *www.tfibcm.com*

| Manager | Full Year 2003 | | Full Year 2002 | | |
	Amount in Billions	Market Share	Amount in Billions	Rank	Market Share
Salomon Smith Barney*	$ 542.8	10.2%	$ 438.4	1	10.3%
Morgan Stanley	394.8	7.4	293.7	5	6.9
Merrill Lynch	380.3	7.1	340.5	2	8.0
Lehman Brothers	354.1	6.7	280.9	6	6.6
J. P. Morgan Chase	353.9	6.6	293.7	4	6.9
Top-five	$2,025.9	38.0%	$1,648.9	—	38.7%
Industry total	$5,326.2	100%	$4,256.5	—	100.0%

*Part of Citigroup.

mergers and acquisitions financed by new issues of debt and equity underwritten by the M&A advising firm.[5]

1. Investing

Investing involves managing not only pools of assets such as closed- and open-end mutual funds but also pension funds in competition with life insurance companies. Securities firms can manage such funds either as agents for other investors or as principals for themselves. The objective in funds management is to choose asset allocations to beat some return-risk performance benchmark such as the S&P 500 index.[6] Since this business generates fees that are based on the size of the pool of assets managed, it tends to produce a more stable flow of income than does either investment banking or trading (discussed next).

2. Investment Banking

IPO
An initial, or first-time, public offering of debt or equity by a corporation.

Investment banking refers to activities related to underwriting and distributing new issues of debt and equity. New issues can be either primary, the first-time issues of companies (sometimes called **IPOs** [initial public offerings]), or secondary issues (the new issues of seasoned firms whose debt or equity is already trading). In recent years public confidence in the integrity of the IPO process has eroded significantly. Investigations have revealed that certain underwriters of IPOs have engaged in conduct contrary to the best interests of investors and the markets. Among the most harmful practices that have given rise to public concerns are spinning (in which certain underwriters allocate "hot" IPO issues to directors and/or executives of potential investment banking clients in exchange for investment banking business) and biased recommendations by research analysts (due to their compensation being tied to the success of their firms' investment banking business). We discuss these issues and some of the legal proceedings resulting from these practices below.[7]

Table 4–2 lists the top five underwriters of global debt and equity for 2003 and 2002. The top five common stock underwriters represented 38.0 percent of the industry total, suggesting that the industry is dominated by a handful of top-tier underwriting firms. Top-tier rating and the implied reputation this brings has a huge

---

[5] See, for example, L. Allen, J. Jagtiani, S. Peristiani, and A. Saunders, "The Role of Bank Advisors in Mergers and Acquisitions," *Journal of Money, Credit and Banking* 3, no. 2 (April 2004), pp. 197–224.

[6] Or the "securities market line" given the fund's "beta."

[7] R. Aggarwal, N. R. Prabhala, and M. Puri, in "Institutional Allocation in Initial Public Offerings: Empirical Evidence," *The Journal of Finance*, June 2002, pp. 1421–42, document a positive relationship between institutional allocation and day-one IPO returns. The result is partly explained by the practice of giving institutions more shares in IPOs with strong premarket demand.

effect in this business. At times, investment banks have refused to participate in an issue because their name would not be placed where they desired it on the "tombstone" advertisement announcing the issue and its major underwriters.

private placement
A securities issue placed with one or a few large institutional investors.

Securities underwritings can be undertaken through either public offerings or private offerings. In a private offering, the investment banker acts as a **private placement** agent for a fee, placing the securities with one or a few large institutional investors such as life insurance companies.[8] In a public offering, the securities may be underwritten on a best-efforts or a firm commitment basis, and the securities may be offered to the public at large. With best-efforts underwriting, investment bankers act as *agents* on a fee basis related to their success in placing the issue. In firm commitment underwriting, the investment banker acts as a *principal*, purchasing the securities from the issuer at one price and seeking to place them with public investors at a slightly higher price. Finally, in addition to investment banking operations in the corporate securities markets, the investment banker may participate as an underwriter (primary dealer) in government, municipal, and asset-backed securities. Table 4–3 shows the top-ranked underwriters for 2003 and 2002 in the different areas of securities underwriting.[9]

Internet Exercise   Go to the Thomson Financial Investment Banking/Capital Markets group Web site (**www.tfibcm.com**) and find the latest information available for top underwriters of various securities.

Go to the Thomson Financial Investment Banking/Capital Markets group Web site at **www.tfibcm.com**. Click on "View the latest League Table Online." Click on "Debt & Equity." Under Press Releases, click on "Global Capital Markets Press Releases." This will download a file on to your computer that will contain the most recent information on top underwriters for various securities.

---

3. *Market Making*

Market making involves creating a secondary market in an asset by a securities firm or investment bank. Thus, in addition to being primary dealers in government securities and underwriters of corporate bonds and equities, investment bankers make a secondary market in these instruments. Market making can involve either agency or principal transactions. *Agency* transactions are two-way transactions on behalf of *customers*, for example, acting as a *stockbroker* or dealer for a fee or commission. On the NYSE, a market maker in a stock such as IBM may, upon the placement of orders by its customers, buy the stock at $78 from one customer and immediately resell it at $79 to another customer. The $1 difference between the buy and sell price is usually called the bid–ask spread and represents a large portion of the market maker's profit. Many securities firms and investment banks offer online trading services to their customers as well as direct access to a client representative (stockbroker). Thus, customers may now conduct trading

---

[8] See *Federal Reserve Bulletin*, February 1993, for an excellent description of the private placement market. Issuers of privately placed securities do not have to register with the SEC since the placements are made only to large, sophisticated investors.

[9] A. Ljungqvist, F. Marston, and W. J. Wilhelm, Jr., in "Competing for Securities Underwriting Mandates: Banking Relationships and Analyst Recommendations," 2003, Working Paper, New York University, investigate whether analyst behavior influenced the likelihood of banks' winning underwriting business for U.S. debt and equity offerings between December 1993 and June 2002. They find no evidence that aggressive analyst recommendations or recommendation upgrades increased a bank's probability of winning an underwriting mandate.

TABLE 4–3   **Who Is Number 1 in Each Market?**

Type	Full Year 2003		Full Year 2002	
	Amount in Billions	Top-Ranked Manager	Amount in Billions	Top-Ranked Manager
Straight debt	$4,938.0	Salomon S.B.	$3,937.7	Salomon S. B.
Convertible debt	164.5	J. P. Morgan Chase	96.2	Salomon S. B.
Investment-grade debt	658.7	Salomon S.B.	549.0	Salomon S. B.
Mortgage-backed securities	900.2	UBS	805.3	UBS
Asset-backed securities	580.8	Salomon S.B.	455.9	J. P. Morgan Chase
Common stock	388.2	Goldman Sachs	318.5	Goldman Sachs
IPOs	13.8	Goldman Sachs	22.6	Salomon S. B.
Syndicated loans	1,920.2	J. P. Morgan	1,860.7	J. P. Morgan

Source: Reprinted with permission of Thomson Financial Securities Data, 2004. *www.tfibcm.com*

activities from their homes and offices through their accounts at securities firms at a lower cost in terms of fees and commissions. In the early 2000s, there were also more than 100 purely electronic securities trading firms in existence. These firms, where at least $5,000 is generally required to open an account, offer investors (day traders) a desk and a computer with high-speed access to the stock markets. An estimated 5 million people used the facilities offered by electronic trading firms in the early 2000s. Accordingly, technology risk is an increasingly important issue for these FIs (see Chapter 14).

In *principal* transactions, the market maker seeks to profit on the price movements of securities and takes either long or short inventory positions for its own account. (Or an inventory position may be taken to stabilize the market in the securities.)[10] In the example above, the market maker would buy the IBM stock at $78 and hold it in its own portfolio in expectation of a price increase later on. Normally, market making can be a fairly profitable business; however, in periods of market stress or high volatility, these profits can rapidly disappear. For example, on the NYSE, market makers, in return for having monopoly power in market making for individual stocks (e.g., IBM), have an affirmative obligation to buy stocks from sellers even when the market is crashing. This caused a number of actual and near bankruptcies for NYSE market makers at the time of the October 1987 market crash. On NASDAQ, which has a system of competing market makers, liquidity was significantly impaired at the time of the crash and a number of firms had to withdraw from market making.[11] Finally, the recent moves toward decimalization of equities markets in the United States (i.e., expressing quotes in integers of 1 cent [e.g., $50.32] rather than rounding to eighths [e.g., 50 $3/8$]) has cut into traders' profits, as has competition from Internet-based or electronic-based exchanges such at The Island ECN and GlobeNet ECN.[12]

---

[10] In general, full-service investment banks can become market makers in stocks on NASDAQ, but they have been prevented until recently from acting as market-making specialists on the NYSE.

[11] See, for example, W. A. Christie and P. H. Schultz, "Dealer Markets under Stress: The Performance of NASDAQ Market Makers during the November 15, 1991, Market Break," *Journal of Financial Services Research* 13 (June 1998), pp. 205–30.

[12] See, for example, R. Bloomfield, M. O'Hara, and G. Saar, "The Make or Take Decision in an Electronic Market: Evidence on the Evolution of Liquidity," *Journal of Financial Economics*, forthcoming.

4. Trading

Trading is closely related to the market-making activities just described, where a trader takes an active net position in an underlying instrument or asset. There are at least four types of trading activities:

1. *Position trading* involves purchasing large blocks of securities on the expectation of a favorable price move. Such positions also facilitate the smooth functioning of the secondary markets in such securities.

2. *Pure arbitrage* entails buying an asset in one market at one price and selling it immediately in another market at a higher price.

3. *Risk arbitrage* involves buying blocks of securities in anticipation of some information release, such as a merger or takeover announcement or a Federal Reserve interest rate announcement.[13]

4. *Program trading* is defined by the NYSE as the simultaneous buying and selling of a portfolio of at least 15 different stocks valued at more than $1 million, using computer programs to initiate such trades. Program trading is often associated with seeking a risk arbitrage between a cash market price (e.g., the Standard & Poor's 500 Stock Market Index) and the *futures* market price of that instrument.[14]

As with many activities of securities firms, such trading can be conducted on behalf of a customer as an agent (or broker), or on behalf of the firm as a principal.

5. Cash Management

cash management accounts
Money market mutual funds sold by investment banks; most CMAs offer check-writing privileges.

Investment banks offer bank deposit–like **cash management** accounts (CMAs) to individual investors and since the 1999 Financial Services Modernization Act, deposit accounts themselves (Merrill Lynch was the first investment bank to offer a direct deposit account in June 2000, via the two banks it owns). Most of these CMAs allow customers to write checks against some type of mutual fund account (e.g., money market mutual fund). These accounts, when issued in association with commercial banks and thrifts, can even be covered by federal deposit insurance from the FDIC. CMAs were instrumental in the securities industry's efforts to provide commercial banking services prior to the 1999 Financial Services Modernization Act.

6. Mergers and Acquisitions

Investment banks are frequently involved in providing advice or assisting in mergers and acquisitions. For example, they will assist in finding merger partners, underwriting new securities to be issued by the merged firms, assessing the value of target firms, recommending terms of the merger agreement, and even helping target firms prevent a merger (for example, seeing that poison-pill provisions are written into a potential target firm's securities contracts). As noted in the introduction to this chapter, merger and acquisition activity stood at $525 billion in 2003. Table 4–4 lists the top 10 investment bank merger advisers ranked by

---

[13] It is termed *risk arbitrage* because if the event does not actually occur—for example, if a merger does not take place or the Federal Reserve does not change interest rates—the trader stands to lose money.

[14] An example would be buying the cash S&P index and selling futures contracts on the S&P index. Since stocks and futures contracts trade in different markets, their prices are not always equal. Moreover, program trading can occur between futures and cash markets in other assets, for example, commodities.

TABLE 4–4

Ten Largest U.S. Merger and Acquisition Firms Ranked by Value of Mergers, 2003

Source: Thomson Financial Securities Data Company 2004. *www.tfibcm.com*

Rank	Investment Bank	Value (billions of dollars)	Number of Deals
1	Goldman Sachs	$239.4	143
2	Morgan Stanley	117.4	97
3	Salomon Smith Barney (Citigroup)	100.1	154
4	Lehman Brothers	99.4	111
5	Credit Suisse First Boston	94.5	149
6	Bank of America Securities	92.5	64
7	Merrill Lynch	88.9	74
8	J. P. Morgan Chase	69.3	97
9	UBS	63.5	81
10	Bear Stearns	38.1	46
	Industry total	$525.6	7,570

TABLE 4–5

Ten Largest Worldwide Merger and Acquisition Firms Ranked by Total Credit Lent, 2004

Source: Thomson Financial Securities Data, 2004. *www.tfibcm.com*

Rank	Investment Bank	Credit Lent (billions of dollars)	Number of Deals
1	Goldman Sachs	$ 392.7	298
2	Morgan Stanley	239.5	239
3	Salomon Smith Barney	219.6	307
4	Merrill Lynch	213.5	191
5	J. P. Morgan Chase	206.4	291
6	Lazard	154.2	188
7	Credit Suisse First Boston	153.2	294
8	UBS	152.1	257
9	Lehman Brothers	147.2	180
10	Deutsche Bank	126.8	178
	Industry total	$1,333.3	27,753

dollar volume of the mergers in which they were involved.[15] Table 4–5 lists the top 10 investment banks ranked by dollar volume of worldwide M&A activity. Notice that many of the top U.S.-ranked investment banks reported in Table 4–4 are also top-ranked for worldwide activity in Table 4–5.

7. Back-Office and Other Service Functions

These functions include custody and escrow services, clearance and settlement services, and research and other advisory services—for example, giving advice on divestitures and asset sales. In addition, investment banks are making increasing

---

[15] Often, in addition to providing M&A advisory services, an investment banker will be involved in underwriting new securities that help finance an M&A. See L. Allen, J. Jagtiani, S. Peristiani and A. Saunders, "The Role of Financial Advisors in Mergers and Acquisitions," *Journal of Money, Credit, and Banking* 36, no. 2 (April 2004), pp. 197–224. A. Saunders and A. Srinivasan, in "Investment Banking Relationships and Merger Fees," 2002, Working Paper, New York University, investigate the effect of prior investment banking relationships on merger advisory fees paid by acquiring firms. Their findings indicate that acquiring firms perceive benefits of retaining merger advisors with whom they have had a prior relationship (even at a cost of higher fees) and/or they face some other (higher) costs of switching to new bank advisors. Finally, V. Ivashina, V. Nair, A. Saunders, N. Massoud, and R. Stover, in "The Role of Banks in Takeovers," 2004, Working Paper, New York University, show that banks use the information generated in lending to increase the probability of takeovers.

inroads into traditional bank service areas such as small business lending and the trading of loans (see Chapter 21). In performing these functions, a securities firm normally acts as an agent for a fee. As mentioned above, fees charged are often based on the total bundle of services performed for the client by the firm. The portion of the fee or commission allocated to research and advisory services is called soft dollars. When one area in the firm, such as an investment advisor, uses client commissions to buy research from another area in the firm, it receives a benefit because it is relieved from the need to produce and pay for the research itself. Thus, the advisor using soft dollars faces a conflict of interest between the need to obtain research and the client's interest in paying the lowest commission rate available. Because of the conflict of interest that exists, the SEC (the primary regulator of investment banks and securities firms) requires these firms to disclose soft dollar arrangements to their clients.

Nevertheless, in 2001 tremendous publicity was generated concerning conflicts of interest in a number of securities firms between analysts' research recommendations on stocks to buy or not buy and whether the firm played a role in underwriting the securities of the firm the analysts were recommending. After an investigation by the New York State Attorney General, Merrill Lynch agreed to pay a fine of $100 million and to follow procedures more clearly separating analysts' recommendations (and their compensation) from the underwriting activities of the firm. A number of other major Wall Street firms were also placed under investigation (see below). The investigation was triggered by the dramatic collapse of many new technology stocks while analysts were still making recommendations to buy or hold them.

Concept Questions

1. Describe the difference between brokerage services and underwriting services.
2. What are the key areas of activities for securities firms?
3. Describe the difference between a best-efforts offering and a firm commitment offering.
4. What are the trading activities performed by securities firms?

BALANCE SHEET AND RECENT TRENDS

Recent Trends

In this section, we look at the balance sheet and trends in the securities firm and investment banking industry. Trends in this industry depend heavily on the state of the stock market. For example, a major effect of the 1987 stock market crash was a sharp decline in stock market trading volume and thus in brokerage commissions earned by securities firms over the 1987–91 period. Commission income began to recover only after 1992, with record equity trading volumes being achieved in 1995–2000 when the Dow Jones and S&P indexes hit new highs. As stock market values plummeted in 2001 and 2002, so did commission income. However, improvements in the U.S. economy in 2003 and 2004 resulted in an increase in stock market values and trading and thus commission income. The overall decline in brokerage commissions actually began over 25 years ago, in 1977, and is reflective of a long-term fall in the importance of commission income, as a percentage of revenues, for securities firms as a result of the abolition of fixed commissions on securities trades by the Securities and Exchange Commission (SEC) in May 1975 and the fierce competition for wholesale commissions and trades that followed (see Figure 4–2).

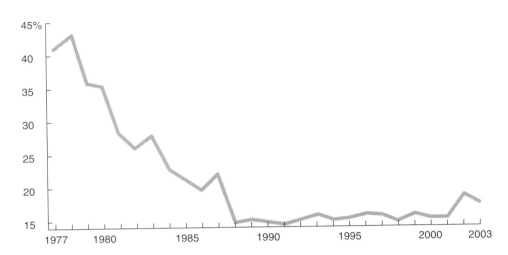

FIGURE 4–2
Commission
Income as a
Percentage of
Total Revenues

Source: Securities and
Exchange Commission,
Standard & Poor's *Industry
Surveys*, and Securities
Industry Association.

TABLE 4–6   U.S. Corporate Underwriting Activity (in billions of dollars)

	Straight Corporate Debt	Con- vertible Debt	Asset- Backed Debt	Total Debt	Common Stock	Preferred Stock	Total Equity	All IPOs	Total Under- writing
1986	$ 149.8	$10.1	$ 67.8	$ 227.7	$ 43.2	$13.9	$ 57.1	$22.3	$ 284.8
1987	117.8	9.9	91.7	219.4	41.5	11.4	52.9	24.0	272.3
1988	120.3	3.1	113.8	237.4	29.7	7.6	37.3	23.6	274.5
1990	107.7	4.7	176.1	288.4	19.2	4.7	23.9	10.1	312.3
1995	466.0	6.9	152.4	625.3	82.0	15.1	97.1	30.2	722.4
2000	1,236.2	17.1	393.4	1,646.6	189.1	15.4	204.5	76.1	1,851.0
2001	1,511.2	21.6	832.5	2,365.4	128.4	41.3	169.7	40.8	2,535.1
2002	1,300.2	8.6	1,115.4	2,427.2	116.4	37.6	154.0	41.2	2,581.1
2003	1,370.7	10.6	1,352.3	2,733.6	118.5	37.8	156.3	43.7	2,889.9
% change (2002 to 2003)	5.2%	23.3%	21.2%	12.6%	1.8%	0.5%	1.5%	6.1%	12.0%

Note: High-yield bonds represent a subset of straight corporate debt. IPOs are a subset of common stock; true and closed-end fund IPOs are subsets of all IPOs.
Source: Thomson Financial Securities Data, 2004. *www.tfibcm.com*

Also affecting the profitability of the securities industry was the decline in new equity issues over the 1987–90 period as well as a decline in bond and equity underwriting in general (see Table 4–6). This was due partly to the stock market crash, partly to a decline in mergers and acquisitions, partly to a general economic recession, and partly to investor concerns about junk bonds after the Michael Milken/Ivan Boesky–Drexel Burnham Lambert scandal, which resulted in that firm's failure in 1989.[16]

[16] Drexel was once the most influential firm on Wall Street because of its pioneering work under Michael Milken in the junk bond market. Drexel went bankrupt, however, after its corporate officials pleaded guilty to six felony counts of federal securities fraud. Drexel and Milken were found to have "plundered" the S&L industry by manipulating the market for junk bonds. The essence of the legal action involved the fact that Milken, working for Drexel, used S&Ls to create a web of buyers that helped give the appearance of a market for junk bonds. This allowed Drexel to sell junk bonds at prices above their fair market values; S&Ls held almost 20 percent of junk bonds outstanding, and when the junk bond market collapsed, many S&Ls, especially those in California, suffered large losses.

FIGURE 4–3

Securities Industry Pretax Profits, 1990–2003

Source: Securities Industry Association, 2003. *www.sia.com*

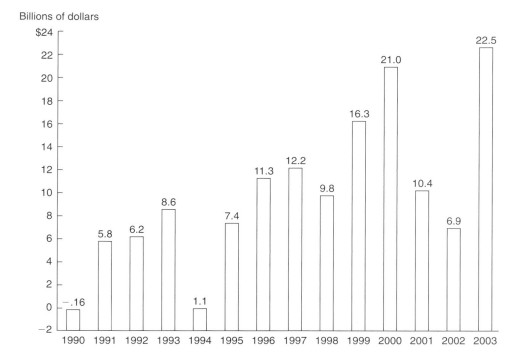

Billions of dollars

Between 1991 and 2001, however, the securities industry showed a resurgence in profitability.[17] For example, domestic underwriting activity over the 1991–2001 period grew from $312.3 billion in 1990 to $2,535.1 billion in 2001 (see Table 4–6). The principal reasons for this were enhanced trading profits and increased growth in new issue underwritings. In particular, corporate debt issues became highly attractive to corporate treasurers because of relatively low long-term interest rates. Moreover, growth in the asset-backed securities market as a result of increased securitization of mortgages (and growth of mortgage debt) added to the value of underwriting.[18]

As a result of enhanced trading profits and growth in new issue underwriting, pretax net income for the industry topped $9 billion each year over the 1997–2000 period (see Figure 4–3). This is despite the collapse of the Russian ruble and bond markets, economic turmoil in Asia, and political uncertainty in Washington during this period. Possibly more surprising is that despite a downturn in the U.S. economy toward the end of 2000, pretax profits soared to an all-time high of $21.0 billion in 2000. The continued slowdown of the U.S. economy in 2001 and the terrorist attacks on the World Trade Center in September 2001, however, brought an end to these record profits. Industry pretax profits for the year 2001 fell 50 percent, to $10.4 billion. The Bank of New York alone estimated costs associated with the terrorist attacks were $125 million. Citigroup estimated it lost

---

[17] Pretax return on equity for broker–dealers rose from 2.2 percent in 1990 to 20.9 and 25.1 percent in 1995 and 2000, respectively. The ratio fell to as low as 8.34 percent in 2002 before recovering to 18.6 percent in 2003.

[18] Another sign of the resurgence in this industry during the 1990s appears in employment figures. Annual U.S. securities industry employment increased by 72 percent (from 486,000 jobs in 1992 to 837,000 in 2000 [peaking at 840,900 in March 2001]).

$100–$200 million in business from branches that were closed and because of the four days the stock market did not trade. Morgan Stanley, the largest commercial tenant in the World Trade Center, said the cost of property damage and relocation of its employees was $150 million.

The slow rate of recovery of the U.S. economy (along with the decline in stock market trading and the fall in M&As and related activities) hampered the ability of the industry to generate profit growth in 2002. As a result, 2002 pretax profits for securities firms were $6.9 billion, the lowest since 1995. Further, employment declined to a two-year low of 793,700 jobs in May 2003 (a decline of 5.6 percent from the high in March 2001). Moreover, the securities industry was rocked by several allegations of securities law violations as well as a loss of investor confidence in Wall Street and corporate America as a result of a number of corporate governance failures and accounting scandals involving Enron, Merck, WorldCom, and other major U.S. corporations.

However, with the recovery of the U.S. economy in late 2002 and 2003, the U.S. securities industry again earned record profits as revenue growth strengthened and became more broadly based. Domestic underwriting surged to $2,889.9 billion in 2003, from $2,535.1 billion in 2001 (see Table 4–6). Further, the industry maintained its profitability mainly through deep cuts in expenses. Total expenses fell 10.4 percent from 2002 levels, largely due to lower interest expenses. Interest expense fell an estimated 22.5 percent from $48.4 billion in 2002 to $37.5 billion in 2003. Operating expenses excluding interest expense fell 4.1 percent in 2003, reflecting the success of cost controls and continued high rates of productivity growth in the securities industry. The results for 2003 were record pretax profits of $22.5 billion (see Figure 4–3).

Balance Sheet

The consolidated balance sheet for the industry is shown in Table 4–7. Note the current importance of securities trading and underwriting in the consolidated balance sheet of all securities firms. Looking at the asset portfolio, we can see that long positions in securities and commodities accounted for 27.0 percent of assets, while reverse repurchase agreements—securities purchased under agreements to resell (i.e., the broker gives a short-term loan to the repurchase agreement seller)—accounted for 24.3 percent of assets. Because of the extent to which this industry's balance sheet consists of financial market securities, the industry is subjected to particularly high levels of market risk (see Chapter 10) and interest rate risk (see Chapters 8 and 9). Further, to the extent that many of these securities are foreign-issued securities, FI managers must also be concerned with foreign exchange risk (see Chapter 15) and sovereign risk (see Chapter 16).

With respect to liabilities, repurchase agreements were the major source of funds; these are securities temporarily lent in exchange for cash received. Repurchase agreements—securities sold under agreements to repurchase—amounted to 39.3 percent of total liabilities and equity. The other major sources of funds were securities and commodities sold short for future delivery and broker-call loans from banks. Equity capital amounted to only 3.8 percent of total assets, while total capital (equity capital plus subordinated liabilities) accounted for 5.7 percent of total assets. These levels are well below those we saw for depository institutions in Chapter 2 (9.10 percent for commercial banks, 9.30 percent for savings associations, 9.64 percent for savings banks, and 9.20 percent for credit unions). One reason for lower capital levels is that securities firms' balance

TABLE 4–7
Assets and
Liabilities of
Broker–Dealers as
of Year-End 2003
(in millions of
dollars)

Source: *Focus Report,* Office
of Economic Analysis, U.S.
Securities and Exchange
Commission, 2004.
www.sec.gov

Assets	
Cash	$ 50,774.0
Receivables from other broker–dealers	1,530,227.0
Receivables from customers	163,159.2
Receivables from noncustomers	18,345.8
Long positions in securities and commodities	1,075,696.7
Securities and investments not readily marketable	11,753.1
Securities purchased under agreements to resell	967,008.0
Exchange membership	1,086.6
Other assets	162,346.1
Total assets	$3,980,375.4
Liabilities	
Bank loans payable	$ 75,548.8
Payables to other broker–dealers	842,983.0
Payables to noncustomers	66,995.6
Payables to customers	407,432.6
Short positions in securities and commodities	510,513.0
Securities sold under repurchase agreements	1,565,003.7
Other nonsubordinated liabilities	286,459.8
Subordinated liabilities	75,921.7
Total liabilities	$3,830,858.1
Capital	
Equity capital	$ 149,517.3
Total capital	$ 225,439.0
Number of firms	6,549

sheets contain mostly tradable (liquid) securities compared with the relatively illiquid loans that constitute a significant proportion of banks' asset portfolios. Securities firms are required to maintain a net worth (capital) to assets ratio in excess of 2 percent (see Chapter 20).

**Concept
Questions**

1. Describe the trend in profitability in the securities industry over the last 10 years.
2. What are the major assets held by broker–dealers?
3. Why do broker–dealers tend to hold less equity capital than do commercial banks and thrifts?

REGULATION

www.sec.gov   The primary regulator of the securities industry is the Securities and Exchange Commission (SEC), established in 1934. The National Securities Markets Improvement Act (NSMIA) of 1996 reaffirmed the significance of the SEC as the primary regulator of securities firms. According to the NSMIA, states are no longer allowed to require federally registered securities firms to be registered in a state as well. States are also now prohibited from requiring registration of securities firms' transactions and from imposing substantive requirements on private placements. Prior to the NSMIA, most securities firms were subject to regulation from the SEC and from each state in which they operated. While the

NSMIA provides that states may still require securities firms to pay fees and file documents to be submitted to the SEC, most of the regulatory burden imposed by states has been removed. Thus, the NSMIA effectively gives the SEC the exclusive regulatory jurisdiction over securities firms. However, the early 2000s saw a reversal of this trend toward the dominance of the SEC with states—especially their attorneys general—increasingly intervening through securities-related investigations. As noted earlier, several highly publicized securities violations resulted in criminal cases brought against securities law violators by state and federal prosecutors. In particular, the New York State Attorney General forced Merrill Lynch to pay a $100 million penalty because of allegations that Merrill Lynch brokers gave investors overly optimistic reports about the stock of its investment banking clients.

Subsequent to these investigations, the SEC instituted rules requiring Wall Street analysts to vouch that their stock picks are not influenced by investment banking colleagues and that analysts disclose details of their compensation that would flag investors to any possible conflicts. If evidence surfaces that analysts have falsely attested to the independence of their work, it could be used to bring enforcement actions. Violators could face a wide array of sanctions, including fines and other penalties, such as a suspension or a bar from the securities industry. In addition, the SEC proposed that top officials from all public companies sign off on financial statements.

In the spring of 2003 the issue culminated in an agreement between regulators and 10 of the nation's largest securities firms to pay a record $1.4 billion in penalties to settle charges involving investor abuse. The long-awaited settlement centered on civil charges that securities firms routinely issued overly optimistic stock research to investors in order to gain favor with corporate clients and win their investment banking business. The agreement also settled charges that at least two big firms, Citigroup and Credit Suisse First Boston, improperly allocated IPO shares to corporate executives to win banking business from their firms. The SEC and other regulators, including the NASD, the NYSE, and state regulators, unveiled multiple examples of how Wall Street stock analysts tailored their research reports and ratings to win investment banking business. The Wall Street firms agreed to the settlement without admitting or denying any wrongdoing. The agreement forced brokerage companies to make structural changes in the way they handle research—preventing analysts, for example, from attending certain investment banking meetings with bankers. The agreement also required securities firms to have separate reporting and supervisory structures for their research and banking operations. Additionally, it required that analysts' pay be tied to the quality and accuracy of their research, rather than the amount of investment banking business they generate. Table 4–8 lists the 10 firms involved in the settlement and the penalties assessed. Within days of this agreement, however, Bear Stearns, one of the 10 firms, was accused of using its analysts to promote a new stock offering (see the Ethical Dilemmas box).

www.nyse.com
www.nasd.com

Along with these changes instituted by the SEC, the U.S. Congress passed the Sarbanes-Oxley Act in July 2002. This act created an independent auditing oversight board under the SEC, increased penalties for corporate wrongdoers, forced faster and more extensive financial disclosure, and created avenues of recourse for aggrieved shareholders. The goal of the legislation was to prevent deceptive accounting and management practices and to bring stability to jittery stock markets battered in the summer of 2002 by corporate governance scandals of Enron, Global Crossings, Tyco, WorldCom, and others.

Ethical **Dilemmas**

BEAR STEARNS USED ANALYST TO TOUT IPO DESPITE PACT WITH REGULATORS

Days after agreeing to a sweeping settlement aimed at overhauling the way Wall Street does business, Bear Stearns Cos. reverted to the practice of using an analyst to promote a new stock offering. When questions about the episode were raised by *The Wall Street Journal*, Bear Stearns took the embarrassing step of delaying the initial public offering of stock in credit card processing firm iPayment Inc., and the securities firm said it would bar the analyst from covering iPayment. Bear Stearns also called the Securities and Exchange Commission and the New York Attorney General's office to tell them about the incident and apologize. . . .

Letting stock research analysts participate in company- or investment banking–sponsored road shows is expressly forbidden under the regulatory pact the 10 securities firms announced with regulators April 28. Documents released in the settlement revealed how firms had routinely used analysts as de facto marketers, having them cite bullish views on IPO candidates during "pitches" to win lucrative underwriting business, and later having them deliver glowing forecasts in road show presentations to investors before the offering.

Virtually before the ink was dry on the settlement, Bear Stearns salespeople on May 2 e-mailed institutional investors a link to a prerecorded "net road show" for iPayment, one of the few stock issues planned by Wall Street in two months amid the worst IPO famine in the U.S. in recent years. In the video clip, Mr. Kissane, a top Bear Stearns computer-services-industry analyst, called it his "pleasure" to introduce three top executives of iPayment and dubbed the Nashville, Tenn., company a smart investment. "I think iPayment represents a great way for investors to play a proven wining strategy in the merchant processing space focused on small business, which I just think is a tremendous growth opportunity," he said. . . .

Source: *The Wall Street Journal*, May 12, 2003, p. A1, by Ann Davis. Reprinted by permission of The Wall Street Journal. © 2003 Dow Jones & Company, Inc. All Rights Reserved Worldwide. *www.wsj.com*

TABLE 4–8
Securities Firm Penalties Assessed for Trading Abuses

Source: Authors' research, 2004.

Firm	Penalty (in millions of dollars)
Citigroup	$400
Credit Suisse First Boston	200
Merrill Lynch	200
Morgan Stanley	125
Goldman Sachs	110
Bear Stearns	80
J. P. Morgan Chase	80
Lehman Brothers	80
UBS Warburg	80
Piper Jaffray	32

shelf-offering
A *shelf offering* allows firms that plan to offer multiple issues of stock over a two-year period to submit one registration statement summarizing the firm's financing plans for the period.

In addition to investigating and prosecuting securities law violations, the SEC also sets rules governing securities firms' underwriting and trading activities. For example, SEC Rule 415 on **shelf-offerings** allows larger corporations to register their new issues with the SEC up to two years in advance.[19] Similarly, SEC Rule 144A defines the boundaries between public offerings of securities and private placements of securities.

[19] They are called shelf-offerings because after registering the issue with the SEC, the firm can take the issue "off the shelf" and sell it to the market when conditions are the most favorable, for example, in the case of debt issues, when interest rates are low.

While the SEC sets the overall regulatory standards for the industry, two self-regulatory organizations are involved in the day-to-day regulation of trading practices. These are the New York Stock Exchange (NYSE) and the National Association of Securities Dealers (NASD)—the latter is responsible for trading in the over-the-counter markets such as NASDAQ. The NYSE and NASD monitor trading abuses (such as insider trading) trading rule violations, and securities firms' capital (solvency) positions. For example, in July 2003, the NYSE fined a veteran floor trader at Fleet Specialist Inc. $25,000 for allegedly mishandling customer orders in General Motors stock when they fell sharply on June 27, 2002, after rumors circulated that the automaker had accounting problems. Instead of buying the stock, the trader sold 10,000 shares from Fleet's own account when there was another known seller on the floor.

Securities firms and investment banks have historically been strongly supportive of efforts to combat money laundering, and the industry has been subject to federal laws that impose extensive reporting and record-keeping requirements. However, the USA Patriot Act, passed in response to the September 11 terrorist attacks, included additional provisions that financial services firms must implement. The new rules, which took effect on October 1, 2003, imposed three requirements on firms in the industry. First, firms must verify the identity of any person seeking to open an account. Second, firms must maintain records of the information used to verify the person's identity. Third, firms must determine whether a person opening an account appears on any list of known or suspected terrorists or terrorist organizations. The new rules are intended to deter money laundering without imposing undue burdens that would constrain the ability of firms to serve their customers.

www.sipc.org   Finally, the Securities Investor Protection Corporation (SIPC) protects investors against losses of up to $500,000 caused by securities firm failures. This guaranty fund was created after the passage of the Securities Investor Protection Act in 1970 and is based on premium contributions from member firms. The fund protects investor accounts against the possibility of the member broker–dealer's not being able to meet its financial obligations to customers. The fund does not, however, protect against losses on a customer's account due to poor investment choices that reduce the value of a portfolio.

While not a primary regulator of securities firms and investment banks, the Federal Reserve, as overseer of the financial system as a whole, also comments on rules and regulations governing the industry and suggests changes to be made. For example, in late 2000, the Federal Reserve called for the securities industry to shorten the time it takes to complete stock trades. Federal Reserve Chairman Alan Greenspan stated that rising volumes of stock trading were straining the capacity of brokerage firms to settle trades in a timely fashion. Delays between the purchase of a stock to completion of the paperwork increase risk to the financial system. The Fed worried that when stock prices plunge, large banks may be vulnerable if investors to whom banks have lent money are unable to come up with more collateral for these loans. A shorter time for the completion of stock sales would lower the risk of defaults on any one trade. Mr. Greenspan noted that the Securities Industry Association, an industry trade group, had been working to shorten the settlement time to one day after the stock sale instead of the current three days.

Concept Questions

1. What is the major result of the NSMIA?
2. What two organizations monitor trading abuses?

TABLE 4–9
Foreign
Transactions in U.S.
Securities Markets
(in billions of
dollars)

Source: *Treasury Bulletin,*
U.S. Treasury, March 2004.
www.ustreas.gov

Year	Corporate Stock Transactions	Corporate Bond Transactions
1991	$ 211.2	$ 85.9
1992	221.2	103.7
1993	319.7	134.7
1994	350.6	130.1
1995	451.7	168.1
1996	578.2	252.8
1997	1,028.4	350.9
1998	1,573.7	381.3
1999	2,340.7	368.7
2000	3,605.2	479.5
2001	3,051.4	741.0
2002	3,209.8	820.7
2003	3,115.2	1,041.2

TABLE 4–10
U.S. Transactions in
Foreign Securities
Markets (in billions
of dollars)

Source: *Treasury Bulletin,*
U.S. Treasury, March 2004.
www.ustreas.gov

Year	Corporate Stock Transactions	Corporate Bond Transactions
1991	$ 152.6	$ 345.1
1992	182.3	529.2
1993	300.2	826.3
1994	434.2	857.6
1995	395.8	927.9
1996	509.6	1,165.4
1997	797.0	1,499.9
1998	932.4	1,345.6
1999	1,161.7	803.9
2000	1,815.3	963.0
2001	1,447.8	1,128.8
2002	1,343.7	1,269.3
2003	2,130.2	1,447.3

GLOBAL ISSUES

Much more so than other sectors of the financial institutions industry, securities firms and investment banks operate globally. This can be seen in Table 4–1, where many recent mergers (such as Deutsche Bank's acquisition of Bankers Trust) involve non-U.S. securities firms. Also, Table 4–3 shows that UBS, a Swiss-based investment bank, was the top underwriter of mortgage-backed securities in the United States. Indeed, in May 2004, UBS announced a further incursion into U.S. financial markets with the creation of a dedicated wealth group aimed at the provision of investment services to the wealthy.[20] Accordingly, as domestic securities trading and underwriting have grown in the 1990s, so have foreign securities trading and underwriting. Tables 4–9 and 4–10 show the foreign transactions in U.S. securities and U.S. transactions in foreign securities from 1991–2003. For example, foreign investors' transactions involving U.S. stocks increased from $211.2 billion in 1991 to $3,115.2 billion in 2003, an increase of 1,375 percent. Similarly, U.S. investors' transactions involving stocks listed on foreign

[20] See "Wall Street Fights over the Rich," *The Wall Street Journal*, May 19, 2004, p. C1.

TABLE 4–11
Value of
International
Security Offerings
(in billions of
dollars)

Source: *Quarterly Review: International Banking and Financial Market Develop-ments,* Bank for International Settlements, various issues. *www.bis.org*

	1995	2001	2002	2003	Percent Change 1995–2003
Total international offerings					
Floating-rate debt	$103.0	$ 642.7	$ 603.3	$ 512.2	397.6%
Straight debt	394.8	1,590.3	1,454.6	2,283.6	478.4
Convertible debt	18.1	72.2	42.7	88.0	386.2
Equity	54.6	149.4	102.3	115.2	111.0
Total offerings	$570.5	$2,454.6	$2,202.9	$2,999.0	427.5
International offerings by U.S. issuers					
Floating-rate debt	$ 50.9	$ 262.3	$ 214.4	$ 220.9	334.0
Straight debt	115.3	836.1	755.0	913.9	692.6
Convertible debt	8.5	32.9	16.5	32.2	278.8
Equity	10.0	24.8	1.2	1.9	−81.0
Total offerings	$184.7	$1,156.1	987.1	$1,168.9	532.9

exchanges grew from $152.6 billion in 1991 to $2,130.2 billion in 2003, an increase of 1,296 percent.

Table 4–11 reports the total dollar value of international security offerings from 1995–2003. Over this period, despite a worldwide economic slowdown, total offerings increased from $570.5 billion to $2,999.0 billion (or by 426 percent). Of the amounts in 2003, U.S. security issuers offered $1,168.9 billion in international markets, up from $184.7 billion in 1995. Nevertheless, concerns about U.S. accounting practices as a result of recent scandals, the burdensome nature of reporting accounting figures using U.S. accounting standards as well as local accounting standards, the decline in the U.S. stock market, and the fall in the value of the U.S. dollar against the euro and yen were all working to weaken the attractiveness of U.S. markets to foreign investors and issuers in the early 2000s.

Concept Questions

1. What have been the trends in foreign transactions in U.S. securities and U.S. transactions in foreign securities in the 1990s and early 2000s?
2. What have been the trends in international securities offerings in the late 1990s and early 2000s?
3. Why do foreign banks operating in the United States compete with both U.S. commercial banks and investment banks?

Summary

This chapter presented an overview of security firms (which offer largely retail services to investors) and investment banking firms (which offer largely wholesale services to corporate customers). Firms in this industry assist in getting new issues of debt and equity to the markets. Additionally, this industry facilitates trading and market making of securities after they are issued as well as corporate mergers and restructurings. We looked at the structure of the industry and changes in the degree of concentration in firm size in the industry over the last decade. We also analyzed balance sheet information which highlighted the major assets and liabilities of firms in the industry. Overall, the industry is in a period of consolidation and globalization as the array and scope of its activities expand.

Questions and Problems

1. Explain how securities firms differ from investment banks. In what ways are they financial intermediaries?

2. In what ways have changes in the investment banking industry mirrored changes in the commercial banking industry?

3. What are the different types of firms in the securities industry, and how does each type differ from the others?

4. What are the key activity areas for securities firms? How does each activity area assist in the generation of profits, and what are the major risks for each area?

5. What is the difference between an IPO and a secondary issue?

6. What is the difference between a private placement and a public offering?

7. What are the risk implications to an investment banker from underwriting on a best-efforts basis versus a firm commitment basis? If you operated a company issuing stock for the first time, which type of underwriting would you prefer? Why? What factors might cause you to choose the alternative?

8. How do agency transactions differ from principal transactions for market makers?

9. An investment banker agrees to underwrite a $500,000,000, 10-year, 8 percent semiannual bond issue for KDO Corporation on a firm commitment basis. The investment banker pays KDO on Thursday and plans to begin a public sale on Friday. What type of interest rate movement does the investment bank fear while holding these securities? If interest rates rise 0.05 percent, or 5 basis points, overnight, what will be the impact on the profits of the investment banker? What if the market interest rate falls 5 basis points?

10. An investment banker pays $23.50 per share for 4,000,000 shares of JCN Company. It then sells those shares to the public for $25 per share. How much money does JCN receive? What is the profit to the investment banker? What is the stock price of JCN?

11. XYZ, Inc., has issued 10,000,000 new shares. An investment banker agrees to underwrite these shares on a best-efforts basis. The investment banker is able to sell 8,400,000 shares for $27 per share, and it charges XYZ $0.675 per share sold. How much money does XYZ receive? What is the profit to the investment banker? What is the stock price of XYZ?

12. One of the major activity areas of securities firms is trading.
    a. What is the difference between pure arbitrage and risk arbitrage?
    b. What is the difference between position trading and program trading?

13. If an investor observes that the price of a stock trading in one exchange is different from the price in another exchange, what form of arbitrage is applicable, and how can the investor participate in that arbitrage?

14. An investor notices that an ounce of gold is priced at $318 in London and $325 in New York.
    a. What action could the investor take to try to profit from the price discrepancy?
    b. Under which of the four trading activities would this action be classified?
    c. If the investor is correct in identifying the discrepancy, what pattern should the two prices take in the short-term future?
    d. What may be some impediments to the success of this transaction?

15. What three factors are given credit for the steady decline in brokerage commissions as a percentage of total revenues over the period beginning in 1977 and ending in 1991?

16. What factors are given credit for the resurgence of profitability in the securities industry beginning in 1991? Are firms that trade in fixed-income securities more or less likely to have volatile profits? Why?

17. Using Table 4–6, which type of security accounts for most underwriting in the United States? Which is likely to be more costly to underwrite: corporate debt or equity? Why?

18. How do the operating activities, and thus the balance sheet structures, of securities firms differ from the operating activities of depository institutions such as commercial banks and insurance firms? How are the balance sheet structures of securities firms similar to those of other financial intermediaries?

19. Based on the data in Table 4–7, what were the second-largest single asset and the largest single liability of securities firms in 2003? Are these asset and liability categories related? Exactly how does a repurchase agreement work?

20. How did the National Securities Markets Improvement Act of 1996 (NSMIA) change the regulatory structure of the securities industry?

21. Identify the major regulatory organizations that are involved in the daily operations of the investment securities industry, and explain their role in providing smoothly operating markets.

22. What are the three requirements of the USA. Patriot Act that financial service firms must implement after October 1, 2003?

Web Questions

23. Go to the Thomson Financial Securities Data Web site at **www.tfibcm.com** and find the most recent data on merger and acquisition volume and number of deals using the following steps. Click on "View the latest league Table Online." Click on "Mergers & Acquisitions." Under Press Releases, click on "Worldwide and US Financial Advisory Press Release." This will download a file onto your computer that will contain the most recent information on top underwriters for various securities. How has the dollar volume and number of deals changed since 2003, as reported in Figure 4–1?

24. Go to the U.S. Treasury Web site at **www.ustreas.gov** and find the most recent data on foreign transactions in U.S. securities and U.S. transactions in foreign securities using the following steps. Click on "Bureaus." Click on "Financial Management Services (FMS)." Under Publications & Guidance, click on "Treasury Bulletins." Click on "Capital Movements Tables (Section V)." This will download a file onto your computer that will contain the most recent information on foreign transactions. How have these number changed since 2003, as reported in Tables 4–9 and 4–10?

S&P Questions

STANDARD &POOR'S

25. Go to the Standard & Poor's Market Insight Web site at **www.mhhe.com/ edumarketinsight** and identify the industry description and industry constituents for investment banking and brokerage using the following steps. Click on "Educational Version of Market Insight." Enter your Site ID and click on "Login." Click on "Industry." From the Industry list, select "Investment Banking & Brokerage." Click on "Go!" Click on "Industry profile" and separately, "Industry Constituents."

STANDARD &POOR'S

26. Go to the Standard & Poor's Market Insight Web site at **www.mhhe.com/edu- marketinsight** and look up the industry financial highlights as posted by S&P for investment banking and brokerage using the following steps. Click on "Educational Version of Market Insight." Enter your Site ID and click on "Login." Click on "Industry." From the Industry list, select "Investment Banking & Brokerage." Click on "Go!" Click on any/all of the items listed under "Industry Financial Highlights."

STANDARD &POOR'S

27. Go to the Standard & Poor's Market Insight Web site at **www.mhhe.com/edu- marketinsight** and look up the most recent balance sheets for Merrill Lynch (MER) and Morgan Stanley Dean Witter (MWD) using the following steps. Click on "Educational Version of Market Insight." Enter your Site ID and click on "Login." Click on "Company." Enter "MER" in the "Ticker:" box and click on "Go!" Click on "Excel Analytics." Click on "FS Ann. Balance Sheet." This will download the Balance Sheet for Merrill Lynch which contains the balances for Total Equity and Total Assets. Repeat the process by entering "MWD" in the "Ticker:" box to get information on Morgan Stanley Dean Witter. Compare the equity ratios for these firms with that for the broker–dealer industry listed in Table 4–7.

Pertinent Web Sites

Board of Governors of the Federal Reserve	www.federalreserve.gov
National Association of Securities Dealers	www.nasd.com
New York Stock Exchange	www.nyse.com
Securities and Exchange Commission	www.sec.gov
Securities Industry Association	www.sia.com
Securities Investor Protection Corporation	www.sipc.org
Thomson Financial Securities Data Company	www.tfibcm.com
The Wall Street Journal	www.wsj.com

Chapter **Five**

The Financial Services Industry: Mutual Funds

INTRODUCTION

Mutual funds are financial intermediaries that pool the financial resources of individuals and companies and invest in diversified portfolios of assets. An open-ended mutual fund (the major type of mutual fund) continuously stands ready to sell new shares to investors and to redeem outstanding shares on demand at their fair market value. Thus, these funds provide opportunities for small investors to invest in financial securities and diversify risk. Mutual funds are also able to generate greater economies of scale by incurring lower transaction costs and commissions than are incurred when individual investors buy securities directly. As a result of the tremendous increase in the market value of financial assets, such as equities, in the 1990s (for example, the S&P 500 index saw a return of over 25 percent in 1997 and 1998) and the relatively low-cost opportunity mutual funds provide to investors (particularly small investors) who want to hold such assets (through either direct mutual fund purchases or contributions to retirement funds sponsored by employers and managed by mutual funds), the mutual fund industry boomed in size and customers in the 1990s.[1] The early 2000s and a slowdown in the U.S. economy brought an end to such a rapid pace of growth. Further, allegations of trading abuses resulted in a loss of confidence in several mutual fund managers. Despite these issues, at the end of 2003 more than 7,100 different stock and bond mutual companies held total assets of $5.36 trillion. If we add money market mutual funds, the number of funds rises close to 8,200 and the 2003 value of assets under management rises to $7.41 trillion.[2]

In this chapter we provide an overview of the services offered by mutual funds and highlight their rapid growth over the last decade. We first look at the size, structure, and composition of the industry. This section highlights historical trends in the industry, the different types of mutual funds, mutual fund objectives, investor returns from mutual fund ownership, and mutual fund costs. We then look

---

[1] Shareholder services offered by mutual funds include free exchanges of investments between a mutual fund company's funds, automatic investing, check-writing privileges on many money market funds and some bond funds, automatic reinvestment of dividends, and automatic withdrawals.

[2] See The Investment Company Institute, *2004 Mutual Fund Fact Book*, May 2004. www.ici.org.

at the industry's balance sheets and recent trends and then at regulations and regulators governing the industry. We conclude the chapter with a discussion of global issues for this industry. The appendix to the chapter discusses investment pools organized as "hedge funds." Because hedge funds limit investors to only the wealthiest individuals, they are examined separately from mutual funds discussed in the chapter that are regulated by the Securities and Exchange Commission.

SIZE, STRUCTURE, AND COMPOSITION OF THE INDUSTRY

Historical Trends

The first mutual fund was founded in Boston in 1924. The industry grew very slowly at first; by 1970, 360 funds held about $50 billion in assets. Since then the number of mutual funds and the asset size of the industry have increased dramatically. This growth is attributed to the advent of money market mutual funds in 1972 (as investors looked for ways to earn market rates on short-term funds when bank deposit rates were constrained by regulatory ceilings), to tax-exempt money market mutual funds first established in 1979, and to an explosion of special-purpose equity, bond, emerging market, and derivative funds (as capital market values soared in the 1990s). Table 5–1 documents the tremendous increase from 1940 though 2003 of mutual funds. For example, total assets invested in mutual funds grew from $0.5 billion in 1940 to $7,414.1 billion in 2003. In addition, the number of mutual fund accounts increased from 296,000 in 1940 to 260.6 million in 2003 and the number of mutual funds increased from 68 in 1940 to 8,126 in 2003. The majority of this growth occurred during the bull market run in the 1990s

TABLE 5–1 Growth of Mutual Fund Industry from 1940 to 2003*

Year	Total Net Assets, billions	Gross Sales, billions	Redemptions, billions	Net Sales, billions	Accounts, thousands	Number of Funds
2003	$7,414.1	$12,451.7	$12,414.8	$36.9	260,650	8,126
2002	6,390.4	13,195.2	13,038.5	156.7	251,224	8,244
2001	6,975.0	12,866.2	12,242.0	624.2	248,804	8,305
2000	6,964.7	11,109.4	10,586.2	523.2	244,768	8,155
1999	6,846.3	9,043.6	8,562.1	481.5	226,413	7,791
1998	5,525.2	7,230.4	6,649.3	581.1	194,074	7,314
1997	4,468.2	5,799.6	5,324.1	475.5	170,264	6,684
1996	3,525.8	4,671.4	4,266.2	405.2	150,042	6,248
1995	2,811.3	3,600.6	3,314.8	285.8	131,219	5,725
1994	2,155.3	3,075.8	2,928.2	147.6	114,383	5,325
1993	2,070.0	3,187.4	2,904.4	283.0	93,214	4,534
1992	1,642.5	2,749.4	2,548.3	201.1	79,931	3,824
1991	1,393.2	2,037.1	1,879.7	157.4	68,332	3,403
1990	1,065.2	1,564.8	1,470.8	94.0	61,948	3,079
1980	134.8	247.4	216.1	31.3	12,088	564
1970	47.6	4.6	3.0	1.6	10,690	361
1960	17.0	2.1	0.8	1.3	4,898	161
1950	2.5	0.5	0.3	0.2	939	98
1940	0.5	N/A	N/A	N/A	296	68

*Data includes money market funds. Institute "gross sales" figures include the proceeds of initial fund underwritings prior to 1970.
Source: Investment Company Institute, *2004 Mutual Fund Fact Book* (Washington, D.C.: Investment Company Institute, May 2004). *www.ici.org*

TABLE 5–2
Net New Cash
Flows to Equity
Mutual Funds
versus Annual
Returns on the
NYSE Composite
Index

Source for the Net New Cash
Flows to Equity Mutual
Funds: Investment Company
Institute, *2004 Mutual Fund
Fact Book* (Washington, D.C.:
Investment Company Insti-
tute, May 2004). Reprinted
by permission of the Invest-
ment Company Institute.
www.ici.org

	Net New Cash Flows to Equity Mutual Funds*	Return on NYSE Composite Index
1985	$ 6.6	26.80%
1986	20.4	13.97
1987	19.2	−0.25
1988	−14.9	13.00
1989	6.8	24.82
1990	12.9	−7.46
1991	39.9	27.12
1992	79.0	4.69
1993	127.3	7.86
1994	114.5	−3.14
1995	124.4	31.31
1996	216.9	19.06
1997	227.1	30.31
1998	157.0	16.55
1999	187.7	9.15
2000	309.4	1.01
2001	32.0	−10.21
2002	−27.7	−19.83
2003	152.3	25.36

*In billions of dollars.

(total assets in 1990 were $1,065.2 billion). Table 5–2 lists the net new investment in equity mutual funds and the return on the New York Stock Exchange (NYSE) composite index from 1985 through 2003. Notice that the net new cash flows into equity mutual funds has been strongly related to the NYSE stock index. Only in 1988 and 2002, as stock markets faltered along with the U.S. economy, did the total net assets invested in mutual funds fall.

As can be seen in Figure 5–1, in terms of asset size, the mutual fund industry is larger than the life insurance industry but smaller than the commercial banking industry. This makes mutual funds the second most important FI group in the United States as measured by asset size.

The tremendous growth in this area of FI services has not gone unnoticed by commercial banks as they have sought to directly compete by either buying existing mutual fund groups or managing mutual fund assets for a fee. Banks' share of all mutual fund assets managed was about 20 percent in 2004. Much of this growth has occurred through banks buying mutual fund companies, for example, Mellon buying Dreyfus, as well as converting internally managed trust funds into open-end mutual funds. Insurance companies are also beginning to enter this booming industry. In March 2001, for example, State Farm began offering a family of 10 mutual funds nationwide. The funds are available from more than 9,000 registered State Farm agents, on the Internet, or by application sent in response to phone requests made to a toll-free number. As of 2004, insurance companies managed 14 percent of the mutual fund industry's assets.

Low barriers to entry in the U.S. mutual fund industry has allowed new entrants to offer funds to compete for investor attention and has kept the industry from being increasingly concentrated. As a result, the share of industry assets held by the largest mutual fund sponsors has changed little since 1990. For example, the

FIGURE 5–1
Assets of Major Financial Intermediaries, 1990 and 2003 (in trillions of dollars)

Source: Federal Reserve Board, "Flow of Fund Accounts," various years. *www.federalreserve.gov*

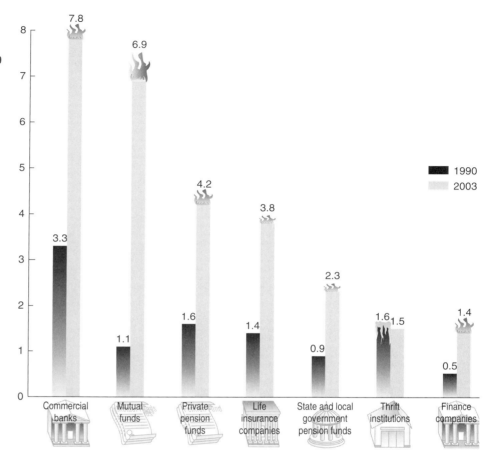

Note: Data for 1990 are at year end; data for 2003 are at year end. Commercial banks include U.S.-chartered commercial banks, foreign banking offices in the United States, bank holding companies, and banks in U.S.-affiliated areas.

bond funds
Funds that contain fixed-income capital market debt securities.

equity funds
Funds that contain common and preferred stock securities.

hybrid funds
Funds that contain bond and stock securities.

money market mutual funds
Funds that contain various mixtures of money market securities.

largest 25 companies that sponsor mutual funds managed 72 percent of the industry's assets in 2003, compared to 76 percent of the industry's assets in 1990. The composition of the list of the 25 largest fund sponsors, however, has changed, with seven of the largest fund companies in 2003 not among the largest in 1990.

Different Types of Mutual Funds

The mutual fund industry is usually divided into two sectors: short-term funds and long-term funds. Long-term funds include **bond funds** (comprised of fixed-income securities with a maturity of over one year), **equity funds** (comprised of common and preferred stock securities), and **hybrid funds** (comprised of both bond and stock securities). Short-term funds include taxable **money market mutual funds** (MMMFs) and tax-exempt money market mutual funds. Tables 5–3 and 5–4 show how the mix of stock, bond, hybrid, and money market fund assets changed between 1980 and 2003. As can be seen, there was a strong trend toward investing in stock mutual funds, reflecting the rise in share values during the 1990s. As a result, in 1999, 74.3 percent of all mutual fund assets were in long-term funds while the remaining funds, or 25.7 percent, were in money market mutual funds. As you can see in Table 5–3, the proportion invested in long-term versus short-term funds can vary considerably over time. For example, the share

TABLE 5–3   Growth in Long-Term versus Short-Term Mutual Funds from 1980 through 2003 (in billions of dollars)

	1980	1990	1995	1997	1999	2000	2001	2002	2003
A. Equity, Hybrid, and Bond Mutual Funds									
Holdings at market value	$61.8	$608.4	$1,852.8	$2,989.4	$4,538.5	$4,434.6	$4,135.5	$3,639.4	$4,664.9
Household sector	45.7	456.7	1,247.8	1,996.7	3,115.2	3,035.8	2,869.7	2,539.2	3,291.6
Nonfinancial corporate business	1.5	9.7	45.7	81.8	133.7	122.8	105.9	90.5	127.9
State and local governments	0.0	4.8	35.0	44.6	25.6	26.4	31.5	33.5	30.5
Commercial banking	0.0	1.9	2.3	8.1	12.4	15.0	21.3	19.6	17.1
Credit unions	0.0	1.4	2.8	2.4	2.5	2.2	3.7	3.5	4.1
Bank personal trusts and estates	6.4	62.7	253.5	342.2	391.5	396.8	359.1	339.1	391.2
Life insurance companies	1.1	30.7	27.7	57.6	103.8	101.9	92.0	80.5	106.7
Private pension funds	7.1	40.5	228.5	456.0	753.8	733.6	651.5	533.5	695.8
B. Money Market Mutual Funds									
Total assets	$76.4	$493.3	$745.3	$1,048.7	$1,578.8	$1,812.1	$2,240.7	$2,223.9	$2,016.0
Household sector	62.1	338.6	451.6	639.0	822.2	967.8	1,116.4	1,076.1	986.0
Nonfinancial corporate business	7.0	26.3	83.0	105.0	195.6	240.8	360.9	390.1	329.1
Bank personal trusts and estates	2.2	26.0	30.2	43.0	53.7	60.6	52.8	54.1	44.9
Life insurance companies	1.9	18.1	22.8	56.5	131.8	142.3	173.3	159.8	151.4
Private pension funds	2.6	17.8	37.5	47.3	75.1	79.6	69.0	71.8	74.7
Funding corporations	0.6	36.6	120.2	157.9	300.5	321.1	468.4	472.0	429.9

Source: Federal Reserve Bulletin, "Flow of Fund Accounts," various issues. *www.federalreserve.gov*

TABLE 5–4
Number of Mutual Funds, 1980, 1990, 2000, and 2003

Source: Investment Company Institute, *2004 Mutual Fund Fact Book* (Washington D.C.: Investment Company Institute, May 2004). Reprinted by permission of the Investment Company Institute. *www.ici.org*

Year	Equity	Hybrid	Bond	Taxable Money Market	Tax-Exempt Money Market	Total
1980*	288	N/A	170	96	10	564
1990	1,099	193	1,046	506	235	3,079
2000	4,385	523	2,208	703	336	8,155
2003	4,601	509	2,043	661	312	8,126

* The definition of equity, hybrid, and bond funds was reclassified in 1989. Thus, 1980 data is not comparable to 1990, 2000, and 2003.

of money market funds was 44.8 percent in 1990 compared to 25.7 percent in 1999. The decline in the growth rate of short-term funds and the increase in the growth rate of long-term funds reflect the increase in equity returns during the period 1992–1999 and the generally low level of short-term interest rates over the period. Notice that in the early 2000, as interest rates rose, the U.S. economy declined, and equity returns fell, the growth in money market funds outpaced the growth in long-term funds. In 2002, the share of long-term funds fell

FIGURE 5–2 **Interest Rate Spread and Net New Cash Flow to Retail Money Market Funds, 1985–2003**
(percent)

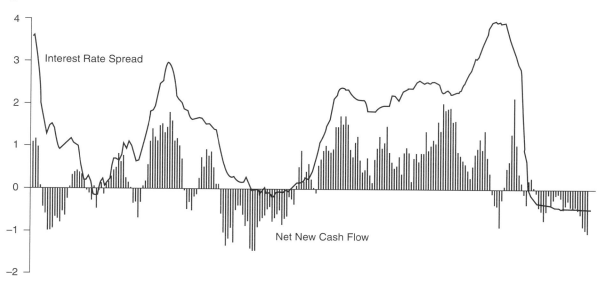

Note: Net new cash flow is a percentage of retail money market fund assets and is shown as a six-month moving average. The interest rate spread is the difference between the taxable money market fund yield and the average interest rate on savings deposits; the series is plotted with a six-month lag.
Source: Investment Company Institute, *2004 Mutual Fund Fact Book* (Washington, D.C.: Investment Company Institute, May 2004). *www.ici.org*

to 62.1 percent and money market funds grew to 37.9 percent. However, in 2003 as the U.S. economy grew and stock values increased, the share of long-term funds grew to 69.8 percent of all funds, while money market funds decreased to 30.2 percent.

Money market mutual funds provide an alternative investment to interest-bearing deposits at commercial banks, which may explain the growth in MMMFs in the 1980s and late 1990s, when the spread earned on MMMF investments relative to deposits was mostly positive (see Figure 5–2). Both investments are relatively safe and earn short-term returns. The major difference between the two is that interest-bearing deposits (below $100,000 in size) are fully insured but due to bank regulatory costs (such as reserve requirements, capital requirements, and deposit insurance premiums) generally offer lower returns than do noninsured MMMFs.[3] Thus, the net gain in switching to MMMFs is higher returns in exchange for the loss of deposit insurance coverage. Many investors appeared willing to give up insurance coverage to obtain additional returns in the 1980s and late 1990s (through 2001). Despite this growth, the decline in the relative importance of short-term funds and the increase in the relative importance of long-term funds in the 1990s reflect the dramatic rise in equity returns over the 1990–2000 period even though MMMF interest spreads over bank deposits were mostly positive. However, a period of low interest rates that began in 2001 and persisted through 2003 resulted in a large relative drop in investments in MMMFs. Many individual and institutional

[3] Some mutual funds are covered by private insurance and/or by implicit or explicit guarantees from mutual fund management companies.

investors moved assets from MMMFs to bank and thrift deposits and open market securities. Indeed, with short-term rates on MMMF too low to cover fund fees, in the early 2000s some MMMFs lowered fees in order to maintain net asset values (discussed below).

Table 5–4 reports the growth in this industry based on the number of mutual funds in 1980, 1990, 2000, and 2003. All categories of funds have increased in number in this time period, from a total of 564 in 1980 to 8,126 in 2003. *Tax*-exempt money market funds first became available in 1979. This was the major reason for their relatively small number (10 funds) in 1980. Also, the number of equity funds has boomed, mainly in the 1990s: Equity funds numbered 4,601 in 2003, up from 1,099 in 1990, while bond funds numbered 2,043 in 2003, up from 1,046 in 1990.

Notice that in Table 5–3 households (i.e., small investors) own the majority of both long- and short-term funds: 70.6 percent for long-term mutual funds and 48.9 percent for short-term mutual funds at year-end 2003. This is to be expected, given that the rationale for the existence of mutual funds is to achieve superior diversification through fund and risk pooling compared to what individual small investors can achieve on their own. Consider that wholesale CDs sell in minimum denominations of $100,000 each and often pay higher interest rates than passbook savings accounts or small time deposits offered by depository institutions. By pooling funds in a money market mutual fund, small investors can gain access to wholesale money markets and instruments and, therefore, to potentially higher interest rates and returns.

Internet Exercise Go to the Federal Reserve Board's Web site at **www.federalreserve.gov**. Find the latest figures for the dollar value of money market and long-term mutual funds and the distribution of mutual fund investment by ownership using the following steps:

Click on "Economic Research and Data." Click on "Statistics: Releases and Historical Data." Click on "Flow of Funds Accounts of the United States, *Releases*." Click on the most recent date. Click on "Level tables." This downloads a file onto your computer that contains the relevant data, in Tables L.206 and L.214.

As of 2003, 53.3 million (47.9 percent of) U.S. households owned mutual funds. This was down from 56.3 million (52.0 percent) in 2001. Table 5–5 lists some characteristics of household mutual fund owners as of 2004. Most are long-term owners, with 50 percent making their first purchases before 1990. Forty-nine percent of all mutual fund holders are members of the Baby Boom Generation (born between 1946 and 1964), 23 percent are from the Silent Generation (born before 1946), 24 percent are Generation Xers (born between 1965 and 1976), and 4 percent are Generation Yers (born after 1976). Interestingly, the number of families headed by a person with less than a college degree investing in mutual funds is 43 percent. In 75 percent of married households owning mutual funds, the spouse also worked full- or part-time. The bull markets of the 1990s, the low transaction costs of purchasing mutual funds shares, as well as the diversification benefits achievable through mutual fund investments are again the likely reasons for these trends. The typical fund-owning household has $48,000 invested in a median number of four mutual funds. Finally, more than a quarter of investors who conducted equity fund transactions used the Internet for some or all of these transactions. This compares to 6 percent in 1998.

Notice from Table 5–5, that compared to 1995, 2004 has seen a slight increase in the median age of mutual fund holders (from 44 to 48 years) and a large increase in

TABLE 5–5
Selected
Characteristics of
Household Owners
of Mutual Funds*

Source: Investment Company Institute, *2004 Mutual Fund Fact Book* and *1996 Mutual Fund Fact Book* (Washington, D.C.: Investment Company Institute, 2004 and 1996). Reprinted by permission of the Investment Company Institute. *www.ici.org*

	2004	1995
Demographic characteristics:		
Median age	48 years	44 years
Median household income	$ 68,700	$60,000
Median household financial assets	$125,000	$50,000
Percent:		
Married or living with a partner	71	71
Employed	77	80
Four-year college degree or more	57	58
Mutual fund ownership characteristics:		
Median mutual fund assets	$ 48,000	$18,000
Median number of funds owned	4	3
Fund types owned (percent):		
Equity	80	73
Bond	44	49[†]
Hybrid	34	N/A
Money market	49	52

*Characteristics of primary financial decision maker in the household.
[†]This number is for bond and income funds.

median household financial assets owned (from $50,000 to $125,000) and median mutual fund assets owned (from $18,000 to $48,000). Further, holdings of equity funds have increased from 73 to 80 percent of all households.

Mutual Fund Objectives

Regulations require that mutual fund managers specify the investment objectives of their funds in a prospectus available to potential investors. This prospectus should include a list of the securities that the fund holds. Many "large" company funds, aiming to diversify across company size, held stocks of relatively "small" companies in the late 1990s, contrary to their stated objectives. Some fund managers justified the inclusion of seemingly "smaller" companies by changing their definition of what a large company was. For example, one fund manager stated the definition of a small company that he used is one that has less than $1 billion in equity capital, in contrast to a large company that has more than $1 billion (the median size of equity capital of firms in the S&P 500 index is $28 billion). The point here is that investors need to read a prospectus carefully before making an investment.

The aggregate figures for long-term equity, bond, and hybrid funds tend to obscure the fact that there are many different funds in these groups. Every mutual fund sponsor offers multiple funds of each type (e.g., long-term equity), differentiated by the securities held in the particular mutual fund as defined by the fund's objective. Table 5–6 classifies 13 major categories of investment objectives (or classifications) for mutual funds. These objectives are shown along with the assets allocated to each major category in 2003. A fund objective provides general information about the types of securities a mutual fund will hold as assets. For example, "capital appreciation" funds hold securities (mainly equities) of high-growth, high-risk firms. Again, within each of these 13 categories of mutual funds are a multitude of different funds offered by mutual fund companies (see also the mutual fund quote section below). Historically, mutual funds have had to send out

TABLE 5–6
Total Net Asset Value of Equity, Hybrid, and Bond Funds by Investment Classification, December 31, 2003

Source: Investment Company Institute, *2004 Mutual Fund Fact Book* (Washington, D.C.: Investment Company Institute, 2004). Reprinted by permission of the Investment Company Institute. *www.ici.org*

Classification of Fund	Combined Assets (in billions of dollars)	Percent of Total
Total net assets	**$7,414.08**	**100.0%**
Capital appreciation	1,858.84	25.1%
World equity	517.70	7.0
Total return	1,308.26	17.6
Total equity funds	**$3,684.80**	**49.7%**
Total hybrid funds	**$436.68**	**5.9%**
Corporate bond	200.06	2.7%
High-yield bond	153.70	2.1
World bond	27.56	0.4
Government bond	224.71	3.0
Strategic income	300.79	4.0
State municipal	150.94	2.0
National municipal	183.16	2.5
Total bond funds	**1,240.92**	**16.7%**
Taxable money market funds	1,763.31	23.8
Tax-exempt money market funds	288.37	3.9
Total money market funds	**$2,051.68**	**27.7%**

lengthy prospectuses describing their objectives and investments. In 1998, the SEC adopted a new procedure in which key sections of all funds' prospectuses must be written in "plain" English instead of legal boilerplate. The idea is to increase the ability of investors to understand the risks related to the investment objectives or profile of a fund.

www.fidelity.com
www.vanguard.com
www.americanfunds.com

Table 5–7 lists the largest (in total assets held) 20 mutual funds available in February 2004, including the fund's objective, 12-month and 5-year returns, net asset value (discussed below), and any initial fees (discussed below). Vanguard's Index: 500 (which is designed to replicate the performance of the S&P 500 Index) was the largest fund at that time. Fidelity, Vanguard, and American Funds offered 19 of the top 20 funds measured by asset size. Many of the top funds list either growth or growth and income as the fund objectives, and all of the top 20 funds performed well as the stock market soared in 2003. The downturn in the U.S. economy and the general drop in stock market values, however, hurt many of the fund returns from 2001 to 2002. Five of the 20 funds experienced negative five-year returns (from February 1999 through January 2004); Fidelity's Blue Chip Fund was the worst performer with a return of −3.40 percent during the five years. It should be noted that the risk of returns [e.g., the fund's total return risk or even its "beta" (or systematic risk)] is rarely mentioned in prospectuses or advertisements. In 1998, the SEC adopted an initiative requiring mutual funds to disclose more information about their return risk as well as the returns themselves. The SEC's rule was intended to better enable investors to compare return-risk trade-offs from investing in different mutual funds.

Investor Returns from Mutual Fund Ownership

The return an investor gets from investing in mutual fund shares reflects three aspects of the underlying portfolio of mutual fund assets. First, income and dividends

TABLE 5–7   The Largest Mutual Funds in Assets Held

Name of Fund	Objective	Total Assets (in millions)	Total Return 12-Month	Total Return 5-Year	NAV	Initial Fees
Vanguard Index:500	Growth/income	$75,345	33.41%	−1.03%	104.54	0.00%
Fidelity Magellan	Growth	67,995	29.19	−1.78	98.99	0.00
American Funds: InvCoA	Growth/income	58,353	30.68	4.14	29.17	5.75
American Funds: WshMut	Growth/income	55,575	30.95	4.17	29.08	5.75
American Funds: Growth	Extreme growth	48,073	37.31	6.27	25.19	5.75
Fidelity Invest: Contra	Growth	36,051	31.55	2.11	49.33	0.00
American Funds: Inc	Balanced	31,955	27.97	7.33	17.29	5.75
Fidelity Invest: Grw/Inc	Growth/income	30,572	23.29	−0.81	36.12	0.00
American Funds: Eupac	International	29,908	41.80	5.15	30.94	5.75
Vanguard Instl Indx:Instl	Balanced	29,457	33.56	−0.92	103.64	0.00
Dodge & Cox Stock	Multicap value	29,437	40.37	13.48	118.28	0.00
American Funds: NewPer	International	29,053	42.55	5.52	24.88	5.75
Fidelity Lw-Prcd Stock	Growth	26,725	46.88	16.69	35.93	0.00
Vanguard: Wellington	Balanced	24,326	24.02	6.62	29.02	0.00
Vanguard Tot Stk Inx; Inv	Growth	24,059	36.87	0.22	26.57	0.00
Fidelity: Eq/Inc	Equity/income	23,520	35.39	3.79	50.27	0.00
Vanguard: Windsor II	Multicap value	22,765	35.57	3.20	27.15	0.00
Fidelity: Growth Company	Growth	22,609	46.26	2.69	51.54	0.00
Fidelity Blue Chip	Growth	22,384	29.62	−3.40	40.45	0.00
Fidelity Puritan	Balanced	21,964	25.84	4.35	18.68	0.00

Source: *The Wall Street Journal,* February 2, 2004. Reprinted by permission of The Wall Street Journal © 2004 Dow Jones & Company, Inc. All Rights Reserved Worldwide. *www.wsj.com*

marked-to-market
Adjusting asset and balance sheet values to reflect current market prices.

are earned on those assets; second, capital gains occur when assets are sold by a mutual fund at prices higher than the purchase price; third, capital appreciation in the underlying values of the assets held in a fund's portfolio add to the value of mutual fund shares. With respect to capital appreciation, mutual fund assets are normally **marked-to-market** daily. This means that the managers of the fund calculate the current value of each mutual fund share by computing the daily market value of the fund's total asset portfolio and then dividing this amount by the number of mutual fund shares outstanding. The resulting value is called the net asset value **(NAV)** of the fund. This is the price the investor gets when selling shares back to the fund that day or buying any new shares in the fund on that day.

NAV
The net asset value of a mutual fund is equal to the market value of the assets in the mutual fund portfolio divided by the number of shares outstanding.

EXAMPLE 5–1
Impact of Capital Appreciation on NAV

Suppose a mutual fund contains 1,000 shares of Sears, Roebuck currently trading at $37.75, 2,000 shares of Exxon/Mobil currently trading at $43.70, and 1,500 shares of Citigroup currently trading at $46.67. The mutual fund currently has 15,000 shares outstanding held by investors. Thus, today, the NAV of the fund is calculated as

$$NAV = ((1,000 \times \$37.75) + (2,000 \times \$43.70) + (1,500 \times \$46.67)) \div 15,000 = \$13.01$$

If next month Sears shares increase to $45, Exxon/Mobil shares increase to $48, and Citigroup shares increase to $50, the NAV (assuming the same number of shares outstanding) would increase to

$$NAV = ((1,000 \times \$45) + (2,000 \times \$48) + (1,500 \times \$50)) \div 15,000 = \$14.40$$

open-end mutual fund
The supply of shares in the fund is not fixed but can increase or decrease daily with purchases and redemptions of shares.

Most mutual funds are **open-end** in that the number of shares outstanding fluctuates up and down daily with the amount of share redemptions and new purchases. With open-end mutual funds, investors buy and sell shares from and to the mutual fund company. Thus, the demand for shares determines the number outstanding and the NAV of shares is determined solely by the market value of the underlying securities held in the mutual fund divided by the number of shareholders outstanding.

EXAMPLE 5–2 *Impact of Investment Size on NAV*	Consider the mutual fund in Example 5–1, but suppose that today 1,000 additional investors buy into the mutual fund at the current NAV of $13.01. This means that the fund manager now has $13,010 in additional funds to invest. Suppose the fund manager decides to use these additional funds to buy additional shares in Sears. At today's market price he or she can buy $13,010 ÷ $37.75 = 344 additional shares of Sears. Thus, the mutual fund's new portfolio of shares would be 1,344 in Sears, 2,000 in Exxon/Mobil, and 1,500 in Citigroup. At the end of the month the NAV of the portfolio would be $$NAV = ((1,344 \times \$45) + (2,000 \times \$48) + (1,500 \times \$50)) \div 16,000 = \$14.47$$ given the appreciation in value of all three stocks over the month. Note that the fund's value changed over the month due to both capital appreciation and investment size. A comparison of the NAV in Example 5–1 with the one in this example indicates that the additional shares alone enabled the fund to gain a slightly higher NAV than had the number of shares remained static ($14.47 versus $14.40).

closed-end investment companies
Specialized investment companies that invest in securities and assets of other firms but have a fixed supply of shares outstanding themselves.

REIT
A real estate investment trust. A closed-end investment company that specializes in investing in mortgages, property, or real estate company shares.

Open-end mutual funds can be compared to most regular corporations traded on stock exchanges and to **closed-end investment companies,** both of which have a fixed number of shares outstanding at any given time. For example, real estate investment trusts **(REITs)** are closed-end investment companies that specialize in investment in real estate company shares and/or in buying mortgages.[4] With closed-end funds, investors must buy and sell the investment company's shares on a stock exchange similar to the trading of corporate stock. Since the number of shares available for purchase at any moment in time is fixed, the NAV of the fund's shares is determined not only by the value of the underlying shares but also by the demand for the investment company's shares themselves. When demand is high, the shares can trade at more than the NAV of the securities held in the fund. In this case, the fund is said to be *trading at a premium,* that is, at more than the fair market value of the securities held. When the value of the closed-end fund's shares are less than the NAV of its assets, its shares are said to be *trading at a discount*, that is, at less than the fair market value of the securities held.

EXAMPLE 5–3 *Market Value of Closed-End Mutual Fund Shares*	Because of high demand for a closed-end investment company's shares, the 50 shares (N_S) are trading at $20 per share ($P_S$). The market value of the equity-type securities in the fund's asset portfolio, however, is $800, or $16 ($800 ÷ 50) per share. The market value balance sheet of the fund is shown below: *(continued)*

---

[4] Many closed-end funds are specialized funds that invest in shares in countries such as Argentina, Brazil, and Mexico. The shares of these closed-end funds are traded on the NYSE or the over-the-counter market. The total market value of funds invested in closed-end funds was $214.0 billion at the end of 2003. This compares to $7,414.1 billion invested in open-end funds at that time.

Assets		Liabilities and Equity	
Market value of asset portfolio	$800	Market value of closed-end fund shares ($P_S \times N_S$)	$1,000
Premium	$200		

The fund's shares are trading at a premium of $4 (200 ÷ 50) per share.

Because of low demand for a *second* closed-end fund, the 100 shares outstanding are trading at $25 per share. The market value of the securities in this fund's portfolio is $3,000, or each share has a NAV of $30 per share. The market value balance sheet of this fund is:

Assets		Liabilities and Equity	
Market value of asset portfolio	$3,000	Market value of closed-end fund shares (100 × $25)	$2,500
Discount	−$500		

www.morningstar. com

Mutual fund investors can get information on the performance of mutual funds from several places. For example, for a comprehensive analysis of mutual funds, Morningstar, Inc., offers information on over 10,000 open-end and closed-end funds. Morningstar does not own, operate, or hold an interest in any mutual fund. Thus, it is recognized as the leading provider of unbiased data and performance analysis (e.g., of returns) for the industry.

Mutual Fund Costs

Mutual funds charge shareholders a price or fee for the services they provide (i.e., management of a diversified portfolio of financial securities). Two types of fees are incurred by investors: sales loads and fund operating expenses. We discuss these next. The total cost to the shareholder of investing in a mutual fund is the sum of the annualized sales load and other fees charged.

Load versus No-Load Funds

load fund
A mutual fund with an up-front sales or commission charge that has to be paid by the investor.

no-load fund
A mutual fund that does not charge up-front fees or commission charges on the sale of mutual fund shares to investors.

An investor who buys a mutual fund share may be subject to a sales charge, sometimes as high as 8.5 percent. In this case, the fund is called a **load fund**.[5] Other funds that directly market shares to investors do not use sales agents working for commissions and have no up-front commission charges; these are called **no-load funds.**

The argument in favor of load funds is that their managers provide investors with more personal attention and advice than managers of no-load funds. However, the cost of this increased attention may not be worthwhile. For example, the last column in Table 5–7 lists initial fees for the largest U.S. stock funds in 2003. Notice that only American Funds group assesses a load fee on mutual fund share purchases. After adjusting for this fee, the 12-month returns on the six American Funds mutual funds fall from 42.55 percent to 27.97 percent (among the highest returns earned by the largest funds) to 36.80 percent to 22.22 percent (among the lowest of the returns on these funds). As Figure 5–3 indicates, investors

---

[5] Another kind of load, called a *back-end load,* is sometimes charged when mutual fund shares are sold by investors. Back-end loads, also referred to as deferred sales charges, are an alternative way to compensate the fund managers or sales force for their services.

FIGURE 5–3
Load versus No-Load Fund Assets as a Share of Fund Assets (percent)

Source: Investment Company Institute, *2004 Mutual Fund Fact Book* (Washington, D.C.: Investment Company Institute, 2004). Reprinted by permission of the Investment Company Institute. *www.ici.org*

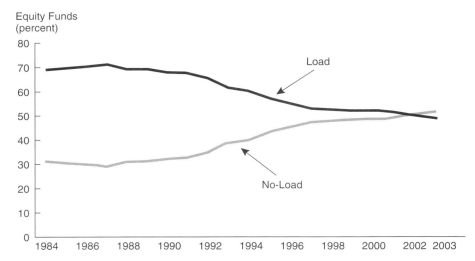

increasingly recognized this cost disadvantage for load funds in the 1990s as stock market values increased broadly and dramatically. In 1985, load funds represented almost 70 percent of equity mutual fund sales, and no-load funds represented just over 30 percent. By 1998 new sales of mutual fund shares exceeded that of load fund shares and by 2002 total assets invested in no-load funds exceeded those invested in load funds.

The demand for no-load funds by mutual fund investors has not gone unnoticed. Many companies, particularly discount brokers, now offer mutual fund supermarkets through which investors can buy and sell mutual fund shares, offered by several different mutual fund sponsors, through a single broker. The most important feature of a fund supermarket is its non–transaction fee program, whereby an investor may purchase mutual funds with no transaction fees from a large number of fund companies. The broker is generally paid for services from the fund's 12b–1 fees (see below). The non–transaction fee offerings at a discount broker often number in the thousands, providing an investor the convenience of purchasing no-load funds from different families at a single location.

Fund Operating Expenses

In contrast to one-time up-front load charges on the initial investment in a mutual fund, annual fees are charged to cover all fund level expenses experienced as a percent of the fund assets. One type of fee (called a management fee) is charged to meet operating costs (such as administration and shareholder services). In addition, mutual funds generally require a small percentage (or fee) of investable funds to meet fund level marketing and distribution costs. Such annual fees are known as **12b–1** fees after the SEC rule covering such charges.[6] Because these fees, charged to cover fund operating expenses, are paid out of the fund's assets, investors indirectly bear these expenses.

12b–1 Fees
Fees relating to the distribution and other operating costs of mutual fund shares.

---

[6] 12b–1 fees are limited to a maximum of 0.25 percent on no-load funds.

EXAMPLE 5–4
Calculation of Mutual Fund Costs

The cost of mutual fund investing to the shareholder includes both the one-time sales load and any annual fees charged. Because the sales load is a one-time charge, it must be converted to an annualized payment incurred by the shareholder over the life of his or her investment. With this conversion, the total shareholder cost of investing in a fund is the sum of the annualized sales load plus any annual fees.

For example, suppose an investor purchases fund shares with a 4 percent front-end load and expects to hold the shares for 10 years. The annualized sales load[7] incurred by the investor is

$$4 \text{ percent}/10 \text{ years} = .4 \text{ percent per year}$$

Further, suppose the fund has a total fund expense ratio (including 12b–1 fees) of 1 percent per year. The annual total shareholder cost for this fund is calculated as

$$.4 \text{ percent} + 1 \text{ percent} = 1.4 \text{ percent per year}$$

Funds sold through financial professionals such as brokers have recently adopted alternative payment methods. These typically include an annual 12b–1 fee based on asset values that also may be combined with a front-end or back-end sales charge. In many cases, funds offer several different share classes (all of which invest in the same underlying portfolio of assets), but each share class may offer investors different methods of paying for broker services. Indeed, in 2002, over half of all mutual funds had two or more share classes, compared to 1980 when all funds had only one share class. Most funds sold in multiple classes offer investors three payment plans through three share classes (A, B, and C), each having different mixes of sales loads and management and 12b–1 fees.

Class A shares represent the traditional means for paying for investment advice. That is, Class A shares carry a front-end load that is charged at the time of purchase as a percent of the sales price. The front-end load on Class A shares is charged on new sales and is not generally incurred when Class A shares are exchanged for another mutual fund within the same fund family. In addition to the front-end load, Class A shares usually have annual management and 12b–1 fees that are used to compensate brokers and sales professionals for ongoing assistance and service provided to fund shareholders. The management and 12b–1 fees for Class A shares are typically between 25 and 35 basis points of the portfolio's assets.

Unlike Class A shares, Class B shares are offered for sale at the NAV without a front-end load. Class B share investors pay for advice and assistance from brokers through a combination of annual management and 12b–1 fees (usually 1 percent) and a back-end load. The back-end load is charged when shares are redeemed (sold) and is typically based on the lesser of the original cost of the shares or the market value at the time of sale. After six to eight years, Class B shares typically convert to Class A shares, lowering the level of the annual management and 12b–1 fees from 1 percent to that of A shares.

Class C shares are offered at the NAV with no front-end load, and typically recover distribution costs through a combination of annual management and 12b–1 fees of 1 percent and a back-end load, set at 1 percent in the first year of purchase. After the first year, no back-end load is charged on redemption. The Class C shares usually do not convert to Class A shares, and thus the annual 1 percent payment to the broker continues throughout the period of time that the shares are held.

---

[7] Convention in the industry is to annualize the sales load without adjusting for the time value of money.

TABLE 5–8 Mutual Fund Quote

NAVs 1/30	Fund Name	Investment Objective	Total Return and Rank					Maximum Initial Charge	Expense Ratio
			January	One Year	Three Years	Five Years	Ten Years		
Vanguard Index Funds									
104.54	500	SP	1.8	34.4 A	−4.7 A	−1.1 A	10.8 A	0.00	0.18
18.58	Balanced	BL	1.7	23.7 B	1.3 B	3.0 B	9.2 B	0.00	0.22
7.70	CalSoc	LC	2.4	36.6 A	−6.1 C	NS . .	NS . .	0.00	0.25
7.92	DevMkt	IL	1.4	46.7 B	−2.6 C	NS . .	NS . .	0.00	NA
12.22	EmerMkt r	EM	3.1	62.4 B	9.4 C	12.0 C	NS . .	0.00	0.53
22.25	Europe	EU	1.1	47.2 C	−2.8 C	−0.2 D	8.5 C	0.00	0.33
27.62	Extnd	MC	3.6	51.9 A	1.5 D	4.6 E	10.1 D	0.00	0.26
25.48	Growth	LC	2.2	32.1 B	−5.9 C	−4.2 D	11.1 A	0.00	0.23
10.77	ITBond	IB	1.1	7.3 A	8.3 A	7.0 A	NS . .	0.00	0.21
11.65	LTBond	AB	1.7	7.5 B	9.3 A	7.1 A	NS . .	0.00	0.21
13.47	MidCp	MC	2.6	41.8 C	4.6 B	10.6 C	NS . .	0.00	0.26
8.19	Pacific	PR	2.0	45.4 D	−1.8 D	1.8 E	−2.1 D	0.00	0.40
23.49	SmCap	SC	3.9	55.6 B	5.8 D	8.1 D	10.2 D	0.00	0.27
13.75	SmGth	SG	5.1	54.4 C	8.0 A	9.2 B	NS . .	0.00	0.27
11.80	SmVal	SV	2.7	46.9 D	8.4 E	11.9 D	NS . .	0.00	0.27
10.29	STBond	SB	0.3	3.7 B	5.6 B	5.8 A	NS . .	0.00	0.21
10.36	TotBd	IB	0.8	4.8 C	6.5 C	6.2 B	6.6 B	0.00	0.22
10.81	TotIntl	IL	1.6	48.1 B	−1.5 B	1.3 C	NS . .	0.00	NA
26.57	TotSt	XC	2.2	37.8 B	−3.1 C	0.2 D	10.4 C	0.00	0.20
19.25	Value	LV	1.6	38.2 A	−3.5 E	1.9 C	10.2 B	0.00	0.23

As discussed below, the lack of complete disclosure and the inability of most mutual fund investors to understand the different fees charged for various classes of mutual fund shares came under scrutiny in the early 2000s. Indeed, the potential for overcharging fees to various classes of mutual fund shareholders led to the SEC creating new rules pertaining to these charges.

Mutual Fund Share Quotes

www.vanguard.com

Table 5–8 presents month-end mutual fund quotes from *The Wall Street Journal* on Monday, February 2, 2004. The quotes for Vanguard Index Funds include information on each fund's NAV, its name, its objective (including the explanation of the objective in the footnote), one-month through 10-year return, and rating (A through E),[8] its maximum initial charge, and annual expenses. The maximum initial charge is listed as "0.00" for each of the Vanguard Index Funds, meaning that they are all *no*-load funds. Index funds attempt to replicate the assets and performance of a broad stock or bond index. For example, Vanguard's 500 Index Fund's objective is to replicate the S&P 500 Index seeking long-term growth of capital and income from dividends. Notice the return on this mutual fund from January 2003 through January 2004 was 34.4 percent. The return on the S&P 500 Index over the same period was 32.2 percent.

---

[8] Funds are ranked by total return within each investment objective defined by *The Wall Street Journal:* A = top 20 percent; B = next 20 percent; C = middle 20 percent; D = next 20 percent; and E = bottom 20 percent.

Mutual-Fund Objectives

Categories compiled by *The Wall Street Journal,* based on classifications by Lipper Inc.

Stock Funds

Emerging Markets (EM)   Funds investing in emerging-market equity securities, where the "emerging market" is defined by a country's GNP per capita and other economic measures.

Equity Income (EI)   Funds seeking high current income and growth of income by investing in equities.

European Region (EU)   Funds investing in markets or operations concentrated in the European region.

Global Stock (GL)   Funds investing in securities traded outside of the United States and may own U.S. securities as well.

Gold Oriented (AU)   Funds investing in gold mines; gold-mining finance houses, gold coins or bullion.

Health/Biotech (HB)   Funds investing in companies related to health care, medicine, and biotechnology.

International Stock (IL) (non-U.S.)   Canadian; International; International Small Cap.

Latin American (LT)   Funds investing in markets or operations concentrated in Latin American region.

Large-Cap Growth (LG)   Funds investing in large companies with long-term earnings that are expected to grow significantly faster than the earnings of stocks in major indexes. Funds normally have above-average price-to-earnings ratios, price-to-book ratios and three-year earnings growth.

Large-Cap Core (LC)   Funds investing in large companies, with wide latitude in the type of shares they buy. On average, the price-to-earnings ratios, price-to-book ratios, and three-year earnings growth are in line with those of the U.S. diversified large-cap funds' universe average.

Large-Cap Value (LV)   Funds investing in large companies that are considered undervalued relative to major stock indexes based on price-to-earnings ratios, price-to-book ratios, or other factors.

Midcap Growth (MG)   Funds investing in midsize companies with long-term earnings that are expected to grow significantly faster than the earnings of stocks in major indexes. Funds normally have above-average price-to-earnings ratios, price-to-book ratios and three-year earnings growth.

Midcap Core (MC)   Funds investing in midsize companies, with wide latitude in the type of shares they buy. On average, the price-to-earnings ratios, price-to-book ratios, and three-year earnings growth are in line with those of the U.S. diversified midcap funds' universe average.

Midcap Value (MV)   Funds investing in midsize companies that are considered undervalued relative to major stock indexes based on price-to-earnings ratios, price-to-book ratios, or other factors.

Multicap Growth (XG)   Funds investing in companies of various sizes, with long-term earnings expected to grow significantly faster than the earnings of stocks in major indexes. Funds normally have above-average price-to-earnings ratios, price-to-book ratios, and three-year earnings growth.

Multicap Core (XC)   Funds investing in companies of various sizes with average price-to-earnings ratios, price-to-book ratios, and earnings growth.

Multicap Value (XV)   Funds investing in companies of various size, normally those that are considered undervalued relative to major stock indexes based on price-to-earnings ratios, price-to-book ratios, or other factors.

Natural Resources (NR)   Funds investing in natural-resource stocks.

Pacific Region (PR)   Funds that invest in China Region: Japan; Pacific Ex-Japan; Pacific Region.

Science & Technology (TK)   Funds investing in science and technology stocks. Includes telecommunication funds.

Sector (SE)   Funds investing in financial services; real estate; specialty & miscellaneous.

S&P 500 Index (SP)   Funds that are passively managed and are designed to replicate the performance of the Standard & Poor's 500-stock Index on a reinvested basis.

Small-Cap Growth (SG)   Funds investing in small companies with long-term earnings that are expected to grow significantly faster than the earnings of stocks in major indexes. Funds normally have above-average price-to-earnings ratios, price-to-book ratios, and three-year earnings growth.

Small-Cap Core (SC)   Funds investing in small companies, with wide latitude in the type of shares they buy. On average, the price-to-earnings ratios, price-to-book ratios, and three-year earnings growth are in line with those of the U.S. diversified small-cap funds' universe average.

Small-Cap Value (SV)   Funds investing in small companies that are considered undervalued relative to major stock indexes based on price-to-earnings ratios, price-to-book ratios, or other factors.

Specialty Equity (SQ)   Funds investing in all market-capitalization ranges, with no restrictions for any one range. May have strategies that are distinctly different from other diversified stock funds.

Utility (UT)   Funds investing in utility stocks.

(continued)

Mutual-Fund Objectives (*continued*)

Taxable-Bond Funds

Short-Term Bond (SB)   Ultra-short Obligation; Short-investment Grade Debt; Short-intermediate investment Grade Debt.

Short-Term U.S. (SU)   Short U.S. Treasury; Short U.S. Government: Short-intermediate U.S. Government debt.

Intermediate Bond (IB)   Funds investing in investment-grade debt issues (rated in the top four grades) with dollar-weighted average maturities of five to 10 years.

Intermediate U.S. (IG)   Intermediate U.S. Government: Intermediate U.S. Treasury.

Long-Term Bond (AB)   Funds investing in corporate- and government-debt issues in the top grades.

Long-Term U.S. (LU)   General U.S. Government; General U.S. Treasury: Target Maturity.

General U.S. Taxable (GT)   Funds investing in general bonds.

High-Yield Taxable (HC)   Funds aiming for high current yields from fixed-income securities and tend to invest in lower-grade debt.

Mortgage (MT)   Adjustable Rate Mortgage: GNMA; U.S. Mortgage.

World Bond (WB)   Emerging Markets Debt: Global Income; International Income; Short World MultiMarket Income.

Municipal-Debt Funds

Short-Term Muni (SM)   California Short-intermediate Muni Debt; Other States Short-intermediate Muni Debt; Short-intermediate Muni Debt; Short Muni Debt.

Intermediate Muni (IM)   Intermediate-term Muni Debt including single states.

General Muni (GM)   Funds investing in muni-debt issues in the top-four credit ratings.

Single-State Municipal (SS)   Funds investing in debt of individual states.

High-Yield Municipal (HM)   Funds investing in lower-rated muni debt.

Insured Muni (NM)   California Insured Muni Debt; Florida Insured Muni Debt; Insured Muni Debt; New York Insured Muni Debt.

Stock & Bond Funds

Balanced (BL)   Primary objective is to conserve principal, by maintaining a balanced portfolio of both stocks and bonds.

Stock/Bond Blend (MP)   Multipurpose funds such as Balanced Target Maturity; Convertible Securities; Flexible Income; Flexible Portfolio; Global Flexible and Income funds, that invest in both stocks and bonds.

Source: *The Wall Street Journal,* February 3, 2004, p. R11. Reprinted by permission of The Wall Street Journal © 2004 Dow Jones & Company, Inc. All Rights Reserved Worldwide. *www.wsj.com*

Concept Questions

1. Where do mutual funds rank in terms of asset size among all FI industries?
2. Describe the difference between short-term and long-term mutual funds.
3. What have been the trends in the number of mutual funds since 1980?
4. What are the three biggest mutual fund companies? How have their funds performed in recent years?
5. Describe the difference between open-end and closed-end mutual funds.

BALANCE SHEET AND RECENT TRENDS

Money Market Funds

Look at the distribution of assets of money market mutual funds from 1990 through 2003 shown in Table 5–9. As you can see, in 2003, $1,395.9 billion (60.2 percent of total assets) were invested in short-term financial securities such as foreign deposits, domestic checkable deposits and currency, time and savings deposits, repurchase agreements (RPs), open market paper (mostly commercial paper), and U.S. government securities. Managers of these funds are particularly subject to credit risk, interest rate risk, foreign exchange risk, and market risk. Short-maturity asset holdings reflect the objective of these funds to retain the depositlike nature of the share liabilities they issue. In fact, most money market mutual fund shares have their values fixed at $1. Asset value fluctuations due to

TABLE 5–9
Distribution of Assets in Money Market Mutual Funds from 1990 through 2003 (in billions of dollars)

Source: Federal Reserve Board, "Flow of Fund Accounts," various issues. *www.federalreserve.gov*

	1990	1995	2000	2003
Total financial assets	$493.3	$745.3	$1,812.1	$2,016.0
Foreign deposits	26.7	19.7	91.1	74.2
Checkable deposits and currency	11.2	−3.5	2.2	−1.9
Time and savings deposits	21.9	52.3	142.4	156.9
Security RPs	58.2	87.8	183.0	251.4
Credit market instruments	371.3	545.5	1,290.9	1,398.5
Open market paper	204.0	235.5	608.6	458.9
U.S. government securities	81.3	160.8	275.6	456.4
Treasury	44.9	70.0	90.4	130.2
Agency	36.4	90.8	185.2	326.2
Municipal securities	84.0	127.7	244.7	297.3
Corporate and foreign bonds	2.0	21.5	161.9	185.9
Miscellaneous assets	4.0	43.4	102.5	137.0

interest rate changes and capital gains or losses on assets are adjusted for by increasing or reducing the number of $1 shares owned by the investor.

EXAMPLE 5–5
Calculation of Number of Shares Outstanding in a Money Market Mutual Fund

Due to a drop in interest rates, the market value of the assets held by a particular MMMF increases from $100 to $110. The market value balance sheet for the mutual fund before and after the drop in interest rates is

Assets		Liabilities and Equity	
(a) Before the interest rate drop:			
Market value of MMMF assets	$100	Market value of MMMF fund shares (100 shares × $1)	$100
(b) After the interest rate drop:			
Market value of MMMF assets	$110	Market value of MMMF fund shares (110 shares × $1)	$110

The interest rate drop results in 10 (110 − 100) new equity-type shares that are held by investors in the MMMF, reflecting the increase in the market value of the MMMF's assets of $10 (i.e., 10 new shares of $1 each).

Long-Term Funds

Note the asset composition of long-term mutual funds shown in Table 5–10. As might be expected, it reflects the popularity of different types of bond or equity funds at that time. Underscoring the attractiveness of equity funds in 2003, was the fact that stocks comprised over 65.6 percent of total long-term mutual fund asset portfolios. Credit market instruments were the next most popular assets (32.3 percent of the asset portfolio). In contrast, look at the distribution of assets in 1990, when the equity markets were not doing so well. Equities made up only 38.3 percent of the long-term mutual fund portfolios. Credit market instruments were the largest asset group at 59.2 percent of total assets.

Concept Questions

1. Describe the major assets held by mutual funds in the 1990s and early 2000s.
2. How does the asset distribution differ between money market mutual funds and long-term mutual funds?

TABLE 5–10
Distribution of Assets in Bond, Income, and Equity Mutual Funds from 1990 through 2003 (in billions of dollars)

Source: Federal Reserve Board, "Flow of Fund Accounts," various issues. *www.federalreserve.gov*

	1990	1995	2000	2003
Total financial assets	$608.4	$1,852.8	$4,434.6	$4,664.9
Security RPs	6.1	50.2	106.4	93.5
Credit market instruments	360.1	771.3	1,097.8	1,056.3
Open market paper	28.5	50.2	106.4	75.3
U.S. government securities	159.7	315.1	399.0	591.6
Treasury	111.1	205.3	123.7	147.3
Agency	48.6	109.9	275.3	444.3
Municipal securities	112.6	210.2	230.5	291.1
Corporate and foreign bonds	59.3	195.7	361.9	548.3
Corporate equities	233.2	1,024.9	3,226.9	3,062.1
Miscellaneous assets	8.9	6.3	3.5	3.1
Total shares outstanding	608.4	1,852.8	4,434.6	4,664.9

REGULATION

www.sec.gov

Because mutual funds manage and invest small investors' savings, this industry is heavily regulated. Indeed, many regulations have been enacted to protect investors against possible abuses by managers of mutual funds. The SEC is the primary regulator of mutual funds. Specifically, the Securities Act of 1933 requires a mutual fund to file a registration statement with the SEC and sets rules and procedures regarding the fund's prospectus sent to investors. In addition, the Securities Exchange Act of 1934 makes the purchase and sale of mutual fund shares subject to various antifraud provisions. This regulation requires that a mutual fund furnish full and accurate information on all financial and corporate matters to prospective fund purchasers. The 1934 act also appointed the National Association of Securities Dealers (NASD) to supervise mutual fund share distributions.

www.nasd.com

In 1940 Congress passed the Investment Advisers Act and the Investment Company Act. The Investment Advisers Act regulates the activities of mutual fund advisers. The Investment Company Act sets out rules to prevent conflicts of interest, fraud, and excessive fees or charges for fund shares.

In recent years, the passage of the Insider Trading and Securities Fraud Enforcement Act of 1988 has required mutual funds to develop mechanisms and procedures to avoid insider trading abuses. In addition, the ability of mutual funds to conduct their business is affected by the Market Reform Act of 1990, which was passed in the wake of the 1987 stock market crash. This act allows the SEC to introduce circuit breakers to halt trading on exchanges and to restrict program trading when it deems necessary. Finally, the National Securities Markets Improvement Act (NSMIA) of 1996 also applies to mutual fund companies. Specifically, the NSMIA exempts mutual fund sellers from oversight by state securities regulators, thus reducing their regulatory burden.

Despite the many regulations imposed on mutual fund companies, several allegations of trading abuses and improper assignment of fees were revealed and prosecuted in the early 2000s. The abusive activities fell into four general categories: market timing, late trading, directed brokerage, and improper assessment of fees to investors.

Market timing involves short-term trading of mutual funds that seeks to take advantage of short-term discrepancies between the price of a mutual fund's shares and out-of-date values on the securities in the fund's portfolio. It is especially common in international funds as traders can exploit differences in time zones. Typically, market timers hold a fund for only a few days. For example, when Asian markets close with losses, but are expected to rebound the following day, market timers can buy a U.S. mutual fund, investing in Asian securities after the loss on that day and then sell the shares for a profit the next day. This single-day investment dilutes the profits of the fund's long-term investors, while market timers profit without much risk. The Ethical Dilemmas box highlights one particularly flagrant case in which a mutual fund allowed selected traders to engage in market timing.

Late trading allegations involved cases in which some investors were able to buy or sell mutual fund shares long after the price had been set at 4:00 PM Eastern time each day (i.e., after the close of the NYSE and NASDAQ). Under existing rules, investors had to place an order with their broker or another FI by 4:00 PM. But the mutual fund company may not have received the order until much later, sometimes as late as 9:00 PM. However, because of this time delay, some large investors had been able to call their broker back after the market closed and alter or cancel their order.

Directed brokerage involves arrangements between mutual fund companies and brokerage houses and whether those agreements improperly influenced which funds brokers recommended to investors. The investigation examined whether some mutual fund companies agreed to direct orders for stock and bond purchases and sales to brokerage houses that agreed to promote sales of the mutual fund company's products.

Finally, regulators claimed that the disclosure of 12b–1 fees allowed some brokers to trick investors into believing they were buying no-load funds. Before 12b–1 fees, all funds sold through brokers carried front-end load fees. As discussed above, with 12b–1 fees, fund companies introduced share classes, some of which carried back-end loads that declined over time and others that charged annual fees of up to 1 percent of asset values. Funds classes that charged annual 12b–1 fees would see performance decrease by that amount and thus not perform as well as an identical fund that carried a lower 12b–1 fee. The shareholder, however, only saw the fund's raw return (before annual fees) and not the dollar amount of the fee paid. Further, regulators discovered in late 2002 that brokers often overcharged customers by failing to provide discounts to fund investors who qualified to receive them. Since discount policies differ from fund to fund, brokers did not always realize which customers qualified for them. Table 5–11 lists some of the mutual fund companies at the center of these abuses, the abuses they were accused of, and outcomes of some of the investigations.

The result of these illegal and abusive activities was new rules and regulations imposed (in 2004) on mutual fund companies. The rules were intended to give investors more information about conflicts of interest, improve fund governance, and close legal loopholes that some fund managers had abused. Many of these new rules involve changes to the way mutual funds operate, including requirements that funds have an independent board headed by an independent chairman. Specifically, the SEC required an increase in the percentage of independent board members to 75 percent from the previous level of 50 percent and required mutual fund companies to have independent board chairs (a move that would displace the sitting chairmen at about 80 percent of the nations mutual funds). The SEC saw independent directors as those who better serve as watchdogs guarding investors' interests. Further, the Sarbanes-Oxley Act of 2002 requires public companies, including mutual fund companies, to make sure their boards' audit committees have at least one individual who is familiar with generally accepted accounting principles and has experience with internal auditing controls, preparing

TABLE 5–11   Mutual Fund Investigations in the Early 2000s

Company	Charge	Results
Alliance Capital	Market timing	$250 million settlement; 2 employees fired
Bank of America	Market timing/late trading	$515 million settlement; 3 employees fired; several more employees resigned
Bank One	Market timing	2 managers resigned
Bear Stearns	Market timing	6 employees fired
Canary Capital	Market timing/late trading	$40 million settlement
Charles Schwab	Late trading	2 employees fired
Citigroup	Market timing/late trading	5 employees fired
Federated Investors	Market timing	Actions pending
Fred Alger & Co.	Market timing/late trading	Vice chairman convicted of felony and fined $400,000; 2 employees fired
Janus Capital	Market timing	$226 million settlement; CEO and others resign; fee reductions of $125 million
Merrill Lynch	Market timing	3 employees fired
MFS Investment Management	Market timing	$225 million settlement; fee reductions of $125 million
Millennium Partners	Late trading	Fund trader pleads guilty and sentenced to up to 4 years in prison
Morgan Stanley	Directed brokerage; improper fees	$50 million settlement
PBHG Funds	Market timing	Co-founders resign
Pilgrim, Baxter & Associates	Market timing	2 founders resign
Prudential Securities	Market timing	12 employees fired; 7 employees facing charges
Putnam Investments	Market timing; improper fees	$110 million settlement; CEO resigns; 6 fund managers resign
Security Trust	Market timing	Company closed; CEO, president, and head of trading operations charged with grand larceny and fraud
Strong Capital Management	Market timing	$140 million settlement; chairman of mutual fund unit resigns; fee reductions of $35 million

Source: Author's research.

or auditing financial statements of "generally comparable issuers," and applying GAAP principles for estimates, accruals, and reserves.

The SEC also took steps to close a loophole that allowed improper trading to go unnoticed at some mutual funds. Prior to the new rules, the SEC required that funds report trading by senior employees in individual stocks but not in shares of mutual funds they manage. The SEC now requires portfolio managers to report trading in funds they manage. Investment advisors also have to protect information about stock selections and client holding and transactions. The SEC and other regulators had found that advisory personnel revealed confidential information about fund portfolio holdings so that others could exploit the funds.

To address the problem of market timing, the SEC now requires funds to provide expanded disclosure of the risks of frequent trading in fund shares and of their policies and procedures regarding such activities. Mutual funds also now have to be more open about their use of fair value pricing (a practice of estimating the value of rarely traded securities or updating the values of non-U.S. securities that last traded many hours before U.S. funds calculate their share prices each day) to guard against stale share prices that could produce profits for market timers. The market timing provisions also require mutual funds to explain when they use fair value pricing. Fair value pricing is one of the most effective ways of combating the market timing that was most common in some mutual funds holding non-U.S. stocks. Many mutual funds had rarely used fair value pricing. Further, new SEC rules require brokers to tell investors about any payments, compensation, or other incentives they receive from fund companies including whether they were paid more to sell a certain fund. Conflicts would have to be disclosed before the sale is completed. Finally, the SEC required that any profits earned by market timers be returned to investors in the mutual funds hurt by the timing.

To ensure that the required rule changes take place, starting October 5, 2004, the SEC required that mutual funds hire chief compliance officers to monitor whether the mutual fund company follows the rules. The chief compliance officer will report directly to mutual fund directors, and not to executives of the fund management company. To further insulate the chief compliance officer from being bullied into keeping quiet about improper behavior, only the fund board can fire the compliance officer. Duties of the compliance officer include policing personal trading by fund managers, ensuring accuracy of information provided to regulators and investors, reviewing fund business practices such as allocating trading commissions, and reporting any wrongdoing directly to fund directors.

Finally, the new SEC rules call for shareholder reports to include the fees shareholders paid during any period covered, as well as management's discussion of the fund's performance over that period. As of September 1, 2004, mutual fund companies must provide clear information to investors on brokerage commissions and discounts, including improved disclosure on upfront sales charges for broker-sold mutual funds. Investors now get a document showing the amount they paid for a fund, the amount their broker was paid, and how the fund compares with industry averages based on fees, sales loads, and brokerage commissions. As of December 2004, mutual funds must provide to investors summary information in a fund prospectus on eligibility for breakpoint discounts and explain what records investors may need to show brokers to demonstrate they qualify for discounts.

While not approved as of mid-2004, the SEC has also proposed that mutual funds or their agents receive all trading orders by 4:00 PM Eastern time, when the fund's daily price is calculated. This "hard closing," which would require fund orders to be in the hands of the mutual fund companies by 4:00 PM, is intended to halt late trading abuses. This proposal had not yet been passed because some argued that the change would cause significant problems for investors who buy funds through brokers. The move requires deadlines several hours earlier at intermediaries such as brokerage firms, forcing them to place orders as early as 10:00 AM so their requests are processed on the same day. Thus, mutual fund investors using brokers for their trades would have less flexibility than direct mutual fund investors.

Ethical Dilemmas

PUTNAM CLAIMS EX-CEO HID ABUSES TO STAY IN POWER

Putnam investments claims ousted Chief Executive Lawrence Lasser concealed improper trading at the mutual fund firm to "maintain his power and absolute control," and to preserve his compensation—more than $100 million over five years—according to an arbitration claim that the company filed in a dispute over his exit package. In November, Putnam's parent, Marsh & McLennan Cos., removed Mr. Lasser as CEO shortly after federal and state regulators accused Putnam of allowing fund managers to trade rapidly in Putnam funds, skimming profits from long-term shareholders. Putnam has said that Mr. Lasser, who ruled it for 18 years and built the firm into an investment titan, knew about the fund-manager trading in 2000, but didn't tell fund trustees, who represent shareholders. In a letter to the chairman of the Putnam funds' trustees, Mr. Lasser disputes that account and has claimed he is being made "a scapegoat.". . .

In harsh language, the SEC's enforcement section called Putnam's conduct "egregious" and "a massive breach of fiduciary duty." . . . In the brief, SEC enforcement attorneys said Mr. Lasser and Putnam had concealed the trading until last year to protect a valuable franchise, and they noted that once the trading was disclosed, investors withdrew $54 billion from Putnam in the fourth quarter of 2003 . . . [T]he SEC attorneys quoted at length from Putnam's arbitration complaint against Mr. Lasser to paint the company's behavior in a harsher light. "When it came time for Mr. Lasser to respond to evidence of market timing by Putnam employees, Lasser made a conscious decision to stick his head in the sand," the SEC quoted Putnam as saying in its arbitration filing. . . . "Mr. Lasser knew that if the market-timing trades were revealed to the Putnam trustees or to anyone at [Marsh], he could be forced to surrender the absolute control with which he had managed Putnam for years," according to Putnam's complaint.

Source: *The Wall Street Journal,* March 24, 2004, p. C1, by John Hechinger. Reprinted by permission of the Wall Street Journal © 2004 Dow Jones & Company, Inc. All Rights Reserved Worldwide. *www.wsj.com*

Concept Questions

1. Who is the primary regulator of mutual fund companies?
2. How did the NSMIA affect mutual funds?

GLOBAL ISSUES

As discussed throughout the chapter, mutual funds have been the fastest growing sector in the U.S. financial institutions industry throughout the 1990s and into the early 2000s. Worldwide investment in mutual funds is shown in Table 5–12. While not as striking as the growth in U.S. funds, worldwide (other than in the United States) investments in mutual funds have increased over 300 percent from $1.626 trillion in 1992 to $6.543 trillion in 2003. This compares to growth of over 350 percent in U.S. funds. The relatively large returns on U.S. stocks is the most likely reason for this growth in U.S. funds relative to other countries. In contrast, as this industry developed in countries throughout the world, the number of mutual funds worldwide (other than in the United States) increased over 150 percent from 18,183 in 1992 to 45,889 in 2003. Much more established in the United States, the number of U.S. mutual funds increased 112 percent over this period.

As may be expected, the worldwide mutual fund market is most active in those countries with the most sophisticated securities markets (e.g., Japan, France,

TABLE 5–12 Worldwide Assets of Open-End Investment Companies[1] (in million of dollars)

Non-U.S. countries	1999	2000	2001	2002	2003
Argentina	$ 6,990	$ 7,425	$ 3,751	$ 1,021	$ 1,916
Australia	N/A	341,955	334,016	356,304	518,411
Austria	56,254	56,549	55,211	66,877	87,982
Belgium	65,461	70,313	68,661	74,983	98,724
Brazil	117,758	148,538	148,189	96,729	171,596
Canada	269,825	279,511	267,863	248,979	338,369
Chile	4,091	4,597	5,090	6,705	8,552
Czech Republic	1,473	1,990	1,778	3,297	4,083
Denmark[2]	27,558	32,485	33,831	40,153	49,533
Finland	10,318	12,698	12,933	16,516	29,967
France	656,132	721,973	713,378	845,147	1,148,446
Germany	237,312	238,029	213,662	209,168	276,319
Greece	36,397	29,154	23,888	26,621	38,394
Hong Kong	182,265	195,924	170,073	164,322	255,811
Hungary	1,725	1,953	2,260	3,992	3,936
India	13,065	13,507	15,284	20,364	29,800
Ireland	95,174	137,024	191,840	250,116	360,425
Italy	475,661	424,014	359,879	378,259	478,734
Japan	502,752	431,996	343,907	303,191	349,148
Korea	167,177	110,613	119,439	149,544	121,488
Liechtenstein	N/A	N/A	N/A	3,847	8,936
Luxembourg	661,084	747,117	758,720	803,869	1,104,112
Mexico	19,468	18,488	31,723	30,759	31,953
Netherlands	94,539	93,580	79,165	84,211	N/A
New Zealand	8,502	7,802	6,564	7,505	9,641
Norway	15,107	16,228	14,752	15,471	21,994
Philippines	117	108	211	474	792
Poland	762	1,546	2,970	5,468	8,576
Portugal	19,704	16,588	16,618	19,969	26,985
Romania	N/A	8	10	27	36
Russia	177	177	297	372	851
South Africa	18,235	16,921	14,561	20,983	34,460
Spain	207,603	172,438	159,899	179,133	255,344
Sweden	83,250	78,085	65,538	57,992	87,746
Switzerland	82,512	83,059	75,973	82,622	90,772
Taiwan	31,153	32,074	49,742	62,153	76,205
Turkey	N/A	N/A	N/A	6,002	14,164
United Kingdom	375,199	361,008	316,702	288,887	396,523
Total non-U.S.	**$ 4,544,799**	**$ 4,906,394**	**$ 4,679,953**	**$ 4,933,771**	**$6,543,480**
Total U.S.	**$ 6,846,339**	**$ 6,964,667**	**$ 6,974,951**	**$ 6,390,360**	**$7,414,084**
Total world	**$11,391,138**	**$11,871,061**	**$11,654,904**	**$11,324,131**	**$13,957,564**

[1] Funds of funds are not included. Data include home-domiciled funds, except for Hong Kong, Korea, and New Zealand.
[2] Before 2003, data include special funds reserved for institutional investors.
Note: Components may not add to total because of rounding.
Source: Investment Company Institute, *2004 and 2004 Mutual Fund Fact Book* (Washington, D.C.: Investment Company Institute, May2004).Reprinted by permission of the Investment Company Institute. *www.ici.org*

Australia, and the United Kingdom). However, in the late 1990s and early 2000s, the faltering Japanese economy resulted in a decrease in both the assets invested in and the number of mutual funds. Assets invested in Japanese mutual funds fell from $502.7 billion in 1999 to $432.0 billion in 2000 (a drop of 14.1 percent) and the number of funds fell from 3,444 to 2,884 (16.3 percent) over the period. Some U.S. FIs saw this decline in the Japanese market as an opportunity. U.S. FIs such as Paine Webber Group (teaming up with Yasuda Life Insurance Co.) and Merrill Lynch (buying the assets of failed Japanese brokerage firm Yamaichi Securities) entered the Japanese mutual fund market in the late 1990s. The U.S. FIs saw Japan as a profitable market for mutual fund sales, noting that about 60 percent of Japan's savings was in low-yielding bank deposits or government-run institutions.[9] The worldwide economic downturn in 2001–2002 also affected the global mutual fund industry. Assets invested in non-U.S. mutual funds fell from $ 4.91 trillion in 1999 to $4.68 trillion in 2001. As the worldwide economic situation improved in 2003, so did assets invested in mutual funds, rising to $6.54 trillion by year-end 2003.

Although U.S. mutual fund companies sponsor funds abroad, barriers to entry overseas are typically higher than in the United States. The U.S. mutual fund industry has worked to lower the barriers that prevent U.S. mutual fund firms from marketing their services more widely and to improve competition in the often-diverse fund markets around the world. The U.S. mutual fund industry, for example, has worked to achieve a true cross-border market for mutual fund companies in Europe and to ensure that publicly offered mutual fund companies can be used as funding vehicles in the retirement fund market in Europe and Japan. The industry also has sought to reduce barriers for U.S. mutual fund sponsors seeking to offer mutual fund company products in China and other Asian countries.

Concept Question

1. What have been the trends in the assets invested in worldwide mutual funds during the 1990s and early 2000s?

Summary

This chapter provided an overview of the mutual fund industry. Mutual funds pool funds from individuals and corporations and invest in diversified asset portfolios. Given the tremendous growth in the market values of financial assets—such as equities—in the 1990s and the cost-effective way in which mutual funds allow small investors to participate in these markets, mutual funds have grown tremendously in size, number of funds, and number of shareholders. We looked at the two major categories of mutual funds—short-term and long-term open-ended funds—highlighting the differences in their growth rates and the composition of their assets. We also looked at the calculation of the net asset values (NAV) of mutual fund shares. Finally, we contrasted open-end mutual funds with closed-end mutual funds.

---

[9] It might be noted that as many European countries move away from state-sponsored pension plans to privately funded pension plans and retirement vehicles the rate of growth in mutual funds in these countries is likely to accelerate rapidly.

Questions and Problems

1. What is a mutual fund? In what sense is it a financial intermediary?

2. What are money market mutual funds? In what assets do these funds typically invest? What factors have caused the strong growth in this type of fund since the late 1970s?

3. What are long-term mutual funds? In what assets do these funds usually invest? What factors caused the strong growth in this type of fund during the 1990s?

4. Using the data in Table 5–3, discuss the growth and ownership holding over the last 20 years of long-term funds versus short-term funds.

5. Why did the proportion of equities in long-term funds increase from 38.3 percent in 1990 to over 70 percent by 2000 and then decrease to 62 percent in 2002? How might an investor's preference for a mutual funds objective change over time?

6. How does the risk of short-term funds differ from the risk of long-term funds?

7. What are the economic reasons for the existence of mutual funds; that is, what benefits do mutual funds provide for investors? Why do individuals rather than corporations hold most mutual funds shares?

8. What are the principal demographics of household owners who own mutual funds? What are the primary reasons why household owners invest in mutual funds?

9. What change in regulatory guidelines occurred in 1998 that had the primary purpose of giving investors a better understanding of the risks and objectives of a fund?

10. What are the three possible components reflected in the return an investor receives from a mutual fund?

11. An investor purchases a mutual fund for $60. The fund pays dividends of $1.75, distributes a capital gain of $3, and charges a fee of $3 when the fund is sold one year later for $67.50. What is the net rate of return from this investment?

12. How is the net asset value (NAV) of a mutual fund determined? What is meant by the term *marked-to-market daily?*

13. A mutual fund owns 400 shares of Fiat, Inc., currently trading at $7, and 400 shares of Microsoft, Inc., currently trading at $70. The fund has 100 shares outstanding.
    a. What is the net asset value (NAV) of the fund?
    b. If investors expect the price of Fiat shares to increase to $9 and the price of Microsoft shares to decrease to $55 by the end of the year, what is the expected NAV at the end of the year?
    c. Assume that the expected price of the Fiat shares is realized at $9. What is the maximum price decrease that can occur to the Microsoft shares to realize an end-of-year NAV equal to the NAV estimated in (a)?

14. What is the difference between open-end and closed-end mutual funds? Which type of fund tends to be more specialized in asset selection? How does a closed-end fund provide another source of return from which an investor may either gain or lose?

15. Open-end Fund A owns 100 shares of AT&T valued at $100 each and 50 shares of Toro valued at $50 each. Closed-end Fund B owns 75 shares of AT&T and 100 shares of Toro. Each fund has 100 shares of stock outstanding.

a. What are the NAVs of both funds using these prices?

b. Assume that in one month the price of AT&T stock has increased to $105 and the price of Toro stock has decreased to $45. How do these changes impact the NAV of both funds? If the funds were purchased at the NAV prices in (a) and sold at month end, what would be the realized returns on the investments?

c. Assume that another 100 shares of AT&T are added to Fund A. What is the effect on Fund A's NAV if the stock prices remain unchanged from the original prices?

16. What is the difference between a load fund and a no-load fund? Is the argument that load funds are more closely managed and therefore have higher returns supported by the evidence presented in Table 5–7?

17. What is a 12b–1 fee? Suppose you have a choice between a load fund with no annual 12b–1 fee and a no-load fund with a maximum 12b–1 fee. How would the length of your expected investment horizon, or holding period, influence your choice between these two funds?

18. Suppose an individual invests $10,000 in a load mutual fund for two years. The load fee entails an up-front commission charge of 4 percent of the amount invested and is deducted from the original funds invested. In addition, annual fund operating expenses (or 12b–1 fees) are 0.85 percent. The annual fees are charged on the average net asset value invested in the fund and are recorded at the end of each year. Investments in the fund return 5 percent each year paid on the last day of the year. If the investor reinvests the annual returns paid on the investment, calculate the annual return on the mutual funds over the two-year investment period.

19. Who are the primary regulators of the mutual fund industry? How do their regulatory goals differ from those of other types of financial institutions?

Web Questions

20. Go to the Fidelity Investments Web site and look up the annual 1-, 5-, and 10-year returns on Fidelity Select Biotechnology Fund using the following steps. The Web site is **www.fidelity.com**. Click on "Investment Products." Click on "Mutual Funds." Click on "Fidelity Funds." Click on "Browse Our Funds." Click on "Fidelity Select Portfolios." Click on "Average Annual Returns." This will bring the file onto your computer that contains the relevant data.

21. Go to the Investment Company Institute Web site and look up the most recent data on the asset values and number of short-term and long-term mutual funds using the following steps. The Web site is **www.ici.org**. Under "Statistics & Research," click on the "Mutual Fund Statistics." Click on "Mutual Fund Fact Book." Click on the most recent year for "XXXX Mutual Fund Fact Book." Go to the "Data Section." This section contains the relevant data. The data on asset values and number of mutual funds is among the first few pages. How have these values increased since those for 2003 reported in Table 5–1?

Pertinent Web Sites

American Funds	www.americanfunds.com
Board of Governors of the Federal Reserve	www.federalreserve.gov
Fidelity Investments	www.fidelity.com
Investment Company Institute	www.ici.org
Morningstar, Inc.	www.morningstar.com
National Association of Securities Dealers	www.nasd.com
Securities and Exchange Commission	www.sec.gov
Vanguard	www.vanguard.com
The Wall Street Journal	www.wsj.com

Appendix 5A

Hedge Funds

Hedge funds are a type of investment pool that solicits funds from (wealthy) individuals and other investors (e.g., commercial banks) and invests these funds on their behalf. Hedge funds, however, are not technically mutual funds in that they are subject to virtually no regulatory oversight (e.g., by the SEC under the Securities Act and Investment Advisors Act) and generally take significant risk. The absence of hedge fund regulations is due to the small number of investors permitted (below that required for SEC registration), as well as the fact that investors are viewed as being sufficiently sophisticated so as not to need overall SEC protection. Hedge funds grew in popularity in the 1990s as investors saw returns of over 40 percent after management fees (often more than 25 percent of the fund's profits).[1] They came to the forefront of the news in the late 1990s when one large hedge fund, Long-Term Capital Management (LTCM), nearly collapsed. The near collapse of LTCM not only hurt its investors, but

arguably came close to damaging the world's financial system. So great was the potential impact of the failure of LTCM that the Federal Reserve felt it was necessary to intervene by brokering a $3.6 billion bailout of LTCM by a consortium of some of the world's largest financial institutions.

Using traditional risk-adjusted measures of performance (such as Sharpe ratios), the performance of hedge funds has been very strong compared to traditional financial investments like stocks and bonds.[2] Many hedge funds posted strong returns during the early 2000s even as stock returns were plummeting. While no hard data exists, industry sources estimate that the total investment in over 7,000 hedge funds was $860 billion at year-end 2003.

Initially, hedge fund managers found mainly wealthy individual investors to invest in their funds. In the late 1990s, however, corporate pension

---

[1] Although S. J. Brown, in "Hedge Funds: Omniscient or Just Plain Wrong," *Pacific Basin Finance Journal* 9 (2001), pp. 301–11, found that over the period 1989–1995, hedge funds earned, on average, 3 percent less than the S&P 500 index over the same period. Further, hedge fund risk was below that of the S&P 500 index.

[2] However, as pointed out by F. R. Edwards and S. Gaon in "Hedge Funds: What Do We Know?" *Journal of Applied Corporate Finance*, Fall 2003, pp. 58–71, data deficiencies in the reporting and collection of hedge fund returns somewhat reduce confidence in all measures of hedge fund performance. Further, the inability to explain returns of individual hedge funds with standard multifactor risk models leaves open the possibility that it is not possible to properly measure the risk associated with at least some hedge fund strategies. If so, risk-adjusted returns earned by hedge funds may be overstated.

plan sponsors, state funds, insurance companies, and university endowment funds became important investors. Most hedge funds require a minimum investment of between $100,000 and $20 million. For example, LTCM required investors to contribute at least $10 million. The funds also line up credit from financial institutions such as banks and brokerages to keep operations moving smoothly. Some funds use these credit lines to increase the size of the investment pool. For example, at its peak LTCM had approximately $5 billion in capital supporting $120 billion in investments.

Some hedge funds take positions (using sophisticated computer models) speculating that some prices will rise faster than others. For example, a hedge fund may buy (take a long position in) a bond expecting that its price will rise. At the same time the fund will borrow (taking a short position) in another bond and sell it, promising to return the borrowed bond in the future. Generally, bond prices tend to move up and down together. Thus, if prices go up as expected, the hedge fund will gain on the bond it purchased while losing money on the bond it borrowed. The hedge fund will make a profit if the gain on the bond it purchased is larger than the loss on the bond it borrowed. If, contrary to expectations, bond prices fall, the hedge fund will make a profit if the gains on the bond it borrowed are greater than the losses on the bond it bought. Thus, regardless of the change in prices, the simultaneous long and short positions in bonds will minimize the risk of overall losses for the hedge fund.

Despite their name, hedge funds do not always "hedge" their investments to protect the fund and its investors against market price declines and other risks. For example, while bond prices generally move in the same direction, the risk in hedge funds is that bond prices may unexpectedly move faster in some markets than others. For example, in 1997 and 1998 computer models used by LTCM detected a price discrepancy between U.S. Treasury markets and other bonds (including high-yield corporate bonds, mortgaged-backed securities, and European government bonds). LTCM consequently shorted U.S. Treasury securities (betting their prices would fall) and took long positions in other types of bonds (betting their prices would rise). However, unexpectedly, in 1998 large drops in many foreign stock markets caused money to pour into the U.S. Treasury markets, driving Treasury security prices up and yields down. This drop in U.S. Treasury yields drove rates on mortgages down, which pushed down the prices of many mortgage-backed securities. Further, the flight to U.S. Treasury security markets meant a drop in funds flowing into European bond markets and high-yield corporate bond markets. With all of their positions going wrong, LTCM experienced huge losses.[3]

In recent years, hedge funds have played an even bigger role in terms of global capital flows. During the early 2000s, riskier securities around the globe became popular investments for hedge funds eagerly searching for higher returns in a low-interest-rate environment. In early 2004 emerging market bond yields started to rise far more rapidly than those on U.S. Treasury bonds, increasing the gap in yields between the two as investors moved out of the riskier emerging country bond market. As a result, as rising interest rates negatively impacted emerging market hedge fund investments, many hedge funds saw decreases in returns. Consequently, there are fears that hedge funds may see a repeat of 1998. This time, however, no one fund is likely to pose a systemic risk since, after LTCM, the amount of borrowing banks extend to any one hedge fund client is far more carefully monitored. But given the copycat nature of hedge fund management, there is concern that similar fund strategies by many hedge funds are combining to create potential systematic LTCM-type problems. Along with the use of similar investment strategies, many hedge funds are using the same risk models. These models are often historically based and are subject to similar errors in predicting the future.

As discussed above, unlike mutual funds, hedge funds are not required to report their holdings to the SEC, to invest in securities with liquid

---

[3] As pointed out in W. Fung and D. A. Hsieh, "The Risk in Hedge Fund Strategies: Theory and Evidence from Fixed Income Traders," working paper, Duke University, 2001, a major reason for LTCM's large loss was that it was so highly leveraged compared to other funds. LTCM was two to four times more leveraged than the typical fund. As expressed in Brittain, "Hedge Funds and the Institutional Investor," *Journal of International Financial Management and Accounting* 12:2, 2001, pp. 225–34, the effort to understand risks experienced in hedge funds often lacks the overall logical framework that is broadly accepted in the traditional investment world.

and active markets, or to adhere to any particular objective or investing style. Hedge funds avoid such regulation by organizing as limited partnerships with no more than 99 limited partners that must have annual incomes of more than $200,000 or net worth exceeding $1 million. (Funds may have up to 499 limited partners if each partner has at least $5 million in invested assets.) The limited partnership structure and stiff financial requirements allow hedge funds to avoid regulation under the theory that individuals with such wealth should be able to evaluate the risk and return on their investments. Further, in order to avoid regulatory restrictions, many hedge funds are headquartered outside the United States (e.g., the Cayman Islands).[4]

Nevertheless, hedge funds are prohibited from abusive trading practices and a number got mixed up in the scandals plaguing the mutual fund industry in the early 2000s. For example, Canary Capital Partners and its managers agreed to pay $30 million from its illicit profits as well as a $10 million penalty to the SEC to settle allegations that it engaged in illegal trading practices with mutual fund companies, including making deals after the market had closed and promising to make substantial investments in various funds managed by the mutual funds. Possibly as a result of the trading abuses in 2003, the SEC began scrutinizing the hedge fund industry more closely. Specifically, the SEC recommended that large hedge funds register as investment advisers with the SEC, subjecting them to periodic audits and inspections. Only about 25 percent of hedge funds were registered with the SEC at the time. Small hedge funds (that manage less than $25 million) would not have to register with the SEC. By requiring hedge funds to register with the SEC, the proposed changes would increase the limits on who can invest in a hedge fund. Investors also would be required to have at least $1.5 million in net worth or over $750,000 invested in the fund. To the relief of many hedge fund managers, the SEC recommendation made no mention of curbing the heavy use of leverage, or the short selling going on in the industry, which is why some argued that these changes will do little to change the way most hedge funds operate, especially larger funds.

---

[4] When compared to domestic hedge funds, offshore hedge funds have been found to trade more intensely than domestic funds, due to the zero or lower capital gains tax for offshore funds. Further, foreign hedge funds tend to engage less often in positive feedback trading (rushing to buy when the market is booming and rushing to sell when the market is declining) than domestic hedge funds. Finally, offshore hedge funds have been found to herd (mimic each other's behavior when trading while ignoring information about the fundamentals of valuation) less than domestic hedge funds. See W. Kim and S. Wei, "Offshore Investment Funds: Monsters in Emerging Markets?" Hong Kong Institute for Monetary Research Working Paper, No. 5/2001, May 2001.

Chapter Six

The Financial Services Industry: Finance Companies

INTRODUCTION

The primary function of finance companies is to make loans to both individuals and corporations. The services provided by finance companies include consumer lending, business lending, and mortgage financing. Some of their loans are similar to commercial bank loans, such as consumer and auto loans, but others are more specialized. Finance companies differ from banks in that they do not accept deposits but instead rely on short- and long-term debt as a source of funds. Additionally, finance companies often lend to customers commercial banks find too risky. In this chapter we look at the services provided by this industry and the competitive and financial situation facing these firms. We discuss the size, structure, and composition of the industry; the services the industry provides; its competitive and financial position; and its regulation. We conclude the chapter with a look at some global issues. From this chapter, the reader should obtain a basic understanding of services provided by finance companies, their performance, and the degree to which they are regulated.

SIZE, STRUCTURE, AND COMPOSITION OF THE INDUSTRY

www.ge.com

The first major finance company was originated during the Depression, when General Electric Corp. created General Electric Capital Corp. (GECC) as a means of financing appliance sales to cash-constrained customers who were unable to get installment credit from banks. Installment credit is a loan that is paid back to the lender with periodic payments (installments) consisting of varying amounts of interest and principal (e.g., auto loans, home mortgages, and student loans). By the late 1950s banks were more willing to make installment loans, and so finance companies began looking outside their parent companies for business. A look at GECC's loan and lease portfolio today shows leases for almost 10,000 locomotive railcars, 25,000 aircraft, over $1 billion in leveraged buyout financing, and $106 billion in a mortgage servicing portfolio (see below), along with over $400 million in loans to General Electric customers.[1]

[1] See GECC's Web site.

TABLE 6–1
Assets and
Liabilities of U.S.
Finance Companies,
2003

Source: *Federal Reserve Bulletin,* June 2003, p. A30.
www.federalreserve.gov

	Billions of Dollars	Percent of Total Assets
Assets		
Accounts receivable gross	$ 934.9	63.7%
Consumer	307.0	21.0
Business	453.9	30.9
Real estate	174.0	11.9
Less reserves for unearned income	(54.2)	(3.7)
Less reserves for losses	(24.0)	(1.6)
Accounts receivable net	$ 856.7	58.4%
All other	610.9	41.6
Total assets	$1,467.6	100.0%
Liabilities and Capital		
Bank loans	$ 47.3	3.2%
Commercial paper	127.3	8.7
Debt due to parent	87.7	6.0
Debt not elsewhere classified	639.1	43.5
All other liabilities	344.4	23.5
Capital, surplus, and undivided profits	221.8	15.1
Total liabilities and capital	$1,467.6	100.0%

www.gmacfs.com
www.fordcredit.com
www.household.com
www.aigag.com
www.citgroup.com

Because of the attractive rates they offer on some loans (such as new car loans, see below), their willingness to lend to riskier borrowers than commercial banks, their often direct affiliation with manufacturing firms, and the relatively limited amount of regulation imposed on these firms, finance companies have been among the fastest growing FI groups in recent years. In 2003 their assets stood at $1,467.6 billion (see Table 6–1). Comparing this to assets at the end of 1977 (reported in Table 6–2) of $104.3 billion, this industry has experienced growth of almost 1,307 percent in the last 26 years. GMAC Commercial Mortgage Corp. (GMACCM), a subsidiary of General Motors Acceptance Corp. (GMAC), is in fact the largest commercial mortgage lender in the United States, with a mortgage portfolio over $160 billion in place. The company announced in the late 1990s that it had plans to expand its product mix to create one of the world's leading "one-stop" commercial finance companies.

sales finance institutions
Institutions that specialize in making loans to the customers of a particular retailer or manufacturer.

The three major types of finance companies are (1) sales finance institutions, (2) personal credit institutions, and (3) business credit institutions. **Sales finance institutions** (e.g., Ford Motor Credit and Sears Roebuck Acceptance Corp.) specialize in making loans to the customers of a particular retailer or manufacturer. Because sales finance institutions can frequently process loans faster and more conveniently (generally at the location of purchase) than depository institutions, this sector of the industry competes directly with depository institutions for consumer loans. **Personal credit institutions** (e.g., Household International Corp. and AIG American General) specialize in making installment and other loans to consumers. Personal credit institutions will make loans to customers that depository institutions find too risky to lend to (due to low income or a bad credit history). These institutions compensate for the additional risk by charging higher interest rates than depository institutions and/or accepting collateral

personal credit institutions
Institutions that specialize in making installment and other loans to consumers.

TABLE 6–2
Assets and
Liabilities of U.S.
Finance Companies
on December 31,
1977

Source: *Federal Reserve Bulletin,* June 1978, p. A39.
www.federalreserve.gov

	Billions of Dollars	Percent of Total Assets
Assets		
Accounts receivable gross	$ 99.2	95.1%
Consumer	44.0	42.2
Business	55.2	52.9
Less reserves for unearned income and losses	(12.7)	(12.2)
Accounts receivable net	$ 86.5	82.9%
Cash and bank deposit	2.6	2.5
Securities	0.9	0.9
All others	14.3	13.7
Total assets	$104.3	100.0%
Liabilities and Capital		
Bank loans	5.9	5.7%
Commercial paper	29.6	28.4
Debt		
Short-term	6.2	5.9
Long-term	36.0	34.5
Other	11.5	11.0
Capital, surplus, and undivided profits	15.1	14.5
Total liabilities and capital	$104.3	100.0%

business credit institutions
Institutions that specialize in making business loans.

factoring
The process of purchasing accounts receivable from corporations (often at a discount), usually with no recourse to the seller if the receivables go bad.

captive finance company
A finance company that is wholly owned by a parent corporation.

(e.g., used cars) that depository institutions do not find acceptable. **Business credit institutions** (e.g., CIT Group and FleetBoston Financial) are companies that provide financing to corporations, especially through equipment leasing and **factoring,** in which the finance company purchases accounts receivable from corporate customers. These accounts are purchased at a discount from their face value, and the finance company specializes in and assumes the responsibility for collecting the accounts receivable. As a result, the corporate customer no longer has the worry of whether the accounts receivable may or may not be delayed and thus receives cash for sales faster than the time it takes customers to pay their bills. Many finance companies perform more than one of these three services (e.g., GMAC).

The industry is quite concentrated, with the largest 20 firms accounting for more than 75 percent of its assets. In addition, many of the largest finance companies, such as GMAC, tend to be wholly owned or captive subsidiaries of major manufacturing companies. A major role of a **captive finance company** is to provide financing for the purchase of products manufactured by the parent, as GMAC does for cars. In turn, the parent company is often a major source of debt finance for the captive finance company.

Table 6–3 lists the top ten finance companies (in terms of total receivables) as of 2003. GECC is the largest with receivables totaling $233.1 billion. In late 2000, Associates First Capital, then the fourth largest finance company and the largest consumer finance company, was acquired by Citigroup for $31.1 billion. The acquisition resulted in Citigroup becoming the industry's third largest receivables financer with receivables of $130.4 billion in 2003 (behind Ford Motor Credit Company with $202.5 billion).

TABLE 6–3
The Largest Finance Companies

Source: Insurance Information Institute.

Company Name	Total Receivables (in $ millions)
General Electric Capital Services	$233,086
Ford Motor Credit Company	202,528
Citigroup	130,400
Household International, Inc.	107,496
MBNA Corp.	107,258
SLM Corp.	79,557
First USA	74,000
American Express	73,800
Capital One Financial	59,746
Discover Bank	51,565

Concept Questions

1. What are the three major types of finance companies? What types of customers does each serve?
2. What is a captive finance company?

BALANCE SHEET AND RECENT TRENDS

Assets

As mentioned above, finance companies provide three basic lending services: customer lending, consumer lending, and business lending. In Table 6–1 we show the balance sheet of finance companies in 2003. As you can see, business and consumer loans (called accounts receivable) are the major assets held by finance companies, accounting for 51.9 percent of total assets. Comparing the figures in Table 6–1 to those in Table 6–2 for 1977, we see that 95.1 percent of total assets were consumer and business loans in 1977. Over the last 26 years, finance companies have replaced consumer and business loans with increasing amounts of real estate loans and other assets, although these loans have not become dominant, as is the case with depository institutions. However, like commercial banks, these activities create credit risk, interest rate risk, and liquidity risk that finance company managers must evaluate and manage.

Table 6–4 shows the breakdown of the industry's loans from 1995 through 2003 for consumer, real estate, and business lending. In recent years, the fastest growing areas of asset business have been in the nonconsumer finance areas, especially leasing and business lending. In December 2003 consumer loans constituted 40.4 percent of all finance company loans, mortgages represented 18.0 percent, and business loans comprised the largest category of loans at 41.6 percent. The growth in leasing was encouraged by tax incentives provided under the 1981 Economic Recovery Tax Act.

Consumer Loans

Consumer loans consist of motor vehicle loans and leases, other consumer loans, and securitized loans from each category. Motor vehicle loans and leases are traditionally the major type of consumer loan (75.3 percent of the consumer loan portfolio in December 2003). As can be seen from Table 6–5, finance companies generally charge higher rates for automobile loans than do commercial banks. In 1995 and 1996, auto finance companies charged interest rates 1.62 to 0.79 percent, respectively, higher than those of commercial banks. Nevertheless, sometimes these rates get lowered dramatically. For example, because new car sales by U.S.

TABLE 6–4
Finance Company
Loans Outstanding
from 1995 through
2003[1] (in billions of
dollars)

Source: Federal Reserve
Board, "Flow of Fund Ac-
counts," various issues.
www.federalreserve.gov

	1995	2000	2003	Percent of Total, 2003
Consumer	$285.8	$ 475.9	$ 538.3	40.4%
Motor vehicle loans	81.1	141.6	197.0	14.8
Motor vehicle leases	80.8	108.2	70.0	5.2
Revolving[2]	28.5	37.6	37.6	2.8
Other[3]	42.6	41.3	51.6	3.9
Securitized assets				
Motor vehicle loans	34.8	97.1	132.8	10.0
Motor vehicle leases	3.5	6.6	5.5	0.4
Revolving	n.a.	27.5	31.6	2.4
Other	14.7	16.0	12.2	0.9
Real estate	72.4	198.9	239.6	18.0
One- to four-family	n.a.	130.6	152.2	11.4
Other	n.a.	41.7	46.7	3.5
Securitized real estate assets[4]				
One- to four-family	n.a.	24.7	36.9	2.8
Other	n.a.	1.9	3.8	0.3
Business	331.2	525.0	553.2	41.6
Motor vehicles	66.5	75.5	74.9	5.6
Retail loans	21.8	18.3	18.2	1.4
Wholesale loans[5]	36.6	39.7	40.4	3.0
Leases	8.0	17.6	16.3	1.2
Equipment	188.0	283.5	277.6	20.9
Loans	58.6	70.2	74.6	5.6
Leases	129.4	213.3	203.0	15.3
Other business receivables[6]	47.2	99.4	105.0	7.9
Securitized assets[4]				
Motor vehicles	20.6	37.8	48.5	3.6
Retail loans	1.8	3.2	2.2	0.2
Wholesale loans	18.8	32.5	44.2	3.3
Leases	n.a.	2.2	2.1	0.1
Equipment	8.1	23.1	22.1	1.7
Loans	5.3	15.5	12.5	1.0
Leases	2.8	7.6	9.6	0.7
Other business receivables[6]	0.8	5.6	25.1	1.9
Total	$689.5	$1,199.8	$1,331.1	100.0%

[1]Owned receivables are those carried on the balance sheet of the institution. Managed receivables are outstanding balances of pools upon which securities have been issued; these balances are no longer carried on the balance sheets of the loan originator.
[2]Excludes revolving credit reported as held by depository institutions that are subsidiaries of finance companies.
[3]Includes personal cash loans, mobile home loans, and loans to purchase other types of consumer goods, such as appliances, apparel, boats, and recreation vehicles.
[4]Outstanding balances of pools on which securities have been issued; these balances are no longer carried on the balance sheets of the loan originator.
[5]Credit arising from transactions between manufacturers and dealers, that is, floor plan financing.
[6]Includes loans on commercial accounts receivable, factored commercial accounts, and receivable dealer capital; small loans used primarily for business or farm purposes; and wholesale and lease paper for mobile homes, campers, and travel trailers.

firms in the late 1990s were lower than normal, auto finance companies owned by the major auto manufacturers slashed interest rates on new car loans (some to as low as 0.9 percent). Moreover, after the terrorist attacks in September 2001, the major auto manufacturers lowered new car rates to 0.0 percent in an attempt to boost sales. Some of these 0.0 percent rates continued to be offered into 2004 as the U.S. economy struggled to recover and the general level of interest rates remained low.

TABLE 6–5 Consumer Credit Interest Rates for 1995 through 2003

Type	1995	1996	1997	2000	2001	2002	2003
Commercial bank new car	9.57%	9.05%	9.02%	9.34%	8.50%	7.62%	6.93%
Auto finance company new car	11.19%	9.84%	7.12%	6.61%	5.65%	4.29%	3.40%
Difference in commercial bank versus finance company rate	1.62%	0.79%	−1.90%	−2.73%	−2.85%	3.33%	3.53%

Source: Federal Reserve Board, "Flow of Fund Accounts," March 2004. *www.federalreserve.gov*

subprime lender
A finance company that lends to high-risk customers.

Notice that the difference between new car loans at commercial banks and finance companies continued to widen throughout the early 2000s. By 2003 finance companies were charging over 3.5 percent less on new car loans than commercial banks. However, other than for new car loans, these types of low rates are fairly rare.

The higher rates finance companies charge for consumer loans are mostly due to the fact that finance companies attract riskier customers than commercial banks. In fact, customers who seek individual (or business) loans from finance companies are often those judged too risky to obtain loans from commercial banks or thrifts.[2] It is, in fact, possible for individuals to get a loan from a **subprime lender** finance company (a finance company that lends to high-risk customers) even with a bankruptcy on their records. For example, in 1997 Jayhawk Acceptance Corp., one of a group of finance companies that lent money to used-car buyers with poor or no credit, began marketing loans for tummy tucks, hair transplants, and other procedures that are not usually covered by health insurance. Jayhawk entered into contracts with doctors to lend money to their patients who were seeking cosmetic surgery or some types of dental procedures. Borrowers who paid the loans within a year paid an annual rate of 9.9 percent, while those who repaid within the maximum of two years paid 13.9 percent per year. Left unanswered, however, was what Jayhawk could repossess if a borrower defaulted on a loan. As discussed below, Jayhawk declared bankruptcy in late 1997. Banks would rarely do this. Most finance companies that offer these types of loans charge rates commensurate with the higher risk, and there are a few **loan shark** companies that prey on desperate consumers, charging exorbitant rates as high as 30 percent per annum or more.

loan sharks
Subprime lenders that charge unfairly exorbitant rates to desperate subprime borrowers.

Other consumer loans include personal cash loans, mobile home loans, and private-label credit card loans (e.g., Discover card) to purchase other types of consumer goods, such as appliances, apparel, general merchandise, and recreational vehicles. In 2003 other consumer loans made up 24.7 percent of the consumer loan portfolio of finance companies.

Mortgages

securitized mortgage assets
Mortgages packaged and used as assets backing secondary market securities.

Residential and commercial mortgages have become a major component in finance company portfolios, although, referring again to Table 6–2, they did not generally deal in mortgages in 1977. However, since finance companies are not subject to as extensive regulations as are banks, they are often willing to issue mortgages to riskier borrowers than commercial banks. They compensate for this additional risk by charging higher interest rates and fees. Mortgages include all loans secured by liens on any type of real estate. Mortgages can be made either directly or as **securitized mortgage assets.** Securitization of mortgages involves the

[2] We look at the analysis of borrower (credit) risk in Chapter 11.

pooling of a group of mortgages with similar characteristics, the removal of these mortgages from the balance sheet, and the subsequent sale of interests in the pool to secondary market investors. Securitization of mortgages results in the creation of mortgage-backed securities (e.g., government agency securities, collateralized mortgage obligations), which can be traded in secondary mortgage markets.[3,4] While removed from its balance sheet, the finance company that originates the mortgage may still service the mortgage portfolio for a fee.

The mortgages in the loan portfolio can be first mortgages or second mortgages in the form of home equity loans. **Home equity loans** allow customers to borrow on a line of credit secured with a second mortgage on their home. Home equity loans have become very profitable for finance companies since the Tax Reform Act of 1986 was passed, disallowing the tax deductibility of consumers' interest payments other than those on home mortgages. Specifically, interest on (first and second) mortgages secured by residential real estate is tax deductible. Interest on other types of individual loans—such as consumer (e.g., credit card) loans—is not eligible for a tax deduction. Also, the bad debt expense and administrative costs on home equity loans are lower than those on other finance company loans. For example, a study by the Consumer Bankers Association found that in 1997–1998 more than 4.2 million households converted $26 billion in credit card debt to home equity loans. Further, in 2003, the average outstanding balance on home equity loans was $69,513, up from $26,627 in 1999.

home equity loans
Loans that let customers borrow on a line of credit secured with a second mortgage on their home.

www.cbanet.org

Business Loans

Business loans represent the largest portion of the loan portfolio of finance companies. Finance companies have several advantages over commercial banks in offering services to small business customers.[5] First, as mentioned earlier, they are not subject to regulations that restrict the types of products and services they can offer. Second, because finance companies do not accept deposits, they have no bank-type regulators looking directly over their shoulders.[6] Third, being in many cases subsidiaries of corporate-sector holding companies, finance companies often have substantial industry and product expertise. Fourth, as mentioned in regard to consumer loans, finance companies are more willing to accept risky customers than are commercial banks. Fifth, finance companies generally have lower overheads than banks have; for example, they do not need tellers or branches for taking deposits.

The major subcategories of business loans are retail and wholesale motor vehicle loans and leases (13.5 percent of all business loans in 2003), equipment loans (50.2 percent), other business loans (19.0 percent), and securitized business assets (17.3 percent). Motor vehicle loans consist of retail loans that assist in transactions between the retail seller of the product and the ultimate consumer (i.e., passenger car fleets and commercial land vehicles for which licenses are required). Wholesale

---

[3] We discuss the securitization of mortgages in more detail in Chapter 28.

[4] Mortgage servicing is a fee-related business whereby, after mortgages are securitized, the flow of mortgage repayments (interest and principal) has to be collected and passed on (by the mortgage servicer) to investors in either whole mortgage loan packages or securitization vehicles such as pass-through securities (see Chapter 28). In undertaking this intermediation activity, the servicer charges a fee.

[5] See also M. Carey et al., "Does Corporate Lending by Banks and Finance Companies Differ? Evidence on Specialization in Private Debt Contracting," *Journal of Finance* 53 (June 1998), pp. 845–78.

[6] Finance companies do, of course, have market participants looking over their shoulders and monitoring their activities.

loans are loan agreements between parties other than the companies' consumers. For example, GMAC provides wholesale financing to GM dealers for inventory floor plans in which GMAC pays for GM dealers' auto inventory received from GM. GMAC puts a lien on each car on the showroom floor. While the dealer pays periodic interest on the floor plan loan, it is not until the car is sold that the dealer pays for the car. These activities extend to retail and wholesale leasing of motor vehicles as well.

Business-lending activities of finance companies also include equipment loans, with the finance company either owning or leasing the equipment directly to its industrial customer or providing the financial backing for a leveraged lease, a working capital loan, or a loan to purchase or remodel the customer's facility. Finance companies often prefer to lease equipment rather than sell and finance the purchase of equipment. One reason for this is that repossession of the equipment in the event of default is less complicated when the finance company retains its title (by leasing). Further a lease agreement generally requires no down payment, making a lease more attractive to the business customer. Finally, when the finance company retains ownership of the equipment (by leasing), it receives a tax deduction in the form of depreciation expense on the equipment. Other business loans include loans to businesses to finance accounts receivable, factored commercial accounts, small farm loans, and wholesale and lease paper for mobile homes, campers, and trailers.

Liabilities and Equity

To finance asset growth, finance companies have relied primarily on short-term commercial paper and other debt (longer-term notes and bonds). Thus, management of liquidity risk is quite different from that in commercial banks that mostly rely on deposits (see Chapter 2). As reported in Table 6–1, in 2003 commercial paper amounted to $127.3 billion (8.7 percent of total assets), while other debt (debt due to parents and debt not elsewhere classified) totaled $726.8 billion (49.5 percent) and bank loans totaled $47.3 billion (3.2 percent). Comparing these figures with those for 1977 (in Table 6–2), commercial paper was used more in 1977 (28.4 percent of total liabilities and capital), while other debt (short- and long-term) was less significant as a source of financing (40.4 percent). Finance companies also now rely less heavily on bank loans for financing. In 1977, bank loans accounted for 5.7 percent of total financing. Much of the change in funding sources is due to the strong economy and low interest rates in the U.S. long-term debt markets in the early 2000s. Finally, in 2003 finance companies' capital-to-assets ratio was 15.1 percent, higher than the 14.5 percent in 1977.[7]

As discussed above, unlike banks and thrifts, finance companies cannot issue deposits. Rather, to finance assets, finance companies rely heavily on short-term commercial paper, with many having direct sale programs in which commercial paper is sold directly to mutual funds and other institutional investors on a continuous day-by-day basis. Indeed, finance companies are now the largest issuers in the short-term commercial paper market. Most commercial paper issues have maturities of 30 days or less, although they can be issued with maturities of up to 270 days.[8]

---

[7] For more on the relative capital adequacy of finance companies versus banks, see M. L. Kwast and S. W. Passmore, "The Subsidy Provided by the Federal Safety Net: Theory, Measurement and Containment," Federal Reserve Board of Governors Working Paper 1997–58.

[8] Commercial paper issued with a maturity longer than 270 days has to be registered with the SEC (i.e., it is treated the same as publicly placed bonds).

Industry Performance

In the early 2000s, the outlook for the industry as a whole is bright. Interest rates are at historical lows. Mortgage refinancing has grown and loan demand among lower- and middle-income consumers is strong. Because many of their potential borrowers have very low savings, no major slowdown in the demand for finance company services is expected. The largest finance companies—those that lend to less risky individual and business customers and with few subprime borrowers (e.g., Household International)—are experiencing strong profits and loan growth. (The industry's assets as a whole grew at a rate of almost 8 percent in 2003.) As such, the most successful finance companies are becoming takeover targets for other financial service as well as industrial firms. For example, as discussed earlier, Citigroup acquired Associates First Capital to create the largest full-service financial institution in the country. In May 2001 American General (the then thirteenth largest finance company) was acquired by American International Group (AIG), one of the country's largest life insurance companies. Finally, in 2003 Household International was acquired by British commercial bank HSBC Holdings for $14.9 billion. This acquisition was one of the largest M&As of any kind in 2003. These are just other examples of integration and consolidation among firms in the financial services sector.

Nevertheless, problems for industry participants who specialize in loans to relatively lower-quality customers have been well publicized. After flourishing for much of the 1990s, subprime lending crashed in the late 1990s, sending some lenders into bankruptcy. For example, Jayhawk Acceptance Corporation, which financed car loans to some of the nation's riskiest buyers, filed for bankruptcy in 1997. A major problem stemmed from finance companies' accounting practices, which let them record fees and profits on loans up front when, in fact, earnings on loans come in gradually, if at all. In the late 1990s, as other lenders began competing for subprime borrowers, customers started repaying "high interest rate" loans early by refinancing them elsewhere.

Indeed, some analysts predicted a shakeout in the market for subprime mortgage issuers as well. For example, Cityscape Financial Corp. of Elmsford, New York, was close to bankruptcy in the late 1990s, as were some of this sector's biggest firms (e.g., Aames Financial Corp., Advanta, and FirstPlus Financial Group). Other leading subprime lenders (e.g., The Money Store and Associates First Capital) ceased trading as they were merged into large financial institutions. For example, in 1998 First Union Bank, the second largest bank home equity lender, acquired The Money Store, the second largest nonbank home equity lender, to create the largest home equity lending firm in the country. Similarly, in September 2000 Citigroup announced plans to buy Associates First Capital, the country's second largest subprime lender, for $31.1 billion. These combinations, however, did not necessarily work out. In June 2000, First Union announced that they were shutting down The Money Store, stating that they had made a bad acquisition. Further, Citigroup is incurring some regulatory and reputation problems as a result of its acquisition of Associates First Capital. Specifically, the Federal Trade Commission filed a complaint in March 2001 against Associates First Capital and Citigroup alleging systematic and widespread abusive lending practices, deceptive marketing practices, and violations of the Truth in Lending Act, the Fair Credit Reporting Act, and the Equal Opportunity Act. The FTC claimed that Associates engaged in widespread deceptive practices, hid essential information from consumers, misrepresented loan terms, and packed optional fees to raise the costs of

www.household.com

www.citigroup.com

www.ftc.gov

the loans. The FTC sought $1 billion in refunds from Citigroup to its customers for the illegal tactics. In September 2002, the FTC agreed to take a $200 million payment from Citigroup to settle allegations of predatory lending. It is problems such as these that may deter future acquisitions, especially of finance companies specializing in the subprime areas.

Another area of this industry that has experienced its ups and downs is the electronic lending area. In the late 1990s electronic lending boomed. Electronic lending allows customers to find, apply for, and close on personal loans (mainly mortgages) completely over the Internet. For example, the first such company, E-Loan, debuted in 1997, initially as a third party, providing an electronic means of matching consumers with lenders (collecting a fee from the lender for bringing the parties together). Upon entering their personal information, customers using electronic lending are presented with multiple options for loans, and sometimes advised on which loan suits their needs best. Customers can keep track of the loan status through the closing—something that often proves difficult when obtaining a loan through the traditional channels. The emphasis with electronic lending is on securing the lowest possible cost for the borrower. While this segment of the industry initially boomed (some estimated that 10 percent of all mortgages would be secured online by 2003), like many dot-com companies, these finance companies took a substantial hit in the early 2000s.

Concept Questions

1. How have the major assets held by finance companies changed in the last 25 years?
2. How do subprime lender finance company customers differ from consumer loan customers at banks?
3. What advantages do finance companies offer over commercial banks to small business customers?

REGULATION

The Federal Reserve defines a finance company as a firm (other than a depository institution) whose primary assets are loans to individuals and businesses.[9] Finance companies, like depository institutions, are financial intermediaries that borrow funds for relending, making a profit on the difference between the interest rate on borrowed funds and the rate charged on the loans. Also like depository institutions, finance companies are subject to any state-imposed usury ceilings on the maximum loan rate assigned to any individual customer and are regulated as to the extent to which they can collect on delinquent loans (e.g., legal mechanisms to be followed). However, because finance companies do not accept deposits, they are not subject to extensive oversight by any specific federal or state regulators as are banks or thrifts—even though they offer services that compete directly with those of depository institutions (e.g., consumer installment loans and mortgages).[10] The lack of regulatory oversight for these companies enables them to offer a wide scope of "bank-like" services and yet avoid the expense of regulatory compliance, such as that imposed on banks and thrifts by the Community Reinvestment Act of 1977, which requires these institutions to keep and file extensive

---

[9] Whereas a bank is defined as an institution that *both* accepts deposits and makes loans.

[10] Like any corporation, they are subject to SEC disclosure rules.

reports showing that they are not discriminating in their lending practices in their local communities.

Further since finance companies are heavy borrowers in the capital markets and do not enjoy the same regulatory "safety net" as banks, they need to signal their solvency and safety to investors.[11] Signals of solvency and safety are usually sent by holding higher equity or capital-asset ratios—and therefore lower leverage ratios—than banks hold. For example, in 2003 the aggregate balance sheet (Table 6–1) shows a capital–assets ratio of 15.1 percent for finance companies. This can be compared to the capital–asset ratio for commercial banks of 9.10 percent reported in Table 2–5 for commercial banks. Larger, captive finance companies also use default protection guarantees from their parent companies and/or guarantees such as letters of credit or lines of credit purchased for a fee from high-quality commercial or investment banks as additional protection against insolvency risk and as a device to increase their ability to raise additional funds in the capital and money markets. Thus, this group will tend to operate with lower capital-to-asset ratios than smaller finance companies. Given that there is little regulatory oversight of this industry, having sufficient capital and access to financial guarantees are critical to their continued ability to raise funds. Thus, finance companies operate more like nonfinancial, nonregulated companies than other types of financial institutions examined in this text.

Concept Questions

1. Since finance companies seem to compete in the same lending markets as banks, why aren't they subject to the same regulations as banks?
2. How do finance companies signal solvency and safety to investors?

GLOBAL ISSUES

Because regulations in most foreign countries are not as restrictive as those in the United States, finance companies in foreign countries are generally subsidiaries of commercial banks or industrial firms. For those finance companies owned by commercial banks, as the bank goes, so does the finance company. For example, the economic recession in Japan in the late 1990s and early 2000s and the resulting huge volume of nonperforming property loans in Japanese commercial banks depleted the banks' capital and restricted their ability to lend to finance company subsidiaries. The result has been some attractive opportunities for others. For example, in January 1999 GE Capital Corporation (GECC) agreed to buy (for $7 billion) Japan Leasing Corporation (JLC), the Japanese lending unit of Long-Term Credit Bank of Japan, in the biggest acquisition ever involving a Japanese company. GECC bought only the healthy assets of JLC shortly after its parent, Long-Term Credit Bank, was declared insolvent and nationalized because of its huge problems with nonperforming property loans. Historically, assets of companies such as JLC would never have been acquired by a foreign investor like GECC, but the extreme size of nonperforming property loans at Japan's biggest banks restricted their ability to undertake any rescue missions like that of JLC.

---

[11] That is, they have no access to the deposit insurance fund or to the Federal Reserve discount window (see Chapters 17 and 19). On the other hand, they do not have to pay deposit insurance premiums or meet regulatory imposed minimum capital standards.

Summary

This chapter provided an overview of the finance company industry. This industry competes directly with depository institutions for its high-quality (prime) loan customers by specializing in consumer loans, real estate loans, and business loans. The industry also services subprime (high-risk) borrowers deemed too risky for most depository institutions. However, because firms in this industry do not accept deposits, they are not regulated to the same extent as are depository institutions. Because they do not have access to deposits for their funding, finance companies rely heavily on short- and long-term debt, especially commercial paper. Currently, the industry is generally growing and profitable, although the subprime lending sector of the industry is experiencing some financial problems as consumer default rates on loans and credit cards rise (see Chapter 11).

Questions and Problems

1. What is the primary function of finance companies? How do finance companies differ from commercial banks?

2. What are the three major types of finance companies? To which market segments do each of these types of companies provide service?

3. What have been the major changes in the accounts receivable balances of finance companies over the 26-year period 1977–2003?

4. What are the major types of consumer loans? Why are the rates charged by consumer finance companies typically higher than those charged by commercial banks?

5. Why have home equity loans become popular? What are securitized mortgage assets?

6. What advantages do finance companies have over commercial banks in offering services to small business customers? What are the major subcategories of business loans? Which category is the largest?

7. What have been the primary sources of financing for finance companies?

8. How do finance companies make money? What risks does this process entail? How do these risks differ for a finance company versus a commercial bank?

9. Compare Tables 6–1 and 4–7. Which firms have higher ratios of capital to total assets: finance companies or securities firms? What does this comparison indicate about the relative strengths of these two types of firms?

10. How does the amount of equity as a percentage of total assets compare for finance companies and commercial banks? What accounts for this difference?

11. Why do finance companies face less regulation than do commercial banks? How does this advantage translate into performance advantages? What is the major performance disadvantage?

Web Question

12. Go to the Federal Reserve's Web site at **www.federalreserve.gov** and get the latest information on finance company consumer, real estate, and business lending using the following steps. Click on "Economic Research and Data." Click on "Statistics: Releases and Historical Data." Click on "Finance Companies:

Releases." Click on the most recent date. This downloads a file onto your computer that contains the relevant data. How have these numbers changed since 2003, reported in Table 6–4?

S&P Questions

13. Go to Standard & Poor's Market Insight Web site at **www.mhhe.com/edumarketinsight** and identify the industry constituents for Capital One Financial Corp. through the Related Links using the following steps. Click on "Educational Version of Market Insight." Enter your Site ID and click on "Login." Click on "Company." Enter "COF" in the "Ticker:" box and click on "Go!" This will take you to the information on Capital One Financial Corp. Click on "Related Links." Click on "Consumer Finance." Click on "GICS Sub-Industry Constituents." This will download the list of industry constituents for Capital One Financial Corp.

14. Go to Standard & Poor's Market Insight Web site at **www.mhhe.com/edumarketinsight** and find the most recent balance sheet for Capital One Financial Corp (COF) and American Express (AXP) using the following steps. Click on "Educational Version of Market Insight." Enter your Site ID and click on "Login." Click on "Company." Enter "COF" in the "Ticker:" box and click on "Go!" Click on "Excel Analytics." Click on "FS Ann. Balance Sheet." This will download the balance sheet for Capital One Financial Corp., which contains the balances for consumer loans, commercial loans, mortgage loans, and total assets. Repeat the process by entering "AXP" in the "Ticker:" box to get information on American Express. Compare the ratios of consumer loans to total assets, business (commercial) loans to total assets, and real estate (mortgage) loans to total assets from these balance sheets with those for the finance company industry listed in Table 6–1.

Pertinent Web Sites

AIG American General Finance	www.aigag.com
Board of Governors of the Federal Reserve	www.federalreserve.gov
CIT Group, Inc.	www.citgroup.com
Citigroup	www.citigroup.com
Consumer Bankers Association	www.cbanet.org
Federal Trade Commission	www.ftc.gov
Ford Motor Credit Corp.	www.fordcredit.com
General Electric Capital Corp.	www.ge.com
General Motors Acceptance Corp.	www.gmacfs.com
Household International	www.household.com

Chapter **Seven**

Risks of Financial Intermediation

INTRODUCTION

A major objective of FI management is to increase the FI's returns for its owners. This often comes, however, at the cost of increased risk. This chapter introduces the various risks facing FIs: interest rate risk, market risk, credit risk, off-balance-sheet risk, technology and operational risk, foreign exchange risk, country or sovereign risk, liquidity risk, and insolvency risk. Table 7–1 presents a brief definition of each of these risks. By the end of this chapter, you will have a basic understanding of the variety and complexity of risks facing managers of modern FIs. In the remaining chapters of the text, we look at the measurement and management of these risks in more detail. As will become clear throughout the rest of the textbook, the effective management of these risks is central to an FI's performance.[1] Indeed, it can be argued that the main business of FIs is to manage these risks.[2]

While over the last decade the profitability of U.S. financial institutions has been robust, the risks of financial intermediation have increased as the U.S. and overseas economies have become more integrated. For example, weakening economic conditions inside and outside the United States—especially in Asia and South America—have presented great risks for those FIs that operate in foreign countries and lend to foreign markets and customers. Even those FIs that do not have foreign customers can be exposed to foreign exchange and sovereign risk if their domestic customers have business dealings with foreign countries. As a result, FI managers must devote significant time to understanding and managing the various risks to which their FIs are exposed.

INTEREST RATE RISK

Chapter 1 discussed asset transformation as a key special function of FIs. Asset transformation involves an FI's buying primary securities or assets and issuing secondary securities or liabilities to fund asset purchases. The primary securities

---

[1] These risks are not necessarily unique to financial institutions. Every global, nonfinancial corporation faces these risks as well, and managers of these firms must deal with these risks just as do managers of FIs.

[2] The book's Web site (**www.mhhe.com/saunders5e**) contains an overview of the evaluation of FI performance and risk exposure (Depository Institutions' Financial Statements and Analysis). Included are several accounting ratio–based, measures of risk.

TABLE 7–1
Risks Faced by Financial Intermediaries

Interest rate risk   The risk incurred by an FI when the maturities of its assets and liabilities are mismatched.

Market risk   The risk incurred from assets and liabilities in an FI's trading book due to changes in interest rates, exchange rates, and other prices.

Credit risk   The risk that promised cash flows from loans and securities held by FIs may not be paid in full.

Off-balance-sheet risk   The risk incurred by an FI as the result of activities related to its contingent assets and liabilities held off the balance sheet.

Technology risk   The risk incurred by an FI when its technological investments do not produce anticipated cost savings.

Operational risk   The risk that existing technology, auditing, monitoring, and other support systems may malfunction or break down.

Foreign exchange risk   The risk that exchange rate changes can affect the value of an FI's assets and liabilities denominated in nondomestic currencies.

Country or sovereign risk   The risk that repayments to foreign lenders or investors may be interrupted because of restrictions, intervention, or interference from foreign governments.

Liquidity risk   The risk that a sudden surge in liability withdrawals may require an FI to liquidate assets in a very short period of time and at less than fair market prices.

Insolvency risk   The risk that an FI may not have enough capital to offset a sudden decline in the value of its assets.

interest rate risk
The risk incurred by an FI when the maturities of its assets and liabilities are mismatched.

purchased by FIs often have maturity and liquidity characteristics different from those of the secondary securities FIs sell. In mismatching the maturities of assets and liabilities as part of their asset-transformation function, FIs potentially expose themselves to **interest rate risk.**

EXAMPLE 7–1
Impact of an Interest Rate Increase on an FI's Profits When the Maturity of Its Assets Exceeds the Maturity of Its Liabilities

Consider an FI that issues $100 million of liabilities of one-year maturity to finance the purchase of $100 million of assets with a two-year maturity. We show this situation in the following time lines:

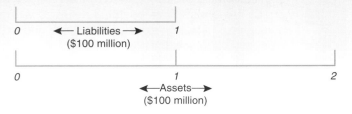

In these time lines the FI can be viewed as being "short-funded." That is, the maturity of its liabilities is less than the maturity of its assets.

Suppose the cost of funds (liabilities) for an FI is 9 percent per annum and the interest return on an asset is 10 percent per annum. Over the first year the FI can lock in a profit spread of 1 percent (10 percent − 9 percent) times $100 million by borrowing short term (for one year) and lending long term (for two years). Thus, its profit is $1 million (.01 × $100 m).

However, its profits for the second year are uncertain. If the level of interest rates does not change, the FI can *refinance* its liabilities at 9 percent and lock in a 1 percent, or $1 million, profit for the second year as well. There is always a risk, however, that interest rates will

refinancing risk
The risk that the cost of rolling over or re-borrowing funds will rise above the returns being earned on asset investments.

change between years 1 and 2. If interest rates were to rise and the FI can borrow new one-year liabilities only at 11 percent in the second year, its profit spread in the second year would actually be negative; that is, 10 percent − 11 percent = −1 percent, or the FI's loss is $1 million (−.01 × $100 m). The positive spread earned in the first year by the FI from holding assets with a longer maturity than its liabilities would be offset by a negative spread in the second year. Note that if interest rates were to rise by more than 1 percent in the second year, the FI would stand to take losses over the two-year period as a whole. As a result, when an FI holds longer-term assets relative to liabilities, it potentially exposes itself to **refinancing risk.** This is the risk that the cost of rolling over or reborrowing funds could be more than the return earned on asset investments. The classic example of this type of mismatch was demonstrated by U.S. savings institutions during the 1980s (see Chapter 2).

EXAMPLE 7–2

Impact of an Interest Rate Decrease When the Maturity of an FI's Liabilities Exceeds the Maturity of Its Assets

An alternative balance sheet structure would have the FI borrowing $100 million for a longer term than the $100 million of assets in which it invests. In the time lines below the FI is "long-funded." The maturity of its liabilities is longer than the maturity of its assets. Using a similar example, suppose the FI borrowed funds at 9 percent per annum for two years and invested the funds in an asset that yields 10 percent for one year. This situation is shown as follows:

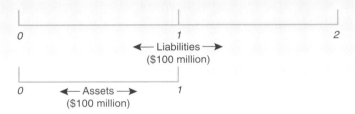

In this case, the FI is also exposed to an interest rate risk; by holding shorter-term assets relative to liabilities, it faces uncertainty about the interest rate at which it can reinvest funds in the second period. As before, the FI locks in a one-year profit spread of 1 percent, or $1 million. At the end of the first year, the asset matures and the funds that have been borrowed for two years have to be reinvested. Suppose interest rates fall between the first and second years so that in the second year the return on $100 million invested in new one-year assets is 8 percent. The FI would face a loss, or negative spread, in the second year of 1 percent (that is, 8 percent asset return minus 9 percent cost of funds), or the FI loses $1 million (−.01 × $100 m). The positive spread earned in the first year by the FI from holding assets with a shorter maturity than its liabilities is offset by a negative spread in the second year. Thus, the FI is exposed to **reinvestment risk;** by holding shorter-term assets relative to liabilities, it faced uncertainty about the interest rate at which it could reinvest funds borrowed for a longer period. In recent years, good examples of this exposure have been provided by banks that have borrowed fixed-rate deposits while investing in floating-rate loans, that is, loans whose interest rates are changed or adjusted frequently.

reinvestment risk
The risk that the returns on funds to be reinvested will fall below the cost of funds.

In addition to a potential refinancing or reinvestment risk that occurs when interest rates change, an FI faces *market value* risk as well. Remember that the market (or fair) value of an asset or liability is conceptually equal to the present value of current and future cash flows from that asset or liability. Therefore, rising interest rates increase the discount rate on those cash flows and reduce the market value of that asset or liability. Conversely, falling interest rates increase the market values of assets and liabilities. Moreover, mismatching maturities by holding longer-term assets than liabilities means that when interest rates rise, the market value of the FI's assets falls by a greater amount than its liabilities. This exposes the FI to the risk of economic loss and, potentially, the risk of insolvency.

If holding assets and liabilities with mismatched maturities exposes FIs to reinvestment (or refinancing) and market value risks, FIs can seek to hedge, or protect against, interest rate risk by matching the maturity of their assets and liabilities.[3] This has resulted in the general philosophy that matching maturities is somehow the best policy to hedge interest rate risk for FIs that are averse to risk. Note, however, that matching maturities is not necessarily consistent with an active asset-transformation function for FIs. That is, FIs cannot be asset transformers (e.g., transforming short-term deposits into long-term loans) and direct balance sheet matchers or hedgers at the same time. While reducing exposure to interest rate risk, matching maturities may also reduce the FI's profitability because returns from acting as specialized risk-bearing asset transformers are reduced. As a result, some FIs emphasize asset–liability maturity mismatching more than others. For example, banks and thrifts traditionally hold longer-term assets than liabilities, whereas life insurance companies tend to match the long-term nature of their liabilities with long-term assets. Finally, matching maturities hedges interest rate risk only in a very approximate rather than complete fashion. The reasons for this are technical, relating to the difference between the average life (or duration) and maturity of an asset or liability and whether the FI partly funds its assets with equity capital as well as debt liabilities. In the preceding simple examples, the FI financed its assets completely with borrowed funds. In the real world, FIs use a mix of debt liabilities and stockholders' equity to finance asset purchases. When assets and debt liabilities are not equal, hedging risk (i.e., insulating FI's stockholder's equity values) may be achieved by not exactly matching the maturities (or average lives) of assets and liabilities. We discuss the causes of interest rate risk and methods used to measure interest rate risk in detail in Chapters 8 and 9. We discuss the methods and instruments used to hedge interest rate risk in Chapters 24 through 26.[4]

Concept Questions

1. What is refinancing risk? What type of FI best illustrated this concept in the 1980s?
2. Why does a rise in the level of interest rates adversely affect the market value of both assets and liabilities?
3. Explain the concept of maturity matching.

---

[3] This assumes that FIs can directly "control" the maturities of their assets and liabilities. As interest rates fall, many mortgage borrowers seek to "prepay" their existing loans and refinance at a lower rate. This prepayment risk—which is directly related to interest rate movements—can be viewed as a further interest rate–related risk. Prepayment risk is discussed in detail in Chapter 28.

[4] We assumed in our examples that interest payments are paid only at the end of each year and could be changed only then. In reality, many loan and deposit rates adjust frequently or float as market rates change. For example, suppose a bank makes a one-year loan whose interest rate and interest rate payments are adjusted each quarter while fully funding the loan with a one-year CD that pays principal and interest at the end of the year, Even though the maturities of the loan and CD are equal to a year, the FI would not be fully hedged in a cash flow sense against interest rate risk since changes in interest rates over the year affect the cash flows (interest payments) on the loan but not those on deposits. In particular, if interest rates were to fall, the FI might lose on the loan in terms of net interest income (interest revenue minus interest expense). The reason for this loss is that the average life of the loan in a cash flow sense is less than that of the deposit because cash flows on the loan are received, on average, earlier than are those paid on the deposit.

TABLE 7–2
The Investment (Banking) Book and Trading Book of a Commercial Bank

	Assets	Liabilities
Banking book	Loans	Capital
	Other illiquid assets	Deposits
Trading book	Bonds (long)	Bonds (short)
	Commodities (long)	Commodities (short)
	FX (long)	FX (short)
	Equities (long)	Equities (short)
	Derivatives* (long)	Derivatives* (short)

*Derivatives are off-balance-sheet items (as discussed in Chapter 13).

MARKET RISK

market risk
The risk incurred in the trading of assets and liabilities due to changes in interest rates, exchange rates, and other asset prices.

Market risk arises when FIs actively trade assets and liabilities (and derivatives) rather than holding them for longer-term investment, funding, or hedging purposes. Market risk is closely related to interest rate, equity return, and foreign exchange risk in that as these risks increase or decrease, the overall risk of the FI is affected. However, market risk adds another dimension resulting from its trading activity. Market risk is the incremental risk incurred by an FI when interest rate, foreign exchange, and equity return risks are combined with an active trading strategy, especially one that involves short trading horizons such as a day. Conceptually, an FI's trading portfolio can be differentiated from its investment portfolio on the basis of time horizon and secondary market liquidity. The trading portfolio contains assets, liabilities, and derivative contracts that can be quickly bought or sold on organized financial markets. The investment portfolio (or in the case of banks, the so-called banking book) contains assets and liabilities that are relatively illiquid and held for longer holding periods. Table 7–2 shows a hypothetical breakdown between banking book and trading book assets and liabilities. As can be seen, the banking book contains the majority of loans and deposits plus other illiquid assets. The trading book contains long and short positions in instruments such as bonds, commodities, foreign exchange (FX), equities, and derivatives.

With the increasing securitization of bank loans (e.g., mortgages), more and more assets have become liquid and tradable. Of course, with time, every asset and liability can be sold. While bank regulators have normally viewed tradable assets as those being held for horizons of less than one year, private FIs take an even shorter-term view. In particular, FIs are concerned about the fluctuation in value—or value at risk (VAR)—of their trading account assets and liabilities for periods as short as one day—so-called daily earnings at risk (DEAR)—especially if such fluctuations pose a threat to their solvency.

To see the type of risk involved in active trading, consider the case of Barings, the 200-year-old British merchant bank that failed as a result of trading losses in February 1995. In this case, the bank (or, more specifically, one trader, Nick Leeson) was betting that the Japanese Nikkei Stock Market Index would rise by buying futures on that index (some $8 billion worth). However, for a number of reasons—including the Kobe earthquake—the index actually fell. As a result, over a period of one month, the bank lost over $1.2 billion on its trading positions, rendering the bank insolvent.[5] That is, the losses on its futures positions exceeded the bank's own

[5] In 1995 Barings was acquired as a subsidiary of ING, a Dutch bank, and was fully integrated into ING in 2000.

equity capital resources. Of course, if the Nikkei Index had actually risen, the bank would have made very large profits and might still be in business. Another good example involves market risk incurred by commercial banks, investment banks, mutual funds, and other FIs as U.S. equity markets fell dramatically in value in July 2002. For instance, in a two-week period (from July 9, 2002, to July 20, 2002) the Dow Jones Industrial Average sank 1,255.64 points, 12.54 percent, from 9,274.90 to 8,019.26.

As the above examples illustrate, market, or trading, risk is present whenever an FI takes an open or unhedged long (buy) or sell (short) position in bonds, equities, and foreign exchange (as well as in commodities and derivative products), and prices change in a direction opposite to that expected. As a result, the more volatile are asset prices in the markets in which these instruments trade, the greater are the market risks faced by FIs that adopt open trading positions. This requires FI management (and regulators) to establish controls to limit positions taken by traders as well as to develop models to measure the market risk exposure of an FI on a day-to-day basis. These market risk measurement models are discussed in Chapter 10.

Concept Questions

1. What is market, or trading, risk?
2. What modern conditions have led to an increase in this particular type of risk for FIs?

CREDIT RISK

credit risk
The risk that the promised cash flows from loans and securities held by FIs may not be paid in full.

Credit risk arises because of the possibility that promised cash flows on financial claims held by FIs, such as loans or bonds, will not be paid in full. Virtually all types of FIs face this risk. However, in general, FIs that make loans or buy bonds with long maturities are more exposed than are FIs that make loans or buy bonds with short maturities. This means, for example, that banks, thrifts, and life insurance companies are more exposed to credit risk than are money market mutual funds and property–casualty insurance companies. If the principal on all financial claims held by FIs was paid in full on maturity and interest payments were made on the promised dates, FIs would always receive back the original principal lent plus an interest return. That is, they would face no credit risk. If a borrower defaults, however, both the principal loaned and the interest payments expected to be received are at risk. As a result, many financial claims issued by corporations and held by FIs promise a limited or fixed upside return (principal and interest payments to the lender) with a high probability and a large downside risk (loss of loan principal and promised interest) with a much smaller probability. Good examples of financial claims issued with these return-risk trade-offs are fixed-income coupon bonds issued by corporations and bank loans. In both cases, an FI holding these claims as assets earns the coupon on the bond or the interest promised on the loan if no borrower default occurs. In the event of default, however, the FI earns zero interest on the asset and may lose all or part of the principal lent, depending on its ability to lay claim to some of the borrower's assets through legal bankruptcy and insolvency proceedings. Accordingly, a key role of FIs involves screening and monitoring loan applicants to ensure that FI managers fund the most creditworthy loans (see Chapter 11).

The effects of credit risk are evident in Figure 7–1, which shows commercial bank charge-off (or write-off) rates for various types of loans. Notice, in particular,

FIGURE 7–1
Charge-Off Rates for Commercial Bank Lending Activities, 1984–2003

Source: FDIC, *Quarterly Banking Profile,* Second Quarter 2003. *www.fdic.gov*

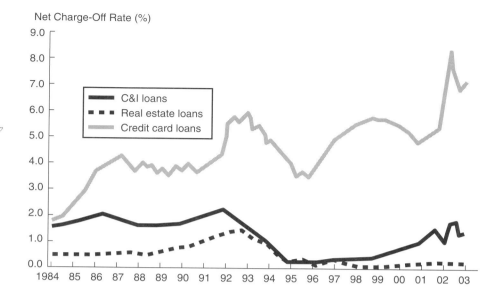

FIGURE 7–2
The Probability Distribution of Dollar Returns on Risky Debt (Loans/Bonds)

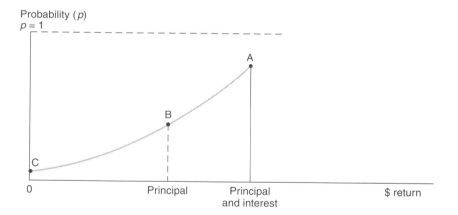

the high rate of charge-offs experienced on credit card loans in the 1980s, most of the 1990s, and the early 2000s. Indeed, credit card charge-offs by commercial banks increased persistently from the mid-1980s until 1993 and again from 1995 through early 1998. By 1998, charge-offs leveled off, and they even declined after 1998. However, a weak economy and an impending change in bankruptcy laws[6] resulted in a surge in credit card charge-offs in the early 2000s. Despite these losses, credit card loans extended by commercial banks (including unused balances) continue to grow, from $1.856 trillion in March 1997 to $4.075 trillion in June 2003.

Figure 7–2 presents the probability distribution of dollar returns for an FI investing in risky loans or bonds. The distribution indicates a high probability (but less than 1) of repayment of principal and promised interest in full (point A).

---

[6] In the early 2000s, the U.S. Congress was considering legislation that would make it more difficult for individuals to declare bankruptcy. This congressional activity brought about a rise in bankruptcy filings before any changes could take effect.

Problems with a borrower's cash flows can result in varying degrees of default risk. These range from partial or complete default on interest payments—the range between point A and point B in Figure 7–2—and partial or complete default on the principal lent, the range between point B and point C. Notice, too, that the probability of a complete default on principal and interest (point C) is often small. Nevertheless, because the probability of partial or complete default on bond and loan interest and principal exists, an FI must estimate expected default risk on these assets and demand risk premiums commensurate with the perceived risk exposure.

The potential loss an FI can experience from lending suggests that FIs need to monitor and collect information about borrowers whose assets are in their portfolios and to monitor those borrowers over time. Thus, managerial monitoring efficiency and credit risk management strategies directly affect the return and risks of the loan portfolio. Moreover, the credit risk distribution in Figure 7–2 is for an investment in a single asset exposed to default risk. One of the advantages FIs have over individual household investors is the ability to diversify some credit risk away by exploiting the law of large numbers in their asset investment portfolios (see Chapter 1). In the framework of Figure 7–2, diversification across assets, such as loans exposed to credit risk, reduces the overall credit risk in the asset portfolio and thus increases the probability of partial or full repayment of principal and/or interest, that is, moderates the long-tailed downside risk of the return distribution.

FIs earn the maximum dollar return when all bonds and loans pay off interest and principal in full. In reality, some loans or bonds default on interest payments, principal payments, or both. Thus, the mean return on the asset portfolio would be less than the maximum possible in a risk-free, no-default case. The effect of risk diversification is to truncate or limit the probabilities of the bad outcomes in the portfolio. In effect, diversification reduces individual **firm-specific credit risk,** such as the risk specific to holding the bonds or loans of General Motors or IBM, while leaving the FI still exposed to **systematic credit risk,** such as factors that simultaneously increase the default risk of all firms in the economy (e.g., an economic recession). We describe methods to measure the default risk of individual corporate claims such as bonds and loans in Chapter 11. In Chapter 12, we investigate methods of measuring the risk in portfolios of such claims. Chapter 27 discusses various methods—for example, loan sales, reschedulings, and a good bank–bad bank structure—to manage and control credit risk exposures better, while Chapters 24 to 26 discuss the role of the recently innovated credit derivative markets in hedging credit risk.

firm-specific credit risk
The risk of default of the borrowing firm associated with the specific types of project risk taken by that firm.

systematic credit risk
The risk of default associated with general economywide or macroconditions affecting all borrowers.

Concept Questions

1. Why does credit risk exist for FIs?
2. How does diversification affect an FI's credit risk exposure?

OFF-BALANCE-SHEET RISK

off-balance-sheet risk
The risk incurred by an FI due to activities related to contingent assets and liabilities.

One of the most striking trends for many modern FIs has been the growth in their off-balance-sheet activities and thus their **off-balance-sheet risk.** While all FIs to some extent engage in off-balance-sheet activities, most attention has been drawn to the activities of banks, especially large banks. By contrast, off-balance-sheet activities have been less of a concern to smaller depository institutions and many insurance companies. An off-balance-sheet activity, by definition, does not appear on an FI's current balance sheet since it does not involve holding a *current primary* claim (asset) or the issuance of a *current secondary* claim (liability). Instead, off-balance-sheet activities affect the *future* shape of an FI's balance sheet in that they involve the creation of contingent assets and liabilities that give rise to their potential (future) placement on the balance sheet. Thus, accountants place them "below the bottom line" of an FI's asset and liability balance sheet. A good example of an off-balance-sheet activity is the issuance of standby **letter of credit** guarantees by insurance companies and banks to back the issuance of municipal bonds. Many state and local governments could not issue such securities without bank or insurance company *letter of credit guarantees* that promise principal and interest payments to investors should the municipality default on its future obligations. Thus, the letter of credit guarantees payment should a municipal government (e.g., New York State) face financial problems in paying the promised interest payments and/or the principal on the bonds it issues. If a municipal government's cash flow is sufficiently strong so as to pay off the principal and interest on the debt it issues, the letter of credit guarantee issued by the FI expires unused. Nothing appears on the FI's balance sheet today or in the future. However, the fee earned for issuing the letter of credit guarantee appears on the FI's income statement.

As a result, the ability to earn fee income while not loading up or expanding the balance sheet has become an important motivation for FIs to pursue off-balance-sheet business. Unfortunately, this activity is not risk free. Suppose the municipal government defaults on its bond interest and principal payments. Then the contingent liability or guaranty the FI issued becomes an actual liability that appears on the FI's balance sheet. That is, the FI has to use its own equity to compensate investors in municipal bonds. Indeed, significant losses in off-balance-sheet activities can cause an FI to fail, just as major losses due to balance sheet default and interest rates risks can cause an FI to fail.

Letters of credit are just one example of off-balance-sheet activities. Others include loan commitments by banks, mortgage servicing contracts by thrifts, and positions in forwards, futures, swaps, and other derivative securities by almost all large FIs. While some of these activities are structured to reduce an FI's exposure to credit, interest rate, or foreign exchange risks, mismanagement or speculative use of these instruments can result in major losses to FIs. We detail the specific nature of the risks of off-balance-sheet activities more fully in Chapter 13.

letter of credit
A credit guaranty issued by an FI for a fee on which payment is contingent on some future event occurring.

Concept Questions

1. Why are letter of credit guarantees an off-balance-sheet item?
2. Why are FIs motivated to pursue off-balance-sheet business? What are the risks?

TECHNOLOGY AND OPERATIONAL RISKS

www.bis.org

Technology and operational risks are closely related and in recent years have caused great concern to FI managers and regulators alike. The Bank for International Settlements (BIS), the principal organization of central banks in the major economies of the world, defines operational risk (inclusive of technological risk) as "the risk of loss resulting from inadequate or failed internal processes, people, and systems or from external events."[7] A number of FIs add reputational risk and strategic risk (e.g., due to a failed merger) as part of a broader definition of operational risk.

[7] See Basel Committee on Bank Supervision, "Sound Practices for the Management and Supervision of Operational Risk," July 2002, p. 2, Basel, Switzerland.

Technological innovation has been a major growth area of FIs in recent years. In the 1980s and 1990s, banks, insurance companies, and investment companies all sought to improve operational efficiency with major investments in internal and external communications, computers, and an expanded technological infrastructure. For example, most banks provide depositors with the capabilities to check account balances, transfer funds between accounts, manage finances, pay bills, and perform other functions from their home personal computers. At the wholesale level, electronic transfer of funds through automated clearing houses (ACH) and wire transfer payment networks such as the Clearing House Interbank Payments Systems (CHIPS) have been developed. Indeed, the global financial services firm Citigroup has operations in more than 100 countries connected in real time by a proprietary-owned satellite system.

economies of scale
The degree to which an FI's average unit costs of producing financial services fall as its outputs of services increase.

The major objectives of technological expansion are to lower operating costs, increase profits, and capture new markets for the FI. In current terminology, the objective is to allow the FI to exploit, to the fullest extent possible, better potential economies of scale and economies of scope in selling its products. **Economies of scale** refer to an FI's ability to lower its average costs of operations by expanding its output of financial services. **Economies of scope** refer to an FI's ability to generate cost synergies by producing more than one output with the same inputs. For example, an FI could use the same information on the quality of customers stored in its computers to expand the sale of both loan products and insurance products. That is, the same information (e.g., age, job, size of family, income) can identify both potential loan and life insurance customers. Indeed, the attempt to better exploit such economies of scope lies behind megamergers such as that of Citicorp with Travelers to create Citigroup, an FI that services over 100 million customers in areas such as banking, securities, and insurance.

economies of scope
The degree to which an FI can generate cost synergies by producing multiple financial service products.

technology risk
The risk incurred by an FI when technological investments do not produce the cost savings anticipated.

Technology risk occurs when technological investments do not produce the anticipated cost savings in the form of either economies of scale or scope. Diseconomies of scale, for example, arise because of excess capacity, redundant technology, and/or organizational and bureaucratic inefficiencies (red tape) that become worse as an FI grows in size. Diseconomies of scope arise when an FI fails to generate perceived synergies or cost savings through major new technology investments. We describe the measurement and evidence of economies of scale and scope in FIs in Chapter 14. Technological risk can result in major losses in the competitive efficiency of an FI and, ultimately, in its long-term failure. Similarly, gains from technological investments can produce performance superior to an FI's rivals as well as allow it to develop new and innovative products, enhancing its long-term survival chances.

operational risk
The risk that existing technology or support systems may malfunction or break down.

Operational risk is partly related to technology risk and can arise whenever existing technology malfunctions or back-office support systems break down. For example, a failure of a back-office system, as well as the downside of operational risk, was evident in the Wells Fargo/First Interstate merger in 1996. Wells Fargo wanted to make the merger process easy for First Interstate customers by allowing them to use up their old checks and deposit forms. Unfortunately, because of the merger, customer account numbers had been changed. As a result, some deposits were not posted to the proper accounts and there was a deluge of checks improperly bounced. Further, Wells Fargo's back-office operations were thinly staffed and unable to find where all the misplaced deposits had gone. Promising to reimburse all customers for its accounting mistakes, Wells Fargo eventually corrected the problems, incurring an operating loss of some $180 million.

More recently, a failure of a back-office system occurred in September 2001 when Citibank's (a subsidiary of Citigroup) ATM system crashed for an extended period of time. Citibank's 2,000 nationwide ATMs, its debit card system, and its online banking functions went down for almost two business days. Even though such computer breakdowns are rare, their occurrence can cause major dislocations in the FIs involved and potentially disrupt the financial system in general.

Operational risk is not exclusively the result of technological failure. For example, employee fraud and errors constitute a type of operational risk that often negatively affects the reputation of an FI (see Chapter 14). For instance, as noted in Chapters 1 and 4, several highly publicized securities violations by employees of major investment banks resulted in criminal cases brought against securities law violators by state and federal prosecutors. In particular, the New York State attorney general forced Merrill Lynch to pay a $100 million penalty because of allegations that Merrill Lynch brokers gave investors overly optimistic reports about the stock of its investment banking clients. Also, a federal judge threw money manager Alan Bond in jail after he was convicted on charges of allocating winning trades to his own brokerage account and saddling his clients with losers. Finally, federal investigators brought criminal and civil charges against stock broker Frank Gruttadauria for theft of his investors' accounts. These fraudulent activities by employees of FIs resulted in an overall loss of reputation and, in turn, business for the FI employers.

Concept Questions

1. What is the difference between economies of scale and economies of scope?
2. How is operational risk related to technology risk?
3. How does technological expansion help an FI better exploit economies of scale and economies of scope? When might technology risk interfere with these goals?

FOREIGN EXCHANGE RISK

Increasingly, FIs have recognized that both direct foreign investment and foreign portfolio investments can extend the operational and financial benefits available from purely domestic investments. Thus, U.S. pension funds that held approximately 5 percent of their assets in foreign securities in the early 1990s now hold close to 10 percent of their assets in foreign securities. Japanese pension funds currently hold more than 30 percent of their assets in foreign securities plus an additional 10 percent in foreign currency deposits. At the same time, many large U.S. banks, investment banks, and mutual funds have become more global in their orientation. To the extent that the returns on domestic and foreign investments are imperfectly correlated, there are potential gains for an FI that expands its asset holdings and liability funding beyond the domestic frontier.

The returns on domestic and foreign direct investing and portfolio investments are not perfectly correlated for two reasons. The first is that the underlying technologies of various economies differ, as do the firms in those economies. For example, one economy may be based on agriculture while another is industry based. Given different economic infrastructures, one economy could be expanding while another is contracting. In the late 1990s, for example, the U.S. economy was rapidly expanding while the Japanese economy was contracting. The second reason is that exchange rate changes are not perfectly correlated across countries. This means the dollar–euro exchange rate may be appreciating while the dollar–yen exchange rate may be falling.

One potential benefit from an FI's becoming increasingly global in its outlook is an ability to expand abroad directly through branching or acquisitions or by developing a financial asset portfolio that includes foreign securities as well as domestic securities. Even so, foreign investment exposes an FI to **foreign exchange risk.** Foreign exchange risk is the risk that exchange rate changes can adversely affect the value of an FI's assets and liabilities denominated in foreign currencies.

foreign exchange risk
The risk that exchange rate changes can affect the value of an FI's assets and liabilities located abroad.

To understand how foreign exchange risk arises, suppose that a U.S. FI makes a loan to a British company in pounds sterling (£). Should the British pound depreciate in value relative to the U.S. dollar, the principal and interest payments received by U.S. investors would be devalued in dollar terms. Indeed, were the British pound to fall far enough over the investment period, when cash flows are converted back into dollars, the overall return could be negative. That is, on the conversion of principal and interest payments from sterling into dollars, foreign exchange losses can offset the promised value of local currency interest payments at the original exchange rate at which the investment occurred.

In general, an FI can hold assets denominated in a foreign currency and/or issue foreign liabilities. Consider a U.S. FI that holds £100 million British pound loans as assets and funds £80 million of them with British pound certificates of deposit. The difference between the £100 million in pound loans and £80 million in pound CDs is funded by dollar CDs (i.e., £20 million pounds' worth of dollar CDs). See Figure 7–3. In this case, the U.S. FI is *net long* £20 million in British assets; that is, it holds more foreign assets than liabilities. The U.S. FI suffers losses if the exchange rate for pounds falls or depreciates against the dollar over this period. In dollar terms, the value of the British pound loan assets falls or decreases in value by more than the British pound CD liabilities do. That is, the FI is exposed to the risk that its net foreign assets may have to be liquidated at an exchange rate lower than the one that existed when the FI entered into the foreign asset–liability position.

Instead, the FI could have £20 million more foreign liabilities than assets; in this case, it would be holding a *net short* position in foreign assets, as shown in Figure 7–4. Under this circumstance, the FI is exposed to foreign exchange risk if the pound appreciates against the dollar over the investment period. This occurs because the value of its British pound liabilities in dollar terms rose faster than the

FIGURE 7–3
The Foreign Asset and Liability Position: Net Long Asset Position in Pounds

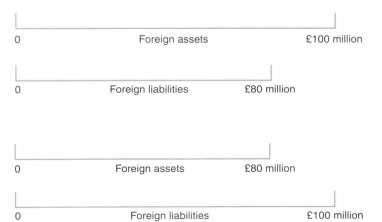

FIGURE 7–4
The Foreign Asset and Liability Position: Net Short Asset Position in Pounds

return on its pound assets. Consequently, to be approximately hedged, the FI must match its assets and liabilities in each foreign currency.

Note that the FI is fully hedged only if we assume that it holds foreign assets and liabilities of exactly the same maturity.[8] Consider what happens if the FI matches the size of its foreign currency book (British pound assets = British pound liabilities = £100 million in that currency) but mismatches the maturities so that the pound sterling assets are of six-month maturity and the liabilities are of three-month maturity. The FI would then be exposed to foreign interest rate risk—the risk that British interest rates would rise when it has to roll over its £100 million British CD liabilities at the end of the third month. Consequently, an FI that matches both the size and maturities of its exposure in assets and liabilities of a given currency is hedged, or immunized, against foreign currency and foreign interest rate risk. To the extent that FIs mismatch their portfolio and maturity exposures in different currency assets and liabilities, they face both foreign currency and foreign interest rate risks. As already noted, if foreign exchange rate and interest rate changes are not perfectly correlated across countries, an FI can diversify away part, if not all, of its foreign currency risk. We discuss the measurement and evaluation of an FI's foreign currency risk exposure in depth in Chapter 15.

Concept Questions

1. Explain why the returns on domestic and foreign portfolio investments are not, in general, perfectly correlated.
2. A U.S. bank is net long in European assets. If the euro appreciates against the dollar, will the bank gain or lose?
3. A U.S. bank is net short in European assets. If the euro appreciates against the dollar, will the bank gain or lose?

COUNTRY OR SOVEREIGN RISK

country or sovereign risk
The risk that repayments from foreign borrowers may be interrupted because of interference from foreign governments.

As we noted in the previous section, a globally oriented FI that mismatches the size and maturities of its foreign assets and liabilities is exposed to foreign currency and foreign interest rate risks. Even beyond these risks, and even when investing in dollars, holding assets in a foreign country can expose an FI to an additional type of foreign investment risk called **country or sovereign risk.** Country or sovereign risk is a different type of credit risk that is faced by an FI that purchases assets such as the bonds and loans of foreign corporations. For example, when a domestic corporation is unable or unwilling to repay a loan, an FI usually has recourse to the domestic bankruptcy courts and eventually may recoup at least a portion of its original investment when the assets of the defaulted firm are liquidated or restructured. By comparison, a foreign corporation may be unable to repay the principal or interest on a loan even if it would like to. Most commonly, the government of the country in which the corporation is headquartered may prohibit or limit debt payments because of foreign currency shortages and adverse political reasons.

For example, in 1982, the Mexican and Brazilian governments announced a debt moratorium (i.e., a delay in their debt repayments) to Western creditors. The largest U.S. banks had made substantial loans to these countries and their

---

[8] Technically speaking, hedging requires matching the durations (average lives of assets and liabilities) rather than simple maturities (see Chapter 9).

government-owned corporations (such as Pemex, the Mexican state-run oil company). As a result, banks such as Citicorp (now Citigroup) eventually had to make additions to their loan loss reserves to meet expected losses on these loans. In 1987 alone, Citicorp set aside more than $3 billion to cover expected losses (again, note the interaction between credit risk and country risk) on South American loans made in 1982 or earlier. More recently, U.S., European, and Japanese banks had enhanced sovereign risk exposures to countries such as Argentina, Russia, Thailand, South Korea, Malaysia, and Indonesia. Financial support given to these countries by the International Monetary Fund (IMF), the World Bank, and the U.S., Japanese, and European governments enabled the banks to avoid the full extent of the losses that were possible. Nevertheless, Indonesia had to declare a moratorium on some of its debt repayments, while Russia defaulted on payments on its short-term government bonds. In 1999, some banks agreed to settle their claims with the Russian government, receiving less than five cents for every dollar owed them. Finally, in 2001, the government of Argentina, which had pegged its peso to the dollar on a one-to-one basis since the early 1990s, had to default on its government debt largely because of an overvalued peso and the adverse effect this had on its exports and foreign currency earnings. In December 2001, Argentina ended up defaulting on $130 billion in government-issued debt and, in 2002, passed legislation that led to defaults on $30 billion of corporate debt owed to foreign creditors. Argentina's economic problems continued into 2003; in September 2003 it defaulted on a $3 billion loan repayment to the IMF.

In the event of such restrictions, reschedulings, or outright prohibitions on the payment of debt obligations by sovereign governments, the FI claimholder has little, if any, recourse to the local bankruptcy courts or an international civil claims court. The major leverage available to an FI to ensure or increase repayment probabilities and amounts is its control over the future supply of loans or funds to the country concerned. However, such leverage may be very weak in the face of a country's collapsing currency and government. Chapter 16 discusses how country or sovereign risk is measured and considers possible financial market solutions to the country risk exposure problems of a globally oriented FI.

Concept Questions

1. Can a bank be subject to sovereign risk if it lends only to AAA or the highest-quality foreign corporations?
2. What is one major way an FI can discipline a country that threatens not to repay its loans?

LIQUIDITY RISK

liquidity risk
The risk that a sudden surge in liability withdrawals may leave an FI in a position of having to liquidate assets in a very short period of time and at low prices.

Liquidity risk arises when an FI's liability holders, such as depositors or insurance policyholders, demand immediate cash for the financial claims they hold with an FI or when holders of off-balance-sheet loan commitments (or credit lines) suddenly exercise their right to borrow (draw down their loan commitments). In recent years, the Federal Reserve has expressed concerns about both liability side and asset side (loan commitment) liquidity risks.[9] When liability holders demand

[9] See, for example, "Regulators Press for Safeguards" and "Years of Living Dangerously Set to Haunt Banks," *Financial Times*, June 4, 2001.

cash immediacy—that is, "put" their financial claims back to the FI—the FI must either borrow additional funds or sell assets to meet the demand for the withdrawal of funds. The most liquid asset of all is cash, which FIs can use to directly meet liability holders' demands to withdraw funds. Although FIs limit their cash asset holdings because cash earns no interest, low cash holdings are usually not a problem. Day-to-day withdrawals by liability holders are generally predictable, and FIs can normally expect to borrow additional funds to meet any sudden shortfalls of cash on the money and financial markets.

However, there are times when an FI can face a liquidity crisis. Because of a lack of confidence by liability holders in the FI or some unexpected need for cash, liability holders may demand *larger* withdrawals than normal. When all, or many, FIs face abnormally large cash demands, the cost of additional purchased or borrowed funds rises and the supply of such funds becomes restricted. As a consequence, FIs may have to sell some of their less liquid assets to meet the withdrawal demands of liability holders. This results in a more serious liquidity risk, especially as some assets with "thin" markets generate lower prices when the asset sale is immediate than when the FI has more time to negotiate the sale of an asset. As a result, the liquidation of some assets at low or fire-sale prices (the price an FI receives if an asset must be liquidated immediately at less than its fair market value) could threaten an FI's profitability and solvency. Good examples of such illiquid assets are bank loans to small firms. Such serious liquidity problems may eventually result in a run in which all liability claim-holders seek to withdraw their funds simultaneously from the FI because they fear that it will be unable to meet their demands for cash in the near future. This turns the FI's liquidity problem into a solvency problem and can cause it to fail.[10]

We examine the nature of normal, abnormal, and run-type liquidity risks and their impact on banks, thrifts, insurance companies, and other FIs in more detail in Chapter 17. In addition, we look at ways an FI can better manage liquidity and liability risk exposures in Chapter 18. Chapter 19 discusses the roles of deposit insurance and other liability guarantee schemes in deterring deposit (liability) runs.

Concept Questions

1. Why might an FI face a sudden liquidity crisis?
2. What circumstances might lead an FI to liquidate assets at fire-sale prices?

INSOLVENCY RISK

Insolvency risk
The risk that an FI may not have enough capital to offset a sudden decline in the value of its assets relative to its liabilities.

Insolvency risk is a consequence or outcome of one or more of the risks described above: interest rate, market, credit, off-balance-sheet, technology, foreign exchange, sovereign, and liquidity risks. Technically, insolvency occurs when the capital or

[10] The situation of several Ohio savings institutions in 1985 is an extreme example of liquidity risk. A group of 70 Ohio savings institutions was insured by a private fund, the Ohio Deposit Guarantee Fund (ODGF). One of these savings banks, Home State Savings Bank (HSSB), had invested heavily in a Florida-based government securities dealer, EMS Government Securities, Inc., which eventually defaulted on its debts to HSSB (note the interaction between credit risk and liquidity risk). This in turn made it difficult for HSSB to meet deposit withdrawals of its customers. HSSB's losses from the ESM default were, in fact, so large that the ODGF could not cover them. Not only was HSSB unable to cover the deposit withdrawals, but other Ohio savings institutions insured by ODGF were inundated with deposit withdrawals to the extent that they could not cover them as well. As a result, ODGF-insured institutions were temporarily closed and the Ohio state legislature had to step in to cover depositors' claims.

equity resources of an FI's owners are driven to, or near to, zero because of losses incurred as the result of one or more of the risks described above. Consider the case of the 1984 failure of Continental Illinois National Bank and Trust Company. Continental's strategy in the late 1970s and early 1980s had been to pursue asset growth through aggressive lending, especially to the oil and gas sector. Continental's loan portfolio grew at an average rate of 19.8 percent per year from 1977 to 1981. The downturn in the U.S. economy at the beginning of the 1980s resulted in the default of many of these loans (credit risk). In addition, Continental had a very small core deposit base, relying instead on purchased and borrowed funds such as fed funds, RPs, and Eurodollar deposits. The increasing number of defaults in Continental's loan portfolio fueled concerns about the bank's ability to meet its liability payments, resulting in the refusal by a number of major lenders to renew or roll over the short-term funds they had lent to Continental (liquidity risk). The substantial defaults on Continental's loans combined with its inability to obtain new or retain existing funds resulted in the rapid deterioration of Continental's capital position (insolvency risk). Continental was unable to survive, and federal regulators assumed control in 1984.[11]

In general, the more equity capital to borrowed funds an FI has—that is, the lower its leverage—the better able it is to withstand losses, whether due to adverse interest rate changes, unexpected credit losses, or other reasons. Thus, both management and regulators of FIs focus on an FI's capital (and adequacy) as a key measure of its ability to remain solvent and grow in the face of a multitude of risk exposures. The issue of what is an adequate level of capital to manage an FI's overall risk exposure is discussed in Chapter 20.

Concept Questions

1. When does insolvency risk occur?
2. How is insolvency risk related to the other risks discussed in this chapter?

OTHER RISKS AND THE INTERACTION OF RISKS

In this chapter we have concentrated on nine major risks continuously impacting an FI manager's decision-making process and risk management strategies. These risks were interest rate risk, market risk, credit risk, off-balance-sheet risk, technology and operational risk, foreign exchange risk, country or sovereign risk, liquidity risk, and insolvency risk. Even though the discussion generally described each independently, in reality, these risks are often interdependent. For example, when interest rates rise, corporations and consumers find maintaining promised payments on their debt more difficult.[12] Thus, over some range of interest rate movements, credit, interest rate, and off-balance-sheet risks are positively correlated. Furthermore, the FI may have been counting on the funds from promised payments on its loans for liquidity management purposes. Thus, liquidity risk is also correlated with interest rate and credit risks. The inability of a customer to make promised payments also affects the FI's income and profits and, consequently, its

---

[11] See Itzhak Swary, "The Stock Market Reaction to Regulatory Action in the Continental Illinois Crisis," *Journal of Business,* no. 3, 1986, pp. 451–74.

[12] Rising interest rates may also negatively impact derivative contract holders, who may then be inclined to default. This credit risk on derivatives is often called counter-party risk.

equity or capital position. Thus, each risk and its interaction with other risks ultimately affects solvency risk. Similarly, foreign exchange rate changes and interest rate changes are also highly correlated. When the Federal Reserve changes a key interest rate (such as the Fed funds rate) through its monetary policy actions, exchange rates are also likely to change.

Various other risks, often of a more discrete or event type, also impact an FI's profitability and risk exposure, although, as noted earlier, many view discrete or event risks as part of operational risks. Discrete risks might include events external to the FI, such as a sudden change in taxation. For example, the Tax Reform Act of 1986 subjected banks to a minimum corporate tax rate of 20 percent (the alternative minimum tax) and limited their ability to expense the cost of funds used to purchase tax-free municipal bonds. Such changes can affect the attractiveness of some types of assets over others, as well as the liquidity of an FI's balance sheet. For example, banks' demand for municipal bonds fell quite dramatically following the 1986 tax law change. As a result, the municipal bond market became quite illiquid for a time.

Changes in regulatory policy constitute another type of external, discrete, or event risk. These include lifting the regulatory barriers to lending or to entry or on products offered (see Chapter 21). The 1994 regulatory change allowing interstate branching after 1997 is one example, as is the 1999 Financial Services Modernization Act. Other discrete or event risks involve sudden and unexpected changes in financial market conditions due to war, revolution, or sudden market collapse, such as the 1929 and 1987 stock market crashes or the September 2001 terrorist attacks in the United States. These can have a major impact on an FI's risk exposure. Other event risks include fraud, theft, earthquakes, storms, malfeasance, and breach of fiduciary trust; all of these can ultimately cause an FI to fail or be severely harmed. Yet each is difficult to model and predict.

Finally, more general macroeconomic or systematic risks, such as increased inflation, inflation volatility, and unemployment, can directly and indirectly impact an FI's level of interest rate, credit, and liquidity risk exposure. For example, inflation was very volatile in the 1979–82 period in the United States. Interest rates reflected this volatility. During periods in which FIs face high and volatile inflation and interest rates, interest rate risk exposure from mismatching balance sheet maturities tends to rise. Credit risk exposure also rises because borrowing firms with fixed-price product contracts often find it difficult to keep up their loan payments when inflation and interest rates rise abruptly.

Concept Questions

1. What is meant by the term *event risk*?
2. What are some examples of event and general macroeconomic risks that impact FIs?

Summary

This chapter provided an introductory view of nine major risks faced by modern FIs. They face *interest rate risk* when their assets and liabilities maturities are mismatched. They incur *market risk* on their trading assets and liabilities if there are adverse movements in interest rates, exchange rates, or other asset prices. They face *credit risk* or default risk if their clients default on their loans and other obligations. Modern-day FIs also engage in a significant number of off-balance-sheet activities that expose them to *off-balance-sheet risks:* contingent asset and liability risks. The advent of sophisticated technology and automation exposes FIs to both *technological risk* and *operational risk*. If FIs conduct foreign business, they are subject to additional risks, namely *foreign exchange* and *sovereign risks*. *Liquidity risk* is a result of a serious run on an FI because of excessive withdrawals or problems in refinancing. Finally, *insolvency risk* occurs when an FI's capital is insufficient to withstand a decline in the value of assets relative to liabilities. The effective management of these risks determines the success or failure of a modern FI. The chapters that follow analyze each of these risks in greater detail.

Questions and Problems

1. What is the process of *asset transformation* performed by a financial institution? Why does this process often lead to the creation of *interest rate risk?* What is interest rate risk?

2. What is *refinancing risk?* How is refinancing risk part of interest rate risk? If an FI funds long-term assets with short-term liabilities, what will be the impact on earnings of an increase in the rate of interest? A decrease in the rate of interest?

3. What is *reinvestment risk?* How is reinvestment risk part of interest rate risk? If an FI funds short-term assets with long-term liabilities, what will be the impact on earnings of a decrease in the rate of interest? An increase in the rate of interest?

4. The sales literature of a mutual fund claims that the fund has no risk exposure since it invests exclusively in federal government securities which are free of default risk. Is this claim true? Explain why or why not.

5. What is *economic or market value risk?* In what manner is this risk adversely realized in the economic performance of an FI?

6. A financial institution has the following balance sheet structure:

Assets		Liabilities and Equity	
Cash	$ 1,000	Certificate of deposit	$10,000
Bond	10,000	Equity	1,000
Total assets	$11,000	Total liabilities and equity	$11,000

The bond has a 10-year maturity and a fixed-rate coupon of 10 percent. The certificate of deposit has a 1-year maturity and a 6 percent fixed rate of interest. The FI expects no additional asset growth.

a. What will be the net interest income at the end of the first year? *Note:* Net interest income equals interest income minus interest expense.

b. If at the end of year 1, market interest rates have increased 100 basis points (1 percent), what will be the net interest income for the second year? Is this result caused by reinvestment risk or refinancing risk?

c. Assuming that market interest rates increase 1 percent, the bond will have a value of $9,446 at the end of year 1. What will be the market value of equity for the FI?

d. If market interest rates had decreased 100 basis points by the end of year 1, would the market value of equity be higher or lower than $1,000? Why?

e. What factors have caused the changes in operating performance and market value for this firm?

7. How does the policy of matching the maturities of assets and liabilities work (a) to minimize interest rate risk and (b) against the asset-transformation function of FIs?

8. Corporate bonds usually pay interest semiannually. If a company decided to change from semiannual to annual interest payments, how would this affect the bond's interest rate risk?

9. Two 10-year bonds are being considered for an investment that may have to be liquidated before the maturity of the bonds. The first bond is a 10-year premium bond with a coupon rate higher than its required rate of return, and the second bond is a zero-coupon bond that pays only a lump-sum payment after 10 years with no interest over its life. Which bond would have more interest rate risk? That is, which bond's price would change by a larger amount for a given change in interest rates? Explain your answer.

10. Consider again the two bonds in problem 9. If the investment goal is to leave the assets untouched until maturity, such as for a child's education or for one's retirement, which of the two bonds has more interest rate risk? What is the source of this risk?

11. A money market mutual fund bought $1,000,000 of two-year Treasury notes six months ago. During this time, the value of the securities has increased, but for tax reasons the mutual fund wants to postpone any sale for two more months. What type of risk does the mutual fund face for the next two months?

12. A bank invested $50 million in a two-year asset paying 10 percent interest per annum and simultaneously issued a $50 million, one-year liability paying 8 percent interest per annum. What will be the impact on the bank's net interest income if at the end of the first year all interest rates have increased by 1 percent (100 basis points)?

13. What is *market risk?* How do the results of this risk surface in the operating performance of financial institutions? What actions can be taken by an FI's management to minimize the effects of this risk?

14. What is *credit risk?* Which types of FIs are more susceptible to this type of risk? Why?

15. What is the difference between *firm-specific credit risk* and *systematic credit risk?* How can an FI alleviate firm-specific credit risk?

16. Many banks and savings institutions that failed in the 1980s had made loans to oil companies in Louisiana, Texas, and Oklahoma. When oil prices fell, these companies, the regional economy, and the banks and savings institutions all experienced financial problems. What types of risk were inherent in the loans that were made by these banks and savings institutions?

17. What is the nature of an off-balance-sheet activity? How does an FI benefit from such activities? Identify the various risks that these activities generate for an FI, and explain how these risks can create varying degrees of financial stress for the FI at a later time.

18. What is *technology risk?* What is the difference between *economies of scale* and *economies of scope?* How can these economies create benefits for an FI? How can these economies prove harmful to an FI?

19. What is the difference between technology risk and *operational risk?* How does internationalizing the payments system among banks increase operational risk?

20. What two factors provide potential benefits to FIs that expand their asset holdings and liability funding sources beyond their domestic economies?

21. What is *foreign exchange risk?* What does it mean for an FI to be *net long* in foreign assets? What does it mean for an FI to be *net short* in foreign assets? In each case, what must happen to the foreign exchange rate to cause the FI to suffer losses?

22. If the Swiss franc is expected to depreciate in the near future, would a U.S.-based FI in Bern City prefer to be net long or net short in its asset positions? Discuss.

23. If international capital markets are well integrated and operate efficiently, will FIs be exposed to foreign exchange risk? What are the sources of foreign exchange risk for FIs?

24. If an FI has the same amount of foreign assets and foreign liabilities in the same currency, has that FI necessarily reduced to zero the risk involved in these international transactions? Explain.

25. A U.S. insurance company invests $1,000,000 in a private placement of British bonds. Each bond pays £300 in interest per year for 20 years. If the current exchange rate is £1.7612/$, what is the nature of the insurance company's exchange rate risk? Specifically, what type of exchange rate movement concerns this insurance company?

26. Assume that a bank has assets located in London that are worth £150 million on which it earns an average of 8 percent per year. The bank has £100 million in liabilities on which it pays an average of 6 percent per year. The current spot rate is £1.50/$.

    a. If the exchange rate at the end of the year is £2.00/$, will the dollar have appreciated or depreciated against the pound?

    b. Given the change in the exchange rate, what is the effect in dollars on the net interest income from the foreign assets and liabilities? *Note:* The net interest income is interest income minus interest expense.

    c. What is the effect of the exchange rate change on the value of assets and liabilities in dollars?

27. Six months ago, Qualitybank, LTD., issued a $100 million, one-year maturity CD denominated in euros. On the same date, $60 million was invested in a €-denominated loan and $40 million was invested in a U.S. Treasury bill. The exchange rate on this date was €1.7382/$. Assume no repayment of principal and an exchange rate today of €1.3905/$.

    a. What is the current value of the CD principal (in dollars and euros)?

    b. What is the current value of the euro-denominated loan principal (in dollars and euros)?

    c. What is the current value of the U.S. Treasury bill (in dollars and euros)?

    d. What is Qualitybank's profit/loss from this transaction (in dollars and euros)?

28. Suppose you purchase a 10-year, AAA-rated Swiss bond for par that is paying an annual coupon of 8 percent. The bond has a face value of 1,000 Swiss francs (SF). The spot rate at the time of purchase is SF1.50/$. At the end of the year, the bond is downgraded to AA and the yield increases to 10 percent. In addition, the SF appreciates to SF1.35/$.

    a. What is the loss or gain to a Swiss investor who holds this bond for a year? What portion of this loss or gain is due to foreign exchange risk? What portion is due to interest rate risk?

b. What is the loss or gain to a U.S. investor who holds this bond for a year? What portion of this loss or gain is due to foreign exchange risk? What portion is due to interest rate risk?

29. What is *country or sovereign risk?* What remedy does an FI realistically have in the event of a collapsing country or currency?

30. Characterize the risk exposure(s) of the following FI transactions by choosing one or more of the risk types listed below:

a. Interest rate risk   d. Technology risk

b. Credit risk   e. Foreign exchange risk

c. Off-balance-sheet risk   f. Country or sovereign risk

(1) A bank finances a $10 million, six-year fixed-rate commercial loan by selling one-year certificates of deposit.

(2) An insurance company invests its policy premiums in a long-term municipal bond portfolio.

(3) A French bank sells two-year fixed-rate notes to finance a two-year fixed-rate loan to a British entrepreneur.

(4) A Japanese bank acquires an Austrian bank to facilitate clearing operations.

(5) A mutual fund completely hedges its interest rate risk exposure by using forward contingent contracts.

(6) A bond dealer uses his own equity to buy Mexican debt on the less-developed country (LDC) bond market.

(7) A securities firm sells a package of mortgage loans as mortgage-backed securities.

31. Consider these four types of risks: credit, foreign exchange, market, and sovereign. These risks can be separated into two pairs of risk types in which each pair consists of two related risk types, with one being a subset of the other. How would you pair off the risk types, and which risk type could be considered a subset of the other type in the pair?

32. What is *liquidity risk?* What routine operating factors allow FIs to deal with this risk in times of normal economic activity? What market reality can create severe financial difficulty for an FI in times of extreme liquidity crises?

33. Why can *insolvency risk* be classified as a consequence or outcome of any or all of the other types of risks?

34. Discuss the interrelationships among the different sources of bank risk exposure. Why would the construction of a bank risk-management model to measure and manage only one type of risk be incomplete?

Pertinent Web Sites

Bank for International Settlements	**www.bis.org**
Federal Deposit Insurance Corporation	**www.fdic.gov**

www.mhhe.com/saunders5e

Measuring Risk

Chapter Eight

Interest Rate Risk I

INTRODUCTION

net worth
The value of an FI to its owners; this is equal to the difference between the market value of assets and that of liabilities.

www.federalreserve.gov

www.bis.org

In Chapter 7 we established that while performing their asset-transformation functions, FIs often mismatch the maturities of their assets and liabilities. In so doing, they expose themselves to interest rate risk. For example, in the 1980s a large number of thrifts suffered economic insolvency (i.e., the **net worth** or equity of their owners was eradicated) when interest rates unexpectedly increased. All FIs tend to mismatch their balance sheet maturities to some degree. However, measuring interest rate risk exposure by looking only at the size of the maturity mismatch can be misleading. The next two chapters present techniques used by FIs to measure their interest rate risk exposures.

This chapter discusses the Federal Reserve's monetary policy, which is a key determinant of interest rate risk. This chapter also analyzes two of the simpler methods to measure an FI's interest rate risk: *the repricing model* and *the maturity model*. The repricing, or funding gap, model concentrates on the impact of interest rate changes on an FI's net interest income (NII), which is the difference between an FI's interest income and interest expense. Because of its simplicity, smaller depository institutions still use this model as their primary measure of interest rate risk. The discussion compares and contrasts this model with the market value–based maturity model, which includes the impact of interest rate changes on the overall market value of an FI's assets and liabilities and, ultimately, its net worth. Until recently, U.S. bank regulators had been content to base their evaluations of bank interest rate risk exposures on the repricing model. As explained later in this chapter, however, the repricing model has some serious weaknesses. Recently, the Bank for International Settlements (the organization of the world's major Central Banks) has issued a consultative document[1] suggesting a standardized model to be used by regulators in evaluating a bank's interest rate risk exposure. Rather than being based on the repricing model, the approach suggested is firmly based on market value accounting and the duration model (see Chapter 9). As regulators move to adopt these models, bigger banks have adopted them as their primary measure of interest rate risk. Moreover, where relevant, banks may be allowed to use their own value-at-risk models (see Chapter 10) to assess the interest rate risk of the banking book.[2] Appendix A to this chapter looks at the term structure of interest rates that compares the market yields or interest rate on securities, assuming that all characteristics except maturity are the same. Explanations for the shape of the yield curve are also discussed in Appendix A to the chapter. Appendix B to the chapter,

---

[1] See Basel Committee on Banking Supervision, "Principles for the Management and Supervision of Interest Rate Risk," Bank for International Settlements, Basel, Switzerland, January 2001.

[2] In this case, a longer horizon (e.g., one year) would be taken compared with that used to measure interest rate risk in the trading book (e.g., one day).

located at the book's Web site (**www.mhhe.com/saunders5e**), presents a review of bond pricing and price volatility.

THE CENTRAL BANK AND INTEREST RATE RISK

*Fed controls
1. money supply
2. inflation
3) Level of interest Rates*

The Central Bank's monetary policy strategy underlies the movement of interest rates that affect an FI's cost of funds and return on assets. The Central Bank in the United States is the Federal Reserve (the Fed). Through its daily open market operations, such as buying and selling Treasury bonds and Treasury bills, the Fed seeks to influence the money supply, inflation, and the level of interest rates (particularly short-term interest rates). In turn, changing interest rates impact economic decisions, such as whether to consume or save. When the Fed finds it necessary to slow down the economy, it tightens monetary policy by raising interest rates. The normal result is a decrease in business and household spending (especially that financed by credit or borrowing). Conversely, if business and household spending decline to the extent that the Fed finds it necessary to stimulate the economy, it allows interest rates to fall (an expansionary monetary policy). The drop in rates promotes borrowing and spending. For example, in 2001, as the U.S. economy showed initial signs of weakness, the Fed began lowering interest rates aggressively. As the economy slid into a recession in 2001 and after the terrorist attacks on the World Trade Center and the Pentagon in September 2001, the Fed continued its aggressive actions, lowering interest rates 11 times during the year. Even as the economy began to recover in the summer and fall of 2003, the Fed kept interest rates at these low levels. Citing deflation as a greater concern than inflation, the Fed insisted that interest rates could remain low for a considerable period.

Furthermore, if the Federal Reserve smooths or targets the level of interest rates, unexpected interest rate movements or shocks and interest rate volatility over time tend to be small. Accordingly, in a low interest rate volatility environment, the risk exposure to an FI from mismatching the maturities of its assets and liabilities also tends to be low. However, to the extent that the Federal Reserve targets the supply of bank reserves and is willing to let interest rates find their own levels, the volatility of interest rates can be very high. Figure 8–1 shows the interest rate on U.S. 91-day T-bills for the period 1965–2003. The first observation to make from this figure is that the degree of interest rate volatility appears to have decreased in recent years. The second is that the relative degree of volatility, or interest rate uncertainty, is directly linked to the Federal Reserve's monetary policy strategy. Specifically, between October 1979 and October 1982, the Federal Reserve targeted bank reserves during the so-called nonborrowed reserves target regime.[3] The volatility of interest rates in this period was far greater than it was in the two regimes surrounding this period. Note how the Federal Reserve targeted interest rates during the 1965 to October 1979 period and smoothed interest rates after October 1982 under the so-called borrowed reserves targeting regime. Indeed, the 1979–82 period was the genesis for the interest rate risk problems facing those thrifts that specialized in making long-term conventional mortgage loans funded by short-term deposits such as CDs.[4] The borrowed reserve targeting system lasted from October

---

[3] For more details, see A. Saunders and T. Urich, "The Effects of Shifts in Monetary Policy and Reserve Accounting Regimes on Bank Reserve Management Behavior in the Federal Funds Market," *Journal of Banking and Finance* 12 (1988), pp. 523–35.

[4] Certificates of deposit usually are issued with maturities of less than one year.

FIGURE 8–1
Interest Rate on U.S. 91-Day Treasury Bills, 1965–2003

Source: Federal Reserve Board Web site, various dates. *www.federalreserve.gov*

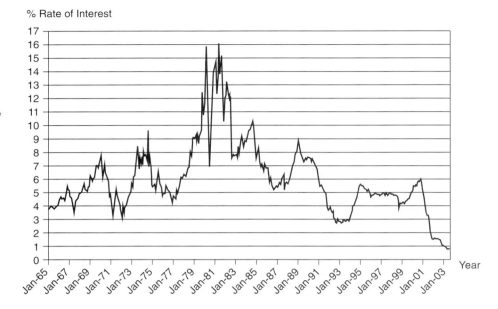

% Rate of Interest

1982 until 1993, when the Federal Reserve announced that it would no longer target bank reserves and money supply growth at all. At that time, the Fed announced that it would use interest rates—the federal funds rate—as the main target variable to guide monetary policy. Under this regime the Fed simply announces after each monthly meeting whether the federal funds rate target has been increased, decreased, or left unchanged.[5] It also should be noted that while Federal Reserve actions are targeted mostly at short-term rates (especially the federal funds rate), changes in short-term rates usually feed through to the whole term structure of interest rates. The linkages between short-term rates and long-term rates and theories of the term structure of interest rates are discussed in Appendix A to this chapter.

Internet Exercise   Go to the Federal Reserve Board's Web site and find the latest information available on three-month CD rates versus the prime rate. Go to the Federal Reserve's Web site at **www.federalreserve.gov.** Click on "Economic Research and Data." Click on "Statistics: Releases and Historical Data." Under "Weekly Releases," click on "Selected Interest Rates—Releases." Click on the most recent date. This will download the data onto your computer that will contain the most recent information on three-month CD rates and the prime rate.

In addition to the Fed's impact on interest rates via its monetary policy strategy, the increased level of financial market integration over the last decade has also affected interest rates. Financial market integration increases the speed with which

[5] In September 2003, Federal Reserve Board Chairman Alan Greenspan termed this form of interest rate management "risk management." He said that when the Fed sets interest rates, it considers not just the most probable forecast of the economy's growth, but also improbable outcomes with big consequences, such as deflation or a financial collapse. See "Greenspan Confronts Criticism of Fed Decision-Making Methods," *The Wall Street Journal*, September 2, 2003, p. A3.

interest rate changes and associated volatility are transmitted among countries, making the control of U.S. interest rates by the Federal Reserve more difficult and less certain than before. The increased globalization of financial market flows in recent years has made the measurement and management of interest rate risk a prominent concern facing many modern FI managers. For example, investors across the world carefully evaluate the statements made by Alan Greenspan (chairman of the Federal Reserve Board of Governors) before Congress. Even hints of increased U.S. interest rates may have a major effect on world interest rates (as well as foreign exchange rates and stock prices).

The volatility of interest rates, the risk that the Federal Reserve may return to a more overtly reserve-targeting regime similar to that in 1979–82, and the increase in worldwide financial market integration make the measurement and management of interest rate risk one of the key issues facing FI managers. Further, the Bank for International Settlements (a worldwide Central Bank) has called for regulations that require depository institutions (DIs) to have interest rate risk measurement systems that assess the effects of interest rate changes on both earnings and economic value. These systems should provide meaningful measures of a DI's current levels of interest rate risk exposure and should be capable of identifying any excessive exposures that might arise (see Chapter 20). In this chapter and in Chapter 9, we analyze the different ways an FI might measure the exposure it faces in running a mismatched maturity book (or gap) between its assets and its liabilities in a world of interest rate volatility.

In particular, we concentrate on three ways, or models, of measuring the asset–liability gap exposure of an FI:

The repricing (or funding gap) model.

The maturity model.

The duration model.

<table>
<tr><td>Concept Questions</td><td>1. How is the Federal Reserve's monetary policy linked to the degree of interest rate uncertainty faced by FIs?</td></tr>
<tr><td></td><td>2. What actions has the Federal Reserve taken to reduce the amount of unexpected versus expected interest rate movements or shocks?</td></tr>
<tr><td></td><td>3. How did the Federal Reserve's monetary policy strategy affect FIs over the period October 1979 to October 1982?</td></tr>
</table>

THE REPRICING MODEL

repricing gap
The difference between assets whose interest rates will be repriced or changed over some future period (rate-sensitive assets) and liabilities whose interest rates will be repriced or changed over some future period (rate-sensitive liabilities).

The repricing, or funding gap, model is essentially a book value accounting cash flow analysis of the **repricing gap** between the interest revenue earned on an FI's assets and the interest paid on its liabilities (or its net interest income) over a particular period of time. This contrasts with the market value–based maturity and duration models discussed later in this chapter and in Chapter 9.

In recent years, the Federal Reserve has required commercial banks to report quarterly on their call reports the repricing gaps for assets and liabilities with these maturities:

1. One day.

2. More than one day to three months.

3. More than three months to six months.

TABLE 8–1
Repricing Gap (in millions of dollars)

	1 Assets	2 Liabilities	3 Gaps	4 Cumulative Gap
1. One day	$ 20	$ 30	$−10	$−10
2. More than one day–three months	30	40	−10	−20
3. More than three months–six months	70	85	−15	−35
4. More than 6 months–12 months	90	70	+20	−15
5. More than one year–five years	40	30	+10	−5
6. Over five years	10	5	+5	0
	$260	$260		

4. More than 6 months to 12 months.

5. More than one year to five years.

6. More than five years.

Under the repricing gap approach, a bank reports the gaps in each maturity bucket by calculating the rate sensitivity of each asset (RSA) and each liability (RSL) on its balance sheet. **Rate sensitivity** here means that the asset or liability is repriced at or near current market interest rates within a certain time horizon (or maturity bucket). More simply, it means how long the FI manager must wait to change the posted interest rates on any asset or liability. In many cases this occurs on a date prior to maturity.

Table 8–1 shows the asset and liability repricing gaps of an FI, categorized into each of the six previously defined maturity buckets. Although the cumulative repricing gap over the whole balance sheet must, by definition, be zero [see Table 8–1, column (4)], the advantage of the repricing model lies in its information value and its simplicity in pointing to an FI's *net interest income exposure* (or profit exposure) to interest rate changes in different maturity buckets.[6]

For example, suppose that an FI has a negative $10 million difference between its assets and liabilities being repriced in one day (one-day bucket). Assets and liabilities that are repriced each day are likely to be interbank borrowings on the federal funds or repurchase agreement market (see Chapter 2). Thus, a negative gap (RSA < RSL) exposes the FI to **refinancing risk,** in that a rise in these short-term rates would lower the FI's *net interest income* since the FI has more rate-sensitive liabilities than assets in this bucket. In other words, assuming equal changes in interest rates on RSAs and RSLs, interest expense will increase by more than interest revenue. Conversely, if the FI has a positive $20 million difference between its assets and liabilities being repriced in 6 months to 12 months, it has a positive gap (RSA > RSL) for this period and is exposed to **reinvestment risk,** in that a drop in rates over this period would lower the FI's net interest income; that is, interest income will decrease by more than interest expense. Specifically, let:

ΔNII_i = Change in net interest income in the ith bucket

GAP_i = Dollar size of the gap between the book value of rate-sensitive assets and rate-sensitive liabilities in maturity bucket i

ΔR_i = Change in the level of interest rates impacting assets and liabilities in the ith bucket

rate-sensitive asset or liability
An asset or liability that is repriced at or near current market interest rates within a maturity bucket.

refinancing risk
The risk that the cost of rolling over or re-borrowing funds will rise above the returns being earned on asset investments.

reinvestment risk
The risk that the returns on funds to be reinvested will fall below the cost of the funds.

[6] If we include equity capital as a long-term (over five years) liability.

Then:

$$\Delta NII_i = (GAP_i)\, \Delta R_i = (RSA_i - RSL_i)\, \Delta R_i$$

In this first bucket, if the gap is negative $10 million and short-term interest rates (such as fed fund and/or repo rates) rise 1 percent, the annualized change in the FI's future net interest income is:[7]

$$\Delta NII_i = (-\$10 \text{ million}) \times .01 = -\$100,000$$

This approach is very simple and intuitive. Remember, however, from Chapter 7 and our overview of interest rate risk that capital or market value losses also occur when rates rise. The capital loss effect that is measured by both the maturity and duration models developed later in this chapter and in Chapter 9 is not accounted for in the repricing model. The reason is that in the book value accounting world of the repricing model, assets and liability values are reported at their *historic* values or costs. Thus, interest rate changes affect only current interest income or interest expense—that is, net interest income on the FI's income statement—rather than the market value of assets and liabilities on the balance sheet.[8]

The FI manager can also estimate cumulative gaps (CGAP) over various repricing categories or buckets. A common cumulative gap of interest is the one-year repricing gap estimated from Table 8–1 as:

$$CGAP = (-\$10) + (-\$10) + (-\$15) + \$20 = -\$15 \text{ million}$$

If ΔR_i is the average interest rate change affecting assets and liabilities that can be repriced within a year, the cumulative effect on the bank's net interest income is:[9]

$$\Delta NII_i = (CGAP)\, \Delta R_i$$
$$= (-\$15 \text{ million})(.01) = -\$150,000$$

We can now look at how an FI manager would calculate the cumulative one-year gap from a balance sheet. Remember that the manager asks: Will or can this asset or liability have its interest rate changed within the next year? If the answer is yes, it is a rate-sensitive asset or liability; if the answer is no, it is not rate sensitive.

Consider the simplified balance sheet facing the FI manager in Table 8–2. Instead of the original maturities, the maturities are those remaining on different assets and liabilities at the time the repricing gap is estimated.

Rate-Sensitive Assets

Looking down the asset side of the balance sheet in Table 8–2, we see the following one-year rate-sensitive assets (RSAs):

1. *Short-term consumer loans: $50 million.* These are repriced at end of the year and just make the one-year cutoff.

2. *Three-month T-bills: $30 million.* These are repriced on maturity (rollover) every three months.

---

[7] One can also calculate an "average" gap. If it is assumed that assets and liabilities reprice on *average* halfway through the period, the one-year gap measure calculated above will be divided by 2.

[8] For example, a 30-year bond purchased 10 years ago when rates were 13 percent would be reported as having the same book (accounting) value as when rates are 7 percent. Using market value, gains and losses to asset and liability values would be reflected in the balance sheet as rates changed.

[9] Note that a change in the dollar value and mix of rate-sensitive assets and liabilities (or a change in CGAP) also affects the FI's net income.

[handwritten: Amount of interest Rev generated by Assets.]

[handwritten: Rate sensitive liabilities (RSL)]

[handwritten: Rate Sensitive Assets (RSA)]

TABLE 8–2
Simple FI Balance Sheet (in millions of dollars)

Assets		Liabilities	
1. Short-term consumer loans (one-year maturity)	$ 50	1. Equity capital (fixed)	$ 20
2. Long-term consumer loans (two-year maturity)	25	2. Demand deposits	40
3. Three-month Treasury bills	30	3. Passbook savings	30
4. Six-month Treasury notes	35	4. Three-month CDs	40
5. Three-year Treasury bonds	70	5. Three-month bankers acceptances	20
6. 10-year, fixed-rate mortgages	20	6. Six-month commercial paper	60
7. 30-year, floating-rate mortgages (rate adjusted every nine months)	40	7. One-year time deposits	20
		8. Two-year time deposits	40
	$270		$270

3. *Six-month T-notes: $35 million.* These are repriced on maturity (rollover) every six months.

4. *30-year floating-rate mortgages: $40 million.* These are repriced (i.e., the mortgage rate is reset) every nine months. Thus, these long-term assets are rate-sensitive assets in the context of the repricing model with a one-year repricing horizon.

Summing these four items produces total one-year rate-sensitive assets (RSAs) of $155 million. The remaining $115 million of assets are not rate sensitive over the one-year repricing horizon—that is, a change in the level of interest rates will not affect the size of the interest revenue generated by these assets over the next year.[10] Although the $115 million in long-term consumer loans, 3-year Treasury bonds, and 10-year, fixed-rate mortgages generate interest revenue, the size of revenue generated will not change over the next year, since the interest rates on these assets are not expected to change (i.e., they are fixed over the next year).

Rate-Sensitive Liabilities

Looking down the liability side of the balance sheet in Table 8–2, we see the following liability items clearly fit the one-year rate or repricing sensitivity test:

1. *Three-month CDs: $40 million.* These mature in three months and are repriced on rollover.

2. *Three-month bankers acceptances: $20 million.* These also mature in three months and are repriced on rollover.

3. *Six-month commercial paper: $60 million.* These mature and are repriced every six months.

4. *One-year time deposits: $20 million.* These get repriced right at the end of the one-year gap horizon.

Summing these four items produces one-year rate-sensitive liabilities (RSLs) of $140 million. The remaining $130 million is not rate sensitive over the one-year period. The $20 million in equity capital and $40 million in demand deposits (see the following discussion) do not pay interest and are therefore classified as non-interest-paying. The $30 million in passbook savings (see the following discussion) and

---

[10] We are assuming that the assets are noncallable over the year and that there will be no prepayments (runoffs, see below) on the mortgages within a year.

$40 million in two-year time deposits generate interest expense over the next year, but the level of the interest expense generated will not change if the general level of interest rates changes. Thus, we classify these items as rate-insensitive liabilities.

Note that demand deposits (or transaction accounts in general) were not included as RSLs. We can make strong arguments for and against their inclusion as rate-sensitive liabilities.

Against Inclusion

The explicit interest rate on demand deposits is zero by regulation. Further, although explicit interest is paid on transaction accounts such as NOW accounts, the rates paid by FIs do not fluctuate directly with changes in the general level of interest rates (particularly when the general level of rates is rising). Moreover, many demand deposits act as **core deposits** for FIs, meaning they are a long-term source of funds.

core deposits
Those deposits that act as an FI's long-term sources of funds.

For Inclusion

Even though they pay no explicit interest rates, demand deposits pay implicit interest because FIs do not charge fees that fully cover their costs for checking services. Further, if interest rates rise, individuals draw down (or run off) their demand deposits, forcing the bank to replace them with higher-yielding, interest-bearing, rate-sensitive funds. This is most likely to occur when the interest rates on alternative instruments are high. In such an environment, the opportunity cost of holding funds in demand deposit accounts is likely to be larger than it is in a low–interest rate environment.

Similar arguments for and against inclusion of retail passbook savings accounts can be made. Although Federal Reserve Regulation Q ceilings on the maximum rates to be charged for these accounts were abolished in March 1986, banks still adjust these rates only infrequently. However, savers tend to withdraw funds from these accounts when rates rise, forcing banks into more expensive fund substitutions.[11]

The four repriced liabilities ($40 + $20 + $60 + $20) sum to $140 million, and the four repriced assets ($50 + $30 + $35 + $40) sum to $155 million. Given this, the cumulative one-year repricing gap (CGAP) for the bank is:

$$CGAP = \text{One-year rate-sensitive assets} - \text{one-year rate-sensitive liabilities}$$

$$= RSA - RSL$$

$$= \$155 - \$140 = \$15 \text{ million}$$

Interest rate sensitivity can also be expressed as a percentage of assets (A) (typically called the *gap ratio*):

$$\frac{CGAP}{A} = \frac{\$15 \text{ million}}{\$270 \text{ million}} = .056 = 5.6\%$$

Expressing the repricing gap in this way is useful since it tells us (1) the direction of the interest rate exposure (positive or negative CGAP) and (2) the scale of that exposure as indicated by dividing the gap by the asset size of the institution.

---

[11] The Federal Reserve's repricing report has traditionally viewed transaction accounts and passbook savings accounts as rate-*in*sensitive liabilities, as we have done in this example. However, with the growth of the Internet and competition from money market mutual funds, the mobility of these funds is highly sensitive to (relative) rates paid by banks versus other nonbank FIs (such as money market mutual funds). See "Regulators Press for Safeguards," *Financial Times,* June 4, 2001, p. 24.

TABLE 8–3
Impact of CGAP on the Relation between Changes in Interest Rates and Changes in Net Interest Income, Assuming Rate Changes for RSAs Equal Rate Changes for RSLs

Row	CGAP	Change in Interest Rates	Change in Interest Revenue		Change in Interest Expense	Change in NII
1	>0	⇑	⇑	>	⇑	⇑
2	>0	⇓	⇓	>	⇓	⇓
3	<0	⇑	⇑	<	⇑	⇓
4	<0	⇓	⇓	<	⇓	⇑

[handwritten: CGAP provides measure of FI's sensitivity]

In our example the bank has 5.6 percent more RSAs than RSLs in one-year-and-less buckets as a percentage of total assets.

Equal Changes in Rates on RSAs and RSLs

The CGAP provides a measure of an FI's interest rate sensitivity. Table 8–3 highlights the relation between CGAP and changes in NII when interest rate changes for RSAs are equal to interest rate changes for RSLs. For example, when CGAP (or the gap ratio) is positive (or the FI has more RSAs than RSLs), NII will rise when interest rates rise (row 1, Table 8–3), since interest revenue increases more than interest expense does.

EXAMPLE 8–1
Impact of Rate Changes on Net Interest Income When CGAP Is Positive

Suppose that interest rates rise by 1 percent on both RSAs and RSLs. The CGAP would project the expected annual change in net interest income (ΔNII) of the bank as approximately:

$$\Delta NII = CGAP \times \Delta R$$
$$= (\$15 \text{ million}) \times .01$$
$$= \$150,000$$

Similarly, if interest rates fall equally for RSAs and RSLs (row 2, Table 8–3), NII will fall when CGAP is positive. As rates fall, interest revenue falls by more than interest expense. Thus, NII falls. Suppose that for our FI, rates fall by 1 percent. The CGAP predicts that NII will fall by approximately:

$$\Delta NII = CGAP \times \Delta R$$
$$= (\$15 \text{ million}) \times -.01$$
$$= -\$150,000$$

It is evident from this equation that the larger the absolute value of CGAP, the larger the expected change in NII (i.e., the larger the increase or decrease in the FI's interest revenue relative to interest expense). In general, when CGAP is positive, the change in NII is positively related to the change in interest rates. Conversely, when CGAP (or the gap ratio) is negative, if interest rates rise by equal amounts for RSAs and RSLs (row 3, Table 8–3), NII will fall (since the FI has more RSLs than RSAs). Thus, an FI would want its CGAP to be positive when interest rates are expected to rise. Similarly, if interest rates fall equally for RSAs and RSLs (row 4, Table 8–3), NII will increase when CGAP is negative. As rates fall, interest expense decreases by more than interest revenue. In general then, when CGAP is negative, the change in NII is negatively related to the change in interest rates. Thus, an FI

FIGURE 8–2
Three-Month CD Rates versus Prime Rates for 1990–2003

Source: *Federal Reserve Bulletin,* various issues. *www.federalreserve.gov*

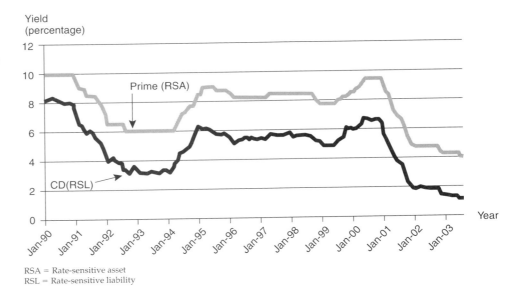

RSA = Rate-sensitive asset
RSL = Rate-sensitive liability

CGAP effects
The relations between changes in interest rates and changes in net interest income.

would want its CGAP to be negative when interest rates are expected to fall. We refer to these relationships as **CGAP effects.**

Unequal Changes in Rates on RSAs and RSLs

The previous section considered changes in net interest income as interest rates changed, assuming that the change in rates on RSAs was exactly equal to the change in rates on RSLs (in other words, assuming the interest rate spread between rates on RSAs and RSLs remained unchanged). This is not often the case; rather, rate changes on RSAs generally differ from those on RSLs (i.e., the spread between interest rates on assets and liabilities changes along with the levels of these rates). See Figure 8–2, which plots quarterly CD rates (liabilities) and prime lending rates (assets) for the period 1990–2003. Notice that although the rates generally move in the same direction, they are not perfectly correlated. In this case, as we consider the impact of rate changes on NII, we have a spread effect in addition to the CGAP effects.[12]

EXAMPLE 8–2
Impact of Spread Effect on Net Interest Income

To understand spread effect, assume for a moment that RSAs equal RSLs equals $155 million. Suppose that rates rise by 1.2 percent on RSAs and by 1 percent on RSLs (i.e., the spread between the rates on RSAs and RSLs increases by 1.2 percent − 1 percent = 0.2 percent). The resulting change in NII is calculated as:

$$\Delta NII = (RSA \times \Delta R_{RSA}) - (RSL \times \Delta R_{RSL})$$
$$= \Delta \text{Interest revenue} - \Delta \text{Interest expense}$$
$$= (\$155 \text{ million} \times 1.2\%) - (\$155 \text{ million} \times 1.0\%)$$
$$= \$155 \text{ million} (1.2\% - 1.0\%)$$
$$= \$310,000$$

[12] The spread effect therefore presents a type of basis risk for the FI. The FI's net interest income varies as the difference (basis) between interest rates on RSAs and interest rates on RSLs varies. We discuss basis risk in detail in Chapter 24.

TABLE 8–4
Impact of CGAP on the Relation between Changes in Interest Rates and Changes in Net Interest Income, Allowing for Different Rate Changes for RSAs and RSLs

Row	CGAP	Change in Interest Rates	Change in Spread	NII
1	>0	⇑	⇑	⇑
2	>0	⇑	⇓	⇑⇓
3	>0	⇓	⇑	⇑⇓
4	>0	⇓	⇓	⇓
5	<0	⇑	⇑	⇑⇓
6	<0	⇑	⇓	⇓
7	<0	⇓	⇑	⇑
8	<0	⇓	⇓	⇑⇓

spread effect
The effect that a change in the spread between rates on RSAs and RSLs has on net interest income as interest rates change.

If the spread between the rate on RSAs and RSLs increases, when interest rates rise (fall), interest revenue increases (decreases) by more (less) than interest expense. The result is an increase in NII. Conversely, if the spread between the rates on RSAs and RSLs decreases, when interest rates rise (fall), interest revenue increases (decreases) less (more) than interest expense, and NII decreases. In general, the **spread effect** is such that, regardless of the direction of the change in interest rates, a positive relation occurs between changes in the spread (between rates on RSAs and RSLs) and changes in NII. Whenever the spread increases (decreases), NII increases (decreases).

See Table 8–4 for various combinations of CGAP and spread changes and their effects on NII. The first four rows in Table 8–4 consider an FI with a positive CGAP; the last four rows consider an FI with a negative CGAP. Notice in Table 8–4 that both the CGAP and spread effects can have the same effect on NII. In these cases, FI managers can accurately predict the direction of the change in NII as interest rates change. When the two work in opposite directions, however, the change in NII cannot be predicted without knowing the size of the CGAP and expected change in the spread.

Some FIs accept quite large interest rate exposures relative to their asset sizes. For example, the average one-year repricing gap ratio of State Street (Boston) Corporation was –14.4 percent at the end of 2000 (i.e., it had considerably more RSLs than RSAs). If interest rates had fallen in 2001, its net interest income would have risen. If rates had risen, however, State Street would have been exposed to significant net interest income losses due to the cost of refinancing its large amount of RSLs (relative to RSAs) at higher rates. As it turned out, State Street was lucky—or its interest rate forecasts were correct—because rates actually fell dramatically during all of 2001. As interest rates hit 50-year lows in 2002 and 2003, State Street adjusted its gap ratio to +9.1 percent. Commercial banks have recently paid much closer attention to interest rate risk exposure, significantly reducing the gaps between RSAs and RSLs.

The repricing gap is the measure of interest rate risk historically used by FIs, and it is still the main measure of interest rate risk used by small community banks and thrifts. In contrast to the market value–based models of interest rate risk discussed below and in Chapter 9, the repricing gap model is conceptually easy to understand and can easily be used to forecast changes in profitability for a given change in interest rates. The repricing gap can be used to allow an FI to structure its assets and liabilities or to go off the balance sheet to take advantage of a projected interest rate change. However, the repricing gap model has some major weaknesses that have resulted in regulators' calling for the use of more comprehensive models (e.g., the duration gap model) to measure interest rate risk. We next discuss some of the major weaknesses of the repricing model.[13]

Concept Questions

1. Why is it useful to express the repricing gap in terms of a percentage of assets? What specific information does this provide?
2. How can banks change the size and the direction of their repricing gap?
3. Summarize the case for and against the inclusion of demand deposits as a rate-sensitive liability.

WEAKNESSES OF THE REPRICING MODEL

The repricing model has four major shortcomings: (1) It ignores market value effects of interest rate changes, (2) it is overaggregative, (3) it fails to deal with the problem of rate-insensitive asset and liability runoffs and prepayments, and (4) it ignores cash flows from off-balance-sheet activities. In this section we discuss each of these weaknesses in more detail.

Market Value Effects

As was discussed in the overview of FI risks (Chapter 7), interest rate changes have a market value effect in addition to an income effect on asset and liability values. That is, the present value of the cash flows on assets and liabilities changes, in addition to the immediate interest received or paid on them, as interest rates change. In fact, the present values (and where relevant, the market prices) of virtually all assets and liabilities on an FI's balance sheet change as interest rates change. The repricing model ignores the market value effect—implicitly assuming a book value accounting approach. As such, the repricing gap is only a *partial* measure of the true interest rate exposure of an FI. As we discuss the market value–based measures of interest rate risk (below and in Chapter 9), we will highlight the impact that ignoring the market value effect has on the ability to accurately measure the overall interest rate risk of an FI.

Overaggregation

The problem of defining buckets over a range of maturities ignores information regarding the distribution of assets and liabilities within those buckets. For example, the dollar values of RSAs and RSLs within any maturity bucket range may be equal; however, on average, liabilities may be repriced toward the end of the bucket's range, while assets may be repriced toward the beginning, in which case a change in interest rates will have an effect on asset and liability cash flows that will not be accurately measured by the repricing gap approach.

Look at the simple example for the three-month to six-month bucket in Figure 8–3. Note that $50 million more RSAs than RSLs are repriced between months and 4, while $50 million more RSLs than RSAs are repriced between months 5 and 6. The bank in its call report would show a zero repricing gap for the three-month to six-month bucket ($+50 + (-50) = 0$). But as you can easily see, the bank's assets and liabilities are *mismatched* within the bucket. Clearly, the

---

[13] See E. Brewer, "Bank Gap Management and the Use of Financial Futures," Federal Reserve Bank of Chicago, *Economic Perspectives,* March–April 1985, for an excellent analysis of the repricing model and its strengths and weaknesses.

FIGURE 8–3
The Over-
aggregation
Problem: The
Three-Month to
Six-Month Bucket

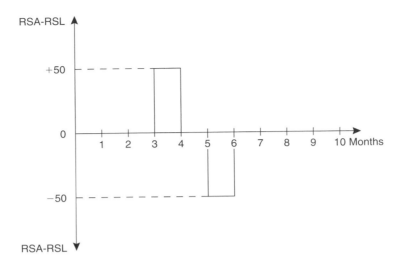

shorter the range over which bucket gaps are calculated, the smaller this problem is. If an FI manager calculated one-day bucket gaps out into the future, this would give a more accurate picture of the net interest income exposure to rate changes. Reportedly, many large banks have internal systems that indicate their repricing gaps on any given day in the future (252 days' time, 1,329 days' time, etc.). This suggests that although regulators require the reporting of repricing gaps over only relatively wide maturity bucket ranges, FI managers could set in place internal information systems to report the daily future patterns of such gaps.[14]

The Problem of Runoffs

In the simple repricing model discussed above, we assumed that all consumer loans matured in 1 year or that all conventional mortgages matured in 30 years. In reality, the FI continuously originates and retires consumer and mortgage loans as it creates and retires deposits. For example, today, some 30-year original maturity mortgages may have only 1 year left before they mature; that is, they are in their 29th year. In addition, these loans may be listed as 30-year mortgages (and included as not rate sensitive), yet they will sometimes be prepaid early as mortgage holders refinance their mortgages and/or sell their houses. Thus, the resulting proceeds will be reinvested at current market rates within the year. In addition, even if an asset or liability is rate insensitive, virtually all assets and liabilities (e.g., long-term mortgages) pay some principal and/or interest back to the FI in any given year. As a result, the FI receives a **runoff** cash flow from its rate-insensitive portfolio that can be reinvested at current market rates; that is,

runoff
Periodic cash flow of
interest and principal
amortization pay-
ments on long-term
assets, such as con-
ventional mortgages,
that can be reinvested
at market rates.

[14] Another way to deal with the overaggregation problem is by adjusting the buckets for the time to interest rate repricing within the bucket. Let RSA and RSL be rate-sensitive assets and liabilities in a bucket, let R denote initial interest rates on an asset or liability, and let K denote new interest rates after repricing. Let t be the proportion of the bucket period for which the asset's (liability's) old interest rate (R) is in effect, and thus, $1 - t$ is the proportion of the bucket period in which the new interest rate (K) is in operation:

$$\Delta NII = RSA[\{(1 + R_A)^{tA} \times (1 + K_A)^{1-tA}\} - (1 + R_A)] - RSL[\{(1 + R_L)^{tL} \times (1 + K_L)^{1-tL}\} - (1 + R_L)]$$

See Brewer, "Bank Gap Management," for more details.

TABLE 8–5 Runoffs of Different Assets and Liabilities (in millions of dollars)

Assets			Liabilities		
Item	$ Amount Runoff in Less Than One Year	$ Amount Runoff in More Than One Year	Item	$ Amount Runoff in Less Than One Year	$ Amount Runoff in More Than One Year
1. Short-term consumer loans	$ 50	—	1. Equity	—	$20
2. Long-term consumer loans	5	$20	2. Demand deposits	$ 30	10
3. Three-month T-bills	30	—	3. Passbook savings	15	15
4. Six-month T-bills	35	—	4. Three-month CDs	40	—
5. Three-year notes	10	60	5. Three-month bankers acceptances	20	—
6. 10-year mortgages	2	18	6. Six-month commercial paper	60	—
7. 30-year floating-rate mortgages	40	—	7. One-year time deposits	20	—
			8. Two-year time deposits	20	20
	$172	$98		$205	$65

this runoff cash flow component of a rate-insensitive asset or liability is itself rate sensitive. The FI manager can deal easily with this in the repricing model by identifying for each asset and liability item the estimated dollar cash flow that will run off within the next year and adding these amounts to the value of rate-sensitive assets and liabilities.

Consider Table 8–5. Notice in this table that while the original maturity of an asset or liability may be long term, these assets and liabilities still generate some cash flows that can be reinvested at market rates. Table 8–5 is a more sophisticated measure of the one-year repricing gap that takes into account the cash flows received on each asset and liability item during that year. Adjusted for runoffs, the repricing gap (in millions) is:

$$GAP = \$172 - \$205 = -\$33$$

As implied above, the runoffs themselves are not independent of interest rate changes. Specifically, when interest rates rise, many people may delay repaying their mortgages (and the principal on those mortgages), causing the runoff amount of $2 million on 10-year mortgages in Table 8–5 to be overly optimistic. Similarly, when interest rates fall, people may prepay their fixed-rate mortgages to refinance at a lower interest rate. Then runoffs could balloon to a number much greater than $2 million. This sensitivity of runoffs to interest rate changes is a further weakness of the repricing model.[15]

Cash Flows from Off-Balance-Sheet Activities

The RSAs and RSLs used in the repricing model generally include only the assets and liabilities listed on the balance sheet. Changes in interest rates will affect the cash flows on many off-balance-sheet instruments as well. For example, an FI might have hedged its interest rate risk with an interest rate futures contract (see

---

[15] In the case of fixed-rate mortgage loans, the FI manager would need to estimate potential prepayments of principal during the year based on interest rate forecasts and mortgage holders' sensitivity to the forecasted change in rates (see Chapter 28 on prepayment models).

Chapter 24). As interest rates change, these futures contracts—as part of the marking-to-market process—produce a daily cash flow (either positive or negative) for the FI that may offset any on-balance-sheet gap exposure. These offsetting cash flows from futures contracts are ignored by the simple repricing model and should (and could) be included in the model.

Concept Questions

1. What are four major weaknesses of the repricing model?
2. What does runoff mean?

THE MATURITY MODEL

book value accounting
Accounting method in which the assets and liabilities of the FI are recorded at historic values.

market value accounting
Accounting method in which the assets and liabilities of the FI are revalued according to the current level of interest rates.

marking to market
Valuing securities at their current market price.

As mentioned above, a weakness of the repricing model is its reliance on book values rather than market values of assets and liabilities. Indeed, in most countries, FIs report their balance sheets by using **book value accounting.** This method records the historic values of securities purchased, loans made, and liabilities sold. For example, for U.S. banks, investment assets (i.e., those expected to be held to maturity) are recorded at book values, while those assets expected to be used for trading (trading securities or available-for-sale securities) are reported according to market value.[16] The recording of market values means that assets and liabilities are revalued to reflect current market conditions. Thus, if a fixed-coupon bond had been purchased at $100 per $100 of face value in a low–interest rate environment, a rise in current market rates reduces the present value of the cash flows from the bond to the investor. Such a rise also reduces the price—say, to $97—at which the bond could be sold in the secondary market today. That is, the **market value accounting** approach reflects economic reality, or the true values of assets and liabilities if the FI's portfolio were to be liquidated at today's securities prices rather than at the prices when the assets and liabilities were originally purchased or sold. This practice of valuing securities at their market value is referred to as **marking to market.** We discuss book value versus market value accounting and the impact that the use of the alternate methods has in measuring the value of an FI in more detail in Chapter 20. In the maturity and duration model, developed below and in Chapter 9, the effects of interest rate changes on the market values of assets and liabilities are explicitly taken into account. This contrasts with the repricing model, discussed above, in which such effects are ignored.

EXAMPLE 8–3
Fixed Income Securities and the Maturity Model

Consider the value of a bond held by an FI that has one year to maturity, a face value of 100 (F) to be paid on maturity, one single annual coupon at a rate of 10 percent of the face value (C) and a current yield to maturity (R) (reflecting current interest rates) of 10 percent. The fair market price of the one-year bond, P_1^B, is equal to the present value of the cash flows on the bond:

$$P_1^B = \frac{F + C}{(1 + R)} = \frac{100 + 10}{1.1} = 100$$

---

[16] More accurately, they are reported at the lower of cost or current market value (LOCOM). However, both the SEC and the Financial Accounting Standards Board (FASB) have strongly advocated that FIs switch to full market value accounting in the near future. Currently, FASB 115 requires FIs to value certain bonds at market prices but not loans.

Suppose the Federal Reserve tightens monetary policy so that the required yield on the bond rises instantaneously to 11 percent. The market value of the bond falls to:

$$P_1^B = \frac{100 + 10}{1.11} = 99.10$$

Thus, the market value of the bond is now only $99.10 per $100 of face value, while its original book value was $100. The FI has suffered a capital loss (ΔP_1) of $0.90 per $100 of face value in holding this bond, or:

$$\Delta P_1 = 99.10 - 100 = -\$0.90$$

Also, the percent change in the price is:

$$\Delta P_1 = \frac{99.10 - 100}{100} = -0.90\%$$

This example simply demonstrates the fact that:

$$\frac{\Delta P}{\Delta R} < 0$$

A rise in the required yield to maturity reduces the price of fixed-income securities held in FI portfolios. Note that if the bond under consideration were issued as a liability by the FI (e.g., a fixed-interest deposit such as a CD) rather than being held as an asset, the effect would be the same—the market value of the FI's deposits would fall. However, the economic interpretation is different. Although rising interest rates that reduce the market value of assets are bad news, the reduction in the market value of liabilities is good news for the FI. The economic intuition is straightforward. Suppose the FI issued a one-year deposit with a promised interest rate of 10 percent and principal or face value of $100.[17] When the current level of interest rates is 10 percent, the market value of the liability is 100:

$$P_1^D = \frac{100 + 10}{(1.1)} = 100$$

Should interest rates on new one-year deposits rise instantaneously to 11 percent, the FI has gained by locking in a promised interest payment to depositors of only 10 percent. The market value of the FI's liability to its depositors would fall to $99.10; alternatively, this would be the price the FI would need to pay the depositor if it repurchased the deposit in the secondary market:

$$P_1^D = \frac{100 + 10}{(1.11)} = 99.10$$

That is, the FI gained from paying only 10 percent on its deposits rather than 11 percent if they were newly issued after the rise in interest rates.

As a result, in a market value accounting framework, rising interest rates generally lower the market values of both assets and liabilities on an FI's balance sheet. Clearly, falling interest rates have the reverse effect: They increase the market values of both assets and liabilities.

---

[17] In this example we assume for simplicity that the promised interest rate on the deposit is 10 percent. In reality, for returns to intermediation to prevail, the promised rate on deposits would be less than the promised rate (coupon) on assets.

EXAMPLE 8–4

Impact of Maturity on Change in Bond Value

In the preceding example, both the bond and the deposit were of one-year maturity. We can easily show that if the bond or deposit had a two-year maturity with the same annual coupon rate, the same increase in market interest rates from 10 to 11 percent would have had a more *negative* effect on the market value of the bond's (and deposit's) price. That is, before the rise in required yield:

$$P_2^B = \frac{10}{(1.1)} + \frac{10 + 100}{(1.1)^2} = 100$$

After the rise in market yields from 10 to 11 percent:

$$P_2^B = \frac{10}{(1.11)} + \frac{10 + 100}{(1.11)^2} = 98.29$$

and

$$\Delta P_2^B = 98.29 - 100 = -1.71$$

The resulting percentage change in the bond's value is:

$$\%\Delta P_2^B = (98.29 - 100)/100 = -1.71\%$$

If we extend the analysis one more year, the market value of a bond with three years to maturity, a face value of $100, and a coupon rate of 10 percent is:

$$P_3^B = \frac{10}{(1.1)} + \frac{10}{(1.1)^2} + \frac{10 + 100}{(1.1)^3} = 100$$

After the rise in market rates from 10 to 11 percent, market value of the bond is:

$$P_3^B = \frac{10}{(1.11)} + \frac{10}{(1.11)^2} + \frac{10 + 100}{(1.11)^3} = 97.56$$

This is a change in the market value of:

$$\Delta P_3^B = 97.56 - 100 = -2.44$$

or

$$\%\Delta P_3^B = \frac{97.56 - 100}{100} = -2.44\%$$

This example demonstrates another general rule of portfolio management for FIs: The *longer* the maturity of a fixed income asset or liability, the larger its fall in price and market value for any given increase in the level of market interest rates. That is:

$$\frac{\Delta P_1}{\Delta R} < \frac{\Delta P_2}{\Delta R} < \cdots < \frac{\Delta P_{30}}{\Delta R}$$

Note that while the two-year bond's fall in price is larger than the fall of the one-year bond's, the difference between the two price falls, $\%\Delta P_2 - \%\Delta P_1$, is $-1.71\% - (-0.9\%) = -0.81\%$. The fall in the three-year, 10 percent coupon bond's price when yield increases to 11 percent is -2.44 percent. Thus, $\%\Delta P_3 - \%\Delta P_2 = -2.44\% - (-1.71\%) = -0.73\%$. This establishes an important result: While P_3 falls more than P_2 and P_2 falls more than P_1, the size of the capital loss increases at a diminishing rate as we move into the higher maturity ranges. This effect is graphed in Figure 8–4.

FIGURE 8–4
The Relationship between ΔR, Maturity, and ΔP (Capital Loss)

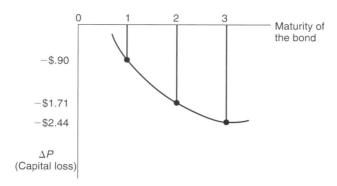

So far, we have shown that for an FI's fixed-income assets and liabilities:

1. A rise (fall) in interest rates generally leads to a fall (rise) in the market value of an asset or liability.
2. The longer the maturity of a fixed-income asset or liability, the larger the fall (rise) in market value for any given interest rate increase (decrease).
3. The fall in the value of longer-term securities increases at a diminishing rate for any given increase in interest rates.

The Maturity Model with a Portfolio of Assets and Liabilities

The preceding general rules can be extended beyond an FI holding an individual asset or liability to a portfolio of assets and liabilities. Let M_A be the weighted-average maturity of an FI's assets and M_L the weighted-average maturity of an FI's liabilities such that:

$$M_i = W_{i1}M_{i1} + W_{i2}M_{i2} + \cdots + W_{in}M_{in}$$

where

M_i = Weighted-average maturity of an FI's assets (liabilities), $i = A$ or L

W_{ij} = Importance of each asset (liability) in the asset (liability) portfolio as measured by the market value of that asset (liability) position relative to the market value of all the assets (liabilities)

M_{ij} = Maturity of the jth asset (or liability), $j = 1 \ldots n$

This equation shows that the maturity of a portfolio of assets or liabilities is a weighted average of the maturities of the assets or liabilities that constitute that portfolio. In a portfolio context, the same three principles prevail as for an individual security:

1. A rise in interest rates generally reduces the market values of an FI's asset and liability portfolios.
2. The longer the maturity of the asset or liability portfolio, the larger the fall in value for any given interest rate increase.
3. The fall in value of the asset or liability portfolio increases with its maturity at a diminishing rate.

maturity gap
Difference between the weighted-average maturity of the FI's assets and liabilities.

Given the preceding, the net effect of rising or falling interest rates on an FI's balance sheet depends on the extent and direction in which the FI mismatches the maturities of its asset and liability portfolios. That is, the effect depends on whether its **maturity gap**, $M_A - M_L$, is greater than, equal to, or less than zero.

TABLE 8–6
The Market Value Balance Sheet of an FI

Assets	Liabilities
Long-term assets (*A*)	Short-term liabilities (*L*)
	Net worth (*E*)

TABLE 8–7
Initial Market Values of an FI's Assets and Liabilities (in millions of dollars)

Assets	Liabilities
$A = \$100$ ($M_A = 3$ years)	$\$90 = L$ ($M_L = 1$ year)
	$10 = E$
$\$100$	$\$100$

Consider the case in which $M_A - M_L > 0$; that is, the maturity of assets is longer than the maturity of liabilities. This is the case of most commercial banks and thrifts. These FIs tend to hold large amounts of relatively longer-term fixed-income assets such as conventional mortgages, consumer loans, commercial loans, and bonds, while issuing shorter-term liabilities, such as certificates of deposit with fixed interest payments promised to the depositors.[18]

Consider the simplified portfolio of a representative FI in Table 8–6 and notice that all assets and liabilities are marked to market; that is, we are using a market value accounting framework. Note that in the real world, reported balance sheets differ from Table 8–6 because historic or book value accounting rules are used. In Table 8–6 the difference between the market value of the FI's assets (*A*) and the market value of its liabilities such as deposits (*L*) is the net worth or true equity value (*E*) of the FI. This is the economic value of the FI owners' stake in the FI. In other words, it is the money the owners would get if they could liquidate the FI's assets and liabilities at today's prices in the financial markets by selling off loans and bonds and repurchasing deposits at the best prices. This is also clear from the balance sheet identity:

$$E = A - L$$

As was demonstrated earlier, when interest rates rise, the market values of both assets and liabilities fall. However, in this example, because the maturity on the asset portfolio is longer than the maturity on the liability portfolio, for any given change in interest rates, the market value of the asset portfolio (*A*) falls by more than the market value of the liability portfolio (*L*). For the balance sheet identity to hold, the difference between the changes in the market value of its assets and liabilities must be made up by the change in the market value of the FI's equity or net worth:

$$\Delta E \quad = \quad \Delta A \quad - \quad \Delta L$$

(change in FI net worth)	(change in market value of assets)	(change in market value of liabilities)

To see the effect on FI net worth of having longer-term assets than liabilities, suppose that initially the FI's balance sheet looks like the one in Table 8–7. The $100 million of assets is invested in three-year, 10 percent coupon bonds, and

---

[18] These assets generate periodic interest payments such as coupons that are fixed over the asset's life. In Chapter 9 we discuss interest payments fluctuating with market interest rates, such as on an adjustable rate mortgage.

TABLE 8–8
An FI's Market
Value Balance Sheet
after a Rise in
Interest Rates of
1 Percent with
Longer-Term Assets

Assets	Liabilities
$A = \$97.56$	$L = \$89.19$
	$E = 8.37$
$\$97.56$	$\$97.56$

or

$$\Delta E = \Delta A - \Delta L$$
$$-\$1.63 = (-\$2.44) - (-\$0.81)$$

the liabilities consist of $90 million raised with one-year deposits paying a promised interest rate of 10 percent. We showed earlier that if market interest rates rise 1 percent, from 10 to 11 percent, the value of three-year bonds falls 2.44 percent while the value of one-year deposits falls 0.9 percent.[19] Table 8–8 depicts this fall in asset and liability market values and the associated effects on FI net worth.

Because the FI's assets have a three-year maturity compared with its one-year maturity liabilities, the value of its assets has fallen by more than has the value of its liabilities. The FI's net worth declines from $10 million to $8.37 million, a loss of $1.63 million, or 16.3 percent! Thus, it is clear that with a *maturity gap* of two years:

$$M_A - M_L = 2 \text{ years}$$
$$(3) - (1)$$

a 1 percentage point rise in interest rates can cause the FI's owners or stockholders to take a big hit to their net worth. Indeed, if a 1 percent rise in interest rates leads to a fall of 16.3 percent in the FI's net worth, it is not unreasonable to ask how large an interest rate change would need to occur to render the FI economically insolvent by reducing its owners' equity stake or net worth to zero. That is, what increase in interest rates would make E fall by $10 million so that all the owners' net worth would be eliminated? For the answer to this question, look at Table 8–9. If interest rates were to rise a full 7 percent, from 10 to 17 percent, the FI's equity (E) would fall by just over $10 million, rendering the FI economically insolvent.[20]

---

[19] The market value of deposits (in millions of dollars) is initially:

$$P_1^D = \frac{9 + 90}{1.1} = 90$$

When rates increase to 11 percent, the market value decreases:

$$P_1^D = \frac{9 + 90}{1.11} = 89.19$$

The resulting change is:

$$\Delta P_1^D = \frac{89.19 - 90}{90} = -0.90\%$$

[20] Here we are talking about economic insolvency. The legal and regulatory definition may vary, depending on what type of accounting rules are used. In particular, under the Federal Deposit Insurance Corporation Improvement Act (FDICIA) (November 1991), a DI is required to be placed in conservatorship by regulators when the book value of its net worth falls below 2 percent. However, the true or market value of net worth may well be less than this figure at that time.

TABLE 8–9
An FI Becomes
Insolvent after a
7 Percent Rate
Increase

Assets	Liabilities
$A = \$84.53$	$L = \$84.62$
	$E = -0.09$
$\$84.53$	$\$84.53$

or
$$\Delta E = \Delta A - \Delta L$$
$$-\$10.09 = -\$15.47 - (-\$5.38)$$

TABLE 8–10
An FI with an
Extreme Maturity
Mismatch (dollars)

Assets	Liabilities
$A = \$100\ (M_A = 30\ \text{years})$	$L = \$90\ (M_L = 1\ \text{year})$
	$E = 10$
$\$100$	$\$100$

TABLE 8–11
The Effect of a
1.5 Percent Rise in
Interest Rates on
the Net Worth of an
FI with an Extreme
Asset and Liability
Mismatch

Assets	Liabilities
$A = \$87.45$	$L = \$88.79$
	$E = -1.34$
$\$87.45$	$\$87.45$

or
$$\Delta E = \Delta A - \Delta L$$
$$-\$11.34 = (-\$12.55) - (-\$1.21)$$

EXAMPLE 8–5
*Extreme
Maturity
Mismatch*

Suppose the FI had adopted an even more extreme maturity gap by investing all its assets in 30-year fixed-rate bonds paying 10 percent coupons while continuing to raise funds by issuing one-year deposits with promised interest payments of 10 percent, as shown in Table 8–10. Assuming annual compounding and a current level of interest rates of 10 percent, the market price of the bonds (in millions of dollars) is initially:

$$P^B_{30} = \frac{\$10}{(1.1)} + \frac{\$10}{(1.1)^2} + \cdots + \frac{\$10}{(1.1)^{29}} + \frac{\$10 + \$100}{(1.1)^{30}} = \$100$$

If interest rates were to rise by 1.5 percent to 11.5 percent, the price (in millions of dollars) of the 30-year bonds would fall to:

$$P^B_{30} = \frac{\$10}{(1.115)} + \frac{\$10}{(1.115)^2} + \cdots + \frac{\$10}{(1.115)^{29}} + \frac{\$10 + \$100}{(1.115)^{30}} = \$87.45,$$

a drop of $12.55, or as a percentage change, $\%\Delta P^B_{30} = (\$87.45 - \$100)/\$100 = -12.55\%$. The market value of the FI's one-year deposits would fall to:

$$P^D_1 = \frac{\$9 + \$90}{1.115} = \$88.79$$

a drop of $1.21 or ($88.79 − $90)/$90 = −1.34%.

Look at Table 8–11 to see the effect on the market value balance sheet and the FI's net worth after a rise of 1 percent in interest rates. It is clear from Table 8–11 that when the mismatch in the maturity of the FI's assets and liabilities is extreme (29 years), a mere 1 percent increase in interest rates completely eliminates the FI's $10 million in net worth and renders it completely and massively insolvent (net worth is –$1.34 million after the rise in rates). In contrast, a smaller maturity gap (such as the two years from above) requires a much larger change in interest rates (i.e., 7 percent) to wipe out the FI's equity. Thus, interest rate risk increases as the absolute value of the maturity gap increases.

Given this example, it is not surprising that savings associations with 30-year fixed-rate mortgages as assets and shorter-term CDs as liabilities suffered badly during the 1979–82 period, when interest rates rose so dramatically (see Figure 8–1). At the time, depository institutions measured interest rate risk almost exclusively according to the repricing model, which captures the impact of interest rate changes on net interest income only. Regulators monitoring this measure only, rather than a market value–based measure, were unable to foresee the magnitude of the impact of rising interest rates on the market values of these FIs' assets and thus on their net worth.

immunize
Fully protect an FI's equity against interest rate risk.

From the preceding examples, you might infer that the best way for an FI to **immunize,** or protect, itself from interest rate risk is for its managers to match the maturities of its assets and liabilities, that is, to construct its balance sheet so that its maturity gap, the difference between the weighted-average maturity of its assets and liabilities, is zero ($M_A - M_L = 0$). However, as we discuss next, maturity matching does not always protect an FI against interest rate risk.

Concept Questions

1. How does book value accounting differ from market value accounting?
2. In a market value accounting framework, what impact do rising interest rates have on the market values of an FI's assets and liabilities?
3. Using the example in Table 8–10, what would be the effect on this FI's net worth if it held one-year discount bonds (with a yield of 10 percent) as assets? Explain your findings.

WEAKNESSES OF THE MATURITY MODEL

The maturity model has two major shortcomings: (1) It does not account for the degree of leverage in the FI's balance sheet, and (2) it ignores the timing of the cash flows from the FI's assets and liabilities. As a result of these shortcomings, a strategy of matching asset and liability maturities moves the FI in the direction of hedging itself against interest rate risk, but it is easy to show that this strategy does not always eliminate all interest rate risk for an FI.

To show the effect of leverage on the ability of the FI to eliminate interest rate risk using the maturity model, assume that the FI is initially set up as shown in Table 8–12. The $100 million in assets is invested in one-year, 10 percent coupon bonds, and the $90 million in liabilities are in one-year deposits paying 10 percent. The maturity gap ($M_A - M_L$) is now zero. A 1 percent increase in interest rates results in the balance sheet in Table 8–13. In Table 8–13, even though the maturity

TABLE 8–12
Initial Market Values of an FI's Assets and Liabilities with a Maturity GAP of Zero (in millions of dollars)

Assets	Liabilities
$A = \$100$ ($M_A = 1$ year)	$L = \$ 90$ ($M_L = 1$ year)
	$E = 10$
$\overline{\$100}$	$\overline{\$100}$

TABLE 8–13
FI's Market Value Balance Sheet after a 1 Percent Rise in Interest Rates (in millions of dollars)

Assets	Liabilities
$A = \$99.09$	$L = \$89.19$
	$E = 9.90$
$\overline{\$99.09}$	$\overline{\$99.09}$

or $\quad \Delta E \;=\; \Delta A \;-\; \Delta L$
$\;\; -0.10 = -0.91 - (-0.81)$

FIGURE 8–5
One-Year CD
Cash Flows

FIGURE 8–6
One-Year Loan
Cash Flows

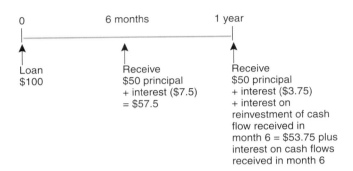

gap is zero, the FI's equity value falls by $0.10 million. The drop in equity value is due to the fact that not all the assets (bonds) were financed with deposits; rather, equity was used to finance a portion of the FI's assets. As interest rates increased, only $90 million in deposits were directly affected, while $100 million in assets were directly affected.

We show next, using a simple example, that an FI choosing to directly match the maturities and values of its assets and liabilities (so that $M_A = M_L$ and $\$A = \$L$) does not necessarily achieve perfect immunization, or protection, against interest rate risk. Consider the example of an FI that issues a one-year CD to a depositor. This CD has a face value of $100 and an interest rate promised to depositors of 15 percent. Thus, on maturity at the end of the year, the FI has to repay the borrower $100 plus $15 interest, or $115, as shown in Figure 8–5.

Suppose the FI lends $100 for one year to a corporate borrower at a 15 percent annual interest rate (thus, $\$A = \$L$). However, the FI contractually requires half of the loan ($50) to be repaid after six months and the last half to be repaid at the end of the year. Note that although the maturity of the loan equals the maturity of the deposit of 1 year and the loan is fully funded by deposit liabilities, the cash flow earned on the loan may be greater or less than the $115 required to pay off depositors, depending on what happens to interest rates over the one-year period. You can see this in Figure 8–6.

At the end of the first six months, the FI receives a $50 repayment in loan principal plus $7.5 in interest ($100 \times 1/2$ year $\times$ 15 percent), for a total midyear cash flow of $57.5. At the end of the year, the FI receives $50 as the final repayment of loan principal plus $3.75 interest ($50 \times 1/2$ year $\times$ 15 percent) plus the reinvestment income earned from relending the $57.5 received six months earlier. If interest rates do not change over the period, the FI's extra return from its ability to reinvest part of the cash flow for the last six months will be ($57.5 \times 1/2 \times$ 15 percent) = 4.3125. We summarize the total cash flow on the FI's one-year loan in Table 8–14.

TABLE 8–14
Cash Flow on a Loan with a 15 Percent Interest Rate

Cash Flow at 1/2 Year	
Principal	$ 50.00
Interest	7.50
Cash Flow at 1 Year	
Principal	$ 50.00
Interest	3.75
Reinvestment income	4.3125
	$115.5625

TABLE 8–15
Cash Flow on the Loan When the Beginning Rate of 15 Percent Falls to 12 Percent

Cash Flow at 1/2 Year	
Principal	$ 50.00
Interest	7.50
Cash Flow at 1 Year	
Principal	$ 50.00
Interest	3.75
Reinvestment income	3.45
	$114.70

As you can see, by the end of the year, the cash paid in on the loan exceeded the cash paid out on the deposit by $0.5625. The reason for this is the FI's ability to reinvest part of the principal and interest over the second half of the year at 15 percent. Suppose that interest rates, instead of staying unchanged at 15 percent throughout the whole one-year period, had fallen to 12 percent over the last six months in the year. This fall in rates would affect neither the promised deposit rate of 15 percent nor the promised loan rate of 15 percent because they are set at time 0 when the deposit and loan were originated and do not change throughout the year. What is affected is the FI's *reinvestment income* on the $57.5 cash flow received on the loan at the end of six months. It can be relent for the final six months of the year only at the new, lower interest rate of 12 percent (see Table 8–15).

The only change to the asset cash flows for the bank comes from the reinvestment of the $57.5 received at the end of six months at the lower interest rate of 12 percent. This produces the smaller reinvestment income of $3.45 ($57.5 × 1/2 × 12 percent) rather than $4.3125 when rates stayed at 15 percent throughout the year. Rather than making a profit of $0.5625 from intermediation, the FI loses $0.3. Note that this loss occurs as a result of interest rates changing, even when the FI had matched the maturity of its assets and liabilities ($M_A = M_L = 1$ year), as well as the dollar amount of loans (assets) and deposits (liabilities) (i.e., $A = $L).

Despite the matching of maturities, the FI is still exposed to interest rate risk because the *timing* of the *cash flows* on the deposit and loan are not perfectly matched. In a sense, the cash flows on the loan are received, on average, earlier than cash flows are paid out on the deposit, where all cash flows occur at the end of the year. The next chapter shows that only by matching the average lives of assets and liabilities—that is, by considering the precise timing of arrival (or payment) of cash flows—can an FI immunize itself against interest rate risk.

Concept Questions

1. Can an FI achieve perfect immunization against interest rate risk by matching the maturities of its assets and liabilities? Explain your answer.
2. Suppose the average maturity of an FI's assets is equal to its liabilities. If interest rates fall, why could an FI's net worth still decline? Explain your answer.

Summary

This chapter introduced two methods of measuring an FI's interest rate risk exposure: the repricing model and the maturity model. The repricing model looks at the difference, or gap, between an FI's rate-sensitive assets and rate-sensitive liabilities to measure interest rate risk, while the maturity model uses the difference between the average maturity of an FI's assets and that of its liabilities to measure interest rate risk. The chapter showed that both the repricing model and the maturity model have difficulty in accurately measuring the interest rate risk of an FI. In particular, the repricing model ignores the market value effects of interest rate changes, while the maturity model ignores the timing of the arrival of cash flows on assets and liabilities. More complete and accurate measures of an FI's exposure are duration and the duration gap, which are explained in the next chapter.

Questions and Problems

1. What was the impact on interest rates of the borrowed reserve targeting regime used by the Federal Reserve from 1982 to 1993?
2. How has the increased level of financial market integration affected interest rates?
3. What is the repricing gap? In using this model to evaluate interest rate risk, what is meant by rate sensitivity? On what financial performance variable does the repricing model focus? Explain.
4. What is a maturity bucket in the repricing model? Why is the length of time selected for repricing assets and liabilities important in using the repricing model?
5. Calculate the repricing gap and the impact on net interest income of a 1 percent increase in interest rates for each of the following positions:
   - Rate-sensitive assets = $200 million
     Rate-sensitive liabilities = $100 million
   - Rate-sensitive assets = $100 million
     Rate-sensitive liabilities = $150 million
   - Rate-sensitive assets = $150 million
     Rate-sensitive liabilities = $140 million

   a. Calculate the impact on net interest income of each of the above situations, assuming a 1 percent decrease in interest rates.
   b. What conclusion can you draw about the repricing model from these results?
6. What are the reasons for not including demand deposits as rate-sensitive liabilities in the repricing analysis for a commercial bank? What is the subtle but potentially strong reason for including demand deposits in the total of rate-sensitive liabilities? Can the same argument be made for passbook savings accounts?
7. What is the gap ratio? What is the value of this ratio to interest rate risk managers and regulators?

8. Which of the following assets or liabilities fit the one-year rate or repricing sensitivity test?

91-day U.S. Treasury bills
1-year U.S. Treasury notes
20-year U.S. Treasury bonds NO
20-year floating-rate corporate bonds with annual repricing
30-year floating-rate mortgages with repricing every two years NO
30-year floating-rate mortgages with repricing every six months
Overnight fed funds
9-month fixed-rate CDs
1-year fixed-rate CDs
5-year floating-rate CDs with annual repricing
Common stock NO

9. Consider the following balance sheet for WatchoverU Savings, Inc. (in millions):

Assets		Liabilities and Equity	
Floating-rate mortgages (currently 10% annually)	$ 50	Demand deposits (currently 6% annually)	$ 70
30-year fixed-rate loans (currently 7% annually)	50	Time deposits (currently 6% annually)	20
		Equity	10
Total assets	$100	Total liabilities and equity	$100

a. What is WatchoverU's expected net interest income at year-end?

b. What will be the net interest income at year-end if interest rates rise 2 percent?

c. Using the cumulative repricing gap model, what is the expected net interest income for a 2 percent increase in interest rates?

10. What are some of the weaknesses of the repricing model? How have large banks solved the problem of choosing the optimal time period for repricing? What is runoff cash flow, and how does this amount affect the repricing model's analysis?

11. Use the following information about a hypothetical government security dealer named M. P. Jorgan. Market yields are in parentheses, and amounts are in millions.

Assets		Liabilities and Equity	
Cash	$ 10	Overnight repos	$170
1-Month T-bills (7.05%)	75	Subordinated debt	150
3-Month T-bills (7.25%)	75	7-year fixed rate (8.55%)	
2-Year T-notes (7.50%)	10 50		
8-Year T-notes (8.96%)	20 100		
5-Year munis (floating rate) (8.20% reset every 6 months)	25	Equity	15
Total assets	$335	Total liabilities and equity	$335

a. What is the funding or repricing gap if the planning period is 30 days? 91 days? 2 years? Recall that cash is a non-interest-earning asset.

b. What is the impact over the next 30 days on net interest income if all interest rates rise 50 basis points? Decrease 75 basis points?

c. The following one-year runoffs are expected: $10 million for two-year T-notes and $20 million for eight-year T-notes. What is the one-year repricing gap?

d. If runoffs are considered, what is the effect on net interest income at year-end if interest rates rise 50 basis points? Decrease 75 basis points?

12. What is the difference between book value accounting and market value accounting? How do interest rate changes affect the value of bank assets and liabilities under the two methods? What is marking to market?

13. Why is it important to use market values as opposed to book values in evaluating the net worth of an FI? What are some of the advantages of using book values as opposed to market values?

14. Consider a $1,000 bond with a fixed-rate, 10 percent annual coupon (Cpn %) and a maturity (N) of 10 years. The bond currently is trading to a market yield to maturity (YTM) of 10 percent. Complete the following table:

N	Cpn %	YTM	Price	From Par, $ Change in Price	From Par, % Change in Price
8	10%	9%			
9	10%	9%			
10	10%	9%			
10	10%	10%	$1,000.00		
10	10%	11%			
11	10%	11%			
12	10%	11%			

Use this information to verify the principles of interest rate–price relationships for fixed-rate financial assets.

15. Consider a 12-year, 12 percent annual coupon bond with a required return of 10 percent. The bond has a face value of $1,000.

a. What is the price of the bond?

b. If interest rates rise to 11 percent, what is the price of the bond?

c. What has been the percentage change in price?

d. Repeat parts (a), (b), and (c) for a 16-year bond.

e. What do the respective changes in bond prices indicate?

16. Consider a five-year, 15 percent annual coupon bond with a face value of $1,000. The bond is trading at a market yield to maturity of 12 percent.

a. What is the price of the bond?

b. If the market yield to maturity increases 1 percent, what will be the bond's new price?

c. Use your answers to parts (a) and (b) to find the percentage change in the bond's price as a result of the 1 percent increase in interest rates.

d. Repeat parts (b) and (c) assuming a 1 percent decrease in interest rates.

e. What do the differences in your answers indicate about the rate–price relationships of fixed-rate assets?

17. What is a maturity gap? How can the maturity model be used to immunize an FI's portfolio? What is the critical requirement that allows maturity matching to have some success in immunizing the balance sheet of an FI?

18. Nearby Bank has the following balance sheet (in millions):

Assets		Liabilities and Equity	
Cash	$ 60	Demand deposits	$140
5-year Treasury notes	60	1-year certificates of deposit	160
30-year mortgages	200	Equity	20
Total assets	$320	Total liabilities and equity	$320

What is the maturity gap for Nearby Bank? Is Nearby Bank more exposed to an increase or a decrease in interest rates? Explain why.

19. County Bank has the following market value balance sheet (in millions, all interest at annual rates):

Assets		Liabilities and Equity	
Cash	$ 20	Demand deposits	$100
15-year commercial loan at 10% interest, balloon payment	160	5-year CDs at 6% interest, balloon payment	210
30-year mortgages at 8% interest, monthly amortizing	300	20-year debentures at 7% interest	120
		Equity	~~50~~
Total assets	$480	Total liabilities and equity	$480 430

a. What is the maturity gap for County Bank?

b. What will be the maturity gap if the interest rates on all assets and liabilities increase 1 percent?

c. What will happen to the market value of the equity?

d. If interest rates increase 2 percent, would the bank be solvent?

20. Given that bank balance sheets typically are accounted in book value terms, why should regulators or anyone else be concerned about how interest rates affect the market values of assets and liabilities?

21. If a bank manager is certain that interest rates are going to increase within the next six months, how should the bank manager adjust the bank's maturity gap to take advantage of this anticipated increase? What if the manager believed rates would fall? Would your suggested adjustments be difficult or easy to achieve?

22. Consumer Bank has $20 million in cash and a $180 million loan portfolio. The assets are funded with demand deposits of $18 million, a $162 million CD, and $20 million in equity. The loan portfolio has a maturity of two years, earns interest at an annual rate of 7 percent, and is amortized monthly. The bank pays 7 percent annual interest on the CD, but the interest will not be paid until the CD matures at the end of two years.

a. What is the maturity gap for Consumer Bank?

b. Is Consumer Bank immunized, or protected, against changes in interest rates? Why or why not?

c. Does Consumer Bank face interest rate risk? That is, if market interest rates increase or decrease 1 percent, what happens to the value of the equity?

d. How can a decrease in interest rates create interest rate risk?

23. FI International holds seven-year Acme International bonds and two-year Beta Corporation bonds. The Acme bonds are yielding 12 percent and the Beta bonds are yielding 14 percent under current market conditions.

    a. What is the weighted-average maturity of FI's bond portfolio if 40 percent is in Acme bonds and 60 percent is in Beta bonds?

    b. What proportion of Acme and Beta bonds should be held to have a weighted-average yield of 13.5 percent?

    c. What will be the weighted-average maturity of the bond portfolio if the weighted-average yield is realized?

24. An insurance company has invested in the following fixed-income securities: (a) $10,000,000 of five-year Treasury notes paying 5 percent interest and selling at par value, (b) $5,800,000 of 10-year bonds paying 7 percent interest with a par value of $6,000,000, and (c) $6,200,000 of 20-year subordinated debentures paying 9 percent interest with a par value of $6,000,000.

    a. What is the weighted-average maturity of this portfolio of assets?

    b. If interest rates change so that the yields on all the securities decrease 1 percent, how does the weighted-average maturity of the portfolio change?

    c. Explain the changes in the maturity values if the yields increase 1 percent.

    d. Assume that the insurance company has no other assets. What will be the effect on the market value of the company's equity if the interest rate changes in (b) and (c) occur?

25. The following is a simplified FI balance sheet:

Assets		Liabilities and Equity	
Loans	$1,000	Deposits	$ 850
		Equity	150
Total assets	$1,000	Total liabilities and equity	$1,000

The average maturity of loans is four years, and the average maturity of deposits is two years. Assume that loan and deposit balances are reported as book value, zero-coupon items.

    a. Assume that the interest rate on both loans and deposits is 9 percent. What is the market value of equity?

    b. What must be the interest rate on deposits to force the market value of equity to be zero? What economic market conditions must exist to make this situation possible?

    c. Assume that the interest rate on both loans and deposits is 9 percent. What must be the average maturity of deposits for the market value of equity to be zero?

26. Gunnison Insurance has reported the following balance sheet (in thousands):

Assets		Liabilities and Equity	
2-year Treasury note	$175	1-year commercial paper	$135
15-year munis	165	5-year note	160
		Equity	45
Total assets	$340	Total liabilities and equity	$340

All securities are selling at par equal to book value. The two-year notes are yielding 5 percent, and the 15-year munis are yielding 9 percent. The one-year commercial paper pays 4.5 percent, and the five-year notes pay 8 percent. All instruments pay interest annually.

a. What is the weighted-average maturity of the assets for Gunnison?

b. What is the weighted-average maturity of the liabilities for Gunnison?

c. What is the maturity gap for Gunnison?

d. What does your answer to part (c) imply about the interest rate exposure of Gunnison Insurance?

e. Calculate the values of all four securities of Gunnison Insurance's balance sheet assuming that all interest rates increase 2 percent. What is the dollar change in the total asset and total liability values? What is the percentage change in these values?

f. What is the dollar impact on the market value of equity for Gunnison? What is the percentage change in the value of the equity?

g. What would be the impact on Gunnison's market value of equity if the liabilities paid interest semiannually instead of annually?

27. Scandia Bank has issued a one-year, $1 million CD paying 5.75 percent to fund a one-year loan paying an interest rate of 6 percent. The principal of the loan will be paid in two installments: $500,000 in six months and the balance at the end of the year.

a. What is the maturity gap of Scandia Bank? According to the maturity model, what does this maturity gap imply about the interest rate risk exposure faced by Scandia Bank?

b. What is the expected net interest income at the end of the year?

c. What would be the effect on annual net interest income of a 2 percent interest rate increase that occurred immediately after the loan was made? What would be the effect of a 2 percent decrease in rates?

d. What do these results indicate about the ability of the maturity model to immunize portfolios against interest rate exposure?

28. EDF Bank has a very simple balance sheet. Assets consist of a two-year, $1 million loan that pays an interest rate of LIBOR plus 4 percent annually. The loan is funded with a two-year deposit on which the bank pays LIBOR plus 3.5 percent interest annually. LIBOR currently is 4 percent, and both the loan and the deposit principal will be paid at maturity.

a. What is the maturity gap of this balance sheet?

b. What is the expected net interest income in year 1 and year 2?

c. Immediately prior to the beginning of year 2, LIBOR rates increase to 6 percent. What is the expected net interest income in year 2? What would be the effect on net interest income of a 2 percent decrease in LIBOR?

d. How would your results be affected if the interest payments on the loan were received semiannually?

e. What implications do these results have for the effectiveness of the maturity model as an immunization strategy?

29. What are the weaknesses of the maturity model?

The following questions and problems are based on material in Appendix A to the chapter.

30. The current one-year Treasury bill rate is 5.2 percent, and the expected one-year rate 12 months from now is 5.8 percent. According to the unbiased expectations theory, what should be the current rate for a two-year Treasury security?

31. A recent edition of *The Wall Street Journal* reported interest rates of 6 percent, 6.35 percent, 6.65 percent, and 6.75 percent for three-year, four-year, five-year, and six-year Treasury notes, respectively. According to the unbiased expectations theory, what are the expected one-year rates for years 4, 5, and 6?

32. How does the liquidity premium theory of the term structure of interest rates differ from the unbiased expectations theory? In a normal economic environment, that is, an upward-sloping yield curve, what is the relationship of liquidity premiums for successive years into the future? Why?

Pertinent Web Sites

Bank for International Settlements	www.bis.org
Board of Governors of the Federal Reserve	www.federalreserve.gov

Chapter Notation

View the Chapter Notation at the Web site for this textbook (**www.mhhe.com/saunders5e**).

Appendix 8A

Term Structure of Interest Rates

To explain the process of estimating the impact of an unexpected shock in short-term interest rates on the entire term structure of interest rates, FIs use the theory of the term structure of interest rates or the yield curve. The *term structure of interest rates* compares the market yields or interest rates on securities, assuming that all characteristics (default risk, coupon rate, etc.) except maturity are the same. The yield curve for U.S. Treasury securities is the most commonly reported and analyzed yield curve. The shape of the yield curve on Treasury securities has taken many forms over the years. Figure 8A–1 presents the Treasury yield curve as of October 3, 2003. As can be seen, the yield curve on this date reflected the normal upward-sloping relationship between yield and maturity. Explanations for the shape of the yield curve fall predominantly into three theories: the unbiased expectations theory, the liquidity premium theory, and the market segmentation theory.

UNBIASED EXPECTATIONS THEORY

According to the unbiased expectations theory for the term structure of interest rates, at a given point in time the yield curve reflects the market's current expectations of future short-term rates. Thus, an upward-sloping yield curve reflects the market's expectation that short-term rates will rise throughout the relevant time period (e.g., the Federal Reserve is expected to tighten monetary policy in the future). Similarly, a flat yield curve reflects the expectation that short-term rates will remain constant over the relevant time period.

The intuition behind the unbiased expectations theory is that if investors have a 30-year investment horizon, they could either buy a current 30-year bond and earn the current yield on a 30-year bond (R_{30}, if held to maturity) each year, or could invest in 30 successive one-year bonds (of which they know only the current one-year rate, R_1, but form expectations of the unknown future one-year rates). In equilibrium, the return to holding a 30-year bond to maturity should equal the expected return to investing in 30 successive one-year bonds. Similarly, the return on a 29-year bond should equal the expected return on investing in 29 successive one-year bonds. If future one-year rates are expected to rise each successive year into the future, then the yield curve will slope upward. Specifically, the current 30-year T-bond rate or return will exceed the 29-year bond rate, which will exceed the 28-year bond rate, and so on. Similarly, if future one-year rates are expected to remain constant each successive year into the future, then the 30-year bond rate will be equal to the 29-year bond rate; that is, the term structure of interest rates will remain constant over the relevant time period. Specifically, the unbiased expectations theory posits that long-term rates are a geometric average of current and expected short-term interest rates. That is, the interest rate that equates the return on a series of short-term security investments with the return on a long-term security with an equivalent maturity reflects the market's forecast of future interest rates. The mathematical equation representing this relationship is:

FIGURE 8A–1
Treasury Yield Curve, October 3, 2003

Source: Board of Governors of the Federal Reserve, "Selected Interest Rates," October 2003. *www.federalreserve.gov*

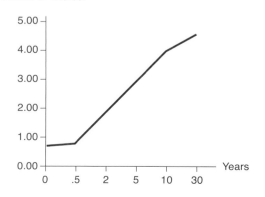

$$(1 + {}_1R_N)^N = (1 + {}_1R_1)(1 + E({}_2r_1)) \ldots (1 + E({}_Nr_1))$$

where

$$_1R_N = \text{Actual N-period rate}$$
$$N = \text{Term to maturity}$$
$$_1R_1 = \text{Current one-year rate}$$
$$E(_tr_1) = \text{Expected one-year (forward) yield during period } t$$

Notice that uppercase interest rate terms $_1R_t$ are the actual current interest rates on securities purchased today with a maturity of t years. Lowercase interest rate terms $_tr_1$ are estimates of future one-year interest rates starting t years into the future. For example, suppose the current one-year spot rate and expected one-year Treasury bill rates over the following three years (i.e., years 2, 3, and 4, respectively) are as follows:

$$_1R_1 = 6\%, \quad E(_2r_1) = 7\%,$$
$$E(_3r_1) = 7.5\%, \quad E(_4r_1) = 7.85\%$$

This would be consistent with the market's expecting the Federal Reserve to increasingly tighten monetary policy. With the unbiased expectations theory, current long-term rates for one-, two-, three-, and four-year maturity Treasury securities should be:

$$_1R_1 = 6\%$$
$$_1R_2 = [(1+.06)(1+.07)]^{1/2} - 1 = 6.499\%$$
$$_1R_3 = [(1+.06)(1+.07)(1+.075)]^{1/3} - 1 = 6.832\%$$
$$_1R_4 = [(1+.06)(1+.07)(1+.075)(1+.0785)]^{1/4} - 1$$
$$= 7.085\%$$

And the yield curve should look like this:

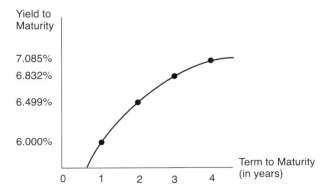

Thus, the upward-sloping yield curve reflects the market's expectation of consistently rising one-year (short-term) interest rates in the future.

LIQUIDITY PREMIUM THEORY

The unbiased expectations theory has the shortcoming that it neglects to recognize that forward rates are not perfect predictors of future interest rates. If forward rates were perfect predictors of future interest rates, future prices of Treasury securities would be known with certainty. The return over any investment period would be certain and independent of the maturity of the instrument initially purchased and of the time at which the investor needs to liquidate the security. However, with uncertainty about future interest rates (and future monetary policy actions) and hence about future security prices, these instruments become risky in the sense that the return over a future investment period is unknown. In other words, because of future uncertainty of return, there is a risk in holding long-term securities, and that risk increases with the security's maturity.

The liquidity premium theory of the term structure of interest rates allows for this future uncertainty. It is based on the idea that investors will hold long-term maturities only if they are offered a premium to compensate for the future uncertainty in a security's value, which increases with an asset's maturity. In other words, the liquidity premium theory states that long-term rates are equal to the geometric average of current and expected short-term rates plus a liquidity or risk premium that increases with the maturity of the security. Figure 8A–2 illustrates the difference in the shape of the yield curve under the unbiased expectations theory versus the liquidity premium theory. For example, according to the liquidity premium theory, an upward-sloping yield curve may reflect the investor's expectations that future short-term rates will rise, be flat, or fall, but because the liquidity premium increases with maturity, the yield curve will nevertheless increase with the term to maturity. The liquidity premium theory may be mathematically represented as:

$$_1R_N = [(1 + {}_1R_1)(1 + E(_2r_1) + LP_2) \cdots$$
$$(1 + E(_Nr_1) + LP_N)]^{1/N} - 1$$

where

$LP_t = $ liquidity premium for a period t and $LP_2 < LP_3 < \cdots < LP_N.$

FIGURE 8A–2 Yield Curve under the Unbiased Expectations Theory (UET) versus the Liquidity-Premium Theory (LPT)

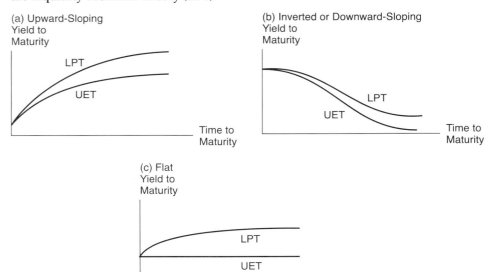

(a) Upward-Sloping Yield to Maturity

LPT
UET
Time to Maturity

(b) Inverted or Downward-Sloping Yield to Maturity

LPT
UET
Time to Maturity

(c) Flat Yield to Maturity

LPT
UET
Time to Maturity

MARKET SEGMENTATION THEORY

Market segmentation theory argues that individual investors have specific maturity preferences. Accordingly, securities with different maturities are not seen as perfect substitutes under the market segmentation theory. Instead, individual investors have preferred investment horizons dictated by the nature of the assets and liabilities they hold. For example, banks might prefer to hold relatively short-term U.S. Treasury bills because of the short-term nature of their deposit liabilities, while insurance companies might prefer to hold long-term U.S. Treasury bonds because of the long-term nature of their life insurance contractual liabilities. As a result, interest rates are determined by distinct supply and demand conditions within a particular maturity bucket or market segment (e.g., the short end and the long end of the market). The market segmentation theory assumes that neither investors nor borrowers are willing to shift from one maturity sector to another to take advantage of opportunities arising from changes in yields. Figure 8A–3 demonstrates how changes in the supply curve for short- versus long-term bonds result in changes in the shape of the yield curve. Such a change may occur if the U.S. Treasury decides to issue fewer short-term bonds and more long-term

bonds (i.e., to lengthen the average maturity of government debt outstanding). Specifically in Figure 8A–3, the higher the yield on securities, the higher the demand for them. Thus, as the supply of securities decreases in the short-term market and increases in the long-term market, the slope of the yield curve becomes steeper. If the supply of short-term securities had increased while the supply of long-term securities had decreased, the yield curve would have become flatter (and may even have sloped downward). Indeed, the large-scale repurchases of long-term Treasury bonds (i.e., reductions in supply) by the U.S. Treasury in 2000 have been viewed as the major cause of the inverted yield curve that appeared in February 2000.

FORECASTING INTEREST RATES

As interest rates change, so do the values of financial securities. Accordingly, the ability to predict or forecast interest rates is critical to the profitability of FIs. For example, if interest rates rise, the value of investment portfolios of FIs will fall, resulting in a loss of wealth. Thus, interest rate forecasts are extremely important for the financial wealth of FIs. The discussion of the unbiased expectations theory above indicated that the shape of the yield curve is determined by the market's

FIGURE 8A–3   Market Segmentation and Determination of the Slope of the Yield Curve

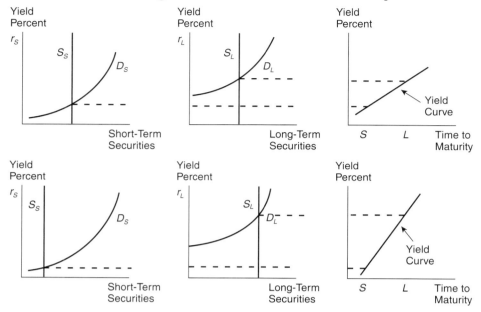

current expectations of future short-term interest rates. For example, an upward-sloping yield curve suggests that the market expects future short-term interest rates to increase. Given that the yield curve represents the market's current expectations of future short-term interest rates, the unbiased expectations theory can be used to forecast (short-term) interest rates in the future (i.e., forward one-year interest rates). A forward rate is an expected or implied rate on a short-term security that is to be originated at some point in the future. With the equations representing unbiased expectations theory, the market's expectation of forward rates can be derived directly from existing or actual rates on securities currently traded in the spot market.

To find an implied forward rate on a one-year security to be issued one year from today, we can rewrite the unbiased expectation theory equation as follows:

$$_1R_2 = [(1 + {_1R_1})(1 + ({_2f_1}))]^{1/2} - 1$$

where

  $_2f_1$ = Expected one-year rate for year 2, or the implied forward one-year rate for next year

Therefore, $_2f_1$ is the market's estimate of the expected one-year rate for year 2. Solving for $_2f_1$,

we get:

$$_2f_1 = [(1 + {_1R_2})^2/(1 + ({_1R_1})] - 1$$

In general, we can find the one-year forward rate for any year, N years into the future using the following equation:

$$_Nf_1 = [(1 + {_1R_N})^N/(1 + ({_1R_{N-1}}))^{N-1}] - 1$$

For example, on October 3, 2003, the existing or current (spot) one-year, two-year, three-year, and four-year zero-coupon Treasury security rates were as follows:

$$_1R_1 = 2.47\%, \quad _1R_2 = 3.66\%,$$
$$_1R_3 = 4.29\%, \quad _1R_4 = 4.69\%$$

With the unbiased expectation theory, one-year forward rates on zero-coupon Treasury bonds for years 2, 3, and 4 as of October 3, 2003, were:

$$_2f_1 = [(1.0366)^2/(1.0247)] - 1 \ = 4.864\%$$
$$_3f_1 = [(1.0429)^3/(1.0366)^2] - 1 = 5.561\%$$
$$_4f_1 = [(1.0469)^4/(1.0429)^3] - 1 = 5.900\%$$

Thus, the expected one-year rate one year into the future was 4.864 percent; the expected one-year rate two years into the future was 5.561 percent; and the expected one-year rate three years into the future was 5.900 percent.

Appendix 8B

The Basics of Bond Valuation

View Appendix 8B at the Web site for this textbook (**www.mhhe.com/saunders5e**).

Chapter **Nine**

Interest Rate Risk II

INTRODUCTION

In this second chapter on measuring interest rate risk, we present a second market value–based model of managing interest rate risk: the duration model. We explain the concept of *duration* and see that duration and the duration gap are more accurate measures of an FI's interest rate risk exposure than is the simple maturity model described in Chapter 8. Unlike the repricing model, duration gap considers market values and the maturity distributions of an FI's assets and liabilities. Further, unlike the maturity model, duration gap considers the degree of leverage on an FI's balance sheet as well as the timing of the payment or arrival of cash flows of assets and liabilities. Thus, duration gap is a more comprehensive measure of an FI's interest rate risk. As a result, regulators are increasingly focusing on this model in determining an appropriate level of capital reserves for an FI exposed to interest rate risk (Chapter 20). We begin the chapter by presenting the basic arithmetic needed to calculate the duration of an asset or liability. Then we analyze the economic meaning of the number we calculate for duration. This number, which measures the average life of an asset or liability, also has *economic* meaning as the interest sensitivity (or interest elasticity) of that asset or liability's value. Next, we show how the duration measure can be used to protect an FI (or immunize its portfolio) against interest rate risk. Finally, we examine some problems in applying the duration measure to real-world FIs' balance sheets. The more advanced issues associated with these problems are presented in the Appendix to the chapter.

DURATION

Duration is a more complete measure of an asset or liability's interest rate sensitivity than is maturity because duration takes into account the time of arrival (or payment) of all cash flows as well as the asset's (or liability's) maturity. Consider the example of the one-year loan at the end of Chapter 8. This loan had a 15 percent interest rate and required repayment of half the $100 in principal at the end of six months and the other half at the end of the year. The promised cash flows *(CF)* received by the FI from the borrower at the end of one-half year and at the end of the year appear in Figure 9–1.

$CF_{1/2}$ is the $50 promised repayment of principal plus the $7.50 promised interest payment ($100 \times \frac{1}{2} \times 15\%$) received after six months. CF_1 is the promised cash flow at the end of the year and is equal to the second $50 promised principal repayment plus $3.75 promised interest ($50 \times \frac{1}{2} \times 15\%$). To compare the relative sizes of these two cash flows, we should put them in the same dimensions. This is the case because $1 of principal or interest received at the end of a year is worth

FIGURE 9–1
Promised Cash
Flows on the One-
Year Loan

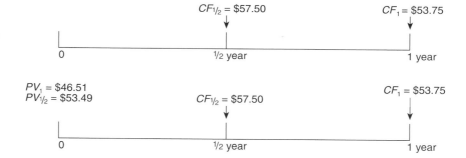

FIGURE 9–2
PV of the Cash
Flows from the
Loan

less to the FI in terms of the time value of money than $1 of principal or interest received at the end of six months. Assuming that the current required interest rates are 15 percent per annum, we calculate the present values (PV) of the two cash flows (CF) shown in Figure 9–2 as:

$$CF_{1/2} = \$57.5 \qquad\qquad PV_{1/2} = \$57.5/(1.075) = \$53.49$$
$$CF_1 = \$53.75 \qquad\qquad PV_1 = \$53.75/(1.075)^2 = \$46.51$$
$$CF_{1/2} + CF_1 = \$111.25 \qquad PV_{1/2} + PV_1 = \$100.00$$

Note that since $CF_{1/2}$, the cash flows received at the end of one-half year, are received earlier, they are discounted at $(1 + \frac{1}{2} R)$, where R is the current annual interest rate on the loan. This is smaller than the discount rate on the cash flow received at the end of the year $(1 + \frac{1}{2} R)^2$.[1] Figure 9–2 summarizes the PVs of the cash flows from the loan.

duration
The weighted-
average time to
maturity on an
investment.

Technically speaking, **duration** is the *weighted-average* time to maturity on the loan using the relative present values of the cash flows as weights. On a time value of money basis, duration measures the period of time required to recover the initial investment on the loan. Any cash flows received prior to the loan's duration reflect recovery of the initial investment, while cash flows received after the period of the loan's duration and before its maturity are the profits, or return, earned by the FI. As Figure 9–2 shows, the FI receives some cash flows at one-half year and some at one year. Duration analysis weights the time at which cash flows are received by the relative importance in present value terms of the cash flows arriving at each point in time. In present value terms, the relative importance of the cash flows arriving at time $t = \frac{1}{2}$ year and time $t = 1$ year are as follows:

Time (t)	Weight (x)		
1/2 year	$X_{1/2} = \dfrac{PV_{1/2}}{PV_{1/2} + PV_1}$	$= \dfrac{53.49}{100.00}$	$= .5349 = 53.49\%$
1 year	$X_1 = \dfrac{PV_1}{PV_{1/2} + PV_1}$	$= \dfrac{46.51}{100.00}$	$= .4651 = 46.51\%$
			$1.0 \qquad 100\%$

That is, in present value terms, the FI receives 53.49 percent of cash flows on the loan with the first payment at the end of six months ($t = \frac{1}{2}$) and 46.51 percent with

[1] We use here the Treasury formula for calculating the present values of cash flows on a security that pays cash flows semiannually. This approach is more accurate, since it reflects the semiannual payment and compounding of interest on the loan.

FIGURE 9–3
PV of the Cash
Flows of the
Deposit

$PV_1 = \$100$ $CF_1 = \$115$

0   1 year

the second payment at the end of the year ($t = 1$). By definition, the sum of the (present value) cash flow weights must equal 1:

$$X_{1/2} + X_1 = 1$$

$$.5349 + .4651 = 1$$

We can now calculate the duration (D), or the weighted-average time to maturity, of the loan using the present value of its cash flows as weights:

$$D_1 = X_{1/2}(^1/_2) + X_1(1)$$

$$= .5349(^1/_2) + .4651(1) = .7326 \text{ years}$$

Thus, while the maturity of the loan is one year, its duration, or average life in a cash flow sense, is only .7326 years. On a time value of money basis, the initial investment in the loan is recovered (albeit not realized) after .7326 years. After that time the FI earns a profit, or return, on the loan. The duration is less than the maturity of the loan because in present value terms 53.49 percent of the cash flows are received at the end of one-half year. Note that duration is measured in years since we weight the time (t) at which cash flows are received by the relative present value importance of cash flows ($X_{1/2}$, X_1, etc.).

To learn why the FI was still exposed to interest rate risk while matching maturities under the maturity model in the example at the end of Chapter 8, we next calculate the duration of the one-year, $100, 15 percent interest certificate of deposit. The FI promises to make only one cash payment to depositors at the end of the year; that is, $CF_1 = \$115$, which is the promised principal ($100) and interest repayment ($15) to the depositor. Since weights are calculated in present value terms:[2]

$$CF_1 = \$115, PV_1 = \$115/1.15 = \$100$$

We show this in Figure 9–3. Because all cash flows are received in one payment at the end of the year, $X_1 = PV_1/PV_1 = 1$, the duration of the deposit is:

$$D_D = X_1 \times (1)$$

$$D_D = 1 \times (1) = 1 \text{ year}$$

Thus, only when all cash flows are limited to one payment at the end of the period with no intervening cash flows does duration equal maturity. This example also illustrates that while the maturity gap between the loan and the deposit is zero, the duration gap is negative:

$$M_L - M_D = 1 - 1 = 0$$

$$D_L - D_D = .7326 - 1 = -.2674 \text{ years}$$

As will become clearer, to measure and to hedge interest rate risk, the FI needs to manage its duration gap rather than its maturity gap.

---

[2] Since the CD is like an annual coupon bond, the annual discount rate is $1/(1 + R) = 1/1.15$.

Concept Questions

1. Why is duration considered a more complete measure of an asset or liability's interest rate sensitivity than maturity?
2. When is the duration of an asset equal to its maturity?

A GENERAL FORMULA FOR DURATION

You can calculate the duration for any fixed-income security that pays interest annually using the following general formula:[3]

*(handwritten: PV of cash flows * Length of time Recieving cash Flow)*

$$D = \frac{\sum_{t=1}^{N} CF_t \times DF_1 \times t}{\sum_{t=1}^{N} CF_t \times DF_t} = \frac{\sum_{t=1}^{N} PV_t \times t}{\sum_{t=1}^{N} PV_t}$$

where

(handwritten: PV of cash flows (market Price))

D = Duration measured in years

CF_t = Cash flow received on the security at end of period t

N = Last period in which the cash flow is received

DF_t = Discount factor = $1/(1 + R)^t$, where R is the annual yield or current level of interest rates in the market

$\sum_{t=1}^{N}$ = Summation sign for addition of all terms from $t = 1$ to $t = N$

PV_t = Present value of the cash flow at the end of the period t, which equals $CF_t \times DF_t$

For bonds that pay interest semiannually, the duration equation becomes:[4]

$$D = \frac{\sum_{t=1/2}^{N} \dfrac{CF_t \times t}{(1 + R/2)^{2t}}}{\sum_{t=1/2}^{N} \dfrac{CF_t}{(1 + R/2)^{2t}}}$$

where $t = 1/2, 1, 1\frac{1}{2}, \ldots, N$

Notice that the denominator of the duration equation is the present value of the cash flows on the security (which in an efficient market will be equal to the current market price). The numerator is the present value of each cash flow received on the security multiplied or weighted by the length of time required to receive the cash flow. To help you fully understand this formula, we next look at some examples.

[3] In the following material a number of useful examples and formulas were suggested by G. Hawawini of INSEAD. For more discussion of the duration model and a number of those examples, see G. Hawawini, "Controlling the Interest Rate Risk of Bonds: An Introduction to Duration Analysis and Immunization Strategies," *Financial Markets and Portfolio Management* 1 (1986–87), pp. 8–18.

[4] In general, the duration equation is written as:

$$D = \frac{\sum_{t=1/m}^{N} \dfrac{CF_t \times t}{(1 + R/m)^{mt}}}{\sum_{t=1/m}^{N} \dfrac{CF_t}{(1 + R/m)^{mt}}}$$

where m = number of times per year interest is paid.

$$\frac{1}{(1+t)^t}$$

TABLE 9–1
The Duration of a
Six-Year Eurobond
with 8 Percent
Coupon and Yield

t	CF_t	DF_t	$CF_t \times DF_t$	$CF_t \times DF_t \times t$
1	80	0.9259	74.07	74.07
2	80	0.8573	68.59	137.18
3	80	0.7938	63.51	190.53
4	80	0.7350	58.80	235.20
5	80	0.6806	54.45	272.25
6	1,080	0.6302	680.58	4,083.48
			1,000.00	4,992.71

$$D = \frac{4,992.71}{1,000} = 4.993 \text{ years}$$

$$\frac{1}{\left(1+\frac{R}{2}\right)^{t*2}}$$

TABLE 9–2
The Duration of
a Two-Year U.S.
Treasury Bond with
8 Percent Coupon
and 12 Percent Yield

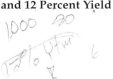

t	CF_t	DF_t	$CF_t \times DF_t$	$CF_t \times DF_t \times t$
½	40	.9434	37.74	18.87
1	40	.8900	35.60	35.60
1½	40	.8396	33.58	50.37
2	1,040	.7921	823.78	1,647.56
			930.70	1,752.40

$$D = \frac{1,752.40}{930.70} = 1.883 \text{ years}$$

The Duration of Interest-Bearing Bonds

EXAMPLE 9–1

*The Duration
of a Six-Year
Eurobond*

Eurobonds pay coupons *annually.* Suppose the annual coupon is 8 percent, the face value of the bond is $1,000, and the current yield to maturity (R) is also 8 percent. We show the calculation of its duration in Table 9–1.

As the calculation indicates, the duration or weighted-average time to maturity on this bond is 4.993 years. In other words, on a time value of money basis, the initial investment of $1,000 is recovered after 4.993 years. Between 4.993 years and maturity (6 years), the bond produces a profit or return to the investor.

EXAMPLE 9–2

*The Duration of
a Two-Year U.S.
Treasury Bond*

U.S. Treasury bonds pay coupon interest semiannually. Suppose the annual coupon rate is 8 percent, the face value is $1,000, and the annual yield to maturity (R) is 12 percent. See Table 9–2 for the calculation of the duration of this bond.[5] As the calculation indicates, the duration, or weighted-average time to maturity, on this bond is 1.883 years. Table 9–3 shows that if the annual coupon rate is lowered to 6 percent, duration rises to 1.909 years. Since 6 percent coupon payments are lower than 8 percent, it takes longer to recover the initial investment in the bond. In Table 9–4 duration is calculated for the original 8 percent bond, assuming that the yield to maturity increases to 16 percent. Now duration falls from 1.883 years (in Table 9–2) to 1.878 years. The higher the yield to maturity on the bond, the more the investor earns on reinvested coupons and the shorter the time needed to recover the initial investment. Finally, when the maturity on a bond decreases to 1 year (see Table 9–5), its duration falls to 0.980 years. Thus, the shorter the maturity on the bond, the more quickly the initial investment is recovered.

[5] Here we use the Treasury formula for discounting bonds with semiannual coupons: $(1 + R/2)^x$ where x is the number of semiannual coupon payments. Thus, at $t = 1/2$, the discount rate is (1.06), at $t = 1$ the discount rate is $(1.06)^2$, and so on.

TABLE 9–3
Duration of a Two-Year U.S. Treasury Bond with 6 Percent Coupon and 12 Percent Yield

t	CF_t	DF_t	$CF_t \times DF_t$	$CF_t \times DF_t \times t$
$1/2$	30	0.9434	28.30	14.15
1	30	0.8900	26.70	26.70
$1\,1/2$	30	0.8396	25.19	37.78
2	1,030	0.7921	815.86	1,631.71
			896.05	1,710.34

$$D = \frac{1{,}710.34}{896.05} = 1.909 \text{ years}$$

TABLE 9–4
Duration of a Two-Year U.S. Treasury Bond with 8 Percent Coupon and 16 Percent Yield

t	CF_t	DF_t	$CF_t \times DF_t$	$CF_t \times DF_t \times t$
$1/2$	40	0.9259	37.04	18.52
1	40	0.8573	34.29	34.29
$1\,1/2$	40	0.7938	31.75	47.63
2	1,040	0.7350	764.43	1,528.86
			867.51	1,629.30

$$D = \frac{1{,}629.30}{867.51} = 1.878 \text{ years}$$

TABLE 9–5
Duration of a One-Year U.S. Treasury Bond with 8 Percent Coupon and 12 Percent Yield

t	CF_t	DF_t	$CF_t \times DF_t$	$CF_t \times DF_t \times t$
$1/2$	40	0.9434	37.74	18.87
1	1,040	0.8900	925.60	925.60
			963.34	944.47

$$D = \frac{944.47}{963.34} = 0.980 \text{ years}$$

Next, we look at two other types of bonds that are useful in understanding duration.

The Duration of a Zero-Coupon Bond

The U.S. Treasury has created zero-coupon bonds that allow securities firms and other investors to strip individual coupons and the principal from regular Treasury bonds and sell them to investors as separate securities. Elsewhere, such as in the Eurobond markets, corporations have issued discount or zero-coupon bonds directly. U.S. T-bills and commercial paper usually are issued on a discount basis and are additional examples of discount bonds. These bonds sell at a discount from face value on issue, pay the face value (e.g., $1,000) on maturity, and have no intervening cash flows, such as coupon payments, between issue and maturity. The current price an investor is willing to pay for such a bond is equal to the present value of the single, fixed (face value) payment on the bond that is received on maturity (here, $1,000), or:

$$P = \frac{1{,}000}{(1 + R)^N}$$

where R is the required annually compounded yield to maturity, N is the number of years to maturity, and P is the price. Because there are no intervening cash flows such as coupons between issue and maturity, the following must be true:

$$D_B = M_B$$

That is, the duration of a zero-coupon bond equals its maturity. Note that only for zero-coupon bonds are duration and maturity equal. Indeed, for any bond that pays some cash flows prior to maturity, its duration will always be less than its maturity.

The Duration of a Consol Bond (Perpetuities)

consol bond
A bond that pays a fixed coupon each year forever.

Although consol bonds have yet to be issued in the United States, they are of theoretical interest in exploring the differences between maturity and duration. A **consol bond** pays a fixed coupon each year. The novel feature of this bond is that it *never* matures; that is, it is a perpetuity:

$$M_c = \infty$$

In fact, consol bonds that were issued by the British government in the 1890s to finance the Boer Wars in South Africa are still outstanding. However, while its maturity is theoretically infinity, the formula for the duration of a consol bond is:[6]

$$D_c = 1 + \frac{1}{R}$$

where R is the required yield to maturity. Suppose that the yield curve implies $R = 5$ percent annually; then the duration of the consol bond would be:

$$D_c = 1 + \frac{1}{.05} = 21 \text{ years}$$

Thus, while maturity is infinite, duration is finite. Specifically, on the basis of the time value of money, recovery of the initial investment on this perpetual bond takes 21 years. After 21 years, the bond produces profit for the bondholder. Moreover, as interest rates rise, the duration of the consol bond falls. Consider the 1979–82 period, when some yields rose to around 20 percent on long-term government bonds. Then:

$$D_c = 1 + \frac{1}{.2} = 6 \text{ years}$$

Concept Questions

1. What does the denominator of the duration equation measure?
2. What does the numerator of the duration equation measure?
3. Calculate the duration of a one-year, 8 percent coupon, 10 percent yield bond that pays coupons quarterly.
4. What is the duration of a zero-coupon bond?
5. What feature is unique about a consol bond compared with other bonds?

[6] For reasons of space, we do not provide a formal proof here. Interested readers might refer to G. Hawawini, "Controlling the Interest Rate Risk of Bonds: An Introduction to Duration Analysis and Immunization Strategies," *Financial Markets and Portfolio Management* 1 (1986–87), pp. 8–18.

FEATURES OF DURATION

From the preceding examples, we derive three important features of duration relating to the maturity, yield, and coupon interest of the security being analyzed.

Duration and Maturity

A comparison of Tables 9–5, 9–2, and 9–6 indicates that duration *increases* with the maturity of a fixed-income asset or liability, but at a *decreasing* rate:

$$\frac{\partial D}{\partial M} > 0 \qquad \frac{\partial D^2}{\partial^2 M} < 0$$

To see this, look at Figure 9–4, where we plot duration against maturity for a three-year, a two-year, and a one-year U.S. Treasury bond using the *same yield of 12 percent* for all three and assuming an annual coupon of 8 percent (with semiannual payments of 4 percent) on each bond. As the maturity of the bond increases from one year to two years (Tables 9–5 and 9–2), duration increases by 0.903 years, from 0.980 years to 1.883 years. Increasing maturity an additional year, from two years to three years (Tables 9–2 and 9–6), increases duration by 0.826, from 1.883 years to 2.709 years.

Duration and Yield

A comparison of Tables 9–2 and 9–4 indicates that duration decreases as yield increases:

$$\frac{\partial D}{\partial R} < 0$$

TABLE 9–6
Duration of a Three-Year U.S. Treasury Bond with 8 Percent Coupon and 12 Percent Yield (coupon interest paid semiannually)

t	CF_t	DF_t	$CF_t \times DF_t$	$CF_t \times DF_t \times t$
$\frac{1}{2}$	40	0.9434	37.74	18.87
1	40	0.8900	35.60	35.60
$1\frac{1}{2}$	40	0.8396	33.58	50.37
2	40	0.7921	31.68	63.36
$2\frac{1}{2}$	40	0.7473	29.89	74.72
3	1,040	0.7050	733.16	2,199.48
			901.65	2,442.40

$$D = \frac{2,442.40}{901.65} = 2.709 \text{ years}$$

FIGURE 9–4
Duration versus Maturity

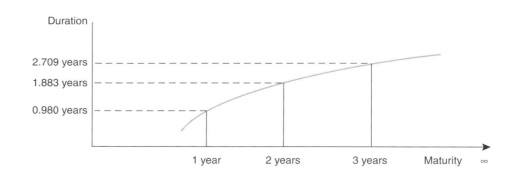

As the yield on the Treasury bond increased from 12 percent to 16 percent (Tables 9–2 and 9–4), the duration on the bond decreased from 1.883 years to 1.878 years. This makes sense intuitively because higher yields discount later cash flows more heavily and the relative importance, or weights, of those later cash flows decline when compared with earlier cash flows on an asset or liability.

Duration and Coupon Interest

A comparison of Tables 9–3 and 9–2 indicates that the higher the coupon or promised interest payment on the security, the lower its duration:

$$\frac{\partial D}{\partial C} < 0$$

As the coupon rate on the U.S. Treasury bond increased from 6 percent to 8 percent in Tables 9–3 and 9–2, the duration on the bond decreased from 1.909 years to 1.883 years. This is due to the fact that the larger the coupons or promised interest payments, the more quickly cash flows are received by investors and the higher are the present value weights of those cash flows in the duration calculation. On a time value of money basis, the investor recoups the initial investment faster when coupon payments are larger.

Concept Questions

1. Which has the longest duration, a 30-year, 8 percent, zero-coupon or discount bond or an 8 percent infinite maturity consol bond?
2. What is the relationship between duration and yield to maturity on a financial security?
3. Do high-coupon bonds have high or low durations?

THE ECONOMIC MEANING OF DURATION

So far we have calculated duration for a number of different fixed-income assets and liabilities. Now we are ready to make the direct link between the number measured in years we call duration and the interest rate sensitivity of an asset or liability or of an FI's entire portfolio.

In addition to being a measure of the average life, in a cash flow sense, of an asset or liability, duration is also a *direct* measure of the interest rate sensitivity, or elasticity, of an asset or liability. In other words, the larger the numerical value of D, the more sensitive the price of that asset or liability is to changes or shocks in interest rates.

Consider the following equation showing that the current price of a bond is equal to the present value of the coupons and principal payment on the bond:

$$P = \frac{C}{(1 + R)} + \frac{C}{(1 + R)^2} + \cdots + \frac{C + F}{(1 + R)^N} \qquad \textbf{(1)}$$

where

P = Price on the bond
C = Coupon (annual)
R = Yield to maturity
N = Number of periods to maturity
F = Face value of the bond

We want to find out how the price of the bond (*P*) changes when yields (*R*) rise. We know that bond prices fall, but we want to derive a direct measure of the size of this fall (i.e., its degree of price sensitivity).

Taking the derivative of the bond's price (*P*) with respect to the yield to maturity (*R*), we can show that:[7]

$$\frac{dP}{dR} = -\frac{1}{1 + R}[P \times D] \qquad \textbf{(2)}$$

By cross multiplying:

$$\frac{dP}{dR} \times \frac{1 + R}{P} = -D \qquad \textbf{(3)}$$

or, alternatively:

$$\frac{\frac{dP}{P}}{\frac{dR}{(1 + R)}} = -D \qquad \textbf{(4)}$$

interest elasticity
The percentage change in the price of a bond for any given change in interest rates.

The economic interpretation of equation (2) is that the number *D* is the **interest elasticity,** or sensitivity, of the security's price to small interest rate changes. That

---

[7] The first derivative of the bond's price in equation (1) with respect to the yield to maturity (*R*) is:

$$\frac{dP}{dR} = \frac{-C}{(1 + R)^2} + \frac{-2C}{(1 + R)^3} + \cdots + \frac{-N(C + F)}{(1 + R)^{N+1}} \qquad \textbf{(A)}$$

By rearranging, we get:

$$\frac{dP}{dR} = -\frac{1}{1 + R}\left[\frac{C}{(1 + R)} + \frac{2C}{(1 + R)^2} + \cdots + \frac{N(C + F)}{(1 + R)^N}\right] \qquad \textbf{(B)}$$

We have shown that duration (*D*) is the weighted-average time to maturity using the present value of cash flows as weights; that is, by definition:

$$D = \frac{1 \times \frac{C}{(1 + R)} + 2 \times \frac{C}{(1 + R)^2} + \cdots + N \times \frac{(C + F)}{(1 + R)^N}}{\frac{C}{(1 + R)} + \frac{C}{(1 + R)^2} + \cdots + \frac{(C + F)}{(1 + R)^N}} \qquad \textbf{(C)}$$

Since the denominator of the duration equation is simply the price (P) of the bond that is equal to the present value of the cash flows on the bond, then:

$$D = \frac{1 \times \frac{C}{(1 + R)} + 2 \times \frac{C}{(1 + R)^2} + \cdots + N \times \frac{(C + F)}{(1 + R)^N}}{P} \qquad \textbf{(D)}$$

Multiplying both sides of this equation by *P*, we get:

$$P \times D = 1 \times \frac{C}{(1 + R)} + 2 \times \frac{C}{(1 + R)^2} + \cdots + N \times \frac{C + F}{(1 + R)^N} \qquad \textbf{(E)}$$

The term on the right side of equation (E) is the same term as that in square brackets in equation (B). Substituting equation (E) into equation (B), we get:

$$\frac{dP}{dR} = -\frac{1}{1 + R}[P \times D]$$

FIGURE 9–5
Proportional Relationship between Price Changes and Yield Changes on a Bond Implied by the Duration Model

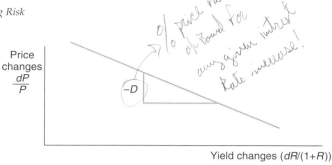

Price changes $\dfrac{dP}{P}$

$-D$

0% price fall of bond for any given interest rate increase!

Yield changes ($dR/(1+R)$)

is, D describes the percentage price fall of the bond (dP/P) for any given (present value) increase in required interest rates or yields ($dR/(1 + R)$).

Equation (4) can be rearranged in another useful way for interpretation regarding interest sensitivity:

$$\frac{dP}{P} = -D\left[\frac{dR}{1 + R}\right] \qquad (5)$$

Equation (5) and Figure 9–5, its graphic representation, show that for small changes in interest rates, bond prices move *in an inversely proportional* fashion according to the size of D. Clearly, for any given change in interest rates, long-duration securities suffer a larger capital loss (or receive a higher capital gain) should interest rates rise (fall) than do short-duration securities. By implication, gains and losses under the duration model are *symmetric*. That is, if we repeated the above examples but allowed interest rates to *decrease* by one basis point annually (or 1/2 basis point semiannually), the percentage increase in the price of the bond (dP/P) would be proportionate with D. Further, the capital gains would be a mirror image of the capital losses for an equal (small) increase in interest rates.

The duration equation can be rearranged, combining D and $(1 + R)$ into a single variable $D/(1 + R)$, to produce what practitioners call **modified duration** (MD). For annual compounding of interest:

modified duration
Duration divided by 1 plus the interest rate.

$$\frac{dP}{P} = -MD\,dR$$

where

$$MD = \frac{D}{1 + R}$$

This form is more intuitive because we multiply MD by the simple change in interest rates rather than the discounted change in interest rates as in the general duration equation. Next, we use duration to measure the interest sensitivity of an asset or liability.

EXAMPLE 9–3
The Six-Year Eurobond

Consider Example 9–1 for the six-year Eurobond with an 8 percent coupon and 8 percent yield. We determined in Table 9–1 that its duration was approximately $D = 4.993$ years. Suppose that yields were to rise by one basis point (1/100th of 1 percent) from 8 to 8.01 percent. Then

yield Rises

$$\frac{dP}{P} = -(4.993)\left[\frac{.0001}{1.08}\right]$$

1 Basis point = $\left(\frac{1}{100} * .01\right)$

$$= -.000462$$

$$\text{or } -0.0462\%$$

The bond price had been $1,000, which was the present value of a six-year bond with 8 percent coupons and 8 percent yield. However, the duration model predicts that the price of the bond would fall to $999.538 after the increase in yield by one basis point. That is, the price would fall by .0462 percent, or by $0.462.[8]

EXAMPLE 9–4
The Consol Bond

Consider a consol bond with an 8 percent coupon paid annually, an 8 percent yield, and a calculated duration of 13.5 years ($D_c = 1 + 1/.08 = 13.5$). Thus, for a one basis point change in the yield (from 8 percent to 8.01 percent):

$$\frac{dP}{P} = -(13.5)\left[\frac{.0001}{1.08}\right]$$

$$= -.00125$$

$$\text{or } -0.125\%$$

As you can see, for any given change in yields, long-duration securities suffer a greater capital loss or receive a greater capital gain than do short-duration securities.

Semiannual Coupon Bonds

For fixed-income assets or liabilities whose interest payments are received semiannually or more frequently than annually, the formula in equation (5) has to be modified slightly. For semiannual payments:

$$\frac{dP}{P} = -D\left[\frac{dR}{1 + \frac{1}{2}R}\right] \tag{6}$$

The only difference between equation (6) and equation (5) is the introduction of a $\frac{1}{2}$ in the discount rate term $1 + 1/2R$ to take into account the semiannual payments of interest.

EXAMPLE 9–5
Semiannual Coupon, Two-Year Maturity Treasury Bonds

Recall from Example 9–2 the two-year T-bond with semiannual coupons whose duration we derived in Table 9–2 as 1.883 years when annual yields were 12 percent. A one-basis-point rise in interest rates would have the following predicted effect on its price:

$$\frac{dP}{P} = -1.883\left[\frac{.0001}{1.06}\right]$$

$$= -.000178$$

or the price of the bond would fall by 0.0178 percent from $930.70 to $930.53. That is, a price fall of 0.0178 percent in this case translates into a dollar fall of $0.17.[9]

[handwritten annotations:]
dollar Fall = (P)(−D)(dR/1+R)
(PRICE)(−DURATION)(Basis points/1+Rate) = dollar change in value!

---

[8] To calculate the dollar change in value, we can rewrite the equation as $dP = (P)(-D)(dR/(1 + R)) = (\$1{,}000)(-4.993)(.0001/1.08) = -\$0.462$.

[9] To calculate the dollar change in value, we can rewrite the equation as $dP = (P)(-D)(dR/(1 + R/2)) = (\$930.70)(-1.883)(.0001/1.06) = -\$0.17$.

Concept Questions

1. What is the relation between the duration of a bond and the interest elasticity of a bond?
2. How would the formula in equation (6) have to be modified to take into account quarterly coupon payments and monthly coupon payments?

DURATION AND IMMUNIZATION

[handwritten: Measure of Asset or liabs Interest Rate Sensitivity [Elasticity]]

So far, you have learned how to calculate duration and you understand that the duration measure has economic meaning because it indicates the interest sensitivity, or elasticity, of an asset or liability's value. For FIs, the major relevance of duration is as a measure for managing interest rate risk exposure. Also important is the role of duration in allowing the FI to immunize its balance sheet or some subset of that balance sheet against interest rate risk. In the following sections we consider two examples of how FIs can use the duration measure for immunization purposes. The first is its use by insurance company and pension fund managers to help meet promised cash flow payments to policyholders or beneficiaries at a particular time in the future. The second is its use to immunize or insulate the whole balance sheet of an FI against interest rate risk.

Duration and Immunizing Future Payments

Frequently, pension fund and life insurance company managers face the problem of structuring their asset investments so they can pay out a given cash amount to policyholders in some future period. The classic example of this is an insurance policy that pays the holder some lump sum on reaching retirement age. The risk to the life insurance company manager is that interest rates on the funds generated from investing the holder's premiums could fall. Thus, the accumulated returns on the premiums invested could not meet the target or promised amount. In effect, the insurance company would be forced to draw down its reserves and net worth to meet its payout commitments. (See Chapter 3 for a discussion of this risk.)

Suppose that we are in 2007 and the insurer has to make a guaranteed payment to a policyholder in five years, 2012. For simplicity, we assume that this target guaranteed payment is $1,469, a lump-sum policy payout on retirement, equivalent to investing $1,000 at an annually compounded rate of 8 percent over five years. Of course, realistically, this payment would be much larger, but the underlying principles of the example do not change by scaling up or down the payout amount.

To immunize, or protect, itself against interest rate risk, the insurer needs to determine which investments would produce a cash flow of exactly $1,469 in five years regardless of what happens to interest rates in the immediate future. The FI investing either in a five-year maturity and duration zero-coupon bond or in a coupon bond with a five-year duration would produce a $1,469 cash flow in five years no matter what happened to interest rates in the immediate future. Next, we consider the two strategies: buying five-year maturity (and duration) deep-discount bonds and buying five-year duration coupon bonds.

Buy Five-Year Maturity Discount Bonds

Given a $1,000 face value and an 8 percent yield and assuming annual compounding, the current price per five-year discount bond would be $680.58 per bond:

$$P = 680.58 = \frac{1,000}{(1.08)^5}$$

Duration matches target horizon (handwritten margin note)

If the insurer bought 1.469 of these bonds at a total cost of $1,000 in 2007, these investments would produce exactly $1,469 on maturity in five years ($1,000 × (1.08)^5 = $1,469). The reason is that the duration of this bond portfolio exactly matches the target horizon for the insurer's future liability to its policyholder. Intuitively, since no intervening cash flows or coupons are paid by the issuer of the zero-coupon discount bonds, future changes in interest rates have no reinvestment income effect. Thus, the return would be unaffected by intervening interest rate changes.

Suppose no five-year discount bonds exist. Then the portfolio manager may seek to invest in appropriate duration coupon bonds to hedge interest rate risk. In this example the appropriate investment would be in five-year duration coupon-bearing bonds.

Buying a coupon bond whose duration matches time horizon of insurer immunizes against Interest Rates changes! (handwritten margin note)

Buy a Five-Year Duration Coupon Bond

We demonstrated earlier in Table 9–1 that a six-year maturity Eurobond paying 8 percent coupons with an 8 percent yield to maturity had a duration of 4.993 years, or approximately five years. If we buy this six-year maturity, five-year duration bond in 2007 and hold it for five years, until 2012, the term exactly matches the target horizon of the insurer. The cash flows generated at the end of five years will be $1,469 whether interest rates stay at 8 percent or instantaneously (immediately) rise to 9 percent or fall to 7 percent. Thus, buying a coupon bond whose duration exactly matches the time horizon of the insurer also immunizes the insurer against interest rate changes.

EXAMPLE 9–6 *Interest Rates Remain at 8 Percent*	The cash flows received by the insurer on the bond if interest rates stay at 8 percent throughout the five years would be

1.	Coupons, 5 × $80	$ 400
2.	Reinvestment income	69
3.	Proceeds from sale of bond at end of fifth year	1,000
		$1,469

We calculate each of the three components of the insurer's income from the bond investment as follows:

1. *Coupons.* The $400 from coupons is simply the annual coupon of $80 received in each of the five years.
2. *Reinvestment income.* Because the coupons are received annually, they can be reinvested at 8 percent as they are received, generating an additional cash flow of $69.[10]

---

[10] Receiving annual coupons of $80 is equivalent to receiving an annuity of $80. There are tables and formulas that help us calculate the value of $1 received each year over a given number of years that can be reinvested at a given interest rate. The appropriate terminal value of receiving $1 a year for five years and reinvesting at 8 percent can be determined from the Future Value of an Annuity Factor (FVAF) Tables, whose general formula is:

$$FVAF_{n,R} = \left[\frac{(1 + R)^n - 1}{R} \right]$$

In our example:

$$FVAF_{5,\,8\%} = \left[\frac{(1 + .08)^5 - 1}{.08} \right] = 5.867$$

Thus, the reinvestment income for $80 of coupons per year is:

$$\text{Reinvestment income} = (80 \times 5.867) - 400 = 469 - 400 = 69$$

Note that we take away $400 since we have already counted the simple coupon income (5 × $80).

3. *Bond sale proceeds.* The proceeds from the sale are calculated by recognizing that the six-year bond has just one year left to maturity when it is sold by the insurance company at the end of the fifth year. That is:

↓ *Sell*   *$1,080*

Year 5   *Year 6*
(2012)   *(2013)*

What fair market price can the insurer expect to get when selling the bond at the end of the fifth year with one year left to maturity? A buyer would be willing to pay the present value of the $1,080—final coupon plus face value—to be received at the end of the one remaining year (i.e., in 2013), or:

$$P_5 = \frac{1,080}{1.08} = \$1,000$$

Thus, the insurer would be able to sell the one remaining cash flow of $1,080, to be received in the bond's final year, for $1,000.

Next, we show that since this bond has a duration of five years, matching the insurer's target period, even if interest rates were to instantaneously fall to 7 percent or rise to 9 percent, the expected cash flows from the bond would still exactly sum to $1,469. That is, the coupons + reinvestment income + principal at the end of the fifth year would be immunized. In other words, the cash flows on the bond are protected against interest rate changes.

EXAMPLE 9–7

Interest Rates Fall to 7 Percent

In this example with falling interest rates, the cash flows over the five years would be:

1. Coupons, 5 × $80	$ 400
2. Reinvestment income	60
3. Bond sale proceeds	1,009
	$1,469

The total proceeds over the five years are unchanged from what they were when interest rates were 8 percent. To see why this occurs, consider what happens to the three parts of the cash flow when rates fall to 7 percent:

1. *Coupons.* Are unchanged since the insurer still gets five annual coupons of $80 = $400.
2. *Reinvestment income.* The coupons can now only be reinvested at the lower rate of 7 percent. Reinvestment income is only $60.[11]
3. *Bond sale proceeds.* When the six-year maturity bond is sold at the end of the fifth year with one cash flow of $1,080 remaining, investors are now willing to pay more:

$$P_5 = \frac{1,080}{1.07} = 1,009$$

---

[11] This reinvestment income is calculated as follows.

$$FVAF_{5,\,7\%} = \left[\frac{(1 + .07)^5 - 1}{.07} \right] = 5.751$$

Reinvestment income = (5.751 × 80) − 400 = 60, which is $9 less than it was when rates were 8 percent.

That is, the bond can be sold for $9 more than it could have when rates were 8 percent. The reason for this is that investors can get only 7 percent on newly issued bonds, while this older bond was issued with a higher coupon of 8 percent.

A comparison of reinvestment income with bond sale proceeds indicates that the fall in rates has produced a *gain* on the bond sale proceeds of $9. This exactly offsets the loss of reinvestment income of $9 due to reinvesting at a lower interest rate. Thus, total cash flows remain unchanged at $1,469.

EXAMPLE 9–8

Interest Rates Rise to 9 Percent

In this example with rising interest rates, the proceeds from the bond investment are:

1. Coupons, 5 × $80	$ 400
2. Reinvestment income [(5.985 × 80) − 400]	78
3. Bond sale proceeds (1,080/1.09)	991
	$1,469

Notice that the rise in interest rates from 8 percent to 9 percent leaves the final terminal cash flow unaffected at $1,469. The rise in rates has generated $9 extra reinvestment income ($78 − $69), but the price at which the bond can be sold at the end of the fifth year has declined from $1,000 to $991, equal to a capital loss of $9. Thus, the gain in reinvestment income is exactly offset by the capital loss on the sale of the bond.

These examples demonstrate that matching the duration of a coupon bond—or any other fixed–interest rate instrument, such as a loan or mortgage—to the FI's target or investment horizon *immunizes* the FI against instantaneous shocks to interest rates. The gains or losses on reinvestment income that result from an interest rate change are exactly offset by losses or gains from the bond proceeds on sale.

Immunizing the Whole Balance Sheet of an FI

So far we have looked at the durations of individual instruments and ways to select individual fixed-income securities to protect FIs such as life insurance companies and pensions funds with precommitted liabilities such as future pension plan payouts. The duration model can also evaluate the overall interest rate exposure for an FI, that is, measure the **duration gap** on its balance sheet.

duration gap
A measure of overall interest rate risk exposure for an FI.

The Duration Gap for a Financial Institution

To estimate the overall duration gap of an FI, we determine first the duration of an FI's asset portfolio (A) and the duration of its liability portfolio (L). These can be calculated as:

$$D_A = X_{1A}D_1^A + X_{2A}D_2^A + \cdots + X_{nA}D_n^A$$

and

$$D_L = X_{1L}D_1^L + X_{2L}D_2^L + \cdots + X_{nL}D_n^L$$

where

$$X_{1j} + X_{2j} + \cdots + X_{nj} = 1 \quad \text{and} \quad j = A, L$$

The X_{ij}'s in the equation are the market value proportions of each asset or liability held in the respective asset and liability portfolios. Thus, if new 30-year

Treasury bonds were 1 percent of a life insurer's portfolio and D_1^A (the duration of those bonds) was equal to 9.25 years, then $X_{1A}D_1^A = .01(9.25) = 0.0925$. More simply, the duration of a portfolio of assets or liabilities is a market value weighted average of the individual durations of the assets or liabilities on the FI's balance sheet.[12]

Consider an FI's simplified market value balance sheet:

Assets ($)	Liabilities ($)
$A = 100$	$L = 90$
	$E = \underline{10}$
$\underline{100}$	100

From the balance sheet:

$$A = L + E$$

and

$$\Delta A = \Delta L + \Delta E$$

or

$$\Delta E = \Delta A - \Delta L$$

That is, when interest rates change, the change in the FI's equity or net worth (E) is equal to the difference between the change in the market values of assets and liabilities on each side of the balance sheet. This should be familiar from our discussion of the maturity model in Chapter 8. The difference here is that we want to relate the sensitivity of an FI's net worth (ΔE) to its duration mismatch rather than to its maturity mismatch. As we have already shown, duration is a more accurate measure of the interest rate sensitivity of an asset or liability than is maturity.

Since $\Delta E = \Delta A - \Delta L$, we need to determine how ΔA and ΔL—the changes in the market values of assets and liabilities on the balance sheet—are related to duration.[13]

From the duration model (assuming annual compounding of interest):

$$\frac{\Delta A}{A} = -D_A \frac{\Delta R}{(1 + R)} \tag{7}$$

$$\frac{\Delta L}{L} = -D_L \frac{\Delta R}{(1 + R)} \tag{8}$$

Here we have simply substituted $\Delta A/A$ or $\Delta L/L$, the percentage change in the market values of assets or liabilities, for $\Delta P/P$, the percentage change in any single bond's price and D_A or D_L, the duration of the FI's asset or liability portfolio, for D_i, the duration on any given bond, deposit, or loan. The term $\Delta R/(1 + R)$ reflects

[12] This derivation of an FI's duration gap closely follows G. Kaufman, "Measuring and Managing Interest Rate Risk: A Primer," Federal Reserve Bank of Chicago, *Economic Perspectives*, 1984, pp. 16–29.

[13] In what follows, we use the Δ (change) notation instead of d (derivative notation) to recognize that interest rate changes tend to be discrete rather than infinitesimally small. For example, in real-world financial markets, the smallest observed rate change is usually one basis point, or 1/100th of 1 percent.

the shock to interest rates as before.[14] To show dollar changes, these equations can be rewritten as:

$$\Delta A = -D_A \times A \times \frac{\Delta R}{(1 + R)} \qquad \textbf{(9)}$$

and

$$\Delta L = -D_L \times L \times \frac{\Delta R}{(1 + R)} \qquad \textbf{(10)}$$

We can substitute these two expressions into the equation $\Delta E = \Delta A - \Delta L$. Rearranging and combining this equation[15] results in a measure of the change in the market value of equity:

$$\Delta E = -[D_A - D_L k] \times A \times \frac{\Delta R}{1 + R}$$

where $k = L/A$ is a measure of the FI's leverage, that is, the amount of borrowed funds or liabilities rather than owners' equity used to fund its asset portfolio. The effect of interest rate changes on the market value of an FI's equity or net worth (ΔE) breaks down into three effects:

1. *The leverage adjusted duration gap* $= [D_A - D_L k]$. This gap is measured in years and reflects the degree of duration mismatch in an FI's balance sheet. Specifically, the larger this gap is *in absolute terms,* the more exposed the FI is to interest rate shocks.
2. *The size of the FI.* The term A measures the size of the FI's assets. The larger the scale of the FI, the larger the dollar size of the potential net worth exposure from any given interest rate shock.
3. *The size of the interest rate shock* $= \Delta R/(1 + R)$. The larger the shock, the greater the FI's exposure.

---

[14] We assume that the level of rates and the expected shock to interest rates are the same for both assets and liabilities, which means that the FI's spread (the difference between the rate on earning assets and interest-bearing liabilities) is zero. However, as long as the FI has more earning assets than interest-bearing liabilities, it will have a positive level for net interest income. This assumption is standard in Macauley duration analysis. While restrictive, this assumption can be relaxed. However, if this is done, the duration measure changes, as is discussed later in Appendix A to this chapter.

[15] We do this as follows:

$$\Delta E = \left[-D_A \times A \times \frac{\Delta R}{(1 + R)} \right] - \left[-D_L \times L \times \frac{\Delta R}{(1 + R)} \right]$$

Assuming that the level of rates and the expected shock to interest rates are the same for both assets and liabilities:

$$\Delta E = [-D_A A + D_L L] \frac{\Delta R}{(1 + R)}$$

or

$$\Delta E = -[D_A A - D_L L] \frac{\Delta R}{(1 + R)}$$

To rearrange the equation in a slightly more intuitive fashion, we multiply and divide both $D_A A$ and $D_L L$ by A (assets):

$$\Delta E = -\left[D_A \frac{A}{A} - D_L \frac{L}{A} \right] \times A \times \frac{\Delta R}{(1 + R)}$$

$$\text{or} \quad \Delta E = -[D_A - D_L k] \times A \times \frac{\Delta R}{(1 + R)}$$

Given this, we express the exposure of the net worth of the FI as:

$$\Delta E = -[\text{Leverage adjusted duration gap}] \times \text{Asset size} \times \text{Interest rate shock}$$

Interest rate shocks are largely external to the FI and often result from changes in the Federal Reserve's monetary policy (as discussed in the first section of Chapter 8). The size of the duration gap and the size of the FI, however, are under the control of management. The Industry Perspectives box highlights how a sharp drop in mortgage rates left Fannie Mae with its highest-ever reported duration gap.

Using an example, the next section explains how a manager can use information on an FI's duration gap to restructure the balance sheet to immunize stockholders' net worth against interest rate risk (i.e., to set the balance sheet up *before* a change in interest rates, so that ΔE is nonnegative for an expected change in interest rates).

EXAMPLE 9–9

Duration Gap Measurement and Exposure

Suppose the FI manager calculates that:

$$D_A = 5 \text{ years}$$
$$D_L = 3 \text{ years}$$

Then the manager learns from an economic forecasting unit that rates are expected to rise from 10 to 11 percent in the immediate future; that is:

$$\Delta R = 1\% = .01$$
$$1 + R = 1.10$$

The FI's initial balance sheet is assumed to be:

Assets ($ millions)	Liabilities ($ millions)
$A = 100$	$L = 90$
	$E = 10$
100	100

The FI's manager calculates the potential loss to equity holders' net worth (E) if the forecast of rising rates proves true as follows:

$$\Delta E = -(D_A - kD_L) \times A \times \frac{\Delta R}{(1 + R)}$$

$$= -(5 - (.9)(3)) \times \$100 \text{ million} \times \frac{.01}{1.1} = -\$2.09 \text{ million}$$

The FI could lose $2.09 million in net worth if rates rise 1 percent. Since the FI started with $10 million in equity, the loss of $2.09 million is almost 21 percent of its initial net worth. The market value balance sheet after the rise in rates by 1 percent would look like this:[16]

Assets ($ millions)	Liabilities ($ millions)
$A = 95.45$	$L = 87.54$
	$E = 7.91$
95.45	95.45

---

[16] These values are calculated as follows:

$$\Delta A/A = -5(.01/1.1) = -.04545 = -4.545\%$$
$$100 + (-.04545)100 = 95.45$$

and

$$\Delta L/L = -3(.01/1.1) = -.02727 = -2.727\%$$
$$90 + (-.02727)90 = 87.54$$

Industry Perspectives

MORTGAGE MISMATCH: HOME REFINANCINGS WIDEN FANNIE'S RISK

A key measure of interest rate risk at Fannie Mae widened sharply last month, boosting part of the bond market but raising new questions about the effects of the home-refinancing boom on Fannie's own finances. In its monthly release of financial data, the giant government-sponsored mortgage company acknowledged that what is known as the "duration gap" between its mortgage assets and debt liabilities ended August at the highest level the company has ever reported publicly, "reflecting the recent sharp drop in mortgage rates." But the company said it can handle the added risk, and its profit projections remain the same.

Nevertheless, the disclosure somewhat rattled Fannie investors. As of 4 PM in the New York Stock Exchange composite trading, Fannie Mae shares fell $1.72 to $70.98 each. The disclosure creates "a general level of concern when you see a huge financial institution reporting what seems to be a mis-hedging of their assets and liabilities," says Robert Young, a mortgage analyst at Salomon Smith Barney. "It looks like a pretty sizable gap."

Fannie Mae's current predicament is related to the recent refinancing boom. With mortgage rates at their lowest levels in a generation, more borrowers are paying off their mortgages early and taking

out new ones with lower rates. When that happens, Fannie replaces those mortgages with new loans that could have lower interest rates—creating a possible mismatch between the mortgages it now owns and the debt on its books. The duration gap is one way the company measures its success in matching its mortgage assets and its liabilities. The gap swung from negative nine months in July to negative 14 months in August. That doesn't mean that the company is in trouble. But it does mean Fannie Mae's huge $747 billion loan portfolio has greater exposure to a sudden shift in interest rates. Fannie Mae likes to have the duration of [its] assets and liabilities more closely matched; its stated target is to maintain a duration gap of within plus or minus six months.

Bond market investors care about the disclosure because it suggests Fannie Mae will have to take steps to get its assets and liabilities back in line, with possible implications for the rest of the bond market. Treasury prices rose yesterday, in part on expectations that Fannie Mae might soon become a big buyer of longer-dated Treasury debt in a move to better hedge its portfolio. . . .

Source: *The Wall Street Journal*, September 17, 2002, p. C1, by Patrick Barta. Reprinted by permission of *The Wall Street Journal*. © 2002 Dow Jones & Company, Inc. All Rights Reserved Worldwide. *www.wsj.com*

Even though the rise in interest rates would not push the FI into economic insolvency, it reduces the FI's net worth–to–assets ratio from 10 (10/100) to 8.29 percent (7.91/95.45). To counter this effect, the manager might reduce the FI's adjusted duration gap. In an extreme case, the gap might be reduced to zero:

$$\Delta E = -[0] \times A \times \Delta R/(1 + R) = 0$$

To do this, the FI should not directly set $D_A = D_L$, which ignores the fact that the FI's assets (A) do not equal its borrowed liabilities (L) and that k (which reflects the ratio L/A) is not equal to 1. To see the importance of factoring in leverage, suppose the manager increased the duration of the FI's liabilities to five years, the same as D_A. Then:

$$\Delta E = -[5 - (.9)(5)] \times \$100 \text{ million} \times (.01/1.1) = -\$0.45 \text{ million}$$

The FI is still exposed to a loss of $0.45 million if rates rise by 1 percent. An appropriate strategy would involve changing D_L until:

$$D_A = kD_L = 5 \text{ years}$$

For example,

$$\Delta E = -[5 - (.9)5.55] \times \$100 \text{ million} \times (.01/1.1) = 0$$

In this case the FI manager sets $D_L = 5.55$ years, or slightly longer than $D_A = 5$ years, to compensate for the fact that only 90 percent of assets are funded by borrowed liabilities, with the other 10 percent funded by equity. Note that the FI manager has at least three other ways to reduce the adjusted duration gap to zero:

1. *Reduce D_A.* Reduce D_A from 5 years to 2.7 years (equal to kD_L or (.9)3) such that:

$$[D_A - kD_L] = [2.7 - (.9)(3)] = 0$$

2. *Reduce D_A* and *increase D_L.* Shorten the duration of assets and lengthen the duration of liabilities at the same time. One possibility would be to *reduce D_A* to 4 years and to *increase D_L* to 4.44 years such that:

$$[D_A - kD_L] = [4 - (.9)(4.44)] = 0$$

3. *Change k and D_L.* Increase k (leverage) from .9 to .95 and increase D_L from 3 years to 5.26 years such that:

$$[D_A - kD_L] = [5 - (.95)(5.26)] = 0$$

Concept Questions

1. Refer to the example of the insurer in Examples 9–6 through 9–8. Suppose rates fell to 6 percent. Would the FI's portfolio still be immunized? What if rates rose to 10 percent?
2. How is the overall duration gap for an FI calculated?
3. How can a manager use information on an FI's duration gap to restructure, and thereby immunize, the balance sheet against interest rate risk?
4. Suppose $D_A = 3$ years, $D_L = 6$ years, $k = .8$, and $A = \$100$ million. What is the effect on owners' net worth if $\Delta R/(1 + R)$ rises 1 percent? ($\Delta E = \$1,800,000$)

IMMUNIZATION AND REGULATORY CONSIDERATIONS

In the above section we assumed that the FI manager wants to structure the duration of assets and liabilities to immunize the equity or net worth stake (E) of the FI's equity owners from interest rate shocks. However, regulators periodically monitor the solvency or capital position of FIs. As we discuss in greater detail in Chapter 20 on capital adequacy, regulators set minimum target ratios for an FI's capital (or net worth) to assets. The simplest is the ratio of FI capital to its assets, or:

$$\frac{E}{A} = \text{Capital (net worth) ratio}$$

www.sec.gov   While this target has normally been formulated in book value accounting terms for depository institutions, it is evaluated in a market value context for investment banks. Also, the SEC has long advocated a capital ratio based on market value accounting for U.S. depository institutions.

Given these regulations imposed on the minimum level of the capital ratio, if an FI's asset levels change significantly through time, FI managers may be most interested in immunizing against changes in the capital ratio ($\Delta(E/A)$) due to interest rate risk rather than changes in the level of capital (ΔE). For example, suppose the FI manager is close to the minimum regulatory required E/A (or capital) ratio (e.g., 4 percent for depository institutions) and wants to immunize the FI against any fall in this ratio if interest rates rise.[17] That is, the immunization target is no longer $\Delta E = 0$ when rates change but $\Delta(E/A) = 0$.

Obviously, immunizing ΔE against interest rate risk cannot result in the same management strategy as immunizing $\Delta(E/A)$. A portfolio constructed to immunize ΔE would have a different duration match from that required to immunize $\Delta(E/A)$. Or, more simply, the manager could satisfy either the FI's stockholders or the regulators *but not both* simultaneously.

More specifically, when the objective is to immunize equity capital against interest rate risk, that is, to set $\Delta E = 0$, the FI manager should structure the balance sheet so that the leverage adjusted duration gap is zero:

$$\Delta E = 0 = D_A - kD_L$$

or set

$$D_A = kD_L$$

By comparison, to immunize the capital ratio, that is, to set $\Delta(E/A) = 0$ the manager needs to set:[18]

$$D_A = D_L$$

In this scenario, the leverage adjustment effect (k) drops out. If $D_A = 5$, then immunizing the capital ratio would require setting $D_L = 5$.

Concept Questions

1. What minimum target ratio is typically used by regulators to measure a bank's net worth relative to its assets?
2. Is immunizing a bank's net worth the same as immunizing its net worth–assets ratio? If not, why not?

In the next section, we analyze weaknesses of the duration model. Specifically, there are several practical problems in estimating duration and duration gaps for real-world FIs.

DIFFICULTIES IN APPLYING THE DURATION MODEL

www.bis.org Critics of the duration model have often claimed that it is difficult to apply in real-world situations. However, duration measures and immunization strategies are useful in most real-world situations. In fact, the model proposed by the Bank for International Settlements to monitor bank interest rate risk taking is based heavily on the duration model. In this section, we look at the various criticisms of the duration model and discuss ways a modern FI manager would deal with them in practice. In the Appendix to the chapter, we present some of the more advanced issues associated with these weaknesses.

Duration Matching Can Be Costly

Critics charge that although in principle an FI manager can change D_A and D_L to immunize the FI against interest rate risk, restructuring the balance sheet of a large and complex FI can be both time-consuming and costly. While this argument may have been true historically, the growth of purchased funds, asset

---

[17] In actuality, depository institutions face three required minimum capital ratios. The 4 percent rule used in this example is for the leverage ratio (see Chapter 20 for more details).
[18] See Kaufman, "Measuring and Managing Interest Rate Risk: A Primer," for a proof.

securitization, and loan sales markets has considerably eased the speed and lowered the transaction costs of major balance sheet restructurings. (See Chapters 27 and 28 for a discussion of these strategies.) Moreover, an FI manager could still manage risk exposure using the duration model by employing techniques other than direct portfolio rebalancing to immunize against interest rate risk. Managers can get many of the same results of direct duration matching by taking hedging positions in the markets for derivative securities, such as futures and forwards (Chapter 24); options, caps, floors, and collars (Chapter 25); and swaps (Chapter 26).[19]

Immunization Is a Dynamic Problem

Immunization is an aspect of the duration model that is not well understood. Let's go back to the earlier immunization example in which an insurer sought to buy bonds to provide an accumulated cash flow of $1,469 in five years no matter what happened to interest rates. We showed that buying a six-year maturity, 8 percent coupon bond with a five-year duration immunizes the insurer against an instantaneous change in interest rates. The word *instantaneous* is very important here; it means a change in interest rates immediately after purchasing the bond. However, interest rates can change at any time over the holding period. Further, the duration of a bond changes as time passes, that is, as it approaches maturity or the target horizon date. In addition, duration changes at a different rate than does real or calendar time.

To understand this time effect, consider the initially hedged position in which the insurer bought the five-year duration (six-year maturity), 8 percent coupon bond in 2007 to match its cash flow target of $1,469 in 2012. Suppose the FI manager puts the bond in the bottom drawer of a desk and does not think about it for a year, believing that the insurance company's position is fully hedged. After one year has passed (in 2008), suppose interest rates (yields) have fallen from 8 percent to 7 percent and the manager opens the drawer of the desk and finds the bond. Knowing the target date is now only four years away, the manager recalculates the duration of the bond. Imagine the manager's shock on finding that the same 8 percent coupon bond with a 7 percent yield and only five years left to maturity has a duration of 4.33 years. This means the insurance company is no longer hedged; the 4.33-year duration of this bond portfolio *exceeds* the investment horizon of four years. As a result, the manager has to restructure the bond portfolio to remain immunized. One way to do this is to sell some of the five-year bonds (4.33-year duration) and buy some bonds of shorter duration so that the overall duration of the investment portfolio is four years.

For example, suppose the insurer sold 50 percent of the five-year bonds with a 4.33-year duration and invested the proceeds in 3.67-year duration and maturity zero-coupon bonds. Because duration and maturity are the same for discount bonds, the duration of the asset portfolio is:

$$D_A = [4.33 \times .5] + [3.67 \times .5] = 4 \text{ years}$$

This simple example demonstrates that immunization based on duration is a dynamic strategy. In theory, the strategy requires the portfolio manager to rebalance the portfolio continuously to ensure that the duration of the investment

---

[19] In particular, instead of direct immunization of a positive duration gap ($D_A > D_L$), an FI manager could sell futures (forwards), take the fixed-rate side of an interest rate swap, buy put options on bonds, and/or buy an interest rate cap.

FIGURE 9–6
Duration versus
True Relationship

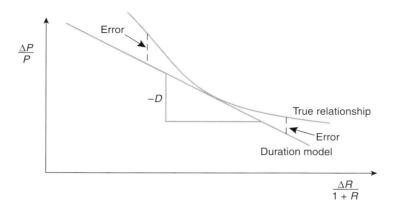

May cost more than what its worth to stay immunized on a portfolio

portfolio exactly matches the investment horizon (i.e., the duration of liabilities). Because continuous rebalancing may not be easy to do and involves costly transaction fees, most portfolio managers seek to be only approximately dynamically immunized against interest rate changes by rebalancing at discrete intervals, such as quarterly. That is, there is a trade-off between being perfectly immunized and the transaction costs of maintaining an immunized balance sheet dynamically.

Large Interest Rate Changes and Convexity

Duration accurately measures the price sensitivity of fixed-income securities for small changes in interest rates of the order of one basis point. But suppose interest rate shocks are much larger, of the order of 2 percent, or 200 basis points. Then duration becomes a less accurate predictor of how much the prices of securities will change and therefore a less accurate measure of interest rate sensitivity. Looking at Figure 9–6, you can see the reason for this. Note first the change in a bond's price due to yield changes according to the duration model and second, the true relationship, as calculated directly, using the exact present value calculation for bond valuation.

The duration model predicts that the relationship between interest rate shocks and bond price changes will be proportional to D (duration). However, by precisely calculating the true change in bond prices, we would find that for large interest rate increases, duration overpredicts the *fall* in bond prices, while for large interest rate decreases, it underpredicts the *increase* in bond prices. That is, the duration model predicts symmetric effects for rate increases and decreases on bond prices. As Figure 9–6 shows, in actuality, for rate increases, the *capital loss effect* tends to be smaller than the *capital gain effect* is for rate decreases. This is the result of the bond price–yield relationship exhibiting a property called *convexity* rather than *linearity*, as assumed by the basic duration model.

convexity
The degree of curvature of the price–yield curve around some interest rate level.

Note that **convexity** is a desirable feature for an FI manager to capture in a portfolio of assets. Buying a bond or a portfolio of assets that exhibits a lot of convexity, or curvature, in the price–yield curve relationship is similar to buying partial interest rate risk insurance. Specifically, high convexity means that for equally large changes of interest rates up and down (e.g., plus or minus 2 percent), the capital gain effect of a rate decrease more than offsets the capital loss effect of a rate increase. As we show in the Appendix to the chapter, all fixed-income assets or liabilities exhibit some convexity in their price–yield relationships.[20]

[20] To be more precise, fixed-income securities without special option features such as callable bonds and mortgage-backed securities exhibit convexity. A callable bond tends to exhibit negative convexity (or concavity), as do some mortgage-backed securities.

FIGURE 9–7

The Price–Yield Curve for the Six-Year Eurobond

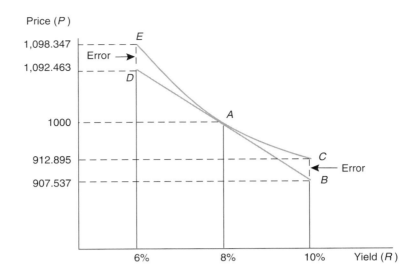

To see the importance of accounting for the effects of convexity in assessing the impact of large rate changes on an FI's portfolio, consider the six-year Eurobond with an 8 percent coupon and yield. According to Table 9–1 (on page 220), its duration is 4.993 years and its current price P_0 is $1,000 at a yield of 8 percent:

$$P_0 = \frac{80}{(1.08)} + \frac{80}{(1.08)^2} + \frac{80}{(1.08)^3}$$

$$+ \frac{80}{(1.08)^4} + \frac{80}{(1.08)^5} + \frac{1,080}{(1.08)^6} = \$1,000$$

This is point A on the price–yield curve in Figure 9–7.

If rates rise from 8 to 10 percent, the duration model predicts that the bond price will fall by 9.2463 percent; that is:

$$\frac{\Delta P}{P} = -4.993 \left[\frac{.02}{1.08} \right] = -9.2463\%$$

or, from a price of $1,000 to $907.537 (see point B in Figure 9–7). However, calculating the exact change in the bond's price after a rise in yield to 10 percent, we find that its true value is:

$$P_0 = \frac{80}{(1.1)} + \frac{80}{(1.1)^2} + \frac{80}{(1.1)^3}$$

$$+ \frac{80}{(1.1)^4} + \frac{80}{(1.1)^5} + \frac{1,080}{(1.1)^6} = \$912.895$$

This is point C in Figure 9–7. As you can see, the true or actual fall in price is less than the predicted fall by $5.358. This means that there is over a 0.5 percent error using the duration model. The reason for this is the natural convexity to the price–yield curve as yields rise.

Reversing the experiment reveals that the duration model would predict the bond's price to rise by 9.2463 percent if yields fell from 8 to 6 percent, resulting in a predicted price of $1,092.463 (see point D in Figure 9–7). By comparison, the true or actual change in price can be computed as $1,098.347 by estimating the present value of the bond's coupons and its face value with a 6 percent yield (see point *E* in Figure 9–7). The duration model has underpredicted the bond price increase by $5.884, or by over 0.5 percent of the true price increase.

An important question for the FI manager is whether a 0.5 percent error is big enough to be concerned about. This depends on the size of the interest rate change and the size of the portfolio under management. Clearly, 0.5 percent of a large number will still be a large number!

Summary

This chapter analyzed the duration model approach to measuring interest rate risk. The duration model is superior to the simple maturity model in that it incorporates the timing of cash flows as well as maturity effects into a simple measure of interest rate risk. The duration measure could be used to immunize a particular liability as well as the whole FI balance sheet. However, as the concluding section of the chapter indicates, a number of potential problems exist in applying the duration model in real-world scenarios. Despite these weaknesses, the duration model is fairly robust and can deal with a large number of real-world complexities, such as credit risk, convexity, floating interest rates, and uncertain maturities.

Questions and Problems

1. What are the two different general interpretations of the concept of duration, and what is the technical definition of this term? How does duration differ from maturity?

2. Two bonds are available for purchase in the financial markets. The first bond is a two-year, $1,000 bond that pays an annual coupon of 10 percent. The second bond is a two-year, $1,000 zero-coupon bond.

    a. What is the duration of the coupon bond if the current yield to maturity (YTM) is 8 percent? 10 percent? 12 percent? (*Hint:* You may wish to create a spreadsheet program to assist in the calculations.)

    b. How does the change in the current YTM affect the duration of this coupon bond?

    c. Calculate the duration of the zero-coupon bond with a YTM of 8 percent, 10 percent, and 12 percent.

    d. How does the change in the current YTM affect the duration of the zero-coupon bond?

    e. Why does the change in the YTM affect the coupon bond differently than it affects the zero-coupon bond?

3. A one-year, $100,000 loan carries a market interest rate of 12 percent. The loan requires payment of accrued interest and one-half of the principal at the end of six months. The remaining principal and the accrued interest are due at the end of the year.

    a. What is the duration of this loan?

    b. What will be the cash flows at the end of six months and at the end of the year?

    c. What is the present value of each cash flow discounted at the market rate? What is the total present value?

    d. What proportion of the total present value of cash flows occurs at the end of six months? What proportion occurs at the end of the year?

e. What is the weighted-average life of the cash flows on the loan?

f. How does this weighted-average life compare with the duration calculated in part (a) above?

4. What is the duration of a five-year, $1,000 Treasury bond with a 10 percent semiannual coupon selling at par? Selling with a YTM of 12 percent? 14 percent? What can you conclude about the relationship between duration and yield to maturity? Plot the relationship. Why does this relationship exist?

5. Consider three Treasury bonds each of which has a 10 percent semiannual coupon and trades at par.

a. Calculate the duration for a bond that has a maturity of four years, three years, and two years.

b. What conclusions can you reach about the relationship between duration and the time to maturity? Plot the relationship.

6. A six-year, $10,000 CD pays 6 percent interest annually. What is the duration of the CD? What would be the duration if interest were paid semiannually? What is the relationship of duration to the relative frequency of interest payments?

7. What is a consol bond? What is the duration of a consol bond that sells at a YTM of 8 percent? 10 percent? 12 percent? Would a consol trading at a YTM of 10 percent have a greater duration than a 20-year zero-coupon bond trading at the same YTM? Why?

8. Maximum Pension Fund is attempting to balance one of the bond portfolios under its management. The fund has identified three bonds that have five-year maturities and trade at a YTM of 9 percent. The bonds differ only in that the coupons are 7 percent, 9 percent, and 11 percent.

a. What is the duration for each bond?

b. What is the relationship between duration and the amount of coupon interest that is paid? Plot the relationship.

9. An insurance company is analyzing three bonds and is using duration as the measure of interest rate risk. All three bonds trade at a YTM of 10 percent and have $10,000 par values. The bonds differ only in the amount of annual coupon interest they pay: 8, 10, and 12 percent.

a. What is the duration for each five-year bond?

b. What is the relationship between duration and the amount of coupon interest that is paid?

10. You can obtain a loan for $100,000 at a rate of 10 percent for two years. You have a choice of paying the principal at the end of the second year or amortizing the loan, that is, paying interest and principal in equal payments each year. The loan is priced at par.

a. What is the duration of the loan under both methods of payment?

b. Explain the difference in the two results.

11. How is duration related to the interest elasticity of a fixed-income security? What is the relationship between duration and the price of the fixed-income security?

12. You have discovered that the price of a bond rose from $975 to $995 when the YTM fell from 9.75 percent to 9.25 percent. What is the duration of the bond?

13. Calculate the duration of a two-year, $1,000 bond that pays an annual coupon of 10 percent and trades at a yield of 14 percent. What is the expected change

in the price of the bond if interest rates decline by 0.50 percent (50 basis points)?

14. The duration of an 11-year, $1,000 Treasury bond paying a 10 percent semiannual coupon and selling at par has been estimated at 6.9 years.

   a. What is the modified duration of the bond (modified duration = $D/(1 + R)$)?

   b. What will be the estimated price change of the bond if market interest rates increase 0.10 percent (10 basis points)? If rates decrease 0.20 percent (20 basis points)?

   c. What would the actual price of the bond be under each rate change situation in part (b) using the traditional present value bond pricing techniques? What is the amount of error in each case?

15. Suppose you purchase a five-year, 13.76 percent bond that is priced to yield 10 percent.

   a. Show that the duration of this annual payment bond is equal to four years.

   b. Show that if interest rates rise to 11 percent within the next year and your investment horizon is four years from today, you will still earn a 10 percent yield on your investment.

   c. Show that a 10 percent yield also will be earned if interest rates fall next year to 9 percent.

16. Consider the case in which an investor holds a bond for a period of time longer than the duration of the bond, that is, longer than the original investment horizon.

   a. If market interest rates rise, will the return that is earned exceed or fall short of the original required rate of return? Explain.

   b. What will happen to the realized return if market interest rates decrease? Explain.

   c. Recalculate parts (b) and (c) of problem 15 above, assuming that the bond is held for all five years, to verify your answers to parts (a) and (b) of this problem.

   d. If either calculation in part (c) is greater than the original required rate of return, why would an investor ever try to match the duration of an asset with his or her investment horizon?

17. Two banks are being examined by the regulators to determine the interest rate sensitivity of their balance sheets. Bank A has assets composed solely of a 10-year, 12 percent $1 million loan. The loan is financed with a 10-year, 10 percent $1 million CD. Bank B has assets composed solely of a 7-year, 12 percent zero-coupon bond with a current (market) value of $894,006.20 and a maturity (principal) value of $1,976,362.88. The bond is financed with a 10-year, 8.275 percent coupon $1,000,000 face value CD with a YTM of 10 percent. The loan and the CDs pay interest annually, with principal due at maturity.

   a. If market interest rates increase 1 percent (100 basis points), how do the market values of the assets and liabilities of each bank change? That is, what will be the net effect on the market value of the equity for each bank?

   b. What accounts for the differences in the changes in the market value of equity between the two banks?

c. Verify your results above by calculating the duration for the assets and liabilities of each bank, and estimate the changes in value for the expected change in interest rates. Summarize your results.

18. If you use only duration to immunize your portfolio, what three factors affect changes in the net worth of a financial institution when interest rates change?

19. Financial Institution XY has assets of $1 million invested in a 30-year, 10 percent semiannual coupon Treasury bond selling at par. The duration of this bond has been estimated at 9.94 years. The assets are financed with equity and a $900,000, two-year, 7.25 percent semiannual coupon capital note selling at par.

   a. What is the leverage adjusted duration gap of Financial Institution XY?
   b. What is the impact on equity value if the relative change in all market interest rates is a decrease of 20 basis points? *Note:* The relative change in interest rates is $\Delta R/(1 + R/2) = -0.0020$.
   c. Using the information you calculated in parts (a) and (b), infer a general statement about the desired duration gap for a financial institution if interest rates are expected to increase or decrease.
   d. Verify your inference by calculating the change in market value of equity assuming that the relative change in all market interest rates is an increase of 30 basis points.
   e. What would the duration of the assets need to be to immunize the equity from changes in market interest rates?

20. The balance sheet for Gotbucks Bank, Inc. (GBI) is presented below ($ millions).

Assets		Liabilities and Equity	
Cash	$ 30	Core deposits	$ 20
Federal funds	20	Federal funds	50
Loans (floating)	105	Euro CDs	130
Loans (fixed)	65	Equity	20
Total assets	$220	Total liabilities and equity	$220

Notes to the balance sheet: The fed funds rate is 8.5 percent, the floating loan rate is LIBOR + 4 percent, and currently LIBOR is 11 percent. Fixed-rate loans have five-year maturities, are priced at par, and pay 12 percent annual interest. Core deposits are fixed rate for two years at 8 percent paid annually. Euros currently yield 9 percent.

   a. What is the duration of the fixed-rate loan portfolio of Gotbucks Bank?
   b. If the duration of the floating-rate loans and fed funds is 0.36 years, what is the duration of GBI's assets?
   c. What is the duration of the core deposits if they are priced at par?
   d. If the duration of the Euro CDs and fed funds liabilities is 0.401 years, what is the duration of GBI's liabilities?
   e. What is GBI's duration gap? What is its interest rate risk exposure?
   f. What is the impact on the market value of equity if the relative change in all market interest rates is an increase of 1 percent (100 basis points)? Note that the relative change in interest rates is $\Delta R/(1 + R) = 0.01$.
   g. What is the impact on the market value of equity if the relative change in all market interest rates is a decrease of 0.5 percent (−50 basis points)?

h. What variables are available to GBI to immunize the bank? How much would each variable need to change to get DGAP to equal zero?

21. Hands Insurance Company issued a $90 million, one-year zero-coupon note at 8 percent add-on annual interest (paying one coupon at the end of the year). The proceeds were used to fund a $100 million, two-year commercial loan at 10 percent annual interest. Immediately after these transactions were simultaneously closed, all market interest rates increased 1.5 percent (150 basis points).

   a. What is the true market value of the loan investment and the liability after the change in interest rates?

   b. What impact did these changes in market value have on the market value of the FI's equity?

   c. What was the duration of the loan investment and the liability at the time of issuance?

   d. Use these duration values to calculate the expected change in the value of the loan and the liability for the predicted increase of 1.5 percent in interest rates.

   e. What was the duration gap of Hands Insurance Company after the issuance of the asset and note?

   f. What was the change in equity value forecasted by this duration gap for the predicted increase in interest rates of 1.5 percent?

   g. If the interest rate prediction had been available during the time period in which the loan and the liability were being negotiated, what suggestions would you have offered to reduce the possible effect on the equity of the company? What are the difficulties in implementing your ideas?

22. The following balance sheet information is available (amounts in thousands of dollars and duration in years) for a financial institution:

	Amount	Duration
T-bills	$ 90	0.50
T-notes	55	0.90
T-bonds	176	x
Loans	2,724	7.00
Deposits	2,092	1.00
Federal funds	238	0.01
Equity	715	

Treasury bonds are five-year maturities paying 6 percent semiannually and selling at par.

   a. What is the duration of the T-bond portfolio?

   b. What is the average duration of all the assets?

   c. What is the average duration of all the liabilities?

   d. What is the leverage adjusted duration gap? What is the interest rate risk exposure?

   e. What is the forecasted impact on the market value of equity caused by a relative upward shift in the entire yield curve of 0.5 percent [i.e., $\Delta R/(1 + R) = 0.0050$]?

   f. If the yield curve shifts downward 0.25 percent [i.e., $\Delta R/(1 + R) = -0.0025$], what is the forecasted impact on the market value of equity?

g. What variables are available to the financial institution to immunize the balance sheet? How much would each variable need to change to get DGAP to equal 0?

23. Assume that a goal of the regulatory agencies of financial institutions is to immunize the ratio of equity to total assets, that is, $\Delta(E/A) = 0$. Explain how this goal changes the desired duration gap for the institution. Why does this differ from the duration gap necessary to immunize the total equity? How would your answers to part (h) in problem 20 and part (g) in problem 22 change if immunizing equity to total assets was the goal?

24. Identify and discuss three criticisms of using the duration model to immunize the portfolio of a financial institution.

25. In general, what changes have occurred in the financial markets that would allow financial institutions to restructure their balance sheets more rapidly and efficiently to meet desired goals? Why is it critical for an investment manager who has a portfolio immunized to match a desired investment horizon to rebalance the portfolio periodically? What is convexity? Why is convexity a desirable feature to capture in a portfolio of assets?

26. A financial institution has an investment horizon of two years, 9.5 months. The institution has converted all assets into a portfolio of 8 percent, $1,000 three-year bonds that are trading at a YTM of 10 percent. The bonds pay interest annually. The portfolio manager believes that the assets are immunized against interest rate changes.

    a. Is the portfolio immunized at the time of the bond purchase? What is the duration of the bonds?

    b. Will the portfolio be immunized one year later?

    c. Assume that one-year, 8 percent zero-coupon bonds are available in one year. What proportion of the original portfolio should be placed in zeros to rebalance the portfolio?

27. MLK Bank has an asset portfolio that consists of $100 million of 30-year, 8 percent coupon $1,000 bonds that sell at par.

    a. What will be the bonds' new prices if market yields change immediately by $+/- 0.10$ percent? What will be the new prices if market yields change immediately by $+/-2.00$ percent?

    b. The duration of these bonds is 12.1608 years. What are the predicted bond prices in each of the four cases using the duration rule? What is the amount of error between the duration prediction and the actual market values?

    c. Given that convexity is 212.4, what are the bond price predictions in each of the four cases using the duration plus convexity relationship? What is the amount of error in these predictions?

    d. Diagram and label clearly the results in parts (a), (b), and (c).

The following questions and problems are based on material in Appendix 9A to the chapter.

28. Estimate the convexity for each of the following three bonds, all of which trade at YTM of 8 percent and have face values of $1,000.

    A 7-year, zero-coupon bond

    A 7-year, 10 percent annual coupon bond

A 10-year, 10 percent annual coupon bond that has a duration value of 6.994 years (i.e., approximately 7 years)

Rank the bonds in terms of convexity, and express the convexity relationship between zeros and coupon bonds in terms of maturity and duration equivalencies.

29. A 10-year, 10 percent annual coupon $1,000 bond trades at a YTM of 8 percent. The bond has a duration of 6.994 years. What is the modified duration of this bond? What is the practical value of calculating modified duration? Does modified duration change the result of using the duration relationship to estimate price sensitivity?

Pertinent Web Sites

Bank for International Settlements	**www.bis.org**
Securities and Exchange Commission	**www.sec.gov**
The Wall Street Journal	**www.wsj.com**

Chapter Notation

View Chapter Notation at the Web site for the textbook (**www.mhhe.com/saunders5e**).

Appendix 9A

Incorporating Convexity into the Duration Model[1]

In the main body of the chapter, we established these three characteristics of convexity:

1. *Convexity is desirable.* The greater the convexity of a security or a portfolio of securities, the more insurance or interest rate protection an FI manager has against rate increases and the greater the potential gains after interest rate falls.

2. *Convexity and duration.* The larger the interest rate changes and the more convex a fixed-income security or portfolio, the greater the error the FI manager faces in using just duration (and duration matching) to immunize exposure to interest rate shocks.

3. *All fixed-income securities are convex.*[2] To see this, we can take the six-year, 8 percent coupon, 8 percent yield bond and look at two extreme price–yield scenarios. What is the price on the bond if yields falls to zero, and what is its price if yields rise to some very large number, such as infinity?

When $R = 0$:

$$P = \frac{80}{(1 + 0)} + \cdots + \frac{1,080}{(1 + 0)^6} = \$1,480$$

The price is just the simple undiscounted sum of the coupon values and the face value. Since yields can never go below zero, $1,480 is the maximum possible price for the bond.

When $R = \infty$:

$$P = \frac{80}{(1 + \infty)} + \cdots + \frac{1,080}{(1 + \infty)^6} \simeq 0$$

As the yield goes to infinity, the bond price falls asymptotically toward zero, but by definition a bond's price can never be negative. Thus, zero must be the minimum bond price (see Figure 9A–1).

Since convexity is a desirable feature for assets, the FI manager might ask: Can we measure convexity? And can we incorporate this measurement in the duration model to adjust for or offset the error in prediction due to its presence? The answer to both questions is yes.

Theoretically speaking, duration is the slope of the price–yield curve, and convexity, or curvature, is the change in the slope of the price–yield curve. Consider the total effect of a change in interest rates on a bond's price as being broken into a number of separate effects. The precise mathematical derivation of these separate effects is based on a Taylor series expansion that you might remember from your math classes. Essentially, the first-order effect (dP/dR) of an interest rate change on the bond's price is the price–yield curve slope effect, which is measured by duration. The second-order effect (dP^2/d^2R) measures the change in the slope of the price–yield curve; this is the curvature, or convexity, effect. There are also third-, fourth-, and higher-order effects from the Taylor series expansion, but for all practical purposes these effects can be ignored.

We have noted that overlooking the curvature of the price–yield curve may cause errors in predicting the interest sensitivity of a portfolio of assets and liabilities, especially when yields change by large amounts. We can adjust for this by explicitly recognizing the second-order effect of yield changes by measuring the change in the slope of the price–yield curve around a given point. Just as D (duration) measures the slope effect (dP/dR), we introduce a new parameter (CX) to measure the curvature effect (dP^2/d^2R) of the price–yield curve.

The resulting equation, predicting the change in a security's price $(\Delta P/P)$, is:

$$\frac{\Delta P}{P} = -D\frac{\Delta R}{(1 + R)} + \frac{1}{2}CX(\Delta R)^2 \quad \textbf{(1)}$$

or:

$$\frac{\Delta P}{P} = -MD\Delta R + \frac{1}{2}CX(\Delta R)^2 \quad \textbf{(2)}$$

The first term in equation (1) is the simple duration model that over- or underpredicts price changes for large changes in interest rates, and the second term is the second-order effect of interest

---

[1] This section contains more technical details, which may be included or dropped from the chapter reading depending on the rigor of the course.

[2] This applies to fixed-income securities without special option features such as calls and puts.

FIGURE 9A–1
The Natural Convexity of Bonds

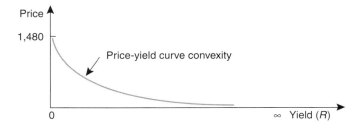

FIGURE 9A–2
Convexity and the Price–Yield Curve

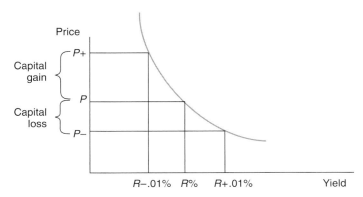

rate changes, that is, the convexity or curvature adjustment. In equation (1), the first term D can be divided by $1 + R$ to produce what we called earlier modified duration (MD). You can see this in equation (2). This form is more intuitive because we multiply MD by the simple change in R (ΔR) rather than by the discounted change in R ($\Delta R/(1 + R)$). In the convexity term, the number $1/2$ and $(\Delta R)^2$ result from the fact that the convexity effect is the second-order effect of interest rate changes while duration is the first-order effect. The parameter CX reflects the degree of curvature in the price–yield curve at the current yield level, that is, the degree to which the *capital gain effect* exceeds the *capital loss effect* for an equal change in yields up or down. At best, the FI manager can only approximate the curvature effect by using a parametric measure of CX. Even though calculus is based on infinitesimally small changes, in financial markets the smallest change in yields normally observed is one basis point, or a $1/100$th of 1 percent change. One possible way to measure CX is introduced next.

As just discussed, the convexity effect is the degree to which the capital gain effect more than offsets the capital loss effect for an equal increase and decrease in interest rates at the current interest rate level. In Figure 9A–2 we depict yields changing upward by one basis point ($R + .01\%$) and downward by one basis point ($R - .01\%$).

Because convexity measures the curvature of the price–yield curve around the rate level R percent, it intuitively measures the degree to which the capital gain effect of a small yield decrease exceeds the capital loss effect of a small yield increase.[3] Definitionally, the CX parameter equals:

$$CX = \begin{array}{c}\text{Scaling}\\\text{factor}\end{array}\left[\begin{array}{cc}\text{Capital} & \text{Capital}\\\text{loss from a} & \text{gain from a}\\\text{one-basis-point} + & \text{one-basis-point}\\\text{rise in yield} & \text{fall in yield}\\\text{(negative effect)} & \text{(positive effect)}\end{array}\right]$$

The sum of the two terms in the brackets reflects the degree to which the capital gain effect exceeds the capital loss effect for a small one-basis-point interest rate change down and up. The scaling factor normalizes this measure to account for a larger 1 percent change in rates. Remember, when interest rates change by a large amount, the convexity effect is important to measure. A commonly used scaling factor is 10^8 so that:[4]

$$CX = 10^8\left[\frac{\Delta P-}{P} + \frac{\Delta P+}{P}\right]$$

[3] We are trying to approximate as best we can the change in the slope of the price–yield curve at R percent. In theory, the changes are infinitesimally small (dR), but in reality, the smallest yield change normally observed is one basis point (ΔR).

[4] This is consistent with the effect of a 1 percent (100 basis points) change in rates.

TABLE 9A–1   **Properties of Convexity**

1. Convexity Increases with Bond Maturity			2. Convexity Varies with Coupon		3. For Same Duration, Zero-Coupon Bonds Are Less Convex Than Coupon Bonds	
Example			Example		Example	
A	B	C	A	B	A	B
$N = 6$	$N = 18$	$N = \infty$	$N = 6$	$N = 6$	$N = 6$	$N = 5$
$R = 8\%$	$R = 8\%$	$R = 8\%$	$R = 8\%$	$R = 8\%$	$R = 8\%$	$R = 8\%$
$C = 8\%$	$C = 8\%$	$C = 8\%$	$C = 8\%$	$C = 0\%$	$C = 8\%$	$C = 0\%$
$D = 5$	$D = 10.12$	$D = 13.5$	$D = 5$	$D = 6$	$D = 5$	$D = 5$
$CX = 28$	$CX = 130$	$CX = 312$	$CX = 28$	$CX = 36$	$CX = 28$	$CX = 25.72$

Calculation of CX

To calculate the convexity of the 8 percent coupon, 8 percent yield, six-year maturity Eurobond that had a price of $1,000:[5]

$$CX = 10^8 \left[\frac{999.53785 - 1,000}{1,000} + \frac{1,000.46243 - 1,000}{1,000} \right]$$

$$\underbrace{\text{Capital loss from a one-basis-point increase in rates}}_{} + \underbrace{\text{Capital gain from a one-basis-point decrease in rates}}_{}$$

$$CX = 10^8 [0.00000028]$$

$$CX = 28$$

This value for CX can be inserted into the bond price prediction equation (2) with the convexity adjustment:

$$\frac{\Delta P}{P} = -MD\Delta R + \frac{1}{2}(28)\Delta R^2$$

Assuming a 2 percent increase in R (from 8 to 10 percent),

$$\frac{\Delta P}{P} = -\left[\frac{4.993}{1.08}\right].02 + \frac{1}{2}(28)(.02)^2$$

$$= -.0925 + .0056$$

$$= -.0869 \text{ or } -8.69\%$$

The simple duration model (the first term) predicts that a 2 percent rise in interest rates will cause the bond's price to fall 9.25 percent. However, for large changes in yields, the duration model overpredicts the price fall. The duration model with the second-order convexity adjustment predicts a price fall of 8.69 percent; it adds back 0.56 percent because of the convexity effect. This is much closer to the true fall in the six-year, 8 percent coupon bond's price if we calculated this using 10 percent to discount the coupon and face value cash flows on the bond. The true value of the bond price fall is 8.71 percent. That is, using the convexity adjustment reduces the error between predicted value and true value to just a few basis points.[6]

In Table 9A–1 we calculate various properties of convexity, where

N = Time to maturity
R = Yield to maturity
C = Annual coupon
D = Duration
CX = Convexity

Part 1 of Table 9A–1 shows that as the bond's maturity (N) increases, so does its convexity (CX). As a result, long-term bonds have more convexity—which is a desirable property—than do short-term bonds. This property is similar to that possessed by duration.[7]

---

[5] You can easily check that $999.53785 is the price of the six-year bond when rates are 8.01 percent and $1,000.46243 is the price of the bond when rates fall to 7.99 percent. Since we are dealing in small numbers and convexity is sensitive to the number of decimal places assumed, we use at least five decimal places in calculating the capital gain or loss. In fact, the more decimal places used, the greater the accuracy of the CX measure.

[6] It is possible to use the third moment of the Taylor series expansion to reduce this small error (8.71 percent versus 8.69 percent) even further. In practice, few people do this.

[7] Note that the CX measure differs according to the level of interest rates. For example, we are measuring CX in Table 9A–1 when yields are 8 percent. If yields were 12 percent, the CX number would change. This is intuitively reasonable, as the curvature of the price–yield curve differs at each point on the price–yield curve. Note that duration also changes with the level of interest rates.

FIGURE 9A–3
Convexity of a
Coupon versus a
Discount Bond with
the Same Duration

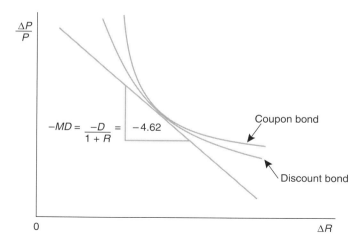

Part 2 of Table 9A–1 shows that coupon bonds of the same maturity (N) have less convexity than do zero-coupon bonds. However, for coupon bonds and discount or zero-coupon bonds of the same duration, part 3 of the table shows that the coupon bond has more convexity. We depict the convexity of both in Figure 9A–3.

Finally, before leaving convexity, we might look at one important use of the concept by managers of insurance companies, pension funds, and mutual funds. Remembering that convexity is a desirable form of interest rate risk insurance, FI managers could structure an asset portfolio to maximize its desirable effects. Consider a pension fund manager with a 15-year payout horizon. To immunize the risk of interest rate changes, the manager purchases bonds with a 15-year duration. Consider two alternative strategies to achieve this:

Strategy 1: Invest 100 percent of resources in a 15-year deep-discount bond with an 8 percent yield.

Strategy 2: Invest 50 percent in the very short-term money market (Federal funds) and 50 percent in 30-year deep-discount bonds with an 8 percent yield.

The duration (D) and convexities (CX) of these two asset portfolios are:

Strategy 1: $D = 15$, $CX = 206$
Strategy 2:[8] $D = \frac{1}{2}(0) + \frac{1}{2}(30) = 15$, $CX = \frac{1}{2}(0) + \frac{1}{2}(797) = 398.5$

[8] The duration and convexity of one-day federal funds are approximately zero.

Strategies 1 and 2 have the same durations, but strategy 2 has a greater convexity. Strategy 2 is often called a barbell portfolio, as shown in Figure 9A–4 by the shaded bars.[9] Strategy 1 is the unshaded bar. To the extent that the market does not price (or fully price) convexity, the barbell strategy dominates the direct duration-matching strategy (strategy 1).[10]

More commonly, an FI manager may seek to attain greater convexity in the asset portfolio than in the liability portfolio, as shown in Figure 9A–5. As a result, both positive and negative shocks to interest rates would have beneficial effects on the FI's net worth.[11]

[9] This is called a barbell because the weights are equally loaded at the extreme ends of the duration range, or bar, as in weight lifting.

[10] In a world in which convexity is priced, the long-term 30-year bond's price would rise to reflect the competition among buyers to include this more convex bond in their barbell asset portfolios. Thus, buying bond insurance—in the form of the barbell portfolio—would involve an additional cost to the FI manager. In addition, for the FI to be hedged in both a duration sense and a convexity sense, the manager should not choose the convexity of the asset portfolio without seeking to match it to the convexity of the liability portfolio. For further discussion of the convexity trap that results when an FI mismatches its asset and liability convexities, see J. H. Gilkeson and S. D. Smith, "The Convexity Trap: Pitfalls in Financing Mortgage Portfolios and Related Securities," Federal Reserve Bank of Atlanta, *Economic Review*, November–December 1992, pp. 17–27.

[11] Another strategy would be for the FI to issue callable bonds as liabilities. Callable bonds have limited upside capital gains because if rates fall to a low level, then the issuer calls the bond in early (and reissues new lower coupon bonds). The effect of limited upside potential for callable bond prices is that the price–yield curve for such bonds exhibits negative convexity. Thus, if asset investments have positive convexity and liabilities negative convexity, then yield shocks (whether positive or negative) are likely to produce net worth gains for the FI.

FIGURE 9A–4
Barbell Strategy

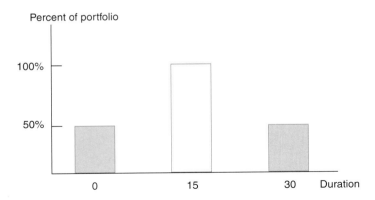

FIGURE 9A–5
Assets Are More
Convex Than
Liabilities

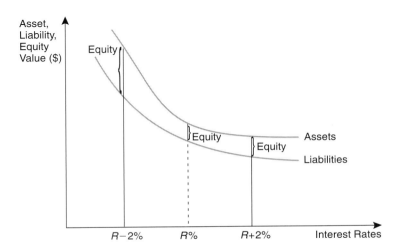

THE PROBLEM OF THE FLAT TERM STRUCTURE

We have been calculating simple, or Macauley, duration, which was named after an economist who was among the first to develop the *duration* concept. A key assumption of the simple duration model is that the yield curve or the term structure of interest rates is flat and that when rates change, the yield curve shifts in a parallel fashion. We show this in Figure 9A–6.

In the real world, the yield curve can take many shapes and at best may only approximate a flat yield curve. If the yield curve is not flat, using simple duration could be a potential source of error in predicting asset and liability interest rate sensitivities. Many models can deal with this problem. These models differ according to the shapes and shocks to the yield curve that are assumed.

Suppose the yield curve is not flat but shifts in such a manner that the yields on different maturity discount bonds change in a proportional fashion.[12] Consider calculating the duration of the six-year Eurobond when the yield curve is not flat at 8 percent. Instead, the yield curve looks like the one in Figure 9A–7.

Suppose the yield on one-year discount bonds rises. Assume also that the discounted changes in longer-maturity discount bonds yields are just proportional to the change in the one-year discount bond yield:

$$\frac{\Delta R_1}{1 + R_1} = \frac{\Delta R_2}{1 + R_2} = \cdots = \frac{\Delta R_6}{1 + R_6}$$

[12] We are interested in the yield curve on discount bonds because these yields reflect the time value of money for single payments at different maturity dates. Thus, we can use these yields as discount rates for cash flows on a security to calculate appropriate present values of its cash flows and its duration.

FIGURE 9A–6
Yield Curve Underlying Macauley Duration

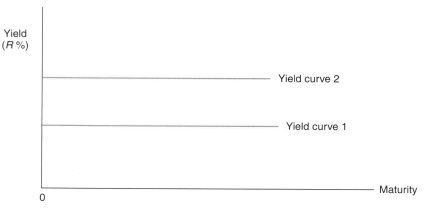

FIGURE 9A–7
Nonflat Yield Curve

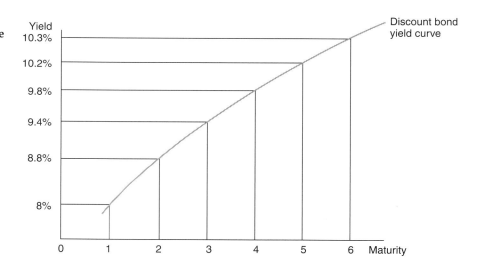

Given this quite restrictive assumption, it can be proved that the appropriate duration measure of the bond—call it D^*—can be derived by discounting the coupons and principal value of the bond by the discount rates or yields on appropriate maturity zero-coupon bonds. Given the discount bond yield curve plotted in Figure 9A–7, D^* is calculated in Table 9A–2.[13]

Notice that D^* is 4.916 years, while simple Macauley duration (with an assumed flat 8 percent

yield curve) is 4.993 years. D^* and D differ because, by taking into account the upward-sloping yield curve in Figure 9A–7, the later cash flows are discounted at higher rates than they are under the flat yield curve assumption underlying Macauley's measure D.

With respect to the FI manager's problem, choosing to use D^* instead of D does not change the basic problem except for a concern with the gap between the D^* on assets and leverage-weighted liabilities:

$$D_A^* - kD_L^*$$

However, remember that the D^* was calculated under very restrictive assumptions about the

[13] For more details, see Hawawini, "Controlling the Interest Rate Risk"; and G. O. Bierwag, G. G. Kaufman, and A. Toevs, "Duration: Its Development and Use in Bond Portfolio Management," *Financial Analysts Journal* 39 (1983), pp. 15–35.

TABLE 9A–2
Duration with an
Upward-Sloping
Yield Curve

t	CF	DF	CF × DF	CF × DF × t
1	80	$\frac{1}{(1.08)} = 0.9259$	74.07	74.07
2	80	$\frac{1}{(1.088)^2} = 0.8448$	67.58	135.16
3	80	$\frac{1}{(1.094)^3} = 0.7637$	61.10	183.30
4	80	$\frac{1}{(1.098)^4} = 0.6880$	55.04	220.16
5	80	$\frac{1}{(1.102)^5} = 0.6153$	49.22	246.10
6	1,080	$\frac{1}{(1.103)^6} = 0.5553$	599.75	3,598.50
			906.76	4,457.29

$$D^* = \frac{4,457.29}{906.76} = 4.91562$$

TABLE 9A–3
Duration and
Rescheduling

t	CF	DF	CF × DF	CF × DF × t
1	0	.9259	0	0
2	160	.8573	137.17	274.34
3	80	.7938	63.51	190.53
4	80	.7350	58.80	235.21
5	80	.6806	54.45	272.25
6	1,080	.6302	680.58	4,083.48
			994.51	5,055.81

$$D = \frac{5,055.81}{994.51} = 5.0837 \text{ years}$$

yield curve. If we change these assumptions in any way, the measure of D^* changes.[14]

THE PROBLEM OF DEFAULT RISK

The models and the duration calculations we have looked at assume that the issuer of bonds or the borrower of a loan pays the promised interest and principal with a probability of 1; we assume no default or delay in the payment of cash flows. In the real world, problems with principal and interest payments are common and lead to restructuring and workouts on debt contracts as bankers and bond trustees renegotiate with borrowers; that is,

the borrower reschedules or recontracts interest and principal payments rather than defaulting outright. If we view default risk as synonymous with the rescheduling of cash flows to a later date, this is quite easy to deal with in duration models.

Consider the six-year, 8 percent coupon, 8 percent yield Eurobond. Suppose the issuer gets into difficulty and cannot pay the first coupon. Instead, the borrower and the FI agree that the unpaid interest can be paid in year 2. This alleviates part of the cash flow pressure on the borrower while lengthening the duration of the bond from the FI's perspective (see Table 9A–3). The effect of rescheduling the first interest payment is to increase duration from approximately 5 years to 5.08 years.

More commonly, an FI manager unsure of the future cash flows because of future default risk might multiply the promised cash flow (CF_t) by

[14] A number of authors have identified other nonstandard measures of duration for more complex yield curve shapes and shifts. See, for example, Bierwag, Kaufman, and Toevs, "Duration: Its Development and Use." *Financial Analysts Journal* 39 (1983), pp. 15–35.

FIGURE 9A–8
Floating-Rate Note

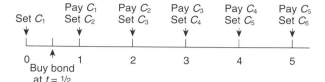

the probability of repayment (p_t) in year t to generate expected cash flows in year t—$E(CF_t)$.[15]

$$E(CF_t) = p_t \times CF_t$$

Chapter 11 suggests a number of ways to generate these repayment probabilities. Once the cash flows have been adjusted for default risk, a duration measure can be directly calculated in the same manner as the Macauley formula (or D^*) except that $E(CF_t)$ replaces CF_t.[16]

FLOATING-RATE LOANS AND BONDS

The duration models we have looked at assume that the interest rates on loans or the coupons on bonds are fixed at issue and remain unchanged until maturity. However, many bonds and loans carry floating interest rates. Examples include loan rates indexed to LIBOR (London Interbank Offered Rate) and adjustable rate mortgages (ARMs) whose rates can be indexed to Treasury or other securities yields. Moreover, in the 1980s, many banks and security firms either issued or underwrote perpetual floating-rate notes (FRNs). These are like consol bonds in that they never mature; unlike consols, their coupons fluctuate with market rates. The FI manager, who wants to analyze overall gap exposure, may ask: What are the durations of such floating-rate securities? The duration of a floating-rate instrument is generally the time interval between the purchase of the security and the time when the next coupon or interest payment is readjusted to reflect current interest rate conditions. We call this the time to repricing of the instrument.

For example, suppose the investor bought a perpetual floating-rate note. These floating-rate notes never mature. At the beginning of each year, the FI sets the coupon rate, which is paid at the end of that year. Suppose the investor buys the bond in the middle of the first year ($t = 1/2$) rather than at the beginning (see Figure 9A–8).

The present value of the bond from time of purchase is:[17]

$$P = \frac{C_1}{(1 + 1/2R)} + \frac{C_2}{(1 + 1/2R)(1 + R)}$$

$$+ \frac{C_3}{(1 + 1/2R)(1 + R)^2} + \frac{C_4}{(1 + 1/2R)(1 + R)^3}$$

$$+ \frac{C_5}{(1 + 1/2R)(1 + R)^4} + \cdots$$

$$+ \frac{C_\infty}{(1 + 1/2R)(1 + R)^{\infty - 1}}$$

Note three important aspects of this present value equation. First, the investor has to wait only a half year to get the first coupon payment—hence, the discount rate is $(1 + \frac{1}{2}R)$. Second, the investor knows with certainty only the size of the first coupon C_1, which was preset at the beginning of the first coupon period to reflect interest rates at that time. The FI set the first coupon rate six months before the investor bought the bond. Third, the other coupons on the bond, C_2, C_3, C_4, C_5, . . . C_∞, are unknown at the time the bond is purchased because they depend on the level of interest rates at the time they are reset (see Figure 9A–8).

---

[15] The probability of repayment is between 0 and 1.

[16] Alternatively, the promised cash flow could be discounted by the appropriate discount yield on a risk-free Treasury security plus an appropriate credit-risk spread; that is, $CF_t /(1 + d_t + S_t)t$, where CF_t is the promised cash flow in year t, d_t is the yield on a t-period zero-coupon Treasury bond, and S_t is a credit-risk premium.

[17] This formula follows the Eurobond convention that any cash flows received in less than one full coupon period's time are discounted using simple interest. Thus, we use $1 + 1/2R$ rather than $(1 + R)^{1/2}$ for the first coupon's cash flow in the example above. Also see R. A. Grobel, "Understanding the Duration of Floating Rate Notes," MIMED (New York: Salomon Brothers, 1986).

To derive the duration of the bond, rewrite the cash flows at one-half year onward as:

$$P = \frac{C_1}{(1 + 1/2R)} + \frac{1}{(1 + 1/2R)}$$

$$\left[\frac{C_2}{(1 + R)} + \frac{C_3}{(1 + R)^2} + \frac{C_4}{(1 + R)^3} \right.$$

$$\left. \frac{C_5}{(1 + R)^4} + \cdots + \frac{C_\infty}{(1 + R)^{\infty - 1}} \right]$$

where P is the present value of the bond (the bond price) at one-half year, the time of purchase.

The term in brackets is the present value or fair price (P_1) of the bond if it were sold at the end of year 1, the beginning of the second coupon period. As long as the variable coupons exactly match fluctuations in yields or interest rates, the present value of the cash flow in the square brackets is unaffected by interest rate changes. Thus,

$$P = \frac{C_1}{(1 + 1/2R)} + \frac{P_1}{(1 + 1/2R)}$$

Since C_1 is a fixed cash flow preset before the investor bought the bond and P_1 is a fixed cash flow in present value terms, buying this bond is similar to buying two single-payment deep-discount bonds each with a maturity of six months. Because the duration of a deep-discount bond is the same as its maturity, this FRN bond has:

$$D = \tfrac{1}{2} \text{ year}$$

As indicated earlier, a half year is exactly the interval between the time when the bond was purchased and the time when it was first repriced.[18]

---

[18] In another case an FI manager might buy a bond whose coupon floated but repaid fixed principal (many loans are priced like this). Calculating the duration on this bond or loan is straightforward. First, we have to think of it as two bonds: a floating-rate bond that pays a variable coupon (C) every year and a deep-discount bond that pays a fixed amount (F) on maturity. The duration of the first bond is the time between purchase and the first coupon reset date; $D = \tfrac{1}{2}$ year in the preceding example. While the duration of the deep-discount bond equals its maturity, $D =$ three years for a three-year bond. The duration of the bond as a whole is the weighted average of a half year and three years, where the weights (w_1) and ($1 - w_1$) reflect the present values of, respectively, the coupon cash flows and face value cash flow to the present value of the total cash flows (the sum of the two present values). Thus,

$$D = w_1(\tfrac{1}{2}) + (1 - w_1)(3)$$

DEMAND DEPOSITS AND PASSBOOK SAVINGS

Many banks and thrifts hold large amounts of checking and passbook savings account liabilities. This is especially true for smaller banks. The problem in assessing the duration of such claims is that their maturities are open-ended and many demand deposit accounts do not turn over very frequently. Although demand deposits allow holders to demand cash immediately—suggesting a very short maturity—many customers tend to retain demand deposit balances for lengthy periods. In the parlance of banking, they behave as if they were a bank's core deposits. A problem arises because defining the duration of a security requires defining its maturity. Yet demand deposits have open-ended maturities. One way for an FI manager to get around this problem is to analyze the runoff, or the turnover characteristics, of the FI's demand and passbook savings account deposits. For example, suppose the manager learned that on average each dollar in demand deposit accounts turned over five times a year. This suggests an average turnover or maturity per dollar of around 73 days.[19]

A second method is to consider demand deposits as bonds that can be instantaneously put back to the bank in return for cash. As instantaneously putable bonds, the duration of demand deposits is approximately zero.

A third approach is more directly in line with the idea of duration as a measure of interest rate sensitivity. It looks at the percentage change of demand deposits ($\Delta DD/DD$) to interest rate changes (ΔR). Because demand deposits and, to a lesser extent, passbook savings deposits pay either low explicit or implicit interest—where implicit interest takes forms such as subsidized checking fees—there tend to be enhanced withdrawals and switching into higher-yielding instruments as rates rise. You can use a number of quantitative techniques to test this sensitivity, including linear and nonlinear time series regression analysis.

A fourth approach is to use simulation analysis. This is based on forecasts of future interest rates and the net withdrawals by depositors from their

---

[19] That is, 365 days/5 = 73 days.

accounts over some future time period. Taking the discounted present values of these cash flows allows a duration measure to be calculated.[20]

MORTGAGES AND MORTGAGE-BACKED SECURITIES

Calculating the durations of mortgages and mortgage-backed securities is difficult because of prepayment risk. Essentially, as the level of interest rates falls, mortgage holders have the option to prepay their old mortgages and refinance with a new mortgage at a lower interest rate. In the terminology of finance, fixed-rate mortgages and mortgage-backed securities contain an embedded option. Calculating duration requires projecting the future cash flows on an asset. Consequently, to calculate the duration of mortgages, we need to

model the prepayment behavior of mortgage holders. Possible ways to do this are left to Chapter 28 on mortgage asset securitization.

FUTURES, OPTIONS, SWAPS, CAPS, AND OTHER CONTINGENT CLAIMS

When interest rates change, so do the values of (off-balance-sheet) derivative instruments such as futures, options, swaps, and caps (see Chapter 13). Market value gains and losses on these instruments can also have an impact on the net worth (E) of an FI. The calculation of the durations of these instruments is left to Chapters 24 to 26. However, it should be noted that a fully fledged duration gap model of an FI should take into account the durations of its derivatives portfolio as well as the duration of its on-balance-sheet assets and liabilities. This is especially so today as more and more FIs take positions in derivative contracts.

---

[20] For a very sophisticated model along these lines, see E. W. Irmler, "The OTS Net Portfolio Value Model" (Washington, DC: OTS, 1994).

Chapter **Ten**

Market Risk

INTRODUCTION

In recent years, the trading activities of FIs have raised considerable concern among regulators and FI analysts alike. For example, in February 1995, Barings, the U.K. merchant bank, was forced into insolvency as a result of losses on its trading in Japanese stock index futures. In September 1995, a similar incident took place at the New York branch of a leading Japanese bank, Daiwa Bank. The largest trading loss in recent history involving a "rogue trader" occurred in June 1996 when Sumitomo Corp. (a Japanese bank) lost $2.6 billion in commodity futures trading. Another relatively turbulent year, 1997, featured considerable currency and financial market volatility in Eastern Europe and Asia. This volatility was magnified further throughout 1998 with additional losses on Russian bonds as the ruble fell in value and the prices of Russian bonds collapsed. The problems in Russia forced big U.S. banks such as Bank of America and Chase Manhattan (now J. P. Morgan Chase) to write off hundreds of millions of dollars in losses on their holdings of Russian government securities. More recently, a single trader's actions in the FX markets resulted in almost $700 million in losses to Allfirst, the U.S. subsidiary of Allied Irish Bank. The Technology in the News box highlights how the use of software technology that monitors market risk could have prevented these losses. As traditional commercial and investment banking franchises shrink and markets become more complex (e.g., emerging country equity and bond markets and new sophisticated derivative contracts), concerns are only likely to increase regarding the threats to FI solvency from trading.

Conceptually, an FI's trading portfolio can be differentiated from its investment portfolio on the basis of time horizon and liquidity. The trading portfolio contains assets, liabilities, and derivative contracts that can be quickly bought or sold on organized financial markets (such as long and short positions in bonds, commodities, foreign exchange, equity securities, interest rate swaps, and options). The investment portfolio (or in the case of banks, the so-called banking book) contains assets and liabilities that are relatively illiquid and held for longer holding periods (such as consumer and commercial loans, retail deposits, and branches). Table 10–1 shows a hypothetical breakdown between banking book and trading book assets and liabilities. Note that capital produces a cushion against losses on either the banking or trading books—see Chapter 20.

With the increasing securitization of bank loans (e.g., mortgages), more and more assets have become liquid and tradable (e.g., mortgage-backed securities). Of course, with time, every asset and liability can be sold. While bank regulators have normally viewed tradable assets as those being held for horizons of less than one

Technology in the News

COULD SOFTWARE HAVE SAVED ALLFIRST $690 MILLION?

Mark Brickell claims the derivatives trading system . . . might have stopped the trades that cost Allfirst Bank $691 million. . . . The technology gives bankers more real-time control, Mr. Brickell said in an interview last month. "The credit risk of the other party is often an important factor in your decision to make the trade," he said. "When you're dealing with someone on an FX forward or an interest rate swap, then you care about the credit risk of your counterparty and his ability to perform over time." The . . . software checks counterparties' credit rules to determine whether each will accept the other for a particular trade. User firms input their credit rules—for example, putting a dollar limit on trades with one counterparty, or a five-year limit on futures transactions with another. On a trader's computer screen, a proposed trade is displayed in red if the trader's own firm would not accept the counterparty's credit risk for it. The trade is coded in yellow if the other firm would block it and in green if it meets the criteria both specified. "Our system measures in the value-at-risk of the transaction your trader is considering," Mr. Brickell said. "If he tries to click on a red or yellow price, the system won't let him make that mistake."

Mr. Brickell . . . said such a system could have prevented the kind of losses that came to light at Allfirst Bank in Baltimore. A single trader, John Rusnak, allegedly lost $691 million of the bank's money as he tried to cover up losses by manufacturing scores of false trades, which led to even steeper losses. Mr. Rusnak has been suspended, though he has not been charged with any crime. An internal investigation for Allied Irish Banks PLC, which owns Allfirst, found that computer deficiencies may have contributed to the bank's trading losses and that deficiencies in credit-risk management played a part. . . . "There was undue reliance on the trader to establish the status of a counterparty," their report said. "The impact of this is that Allfirst traders repeatedly entered into transactions with counterparties for whom there were no valid limits."

But Allfirst failed in other areas as well, according to the report. Senior managers failed to supervise Mr. Rusnak's activities, the report found. Among other things, they let him conduct trades while he was on vacation—a two-week vacation being mandatory precisely to prevent bank employees from hiding improper conduct. The report urged management to continue to cooperate with government investigations in the case. . . . Mr. Brickell . . . said the security features of its trading software are no panacea but create a record, updating the general ledger and keeping track of credit and market risk "so anybody will have an accurate record of the deal." . . .

Source: Steve Bills, *The American Banker*, April 5, 2002, p. 12. *www.americanbanker.com*

---

year, private FIs take an even shorter-term view. In particular, FIs are concerned about the fluctuation in value—or value at risk (VAR)—of their trading account assets and liabilities for periods as short as one day (so-called daily earnings at risk [DEAR])—especially if such fluctuations pose a threat to their solvency.

market risk
Risk related to the uncertainty of an FI's earnings on its trading portfolio caused by changes in market conditions.

Market risk (or value at risk) can be defined as the risk related to the uncertainty of an FI's earnings on its trading portfolio caused by changes in market conditions such as the price of an asset, interest rates, market volatility, and market liquidity.[1,2] Thus, risks such as interest rate risk (discussed in the last two chapters) and foreign exchange risk (discussed in Chapter 15) affect market risk. However,

---

[1] J. P. Morgan, *Introduction to RiskMetrics* (New York: J. P. Morgan, October 1994), p. 2. There is an ongoing debate about whether spread risk is a part of market risk or credit risk. J. P. Morgan, includes spread risk as credit risk (and includes it in the CreditMetrics measure [see Chapter 11]) rather than as part of market risk.

[2] Market risk used by FI managers and regulators is not synonymous with systematic market risk analyzed by investors in securities markets. Systematic (market) risk reflects the comovement of a security with the market portfolio (reflected by the security's beta), although beta is used to measure the market risk of equities, as noted below.

TABLE 10–1
The Investment
(Banking) Book and
Trading Book of a
Commercial Bank

	Assets	Liabilities
Banking Book	Loans	Capital
	Other illiquid assets	Deposits
Trading Book	Bonds (long)	Bonds (short)
	Commodities (long)	Commodities (short)
	FX (long)	FX (short)
	Equities (long)	Equities (short)
	Derivatives* (long)	Derivatives* (short)

*Derivatives are off balance sheet (as discussed in Chapter 7).

market risk emphasizes the risks to FIs that actively trade assets and liabilities (and derivatives) rather than hold them for longer-term investment, funding, or hedging purposes. Income from trading activities is increasingly replacing income from traditional FI activities of deposit taking and lending. The resulting earnings uncertainty can be measured over periods as short as a day or as long as a year. Moreover, market risk can be defined in absolute terms as a *dollar* exposure amount or as a relative amount against some benchmark. The sections that follow concentrate on absolute dollar measures of market risk. We look at three major approaches that are being used to measure market risk: RiskMetrics, historic or back simulation, and Monte Carlo simulation.

So important is market risk in determining the viability of an FI that since 1998, U.S. regulators have included market risk in determining the required level of capital an FI must hold.[3] The link between market risk and required capital levels is also discussed in the chapter.

MARKET RISK MEASUREMENT

There are at least five reasons market risk measurement (MRM) is important:

1. *Management information.* MRM provides senior management with information on the risk exposure taken by FI traders. Management can then compare this risk exposure to the FI's capital resources.

2. *Setting limits.* MRM considers the market risk of traders' portfolios, which will lead to the establishment of economically logical position limits per trader in each area of trading.

3. *Resource allocation.* MRM involves the comparison of returns to market risks in different areas of trading, which may allow the identification of areas with the greatest potential return per unit of risk into which more capital and resources can be directed.

4. *Performance evaluation.* MRM, relatedly, considers the return-risk ratio of traders, which may allow a more rational bonus (compensation) system to be put in place. That is, those traders with the highest returns may simply be the ones who have taken the largest risks. It is not clear that they should receive higher compensation than traders with lower returns and lower risk exposures.

[3] This requirement was introduced earlier (in 1996) in the EU.

5. *Regulation.* With the Bank for International Settlements (BIS) and Federal Reserve currently regulating market risk through capital requirements (discussed later in this chapter), private sector benchmarks are important, since it is possible that regulators will overprice some risks. MRM conducted by the FI can be used to point to potential misallocations of resources as a result of prudential regulation. As a result, in certain cases regulators are allowing banks to use their own (internal) models to calculate their capital requirements.[4]

**Concept
Questions**

1. What is market risk?
2. Why is market risk measurement important for FIs?

CALCULATING MARKET RISK EXPOSURE

Large commercial banks, investment banks, insurance companies, and mutual funds have all developed market risk models. In the development of these models—so-called internal models—three major approaches have been followed:

- RiskMetrics (or the variance/covariance approach).
- Historic or back simulation.
- Monte Carlo simulation.

We consider RiskMetrics[5] first and then compare it with other internal model approaches, such as historic or back simulation.

THE RISKMETRICS MODEL

The ultimate objective of market risk measurement models can best be seen from the following quote by Dennis Weatherstone, former chairman of J. P. Morgan (JPM), now J. P. Morgan Chase: "At close of business each day tell me what the market risks are across all businesses and locations." In a nutshell, the chairman of J. P. Morgan wants a single *dollar* number at 4:15 PM New York time that tells him J. P. Morgan's market risk exposure the next day—especially if that day turns out to be a "bad" day.

This is nontrivial, given the extent of JPM's trading business. As shown in Table 10–2, when JPM developed its RiskMetrics Model in 1994 it had 14 active trading locations with 120 independent units trading fixed-income securities, foreign exchange, commodities, derivatives, emerging-market securities, and proprietary assets, with a total daily volume exceeding $50 billion. This scale and variety of activities is typical of the major money center banks, large overseas banks (e.g., Deutsche Bank and Barclays), and major insurance companies and investment banks.

Here, we will concentrate on measuring the market risk exposure of a major FI on a daily basis using the RiskMetrics approach. As will be discussed later, measuring

---

[4] Since regulators are concerned with the social costs of a failure or insolvency, including contagion effects and other externalities, regulatory models will normally tend to be more conservative than private sector models that are concerned only with the private costs of failure.

[5] J. P. Morgan (JPM) first developed RiskMetrics in 1994. In 1998 the development group formed a separate company, partly owned by JPM. The material presented in this chapter is an overview of the RiskMetrics model. The details, additional discussion, and examples are found in "Return to RiskMetrics: The Evolution of a Standard," April 2001, available at the J. P. Morgan Chase Web site, **www.jpmorganchase.com** or **www.riskmetrics.com**.

TABLE 10–2   **JPM's Trading Business**

	Fixed Income	Foreign Exchange STIRI*	Commodities	Derivatives	Equities	Emergency Markets	Proprietary	Total
Number of active locations	14	12	5	11	8	7	11	14
Number of independent risk-taking units	30	21	8	16	14	11	19	120
Thousands of transactions per day	>5	>5	<1	<1	>5	<1	<1	>20
Billions of dollars in daily trading volume	>10	>30	1	1	<1	1	8	>50

*Short-term interest rate instruments.

Source: J. P. Morgan, *Introduction to RiskMetrics* (New York: J. P. Morgan, October 1994). *www.jpmorganchase.com*

the risk exposure for periods longer than a day (e.g., five days) is under certain assumptions a simple transformation of the daily risk exposure number.

Essentially, the FI is concerned with how much it can potentially lose if market conditions move adversely tomorrow; that is:

Market risk = Estimated potential loss under adverse circumstances

daily earnings at risk (DEAR)
Market risk exposure over the next 24 hours.

More specifically, the market risk is measured in terms of the FI's **daily earnings at risk (DEAR)** and has three components:

$$\begin{matrix}\text{Daily earnings} \\ \text{at risk}\end{matrix} = \begin{pmatrix}\text{Dollar market} \\ \text{value of} \\ \text{the position}\end{pmatrix} \times \begin{pmatrix}\text{Price} \\ \text{sensitivity of} \\ \text{the position}\end{pmatrix} \times \begin{pmatrix}\text{Potential} \\ \text{adverse move} \\ \text{in yield}\end{pmatrix} \quad \textbf{(1)}$$

Since price sensitivity multiplied by adverse yield move measures the degree of price volatility of an asset, we can also write equation (1) as equation (2):

$$\begin{matrix}\text{Daily earnings} \\ \text{at risk}\end{matrix} = \begin{pmatrix}\text{Dollar market} \\ \text{value of} \\ \text{the position}\end{pmatrix} \times \begin{pmatrix}\text{Price} \\ \text{volatility}\end{pmatrix} \quad \textbf{(2)}$$

How price sensitivity and an adverse yield move will be measured depends on the FI and its choice of a price-sensitivity model as well as its view of what exactly is a potentially adverse price (yield) move.

We concentrate on how the RiskMetrics model calculates daily earnings at risk in three trading areas—fixed income, foreign exchange (FX), and equities—and then on how it estimates the aggregate risk of the entire trading portfolio to meet Dennis Weatherstone's objective of a single aggregate dollar exposure measure across the whole bank at 4:15 PM each day.[6]

---

[6] It is clear from the above discussion that interest rate risk (see Chapters 8 and 9) is part of market risk. However, in market risk models, we are concerned with the interest rate sensitivity of the fixed-income securities held as part of an FI's active trading portfolio. Many fixed-income securities are held as part of an FI's investment portfolio. While the latter are subject to interest rate risk, they will not be included in a market risk calculation.

The Market Risk of Fixed-Income Securities

Suppose an FI has a $1 million market value position in zero-coupon bonds of seven years to maturity with a face value of $1,631,483.[7] Today's yield on these bonds is 7.243 percent per annum. These bonds are held as part of the trading portfolio. Thus,

$$\text{Dollar market value of position} = \$1 \text{ million}$$

The FI manager wants to know the potential exposure the FI faces should interest rates move against the FI as the result of an adverse or reasonably bad market move the next day. How much the FI will lose depends on the bond's price volatility. From the duration model in Chapter 9 we know that:

$$\text{Daily price volatility} = (\text{Price sensitivity to a small change in yield})$$
$$\times (\text{Adverse daily yield move})$$
$$= (MD) \times (\text{Adverse daily yield move}) \qquad (3)$$

The modified duration (MD) of this bond is:[8]

$$MD = \frac{D}{1+R} = \frac{7}{(1.07243)} = 6.527$$

given that the yield on the bond is $R = 7.243$ percent. To estimate price volatility, multiply the bond's MD by the expected adverse daily yield move.

EXAMPLE 10–1

Daily Earnings at Risk on Fixed-Income Securities

Suppose we define bad yield changes such that there is only a 5 percent chance that the yield changes will exceed this amount in either direction—or, since we are concerned only with bad outcomes, and we are long in bonds, that there is 1 chance in 20 (or a 5 percent chance) that the next day's yield increase (or shock) will exceed this given adverse move.

If we assume that yield changes are normally distributed,[9] we can fit a normal distribution to the histogram of recent past changes in seven-year zero-coupon interest rates (yields) to get an estimate of the size of this adverse rate move. From statistics, we know that (the middle) 90 percent of the area under the normal distribution is to be found within ± 1.65 standard deviations (σ) from the mean—that is, 1.65σ—and 10 percent of the area under the normal distribution is found beyond $\pm 1.65\sigma$ (5 percent under each tail, -1.65σ and $+1.65\sigma$, respectively). Suppose that during the last year the mean change in daily yields on seven-year zero-coupon bonds was 0 percent[10] while the standard deviation was 10 basis

(continued)

---

[7] The face value of the bonds is $1,631,483—that is, $1,631,483/(1.07243)^7 = $1,000,000 market value. In the original model, prices were determined using a discrete rate of return, R_j. In the 2001 document "Return to RiskMetrics: The Evolution of a Standard," April 2001, prices are determined using a continuously compounded return, e^{-rt}. The change was implemented because continuous compounding has properties that facilitate mathematical treatment. For example, the logarithmic return on a zero-coupon bond equals the difference of interest rates multiplied by the maturity of the bond. That is:

$$\log \left(\frac{e^{-\tilde{r}t}}{e^{-rt}} \right) = -(\tilde{r} - r)t$$

where $\tilde{r}$ is the expected return.

[8] Assuming annual compounding for simplicity.

[9] In reality, many asset return distributions—such as exchange rates and interest rates—have "fat tails." Thus, the normal distribution will tend to underestimate extreme outcomes. This is a major criticism of the RiskMetrics modeling approach. (See later footnote and references.)

[10] If the mean were nonzero (e.g., -1 basis point), this could be added to the 16.5 bp (i.e., 15.5 bp) to project the yield shock

points (or 0.001). Thus, 1.65σ is 16.5 basis points (bp).[11] In other words, over the last year, daily yields on seven-year, zero-coupon bonds have fluctuated (either positively or negatively) by more than 16.5 bp 10 percent of the time. Adverse moves in yields are those that decrease the value of the security (i.e., the yield increases). These occurred 5 percent of the time, or 1 in 20 days. This is shown in Figure 10–1.

We can now calculate the potential daily price volatility on seven-year discount bonds using equation (3) as:

$$\text{Price volatility} = (MD) \times (\text{Potential adverse move in yield})$$

$$= (6.527) \times (.00165)$$

$$= .01077 \text{ or } 1.077\%$$

Given this price volatility and the initial market value of the seven-year bond portfolio, then equation (2) can be used to calculate the daily earnings at risk as:[12]

$$\text{Daily earnings at risk} = (\text{Dollar market value of position}) \times (\text{Price volatility})$$

$$= (\$1,000,000) \times (.01077)$$

$$= \$10,770$$

That is, the potential daily loss on the $1 million position is $10,770 if the 1 bad day in 20 occurs tomorrow.

We can extend this analysis to calculate the potential loss over 2, 3, . . . N days. If we assume that yield shocks are independent and daily volatility is approximately constant,[13] and that the FI is locked in to holding this asset for N number of days, then the N-day market value at risk (VAR) is related to daily earnings at risk (DEAR) by:

$$VAR = DEAR \times \sqrt{N}$$

That is, the earnings the FI has at risk, should interest rate yields move against the FI, are a function of the value or earnings at risk for one day (DEAR) and the (square root of the) number of days that the FI is forced to hold the securities because of an illiquid market. Specifically, DEAR assumes that the FI can sell all the bonds tomorrow, even at the new lower price. In reality, it may take many days for the FI to unload its position. This relative illiquidity of a market exposes the

---

[11] RiskMetrics weights more recent observations more highly than past observations (this is called *exponential weighting*). This allows more recent news to be more heavily reflected in the calculation of σ. Regular σ calculations put an equal weight on all past observations.

[12] Since we are calculating loss, we drop the minus sign here.

[13] The assumptions that daily volatility is constant and that there is no autocorrelation in yield shocks are strong assumptions. Much recent literature suggests that shocks are autocorrelated in many asset markets over relatively long horizons. To understand why we take the square root of N, consider a five-day holding period. The σ_5^2, or five-day variance of asset returns, will equal the current one-day variance σ_1^2 times 5 under the assumptions of constant daily variance and no autocorrelation in shocks, or:

$$\sigma_5^2 = \sigma_1^2 \times 5$$

The standard deviation of this equation is:

$$\sigma_5 = \sigma_1 \times \sqrt{5}$$

or since DEAR is measured in the same dimensions as a standard deviation (σ), in the terminology of RiskMetrics, the five-day value at risk (VAR_5) is:

$$VAR_5 = DEAR \times \sqrt{5}$$

FIGURE 10–1
Adverse Rate Move,
Seven-Year Rates

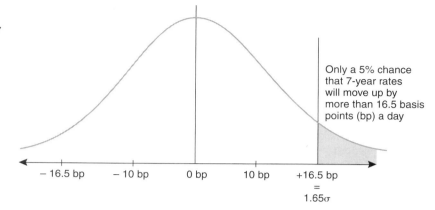

Only a 5% chance
that 7-year rates
will move up by
more than 16.5 basis
points (bp) a day

−16.5 bp   −10 bp   0 bp   10 bp   +16.5 bp
=
1.65σ

FI to magnified losses (measured by the square root of *N*).[14] If *N* is five days, then:

$$VAR = \$10,770 \times \sqrt{5} = \$24,082$$

If *N* is 10 days, then:[15]

$$VAR = \$10,770 \times \sqrt{10} = \$34,057$$

In the above calculations, we estimated price sensitivity using modified duration. However, the RiskMetrics model generally prefers using the present value of cash flow changes as the price-sensitivity weights over modified durations. Essentially, each cash flow is discounted by the appropriate zero-coupon rate to generate the daily earnings at risk measure. If we used the direct cash flow calculation in this case, the loss would be $10,771.2.[16] The estimates in this case are very close.

Foreign Exchange

Like other large FIs, J. P. Morgan Chase actively trades in foreign exchange (FX). Remember that:

$$DEAR = (\text{Dollar value of position}) \times (\text{Price volatility})$$

EXAMPLE 10–2
Daily Earnings at Risk of Foreign Exchange Contracts

Suppose the FI had a €1.6 million trading position in spot euros at the close of business on a particular day. The FI wants to calculate the daily earnings at risk from this position (i.e., the risk exposure on this position should the next day be a bad day in the FX markets with respect to the value of the euro against the dollar).

The first step is to calculate the dollar value of the position:

Dollar equivalent value of position = (FX position) × (€/$ spot exchange rate)

= (€1.6 million) × ($ per unit of foreign currency)

(continued)

---

[14] In practice, a number of FIs calculate *N* internally by dividing the position held in a security by the median daily volume of trading of that security over recent days. Thus, if trading volume is low because of a "one-way market," in that most people are seeking to sell rather than buy, then *N* can rise substantially; that is, *N* = ($ position in security/median daily $ volume of trading).

[15] Under the BIS 1998 market risk capital requirements, a 10-day holding period (*N* = 10) is assumed to measure exposure.

[16] The initial market value of the seven-year zero was $1,000,000, or $1,631,483/(1.07243)[7]. The (loss) effect on each $1 (market value) invested in the bond of a rise in rates by 1 bp from 7.243 percent to 7.253 percent is .0006528. However, the adverse rate move is 16.5 bp. Thus:

$$DEAR = (\$1 \text{ million}) \times (.0006528) \times (16.5) = \$10,771.2$$

If the exchange rate is €1.60/$1 or $0.625/€ at the daily close, then

$$\text{Dollar value of position} = (€\ 1.6\ \text{million}) \times (\$0.625/€)$$

$$= \$1\ \text{million}$$

Suppose that, looking back at the daily changes in the €/$ exchange rate over the past year, we find that the volatility, or standard deviation (σ), of daily changes in the spot exchange rate was 56.5 bp. However, suppose that the FI is interested in adverse moves—that is, bad moves that will not occur more than 5 percent of the time, or 1 day in every 20. Statistically speaking, if changes in exchange rates are historically "normally" distributed, the exchange rate must change in the adverse direction by 1.65σ (1.65×56.5 bp) for this change to be viewed as likely to occur only 1 day in every 20 days:[17]

$$\text{FX volatility} = 1.65 \times 56.5\ \text{bp} = 93.2\ \text{bp or } 0.932\%$$

In other words, during the last year, the euro declined in value against the dollar by 93.2 bp 5 percent of the time. As a result:

$$DEAR = (\text{Dollar value of position}) \times (\text{FX volatility})$$

$$= (\$1\ \text{million}) \times (.00932)$$

$$= \$9,320$$

This is the potential daily earnings exposure to adverse euro to dollar exchange rate changes for the FI from the €1.6 million spot currency holdings.

Equities

Many large FIs also take positions in equities. As is well known from the Capital Asset Pricing Model (CAPM), there are two types of risk to an equity position in an individual stock i:[18]

$$\text{Total risk} = \text{Systematic risk} + \text{Unsystematic risk}$$

$$(\sigma_{it}^2) = (\beta_i^2\,\sigma_{mt}^2) + (\sigma_{eit}^2)$$

beta
Systematic (undiversifiable) risk reflecting the comovement of the returns on a specific stock with returns on the market portfolio.

Systematic risk reflects the comovement of that stock with the market portfolio reflected by the stock's **beta** (β_i) and the volatility of the market portfolio (σ_{mt}), while unsystematic risk is specific to the firm itself (σ_{eit}).

In a very well diversified portfolio, unsystematic risk (σ^2_{eit}) can be largely diversified away (i.e., will equal zero), leaving behind systematic (undiversifiable) market risk ($\beta^2_i\sigma^2_{mt}$). If the FI's trading portfolio follows (replicates) the returns on the stock market index, the β of that portfolio will be 1, since the movement of returns on the FI's portfolio will be one to one with the market,[19] and the standard deviation of the portfolio, σ_{it}, will be equal to the standard deviation of the stock market index, σ_{mt}.

---

[17] Technically, 90 percent of the area under a normal distribution lies between +/− 1.65σ from the mean. This means that 5 percent of the time, daily exchange rate changes will increase by more than 1.65σ, and 5 percent of the time, will decrease by 1.65σ. This case concerns only adverse moves in the exchange rate of euros to dollars (i.e., a depreciation of 1.65σ).

[18] This assumes that systematic and unsystematic risks are independent of each other.

[19] If $\beta \neq 1$, as in the case of most individual stocks, DEAR = dollar value of position × β_i × $1.65\sigma_m$, where β_i is the systematic risk of the ith stock.

EXAMPLE 10–3
Daily Earnings at Risk on Equities

Suppose the FI holds a $1 million trading position in stocks that reflect a U.S. stock market index (e.g., the Wilshire 5000). Then $\beta = 1$ and the DEAR for equities is:

$$\text{DEAR} = (\text{Dollar market value of position}) \times (\text{Stock market return volatility})$$
$$= (\$1,000,000) \times (1.65\ \sigma_m)$$

If, over the last year, the σ_m of the daily returns on the stock market index was 2 percent, then $1.65\ \sigma_m = 3.3$ percent (i.e., the adverse change or decline in the daily return on the stock market exceeded 3.3 percent only 5 percent of the time). In this case:

$$\textit{DEAR} = (\$1,000,000) \times (0.033)$$
$$= \$33,000$$

That is, the FI stands to lose at least $33,000 in earnings if adverse stock market returns materialize tomorrow.[20]

In less well diversified portfolios or portfolios of individual stocks, the effect of unsystematic risk σ_{eit} on the value of the trading position would need to be added. Moreover, if the CAPM does not offer a good explanation of asset pricing compared with, say, multi-index arbitrage pricing theory (APT), a degree of error will be built into the DEAR calculation.[21]

Portfolio Aggregation

The preceding sections analyzed the daily earnings at risk of individual trading positions. The examples considered a seven-year, zero-coupon, fixed-income security ($1 million market value); a position in spot euros ($1 million market value); and a position in the U.S. stock market index ($1 million market value). The individual DEARs were:

1. Seven-year zero-coupon bonds = $10,770
2. Euro spot = $9,320
3. U.S. equities = $33,000

However, senior management wants to know the aggregate risk of the entire trading position. To calculate this, we *cannot* simply sum the three DEARs— $10,770 + $9,320 + $33,000 = $53,090—because that ignores any degree of offsetting covariance or correlation among the fixed-income, FX, and equity trading positions. In particular, some of these asset shocks (adverse moves) may be negatively correlated. As is well known from modern portfolio theory, negative correlations among asset shocks will reduce the degree of portfolio risk.

---

[20] If we consider a single equity security with a beta (β) = 1.25 (i.e., one that is more sensitive than the market, such that as market returns increase [decrease] by 1 percent, the security's return increases [decreases] by 1.25 percent), then with a $1 million investment and the same (assumed) volatility (σ) of 2 percent (such that $1.65 \times .02 = 0.033$, or 3.3 percent), the FI would stand to lose at least $41,250 in daily earnings if adverse stock returns materializes (i.e., DEAR = $1,000,000 \times 1.25 \times 0.033 = $41,250).

[21] As noted in the introduction, derivatives are also used for trading purposes. In the calculation of its DEAR, a derivative has to be converted into a position in the underlying asset (e.g., bond, FX, or equity).

TABLE 10–3
Correlations (ρ_{ij}) among Assets

	Seven-Year Zero	€/\$1	U.S. Stock Index
Seven-year zero	—	−.2	.4
€/\$1		—	.1
U.S. stock index			—

EXAMPLE 10–4

Calculation of the DEAR of a Portfolio

Table 10–3 shows a hypothetical correlation matrix between daily seven-year zero-coupon bond yield changes, €/\$ spot exchange rate changes, and changes in daily returns on a U.S. stock market index (Wilshire 5000). From Table 10–3, the correlation between the seven-year zero-coupon bonds and €/\$ exchange rates, $\rho_{z,\epsilon}$, is negative (−.2), while the seven-year zero-coupon yield changes with, respectively, U.S. stock returns, $\rho_{z,U.S.}$, (.4) and €/\$ shocks, $\rho_{U.S.,\epsilon}$, (.1) are positively correlated.

Using this correlation matrix along with the individual asset DEARs, we can calculate the risk or standard deviation of the whole (three-asset) trading portfolio as:[22]

$$DEAR \text{ portfolio} = \begin{bmatrix} (DEAR_z)^2 + (DEAR_\epsilon)^2 + (DEAR_{U.S.})^2 \\ + (2 \times \rho_{z\epsilon} \times DEAR_z \times DEAR_\epsilon) \\ + (2 \times \rho_{z,U.S.} \times DEAR_z \times DEAR_{U.S.}) \\ + (2 \times \rho_{U.S.,\epsilon} \times DEAR_{U.S.} \times DEAR_\epsilon) \end{bmatrix}^{1/2} \quad (4)$$

This is a direct application of modern portfolio theory (MPT) since DEARs are directly similar to standard deviations. Substituting into this equation the calculated individual DEARs (in thousands of dollars), we get:

$$DEAR \text{ portfolio} = \begin{bmatrix} (10.77)^2 + (9.32)^2 + (33)^2 + 2(-.2)(10.77)(9.32) \\ + 2(.4)(10.77)(33) + 2(.1)(9.32)(33) \end{bmatrix}^{1/2}$$

$$= \$39,969$$

The equation indicates that considering the risk of each trading position as well as the correlation structure among those positions' returns results in a lower measure of portfolio trading risk (\$39,969) than when risks of the underlying trading positions (the sum of which was \$53,090) are added. A quick check will reveal that had we assumed that all three assets were perfectly positively correlated (i.e., $\rho_{ij} = 1$), DEAR for the portfolio would have been \$53,090 (i.e., equal to the sum of the three DEARs). Clearly, even in abnormal market conditions, assuming that asset returns are perfectly correlated will exaggerate the degree of actual trading risk exposure.

Table 10–4 shows the type of spreadsheet used by FIs such as J. P. Morgan Chase to calculate DEAR. As you can see, in this example, positions can be taken in 13 different country (currency) bonds in eight different maturity buckets.[23] There is also a

---

[22] This is a standard relationship from modern portfolio theory in which the standard deviation or risk of a portfolio of three assets is equal to the square root of the sum of the variances of returns on each of the three assets individually plus two times the covariances among each pair of these assets. With three assets there are three covariances. Here we use the fact that a correlation coefficient times the standard deviations on each pair of assets equals the covariance between each pair of assets. Note that DEAR is measured in dollars and has the same dimensions as a standard deviation. We discuss Modern Portfolio Theory in more detail in Chapter 12.

[23] Bonds held with different maturity dates (e.g., six years) are split into two and allocated to the nearest two of the eight maturity buckets (here, five years and seven years) using three criteria: (1) The sum of the current market *value* of the two resulting cash flows must be identical to the market value of the original cash flow; (2) the market *risk* of the portfolio of two cash flows must be identical to the overall market risk of the original cash flow; and (3) the two cash flows have the same *sign* as the original cash flow. See J. P. Morgan, "RiskMetrics—Technical Document," November 1994, and "Return to RiskMetrics: The Evolution of a Standard," April 2001. www.jpmorganchase.com or www.riskmetrics.com.

TABLE 10–4   Portfolio DEAR Spreadsheet

	Interest Rate Risk Notional Amounts (U.S. $ millions equivalents)									FX Risk			Total	
	1 Month	1 Year	2 Years	3 Years	4 Years	5 Years	7 Years	10 Years	Interest DEAR	Spot FX	FX DEAR	Portfolio Effect	Total DEAR
Australia										AUD			
Brazil										BRL			
Canada										CAD			
Denmark	19			−30				11	48	DKK			48
European Union	−19			30				−11	27	EUR			27
Hong Kong										HKD			
Japan										YEN			
Mexico										MXN			
Singapore										SGD			
Sweden										SEK			
Switzerland										CHF			
United Kingdom										GBP			
United States						10		10	76	USD			76
Total						10		10	151				151
						Portfolio effect			(62)				(62)
RISK	DATA PRINT CLOSE					Total DEAR ($000s)			89				89

Source: J. P. Morgan, *RiskMetrics* (New York: J. P. Morgan, 1994). *www.jpmorgan.com*, *www.riskmetrics.com*

column for FX risk (and, if necessary, equity risk) in these different country markets, although in this example, the FI has no FX risk exposure (all the cells are empty).

In the example in Table 10–4, while the FI is holding offsetting long and short positions in both Danish and Euro bonds, it is still exposed to trading risks of $48,000 and $27,000, respectively (see the column Interest DEAR). This happens because the European Union yield curve is more volatile than the Danish and shocks at different maturity buckets are not equal. The DEAR figure for a U.S. bond position of long $20 million is $76,000. Adding these three positions yields a DEAR of $151,000. However, this ignores the fact that Danish, European Union, and U.S. yield shocks are not perfectly correlated. Allowing for diversification effects (the portfolio effect) results in a total DEAR of only $89,000. This would be the number reported to the FI's senior management. Most financial institutions establish limits for value at risk, daily earnings at risk, position limits, and dollar trading loss limits for their trading portfolios. Actual activity compared with these limits is then monitored daily. Should a risk exposure level exceed approved limit levels, management must provide a strategy for bringing risk levels within approved limits. Table 10–5 reports the average, minimum, and maximum daily earnings at risk for several large U.S. commercial banks during 2002. For example, J. P. Morgan Chase was exposed to a maximum of $160 million in 2002.

Currently, the number of markets covered by J. P. Morgan Chase's traders and the number of correlations among those markets require the daily production and updating of over 450 volatility estimates (σ) and correlations (ρ). These data are updated daily.

Concept Questions

1. What is the ultimate objective of market risk measurement models?
2. Refer to Example 10–1. What is the DEAR for this bond if σ is 15 bp?
3. Refer to Example 10–4. What is the DEAR of the portfolio if the returns on the three assets are independent of each other?

TABLE 10–5
Daily Earnings at Risk for Large U.S. Commercial Banks, 2002* (in millions of dollars)

Source: Year 2002 10-K reports for the respective companies.

Name	Average DEAR for the year 2002	Minimum DEAR during 2002	Maximum DEAR during 2002
Bank of America	$ 40	$ 19	$ 70
Bank One	13	11	16
Citicorp	66	58	184
Wachovia	12	10	17
FleetBoston Financial	72	28	135
J. P. Morgan Chase	120	88	160

*The figures are based on these banks' internal models, i.e., they may be based on methodologies other than RiskMetrics—see below.

HISTORIC (BACK SIMULATION) APPROACH

A major criticism of RiskMetrics is the need to assume a symmetric (normal) distribution for all asset returns.[24] Clearly, for some assets, such as options and short-term securities (bonds), this is highly questionable. For example, the most an investor can lose if he or she buys a call option on an equity is the call premium; however, the investor's potential upside returns are unlimited. In a statistical sense, the returns on call options are nonnormal since they exhibit a positive skew.[25]

Because of these and other considerations discussed below, the large majority of FIs that have developed market risk models have employed a historic or back simulation approach. The advantages of this approach are that (1) it is simple, (2) it

[24] Another criticism is that VAR models like RiskMetrics ignore the (risk in the) payments of accrued interest on an FI's debt securities. Thus, VAR models will underestimate the true probability of default and the appropriate level of capital to be held against this risk (see P. Kupiec, "Risk Capital and VAR," *The Journal of Derivatives,* Winter 1999, pp. 41–52). Also, Johansson, Seiles, and Tjarnberg find that because of the distributional assumptions, while RiskMetrics produces reasonable estimates of downside risk for FIs with highly diversified portfolios, FIs with small, undiversified portfolios will significantly underestimate their true risk exposure using RiskMetrics (see, F. Johansson, M. J. Seiles, and M. Tjarnberg, "Measuring Downside Portfolio Risks," *The Journal of Portfolio Management,* Fall 1999, pp. 96–107). Further, a number of authors have argued that many asset distributions have "fat tails" and that RiskMetrics, by assuming the normal distribution, underestimates the risk of extreme losses. See, for example, Salih F. Neftci, "Value at Risk Calculations, Extreme Events and Tail Estimations," *Journal of Derivatives,* Spring 2000, pp. 23–37. One alternative approach to dealing with the "fat-tail" problem is extreme value theory. Simply put, one can view an asset distribution as being explained by two distributions. For example, a normal distribution may explain returns up to the 95 percent threshold, but for losses beyond that threshold another distribution, such as the generalized Pareto distribution, may provide a better explanation of loss outcomes such as the 99 percent level and beyond. In short, the normal distribution is likely to underestimate the importance and size of observations in the tail of the distribution, which is, after all, what value at risk models are meant to be measuring (see also Alexander J. McNeil, "Extreme Value Theory for Risk Managers," Working Paper, Department of Mathematics, ETH Zentrom, Ch-8092, Zurich, Switzerland, May 17, 1999). Finally, VAR models by definition concern themselves with risk rather than return. It should be noted that minimizing risk may be highly costly in terms of the return the FI gives up. Indeed, there may be many more return–risk combinations preferable to that achieved at the minimum risk point in the trading portfolio. Recent upgrades to RiskMetrics (see the RiskMetrics Web site at **www.riskmetrics.com**) allow management to incorporate a return dimension to VAR analysis so that management can evaluate how trading portfolio returns differ as VAR changes.

[25] For a normal distribution, its skew (which is the third moment of a distribution) is zero.

does not require that asset returns be normally distributed, and (3) it does not require that the correlations or standard deviations of asset returns be calculated.

The essential idea is to take the current market portfolio of assets (FX, bonds, equities, etc.) and revalue them on the basis of the actual prices (returns) that existed on those assets yesterday, the day before that, and so on. Frequently, the FI will calculate the market or value risk of its current portfolio on the basis of prices (returns) that existed for those assets on each of the last 500 days. It will then calculate the 5 percent worst case—the portfolio value that has the 25th lowest value out of 500. That is, on only 25 days out of 500, or 5 percent of the time, would the value of the portfolio fall below this number based on recent historic experience of exchange rate changes, equity price changes, interest rate changes, and so on.

Consider the following simple example in Table 10–6, where a U.S. FI is trading two currencies: the Japanese yen and the Swiss franc. At the close of trade on December 1, 2006, it has a long position in Japanese yen of 500,000,000 and a long position in Swiss francs of 20,000,000. It wants to assess its VAR. That is, if tomorrow is that 1 bad day in 20 (the 5 percent worst case), how much does it stand to lose on its total foreign currency position? As shown in Table 10–6, six steps are required to calculate the VAR of its currency portfolio. It should be noted that the same methodological approach would be followed to calculate the VAR of any asset, liability, or derivative (bonds, options, etc.) as long as market prices were available on those assets over a sufficiently long historic time period.

- *Step 1: Measure exposures.* Convert today's foreign currency positions into dollar equivalents using today's exchange rates. Thus, an evaluation of the FX position of the FI on December 1, 2006, indicates that it has a long position of $3,846,154 in yen and $14,285,714 in Swiss francs.

- *Step 2: Measure sensitivity.* Measure the sensitivity of each FX position by calculating its delta, where delta measures the change in the dollar value of each FX position if the yen or the Swiss franc depreciates (declines in value) by 1 percent against the dollar.[26] As can be seen from Table 10–6, line 6, the delta for the Japanese yen position is −$38,081, and for the Swiss franc position, it is − $141,442.

- *Step 3: Measure risk.* Look at the actual percentage changes in exchange rates, yen/$ and SF/$, on each of the past 500 days. Thus, on November 30, 2006, the yen declined in value against the dollar over the day by 0.5 percent while the Swiss franc declined in value against the dollar by 0.2 percent. (It might be noted that if the currencies were to appreciate in value against the dollar, the sign against the number in row 7 of Table 10–6 would be negative; that is, it takes fewer units of foreign currency to buy a dollar than it did the day before). As can be seen in row 8, combining the delta and the actual percentage change in each FX rate means a total loss of $47,328.9 if the FI had held the current ¥500,000,000 and SF 20,000,000 positions on that day (November 30, 2006).

- *Step 4: Repeat Step 3.* Step 4 repeats the same exercise for the yen and Swiss franc positions but uses actual exchange rate changes on November 29, 2006; November 28, 2006; and so on. That is, we calculate the FX losses and/or gains on each of the past 500 trading days, excluding weekends and holidays, when the FX market is closed. This amounts to going back in time over two years. For

---

[26] That is, in the case of FX, delta measures the dollar change in FX holdings for a 1 percent change in the foreign exchange rate. In the case of equities, it would measure the change in the value of those securities for a 1 percent change in price, while for bonds, it measures the change in value for a 1 percent change in the price of the bond (note that delta measures sensitivity of a bond's value to a change in yield, not price).

TABLE 10–6   Hypothetical Example of the Historic, or Back Simulation, Approach Using Two Currencies, as of December 1, 2006

	Yen	Swiss Franc
Step 1. Measure Exposures		
1. Closing position on December 1, 2006	500,000,000	20,000,000
2. Exchange rate on December 1, 2006	¥130/$1	SF 1.4/$1
3. U.S. $ equivalent position on December 1, 2006	3,846,154	14,285,714
Step 2. Measure Sensitivity		
4. 1.01 × current exchange rate	¥131.3	SF 1.414
5. Revalued position in $s	3,808,073	14,144,272
6. Delta of position ($s) (measure of sensitivity to a 1% adverse change in exchange rate, or row 5 minus row 3)	−38,081	−141,442

Step 3. Measure risk of December 1, 2006, closing position using exchange rates that existed on each of the last 500 days

November 30, 2006	Yen	Swiss Franc
7. Change in exchange rate (%) on November 30, 2006	0.5%	0.2%
8. Risk (delta × change in exchange rate)	−19,040.5	−28,288.4
9. Sum of risks = −$47,328.9		

Step 4. Repeat Step 3 for each of the remaining 499 days

November 29, 2006

    ⋮

April 15, 2005

    ⋮

November 30, 2004

    ⋮

Step 5. Rank days by risk from worst to best

Date	Risk ($)
1. May 6, 2005	−$105,669
2. Jan 27, 2006	−$103,276
3. Dec 1, 2004	−$ 90,939
⋮	⋮
25. Nov 30, 2006	−$ 47,328.9
⋮	⋮
499. April 8, 2006	+$ 98,833
500. July 28, 2005	+$108,376

Step 6. VAR (25th worst day out of last 500)

VAR = −$47,328.9 (November 30, 2006)

each of these days the actual change in exchange rates is calculated (row 7) and multiplied by the deltas of each position (the numbers in row 6 of Table 10–6). These two numbers are summed to attain total risk measures for each of the past 500 days.

- *Step 5: Rank days by risk from worst to best.* These risk measures can then be ranked from worst to best. Clearly the worst-case loss would have occurred on this position on May 6, 2005, with a total loss of $105,669. While this worst-case scenario is of interest to FI managers, we are interested in the 5 percent worst case, that is, a loss that does not occur more than 25 days out of the 500 days (25 ÷ 500 equals 5 percent). As can be seen, in our example, the 25th worst loss out of 500 occurred on November 30, 2006. This loss amounted to $47,328.9.

- *Step 6: VAR.* If it is assumed that the recent past distribution of exchange rates is an accurate reflection of the likely distribution of FX rate changes in the future—that exchange rate changes have a stationary distribution—then the $47,328.9 can be viewed as the FX value at risk (VAR) exposure of the FI on December 1, 2006. That is, if tomorrow (in our case, December 2, 2006) is a bad day in the FX markets, and given the FI's position of long yen 500 million and long Swiss francs 20 million, the FI can expect to lose $47,328.9 (or more) with a 5 percent probability. This VAR measure can then be updated every day as the FX position changes and the delta changes. For example, given the nature of FX trading, the positions held on December 5, 2006, could be very different from those held on December 1, 2006.[27]

The Historic (Back Simulation) Model versus RiskMetrics

One obvious benefit of the historic, or back simulation, approach is that we do not need to calculate standard deviations and correlations (or assume normal distributions for asset returns) to calculate the portfolio risk figures in row 9 of Table 10–6.[28] A second advantage is that it directly provides a worst-case scenario number, in our example, a loss of $105,669—see step 5. RiskMetrics, since it assumes asset returns are normally distributed—that returns can go to plus and minus infinity—provides no such worst-case scenario number.[29]

The disadvantage of the back simulation approach is the degree of confidence we have in the 5 percent VAR number based on 500 observations. Statistically speaking, 500 observations are not very many, so there will be a very wide confidence band (or standard error) around the estimated number ($47,328.9 in our example). One possible solution to the problem is to go back in time more than 500 days and estimate the 5 percent VAR based on 1,000 past daily observations (the 50th worst case) or even 10,000 past observations (the 500th worst case). The problem is that as one goes back farther in time, past observations may become decreasingly relevant in predicting VAR in the future. For example, 10,000 observations may require the FI to analyze FX data going back 40 years. Over this period we have moved through many very different FX regimes: from relatively

---

[27] As in RiskMetrics, an adjustment can be made for illiquidity of the market, in this case, by assuming the FI is locked into longer holding periods. For example, if it is estimated that it will take five days for the FI to sell its FX position, then the FI will be interested in the weekly (i.e., five trading days) changes in FX rates in the past. One immediate problem is that with 500 past trading days, only 100 weekly periods would be available, which reduces the statistical power of the VAR estimate (see below).

[28] The reason is that the historic, or back simulation, approach uses actual exchange rates on each day that explicitly include correlations or comovements with other exchange rates and asset returns on that day.

[29] The 5 percent number in RiskMetrics tells us that we will lose more than this amount on 5 days out of every 100; it does not tell us the maximum amount we can lose. As noted in the text, theoretically, with a normal distribution, this could be an infinite amount.

fixed exchange rates in the 1950–70 period, to relatively floating exchange rates in the 1970s, to more managed floating rates in the 1980s and 1990s, to the abolition of exchange rates and the introduction of the euro in January 2002. Clearly, exchange rate behavior and risk in a fixed–exchange rate regime will have little relevance to an FX trader or market risk manager operating and analyzing risk in a floating–exchange rate regime.

This seems to confront the market risk manager with a difficult modeling problem. There are, however, at least two approaches to this problem. The first is to weight past observations in the back simulation unequally, giving a higher weight to the more recent past observations.[30] The second is to use a Monte Carlo simulation approach, which generates additional observations that are consistent with recent historic experience. The latter approach, in effect, amounts to simulating or creating artificial trading days and FX rate changes.

The Monte Carlo Simulation Approach[31]

To overcome the problems imposed by a limited number of actual observations, we can generate additional observations (in our example, FX changes). Normally, the simulation or generation of these additional observations is structured using a Monte Carlo simulation approach so that returns or rates generated reflect the probability with which they have occurred in recent historic time periods. The first step is to calculate the historic variance–covariance matrix (Σ) of FX changes. This matrix is then decomposed into two symmetric matrices, A and A'.[32] This allows the FI to generate scenarios for the FX position by multiplying the A' matrix, which reflects the historic volatilities and correlations among FX rates, by a random number vector z:[33] 10,000 random values of z are drawn for each FX exchange rate.[34] This simulation approach results in realistic FX scenarios being generated as historic volatilities and correlations among FX rates are multiplied by the randomly drawn values of z. The VAR of the current position is then calculated as in Table 10–6, except that in the Monte Carlo approach, the VAR is the 500th worst simulated loss out of 10,000.[35]

Concept Questions

1. What are the advantages of the historic, or bank simulation, approach over RiskMetrics to measure market risk?
2. What are the steps involved with the historic, or back simulation, approach to measuring market risk?
3. What is the Monte Carlo simulation approach to measuring market risk?

---

[30] See L. Allen, J. Boudoukh, and A. Saunders, *Understanding Market, Credit and Operational Risk: The Value at Risk Approach* (New York: Blackwell, 2004), Chapters 1–3.

[31] This section, which contains more technical details, may be included in or dropped from the chapter reading depending on the rigor of the course.

[32] The only difference between A and A' is that the numbers in the rows of A become the numbers in the columns of A'. The technical term for this procedure is the Cholesky decomposition, where $\Sigma = AA'$.

[33] Where z is assumed to be normally distributed with a mean of zero and a standard deviation of 1 or $z \sim N(0, 1)$.

[34] Technically, let y be an FX scenario; then $y = A'z$. For each FX rate, 10,000 values of z are randomly generated to produce 10,000 values of y. The y values are then used to revalue the FX position and calculate gains and losses.

[35] See, for example, J. P. Morgan, *RiskMetrics*, Technical Document, 4th ed., 1997.

REGULATORY MODELS: THE BIS STANDARDIZED FRAMEWORK

www.bis.org

www.federalreserve. gov

The development of internal market risk models by FIs such as J. P. Morgan Chase was partly in response to proposals by the Bank for International Settlement (BIS) in 1993 to measure and regulate the market risk exposures of banks by imposing capital requirements on their trading portfolios.[36] As noted in Chapter 7, the BIS is a organization encompassing the largest central banks in the world. After refining these proposals over a number of years, the BIS (including the Federal Reserve) decided on a final approach to measuring market risk and the capital reserves necessary for an FI to hold to withstand and survive market risk losses. These required levels of capital held to protect against market risk exposure are in addition to the minimum level of capital banks are required to hold for credit risk purposes (see Chapter 20). Since January 1998[37] banks in the countries that are members of the BIS can calculate their market risk exposures in one of two ways. The first is to use a simple standardized framework (to be discussed below). The second, with regulatory approval, is to use their own internal models, which are similar to the models described above. However, if an internal model is approved for use in calculating capital requirements for the FI, it is subject to regulatory audit and certain constraints. Before looking at these constraints, we examine the BIS standardized framework for fixed-income securities, foreign exchange, and equities. Additional details of this model can be found at the BIS Web site, **www.bis.org**.

Fixed Income

We can examine the BIS standardized framework for measuring the market risk on the fixed-income (or debt security) trading portfolio by using the example for a typical FI provided by the BIS (see Table 10–7). Panel A in Table 10–7 lists the security holdings of an FI in its trading account. The FI holds long and short positions in [column (3)] various quality debt issues [column (2)] with maturities ranging from one month to over 20 years [column (1)]. Long positions have positive values; short positions have negative values. To measure the risk of this trading portfolio, the BIS uses two capital charges: (1) a specific risk charge [columns (4) and (5)] and (2) a general market risk charge [columns (6) and (7)].

Specific Risk Charge

specific risk charge
A charge reflecting the risk of a decline in the liquidity or credit risk quality of the trading portfolio.

The **specific risk charge** is meant to measure the risk of a decline in the liquidity or credit risk quality of the trading portfolio over the FI's holding period. As column (4) in panel A of Table 10–7 indicates, Treasuries have a zero risk weight, while junk bonds (e.g., 10- to 15-year nonqualifying "Non Qual" corporate debt) have a risk weight of 8 percent. As shown in Table 10–7, multiplying the absolute dollar values of all the long and short positions in these instruments [column (3)] by the specific risk weights [column (4)] produces a specific risk capital or requirement charge for each position [column (5)]. Summing the individual charges for specific risk gives the total specific risk charge of $229.[38]

---

[36] BIS, Basel Committee on Banking Supervision, "The Supervisory Treatment of Market Risks," Basel, Switzerland, April 1993; "Proposal to Issue a Supplement to the Basel Accord to Cover Market Risks," Basel, Switzerland, April 1995; and "The New Basel Capital Accord: Third Consultive Paper," Basel, Switzerland, April 2003.

[37] The requirements were introduced earlier in 1996 in the European Union.

[38] Note that the risk weights for specific risks are not based on obvious theory, empirical research, or past experience. Rather, the weights are based on regulators' perceptions of what was appropriate when the model was established.

TABLE 10–7 BIS Market Risk Calculation (Debt Securities, Sample Market Risk Calculation)

Panel A: FI Holdings and Risk Charges

(1) Time Band	(2) Issuer	(3) Position ($)	Specific Risk (4) Weight (%)	Specific Risk (5) Charge	General Market Risk (6) Weight (%)	General Market Risk (7) Charge
0–1 month	Treasury	5,000	0.00%	0.00	0.00%	0.00
1–3 months	Treasury	5,000	0.00	0.00	0.20	10.00
3–6 months	Qual Corp	4,000	0.25	10.00	0.40	16.00
6–12 months	Qual Corp	(7,500)	1.00	75.00	0.70	(52.50)
1–2 years	Treasury	(2,500)	0.00	0.00	1.25	(31.25)
2–3 years	Treasury	2,500	0.00	0.00	1.75	43.75
3–4 years	Treasury	2,500	0.00	0.00	2.25	56.25
3–4 years	Qual Corp	(2,000)	1.60	32.00	2.25	(45.00)
4–5 years	Treasury	1,500	0.00	0.00	2.75	41.25
5–7 years	Qual Corp	(1,000)	1.60	16.00	3.25	(32.50)
7–10 years	Treasury	(1,500)	0.00	0.00	3.75	(56.25)
10–15 years	Treasury	(1,500)	0.00	0.00	4.50	(67.50)
10–15 years	Non Qual	1,000	8.00	80.00	4.50	45.00
15–20 years	Treasury	1,500	0.00	0.00	5.25	78.75
> 20 years	Qual Corp	1,000	1.60	16.00	6.00	60.00
Specific risk				229.00		
Residual general market risk						66.00

Panel B: Calculation of Capital Charge

(1)	(2)	(3)	(4)	(5)	(6)	(7) Charge
1. Specific Risk						229.00

2. Vertical Offsets within Same Time Bands

Time Band	Longs	Shorts	Residual*	Offset	Disallowance	Charge
3–4 years	56.25	(45.00)	11.25	45.00	10.00%	4.50
10–15 years	45.00	(67.50)	(22.50)	45.00	10.00	4.50

3. Horizontal Offsets within Same Time Zones

Zone 1						
0–1 month	0.00					
1–3 months	10.00					
3–6 months	16.00					
6–12 months		(52.50)				
Total zone 1	26.00	(52.50)	(26.50)	26.00	40.00%	10.40
Zone 2						
1–2 years		(31.25)				
2–3 years	43.75					
3–4 years	11.25					
Total zone 2	55.00	(31.25)	23.75	31.25	30.00%	9.38
Zone 3						
4–5 years	41.25					
5–7 years		(31.50)				
7–10 years		(56.25)				
10–15 years		(22.50)				
15–20 years	78.75					
>20 years	60.00					
Total zone 3	180.00	(111.25)	68.75	111.25	30.00%	33.38

(continued)

TABLE 10–7 (*concluded*)

Time Band	Longs	Shorts	Residual*	Offset	Disallowance	Charge
4. Horizontal Offsets between Time Zones						
Zones 1 and 2	23.75	(26.50)	(2.75)	23.75	40.00%	9.50
Zones 1 and 3	68.75	(2.75)	66.00	2.75	150.00%	4.12
5. Total Capital Charge						
Specific risk						229.00
Vertical disallowances						9.00
Horizontal disallowances						
Offsets within same time zones						53.16
Offsets between time zones						13.62
Residual general market risk after all offsets						66.00
Total						370.78

*Residual amount carried forward for additional offsetting as appropriate.

Note: Qual Corp is an investment grade debt issue (e.g., rated BBB and above). Non Qual is a below investment grade debt issue (e.g., rated BB and below), that is, a junk bond.

General Market Risk Charge

general market risk charges
Charges reflecting the modified duration and interest rate shocks for each maturity.

The **general market risk charges** or weights—column (6)—reflect the product of the modified durations and interest rate shocks expected for each maturity.[39] The weights in Table 10–7 range from zero for the 0 to 1-month Treasuries to 6 percent for the long-term (longer than 20 years to maturity) quality corporate debt securities. The positive or negative dollar values of the positions in each instrument [column (3)] are multiplied by the general market risk weights [column (6)] to determine the general market risk charges for the individual holdings [column (7)]. Summing these gives the total general market risk charge of $66 for the whole fixed-income portfolio.

Vertical Offsets

The BIS model assumes that long and short positions, in the same maturity bucket but in different instruments, cannot perfectly offset each other. Thus, the $66 general market risk charge tends to underestimate interest rate or price risk exposure. For example, the FI is short $1,500 in 10- to 15-year U.S. Treasuries producing a market risk charge of $67.50 and is long $1,000 in 10- to 15-year junk bonds (with a risk charge of $45). However, because of basis risk—that is, the fact that the rates on Treasuries and junk bonds do not fluctuate exactly together—we cannot assume that a $45 short position in junk bonds is hedging an equivalent ($45) risk value of U.S. Treasuries of the same maturity. Similarly, the FI is long $2,500 in three- to four-year Treasuries (with a general market risk charge of $56.25) and short $2,000 in three- to four-year quality corporate bonds (with a risk charge of $45). To account for this, the BIS requires additional capital charges for basis risk, called **vertical offsets** or disallowance factors. We show these calculations in part 2 of panel B in Table 10–7.

vertical offsets
Additional capital charges assigned because long and short positions in the same maturity bucket but in different instruments cannot perfectly offset each other.

[39] For example, for 15- to 20-year Treasuries in Table 10–7, the modified duration is assumed to be 8.75 years, and the expected interest rate shock is 0.60 percent. Thus, 8.75 × 0.6 = 5.25, which is the general market risk weight for these securities shown in Table 10–7. Multiplying 5.25 by the $1,500 long position in these securities results in a general market risk charge of $78.75. Note that the shocks assumed for short-term securities, such as three-month T-bills, are larger (at 1 percent) than those assumed for longer-maturity securities. This reflects the fact that short-term rates are more impacted by monetary policy. Finally, note that the standardized model combines unequal rate shocks with estimated modified durations to calculate market risk weights. Technically, this violates the underlying assumptions of the duration model, which assumes parallel yield shifts (see Chapter 9) at each maturity.

In panel B, column 1 lists the time bands for which the bank has both a long and short position. Columns (2) and (3) list the general market risk charges—from column (7) of panel A—resulting from the positions, and column (4) lists the difference (or residual) between the charges. Column (5) reports the smallest value of the risk charges for each time band (or offset). As listed in column (6), the BIS disallows 10 percent[40] of the $45 position in corporate bonds in hedging $45 of the Treasury bond position. This results in an additional capital charge of $4.50 ($45 × 10 percent).[41] The total charge for all vertical offsets is $9.

Horizontal Offsets within Time Zones

horizontal offsets
Additional capital charges required because long and short positions of different maturities do not perfectly hedge each other.

In addition, the debt trading portfolio is divided into three maturity zones: zone 1 (1 month to 12 months), zone 2 (more than 1 year to 4 years), and zone 3 (more than 4 years to 20 years plus). Again because of basis risk (i.e., the imperfect correlation of interest rates on securities of different maturities), short and long positions of different maturities in these zones will not perfectly hedge each other. This results in additional (horizontal) disallowance factors of 40 percent (zone 1), 30 percent (zone 2), and 30 percent (zone 3).[42] Part 3 of the bottom panel in Table 10–7 shows these calculations. The **horizontal offsets** are calculated using the sum of the general market risk charges from the long and short positions in each time zone—columns (2) and (3). As with the vertical offsets, the smallest of these totals is the offset value against which the disallowance is applied. For example, the total zone 1 charges for long positions equal $26.00 and for short positions ($52.50). A disallowance of 40 percent of the offset value (the smaller of these two values), $26.00, is charged, that is, $10.40 ($26 × 40 percent). Repeating this process for each of the three zones produces additional (horizontal offset) charges totaling $53.16.

Horizontal Offsets between Time Zones

Finally, because interest rates on short maturity debt and long maturity debt do not fluctuate exactly together, a residual long or short position in each zone can only partly hedge an offsetting position in another zone. This leads to a final set of offsets, or disallowance factors, between time zones, part 4 of panel B of Table 10–7. Here the BIS model compares the residual charges from zones 1 ($26.50) and 2 ($23.75). The difference, $2.75, is then compared with the residual from zone 3 ($68.75). The smaller of each zone comparison is again used as the offset value against which a disallowance of 40 percent for adjacent zones[43] and 150 percent[44] for nonadjacent zones, respectively, is applied. The additional charges here total $13.62.

Summing the specific risk charges ($229), the general market risk charge ($66), and the basis risk or disallowance charges ($9.00 + $53.16 + $13.62) produces a total capital charge of $370.78 for this fixed-income trading portfolio.[45]

---

[40] Note again that the disallowance factors were set subjectively by regulators.

[41] Intuitively, this implies that long-term U.S. Treasury rates and long-term junk bond rates are approximately 90 percent correlated. However, in the final plan, it was decided to cut vertical disallowance factors in half. Thus, a 10 percent disallowance factor becomes a 5 percent disallowance factor, and so on.

[42] The zones were also set subjectively by regulators.

[43] For example, zones 1 and 2 are adjacent to each other in terms of maturity. By comparison, zones 1 and 3 are not adjacent to each other.

[44] This adjustment of 150 percent was later reduced to 100 percent.

[45] This number can also be recalculated in risk-adjusted asset terms to compare with risk-adjusted assets on the banking book. Thus, if capital is meant to be a minimum of 8 percent of risk-adjusted assets, then $370.78 × (1/1.08), or $370.78 × 12.5 = $4,634.75 is the equivalent amount of trading book risk-adjusted assets supported by this capital requirement.

TABLE 10–8
Example of the BIS Standardized Framework Measure of Foreign Exchange Risk (in millions of dollars)

Source: BIS, 1993.
www.bis.org

Once a bank has calculated its net position in each foreign currency, it converts each position into its reporting currency and calculates the risk (capital) measure as in the following example, in which the position in the reporting currency (dollars) has been excluded:

Yen*	Euros	GB£	A$	SF
+50	+100	+150	−20	−180

+300   −200

The capital charge would be 8 percent of the higher of the longs and shorts (i.e., 300).

*All currencies in $ equivalents.

Foreign Exchange

The standardized model or framework requires the FI to calculate its net exposure in each foreign currency—yen, euros, and so on—and then convert this into dollars at the current spot exchange rate. As shown in Table 10–8, the FI is net long (million-dollar equivalent) $50 yen, $100 euros, and $150 pounds while being short $20 Australian dollars and $180 Swiss francs. Its total currency long position is $300, and its total short position is $200. The BIS standardized framework imposes a capital requirement equal to 8 percent times the maximum absolute value of the aggregate long or short positions. In this example, 8 percent times $300 million = $24 million. This method of calculating FX exposure assumes some partial, but not complete, offsetting of currency risk by holding opposing long or short positions in different currencies.

Equities

As discussed in the context of the RiskMetrics market value model, the two sources of risk in holding equities are (1) a firm-specific, or unsystematic, risk element and (2) a market, or systematic, risk element. The BIS charges for unsystematic risk by adding the long and short positions in any given stock and applying a 4 percent charge against the gross position in the stock (called the *x* factor). Suppose stock number 2, in Table 10–9, is IBM. The FI has a long $100 million and short $25 million position in that stock. Its gross position that is exposed to unsystematic (firm-specific) risk is $125, which is multiplied by 4 percent to give a capital charge of $5 million.

Market, or systematic, risk is reflected in the net long or short position (the so-called *y* factor). In the case of IBM, this risk is $75 million ($100 long minus $25 short). The capital charge would be 8 percent against the $75 million, or $6 million. The total capital charge (*x* factor + *y* factor) is $11 million for this stock.

This approach is very crude, basically assuming the same systematic risk factor (β) for every stock. It also does not fully consider the benefits from portfolio diversification (i.e., that unsystematic risk can be diversified away).

Concept Questions

1. What is the difference between the BIS specific risk and general market risk in measuring trading portfolio risk?
2. What methods did the BIS model propose for calculating FX trading exposure?
3. How are unsystematic and systematic risks in equity holdings by FIs reflected in charges assessed under the BIS model?

TABLE 10–9   BIS Capital Requirement for Equities (Illustration of x plus y Methodology)

Under the proposed two-part calculation, there would be separate requirements for the position in each individual equity (i.e., the gross position) and for the net position in the market as a whole. Here we show how the system would work for a range of hypothetical portfolios, assuming a capital charge of 4 percent for the gross positions and 8 percent for the net positions.

			x Factor		*y* Factor		
Stock	Sum of Long Positions	Sum of Short Positions	Gross Position (sum of cols. 2 and 3)	4 Percent of Gross	Net Position (difference between cols. 2 and 3)	8 Percent of Net	Capital Required (gross + net)
1	100	0	100	4	100	8	12
2	100	25	125	5	75	6	11
3	100	50	150	6	50	4	10
4	100	75	175	7	25	2	9
5	100	100	200	8	0	0	8
6	75	100	175	7	25	2	9
7	50	100	150	6	50	4	10
8	25	100	125	5	75	6	11
9	0	100	100	4	100	8	12

Source: BIS, 1993. *www.bis.org*

THE BIS REGULATIONS AND LARGE BANK INTERNAL MODELS

As discussed above, the BIS capital requirement for market risk exposure introduced in January 1998 allows large banks (subject to regulatory permission) to use their own internal models to calculate market risk instead of the standardized framework. (We examine the initiatives taken by the BIS and the major central banks, e.g., the Federal Reserve, in controlling bank risk exposure through capital requirements in greater detail in Chapter 20.) However, the required capital calculation has to be relatively conservative compared with that produced internally. A comparison of the BIS requirement for large banks using their internal models with RiskMetrics indicates the following, in particular:

1. In calculating DEAR, the FI must define an adverse change in rates as being in the 99th percentile rather than in the 95th percentile (multiply σ by 2.33 rather than by 1.65 as under RiskMetrics).

2. The FI must assume the minimum holding period to be 10 days (this means that RiskMetrics' daily DEAR would have to be multiplied by $\sqrt{10}$).[46]

The FI must consider its proposed capital charge or requirement as the *higher* of:

1. The previous day's VAR (value at risk or DEAR $\times \sqrt{10}$).

2. The average daily VAR over the previous 60 days times a multiplication factor with a minimum value of 3, i.e., capital charge = (DEAR) $\times (\sqrt{10}) \times (3)$. In general, the multiplication factor makes required capital significantly higher than VAR produced from private models.

[46] It is proposed that this will be changed to a minimum holding period of five days under Basel II (at the end of 2006). See "The New Basel Capital Accord: Third Consultive Paper," Basel, Switzerland, April 2003. Note that this will reduce market risk capital requirements.

However, to reduce the burden of capital needs, an additional type of capital can be raised by FIs to meet the capital charge (or requirement). Suppose the portfolio DEAR was $10 million using the 1 percent worst case (or 99th percentile).[47] The minimum capital charge would be:[48]

$$\text{Capital charge} = (\$10 \text{ million}) \times (\sqrt{10}) \times (3) = \$94.86 \text{ million}$$

As explained in Chapters 7 and 20, capital provides an internal insurance fund to protect an FI, its depositors and other liability holders, and the insurance fund (e.g., the FDIC fund) against losses. The BIS permits three types of capital to be held to meet this capital requirement: Tier 1, Tier 2, and Tier 3. Tier 1 capital is essentially retained earnings and common stock, Tier 2 is essentially long-term subordinated debt (over five years), and Tier 3 is short-term subordinated debt with an original maturity of at least two years. Thus, the $94.86 million in the example above can be raised by any of the three capital types subject to the two following limitations: (1) Tier 3 capital is limited to 250 percent of Tier 1 capital, and (2) Tier 2 capital can be substituted for Tier 3 capital up to the same 250 percent limit. For example, suppose Tier 1 capital was $27.10 million and the FI issued short-term Tier 3 debt of $67.76 million. Then the 250 percent limit would mean that no more Tier 3 (or Tier 2) debt could be issued to meet a target above $94.86 ($27.1 × 2.5 = $67.76) without additional Tier 1 capital being added. This capital charge for market risk would be added to the capital charge for credit risk and operational risk to get the FI's total capital requirement. The different types of capital and capital requirements are discussed in more detail in Chapter 20.

Table 10–10 lists the market risk capital requirement to the total capital requirement for several large U.S. bank holding companies in the early 2000s. Notice how small the market risk capital requirement is relative to the total capital requirement for these banks. Only Bank of America and CIBC have ratios greater than 4 percent. The average ratio of market risk capital required to total capital required for the 18 bank holding companies is only 1.61 percent.[49] Moreover, very few banks, other than the very largest (above), report market risk exposures at all.

Concept Questions

1. What is the BIS standardized framework for measuring market risk?
2. What is the effect of using the 99th percentile (1 percent worst case) rather than the 95th percentile (5 percent worst case) on the measured size of an FI's market risk exposures?

---

[47] Using 2.33σ rather than 1.65σ.

[48] The idea of a minimum multiplication factor of 3 is to create a scheme that is "incentive compatible." Specifically, if FIs using internal models constantly underestimate the amount of capital they need to meet their market risk exposures, regulators can punish those FIs by raising the multiplication factor to as high as 4. Such a response may effectively put the FI out of the trading business. The degree to which the multiplication factor is raised above 3 depends on the number of days an FI's model underestimates its market risk over the preceding year. For example, an underestimation error that occurs on more than 10 days out of the past 250 days will result in the multiplication factor's being raised to 4.

[49] D. Hendricks and B. Hirtle, in "Bank Capital Requirements for Market Risk: The Internal Models Approach," Federal Reserve Bank of New York Economic Policy Review, December 1997, pp. 1–12, also find that the impact of the market risk capital charges on required capital ratios using internal models is small. They calculate an increase in the level of required capital from the general market risk component to range between 1.5 and 7.5 percent for the banks they examined. B. Hirtle, in "What Market Risk Capital Reporting Tells Us about Bank Risk," Federal Reserve Bank of New York, Economic Policy Review, September 2003, pp. 37–54, finds that since the implementation of the market risk capital standards at the beginning of 1998, the bank holding companies that were subject to the market capital requirements accounted for more than 98 percent of the trading positions held by all U.S. banking organizations. For these banks, market risk capital represented just 1.9 percent of overall capital requirements of the median bank.

TABLE 10–10
Ratio of Market Risk Capital Required to Total Capital Required for Bank Holding Companies Using Internal Models

Source: Federal Reserve Board, FR Y-9C Reports, 2002.

Name	Market Risk Capital Requirement to Total Capital Requirement (%)
KeyCorp	0.266%
Suntrust	0.274
U.S. Bancorp	0.278
PNC Financial	0.304
Bank of New York	0.664
Wells Fargo	0.666
ABN Amro	0.676
Bank One	0.725
State Street	1.000
Wachovia	1.397
Taunus	1.437
HSBC North America	1.568
FleetBoston Financial	1.575
Mellon Financial	1.736
Citigroup	2.985
J.P. Morgan Chase	3.474
Bank of America	4.733
CIBC	5.234

Summary

In this chapter we analyzed the importance of measuring an FI's market risk exposure. This risk is likely to continue to grow in importance as more and more loans and previously illiquid assets become marketable and as the traditional franchises of commercial banks, insurance companies, and investment banks shrink. Given the risks involved, both private FI management and regulators are investing increasing resources in models to measure and track market risk exposures. We analyzed in detail three approaches FIs have used to measure market risk: RiskMetrics, the historic (or back simulation) approach, and the Monte Carlo simulation approach. The three approaches were also compared in terms of simplicity and accuracy. Market risk is also of concern to regulators. Beginning in January 1998, banks in the United States have had to hold a capital requirement against the risk of their trading positions. The novel feature of the regulation of market risk is that the Federal Reserve and other central banks (subject to regulatory approval) have given large FIs the option to calculate capital requirements based on their own internal models rather than the regulatory model.

Questions and Problems

1. What is meant by *market risk?*

2. Why is the measurement of market risk important to the manager of a financial institution?

3. What is meant by *daily earnings at risk (DEAR)?* What are the three measurable components? What is the price volatility component?

4. Follow Bank has a $1 million position in a five-year, zero-coupon bond with a face value of $1,402,552. The bond is trading at a yield to maturity of 7.00 percent. The historical mean change in daily yields is 0.0 percent, and the standard deviation is 12 basis points.

   a. What is the modified duration of the bond?

   b. What is the maximum adverse daily yield move given that we desire no more than a 5 percent chance that yield changes will be greater than this maximum?

   c. What is the price volatility of this bond?

   d. What is the daily earnings at risk for this bond?

5. What is meant by *value at risk* (VAR)? How is VAR related to DEAR in J. P. Morgan's RiskMetrics model? What would be the VAR for the bond in problem 4 for a 10-day period? With what statistical assumption is our analysis taking liberties? Could this treatment be critical?

6. The DEAR for a bank is $8,500. What is the VAR for a 10-day period? A 20-day period? Why is the VAR for a 20-day period not twice as much as that for a 10-day period?

7. The mean change in the daily yields of a 15-year, zero-coupon bond has been five basis points (bp) over the past year with a standard deviation of 15 bp. Use these data and assume that the yield changes are normally distributed.

   a. What is the highest yield change expected if a 90 percent confidence limit is required; that is, adverse moves will not occur more than 1 day in 20?

   b. What is the highest yield change expected if a 95 percent confidence limit is required?

8. In what sense is duration a measure of market risk?

9. Bank Alpha has an inventory of AAA-rated, 15-year zero-coupon bonds with a face value of $400 million. The bonds currently are yielding 9.5 percent in the over-the-counter market.

   a. What is the modified duration of these bonds?

   b. What is the price volatility if the potential adverse move in yields is 25 basis points?

   c. What is the DEAR?

   d. If the price volatility is based on a 90 percent confidence limit and a mean historical change in daily yields of 0.0 percent, what is the implied standard deviation of daily yield changes?

10. Bank Two has a portfolio of bonds with a market value of $200 million. The bonds have an estimated price volatility of 0.95 percent. What are the DEAR and the 10-day VAR for these bonds?

11. Bank of Southern Vermont has determined that its inventory of 20 million euros (€) and 25 million British pounds (£) is subject to market risk. The spot exchange rates are $0.40/€ and $1.28/£, respectively. The σ's of the spot exchange rates of

the € and £, based on the daily changes of spot rates over the past six months, are 65 bp and 45 bp, respectively. Determine the bank's 10-day VAR for both currencies. Use adverse rate changes in the 95th percentile.

12. Bank of Alaska's stock portfolio has a market value of $10,000,000. The beta of the portfolio approximates the market portfolio, whose standard deviation (σ_m) has been estimated at 1.5 percent. What is the five-day VAR of this portfolio using adverse rate changes in the 99th percentile?

13. Jeff Resnick, vice president of operations of Choice Bank, is estimating the aggregate DEAR of the bank's portfolio of assets consisting of loans (L), foreign currencies (FX), and common stock (EQ). The individual DEARs are $300,700; $274,000; and $126,700, respectively. If the correlation coefficients (ρ_{ij}) between L and FX, L and EQ, and FX and EQ are 0.3, 0.7, and 0.0, respectively, what is the DEAR of the aggregate portfolio?

14. Calculate the DEAR for the following portfolio with and without the correlation coefficients.

Assets	Estimated DEAR	$(\rho_{S,\ FX})$	$(\rho_{S,\ B})$	$(\rho_{FX,\ B})$
Stocks (S)	$300,000	−0.10	0.75	0.20
Foreign Exchange (FX)	200,000			
Bonds (B)	250,000			

What is the amount of risk reduction resulting from the lack of perfect positive correlation between the various asset groups?

15. What are the advantages of using the back simulation approach to estimate market risk? Explain how this approach would be implemented.

16. Export Bank has a trading position in Japanese yen and Swiss francs. At the close of business on February 4, the bank had ¥300,000,000 and SF 10,000,000. The exchange rates for the most recent six days are given below.

Exchange Rates per U.S. Dollar at the Close of Business

	2/4	2/3	2/2	2/1	1/29	1/28
Japanese yen	112.13	112.84	112.14	115.05	116.35	116.32
Swiss francs	1.4140	1.4175	1.4133	1.4217	1.4157	1.4123

a. What is the foreign exchange (FX) position in dollar equivalents using the FX rates on February 4?

b. What is the definition of delta as it relates to the FX position?

c. What is the sensitivity of each FX position; that is, what is the value of delta for each currency on February 4?

d. What is the daily percentage change in exchange rates for each currency over the five-day period?

e. What is the total risk faced by the bank on each day? What is the worst-case day? What is the best-case day?

f. Assume that you have data for the 500 trading days preceding February 4. Explain how you would identify the worst-case scenario with a 95 percent degree of confidence.

g. Explain how the 5 percent value at risk (VAR) position would be interpreted for business on February 5.

h. How would the simulation change at the end of the day on February 5? What variables and/or processes in the analysis may change? What variables and/or processes will not change?

17. What is the primary disadvantage of the back simulation approach in measuring market risk? What effect does the inclusion of more observation days have as a remedy for this disadvantage? What other remedies can be used to deal with the disadvantage?

18. How is Monte Carlo simulation useful in addressing the disadvantages of back simulation? What is the primary statistical assumption underlying its use?

19. In the BIS standardized framework for regulating risk exposure for the fixed-income portfolios of banks, what do the terms *specific risk* and *general market risk* mean? Why does the capital charge for general market risk tend to underestimate the true interest rate or price risk exposure? What additional offsets, or disallowance factors, are included in the analysis?

20. An FI has the following bonds in its portfolio: long 1-year U.S. Treasury bills, short 3-year Treasury bonds, long 3-year AAA-rated corporate bonds, and long 12-year B-rated (nonqualifying) bonds worth $40, $10, $25, and $10 million, respectively (market values). Using Table 10–7, determine the following:

a. Charges for specific risk.

b. Charges for general market risk.

c. Charges for basis risk: vertical offsets within same time bands only (i.e., ignoring horizon effects).

d. The total capital charge, using the information from parts (a) through (c).

21. Explain how the capital charge for foreign exchange risk is calculated in the BIS standardized model. If an FI has an $80 million long position in euros, a $40 million short position in British pounds, and a $20 million long position in Swiss francs, what will be the capital charge required against FX market risk?

22. Explain the BIS capital charge calculation for unsystematic and systematic risk for an FI that holds various amounts of equities in its portfolio. What would be the total capital charge required for an FI that holds the following portfolio of stocks? What criticisms can be levied against this treatment of measuring the risk in the equity portfolio?

Company	Long	Short
Texaco	$45 million	$25 million
Microsoft	$55 million	$12 million
Robeco	$20 million	
Cifra		$15 million

23. What conditions were introduced by BIS in 1998 to allow large banks to use internally generated models for the measurement of market risk? What types of capital can be held to meet the capital charge requirements?

24. Dark Star Bank has estimated its average VAR for the previous 60 days to be $35.5 million. DEAR for the previous day was $30.2 million.

a. Under the latest BIS standards, what is the amount of capital required to be held for market risk?

b. Dark Star has $15 million of Tier 1 capital, $37.5 million of Tier 2 capital, and $55 million of Tier 3 capital. Is this amount of capital sufficient? If not, what minimum amount of new capital should be raised? Of what type?

Pertinent Web Sites

American Banker	www.americanbanker.com
Bank of America	www.bankofamerica.com
Bank for International Settlements	www.bis.org
Board of Governors of the Federal Reserve	www.federalreserve.gov
J. P. Morgan Chase	www.jpmorganchase.com
RiskMetrics	www.riskmetrics.com

Chapter Notation

View Chapter Notation at the Web site for the textbook (**www.mhhe.com/saunders5e**).

Chapter **Eleven**

Credit Risk: Individual Loan Risk

INTRODUCTION

As discussed in Chapter 1, financial intermediaries (FIs) are special because of their ability to efficiently transform financial claims of household savers into claims issued to corporations, individuals, and governments. An FI's ability to evaluate information and to control and monitor borrowers allows it to transform these claims at the lowest possible cost to all parties. One of the specific types of financial claim transformation discussed in Chapter 1 is credit allocation. That is, FIs transform claims of household savers (in the form of deposits) into loans issued to corporations, individuals, and governments. The FI accepts the credit risk on these loans in exchange for a fair return sufficient to cover the cost of funding (e.g., covering the costs of borrowing, or issuing deposits) to household savers and the credit risk involved in lending.

In this chapter, the first of two chapters on credit risk, we discuss various approaches to analyzing and measuring the credit or default risk on individual loans (and bonds). In the next chapter, we consider methods for evaluating the risk of loan portfolios, or loan concentration risk. Methods for hedging and managing an FI's credit risk are left to Chapters 24 to 28. Measurement of the credit risk on individual loans or bonds is crucial if an FI manager is to (1) price a loan or value a bond correctly and (2) set appropriate limits on the amount of credit extended to any one borrower or the loss exposure it accepts from any particular counterparty. The Ethical Dilemmas box highlights how the default of one major borrower can have a significant impact on the value and reputation of many FIs. Thus, managers need to manage the FI's loan portfolio to protect the overall FI from the failure of a single borrower. Management of the overall loan portfolio is equally important. In recent years Japanese FIs have suffered losses from an overconcentration of loans in real estate and in Asia. Indeed, in the early 2000s bad loans of the top eight Japanese banks exceeded $43 billion, and a majority of Japanese banks reported losses as a result of having to write off these loans. In addition, Japanese life insurers were heavily exposed through their over 14 trillion yen ($129 billion) loan exposure to Japanese banks.

We begin this chapter with a look at the types of loans (commercial and industrial [C&I], real estate, individual, consumer, and others) as well as the characteristics of those loans—made by U.S. FIs. We then look at how both interest and fees are incorporated to calculate the return on a loan. This is followed by a discussion of how the return on a loan versus the quantity of credit made available for lending is used by FIs to make decisions on wholesale (C&I) versus retail (consumer) lending. Finally,

Ethical Dilemmas

BANKS' WORLDCOM RISK SAID BELOW ENRON LEVELS

Fueled by memories of bad loans to the bankrupt energy trader Enron Corp., investors on Wednesday ignored analyst warnings not to flee bank stocks in response to the news of alleged accounting fraud at WorldCom Inc. Late Tuesday the Clinton, Miss.–based company, which operates MCI, the country's second biggest long-distance telephone company, said that it had improperly booked $3.9 billion of expenses. Some observers said that it may be forced to file for bankruptcy. . . .

WorldCom currently has $2.65 billion of outstanding loans, and U. S. banking companies are on the book for about a third of that. Though analysts disagree about the total U.S. bank exposure, forecasts range from $670 million to $955 million. All day Wednesday, analysts kept revising their estimates for bank exposure. They also downplayed the fraud's impact on the large commercial banking companies that extended credit to WorldCom, including Mellon Financial Corp., J. P. Morgan Chase & Co., Citigroup Inc., FleetBoston Financial Corp., Bank One Corp., Bank of America Corp., and Wells Fargo & Co.

While most of the banks, citing client confidentiality, would not comment on their exposure, Mellon said it has $100 million of exposure to WorldCom. Lori Appelbaum, an analyst at Goldman Sachs Group Inc., said it would lower Mellon's earnings per share this year by 12 cents, or 6 percent. Of the U. S. banking companies involved in the internationally shared credit, Mellon has the most exposure in proportion to its size, said Ms. Appelbaum. . . . In a report issued Wednesday, Ms. Applebaum estimated that WorldCom exposure would lower Morgan Chase's earnings per share by 5 cents, or nearly 2 percent; Fleet's by 5 cents, or nearly 2 percent; Bank One's by 3 cents, or 1 percent; Bank of America's by 5 cents, or 1 percent; Wells Fargo's by 2 cents, or 0.7 percent; and Citi's by 1 cent, or 0.3 percent. Some banks will be able to cover their charge-offs with existing reserves, she said.

Morgan Chase could have the most exposure to WorldCom, with $133 million of outstanding loans and $268 million of undrawn commitments, according to Ruchi Madan, an analyst at Citi's Salomon Smith Barney. In a report Wednesday, Ms. Madan estimated that WorldCom has $5.4 billion of credit lines outstanding. Analysts agree that banks probably will not be obligated to honor these lines. Because the company has admitted to improper accounting, it is prevented from drawing down untapped credit lines. . . .

Source: Veronica Agosta, *The American Banker*, June 27, 2002, p. 20. *www.americanbanker.com*

we examine various models used to measure credit risk, including qualitative models, credit scoring models, and newer models of credit risk measurement. Indeed, technological advances have been at least one driving force behind the advances and new models of credit risk measurement and management in recent years. Appendixes A and B examine two privately developed credit risk measurement models: CreditMetrics and Credit Risk +. Appendix C, located at the book's website (**www.mhhe.com/saunders5e**) discusses cash flow and financial ratio analysis widely used in the credit analysis process for mortgage, consumer, and commercial loans.

CREDIT QUALITY PROBLEMS

junk bond
A bond rated as speculative or less than investment grade by bond-rating agencies such as Moody's.

Over the past two decades the credit quality of many FIs' lending and investment decisions has attracted a great deal of attention. In the 1980s there were tremendous problems with bank loans to less developed countries (LDCs) as well as with thrift and bank residential and farm mortgage loans. In the early 1990s attention switched to the problems of commercial real estate loans (to which banks, thrifts, and insurance companies were all exposed) as well as **junk bonds** (rated as speculative or less than investment grade securities by bond-rating agencies such as Moody's or Standard & Poors). In the late 1990s concerns shifted to the rapid growth in low-quality auto loans and credit cards as well as the declining quality in commercial lending standards as loan delinquencies started to increase. In the late 1990s and early 2000s, attention has focused on problems with telecommunication companies, new technology companies, and a variety of sovereign countries including at various times Argentina, Brazil, Russia, and South Korea.

www.moodys.com
www.standardand-poors.com

Nevertheless, over the last decade the credit quality of most U.S. FIs has continued to improve even in the face of a prolonged spurt in the growth of loans (see Figure 11–1). This improvement in asset quality—measured by the decline in the ratio of nonperforming loans[1] to loans from 3.9 percent in 1991 to 0.74 percent in 2000—reflects, in part, the expansion of the U.S. economy in the 1990s as well as improvements in the way FIs measure and manage credit risk (see below). However, the recession in the U.S. economy in the early 2000s led to a turnaround in this pattern as nonperforming loan rates increased to 1.5 percent. For example, J. P. Morgan Chase and Citigroup had combined loans of $1.4 billion outstanding to Enron when it declared bankruptcy in December 2001.

Internet Exercise

Go to the Federal Deposit Insurance Corporation Web site and find the latest information available for nonperforming loans at commercial banks in the United States, using the following steps.

Go to the Federal Deposit Insurance Corporation Web Site a **www.fdic.gov.** Click on the "*Analysts.*" Click on "FDIC Quarterly Banking Profile." Click on "Quarterly Banking Profile." Click on the most recent date and "Commercial Bank Section." Click on "TABLE V-A. Loan Performance." This will download a file on to your computer that will contain the most recent information as "Percent of Loans Noncurrent: Total Loans and Leases."

Credit quality problems, in the worst case, can cause an FI to become insolvent or can result in such a significant drain on capital[2] and net worth that they adversely affect its growth prospects and ability to compete with other domestic and international FIs.[3]

However, credit risk does not apply only to traditional areas of lending and bond investing. As banks and other FIs have expanded into credit guarantees

---

[1] Nonperforming loans are loans that are 90 days or more past due or are not accruing interest.

[2] Losses drain capital through the income statement item "provision for loan losses." The provision for loan losses is a noncash, tax-deductible expense representing the FI management's prediction of loans at risk of default for the current period. As credit quality problems arise, the FI recognizes its expected bad loans by recording this expense, which reduces net income and, in turn, the FI's capital. The provision for loan losses is then allocated to the allowance for loan losses listed on the balance sheet. The allowance for loan and lease losses is a cumulative estimate by the FI's management of the percentage of the gross loans (and leases) that will not be repaid to the FI. Although the maximum amount of the provision of loan losses and the reserve for loan losses is influenced by tax laws, the FI's management actually sets the level based on loan growth and recent loan loss experience. The allowance for loan losses is an accumulated reserve that is adjusted each period as management recognizes the possibility of additional bad loans and makes appropriate provisions for such losses. Actual losses are then deducted from, and recoveries are added to (referred to as net write-offs), their accumulated loans and lease loss reserve balance. See Appendix 2C, "Financial Statements and Analysis" (located at the book's Web site, **www.mhhe. com/saunders5e**) for a more detailed discussion of these items.

[3] Not only is the book value of the FI's capital affected by credit quality problems in its loan portfolio, but studies have found that returns on commercial banks' common stocks decrease significantly on the announcement of bankruptcy and default by borrowers of their bank. See S. Dahiya, A. Saunders, and A. Srinivasan, "Financial Distress and Bank Lending Relationships," *Journal of Finance*, February 2003, pp. 375–401.

FIGURE 11–1   Loan Growth and Asset Quality

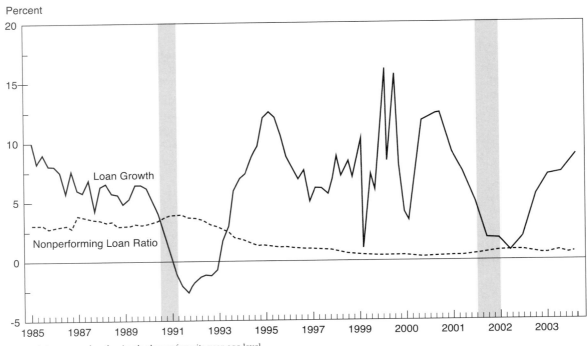

Loan growth is measured as the simple change from its year-ago level.
Shaded area represents a business recession.

Source: Federal Reserve Bank of St. Louis, *Monetary Trends*, April 1998; and Federal Deposit Insurance Corporation, *Quarterly Banking Profile*, Second Quarter 2003, *www.stls.frb.org* and *www.fdic.gov*

and other off-balance-sheet activities (see Chapter 13), new types of credit risk exposure have arisen, causing concern among managers and regulators. Thus, credit risk analysis is now important for a whole variety of contractual agreements between FIs and counterparties.[4]

Concept Questions

1. What are some of the credit quality problems faced by FIs over the last two decades?
2. What are some of the newer, nontraditional activities that create credit risk for today's FIs?

TYPES OF LOANS

Although most FIs make loans, the types of loans made and the characteristics of those loans differ considerably. This section analyzes the major types of loans made by U.S. commercial banks. Remember from Chapters 2 through 6, however, that other FIs, such as thrifts, finance companies, and insurance companies, also engage heavily in lending, especially in the real estate area. We also discuss important aspects of other FIs' loan portfolios.

Table 11–1 shows a recent breakdown of the aggregate loan portfolio of U.S. commercial banks into four broad classes: commercial and industrial (C&I), real estate, individual, and all others. We look briefly at each of these loan classes in turn.

Commercial and Industrial Loans

The figures in Table 11–1 disguise a great deal of heterogeneity in the commercial and industrial loan portfolio. Indeed, commercial loans can be made for periods as

[4] This is one of the reasons for bank regulators' setting capital requirements against credit risk (see Chapter 20).

TABLE 11–1
Types of U.S. Bank Loans, October 2003 (in billions of dollars)

Source: Federal Reserve Board, *Assets and Liabilities of Commercial Banks*, October 2003. *www.federalreserve.gov*

	Amount	Percent
Total loans*	$4,348.3	100.0%
C&I	1,106.2	25.4
Real estate	2,221.6	51.1
Individual	594.9	13.7
Other	425.6	9.8

*Excluding interbank loans.

syndicated loan
A loan provided by a group of FIs as opposed to a single lender.

secured loan
A loan that is backed by a first claim on certain assets (collateral) of the borrower if default occurs.

unsecured loan
A loan that has only a general claim to the assets of the borrower if default occurs.

spot loan
The loan amount is withdrawn by the borrower immediately.

loan commitment
A credit facility with a maximum size and a maximum period of time over which the borrower can withdraw funds; a line of credit.

short as a few weeks to as long as eight years or more. Traditionally, short-term commercial loans (those with an original maturity of one year or less) are used to finance firms' working capital needs and other short-term funding needs, while long-term commercial loans are used to finance credit needs that extend beyond one year, such as the purchase of real assets (machinery), new venture start-up costs, and permanent increases in working capital. They can be made in quite small amounts, such as $100,000, to small businesses or in packages as large as $10 million or more to major corporations. Large C&I loans are often syndicated. A **syndicated loan** is provided by a group of FIs as opposed to a single lender. A syndicated loan is structured by the lead FI (or agent) and the borrower. Once the terms (rates, fees, and covenants) are set, pieces of the loan are sold to other FIs. In addition, C&I loans can be secured or unsecured. A **secured loan** (or asset-backed loan) is backed by specific assets of the borrower; if the borrower defaults, the lender has a first lien or claim on those assets. In the terminology of finance, secured debt is senior to an **unsecured loan** (or junior debt) that has only a general claim on the assets of the borrower if default occurs. As we explain later in this chapter, there is normally a trade-off between the security or collateral backing of a loan and the loan interest rate or risk premium charged by the lender on a loan.[5]

In addition, commercial loans can be made at either fixed or floating rates of interest. A fixed-rate loan has the rate of interest set at the beginning of the contract period. This rate remains in force over the loan contract period no matter what happens to market rates. Suppose, for example, IBM borrowed $10 million at 10 percent for one year, but the FI's cost of funds rose over the course of the year. Because this is a fixed-rate loan, the FI bears all the interest rate risk. This is why many loans have floating-rate contractual terms. The loan rate can be periodically adjusted according to a formula so that the interest rate risk is transferred in large part from the FI to the borrower. As might be expected, longer-term loans are more likely to be made under floating-rate contracts than are relatively short-term loans.[6]

Finally, loans can be made either spot or under commitment. A **spot loan** is made by the FI, and the borrower uses or takes down the entire loan amount immediately. With a **loan commitment,** or line of credit, by contrast, the lender makes an amount of credit available, such as $10 million; the borrower has the option to

---

[5] Such a trade-off has been confirmed in A. Berger and G. Udell, "Lines of Credit, Collateral and Relationship Lending in Small Firm Finance," *Journal of Business* 68 (July 1995), pp. 351–82.

[6] However, floating-rate loans are more credit risky than fixed-rate loans, holding all other contractual features the same. This is because floating-rate loans pass the risk of all interest rate changes onto borrowers. Thus, in rising interest rate environments, floating-rate borrowers may find themselves unable to pay the interest on their loans and may be forced to default. The benefit of floating-rate loans to lenders is that they better enable FIs to hedge the cost of rising interest rates on liabilities (such as deposits). This suggests that controlling interest rate risk may be at the expense of enhanced credit risk.

TABLE 11–2   Characteristics of Commercial Loan Portfolios, August 4–8, 2003

	Long-Term Loans	Short-Term Loans			
		Zero*	Daily	2 to 30 days	31 to 365 days
Amount outstanding (in billions of dollars)	$2.89	$15.48	$20.86	$9.14	$10.08
Average size of loan	$210,000	$253,000	$646,000	$644,000	$627,000
Weighted-average maturity	60 months	41 days	231 days	416 days	608 days
Percent of which made under commitment	59.2%	86.1%	72.6%	75.9%	84.0%
Percent of loans secured by collateral	66.9%	41.1%	28.0%	34.3%	45.2%

*Floating-rate loans that are subject to repricing at any time.

Source: Federal Reserve Board Web site, October 2003. *www.federalreserve.gov*

take down any amount up to the $10 million at any time over the commitment period. In a fixed-rate loan commitment, the interest rate to be paid on any takedown is established when the loan commitment contract originates. In a floating-rate commitment, the borrower pays the loan rate in force when the loan is actually taken down. For example, suppose the $10 million IBM loan was made under a one-year loan commitment. When the loan commitment was originated (say, January 2006), IBM borrows nothing. Instead, it waits until six months have passed (say, July 2006) before it takes down the entire $10 million. IBM pays the loan rate in force as of July 2006. We discuss the special features of loan commitments more fully in Chapter 13.

To determine the basic characteristics of C&I loans, the Federal Reserve surveys more than 400 banks each quarter. Table 11–2 shows the major characteristics in a recent lending survey. As you can see, more short-term (under one year) C&I loans than long-term loans were reported. Also, short-term loans are more likely to be made under commitment than long-term loans and are less likely to be backed or secured by collateral.

Finally, as we noted in Chapter 2, commercial loans are declining in importance in bank loan portfolios. The major reason for this has been the rise in nonbank loan substitutes, especially commercial paper. **Commercial paper** is an unsecured short-term debt instrument issued by corporations either directly or via an underwriter to purchasers in the financial markets, such as money market mutual funds. By using commercial paper, a corporation can sidestep banks and the loan market to raise funds often at rates below those banks charge. As of October 2003, the total commercial paper outstanding in the United States was $1,324.7 billion compared with C&I loans of $1,287.8 billion.[7] Moreover, since only the largest corporations can tap the commercial paper market, banks are often left with a pool of increasingly smaller and riskier borrowers in the C&I loan market. For example, as the U.S. economy slowed in the early 2000s, noncurrent (loans that are 90 days or more past due or are not accruing interest) C&I loans increased from $14 billion (in the fourth quarter of 1999) to almost $24 billion (in the second quarter of 2003).

commercial paper
Unsecured short-term debt instrument issued by corporations.

---

[7] With the advent of Section 20 subsidiaries in 1987, large banks have enjoyed much greater powers to underwrite commercial paper (and other securities) directly without legal challenges by the securities industry that underwriting by banks was contrary to the Glass–Steagall Act. With the passage of the Financial Services Modernization Act of 1999 (see Chapter 21) and the abolition of the Glass–Steagall Act, the need to issue bank loans as an imperfect substitute for commercial paper underwriting has now become much less important.

TABLE 11–3
Distribution of U.S. Commercial Bank Real Estate Mortgage Debt, Second Quarter 2003

	Percent
One- to four-family residences	76.8%
Multifamily residences	5.7
Commercial	16.1
Farm	1.4
	100.0%

Source: Federal Reserve Board Web site, September 2003. *www.federalreserve.gov*

However, in late 2001 and early 2002, the slowdown in the U.S. economy also resulted in ratings downgrades for some of the largest commercial paper issuers. For example, the downgrade of General Motors and Ford from a tier-one (the best) to a tier-two (second-best) commercial paper issuer had a huge impact on the commercial paper markets. Tyco International, another major commercial paper issuer, fell from a tier-one to a tier-three (third-best) issuer, a level for which there is virtually no demand.[8] The result is that these commercial paper issuers have been forced to give up the cost advantage of commercial paper and to move to the bank loan market or the long-term debt markets to ensure they have access to cash. Thus, while commercial paper is still the largest money market instrument outstanding, the decrease in the number of eligible commercial paper issuers in 2001–2003 resulted in a decrease in the size of the commercial paper market for the first time in 40 years.

Real Estate Loans

Real estate loans are primarily mortgage loans and some revolving home equity loans (approximately 12 percent of the real estate loan portfolio in October 2003).[9] We show the distribution of mortgage debt for U.S. banks for the second quarter of 2003 in Table 11–3. For banks (as well as thrifts), residential mortgages are still the largest component of the real estate loan portfolio; until recently, however, commercial real estate mortgages were the fastest-growing component of real estate loans. Moreover, commercial real estate loans make up more than 80 percent of life insurance companies' real estate portfolios. These loans caused banks, thrifts, and insurance companies significant default and credit risk problems in the early 1990s.

As with C&I loans, the characteristics of residential mortgage loans differ widely. These characteristics include the size of the loan, the ratio of the loan to the property's price (the loan price or loan value ratio), and the maturity of the mortgage. Other important characteristics are the mortgage interest (or commitment) rate and fees and charges on the loan, such as commissions, discounts, and points paid by the borrower or the seller to obtain the loan.[10] In addition, the mortgage rate differs according to whether the mortgage has a fixed rate or a floating rate, also called an adjustable rate. **Adjustable rate mortgages (ARMs)** have their contractual rates periodically adjusted to some underlying index, such as the one-year T-bond rate. The proportion of fixed-rate mortgages to ARMs in FI portfolios varies with the

adjustable rate mortgage (ARM)
A mortgage whose interest rate adjusts with movements in an underlying market index interest rate.

[8] The market and investors view this type of commercial paper as the short-term equivalent of junk bonds.

[9] Under home equity loans, borrowers use their homes as collateral backing for loans.

[10] Points are a certain percentage of the face value of the loan paid up front, as a fee, by the borrower to the lender.

FIGURE 11–2   ARMs' Share of Total Loans Closed, 1992–2003

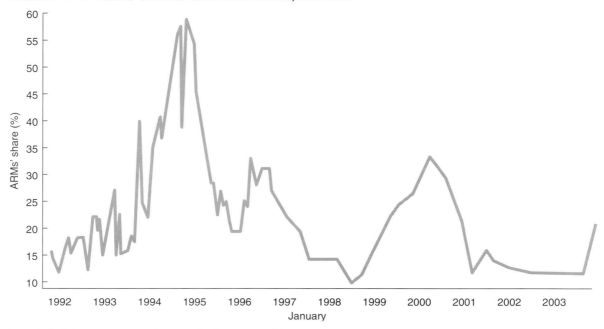

Source: Federal Housing Finance Board Web site, October 2003. *www.fhfb.gov*

TABLE 11–4
Contractual Terms on Conventional New Home Mortgages, June 2003

Source: *Federal Reserve Bulletin*, September 2003, Table 1.53.
www.federalreserve.gov

Purchase price (in thousands of dollars)	$283.3
Amount of loan (in thousands of dollars)	$213.7
Loan-to-value ratio (percent)	78.0%
Maturity (years)	28.8
Fees and charges (percent of loan amount)	0.64%
Contract rate (percent)	5.42%

interest rate cycle. In low–interest rate periods, borrowers prefer fixed-rate to adjustable rate mortgages. As a result, the proportion of ARMs to fixed-rate mortgages can vary considerably over the rate cycle. In Figure 11–2, note the behavior of ARMs over one recent interest rate cycle—1992 to 2002—when interest rates rose, then fell, and then rose and fell again. Table 11–4 presents a summary of the major contractual terms on conventional fixed-rate mortgages as of June 2003.

Residential mortgages are very long-term loans with an average maturity of almost 29 years. To the extent that house prices can fall below the amount of the loan outstanding—that is, the loan-to-value ratio rises—the residential mortgage portfolio can also be susceptible to default risk. For example, during the collapse in real estate prices in Houston, Texas, in the late 1980s, many house prices actually fell below the prices of the early 1980s. This led to a dramatic surge in the proportion of mortgages defaulted on and eventually foreclosed by banks and thrifts.

Individual (Consumer) Loans

Another major type of loan is the individual, or consumer, loan, such as personal and auto loans. Commercial banks, finance companies, retailers, savings institutions,

FIGURE 11–3 Payment Flows in a Typical Credit Card Transaction

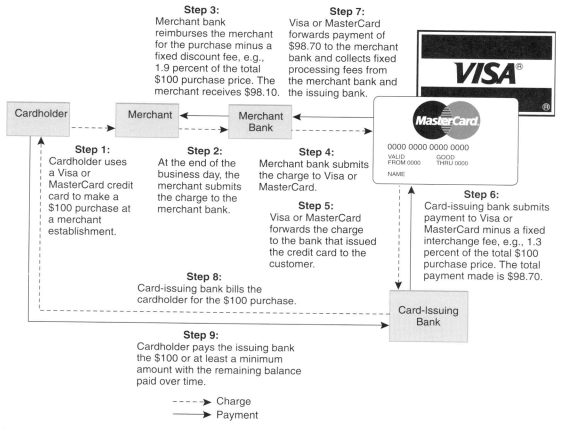

Step 3:
Merchant bank reimburses the merchant for the purchase minus a fixed discount fee, e.g., 1.9 percent of the total $100 purchase price. The merchant receives $98.10.

Step 7:
Visa or MasterCard forwards payment of $98.70 to the merchant bank and collects fixed processing fees from the merchant bank and the issuing bank.

Cardholder — Merchant — Merchant Bank

Step 1:
Cardholder uses a Visa or MasterCard credit card to make a $100 purchase at a merchant establishment.

Step 2:
At the end of the business day, the merchant submits the charge to the merchant bank.

Step 4:
Merchant bank submits the charge to Visa or MasterCard.

Step 5:
Visa or MasterCard forwards the charge to the bank that issued the credit card to the customer.

Step 6:
Card-issuing bank submits payment to Visa or MasterCard minus a fixed interchange fee, e.g., 1.3 percent of the total $100 purchase price. The total payment made is $98.70.

Step 8:
Card-issuing bank bills the cardholder for the $100 purchase.

Card-Issuing Bank

Step 9:
Cardholder pays the issuing bank the $100 or at least a minimum amount with the remaining balance paid over time.

- - - → Charge
——→ Payment

Source: GAO (1994) (GAO/GGD-94-23), p. 57.

TABLE 11–5
Biggest Credit Card Issuers as of December 2002

Source: Card Source One Web site, November 2003. *www.cardsourceone.com*

Card Issuer	Total Outstanding Balances (in billions of dollars)	Change from Year Earlier (percent)
Citigroup	$116.6	+7%
MBNA America	92.4	+9
BankOne	74.0	+8
Capital One Financial	57.7	+27
Discover Financial Services	55.8	+13

credit unions, and oil companies also provide consumer loan financing through credit cards, such as Visa, MasterCard, and proprietary credit cards issued by, for example, Sears and AT&T. A typical credit card transaction is illustrated in Figure 11–3. The five largest credit card issuers and their outstanding balances in 2003 are shown in Table 11–5.

In Table 11–6 are the two major classes of consumer loans at U.S. banks. The largest class of loans is nonrevolving consumer loans, which include new and used automobile loans, mobile home loans, and fixed-term consumer loans such

TABLE 11–6

Types of Consumer Loans at Commercial Banks, August 2003

	Percent
Revolving	37.2%
Nonrevolving	62.8
	100.0%

Source: Federal Reserve Board Web site, Consumer Credit, October 2003. *www.federalreserve.gov*

FIGURE 11–4   **Annual Net Charge-Off Rates on Loans**

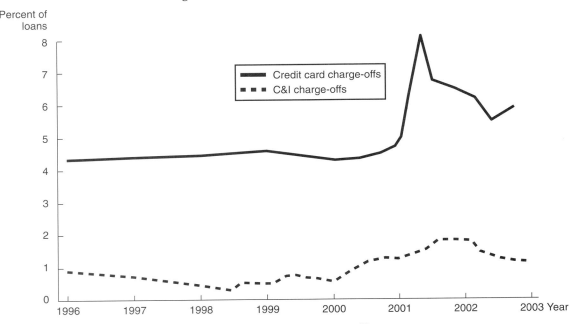

Source: Federal Deposit Insurance Corporation, *Quarterly Banking Profile,* various issues. *www.fdic.gov*

revolving loan
A credit line on which a borrower can both draw and repay many times over the life of the loan contract.

as 24-month personal loans. The other major class of consumer loans is revolving loans, such as credit card debt. With a **revolving loan,** the borrower has a credit line on which to draw as well as to repay up to some maximum over the life of the credit contract. In recent years, banks have faced charge-off rates between 4 and 8 percent on their credit card loan outstanding. These charge-off rates are significantly higher than those on commercial loans (see Figure 11–4). Such relatively high default rates again point to the importance of risk evaluation prior to the credit decision.

In Table 11–7 we show indicative interest rates on car, personal, and credit card loans as of August 2003. These rates differ widely depending on features such as collateral backing, maturity, default rate experience, and non–interest rate fees. In addition, competitive conditions in each market as well as regulations such as state- or city-imposed **usury ceilings** (maximum rates FIs can charge on consumer and mortgage debt) all affect the rate structure for consumer loans. For example, in April 2001, Philadelphia enacted a statute, targeting non-bank lenders, prohibiting the issuance of mortgage loans with an interest rate

usury ceilings
State- or city-imposed ceilings on the maximum rate FIs can charge on consumer and mortgage debt.

TABLE 11–7
Interest Rate Terms on Consumer Loans, August 2003

Source: Federal Reserve Board Web site, Consumer Credit, October 2003. *www.federalreserve.gov*

	Percent
48-month car loan	6.77%
24-month personal loan	11.94
Credit card	12.94

more than 6.5 percent above the yield on comparable maturity Treasury securities and with total fees greater than 4 percent of the total loan amount.

Other Loans

The "other loans" category can include a wide variety of borrowers and types, including farmers, other banks, nonbank financial institutions (such as call loans to investment banks[11]), broker margin loans (loans financing a percentage of an individual investment portfolio), state and local governments, foreign banks, and sovereign governments. We discuss sovereign loans in Chapter 16.

Concept Questions

1. What are the four major types of loans made by U.S. commercial banks? What are the basic distinguishing characteristics of each type of loan?
2. Will more ARMs be originated in high- or low-interest-rate environments? Explain your answer.
3. In Table 11–7, explain why credit card loan rates are much higher than car loan rates.

CALCULATING THE RETURN ON A LOAN

An important element in the credit management process, once the decision to make a loan has been made, is its pricing. This includes adjustments for the perceived credit risk or default risk of the borrower as well as any fees and collateral backing the loan.[12] This section demonstrates one method used to calculate the return on a loan: the traditional *return on assets approach*. Although we demonstrate the return calculations using examples of commercial and industrial loans, the techniques can be used to calculate the return on other loans (such as credit card or mortgage loans) as well.

The Contractually Promised Return on a Loan

The previous description of loans makes it clear that a number of factors impact the promised return an FI achieves on any given dollar loan (asset) amount. These factors include the following:

1. The interest rate on the loan.
2. Any fees relating to the loan.

---

[11] A call loan is a loan contract enabling the lender (e.g., the bank) to request repayment of a loan at any time in the contract period. A noncallable loan leaves the timing of the repayment in the hands of the borrower subject to the limit of the maturity of the loan. For example, most broker loans to investment banks are callable within the day and have to be repaid immediately at the bank lender's request.

[12] FIs have recently developed relationship pricing programs, which offer discounts on interest rates for customers based on the total amount of fee-based services used and investments held at the FI. Relationship pricing is in contrast to (the more traditional) transaction pricing, in which customers pay a stated rate for a service regardless of the total amount of other (nonloan) business conducted with the FI.

3. The credit risk premium on the loan.
4. The collateral backing of the loan.
5. Other nonprice terms (especially compensating balances and reserve requirements).

First, let us consider an example of how to calculate the promised return on a C&I loan. Suppose that an FI makes a spot one-year, $1 million loan. The loan rate is set as follows:

$$\text{Base lending rate } (BR) = 12\%$$
$$+ \text{ Credit risk premium or margin } (m) = \underline{\ \ 2\%}$$
$$BR + m = 14\%$$

The base lending rate (BR) could reflect the FI's weighted-average cost of capital or its marginal cost of funds, such as the commercial paper rate, the federal funds rate, or **LIBOR**—the London Interbank Offered Rate, which is the rate for interbank dollar loans of a given maturity in the Eurodollar market. The center of the Eurodollar market is London. Alternatively, it could reflect the **prime lending rate.** The prime rate is most commonly used in pricing longer-term loans, while the fed funds rate and LIBOR rate are most commonly used in pricing short-term loans. Traditionally, the prime rate has been the rate charged to the FI's lowest-risk customers. Now, it is more of a base rate to which positive or negative risk premiums can be added. In other words, the best and largest borrowers now commonly pay below prime rate to be competitive with the commercial paper market.[13]

Direct and indirect fees and charges relating to a loan generally fall into three categories:

1. A loan origination fee (*of*) charged to the borrower for processing the application.
2. A compensating balance requirement (*b*) to be held as non-interest-bearing demand deposits. **Compensating balances** are a percentage of a loan that a borrower cannot actively use for expenditures. Instead, these balances must be kept on deposit at the FI. For example, a borrower facing a 10 percent compensating balance requirement on a $100 loan would have to place $10 on deposit (traditionally on demand deposit) with the FI and could use only $90 of the $100 borrowed. This requirement raises the effective cost of loans for the borrower since less than the full loan amount ($90 in this case) can actually be used by the borrower and the deposit rate earned on compensating balances is less than the borrowing rate. Thus, compensating balance requirements act as an additional source of return on lending for an FI.[14]
3. A reserve requirement (*RR*) imposed by the Federal Reserve on the FI's (specifically depository institution's) demand deposits, including any compensating balances.

While credit risk may be the most important factor ultimately affecting the return on a loan, these other factors should not be ignored by FI managers in evaluating loan profitability and risk. Indeed, FIs can compensate for high credit risk in a number of ways other than charging a higher explicit interest rate or risk premium on a loan or restricting the amount of credit available. In particular, higher

LIBOR
The London Interbank Offered Rate, which is the rate for interbank dollar loans of a given maturity in the offshore or Eurodollar market.

prime lending rate
The base lending rate periodically set by banks.

compensating balance
A percentage of a loan that a borrower is required to hold on deposit at the lending institution.

---

[13] For more information on the prime rate, see P. Nabar, S. Park, and A. Saunders, "Prime Rate Changes: Is There an Advantage in Being First?" *Journal of Business* 66 (1993), pp. 69–92; and L. Mester and A. Saunders, "When Does the Prime Rate Change?" *Journal of Banking and Finance* 19 (1995), pp. 743–64.

[14] They also create a more stable supply of deposits and thus mitigate liquidity problems.

fees, high compensating balances, and increased collateral backing all offer implicit and indirect methods of compensating an FI for lending risk.

The contractually promised gross return on the loan, k, per dollar lent—or ROA per dollar lent—equals:[15]

$$1 + k = 1 + \frac{of + (BR + m)}{1 - [b(1 - RR)]}$$

This formula may need some explanation. The numerator is the promised gross cash inflow to the FI per dollar, reflecting direct fees (of) plus the loan interest rate ($BR + m$). In the denominator, for every \$1 in loans the FI lends, it retains b as non-interest-bearing compensating balances. Thus, $1 - b$ is the net proceeds of each \$1 of loans received by the borrower from the FI, ignoring reserve requirements. However, since b (compensating balances) are held by the borrower at the FI as demand deposits, the Federal Reserve requires depository institutions to hold non-interest-bearing reserves at the rate RR against these compensating balances. Thus, the FI's net benefit from requiring compensating balances must consider the cost of holding additional non-interest-bearing reserve requirements. The net outflow by the FI per \$1 of loans is $1 - [b(1 - RR)]$ or, 1 minus the reserve adjusted compensating balance requirement.

EXAMPLE 11–1
Calculation of ROA on a Loan

Suppose a bank does the following:

1. Sets the loan rate on a prospective loan at 14 percent (where $BR = 12\%$ and $m = 2\%$).
2. Charges a 1/8 percent (or 0.125 percent) loan origination fee to the borrower.
3. Imposes a 10 percent compensating balance requirement to be held as non-interest-bearing demand deposits.
4. Sets aside reserves, at a rate of 10 percent of deposits, held at the Federal Reserve (i.e., the Fed's cash-to-deposit reserve ratio is 10 percent).

Plugging the numbers from our example into the return formula, we have:[16]

$$1 + k = 1 + \frac{.00125 + (.12 + .02)}{1 - [(.10)(.9)]}$$

$$1 + k = 1 + \frac{.14125}{.91}$$

$$1 + k = 1.1552 \text{ or } k = 15.52\%$$

This is, of course, greater than the simple promised interest return on the loan, $BR + m = 14\%$.

In the special case where fees (of) are zero and the compensating balance (b) is zero:

$$of = 0$$

$$b = 0$$

---

[15] This formula ignores present value aspects that could easily be incorporated. For example, fees are earned in up-front undiscounted dollars while interest payments and risk premiums are normally paid on loan maturity and thus should be discounted by the FI's cost of funds.

[16] If we take into account the present value effects on the fees and the interest payments and assume that the bank's discount rate (d) was $12\frac{1}{2}$ percent, then the $BR + m$ term needs to be discounted by $1 + d = 1.125$ while fees (as up-front payments) are undiscounted. In this case, k is 13.81 percent.

the contractually promised return formula reduces to:

$$1 + k = 1 + (BR + m)$$

That is, the credit risk premium or margin (m) is the fundamental factor driving the promised return on a loan once the base rate on the loan is set.

Note that as commercial lending markets have become more competitive, both origination fees (of) and compensating balances (b) are becoming less important. For example, where compensating balances are still charged, the bank may now allow them to be held as time deposits, and they earn interest. As a result, borrowers' opportunity losses from compensating balances have been reduced to the difference between the loan rate and the compensating balance time-deposit rate. Further, compensating balance requirements are very rare on international loans such as Eurodollar loans.[17] Finally, note that for a given promised gross return on a loan, k, FI managers can use the pricing formula to find various combinations of fees, compensating balances, and risk premiums they may offer their customers that generate the same returns.

The Expected Return on a Loan

The promised return on the loan ($1 + k$) that the borrower and lender contractually agree on includes both the loan interest rate and non-interest rate features such as fees. The promised return on the loan, however, may well differ from the expected and, indeed, actual return on a loan because of default risk. **Default risk** is the risk that the borrower is unable or unwilling to fulfill the terms promised under the loan contract. Default risk is usually present to some degree in all loans. Thus, at the time the loan is made, the expected return [$E(r)$] per dollar lent is related to the promised return as follows:

$$E(r) = p(1 + k) - 1$$

default risk
The risk that the borrower is unable or unwilling to fulfill the terms promised under the loan contract.

where p is the probability of repayment of the loan. To the extent that p is less than 1, default risk is present. This means the FI manager must (1) set the risk premium (m) sufficiently high to compensate for this risk and (2) recognize that setting high risk premiums as well as high fees and base rates may actually reduce the probability of repayment (p). That is, k and p are not independent. Indeed, over some range, as fees and loan rates increase, the probability that the borrower pays the promised return may decrease (i.e., k and p may be negatively related). As a result, FIs usually have to control for credit risk along two dimensions: the price or promised return dimension ($1 + k$) and the quantity or credit availability dimension. Further, even after adjusting the loan rate (by increasing the risk premium on the loan) for the default risk of the borrower, there is no guarantee that the FI will actually receive the promised payments. The measurement and pricing approaches discussed in the chapter consider credit risk based on probabilities of receiving promised payments on the loan. The actual payment or default on a loan once it is issued may vary from the probability expected.

---

[17] For a number of interesting examples using similar formulas, see J. R. Brick, *Commercial Banking: Text and Readings* (Haslett, Mich.: Systems Publications Inc., 1984), chap. 4. If compensating balances held as deposits paid interest at 8 percent ($r_d = 8\%$), then the numerator (cash flow) of the bank in the example would be reduced by $b \times r_d$, where $r_d = .08$ and $b = .1$. In this case, the $k = 14.64$ percent. This assumes that the reserve requirement on compensating balances held as time deposits (RR) is 10 percent. However, while currently reserve requirements on demand deposits are 10 percent, the reserve requirement on time deposits is 0 percent (zero). Recalculating but assuming $RR = 0$ and interest of 8 percent on compensating balances, we find $k = 14.81$ percent.

In general, compared with wholesale (e.g., C&I) loans, the quantity dimension controls credit risk differences on retail (e.g., consumer) loans more than the price dimension does. We discuss the reasons for this in the next section. That is followed by a section that evaluates various ways FI managers can assess the appropriate size of m, the risk premium on a loan. This is the key to pricing wholesale loan and debt risk exposures correctly.

Concept Questions

1. Calculate the promised return (k) on a loan if the base rate is 13 percent, the risk premium is 2 percent, the compensating balance requirement is 5 percent, fees are $^1/_2$ percent, and reserve requirements are 10 percent. (16.23%)
2. What is the expected return on this loan if the probability of default is 5 percent. (10.42%)

RETAIL VERSUS WHOLESALE CREDIT DECISIONS

Retail

Because of the small dollar size of the loans in the context of an FI's overall investment portfolio and the higher costs of collecting information on household borrowers (consumer loans), most loan decisions made at the retail level tend to be accept or reject decisions. Borrowers who are accepted are often charged the same rate of interest and by implication the same credit risk premium. For example, a wealthy individual borrowing from a credit union to finance the purchase of a Rolls-Royce is likely to be charged the same auto loan rate as a less wealthy individual borrowing from that credit union to finance the purchase of a Honda. In the terminology of finance, retail customers (consumer loans) are more likely to be sorted or rationed by loan quantity restrictions than by price or interest rate differences.[18] That is, at the retail level an FI controls its credit risks by **credit rationing** rather than by using a range of interest rates or prices. Thus, the FI may offer the wealthy individual a loan of up to $60,000, while the same FI may offer the less wealthy individual a loan of up to $10,000, both at the same interest rate. Residential mortgage loans provide another good example. While two borrowers may be accepted for mortgage loans, an FI discriminates between them according to the loan-to-value ratio—the amount the FI is willing to lend relative to the market value of the house being acquired—rather than by setting different mortgage rates.[19]

credit rationing
Restricting the quantity of loans made available to individual borrowers.

Wholesale

In contrast to the retail level, at the wholesale (C&I) level FIs use both interest rates and credit quantity to control credit risk. Thus, when FIs quote a prime lending rate (BR) to C&I borrowers, lower-risk borrowers may be charged a lending rate below the prime lending rate. Higher-risk borrowers are charged a markup on the prime rate, or a credit (default) risk premium (m), to compensate the FI for the additional credit risk involved.

---

[18] This does not mean that rates cannot vary across FIs. For example, finance companies associated with car manufacturers (e.g., GMAC) offered 0.0 percent financing on car loans for much of the early 2000s. Unrecognized by many car buyers, the lenders' costs of funds were incorporated into an increased price for the car. Depository institutions, not able to recover their costs of funds in this manner, offered varying rates in an attempt to compete with finance companies. However, for a given FI, the rate offered on car loans would be the same for all borrowers.

[19] However, as the cost of information falls and comprehensive databases on individual households' creditworthiness are developed, the size of a loan for which a single interest rate becomes optimal will shrink.

FIGURE 11–5

Relationship between the Promised Loan Rate and the Expected Return on the Loan

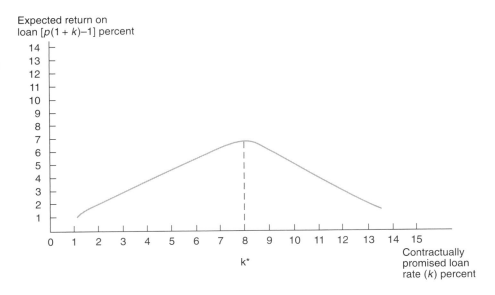

As long as they are compensated with sufficiently high interest rates (or credit risk premiums), over some range of credit demand, FIs may be willing to lend funds to high-risk wholesale borrowers. However, as discussed earlier, increasing loan interest rates (k) may decrease the probability (p) that a borrower will pay the promised return. For example, a borrower who is charged 15 percent for a loan—a prime rate of 10 percent plus a credit risk premium of 5 percent—may be able to make the promised payments on the loan only by using the funds to invest in high-risk investments with some small chance of a big payoff. However, by definition, high-risk projects have relatively high probabilities that they will *fail* to realize the big payoff. If the big payoff does not materialize, the borrower may have to default on the loan. In an extreme case, the FI receives neither the promised interest and fees on the loan nor the original principal lent. This suggests that very high contractual interest rate charges on loans may actually reduce an FI's expected return on loans because high interest rates induce the borrower to invest in risky projects.[20] Alternatively, only borrowers that intend to use the borrowed funds to invest in high-risk projects (high-risk borrowers) may be interested in borrowing from FIs at high interest rates. Low-risk borrowers drop out of the potential borrowing pool at high-rate levels. This lowers the average quality of the pool of potential borrowers. We show these effects in Figure 11–5.[21]

At very low contractually promised interest rates (k), borrowers do not need to take high risks in their use of funds and those with relatively safe investment projects use FI financing. As interest rates increase, borrowers with fairly low-risk, low-return projects no longer think it is profitable to borrow from FIs and drop out of the pool of potential borrowers. Alternatively, borrowers may switch their use of the borrowed funds to high-risk investment projects to have a (small) chance of being able to pay off the loan. In terms of Figure 11–5, when interest rates rise

---

[20] In the context of the previous section, a high k on the loan reflecting a high base rate (BR) and risk premium (m) can lead to a lower probability of repayment (p) and thus a lower $E(r)$ on the loan, where $E(r) = p(1 + k) - 1$. Indeed, for very high k, the expected return on the loan can become negative.

[21] See also J. Stiglitz and A. Weiss, "Credit Rationing in Markets with Imperfect Information," *American Economic Review* 71 (1981), pp. 393–410.

above k^* (8 percent), the additional expected return earned by the FI through higher contractually promised interest rates (k) is increasingly offset by a lower probability of repayment on the loan (p). In other words, because of the potential increase in the probability of default when contractually promised loan rates are high, an FI charging wholesale borrowers loan rates in the 9 to 14 percent region can earn a *lower* expected return than will an FI charging 8 percent.

This relationship between contractually promised interest rates and the expected returns on loans suggests that beyond some interest rate level, it may be best for the FI to *credit ration* its wholesale loans, that is, to not make loans or to make fewer loans. Rather than seeking to ration by price (by charging higher and higher risk premiums to borrowers), the FI can establish an upper ceiling on the amounts it is willing to lend to maximize its expected returns on lending.[22] In the context of Figure 11–5, borrowers may be charged interest rates up to 8 percent, with the most risky borrowers also facing more restrictive limits or ceilings on the amounts they can borrow at any given interest rate.

Concept Questions

1. Can an FI's return on its loan portfolio increase if it cuts its loan rates?
2. What might happen to the expected return on a wholesale loan if an FI eliminates its fees and compensating balances in a low–interest rate environment?

MEASUREMENT OF CREDIT RISK

To calibrate the default risk exposure of credit and investment decisions as well as to assess the credit risk exposure in off-balance-sheet contractual arrangements such as loan commitments, an FI manager needs to measure the probability of borrower default. The ability to do this depends largely on the amount of information the FI has about the borrower. At the retail level, much of the information needs to be collected internally or purchased from external credit agencies. At the wholesale level, these information sources are bolstered by publicly available information, such as certified accounting statements, stock and bond prices, and analysts' reports. Thus, for a publicly traded company, more information is produced and is available to an FI than is available for a small, single-proprietor corner store. The availability of more information, along with the lower average cost of collecting such information, allows FIs to use more sophisticated and usually more quantitative methods in assessing default probabilities for large borrowers compared with small borrowers. However, advances in technology and information collection are making quantitative assessments of even smaller borrowers increasingly feasible and less costly.[23] The simpler details (such as cash flow and ratio analysis) associated with the measurement of credit risk at the retail and the wholesale levels are discussed in Appendix 11C to the chapter, located at the book's Web site (**www.mhhe.com/saunders5e**).

---

[22] Indeed, it has been found that the availability of bank credit depends not just on interest rates, but on the borrower's credit quality as well. Specifically, banks sometimes tighten their credit standards (forgoing riskier loans even when higher interest rates can be charged) to maximize their expected return on lending. See C. S. Lown, D. P. Morgan, and S. Rohatgin, "Listening to Loan Officers: The Impact of Commercial Credit Standards on Lending and Output," *FRBNY Economic Policy Review*, July 2000, pp. 1–16. In addition, the degree of competition in the wholesale loan market, and hence the price elasticity of demand for loans, will affect the availability of bank credit. That is, as competition for loans increases, the point (interest rate) at which banks switch from risk-based pricing to credit rationing may increase as well, and vice versa.

[23] These advances include database services and software for automating credit assessment provided by companies such as Dun & Bradstreet.

covenants
Restrictions written into bond and loan contracts either limiting or encouraging the borrower's actions that affect the probability of repayment.

In principle, FIs can use very similar methods and models to assess the probabilities of default on both bonds and loans. Even though loans tend to involve fewer lenders to any single borrower as opposed to multiple bondholders, in essence, both loans and bonds are contracts that promise fixed (or indexed) payments at regular intervals in the future. Loans and bonds stand ahead of the borrowing firm's equity holders in terms of the priority of their claims if things go wrong. Also, bonds, like loans, include **covenants** restricting or encouraging various actions to enhance the probability of repayment. Covenants can include limits on the type and amount of new debt, investments, and asset sales the borrower may undertake while the loan or bonds are outstanding. Financial covenants are also often imposed restricting changes in the borrower's financial ratios such as its leverage ratio or current ratio. For example, a common restrictive covenant included in many bond and loan contracts limits the amount of dividends a firm can pay to its equity holders. Clearly, for any given cash flow, a high dividend payout to stockholders means that less is available for repayments to bondholders and lenders. Moreover, bond yields, like wholesale loan rates, usually reflect risk premiums that vary with the perceived credit quality of the borrower and the collateral or security backing of the debt. Given this, FIs can use many of the following models that analyze default risk probabilities either in making lending decisions or when considering investing in corporate bonds offered either publicly or privately.[24]

Concept Questions

1. Is it more costly for an FI manager to assess the default risk exposure of a publicly traded company or a small, single-proprietor firm? Explain your answer.
2. How do loan covenants help protect an FI against default risk?

DEFAULT RISK MODELS

Economists, analysts, and FI managers have employed many different models to assess the default risk on loans and bonds. These vary from relatively qualitative to the highly quantitative models. Further, these models are not mutually exclusive; an FI manager may use more than one model to reach a credit pricing or loan quantity rationing decision. As will be discussed below in more detail, a great deal of time and effort has recently been expended by FIs in building highly technical credit risk evaluation models. Many of these models use ideas and techniques similar to the market risk models discussed in Chapter 10. We analyze a number of models in three broad groups: qualitative models, credit scoring models, and newer models.

Qualitative Models

In the absence of publicly available information on the quality of borrowers, the FI manager has to assemble information from private sources—such as credit and deposit files—and/or purchase such information from external sources—such as credit rating agencies. This information helps a manager make an informed judgment on the probability of default of the borrower and price the loan or debt correctly.

In general, the amount of information assembled varies with the size of the potential debt exposure and the costs of collection. However, a number of key factors

---

[24] For more discussion of the similarities between bank loans and privately placed debt, see M. Berlin and L. Mester, "Debt Covenants and Renegotiation," *Journal of Financial Intermediation* 2 (1992), pp. 95–133; M. Carey et al., "The Economics of Private Placement: A New Look," *Financial Markets, Institutions and Instruments* 2, no. 3 (1993); and M. Carey et al., "Does Corporate Lending by Banks and Finance Companies Differ? Evidence on Specialization in Private Debt Contracting," *Journal of Finance* 53 (June 1998), pp. 845–78.

FIGURE 11–6
Relationship between the Cost of Debt, the Probability of Default, and Leverage

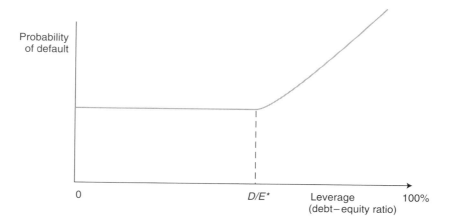

enter into the credit decision. These include (1) *borrower-specific* factors which are idiosyncratic to the individual borrower, and (2) *market-specific* factors, which have an impact on all borrowers at the time of the credit decision. The FI manager then weights these factors subjectively to come to an overall credit decision. Because of their reliance on the subjective judgment of the FI manager, these models are often called expert systems. Commonly used borrower-specific and market-specific factors are discussed next.

Borrower-Specific Factors

Reputation The borrower's reputation involves the borrowing–lending history of the credit applicant. If, over time, the borrower has established a reputation for prompt and timely repayment, this enhances the applicant's attractiveness to the FI. A long-term customer relationship between a borrower and lender forms an **implicit contract** regarding borrowing and repayment that extends beyond the formal explicit legal contract on which borrower–lender relationships are based. The importance of reputation, which can be established only over time through repayment and observed behavior, works to the disadvantage of small, newer borrowers. This is one of the reasons initial public offerings of debt securities by small firms often require higher yields than do offerings of older, more seasoned firms.[25]

Leverage A borrower's **leverage** or capital structure—the ratio of debt to equity—affects the probability of its default because large amounts of debt, such as bonds and loans, increase the borrower's interest charges and pose a significant claim on its cash flows. As shown in Figure 11–6, relatively low debt–equity ratios may not significantly impact the probability of debt repayment. Yet beyond some point, the risk of bankruptcy increases, as does the probability of some loss of interest or principal for the lender. Thus, highly leveraged firms, such as firms recently engaged in leveraged buyouts (LBOs) financed in part by FIs' provision of junk bonds or below-investment-grade debt, may find it necessary to pay higher risk premiums on their borrowings if they are not rationed in the first place.[26]

implicit contract
Long-term customer relationship between a borrower and lender based on reputation.

leverage
The ratio of a borrower's debt to equity.

[25] For the link between bank finance and the cost of initial public offerings of securities, see C. James and P. Weir, "Borrowing Relationships, Intermediation, and the Costs of Issuing Public Securities," *Journal of Financial Economics* 28 (1992), pp. 149–71.

[26] However, S. J. Grossman and O. D. Hart argue that high debt (leverage) may be a signal of managerial efficiency and may in fact lower bankruptcy risk. Similar arguments have been made about the efficiency incentives for managers in junk bond–financed LBOs. That is, firms with a lot of debt have to be "lean and mean" to meet their repayment commitments. See "Corporate Financial Structure and Managerial Incentives," in *The Economics of Information and Uncertainty*, ed. J. McCall (Chicago: Chicago University Press, 1982).

Volatility of Earnings   As with leverage, a highly volatile earnings stream increases the probability that the borrower cannot meet fixed interest and principal charges for any given capital structure. Consequently, newer firms or firms in high-tech industries with a high earnings variance over time are less attractive credit risks than are those with long and more stable earnings histories.

Collateral   As discussed earlier, a key feature in any lending and loan-pricing decision is the degree of collateral, or assets backing the security of the loan. Many loans and bonds are backed by specific assets should a borrower default on repayment obligations. Mortgage bonds give the bondholder first claim to some specific piece of property of the borrower, normally machinery or buildings; debentures give a bondholder a more general and more risky claim to the borrower's assets. Subordinated debentures are even riskier because their claims to the assets of a defaulting borrower are junior to those of both mortgage bondholders and debenture bondholders. Similarly, loans can be either secured (collateralized) or unsecured (uncollateralized).[27]

Market-Specific Factors

The Business Cycle   The position of the economy in the business cycle phase is enormously important to an FI in assessing the probability of borrower default. For example, during recessions, firms in the consumer durable goods sector that produce autos, refrigerators, or houses do badly compared with those in the nondurable goods sector producing tobacco and foods. People cut back on luxuries during a recession but are less likely to cut back on necessities such as food. Thus, corporate borrowers in the consumer durable goods sector of the economy are especially prone to default risk. Because of cyclical concerns, FIs are more likely to increase the relative degree of credit rationing in recessionary phases. This has especially adverse consequences for smaller borrowers with limited or no access to alternative credit markets such as the commercial paper market.[28]

The Level of Interest Rates   High interest rates indicate restrictive monetary policy actions by the Federal Reserve. FIs not only find funds to finance their lending decisions scarcer and more expensive but also must recognize that high interest rates are correlated with higher credit risk in general. As discussed earlier, high interest rate levels may encourage borrowers to take excessive risks and/or encourage only the most risky customers to borrow.

So far, we have delineated just a few of the qualitative borrower- and economy-specific factors an FI manager may take into account in deciding on the probability of default on any loan or bond.[29] Rather than letting such factors enter into the decision process in a purely subjective fashion, the FI manager may weight these

www.federalreserve.
gov

---

[27] However, collateralized loans are still subject to some default risk unless these loans are significantly overcollateralized; that is, assets are pledged with market values exceeding the face value of the debt instrument. There is also some controversy as to whether posting collateral signifies a high- or low-risk borrower. Arguably, the best borrowers do not need to post collateral since they are good credit risks, whereas only more risky borrowers need to post collateral. That is, posting collateral may be a signal of more rather than less credit risk. See, for example, A. Berger and G. Udell, "Lines of Credit, Collateral and Relationship Lending in Small Firm Finance," *Journal of Business*, 1995, pp. 351–381.

[28] For a good discussion of the sensitivity of different U.S. industries' default rates to the business cycle, see J. D. Taylor, "Cross-Industry Differences in Business Failure Rates: Implications for Portfolio Management," *Commercial Lending Review*, 1998, pp. 36–46.

[29] More generally, J. F. Sinkey identifies five Cs of credit that should be included in any subjective (qualitative) credit analysis: character (willingness to pay), capacity (cash flow), capital (wealth), collateral (security), and conditions (economic conditions). See *Commercial Bank Financial Management—In the Financial Services Industry*, 5th ed. (New York: Macmillan, 1998).

www.rmahq.org

factors in a more objective or quantitative manner. We discuss quantitative credit scoring models used to measure credit risk next. One frequently used source of much of this information is Robert Morris Associates (RMA). RMA has become a standard reference for thousands of commercial lenders by providing average balance sheet and income data for more than 400 industries, common ratios computed for each size group and industry, five-year trend data, and financial statement data for more than 100,000 commercial borrowers.

**Concept
Questions**

1. Make a list of 10 key borrower characteristics you would assess before making a mortgage loan.
2. How should the risk premium on a loan be affected if there is a reduction in a borrower's leverage?

Credit Scoring Models

**credit scoring
models**
Mathematical models that use observed loan applicant's characteristics either to calculate a score representing the applicant's probability of default or to sort borrowers into different default risk classes.

Credit scoring models are quantitative models that use observed borrower characteristics either to calculate a score representing the applicant's probability of default or to sort borrowers into different default risk classes. By selecting and combining different economic and financial borrower characteristics, an FI manager may be able to:

1. Numerically establish which factors are important in explaining default risk.
2. Evaluate the relative degree or importance of these factors.
3. Improve the pricing of default risk.
4. Be better able to screen out bad loan applicants.
5. Be in a better position to calculate any reserves needed to meet expected future loan losses.

The primary benefit from credit scoring is that credit lenders can more accurately predict a borrower's performance without having to use more resources. With commercial loan credit scoring models taking into account all necessary regulatory parameters and posting an 85 percent accuracy rate on average, according to credit scoring experts,[30] using these models means fewer defaults and write-offs for commercial loan lenders. Indeed, many commercial credit grantors are implementing credit scoring models as a way to come in accordance with the Sarbanes–Oxley Act of 2002, which sets guidelines for corporate governance in several areas, including risk management and control assessment.

To use credit scoring models, the manager must identify objective economic and financial measures of risk for any particular class of borrower. For consumer debt, the objective characteristics in a credit scoring model might include income, assets, age, occupation, and location. For commercial debt, cash flow information and financial ratios such as the debt–equity ratio are usually key factors.[31] After data are identified, a statistical technique quantifies, or scores, the default risk probability or default risk classification.

---

[30] See "Credit Scoring Heats Up," *Collections and Credit Risk,* September 2003, p. 34.

[31] A. N. Berger, W. S. Frame, and N. H. Miller, in "Credit Scoring and the Availability, Price, and Risk of Small Business Credit," 2002, Working Paper, Federal Reserve Board, find that small business credit scoring is associated with expanded credit supply, higher average interest rates, and greater risk levels for small business loans. Their findings are consistent with a net increase in lending to small businesses that would otherwise not receive credit without the use of credit scoring.

Credit scoring models include these three broad types: (1) linear probability models, (2) logit models, and (3) linear discriminant analysis. Appendix: 11C to the chapter (located at the book's Web site, **www.mhhe.com/saunders5e**) looks at credit scoring models used to evaluate mortgages and consumer loans. In this section we look at credit scoring models used to evaluate commercial loans.

Linear Probability Model and Logit Model

The linear probability model uses past data, such as financial ratios, as inputs into a model to explain repayment experience on old loans. The relative importance of the factors used in explaining past repayment performance then forecasts repayment probabilities on new loans. That is, factors explaining past repayment performance can be used for assessing p, the probability of repayment discussed earlier in this chapter (a key input in setting the credit premium on a loan or determining the amount to be lent) and the probability of default (PD).

Briefly, we divide old loans (i) into two observational groups: those that defaulted ($PD_i = 1$) and those that did not default ($PD_i = 0$). Then we relate these observations by linear regression to a set of j causal variables (X_{ij}) that reflect quantitative information about the ith borrower, such as leverage or earnings. We estimate the model by linear regression of this form:

$$PD_i = \sum_{j=1}^{n} \beta_j X_{ij} + \text{error}$$

where β_j is the estimated importance of the jth variable (leverage) in explaining past repayment experience.

If we then take these estimated β_js and multiply them by the observed X_{ij} for a prospective borrower, we can derive an expected value of PD_i for the prospective borrower. That value can be interpreted as the probability of default for the borrower: $E(PD_i) = (1 - p_i) = $ expected probability of default, where p_i is the probability of repayment on the loan.

EXAMPLE 11–2 *Estimating the Probability of Repayment on a Loan Using Linear Probability Credit Scoring Models*	Suppose there were two factors influencing the past default behavior of borrowers: the leverage or debt–equity ratio (*D/E*) and the sales–asset ratio (*S/A*). Based on past default (repayment) experience, the linear probability model is estimated as: $$PD_i = .5(D/E_i) + .1(S/A_i)$$ Assume a prospective borrower has a *D/E* = .3 and an *S/A* = 2.0. Its expected probability of default (PD$_i$) can then be estimated as: $$PD_i = .5(.3) + .1(2.0) = .35$$

While this technique is straightforward as long as current information on the X_{ij} is available for the borrower, its major weakness is that the estimated probabilities of default can often lie outside the interval 0 to 1. The logit model overcomes this weakness by restricting the estimated range of default probabilities from the linear regression model to lie between 0 and 1.[32]

[32] Essentially this is done by plugging the estimated value of PD_i from the linear probability model (in our example, $PD_i = .35$) into the following formula:

$$F(PD_i) = \frac{1}{1 + e^{-PD_i}}$$

where e is exponential (equal to 2.718) and $F(PD_i)$ is the logistically transformed value of PD_i.

Linear Discriminant Models

While linear probability and logit models project a value for the expected probability of default if a loan is made, discriminant models divide borrowers into high or low default risk classes contingent on their observed characteristics (X_j).

Consider the discriminant analysis model developed by E. I. Altman for publicly traded manufacturing firms in the United States. The indicator variable Z is an overall measure of the default risk classification of a commercial borrower.[33] This in turn depends on the values of various financial ratios of the borrower (X_j) and the weighted importance of these ratios based on the past observed experience of defaulting versus nondefaulting borrowers derived from a discriminant analysis model.[34]

Altman's discriminant function (credit-classification model) takes the form:

$$Z = 1.2X_1 + 1.4X_2 + 3.3X_3 + 0.6X_4 + 1.0X_5$$

where

X_1 = Working capital/total assets ratio
X_2 = Retained earnings/total assets ratio
X_3 = Earnings before interest and taxes/total assets ratio
X_4 = Market value of equity/book value of long-term debt ratio
X_5 = Sales/total assets ratio

The higher the value of Z, the lower the default risk classification of the borrower.[35] Thus, low or negative values of Z may be evidence of the borrower being a member of a relatively high default risk class.

EXAMPLE 11–3

Calculation of Altman's Z Score

Suppose that the financial ratios of a potential borrowing firm took the following values:

$X_1 = .2$
$X_2 = 0$
$X_3 = -.20$
$X_4 = .10$
$X_5 = 2.0$

The ratio X_2 is zero and X_3 is negative, indicating that the firm has had negative earnings or losses in recent periods. Also, X_4 indicates that the borrower is highly leveraged. However, the working capital ratio (X_1) and the sales/assets ratio (X_5) indicate that the firm is reasonably liquid and is maintaining its sales volume. The Z score provides an overall score or indicator of the borrower's credit risk since it combines and weights these five factors according to their past importance in explaining borrower default. For the borrower in question:

$$Z = 1.2\,(.2) + 1.4(0) + 3.3(-.20) + 0.6(.10) + 1.0\,(2.0)$$
$$= 0.24 + 0 - .66 + 0.06 + 2.0$$
$$= 1.64$$

(continued)

---

[33] The Z score is a default indicator and is not a direct probability of default (*PD*) measure.

[34] E. I. Altman, "Managing the Commercial Lending Process," in *Handbook of Banking Strategy,* eds. R. C. Aspinwall and R. A. Eisenbeis (New York: John Wiley & Sons, 1985), pp. 473–510.

[35] Working capital is current assets minus current liabilities.

According to Altman's credit scoring model, any firm with a *Z* score less than 1.81 should be placed in the high default risk region.[36] Thus, the FI should not make a loan to this borrower until it improves its earnings.

There are a number of problems in using the discriminant analysis model to make credit risk evaluations.[37] The first problem is that these models usually discriminate only between two extreme cases of borrower behavior: no default and default. As discussed in Chapter 7, in the real world various gradations of default exist, from nonpayment or delay of interest payments (nonperforming assets) to outright default on all promised interest and principal payments. This problem suggests that a more accurate or finely calibrated sorting among borrowers may require defining more classes in the discriminant analysis model.

The second problem is that there is no obvious economic reason to expect that the weights in the discriminant function—or, more generally, the weights in any credit scoring model—will be constant over any but very short periods. The same concern also applies to the variables (X_j). Specifically, because of changing real and financial market conditions, other borrower-specific financial ratios may come to be increasingly relevant in explaining default risk probabilities. Moreover, the linear discriminant model assumes that the X_j variables are independent of one another.[38]

The third problem is that these models ignore important, hard-to-quantify factors that may play a crucial role in the default or no default decision. For example, reputation of the borrower and the nature of long-term borrower–lender relationships could be important borrower-specific characteristics, as could macrofactors such as the phase of the business cycle. These variables are often ignored in credit scoring models. Moreover, traditional credit scoring models rarely use publicly available information, such as the prices of outstanding public debt and equity of the borrower.[39]

A fourth problem relates to default records kept by FIs. Currently, no centralized database on defaulted business loans for proprietary and other reasons exists. Some task forces set up by consortiums of commercial banks, insurance companies, and consulting firms are currently seeking to construct such databases largely in response to proposed reforms to bank capital requirements (see Chapter 20). However, it may well be many years before they are developed.[40] This constrains the

---

[36] Discriminant analysis models produce such a switching point, $Z = 1.81$. This is the mean difference between the average *Z* scores of the defaulting firms and the nondefaulting firms. For example, suppose the average *Z* for nondefaulting firms was 2.01 and for defaulting firms it was 1.61. The mean of these two scores is 1.81. See G. Turvey, "Credit Scoring for Agricultural Loans: A Review with Applications," *Agricultural Finance Review* 51 (1991), pp. 43–54, for more details.

[37] Most of these criticisms also apply to the linear probability and logit models.

[38] Recent work in nonlinear discriminant analysis has sought to relax this assumption. Moreover, work with neural networks, which are complex computer algorithms seeking links or correlations between the X_j variables to improve on *Z* classifications, shows some promise. See P. K. Coats and L. F. Fant, "Recognizing Financial Distress Patterns: Using a Neural Network Tool," *Financial Management,* Summer 1993, pp. 142–55; and "New Tools for Routine Jobs," *The Financial Times,* September 24, 1994.

[39] For example, S. C. Gilson, K. John, and L. Lang show that three years of low or negative stock returns can usefully predict bankruptcy probabilities. In fact, this market-based approach is supplementary to the market-based information models discussed in later sections of this chapter. See "An Empirical Study of Private Reorganization of Firms in Default," *Journal of Financial Economics,* 1990, pp. 315–53.

[40] A recent, successful example of such a database is "1986–1992 Credit-Loss Experience Study: Private Placement Bonds," *Society of Actuaries,* Schaumburg, IL, 1996. For an analysis of these data, see M. Carey, "Credit Risk in Private Debt Portfolios," *Journal of Finance,* June 1998, pp. 1363–87.

ability of many FIs to use traditional credit scoring models (and quantitative models in general) for larger business loans—although their use for smaller consumer loans, such as credit card loans, where much better centralized databases exist, is well established.

The newer credit risk models use *financial theory* and more widely available *financial market* data to make inferences about default probabilities on debt and loan instruments. Consequently, these models are most relevant in evaluating loans to larger borrowers in the corporate sector. This is the area in which a great deal of current research is taking place by FIs, as noted in Appendixes 11A and 11B. Below we consider a number of these newer approaches or models of credit risk, including:

1. Term structure of credit risk approach.
2. Mortality rate approach.
3. RAROC models.
4. Option models (including the KMV credit monitor model).
5. CreditMetrics (see Appendix 11A).
6. Credit Risk+ (see Appendix 11B).

While some of these models focus on different aspects of credit risk, they are all linked by a strong reliance on modern financial theory and financial market data.[41]

Concept Questions

1. Suppose the estimated linear probability model looked as follows: $Z = 0.3X_1 + 0.1X_2 +$ error, where

$$X_1 = \text{Debt–equity ratio; and } X_2 = \text{Total assets} - \text{Working capital ratio}$$

Suppose, for a prospective borrower, $X_1 = 1.5$ and $X_2 = 3.0$. What is the projected probability of default for the borrower? (75%)
2. Suppose $X_3 = .5$ in Example 11–3. Show how this would change the default risk classification of the borrower. ($Z = 3.95$)
3. What are two problems in using discriminant analysis to evaluate credit risk?

NEWER MODELS OF CREDIT RISK MEASUREMENT AND PRICING

Term Structure Derivation of Credit Risk

One market-based method of assessing credit risk exposure and default probabilities is to analyze the risk premiums inherent in the current structure of yields on corporate debt or loans to similar risk-rated borrowers. Rating agencies such as Standard & Poor's (S&P) categorize corporate bond issuers into at least seven major classes according to perceived credit quality. The first four quality ratings— AAA, AA, A, and BBB—indicate investment-quality borrowers. For example, the Office of the Comptroller of the Currency, which regulates national banks, restricts the ability of banks to purchase securities rated outside these classes. By comparison, insurance company regulators have permitted these FIs to purchase non-investment-grade securities with ratings such as BB, B, and CCC, but with restrictions on the aggregate amounts they can include in their portfolios. These three classes are known as high-yield or junk bonds. Different quality ratings are reflected in the degree to which corporate bond yields exceed those implied by the Treasury (credit risk–free) yield curve.

www.standardand-poors.com

www.occ.treas.gov

---

[41] For further details on these newer models, see A. Saunders and L. Allen, *Credit Risk Measurement: New Approaches to Value at Risk and Other Paradigms*, 2nd ed. (John Wiley and Sons: New York, 2002).

FIGURE 11–7
Corporate and
Treasury Discount
Bond Yield Curves

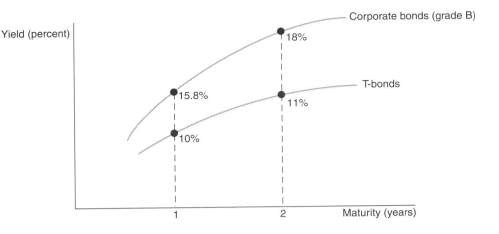

Look at the spreads shown in Figure 11–7 for zero-coupon corporate (grade B) bonds over similar maturity zero-coupon Treasuries (called Treasury strips). Because **Treasury strips and zero-coupon corporate bonds** are single-payment discount bonds, it is possible to extract required credit risk premiums and implied probabilities of default from actual market data on interest rates. That is, the spreads between risk-free discount bonds issued by the Treasury and discount bonds issued by corporate borrowers of differing quality reflect perceived credit risk exposures of corporate borrowers for single payments at different times in the future. FIs can use these credit risk probabilities on existing debt to decide whether or not to issue additional debt to a particular credit risk borrower.

Next, we look at the simplest case of extracting an implied probability of default for an FI considering buying one-year bonds from or making one-year loans to a risky borrower. Then, we consider multiyear loans and bonds. In each case, we show that we can extract a market view of the credit risk—the expected probability of default—of an individual borrower.[42]

Treasury strips and zero-coupon corporate bonds
Bonds that are created or issued bearing no coupons and only a face value to be paid on maturity. As such, they are issued at a large discount from face value. (Also called deep-discount bonds.)

Probability of Default on a One-Period Debt Instrument

Assume that the FI requires an expected return on a one-year (zero-coupon) corporate debt security equal to at least the risk-free return on one-year (zero-coupon) Treasury bonds. Let p be the probability that the corporate debt, both principal and interest, will be repaid in full; therefore, $1 - p$ is the probability of default. If the borrower defaults, the FI is (for now) assumed to get nothing (i.e., the recovery rate is zero or the loss given default is 100 percent).[43] By denoting the contractually promised return on the one-year corporate debt security as $1 + k$ and on the credit

---

[42] Technically, these credit risk models are often called intensity-based models or reduced form models. For a full review, see A. Saunders and L. Allen, *Credit Risk Measurement: New Approaches to Value at Risk and Other Paradigms,* 2nd ed. (John Wiley and Sons: New York, 2002), chap. 5.

[43] This is a key assumption. If the recovery rate is nonzero (which in reality is true, since in recent years banks have recovered on average up to 40 percent of a defaulted loan and 50 percent of a senior secured bond), then the spread between the corporate bond return and the Treasury bond return will reflect both the probability of default as well as the loss given default (the latter is equal to 1 minus the recovery rate). To disentangle the probability of default from the loss given default, we need to make assumptions about the size of the loss given default (LGD) or the statistical process that either the PD and/or the LGD follow, such as the Poisson process. One simple case assuming LGD is known is discussed later in this chapter.

risk–free one-year Treasury security as $1 + i$, the FI manager would just be indifferent between corporate and Treasury securities when[44]

$$p(1 + k) = 1 + i$$

or, the expected return on corporate securities is equal to the risk-free rate.

EXAMPLE 11–4

Calculating the Probability of Default on a One-Year Bond (Loan) Using Term Structure Derivation of Credit Risk

Suppose, as shown in Figure 11–7, the interest rates in the market for one-year zero-coupon Treasury bonds and for one-year zero-coupon grade B corporate bonds are, respectively:

$$i = 10\%$$

and

$$k = 15.8\%$$

This implies that the probability of repayment on the security as perceived by the market is:

$$p = \frac{1 + i}{1 + k} = \frac{1.100}{1.158} = .95$$

If the probability of repayment is .95, this implies a probability of default $(1 - p)$ equal to .05. Thus, in this simple one-period framework, a probability of default of 5 percent on the corporate bond (loan) requires the FI to set a risk premium (ϕ) of 5.8 percent.[45]

$$\phi = k - i = 5.8\%$$

Clearly, as the probability of repayment (p) falls and the probability of default $(1 - p)$ increases, the required spread ϕ between k and i increases.

This analysis can easily be extended to the more realistic case in which the FI does not expect to lose all interest and all principal if the corporate borrower defaults.[46] Realistically, the FI lender can expect to receive some partial repayment even if the borrower goes into bankruptcy. For example, Altman and Bana estimated that when firms defaulted on their bonds in 2002, the investor lost on average 74.7 cents on the dollar (i.e., recovered around 25.3 cents on the dollar).[47] Table 11–8 gives recovery rates on defaulted debt by seniority from 1978–2002. As discussed earlier in this chapter, many loans and bonds are secured or collateralized by first liens on various pieces of property or real assets should a borrower default. Let γ be the

---

[44] This assumes that the FI manager is not risk averse; that is, this is a risk-neutral valuation method and the probabilities so derived are called risk-neutral probabilities. In general these will differ from probabilities estimated from historic data on defaults. See Saunders and Allen, *Credit Risk Management,* chap. 5.

[45] In the real world a bank could partially capture this required spread in higher fees and compensating balances rather than only in the risk premium. In this simple example, we are assuming away compensating balances and fees. However, they could easily be built into the model. For additional information on this model, see A. Ginzburg, K. J. Maloney, and R. Wilner, "Risk Rating Migration and the Valuation of Floating Rate Debt," Citicorp Working Paper, March 1994; and R. Litterman and T. Iben, "Corporate Bond Valuation and the Term Structure of Credit Spreads," *Journal of Portfolio Management,* 1989, pp. 52–64.

[46] See J. B. Yawitz, "Risk Premia on Municipal Bonds," *Journal of Financial and Quantitative Analysis* 13 (1977), pp. 475–85; and J. B. Yawitz, "An Analytical Model of Interest Rate Differentials and Different Default Recoveries," *Journal of Financial and Quantitative Analysis* 13 (1977), pp. 481–90.

[47] E. I. Altman and G. Bana, "Defaults and Returns on High-Yield Bonds: The Year 2002 in Review and the Market Outlook," Working Paper, New York University Salomon Center, February 2003.

TABLE 11–8   Recovery Rates (RR) on Defaulted Debt by Seniority, 1978–2002

Year	Senior Secured		Senior Unsecured		Senior Subordinated		Subordinated		Discount and Zero Coupon		All Securities	
	Number	RR	Number	RR	Number	RR	Number	RR	Number	RR	Number	RR
2002	37	52.81%	254	21.82%	21	32.79%	—	—	28	26.47%	340	25.32%
2001	9	40.95	187	28.84	48	18.37	—	—	37	15.05	281	25.48
2000	13	39.58	47	25.40	61	25.96	26	26.62%	17	23.61	164	25.83
1999	14	26.90	60	42.54	40	23.56	2	13.88	11	17.30	127	31.14
1998	6	70.38	21	39.57	6	17.54	—	—	1	17.00	34	37.27
1997	4	74.90	12	70.94	6	31.89	1	60.66	2	19.00	25	53.89
1996	4	59.08	4	50.11	9	48.99	4	44.23	3	11.99	24	51.91
1995	5	44.64	9	50.50	17	39.01	1	20.00	1	17.50	33	41.77
1994	5	48.66	8	51.14	5	19.81	3	37.04	1	5.00	22	39.44
1993	2	55.75	7	33.38	10	51.50	9	28.38	4	31.75	32	38.83
1992	15	59.85	8	35.61	17	58.20	22	49.13	5	19.82	67	50.03
1991	4	44.12	69	55.84	37	31.91	38	24.30	9	27.89	157	40.67
1990	12	32.18	31	29.02	38	25.01	24	18.83	11	15.63	116	24.66
1989	9	82.69	16	53.70	21	19.60	30	23.95	—	—	76	35.97
1988	13	67.96	19	41.99	10	30.70	20	35.27	—	—	62	43.45
1987	4	90.68	17	72.02	6	56.24	4	35.25	—	—	31	66.63
1986	8	48.32	11	37.72	7	35.20	30	33.39	—	—	56	36.60
1985	2	74.25	3	34.81	7	36.18	15	41.45	—	—	27	41.78
1984	4	53.42	1	50.50	2	65.88	7	44.68	—	—	14	50.62
1983	1	71.00	3	67.72	—	—	4	41.79	—	—	8	55.17
1982	—	—	16	39.31	—	—	4	32.91	—	—	20	38.03
1981	1	72.00	—	—	—	—	—	—	—	—	1	72.00
1980	—	—	2	26.71	—	—	2	16.63	—	—	4	21.67
1979	—	—	—	—	—	—	1	31.00	—	—	1	31.00
1978	—	—	1	60.00	—	—	—	—	—	—	1	60.00
Total/ Average	172	52.86	806	33.62	368	29.67	247	31.03	130	20.40	1723	32.93

Source: E. I. Altman and G. Bana, "Defaults and Returns on High-Yield Bonds: The Year 2002 in Review and the Market Outlook," Working Paper, New York University Salomon Center, February 2003. *www.stern.nyu.edu/-ealtman*

proportion of the loan's principal and interest that is collectible on default, where in general γ is positive.

The FI manager would set the expected return on the loan to equal the risk-free rate in the following manner:

$$[(1 - p)\, \gamma\, (1 + k)] + [p\, (1 + k)] = 1 + i$$

The new term here is $(1 - p)\, \gamma\, (1 + k)$; this is the payoff the FI expects to get if the borrower defaults.

As might be expected, if the loan has collateral backing such that $\gamma > 0$, the required risk premium on the loan will be less for any given default risk probability $(1 - p)$. Collateral requirements are a method of controlling default risk; they act as a direct substitute for risk premiums in setting required loan rates. To see this, solve for the risk premium ϕ between k (the required yield on risky corporate debt) and i (the risk-free rate of interest):

$$k - i = \phi = \frac{(1 + i)}{(\gamma + p - p\gamma)} - (1 + i)$$

If $i = 10$ percent and $p = .95$ as before but the FI can expect to collect 90 percent of the promised proceeds if default occurs ($\gamma = .9$), then the required risk premium $\phi = 0.6$ percent.[48]

Interestingly, in this simple framework, γ and p are perfect substitutes for each other. That is, a bond or loan with collateral backing of $\gamma = .7$ and $p = .8$ would have the same required risk premium as one with $\gamma = .8$ and $p = .7$. An increase in collateral γ is a direct substitute for an increase in default risk (i.e., a decline in p).

Probability of Default on a Multiperiod Debt Instrument

marginal default probability
The probability that a borrower will default in any given year.

cumulative default probability
The probability that a borrower will default over a specified multiyear period.

We can extend this type of analysis to derive the credit risk or default probabilities occurring in the market for longer-term loans or bonds (i.e., two-year bonds). To do this, the manager must estimate the probability that the bond will default in the second year conditional on the probability that it does not default in the first year. The probability that a bond will default in any given year is clearly conditional on the fact that the default has not occurred earlier. The probability that a bond will default in any given year, t, is the **marginal default probability** for that year, $1 - p_t$. However, for, say, a two-year loan, the marginal probability of default in the second year ($1 - p_2$) can differ from the marginal probability of default in the first year ($1 - p_1$). If we use these marginal default probabilities, the **cumulative default probability** at some time between now and the end of year 2 is:

$$Cp = 1 - [(p_1)(p_2)]$$

EXAMPLE 11–5
Calculating the Probability of Default on a Multiperiod Bond

Suppose the FI manager wanted to find out the probability of default on a two-year bond. For the one-year loan, $1 - p_1 = .05$ is the marginal and total or cumulative probability (Cp) of default in year 1. Later in this chapter we discuss ways in which p_2 can be estimated by the FI manager, but for the moment suppose that $1 - p_2 = .07$. Then:

$$1 - p_1 = .05 = \text{marginal probability of default in year 1}$$
$$1 - p_2 = .07 = \text{marginal probability of default in year 2}$$

The probability of the borrower surviving—not defaulting at any time between now (time 0) and the end of period 2—is $p_1 \times p_2 = (.95)(.93) = .8835$.

$$Cp = 1 - [(.95)(.93)] = .1165$$

There is an 11.65 percent probability of default over this period.

We have seen how to derive the one-year probability of default from yield spreads on one-year bonds. We now want to derive the probability of default in year 2, year 3, and so on. Look at Figure 11–7; as you can see, yield curves are rising for both Treasury issues and corporate bond issues. We want to extract from these yield curves the *market's expectation* of the multiperiod default rates for corporate borrowers classified in the grade B rating class.[49]

---

[48] For example, from Table 11–8 the average recovery rate on bonds that were senior secured in 1987 was 90.68 percent (although these bonds recover on average 52.86 percent), recovery rates are usually calculated in one of two ways: first, by looking at the prices of loans or bonds in the secondary market postdefault or, second (if they are not actively traded), by calculating the net present value of the expected cash flows that are projected to be recovered postdefault.

[49] To use this model, one has to place borrowers in a rating class. One way to do this for unrated firms would be to use the Z score model to calculate a Z ratio for this firm. E. I. Altman has shown that there is a high correlation between Z scores and Standard & Poor's and Moody's bond ratings. Once a firm is placed in a bond rating group (e.g., B) by the Z score model, the term structure model can be used to infer the expected (implied) probabilities of default for the borrower at different times in the future. See "Valuation, Loss Reserves, and Pricing of Commercial Loans," *Journal of Commercial Bank Lending*, August 1993, pp. 9–25.

no arbitrage
The inability to make a profit without taking risk.

Look first at the Treasury yield curve. The condition of efficient markets and thus **no arbitrage** profits by investors requires that the return on buying and holding the two-year Treasury discount bond to maturity just equals the expected return from investing in the current one-year discount T-bond and reinvesting the principal and interest in a new one-year discount T-bond at the end of the first year at the expected one-year **forward rate.** That is:

forward rate
A one-period rate of interest expected on a bond issued at some date in the future.

$$(1 + i_2)^2 = (1 + i_1)(1 + f_1) \qquad \textbf{(1)}$$

The term on the left side is the return from holding the two-year discount bond to maturity. The term on the right side results from investing in two successive one-year bonds, where i_1 is the current one-year bond rate and f_1 is the expected one-year bond rate or forward rate next year. Since we can observe directly from the T-bond yield curve the current required yields on one- and two-year Treasuries, we can directly infer the market's expectation of the one-year T-bond rate next period or the one-year forward rate, f_1:

$$1 + f_1 = \frac{(1 + i_2)^2}{(1 + i_1)} \qquad \textbf{(2)}$$

We can use the same type of analysis with the corporate bond yield curve to infer the one-year forward rate on corporate bonds (grade B in this example). The one-year rate expected on corporate securities (c_1) one year into the future reflects the market's default risk expectations for this class of borrower as well as the more general time value factors also affecting f_1:

$$1 + c_1 = \frac{(1 + k_2)^2}{(1 + k_1)} \qquad \textbf{(3)}$$

The expected rates on one-year bonds can generate an estimate of the expected probability of repayment on one-year corporate bonds in one year's time, or what we have called p_2. Since:

$$p_2 (1 + c_1) = 1 + f_1$$

then:

$$p_2 = \left[\frac{1 + f_1}{1 + c_1} \right] \qquad \textbf{(4)}$$

Thus, the expected probability of default in year 2 is:

$$1 - p_2 \qquad \textbf{(5)}$$

In a similar fashion, the one-year rates expected in two years' time can be derived from the Treasury and corporate term structures so as to derive p_3, and so on.

EXAMPLE 11–6

Calculating the Probability of Default on a Multiperiod Bond Using Term Structure Derivation of Credit Risk

From the T-bond yield curve in Figure 11–7, the current required yields on one- and two-year Treasuries are $i_1 = 10$ percent and $i_2 = 11$ percent, respectively. If we use equation (2), the one-year forward rate, f_1, is:

$$1 + f_1 = \frac{(1.11)^2}{(1.10)} = 1.12$$

or

$$f_1 = 12\%$$

The expected rise in one-year rates from 10 percent (i_1) this year to 12 percent (f_1) next year reflects investors' perceptions regarding inflation and other factors that directly affect the time value of money.

Further, the current yield curve, in Figure 11–7, indicates that appropriate one-year discount bonds are yielding $k_1 = 15.8$ percent and two-year bonds are yielding $k_2 = 18$ percent. Thus, if we use equation (3), the one-year rate expected on corporate securities, c_1, is:

$$1 + c_1 = \frac{(1.18)^2}{(1.158)} = 1.202$$

or

$$c_1 = 20.2\%$$

We summarize these calculations in Table 11–9. As you can see, the expected spread between one-year corporate bonds and Treasuries in one year's time is higher than the spread for current one-year bonds. Thus, the default risk premium increases with the maturity on the corporate (risky) bond.

From these expected rates on one-year bonds, if we use equations (4) and (5), the expected probability of repayment on one-year corporate bonds in one year's time, p_2, is:

$$p_2 = \frac{[1.12]}{[1.202]} = .9318$$

and the expected probability of default in year 2 is:

$$1 - p_2 = 1 - .9318 = .0682$$

or

$$6.82\%$$

The probabilities we have estimated are marginal probabilities conditional on default not occurring in a prior period. We also discussed the concept of the *cumulative probability* of default that would tell the FI the probability of a loan or bond investment defaulting over a particular time period. In the example developed earlier, the cumulative probability that corporate grade-B bonds would default over the next two years is:

$$Cp = 1 - [(p_1)(p_2)]$$

$$Cp = 1 - [(.95)(.9318)] = 11.479\%$$

As with the credit scoring approach, this model creates some potential problems. Its principal advantages are that it is clearly forward-looking and based on market expectations. Moreover, if there are liquid markets for Treasury and corporate discount bonds—such as Treasury strips and corporate zero-coupon bonds—then we can easily estimate expected future default rates and use them to value and price loans. However, while the market for Treasury strips is now quite deep, the market for corporate discount bonds is quite small. Although a discount yield curve for corporate bonds could be extracted mathematically from the corporate bond coupon yield curve (see Chapter 26), these bonds often are not very actively traded and prices are not very transparent. Given this, the FI manager might have to consider an alternative way to use bond or loan data to extract default rate probabilities for all but the very largest corporate borrowers. We consider a possible alternative next.[50]

Concept Questions

1. What is the difference between the marginal default probability and the cumulative default probability?
2. How should the posting of collateral by a borrower affect the risk premium on a loan?

[50] For a discussion of and empirical evidence on the lack of price transparency in the U.S. corporate bond markets, see A. Saunders, A. Srinivasan, and I. Walter, "Price Formation in the OTC Corporate Bond Markets: A Field Study of the Inter-Dealer Market," *Journal of Economics and Business,* January–February 2002, pp. 95–113.

TABLE 11–9
Treasury and
Corporate Rates
and Rate Spreads

	Current One-Year Rate	Expected One-Year Rate
Treasury	10.0%	12.0%
Corporate (B)	15.8	20.2
Spread	5.8	8.2

FIGURE 11–8
Hypothetical
Marginal Mortality
Rate Curve for
Grade B Corporate
Bonds

Source: Excerpted, with permission, from *Default Risk,
Mortality Rates, and the Performance of Corporate Bonds,*
1989. Copyright 1989. Association for Investment Management and Research,
Charlottesville, VA. All
rights reserved.

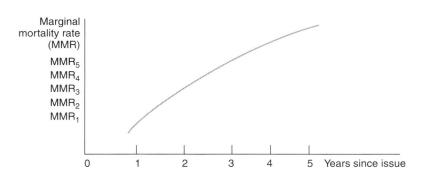

Mortality Rate Derivation of Credit Risk

mortality rate
Historic default rate
experience of a bond
or loan.

**marginal mortality
rate**
The probability of a
bond or loan default-
ing in any given year
after issue.

Rather than extracting *expected* default rates from the current term structure of interest rates, the FI manager may analyze the *historic* or past default risk experience,
the **mortality rates,** of bonds and loans of a similar quality. Consider calculating
p_1 and p_2 using the mortality rate model.[51] Here p_1 is the probability of a grade B
bond or loan surviving the first year of its issue; thus $1 - p_1$ is the **marginal mortality rate,** or the probability of the bond or loan defaulting in the first year of issue. While p_2 is the probability of the loan surviving in the second year given that
default has not occurred during the first year, $1 - p_2$ is the marginal mortality rate
for the second year. Thus, for each grade of corporate borrower quality, a marginal
mortality rate (MMR) curve can show the historical default rate experience of
bonds in any specific quality class in each year after issue on the bond or loan.

Note in Figure 11–8 that as grade B bonds age, their probability of dying increases
in each successive year. Of course, in reality, any shape to the mortality curve is possible. It is possible that MMRs can be flat, decline over time, or show a more complex
functional form. These marginal mortality rates can be estimated from actual data on
bond and loan defaults. Specifically, for grade B quality bonds (loans):

$$MMR_1 = \frac{\text{Total value of grade B bonds defaulting in year 1 of issue}}{\text{Total value of grade B bonds outstanding in year 1 of issue}}$$

$$MMR_2 = \frac{\text{Total value of grade B bonds defaulting in year 2 of issue}}{\begin{array}{c}\text{Total value of grade B bonds outstanding in year 2 of issue}\\\text{adjusted for defaults, calls, sinking fund redemptions, and}\\\text{maturities in the prior year}\end{array}}$$

[51] For further reading, see E. I. Altman, "Measuring Corporate Bond Mortality," *Journal of Finance,*
September1989, pp. 909–22; Altman and Bana, "Defaults and Returns on High-Yield Bonds"; and
Saunders and Allen, *Credit Risk Measurement,* chap. 8.

TABLE 11–10   Mortality Rates by Original Rating—All Rated* Corporate Bonds, 1971–2002

		Years after Issuance									
		1	2	3	4	5	6	7	8	9	10
AAA	Marginal	0.00%	0.00%	0.00%	0.00%	0.03%	0.00%	0.00%	0.00%	0.00%	0.00%
	Cumulative	0.00	0.00	0.00	0.00	0.03	0.03	0.03	0.03	0.03	0.03
AA	Marginal	0.00	0.00	0.33	0.17	0.00	0.00	0.00	0.00	0.03	0.02
	Cumulative	0.00	0.00	0.33	0.50	0.50	0.50	0.50	0.50	0.53	0.55
A	Marginal	0.01	0.10	0.02	0.09	0.04	0.10	0.05	0.20	0.11	0.06
	Cumulative	0.01	0.11	0.13	0.22	0.26	0.36	0.41	0.61	0.72	0.78
BBB	Marginal	0.25	3.42	1.52	1.44	0.92	0.57	0.80	0.26	0.17	0.35
	Cumulative	0.25	3.66	5.13	6.49	7.35	7.88	8.62	8.85	9.01	9.33
BB	Marginal	1.23	2.62	4.53	2.15	2.49	1.14	1.67	0.67	1.76	3.78
	Cumulative	1.23	3.82	8.17	10.15	12.39	13.39	14.83	15.40	16.89	20.03
B	Marginal	3.19	7.14	7.85	8.74	6.22	4.28	3.88	2.39	2.07	0.87
	Cumulative	3.19	10.10	17.16	24.40	29.10	32.14	34.77	36.33	37.65	38.19
CCC	Marginal	6.70	14.57	16.16	11.28	3.36	10.26	5.35	3.25	0.00	4.18
	Cumulative	6.70	20.29	33.17	40.71	42.70	48.58	51.33	52.92	52.92	54.88

*Rated by S&P at issuance.

Source: E. I. Altman and G. Bana, "Defaults and Returns on High-Yield Bonds: The Year 2002 in Review and the Market Outlook," Working Paper, New York University Salomon Center, February 2003.

Table 11–10 shows the estimated mortality and cumulative default rates for samples of 1,513 rated corporate bonds over the 1971–2002 period. From Table 11–10 it can be seen that mortality rates are higher the lower the rating of the bond.

The mortality rate approach has a number of conceptual and applicability problems. Probably the most important of these is that, like the credit scoring model, it produces historic, or backward-looking, measures. Also, the estimates of default rates and therefore implied future default probabilities tend to be highly sensitive to the period over which the FI manager calculates the MMRs. For example, WorldCom had an S&P rating of BBB just prior to its defaulting on its debt in 2002. Note in Table 11–10 the second year's marginal mortality rate for BBB Cords (3.42%) is much higher than those of years 3 and 4 and is even higher than that of the second year mortality rate for BB bonds. This is primarily due to the default of WorldCom in 2002. In addition, the estimates tend to be sensitive to the number of issues and the relative size of issues in each investment grade.[52]

Concept Questions

1. In Table 11–10, the CMR over 3 years for CCC rated corporate bonds is 33.17 percent. Check this calculation using the individual year MMRs.
2. Why would any FI manager buy loans that have a CMR of 33.17 percent? Explain your answer.

RAROC Models

An increasingly popular model used to evaluate (and price) credit risk based on market data is the RAROC model. The **RAROC** (risk-adjusted return on capital) was pioneered by Bankers Trust (acquired by Deutsche Bank in 1998) and has now

RAROC
Risk-adjusted return on capital.

[52] For example, even though the estimates in Table 11–10 are based on 1,513 observations of bonds, these estimates still have quite wide confidence bands. See P. H. McAllister and J. J. Mingo, "Commercial Loan Risk Management, Credit Scoring and Pricing: The Need for a New Shared Data Base," *Journal of Commercial Lending*, May 1994, pp. 6–20; and Saunders and Allen, *Credit Risk Measurement*, chap. 8.

been adopted by virtually all the large banks in the United States and Europe, although with some significant proprietary differences between them.

The essential idea behind RAROC is that rather than evaluating the actual or contractually promised annual ROA on a loan, as on p. 299 (that is, net interest and fees divided by the amount lent), the lending officer balances expected interest and fee income less the cost of funds against the loan's expected risk. Thus, the numerator of the RAROC equation is net income (accounting for the cost of funding the loan) on the loan. Further, rather than dividing annual loan income by assets lent, it is divided by some measure of asset (loan) risk or what is often called capital at risk, since (unexpected) loan losses have to be written off against an FI's capital:[53]

$$RAROC = \frac{\text{One year net income on a loan}}{\text{Loan (asset) risk or capital at risk}}$$

A loan is approved only if RAROC is sufficiently high relative to a benchmark return on capital (ROE) for the FI, where ROE measures the return stockholders require on their equity investment in the FI. The idea here is that a loan should be made only if the risk-adjusted return on the loan adds to the FI's equity value as measured by the ROE required by the FI's stockholders. Thus, for example, if an FI's ROE is 15 percent, a loan should be made only if the estimated RAROC is higher than the 15 percent required by the FI's stockholders as a reward for their investment in the FI. Alternatively, if the RAROC on an existing loan falls below an FI's RAROC benchmark, the lending officer should seek to adjust the loan's terms to make it "profitable" again. Therefore, RAROC serves as both a credit risk measure and a loan pricing tool for the FI manager.

One problem in estimating RAROC is the measurement of loan risk (the denominator in the RAROC equation). Chapter 9 on duration showed that the percentage change in the market value of an asset such as a loan ($\Delta LN/LN$) is related to the duration of the loan and the size of the interest rate shock ($\Delta R/(1 + R)$), where R is the base rate, BR, plus the credit risk premium, m:

$$\frac{\Delta LN}{LN} = -D_{LN}\frac{\Delta R}{1 + R}$$

The same concept is applied here, except that (assuming that the base rate remains constant) interest rate shocks are the consequence of credit quality (or credit risk premium) shocks (i.e., shocks to m). We can thus rewrite the duration equation with the following interpretation to estimate the loan risk or capital at risk on the loan:

ΔLN	$=$	$-D_{LN}$	$\times$	LN	$\times$	$(\Delta R/(1 + R))$
(dollar capital risk exposure or loss amount)		(duration of the loan)		(risk amount or size of loan)		(expected maximum change in the loan rate due to a change in the credit premium (m) or risk factor on the loan)

While the loan's duration (say, 2.7 years) and the loan amount (say, $1 million) are easily estimated, it is more difficult to estimate the maximum change in the credit risk premium on the loan over the next year. Since publicly available data on

---

[53] Traditionally, expected loan losses are covered by a bank's loss reserve (or provisions), while unexpected or extreme loan losses are being met by a bank's capital reserves.

loan risk premiums are scarce, we turn to publicly available corporate bond market data to estimate premiums. First, an S&P credit rating (AAA, AA, A, and so on) is assigned to a borrower. Thereafter, the available risk premium changes of all the bonds traded in that particular rating class over the last year are analyzed. The ΔR in the RAROC equation equals:

$$\Delta R = \text{Max} [\Delta (R_i - R_G) > 0]$$

where $\Delta (R_i - R_G)$ is the change in the yield spread between corporate bonds of credit rating class i (R_i) and matched duration treasury bonds (R_G) over the last year. In order to consider only the worst-case scenario, a maximum change in yield spread is chosen, as opposed to the average change. In general, it is common to pick the 1 percent worst case or 99th percentile of credit risk changes.

EXAMPLE 11–7

Calculation of RAROC on a Loan

Suppose we want to evaluate the credit risk of a loan to a AAA borrower. Assume there are currently 400 publicly traded bonds in that class (i.e., bonds issued by firms of a rating type similar to that of the borrower). The first step is to evaluate the actual changes in the credit risk premiums ($R_i - R_G$) on each of these bonds for the past year (in this example, the year 2006). These (hypothetical) changes are plotted in the frequency curve of Figure 11–9. They range from a fall in the risk premiums of negative 2 percent to an increase of 3.5 percent. Since the largest increase may be a very extreme (unrepresentative) number, the 99 percent worst-case scenario is chosen (i.e., only 4 bonds out of 400 had risk premium increases exceeding the 99 percent worst case). For the example shown in Figure 11–9 this is equal to 1.1 percent.

The estimate of loan (or capital) risk, assuming that the current average level of rates (R) on AAA bonds is 10 percent, is:

$$\Delta LN = -D_{LN} \times LN \times \frac{\Delta R}{1 + R}$$
$$= -(2.7)(\$1 \text{ million})\left(\frac{.011}{1.1}\right)$$
$$= -\$27,000.$$

Thus, while the face value of the loan amount is $1 million, the risk amount, or change in the loan's market value due to a decline in its credit quality, is $27,000.

To determine whether the loan is worth making, the estimated loan risk is compared with the loan's income (spread over the FI's cost of funds plus fees on the loan). Suppose the projected (one-year) spread plus fees is as follows:

$$\text{Spread} = 0.2\% \times \$1 \text{ million} = \$2,000$$
$$\text{Fees} = 0.1\% \times \$1 \text{ million} = \underline{\$1,000}$$
$$\overline{\$3,000}$$

The loan's RAROC is:

$$RAROC = \frac{\text{One-year net income on loan}}{\text{Loan risk (or capital risk)}(\Delta LN)} = \frac{\$3,000}{\$27,000} = 11.1\%$$

Note that RAROC can be either forward looking, comparing the projected income over the next year on the loan with ΔLN, or backward looking, comparing the actual income generated on the loan over the past year with ΔLN.

If the 11.1 percent exceeds the FI's internal RAROC benchmark (based on its cost of capital, or ROE), the loan will be approved. If it is less, the loan will be rejected outright or the borrower will be asked to pay higher fees and/or a higher spread to increase the RAROC to acceptable levels.

FIGURE 11–9
Hypothetical
Frequency
Distribution of
Yield Spread
Changes for All
AAA Bonds in 2006

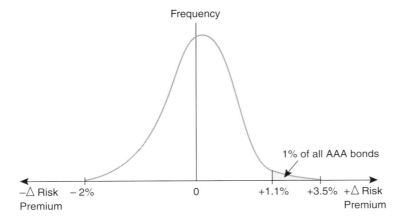

Other FIs have adopted different ways of calculating ΔLN in their versions of RAROC. Some FIs, usually the largest ones with very good loan default databases, divide one-year income by the product of an unexpected loss rate and the proportion of the loan lost on default, also called the loss given default. Thus:

$$RAROC =$$

$$\frac{\text{One-year net income per dollar loaned}}{\text{Unexpected default rate} \times \text{Proportion of loan lost on default (loss given default)}}$$

Suppose expected income per dollar lent is 0.3 cents, or .003. The 99th percentile historic (extreme case) default rate for borrowers of this type is 4 percent, and the dollar proportion of loans of this type that cannot be recaptured is 80 percent. Then:[54]

$$RAROC = \frac{.003}{(.04)(.8)} = \frac{.003}{(.032)} = 9.375\%$$

Concept Question

1. Describe the basic concept behind RAROC models.

Option Models of Default Risk[55]

Theoretical Framework

In recent years, following the pioneering work of Nobel prize winners Merton, Black, and Scholes, we now recognize that when a firm raises funds by issuing bonds or increasing its bank loans, it holds a very valuable default or repayment

[54] Calculating the unexpected default rate commonly involves calculating the standard derivation (σ) of annual default rates on loans of this type and then multiplying σ by a factor such that 99 percent (or higher) of defaults are covered by capital. For example, if the loss distribution was normally distributed, then the σ of default rates would be multiplied by 2.33 to get the extreme 99 percent default rate. For many FIs, default rates are skewed to the right and have fat tails suggesting a multiplier much larger than 2.33. For example, to get coverage of 99.97 percent of defaults, Bank of America has historically used a multiplier of 6. Finally, the denominator can also be adjusted for the degree of correlation of the loan with the rest of the FI's portfolio. See, for example, Edward Zaik et al., "RAROC at Bank of America: From Theory to Practice," *Journal of Applied Corporate Finance*, Summer 1996, pp. 83–93.

[55] This section, which contains more technical details, may be included in or dropped from the chapter reading depending on the rigor of the course. Students unfamiliar with the basics of options may want to review the section "Basic Features of Options" in Chapter 25 of the text.

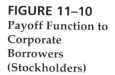

FIGURE 11–10
Payoff Function to Corporate Borrowers (Stockholders)

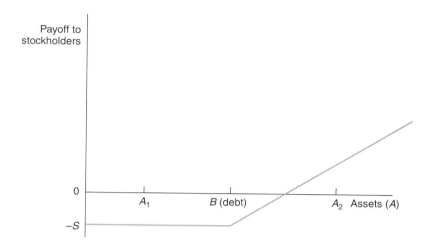

option.[56] That is, if a borrower's investment projects fail so that it cannot repay the bondholder or the bank, it has the option of defaulting on its debt repayment and turning any remaining assets over to the debtholder. Because of limited liability for equity holders, the borrower's loss is limited on the downside by the amount of equity invested in the firm.[57] On the other hand, if things go well, the borrower can keep most of the upside returns on asset investments after the promised principal and interest on the debt have been paid. The KMV Corporation (which was purchased by Moody's in 2002) turned this relatively simple idea into a credit monitoring model. Many of the largest U.S. FIs are now using this model to determine the expected default risk frequency (EDF) of large corporations.[58] Before we look at the KMV credit monitor model, we will take a closer look at the theory underlying the option approach to default risk estimation.

The Borrower's Payoff from Loans

Look at the payoff function for the borrower in Figure 11–10, where S is the size of the initial equity investment in the firm, B is the value of outstanding bonds or loans (assumed for simplicity to be issued on a discount basis), and A is the market value of the assets of the firm.

If the investments in Figure 11–10 turn out badly such that the firm's assets are valued at point A_1, the limited-liability stockholder–owners of the firm will default on the firm's debt, turn its assets (such as A_1) over to the debt holders, and lose only their initial stake in the firm (S). By contrast, if the firm does well and the assets of the firm are valued highly (A_2), the firm's stockholders will pay off the firm's debt and keep the difference ($A_2 - B$). Clearly, the higher A_2 is relative to B, the better off are the firm's stockholders. Given that borrowers face only a limited downside risk of loss of their equity investment but a very large

[56] R. C. Merton, "On the Pricing of Corporate Debt: The Risk Structure of Interest Rates," *Journal of Finance* 29 (1974), pp. 449–70; and F. Black and M. Scholes, "The Pricing of Options and Corporate Liabilities," *Journal of Political Economy* 81 (1973), pp. 637–59.

[57] Given limits to losses in personal bankruptcy, a similar analysis can be applied to retail and consumer loans.

[58] See KMV Corporation Credit Monitor, KMV Corporation, San Francisco, 1994; S. P. Choudhury, "Choosing the Right Box of Credit Tricks," *Risk Magazine,* November 1997 pp. 61–62; and Saunders and Allen, *Credit Risk Measurement,* chap. 4.

FIGURE 11–11
Payoff Function to
the Debt Holder
(the FI) from a Loan

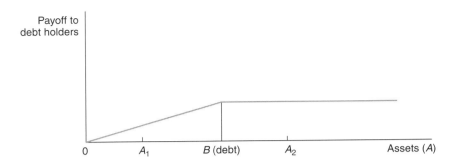

potential upside return if things turn out well, equity is analogous to buying a call option on the assets of the firm (see also Chapter 25 on options).

The Debt Holder's Payoff from Loans

Consider the same loan or bond issue from the perspective of the FI or bondholder. The maximum amount the FI or bondholder can get back is B, the promised payment. However, the borrower who possesses the default or repayment option would rationally repay the loan only if $A > B$, that is, if the market value of assets exceeds the value of promised debt repayments. A borrower whose asset value falls below B would default and turn over any remaining assets to the debt holders. The payoff function to the debt holder is shown in Figure 11–11.

After investment of the borrowed funds has taken place, if the value of the firm's assets lies to the right of B, the face value of the debt—such as A_2—the debt holder or FI will be paid off in full and receive B. On the other hand, if asset values fall in the region to the left of B—such as A_1—the debt holder will receive back only those assets remaining as collateral, thereby losing $B - A_1$. Thus, the value of the loan from the perspective of the lender is always the minimum of B or A, or min $[B,A]$. That is, the payoff function to the debt holder is similar to writing a put option on the value of the borrower's assets with B, the face value of debt, as the *exercise price*. If $A > B$, the loan is repaid and the debt holder earns a small fixed return (similar to the premium on a put option), which is the interest rate implicit in the discount bond. If $A < B$, the borrower defaults and the debt holder stands to lose both interest and principal. In the limit, default for a firm with no assets left results in debt holders' losing all their principal and interest. In actuality, if there are also costs of bankruptcy, the debt holder can potentially lose even more than this.

Applying the Option Valuation Model to the Calculation of Default Risk Premiums

Merton has shown that in the context of the preceding options framework, it is quite straightforward to express the market value of a risky loan made by a lender to a borrower as:[59]

$$F(\tau) = Be^{-i\tau} [(1/d)N(h_1) + N(h_2)] \qquad \textbf{(6)}$$

where

τ = Length of time remaining to loan maturity; that is, $\tau = T - t$, where T is the maturity date and time t is today.

d = Borrower's leverage ratio measured as $Be^{-i\tau}/A$, where the market value of debt is valued at the rate i, the risk-free rate of interest.

[59] See Merton, "On the Pricing of Corporate Debt."

$N(h)$ = Value computed from the standardized normal distribution statistical tables. This value reflects the probability that a deviation exceeding the calculated value of h will occur.

$$h_1 = -[1/2\sigma^2\tau - ln(d)]/\sigma\sqrt{\tau}$$
$$h_2 = -[1/2\sigma^2\tau + ln(d)]/\sigma\sqrt{\tau}$$

σ^2 = Measures the asset risk of the borrower. Technically, it is the variance of the rate of change in the value of the underlying assets of the borrower.

More important, written in terms of a yield spread, this equation reflects an equilibrium default risk premium that the borrower should be charged:

$$k(\tau) - i = (-1/\tau)ln[N(h_2) + (1/d)N(h_1)]$$

where

$k(\tau)$ = Required yield on risky debt (the contractually promised return from earlier)

ln = Natural logarithm

i = Risk-free rate on debt of equivalent maturity (here, one period)

Thus, Merton has shown that the lender should adjust the required risk premium as d and σ^2 change, that is, as leverage and asset risk change.

EXAMPLE 11–8

Calculating the Value of and Interest Rate on a Loan Using the Option Model[60]

Suppose that:

B = $100,000
τ = 1 year
i = 5 percent
d = 90% or .9
σ = 12%

That is, suppose we can measure the market value of a firm's assets (and thus $d = Be^{-i\tau}/A$) as well as the volatility of those assets (σ). Then, substituting these values into the equations for h_1 and h_2 and solving for the areas under the standardized normal distribution, we find that:

$$N(h_1) = .174120$$

$$N(h_2) = .793323$$

where

$$h_1 = \frac{-[\frac{1}{2}(.12)^2 - ln(.9)]}{.12} = -.938$$

and

$$h_2 = \frac{-[\frac{1}{2}(.12)^2 - ln(.9)]}{.12} = +.818$$

The current market value of the loan is:

$$L(t) = Be^{-i\tau}[N(h_2) + (1/d)N(h_1)]$$
$$= \frac{\$100,000}{1.05127}[.793323 + (1.1111)(.17412)]$$

(continued)

---

[60] This numerical example is based on D. F. Babbel, "Insuring Banks against Systematic Credit Risk," *Journal of Futures Markets* 9 (1989), pp. 487–506.

$$= \frac{\$100,000}{1.05127}[.986788]$$

$$= \$93,866.18$$

and the required risk spread or premium is:

$$k(\tau) - i = \left(\frac{-1}{\tau}\right) ln[N(h_2) + (1/d)N(h_1)]$$

$$= (-1)ln[.986788]$$

$$= 1.33\%$$

Thus, the risky loan rate $k(\tau)$ should be set at 6.33 percent when the risk-free rate (i) is 5 percent.

Theoretically, this model is an elegant tool for extracting premiums and default probabilities; it also has important conceptual implications regarding which variables to focus on in credit risk evaluation [e.g., the firm's market value of assets (A) and asset risk (σ^2)]. Even so, this model has a number of real-world implementation problems. Probably the most significant is the fact that neither the market value of a firm's assets (A) nor the volatility of the firm's assets (σ^2) is directly observed.

The KMV model in fact recognizes this problem by using an option pricing model (OPM) approach to extract the implied market value of assets (A) and the asset volatility of a given firm's assets (σ^2).[61] The KMV model uses the value of equity in a firm (from a stockholder's perspective) as equivalent to holding a call option on the assets of the firm (with the amount of debt borrowed acting similarly to the exercise price of the call option). From this approach, and the link between the volatility of the market value of the firm's equity and that of its assets, it is possible to derive the asset volatility (risk) of any given firm (σ) and the market value of the firm's assets (A).[62] Using the implied value of σ for assets and A, the market value of assets, the likely distribution of possible asset values of the firm relative to its current debt obligations can be calculated over the next year.[63] As shown in Figure 11–12,

www.moodyskmv.com

---

[61] See S. Kealhofer, "Quantifying Credit Risk I: Default Prediction," *Financial Analysts Journal,* January/February 2003, pp. 30–44.

[62] More specifically, it does this by using the equity (stock market) value of the firm's shares (E) and the volatility of the value of the firm's shares (σ_E). Since equity can be viewed as a call option on the firm's assets and the volatility of a firm's equity value will reflect the leverage adjusted volatility of its underlying assets, we have in general form:

$$\bar{E} = f(A, \sigma, \bar{B}, \bar{r}, \bar{\tau})$$

and

$$\bar{\sigma}_E = g(\sigma)$$

where the bars denote values that are directly measurable. Since we have two equations and two unknowns (A, σ), we can directly solve for both A and σ and use these, along with the firm's outstanding short-term liabilities or current liabilities, to calculate the EDF (expected default frequency).

[63] Suppose the value of the firm's assets (A) at the time zero is $100 million and the value of its short-term debt is $80 million. Suppose that the implied volatility (σ) of asset values was estimated at $12.12 million, and it is assumed that asset-value changes are normally distributed. The firm becomes distressed only if the value of its assets falls to $80 million or below (falls by $20 million). Such a fall is equal to 1.65σ, i.e., $1.65 \times \$12.12$ million = $20 million. From statistics, we know that the area of the normal distribution (in each tail) lying ± 1.65 σ from the mean is theoretically 5 percent. Thus, the KMV model would suggest a theoretical 5 percent probability of the firm's going into distress over the next year (by time 1). However, KMV calculates empirical EDFs, since we do not know the true distribution of asset values (A) over time. Essentially, it asks this question: In practice, how many firms that started the year with asset values 1.65 σ distance from default (see Figure 11–12) actually defaulted at the end of the year? This value may or may not equal 5 percent.

FIGURE 11–12
Expected Default Frequency Using the KMV Model

Source: KMV Corporation Credit Monitor. Reprinted by permission of KMV Corporation. *www.moodyskmv.com*

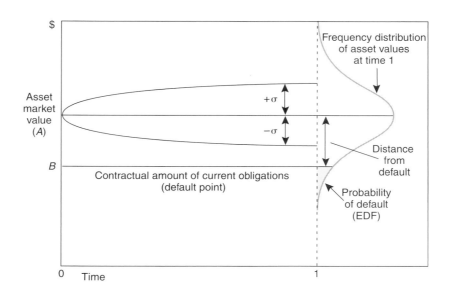

the expected default frequency (EDF) that is calculated reflects the probability that the market value of the firm's assets (*A*) will fall below the promised repayments on its short-term debt liabilities (*B*) in one year. If the value of a firm's assets falls below its debt liabilities, it can be viewed as being economically insolvent. Simulations by KMV have shown that EDF models outperform both Z score–type models and S&P rating changes as predictors of corporate failure and distress.[64] An example for Enron Corp., which filed for Chapter 11 bankruptcy protection on June 25, 2001, is shown in Figure 11–13. Note that the KMV score (expected default frequency) is rising faster than the rating agencies are downgrading the firm's debt. Indeed, the rating agency ratings are very slow to react to, if not totally insensitive to, the increase in Enron's risk. The KMV EDF score starts to rise over a year prior to Enron's bankruptcy. Thus, the KMV EDF score gives a better early warning of impending default.[65]

Concept Questions

1. Which is the only credit risk model discussed in this section that is really forward looking?
2. How should the risk premium on a loan be affected if there is a reduction in a borrower's leverage and the underlying volatility of its earnings?
3. What is the link between the implied volatility of a firm's assets and its expected default frequency?

Summary

This chapter discussed different approaches to measuring credit or default risk on individual loans (bonds). The different types of loans made by FIs and some of their basic characteristics were first examined. The expected return on a loan was shown to depend on factors such as origination fees, compensating balances, interest rates, and maturity. The various models to assess default risk include both qualitative and quantitative models. The qualitative models usually contain both

[64] KMV provides monthly EDFs for over 6,000 U.S. companies and 20,000 companies worldwide.

[65] One reason is that the KMV score is extracted from stock market data that is highly sensitive to new information about a firm's future prospects. Indeed, the acquisition of KMV by Moody's allowed the rating agency to move closer to including market-based information in its rating process. See "Implications of the Acquisition of KMV for Moody's Ratings," Moody's Investors Service, March 2002.

FIGURE 11–13   **KMV and S&P Ratings for Enron Corp.**

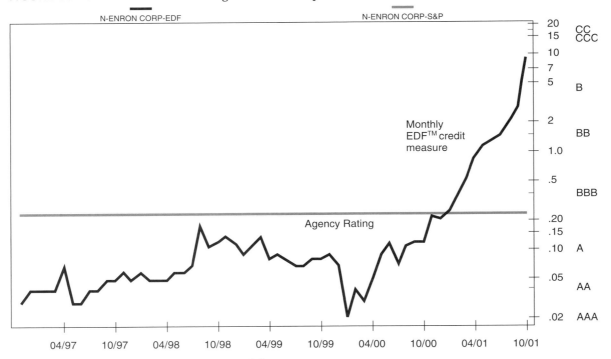

Source: KMV Corporation, San Francisco, California. *www.moodyskmv.com*

firm-specific factors, such as reputation and leverage, and market-specific factors, such as the business cycle and the level of interest rates. Quantitative models, such as the linear probability model, the logit model, and the linear discriminant model, were shown to provide credit scores that can rank or classify loans by expected default risk. The more rigorous of the quantitative models make use of both financial theory and financial data. These include the term structure and mortality rate models as well as the RAROC (risk-adjusted return on capital) and option-based models. (Two additional models, CreditMetrics and Credit Risk+, are discussed in Appendixes 11A and 11B to this chapter.) In the next chapter we look at methods to evaluate the risk of loan portfolios, or loan concentration risk.

Questions and Problems

1. Why is credit risk analysis an important component of FI risk management? What recent activities by FIs have made the task of credit risk assessment more difficult for both FI managers and regulators?

2. Differentiate between a secured loan and an unsecured loan. Who bears most of the risk in a fixed-rate loan? Why would FI managers prefer to charge floating rates, especially for longer-maturity loans?

3. How does a spot loan differ from a loan commitment? What are the advantages and disadvantages of borrowing through a loan commitment?

4. Why is commercial lending declining in importance in the United States? What effect does this decline have on overall commercial lending activities?

5. What are the primary characteristics of residential mortgage loans? Why does the ratio of adjustable rate mortgages to fixed-rate mortgages in the economy vary over the interest rate cycle? When would the ratio be highest?

6. What are the two major classes of consumer loans at U.S. banks? How do revolving loans differ from nonrevolving loans?

7. How does the credit card transaction process assist in the credit monitoring function of financial institutions? Which major parties receive a fee in a typical credit card transaction? Do the services provided warrant the payment of these associated fees?

8. What are compensating balances? What is the relationship between the amount of compensating balance requirement and the return on the loan to the FI?

9. County Bank offers one-year loans with a stated rate of 9 percent but requires a compensating balance of 10 percent. What is the true cost of this loan to the borrower? How does the cost change if the compensating balance is 15 percent? If the compensating balance is 20 percent?

10. Metrobank offers one-year loans with a 9 percent stated or base rate, charges a 0.25 percent loan origination fee, imposes a 10 percent compensating balance requirement, and must pay a 6 percent reserve requirement to the Federal Reserve. The loans typically are repaid at maturity.

   a. If the risk premium for a given customer is 2.5 percent, what is the simple promised interest return on the loan?
   b. What is the contractually promised gross return on the loan per dollar lent?
   c. Which of the fee items has the greatest impact on the gross return?

11. Why are most retail borrowers charged the same rate of interest, implying the same risk premium or class? What is credit rationing? How is it used to control credit risks with respect to retail and wholesale loans?

12. Why could a lender's expected return be lower when the risk premium is increased on a loan? In addition to the risk premium, how can a lender increase the expected return on a wholesale loan? A retail loan?

13. What are covenants in a loan agreement? What are the objectives of covenants? How can these covenants be negative? Affirmative?

14. Identify and define the borrower-specific and market-specific factors that enter into the credit decision. What is the impact of each type of factor on the risk premium?

   a. Which of these factors is more likely to adversely affect small businesses rather than large businesses in the credit assessment process by lenders?
   b. How does the existence of a high debt ratio typically affect the risk of the borrower? Is it possible that high leverage may reduce the risk of bankruptcy (or the risk of financial distress)? Explain.
   c. Why is the volatility of the earnings stream of a borrower important to a lender?

15. Why is the degree of collateral as specified in the loan agreement of importance to the lender? If the book value of the collateral is greater than or equal to the amount of the loan, is the credit risk of the lender fully covered? Why or why not?

16. Why are FIs consistently interested in the expected level of economic activity in the markets in which they operate? Why is monetary policy of the Federal Reserve System important to FIs?

17. What are the purposes of credit scoring models? How could these models possibly assist an FI manager in better administering credit?

18. Suppose the estimated linear probability model is $PD = .3X_1 + .2X_2 - 0.5X_3 +$ error, where $X_1 = 0.75$ is the borrower's debt/equity ratio, $X_2 = 0.25$ is the volatility of borrower earnings, and $X_3 = 0.10$ is the borrower's profit ratio.

   a. What is the projected probability of default for the borrower?

   b. What is the projected probability of repayment if the debt–equity ratio is 2.5?

   c. What is a major weakness of the linear probability model?

19. Describe how a linear discriminant analysis model works. Identify and discuss the criticisms which have been made regarding the use of this type of model to make credit risk evaluations.

20. MNO, Inc., a publicly traded manufacturing firm in the United States, has provided the following financial information in its application for a loan.

Assets		Liabilities and Equity	
Cash	$ 20	Accounts payable	$ 30
Accounts receivable	90	Notes payable	90
Inventory	90	Accruals	30
		Long-term debt	150
Plant and equipment	500	Equity	400
Total assets	$700	Total liabilities and equity	$700

Also assume sales = $500, cost of goods sold = $360, taxes = $56, interest payments = $40, and net income = $44; the dividend payout ratio is 50 percent, and the market value of equity is equal to the book value.

   a. What is the Altman discriminant function value for MNO, Inc.? Recall that:
   Net working capital = Current assets minus current liabilities.
   Current assets = Cash + Accounts receivable + Inventories.
   Current liabilities = Accounts payable + Accruals + Notes payable.
   EBIT = Revenues − Cost of goods sold − Depreciation.
   Taxes = (EBIT − Interest) (Tax rate).
   Net income = EBIT − Interest − Taxes.
   Retained earnings = Net income (1 − Dividend payout ratio).

   b. Should you approve MNO, Inc.'s, application to your bank for a $500 capital expansion loan?

   c. If sales for MNO were $300, the market value of equity was only half of book value, and the cost of goods sold and interest were unchanged, what would be the net income for MNO? Assume the tax credit can be used to offset other tax liabilities incurred by other divisions of the firm. Would your credit decision change?

   d. Would the discriminant function change for firms in different industries? Would the function be different for retail lending in different geographic sections of the country? What are the implications for the use of these types of models by FIs?

21. Consider the coefficients of Altman's Z score. Can you tell by the size of the coefficients which ratio appears most important in assessing creditworthiness of a loan applicant? Explain.

22. If the rate on one-year T-bills currently is 6 percent, what is the repayment probability for each of the following two securities? Assume that if the loan is

defaulted, no payments are expected. What is the market-determined risk premium for the corresponding probability of default for each security?

    a. One-year AA-rated bond yielding 9.5 percent.

    b. One-year BB-rated bond yielding 13.5 percent.

23. A bank has made a loan charging a base lending rate of 10 percent. It expects a probability of default of 5 percent. If the loan is defaulted, the bank expects to recover 50 percent of its money through the sale of its collateral. What is the expected return on this loan?

24. Assume that a one-year T-Bill is currently yielding 5.5 percent and a AAA-rated discount bond with similar maturity is yielding 8.5 percent.

    a. If the expected recovery from collateral in the event of default is 50 percent of principal and interest, what is the probability of repayment of the AAA-rated bond? What is the probability of default?

    b. What is the probability of repayment of the AAA-rated bond if the expected recovery from collateral in the case of default is 94.47 percent of principal and interest? What is the probability of default?

    c. What is the relationship between the probability of default and the proportion of principal and interest that may be recovered in case of default on the loan?

25. What is meant by the phrase *marginal default probability?* How does this term differ from *cumulative default probability?* How are the two terms related?

26. Calculate the term structure of default probabilities over three years using the following spot rates from the Treasury and corporate bond (pure discount) yield curves. Be sure to calculate both the annual marginal and the cumulative default probabilities.

	Spot 1 year	Spot 2 year	Spot 3 year
Treasury bonds	5.0%	6.1%	7.0%
BBB-rated bonds	7.0	8.2	9.3

27. The bond equivalent yields for U.S. Treasury and A-rated corporate bonds with maturities of 93 and 175 days are given below:

	93 days	175 days
U.S. Treasury	8.07%	8.11%
A-rated corporate	8.42	8.66
Spread	0.35	0.55

    a. What are the implied forward rates for both an 82-day Treasury and an 82-day A-rated bond beginning in 93 days? Use daily compounding on a 365-day year basis.

    b. What is the implied probability of default on A-rated bonds over the next 93 days? Over 175 days?

    c. What is the implied default probability on an 82-day A-rated bond to be issued in 93 days?

28. What is the mortality rate of a bond or loan? What are some of the problems with using a mortality rate approach to determine the probability of default of a given bond issue?

29. The following is a schedule of historical defaults (yearly and cumulative) experienced by an FI manager on a portfolio of commercial and mortgage loans.

			Years after Issuance		
Loan Type	1 Year	2 Years	3 Years	4 Years	5 Years
Commercial:					
Annual default	0.00%	———	0.50%	———	0.30%
Cumulative default	———	0.10%	———	0.80%	———
Mortgage:					
Annual default	0.10%	0.25%	0.60%	———	0.80%
Cumulative default	———	———	———	1.64%	———

a. Complete the blank spaces in the table.
b. What are the probabilities that each type of loan will not be in default after five years?
c. What is the measured difference between the cumulative default (mortality) rates for commercial and mortgage loans after four years?

30. The table below shows the dollar amounts of outstanding bonds and corresponding default amounts for every year over the past five years. Note that the default figures are in millions, while those outstanding are in billions. The outstanding figures reflect default amounts and bond redemptions.

			Years after Issuance		
Loan Type	1 Year	2 Years	3 Years	4 Years	5 Years
A-rated: Annual default (millions)	0	0	0	$ 1	$ 2
Outstanding (billions)	$100	$95	$93	$91	$88
B-rated: Annual default (millions)	0	$ 1	$ 2	$ 3	$ 4
Outstanding (billions)	$100	$94	$92	$89	$85
C-rated: Annual default (millions)	$ 1	$ 3	$ 5	$ 5	$ 6
Outstanding (billions)	$100	$97	$90	$85	$79

What are the annual and cumulative default rates of the above bonds?

31. What is RAROC? How does this model use the concept of duration to measure the risk exposure of a loan? How is the expected change in the credit premium measured? What precisely is ΔLN in the RAROC equation?

32. A bank is planning to make a loan of $5,000,000 to a firm in the steel industry. It expects to charge a servicing fee of 50 basis points. The loan has a maturity of 8 years with a duration of 7.5 years. The cost of funds (the RAROC benchmark) for the bank is 10 percent. Assume the bank has estimated the maximum change in the risk premium on the steel manufacturing sector to be approximately 4.2 percent, based on two years of historical data. The current market interest rate for loans in this sector is 12 percent.

a. Using the RAROC model, determine whether the bank should make the loan.
b. What should be the duration in order for this loan to be approved?
c. Assuming that the duration cannot be changed, how much additional interest and fee income will be necessary to make the loan acceptable?
d. Given the proposed income stream and the negotiated duration, what adjustment in the loan rate would be necessary to make the loan acceptable?

33. A firm is issuing two-year debt in the amount of $200,000. The current market value of the assets is $300,000. The risk-free rate is 6 percent, and the standard deviation of the rate of change in the underlying assets of the borrower is 10 percent. Using an options framework, determine the following:

a. The current market value of the loan.

b. The risk premium to be charged on the loan.

34. A firm has assets of $200,000 and total debts of $175,000. With an option pricing model, the implied volatility of the firm's assets is estimated at $10,730. Under the KMV method, what is the expected default frequency (assuming a normal distribution for assets)?

35. Carman County Bank (CCB) has outstanding a $5,000,000 face value, adjustable rate loan to a company that has a leverage ratio of 80 percent. The current risk-free rate is 6 percent, and the time to maturity on the loan is exactly 1/2 year. The asset risk of the borrower, as measured by the standard deviation of the rate of change in the value of the underlying assets, is 12 percent. The normal density function values are given below.

h	N(h)	h	N(h)
−2.55	0.0054	2.50	0.9938
−2.60	0.0047	2.55	0.9946
−2.65	0.0040	2.60	0.9953
−2.70	0.0035	2.65	0.9960
−2.75	0.0030	2.70	0.9965

a. Use the Merton option valuation model to determine the market value of the loan.

b. What should be the interest rate for the last six months of the loan?

The questions and problems that follow refer to Appendixes 11A and 11B. Refer to the example information in Appendix 11A for problems 36 and 37.

36. From Table 11A–1, what is the probability of a loan upgrade? A loan downgrade?

a. What is the impact of a rating upgrade or downgrade?

b. How is the discount rate determined after a credit event has occurred?

c. Why does the probability distribution of possible loan values have a negative skew?

d. How do the capital requirements of the CreditMetrics approach differ from those of the BIS and the Federal Reserve System?

37. A five-year fixed-rate loan of $100 million carries a 7 percent annual interest rate. The borrower is rated BB. Based on hypothetical historical data, the probability distribution given below has been determined for various ratings upgrades, downgrades, status quo, and default possibilities over the next year. Information also is presented reflecting the forward rates of the current Treasury yield curve and the annual credit spreads of the various maturities of BBB bonds over Treasuries.

Rating	Probability Distribution	New Loan Value plus Coupon $	Forward Rate Spreads at Time t		
			t	$r_t\%$	$s_t\%$
AAA	0.01%	$114.82	1	3.00%	0.72%
AA	0.31	114.60	2	3.40	0.96
A	1.45	114.03	3	3.75	1.16
BBB	6.05		4	4.00	1.30
BB	85.48	108.55			
B	5.60	98.43			
CCC	0.90	86.82			
Default	0.20	54.12			

a. What is the present value of the loan at the end of the one-year risk horizon for the case where the borrower has been upgraded from BB to BBB?

b. What is the mean (expected) value of the loan at the end of year 1?

c. What is the volatility of the loan value at the end of year 1?

d. Calculate the 5 percent and 1 percent VARs for this loan assuming a normal distribution of values.

e. Estimate the approximate 5 percent and 1 percent VARs using the actual distribution of loan values and probabilities.

f. How do the capital requirements of the 1 percent VARs calculated in parts (d) and (e) above compare with the capital requirements of the BIS and the Federal Reserve System?

g. Go to the J. P. Morgan Chase Web site (**www.jpmorgan.com/RiskManagement/CreditMetric**). What data set information is provided for use with CreditMetrics?

38. How does the Credit Risk+ model of Credit Suisse Financial Products differ from the CreditMetrics model of J. P. Morgan Chase?

39. An FI has a loan portfolio of 10,000 loans of $10,000 each. The loans have a historical average default rate of 4 percent, and the severity of loss is 40 cents per dollar.

a. Over the next year, what are the probabilities of having default rates of 2, 3, 4, 5, and 8 percent?

b. What would be the dollar loss on the portfolios with default rates of 4 and 8 percent?

c. How much capital would need to be reserved to meet the 1 percent worst-case loss scenario? What proportion of the portfolio's value would this capital reserve be?

Web Questions

40. Go to the Federal Reserve Board's Web site at **www.federalreserve.gov** and update the data in Table 11–1 using the following steps. Click on "Economic Research and Data." Click on "Statistics: Releases and Historical Data." Click on "Assets and Liabilities of Commercial Banks in the United States, Releases." Click on the most recent date. This will bring the file onto your computer that contains the relevant data. How has the data changed since that reported in Table 11–1 for 2003?

41. Go to the Federal Housing Finance Board's Web site at **www.fhfb.gov** and find the most recent data on the percentage of conventional single-family mortgages with adjustable rates using the following steps. Click on "Monthly Interest Rate Summary." Click on "Periodic Summary Tables." Click on "Percentage of Conventional Single Family Mortgages Originated by Major Lenders with Adjustable Rates." This will bring the file onto your computer that contains the relevant data. How has this data changed since 2003?

42. Go to the Federal Reserve Board's Web site at **www.federalreserve.gov** and update Table 11–7 using the following steps. Click on "Economic Research and Data." Click on "Statistics: Releases and Historical Data." Click on "Consumer Credit, Releases." Click on the most recent date. This will bring the file onto

your computer that contains the relevant data. How have consumer loan rates changed since 2003 as reported in Table 11–7?

S&P Question

43. Go to the S&P Educational Version of Market Insight Web site at **www.mhhe. com/edumarketinsight** and find the most recent Balance Sheets for J. P. Morgan Chase (JPM), Bank of New York (BK), and Bank One Corp (ONE) using the following steps. Click on "Educational Version of Market Insight." Enter your Site ID and click on "Login." Click on "Company." Enter "JPM" in the "Ticker:" box and click on "Go!" Click on "Excel Analytics." Click on "FS Ann. Balance Sheet." This will download the Balance Sheet for J. P. Morgan Chase which contains the balances for Total Loans, Consumer Loans, Commercial Loans, Mortgage Loans, and Total Assets. Repeat the process by entering "BK" in the "Ticker:" box to get information on Bank of New York. Repeat the process by entering "ONE" in the "Ticker:" box to get information on Bank One Corp. Calculate the ratios of loans to total assets, real estate (mortgage) loans to total assets, commercial and industrial (business) loans to total assets, and consumer loans to total assets. How do these ratios differ for the three banks?

Pertinent Web Sites

American Banker	www.americanbanker.com
Board of Governors of the Federal Reserve	www.federalreserve.gov
Card Source One	www.cardsource.com
CreditMetrics	www.creditmetrics.com
Federal Deposit Insurance Corporation	www.fdic.gov
Federal Housing Finance Board	www.fhfb.gov
Federal Reserve Bank of St. Louis	www.stls.frb.org
KMV Corporation	www.moodyskmv.com
Moody's	www.moodys.com
Office of the Comptroller of the Currency	www.occ.treas.gov
Robert Morris Associates	www.rmahq.org
Standard & Poor's	www.standardandpoors.com

Chapter Notation

View Chapter Notation at the Web site for this textbook (**www.mhhe.com/ saunders5e**).

Appendix 11A[1]

CreditMetrics

CreditMetrics was introduced in 1997 by J. P. Morgan (www.creditmetrics.com) and its co-sponsors (Bank of America, Union Bank of Switzerland, et al.) as a value at risk (VAR) framework to apply to the valuation and risk of non-tradable assets such as loans and privately placed bonds.[2] Thus, while RiskMetrics seeks to answer the question, if tomorrow is a bad day, how much will I lose on tradable assets such as stocks, bonds, and equities? CreditMetrics asks, if next year is a bad year, how much will I lose on my loans and loan portfolio?[3]

With RiskMetrics (see Chapter 10) we answer this question by looking at the market value or price of an asset and the volatility of that asset's price or return in order to calculate a probability (e.g., 5 percent) that the value of that asset will fall below some given value tomorrow. In the case of RiskMetrics, this involves multiplying the estimated standard deviation of returns on that asset by 1.65 and then revaluing the current market value of the position (P) downward by 1.65σ. That is, VAR for one day (or DEAR) is:

$$VAR = P \times 1.65 \times \sigma$$

Unfortunately, since loans are not publicly traded, we observe neither P (the loan's market value) nor σ (the volatility of loan value over the horizon of interest—assumed to be one year for loans and bonds under CreditMetrics). However, using (1) available data on a borrower's credit rating, (2) the probability of that rating changing over the next year (the rating transition matrix),

(3) recovery rates on defaulted loans, and (4) yield spreads in the bond market, it is possible to calculate a hypothetical P and σ for any non-traded loan or bond and thus a VAR figure for individual loans and the loan portfolio.

Consider the example of a five-year, fixed-rate loan of $100 million made at 6 percent annual interest.[4] The borrower is rated BBB.

RATING MIGRATION

On the basis of historical data collected by S&P, Moody's, and other bond analysts, it is estimated that the probability of a BBB borrower's staying at BBB over the next year is 86.93 percent. There is also some probability that the borrower of the loan will be upgraded (e.g., to A), and there is some probability that it will be downgraded (e.g., to CCC) or even default. Indeed, there are eight possible transitions the borrower can make over the next year, seven of which involve upgrades, downgrades, and no rating changes and one which involves default. The estimated probabilities are shown in Table 11A–1.

TABLE 11A–1   One-Year Transition Probabilities for BBB-Rated Borrower

Rating	Transition Probability	
AAA	0.02%	
AA	0.33	
A	5.95	
BBB	86.93	← Most likely to stay
BB	5.30	in same class
B	1.17	
CCC	0.12	
Default	0.18	

VALUATION

The effect of rating upgrades and downgrades is to impact the required credit risk spreads or premiums on loans and thus the implied market

[1] This Appendix, which contains more technical topics, may be included in or dropped from the chapter reading depending on the rigor of the course.

[2] See CreditMetrics, *Technical Document*, New York, April 2, 1997; and Saunders and Allen, *Credit Risk Measurement*, chap. 6.

[3] In 2002, J. P. Morgan introduced a third measure of credit risk, CreditGrades. The CreditGrades model establishes a framework linking the credit and equity markets. The model employs approximations for the asset value, volatility, and drift, which are used to value credit as an exotic equity derivative. This model is similar in approach to the KMV model described in the chapter. See "CreditGrades: Technical Documents," RiskMetrics Group, Inc., May 2002.

[4] This example is based on the one used in the CreditMetrics, *Technical Document*, April 2, 1997.

value (or present value) of the loan. If a loan is downgraded, the required credit spread premium should rise (remember, the loan rate in our example is fixed at 6 percent) so that the present value of the loan to the FI should fall; the reverse is true for a credit rating upgrade.

Technically, since we are revaluing the five-year $100 million, 6 percent loan at the end of the first year after a credit event has occurred during that year, then (measured in millions of dollars):

$$P = 6 + \frac{6}{(1 + r_1 + s_1)} + \frac{6}{(1 + r_2 + s_2)^2} + \frac{6}{(1 + r_3 + s_3)^3} + \frac{106}{(1 + r_4 + s_4)^4}$$

where the r_i are the risk-free rates on T-bonds expected to exist one year, two years, and so on, into the future (i.e., they reflect forward rates from the current Treasury yield curve—see discussion in the main body of this chapter) and s_i are annual credit spreads for loans of a particular rating class of one year, two years, three years, and four years to maturity (the latter are derived from observed spreads in the corporate bond market over Treasuries). The first coupon or interest payment of $6 million in the above example is undiscounted and can be viewed as being similar to the accrued interest earned on a bond or a loan since we are revaluing the loan at the end (not the beginning) of the first year of its life.

Suppose the borrower gets upgraded during the first year from BBB to A. Then the present value or market value of the loan to the FI at the end of the one-year risk horizon (in millions of dollars) is:

$$P = 6 + \frac{6}{(1.0372)} + \frac{6}{(1.0432)^2} + \frac{6}{(1.0493)^3} + \frac{106}{(1.0532)^4}$$
$$= \$108.66$$

That is, at the end of the first year, if the loan borrower is upgraded from BBB to A, the $100 million (book value) loan has a market value to the FI of $108.66 million. (This is the value the FI would theoretically be able to obtain if it "sold" the loan, with the accrued first year coupon of 6, to another FI at the end of year 1 horizon at the fair market price or value.) Table 11A–2 shows the value of the loan if other credit events occur. Note that the loan has a maximum market value of

TABLE 11A–2 Value of the Loan at the End of One Year under Different Ratings

Year-End Rating	Loan Value ($) (including first-year coupon)
AAA	109.37
AA	109.19
A	108.66
BBB	107.55
BB	102.02
B	98.10
CCC	83.64
Default	51.13

FIGURE 11A–1 Distribution of Loan Values on a Five-Year BBB Loan at the End of Year 1

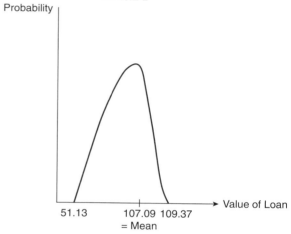

$109.37 (if the borrower is upgraded to AAA) and a minimum value of $51.13 if the borrower defaults. The minimum value is the estimated recovery value of the loan if the borrower declares bankruptcy.

The probability distribution of loan values is shown in Figure 11A–1. As can be seen, the value of the loan has a fixed upside and a long downside (i.e., a negative skew). It is clear that the value of the loan is not symmetrically (or normally) distributed. Thus CreditMetrics produces two VAR measures:

1. Based on the normal distribution of loan values.
2. Based on the actual distribution of loan values.

TABLE 11A–3   VAR Calculations for the BBB Loan

Year-End Rating	Probability of State, %	New Loan Value plus Coupon, $	Probability Weighted Value, $	Difference of Value from Mean, $	Probability Weighted Difference Squared
AAA	0.02%	$109.37	$ 0.02	$2.28	0.0010
AA	0.33	109.19	0.36	2.10	0.0146
A	5.95	108.66	6.47	1.57	0.1474
BBB	86.93	107.55	93.49	0.46	0.1853
BB	5.30	102.02	5.41	(5.06)	1.3592
B	1.17	98.10	1.15	(8.99)	0.9446
CCC	0.12	83.64	1.10	(23.45)	0.6598
Default	0.18	51.13	0.09	(55.96)	5.6358

Mean = $107.09

Variance = 8.94777
σ = Standard deviation = $2.99

Assuming Normal Distribution
$\begin{cases} \text{5\% VAR} = 1.65 \times \sigma = \$4.93 \\ \text{1\% VAR} = 2.33 \times \sigma = \$6.97 \end{cases}$

Assuming Actual Distribution*
$\begin{cases} \text{5\% VAR} = 95\% \text{ of actual distribution} = \$107.09 - \$102.02 = \$5.07 \\ \text{1\% VAR} = 99\% \text{ of actual distribution} = \$107.09 - \$98.10 = \$8.99 \end{cases}$

*5% VAR approximated by 6.77% VAR (i.e., 5.3% + 1.17% + 0.12% + 0.18%) and 1% VAR approximated by 1.47% VAR (i.e., 1.17% + 0.12% + 0.18%).

CALCULATION OF VAR

Table 11A–3 shows the calculation of the VAR based on each approach for both the 5 percent worst-case and the 1 percent worst-case scenarios.

The first step in calculating VAR is to calculate the mean of the loan's value, or its expected value, at year 1, which is the sum of each possible loan value at the end of year 1 times its transition probability. As can be seen, the mean value of the loan is $107.09 (also see Figure 11A–1). However, the FI is concerned about losses or volatility in value. In particular, if next year is a bad year, how much can it expect to lose? We could define a bad year as occurring once every 20 years (the 5 percent VAR) or once every 100 years (the 1 percent VAR)—this is similar to market risk VAR except that for credit risk the horizon is longer: 1 year rather than 1 day as under market risk DEAR.

Assuming that loan values are normally distributed, the variance of loan value around its mean is $8.9477 (squared) and its standard deviation or volatility is the square root of the variance equal to $2.99. Thus the 5 percent VAR for the loan is 1.65 × $2.99 = $4.93 million, while the 1 percent VAR is 2.33 × $2.99 = $6.97 million. However, this is likely to underestimate the actual or true VAR of the loan because, as shown in Figure 11A–1, the distribution of the loan's value

is clearly nonnormal. In particular, it demonstrates a negative skew or a long-tail downside risk. Using the actual distribution of loan values and probabilities, we can see from Table 11A–3 that there is a 6.77 percent probability that the loan value will fall below $102.02, implying an approximate 5 percent actual VAR of over $107.09 − $102.02 = $5.07 million, and that there is a 1.47 percent probability that the loan value will fall below $98.10, implying an approximate 1 percent actual VAR of over $107.09 − $98.10 = $8.99. These actual VARs could be made less approximate by using linear interpolation to get the exact 5 percent and 1 percent VAR measures. For example, since the 1.47 percentile equals 98.10 and the 0.3 percentile equals 83.64, then, using linear interpolation, the 1.00 percentile equals $92.29. This suggests an actual 1 percent VAR of $107.09 − $92.29 = $14.80.

CAPITAL REQUIREMENTS

It is interesting to compare these VAR figures with the capital reserves against loans currently required by the Federal Reserve and the BIS. While these requirements are explained in more detail in Chapter 20, they basically amount to a requirement that a bank (or thrift) hold an 8 percent ratio of the book value of the loan as a capital reserve against unexpected losses. In our example of a $100 million face (book) value BBB loan, the capital requirement would be $8 million. This contrasts to the two market-based VAR measures developed above. Using the 1 percent VAR based on the normal distribution, a capital requirement of $6.97 million would be required (i.e., less than the BIS requirement), while using the 1 percent VAR based on the iterated value from the actual distribution, a $14.80 million capital requirement would be required (which is much greater than the BIS capital requirement).

It should be noted that under the CreditMetrics approach, every loan is likely to have a different

VAR and thus a different implied capital requirement.[5] This contrasts to the current BIS regulations, where all private sector loans of different ratings (AAA through CCC) and different maturities are subject to the same 8 percent capital requirements.

---

[5] Although, as we discuss in Chapter 20, the 8 percent ratio and 100 percent risk weight for all commercial loans will be revised and fully implemented in 2006. Under the foundations and advanced approaches of BIS 2 (proposed), each loan will have an individual capital requirement.

Appendix 11B[1]

Credit Risk+

Credit Risk+ is a model developed by Credit Suisse Financial Products (CSFP).[2] Unlike CreditMetrics, which seeks to develop a full VAR framework, Credit Risk+ attempts to estimate the expected loss of loans and the distribution of those losses with a focus on calculating the FI's required capital reserves to meet losses above a certain level.

The key ideas come from the insurance literature (especially fire insurance), in which the losses incurred by an insurer reflect two things: (1) the probability of a house burning down (what an insurer calls the frequency of the event) and (2) the value of the house lost if it burns down (what the insurer calls severity of the loss). We can apply the same idea to loans, in which the loss distribution on a portfolio of loans reflects the combination (or product) of the frequency of loan defaults and their severity. This framework is shown in Figure 11B–1.

Unlike CreditMetrics, which assumes that there is a fixed probability of a loan defaulting in the next period (defined by its historic transition probability), it is assumed in its simplest form that (1) the probability of any individual loan defaulting in

the portfolio of loans is random and (2) the correlation between the defaults on any pair of loans is zero (i.e., individual loan default probabilities are independent). This framework is therefore most appropriate for analyzing the default risk on large portfolios of small loans (e.g., small business loans, mortgages, and consumer loans) rather than portfolios that contain a few large loans. The model's assumptions about the probability (frequency) of default are shown in Figure 11B–2.

When the probability of default on individual loans is small and this probability is independent

FIGURE 11B–1   **Credit Risk+ Model of the Determinants of Loan Losses**

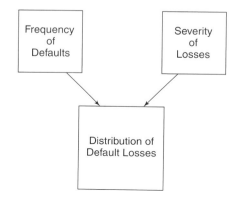

---

[1] This Appendix, which contains more technical topics, may be included in or dropped from the chapter reading depending on the rigor of the course.

[2] See Credit Suisse Financial Products, "Credit Risk+; Credit Risk Management Framework," October 1997, New York/London; and Saunders and Allen, *Credit Risk Measurement*, chap. 7.

FIGURE 11B–2
Frequency of
Default on a Loan
Assumed by Credit
Risk+

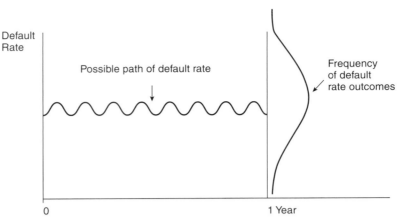

FIGURE 11B–3
Frequency
Distribution of
Default Rates from
Example

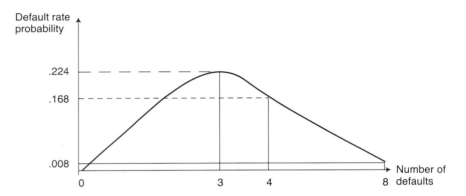

across loans in the portfolio, the frequency distribution of default rates can be modeled by a Poisson distribution. Below we look at an example.

Assume that:

1. The FI makes 100 loans of $100,000 each.
2. Historically, 3 percent (3 of 100) of loans have defaulted on average.
3. On default, the severity of loss on each of these loans is the same, at 20 cents per $1 (or $20,000 per $100,000 loan).

THE FREQUENCY DISTRIBUTION OF DEFAULT RATES

From the Poisson distribution, we can easily generate the probability of different numbers of defaults (in a 100-loan portfolio) occurring:

$$\text{Probability of } n \text{ defaults} = \frac{e^{-m}m^n}{n!}$$

Where e is exponential (2.71828), m is the historic average number of defaults (3 of 100, or 3 percent) for loans of this type, and $n!$ is n factorial, where n is the number of loans for which we are trying to determine the probability of default.

For example, the probability of 3 of 100 loans defaulting over the next year is:

$$\frac{(2.71828)^{-3} \times 3^3}{1 \times 2 \times 3} = .224$$

That is, there is a 22.4 percent probability of 3 loans defaulting. We can also determine the probability of 4 of the 100 loans defaulting:

$$\frac{(2.71828)^{-3} \times 3^4}{1 \times 2 \times 3 \times 4} = .168$$

or 16.8 percent. The frequency distribution of default rates is shown in Figure 11B–3.

We can multiply these default numbers by loss severity to get the distribution of dollar *losses* on the loan:

Dollar loss of 3 loans defaulting = 3 × 20c× $100,000
= $60,000

FIGURE 11B–4
Frequency Distribution of Losses on Loan Portfolio from Example

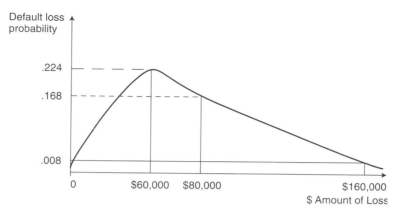

Dollar loss of 4 loans defaulting $= 4 \times 20c \times \$100,000$

$$= \$80,000$$

The distribution of dollar losses is shown in Figure 11B–4.

As under CreditMetrics, we may ask what the 1 percent worst-case loss scenario (i.e., the 99th worst year's loss out of 100 years) is. From the Poisson distribution, the probability of having 8 losses per 100 loans is approximately 1 percent; thus, there is a 1 percent chance of losing $160,000.[3] In the framework of Credit Risk+ the FI would hold a capital reserve to meet the difference between the unexpected (1 percent) loss rate and the average or expected loss rate (the losses associated with three defaults), with expected losses being covered by loan loss provisions and pricing. In our example the capital reserve would be $160,000 − $60,000 = $100,000, or approxi-

mately 1 percent of the value of the portfolio. One reason capital reserves are low in this case is that the severity of loss is assumed to be low and equal in each case (i.e., only 20 percent). If, for example, each of the loans in the portfolio lost 80 cents on default, the required capital reserve would rise to 4 percent of the loan portfolio's value. Moreover, in general, the severity of the losses themselves has a distribution. For example, if loan 1 defaults, the FI might lose 20 cents in $1, while if loan 2 defaults, it may lose 30 cents in $1, and so on. Allowing for a distribution in the severity of losses as well as in the number of defaults can easily be built into the Credit Risk+ framework, as can allowing the mean default rate itself to be variable (see the CSFP technical document for more details).[4]

---

[4] If the (variable) mean default rate is incorporated into the model, this allows the FI to analyze unexpected loan losses in recessions versus expansions. In general, allowing the mean default rate to vary over time increases unexpected losses and required capital reserves.

---

[3] In actual practice, the probability of eight losses is 0.8 percent.

Appendix 11C

Credit Analysis

View Appendix 11C at the Web site for this textbook (**www.mhhe.com/saunders5e**).

Chapter **Twelve**

Credit Risk: Loan Portfolio and Concentration Risk

INTRODUCTION

The models discussed in the previous chapter describe alternative ways by which an FI manager can measure the default risks on *individual* debt instruments such as loans and bonds. Rather than looking at credit risk one loan at a time, this chapter concentrates on the ability of an FI manager to measure credit risk in a loan (asset) *portfolio context* and the benefit from loan (asset) portfolio diversification. We discuss and illustrate several models that are used by FI managers to assess the risk of the overall loan portfolio. The risk-return characteristics of each loan in the portfolio are a concern for the FI, but the risk-return of the overall loan portfolio, with some of the risk of the individual loans diversified, affects an FI's overall credit risk exposure. Additionally, we look at the potential use of loan portfolio models in setting maximum concentration (borrowing) limits for certain business or borrowing sectors (e.g., sectors identified by their Standard Industrial Classification [SIC] codes).

This chapter also discusses regulatory methods for measuring default risk of a portfolio. In particular, the FDIC Improvement Act of 1991 required bank regulators to incorporate credit concentration risk into their evaluation of bank insolvency risk. Moreover, a debate currently is being conducted among bankers and regulators about how this could be done. One possibility is that banks will be allowed to use their own internal models, such as CreditMetrics and Credit Risk+ (discussed in the Chapter 11 Appendixes) and KMV's Portfolio Manager (discussed later in this chapter), to calculate their capital requirements against insolvency risk from excessive loan concentrations. Further, the National Association of Insurance Commissioners (NAIC) has developed limits for different types of assets and borrowers in insurers' portfolios—a so-called pigeonhole approach.

www.naic.org

SIMPLE MODELS OF LOAN CONCENTRATION RISK

FIs widely employ two simple models to measure credit risk concentration in the loan portfolio beyond the purely subjective model of "we have already lent too

TABLE 12–1
A Hypothetical
Rating Migration,
or Transition,
Matrix

			Risk Rating at End of Year		
		1	2	3	D*
Risk rating at beginning of year	1	.85	.10	.04	.01
	2	.12	.83	.03	.02
	3	.03	.13	.80	.04

*D = default.

migration analysis
A method to measure
loan concentration
risk by tracking credit
ratings of firms in
particular sectors or
ratings class for un-
usual declines.

www.standardand-poors.com

www.moodys.com

**loan migration
matrix**
A measure of the
probability of a loan
being upgraded,
downgraded, or de-
faulting over some
period.

much to this borrower."[1] The first is **migration analysis,** where lending officers track S&P, Moody's, or their own internal credit ratings of certain pools of loans or certain sectors—for example, machine tools. If the credit ratings of a number of firms in a sector or rating class decline faster than has been historically experienced, FIs curtail lending to that sector or class.

A **loan migration matrix** (or transition matrix) seeks to reflect the historic experience of a pool of loans in terms of their credit rating migration over time. As such, it can be used as a benchmark against which the credit migration patterns of any new pool of loans can be compared. Table 12–1 shows a hypothetical credit migration matrix, or table, in which loans are assigned to one of three rating classes (most FIs use 10 to 13 rating classes).[2] The rows in Table 12–1 list the rating at which the portfolio of loans began the year, and the columns list the rating at which the portfolio ended the year. The numbers in the table are called transition probabilities, reflecting the average experience (proportions) of loans that began the year, say, as rating 2 remaining rating 2 at the end of the year, being upgraded to a 1, being downgraded to a 3, or defaulting (*D*).

For example, for loans that began the year at rating 2, historically (on average) 12 percent have been upgraded to 1; 83 percent have remained at 2; 3 percent have been downgraded to 3; and 2 percent have defaulted by the end of the year. Suppose that the FI is evaluating the credit risk of its current portfolio of loans of borrowers rated 2 and that over the last few years, a much higher percentage (say, 5 percent) of loans has been downgraded to 3 and a higher percentage (say, 3 percent) has defaulted than is implied by the historic transition matrix. The FI may then seek to restrict its supply of lower-quality loans (e.g., those rated 2 and 3), concentrating more of its portfolio on grade 1 loans.[3] At the very least, the FI should seek higher credit risk premiums on lower-quality (rated) loans. Not only is migration analysis used to evaluate commercial loan portfolios, it is widely used to analyze credit card portfolios and consumer loans as well.[4]

[1] See Board of Governors of the Federal Reserve, "Revisions to Risk-Based Capital Standards to Account for Concentration of Credit Risk and Risks of Non-Traditional Activities," Section 305, FDICIA, Washington, DC, March 26, 1993.

[2] A recent survey of credit portfolio management by FIs found the range of credit rating classes to be 5 to 22. See "2002 Survey of Credit Portfolio Management Practices," International Association of Credit Portfolio Managers, International Swaps and Derivatives Association, and Risk Management Association, October 2002.

[3] The theory underlying the use of the average one-year transition matrix (based on historic data) as a benchmark is that actual transactions will fluctuate randomly around these average transitions. In the terminology of statistics, actual transitions follow a stable Markov (chain) process.

[4] See, for example, J. Kallberg and A. Saunders, "Markov Chain Approaches to the Analysis of Payment Behavior of Retail Credit Customers," *Financial Management,* 1983, pp. 5–14.

concentration limits
External limits set on the maximum loan size that can be made to an individual borrower.

The second simple model requires management to set some firm external limit on the maximum amount of loans that will be made to an individual borrower or sector. The FI determines **concentration limits** on the proportion of the loan portfolio that can go to any single customer by assessing the borrower's current portfolio, its operating unit's business plans, its economists' economic projections, and its strategic plans. Typically, FIs set concentration limits to reduce exposures to certain industries and increase exposures to others. When two industry groups' performances are highly correlated, an FI may set an aggregate limit of less than the sum of the two individual industry limits. FIs also typically set geographic limits. They may set aggregate portfolio limits or combinations of industry and geographic limits.

EXAMPLE 12–1

Calculating Concentration Limits for a Loan Portfolio

Suppose management is unwilling to permit losses exceeding 10 percent of an FI's capital to a particular sector. If management estimates that the amount lost per dollar of defaulted loans in this sector is 40 cents, the maximum loans to a single sector as a percent of capital, defined as the concentration limit, is:

$$\text{Concentration limit} = \text{Maximum loss as a percent of capital} \times \frac{1}{\text{Loss rate}}$$

$$= 10\% \times [1/.4]$$

$$= 25\%$$

Bank regulators in recent years have limited loan concentrations to *individual borrowers* to a maximum of 10 percent of a bank's capital.[5]

Concept Questions

1. What would the concentration limit be if the loss rate on bad loans is 25 cents on the dollar?
2. What would the concentration limit be if the maximum loss (as a percent of capital) is 15 percent instead of 10 percent?

Next we look at the use of more sophisticated portfolio theory–based models to set concentration limits. While these models have a great deal of potential, data availability and other implementation problems have, until recently, hindered their use. The basic idea is to select the portfolio of loans that maximizes the return on the loan portfolio for any given level of risk (or that minimizes the degree of portfolio risk for any given level of returns).

LOAN PORTFOLIO DIVERSIFICATION AND MODERN PORTFOLIO THEORY (MPT)

To the extent that an FI manager holds widely traded loans and bonds as assets or, alternatively, can calculate loan or bond returns, portfolio diversification models can be used to measure and control the FI's aggregate credit risk exposure. Suppose the manager can estimate the expected returns of each loan or bond ($\overline{R}_i$) in the FI's portfolio.

---

[5] In some countries, such as Chile, limits are mandated by sector or industry.

After calculating the individual security return series, the FI manager can compute the expected return ($\overline{R}_p$) on a portfolio of assets as:

$$\overline{R}_p = \sum_{i=1}^{N} X_i \overline{R}_i \tag{1}$$

In addition, the variance of returns or risk of the portfolio (σ_i^2) can be calculated as:

$$\sigma_p^2 = \sum_{i=1}^{n} X_i^2 \sigma_i^2 + \sum_{i=1}^{n}\sum_{\substack{j=1 \\ i \neq j}}^{n} X_i X_j \sigma_{ij} \tag{2}$$

or:

$$\sigma_p^2 = \sum_{i=1}^{n} X_i^2 \sigma_i^2 + \sum_{i=1}^{n}\sum_{\substack{j=1 \\ i \neq j}}^{n} X_i X_j \rho_{ij} \sigma_i \sigma_j \tag{3}$$

where

$\overline{R}_p$ = Expected or mean return on the asset portfolio
Σ = Summation sign
$\overline{R}_i$ = Mean return on the ith asset in the portfolio
X_i = Proportion of the asset portfolio invested in the ith asset (the desired concentration amount)
σ_i^2 = Variance of returns on the ith asset
σ_{ij} = Covariance of returns between the ith and jth assets
ρ_{ij} = Correlation between the returns on the ith and jth assets[6]

The fundamental lesson of modern portfolio theory (MPT) is that by taking advantage of its size, an FI can diversify considerable amounts of credit risk as long as the returns on different assets are imperfectly correlated with respect to their default risk adjusted returns.[7]

Consider the σ_p^2 in equation (2). If many loans have negative covariances or correlations of returns (ρ_{ij} are negative)—that is, when one borrower's loans do badly and another's do well—the sum of the individual credit risks of loans viewed independently overestimates the risk of the whole portfolio. This is what we meant in Chapter 5 when we stated that by pooling funds, FIs can reduce risk by taking advantage of the law of large numbers in their investment decisions.

---

[6] The correlation coefficient reflects the joint movement of asset returns or default risks in the case of loans and lies between the values $-1 \leq \rho \leq +1$, where ρ is the correlation coefficient. As can be seen from equations (2) and (3), the covariance between any two assets (σ_{ij}) is related to the correlation coefficient (ρ_{ij}) by $\sigma_{ij} = \rho_{ij}\, \sigma_i\, \sigma_j$.

[7] One objection to using modern portfolio theory for loans is that the returns on individual loans are not normally or symmetrically distributed. In particular, most loans have limited upside returns and long-tail downside risks; see the discussion in Chapter 11, Appendix A, "CreditMetrics," and chapter 9 in A. Saunders and L. Allen, *Credit Risk Measurements: New Approaches to Value at Risk and Other Paradigms*, 2nd ed. (New York: John Wiley & Sons, 2002). Also, concerns about maintaining relationships with traditional customers may limit the ability of an FI to diversify. The relationship limit on diversification has been called the "paradox of credit." That is, banks specialize in monitoring and generating information about their key customers (see Chapter 1), yet such monitoring specialization may lead to a highly concentrated loan portfolio. Relationship concerns may inhibit the loan portfolio's being managed in a fashion similar to a mutual fund's management of an equity portfolio.

FIGURE 12–1
FI Portfolio
Diversification

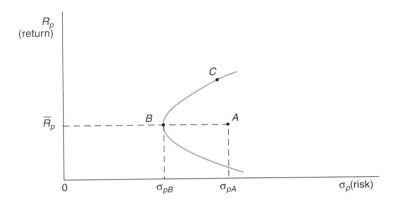

EXAMPLE 12–2

Calculation of Return and Risk on a Two-Asset Portfolio

Suppose that an FI holds two loans with the following characteristics:[8]

Loan i	X_i	$\overline{R}_i$	σ_i	σ_i^2	
1	.40	10%	.0980	.0096	$\rho_{12} = -.84$
2	.60	12	.0857	.007344	$\sigma_{12} = .70548$

The return on the loan portfolio is:

$$R_p = .4\,(10\%) + .6\,(12\%) = 11.2\%$$

while the risk of the portfolio is:

$$\sigma_p^2 = (.4)^2\,(.0096) + (.6)^2\,(.007344) + 2\,(.4)(.6)(-.84)(.098)(.0857) = .0007935$$

thus, $\sigma_p = \sqrt{.0007935} = .0282 = 2.82\%$.

Notice that the risk (or standard deviation of returns) of the portfolio, σ_p (2.82 percent), is less than the risk of either individual asset (9.8 percent and 8.57 percent, respectively). The negative correlation between the returns of the two loans ($-.84$) results in an overall reduction of risk when they are put together in an FI's portfolio.

To see more generally the advantages of diversification, consider Figure 12–1. Note that A is an undiversified portfolio with heavy investment concentration in just a few loans or bonds. By fully exploiting diversification potential with bonds or loans whose returns are negatively correlated or that have a low positive correlation with those in the existing portfolio, the FI manager can lower the credit risk on the portfolio from σ_{pA} to σ_{pB} while earning the same expected return. That is, portfolio B is the efficient (lowest-risk) portfolio associated with portfolio return level $\overline{R}_p$. By varying the proportion of the asset portfolio invested in each asset (in other words, by varying the required portfolio return level $\overline{R}_p$ up and down), the manager can identify an entire frontier of efficient portfolio mixes (weights) of loans and bonds. Each portfolio mix is efficient in the sense that it offers the lowest risk level to the FI manager at each possible level of portfolio returns. However, as you can see in Figure 12–1, of all possible efficient portfolios that can be generated, portfolio B produces the lowest possible risk level for the FI manager. That is, it maximizes the gains from diversifying across all available loans and bonds so that the manager cannot reduce the risk of the portfolio below σ_{pB}. For this reason, σ_{pB} is usually labeled the **minimum risk portfolio.**

Even though B is clearly the minimum risk portfolio, it does not generate the highest returns. Consequently, portfolio B may be chosen only by the most

minimum risk portfolio
Combination of assets that reduces the variance of portfolio returns to the lowest feasible level.

[8] Note that variance (σ^2) is measured in percent squared; standard deviation (σ) is measured in percent.

risk-averse FI managers, whose sole objective is to minimize portfolio risk regardless of the portfolio's return. Most portfolio managers have some desired return-risk trade-off in mind; they are willing to accept more risk if they are compensated with higher expected returns.[9] One such possibility would be portfolio *C* in Figure 12–1. This is an efficient portfolio in that the FI manager has selected loan proportions (X_i) to produce a portfolio risk level that is a minimum for that higher expected return level. This portfolio dominates all other portfolios that can produce the same expected return level.[10]

Portfolio theory is a highly attractive tool. Still, over and above the intuitive concept that diversification is generally good, a question arises as to its applicability for banks, insurance companies, and thrifts. These FIs often hold significant amounts of regionally specific nontraded or infrequently traded loans and bonds.

Concept Questions

1. What is the main point in using MPT for loan portfolio risk?
2. Why would an FI not always choose to operate with a minimum risk portfolio?

KMV Portfolio Manager Model

www.moodyskmv.com

KMV Portfolio Manager
A model that applies modern portfolio theory to the loan portfolio.

Despite the nontraded aspect of many loans, a great deal of recent research has gone into developing modern portfolio theory models for loans. Below we look at one approach developed by KMV Corporation (which was purchased by Moody's in 2002) called **Portfolio Manager.**[11]

Any model that seeks to estimate an efficient frontier for loans, as in Figure 12–1, and thus the optimal or best proportions (X_i) in which to hold loans made to different borrowers, needs to determine and measure three things [see equations (1), (2), and (3)]: the expected return on a loan to borrower i (R_i), the risk of a loan to borrower i (σ_i), and the correlation of default risks between loans made to borrowers i and j (ρ_{ij}).

---

[9] The point that is chosen depends on the risk aversion of managers and the degree of separation of ownership from control. If the FI is managed by agents who perform the task of maximizing the value of the firm, they act as risk-neutral agents. They would know that stockholders, who are well diversified, could, through homemade diversification, hold the shares of many firms to eliminate borrower-specific risk. Thus, managers would seek to maximize expected return subject to any regulatory constraints on risk-taking behavior (i.e., they probably would pick a point in region *C* in Figure 12–1). However, if managers are risk averse because of their human capital invested in the FI and make lending decisions based on their own risk preferences rather than those of the stockholders, they are likely to choose a relatively low-risk portfolio, something closer to the minimum risk portfolio. For more on agency issue and bank risk taking, see A. Saunders, E. Strock, and N. G., Travlos, "Ownership Structure, Deregulation, and Bank Risk Taking," *Journal of Finance* 45 (1990), pp. 643–54. The trade-off between portfolio return and portfolio risk can now be solved using new methods of optimization called genetic algorithm-based techniques. See A. Mukherjee, R. Bisuras, K. Deb, and A. Mathur, "Multi-Objective Evolutionary Algorithms for the Risk-Return Trade-off in Bank Loan Management," KanGAL Report Number 200/005.

[10] Rather than selecting a point on the loan efficient frontier that reflects managerial risk aversion, as in Figure 12–1 point *C* (see footnote 9), the FI manager would pick a point that maximizes firm value. This would be the point where the return of the portfolio minus the risk-free rate divided by the standard deviation of portfolio returns is maximized, that is the maximum of $[(R_p - R_f/\sigma_p)]$. In MPT this is often called the Sharpe ratio. Diagramatically, this is a point on the efficient frontier where a straight line drawn from the vertical axis, from a point equal to R_f, is just tangential to the efficient frontier. At this tangency point, it is impossible to improve upon the risk-return trade-off.

[11] Other portfolio models have been developed, including CreditMetrics, Credit Risk+, and Credit Portfolio View (McKinsey and Company). See Saunders and Allen, *Credit Risk Measurement*. A recent survey of credit portfolio management by FIs found that 69 percent of the financial institutions that used a credit portfolio model used Portfolio Manager. See "2002 Survey of Credit Portfolio Management Practices," International Association of Credit Portfolio Managers, International Swaps and Derivatives Association, and Risk Management Association, October 2002.

In its simplest model, KMV measures each of these as follows:

$$R_i = AIS_i - E(L_i) = AIS_i - [EDF_i \times LGD_i] \qquad \textbf{(4)}$$

$$\sigma_i = UL_i = \sigma_{Di} \times LGD_i = \sqrt{EDF_i(1 - EDF_i)} \times LGD_i \qquad \textbf{(5)}$$

ρ_{ij} = Correlation between the systematic return components
of the asset returns of borrower i and borrower j.

Each of these needs some explanation.

Return on the Loan (R_i)

The return on a loan is measured by the so-called annual all-in-spread (AIS), which measures annual fees earned on the loan by the FI plus the annual spread between the loan rate paid by the borrower and the FI's cost of funds. Deducted from this is the expected loss on the loan [$E(L_i)$]. This expected loss is equal to the product of the expected probability of the borrower defaulting over the next year, or its expected default frequency (EDF_i)—as discussed in Chapter 11—times the amount lost by the FI if the borrower defaults [the loss given default, or LGD_i]. Also, if desired, the return on the loan can be expressed in excess return form by deducting the risk-free rate on a security of equivalent maturity.

Risk of the Loan (σ_i)

The risk of the loan reflects the volatility of the loan's default rate (σ_{Di}) around its expected value times the amount lost given default (LGD_i). The product of the volatility of the default rate and the LGD is called the unexpected loss on the loan (UL_i) and is a measure of the loan's risk, or σ_i. To measure the volatility of the default rate, assume that loans can either default or repay (no default); then defaults are binomially distributed, and the standard deviation of the default rate for the ith borrower (σ_{Di}) is equal to the square root of the probability of default times 1 minus the probability of default ($\sqrt{(EDF)(1 - EDF)}$).

Correlation (ρ_{ij})

To measure the unobservable default risk correlation between any two borrowers, the KMV Portfolio Manager model uses the systematic asset return components of the two borrowers and calculates a correlation that is based on the historical co-movement between those returns. According to KMV, default correlations tend to be low and lie between .002 and .15. This makes intuitive sense. For example, what is the probability that both IBM and General Motors will go bankrupt at the same time? For both firms, their asset values would have to fall below their debt values at the same time over the next year! The likelihood of this is small except in a very severe or extreme recession or extremely high growth in each firm's short-term debt obligations. The generally low (positive) correlations between the default risks of borrowers is also good news for FI managers in that it implies that by spreading loans across many borrowers, they can reduce portfolio risk significantly.[12]

---

[12] The Portfolio Manager model of KMV also can be used to assess the risk of extending more loans to any one borrower. If more loans are extended to one borrower, fewer loans can be made to others (assuming a fixed amount of loans). Technically, since the variance of the loan portfolio is:

$$UL_p^2 = \sum_{i=1}^{n} X_i^2 UL_i^2 + \sum_{i=1}^{n} \sum_{\substack{j=1 \\ i \neq j}}^{n} X_i X_j UL_i UL_j \rho_{ij}$$

The marginal risk contribution of a small amount of additional loans to borrower i can be calculated as:

$$\text{Marginal risk contribution} = \frac{dUL_p}{dX_i}$$

EXAMPLE 12–3
Calculation of Return and Risk on a Two-Asset Portfolio Using KMV Portfolio Manager

Suppose that an FI holds two loans with the following characteristics:

Loan i	X_i	Annual Spread between Loan Rate and FI's Cost of Funds	Annual Fees	Loss to FI Given Default	Expected Default Frequency	
1	.60	5%	2%	25%	3%	$\rho_{12} = -.25$
2	.40	4.5	1.5	20	2	

The return and risk on loan 1 are:

$$R_1 = (.05 + .02) - [.03 \times .25] = 0.0625 \text{ or } 6.25\%$$

$$\sigma_1 = [\sqrt{.03(.97)}] \times .25 = .04265 \text{ or } 4.265\%$$

The return and risk on loan 2 are:

$$R_2 = (.045 + .015) - [.02 \times .20] = 0.056 \text{ or } 5.60\%$$

$$\sigma_2 = [\sqrt{.02(.98)}] \times .20 = .028 \text{ or } 2.80\%$$

The return and risk of the portfolio are then:

$$R_p = .6 (6.25\%) + .4 (5.60\%) = 5.99\%$$

$$\sigma_p^2 = (.6)^2 (.04265)^2 + (.4)^2 (.028)^2 + 2 (.6)(.4)(-.25)(.04265)(.028) = .0006369$$

thus, $\sigma_p = \sqrt{.0006369} = .0252 = 2.52\%$.

Reportedly, a number of large FIs are using the KMV model (and other similar models) to actively manage their loan portfolios.

Concept Questions

1. How does KMV measure the return on a loan?
2. If *EDF* = 0.1 percent and *LGD* = 50 percent, what is the unexpected loss (σ_i) on the loan?
3. How does KMV calculate loan default correlations?

Partial Applications of Portfolio Theory

Loan Volume–Based Models

As discussed above, direct application of modern portfolio theory is often difficult for FIs lacking information on market prices of assets because many of the assets—such as loans—are not bought and sold in established markets. However, sufficient loan volume data may be available to allow managers to construct a

---

where UL_p is the standard deviation (in dollars) of the loan portfolio. Clearly, the marginal risk contribution (dUL_p) of an additional amount of loans to borrower i, (dX_i), will depend not just on the risk of loan i on a stand-alone basis, but also on (i) the correlation of loan i with j other loans, (ii) the risk of the j other loans, and (iii) where the funds to increase loan i come from. In particular, if $dX_i > 0$, then the sum of the proportion of all remaining loans must decrease unless new funds are raised. Indeed, in the presence of a binding funding constraint $\sum_{i=1}^{n} dx_i < 0$ where $j \neq i$, the key insight is that a loan to a BBB-rated borrower may well be more valuable to an FI (in an MPT sense) if it has a lower correlation with other loans than a loan to an A-rated borrower; that is, it is the loan's marginal risk contribution to total portfolio risk that is important, not its stand-alone risk.

TABLE 12–2
Allocation of the
Loan Portfolio to
Different Sectors
(in percentages)

	(1) National	(2) Bank A	(3) Bank B
Real estate	45%	65%	10%
C&I	30	20	25
Individuals	15	10	55
Others	10	5	10
	100%	100%	100%

modified or partial application of MPT to analyze the overall concentration or credit risk exposure of the FI.[13] Such loan volume data include:

1. *Commercial bank call reports*. These reports to the Federal Reserve classify loans as real estate, agriculture, commercial and industrial (C&I), depository institution, individual, state and political subdivision, and international. Produced for individual banks, these data can be aggregated to estimate the notional allocation of loans among categories or types.[14]

2. *Data on shared national credits*. A national database on large commercial and industrial loans that categorizes loan volume by two-digit Standard Industrial Classification (SIC) codes. For example, loans made to SIC code 49 are loans to public utilities. Because this database provides a national picture of the allocation of large loans across sectors, it is analogous to the market portfolio or basket of commercial and industrial loans.

3. *Commercial databases*. Data on 100,000-plus loans by bank and by borrower on the *Loan Pricing Corporations*, *Dealscan* database.[15]

These data therefore provide *market benchmarks* against which an individual FI can compare its own internal allocations of loans across major lending sectors such as real estate and C&I. For example, the Shared National Credit (SNC) database provides a market benchmark of the allocation of loans across various industries or borrowers.

By comparing its own allocation, or the proportions (X_{ij}), of loans in any specific area with the national allocations across borrowers $(X_i,$ where i designates different loan groups), the jth FI can measure the extent to which its loan portfolio deviates from the market portfolio benchmark. This indicates the degree to which the FI has developed *loan concentrations* or relatively undiversified portfolios in various areas.

Consider Table 12–2. In this table we evaluate the first level of the loan asset allocation problem, which is the amount to be lent to each major loan sector or type. Here we show hypothetical numbers for four types of loans: real estate, commercial and industrial, individual, and others. Column (1) shows the loan allocation proportions at the national level for all banks; this is the market portfolio allocation. Column (2) lists the allocations assumed to be chosen by bank A, and column (3) shows the allocations chosen by bank B.

---

[13] This partial application of portfolio theory was first suggested by L. B. Morgan, "Managing a Loan Portfolio like an Equity Fund," *Bankers Magazine*, January–February 1989, pp. 228–35.

[14] Some countries, like Italy, go further and break down a bank's loan portfolio into greater detail including industry and geographic concentrations.

[15] *Dealscan* also provides data on pricing of new loans. See the discussion in E. Altman, A. Gande, and A. Saunders, "Informational Efficiency of Loans versus Bonds: Evidence from Secondary Market Prices," Stern School of Business Working Paper, 2003; and S. Dahiya et al., "Financial Distress and Bank Lending Relationships," *Journal of Finance*, 2003, pp. 375–90. As these databases expand, tests of full MPT models for loans become easier.

Note that bank A has concentrated loans more heavily in real estate lending than the national average, while bank B has concentrated loans more heavily in lending to individuals. To calculate the extent to which each bank deviates from the national benchmark, we use the standard deviation of bank A's and bank B's loan allocations from the national benchmark. Of course, the national benchmark may be inappropriate as the relevant market portfolio for a very small regional bank, insurance company, or thrift. In this case, the FI could construct a regional benchmark from the call report data of banks (or similar data collected by insurance company and thrift regulators) in a given regional area, such as the American Southwest, or, alternatively, a peer group benchmark of banks of a similar asset size and location.

We calculate the relative measure of loan allocation deviation as:[16]

$$\sigma_j = \sqrt{\frac{\sum_{i=1}^{N}(X_{ij} - X_i)^2}{N}} \tag{6}$$

where

σ_j = Standard deviation of bank j's asset allocation proportions from the national benchmark

X_{ij} = Asset allocation proportions of the jth bank

X_i = National asset allocations

N = Number of observations or loan categories, $N = 4$

EXAMPLE 12–4 *Calculating Loan Allocation Deviation*	Refer again to Table 12–2. Applying equation (6) to bank A's loan portfolio, we get the deviation in its loan portfolio allocation as follows: $(X_{1A} - X_1)^2 = (.65 - .45)^2 = .0400$ $(X_{2A} - X_2)^2 = (.20 - .30)^2 = .0100$ $(X_{3A} - X_3)^2 = (.10 - .15)^2 = .0025$ $(X_{4A} - X_4)^2 = (.05 - .10)^2 = \underline{.0025}$ and $\sum_{i=1}^{4} = .0550$ Therefore, $\sigma_A = (.0550/4)^2 = 11.73\%$. Repeating this process for bank B's loan portfolio, we get: $(X_{1B} - X_1)^2 = (.10 - .45)^2 = .1225$ $(X_{2B} - X_2)^2 = (.25 - .30)^2 = .0025$ $(X_{3B} - X_3)^2 = (.55 - .15)^2 = .1600$ $(X_{4B} - X_4)^2 = (.10 - .10)^2 = \underline{.0000}$ and $\sum_{i=1}^{4} = .2850$ *(continued)*

[16] For small samples such as this, it is really more appropriate for the divisor of equation (6) to be $N - 1$ rather than N.

Therefore, $\sigma_B = (.2850/4)^2 = 26.69\%$. As you can see, bank B deviates more significantly from the national benchmark than bank A because of its heavy concentration on loans to individuals.

Deviation from the national benchmark is not necessarily bad; a bank may specialize in this area of lending because of its comparative advantage in information collection and monitoring of personal loans (perhaps due to its size or location). The standard deviation simply provides a manager with a measure of the degree to which an FI's loan portfolio composition deviates from the national average or benchmark. Nevertheless, to the extent that the national composition of a loan portfolio represents a more diversified market portfolio, because it aggregates across all banks, the asset proportions derived nationally (the X_i) are likely to be closer to the *most efficient portfolio composition* than the X_{ij} of the individual bank. This partial use of modern portfolio theory provides an FI manager with a sense of the relative degree of loan concentration carried in the asset portfolio. Finally, although the preceding analysis has referred to the loan portfolio of banks, any FI can use this portfolio theory for any asset group or, indeed, the whole asset portfolio, whether the asset is traded or not. The key data needed are the allocations of a peer group of regional or national financial institutions faced with similar investment decision choices.

Loan Loss Ratio–Based Models

systematic loan loss risk
A measure of the sensitivity of loan losses in a particular business sector relative to the losses in an FI's loan portfolio.

A second partial application of MPT is a model based on historic loan loss ratios.[17] This model involves estimating the **systematic loan loss risk** of a particular (SIC) sector or industry relative to the loan loss risk of an FI's total loan portfolio. This systematic loan loss can be estimated by running a time-series regression of quarterly losses of the ith sector's loss rate on the quarterly loss rate of an FI's total loans:

$$\left(\frac{\text{Sectoral losses in the } i\text{th sector}}{\text{Loans to the } i\text{th sector}}\right) = \alpha + \beta_i \left(\frac{\text{Total loan losses}}{\text{Total loans}}\right)$$

where α measures the loan loss rate for a sector that has no sensitivity to losses on the aggregate loan portfolio (i.e., its $\beta = 0$) and β_i measures the systematic loss sensitivity of the ith sector loans to total loan losses. For example, regression results showing that the consumer sector has a β of 0.2 and the real estate sector has a β of 1.4, suggest that loan losses in the real estate sector are systematically higher relative to the total loan losses of the FI (by definition, the loss rate β for the whole loan portfolio is 1). Similarly, loan losses in the consumer sector are systematically lower relative to the total loan losses of the FI. Consequently, it may be prudent for the FI to maintain lower concentration limits for the real estate sector as opposed to the consumer sector, especially as the economy moves toward a recession and total loan losses start to rise. The implication of this model is that sectors with lower βs could have higher concentration limits than high β sectors—since low β loan sector risks (loan losses) are less systematic, that is, are more diversifiable in a portfolio sense.[18]

[17] See E. P. Davis, "Bank Credit Risk," Bank of England, Working Paper Series no. 8, April 1993.

[18] This type of approach suggests a possible extension to factor analysis (on the lines of multifactor models). Basically, it involves regressing SIC sector losses against various factors (market risk, interest rate risk, etc.) to see which sectors have the greatest (least) factor sensitivity. See also J. Neuberger, "Conditional Risk and Return in Bank Holding Company Stocks: A Factor-GARCH Approach," Federal Reserve Bank of San Francisco, Working Paper, May 1994.

EXAMPLE 12–5
Calculating Loan Loss Ratios

Using regression analysis on historical loan losses, a finance company has estimated the following:

$$X_{C\&I} = 0.003 + 0.75X_L \quad \text{and} \quad X_{con} = 0.005 + 1.25X_L$$

where $X_{C\&I}$ = the loss rate in the commercial and industrial loan sector, X_{con} = the loss rate in the consumer loan sector, and X_L = the loss rate for the finance company's loan portfolio. If the finance company's total loan loss rate increases by 15 percent, the expected loss rate increase in the commercial and industrial loan sector will be:

$$X_{C\&I} = 0.003 + 0.75\,(.15) = 11.55\%$$

and in the consumer loan sector will be:

$$X_{con} = 0.005 + 1.25\,(.15) = 19.25\%$$

To protect against this increase in losses, the finance company should consider reducing its concentration of consumer loans.

Regulatory Models

www.federalreserve.gov

As noted in the introduction to this chapter, bank and insurance regulators have also been investigating ways to measure concentration risk. After examining various quantitative approaches, the Federal Reserve in 1994 issued a final ruling on its proposed measure of credit concentration risk. The method adopted is largely subjective and is based on examiner discretion. The reasons given for rejecting the more technical models were that (1) at the time, the methods for identifying concentration risk were not sufficiently advanced to justify their use and (2) insufficient data were available to estimate more quantitative-type models, although the development of models like KMV (as well as CreditMetrics and Credit Risk+, discussed in the Appendixes in Chapter 11) may make bank regulators change their minds. In Chapter 20, we look at the details of how credit risk is one component used to determine depository institutions' required level of capital.

www.naic.org

Life and property–casualty insurance regulators have also been concerned with excessive industry sector and borrower concentrations. The Model Act established by the National Association of Insurance Commissioners (NAIC) for state regulators (remember that insurance companies are regulated at the state level—see Chapter 3) sets maximums on the investments an insurer can hold in securities or obligations of any single issuer.[19] These so-called **general diversification limits** are set at 3 percent for life–health insurers and 5 percent for property–casualty insurers—implying that the minimum numbers of different issues is 33 for life–health companies and for PC companies is 20. The rationale for such a simple rule comes from modern portfolio theory, which shows that *equal* investments across approximately 15 or more stocks can provide significant gains from diversification, that is, a lowering of portfolio risk or the variance of returns.

general diversification limits
Maximums set on the amount of investments an insurer can hold in securities of any single issuer.

Concept Questions

1. Suppose the returns on different loans were independent. Would there be any gains from loan portfolio diversification?
2. How would you find the minimum risk loan portfolio in a modern portfolio theory framework?
3. Should FI managers select the minimum risk loan portfolio? Why or why not?

[19] See *Investments of Insurers Model Act*, NAIC, draft, Washington DC, August 12, 1994.

4. Explain the reasoning behind the Federal Reserve's 1994 decision to rely more on a subjective rather than a quantitative approach to measuring credit concentration risk. Is that view valid today?

Summary

This chapter discussed the various approaches available to an FI manager to measure credit portfolio and concentration risk. It showed how portfolio diversification can reduce the loan risk exposure of an FI. Two simple models that allow an FI to monitor and manage its loan concentration risk were also discussed: migration analysis, which relies on rating changes to provide information on desirable and undesirable loan concentrations, and a model that sets concentration limits based on an FI's capital exposure to different lending sectors. The application of the fully fledged MPT model to the credit (loan) concentration issue was also analyzed as was the KMV Portfolio Manager model. In addition, a model that applies portfolio theory to loan loss ratios in different sectors to determine loan concentrations was discussed. Finally, the approaches of regulators, such as the Federal Reserve and the NAIC, to measuring loan concentrations were described.

Questions and Problems

1. How do loan portfolio risks differ from individual loan risks?

2. What is migration analysis? How do FIs use it to measure credit risk concentration? What are its shortcomings?

3. What does loan concentration risk mean?

4. A manager decides not to lend to any firm in sectors that generate losses in excess of 5 percent of equity.

   a. If the average historical losses in the automobile sector total 8 percent, what is the maximum loan a manager can lend to a firm in this sector as a percentage of total capital?

   b. If the average historical losses in the mining sector total 15 percent, what is the maximum loan a manager can make to a firm in this sector as a percentage of total capital?

5. An FI has set a maximum loss of 12 percent of total capital as a basis for setting concentration limits on loans to individual firms. If it has set a concentration limit of 25 percent to a firm, what is the expected loss rate for that firm?

6. Explain how modern portfolio theory can be applied to lower the credit risk of an FI's portfolio.

7. The Bank of Tinytown has two $20,000 loans with the following characteristics: Loan A has an expected return of 10 percent and a standard deviation of returns of 10 percent. The expected return and standard deviation of returns for loan B are 12 percent and 20 percent, respectively.

   a. If the covariance between A and B is .015 (1.5 percent), what are the expected return and the standard deviation of this portfolio?

   b. What is the standard deviation of the portfolio if the covariance is −.015 (−1.5 percent)?

   c. What role does the covariance, or correlation, play in the risk reduction attributes of modern portfolio theory?

8. Why is it difficult for small banks and thrifts to measure credit risk using modern portfolio theory?

9. What is the minimum risk portfolio? Why is this portfolio usually not the portfolio chosen by FIs to optimize the return-risk trade-off?

10. The obvious benefit to holding a diversified portfolio of loans is to spread risk exposures so that a single event does not result in a great loss to the bank. Are there any benefits to not being diversified?

11. A bank vice president is attempting to rank, in terms of the risk-reward trade-off, the loan portfolios of three loan officers. Information on the portfolios is noted below. How would you rank the three portfolios?

Portfolio	Expected Return	Standard Deviation
A	10%	8%
B	12	9
C	11	10

12. CountrySide Bank uses the KMV Portfolio Manager model to evaluate the risk-return characteristics of the loans in its portfolio. A specific $10 million loan earns 2 percent per year in fees, and the loan is priced at a 4 percent spread over the cost of funds for the bank. Because of collateral considerations, the loss to the bank if the borrower defaults will be 20 percent of the loan's face value. The expected probability of default is 3 percent. What is the anticipated return on this loan? What is the risk of the loan?

13. What databases are available that contain loan information at the national and regional levels? How can they be used to analyze credit concentration risk?

14. Information concerning the allocation of loan portfolios to different market sectors is given below.

Allocation of Loan Portfolios in Different Sectors (%)

Sectors	National	Bank A	Bank B
Commercial	30%	50%	10%
Consumer	40	30	40
Real Estate	30	20	50

Bank A and bank B would like to estimate how much their portfolios deviate from the national average.

a. Which bank is further away from the national average?

b. Is a large standard deviation necessarily bad for a bank using this model?

15. Assume that the averages for national banks engaged primarily in mortgage lending have their assets diversified in the following proportions: 20 percent residential, 30 percent commercial, 20 percent international, and 30 percent mortgage-backed securities. A local bank has the following ratios: 30 percent residential, 40 percent commercial, and 30 percent international. How does the local bank differ from national banks?

16. Using regression analysis on historical loan losses, a bank has estimated the following:

$$X_C = 0.002 + 0.8X_L, \quad \text{and} \quad X_h = 0.003 + 1.8X_L$$

where X_C = loss rate in the commercial sector, X_h = loss rate in the consumer (household) sector, and X_L = loss rate for its total loan portfolio.

    a. If the bank's total loan loss rates increase by 10 percent, what are the expected loss rate increases in the commercial and consumer sectors?

    b. In which sector should the bank limit its loans and why?

17. What reasons did the Federal Reserve Board offer for recommending the use of subjective evaluations of credit concentration risk instead of quantitative models?

18. What rules on credit concentrations has the National Association of Insurance Commissioners proposed? How are they related to modern portfolio theory?

19. An FI is limited to holding no more than 8 percent of the securities of a single issuer. What is the minimum number of securities it should hold to meet this requirement? What if the requirements are 2 percent, 4 percent, and 7 percent?

Pertinent Web Sites

Board of Governors of the Federal Reserve	**www.federalreserve.gov**
KMV Corporation	**www.moodyskmv.com**
Moody's	**www.moodys.com**
National Association of Insurance	
Commissioners	**www.naic.org**
Standard & Poor's	**www.standardandpoors.com**

Chapter Notation

View Chapter Notation at the Web site for this textbook (**www.mhhe.com/saunders5e**).

Chapter **Thirteen**

Off-Balance-Sheet Risk

INTRODUCTION

Off-balance-sheet (OBS) activities can involve risks that add to an FI's overall risk exposure. While some part of OBS risk is related to interest rate risk, credit risk, and other risks, these items also introduce unique risks that must be managed by FIs. Indeed, the failure of the U.K. investment bank Barings, the legal problems of Bankers Trust (relating to swap deals involving Procter & Gamble and Gibson Greeting Cards), the $2.6 billion loss incurred by Sumitomo Corp. (of Japan) from commodity futures trading, and the $1.5 billion in losses and eventual bankruptcy of Orange County in California have all been linked to FI off-balance-sheet activities in derivatives. For example, in May 1998 Credit Suisse First Boston paid $52 million to Orange County to settle a lawsuit alleging that it had been in part responsible for that county's investments in risky securities and derivatives transactions. Twenty other banks and securities firms have been similarly sued. The Ethical Dilemmas box discusses how more recently, questionable off-balance-sheet transactions between Citigroup, J. P. Morgan Chase, and Enron (in addition to other questionable accounting practices by many other firms) resulted in regulatory changes in 2002 regarding how off-balance-sheet activities are recorded by all public companies. Table 13–1 lists some other big losses for FIs from trading in derivatives. (Derivative securities [futures, forwards, options, and swaps] are examined in detail in chapters 24 through 26.) In addition to increasing an FI's risk, OBS activities can hedge or reduce the interest rate, credit, and foreign exchange risks of FIs. That is, OBS activities have both risk-increasing and risk-reducing attributes. In addition. OBS activities are now an important source of fee income for many FIs.[1]

This chapter examines the various OBS activities (listed in Table 13–2) of FIs. We first discuss the effect of OBS activities on an FI's risk exposure, return performance, and solvency. We then describe the different types of OBS activities and the risks associated with each. While the discussion emphasizes that these activities may add to an FI's riskiness, the chapter concludes with a discussion of the role of OBS activities in reducing the risk of an FI.

---

[1] This fee income can have both direct (e.g., a fee from the sale of a letter of credit) and indirect (through improved customer relationships) effects that have a positive income impact in other product areas. In cases where customers feel aggrieved with respect to derivatives purchased from a dealer FI, off-balance-sheet activities can have important negative reputational effects that have an adverse impact on the future flow of fees and other income (see "Bankers Trust Clients Complaining," *New York Times,* January 20, 1995, p. D1).

Ethical **Dilemmas**

IN FOCUS: SEC PROPOSAL COULD CLOUD OFF-BALANCE-SHEET PICTURE

. . . The SEC on Wednesday proposed to toughen its rules for disclosing off-balance-sheet items by all public companies. Though others have offered more sweeping reforms—such as a Financial Accounting Standards Board plan that would restrict the use of off-the-books partnerships—experts said the SEC plan threatens to complicate the operation of special-purpose entities and similar arrangements popular with banks. "Banks that have standby letters of credit, swap agreements, reverse-repurchase agreements, and hedging devices will have to assess the disclosure requirements carefully," said V. Gerard Comizio, a partner in the corporate and financial institutions practice at Thacher, Proffitt & Wood. . . .

The corporate accounting scandals of the last year have put a sometimes unflattering spotlight on banks' and other public companies' use of off-the-books entities. For example, lawmakers and news reports have asked whether Citigroup Inc. and J. P. Morgan Chase & Co. used special-purpose entities to help Enron disguise its debt. In response to those concerns, the Sarbanes-Oxley Act directed the SEC to come up with disclosure requirements for off-balance-sheet arrangements that "may" be of material concern to the markets. Under the SEC's proposal, companies would disclose any transactions meeting the materiality standard in the management's discussion and analysis section of public filings. They would also describe the nature of the arrangements, aggregate contractual obligations in a table, and provide an overview of contingent liabilities and commitments. Those steps, the SEC said, would give a "total picture in a single location" of off-balance-sheet exposure.

Though securities rules already require issuers to disclose off-balance-sheet arrangements that are "reasonably likely" to be material, the agency interpreted Sarbanes-Oxley as dictating a stricter standard. It plans to have the standard be transactions that have a "more than remote" chance of being material.

Source: Todd Davenport, *The American Banker*, November 4, 2002, p. 1. *www.americanbanker.com*

TABLE 13–1 Some Big Losses on Derivatives

- September–October 1994: Bankers Trust is sued by Gibson Greeting and Procter & Gamble over derivative losses which amounted to $21 million for Gibson and a $200 million settlement for Procter & Gamble.

- February 1995: Barings, Britain's oldest investment bank, announces a loss which ultimately totals $1.38 billion, related to derivatives trading in Singapore by trader Nicholas Leeson.

- December 1996: NatWest Bank finds losses of £77 million caused by mispricing of derivatives in its investment-banking arm. Former trader Kyriacos Papouis was blamed for the loss, caused by two years of unauthorized trading by him, but NatWest Markets chief Martin Owen resigned over the incident.

- March 1997: Damian Cope, a former trader at Midland Bank's New York branch, was banned by the Federal Reserve Board over the falsification of books and records relating to his interest-rate derivatives trading activities. Midland parent HSBC said the amount of money involved was not significant.

- November 1997: Chase Manhattan was found to have lost up to $200 million on trading emerging-market debt; part of the problem was reportedly due to exposure to emerging markets through complex derivatives products.

- January 1998: Union Bank of Switzerland was reported sitting on unquantified derivatives losses; UBS pledged full disclosure at a later date.

- August–September 1998: Long-Term Capital Management, a hedge fund with an exposure exceeding $1.25 trillion in derivatives and other securities, had to be rescued by a consortium of commercial and investment banks that infused an additional $3.65 billion of equity into the fund.

- December 2001–January 2002: Allied Irish Banks incurs a $750 million loss from foreign exchange trades by rogue trader John Rusnak.

- July 2001: J. P. Morgan Chase and Citigroup exposed to $2.25 billion in losses on credit derivatives issued to a failing Enron.

Source: Dan Atkinson, "UBS Pledged Derivatives Explanation," *Manchester Guardian*, 1998; and update by author.

TABLE 13–2
Major Types of
Off-Balance-Sheet
Activities

Schedule L Activities*

  Loan commitment   Contractual commitment to make a loan up to a stated amount at a given interest rate in the future.

  Letters of credit   Contingent guarantees sold by an FI to underwrite the trade, commercial, or more severe and less predictable contingent performance of the buyer of the guaranty.

  Derivative contract   Agreement between two parties to exchange a standard quantity of an asset at a predetermined price at a specified date in the future.

  When issued trading   Trading in securities prior to their actual issue.

  Loans sold   Loans originated by an FI and then sold to other investors that (in some cases) can be returned to the originating institution in the future if the credit quality of the loans deteriorates.

Non–Schedule L Activities*

  Settlement risk   Intraday credit risk associated with CHIPS wire transfer activities.

  Affiliate risk   Risk imposed on one holding company affiliate as a result of the potential failure of the other holding company affiliates.

* As discussed later in the chapter, Schedule L activities are those that banks have to report to the Federal Reserve as part of their quarterly Call Reports. Non–Schedule L activities are those not subject to this requirement.

OFF-BALANCE-SHEET ACTIVITIES AND FI SOLVENCY

contingent assets and liabilities
Assets and liabilities off the balance sheet that potentially can produce positive or negative future cash flows for an FI.

One of the most important choices facing an FI manager is the relative scale of an FI's on- and off-balance-sheet activities. Most of us are aware of on-balance-sheet activities because they appear on an FI's published asset and liability balance sheets. For example, an FI's deposits and holdings of bonds and loans are on-balance-sheet activities. By comparison, off-balance-sheet activities are less obvious and often are invisible to all but the best-informed investor or regulator. In accounting terms, *off-balance-sheet items* usually appear "below the bottom line," frequently just as footnotes to financial statements. In economic terms, however, off-balance-sheet items are **contingent assets and liabilities** that affect the future, rather than the current, shape of an FI's balance sheet. As such, they have a direct impact on the FI's future profitability and solvency performance. Consequently, efficient management of these OBS items is central to controlling overall risk exposure in a modern FI.

off-balance-sheet asset
An item or activity that, when a contingent event occurs, moves onto the asset side of the balance sheet.

From a valuation perspective, OBS assets and liabilities have the potential to produce positive or negative *future* cash flows. As a result, the true value of an FI's capital or net worth is not simply the difference between the market value of assets and liabilities on its balance sheet today but also reflects the difference between the current market value of its off-balance-sheet or contingent assets and liabilities.

An item or activity is an **off-balance-sheet asset** if, when a contingent event occurs, the item or activity moves onto the asset side of the balance sheet. Conversely, an item or activity is an **OBS liability** if, when the contingent event occurs, the item or activity moves onto the liability side of the balance sheet. For example, as we discuss in more detail later, FIs sell various performance guarantees, especially guarantees that their customers will not default on their financial and other obligations. Examples of such guarantees include letters of credit and standby letters of credit. Should a customer default occur, the FI's contingent liability (its guaranty) becomes an actual liability and it moves onto the liability side of the balance sheet. Indeed, FI managers and regulators are just beginning to recognize and measure the risk of OBS activities and their impact on the FI's value.

off-balance-sheet liability
An item or activity that, when a contingent event occurs, moves onto the liability side of the balance sheet.

Since off-balance-sheet items are contingent assets and liabilities and move onto the balance sheet with a probability less than 1, their valuation is difficult and often highly complex. Because many off-balance-sheet items involve option features, the most common methodology has been to apply contingent claims/option pricing theory models of finance. For example, one relatively simple way to estimate the value of an OBS position in options is by calculating the **delta of an option**—the sensitivity of an option's value to a unit change in the price of the underlying security, which is then multiplied by the notional value of the option's position. (The delta of an option lies between 0 and 1.) Thus, suppose an FI has bought call options on bonds (i.e., it has an OBS asset) with a face or **notional value** of $100 million and the delta is calculated at .25.[2] Then the contingent asset value of this option position would be $25 million:

delta of an option
The change in the value of an option for a unit change in the price of the underlying security.

notional value of an OBS item
The face value of an OBS item.

$$d = \text{Delta of an option} = \frac{\text{Change in the option's price}}{\text{Change in price of underlying security}} = \frac{dO}{dS} = .25$$

$$F = \text{Notional or face value of options} = \$100 \text{ million}$$

The delta equivalent or contingent asset value = delta × face value of option = .25 × $100 million = $25 million. Of course, to figure the value of delta for the option, one needs an option pricing model such as Black-Scholes or a binomial model. In general, the delta of the option varies with the level of the price of the underlying security as it moves in and out of the money;[3] that is, $0 < d < 1$.[4] Note that if the FI sold options, they would be valued as a contingent liability.[5]

Loan commitments and letters of credit are also off-balance-sheet activities that have option features.[6] Specifically, the holder of a loan commitment or credit line who decides to draw on that credit line is exercising an *option to borrow*. When the buyer of a guaranty defaults, this buyer is exercising a *default* option. Similarly, when the counterparty to a derivatives transaction is unable or unwilling to meet its obligation to pay (e.g., in a swap), this is considered an exercise of a default option.

With respect to swaps, futures, and forwards, a common approach is to convert these positions into an equivalent value of the underlying assets. For example, a $20 million, 10-year, fixed–floating interest rate swap in which an FI

---

[2] A 1-cent change in the price of the bonds underlying the call option leads to a 0.25 cent (or quarter-cent) change in the price of the option.

[3] For example, for an in-the-money call option the price of the underlying security exceeds the option's exercise price. For an out-of-the money call option, the price of the underlying security is less than the option's exercise price. In general, the relationship between the value of an option and the underlying value of a security is nonlinear. Thus, using the delta method to derive the market value of an option is at best an approximation. To deal with the nonlinearity of payoffs on options, some analysts take into account the gamma as well as the delta of the option (gamma measures the change in delta as the underlying security price varies). For example, the standardized model of the BIS used to calculate the market risk of options incorporates an option's delta, its gamma, and its vega (a measure of volatility risk). See Bank for International Settlements, *Standardized Model for Market Risk* (Basel, Switzerland, BIS, 1996). See also J. P. Morgan, *RiskMetrics,* 4th ed., 1996.

[4] In the context of the Black-Scholes model, the value of the delta on a call option is $d = N(d_1)$, where $N(.)$ is the cumulative normal distribution function and $d_1 = [ln(S/X) + (r + \sigma^2/2\tau]/\sigma \sqrt{T}$.

[5] Note that a cap or a floor is a complex option—that is, a collection of individual options (see Chapter 25).

[6] See S. I. Greenbaum, H. Hong, and A. Thakor, "Bank Loan Commitments and Interest Rate Volatility," *Journal of Banking and Finance* 5 (1981), pp. 497–510; T. Ho and A. Saunders, "Fixed Rate Loan Commitments, Takedown Risk, and the Dynamics of Hedging with Futures," *Journal of Financial and Quantitative Analysis* 18 (1983), pp. 499–516; and O. E. Ergungor, "Theories of Bank Loan Commitments: A Literature Review," Working Paper, Federal Reserve Bank of Cleveland, September 2000.

TABLE 13–3
Traditional Valuation of an FI's Net Worth

Assets		Liabilities	
Market value of assets (A)	100	Market value of liabilities (L)	90
		Net worth (E)	10
	100		100

TABLE 13–4
Valuation of an FI's Net Worth with On- and Off-Balance-Sheet Activities Valued

Assets		Liabilities	
Market value of assets (A)	100	Market value of liabilities (L)	90
		Net worth (E)	5
Market value of contingent assets (CA)	50	Market value of contingent liabilities (CL)	55
	150		150

receives 20 semiannual fixed interest rate payments of 8 percent per annum (i.e., 4 percent per half year) and pays floating rate payments every half year indexed to LIBOR, can be viewed as the equivalent, in terms of valuation, of an on-balance-sheet position in two $20 million bonds. That is, the FI can be viewed as being long $20 million (holding an asset) in a 10-year bond with an annual coupon of 8 percent per annum and short $20 million (holding a liability) in a floating-rate bond of 10 years' maturity whose rate is adjusted every six months.[7] The market value of the swap can be viewed as the present value of the difference between the cash flows on the fixed-rate bond and the expected cash flows on the floating-rate bond. This market value is usually a very small percent of the notional value of the swap. In our example of a $20 million swap, the market value is about 3 percent of this figure, or $600,000.[8]

Given these valuation models, we can calculate, in an approximate sense, the current or market value of each OBS asset and liability and its effect on an FI's solvency. Consider Tables 13–3 and 13–4. In Table 13–3 the value of the FI's net worth (E) is calculated in the traditional way as the difference between the market values of its on-balance-sheet assets (A) and liabilities (L). As we discussed in Chapter 8:

$$E = A - L$$
$$10 = 100 - 90$$

Under this calculation, the market value of the stockholders' equity stake in the FI is 10 and the ratio of the FI's capital to assets (or capital–assets ratio) is 10 percent. Regulators and FIs often use the latter ratio as a simple measure of solvency (see Chapter 20 for more details).

A truer picture of the FI's economic solvency should consider the market value of both its visible on-balance-sheet and OBS activities. Specifically, the FI manager should value contingent or future assets and liability claims as well as current assets and liabilities. In our example, the current market value of the FI's contingent assets (CA) is 50, while the current market value of its contingent liabilities (CL) is 55. Since the market value of contingent liabilities exceeds the market value of

[7] An interest rate swap does not normally involve principal payments on maturity. In the case above, the two principal amounts on the fixed- and floating-rate bonds cancel each other out.

[8] This is based on calculations by J. Kambhu, F. Keane, and C. Benadon, "Price Risk Intermediation in the Over-the-Counter Derivatives Markets: Interpretation of a Global Survey," Federal Reserve Bank of New York, *Economic Policy Review,* April 1996, pp. 1–15.

contingent assets by 5, this difference is an additional obligation, or claim, on the net worth of the FI. That is, stockholders' true net worth (E) is really:

$$E = (A - L) + (CA - CL)$$
$$= (100 - 90) + (50 - 55)$$
$$= 5$$

rather than 10, as it was when we ignored off-balance-sheet activities. Thus, economically speaking, contingent assets and liabilities are contractual claims that directly impact the economic value of the FI. Indeed, from both the stockholders' and regulators' perspectives, large increases in the value of OBS liabilities can render an FI economically insolvent just as effectively as can losses due to mismatched interest rate gaps and default or credit losses from on-balance-sheet activities. For example, in 1998, J. P. Morgan had to recognize $587 million in currency swaps as nonperforming, of which $489 million were related to currency swaps with SK, a Korean investment company. Two of those swaps involved the exchange of Thai baht for Japanese yen in which SK would benefit if the Thai baht rose in value. As it turned out, soon after the contract was entered into, the baht collapsed and SK disputed the legality of the contract.[9] In 2001, U.S. Bancorp announced a special $1 billion charge to boost its loan loss reserves, specifying that part of the reserve addition would be allocated against exposure to undrawn loan commitments.

Concept Questions

1. Define a contingent asset and a contingent liability.
2. Suppose an FI had a market value of assets of 95 and a market value of liabilities of 88. In addition, it had contingent assets valued at 10 and contingent liabilities valued at 7. What is the FI's true net worth position?

RETURNS AND RISKS OF OFF-BALANCE-SHEET ACTIVITIES

In the 1980s, rising losses on loans to less developed and Eastern European countries, increased interest rate volatility, and squeezed interest margins for on-balance-sheet lending due to nonbank competition induced many large commercial banks to seek profitable OBS activities. By moving activities off the balance sheet, banks hoped to earn more fee income to offset declining margins or spreads on their traditional lending business. At the same time, they could avoid regulatory costs or taxes, since reserve requirements, deposit insurance premiums, and capital adequacy requirements were not levied on off-balance-sheet activities. Thus, banks had both earnings and regulatory tax-avoidance incentives to move activities off their balance sheets.[10]

www.federalreserve. gov

The dramatic growth in OBS activities caused the Federal Reserve to introduce a tracking scheme in 1983. As part of their quarterly call reports, banks began submitting schedule L on which they listed the notional size and variety of their OBS activities. We show these off-balance-sheet activities for U.S. commercial banks and their distribution and growth for 1992 and 2003 in Table 13–5. We also show the 2003 distribution of OBS activities for Bank One Corporation in Table 13–5.

In Table 13–5 notice the relative growth of off-balance-sheet activities. In 1992, the notional or face value of OBS bank activities was $10,200.3 billion compared with

---

[9] See "J. P. Morgan in Korean Battle on Derivatives," *New York Times*, February 27, 1998, p. D1.

[10] For a modeling of the incentives to go off balance sheet due to capital requirements, see G. G. Pennacchi, "Loan Sales and the Cost of Bank Capital," *Journal of Finance* 43 (1988), pp. 375–96. Also, Chapter 27 goes into further details on incentives relating to loan sales.

TABLE 13–5   Aggregate Volume of Off-Balance-Sheet Commitments and Contingencies by U.S. Commercial Banks (in billions of dollars)

	1992	2003*	Distribution 2003	Bank One 2003*
Commitments to lend	$ 1,272.0	$ 5,527.5	7.3%	$ 490.8
Future and forward contracts (exclude FX)				
On commodities and equities	26.3	105.0	0.1	0.7
On interest rates	1,738.1	6,890.5	9.2	193.1
Notional amount of credit derivatives				
Bank is guarantor	4.1	405.8	0.5	6.5
Bank is beneficiary	4.5	463.2	0.6	10.2
Standby contracts and other option contracts				
Written option contracts on interest rates	504.7	5,982.5	8.0	75.6
Purchased option contracts on interest rates	508.0	5,977.4	7.9	82.1
Written option contracts on foreign exchange	245.7	705.0	0.9	18.9
Purchased option contracts on foreign exchange	249.1	714.7	0.9	17.8
Written option contracts on commodities	30.9	406.5	0.5	1.1
Purchased option contracts on commodities	29.4	393.5	0.5	2.7
Commitments to buy FX (includes $U.S.), spot, and forward	3,015.5	5,168.8	6.9	104.4
Standby LCs and foreign office guarantees	162.5	360.0	0.5	25.2
(Amount of these items sold to others via participations)	(14.9)	(57.2)		(17.0)
Commercial LCs	28.1	23.3	0.0	0.6
Participations in acceptances sold to others	0.8	0.3	0.0	0.0
Participations in acceptances bought from others	0.2	0.2	0.0	0.0
Securities lent	96.4	767.6	1.0	3.8
Other significant commitments and contingencies	19.5	58.1	0.1	0.0
Notional value of all outstanding interest rate and FX swaps	2,122.0	41,205.5	54.8	732.2
Mortgages sold, with recourse				
Outstanding principal balance of mortgages sold or swapped	10.7	2.4	0.0	0.0
Amount of recourse exposure on these mortgages	6.3	0.2	0.0	0.0
Total	$10,200.3	$75,158.0	100.0%	$1,765.7
Total assets (on-balance-sheet items)	$ 3,476.4	$ 7,474.3		$ 300.1

FX = Foreign exchange, LC = Letter of credit.
*Third quarter.
Source: FDIC, *Statistics on Banking*, various issues. *www.fdic.gov*

$3,476.4 billion in on-balance-sheet activities. By the third quarter of 2003, the notional value of these OBS bank activities was $75,158.0 billion (an increase of 637 percent in 11 years) compared with $7,474.3 billion of on-balance-sheet activities (an increase of 115 percent). Likewise, in 2003 Bank One had total OBS activities of $1,765.7 billion ($1,140.9 of which were derivative contracts [futures, forwards, swaps, options, and credit derivatives]) compared with on-balance-sheet assets of $300.1 billion. Table 13–6 shows that much of the growth in OBS activities during the period 1992–2003 was due to derivative contracts. Bank holdings of these contracts increased 796 percent, from $8,765 billion in 1992 to $65,838 billion in the second quarter of 2003. The vast majority of these OBS activities are conducted by just a very few banks. For example, in 2003 approximately 530 of the over 7,800 U.S. banks held the OBS derivatives reported in Table 13–5, and the largest 25 banks

TABLE 13–6
Derivative Contracts Held by Commercial Banks, by Contract Product (in billions of dollars)*

Source: Office of the Comptroller of the Currency Web site, Second Quarter 2003. *www.occ.treas.gov*

	1992	1996	2000	2003 (second quarter)
Futures and forwards	$4,780	$ 8,041	$ 9,877	$12,658
Swaps	2,417	7,601	21,949	38,074
Options	1,568	4,393	8,292	14,304
Credit derivatives	—	—	426	802
Total	$8,765	$20,035	$40,544	$65,838

* Notional amount of futures, total exchange traded options, total over-the-counter options, total forwards, and total swaps. Note that data after 1994 do not include spot FX in the total notional amount of derivatives. Credit derivatives were reported for the first time in the first quarter of 1997. Currently, the Call Report does not differentiate credit derivatives by product and thus they have been added as a separate category.

held 99.5 percent of the derivatives outstanding. While, as noted above, the notional value of OBS items overestimates their current market or contingent claims values, the growth of these activities is still nothing short of phenomenal. Indeed, this phenomenal increase has pushed regulators to impose capital requirements on such activities and to explicitly recognize FIs' solvency risk exposure from pursuing such activities. These capital requirements came into affect on January 1, 1993; we describe them in Chapter 20.

From Tables 13–5 and 13–6, the major types of OBS activities for U.S. banks are:

- Loan commitments.
- Standby letters of credit and letters of credit.
- Futures, forward contracts, swaps, and options.
- When issued securities.
- Loans sold.

Larger thrifts and insurance companies engage in most of these OBS activities as well.[11]

The next section analyzes these OBS activities in more detail and pays particular attention to the types of risk exposure an FI faces when engaging in such activities. As we discussed earlier, precise market valuation of these contingent assets and liabilities can be extremely difficult because of their complex contingent claim features and option aspects. At a very minimum, FI managers should understand not only the general features of the risk exposure associated with each major OBS asset and liability but also how each one can impact the return and profitability of an FI.

loan commitment agreement
A contractual commitment to make a loan up to a stated amount at a given interest rate in the future.

Loan Commitments

These days, most commercial and industrial loans are made by firms that take down (or borrow against) prenegotiated lines of credit or loan commitments rather than borrow spot loans (see Chapter 11's discussion on C&I loans).[12] A recent Federal Reserve study estimated that 79 percent of all C&I lending is made under commitment contracts.[13] A **loan commitment agreement** is a contractual commitment

---

[11] See, for example, M. K. Hassan and W. H. Sackley, "Determinants of Thrift Institution Off-Balance-Sheet Activities: An Empirical Investigation," Working Paper 70148, Department of Finance, University of New Orleans, LA.

[12] For example, see Hassan and Sackley, "Determinants of Thrift Institution Off-Balance-Sheet Activities"; S. Figlewski, "The Use of Futures and Options by Life Insurance Companies," *Best's Review,* 1989; and R. L. Shockley and A. V. Thakor, "Bank Loan Commitment Contracts: Data, Theory and Tests," *Journal of Money, Credit and Banking* 29 (November 1997) (part 1), pp. 517–34.

[13] See O. E. Ergungor, "Theories of Bank Loan Commitments: A Literature Review," Working Paper, Federal Reserve Bank of Cleveland, September 2000.

FIGURE 13–1
Structure of a Loan Commitment

by an FI to lend to a firm a certain maximum amount (say, $10 million) at given interest rate terms (say, 12 percent). The loan commitment agreement also defines the length of time over which the borrower has the option to take down this loan. In return for making this loan commitment, the FI may charge an **up-front fee** (or facility fee) of, say, $\frac{1}{8}$ percent of the commitment size, or $12,500 in this example. In addition, the FI must stand ready to supply the full $10 million at any time over the commitment period—say, one year. Meanwhile, the borrower has a valuable option to take down any amount between $0 and $10 million. The FI also may charge the borrower a **back-end fee** (or commitment fee) on any unused balances in the commitment line at the end of the period.[14] In this example, if the borrower takes down only $8 million in funds over the year and the fee on *unused* commitments is $\frac{1}{4}$ percent, the FI will generate additional revenue of $\frac{1}{4}$ percent times $2 million, or $5,000. Figure 13–1 presents a summary of the structure of this loan commitment.

up-front fee
The fee charged for making funds available through a loan commitment.

back-end fee
The fee imposed on the unused balance of a loan commitment.

EXAMPLE 13–1

Calculation of the Promised Return on a Loan Commitment

It is quite easy to show how the unique features of loan commitments affect the promised return $(1 + k)$ on a loan. In Chapter 11 we developed a model for determining $(1 + k)$ on a spot loan. This can be extended by allowing for partial takedown and the up-front and back-end fees commonly found in loan commitments. For a one-year loan commitment, let:

BR = Interest on the loan = 12%
m = Risk premium = 2%
f_1 = Up-front fee on the whole commitment = $\frac{1}{8}$%
f_2 = Back-end fee on the unused commitment = $\frac{1}{4}$%
b = Compensating balance = 10%
RR = Reserve requirements = 10%
td = Expected (average) takedown rate $(0 < td < 1)$ on the loan commitment = 75%

Then the general formula for the promised return $(1 + k)$ of the loan commitment is:[15]

$$1 + k = 1 + \frac{f_1 + f_2(1 - td) + (BR + m)td}{td - [b(td)(1 - RR)]}$$

$$1 + k = 1 + \frac{.00125 + .0025(.25) + (.12 + .02).75}{.75 - [(.10)(.75)(.9)]}$$

$$1 + k = 1 + \frac{.106875}{.682500} = 1.1566 \text{ or } k = 15.66\%$$

---

[14] This can be viewed as an excess capacity charge; see A. V. Thakor and G. Udell, "An Economic Rationale for the Pricing Structure of Bank Loan Commitments," *Journal of Banking and Finance* 11 (1987), pp. 271–90.

[15] This formula closely follows that in John R. Brick, *Commercial Banking: Text and Readings* (Haslett, MI: Systems Publication, Inc., 1984), chap. 4. Note that for simplicity we have used undiscounted cash flows. Taking into account the time value of money means that we would need to discount both f_2 and $BR + m$ since they are paid at the end of the period. If the discount factor (cost of funds) is $d = 10$ percent, then $k = 14.25$ percent.

Note that only when the borrower actually draws on the commitment do the loans made under the commitment appear on the balance sheet. Thus, only when the $8 million loan is taken down exactly halfway through the one-year commitment period (i.e., six months later), does the balance sheet show a new $8 million loan being created. When the $10 million commitment is made at time 0, nothing shows on the balance sheet. Nevertheless, the FI must stand ready to make the full $10 million in loans on any day within the one-year commitment period; that is, at time 0 a new contingent claim on the resources of the FI was created.

This raises the question: What contingent risks are created by the loan commitment provision? At least four types of risk are associated with the extension of loan commitments: interest rate risk, takedown risk, credit risk, and aggregate funding risk.

Interest Rate Risk

Interest rate risk is a contingent risk emanating from the fact that the FI precommits to make loans available to a borrower over the commitment period at either (1) some fixed interest rate as a fixed-rate loan commitment or (2) some variable rate as a variable-rate loan commitment. Suppose the FI precommits to lend a maximum of $10 million at a fixed rate of 12 percent over the year and its cost of funds rises. The cost of funds may well rise to a level that makes the spread between the 12 percent commitment rate and the FI's cost of funds negative or very small. Moreover, 12 percent may be much less than the rate the customer would have to pay if forced to borrow on the spot loan market under current interest rate conditions. When rates do rise over the commitment period, the FI stands to lose on its portfolio of fixed-rate loan commitments as borrowers exercise to the full amount their very valuable options to borrow at below-market rates.[16]

One way the FI can control this risk is by making commitment rates float with spot loan rates, for example, by indexing loan commitments to the prime rate. If the prime rate rises during the commitment period, so does the cost of commitment loans to the borrower—the borrower pays the market rate in effect when the commitment is drawn on. Nevertheless, this fixed formula rate solution does not totally eradicate interest rate risk on loan commitments. For example, suppose that the prime rate rises 1 percent but the cost of funds rises 1.25 percent; the spread between the indexed commitment loan and the cost of funds narrows by .25 percent. This spread risk is often called **basis risk.**[17]

basis risk
The variable spread between a lending rate and a borrowing rate or between any two interest rates or prices.

Takedown Risk

Another contingent risk is takedown risk. Specifically, in making the loan commitment, the FI must always stand ready to provide the maximum of the commitment line—$10 million in our example. The borrower has the flexible option to borrow anything between $0 and the $10 million ceiling on any business day in the commitment period. This exposes the FI to a degree of future liquidity risk or uncertainty (see Chapter 17). The FI can never be absolutely sure when, during the commitment period, the borrower will demand the full $10 million or some proportion thereof in cash.[18] For example, in February 2002, Tyco International unexpectedly drew down $14.4 billion in

---

[16] In an options sense, the loans are in the money to the borrower.

[17] Basis risk arises because loan rates and deposit rates are not perfectly correlated in their movements over time.

[18] Indeed, the borrower could come to the bank and borrow different amounts over the period ($1 million in month 1, $2 million in month 2, etc.). The only constraint is the $10 million ceiling. See Ho and Saunders, "Fixed Rate Loan Commitments," for a modeling approach to takedown risk. We discuss this liquidity risk aspect of loan commitments further in Chapter 17.

credit lines from banks such as Bank of America and J. P. Morgan Chase after being shut out of the commercial paper market when investors began to doubt its accounting practices. To some extent, at least, the back-end fee on unused amounts is designed to create incentives for the borrower to take down lines in full to avoid paying this fee. However, in actuality, many lines are only partially drawn upon.[19]

Credit Risk

FIs also face a degree of contingent credit risk in setting the interest or formula rate on a loan commitment. Specifically, the FI often adds a risk premium based on its current assessment of the creditworthiness of the borrower. For example, the borrower may be judged as a AA credit risk paying 1 percent above prime rate. However, suppose that over the one-year commitment period the borrowing firm gets into difficulty; its earnings decline so that its creditworthiness is downgraded to BBB. The FI's problem is that the credit risk premium on the commitment had been preset to the AA level for the one-year commitment period. To avoid being exposed to dramatic declines in borrower creditworthiness over the commitment period, most FIs include an *adverse material change in conditions clause* by which the FI can cancel or reprice a loan commitment. However, exercising such a clause is really a last resort tactic for an FI because it may put the borrower out of business and result in costly legal claims for breach of contract.[20]

Aggregate Funding Risk

Many large borrowing firms, such as GM, Ford, and IBM, take out multiple commitment or credit lines with many FIs as insurance against future credit crunches.[21] In a credit crunch, the supply of spot loans to borrowers is restricted, possibly as a result of restrictive monetary policy actions of the Federal Reserve. Another cause is an FI's increased aversion toward lending, that is, a shift to the left in the loan supply function at all interest rates. In such credit crunches, borrowers with long-standing loan commitments are unlikely to be as credit constrained as those without loan commitments. However, this also implies that borrowers' aggregate demand to take down loan commitments is likely to be greatest when the FI's borrowing and funding conditions are most costly and difficult. In difficult credit conditions, this aggregate commitment takedown effect can increase the cost of funds above normal levels while many FIs scramble for funds to meet their commitments to customers. This is similar to the *externality effect* common in many markets when all participants simultaneously act together and adversely affect the costs of each individual participant.

---

[19] See A. Melnick and S. Plaut, "Loan Commitment Contracts, Terms of Lending, and Credit Allocations," *Journal of Finance* 41 (1986), pp. 425–36; R. L. Shockley and A. V. Thakor, "Bank Loan Commitment Contracts"; and E. Asarnow and J. Marker, "Historical Performance of the U.S. Corporate Loan Market 1988–1993," *Journal of Commercial Lending,* Spring 1995, pp. 13–22. Asarnow and Marker show that the average takedown rates vary widely by borrower credit rating, from a takedown rate of only 0.1 percent by a AAA borrower to 20 percent for BBB and 75 percent for CCC.

[20] Potential damage claims can be enormous if the borrower goes out of business and attributes this to the cancelation of loans under the commitment contract. There are also important reputational costs to take into account in canceling a commitment to lend.

[21] Recent research by Donald P. Morgan, "The Credit Effects of Monetary Policy: Evidence Using Loan Commitments," *Journal of Money, Credit, and Banking* 30 (February 1998), pp. 102–18, has found evidence of this type of insurance effect. Specifically, in credit crunches, spot loans may decline, but loans made under commitment do not.

The four contingent risk effects just identified—interest rate risk, takedown risk, credit risk, and aggregate funding risk—appear to imply that loan commitment activities increase the insolvency exposure of FIs that engage in such activities. However, an opposing view holds that loan commitment contracts may make an FI less risky than had it not engaged in them. This view maintains that to be able to charge fees and sell loan commitments or equivalent credit rationing insurance, the FI must convince borrowers that it will still be around to provide the credit needed in the *future*[22] To convince borrowers that an FI will be around to meet its future commitments, managers may have to adopt *lower*-risk portfolios *today* than would otherwise be the case. By adopting lower-risk portfolios, managers increase the probability that the FI will be able to meet all its long-term on- and off-balance-sheet obligations. Interestingly, empirical studies have confirmed that banks making more loan commitments have lower on-balance-sheet portfolio risk characteristics than those with relatively low levels of commitments; that is, safer banks have a greater tendency to make loan commitments.[23]

Commercial Letters of Credit and Standby Letters of Credit

commercial letters of credit

Contingent guarantees sold by an FI to underwrite the trade or commercial performance of the buyer of the guaranty.

In selling **commercial letters of credit** (LCs) and **standby letters of credit** (SLCs) for fees, FIs add to their contingent future liabilities. Both LCs and SLCs are essentially *guarantees* sold by an FI to underwrite the *performance* of the buyer of the guaranty (such as a corporation). In economic terms, the FI that sells LCs and SLCs is selling insurance against the frequency or severity of some particular future occurrence. Further, similar to the different lines of insurance sold by property–casualty insurers, LC and SLC contracts differ as to the severity and frequency of their risk exposures. We look next at an FI's risk exposure from engaging in LC and SLC off-balance-sheet activities.

standby letters of credit

Guarantees issued to cover contingencies that are potentially more severe and less predictable than contingencies covered under trade-related or commercial letters of credit.

Commercial Letters of Credit

Commercial letters of credit are widely used in both domestic and international trade. For example, they ease the shipment of grain between a farmer in Iowa and a purchaser in New Orleans or the shipment of goods between a U.S. importer and a foreign exporter. The FI's role is to provide a formal guaranty that payment for goods shipped or sold will be forthcoming regardless of whether the buyer of the goods defaults on payment. We show a very simple LC example in Figure 13–2 for an international transaction between a U.S. importer and a German exporter.

Suppose the U.S. importer sent an order for $10 million worth of machinery to a German exporter, as shown by arrow 1 in Figure 13–2. However, the German exporter may be reluctant to send the goods without some assurance or guaranty of being paid once the goods are shipped. The U.S. importer may promise to pay for the goods in 90 days, but the German exporter may feel insecure either because it knows little about the creditworthiness of the U.S. importer or because the U.S. importer has a low credit rating (say, B or BB). To persuade the German exporter to ship the goods, the U.S. importer may have to turn to a large U.S. FI with which it has developed a long-term customer relationship. In its role as a lender and monitor, the U.S. FI can better appraise the U.S. importer's creditworthiness. The U.S. FI can issue a contingent payment guaranty—that is, an LC to the German

---

[22] A. W. A. Boot and A. V. Thakor, "Off-Balance-Sheet Liabilities, Deposit Insurance, and Capital Regulation," *Journal of Banking and Finance* 15 (1991), pp. 825–46.

[23] See, for example, R. B. Avery and A. N. Berger, "Loan Commitments and Bank Risk Exposure," *Journal of Banking and Finance* 15 (1991), pp. 173–92.

FIGURE 13–2
Simple Letter of Credit Transaction

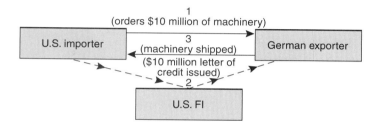

exporter on the importer's behalf—in return for an LC fee paid by the U.S. importer.[24] In our example, the FI would send to the German exporter an LC guaranteeing payment for the goods in 90 days regardless of whether the importer defaults on its obligation to the German exporter (see arrow 2 in Figure 13–2). Implicitly, the FI is replacing the U.S. importer's credit risk with its own credit risk guaranty. For this substitution to work effectively, in guaranteeing payment, the FI must have a higher credit standing or better credit quality reputation than the U.S. importer.[25] Once the FI issues the LC and sends it to the German exporter, the exporter ships the goods to the U.S. importer, as shown by arrow 3. The probability is very high that in 90 days' time, the U.S. importer will pay the German exporter for the goods sent and the FI keeps the LC fee as profit. The fee is, perhaps, 10 basis points of the face value of the letter of credit, or $10,000 in this example.

A small probability exists, however, that the U.S. importer will be unable to pay the $10 million in 90 days and will default. Then the FI would be obliged to make good on its guaranty. The cost of such a default could mean an FI must pay $10 million, although it would have a creditor's claim against the importer's assets to offset this loss. Clearly, the LC fee should exceed the expected default risk on the LC, which is equal to the probability of default times the expected net payout on the LC, after adjusting for the FI's ability to reclaim assets from the defaulting importer and any monitoring costs.[26] A more detailed version of an LC transaction is presented in Appendix 13A to the chapter, located at the book's Web site (**www.mhhe.com/saunders5e**).

Standby Letters of Credit

Standby letters of credit perform an insurance function similar to that of commercial and trade letters of credit. However, the structure and type of risks covered are different. FIs may issue SLCs to cover contingencies that are potentially more *severe,*

---

[24] The FI subsequently notifies the German exporter that, upon meeting the delivery requirements, the exporter is entitled to draw a time draft against the letter of credit at the importer's FI (i.e., withdraw money) for the amount of the transaction. After the export order is shipped, the German exporter presents the time draft and the shipping papers to its own (foreign) FI, who forwards these to the U.S. importer's U.S. FI. The U.S. FI stamps the time draft as accepted and the draft becomes a banker's acceptance listed *on the balance sheet.* At this point, the U.S. FI either returns the stamped time draft (now a banker's acceptance) to the German exporter's FI and payment is made on the maturity date (e.g., in 90 days), or the U.S. FI immediately pays the foreign FI (and implicitly the exporter) the discounted value of the banker's acceptance. In either case, the foreign FI pays the German exporter for the goods. When the banker's acceptance matures, the U.S. importer must pay its U.S. FI for the purchases, and the U.S. FI sends the U.S. importer the shipping papers.

[25] In fact, research has found that, when the market becomes aware that a line of credit is granted, the FI customer experiences a significant increase in its stock price. See M. Mosebach, "Market Response to Banks Granting Lines of Credit," *Journal of Banking and Finance* 23 (1999), pp. 1701–23.

[26] Hassan finds that stockholders view commercial letter of credit activities by banks as risk reducing. See M. K. Hassan, "The Market Perception of the Riskiness of Large U.S. Bank Commercial Letters of Credit," *Journal of Financial Services Research* 6 (1992), pp. 207–21.

less *predictable* or frequent, and not necessarily trade related.[27] These contingencies include performance bond guarantees whereby an FI may guarantee that a real estate development will be completed in some interval of time. Alternatively, the FI may offer default guarantees to back an issue of commercial paper (CP) or municipal revenue bonds to allow issuers to achieve a higher credit rating and a lower funding cost than would otherwise be the case.

Without credit enhancements, for example, many firms would be unable to borrow in the CP market or would have to borrow at a higher funding cost. P1 borrowers, who offer the highest-quality commercial paper, normally pay 40 basis points less than P2 borrowers, the next quality grade. By paying a fee of perhaps 25 basis points to an FI, the FI guarantees to pay CP purchasers' principal and interest on maturity should the issuing firm itself be unable to pay. The SLC backing of CP issues normally results in the paper's placement in the lowest default risk class (P1) and the issuer's savings of up to 15 basis points on issuing costs—40 basis points (the P2–P1 spread) minus the 25-basis-point SLC fee equals 15 basis points.

Note that in selling the SLCs, FIs are competing directly with another of their OBS products, loan commitments. Rather than buying an SLC from an FI to back a CP issue, the issuing firm might pay a fee to an FI to supply a loan commitment. This loan commitment would match the size and maturity of the CP issue, for example, a $100 million ceiling and 45 days maturity. If, on maturity, the CP issuer has insufficient funds to repay the CP holders, the issuer has the right to take down the $100 million loan commitment and to use those funds to meet CP repayments. Often, the up-front fees on such loan commitments are less than those on SLCs; therefore, many CP-issuing firms prefer to use loan commitments.

It needs to be stressed that U.S. banks are not the only issuers of SLCs. Not surprisingly, performance bonds and financial guarantees are an important business line of property–casualty insurers. The growth in these lines for property–casualty insurers has come at the expense of U.S. banks. Moreover, foreign banks increasingly are taking a share of the U.S. market in SLCs. The reason for the loss in this business line by U.S. banks is that to sell guarantees such as SLCs credibly, the seller must have a better credit rating than the customer. In recent years, few U.S. banks or their parent holding companies have had AA ratings. Other domestic FIs and foreign banks, on the other hand, have more often had AA ratings. High credit ratings not only make the guarantor more attractive from the buyer's perspective but also make the guarantor more competitive because its cost of funds is lower than that of less creditworthy FIs.

Derivative Contracts: Futures, Forwards, Swaps, and Options

FIs can be either users of derivative contracts for hedging (see Chapters 24 through 26) and other purposes or dealers that act as counterparties in trades with customers for a fee. In 2003, approximately 530 U.S. banks were users of derivatives, with three big dealer banks (J. P. Morgan Chase, Bank of America, and Citigroup) accounting for some 87 percent of the $65,838 billion derivatives held by the user banks and reported in Table 13–6. In the second quarter of 2003 these 530 banks earned over $3.1 billion in trading revenue from their derivatives portfolios. However, as noted in Table 13–1, risk on these securities can lead to large losses.

Contingent credit risk is likely to be present when FIs expand their positions in forwards, futures, swaps, and option contracts. This risk relates to the fact that the

www.jpmorganchase.
com
www.bankofamerica.
com
www.citigroup.com

---

[27] G. O. Koppenhaver uses a similar definition to distinguish between LCs and SLCs. See "Standby Letters of Credit," Federal Reserve Bank of Chicago, *Economic Perspectives*, 1987, pp. 28–38.

counterparty to one of these contracts may default on payment obligations, leaving the FI unhedged and having to replace the contract at today's interest rates, prices, or exchange rates.[28] Further, such defaults are most likely to occur when the counterparty is losing heavily on the contract and the FI is in the money on the contract. As noted earlier, J. P. Morgan suffered significantly increased default exposure on its derivative positions in 1998. This type of default risk is much more serious for forward (and swap) contracts than for futures contracts. This is so because **forward contracts**[29] are nonstandard contracts entered into bilaterally by negotiating parties such as two FIs, and all cash flows are required to be paid at one time (on contract maturity). Thus, they are essentially over-the-counter (OTC) arrangements with no external guarantees should one or the other party default on the contract. For example, the contract seller might default on a forward foreign exchange contract that promises to deliver £10 million in three months' time at the exchange rate of $1.40 to £1 if the cost to purchase £1 for delivery is $1.60 when the forward contract matures. By contrast, **futures contracts** are standardized contracts guaranteed by organized exchanges such as the New York Futures Exchange (NYFE), a part of the New York Board of Trade (NYBOT). Futures contracts, like forward contracts, make commitments to deliver foreign exchange (or some other asset) at some future date. If a counterparty defaults on a futures contract, however, the exchange assumes the defaulting party's position and the payment obligations. For example, when Barings, the British merchant bank, was unable to meet its margin calls on Nikkei Index futures traded on the Singapore futures exchange (SIMEX) in 1995, the exchange stood ready to assume Barings' $8 billion position in futures contracts and ensure that no counterparty lost money. Thus, unless a systematic financial market collapse threatens the exchange itself, futures are essentially default risk free.[30] In addition, default risk is reduced by the daily marking to market of contracts. This prevents the accumulation of losses and gains that occurs with forward contracts. These differences are discussed in more detail in Chapter 24.

An option is a contract that gives the holder the right, but not the obligation, to buy (a call option) or sell (a put option) an underlying asset at a prespecified price for a specified time period. Option contracts can also be purchased or sold by an FI, trading either over the counter (OTC) or bought/sold on organized exchanges. If the options are standardized options traded on exchanges, such as bond options, they are virtually default risk free.[31] If they are specialized options purchased OTC such as interest rate caps (see Chapter 25), some element of default risk exists.[32]

forward contracts
Nonstandard contracts between two parties to deliver and pay for an asset in the future.

futures contracts
Standardized contract guaranteed by organized exchanges to deliver and pay for an asset in the future.

www.nybot.com

---

[28] In fact, J. F. Sinkey, Jr., and D. A. Carter, in "The Reaction of Bank Stock Prices to News of Derivative Losses by Corporate Clients," *Journal of Banking and Finance* 23 (1999), pp. 1725–43, find that when large nonfinancial firms announced losses from derivative deals, the FI serving as the derivatives dealer experiences significant stock price declines. Thus, FIs are exposed to OBS risk as a party to a derivatives contract as well as a derivative dealer (acting as a third party, but not a direct party, to the contract).

[29] Conceptually, a swap contract can be viewed as a succession of forward contracts.

[30] More specifically, there are at least four reasons why the default risk of a futures contract is less than that of a forward contract: (1) daily marking to market of futures, (2) margin requirements on futures that act as a security bond, (3) price limits that spread out over extreme price fluctuations, and (4) default guarantees by the futures exchange itself.

[31] Note that the options can still be subject to interest rate risk; see our earlier discussion of the delta on a bond option.

[32] Under an interest rate cap, in return for a fee, the seller promises to compensate the buyer if interest rates rise above a certain level. If rates rise a lot more than expected, the cap seller may have an incentive to default to truncate the losses. Thus, selling a cap is similar to an FI selling interest rate risk insurance (see Chapter 25 for more details).

FIGURE 13–3
T-Bill Auction
Time Line

Tuesday	Monday
Size of	Allotment of bills
auction announced	among bidders

A swap is an agreement between two parties (called counterparties) to exchange specified periodic cash flows in the future based on some underlying instrument or price (e.g., a fixed or floating rate on a bond or note). Similar to options, swaps are OTC instruments normally susceptible to counterparty risk (see Chapter 26). If interest rates (or foreign exchange rates) move a lot, one party can be faced with considerable future loss exposure, creating incentives to default.

Credit derivatives are a new, popular derivative security, growing in volume by over 100 percent per year since 1996. Credit derivatives (including forwards, options, and swaps) allow FIs to hedge their credit risk. They can be used to hedge the credit risk on individual loans or bonds or portfolios of loans and bonds. As shown in Table 13–6, commercial banks had over $800 billion of notional value in credit derivatives outstanding in 2003. The emergence of these new derivatives is important since more FIs fail as a result of credit risk exposures than either interest rate or FX risk exposures. We discuss these derivatives in more detail in Chapters 24 through 26.

In general, default risk on OTC contracts increases with the time to maturity of the contract and the fluctuation of underlying prices, interest rates, or exchange rates.[33] Most empirical evidence suggests that derivative contracts have generally reduced FI risk or left it unaffected.[34]

Forward Purchases and Sales of When Issued Securities

when issued (WI) trading
Trading in securities prior to their actual issue.

www.federalreserve. gov
www.ustreas.gov

Very often banks and other FIs—especially investment banks—enter into commitments to buy and sell securities before issue. This is called **when issued (WI) trading.** These OBS commitments can expose an FI to future or contingent interest rate risk. Commercial banks often include these securities as a part of their holdings of forward contracts.

Good examples of WI commitments are those taken on with new T-bills in the week prior to the announcement of T-bill auction results. Every Tuesday the Federal Reserve, on behalf of the Treasury, announces the auction size of new three- and six-month bills to be allotted the following Monday (see Figure 13–3). Between

[33] Reputational considerations and the need for future access to markets for hedging deter the incentive to default (see Chapter 26 as well).

[34] See, for example, L. Angbazo, "Commercial Bank Net Interest Margins, Default Risks, Interest Rate Risk and Off-Balance-Sheet Banking," *Journal of Banking and Finance* 21 (January 1997), pp. 55–87, who finds no link between interest rate risk and FIs' use of derivatives; and G. Gorton and R. Rosen, "Banks and Derivatives," Working Paper, University of Pennsylvania, Wharton School, February 1995. Gorton and Rosen find that swap contracts have generally reduced the systemic risk of the U.S. banking system. J. T. Harper and J. R. Wingender, "An Empirical Test of Agency Cost Reduction Using Interest Rate Swaps," *Journal of Banking and Finance* 24 (2000), pp. 1419–31, find that the use of interest rate swaps is positively related to a reduction in a firm's agency costs. Nevertheless, B. Hirtle, "Derivatives, Portfolio Composition and Bank Holding Company Interest Rate Risk Exposure," *Journal of Financial Services Research,* 1997, pp. 243–66, finds that the use of interest rate derivatives corresponded to greater interest rate risk exposure during the 1991–94 period for U.S. bank holding companies. Finally, N. Y. Naik and P. K. Yadav, "Risk Management with Derivatives by Dealers and Market Quality in Government Bond Markets," *Journal of Finance* 58 (2003), pp. 1873–1904, find that intermediaries use futures contracts to offset or hedge changes in their spot positions. They find that larger intermediaries engage in greater amounts of market risk taking and hedge their spot exposure to a lesser extent than smaller intermediaries. They do not find that larger intermediaries earn more profit from their selective risk taking than smaller intermediaries.

FIGURE 13–4
Loans Sold with and without Recourse

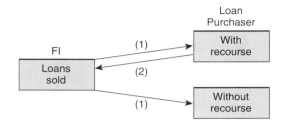

the announcement of the total auction size on Tuesday and the announcement of the winning bill allotments on the following Monday, major T-bill dealers sell WI contracts. Normally, large investment banks and commercial banks are major WI T-bill dealers (currently, approximately 40 such banks). They sell the yet-to-be-issued T-bills for forward delivery to customers in the secondary market at a small margin above the price they expect to pay at the primary auction. This can be profitable if the primary dealer gets all the bills needed at the auction at the appropriate price or interest rate to fulfill these forward WI contracts. A primary dealer that makes a mistake regarding the tenor of the auction (i.e., the level of interest rates) faces the risk that the commitments entered into to deliver T-bills in the WI market can be met only at a loss. For example, an overcommitted dealer may have to buy T-bills from other dealers at a loss right after the auction results are announced to meet the WI T-bill delivery commitments made to its customers.[35]

Loans Sold

We discuss in more detail in Chapter 27 the types of loans FIs sell, their incentives to sell, and the way they can be sold. Increasingly, banks and other FIs originate loans on their balance sheets, but rather than holding them to maturity, they quickly sell them to outside investors. These outside investors include other banks, insurance companies, mutual funds, and even corporations. In acting as loan originators and loan sellers, FIs are operating more in the fashion of loan brokers than as traditional asset transformers (see Chapter 1).

recourse
The ability to put an asset or loan back to the seller if the credit quality of that asset deteriorates.

When an outside party buys a loan with absolutsely no **recourse** to the seller of the loan should the loan eventually go bad, loan sales have no OBS contingent liability implications for FIs. Specifically, *no recourse* means that if the loan the FI sells goes bad, the buyer of the loan must bear the full risk of loss (see arrow 1 in Figure 13–4). In particular, the buyer cannot put the bad loan back to the seller or originating bank. Suppose the loan is sold with recourse. Then, loan sales present a long-term contingent credit risk to the seller. Essentially, the buyer of the loan holds a long-term option to put the loan back to the seller (arrow 2), which the buyer can exercise should the credit quality of the purchased loan deteriorate. In reality, the recourse or nonrecourse nature of loan sales is often ambiguous. For example, some have argued that FIs generally are willing to repurchase bad no recourse loans to preserve their reputations with their customers.[36] Obviously,

---

[35] This problem occurred when Salomon Brothers cornered or squeezed the market for new two-year Treasury bonds in 1990. Under the auction rules, no bidder could bid for or attain more than 35 percent of an issue. However, by bidding using customers' names (without their knowledge) in addition to bidding under its own name, Salomon vastly exceeded the 35 percent limit. This put extreme pressure on other dealers, who were unable to meet their selling commitments.

[36] G. Gorton and G. Pennacchi, "Are Loan Sales Really Off Balance Sheet?" in *Off-Balance-Sheet Activities*, ed. J. Ronen, A. Saunders, and A. C. Sondhi (New York: Quorum Books, 1989), pp. 19–40. We discuss loan sales in more detail in Chapter 27.

reputational concerns may extend the size of a selling FI's contingent liabilities for OBS activities.[37]

Concept Questions

1. What are the four risks related to loan commitments?
2. What is the major difference between a commercial letter of credit and a standby letter of credit?
3. What is meant by counterparty risk in a forward contract?
4. Which is more risky for an FI, loan sales with recourse or loan sales without recourse?

NON–SCHEDULE L OFF-BALANCE-SHEET RISKS

So far we have looked at five different OBS activities that banks have to report to the Federal Reserve each quarter as part of their Schedule L section of the call report. Remember that many other FIs engage in these activities as well. Thus, thrifts, insurance companies, and investment banks all engage in futures, forwards, swaps, and options transactions of varying forms. Life insurers are heavily engaged in making loan commitments in commercial mortgages, property–casualty companies underwrite large amounts of financial guarantees, and investment banks engage in when issued securities trading. Moreover, the five activities just discussed are not the only OBS activities that can create contingent liabilities or risks for an FI. Next, we briefly introduce two other activities that can create them; we discuss the activities at greater length in later chapters.

Settlement Risk

www.federalreserve. gov

www.chips.org

FIs send the bulk of their wholesale dollar payments along wire transfer systems such as Fedwire and the Clearing House InterBank Payments System (CHIPS). The Federal Reserve owns Fedwire, a domestic wire transfer network. CHIPS is an international and private network owned by 55 or so participating or member banks. Currently, these two networks transfer over $3.0 trillion a day.

Unlike the domestic Fedwire system, funds or payment messages sent on the CHIPS network *within* the day are provisional messages that become final and are settled only at the *end* of the day. For example, bank X sends a fund transfer payment message to bank Z at 11 AM EST. The actual cash settlement and the physical transfer of funds between X and Z take place at the end of the day, normally by transferring cash held in reserve accounts at the Federal Reserve banks. Because the transfer of funds is not finalized until the end of the day, bank Z—the message-receiving bank—faces an *intraday,* or within-day, **settlement risk.** Specifically, bank Z assumes that the funds message received at 11 AM from bank X will result in the actual delivery of the funds at the end of the day and may lend them to Bank Y at 11:15 AM. However, if bank X does not deliver (settle) the promised funds at the end of the day, bank Z may be pushed into a serious net funds deficit position and may therefore be unable to meet its payment commitment to bank Y. Conceivably, Bank Z's net debtor position may be large enough to exceed its capital and reserves, rendering it technically insolvent. Such a disruption can occur only if a major fraud were discovered in bank X's books during the day and bank regulators closed it the

settlement risk
Intraday credit risk associated with CHIPS wire transfer activities.

---

[37] However, C. Pavel finds that there is little relationship between bank loan sales and bank risk. See C. Pavel, "Loan Sales Have Little Effect on Bank Risk," *Economic Perspectives,* Federal Reserve Bank of Chicago, May–June 1988, pp. 23–31.

FIGURE 13–5
One-Bank and
Multibank Holding
Company
Structures

same day. That situation would make payment to bank Z impossible to complete at the end of the day. Alternatively, bank X might transmit funds it does not have in the hope of keeping its "name in the market" to be able to raise funds later in the day. However, other banks may revise their credit limits for this bank during the day, making Bank X unable to deliver all the funds it promised to bank Z.

The essential feature of settlement risk is that an FI is exposed to a within-day, or intraday, credit risk that does not appear on its balance sheet. The balance sheet at best summarizes only the end-of-day closing position or book of an FI. Thus, intra-day settlement risk is an additional form of OBS risk that FIs participating on private wholesale wire transfer system networks face. (See Chapter 14 for a more detailed analysis of this risk and recent policy changes designed to reduce this risk.)

Affiliate Risk

Many FIs operate as holding companies. A *holding company* is a corporation that owns the shares (normally more than 25 percent) of other corporations. For example, Citigroup is a one-bank holding company (OBHC) that owns all the shares of Citibank. Citigroup engages in certain permitted nonbank activities such as data processing through separately capitalized affiliates or companies that it owns. Similarly, a number of other holding companies are multibank holding companies (MBHCs) that own shares in a number of different banks. J. P. Morgan Chase is an MBHC that holds shares in banks nationwide. The organizational structures for these two holding companies are presented in Figure 13–5.

Legally, in the context of OBHCs, the bank and the nonbank affiliate are separate companies, as are bank 1 and bank 2 in the context of MBHCs. Thus, in Figure 13–5, the failure of the nonbank affiliate and bank 2 should have no effect on the financial resources of the bank in the OBHC or on bank 1 in the MBHC. This is the essence of the principle of corporate separateness underlying a legal corporation's limited liability in the United States. In reality, the failure of an affiliated firm or bank imposes **affiliate risk** on another bank in a holding company structure in a number of ways. We discuss two ways next.

affiliate risk
Risk imposed on one holding company affiliate due to the potential failure of the other holding company affiliates.

First, *creditors* of the failed affiliate may lay claim to the surviving bank's resources on the grounds that operationally, in name or in activity, the bank is not really a separate company from its failed affiliate. This "estoppel argument" made under the law is based on the idea that the customers of the failed institution are relatively unsophisticated in their financial affairs. They probably cannot distinguish between the failing corporation and its surviving affiliate because of name similarity or some similar reason.[38] Second, *regulators* have tried to enforce a source of strength doctrine in recent years for large MBHC failures. Under this doctrine, which directly challenges the principle of corporate separateness, the resources of

---

[38] For example, suppose the failing nonbank affiliate was called Town Data Processing and the affiliated bank was called Town Bank.

sound banks may be used to support failing banks. However, regulators have tried to implement this principle, but the courts have generally prevented this.[39]

If either of these breaches of corporate separateness are legally supported, the risks related to the activities of the nonbank affiliate or an affiliated bank's activities impose an additional contingent OBS liability on a healthy bank. This is true for banks and potentially true for many other FIs, such as insurance companies, investment banks, and financial service conglomerates that adopt holding company organizational structures in which corporate separateness is in doubt.[40]

In 1999, the U.S. Congress passed the Financial Services Modernization Act (FSMA, see Chapter 21). This act, viewed as the biggest change in the regulation of financial institutions in nearly 70 years, allowed the creation of a "financial holding company" that could engage in banking activities *and* securities underwriting *and* insurance activities. Prior to the passage of the act, such combinations of commercial banks and other FI activities were highly restricted. One result of the act has been an increase in the formation of full-service financial institutions, and thus, by implication, an increase in affiliate risk. As of year-end 2003, 639 financial institutions (such as ABN AMRO, Citigroup, and Charles Schwab) have elected to become financial holding companies. Certainly, not all of these are currently undertaking the full spectrum of financial activities allowed with FSMA, but with the new framework, all are sure to explore the opportunities available.

Concept Questions

1. What is the source of settlement risk on the CHIPS payments system?
2. What are two major sources of affiliate risk?

THE ROLE OF OBS ACTIVITIES IN REDUCING RISK

This chapter has emphasized that OBS activities may add to the riskiness of an FI's activities. Indeed, most contingent assets and liabilities have various characteristics that may accentuate an FI's default and/or interest rate risk exposures. Even so, FIs use some OBS instruments—especially forwards, futures, options, and swaps—to reduce or manage their interest rate risk, foreign exchange risk, and credit risk exposures in a manner superior to what would exist in their absence.[41] When used to hedge on-balance-sheet interest rate, foreign exchange, and credit risks, these instruments can actually work to reduce FIs' overall insolvency risk.[42] Although we

---

[39] Nevertheless, the attempts by regulators to impose the source of strength doctrine appear to have had an adverse effect on the equity values of bank holding companies operating with a larger number of subsidiaries. Also, the number of subsidiaries of bank holding companies has fallen each year since 1987, the first year in which the Fed tried to impose the source of strength doctrine (Hawkeye BanCorp of Iowa). See J. Houston, "Corporate Separateness and the Organizational Structure of Bank Holding Companies," Working Paper, Department of Finance, University of Florida–Gainesville, April 1993.

[40] A good example is the failure of Drexel Burnham Lambert in February 1991. For a good discussion of affiliate risk in this case, see W. S. Haraf, "The Collapse of Drexel Burnham Lambert: Lessons for Bank Regulators," *Regulation,* Winter 1991, pp. 23–25.

[41] As we discuss in Chapter 24, there are strong tax disincentives to using derivatives for purposes other than direct hedging.

[42] For example, the London International Financial Futures and Options Exchange (LIFFE) introduced in 2001 a swapnote, which is a futures contract whose settlement price is based on swap market rates. Swapnotes provide an effective mechanism for FIs to hedge interest rate risk with minimal basis risk (see Chapter 26).

do not fully describe the role of these instruments as hedging vehicles in reducing an FI's insolvency exposure until Chapters 24 through 26, you can now recognize the inherent danger in the overregulation of OBS activities and instruments. For example, the risk that a counterparty might default on a forward foreign exchange contract risk is very small. It is probably much lower than the insolvency risk an FI faces if it does not use forward contracts to hedge its foreign exchange assets against undesirable fluctuations in exchange rates. (See Chapters 15 and 24 for some examples of this.)

Despite the risk-reducing attributes of OBS derivative securities held by FIs, the expanded use of derivatives has caused many regulators to focus on the risk-increasing attributes of these securities and the possible detrimental effect the risk may have on global financial markets. The result has been an increase in the amount of regulation proposed for these activities. For example, the Derivatives Safety and Soundness Supervision Act (DSSSA) of 1994 mandated increased regulatory oversight for FIs holding derivative securities, including increased regulation of capital, disclosure, and accountability; enhanced supervision of risk management processes; and additional reporting requirements. Also in 1994, the General Accounting Office (GAO) released a report to Congress on derivative use by FIs and the regulatory actions needed to ensure the integrity of the financial system. The GAO specifically recommended that derivative activities of unregulated securities and insurance firm affiliates of banking organizations be brought under the purview of one or more existing regulatory bodies. Despite these rules and regulations passed in the early 1990s, huge losses on derivative securities by FIs such as Bankers Trust (in 1994), Barings (in 1995), and Long Term Capital Management (in 1998) have resulted in the call for additional regulation. Partially as a result of these concerns, the regulatory costs of hedging have risen (e.g., through the imposition of special capital requirements or restrictions on the use of such instruments [see Chapter 20]). As a result, FIs may have a tendency to underhedge, thereby increasing, rather than decreasing, their insolvency risk.

Finally, fees from OBS activities provide a key source of noninterest income for many FIs, especially the largest and most creditworthy ones. The importance of noninterest incomes for large banks is shown in Table 14–1 in the next chapter. Thus, increased OBS earnings can potentially compensate for increased OBS risk exposure and actually reduce the probability of insolvency for some FIs.[43]

Concept Questions

1. While recognizing that OBS instruments may add to the riskiness of an FI's activities, explain how they also work to reduce the overall insolvency risk of FIs.
2. Other than hedging and speculation, what reasons do FIs have for engaging in OBS activities?

Summary

This chapter showed that an FI's net worth or economic value is linked not only to the value of its traditional on-balance-sheet activities but also to the contingent asset and liability values of its off-balance-sheet activities. The risks and returns of several off-balance-sheet items were discussed in detail: loan commitments; commercial and standby letters of credit; derivative contracts such as futures, options, and

---

[43] In addition, by allowing risk-averse managers to hedge risk, derivatives may induce the managers to follow more value-maximizing investment strategies. That is, derivatives may allow manager–stockholder agency conflicts over the level of risk taking to be reduced. See, for example, D. R. Nance, C. W. Smith, Jr., and C. W. Smithson, "On the Determinants of Corporate Hedging," *Journal of Finance*, 1993, pp. 267–84.

swaps; forward purchases; and sales of when issued securities and loans sold. In all cases, it is clear that these instruments have a major impact on the future profitability and risk of an FI. Two other risks associated with off-balance-sheet activities—settlement risk and affiliate risk—were also discussed. The chapter concluded by pointing out that although off-balance-sheet activities can be risk increasing, they can also be used to hedge on-balance-sheet exposures, resulting in lower risks as well as generating fee income to the FI.

Questions and Problems	

1. Classify the following items as (1) on-balance-sheet assets, (2) on-balance-sheet liabilities, (3) off-balance-sheet assets, (4) off-balance-sheet liabilities, or (5) capital account.
   a. Loan commitments.
   b. Loan loss reserves.
   c. Letter of credit.
   d. Bankers acceptance.
   e. Rediscounted bankers acceptance.
   f. Loan sales without recourse.
   g. Loan sales with recourse.
   h. Forward contracts to purchase.
   i. Forward contracts to sell.
   j. Swaps.
   k. Loan participations.
   l. Securities borrowed.
   m. Securities lent.
   n. Loss adjustment expense account (PC insurers).
   o. Net policy reserves.

2. How does one distinguish between an off-balance-sheet asset and an off-balance-sheet liability?

3. Contingent Bank has the following balance sheet in market value terms (in millions of dollars).

Assets		Liabilities	
Cash	$ 20	Deposits	$220
Mortgages	220	Equity	20
Total assets	$240	Total liabilities and equity	$240

In addition, the bank has contingent assets with $100 million market value and contingent liabilities with $80 million market value. What is the true stockholder net worth? What does the term *contingent* mean?

4. Why are contingent assets and liabilities like options? What is meant by the delta of an option? What is meant by the term *notional value?*

5. An FI has purchased options on bonds with a notional value of $500 million and has sold options on bonds with a notional value of $400 million. The purchased options have a delta of 0.25, and the sold options have a delta of 0.30. What is (a) the contingent asset value of this position, (b) the contingent liability value of this position, and (c) the contingent market value of net worth?

6. What factors explain the growth of off-balance-sheet activities in the 1980s through the early 2000s among U.S. FIs?

7. What role does Schedule L play in reporting off-balance-sheet activities? Refer to Table 13–5. What was the annual growth rate over the 11-year period 1992–2003 in the notional value of off-balance-sheet items compared with on-balance-sheet items? Which contingencies have exhibited the most rapid growth?

8. What are the characteristics of a loan commitment that an FI may make to a customer? In what manner and to whom is the commitment an option? What are the various possible pieces of the option premium? When does the option or commitment become an on-balance-sheet item for the FI and the borrower?

9. A FI makes a loan commitment of $2,500,000 with an up-front fee of 50 basis points and a back-end fee of 25 basis points on the unused portion of the loan. The takedown on the loan is 50 percent.

   a. What total fees does the FI earn when the loan commitment is negotiated?

   b. What are the total fees earned by the FI at the end of the year, that is, in future value terms? Assume the cost of capital for the FI is 6 percent.

10. A FI has issued a one-year loan commitment of $2,000,000 for an up-front fee of 25 basis points. The back-end fee on the unused portion of the commitment is 10 basis points. The FI requires a compensating balance of 5 percent as demand deposits. The FI's cost of funds is 6 percent, the interest rate on the loan is 10 percent, and reserve requirements on demand deposits are 8 percent. The customer is expected to draw down 80 percent of the commitment at the beginning of the year.

    a. What is the expected return on the loan without taking future values into consideration?

    b. What is the expected return using future values? That is, the net fee and interest income are evaluated at the end of the year when the loan is due.

    c. How is the expected return in part (b) affected if the reserve requirements on demand deposits are zero?

    d. How is the expected return in part (b) affected if compensating balances are paid a nominal interest rate of 5 percent?

    e. What is the expected return using future values but with the funding of demand deposits replaced by certificates of deposit that have an interest rate of 5.5 percent and no reserve requirements?

11. Suburb Bank has issued a one-year loan commitment of $10,000,000 for an up-front fee of 50 basis points. The back-end fee on the unused portion of the commitment is 20 basis points. The bank requires a compensating balance of 10 percent on demand deposits, has a cost of funds of 7 percent, will charge an interest rate on the loan of 9 percent, and must maintain reserve requirements on demand deposits of 10 percent. The customer is expected to draw down 60 percent of the commitment.

    a. What is the expected return on this loan?

    b. What is the expected return per annum on the loan if the draw-down on the commitment does not occur until the end of six months?

12. How is an FI exposed to interest rate risk when it makes loan commitments? In what way can an FI control for this risk? How does basis risk affect the implementation of the control for interest rate risk?

13. How is an FI exposed to credit risk when it makes loan commitments? How is credit risk related to interest rate risk? What control measure is available to an FI for the purpose of protecting against credit risk? What is the realistic opportunity to implement this control feature?

14. How is an FI exposed to takedown risk and aggregate funding risk? How are these two contingent risks related?

15. Do the contingent risks of interest rate, takedown, credit, and aggregate funding tend to increase the insolvency risk of an FI? Why or why not?

16. What is a letter of credit? How is a letter of credit like an insurance contract?

17. A German bank issues a three-month letter of credit on behalf of its customer in Germany, who is planning to import $100,000 worth of goods from the United States. It charges an up-front fee of 100 basis points.

    a. What up-front fee does the bank earn?

    b. If the U.S. exporter decides to discount this letter of credit after it has been accepted by the German bank, how much will the exporter receive, assuming that the interest rate currently is 5 percent and that 90 days remain before maturity?

    c. What risk does the German bank incur by issuing this letter of credit?

18. How do standby letters of credit differ from commercial letters of credit? With what other types of FI products do SLCs compete? What types of FIs can issue SLCs?

19. A corporation is planning to issue $1,000,000 of 270-day commercial paper for an effective annual yield of 5 percent. The corporation expects to save 30 basis points on the interest rate by using either an SLC or a loan commitment as collateral for the issue.

    a. What are the net savings to the corporation if a bank agrees to provide a 270-day SLC for an up-front fee of 20 basis points (of the face value of the loan commitment) to back the commercial paper issue?

    b. What are the net savings to the corporation if a bank agrees to provide a 270-day loan commitment to back the issue? The bank will charge 10 basis points for an up-front fee and 10 basis points for a back-end fee for any unused portion of the loan. Assume the loan is not needed, and that the fees are on the face value of the loan commitment.

    c. Should the corporation be in different to the two alternative collateral methods at the time the commercial paper is issued?

20. Explain how the use of derivative contracts such as forwards, futures, swaps, and options creates contingent credit risk for an FI. Why do OTC contracts carry more contingent credit risk than do exchange-traded contracts? How is the default risk of OTC contracts related to the time to maturity and the price and rate volatilities of the underlying assets?

21. What is meant by when issued trading? Explain how forward purchases of when issued government T-bills can expose FIs to contingent interest rate risk.

22. Distinguish between loan sales with and without recourse. Why would banks want to sell loans with recourse? Explain how loan sales can leave banks exposed to contingent interest rate risks.

23. The manager of Shakey Bank sends a $2 million funds transfer payment message via CHIPS to the Trust Bank at 10 AM. Trust Bank sends a $2 million funds transfer message via CHIPS to Hope Bank later that same day. What type of risk is inherent in this transaction? How will the risk become reality?

24. Explain how settlement risk is incurred in the interbank payment mechanism and how it is another form of off-balance-sheet risk.

25. What is the difference between a one-bank holding company and a multibank holding company? How does the principle of corporate separateness ensure that a bank is safe from the failure of its affiliates?

26. Discuss how the failure of an affiliate can affect the holding company or its affiliates even if the affiliates are structured separately.

27. Defend the statement that although off-balance-sheet activities expose FIs to several forms of risks, they also can alleviate the risks of FIs.

Web Questions

28. Go to the FDIC Web site at **www.fdic.gov** and find the total amount of unused commitments and letters of credit and the notional value of interest rate swaps of FDIC-insured commercial banks for the most recent quarter available using the following steps. Click on "Analysts." From there click on "Statistics on Banking." Next click on "Commitments and Contingencies" and "Run Report." Select "Total Unused Commitments," then "Letters of Credit," and finally "Derivatives" to get the relevant data. This will bring the three files up on your computer that contain the relevant data. What is the dollar value increase in these amounts over the third-quarter 2003 values reported in Table 13–5?

29. Go to the Web site of the Office of the Comptroller of the Currency at **www.occ.treas.gov** and update Table 13–6 using the following steps. Click on "Publications." Click on "Qrtrly. Derivative Fact Sheet." Click on the most recent date. Click on "Tables." This will bring the file onto your computer that contains the relevant data. What is the dollar value increase in these values over those reported in Table 13–6?

Pertinent Web Sites

Chapter Notation

View Chapter Notation at the Web site to the textbook (**www.mhhe.com/saunders5e**).

Appendix 13A

A Letter of Credit Transaction

View Appendix 13A at the Web site for this textbook (**www.mhhe.com/saunders5e**)

Chapter **Fourteen**

Technology and Other Operational Risks

INTRODUCTION

Chapters 7 through 13 concentrated on the financial risks that arise as FIs perform their asset-transformation and/or brokerage functions on or off the balance sheet. However, financial risk is only one part of a modern FI's risk profile. As with regular corporations, FIs have a real or production side to their operations that results in additional costs and revenues. This chapter focuses on (1) factors that impact the operational returns and risks of FIs (with an emphasis on technology) and (2) on the importance of optimal management and control of labor, capital, and other input sources and their costs. In particular, well-managed FIs can use operational cost savings to increase profits and thus reduce the probability of insolvency.

Central to FIs' decision-making processes is the cost of inputs, or factors used to produce services both on and off the balance sheet. Two important factors are labor (tellers, credit officers) and capital (buildings, machinery, furniture). Crucial to the efficient management and combination of these inputs (which result in financial outputs at the lowest cost) is technology. Technological innovation has been a major concern of FIs in recent years. Since the 1980s, banks, insurance companies, and investment companies have sought to improve operational efficiency with major investments in internal and external communications, computers, and an expanded technological infrastructure. Internet and wireless communications technologies are having a profound effect on financial services. These technologies are more than just new distribution channels—they are a completely different way of providing financial services. Indeed, a global financial service firm such as Citigroup has operations in more than 100 countries connected in real time by a proprietary-owned satellite system. Operational risk is partly related to technology risk and can arise when existing technology malfunctions or back-office support systems break down. Further, back-office support systems combine labor and technology to provide clearance, settlement, and other services to back FIs' underlying on- and off-balance-sheet transactions.

According to Hitachi Data Systems, back-office system failures usually occur four times per year in the average firm. Recovery time from system failures average 12 hours. The terrorist attacks on the World Trade Center and the Pentagon created back-office system failures of an unforeseen magnitude. For example, over a week after the attacks, Bank of New York was still having trouble with some crucial communications links, such as its connection to the Government Securities Clearing Corp., a central part of the government bond market. Though trades were eventually posted, Bank of New York clients were deprived of instantaneous reports on their positions.

As should already be apparent, technology and operational risks are closely related and in recent years have caused great concern to FI managers and regulators alike. The Bank for International Settlements (BIS), the principal organization of central banks in the major economies of the world, has defined operational risk (inclusive of technological risk) as "the risk of losses resulting from inadequate or failed internal processes, people, and systems or from external events."[1] A number of FIs add reputational risk and strategic risk (e.g., due to a failed merger) as part of a broader definition of operational risk. Indeed, so significant has operational risk become that the BIS has proposed that, as of 2006, banks should be made to carry a capital cushion against losses from this risk. We discuss these proposals briefly in this chapter and in more detail in Chapter 20.

www.bis.org

WHAT ARE THE SOURCES OF OPERATIONAL RISK?

These are at least five sources of operational risk:[2]

1. Technology (e.g., technological failure and deteriorating systems).
2. Employees (e.g., human error and internal fraud).
3. Customer relationships (e.g., contractual disputes).
4. Capital assets (e.g., destruction by fire or other catastrophes).
5. External (e.g., external fraud).

Increasingly important to the profitability and riskiness of modern FIs has been item 1: technology.

TECHNOLOGICAL INNOVATION AND PROFITABILITY

technology
Computers, audio and visual communication systems, and other information systems, which can be applied to an FI's production of services.

Broadly defined, **technology** includes computers, visual and audio communication systems, and other information technology (IT). In recent years U.S. banks alone have spent $20 billion per annum in technology related expenditures.[3]

An efficient technological base for an FI can result in:

1. Lower costs, by combining labor and capital in a more efficient mix.
2. Increased revenues, by allowing a wider array of financial services to be produced or innovated and sold to customers.

---

[1] See Basel Committee on Bank Supervision, "Overview of the New Basel Capital Accord," Bank for International Settlements, April 2003, p.120.

[2] See, for example, D. Hoffman and M. Johnson, "Operating Procedures," *Risk Magazine*, October 1996, pp. 60–63.

[3] A 2003 survey by the American Bankers Association and the Tower Group found that the top five technology infrastructure investments planned for 2004 included communications network replacement and enhancements, PC and server hardware/software upgrades, mainframe computer upgrades, computer operations center replacement, and IP telephony (the transmission of telephone calls over a data network line).

TABLE 14–1
Earnings and Other Data for All Insured Banks (in millions of dollars)

Source: Federal Deposit Insurance Corporation Web site, various dates. *www.fdic.gov*

Financial Data	1991	1995	2000	2003*
Interest income	$289,166	$302,663	$427,985	$252,084
Interest expense	−167,265	−148,441	−224,195	−73,555
Net interest income	121,901	154,222	203,790	178,529
Provision for loan losses	−34,274	−12,550	−29,254	−26,346
Fiduciary activities	9,089	12,303	21,370	15,494
Deposit service charges	12,811	16,045	23,778	23,610
Trading account gains and fees	5,829	6,321	12,444	9,330
All other	31,974	47,771	95,159	89,705
Noninterest income	59,703	82,440	152,751	138,139
Salaries and employee benefits	−53,079	−63,440	−88,507	−80,860
Premises and equipment	−17,718	−19,618	−26,765	−23,228
All other	−53,854	−66,613	−100,481	−78,269
Noninterest expenses	−124,651	−149,671	−215,753	−182,357
Net securities gains or losses	2,966	545	−2,285	5,282
Extraordinary items	687	26	−30	29
Taxes	−8,285	−26,176	−38,043	−37,163
Net earnings	$ 18,047	$ 48,836	$ 71,176	$ 76,113
Average total assets ($ billion)	$ 3,430.1	$ 4,312.7	$ 6,238.7	$ 7,299.4
Return on assets (%)	0.53%	1.13%	1.14%	1.04%

*As of the third quarter.

The importance of an FI's operating costs and the efficient use of technology impacting these costs is clearly demonstrated by this simplified profit function:

Earnings or profit before taxes = (Interest income − Interest expense)
+ (Other income − Noninterest expense) − Provision for loan losses

Table 14–1 breaks down the profit data for U.S. banks over the 1991–2003 period into the different components impacting profits. For example, through the third quarter of 2003, interest income of $252,084 million and interest expense of $73,555 million produced net interest income of $178,529 million. However, U.S. banks also had total noninterest income of $138,139 million (including service charges on deposits of $23,610 million) and noninterest expenses of $182,357 million (including salaries and employee benefits of $80,860 million and premises and equipment expenses of $23,228 million). Thus, banks' net noninterest income was −$44,218. After considering provisions for loan losses of $26,346 million, net securities gains ($5,282 million), extraordinary gains ($29 million), and taxes ($37,163 million), after-tax net profits were $76,113 million. Underscoring the importance of operating costs is the fact that noninterest expenses amounted to 248 percent of interest expense and were 2.4 times net profits in 2003.

Internet Exercise Go to the Federal Deposit Insurance Corporation's Web site, and find the latest information available for earnings at U.S. commercial banks.

Go to the Federal Deposit Insurance Corporation's Web site at **www.fdic.gov**. Click on "Analysts." Click on "Statistics on Banking." Select "o Income and Expense" and click on "Run Report." This will download a file on to your computer that will contain the most recent information.

Technology is important because well-chosen technological investments have the potential to increase both the FI's net interest margin, or the difference between interest income and interest expense, and other net income. Therefore, technology can directly improve profitability, as the following examples show:

1. *Interest income* can increase if the FI sells a broader array of financial services as a result of technological developments. These may include cross selling financial products by having the computer identify customers and then having the FI telemarket financial service products such as life insurance and bank products directly and over the Internet.[4]

2. *Interest expense* can be reduced if access to markets for liabilities is directly dependent on the FI's technological capability. For example, Fedwire and CHIPS (two wire transfer systems discussed later in the chapter) link the domestic and international interbank lending markets; they are based on interlocking computer network systems. Moreover, an FI's ability to originate and sell commercial paper is increasingly computer driven. Thus, failure to invest in the appropriate technology may lock an FI out of a lower-cost funding market.[5]

3. *Other income* increases when fees for FI services, especially those from off-balance-sheet activities, are linked to the quality of the FI's technology. For example, letters of credit are now commonly originated electronically by customers; swaps, caps, options, and other complex derivatives are usually traded, tracked, and valued using high-powered computers and algorithms. FIs could not offer innovative derivative products to customers without investments in suitable IT. Further, new technology has resulted in an evolution of the U.S. (and international) payment systems (see below), which has increased the amount of fee income (noninterest income) as a percent of total operating income (interest income plus noninterest income) for FIs. For example, referring again to Table 14–1, we see that noninterest income as a percent of total operating income was 17.11 percent in 1991 and increased to 35.40 percent by 2003.[6]

4. *Noninterest expenses* can be reduced if the collection and storage of customer information as well as the processing and settlement of numerous financial products are computer based rather than paper based. This is particularly true of security-related back-office activities.

Concept Questions

1. What are some of the advantages of an efficient technological base for an FI? How can it be used to directly improve profitability?
2. Looking at Table 14–1, determine if noninterest expenses and noninterest income have been increasing or decreasing as a percent of total bank costs over the 1991–2003 period.

---

[4] The Financial Services Modernization Act of 1999 requires FIs to notify customers and allow them to opt out of the sharing of nonpublic personal information between an FI's affiliates or third parties (see Chapter 21).

[5] Not only corporations sell commercial paper. In recent years approximately 75 percent of all commercial paper has been sold by financial firms such as bank holding companies, investment banks, and finance companies. Thus, commercial paper is now an important source of funds for many FIs.

[6] The growth of fee income has been particularly large for the biggest FIs. L. F. Radecki, in "Banks' Payments-Driven Results," Working Paper, Federal Reserve Bank of New York, 2000, finds that payment services bring in from one-third to two-fifths of the combined operating income of the 25 largest bank holding companies.

THE IMPACT OF TECHNOLOGY ON WHOLESALE AND RETAIL FINANCIAL SERVICE PRODUCTION

The previous discussion established that modern technology has the potential to directly affect a modern FI's profit-producing areas. The following discussion focuses on some specific technology-based products found in modern retail and wholesale financial institutions.[7] Note that this is far from a complete list.

Wholesale Financial Services

Probably the most important area in which technology has had an impact on wholesale or corporate customer services is an FI's ability to provide cash management or working capital services. Cash management services include "services designed to collect, disburse and transfer funds—on a local, regional, national or international basis—and to provide information about the location and status of those funds."[8] Cash management service needs have largely resulted from (1) corporate recognition that excess cash balances result in a significant opportunity cost due to lost or forgone interest and (2) corporate need to know cash or working capital position on a real-time basis. Among the services modern FIs provide to improve the efficiency with which corporate clients manage their financial positions are the following:

1. *Controlled disbursement accounts.* An account feature that establishes in the morning almost all payments to be made by the customer in a given day. The FI informs the corporate client of the total funds it needs to meet disbursements, and the client wire transfers the amount needed. These checking accounts are debited early each day so that corporations can obtain an early insight into their net cash positions.

2. *Account reconciliation.* A checking feature that records which of the firm's checks have been paid by the FI.[9]

float
The interval between the deposit of a check and when funds become available for depositor use; that is, the time is takes a check to clear at a bank.

3. *Wholesale lockbox.* A centralized collection service for corporate payments to reduce the delay in check clearing, or the **float.** In a typical lockbox arrangement, a local FI sets up a lockbox at the post office for a corporate client located outside the area. Local customers mail payments to the lockbox rather than to the out-of-town corporate headquarters. The FI collects these checks several times per day and deposits them directly into the customer's account. Details of the transaction are wired to the corporate client.

4. *Electronic lockbox.* Same type of service as item 3 but receives online payments for public utilities and similar corporate clients.

5. *Funds concentration.* Redirects funds from accounts in a large number of FIs or branches to a few centralized accounts at one FI.

---

[7] A. K. Pennathur, in "'Clicks and Bricks': e-Risk Management for Banks in the Age of the Internet," *Journal of Banking and Finance* 25 (2001), pp. 2103–23, outlines various risks associated with the provision of these services.

[8] Salomon Brothers, "Transaction Processing: Raising the Technological Hurdle," U.S. Equity Research (Commercial Banks), January 6, 1997, p. 5.

[9] The Check Clearing for the 21st Century Act, passed by Congress in 2003, allows FIs to replace the delivery of an original, paper-based check back to deposit customers with electronically transmitted copies of the checks. In doing so, check processing time and handling costs can be reduced significantly for FIs.

6. *Electronic funds transfer.* Includes overnight payments via CHIPS or Fedwire, automated payment of payrolls or dividends via automated clearinghouses (ACHs), and automated transmission of payments messages by SWIFT, an international electronic message service owned and operated by U.S. and European FIs that instructs FIs to make specific payments.

7. *Check deposit services.* Encoding, endorsing, microfilming, and handling customers' checks.

8. *Electronic initiation of letters of credit.* Allows customers in a network to access FI computers to initiate letters of credit.

9. *Treasury management software.* Allows efficient management of multiple currency and security portfolios for trading and investment purposes.[10]

10. *Electronic data interchange.* A specialized application of electronic mail, allowing businesses to transfer and transact invoices, purchase orders, and shipping notices automatically, using FIs as clearinghouses.

11. *Facilitation of business-to-business e-commerce.* A few of the largest commercial banks have begun to offer firms the technology for electronic business-to-business commerce. The banks are essentially undertaking automation of the entire information flow associated with the procurement and distribution of goods and services among businesses.

12. *Electronic billing.* Provides the presentment and collection services for companies that send out substantial volumes of recurring bills. Banks combine the e-mail capability of the Internet to send out bills with their ability to process payments electronically through the interbank payment networks.[11]

13. *Verification of identities.* Using encryption technology, banks certify the identities of its own account holders and serve as the intermediary through which its business customers can verify the identities of account holders at other banks. After the September 11, 2001, terrorist attacks, some legislators called for restrictions on encryption technology unless it permits law enforcement access to otherwise coded data.

14. *Assistance to small businesses entering into e-commerce.* Help to smaller firms in setting up the infrastructure—interactive Web site and payment capabilities—for engaging in e-commerce.

Retail Financial Services

Retail customers have demanded efficiency and flexibility in their financial transactions. Using only checks or holding cash is often more expensive and time-consuming than using retail-oriented electronic payments technology and, increasingly, the Internet. Further, securities trading is increasingly moving toward electronic platforms not tied to any specific location. Electronic trading networks have lowered the costs of trading and allowed for better price determination. For example, with a single click of a mouse, Merrill Lynch customers can obtain

---

[10] Computerized pension fund management and advisory services could be added to this list.

[11] Firms and households have been slow to embrace this technology because of the presence of coordination problems in the electronic payments sector. These systems involve significant up-front costs for billers and customers. If billers believe that most of their customers will not establish connections to the system, they will not purchase the equipment for fear that they will be unable to recover their fixed investment costs. See "Why Hasn't Electronic Bill Presentment and Payment Taken Off?" *Current Issues in Economics and Finance*, Federal Reserve Bank of New York, July/August 2002.

information on all research (conducted by Merrill Lynch) on a company. Another click gives the customer information on the best terms available on a trade, and a final click executes a customer's trade. A typical customer transaction through a branch or phone call costs a customer about $1, while a similar online transaction costs just $0.02. Some of the most important retail payment product innovations include:

1. *Automated teller machines (ATMs).* Allows customers 24-hour access to their deposit accounts. They can pay bills as well as withdraw cash from these machines. In addition, if the FI's ATMs are part of a bank network (such as CIRRUS), retail depositors can gain direct nationwide—and in many cases international—access to their deposit accounts by using the ATMs of other banks in the network to draw on their accounts.[12]

2. *Point-of-sale (POS) debit cards.* Allows customers who choose not to use cash, checks, or credit cards for purchases to buy merchandise using debit card/point-of-sale (POS) terminals. The merchant avoids the check float and any delay in payment associated with credit card receivables since the FI offers the debit card/POS service immediately and transfers funds directly from the customer's deposit account to the merchant's deposit account at the time of card use. Unlike check or credit card transactions the use of a debit card results in an immediate transfer of funds from the customers' account to the merchant's account.[13] Moreover, the customer never runs up a debit to the card issuer as is common with a credit card.

3. *Home banking.* Connects customers to their deposit and brokerage accounts and provides services such as electronic securities trading and bill paying via personal computers.

4. *Preauthorized debits/credits.* Includes direct deposits of payroll checks into bank accounts as well as direct payments of mortgage and utility bills.

5. *Payment of bills via telephone.* Allows direct transfer of funds from the customer's FI account to outside parties either by voice command or by touch-tone telephone.

6. *E-mail billing.* Allows customers to receive and pay bills using the Internet, thus saving postage and paper.[14]

---

[12] Using another bank's ATM usually results in an access fee to the customer that averages $1 but can be as high as $5. See J. J. McAndrews, "ATM Surcharges," *Current Issues in Economics and Finance,* Federal Reserve Bank of New York, April 1998. N. Massoud, A. Saunders, and B. Scholnick, in "The Impact of ATM Surcharges on Large versus Small Banks: Is There a Customer Relationship Effect?" Department of Finance, New York University Working Paper, 2003, find that if both large and small banks impose the same ATM surcharge, there will be an increase in the market share of deposits of the larger banks and a decrease in the market share of the smaller banks. Also, ATM surcharges positively impact the profitability of larger, but not smaller, banks.

[13] In the case of bank-supplied credit cards, the merchant normally gets compensated very quickly but not instantaneously by the credit card issuer (usually one or two days). The bank then holds an account receivable against the card user. However, even a short delay can represent an opportunity cost for the merchant. In 2003, MasterCard and Visa agreed to settle an antitrust suit consenting to lower fees, modify card policies, and pay over $3 billion in damages to about 5 million merchants (including Wal-Mart and Sears). The merchants argued that these card associations illegally tied their debit cards to their credit cards, forcing retailers for pay higher fees. The debit transactions are processed on ATM/POS networks.

[14] For example, the U.S. Postal Service estimated that $2.4 billion was spent on postage for bills and bank statements in 1995. See "Paying Bills without Any Litter," *New York Times,* July 5, 1996, pp. D1–D3; and K. N. Kuttner and J. J. McAndrews, "Personal On-Line Payments, *Economic Policy Review,* Federal Reserve Bank of New York, December 2001, pp. 35–50.

7. *Online banking.* Allows customers to conduct retail banking and investment services offered via the Internet.[15,16,17] In some cases this involves building a new online Internet-only "bank," such as NetBank of Atlanta.

8. *Smart cards (store-value cards).* Allows the customer to store and spend money for various transactions using a card that has a chip storage device, usually in the form of a strip. These have become increasingly popular at universities.[18,19]

Concept Questions

1. Describe some of the wholesale financial services provided to corporate customers that have been improved by technology.
2. Describe some of the automated retail payment products available today. What advantages do these products offer the retail customer?

THE EFFECT OF TECHNOLOGY ON REVENUES AND COSTS

The previous section presented an extensive yet incomplete list of current products or services being offered by FIs that are built around a strong technological base and, increasingly, the Internet. Technological advances allow an FI to offer such products to its customers and potentially to earn higher profits. The investment of resources in many of these products is risky, however, because product innovations may fail to attract sufficient business relative to the initial cash outlay and the future costs related to these investments once they are in place. In the terminology of finance, a number of technologically based product innovations may turn out to be *negative* net present value projects because of uncertainties over revenues and costs and how quickly rivals will mimic or copy any innovation. Another factor is agency conflicts, in which managers undertake growth-oriented investments to increase an FI's size; such investments may be inconsistent with stockholders' value-maximizing objectives. As a result, losses on technological innovations and new technology could weaken an FI because scarce capital resources were invested in value-decreasing products.[20]

---

[15] In 2003 Wells Fargo said its online Banking customer base jumped 52 percent over 2002 levels. Bank of America reported a 50 percent increase to 6.2 million online customers, and Bank One saw a 65 percent increase to 2.2 million online customers. See "Security Worries Keep Many from Banking Online," *Dallas Morning News*, December 1, 2003, p. 5.

[16] K. Furst, W. W. Lang, and D. E. Nolle find that, as of the third quarter of 1999, while only 20 percent of U.S. national banks offered Internet banking, these transactions accounted for almost 90 percent of the national banking system's assets and 84 percent of the total number of small deposit accounts. See "Internet Banking: Developments and Prospects," Office of the Comptroller of the Currency, Economic and Policy Analysis Working Paper 2000–2009, September 2000.

[17] In addition to cash management services, technology also enhances the ability of FIs to offer security services (e.g., local and global custody and transfer).

[18] Another example is Mondex, under which employees of Wells Fargo Bank use store-value cards at nearby merchants. See B. A. Good, "Electronic Money," Federal Reserve Bank of Cleveland, Working Paper 97–16, 1997.

[19] Note that the provision of electronic funds and the public and policy issues that arise relating to their provision fall under Regulation E of the Federal Reserve.

[20] Standard capital budgeting techniques can be applied to technological innovations and new FI products. Let:

I_0 = Initial capital outlay for developing an innovation or product at time 0

R_i = Expected net revenues or cash flows from product sales in future years i, $i = 1 \ldots N$

d = FI's discount rate reflecting its risk-adjusted cost of capital

This leads one to consider whether direct or indirect evidence is available that indicates whether technology investments to update the operational structure of FIs have increased revenues or decreased costs. Most of the direct or indirect evidence has concerned the effects of size on financial firms' operating costs; indeed, it is the largest FIs that appear to be investing most in IT and other technological innovations.

We first discuss the evidence on the product revenue side and then discuss the evidence on the operating cost side. However, before looking at these revenue and cost aspects, we should stress that the success of technologically related innovation cannot be evaluated independently from regulation and regulatory changes. To a large extent, the growth and success of the retail and wholesale cash management products just described above depend on trends in FI consolidation and interstate banking (see Chapters 21 through 23). Historically, restrictions on U.S. banks' ability to branch across state lines created problems for large corporations with national and international franchises; these firms needed to consolidate and centralize their deposit funds for working capital purposes. Innovations such as wholesale lockboxes and funds concentration have eased these problems. It is more than coincidence that cash management services have not attracted customers in Europe to the degree that they have in the United States. One reason is that in European countries, nationwide branching and banking have been far more prevalent and interregional banking restrictions notably absent. As a result, the 1997 introduction of full interstate banking for banks in the United States, as well as the rapid consolidation in the U.S. financial services industry (e.g., as a result of mergers of large banks and the development of national branch systems), may well reduce the demand for such services in the future.

Technology and Revenues

One potential benefit of technology is that it allows an FI to cross-market both new and existing products to customers. Such joint selling does not require the FI to produce all the services sold within the same branch or financial services outlet.[21] For example, a commercial bank may link up with an insurance company to jointly market each other's loan, credit card, and insurance products. This arrangement has proved popular in Germany, where some of the largest banks have developed sophisticated cross-marketing arrangements with large insurance companies.

Thus, a negative net present value (NPV) project would result if:

$$I_0 > \frac{R_1}{(1+d)} + \cdots + \frac{R_N}{(1+d)^N}$$

Clearly, the profitability of any product innovation is negatively related to the size of the initial setup and development costs (I_0) and the FI's cost of capital (d), and positively related to the size of the stream of expected net cash flows (R_i) from selling the services.

For example, home banking might reasonably be viewed—to date—as a negative NPV product for banks such as Bank of America. Considerable resources (I_0) were sunk into its development in the 1980s at a time when banks' cost of capital (d) was high. The realized net revenue streams (R_i) from home banking have been disappointing so far—although, as is described in the text, home banking has become increasingly important as the Internet takes a hold in determining the size and direction of retail financial service transactions.

[21] Title V of the Financial Services Modernization Act 1999, however, allows FI customers to opt out of any nonpublic personal information sharing with nonaffiliated third parties. The act also requires FIs to disclose their privacy policies regarding the sharing of nonpublic personal information with both affiliates and third parties.

In the United States, Citicorp's merger with Travelers to create Citigroup was explicitly designed to cross-market banking, insurance, and securities products in over 100 countries. However, Citigroup management admitted after the completion of the merger that it may take 10 or more years to integrate computer systems to a sufficient degree to achieve this objective.

Technology also increases the rate of innovation of new financial products. In recent years, many notable failures as well as successes have occurred. For example, despite large investments by banks, product innovations such as POS/debit cards have not found a sufficiently large market in the United States. On the other hand, electronic securities trading, bill paying via telephone,[22] and using preauthorized debits and credits, including direct payroll systems, are proving to be high-growth areas in modern FIs.

Finally, we cannot ignore the issue of *service quality* and convenience. For example, while ATMs and Internet banking may potentially lower FI operating costs compared with employing full-service tellers, the inability of machines to address customers' concerns and questions flexibly may drive retail customers away; revenue losses may counteract any cost-savings effects. Customers still want to interact with a person for many transactions. For example, a survey of the home buying and mortgage process by the Mortgage Bankers Association (in the early 2000s) found that, while 73 percent of home buyers used the Internet to obtain information on mortgage interest rates, only 12 percent applied for a mortgage via the Internet and only 3 percent actually closed on a mortgage on the Internet. The survival of small banks in the face of growing nationwide branching may well be due in part to customers' belief that overall service quality is higher with tellers who provide a human touch rather than the Internet banking and ATMs more common at bigger banks. Even Internet-only banks are recognizing this as "virtual" FIs such as Atlanta's NetBank added 42 offices in several states in 2001. Further, a new type of customer service will be needed; customers require prompt, well-informed support on technical issues as they increasingly conduct their financial business electronically.[23]

Technology and Costs

Traditionally, FIs have considered the major benefits of technological advances to be on the cost side rather than the revenue side. After a theoretical look at how technology favorably or unfavorably affects an FI's costs, we look at the direct and indirect evidence of technology-based cost savings for FIs. In general, technology may favorably affect an FI's cost structure by allowing it to exploit either economies of scale or economies of scope.

Economies of Scale

As financial firms become larger, the potential scale and array of the technology in which they can invest generally expands.[24] As noted above, the largest FIs make the largest expenditures on technology-related innovations. For example, the Tower Group (a consulting firm specializing in information technology) estimated that technology expense as a percent of noninterest expense was 22 percent

---

[22] See Bob Tedeschi, "E-Commerce Report," *The New York Times*, May 17, 1999, p. C4.

[23] See "Horizons Narrowing for Internet-Only Banks," *The American Banker*, December 17, 2002, p. 10A.

[24] Economies of scale and scope can result from a variety of factors other than technology (e.g., interstate bank expansion). In this section, however, we demonstrate these economies using a framework of technological investments.

FIGURE 14–1
Economies of Scale in FIs

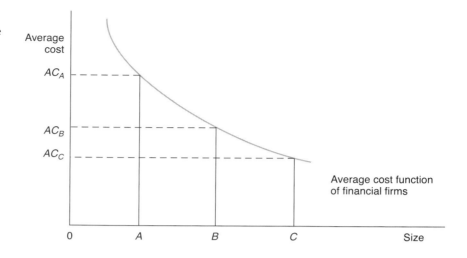

economy of scale

A drop in the average costs of production as the output of an FI increases.

at the largest U.S. banks over the period 1999–2004. If enhanced or improved technology lowers an FI's average costs of financial service production, larger FIs may have an **economy of scale** advantage over smaller financial firms. Economies of scale imply that the unit or average cost of producing FI services in aggregate (or some specific service such as deposits or loans) falls as the size of the FI expands.

Figure 14–1 shows economies of scale for three different-sized FIs. The average cost of producing an FI's output of financial services is measured as:

$$AC_i = \frac{TC_i}{S_i}$$

where

AC_i = Average costs of the ith FI

TC_i = Total costs of the ith FI

S_i = Size of the FI measured by assets, deposits, or loans.[25]

The largest FI in Figure 14–1 (size C) has a lower average cost of producing financial services than do smaller firms B and A. This means that at any given price for financial service firm products, firm C can make a bigger profit than either B or A. Alternatively, firm C can undercut B and A in price and potentially gain a larger market share. For example, First Union Corporation's $3.2 billion acquisition of Signet Banking Corporation was billed as a cost-savings acquisition. Because of overlapping operations with Signet, First Union said it expected annual cost savings of approximately $240 million. In the framework of Figure 14–1, Signet, firm A, might be operating at AC_A and First Union might be represented as firm B operating at AC_B. First Union and Signet had significant back-office operations in Virginia that could be combined and consolidated. The consolidation of such overlapping activities would lower the average costs for the combined (larger) bank to point C in Figure 14–1, operating at AC_C. The long-run implication of economies of scale on the FI sector is that the larger and most cost-efficient FIs will drive out smaller FIs, leading to increased large-firm dominance and concentration in financial services

---

[25] It is arguable that the size of a modern FI should be measured by including off-balance-sheet assets (contingent value) as well.

FIGURE 14–2
Effects of
Technological
Improvement

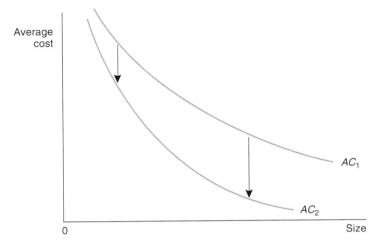

FIGURE 14–3
Diseconomies of
Scale

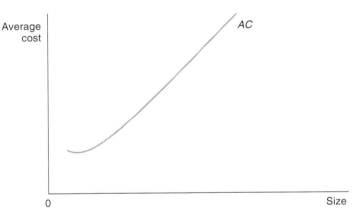

production. Such an implication is reinforced if time-related operating or technological improvements increasingly benefit larger FIs more than smaller FIs. For example, satellite technology and supercomputers, in which enormous technological advances are being made, may be available to only the largest FIs. The effect of improving technology over time, which is biased toward larger projects, is to shift the AC curve downward over time but with a larger downward shift for large FIs (see Figure 14–2). In Figure 14–2, AC_1 is the hypothetical AC curve prior to cost-reducing technological innovations. AC_2 reflects the cost-lowering effects of technology on FIs of all sizes but with the greatest benefit accruing to those of the largest size.

As noted earlier, technological investments are risky; if their future revenues do not cover their costs of development, they reduce the value of the FI and its net worth to the FI's owners. On the cost side, large-scale investments may result in excess capacity problems and integration problems as well as cost overruns and cost control problems. Then small FIs with simple and easily managed computer systems and/or those leasing time on large FIs' computers without bearing the fixed costs of installation and maintenance may have an average cost advantage. In this case, technological investments of large-sized FIs result in higher average costs of financial service production, causing the industry to operate under conditions of **diseconomies of scale** (see Figure 14–3). Diseconomies of scale imply that

diseconomies of scale
Increase in the average costs of production as the output of an FI increases.

FIGURE 14–4
Other Average Cost Functions

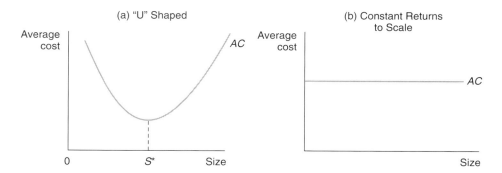

small FIs are more cost efficient than large FIs and that in a freely competitive environment for financial services, small FIs prosper.

At least two other possible shapes for the AC function exist (see Figure 14–4). In panel (a) of Figure 14–4, the financial services industry reflects economies of scale at first and then diseconomies of scale as firms grow larger. This suggests that a best or most efficient size for an FI exists at point S^* and that too much technology investment can be as bad as too little. Panel (b) of Figure 14–4 represents constant returns to scale. Any potential cost-reducing effects of technology are spread evenly over FIs of all sizes. That is, technology investments are neutral rather than favoring one size of FI over another.

Economies of Scope

While technological investments may have positive or negative effects on FIs in general and these effects may well differ across FIs of different size, technology tends to be applied more in some product areas than in others. That is, FIs are multiproduct firms producing services involving different technological needs. Moreover, technological improvements or investments in one financial service area (such as lending) may have incidental and synergistic benefits in lowering the costs of producing financial services in other areas (such as securities underwriting and brokerage). Specifically, computerization allows the storage and joint use of important information on customers and their needs. The simple *economy of scale* concept ignores these interrelationships among products and the "jointness" in the costs of producing financial products. In particular, FIs' abilities to generate synergistic cost savings through joint use of inputs in producing multiple products is called *economies of scope* as opposed to economies of scale.

Technology may allow two FIs to jointly use their input resources, such as capital and labor, to produce a set of financial services at a lower cost than if financial service products were produced independently of one another. Specifically, let X_1 and X_2 be two financial products; each is produced by one firm as a specialized producer. That is, firm A produces only X_1 and no X_2, and firm B produces only X_2 and no X_1. The average cost functions (AC) of these firms are:

$$AC_A[X_1, 0] \quad \text{and} \quad AC_B[0, X_2]$$

economies of scope
The ability of FIs to generate synergistic cost savings through joint use of inputs in producing multiple products.

Economies of scope exist if these firms merge and jointly produce X_1 and X_2, resulting in:

$$AC_{A+B}[X_1, X_2] < AC_A[X_1, 0] + AC_B[0, X_2]$$

That is, the cost of joint production via cost synergies is less than the separate and independent production of these services.

EXAMPLE 14–1

Calculation of Average Costs

Let TC_B be a specialized commercial bank's total cost of producing lending services to a corporate client. Suppose that the total operating costs of producing these services is $50,000 for a loan volume (L_B) of $10 million. Such costs include information collection and monitoring as well as account maintenance and processing. Thus, the average cost (AC_B) of loan production for the bank is:

$$AC_B = \frac{TC_B}{L_B} = \frac{\$50,000}{\$10,000,000} = .005 = .5\%$$

At the same time, a specialized investment bank is selling commercial paper for the same corporate customer. The investment bank's total cost (TC_S) of running the commercial paper operation is $10,000 for a $1 million issue ($P_S$). These costs include the cost of underwriting the issue as well as placing the issue with outside buyers. Thus:

$$AC_S = \frac{TC_S}{P_S} = \frac{\$10,000}{\$1,000,000} = .01 = 1\%$$

Consequently, the total average cost (*TAC*) of separately producing the loan services through the commercial bank and the commercial paper issuance through the investment bank is:

$$TAC = \frac{\$60,000}{\$11,000,000} = 0.54\%$$

Suppose, instead, a single FI produces both $10 million of lending services and $1 million commercial paper issuance services for the same customer (i.e., P_{FS} = $11 million). Loans and commercial paper are substitute sources of funds for corporate customers. For an FI to originate a loan and commercial paper requires very similar expertise both in funding that issue and in credit risk assessment and monitoring. Common technologies in the loan and commercial paper production functions suggest that a single FI simultaneously (or jointly) producing both loan and commercial paper services for the same client at a total cost TC_{FS} should be able to do this at a lower average cost than could the specialized FIs that separately produce these services. That is, the single FI should be able to produce the $11,000,000 ($P_{FS}$) of financial services at a lower cost (say TC_{FS} = $51,000), than should two specialized FIs. Accordingly:

$$AC_{FS} = \frac{TC_{FS}}{P_{FS}} = \frac{\$51,000}{\$11,000,000} = 0.46\% < 0.54\%$$

Formally, if AC_{FS} is the total average cost of a nonspecialized financial services firm, then economies of scope imply that:

$$AC_{FS} < TAC$$

diseconomies of scope
The costs of joint production of FI services are higher than they would be if they were produced independently.

Nevertheless, **diseconomies of scope** may occur instead; FIs find costs actually higher from joint production of services than if they were produced independently. For example, suppose an FI purchases some very specialized information-based technology to ease the loan production and processing function. The FI could use any excess capacity this system has in other service areas. However, this process could be a relatively inefficient technology for other service areas and could add to the overall costs of production compared with using a specialized technology for each service or product area.

Concept Questions

1. What are two risk factors involved in an FI's investment of resources in innovative technological products?
2. What is the link between interstate banking restrictions and the retail demand for electronic payment services?

3. Does the existence of economies of scale for FIs mean that in the long run small FIs cannot survive?
4. If there are diseconomies of scope, do specialized FIs have a relative cost advantage or disadvantage over product-diversified FIs?
5. Make a list of the potential economies of scope or cost synergies if a commercial bank merged with an investment bank.

TESTING FOR ECONOMIES OF SCALE AND ECONOMIES OF SCOPE

To test for economies of scale and economies of scope, FIs must clearly specify both the inputs to their production process and the cost of those inputs. Basically, the two approaches to analyzing the cost functions of FIs are the production and the intermediation approaches.

The Production Approach

The production approach views FIs' outputs of services as having two underlying inputs: labor and capital. If w = wage costs of labor, r = rental costs of capital, and y = output of services, the total cost function (C) for the FI is:

$$C = f(y, w, r)$$

The Intermediation Approach

The intermediation approach views the output of financial services as being produced by labor and capital as well as funds the intermediary uses to produce intermediated services. Thus, deposit costs would be an input in the banking and thrift industries, while premiums or reserves would be inputs in the insurance industry, and:

$$C = f(y, w, r, k)$$

where k reflects the cost of funds for the FI.

Concept Questions

1. Describe the basic concept behind the production approach to testing for economies of scale and economies of scope.
2. How does the intermediation approach differ from the production approach?

EMPIRICAL FINDINGS ON COST ECONOMIES OF SCALE AND SCOPE AND IMPLICATIONS FOR TECHNOLOGY EXPENDITURES

A large number of studies have examined economies of scale and scope in different financial service industry sectors.[26] With respect to banks, most of the early studies failed to find economies of scale for any but the smallest banks. More recently,

---

[26] Good reviews are found in J. A. Clark, "Economies of Scale and Scope at Depository Financial Institutions: A Review of the Literature," Federal Reserve Bank of Kansas City, *Economic Review,* September–October 1988, pp. 16–33; L. Mester, "Efficient Production of Financial Services: Scale and Scope Economies," Federal Reserve Bank of Philadelphia, *Economic Review,* January–February 1987, pp. 15–25; A. Berger, W. C. Hunter, and S. B. Timme, "The Efficiency of Financial Institutions: A Review and Preview of Research Past, Present and Future," *Journal of Banking and Finance* 17 (1993), pp. 221–49; and R. DeYoung, "Learning-by-Doing, Scale Efficiencies, and Financial Performance at Internet-Only Banks," Federal Reserve Bank of Chicago Working Paper, June 2002. Three major production function forms have been tested: The Cobb-Douglas, the trans-log, and the Box-Cox flexible functional form.

better data sets and improved methodologies have suggested that economies of scale may exist for banks up to the $10 billion to $25 billion size range. Many large regional and super regional banks fall in this size range. With respect to economies of scope either among deposits, loans, and other traditional banking product areas or between on-balance-sheet products and off-balance-sheet products such as loan sales, the evidence that cost synergies exist is at best very weak. Similarly, the smaller number of studies involving nonbank financial service firms such as thrifts, insurance companies, and securities firms almost always report neither economies of scale nor economies of scope.[27]

Economies of Scale and Scope and X-Inefficiencies

A number of more recent studies have looked at the *dispersion* of costs in any given FI size class rather than the shape of the average cost functions. These efficiency studies find quite dramatic cost differences of 20 percent or more among banks, thrifts, and insurance companies in any given size class ($100 million asset size class, $200 million asset size class, etc.). Moreover, these studies find that only a small part of the cost differences among FIs in any size class can be attributed to economies of scale or scope.[28] This suggests that cost inefficiencies related to managerial performance and other hard-to-quantify factors (so-called *X-inefficiencies*) may better explain cost differences and operating cost efficiencies among financial firms than technology-related investments per se.[29]

There is little strong, direct evidence that larger multiproduct financial service firms enjoy cost advantages over smaller, more specialized financial firms. Nor do economies of scope and scale explain many of the cost differences among FIs of the same size. These empirical findings raise questions about the benefits of technology investments and technological innovation. While a majority of the studies tested for economies of scope and scale rather than the benefits of technology, these results are consistent with the relatively low payoff from technological innovation. To the extent that large FIs obtain benefits, they may well be on the revenue generation/new product innovation side rather than on the cost side. Indeed, recent studies looking at output and input efficiencies for banks and insurance companies derived from revenue and profit functions found that large FIs tend to be more efficient in revenue generation than smaller FIs and that such efficiencies may well offset scope and scale cost inefficiencies related to size.[30]

[27] A. Berger, D. Humphrey, and L. B. Pulley, "Do Consumers Pay for One-Stop Banking? Evidence from an Alternative Revenue Function," *Journal of Banking and Finance* 20 (1996), pp. 1601–21, look at revenue economies of scope (rather than cost economies of scope) between loans and deposits over the 1978–90 period and find no evidence of revenue economies of scope. J. D. Cummins, S. Tennyson, and M. A. Weiss, "Consolidation and Efficiency in the U.S. Life Insurance Industry," *Journal of Banking and Finance* 23 (1999), pp. 325–57, find that mergers and acquisitions in the insurance industry do produce economies of scale, while efficiency gains are significantly smaller in non-M&A life insurers.

[28] See A. N. Berger and L. J. Mester, "Inside the Black-Box: What Explains Differences in the Efficiencies of Financial Institutions," *Journal of Banking and Finance* 21 (1997), pp. 895–947, for an extensive review of these efficiency studies. See also K. Mukherjee, S. C. Ray, and S. M. Miller, "Productivity Growth in Large U.S. Commercial Banks: The Initial Post-Deregulation Experience," *Journal of Banking and Finance* 25 (2001), pp. 913–39; and A. Akhigbe and J. E. McNulty, "The Profit Efficiency of Small U.S. Commercial Banks," *Journal of Banking and Finance* 27 (2003), pp. 307–25.

[29] See, for example, T. T. Milbourn, A. W. A. Boot, and A. V. Thakor, "Megamergers and Expanded Scope: Theories of Bank Size and Activity Diversity," *Journal of Banking and Finance* 23 (1999), pp. 195–214.

[30] See Berger and Mester, "Inside the Black-Box"; J. Cummins, S. Tennyson, and M. A. Weiss, "Efficiency, Scale Economies and Consolidation in the U.S. Life Insurance Industry," *Journal of Banking and Finance,*

Finally, the real benefits of technological innovation may be long term and dynamic, related to the evolution of the U.S. payments system away from cash and checks and toward electronic means of payment.[31] Such benefits are difficult to obtain in traditional economy of scale and scope studies, which are largely static and ignore the more dynamic aspects of efficiency gains. This dynamic technological evolution not only has affected the fundamental role of FIs in the financial system but also has generated some new and subtle types of risks for FIs and their regulators. In the next section we take a closer look at the effects of technology on the payments system.

Concept Questions

1. What does the empirical evidence reveal about economies of scale and scope?
2. What conclusion is suggested by recent studies that have focused on the dispersion of costs across banks of a given asset size?

TECHNOLOGY AND THE EVOLUTION OF THE PAYMENTS SYSTEM

To better understand the changing nature of the U.S. payments system, look at Tables 14–2 to 14–4. Nonelectronic methods—mostly checks—accounted for 53.5 percent of noncash transactions, but this represented only 4.9 percent of the dollar *value* of noncash transactions. By comparison, while electronic methods of payment—automated clearinghouses (ACH), credit cards, debit cards, and wire transfer systems—accounted for only 46.5 percent in volume, they accounted for 95.1 percent in value. Wire transfer systems alone accounted for 92.6 percent of all dollar transactions measured in value.[32]

As can be seen from Tables 14–3 and 14–4, the use of electronic methods of payment is far higher in other major developed countries. For example, in Canada, Germany, and the United Kingdom electronic transactions account for over 74 percent of total transactions measured by number of transactions. To some extent, the United States is only now starting to catch up with these countries. Part of the reason for this involves culture and tradition in the United States. For example, checks have been obsolete in Germany for some time, but in the United States people still prefer to write checks. As a result, U.S. FIs have been slow in adopting and using online banking and electronic payment methods extensively. The speed with which this electronic payments gap will be closed will in large part depend on two factors: the speed with which the trend toward consolidation and automated banking continues and the degree and speed of technological innovation. Note that in terms of dollar values of transactions completed electronically (Table 14–4),

---

February 1999, pp. 325–57; and R. DeYoung and K. P. Roland, "Product Mix and Earnings Volatility at Commercial Banks: Evidence from a Degree of Total Leverage Model," *Journal of Financial Intermediation* 10 (2001), pp. 54–84. In contrast to the majority of the research, a recent study of 201 large U.S. commercial banks in the postderegulation period (after 1984) finds overall productivity growth at a rate of about 4.5 percent per year on average. The growth in productivity reflected largely adjustments in technology. See Mukherjee et al., "Productivity Growth in Large U.S. Commercial Banks."

[31] For example, D. Hancock, D. B. Humphrey, and J. A. Wilcox, "Cost Reductions in Electronic Payments: The Roles of Consolidation, Economies of Scale, and Technical Change," *Journal of Banking and Finance* 23 (1999), pp. 391–421, find that when the Fed consolidated its Fedwire electronic funds transfer operations, reductions in production costs were partially attributable to technological advances.

[32] Although these data are for commercial banks, many mutual funds and security firms permit customers to automatically deposit their paychecks in cash management accounts, from which check writing capabilities are allowed. Further, these accounts can also be linked to credit cards that also function as debit cards at ATMs.

TABLE 14–2
U.S. Cashless
Payments System:
Volume, Value, and
Average Transaction
Amount

Source: Bank for International Settlements, *Statistics on Payment Systems in Selected Countries*, Basel, Switzerland, May 2003. *www.bis.org*

	Volume, billions	Percent	Value, billions	Percent	Transaction Average Value
Check	41.2	53.5%	$ 38,909	4.9%	$944
Credit card	17.1	22.2	1,514	0.2	89
Debit card	12.4	16.1	572	0.1	46
ACH	6.1	7.9	17,637	2.2	2,891
Wire transfer	0.2	0.3	735,573	92.6	3,677,865
	77.0		$794,205		

TABLE 14–3
Percentage of Total
Noncash Paper and
Electronic
Transactions

Source: Bank for International Settlements, *Statistics on Payment Systems in Selected Countries*, Basel, Switzerland, May 2003. *www.bis.org*

	Paper (Check)	Debit and Credit Cards	Credit Transfers	Direct Debits	Electronic
United States	53.5%	38.3%	5.0%	3.1%	46.5%
Canada	25.5	57.1	9.5	7.8	74.5
Germany	2.3	11.3	49.8	36.4	97.7
United Kingdom	23.5	39.0	17.7	19.7	76.5

TABLE 14–4
Percentage of Total
Value of Noncash
Transactions, 2002

Source: Bank for International Settlements, *Statistics on Payment Systems in Selected Countries*, Basel, Switzerland, May 2003. *www.bis.org*

	Paper (Check)	Debit and Credit Cards	Credit Transfers	Direct Debit	Electronic
United States	4.9%	0.3%	93.7%	1.1%	95.1%
Canada	12.7	0.5	86.2	0.6	87.3
Germany	2.7	0.4	84.2	12.8	97.3
United Kingdom	2.2	0.2	97.0	0.6	97.8

*See notes to Table 14–5.

the United States is comparable with the other reported countries; 95.1 percent in the United States compared with 87.3 percent, 97.3 percent, and 97.8 percent in Canada, Germany, and the United Kingdom, respectively.

The two wire transfer systems that dominate the U.S. payments system are Fedwire and the Clearing House Interbank Payments System (CHIPS). Fedwire is a wire transfer network linking more than 8,000 domestic banks with the Federal Reserve System. Banks use this network to make deposit and loan payments, to transfer book entry securities among themselves, and to act as payment agents on behalf of large corporate customers, including other financial service firms. CHIPS is a privately operated payments network. At the core of the CHIPS system are approximately 55 large U.S. and foreign banks acting as correspondent banks for a larger number of domestic and international banks in clearing mostly international payments (such as foreign exchange, Eurodollar loans, certificates of deposit).

Together, these two wire transfer networks have been growing at around 10 percent per annum. Indeed, in 2003 the combined value of payments sent over these two networks often exceeded $3.0 trillion a day.[33] Another way to see the tremendous growth in these wire transfer payment networks is to compare their

www.chips.org

---

[33] For example, in 2003, the average daily Fedwire funds value was $1.7 trillion and the average daily CHIPS value was $1.3 trillion. Volume on Fedwire averaged 488,800 transactions and on CHIPS, 255,000 transactions.

TABLE 14–5
Ratio of Fedwire
and CHIPS Dollar
Payments to Bank
Reserves

Source: David B. Humphrey,
"Future Directions in
Payment Risk Reduction,"
Journal of Cash Management,
1988; and Federal Reserve
figures.

	Ratio of Average Daily Fedwire and CHIPS Payments ($) to Bank Reserves
1970	2 times
1980	17
1983	38
1985	42
1990	80
1994	81
1997	63
2000	66
2003	57

TABLE 14–6
Wholesale Wire
Transfer Systems in
Selected Countries
2002

Source: The Bank for International Settlements, *Statistics on Payment Systems in Selected Countries*, Basel, Switzerland, May 2003, Table 10b. *www.bis.org*

	Number of Transactions (thousands)	Annual Value of Transactions (US$ billions)	Ratio of Transactions Value to GDP (at annual rate)
Japan			
FXYCS	9,564	$ 56,587	13.6%
BOJ-NET	5,046	156,640	37.5
Netherlands			
Interpay	2,558,284	1,409	3.7
Top	4,023	18,514	48.2
Sweden			
K-RIX	655	10,962	52.3
Bank Giro System	345,200	376	1.8
Switzerland			
SIC	161,200	26,905	109.4
DTA/LSV	103,700	225	0.9
United Kingdom			
CHAPS-Sterling	23,962	76,189	53.6
BACS	3,527,340	3,119	2.2
Check/credit	1,940,000	2,073	1.5
United States			
Fedwire	112,500	423,867	42.0
CHIPS	60,400	311,707	30.9
European Union			
TARGET	53,664	368,469	—
Euro 1	28,633	58,101	—

dollar payment values with bank reserves, as we do in Table 14–5. Thus, the value of wire transfers increased more than 80-fold relative to bank reserves in the mid-1990s before falling back to almost 60-fold in the early 2000s. According to data in Table 14–6, the United States is not the only country in which wholesale wire transfer systems have come to dominate the payment systems. The United Kingdom, Switzerland, and Japan also have very large wire transfer systems measured as a percentage of local gross domestic product (GDP). In 2001 as a result of the single currency (the euro) and the European Monetary Union, a single wholesale wire transfer system for Europe fully emerged, linking all countries that are members of

FIGURE 14–5
Daylight Overdrafts on Fedwire

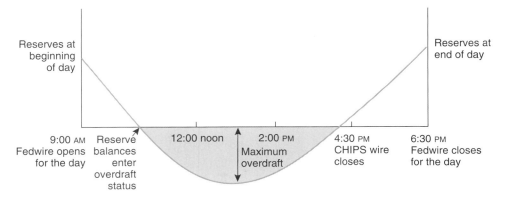

the European Monetary Union. The transactional system is called TARGET (Trans-European Automated Real-Time Gross-Settlement Express Transfer).

Risks That Arise in an Electronic Transfer Payment System

At least six important risks have arisen along with the growth of wire transfer systems. We mentioned some of these while discussing off-balance-sheet activities in Chapter 13; here, we go into more detail.

Daylight Overdraft Risk

Some analysts and regulators view settlement, or daylight, overdraft risk as one of the greatest potential sources of instability in the financial markets today. To understand daylight overdrafts better, look at Figure 14–5. It shows a typical daily pattern of net wire payment transfers—payment messages sent (debits) minus payment messages received (credits)—for a large money center bank using Fedwire (the Federal Reserve's wire transfer network).

Under the Federal Reserve Act, banks must maintain cash reserves on deposit at the Fed; Fedwire settlement occurs at the end of the banking day at 6:30 PM EST. At that time, the Fed adjusts each member bank's reserve account to reflect its net debit (credit) position with other banks.[34] Under current regulations, the member bank's end-of-day reserve position cannot be negative. However, what is true at the end of the day is not true during the day; that is, the Fed allows banks to run real-time **daylight overdrafts** (or negative intraday balances) on their reserve accounts. These negative reserve balances occur under the current payments system because large banks and their customers often send payment messages repaying overnight loans and making interest payments at the beginning of the banking day and borrow funds and receive payment messages toward the end of the banking day. For periods during the day, banks frequently run daylight overdrafts on their reserve accounts at the Fed by having their payment outflow messages exceed their payment inflow messages (see Figure 14–5).

In effect, the Fed is implicitly lending banks within-day reserves. This process involves two other important institutional factors. First, until recently, the Fed did not charge banks an explicit interest rate or fee for these daylight overdrafts. As a result, neither banks nor their large corporate customers had any incentive to economize on these transactions. Daylight Fedwire overdrafts were effectively free and

daylight overdraft
A bank's negative intraday balance in its reserve account at the Fed.

---

[34] Technically, CHIPS transactions settle on Fedwire by 4:30 PM, before Fedwire closes.

therefore oversupplied.[35] Second, under Regulation J, the Fed guarantees payment finality for every wire transfer message. Therefore, if the representative bank in Figure 14–5 were to fail at 12:00 noon, the Fed would be liable for all of the bank's Fedwire transactions made that day by that bank until 12 noon. This eliminates any risk that a payment message–receiving bank or its customers would be left short of funds at the end of the day. Essentially, the Fed bears the Fedwire credit risk of bank failures by granting overdrafts without charging a market interest rate.

On CHIPS, net payment flows often reflect a daily pattern similar to that in Figure 14–5 except that, as a privately owned pure net settlement system, the beginning-of-day position must be zero for all banks. As on Fedwire, big banks often run a daylight overdraft, but this is generally larger and more pronounced early in the morning than it is on Fedwire. Again, large banks then seek to borrow funds in the afternoon to cover net debit positions created earlier in the day. CHIPS does not charge banks explicit fees for running daylight overdrafts, but it treats a bank's failure to settle at the end of the day very differently than does Fedwire. On Fedwire, all payments are in good funds; that is, the Fed guarantees the finality of any wire transfer at the time it is made. By contrast, because CHIPS is a private network, all within-day transfers are provisional and become final only on settlement among CHIPS members at the end of the day. In this case, if a bank (bank Z) with a daylight overdraft were to fail, CHIPS might have to resolve this by unwinding all the failing bank's transactions over that day with the other $(N - 1)$ remaining banks. Bank Z's individual failure could result in a systemic crisis in the banking and financial system among the remaining $(N - 1)$ banks in the system. While no settlement failure has occurred recently on CHIPS,[36] any such failure could be potentially disastrous, with financial ramifications far exceeding those of the October 1987 stock market crash[37] or the 1997 Asian financial market crisis.[38]

---

[35] Beginning in 1993, a small per annum interest charge (penalty) was levied on a bank's daily overdraft amount in excess of a deductible amount (10 percent of its regulatory capital). The interest charge is an annualized 15 basis points. As a result, this interest charge is very small. For example, it is estimated that only 90 financial institutions had to pay a penalty exceeding $100 over any two-week period in 1995. See H. W. Richards, "Daylight Overdraft Fees and the Federal Reserves Payment System Risk Policy," *Federal Reserve Bulletin,* December 1995, pp. 1065–77.

[36] There was a failure in 1974 by the Herstatt Bank of Germany.

[37] Simulations by D. B. Humphrey of CHIPS unwinding following an assumed bank failure show that up to 50 banks might be unable to meet their payment obligations on CHIPS following any one bank's failure to settle, implying a massive systematic collapse of the payment system. See "Payments Finality and Risk Settlement Failure," in *Technology and the Regulation of Financial Markets: Securities, Futures, and Banking,* ed. A. Saunders and L. J. White (Lexington, MA: Lexington Books, 1986), pp. 97–120. Interestingly, in a paper conducting similar simulations for Italy (P. Angelini, G. Maresca, and D. Russo, "An Assessment of Systemic Risk in the Italian Clearing System," *Bank of Italy,* Discussion Paper No. 207, 1993), these systemic costs were much lower. This was largely due to the lower importance of wholesale wire transfers in Italy. For example, there are only 288 participants, versus 10,000 on Fedwire. In fact, only the failure of 4 out of 288 banks triggers a systemic crisis in simulations for January 1992.

[38] To lower this settlement risk problem and to introduce an element of payment finality, CHIPS members have contributed more than $4 billion to a special escrow fund that became operational in October 1990. CHIPS members can use this fund to replace the message commitments of any failed bank, therefore preventing the potentially disastrous unwinding effects just described. However, it is estimated that this fund is sufficient to cover only the failure of its two largest financial institution members. At the end of the day, the Fed and other central banks would have to mount a rescue to prevent an international failure contagion from spreading throughout the domestic and international financial system. Of course, this implies yet another subsidy from U.S. regulators and taxpayers to the private domestic and international banking system. See Computer Sciences Corp., *Sustaining Stable Financial Markets throughout the Millennium* (Waltham, MA: CSC, 1998).

Because of these concerns, the FDIC Improvement Act, passed in 1991, required the Federal Reserve to implement Regulation F, under which banks, thrifts, and foreign banks must develop internal procedures or benchmarks to limit their settlement and other credit exposures to depository institutions with which they do business (so-called correspondent banks). Accordingly, since December 1992, banks have been required to limit their exposure to an individual corespondent to no more than 25 percent of the correspondent bank's capital. However, for adequately capitalized banks, this can be raised to 50 percent, while no set benchmark is required for well-capitalized banks. Thus, it is now easier for the most solvent banks to transact on the wire transfer networks and run daylight overdrafts than for less well-capitalized banks.[39] In addition, as long as the benchmarks are adhered to, regulators' exposure to settlement risk is reduced.[40]

International Technology Transfer Risk

In recent years the United States has been at the forefront in making technology investments and financial service innovations in the payments system. For example, the United States has been a major pioneer of ATMs, yet such networks have grown relatively slowly in countries such as Sweden and Belgium, often because of prohibitive charges imposed for the use and leasing of domestic telephone lines (see Table 14–7).

This suggests that U.S. financial service firms have often been unable to transfer profitably their domestic technological innovations to international markets to gain competitive advantage, at least in the short term.[41] In contrast, foreign financial service firms entering the U.S. market gain direct access to, and knowledge of, U.S. technology–based products at a very low cost. For example, since the passage of the International Banking Act in 1978, foreign banks have had direct access to U.S. Fedwire.

Crime and Fraud Risk

The increased replacement of checks and cash by wire transfers as methods of payment or exchange has resulted in an increase in the efficiency of the execution of transactions, but it has also resulted in new problems regarding theft, data snooping, and white-collar crime. Because huge sums are transferred across the wire networks each day and some bank employees have specialized knowledge of personal identification numbers (PINS) and other entry codes, the incentive for white-collar crime appears to have increased. For example, a manager at the Sri Lankan branch of the now defunct BCCI reportedly stole a computer chip from a telex machine in the bank's Oman branch and used it to transfer $10 million from three banks in the United States and Japan to his own account in Switzerland.[42]

---

[39] See Federal Reserve Board of Governors press release, July 14, 1992, for more details and Chapter 20 for definitions of "adequately" and "well-capitalized" banks.

[40] One way to eliminate payment systems risk is to go to continuous real-time gross settlement (RTGS) rather than end-of-day settlement. Such a system is used in Switzerland. However, such a system imposes a danger of payment system gridlock. See New York Clearing House Association, New York, January 1995; and W. R. Emmons, "Recent Developments in Wholesale Payment Systems," *Federal Reserve Bank of St. Louis Review,* November–December 1997, pp. 23–43.

[41] Long-term benefits may yet be realized as a result of telecommunications deregulation globally and through better customer recruitment and marketing of products in foreign environments. See S. Claessens, T. Glaessner, and D. Klingebiel, "E-finance in Emerging Markets: Is Leapfrogging Possible?" *Financial Markets Institutions & Instruments*, February 2002, pp. 1–124, for an update on e-banking in emerging markets.

[42] Office of Technology Assessment, *U.S. Banks and International Telecommunications*, October 1992, chap. 5, pp. 27–35.

TABLE 14–7
Cash Dispensers
and ATMs

Source: The Bank for International Settlements, *Statistics on Payment Systems in Selected Countries*, Basel, Switzerland, May 2003, Table 5. *www.bis.org*

	1991	1995	1999	2001
Number of Machines per 1,000,000 Inhabitants				
Belgium	105	360	606	669
Canada[†]	467	600	873	1,142
France	284	395	538	606
Germany	161	436	563	603
Italy	204	378	524	593
Japan	795	1,013	944	918
Netherlands	222	378	422	445
Singapore	—	—	470	435
Sweden	258	267	291	289
Switzerland	347	532	655	694
United Kingdom	309	358	460	612
United States	331	466	832	1,137
Number of Transactions per Inhabitant				
Belgium	8.1	14.3	17.4	21.5
Canada[†]	33.6	45.7	47.2	47.8
France	11.0	15.8	17.0	19.1
Germany	—	13.4	18.4	19.4
Italy	2.9	5.8	8.7	9.7
Japan	2.4	3.8	3.1	3.1
Netherlands	13.7	23.2	28.5	28.0
Singapore	—	—	2.6	2.1
Sweden	24.1	31.8	35.0	37.7
Switzerland	6.6	10.0	12.2	19.6
United Kingdom	18.5	25.2	33.1	36.6
United States	25.3	36.9	39.9	47.7
Average Value of Transactions (US$)*				
Belgium	117.4	138.1	111.3	92.8
Canada[†]	56.7	51.0	65.3	69.5
France	82.7	81.3	64.8	54.7
Germany	—	196.6	155.9	140.2
Italy	239.2	198.3	170.6	144.9
Japan	356.5	450.6	501.3	474.4
Netherlands	92.2	119.3	93.7	88.2
Singapore	—	—	140.0	124.7
Sweden	120.6	112.6	100.2	81.4
Switzerland	224.6	246.9	173.2	111.9
United Kingdom	81.0	77.3	88.8	84.0
United States	67.0	67.7	68.0	68.0

* Converted at yearly average exchange rates.
[†] Average value of a cash withdrawal only.

Moreover, considerable security problems exist in trying to develop the Internet as a form of electronic payment system. Internet transactions can be intercepted by third parties. Financial institutions are accordingly concerned about open credit or debit card details on the Internet. Any version of electronic payment via the Internet must not only meet the requirements of recognition and acceptability associated with physical cash but also provide the same high level of security that is demanded of cash payments but which the Internet itself cannot guarantee. After the terrorist attacks on September 11, 2001, the U.S. Congress passed the USA Patriot Act of 2001. The act contains a number of specific amendments to existing criminal

Technology in the News   1

PATRIOT ACT ARRIVES FOR FUND COMPANIES

Nearly two years after passage of the USA Patriot Act, another piece of the law kicked in this month, requiring mutual funds to bring their customer identification programs into compliance with rules issued by the Treasury Department and the Securities and Exchange Commission. The USA Patriot Act, which amended the Bank Secrecy Act in establishing minimum standards for identifying customers who open accounts at financial institutions, became effective in June, but banks and financial institutions had until 1 October to comply.

In the mutual fund business, every fund provider's so-called customer identification program (CIP) must define its methods for profiling new individual and corporate customers who are opening accounts, as well as define its methods for maintaining data on them. Fund companies must obtain and verify the following pieces of data from each new customer: name; street address; date of birth (for individuals); and a Social Security number, tax identification number or, for non-US investors, a foreign government–issued ID card. . . .

Patriot Act compliance will undoubtedly cost mutual fund companies millions, in compliance costs, which in turn will place ever-greater earnings pressure on an already beleaguered industry. TowerGroup, the Needham, Massachusetts–based financial consultancy, estimated in a recent report, for example, that U.S. funds will spend at least $288 million on Patriot Act compliance in the first year, and $140 million in each succeeding year for the foreseeable future. Such hefty costs will likely be absorbed by the major players, but smaller funds may have no choice but to pass them on to customers. The cost of compliance actually represents less than 0.2 percent of annual mutual fund fees, but in an environment of increasing regulatory scrutiny "it's one more straw on the camel's back," the TowerGroup report states.

Funds have little choice but to comply: The Patriot Act provides for both civil and criminal penalties for noncompliance. Fund company officials say they're concerned about those penalties, but are optimistic that they will avoid them. . . .

Source: *Funds International,* Lafferty Publications Limited, October 29, 2003, p. 4.

---

laws designed to streamline early detection and investigation of suspected terrorist activity conducted through financial institutions. For example, in accordance with the Patriot Act, in April 2004 the FBI and federal regulators began a probe into large cash withdrawals from Riggs National Bank by Saudi Arabian citizens/customers and accused Riggs of failing to alert regulators of suspicious transactions. The Office of the Comptroller of the Currency (OCC) also classified Riggs as a "troubled institution" for failing to adequately tighten its money laundering controls despite an order from the OCC to do so. Regulators also pursued a second line of inquiry into whether Riggs violated "know your customer" record keeping laws in its dealings with foreign customers. Treasury Department investigators were looking into the relationship between Riggs and high risk foreign customers. But as Technology in the News box 1 points out, compliance with the Patriot Act can be quite costly for FIs.

In the future, greater bank and regulatory resources will have to be spent on surveillance and employee monitoring as well as on developing fail-safe and unbreakable entry codes to wire transfer accounts, especially as a number of countries have passed data privacy laws. Surprisingly, however, a study on the problems arising with U.S. online banking found that only 1 percent of those problems could be attributed to employee sabotage or internal fraudulent attacks.[43]

[43] General Accounting Office, *Electronic Banking: Experiences Reported by Banks in Implementing On-line Banking,* January 1998, GAO/GGD 98–34.

Regulatory Risk

The improvement in FIs' computer and telecommunications networks also enhances the power of FIs' vis-à-vis regulators, effectively aiding regulatory avoidance. Thus, as implied earlier, regulation not only can affect the profitability of technological innovations, but also can spur or hinder the rate and types of innovation.[44, 45] For example, many states in the United States impose usury ceilings on FIs. **Usury ceilings** place caps and controls on the fees and interest rates that many FIs can charge on credit cards, consumer loans, and residential mortgages. Because credit card operations are heavily communications based and do not need to be located directly in an FI's market, the two states that now dominate the credit card market are South Dakota and Delaware. These two states are among the most liberal regarding credit card fee and interest rate usury regulations.[46] As a result of regulation in the United States, banking in the relatively unregulated Cayman Islands has experienced considerable growth. The 500 or more FIs located there do most of their business via public and private telecommunications networks.[47] The use of telecommunications networks and technological improvements has changed, perhaps irreversibly, the balance of power between large multinational FIs and governments—both local and national—in favor of the former. Such a shift in power may create incentives for countries to lower their regulations to attract entrants; that is, the shift may increase the incentives for competitive deregulation. This trend may be potentially destabilizing to the market in financial services, with the weakest regulators attracting the most entrants.[48]

Tax Avoidance

The development of international wire networks as well as international financial service firm networks has enabled FIs to shift funds and profits by using internal pricing mechanisms, thereby minimizing their overall U.S. tax burden and maximizing their foreign tax credits. For example, prior to 1986, many large U.S. banks paid almost no corporate income taxes, despite large reported profits, by rapidly moving profits and funds across different tax regimes. This raised considerable public policy concerns and was a major reason underlying the 1986 tax reforms in the United States. These reforms imposed a minimum corporate income tax rate of

usury ceilings
Caps or ceilings on consumer and mortgage interest rates imposed by state governments.

---

[44] A further example of regulatory risk impacts on technology and operating costs in general is the cost of converting European banks' systems from local currencies into the euro. This may cost European banks $150 billion or more. See "A Year before the Millennium Bug, There's the Euro Problem," *New York Times,* March 9, 1998, p. 1.

[45] The importance of accounting for technological change in the design of regulatory policies has been emphasized by the Chairman of the Federal Reserve. See A. Greenspan, "Technological Change and the Design of Bank Supervising Policies," in *33rd Annual Conference on Bank Structure and Competition* (Federal Reserve Bank of Chicago, May 1997), pp. 1–8.

[46] For example, Citigroup, the U.S. financial services firm with the largest credit card franchise, has located its credit card operations in South Dakota. See also I. Walter and A. Saunders for a discussion of trends in financial service firms leaving New York: "Global Competitiveness of New York City as a Financial Center," Occasional Papers in Business and Finance, Stern Business School, New York University, 1992.

[47] A major reason for the growth in Cayman Islands banking was the desire of large U.S. banks to avoid or reduce the cost of the Federal Reserve's non-interest-bearing reserve requirements. Many attribute its current popularity to drug- or crime-related secret money transactions. See I. Walter, *Secret Money: The World of International Financial Secrecy* (London: Allen and Unwin, 1985).

[48] A closely associated risk for regulators is that increased use of international wire transfer systems weakens the power of central banks to control the domestic money supply.

20 percent on U.S. banks and limited their ability to use foreign tax credits to off-set their domestic income tax burdens.

Competition Risk

As financial services become more technologically based, they are increasingly competing with nontraditional financial service suppliers. For example, in addition to offering its own enhanced credit card in competition with bank-supplied credit cards, AT&T owns a finance company.[49] Also, once established, nonfinancial firms can easily purchase financial services technology. For example, General Motors has established a credit card operation linked to the purchase of its vehicles at a discount. Currently, banks issue less than half of all new credit cards; much of the new business is going to nontraditional firms such as AT&T and General Motors. Another example is the dramatic rise in industrial loan corporations (ILCs) in Utah, owned by nonbanking companies such as AMEX, General Electric, and Pitney Bowes. ILCs provide loans to low-quality, high–interest rate corporations that banks avoid. The deposits of these ILCs are insured by the FDIC, yet ILCs are regulated by neither the Federal Reserve nor the Office of the Comptroller of the Currency. While being based in Utah (where the regulatory environment is favorable) technology has helped ILCs expand their services nationwide. As a result, assets under management have grown from $2.9 billion at the end of 1995 to $103 billion in 2003.[50] This can be compared with total C&I loans at commercial banks of $870 billion. Thus, technology exposes existing FIs to the increased risk of erosion of their franchises as costs of entry fall and the competitive landscape changes.[51]

Concept Questions

1. Describe the six risks faced by FIs with the growth of wire transfer payment systems.
2. Why do daylight overdrafts create more of a risk problem for banks on CHIPS than on Fedwire?
3. What steps have the members of CHIPS taken to lower settlement, or daylight overdraft, risk?

OTHER OPERATIONAL RISKS

While technology risk has become increasingly important to the profitability and riskiness of modern FIs, it is not the sole source of operational risk. Early in the chapter we listed four other sources of operational risk. These are employees, customer relationships, capital assets, and external risks. Table 14–8 lists a summary of the problems these sources of operational risk can create, including how the other sources of operational risk interact with technology risk. For example, employee risk includes employee turnover and fraud, as well as programming errors by employees. The Ethical Dilemmas box examines an alleged infraction by a rule several Wall Street firms that requires securities firms to retain e-mail for three

[49] AT&T's universal card began operation in March 1990. It is both a credit card and a calling card. Its finance company subsidiary—AT&T Capital Corp.—does leasing, project financing, and small business lending.

[50] See "From Mormon to Mammon," *The Economist,* June 9, 2001, pp. 86–87; and "Success Brings CRA Quandry at Utah's ILCs: Windfall for a State Is Running Out of Places to Invest," *The American Banker*, April 25, 2003, p. 1.

[51] For an excellent overview of the issues relating to the risks of payment systems, see D. Hancock and D. B. Humphrey, "Payment Transactions, Instruments and Systems: A Survey," *Journal of Banking and Finance* 21 (December 1997), pp. 1573–1624.

TABLE 14–8
A Summary of
Operational Risks
Faced by FIs

Source: C. Marshall,
*Measuring and Managing
Operational Risks in Financial
Institutions: Tools,
Techniques and Other
Resources* (Singapore: John
Wiley and Sons, 2001).

Source of Risk	Specific Problem
Employee risk	Employee turnover
	Key personnel risk
	Fraud risk
	Error
	Rogue trading
	Money laundering
	Confidentiality breach
Technology risk	Programming error
	Model risk
	Mark-to-market error
	Management information
	IT systems outage
	Telecommunications failure
	Technology provider failure
	Contingency planning
Customer risk	Contractual disagreement
	Dissatisfaction
	Default
Capital asset risk	Safety
	Security
	Operating costs
	Fire/flood
External risk	External fraud
	Taxation risk
	Legal risk
	War
	Collapse of markets
	Reputation risk
	Relationship risk

years. Similarly, the failure of a third-party technology provider to perform as promised, resulting an FI's online banking services being interrupted, may cause the FI to lose customers.[52]

Like technology risk, these other sources of operational risk can result in direct costs (e.g., loss of income), indirect costs (e.g., client withdrawals and legal costs), and opportunity costs (e.g., forgone business opportunities) for an FI that reduce profitability and value. To offset these costs, FI managers spend considerable effort and resources to prevent, control, finance, and insulate the FI from losses due to operational risk. These efforts include (see Marshall, 2001):

1. *Loss prevention:* Training, development, and review of employees.
2. *Loss control:* Planning, organization, backup (e.g., computer systems).
3. *Loss financing:* External insurance (e.g., catastrophe insurance).
4. *Loss insulation:* FI capital.

[52] See "E Is for Risk," *Risk: Operational Risk Special Report,* November 1999, pp. 6–9. This section is based in part on Christopher Marshall, *Measuring and Managing Operational Risks in Financial Institutions: Tools, Techniques, and Other Resources* (Singapore: John Wiley and Sons, 2001).

Ethical **Dilemmas**

WALL STREET HAS E-MAIL PROBLEMS

Wall Street firms seem to have found another way to anger securities regulators and risk shaking investor confidence. Regulators are seeking to fine six securities firms, including Citigroup Inc.'s Salomon Smith Barney, Morgan Stanley, Goldman Sachs Group Inc. and Merrill Lynch & Co., a total of $10 million for allegedly failing to keep e-mails and produce them in pending investigations of Wall Street abuses, according to people familiar with the matter.

At an unusual meeting Tuesday at the Securities and Exchange Commission, regulators demanded the penalties from the six securities firms, which also include Deutsche Bank AG and US Bancorp's Piper Jaffray unit. Each firm has received notices from the SEC, the National Association of Securities Dealers and the New York Stock Exchange that their enforcement staffs have recommended sanctioning the companies for failing to produce the e-mails. . . .

The regulators currently are conducting investigations of these firms for possible rule violations in doling out sought-after initial public offerings and conflicts of interest among their stock research analysts, among other matters. Regulators haven't been able to retrieve at least some key pieces of evidence because they hadn't been kept by the firms. . . . As part of the sanctions, the firms would be censured and promise not to repeat the offense, which violates securities law.

Regulatory rules require securities firms to retain e-mails and other records that pertain to their business for two years in an easily accessible location, and for an additional year in a manner that doesn't have to be easily accessible. The rules also require the firms to be able to produce the records promptly if needed for an investigation. . . . E-mails, for instance, which are often written in blunt, colloquial and colorful language, have played a prominent role in at least two recent regulatory cases. The charges of analysts' conflicts of interest against Merrill Lynch brought in April . . . were buttressed by numerous e-mails in which Merrill Internet analysts privately derided stocks they were recommending in what (was) charged as an attempt to win investment banking business. Some of the e-mails included words like "dog" or "crap" to describe specific stocks. . . . And in another $100 million settlement, with Credit Suisse First Boston, announced in January, the NASD and SEC both included extensive e-mail evidence that described how the securities unit of Credit Suisse Group illegally charged some clients commissions based on the amount of their profits on IPOs they received from CFSB.

The latest regulatory action suggests that e-mail destruction has been pervasive on Wall Street. . . .

Source: *The Wall Street Journal*, August 2, 2002, p. C1, by Randall Smith. Reprinted by permission of *The Wall Street Journal*, © 2002 Dow Jones & Company, Inc. All Rights Reserved Worldwide. *www.wsj.com*

Risk management efforts, of course, come at a cost to the FI. As illustrated in Figure 14–6, the greater the commitment of resources to risk management efforts, the lower the costs resulting from operational risks. However, the resources spent in preventing costs of operational risk may, at some point, be greater than the cost of the risk itself. In maximizing profits and value, FIs will invest in these risk management efforts until the costs of such efforts just offset operating losses from not undertaking such efforts (point RME* in Figure 14–6). See Marshall (2001), p. 317.

Concept Questions

1. What are some examples of operational risk coming from employees, customer relationships, capital assets, and external risk?
2. What risk management efforts are involved in controlling operational risk?

FIGURE 14–6
Optimal Risk Management Effort

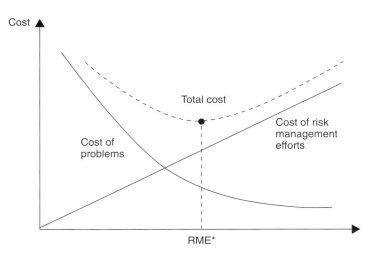

Extent of risk managment efforts

REGULATORY ISSUES AND TECHNOLOGY AND OPERATIONAL RISKS

As stated earlier, operational risk is the risk of direct or indirect loss resulting from inadequate or failed internal processes, people, or systems, and from external events. Certainly, as FIs' use of technology increases, operational risk increases as well. However, little has been done to oversee or regulate these increasing risks. In this section, we look at two areas that have been directly impacted by the increase in operational risk.

1. *Operational Risk and FI Insolvency.* Research by Operational Research Inc., an operational risk consultancy firm, estimates that since 1980, FIs have lost over $200 billion due to operational risk.[53] Regulators have recognized the significance of operational risk for FIs. Specifically, in 1999 the Basel Committee (of the BIS) on Banking Supervision said that operational risks "are sufficiently important for banks to devote necessary resources to quantify the level of such risks and to incorporate them (along with market and credit risk) into their assessment of their overall capital adequacy."[54] In its follow-up consultative documents released in January 2001 and April 2003, the Basel Committee proposed three specific methods by which depository institutions (DIs) could calculate the required capital (effective 2006) to protect themselves against operational risk. These methods are the Basic Indicator Approach, the Standardized Approach, and the Advanced Measurement Approach.[55] We discuss each of the methods in more detail in Chapter 20.

---

[53] See C. Smithson,"Measuring Operational Risk," *Risk,* March 2000, pp. 58–59.

[54] See "Basel Committee on Banking Supervision, 1999; A New Capital Adequacy Framework," Bank for International Settlements, Basel, Switzerland, June 1999, p. 50.

[55] See "Basel Committee on Banking Supervision, 2001; The New Basel Capital Accord," January 2001, and "Overview of The New Basel Capital Accord," April 2003, Bank for International Settlements, Basel, Switzerland, (www.bis.org). The Advanced Measurement Approach offers three alternative methodologies for capital reserve calculations for the most sophisticated and largest banks in the world.

Technology in the News   2

WEB FRAUD UNDETECTED? NOT FOR LONG

Bank robbery is still big business in America. From Jesse James to John Dillinger and Willie Sutton, bank robbers have always been among America's most infamous figures, and holdups still make the evening news every time. But surveillance cameras, guards, alarms, dye packs and cooperative law enforcement efforts stack the odds very high against any aspiring robber who walks into a bank, if he walks in. That's the very expensive problem—bank robbery no longer requires the actual presence of the thief. Thanks to Internet banking and high-tech credit card fraud, it is now possible to anonymously steal large amounts of money from a financial institution by remote control.

It's happening all over the world. Italian police broke up a Mafia scheme to "clone" an online branch of the Banco di Sicilia and siphon hundreds of millions of dollars from an account belonging to the Sicilian regional government. The gang, with help from two bank employees and a couple of Telecom Italia technicians, used stolen computer files, codes and passwords to penetrate the bank's systems. In another case three Englishmen were caught attempting to defraud the Internet financial services group Egg by submitting multiple phony applications for online loans and savings accounts. British police found evidence the thieves had previously robbed two other online banks undetected. And finally a New Orleans bank employee stole thousands of dollars via dozens of Internet bank and credit card accounts he opened under the names of prominent local citizens by accessing their personal information on the bank's computer.

Perhaps the most vulnerable part of any financial services enterprise is the credit card division, which, among other functions, fields online card applications. The U.S. Secret Service calls credit card fraud "the bank robbery of the future" because criminals have realized that banking and card systems are easy pickings. A recent study by the Internet Fraud Prevention Advisory Council estimates that online fraud as a percentage of business revenues may be as much as 40 times higher than "real world" fraud. Online credit card fraud cost businesses an estimated $9 billion in 2001; that figure could reach $60 billion by 2005, according to Meridien Research. . . .

Every industry survey shows the biggest concern for online financial customers is the safety and security of their money, account information and transactions—small wonder when they read every day about fraud perpetrated through stolen online accounts or credit card numbers. And banks will soon bear an even larger financial responsibility for online crime. Both MasterCard and Visa are rolling out new verification programs that shift online credit card fraud liability from merchants to issuing banks.

Source: Marie Alexander, "American Banker-Bond Buyer," *US Banker*, June 2003, p. 80. *www.us-banker.com*

2. *Consumer Protection.* A KPMG Information Security Survey 2000 reported that business customers hesitate to put their personal and financial information on the Internet for two reasons. First, they are worried about who has access to this information and how it will be used. Second, they worry that credit card or bank account details will be stolen or used fraudulently.[56] As Technology in the News box 2 points out, these worries are well founded. The advent of electronic banking is making consumer protection an increasingly important responsibility for regulators of FIs. As mentioned earlier, the 1999 Financial Services Modernization Act allows FI customers to opt out of any private information sharing an FI may want to pursue. Thus, FI customers have some control over who will see and have access to their private information. However, this regulation does not include the sharing of information by nonfinancial firms that have entered the financial services industry. Indeed, global standards and protocols that can be

[56] See R. Coles, "Safety Net," *The Banker,* September 2000, pp. 7–8; and "E Is for Risk."

credibly enforced will become increasingly necessary to assure the customer's desired degree of privacy.

With respect to security risk, because Internet transactions involve open systems, they are susceptible to interception and fraud. Cryptographic techniques for ensuring transaction security are rapidly improving and are almost fully secure for consumer transactions. Further, technological developments are soon expected that will provide protection needed for large transactions as well. Availability of these technologies does not ensure that FIs will use them (especially if their costs are high). Consequently, regulators may need to oversee (or even mandate) the implementation of these technologies if FIs are slow to use them operationally.

Concept Questions

1. What are the three approaches proposed by the Basel Committee on Banking Supervision for measuring capital requirements associated with operational risk?
2. What steps have been or are being taken to ensure privacy and protection against fraud in the use of personal and financial consumer information placed on the Internet?

Summary

This chapter analyzed the operating cost side of FIs' activities, including the effects of the growth of technology-based innovations. The impact of technology was first examined separately for wholesale and retail services before an analysis was presented of its impact on cost and revenues. Technology-based investments can potentially result in new product innovations and lower costs, but the evidence for such cost savings is mixed. Moreover, new and different risks appear to have been created by modern technology. These include settlement or daylight overdraft risk, international technology transfer risk, crime or fraud risk, regulatory avoidances risk, taxation avoidance risk, and competition risk. Nevertheless, although the chapter focuses on the cost and benefits of technology to an FI, a more fundamental issue may not be technology's costs and benefits but the need to invest in technology to survive as a modern full-service FI.

Questions and Problems

1. Explain how technological improvements can increase an FI's interest and noninterest income and reduce interest and noninterest expenses. Use some specific examples.
2. Table 14–1 shows data on earnings, expenses, and assets for all insured banks. Calculate the annual growth rates in the various income, expense, earnings, and asset categories from 1991 to 2003. If part of the growth rates in assets, earnings, and expenses can be attributed to technological change, in what areas of operating performance has technological change appeared to have the greatest impact? What growth rates are more likely to be caused by economy-wide economic activity?
3. Compare the effects of technology on an FI's wholesale operations with the effects of technology on an FI's retail operations. Give some specific examples.
4. What are some of the risks inherent in being the first to introduce a financial innovation?
5. The operations department of a major FI is planning to reorganize several of its back-office functions. Its current operating expense is $1,500,000, of which $1,000,000 is for staff expenses. The FI uses a 12 percent cost of capital to evaluate cost-saving projects.

www.mhhe.com/saunders5e

a. One way of reorganizing is to outsource overseas a portion of its data entry functions. This will require an initial investment of approximately $500,000 after taxes. The FI expects to save $150,000 in annual operating expenses after tax for the next 7 years. Should it undertake this project, assuming that this change will lead to permanent savings?

b. Another option is to automate the entire process by installing new state-of-the-art computers and software. The FI expects to realize more than $500,000 per year in after-tax savings, but the initial investment will be approximately $3,000,000. In addition, the life of this project is limited to seven years, at which time new computers and software will need to be installed. Using this seven-year planning horizon, should the FI invest in this project? What level of after-tax savings would be necessary to make this plan comparable in value creation to the plan in part (a)?

6. City Bank upgrades its computer equipment every five years to keep up with changes in technology. Its next upgrade is two years from today and is budgeted to cost $1,000,000. Management is considering moving up the date by two years to install some new computers with a breakthrough software that could generate significant cost savings. The cost for this new equipment also is $1,000,000. What should be the savings per year to justify moving up the planned upgrade by two years? Assume a cost of capital of 15 percent.

7. Identify and discuss three benefits of technology in generating revenue for FIs.

8. Distinguish between economies of scale and economies of scope.

9. What information on the operating costs of FIs does the measurement of economies of scale provide? If economies of scale exist, what implications do they have for regulators?

10. What are diseconomies of scale? What are the risks of large-scale technological investments, especially to large FIs? Why are small FIs willing to outsource production to large FIs against which they are competing? Why are large FIs willing to accept outsourced production from smaller FI competition?

11. What information on the operating costs of FIs is provided by the measurement of economies of scope? What implications do economies of scope have for regulators?

12. Buy Bank had $130 million in assets and $20 million in expenses before the acquisition of Sell Bank, which had assets of $50 million and expenses of $10 million. After the merger, the bank had $180 million in assets and $35 million in costs. Did this acquisition generate either economies of scale or economies of scope?

13. A bank with assets of $2 billion and costs of $200 million has acquired an investment banking firm subsidiary with assets of $40 million and expenses of $15 million. After the acquisition, the costs of the bank are $180 million and the costs of the subsidiary are $20 million. Does the resulting merger reflect economies of scale or economies of scope?

14. What are diseconomies of scope? How could diseconomies of scope occur?

15. A survey of a local market has provided the following average cost data: Mortgage Bank A (MBA) has assets of $3 million and an average cost of 20 percent. Life Insurance Company B (LICB) has assets of $4 million and an average cost of 30 percent. Corporate Pension Fund C (CPFC) has assets of $4 million and an average cost of 25 percent. For each firm, average costs are measured as a proportion of assets. MBA is planning to acquire LICB and CPFC with the

expectation of reducing overall average costs by eliminating the duplication of services.

   a. What should be the average cost after acquisition for the bank to justify this merger?

   b. If MBA plans to reduce operating costs by $500,000 after the merger, what will be the average cost of the new firm?

16. What is the difference between the production approach and the intermediation approach to estimating cost functions of FIs?

17. What are some of the conclusions of empirical studies on economies of scale and scope? How important is the impact of cost reductions on total average costs? What are X-inefficiencies? What role do these factors play in explaining cost differences among FIs?

18. Why does the United States lag behind most other industrialized countries in the proportion of annual electronic noncash transactions per capita? What factors probably will be important in causing the gap to decrease?

19. What are the differences between the Fedwire and CHIPS payment systems?

20. What is a daylight overdraft? How do an FI's overdraft risks incurred during the day differ for each of the two competing electronic payment systems, Fedwire and CHIPS? What provision has been taken by the members of CHIPS to introduce an element of insurance against the settlement risk problem?

21. How does Regulation F of the 1991 FDICIA reduce the problem of daylight overdraft risk?

22. Why do FIs in the United States face a higher degree of international technology risk than do the FIs in other countries, especially some European countries?

23. What has been the impact of rapid technological improvements in the electronic payment systems on crime and fraud risk?

24. What are usury ceilings? How does technology create regulatory risk?

25. How has technology altered the competition risk of FIs?

26. What actions has the BIS taken to protect depository institutions from insolvency due to operational risk?

Web Questions

27. Go to the BIS Web site at **www.bis.org** and find the most recent data on the volume and value of payment system transactions in the United States (Table 14–2) using the following steps. Click on "Publications and Statistics." Click on "Publications of the Committee on Payment and Settlement Systems." Click on the most recent release of "Statistics on Payment Systems in Selected Countries." Click on "Full Publication." Under Bookmarks, click on "United States." This will bring the file onto your computer that contains the relevant data (in Tables 9 and 10). How these numbers changed since 2002 as reported in Table 14–2?

28. Go to the BIS Web site at **www.bis.org** and find the most recent data on the volume and value of worldwide wire transfer systems (Table 14–6). Click on "Publications and Statistics." Click on "Publications of the Committee on Payment and Settlement Systems." Click on the most recent release of "Statistics

on Payment Systems in Selected Countries." Click on "Comparative tables only." This will bring the file onto your computer that contains the relevant data (in Table 15). How have these numbers changed since 2002 as reported in Table 14–6?

Pertinent Web Sites

Bank for International Settlements	www.bis.org
Clearing House Interbank Payments System	www.chips.org
Federal Deposit Insurance Corp.	www.fdic.gov
The Wall Street Journal	www.wsj.com
U.S. Banker	www.us-banker.com

Chapter Notation

View Chapter Notation at the Web site to the textbook (**www.mhhe.com/saunders5e**).

Chapter **Fifteen**

Foreign Exchange Risk

INTRODUCTION

The globalization of the U.S. financial services industry has meant that FIs are increasingly exposed to foreign exchange (FX) risk. FX risk can occur as a result of trading in foreign currencies, making foreign currency loans (such as a loan in sterling to a corporation), buying foreign-issued securities (U.K. sterling–denominated gilt-edged bonds or German euro–government bonds), or issuing foreign currency–denominated debt (sterling certificates of deposit) as a source of funds. Extreme foreign exchange risk was evident in 1997 when a currency crisis occurred in Asia. The crisis began July 2 when the Thai baht fell nearly 50 percent in value relative to the U.S. dollar, which led to contagious drops in the value of other Asian currencies and eventually affected currencies other than those in Asia (e.g., the Brazilian real and Russian ruble). On November 20, 1997, almost five months after the baht's drop in value, the value of the South Korean won dropped by 10 percent relative to the dollar. As a result of these currency shocks, the earnings of some U.S. FIs were adversely impacted. For example, in November 1997, Chase Manhattan Corp. announced a $160 million loss in October from foreign currency trading and holdings of foreign currency bonds. More recently, a single trader at Allfirst Bank covered up $211 million in losses from foreign currency trading. After five years in which these losses were successfully hidden, the activities were discovered in 2002. The Ethical Dilemmas box reviews alleged illegal foreign currency trading by several FX traders. In an attempt to control interest rate risk, in February 2004, key European nations pressed the U.S. for a more aggressive campaign to stabilize the sliding dollar. The effort to boost the falling dollar was particularly promoted by the Europeans and Japanese as the dollar's decline dampened their country's economic growth.

This chapter looks at how FIs evaluate and measure the risks faced when their assets and liabilities are denominated in foreign (as well as in domestic) currencies and when they take major positions as traders in the spot and forward foreign currency markets.

SOURCES OF FOREIGN EXCHANGE RISK EXPOSURE

The nation's largest commercial banks are major players in foreign currency trading and dealing, with large money center banks such as Citigroup and J. P. Morgan Chase also taking significant positions in foreign currency assets and liabilities (see also Chapter 10 on market risk, where we looked at methods of calculating value at risk on foreign exchange contracts). Table 15–1 shows the outstanding dollar

417

Ethical **Dilemmas**

FEDS DROP DIME ON DOLLAR SCAMS

An 18-month government sting operation produced a series of fraud charges in the lightly regulated foreign-exchange market, including allegations that five currency traders at such prominent dealers as J. P. Morgan Chase & Co. and UBS AG duped their employers via bogus trades. About $30 million was involved in the alleged fraud, a fraction of the hundreds of billions of dollars traded every day in foreign-currency markets. Forty-seven traders and executives were charged in the case after a series of arrests, covered by television news crews alerted to a roundup that began Tuesday afternoon. . . .

The five traders at the major dealers allegedly arranged transactions that lost money for their employers while producing profits for customers. The traders then secretly shared in the customers' profits, totaling $650,000 via kickbacks obtained from employees at four other dealers, according to charges filed yesterday by regulators led by U.S. Attorney James Comey. . . . One of the traders, charged with conspiracy, bank fraud and wire fraud in the alleged kickback scheme involving the major dealers, was Stephen Moore, chief executive of Itradecurrency USA LLC, who was a member of the foreign-exchange committee of the Federal Reserve Bank of New York in the mid-1980s. . . .

The sting operation also resulted in civil charges by the Commodity Futures Trading Commission against four so-called "boiler room" operations that collected more than $25 million from more than 900 customers who sought to trade in currency markets, but then allegedly misappropriated much of the money collected. . . . The Securities and Exchange Commission also joined the case by bringing civil charges against United Currency Group Inc. and its chief executive, Adam Swickle, for conducting a fraudulent offering of worthless stock in the purported currency-trading firm.

Mr. Comey said the probe turned up two distinct schemes. In one, operators of foreign-currency boiler rooms bilked mom-and-pop investors through high-pressure sales tactics. . . . In the second scheme, low-level currency traders at large banks such as J. P. Morgan and UBS engaged in rigged trades in return for kickbacks. . . .

Source: *The Wall Street Journal*, November 20, 2003, p. C1, by Randall Smith and Kara Scannell. Reprinted by permission of *The Wall Street Journal*, © 2003 Dow Jones & Company, Inc. All Rights Reserved Worldwide. *www.wsj.com*

TABLE 15–1   Liabilities to and Claims on Foreigners Reported by Banks in the United States, Payable in Foreign Currencies (millions of dollars, end of period)*

Item	1994	1995	1996	1997	1998	2000	2003
Banks' liabilities	$89,284	$109,713	$103,383	$117,524	$101,125	$76,120	$88,583
Banks' claims	60,689	74,016	66,018	83,038	78,162	56,867	81,242
Deposits	19,661	22,696	22,467	28,661	45,985	22,907	54,194
Other claims	41,028	51,320	43,551	54,377	32,177	33,960	27,048
Claims of banks' domestic customers†	10,878	6,145	10,978	8,191	20,718	29,782	27,706

Note: Data on claims exclude foreign currencies held by U.S. monetary authorities.

* 2003 data are for end of March.

† Assets owned by customers of the reporting bank located in the United States that represent claims on foreigners held by reporting banks for the accounts of the domestic customers.

Source: *Federal Reserve Bulletin*, Table 3.16, various issues. *www.federalreserve.gov*

TABLE 15–2
Monthly U.S. Bank Positions in Foreign Currencies and Foreign Assets and Liabilities, September 2003 (in currency of denomination)

Source: *Treasury Bulletin,* December 2003, pp. 99–109. *www.ustreas.gov*

	(1) Assets	(2) Liabilities	(3) FX Bought*	(4) FX Sold*	(5) Net Position†
Canadian dollars (millions)	126,812	130,875	367,077	369,335	−6,321
Japanese yen (billions)	43,969	43,869	183,081	187,711	−4,530
Swiss francs (millions)	52,152	57,423	377,101	384,344	−12,514
British pounds (millions)	225,987	223,079	519,818	528,657	−5,931
Euros (millions)	1,113,381	1,072,384	1,848,576	1,867,959	21,614

* Includes spot, future, and forward contracts.
† Net position = (Assets − Liabilities) + (FX bought − FX sold).

value of U.S. banks' foreign assets and liabilities for the period 1994 to March 2003. The 2003 figure for foreign assets (claims) was $81.2 billion, with foreign liabilities of $88.6 billion. As you can see, both foreign currency liabilities and assets were growing until 1997. The financial crises in Asia and Russia in 1997 and 1998 and in Argentina in the early 2000s are likely reasons for the decrease in foreign assets and liabilities since 1997.

Table 15–2 gives the categories of foreign currency positions (or investments) of all U.S. banks in major currencies as of September 2003. Columns (1) and (2) refer to the assets and liabilities denominated in foreign currencies that are held in the portfolios at U.S. banks. Columns (3) and (4) refer to foreign currency trading activities (the **spot** and **forward foreign exchange** contracts bought—a long position—and sold—a short position—in each major currency). Foreign currency trading dominates direct portfolio investments. Even though the aggregate trading positions appear very large—for example, U.S. banks bought 183,081 billion yen—their overall or net exposure positions can be relatively small (e.g., the net position in yen was −4,530 billion yen).

An FIs' overall FX exposure in any given currency can be measured by the **net position exposure,** which is measured in column (5) of Table 15–2 as:

$$\text{Net exposure}_i = (\text{FX assets}_i - \text{FX liabilities}_i) + (\text{FX bought}_i - \text{FX sold}_i)$$
$$= \text{Net foreign assets}_i + \text{Net FX bought}_i$$

where

$$i = i\text{th currency}$$

Clearly, an FI could match its foreign currency assets to its liabilities in a given currency and match buys and sells in its trading book in that foreign currency to reduce its foreign exchange net exposure to zero and thus avoid FX risk. It could also offset an imbalance in its foreign asset–liability portfolio by an opposing imbalance in its trading book so that its net exposure position in that currency would be zero.

Notice in Table 15–2 that U.S. banks had positive net FX exposures in one of the five major currencies, euros, in September 2003.[1] A *positive* net exposure position implies a U.S. FI is overall **net long in a currency** (i.e., the FI has bought more foreign currency than it has sold) and faces the risk that the foreign

spot market for FX
The market in which foreign currency is traded for immediate delivery.

forward market for FX
The market in which foreign currency is traded for future delivery.

net exposure
The degree to which an FI is net long (positive) or net short (negative) in a given currency.

net long (short) in a currency
Holding more (fewer) assets than liabilities in a given currency.

[1] A. D. Martin and L. J. Mauer, in "Exchange Rate Exposures of US Banks: A Cash Flow-based Methodology," *Journal of Banking and Finance* 27 (2003) pp. 851–65, examine foreign exchange rate exposure in 105 individual U.S. banks over the period 1988–1998. They find that 72 percent of internationally oriented and 88 percent of domestically oriented banks in the sample have significant exposure to at least one of five currency pairs examined. They conclude that domestic banks are exposed and should be concerned about the impact of exchange rate risk.

currency will fall in value against the U.S. dollar, the domestic currency. A *negative* net exposure position implies that a U.S. FI is **net short in a foreign currency** (i.e., the FI has sold more foreign currency than it has purchased) and faces the *risk* that the foreign currency could rise in value against the dollar. Thus, failure to maintain a fully balanced position in any given currency exposes a U.S. FI to fluctuations in the FX rate of that currency against the dollar. Indeed, the greater the volatility of foreign exchange rates given any net exposure position, the greater the fluctuations in value of an FI's foreign exchange portfolio (see Chapter 10, where we discussed market risk).

We have given the FX exposures for U.S. banks only, but most large nonbank FIs also have some FX exposure either through asset–liability holdings or currency trading. The absolute sizes of these exposures are smaller than those for major U.S. money center banks. The reasons for this are threefold: smaller asset sizes, prudent person concerns,[2] and regulations.[3] For example, U.S. pension funds invest approximately 15 percent of their asset portfolios in foreign securities, and U.S. life insurance companies generally hold less than 10 percent of their assets in foreign securities. Interestingly, U.S. FIs' holdings of overseas assets are less than those of FIs in Japan and Britain. For example, in Britain, pension funds have traditionally invested over 20 percent of their funds in foreign assets.

While the levels of claims and positions in foreign currencies held by financial institutions have increased in recent years, the volume of foreign currency trading has decreased. For example, the Bank for International Settlements reported that average daily turnover in the foreign exchange markets was $1,200 billion in 2003, down from $1,958 billion in 1996. The United Kingdom is the most active country trading in foreign exchange (about one-third of all trades). Yet in the United Kingdom the number of foreign exchange traders decreased from 32,000 to 28,000 traders during the 1990s. There are a number of reasons for the decline in FX trading. First, investment bank mergers have reduced the number of computer terminals and thus the number of traders. Second, increased use of technology links worldwide has increased the efficiency of each foreign exchange trader, reducing the need for as many. Third, reduced volatility in European foreign exchange rates in the 1990s and the movement toward a single currency in Europe as part of the 1999 European Monetary Union (EMU) agreement reduced the need for foreign exchange trading within EMU currencies (e.g., the deutsche mark for the French franc). With the introduction of the euro in January 2002, the cross-trading of member currencies within the EMU bloc has completely disappeared. For example, with the euro in place, cash flows from subsidiaries based in one European country can be put directly into the accounts of a parent company without complicated foreign exchange adjustments. As a result, with the EMU fully implemented, large multinational companies are likely to continue to reduce the number of banking relationships and foreign exchange transactions they need.

www.bis.org

Foreign Exchange Rate Volatility and FX Exposure

As Chapter 10 on market risk discussed, we can measure the potential size of an FI's FX exposure by analyzing the asset, liability, and currency trading mismatches on its balance sheet and the underlying volatility of exchange rate movements.

---

[2] Prudent person concerns are especially important for pension funds.

[3] For example, New York State restricts foreign asset holdings of New York–based life insurance companies to less than 10 percent of their assets.

Specifically, we can use the following equation:

Dollar loss/gain in currency i = [Net exposure in foreign currency i measured in U.S. dollars] × Shock (volatility) to the $/Foreign currency i exchange rate

The larger the FI's net exposure in a foreign currency and the larger the foreign currency's exchange rate volatility,[4] the larger is the potential dollar loss or gain to an FI's earnings (i.e., the greater its daily earnings at risk [*DEAR*]). The underlying causes of FX volatility reflect fluctuations in the demand for and supply of a country's currency. That is, conceptually, an FX rate is like the price of any good and will appreciate in value relative to other currencies when demand is high or supply is low and will depreciate in value when demand is low or supply is high. For example, in October 1998 the dollar fell (depreciated) in value on one day from 121 yen/$ to 112 yen/$, or by over 7 percent. The major reason for this was the purchase of yen by hedge funds and the sale of dollars to repay Japanese banks for the yen loans they had borrowed at low interest rates earlier in 1998. While not as rapid a decline, in the early 2000s the dollar fell in value by almost 20 percent relative to the yen (from 134.0 in early 2002 to 107.8 in October 2003), much of which was due to an improving Japanese economy and intervention by Japan's Central Bank. A final example is the devaluation of the Argentinian peso in 2002 that resulted in a $595 million loss to Citigroup. See Chapter 10 for more details on measuring FX exposure.

Concept Questions

1. How is the net foreign currency exposure of an FI measured?
2. If a bank is long in British pounds (£), does it gain or lose if the dollar appreciates in value against the pound?
3. A bank has £10 million in assets and £7 million in liabilities. It has also bought £52 million in foreign currency trading. What is its net exposure in pounds? (£55 million)

FOREIGN CURRENCY TRADING

The FX markets of the world have become one of the largest of all financial markets, with trading turnover averaging as high as $1.8 trillion a day in recent years, 90 times the daily trading volume on the New York Stock Exchange.[5] London continues to be the largest market, followed by New York and Tokyo.[6] Foreign exchange trading has been called the fairest market in the world because of its immense volume and the fact that no single institution can control the market's direction. Although professionals refer to global foreign exchange trading as a market, it is not really one in the traditional sense of the word. There is no central location where foreign exchange trading takes place. Moreover, the FX market is essentially a 24-hour market, moving among Tokyo, London, and New York throughout the day. Therefore, fluctuations in exchange rates and thus FX trading risk exposure continues into the night even when other FI operations are closed.

---

[4] In the case of RiskMetrics the shock (or volatility) measure would equal 1.65 times the historic volatility (standard deviation) of the currency's exchange rate with the dollar. This shock, when multiplied by the net exposure in that currency (measured in dollars), provides an estimate of the loss exposure of the FI if tomorrow is that "1 bad day in 20" (see Chapter 10 for more details).

[5] The early 2000s saw a drop in FX trading, with daily volume falling to $1.2 trillion in 2003. Up to 95 percent of all currency trading is now conducted via electronic brokers (resulting in a reduction in the number of people working in the industry).

[6] On a global basis, approximately 30 percent of trading in FX occurs in London, 16 percent in New York, and 10 percent in Tokyo. The remainder is spread throughout the world.

This clearly adds to the risk from holding mismatched FX positions. Most of the volume is traded among the top international banks, which process currency transactions for everyone from large corporations to governments around the world. Online foreign exchange trading is increasing, and the transnational nature of the electronic exchange of funds makes secure, Internet-based trading an ideal platform. Online trading portals—terminals where currency transactions are being executed—are a low-cost way of conducting spot and forward foreign exchange transactions. Reuters speculates that the number of global FIs using online trading systems will grow from 200 banks in 2003 to 700 banks by 2007.[7]

FX Trading Activities

An FI's position in the FX markets generally reflects four trading activities:

1. The purchase and sale of foreign currencies to allow customers to partake in and complete international commercial trade transactions.
2. The purchase and sale of foreign currencies to allow customers (or the FI itself) to take positions in foreign real and financial investments.
3. The purchase and sale of foreign currencies for hedging purposes to offset customer (or FI) exposure in any given currency.
4. The purchase and sale of foreign currencies for speculative purposes through forecasting or anticipating future movements in FX rates.

In the first two activities, the FI normally acts as an *agent of* its customers for a fee but does not assume the FX risk itself. Citigroup is the dominant supplier of FX to retail customers in the United States. As of 2003, the aggregate value of Citigroup's principal amount of foreign exchange contracts totaled $1,435 billion. In the third activity, the FI acts defensively as a hedger to reduce FX exposure. For example, it may take a short (sell) position in the foreign exchange of a country to offset a long (buy) position in the foreign exchange of that same country. Thus, FX risk exposure essentially relates to **open positions** taken as a principal by the FI for speculative purposes, the fourth activity. An FI usually creates an open position by taking an unhedged position in a foreign currency in its FX trading with other FIs. The Federal Reserve estimates that 200 FIs are active market makers in foreign currencies in the U.S. foreign exchange market with about 30 commercial and investment banks making a market in the five major currencies. FIs can make speculative trades directly with other FIs or arrange them through specialist FX brokers. The Federal Reserve Bank of New York estimates that approximately 44 percent of speculative or open position trades are accomplished through specialized brokers who receive a fee for arranging trades between FIs. Speculative trades can be instituted through a variety of FX instruments. Spot currency trades are the most common, with FIs seeking to make a profit on the difference between buy and sell prices (i.e., on movements in the bid–ask prices over time). However, FIs can also take speculative positions in foreign exchange forward contracts, futures, and options.

open position
An unhedged position in a particular currency.

The Profitability of Foreign Currency Trading

Remember from the previous section that most profits or losses on foreign trading come from taking an open position or speculating in currencies. Revenues from market making—the bid–ask spread—or from acting as agents for retail or wholesale customers generally provide only a secondary or supplementary revenue source.

---

[7] See "The Institutional Investor Guide to Foreign Exchange as an Asset Class," *Institutional Investor*, February 2003, p. 4.

TABLE 15–3
Foreign Exchange
Trading Income of
Major U.S. Banks
(in millions of
dollars)

Source: FDIC, *Statistics on Depository Institutions*, various dates. *www.fdic.gov*

	1995	2000	2002
ABN AMRO	$ 5.2	$ −6.7	$ 36.1
Bank of America	303.0	524.0	530.0
Bank of New York	42.0	261.0	164.8
Bank One	5.5	102.0	91.0
Citigroup	1,053.0	1,243.0	1,933.0
FleetBoston	14.7	238.0	183.0
J. P. Morgan Chase	253.0	1,456.0	767.0
KeyCorp	8.0	19.6	33.3
State Street B&TC	140.7	386.5	306.8
Suntrust	0.0	16.9	17.1
Wachovia	6.8	69.0	85.0
Wells Fargo	7.9	122.9	152.0
U.S. Bancorp	7.3	22.4	20.6

www.citigroup.com

www.jpmorganchase.com

Note the trading income from FX trading for some large U.S. banks in Table 15–3. As can be seen, total trading income has grown steadily over recent years. The dominant FX trading banks are Citigroup and J. P. Morgan Chase. This growth of profits has occurred despite the decline in the volatility of FX rates among major European countries. This decline has been offset in part by the greater volatilities of Asian currencies. The decline in European FX volatility is the result of two forces. The first is the reduction in inflation rates in these countries, and the second is the fixity of exchange rates among European countries as they moved toward full monetary union and the replacement of local currencies with the euro. Specifically, in May 1998, 11 countries in the European Union[8] fixed their exchange rates with each other and on January 1, 1999, all FIs and stock exchanges in these countries began using euros (electronically). On January 1, 2002, the euro went into physical circulation, and on July 1, 2002, local currencies were no longer accepted. While, as noted above, there has been increased FX volatility in many emerging-market countries, such as those of Thailand, Indonesia, and Malaysia,[9] the importance of these currencies in the FX trading activities of major FIs remains relatively small.

Concept Questions

1. What are the four major FX trading activities?
2. In which trades do FIs normally act as agents, and in which trades as principals?
3. What is the source of most profits or losses on foreign exchange trading? What foreign currency activities provide a secondary source of revenue?

FOREIGN ASSET AND LIABILITY POSITIONS

The second dimension of an FI's FX exposure results from any mismatches between its foreign financial asset and foreign financial liability portfolios. As discussed earlier, an FI is long a foreign currency if its assets in that currency exceed its liabilities, while it is short a foreign currency if its liabilities in that currency exceed its assets. Foreign financial assets might include Swiss franc–denominated bonds, British pound–denominated gilt-edged securities, or peso-denominated Mexican

[8] These countries were Austria, Belgium, Finland, France, Germany, Ireland, Italy, Luxemburg, Netherlands, Portugal, and Spain.

[9] For example, in 1997 these currencies fell over 50 percent in value relative to the dollar. In the fall of 1998 Malaysia introduced capital controls and restrictions on trading in its currency.

bonds. Foreign financial liabilities might include issuing British pound CDs or a yen-denominated bond in the Euromarkets to raise yen funds. The globalization of financial markets has created an enormous range of possibilities for raising funds in currencies other than the home currency. This is important for FIs that wish to not only diversify their source and use of funds but also exploit imperfections in foreign banking markets that create opportunities for higher returns on assets or lower funding costs.

The Return and Risk of Foreign Investments

This section discusses the extra dimensions of return and risk from adding foreign currency assets and liabilities to an FI's portfolio. Like domestic assets and liabilities, profits (returns) result from the difference between contractual income from or costs paid on a security. With foreign assets and liabilities, however, profits (returns) are also affected by changes in foreign exchange rates.

EXAMPLE 15–1

Calculating the Return of Foreign Exchange Transactions of a U.S. FI

Suppose that an FI has the following assets and liabilities:

Assets	Liabilities
$100 million U.S. loans (one-year) in dollars	$200 million U.S. CDs (one-year) in dollars
$100 million equivalent U.K. loans (one-year) (loans made in sterling)	

The U.S. FI is raising all of its $200 million liabilities in dollars (one-year CDs) but investing 50 percent in U.S. dollar assets (one-year maturity loans) and 50 percent in U.K. pound sterling assets (one-year maturity loans).[10] In this example, the FI has matched the duration of its assets and liabilities ($D_A = D_L = 1$ year) but has mismatched the currency composition of its asset and liability portfolios. Suppose the promised one-year U.S. CD rate is 8 percent, to be paid in dollars at the end of the year, and that one-year, credit risk–free loans in the United States are yielding only 9 percent. The FI would have a positive spread of 1 percent from investing domestically. Suppose, however, that credit risk–free one-year loans are yielding 15 percent in the United Kingdom.

To invest in the United Kingdom, the FI decides to take 50 percent of its $200 million in funds and make one-year maturity U.K. sterling loans while keeping 50 percent of its funds to make U.S. dollar loans. To invest $100 million (of the $200 million in CDs issued) in one-year loans in the United Kingdom, the U.S. FI engages in the following transactions (illustrated in panel (a) of Figure 15–1).

1. At the beginning of the year, sells $100 million for pounds on the spot currency markets. If the exchange rate is $1.60 to £1, this translates into $100 million/1.6 = £62.5 million.

2. Takes the £62.5 million and makes one-year U.K. loans at a 15 percent interest rate.

3. At the end of the year, sterling revenue from these loans will be £62.5(1.15) = £71.875 million.[11]

4. Repatriates these funds back to the United States at the end of the year. That is, the U.S. FI sells the £71.875 million in the foreign exchange market at the spot exchange rate that exists at that time, the end of the year spot rate.

---

[10] For simplicity, we ignore the leverage or net worth aspects of the FI's portfolio.

[11] No default risk is assumed.

Suppose the spot foreign exchange rate has not changed over the year; it remains fixed at $1.60/£1. Then the dollar proceeds from the U.K. investment will be:

$$£71.875 \text{ million} \times \$1.60/£1 = \$115 \text{ million}$$

or, as a return,

$$\frac{\$115 \text{ million} - \$100 \text{ million}}{\$100 \text{ million}} = 15\%$$

Given this, the weighted return on the bank's portfolio of investments would be:

$$(.5)(.09) + (.5)(.15) = .12 \text{ or } 12\%$$

This exceeds the cost of the FI's CDs by 4 percent (12% − 8%).

Suppose, however, that at the end of the year the British pound had fallen in value relative to the dollar, or the U.S. dollar had appreciated in value relative to the pound. The returns on the U.K. loans could be far less than 15 percent even in the absence of interest rate or credit risk. For example, suppose the exchange rate had fallen from $1.60/£1 at the beginning of the year to $1.45/£1 at the end of the year when the FI needed to repatriate the principal and interest on the loan. At an exchange rate of $1.45/£1, the pound loan revenues at the end of the year translate into:

$$£71.875 \text{ million} \times \$1.45/£1 = \$104.22 \text{ million}$$

or as a return on the original dollar investment of:

$$\frac{\$104.22 - \$100}{\$100} = .0422 = 4.22\%$$

The weighted return on the FI's asset portfolio would be:

$$(.5)(.09) + (.5)(.0422) = .0661 = 6.61\%$$

In this case, the FI actually has a loss or has a negative interest margin (6.61% − 8% = −1.39%) on its balance sheet investments.

The reason for the loss is that the depreciation of the pound from $1.60 to $1.45 has offset the attractive high yield on British pound sterling loans relative to domestic U.S. loans. If the pound had instead appreciated (risen in value) against the dollar over the year—say, to $1.70/£1—then the U.S. FI would have generated a dollar return from its U.K. loans of:

$$£71.875 \times \$1.70 = \$122.188 \text{ million}$$

or a percentage return of 22.188 percent. Then the U.S. FI would receive a double benefit from investing in the United Kingdom: a high yield on the domestic British loans plus an appreciation in sterling over the one-year investment period.

Risk and Hedging

Since a manager cannot know in advance what the pound/dollar spot exchange rate will be at the end of the year, a portfolio imbalance or investment strategy in which the FI is *net long* $100 million in pounds (or £62.5 million) is risky. As we discussed, the British loans would generate a return of 22.188 percent if the pound appreciated from $1.60 to $1.70 but would produce a return of only 4.22 percent if the pound depreciated in value against the dollar to $1.45.

In principle, an FI manager can better control the scale of its FX exposure in two major ways: on-balance-sheet hedging and off-balance-sheet hedging. On-balance-sheet hedging involves making changes in the on-balance-sheet assets

FIGURE 15–1
Time Line for a
Foreign Exchange
Transaction

(a) Unhedged Foreign Exchange Transaction

FI lends $100 million for
pounds at $1.6/£1

FI receives £62.5(1.15)
for dollars at $?/£1

0   1 year

(b) Foreign Exchange Transaction Hedged On the Balance Sheet

FI lends $100 million for
pounds at $1

FI receives £62.5(1.15)
for dollars at $?/£1

FI receives (from a CD)
$100 million for pounds at
$1.6/£1

FI pays £62.5(1.11)
with dollars at $?/£1

0   1 year

(c) Foreign Exchange Transaction Hedged with Forwards

FI lends $100 million for
pounds at $1.6/£1

FI sells a one-year pounds
for dollars forward contract
with a stated forward rate of
$1.55/£1 and nominal value
of £62.5 (1.15)

FI receives £62.5(1.15)
from borrower and
delivers funds to forward
buyer receiving £62.5 ×
(1.15) × 1.55 guaranteed.

0   1 year

and liabilities to protect FI profits from FX risk. Off-balance-sheet hedging involves no on-balance-sheet changes but rather involves taking a position in forward or other derivative securities to hedge FX risk.

On-Balance-Sheet Hedging

The following example illustrates how an FI manager can control FX exposure by making changes on the balance sheet.

EXAMPLE 15–2	Suppose that instead of funding the $100 million investment in 15 percent British loans with
Hedging on the *Balance Sheet*	U.S. CDs, the FI manager funds the British loans with $100 million equivalent one-year pound sterling CDs at a rate of 11 percent (as illustrated in panel (b) of Figure 15–1). Now the balance sheet of the bank would look like this:

Assets	Liabilities
$100 million U.S. loans (9%)	$100 million U.S. CDs (8%)
$100 million U.K. loans (15%) (loans made in sterling)	$100 million U.K. CDs (11%) (deposits raised in sterling)

In this situation, the FI has both a matched maturity and currency foreign asset–liability book. We might now consider the FI's profitability or spreads between the return on assets and the cost of funds under two scenarios: first, when the pound depreciates in value against the dollar over the year from $1.60/£1 to $1.45/£ and second, when the pound appreciates in value over the year from $1.60/£1 to $1.70/£1.

The Depreciating Pound

When the pound falls in value to $1.45/£1, the return on the British loan portfolio is 4.22 percent. Consider now what happens to the cost of $100 million in pound liabilities in dollar terms:

1. At the beginning of the year, the FI borrows $100 million equivalent in sterling CDs for one year at a promised interest rate of 11 percent. At an exchange rate of $1.60£, this is a sterling equivalent amount of borrowing of $100 million/1.6 = £62.5 million.
2. At the end of the year, the bank has to pay back the sterling CD holders their principal and interest, £62.5 million (1.11) = £69.375 million.
3. If the pound had depreciated to $1.45/£ over the year, the repayment in dollar terms would be £69.375 million × $1.45/£1 = $100.59 million, or a dollar cost of funds of 0.59 percent.

Thus, at the end of the year the following occurs:

Average return on assets:

$$(0.5)(0.9) + (0.5)(0.422) = .0661 = 6.61\%$$

U.S. asset return + U.K. asset return = Overall return

Average cost of funds:

$$(0.5)(.08) + (0.5)(.0059) = .04295 = 4.295\%$$

U.S. cost of funds + U.K. cost of funds = Overall cost

Net return:

Average return on assets − Average cost of funds

$$6.61\% - 4.295\% = 2.315\%$$

The Appreciating Pound

When the pound appreciates over the year from $1.60/£1 to $1.70/£1, the return on British loans is equal to 22.188. Now consider the dollar cost of British one-year CDs at the end of the year when the U.S. FI has to pay the principal and interest to the CD holder:

$$£69.375 \text{ million} \times \$1.70/£1 = \$117.9375 \text{ million}$$

or a dollar cost of funds of 17.9375 percent. Thus, at the end of the year:

Average return on assets:

$$(0.5)(.09) + (0.5)(.22188) = .15594 \text{ or } 15.594\%$$

Average cost of funds:

$$(0.5)(.08) + (0.5)(.179375) = .12969 \text{ or } 12.969\%$$

Net return:

$$15.594 - 12.969 = 2.625\%$$

Thus, by directly matching its foreign asset and liability book, an FI can lock in a positive return or profit spread whichever direction exchange rates change over the investment period. For example, even if domestic U.S. banking is a relatively low-profit activity (i.e., there is a low spread between the return on assets and the cost of funds), the FI could be quite profitable overall. Specifically, it could lock in a large positive spread—if it exists—between deposit rates and loan rates in foreign markets. In our example, a 4 percent positive spread existed between British one-year loan rates and deposit rates compared with only a 1 percent spread domestically.

Note that for such imbalances in domestic spreads and foreign spreads to continue over long periods of time, financial service firms would have to face significant barriers to entry in foreign markets. Specifically, if real and financial capital is free to move, FIs would increasingly withdraw from the U.S. market and reorient their operations toward the United Kingdom. Reduced competition would widen loan deposit interest spreads in the United States, and increased competition would contract U.K. spreads, until the profit opportunities from foreign activities disappeared. We discuss FIs' abilities, and limits on their abilities, to engage in cross-border financial and real investments further in Chapter 23.[12]

Hedging with Forwards

Instead of matching its $100 million foreign asset position with $100 million of foreign liabilities, the FI might have chosen to remain unhedged on the balance sheet.[13] As a lower-cost alternative, it could hedge by taking a position in the forward market for foreign currencies—for example, the one-year forward market for selling sterling for dollars. We discuss the nature and use of forward contracts by FI managers more extensively in Chapter 24; however, here we introduce them to show how they can insulate the FX risk of the FI in our example. Any forward position taken would not appear on the balance sheet; it would appear as a contingent off-balance-sheet claim, which we described in Chapter 13 as an item below the bottom line. The role of the forward FX contract is to offset the uncertainty regarding the future spot rate on sterling at the end of the one-year investment horizon. Instead of waiting until the end of the year to transfer sterling back into dollars at an unknown spot rate, the FI can enter into a contract to sell forward its *expected* principal and interest earnings on the loan, at today's known **forward exchange rate** for dollars/pounds, with delivery of sterling funds to the buyer of the forward contract taking place at the end of the year. Essentially, by selling the expected proceeds on the sterling loan forward, at a known (forward FX) exchange rate today, the FI removes the future spot exchange rate uncertainty and thus the uncertainty relating to investment returns on the British loan.

forward exchange rate
The exchange rate agreed to today for future (forward) delivery of a currency.

---

[12] In the background of the previous example was the implicit assumption that the FI was also matching the durations of its foreign assets and liabilities. In our example, it was issuing one-year duration sterling CDs to fund one-year duration sterling loans. Suppose instead that it still had a matched book in size ($100 million) but funded the one-year 15 percent British loans with three-month 11 percent sterling CDs.

$$D_{\pounds A} - D_{\pounds L} = 1 - .25 = .75 \text{ years}$$

Thus, sterling assets have a longer duration than do sterling liabilities.

If British interest rates were to change over the year, the market value of sterling assets would change by more than the market value of sterling liabilities. This effect should be familiar from Chapter 9. More importantly, the FI would no longer be locking in a fixed return by matching in the size of its foreign currency book since it would have to take into account its potential exposure to capital gains and losses on its sterling assets and liabilities due to shocks to British interest rates. In essence, an FI is hedged against both foreign exchange rate risk and foreign interest rate risk only if it matches both the size and the durations of its foreign assets and liabilities in a specific currency. For a detailed discussion of this risk, see T. Grammatikos, A. Saunders, and I. Swary, "Returns and Risks of U.S. Bank Foreign Currency Activities," *Journal of Finance* 41 (1986), pp. 670–81; K. C. Mun and G. E. Morgan, "Should Interest and Foreign Exchange Risk Management Be Integrated in International Banking?" Working Paper, Virginia Polytechnic Institute, 1994; and J. J. Choi and E. Elyasiani, "Derivative Exposure and the Interest Rate and Exchange Rate Risks of U.S. Banks," *Journal of Financial Services Research* 12 (1997), pp. 267–86.

[13] An FI could also hedge its on-balance-sheet FX risk by taking off-balance-sheet positions in futures, swaps, and options on foreign currencies. Such strategies are discussed in detail in Chapters 24 through 26.

EXAMPLE 15–3

Hedging with Forwards

Consider the following transactional steps when the FI hedges its FX risk immediately by selling its expected one-year sterling loan proceeds in the forward FX market (illustrated in panel (c) of Figure 15–1).

1. The U.S. FI sells $100 million for pounds at the *spot* exchange rate *today* and receives $100 million/1.6 = £62.5 million.
2. The FI then immediately lends the £62.5 million to a British customer at 15 percent for one year.
3. The FI also sells the expected principal and interest proceeds from the sterling loan forward for dollars at today's forward rate for one-year delivery. Let the current forward one-year exchange rate between dollars and pounds stand at $1.55/£1, or at a 5 cent discount to the spot pound; as a percentage discount:

$$(\$1.55 - \$1.60)/\$1.6 = -3.125\%$$

This means that the forward buyer of sterling promises to pay:

$$£62.5 \text{ million } (1.15) \times \$1.55/£ = £71.875 \text{ million} \times \$1.55/£1 = \$111.406 \text{ million}$$

to the FI (the forward seller) in one year when the FI delivers the £71.875 million proceeds of the loan to the forward buyer.

4. In one year, the British borrower repays the loan to the FI plus interest in sterling (£71.875 million).
5. The FI delivers the £71.875 million to the buyer of the one-year forward contract and receives the promised $111.406 million.

Barring the sterling borrower's default on the loan or the forward buyer's reneging on the forward contract, the FI knows from the very beginning of the investment period that it has locked in a guaranteed return on the British loan of:

$$\frac{\$111.406 - \$100}{\$100} = .11406 = 11.406\%$$

Specifically, this return is fully hedged against any dollar/pound exchange rate changes over the one-year holding period of the loan investment. Given this return on British loans, *the overall expected return* on the FI's asset portfolio is:

$$(.5)(.09) + (.5)(.11406) = .10203 \text{ or } 10.203\%$$

Since the cost of funds for the FI's $200 million U.S. CDs is an assumed 8 percent, it has been able to lock in a risk-free return spread over the year of 2.203 percent regardless of spot exchange rate fluctuations between the initial foreign (loan) investment and repatriation of the foreign loan proceeds one year later.

In the preceding example, it is profitable for the FI to increasingly drop domestic U.S. loans and invest in hedged foreign U.K. loans, since the hedged dollar return on foreign loans of 11.406 percent is so much higher than 9 percent domestic loans. As the FI seeks to invest more in British loans, it needs to buy more spot sterling. This drives up the spot price of sterling in dollar terms to more than $1.60/£1. In addition, the FI would need to sell more sterling forward (the proceeds of these sterling loans) for dollars, driving the forward rate to below $1.55/£1. The outcome would widen the dollar forward–spot exchange rate spread on sterling, making forward hedged sterling investments less attractive than before. This process would continue until the U.S. cost of FI funds just equals the forward hedged return on British loans. That is, the FI could make no further profits by borrowing in U.S. dollars and making forward contract–hedged investments in U.K. loans.

Interest Rate Parity Theorem

interest rate parity theorem
Relationship in which the discounted spread between domestic and foreign interest rates equals the percentage spread between forward and spot exchange rates.

We discussed above that foreign exchange spot market risk can be reduced by entering into forward foreign exchange contracts. In general, spot rates and forward rates for a given currency differ. For example, the spot exchange rate between the British pound and the U.S. dollar was 1.7739 on December 18, 2003, meaning that one pound could be exchanged on that day for 1.7739 U.S. dollars. The three month forward rate between the two currencies, however, was 1.7615 on December 18, 2003. This forward exchange rate is determined by the spot exchange rate and the interest rate differential between the two countries. The specific relationship that links spot exchange rates, interest rates, and forward exchange rates is described as the **interest rate parity theorem** (IRPT). Intuitively, the IRPT implies that by hedging in the forward exchange rate market, an investor realizes the same returns whether investing domestically or in a foreign country. This is a so-called no-arbitrage relationship in the sense that the investor cannot make a risk-free return by taking offsetting positions in the domestic and foreign markets. That is, the hedged dollar return on foreign investments just equals the return on domestic investments. The eventual equality between the cost of domestic funds and the hedged return on foreign assets, or the IRPT, can be expressed as:

$$1 + r_{ust}^{D} = \frac{1}{S_t} \times \left[1 + r_{ukt}^{L}\right] \times F_t$$

Rate on U.S. investment = Hedged return on foreign (U.K.) investment where

$1 + r_{ust}^{D} = 1$ plus the interest rate on U.S. CDs for the FI at time t

$S_t = \$/\£$ spot exchange rate at time t

$1 + r_{ukt}^{L} = 1$ plus the interest rate on U.K. loans at time t

$F_t = \$/\£$ forward exchange at time t

EXAMPLE 15–4

An Application of Interest Rate Parity Theorem

Suppose $r_{ust}^{D} = 8$ percent and $r_{ukt}^{L} = 15$ percent, as in our preceding example. As the FI moves into more British loans, suppose the spot exchange rate for buying pounds rises from \$1.60/\£1 to \$1.63/\£1. In equilibrium, the forward exchange rate would have to fall to \$1.5308/\£1 to eliminate completely the attractiveness of British investments to the U.S. FI manager. That is:

$$(1.08) = \left(\frac{1}{1.63}\right)[1.15](1.5308)$$

This is a *no-arbitrage* relationship in the sense that the hedged dollar return on foreign investments just equals the FI's dollar cost of domestic CDs. Rearranging, the IRPT can be expressed as:

$$\frac{r_{ust}^{D} - r_{ukt}^{L}}{1 + r_{ukt}^{L}} \simeq \frac{F_t - S_t}{S_t}$$

$$\frac{.08 - .15}{1.15} \simeq \frac{1.5308 - 1.63}{1.63}$$

$$-.0609 \simeq -.0609$$

That is, the discounted spread between domestic and foreign interest rates is, in equilibrium, equal to the percentage spread between forward and spot exchange rates.

Suppose that in the preceding example, the annual rate on U.S. time deposits is 8.1 percent (rather than 8 percent). In this case, it would be profitable for the investor to put excess funds in the U.S. rather than the U.K. deposits. In fact, the arbitrage opportunity that exists results in a flow of funds out of U.K. time deposits into U.S. time deposits. According to the IRPT, this flow of funds would quickly drive up the U.S. dollar–British pound exchange rate until the potential profit opportunities from U.S. deposits are eliminated. The implication of IRPT is that in a competitive market for deposits, loans, and foreign exchange, the potential profit opportunities from overseas investment for the FI manager are likely to be small and fleeting.[14] Long-term violations of IRPT are likely to occur only if there are major imperfections in international deposit, loan, and other financial markets, including barriers to cross-border financial flows.

Multicurrency Foreign Asset–Liability Positions

So far, we have used a one-currency example of a matched or mismatched foreign asset–liability portfolio. Many FIs, including banks, mutual funds, and pension funds, hold multicurrency asset–liability positions. As for multicurrency trading portfolios, diversification across many asset and liability markets can potentially reduce the risk of portfolio returns and the cost of funds. To the extent that domestic and foreign interest rates or stock returns for equities do not move closely together over time, potential gains from asset–liability portfolio diversification can offset the risk of mismatching individual currency asset–liability positions.

real interest rate
The difference between a nominal interest rate and the expected rate of inflation.

Theoretically speaking, the one-period nominal interest rate (r_i) on fixed-income securities in any particular country has two major components. First, the **real interest rate** reflects underlying real sector demands and supplies for funds in that currency. Second, the *expected inflation rate* reflects an extra amount of interest lenders demand from borrowers to compensate the lenders for the erosion in the principal (or real) value of the funds they lend due to inflation in goods prices expected over the period of the loan. Formally:[15]

$$r_i = rr_i + i_i^e$$

where

r_i = Nominal interest rate in country i

rr_i = Real interest rate in country i

i_i^e = Expected one-period inflation rate in country i

If real savings and investment demand and supply pressures, as well as inflationary expectations, are closely linked or integrated across countries, we expect to find that nominal interest rates are highly correlated across financial markets. For example, if, as the result of a strong demand for investment funds, German

---

[14] Note that in a fully competitive market for loans and deposits (and free movement of exchange rates), not only would the U.S. deposit rate equal the hedged return on U.K. loans (8 percent in our example), but the U.S. loan rate (for risk-free loans) would also be driven into equality with the U.S. CD rate, that is, would fall from 9 percent to 8 percent.

[15] This equation is often called the Fisher equation after the economist who first publicized this hypothesized relationship among nominal rates, real rates, and expected inflation. As shown, we ignore the small cross-product term between the real rate and the expected inflation rate.

TABLE 15–4
Correlations of Long-Term Government Bond Annual Returns in Local Currencies, January 1986–December 1998

Source: A Saunders and A. Schmeits, "The Determinants of Bank Lending Rates: Evidence from the Netherlands and Other Countries," Working Paper. Stern School of Business, New York University, June 2001.

	United States	United Kingdom	Germany	Netherlands
United States	1.00	.8692	.5882	.6000
United Kingdom	.8692	1.00	.7632	.7705
Germany	.5882	.7632	1.00	.9932
Netherlands	.6000	.7705	.9932	1.00

real interest rates rise, there may be a capital outflow from other countries toward Germany. This may lead to rising real and nominal interest rates in other countries as policymakers and borrowers try to mitigate the size of their capital outflows. On the other hand, if the world capital market is not very well integrated, quite significant nominal and real interest deviations may exist before equilibrating international flows of funds materialize. Foreign asset or liability returns are likely to be relatively weakly correlated, and significant diversification opportunities exist.

Table 15–4 lists the correlations among the returns on long-term government bonds in major bond markets for 1986–1998. Looking at correlations between foreign bond market monthly returns and U.S. bond market monthly returns, you can see that the correlations across bond markets vary from a high of .9932 between Germany and the Netherlands to a low of .5882 between the United States and Germany. Further, these correlations are all positive and they are generally quite high, similar to correlations computed for stock returns among the same countries.[16]

Concept Questions

1. The cost of one-year U.S. dollar CDs is 8 percent, one-year U.S. dollar loans yield 10 percent, and U.K. sterling loans yield 15 percent. The dollar/pound spot exchange is $1.50/£1, and the one-year forward exchange rate is $1.48/£1. Are one-year U.S. dollar loans more or less attractive than U.K. sterling loans?
2. What are two ways an FI manager can control FX exposure?
3. Suppose the one-year expected inflation rate in the United States is 8 percent and nominal one-year interest rates are 10 percent. What is the real rate of interest? (2%)

Summary

This chapter analyzed the sources of FX risk faced by modern FI managers. Such risks arise through mismatching foreign currency trading and/or foreign asset–liability positions in individual currencies. While such mismatches can be profitable if FX forecasts prove correct, unexpected outcomes and volatility can impose significant losses on an FI. They threaten its profitability and, ultimately, its solvency in a fashion similar to interest rate, off-balance-sheet, and technology risks. This chapter discussed possible ways to mitigate such risks, including direct hedging through matched foreign asset–liability books, hedging through forward contracts, and hedging through foreign asset and liability portfolio diversification.

---

[16] From the Fisher relationship, high correlations may be due to high correlations of real interest rates over time and/or inflation expectations.

Questions and Problems

1. What are the four FX risks faced by FIs?

2. What is the spot market for FX? What is the forward market for FX? What is the position of being net long in a currency?

3. X-IM Bank has ¥14 million in assets and ¥23 million in liabilities and has sold ¥8 million in foreign currency trading. What is the net exposure for X-IM? For what type of exchange rate movement does this exposure put the bank at risk?

4. What two factors directly affect the profitability of an FI's position in a foreign currency?

5. The following are the foreign currency positions of an FI, expressed in dollars.

Currency	Assets	Liabilities	FX Bought	FX Sold
Swiss francs (SF)	$125,000	$50,000	$10,000	$15,000
British pound (£)	50,000	22,000	15,000	20,000
Japanese yen (¥)	75,000	30,000	12,000	88,000

   a. What is the FI's net exposure in Swiss francs?

   b. What is the FI's net exposure in British pounds?

   c. What is the FI's net exposure in Japanese yen?

   d. What is the expected loss or gain if the SF exchange rate appreciates by 1 percent?

   e. What is the expected loss or gain if the £ exchange rate appreciates by 1 percent?

   f. What is the expected loss or gain if the ¥ exchange rate appreciates by 2 percent?

6. What are the four FX trading activities undertaken by FIs? How do FIs profit from these activities? What are the reasons for the slow growth in FX profits at major U.S. banks?

7. City Bank issued $200 million of one-year CDs in the United States at a rate of 6.50 percent. It invested part of this money, $100 million, in the purchase of a one-year bond issued by a U.S. firm at an annual rate of 7 percent. The remaining $100 million was invested in a one-year Brazilian government bond paying an annual interest rate of 8 percent. The exchange rate at the time of the transactions was Brazilian real 1/$.

   a. What will be the net return on this $200 million investment in bonds if the exchange rate between the Brazilian real and the U.S. dollar remains the same?

   b. What will be the net return on this $200 million investment if the exchange rate changes to real 1.20/$?

   c. What will the net return on this $200 million investment be if the exchange rate changes to real 0.80/$?

8. Sun Bank USA has purchased a 16 million one-year swiss franc loan that pays 12 percent interest annually. The spot rate for swiss franc is SF1.60/$. Sun Bank has funded this loan by accepting a British pound (£)–denominated deposit for the equivalent amount and maturity at an annual rate of 10 percent. The current spot rate of the British pound is $1.60/£.

   a. What is the net interest income earned in dollars on this one-year transaction if the spot rates at the end of the year are SF1.70/\$ and \$1.85/£?

   b. What should be the £ to US\$ spot rate in order for the bank to earn a net interest margin of 4 percent?

   c. Does your answer to part (b) imply that the dollar should appreciate or depreciate against the pound?

   d. What is the total effect on net interest income and principal of this transaction given the end-of-year spot rates in part (a)?

9. Bank USA recently made a one-year \$10 million loan that pays 10 percent interest annually. The loan was funded with a Swiss francs–denominated one-year deposit at an annual rate of 8 percent. The current spot rate is SF 1.60/\$.

   a. What will be the net interest income in dollars on the one-year loan if the spot rate at the end of the year is SF 1.58/\$?

   b. What will be the net interest return on assets?

   c. How far can the SF appreciate before the transaction will result in a loss for Bank USA?

   d. What is the total effect on net interest income and principal of this transaction given the end-of-year spot rates in part (a)?

10. What motivates FIs to hedge foreign currency exposures? What are the limitations to hedging foreign currency exposures?

11. What are the two primary methods of hedging FX risk for an FI? What two conditions are necessary to achieve a perfect hedge through on-balance-sheet hedging? What are the advantages and disadvantages of off-balance-sheet hedging in comparison to on-balance-sheet hedging?

12. North Bank has been borrowing in the U.S. markets and lending abroad, thus incurring foreign exchange risk. In a recent transaction, it issued a one-year \$2 million CD at 6 percent and funded a loan in euros at 8 percent. The spot rate for the euro was €1.45/\$ at the time of the transaction.

   a. Information received immediately after the transaction closing indicated that the euro will depreciate to €1.47/\$ by year-end. If the information is correct, what will be the realized spread on the loan? What should have been the bank interest rate on the loan to maintain the 2 percent spread?

   b. The bank had an opportunity to sell one-year forward euros at €1.46. What would have been the spread on the loan if the bank had hedged forward its foreign exchange exposure?

   c. What would have been an appropriate change in loan rates to maintain the 2 percent spread if the bank intended to hedge its exposure using forward contracts?

13. A bank purchases a six-month \$1 million Eurodollar deposit at an annual interest rate of 6.5 percent. It invests the funds in a six-month Swedish krone bond paying 7.5 percent per year. The current spot rate is \$0.18/SK.

   a. The six-month forward rate on the Swedish krone is being quoted at \$0.1810/SK. What is the net spread earned on this investment if the bank covers its foreign exchange exposure using the forward market?

   b. What forward rate will cause the spread to be only 1 percent per year?

   c. Explain how forward and spot rates will both change in response to the increased spread.

d. Why will a bank still be able to earn a spread of 1 percent knowing that interest rate parity usually eliminates arbitrage opportunities created by differential rates?

14. Explain the concept of interest rate parity. What does this concept imply about the long-run profit opportunities from investing in international markets? What market conditions must prevail for the concept to be valid?

15. Assume that annual interest rates are 8 percent in the United States and 4 percent in Japan. An FI can borrow (by issuing CDs) or lend (by purchasing CDs) at these rates. The spot rate is $0.60/¥.

    a. If the forward rate is $0.64/¥, how could the FI arbitrage using a sum of $1 million? What is the expected spread?

    b. What forward rate will prevent an arbitrage opportunity?

16. How does the lack of perfect correlation of economic returns between international financial markets affect the risk-return opportunities for FIs holding multicurrency assets and liabilities? Refer to Table 15–4. Which country pairings seem to have the highest correlation of returns on long-term government bonds?

17. What is the relationship between the real interest rate, the expected inflation rate, and the nominal interest rate on fixed-income securities in any particular country? Refer to Table 15–4. What factors may be the reasons for the relatively high correlation coefficients?

18. What is economic integration? What impact does the extent of economic integration of international markets have on the investment opportunities for FIs?

19. An FI has $100,000 of net positions outstanding in British pounds (£) and −$30,000 in Swiss francs (SF). The standard deviation of the net positions as a result of exchange rate changes is 1 percent for the SF and 1.3 percent for the £. The correlation coefficient between the changes in exchange rates of the £ and the SF is 0.80.

    a. What is the risk exposure to the FI of fluctuations in the £/$ rate?

    b. What is the risk exposure to the FI of fluctuations in the SF/$ rate?

    c. What is the risk exposure if both the £ and the SF positions are combined?

20. A money market mutual fund manager is looking for some profitable investment opportunities and observes the following one-year interest rates on government securities and exchange rates: $r_{US} = 12\%$, $r_{UK} = 9\%$, S = $1.50/£, f = $1.6/£, where S is the spot exchange rate and f is the forward exchange rate. Which of the two types of government securities would constitute a better investment?

Web Questions

21. Go to the Web site of the U.S. Treasury at **www.ustreas.gov** and update Table 15–2 using the following steps. Click on "Bureaus." Click on "Financial Management Service (FMS)." Under "Reports & Statements," click on "Treasury Bulletin." Click on "Foreign Currency Positions." This will bring the file onto your computer that contains the relevant data. Which countries have positive versus negative net exposures in foreign currencies?

22. Go to the FDIC Web site at **www.fdic.gov** and find the most recent values for foreign exchange trading revenue at J.P. Morgan Chase and Citigroup using the following steps. Click on "Analysts." Click on "Statistics on Depository Institutions (SDI)." Click on "Enter SDI." Click on "ID Home." Click on "Find Bank Holding Cos." At *BHC Name:,* enter "Citigroup" then click on "find." Under "BHC ID," click on *"1951350."* Under "ID Report Selections:" select "Income and Expenses," then click on "Generate Report." Click on *"Trading account gains & fees."* This will bring the file onto your computer that contains revenue from foreign exchange exposures. Repeat this process for J.P. Morgan Chase and BHC ID *1039502.*

Pertinent Web Sites

Bank for International Settlements	**www.bis.org**
Board of Governors of the Federal Reserve	**www.federalreserve.gov**
Citigroup	**www.citigroup.com**
Federal Deposit Insurance Corporation	**www.fdic.gov**
J. P. Morgan Chase	**www.jpmorganchase.com**
U.S. Treasury	**www.ustreas.gov**
The Wall Street Journal	**www.wsj.com**

Chapter Notation

View Chapter Notation at the Web site to the textbook (**www.mhhe.com/saunders5e**).

Chapter **Sixteen**

Sovereign Risk

INTRODUCTION

debt moratoria
Delay in repaying
interest and/or
principal on debt.

loan loss reserves
Special reserves
created on the balance
sheet against which to
write off bad loans.

In the 1970s, commercial banks in the United States and other countries rapidly expanded their loans to Eastern European, Latin American, and other less developed countries (LDCs). This was largely to meet these countries' demand for funds beyond those provided by the World Bank and the International Monetary Fund (IMF) to aid their development, and to allow commercial banks to recycle petrodollar funds from huge dollar holders such as Saudi Arabia. In many cases, these loans appear to have been made with little judgment regarding the credit quality of the sovereign country in which the borrower resided or whether that body was a government-sponsored organization (such as Pemex) or a private corporation.

The debt repayment problems of Poland and other Eastern European countries at the beginning of the 1980s and the **debt moratoria** announced by the Mexican and Brazilian governments in the fall of 1982 had a major and long-lasting impact on commercial banks' balance sheets and profits. Indeed, at the time of the 1982 moratoria, the 10 largest U.S. money center banks had overall sovereign risk exposure of $56 billion, 80 percent of which was to Latin America. As a result, large banks such as Citicorp (now Citigroup) had to make provisions to their **loan loss reserves** because they had to write down the value of these loans in their portfolios. For example, in 1987, more than 20 U.S. banks announced major additions to their loan loss reserves, with Citicorp alone setting aside $3 billion.

Notwithstanding their experience with LDC lending a decade earlier, U.S. and other FIs began once again to invest considerable amounts in these emerging market countries in the late 1980s to early 1990s. Rather than making loans, however, the FIs concentrated their investments in debt and equity claims. However, with rising trade deficits and declining foreign exchange reserves, as the result of an overvalued peso, Mexico devalued the peso on December 20, 1994.[1] The Mexican devaluation—as with the Mexican loan moratorium 12 years earlier—had devastating short-term repercussions on the Mexican capital markets as well as on other emerging markets. The run on emerging market debt and equity markets was ameliorated only when the Clinton administration, along with the IMF, put together an international aid package for Mexico amounting to some $50 billion. Specifically, the United States provided loan guarantees over three to five years that would amount to up to $20 billion to help restructure Mexican debt. The IMF and the Bank for International Settlements provided loans of $17.8 billion and $10 billion, respectively. Mexican oil revenues were promised as collateral for the U.S.

---

[1] Mexico's foreign exchange reserves fell from $25 billion at the end of 1993 to $6 billion at the end of 1994.

FIGURE 16–1
Foreign Banks'
Share of Asian Debt
in June 1997

Source: Bank for International Settlements, June 1997. *www.bis.org*

Foreign banks' share of total Asian debt at the end of June 1997, excluding Singapore and Hong Kong.

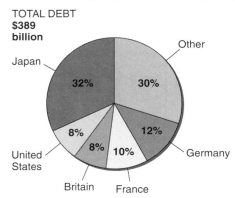

TOTAL DEBT
$389 billion

Japan 32%
Other 30%
United States 8%
Britain 8%
France 10%
Germany 12%

financial guarantees.[2] By January 1997 the Mexican economy had improved to such an extent that the Mexican government was able to pay back all its loans in full to the U.S. government.[3]

Emerging markets in Asia faltered in 1997 when an economic and financial crisis in Thailand, a relatively small country in terms of financial markets, produced worldwide reactions. In early July, the devaluation of the Thai baht resulted in contagious devaluations of currencies throughout Southeast Asia (including those of Indonesia, Singapore, Malaysia, and South Korea) and the devaluations eventually spread to South America and Russia. Hong Kong's pegging of its currency to the U.S. dollar forced its monetary authorities to take precautionary action by increasing interest rates and to use China's foreign currency reserves to stabilize the Hong Kong dollar. In Russia, financial speculation was fueled in part by the belief that the Russian government would not default on its bonds or let any of its major companies default on theirs.[4]

Possibly as a reaction to the events (losses) experienced with the Latin American countries in the 1980s or to improved sovereign risk assessment techniques[5] (see later discussion), U.S. FIs held their exposure in Asia (in the mid- and late 1990s) to approximately one-third of the investment made by Japanese and European banks. As can be seen in Figure 16–1, in June 1997 (just before the beginning of the Thai crisis) foreign banks had $389 billion in loans and other debt outstanding to emerging market Asian countries. Not all U.S. FIs had limited exposure. For example, in November 1997, Chase Manhattan Corp. announced losses from emerging market securities holdings in the $150 million to $200 million range. This was followed by a similar announcement of poor earnings by J. P. Morgan. In 1999, U.S. banks such as Bank of America, Republic New York Corp., and Chase Manhattan (now J. P. Morgan Chase) wrote off hundreds of millions of dollars in losses as they accepted a payoff of less than five cents on the dollar for Russian securities.

[2] See "The Mexican Rescue Plan," *The New York Times,* February 1, 1995, p. 1

[3] See "Mexico Will Close Out Its Debt to U.S.," *The Wall Street Journal,* January 16, 1997, p. A10.

[4] See T. L. O'Brien, "Risk Takers' Safety Net: From Rock 'n' Roll to Russia: Having a Likely Rescuer Fosters Moral Hazard," *The New York Times,* May 1, 1999, p. B11.

[5] See N. Kochan, "Controversial Calls: Credit Rating Agencies May Be Too Negative on Latin American Sovereign Risk Following Their Misjudgements in Asia and Russia," *LatinFinance,* November 1999, pp. 37–39.

TABLE 16–1
Statistics on
External Debt
Outstanding,
Argentina, June
2003

Source: World Bank, Joint
BIS-IMF-OECD-World Bank
Statistics on External Debt,
November 2003.
www.worldbank.org

Type of Debt	Amount Outstanding (in millions of U.S. dollars)
Bank loans	$ 25,052
Debt securities issued abroad	84,740
Brady bonds	6,846
Multilateral claims	30,798
Total	$147,436

In contrast to U.S. FIs, as Asian currencies collapsed, financial institutions in countries such as Japan and Hong Kong failed or were forced to merge or restructure. Investment bank powerhouses such as Yamaichi Securities, Japan's fourth-largest securities firm, and Peregrine Investment Holding, Ltd., one of Hong Kong's largest investment banks, failed as currency values fell. Commercial banks in Japan and Hong Kong that had lent heavily to other Southeast Asian countries failed in record numbers as well. Estimates of problem loans held by Japanese banks totaled $577.5 billion in September 1997, compared with $210 billion in early August 1997.[6] Financial support given to these countries by the International Monetary Fund (IMF) and the U.S., Japanese, and European governments enabled the banks largely to avoid the full extent of the possible losses. Nevertheless, Indonesia had to declare a moratorium on some of its debt repayments, while Russia defaulted on payments on its short-term government bonds.

Most recently, in the early 2000s, concerns were raised about the ability of Argentina and Turkey to meet their debt obligations and the effects this will have on other emerging market countries.[7] For example, in December 2001, Argentina defaulted on $130 billion in government-issued debt, and in 2002, passed legislation that led to defaults on $30 billion of corporate debt owed to foreign creditors. The situation continued to deteriorate, and in November 2002 Argentina's government paid only $79.5 million of an $805 million repayment (that had become more than 30 days delinquent) due to the World Bank. Further, a U.S. Court approved a class-action motion against Argentina in December 2003 that would allow creditors holding $3.5 billion from two series of the country's defaulted bonds to seek legal compensation. Table 16–1 shows the total external debt outstanding for Argentina as of June 2003. In an attempt to resolve the country's problem and restructure its debt, in January 2004 Argentina's government set up a voluntary register for creditors holding the country's defaulted bonds. However, as Argentina pulled out of its crisis, it was offering debtholders only 25 cents on the dollar for their holdings.[8]

[6] See "Japan Plans Crackdown on Bad Loans," *The Wall Street Journal,* December 26, 1997, p. A5.

[7] See "Gloom Over the River Plate," *The Economist,* July 14, 2001, pp. 11, 12; "How the Bug Can Spread," *The Economist,* July 21, 2001, pp. 20, 21; "Austerity or Bust," *The Economist,* July 21, 2001, pp. 29, 30; "Analysts Worry of Ripple Effect in Argentina's Latest Debt Plan," *The New York Times,* November 3, 2001, pp. C1; and "Experts See Record Default in Argentine Debt Revision," *The New York Times,* November 3, 2001, pp. A4.

[8] See "After Huge Default, Argentina Squeezes Small Bondholders," *The Wall Street Journal*, January 14, 2004, p. A1.

MYRAs
Multiyear restructuring agreements, the official terminology for a sovereign loan rescheduling.

Brady bond
Bonds issued by an LDC that are swapped for an outstanding loan to that LDC.

These recurring experiences confirm the importance of assessing the country or sovereign risk of a borrowing country before making lending or other investment decisions such as buying foreign bonds or equities. In this chapter, we first define sovereign or country risk. We next look at measures of sovereign risk that FI managers can use as screening devices before making loans or other investment decisions. Appendix A to this chapter looks at the ways FIs have managed sovereign risk problems, including entering into **multiyear restructuring agreements (MYRAs),** debt–equity swaps, loan sales, and **Brady bond** conversions.

CREDIT RISK VERSUS SOVEREIGN RISK

rescheduling
Changing the contractual terms of a loan, such as its maturity and interest payments.

To understand the difference between the sovereign risk and the credit risk on a loan or a bond, consider what happens to a domestic firm that refuses to repay, or is unable to repay, its loans. The lender would probably seek to work out the loan with the borrower by **rescheduling** its promised interest and principal payments on the loan into the future. Ultimately, continued inability or unwillingness to pay would likely result in bankruptcy proceedings and eventual liquidation of the firm's assets. Consider next a dollar loan made by a U.S. FI to a private Indonesian corporation. Suppose that this first-class corporation always maintained its debt repayments in the past; however, the Indonesian economy and the Indonesian government's dollar reserve position are in bad shape. As a result, the Indonesian government refuses to allow any further debt repayment to be made in dollars to outside creditors. This puts the Indonesian borrower automatically into default even though, when viewed on its own, the company is a good credit risk. The Indonesian government's decision is a *sovereign* or *country risk event* in large part independent of the credit standing of the individual loan to the borrower. Further, unlike the situation in the United States, where the lender might seek a legal remedy in the local bankruptcy courts, there is no international bankruptcy court to which the lender can take the Indonesian government. That is, the lenders' legal remedies to offset a sovereign country's default or moratoria decisions are very limited. For example, lenders can and have sought legal remedies in U.S. courts, but such decisions pertain only to Indonesian government or Indonesian corporate assets held in the United States itself.

This situation suggests that making a lending decision to a party residing in a foreign country is a *two-step* decision. First, lenders must assess the underlying *credit quality* of the borrower, as it would do for a normal domestic loan, including setting an appropriate credit risk premium or credit limits (see Chapter 11). Second, lenders must assess the *sovereign risk quality* of the country in which the borrower resides. Should the credit risk or quality of the borrower be assessed as good but the sovereign risk be assessed as bad, the lender should not make the loan. When making international lending or foreign bond investment decisions, an FI manager should consider sovereign risk above considerations of private credit risk.

Concept Questions

1. What is the difference between credit risk and sovereign risk?
2. In deciding to lend to a party residing in a foreign country, what two considerations must an FI weigh?

DEBT REPUDIATION VERSUS DEBT RESCHEDULING

A good deal of misunderstanding exists regarding the nature of a sovereign risk event. In general, a sovereign country's (negative) decisions on its debt obligations or the obligations of its public and private organizations may take two forms: repudiation and rescheduling.

repudiation
Outright cancelation of all current and future debt obligations by a borrower.

www.worldbank.org

www.imf.org

Debt repudiation. **Repudiation** is an outright cancelation of all a borrower's current and future foreign debt and equity obligations. Since World War II, only China (1949), Cuba (1961), and North Korea (1964) have followed this course.[9] The low level of repudiations partly reflects recent international policy toward the poorest countries in the world. Specifically, in the fall of 1996, the World Bank, the International Monetary Fund, and major governments around the world agreed to forgive the external debt of the world's poorest, most heavily indebted poor countries (HIPCs). The HIPC initiative broke new ground by removing debt obligations from countries that pursue economic and social reform targeted at measurable poverty reduction. By 2003, 6 countries had received irrevocable debt relief under the HIPC initiative, and an additional 20 countries had begun to receive interim debt relief. Together, these countries had their outstanding debt reduced by $40 billion. About 35 countries are expected to ultimately qualify for HIPC assistance. Repudiations on debt obligations were far more common before World War II, as we discuss later in this chapter.

Debt rescheduling. Rescheduling has been the most common form of sovereign risk event. Specifically, a country (or a group of creditors in that country) declares a moratorium or delay on its current and future debt obligations and then seeks to ease credit terms through a rescheduling of the contractual terms, such as debt maturity and/or interest rates. Such delays may relate to the principal and/or the interest on the debt (South Korea in January 1998 and Argentina in 2001[10] are recent examples of debt reschedulings).

One of the interesting questions in the provision of international financial services is why we have generally witnessed international debtor problems (of other than the poorest highly indebted countries) being met by reschedulings in the post–World War II period, whereas a large proportion of debt problems were met with repudiations before World War II. A fundamental reason given for this difference in behavior is that until recently, most postwar international debt has been in *bank loans,* while before the war it was mostly in the form of *foreign bonds.*[11]

International loan rather than bond financing makes rescheduling more likely for reasons related to the inherent nature of international loan versus bond contracts. First, there are generally fewer FIs in any international lending syndicate compared with thousands of geographically dispersed bondholders. The relatively

[9] With respect to equity, repudiation can include direct nationalization of private sector assets.

[10] See "Argentina Plans Debt Swap in Billions, Delaying Payments," *The New York Times,* May 25, 2001, p. C4; and "Cavallo Pawns an Uncertain Future," *The Economist,* June 9, 2001, p. 64.

[11] See B. Eichengreen and R. Portes, "The Anatomy of Financial Crises," in *Threats to International Financial Stability,* ed. R. Portes and A. K. Swoboda (Cambridge: Cambridge University Press, 1987), pp. 10–15.

small number of lending parties makes renegotiation or rescheduling easier and less costly than when a borrower or a bond trustee has to get thousands of bondholders to agree to changes in the contractual terms on a bond.[12]

Second, many international loan syndicates comprise the same groups of FIs, which adds to FI cohesiveness in loan renegotiations and increases the probability of consensus being reached. For example, Citigroup was chosen the lead bank negotiator by other banks in five major loan reschedulings in the 1980s,[13] as well as in both the Mexican and South Korean reschedulings. J. P. Morgan Chase is the lead bank involved in the recent loan reschedulings of Argentina.

Third, many international loan contracts contain cross-default provisions that state that if a country were to default on just one of its loans, all the other loans it has outstanding would automatically be put into default as well. Cross-default clauses prevent a country from selecting a group of weak lenders for special default treatment and make the outcome of any individual loan default decision potentially very costly for the borrower.

A further set of reasons rescheduling is likely to occur on loans relates to the behavior of governments and regulators in lending countries. One of the overwhelming public policy goals in recent years has been to prevent large FI failures in countries such as the United States, Japan, Germany, and the United Kingdom. Thus, government-organized rescue packages for LDCs arranged either directly or indirectly via World Bank/IMF guarantees or the Brady Plan are ways of subsidizing large FIs and/or reducing the incentives for LDCs to default on their loans. To the extent that banks are viewed as special (see Chapter 1), domestic governments may seek political and economic avenues to reduce the probability of foreign sovereign borrowers defaulting on or repudiating their debt contracts. Governments and regulators appear to view the social costs of default on international bonds as less worrisome than those on loans. The reason is that bond defaults are likely to be more geographically and numerically dispersed in their effects, and bondholders do not play a key role in the provision of liquidity services to the domestic and world economy. It should also be noted that the tendency of the IMF/governments to bail out countries and thus, indirectly, FI lenders such as the major U.S., Japanese, and European FIs has not gone without criticism. Specifically, it has been argued that unless FIs and countries are ultimately punished, they will have no incentives to avoid similar risks in the future. This is one reason sovereign debt crises keep recurring.

Concept Questions

1. What is the difference between debt repudiation and debt rescheduling?
2. Provide four reasons we see sovereign loans being rescheduled rather than repudiated.

COUNTRY RISK EVALUATION

In evaluating sovereign risk, an FI can use alternative methods, varying from the highly quantitative to the very qualitative. Moreover, as in domestic credit analysis, an FI may rely on outside evaluation services or develop its own internal evaluation

---

[12] In January 1998 the rescheduling of South Korean loans required the agreement of just over 100 banks.
[13] See T. Grammatikos and A. Saunders, "Additions to Bank Loan Loss Reserves," *Journal of Monetary Economics* 25 (1990), pp. 289–304.

or sovereign risk models. Of course, to make a final assessment, an FI may use many models and sources together because different measures of country risk are not mutually exclusive.

We begin by looking at three country risk assessment services available to outside investors and FIs: the *Euromoney Index*, the *Economist Intelligence Unit*, and the *Institutional Investor Index*. We then look at ways an FI manager might make internal risk assessments regarding sovereign risk.

Outside Evaluation Models

The Euromoney Index

LIBOR
The London Inter-
bank Offered Rate;
the rate charged on
prime interbank loans
on the Eurodollar
market.

www.economist.com

When originally published in 1979, the *Euromoney Index* was based on the spread in the Euromarket of the required interest rate on that country's debt over the London Interbank Offered Rate (**LIBOR**), adjusted for the volume and maturity of the issue. More recently, this has been replaced by an index based on a large number of economic and political factors weighted subjectively according to their perceived relative importance in determining country risk problems.

The Economist Intelligence Unit

A sister index to *The Economist*, The Economist Intelligence Unit (EIU) rates country risk by combined economic and political risk on a 100 (maximum) point scale. The higher the number, the worse the sovereign risk rating of the country. The EIU country risk ratings reported in 2003 are presented in Figure 16–2.

The Institutional Investor Index

Normally published twice a year, this index is based on surveys of the loan officers of major multinational banks. These officers give subjective scores regarding the credit quality of given countries. Originally, the score was based on 10, but since 1980 it has been based on 100, with a score of 0 indicating certainty of default and 100 indicating no possibility of default. The *Institutional Investor* then weighs the scores received from the officers surveyed by the exposure of each bank to the country in question. For a sampling of the *Institutional Investor's* country credit ratings as of September 2003, see Table 16–2. For example, in September 2003, loan officers around the world assessed Switzerland as the country with the least chance of default, while they assessed Somalia as the country with the highest chance of default.

Internal Evaluation Models

Statistical Models

By far, the most common approach to evaluating sovereign country risk among large FIs has been to develop sovereign country risk-scoring models based on key economic ratios for each country, similar to the domestic credit risk–scoring models discussed in Chapter 11.

An FI analyst begins by selecting a set of macro- and microeconomic variables and ratios that might be important in explaining a country's probability of rescheduling. Then the analyst uses past data on rescheduling and nonrescheduling countries to see which variables best discriminate between those countries that rescheduled their debt and those that did not. This helps the analyst identify a set of key variables that best explain rescheduling and a group of weights indicating

FIGURE 16–2

The Economist **Intelligence Unit Country Risk Ratings**

Source: Country Risk Service Risk Ratings, 4th quarter 2003, *The Economist.* *www.eiu.com*

the relative importance of these variables. For example, domestic credit risk analysis can employ discriminant analysis to calculate a Z score rating of the probability of corporate bankruptcy. Similarly, in sovereign risk analysis we can develop a Z score to measure the probability that a country will reschedule (see Chapter 11 for discussion of the Z score model).[14]

The first step in this country risk analysis (CRA) is to pick a set of variables that may be important in explaining rescheduling probabilities. In many cases analysts

---

[14] Alternatively, analysts could employ linear probability, logit, or probit models.

TABLE 16–2
Institutional Investor's 2003 Country Credit Ratings

Source: *Institutional Investor,* September 2003. *www.institutionalinvestor.com*

Rank March 2003	Rank September 2003	Country	Institutional Investor Credit Rating	Six-Month Change	One-Year Change
1	1	Switzerland	94.0	−1.3	−2.2
2	2	Luxembourg	93.3	−1.0	−1.4
5	3	Norway	92.9	0.1	−0.2
3	4	United States	92.8	−0.5	−0.3
5	5	United Kingdom	92.3	−0.5	−1.8
4	6	Netherlands	92.2	−1.0	−2.4
8	7	France	91.7	−0.5	−1.2
10	8	Denmark	91.0	0.7	0.5
12	9	Finland	90.6	0.7	−0.5
9	*10	Austria	90.3	−0.3	−0.4
11	*11	Canada	90.3	0.4	0.9
13	12	Sweden	89.3	0.2	0.0
15	13	Ireland	87.5	0.6	−1.0
14	14	Belgium	87.2	−1.1	−2.3
7	15	Germany	86.8	−5.5	−7.2
16	16	Spain	85.7	−0.4	−1.3
19	17	Australia	84.3	1.0	−0.2
17	18	Singapore	84.2	−1.4	−1.9
18	19	Italy	83.1	−1.2	−3.1
22	20	New Zealand	81.1	1.2	−0.1
21	21	Portugal	80.4	−1.2	−3.8
34	22	Kuwait	79.2	15.6	16.3
20	23	Japan	77.2	−4.8	−5.5
24	24	Taiwan	74.0	−0.3	−0.7
23	25	Greece	73.1	−1.5	−2.2
25	26	Iceland	72.4	−0.8	−1.2
30	27	Slovenia	69.2	2.8	0.8
27	28	South Korea	68.5	0.3	2.9
26	29	Hong Kong	67.8	−0.8	0.1
33	30	Czech Republic	65.6	1.9	1.6
122	*144	Serbia and Montenegro	16.1	−1.4	−0.4
137	*145	Ethiopia	16.1	1.4	0.1
129	*146	Haiti	15.8	−0.5	1.0
—	*147	Madagascar	15.8	—	—
121	148	Côte d'Ivoire	15.7	−2.0	−2.8
135	149	Zambia	15.3	−0.4	−0.5
131	150	Niger	14.7	−1.4	1.1
136	151	Chad	14.4	−0.8	−0.4
141	152	Tajikistan	14.3	1.2	1.6
—	153	Comoros	13.9	—	—
—	154	São Tomé and Principe	13.6	—	—
140	155	Myanmar	13.5	0.4	−0.3
—	156	East Timor	13.1	—	—
—	157	Central African Republic	12.8	—	—
146	158	Congo Republic	12.6	2.2	2.1
139	159	Cuba	12.3	−1.4	−3.4
—	160	Eritrea	12.0	—	—
144	161	Zimbabwe	11.0	0.2	−0.9

TABLE 16–2
(*continued*)

Rank		Country	Institutional Investor Credit Rating	Six-Month Change	One-Year Change
March 2003	September 2003				
—	162	Guinea—Bissau	10.6	—	—
145	*163	Sudan	10.5	0.0	0.8
142	*164	Burundi	10.5	−0.8	−0.8
147	165	Sierra Leone	8.5	−0.7	−1.1
150	166	Iraq	8.4	0.4	−1.8
—	167	Rwanda	8.2	—	—
148	168	Afghanistan	7.6	−1.3	0.7
151	169	North Korea	7.5	0.8	0.2
149	170	Democratic Republic of the Congo	7.3	−1.0	−1.4
143	171	Liberia	6.6	−4.3	−3.0
—	172	Somalia	6.5	—	—
Global average rating			39.6	−2.5	−2.9

*Order determined by actual results before rounding.

select more than 40 variables. Here we identify the variables most commonly included in sovereign risk probability models.[15]

The Debt Service Ratio (DSR)

$$DSR = \frac{\text{Interest plus amortization on debt}}{\text{Exports}}$$

debt service ratio
The ratio of a country's interest and amortization obligations to the value of its exports.

An LDC's exports are its primary way of generating dollars and other hard currencies. The larger the debt repayments in hard currencies are in relation to export revenues, the greater the probability that the country will have to reschedule its debt. Thus, there should be a *positive* relationship between the size of the **debt service ratio** and the probability of rescheduling. Table 16–3 shows the scheduled debt service ratios of various countries. Note that several countries are servicing debt obligations at several times the level of their exports (e.g., Argentina's debt service ratio is 376 percent, Brazil's debt service ratio is 531 percent).

The Import Ratio (IR)

$$IR = \frac{\text{Total imports}}{\text{Total foreign exchange reserves}}$$

[15] See, for example, K. Saini and P. Bates, "Statistical Techniques for Determining Debt-Servicing Capacity for Developing Countries: Analytical Review of the Literature and Further Empirical Results," Federal Reserve Bank of New York Research Paper no. 7818, September 1978, for an early attempt in using statistical models to predict sovereign risk problems. More recent examples can be found in A. Saunders and L. Allen, *Credit Risk Measurement: New Approaches to Value at Risk and Other Paradigms,* 2nd ed. (New York: John, Wiley and Sons, 2002). See also C. W. Calomiris, "Lessons from the Tequila Crisis for Successful Financial Liberalization," *Journal of Banking and Finance* 23 (1999), pp. 1457–61; F. Drudi and R. Giordano, "Default Risk and Optimal Debt Management," *Journal of Banking and Finance* 24 (2000), pp. 861–91; F. Ferri, L. Liu, and F. Majnoni, "The Role of Rating Agency Assessments in Less Developed Countries: Impact of the Proposed Basel Guidelines," *Journal of Banking and Finance* 25 (2001), pp. 115–48; and R. Brooks, R. W. Faff, and D. Hillier, "The National Market Impact of Sovereign Rating Changes," *Journal of Banking and Finance* 28 (2004), pp. 233–50.

TABLE 16–3
Debt Service Ratio
for Various
Countries, 2003

Source: *The Economist* Web
site, December 2003.
www.economist.com

Country	Debt Service Ratio
Argentina	376%
Brazil	531
Chile	221
China	56
Colombia	347
Costa Rica	100
Hong Kong	30
Indonesia	224
Malaysia	57
Philippines	145
Poland	203
Russia	142
Singapore	10
South Korea	76
Turkey	354

Many LDCs must import manufactured goods since their inadequate infrastructure limits their domestic production. In times of famine, even food becomes a vital import. To pay for imports, the LDC must run down its stock of hard currencies—its foreign exchange reserves. The greater its need for imports—especially vital imports—the quicker a country can be expected to deplete its foreign exchange reserves. For example, Chile's import ratio was 113 percent in 2003, implying that Chile imported more goods and services than it had foreign reserves to pay for. Since the first use of reserves is to buy vital imports, the larger the ratio of imports to foreign exchange reserves, the higher the probability that the LDC will have to reschedule its debt repayments. This is so because these countries generally view repaying foreign debtholders as being less important than supplying vital goods to the domestic population. Thus, the **import ratio** and the probability of rescheduling should be *positively* related.

import ratio
The ratio of a country's imports to its total foreign currency reserves.

Investment Ratio (INVR)

$$INVR = \frac{\text{Real investment}}{\text{GNP}}$$

investment ratio
The ratio of a country's real investment to its GNP.

The **investment ratio** measures the degree to which a country is allocating resources to real investment in factories, machines, and so on, rather than to consumption. The higher this ratio, the more productive the economy should be in the future and the lower the probability that the country would need to reschedule its debt: This implies a *negative* relationship between *INVR* and the probability of rescheduling. An opposing view is that a higher investment ratio allows an LDC to build up its investment infrastructure. The higher ratio puts it in a stronger bargaining position with external creditors since the LDC would rely less on funds in the future and would be less concerned about future threats of credit rationing by FIs should it request a rescheduling. This view argues for a *positive* relationship between the investment ratio and the probability of rescheduling, especially if the LDC invests heavily in import competing industries.[16] Just before the collapse of

[16] See S. Acharya and I. Diwan, "Debt Conversion Schemes of Debtor Countries as a Signal of Creditworthiness: Theory and Evidence," *International Economic Review* 34 (1993), pp. 795–815.

their economies (in the mid-1990s) investment ratios in Thailand and Malaysia were 34 and 26 percent, respectively, while Brazil's investment ratio was close to zero. More recently, the investment ratio in the United Kingdom averaged 12 percent in the early 2000s.

Variance of Export Revenue (VAREX)

$$VAREX = \sigma_{ER}^2$$

An LDC's export revenues may be highly variable as a result of two risk factors. *Quantity risk* means that the production of the raw commodities the LDC sells abroad—for example, coffee or sugar—is subject to periodic gluts and shortages. *Price risk* means that the international dollar prices at which the LDC can sell its exportable commodities are subject to high volatility as world demand for and supply of a commodity, such as copper, vary. The more volatile an LDC's export earnings, the less certain creditors can be that at any time in the future it will be able to meet its repayment commitments. That is, there should be a *positive* relationship between σ_{ER}^2 and the probability of rescheduling.

Domestic Money Supply Growth (MG)

$$MG = \frac{\Delta M}{M}$$

The faster the domestic growth rate of an LDC's money supply [$\Delta M/M$, which measures the change in the money supply (ΔM) over its initial level (M)], the higher the domestic inflation rate and the weaker that country's currency becomes in domestic and international markets.[17] When a country's currency loses credibility as a medium of exchange, real output is often adversely impacted, and the country must increasingly rely on hard currencies for both domestic and international payments, the most recent case being Argentina in 2003. These inflation, output, and payment effects suggest a *positive* relationship between domestic money supply growth and the probability of rescheduling.

We can summarize the expected relationships among these five key economic variables and the probability of rescheduling (p) for any country as:

$$p = f(DSR, IR, INVR, VAREX, MG \ldots)$$
$$\quad + \quad ++ \text{ or } - \quad + \quad +$$

After selecting the key variables, the FI manager normally places countries into two groups or populations:

P_1 = Bad (reschedulers)

P_2 = Good (nonreschedulers)

Then the manager uses a statistical methodology such as discriminant analysis (see Chapter 11) to identify which of these variables best discriminates between the population of rescheduling borrowers and that of nonrescheduling borrowers. Once the key variables and their relative importance or weights have been identified, the discriminant function can classify as good or bad current sovereign loans or sovereign loan applicants using currently observed values for the *DSR*, *IR*, and

---

[17] The purchasing power parity (PPP) theorem argues that high relative inflation rates lead to a country's currency depreciating in value against other currencies.

so on. Again, the methodology is very similar to the credit scoring models discussed in Chapter 11.

Problems with Statistical CRA Models

Even though this methodology has been one of the most common forms of CRA used by FIs, it is fraught with problems. This section discusses six major problems in using traditional CRA models and techniques. We do not imply in any way that these techniques should not be used but instead indicate that FI managers should be aware of the potential pitfalls in using such models.

Measurement of Key Variables Very often the FI manager's information on a country's DSR or IR is out of date because of delays in collection of data and errors in measurement. For example, the Bank for International Settlements (BIS) collects aggregate loan volume data for countries; frequently, this information is six months old or more before it is published. This example illustrates the problem: Citigroup may know today the current amount of its outstanding loans to Indonesia, but it is unlikely to know with any great degree of accuracy Indonesia's total outstanding external loans and debt with every other lender in the world.

www.bis.org

Moreover, these measurement problems are compounded by forecast errors when managers use these statistical models to predict the probabilities of rescheduling with future or projected values of key variables such as *DSR* and *IR*.

Population Groups Usually, analysts seek to find variables that distinguish between only two possible outcomes: reschedulers and nonreschedulers. In actuality, a finer distinction may be necessary—for example, a distinction between those countries announcing a moratorium on only interest payments and those announcing a moratorium on both interest and principal payments. Thus, Peru, which in the early 1980s limited its total debt repayments to a small proportion of its export revenues, should be viewed as a higher-risk country than a country that delayed the interest payments on its debt for a few months because of short-term foreign exchange shortages.

Political Risk Factors Traditionally, CRA statistical credit-scoring models incorporate only economic variables. While there may be a strong correlation between an economic variable such as money supply growth and rescheduling, the model may not capture very well purely political risk events such as *strikes, elections, corruption,* and *revolutions.* For example, the election of a strongly nationalist politician may reduce the probability of repayment and increase the probability of rescheduling. Similarly, a considerable part of the debt repayment and banking crisis problems in Southeast Asia has been attributed to cronyism and corruption.

www.heritage.org

Since 1995, the Index of Economic Freedom (compiled by the Heritage Foundation) has provided a measure that summarizes the economic freedom of over 160 countries in the world. The Heritage Foundation defines economic freedom as "the absence of government coercion or constraint on the production, distribution, or consumption of goods and services beyond the extent necessary for citizens to protect and maintain liberty itself."[18] The index includes measures of trade policy, fiscal burden of government, government intervention in the economy, monetary policy, capital flows and foreign investment, banking and finance, wages and prices, prosperity rights, regulation, and black market activities. Each country is assigned a score ranging from 1 to 5 for each of the 10 individual factors as well as an overall score based on the average of these factors. A score of 1 signifies policies most conducive to economic freedom; a score of 5, policies least conducive to

---

[18] See *2004 Index of Economic Freedom* (Washington, DC: Heritage Foundation, 2004), chap. 5, p. 50.

TABLE 16–4
Economic Freedom
Index for Various
Countries

Source: The Heritage Foundation Web site, January 2004. *www.heritage.org*

Country	Overall Economic Freedom Index
Hong Kong	1.45
Singapore	1.50
Luxembourg	1.70
New Zealand	1.70
Ireland	1.75
Denmark	1.80
Estonia	1.80
United States	1.80
Australia	1.85
United Kingdom	1.85
Turkmenistan	4.15
Burma	4.15
Uzbekistan	4.25
Serbia and Montenegro	4.25
Belarus	4.30
Libya	4.30
Laos	4.40
Zimbabwe	4.40
Cuba	4.45
North Korea	5.00

economic freedom. Table 16–4 lists the economic freedom index for the 10 highest- and lowest-rated countries as of 2003.

An alternative quantitative measure of country risk is the Corruption Perceptions Index produced by Transparency International. Figure 16–3 shows the corruption index for 18 out of 133 countries covered for 2003. The least corrupt countries are assigned a score of 10, while the most corrupt countries are assigned a score of 0.[19]

Portfolio Aspects   Traditional CRA considers each country separately. However, many large banks with LDC or sovereign risk exposures hold a portfolio of LDC loans. In a portfolio context, the risk of holding a well-diversified portfolio of LDC sovereign loans may be smaller than that of having a portfolio heavily concentrated in non-oilproducing LDC loans. In particular, the lender may distinguish between those key risk indicator variables having a *systematic* effect on the probability of repayment across a large number of sovereign countries and those variables having an *unsystematic* effect by impacting only one or a few countries.

One way to address this problem is to employ a portfolio framework for sovereign risk analysis. Such an analysis would identify those indicator variables that have a *systematic* impact across all borrowers' probability of repayment and those that tend to be country specific (or *unsystematic*).[20] The indicator variables that the

---

[19] J. deHaan and W. J. Kooi, in "Does Central Bank Independence Really Matter? New Evidence for Developing Countries Using a New Indicator," *Journal of Banking and Finance* 24 (2000), pp. 643–64, find that the turnover rate of central bank governors is also an indicator of central bank independence, which in turn is found to affect the economic health (and, consequently, country risk) of the countries examined. C. Pantzalis, D. A. Stangeland, and H. J. Turtle, in "Political Elections and the Resolution of Uncertainty: The International Evidence," *Journal of Banking and Finance* 24 (2000), pp. 1575–1604, find that stock markets react positively in less-free countries when a political election is won by the opposition or lost by the incumbent government.

[20] See L. S. Goodman, "Diversifiable Risks in LDC Lending: A 20/20 Hindsight View," *Studies in Banking and Finance* 3 (1986), pp. 249–62.

FIGURE 16–3
Corruption
Perceptions Index,
2003

Source: Transparency International, October 2003.
www.transparency.org

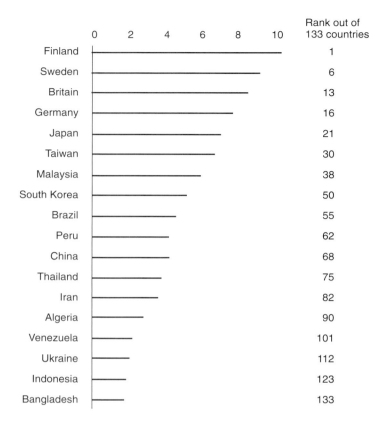

FI manager should really be concerned with are the *systematic* variables since they cannot be diversified away in a multisovereign loan portfolio. By comparison, unsystematic, or country-specific, risks can be diversified away. Consider the following model:

$$X_i = a_i + b_i\overline{X} + e_i$$

where

X_i = Key variable or country risk indicator for country i (e.g., the *DSR* for country i)

$\overline{X}$ = Weighted index of this key risk indicator across all countries to which the lender makes loans (e.g., the *DSR* for each country weighted by the shares of loans for each country in the FI's portfolio)

e_i = Other factors impacting X_i for any given country

Expressing this equation in variance terms, we get:

$$VAR(X_i) = b_i^2 VAR(\overline{X}) + VAR(e_i)$$

Total risk = Systematic risk + Unsystematic risk

From this equation, you can see that the total risk or variability of any given risk indicator for a country, such as the *DSR* for Nigeria, can be divided into a nondiversifiable *systematic* risk element that measures the extent to which that country's *DSR* moves in line with the *DSR*s of all other debtor countries and an unsystematic risk element that impacts the *DSR* for Nigeria independently. The greater the size of the *unsystematic* element relative to the systematic risk element, the less important this variable is to the lender since it can be diversified away by holding a broad array of LDC loans.

L. S. Goodman found that for the 1970–83 period, the *DSR* had a high systematic element across countries, as did export revenue variance (*VAREX*).[21] This implies that when one LDC country was experiencing a growing debt burden relative to its exports, so were all others. Similarly, when commodity prices or world demand collapsed for one debtor country's commodity exports, the same occurred for other debtor countries as well. A possible reason for the high systematic risk of the *DSR* is the sensitivity of this ratio to rising nominal and real interest rates in the developed (or lending) countries. As we discussed in Chapter 15, international interest rates tend to be positively correlated over time. A possible reason for the high systematic risk of the export variance is the tendency of prices and world demands for commodities to reflect simultaneously economic conditions such as recessions and expansions in developed countries.

By comparison, money supply growth ($\Delta M/M$) and the import ratio appear to have low systematic elements.[22] This is not surprising since control over the money supply and the use of domestic reserves are relatively discretionary variables for LDC governments. Thus, while Argentina may choose a money supply growth rate of 50 percent per annum, the Chilean government may choose a target rate of 10 percent per annum. Similarly, the Argentinean and Chilean economies may have very different demands for imports, and the scale of vital imports may differ quite widely across LDCs. Using this type of analysis allows an FI manager to focus on relatively few variables such as the *DSR*s and export variances that affect the risk of the LDC sovereign loan portfolio.

In another study[23] of systematic risk versus nonsystematic risk, for 54 LDCs over the 1974–87 period, looking at *Institutional Investor* ratings of a country as the risk indicator variable, it was found that the systematic versus nonsystematic risk components varied from 97 percent versus 3 percent for Argentina to 41 percent versus 59 percent for Russia. This would suggest, all else being equal, that an FI should hold more Russian than Argentinean loans—although the experience of FIs in 2002 with Russian defaults and in 2003 with Argentinian defaults may call into question the appropriateness of the portfolio approach and especially, the ability of FIs to diversify away unsystematic sovereign risk in a contagious crisis. More recently, value at risk models have been applied to (Dutch) government bond portfolios.[24] Similar to the discussion in Chapter 12, this line of research examines total losses on portfolios of government debt in the worst-case (say, 1 percent) scenario.[25]

---

[21] Ibid.

[22] Ibid.

[23] See M. Palmer and T. B. Sanders, "A Model for Diversifying International Loan Portfolios," *Journal of Financial Services Research*, 1996, pp. 359–71.

[24] See P. J. G. Vlaar, "Value at Risk Models for Dutch Bond Portfolios," *Journal of Banking and Finance* 24 (2000), pp. 1131–54.

[25] VAR models might also be applied to a country's FX revenues—to evaluate its ability to withstand shocks or crises.

Incentive Aspects CRA statistical models often identify variables based on rather loose or often nonexistent analyses of the borrower or lender's incentives to reschedule. Rarely are the following questions asked: What are the *incentives* or *net benefits* to an LDC seeking a rescheduling? What are the incentives or net benefits to an FI that grants a rescheduling? That is, what determines the demand for rescheduling by LDCs and the supply of rescheduling by FIs? Presumably, only when the benefits outweigh the costs for both parties does rescheduling occur. Consider the following benefits and costs of rescheduling for borrowers on the one hand and FIs on the other.

Borrowers

Benefits

- By rescheduling its debt, the borrower lowers the present value of its future payments in hard currencies to outside lenders. This allows it to increase its consumption of foreign imports and/or increase the rate of its domestic investment.

Costs

- By rescheduling now, the borrower may close itself out of the market for loans in the future. As a result, even if the borrower encounters high-growth investment opportunities in the future, it may be difficult or impossible to finance them.

- Rescheduling may result in significant interference with the borrower's international trade since it would be difficult to gain access to instruments such as letters of credit, without which trade may be more costly.[26]

Lenders (FIs)

Benefits

- Once a loan has been made, a rescheduling is much better than a borrower default. With a rescheduling, the FI lender may anticipate some present value loss of principal and interest on the loan; with an outright default, the FI stands to lose all its principal and future interest repayments.

- The FI can renegotiate fees and various other collateral and option features into a rescheduled loan.

- There may be tax benefits to an FI's taking a recognized write-down or loss in value on a rescheduled LDC loan portfolio.[27]

Costs

- Through rescheduling, loans become similar to long-term bonds or even equity, and the FI often becomes locked into a particular loan portfolio structure.

- Those FIs with large amounts of rescheduled loans are subject to greater regulatory attention. For example, in the United States, such FIs may be placed on the regulators' problem list of FIs.[28]

All these relevant economic incentive considerations go into the demand for and the supply of rescheduling; however, it is far from clear how the simple statistical models just described incorporate this complex array of incentives. At a very

---

[26] See Chapter 13 on letters of credit.

[27] For example, in 1998 Deutsche Bank took a loan loss provision of nearly $800 million against its Asian loan portfolio (see "Study Shows How World Banks Panicked Over Asian Troubles," *The New York Times,* January 30, 1998, p. D1).

[28] The problem list singles out banks for special regulatory attention. Normally, examiners rate a problem list bank as 4 or 5 on a rating scale of 1 to 5, where 1 is good and 5 is bad.

minimum, statistical models should clearly reflect the underlying theory of rescheduling.[29]

Stability A final problem with simple statistical CRA models is that of stability. The fact that certain key variables may have explained rescheduling in the past does not mean that they will perform or predict well in the future. Over time, new variables and incentives affect rescheduling decisions, and the relative weights on the key variables change. This suggests that the FI manager must continuously update the CRA model to incorporate all currently available information and ensure the best predictive power possible. This is particularly true in today's new global environment of enhanced trade and competition with major changes in production technology taking place in countries such as China and India.

Using Market Data to Measure Risk: The Secondary Market for LDC Debt

Since the mid-1980s, a secondary market for trading LDC debt has developed among large commercial and investment banks in New York and London. The volume of trading grew dramatically from around $2 billion per year in 1984 to over $6 billion today, with trading often taking place in the high-yield (or junk bond) departments of the participating FIs.[30] Trading declined to $4.2 billion in 1998 after the Russian debt defaults and again in 1999 after Ecuador's failure to pay interest on its Brady bonds (see below). Trading has also been adversely affected by schemes of the more successful emerging market countries to get investors to swap Brady bonds for domestic government bonds (see below). The early 2000s were characterized by increasing trading activity and growing investor confidence in emerging markets, sparked in large part by Brazil's rapid economic recovery and Mexico's upgraded credit rating to investment grade, and Russia's successful debt restructuring.

These markets provide quoted prices for LDC loans and other debt instruments that an FI manager can use for CRA. Before we look at how this might be done, we describe the structure and development of the markets for LDC loans and related debt instruments, including the determinants of market demand and supply.

The Structure of the Market

This secondary market in LDC debt has considerably enhanced the liquidity of LDC loans on bank and other FI balance sheets.[31] The following are the market players that sell and buy LDC loans and debt instruments.

---

[29] See J. Bulow and K. Rogoff, "A Constant Recontracting Model of Sovereign Debt," *Journal of Political Economy* 97 (1989), pp. 155–78.

[30] See "Loads of Debt," *The Economist,* March 22, 1997, p. 5. The Loan Syndication Trading Association has reported that trading in domestic corporate loans plus sovereign loans exceeded $110 billion in total in 2003. The market comprises over 100 traders/dealers.

[31] LDC loans change hands when one creditor assigns the rights to all future interest payments and principal payments to a buyer. In most early market transactions, the buyer had to get the permission of the sovereign debtor country before the loan could be assigned to a new party. The reason for this was that the country might have concerns as to whether the buyer was as committed to any new money deals as part of restructuring agreements as the original lender. Most recent restructuring agreements, however, have removed the right of assignment from the borrower (the sovereign country). This has increased liquidity in the LDC loan market.

Sellers

- Large FIs willing to accept write-downs of loans on their balance sheets.
- Small FIs wishing to disengage themselves from the LDC loan market.
- FIs willing to swap one country's LDC debt for another's to rearrange their portfolios of country risk exposures.

Buyers

- Wealthy investors, hedge funds (see Chapter 5, Appendix A), FIs, and corporations seeking to engage in debt-for-equity swaps or speculative investments.
- FIs seeking to rearrange their LDC balance sheets by reorienting their LDC debt concentrations.

The Early Market for Sovereign Debt

Consider the quote sheet from Salomon Brothers, in Table 16–5, for May 2, 1988—a relatively early stage of LDC loan market development. As indicated in Table 16–5, FIs such as investment banks and major commercial banks act as market makers, quoting two-way bid–ask prices for LDC debt.[32] Thus, an FI or an investor could have bought $100 of Peruvian loans from Salomon for $9 in May 1988, or at a 91 percent discount from face value. However, in selling the same loans to Salomon, the investor would have received only $7 per $100, or a 93 percent discount. The bid–ask spreads for certain countries were very large in this period; for example, Sudan's $2 bid and $10 ask exemplified a serious lack of market demand for the sovereign loans of many countries.

Today's Market for Sovereign Debt

In recent years there have been a large number of changes in the structure of the market. Now there are four market segments: Brady bonds, sovereign bonds, performing loans, and nonperforming loans.

Brady Bonds The first segment of the market (and the largest) is that for Brady bonds. These reflect programs under which the U.S. and other FIs exchanged their dollar loans for dollar bonds issued by the relevant less developed countries (LDCs). These bonds have a much longer maturity than that promised on the original loans and a lower promised original coupon (yield) than the interest rate on the original loan. However, the principal has usually been collateralized through the issuing country's purchasing U.S. treasury bonds and holding them in a special-purpose escrow account. Should that country default on its Brady bonds the buyers of the bonds could access the dollar bonds held as collateral. These loan-for-bond restructuring programs, also called debt-for-debt swaps, were developed under the auspices of the U.S. Treasury's 1989 Brady Plan and international organizations such as the IMF. Once loans were swapped for bonds by banks and other FIs, they could be sold on the secondary market. For example, in March 2002, the 30-year Brazilian discount Brady bonds had a bid price of $90.75 per $100 of face value. These bonds have their principal repayments collateralized by U.S. Treasury bonds. Table 16–6 lists the amount of Brady bonds outstanding for several countries.

Sovereign Bonds The second segment of the LDC debt market is that for sovereign bonds. Beginning in May 1996, as the debt position and economies of some LDCs

---

[32] Major market makers include the Dutch ING bank, as well as Lehman, Citigroup, J. P. Morgan, Bankers Trust, and Merrill Lynch.

TABLE 16–5   Indicative Prices for Less Developed Country Bank Loans

Country	Indicative Cash Prices		Swap Index		Trading Commentary
	Bid	Offer	Sell	Buy	
Algeria	$91.00	$93.00	5.22	6.71	Longer-dated paper resurfacing as cash substitute in swaps.
Argentina	29.00	30.00	0.66	0.67	Less volume this period; consolidation exercise slows note trades.
Bolivia	10.00	13.00	0.52	0.54	Minimal current activity.
Brazil	53.00	54.00	1.00	1.02	Rally topping out as supply catches up with auction interest.
Chile	60.50	61.50	1.19	1.22	Market firm and rising as deal calendar fills.
Colombia	67.00	68.00	1.42	1.47	Resurgence of interest as high-quality exit.
Costa Rica	13.00	16.00	0.54	0.56	Market building reserves of patience to deal with this name again.
Dominican Republic	17.00	20.00	0.57	0.59	Trading picks up at lower levels.
Ecuador	31.00	33.00	0.66	0.70	Occasional swaps surfacing.
Honduras	25.00	28.00	0.63	0.65	Viewed as expensive on a relative value basis.
Ivory Coast	30.00	33.00	0.67	0.70	Newly sighted by fee swappers.
Jamaica	33.00	36.00	0.70	0.73	Slow but serious inquiry continues.
Mexico	52.50	53.50	0.99	1.01	Prices continue upward drift on lower, lumpy flow.
Morocco	50.00	51.00	0.94	0.96	Fee swappers oblige sellers by jumping into the wider breach versus Latins.
Nicaragua	3.00	4.00	0.48	0.49	Avoided by the surviving court tasters.
Nigeria	28.50	30.50	0.66	0.68	Retail stonewalls dealer interest.
Panama	20.00	23.00	0.59	0.61	Recent bidding stirs the mud.
Peru	7.00	9.00	0.51	0.52	Debt-for-debt workouts and debt-for-goods deals continue.
Philippines	52.00	53.00	0.98	1.00	Prices drift higher with good interest in non-CB names.
Poland	43.25	44.50	0.83	0.85	Somewhat slower trading this period.
Romania	82.00	84.00	2.61	2.94	Bidding improves on expectations of 1988 principal payments.
Senegal	40.00	45.00	0.78	0.85	Trading talk more serious.
Sudan	2.00	10.00	0.48	0.52	Still on the mat.
Turkey	97.50	99.00	18.80	47.00	CTLDs remain well bid.
Uruguay	59.50	61.50	1.16	1.22	Remains a patience-trying market.
Venezuela	55.00	55.75	1.04	1.06	Trading stronger as uptick in Chile brings swaps back into range.
Yugoslavia	45.50	47.00	0.86	0.89	More frequent trading.
Zaire	19.00	23.00	0.58	0.61	New interest develops.

Source: Salomon Brothers Inc., May 2, 1988.

improved,[33] a number started buy-back, or repurchase, programs for their Brady bonds. For example, in April 2003 Mexico sold $2.5 billion of sovereign bonds to help finance the repurchase of the country's U.S. dollar–denominated Brady Bonds.

[33] In fact, Mexico has experienced such a turnaround. It is now embroiled in a lawsuit with Citigroup for prepaying on its Brady debt. See "Mexico's Debt Situation Takes a New Twist," *The New York Times*, June 27, 2000, p. 02.

TABLE 16–6
Brady Bonds and
Bank Loans
Outstanding, June
2003 (in billions of
dollars)

Source: World Bank Web
site, January 2004.
www.worldbank.org

Country	Brady Bonds Outstanding	Bank Loans Outstanding
Argentina	$ 6.85	$ 25.05
Brazil	17.78	58.20
Bulgaria	2.44	0.82
Costa Rica	0.43	3.03
Côte d'Ivoire	2.23	2.22
Dominican Republic	0.46	2.70
Ecuador	0.00	1.83
Mexico	1.27	45.69
Nigeria	1.44	1.99
Peru	2.47	4.23
Philippines	1.16	12.26
Poland	2.79	16.81
Russia	0.00	35.32
Uruguay	0.46	2.08
Venezuela	7.67	11.16

The difference between a Brady bond and a sovereign bond is that a Brady bond's value partly reflects the value of the U.S. Treasury bond collateral underlying the principal and/or interest on the issue. By contrast, sovereign bonds are uncollateralized and their price or value reflects the credit risk rating of the country issuing the bonds. The benefit to the country is the "saving" from not having to pledge U.S. Treasury bonds as collateral. The cost is the higher interest spreads required on such bonds. Thus, the $2.8 billion June 1997 issue by Brazil of 30-year dollar-denominated bonds (rated BB – grade by Standard & Poor's) was sold at a yield spread of nearly 4 percent over U.S. Treasuries at the time of issue.[34] In July 2001, Argentinian sovereign bonds were trading at spreads of over 15 percent above U.S. Treasury rates, with the J. P. Morgan Emerging Market Bond Index showing a spread of nearly 10 percent over U.S. Treasuries. This reflected the serious economic problems in Argentina and the contagious effects these were having on other sovereign bond markets.[35]

Performing Loans The third segment of the LDC debt market is that for performing LDC loans. Performing loans are original or restructured outstanding sovereign loans on which the sovereign country is currently maintaining promised payments to lenders or debt holders. Any discounts from 100 percent reflect expectations that these countries may face repayment problems in the future. Table 16–6 reports external bank loans outstanding for several countries as of June 2003.

[34] A. Gande and D. Parsley found that the credit rating on sovereign debt of one country can affect the credit rating and thus the yield spread in other countries' debt. For example, a one-category downgrade (e.g., from BB to B) is associated with a 12–basis point increase in spreads of sovereign bonds. However, positive rating events have no discernible impact on sovereign bond debt (see "News Spillovers in the Sovereign Debt Market," *Journal of Financial Economics,* forthcoming). Further, D. Duffie, L. H. Pedersen, and K. J. Singleton find that Russian yield spreads in the 1990s and 2000 varied significantly over time (responding to political events) and were negatively correlated with Russian foreign currency reserves and oil prices. Their model suggests that Russian sovereign bonds may have been overpriced in September 1997 (see "Modeling Sovereign Yield Spreads: A Case Study of Russian Debt," *Journal of Finance* 58 (February 2003), pp. 119–59).

[35] See "Gloom Over the River Plate," *The Economist,* June 14, 2001, pp. 11–12.

Nonperforming Loans   The fourth and final segment of the LDC market is that for nonperforming loans. Nonperforming loans reflect the secondary market prices for the sovereign loans of countries where there are no interest or principal payments currently being made. These are normally traded at very deep discounts from 100 percent.

LDC Market Prices and Country Risk Analysis

By combining LDC debt prices with key variables, FI managers can potentially predict future repayment problems. For example, in the markets for which LDC debt is quite heavily traded, such as Mexico and Brazil, these prices reflect market consensus regarding the current and expected future cash flows on these loans and, implicitly, the probability of rescheduling or repudiation of these loans. Because market prices on LDC loans have been available monthly since 1985, the FI manager might construct a statistical CRA model to analyze which key economic and political variables or factors have driven changes in secondary market prices. Basically, this would involve regressing periodic changes in the prices of LDC debt in the secondary market on a set of key variables such as those described earlier in this section. Table 16–7 presents the results of a study by E. Boehmer and W. L. Megginson of the factors driving the secondary market prices of 10 LDC countries' loans over a 32-month period, July 1985–July 1988.

As you can see, the most significant variables affecting LDC loan sale prices *(P)* over this period were a country's debt service ratio (TDGNP and TDEX), its import ratio (NIRES), its accumulated debt in arrears (ARR), and the amount by which FIs had already made loan loss provisions against these LDC loans (USP). Also important were variables that reflect the debt moratoria for Peru and Brazil (PDUM and BDUM) and that indicate whether a debt-for-equity swap program was in place. Interestingly, debt-for-equity swap programs appear to depress prices. (We discuss these programs in more detail in Appendix A to the chapter).

Once managers have estimated a statistical model, they can use the estimate of parameters $\beta_1, \beta_2, \ldots \beta_n$ along with forecasts for a given LDC's debt service ratio and other key variables to derive predicted changes in LDC asset prices. That is, this approach might allow the FI manager to come up with another set of forecasts regarding changes in sovereign risk exposure to a number of sovereign debtors.

This approach is subject to many of the same criticisms as the traditional statistical models of country risk prediction. Specifically, the parameters of the model may be unstable; managers can measure variables, such as the *DSR* and the import ratio, only with error; and the LDC loan market may not be price efficient.[36] In addition, the link between these key variables and the change in secondary market price is something of a black box in terms of links to the underlying theoretical incentives of borrowers and lenders to engage in future reschedulings or repudiations of their debt obligations.

---

[36] However, in S. H. Lee, H. M. Sung, and J. L. Urrutia, "The Behavior of Secondary Market Prices of LDC Syndicated Loans," *Journal of Banking and Finance* 20 (1996), pp. 537–54, it is shown that returns on LDC loans traded in the secondary market conform to those expected to exist in an efficient market. In fact, recent research has found that, in general, international and, particularly, emerging markets are becoming increasingly efficient. See B. Eftekhari and S. E. Satchell, "International Investors' Exposure to Risk in Emerging Markets," *Journal of Financial Research,* Spring 1999, pp. 83–106. Additionally, J. J. Choi, S. Hauser, and K. J. Kopecky, in "Does the Stock Market Predict Real Activity? Time Series Evidence from the G-7 Countries," *Journal of Banking and Finance* 23 (1999), pp. 1771–92, found a significant relationship between lagged real stock returns and the growth rate in industrial production for the G-7 countries.

TABLE 16–7
Variables Affecting Secondary Market Prices

Source: E. Boehmer and W. L. Megginson, "Determinants of Secondary Market Prices for Developing Country Syndicated Loans," *Journal of Finance* 45 (1990), pp. 1517–40.

The following regression equation is estimated:

$$P_{it} = \beta_1 \times \text{Intercept} + \beta_2 \times \text{TDGNP}_{it} + \beta_3 \times \text{TDEX}_{it} + \beta_4 \times \text{NETDS}_{it} + \beta_5 \times \text{NIRES}_{it}$$
$$+ \beta_6 \times \text{INT}_{it} + \beta_7 \times \text{ARR}_{it} + \beta_8 \times \text{USP}_{it} + \beta_9 \times \text{BDUM}_{it} + \beta_{10} \times \text{PDUM}_{it}$$
$$+ \beta_{11} \times \text{CONVDUM}_{it} + U_{it}$$

where

P =	LDC secondary market loan prices
TDGNP =	Ratio of total long-term debt to GNP
TDEX =	Ratio of total long-term debt to exports
NETDS =	Ratio of net exports to debt service
NIRES =	Ratio of net imports to hard currency reserves
INT =	Monthly London Interbank Offered Rate (a short-term interest rate)
ARR =	Level of incurred payment arrears
USP =	Cumulative developing country specific loan provisioning by U.S. FIs
BDUM =	Unity for Brazil from January to December of 1987 and zero otherwise to capture the effects of the debt moratorium
PDUM =	Unity for Peru over the whole sampling period and zero otherwise to account for the unilateral limitation of debt service payments
CONVDUM =	Unity for all months in which a country maintained legislation for debt-to-equity conversions

Parameter	Estimate	*t*-Statistic
Intercept	88.51760	13.47
TDGNP	−18.11610	−4.75
TDEX	−0.10437	−3.57
NETDS	−0.30754	−0.50
NIRES	5.79548	1.28
INT	0.22825	0.30
ARR	−0.00574	−2.68
USP	−0.00100	−13.69
BDUM	−10.92820	−6.61
PDUM	−36.07240	−8.31
CONVDUM	−5.43157	−6.75

Degrees of freedom: 309
Adjusted R^2: 0.96

Concept Questions

1. Are the credit ratings of countries in the *Institutional Investor* rating scheme forward looking or backward looking?
2. What variables are most commonly included in sovereign risk prediction models? What does each one measure?
3. What are the major problems involved with using traditional CRA models and techniques?
4. Which sovereign risk indicators are the most important for a large FI, those with a high or those with a low systematic element?
5. Why is the supply of Brady bonds in decline?

Summary

This chapter reviewed the problems FIs face from sovereign or country risk exposures. Sovereign risk is the risk of a foreign government's limiting or preventing domestic borrowers in its jurisdiction from repaying the principal and interest on debt owned to external lenders. In recent years this risk has caused enormous problems for U.S. banks lending to LDCs, and Latin American and Asian countries. We reviewed various models for country risk analysis (CRA), including those produced by external monitoring agencies such as *Euromoney, The Economist* Intelligence Unit, and the *Institutional Investor* and those that could be constructed by an FI manager for internal evaluation purposes. Such statistical CRA models have problems and pitfalls. An alternative approach using secondary market prices on LDC loans and bonds was also described. In Appendix A, we analyze the advantages and disadvantages of using four alternative mechanisms for dealing with problem sovereign credits from the perspective of the lender: debt–equity swaps, MYRAs, loan sales, and bond-for-loan swaps.

Questions and Problems

1. What risks are incurred in making loans to borrowers based in foreign countries? Explain.
2. What is the difference between debt rescheduling and debt repudiation?
3. Identify and explain at least four reasons that rescheduling debt in the form of loans is easier than rescheduling debt in the form of bonds.
4. What three country risk assessment models are available to investors? How is each model compiled?
5. What types of variables normally are used in a CRA Z score model? Define the following ratios and explain how each is interpreted in assessing the probability of rescheduling.
   a. Debt service ratio.
   b. Import ratio.
   c. Investment ratio.
   d. Variance of export revenue.
   e. Domestic money supply growth.
6. An FI manager has calculated the following values and weights to assess the credit risk and likelihood of having to reschedule the loan. From the Z score calculated from these weights and values, is the manager likely to approve the loan? Validation tests of the Z score model indicated that scores below 0.500 were likely to be nonreschedulers, while scores above 0.700 indicated a likelihood of rescheduling. Scores between 0.500 and 0.700 do not predict well.

Variable	Country Value	Weight
DSR	1.25	0.05
IR	1.60	0.10
INVR	0.60	0.35
VAREX	0.15	0.35
MG	0.02	0.15

7. Countries A and B have exports of $2 and $6 billion, respectively. The total interest and amortization on foreign loans for both countries are $1 and $2 billion, respectively.
   a. What is the debt service ratio (DSR) for each country?
   b. Based only on this ratio, to which country should lenders charge a higher risk premium?

c. What are the shortcomings of using only these ratios to determine your answer in (b)?

8. What shortcomings are introduced by using traditional CRA models and techniques? In each case, what adjustments are made in the estimation techniques to compensate for the problems?

9. How do price and quantity risks affect the variability of a country's export revenue?

10. The average σ^2_{ER} (or VAREX = variance of export revenue) of a group of countries has been estimated at 20 percent. The individual VAREX of two countries in the group, Holland and Singapore, has been estimated at 15 percent and 28 percent, respectively. The regression of individual country VAREX on the average VAREX provides the following beta (coefficient) estimates:

$$\beta_H = \text{Beta of Holland} = 0.80$$

$$\beta_S = \text{Beta of Singapore} = 0.20$$

a. Based only on the VAREX estimates, which country should be charged a higher risk premium? Explain.

b. If FIs include unsystematic risk in their estimation of risk premiums, how would your conclusions to (a) be affected? Explain.

11. Explain the following relation:

$$p = f(IR, INVR)$$

$$+, + \text{ or } -$$

where

$$p = \text{Probability of rescheduling}$$
$$IR = \text{Total imports/Total foreign exchange reserves}$$
$$INVR = \text{Real investment/GNP}$$

12. What is systematic risk in terms of sovereign risk? Which of the variables often used in statistical models tend to have high systematic risk? Which variables tend to have low systematic risk?

13. What are the benefits and costs of rescheduling to the following?
   a. A borrower.
   b. A lender.

14. Who are the primary sellers of LDC debt? Who are the buyers? Why are FIs often both sellers and buyers of LDC debt in the secondary markets?

15. Identify and describe the four market segments of the secondary market for LDC debt.

The following questions and problems are based on material presented in Appendix 16A.

16. What are the risks to an investing company participating in a debt-for-equity swap?

17. Chase Bank holds a $200 million loan to Argentina. The loans are being traded at bid-offer prices of 91–93 per 100 in the London secondary market.
   a. If Chase has an opportunity to sell this loan to an investment bank at a 7 percent discount, what are the savings after taxes compared with the revenue selling the loan in the secondary market? Assume the tax rate is 40 percent.

b. The investment bank in turn sells the debt at a 6 percent discount to a real estate company planning to build apartment complexes in Argentina. What is the profit after taxes to the investment bank?

c. The real estate company converts this loan into pesos under a debt-for-equity swap organized by the Argentinean government. The official rate for dollar to peso conversion is P1.05/$. The free market rate is P1.10/$. How much did the real estate company save by investing in Argentina through the debt-for-equity swap program as opposed to directly investing $200 million using the free market rates?

d. How much would Chase benefit from doing a local currency debt-for-equity swap itself? Why doesn't the bank do this swap?

18. Zlick Company plans to invest $20 million in Chile to expand its subsidiary's manufacturing output. Zlick has two options. It can convert the $20 million at the current exchange rate of 410 pesos to a dollar (i.e., P410/$), or it can engage in a debt-for-equity swap with its bank, City Bank, by purchasing Chilean debt and then swapping that debt into Chilean equity investments.

a. If City Bank quotes bid-offer prices of 94–96 for Chilean loans, what is the bank expecting to receive from Zlick Corporation (ignore taxes)? Why would City Bank want to dispose of this loan?

b. If Zlick decides to purchase the debt from City Bank and convert it to equity, it will have to exchange it at the official rate of P400/$. Is this option better than investing directly in Chile at the free market rate of P410/$?

c. What official exchange rate will cause Zlick to be indifferent between the two options?

19. What is concessionality in the process of rescheduling a loan?

20. Which variables typically are negotiation points in an LDC multiyear restructuring agreement (MYRA)? How do changes in these variables provide benefits to the borrower and to the lender?

21. How would the restructuring, such as rescheduling, of sovereign bonds affect the interest rate risk of the bonds? Is it possible that such restructuring would cause the FI's cost of capital not to change? Explain.

22. A bank is in the process of renegotiating a loan. The principal outstanding is $50 million and is to be paid back in two installments of $25 million each, plus interest of 8 percent. The new terms will stretch the loan out to five years with only interest payments of 6 percent, no principal payments, for the first three years. The principal will be paid in the last two years in payments of $25 million along with the interest. The cost of funds for the bank is 6 percent for both the old loan and the renegotiated loan. An up-front fee of 1 percent is to be included for the renegotiated loan.

a. What is the present value of the existing loan for the bank?

b. What is the present value of the rescheduled loan for the bank?

c. Is the concessionality positive or negative for the bank?

23. A bank is in the process of renegotiating a three-year nonamortizing loan. The principal outstanding is $20 million, and the interest rate is 8 percent. The new terms will extend the loan to 10 years at a new interest rate of 6 percent. The cost of funds for the bank is 7 percent for both the old loan and the renegotiated loan. An up-front fee of 50 basis points is to be included for the renegotiated loan.

    a. What is the present value of the existing loan for the bank?

    b. What is the present value of the rescheduled loan for the bank?

    c. What is the concessionality for the bank?

    d. What should be the up-front fee to make the concessionality zero?

24. A $20 million loan outstanding to the Nigerian government is currently in arrears with City Bank. After extensive negotiations, City Bank agrees to reduce the interest rate from 10 percent to 6 percent and to lengthen the maturity of the loan to 10 years from the present 5 years remaining to maturity. The principal of the loan is to be paid at maturity. There will be no grace period, and the first interest payment is expected at the end of the year.

    a. If the cost of funds is 5 percent for the bank, what is the present value of the loan prior to the rescheduling?

    b. What is the present value of the rescheduled loan to the bank?

    c. What is the concessionality of the rescheduled loan if the cost of funds remains at 5 percent and an up-front fee of 5 percent is charged?

    d. What up-front fee should the bank charge to make the concessionality equal zero?

25. A bank was expecting to receive $100,000 from its customer based in Great Britain. Since the customer has problems repaying the loan immediately, the bank extends the loan for another year at the same interest rate of 10 percent. However, in the rescheduling agreement, the bank reserves the right to exercise an option for receiving the payment in British pounds, equal to £81,500.

    a. If the cost of funds to the bank is also assumed to be 10 percent, what is the value of this option built into the agreement if only two possible exchange rates are expected at the end of the year, £1.75/$ or £1.55/$, with equal probability?

    b. How would your answer differ if the probability of the exchange rate being being £1.75/$ is 70 percent and that of £1.55/$ is 30 percent?

    c. Does the currency option have more or less value as the volatility of the exchange rate increases?

26. What are the major benefits and costs of loan sales to an FI?

27. What are the major costs and benefits of converting debt to Brady bonds for an FI?

Web Questions

28. Go to the Heritage Foundation Web site at **www.heritage.org** and find the most recent Economic Freedom Index for the United States using the following steps. Click on "20XX Index of Economic Freedom." Click on "Countries." Click on "United States." This will bring the file onto your computer that contains the relevant data. What factors led to this rating?

29. Go to the World Bank Web site at **www.worldbank.org** and find the amount of Brady bonds currently outstanding in Brazil using the following steps. Click on "Data and Statistics." Click on "Data by Country." Click on "BIS, IMF, OECD, and World Bank Joint Initiative on Debt Reporting." Click on "Joint

Statistics on External Debt (Home)." Click on "25 countries are also available in HTML format." Under Brazil, click on "Joint BIS-IMF-OECD-World Bank Statistics on External Debt." This will bring the file onto your computer that contains the relevant data.

Pertinent Web Sites

Bank for International Settlements	www.bis.org
Heritage Foundation	www.heritage.org
Institutional Investor	www.institutionalinvestor.com
International Monetary Fund	www.imf.org
The Economist	www.economist.com
Transparency International	www.transparency.org
World Bank	www.worldbank.org

Chapter Notation

View Chapter Notation at the Web site to the textbook (**www.mhhe.com/saunders5e**).

Appendix 16A

Mechanisms for Dealing with Sovereign Risk Exposure

In the text of the chapter, we identified methods and models FI managers can use to measure sovereign risk exposure before making credit decisions. In this Appendix, we consider the benefits and costs of using four alternative mechanisms to deal with problem sovereign credits once they have arisen. The four mechanisms are:

1. Debt-for-equity swaps.
2. Multiyear restructuring of loans (MYRAs).
3. Sale of LDC loans on the secondary market.
4. Bond-for-loan swaps (Brady bonds).

While restructuring keeps the loans in the portfolio, the other three mechanisms change the fundamental nature of the FI's claim itself or remove it from the balance sheet.

In this Appendix we look at the mechanics of loan restructuring and debt-for-equity swaps. Because we have already described LDC loan sales and bond-for-loan swaps (e.g., Brady bonds), we only summarize their benefits and costs here. Understanding each of these mechanisms, especially their benefits and costs, is important, since an FI can choose among the four in dealing with a problem sovereign loan or credit.

DEBT-FOR-EQUITY SWAPS

The market for LDC loan sales has a close link to debt-for-equity swap programs arranged by certain LDCs, such as Chile and Mexico, with outside investors that wish to make equity investments in debtor countries.[1] Indeed, while banks are the major sellers of LDC loans, important buyers are parties that wish to engage in long-term equity or real investments in those debtor countries. For example, the 1985 Mexican debt-for-equity swap program allowed Mexican dollar loans to be swapped for Mexican equity in certain priority investment areas. These were the motor, tourism, and chemical industries. For example, American

Express was an FI that exploited the opportunities of the Mexican debt-for-equity swap program by building seven hotels in Mexico. The estimated annual amount of debt-for-equity swaps is currently around $10 billion.[2]

To demonstrate the costs and benefits of a debt-for-equity swap for the FI and other parties participating in the transaction, we present a hypothetical example. Suppose that in November 2003, Citigroup had $100 million loans outstanding to Chile and could have sold those loans on the secondary market for a bid price of $91 million, or $91 per $100. The advantages to Citigroup from selling loans are the removal of these loans from its books and the freeing up of funds for other investments. However, Citigroup has to accept a loss of $9 million on the loan. Given that the rest of the bank is profitable, the bank can offset this loss against other profits. Further, if the corporate tax rate is 34 percent, then Citigroup's after-tax loss will be $9(1 - .34)$ million = $5.94 million.

If Citigroup sold this loan to Merrill Lynch for $91 million, Merrill Lynch, as a market maker, could reoffer the loan to an outside buyer at a slightly higher price—say, $93 million (or $93 per $100 of face value). Suppose IBM wants to build a computer factory in Chile and buys the $100 million face value loan from Merrill Lynch for $93 million to finance its investments in Chile. Thus, Merrill Lynch earns a profit of $93 million - $91 million = $2 million, and IBM knows that Chile has a debt-for-equity swap program. This means that at a given exchange rate, the Chilean government will allow IBM to convert the $100 million dollar loan it has purchased into local currency, or pesos. However, the Chilean government will be willing to do this only if it receives something in return. Thus, it may be willing to convert the dollars into pesos only at a 5 percent discount from the true free market dollar/peso exchange rate. If the free market exchange rate was 380 Chilean pesos to the U.S. dollar, the Chilean government

---

[1] For more details, see R. Grosse, "The Debt/Equity Swap in Latin America—In Whose Interest?" *Journal of International Financial Management and Accounting* 4 (Spring 1992), pp. 13–39.

[2] Countries that have recently employed debt-for-equity swap programs include Argentina, Brazil, Chile, Costa Rica, Ecuador, Jamaica, Mexico, Uruguay, and Venezuela.

FIGURE 16A–1
Debt-for-Equity
Swaps and Loan
Sales

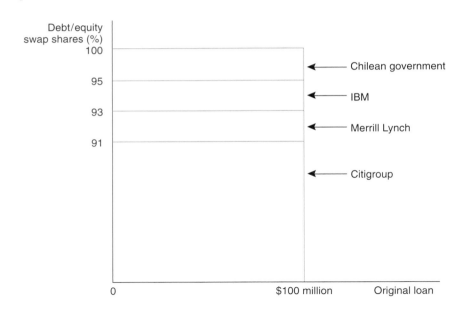

will convert the dollars only at 361 pesos to the U.S. dollar. Thus IBM must bear a 5 percent discount on the face value of the purchased loan; that is, when converting the $100 million loan at the Chilean Central Bank, IBM receives $95 million equivalent in pesos.[3] Remember that IBM had originally bought the loan for only $93 million on the secondary market. Thus, its net savings from this debt-for-equity conversion program is $2 million.[4] However, note that the $95 million is in pesos that must be invested in Chilean equity, such as real estate for factories. In general, debt-for-equity swap investors face long periods before they can repatriate dividends (12 years in the Mexican case) and often large withholding taxes (55 percent in the Mexican case). Moreover, they face the risk of future expropriation or nationalization of those assets as well as peso currency risk. Thus, the $2 million spread reflects IBM's expectations about such risks.

Finally, what does the Chilean government get out of this debt-for-equity swap program? It has retired relatively expensive hard currency dollar debt with local currency pesos at a discount. Implicitly, it has retired a $100 million face value debt at a cost of $95 million in pesos; the difference reflects the debt-for-equity swap official exchange rate (361 pesos/$1) and the true exchange rate (380 pesos/$1). The cost to Chile is printing $95 million more in pesos. This may lead to a higher domestic inflation rate, as well as increased foreign ownership and control of Chilean real assets as a result of IBM's equity purchases.

We illustrate the division of the original $100 million face value loan among the four parties as a result of the loan sale and debt-for-equity swap in Figure 16A–1. Citigroup gets 91 percent of the original face value of the loan; Merrill Lynch, 2 percent; IBM, 2 percent; and Chile, 5 percent. That is, the three parties have the 9 percent discount from face value accepted by Citigroup: the investment bank, the corporation involved in the debt-for-equity swap, and the sponsoring country's government.

One puzzle from the preceding example is why Citigroup does not sidestep both the investment bank and IBM and engage in a local currency debt-for-equity swap itself. That is, why doesn't Citibank directly swap its $100 million loan to Chile for the $95 million equivalent of local equity? The problem is that in the United States, Federal Reserve Regulation K restricts U.S. banks' ability to buy real equity or engage in commerce

---

[3] In practice, debt-for-equity swaps convert into pesos at an official rate. This official rate is often less attractive than the rate quoted in official or unofficial parallel markets for private transactions.

[4] That is, in general, the swap is cheaper than direct local borrowing if this is an available alternative.

in overseas countries.[5] If a U.S. bank can buy and hold Chilean real assets, this might lower its potential losses from restructuring its LDC loan portfolio. Nevertheless, note that although a loan sale directly removes a problem loan from the balance sheet, a debt-for-equity swap replaces that problem loan with a risky long-term peso-denominated equity position on its balance sheet. Thus, the improvement of the liquidity of the balance sheet through such a transaction is far from certain.

MULTIYEAR RESTRUCTURING AGREEMENTS (MYRAS)

If a country is unable to keep its payments on a loan current and an FI chooses to maintain the loan on its balance sheet rather than selling it or swapping it for equity or debt, the loan and its contractual terms would be rescheduled under a multiyear restructuring agreement (MYRA). A good example of a MYRA was the January 1998 agreement reached between South Korea and its major creditors to restructure $24 billion of short-term dollar loans that had been made by banks and corporations (and that were coming due in March 1998). Many of these loans had interest rates as high as 20 percent and maturities of 90 days or less.

As with the loan sale, the debt-for-equity swap, and the debt-for-debt swap, the crucial question for an FI is the amount it is willing to concede or give up to the borrower in the sovereign loan rescheduling process. The benefits and costs of this policy depend on a number of factors that are usually built into any MYRA, including the following:

1. The *fee* charged by the FI to the borrower for the costs of restructuring the loan. This fee may be as high as 1 percent of the face value of the loan if a large lending syndicate is involved in the negotiations.

2. The *interest rate* charged on the new loan. This is generally lower than the rate on the original loan to ease the repayment cash flow problems of the borrower. In the South Korean case, if the loan was rescheduled for one year, the new interest was LIBOR plus 2.25 percent; if it was rescheduled for two years, the new loan interest rate was LIBOR plus 2.5 percent; and if it was rescheduled for three years, the new interest rate was LIBOR plus 2.75 percent.

3. A *grace period* may be involved before interest and/or principal payments begin on the new loan to give the borrower time to accumulate hard currency reserves to meet its future debt interest and principal obligations. In the South Korean case, no grace period was set.

4. The *maturity* of the loan is lengthened, normally to extend the interest and principal payments over a longer period. In the South Korean case the restructured loan maturities were set at between one and three years.

5. *Option and guarantee features* are often built into the MYRA to allow the lender (and sometimes the borrower) to choose the currency for repayment of interest and principal,[6] and/or to protect the lenders against default in the future. In the case of the South Korean loans, the government had to guarantee repayment of the $24 billion.

The magnitude and interaction of these factors determine the degree of the MYRA's concessionality (the net cost) to an FI. In general, the net cost or degree of concessionality can be defined as:

Concessionality

$$= \left(\begin{array}{c}\text{Present value of}\\ \text{original loan}\end{array}\right) - \left(\begin{array}{c}\text{Present value of}\\ \text{restructured loan}\end{array}\right)$$
$$= PV_0 - PV_R$$

The lower the present value of the restructured loan relative to the original loan, the greater are the *concessions* the FI has made to the borrower, that is, the greater the cost of loan restructuring.

[5] Limited amounts of equity purchases are allowed to specialized U.S. bank subsidiaries called Edge Act corporations. Such corporations have been established since 1919 under the Edge Act to allow banks to finance international transactions. In 1987, the Federal Reserve approved bank acquisitions of 100 percent stakes in nonfinancial companies in 33 extremely poor LDCs as part of debt-for-equity swaps. Unfortunately, most of these countries do not operate debt-for-equity programs or have very little equity that is attractive. However, the American Express bank example of building seven hotels in Mexico illustrates a bank engaging in a direct debt-for-equity swap.

[6] For example, the lender may choose to be repaid in dollars or in yen. Such option features add value to the cash flow stream for either the borrower or the lender, depending on who can exercise the currency option.

LOAN SALES

The third mechanism for dealing with problem sovereign loans—LDC loan sales—was discussed earlier in this chapter. Here we summarize the main benefits and costs of the sales to the FI. The first major benefit is the removal of these loans from the balance sheet and, as a result, the freeing up of resources for other investments. Second, being able to sell these loans at a discount or loss signifies that the rest of the FI's balance sheet is sufficiently strong to bear the cost. In fact, a number of studies have found that announcements of FIs taking reserve additions against LDC loans—prior to their charge-off and sale—have a positive effect on bank stock prices.[7] Third, the FI shares part of the loan sale loss with the government because such losses provide a tax write-off for the lender.

The major cost is one of the loss itself—the tax-adjusted difference between the face value of the loan and its market value at the time of the sale.

[7] See, for example, Grammatikos and Saunders, "Additions to Bank Loan Loss Reserves."

BOND-FOR-LOAN SWAPS (BRADY BONDS)

The fourth mechanism is a bond-for-loan swap. The primary benefit of bond-for-loan swaps is that they transform an LDC loan into a highly marketable and liquid instrument—a bond. For example, FIs trade and clear Brady bonds (the most common of these types of swaps) in a fashion similar to most Eurobonds with relatively low transaction costs, small bid–ask spreads, and an efficient clearing and settlement system. In addition, because of full or partial collateral backing, these bonds are normally senior in status to any remaining LDC loans or sovereign bonds of that country. The major cost occurs when the bond is swapped for the loan because the bond usually has a longer stated maturity. Also, the swap of loan face value for debt face value is often less than dollar for dollar. Moreover, posting U.S. dollar debt as collateral can be very expensive for an LDC country with minimal hard currency exchange reserves.

Chapter **Seventeen**

Liquidity Risk

INTRODUCTION

Chapters 8 through 16 examined how the major problems of interest rate risk, market risk, credit risk, off-balance-sheet risk, operational and technology risk, foreign exchange risk, and sovereign risk can threaten the solvency of an FI. This chapter looks at the problems created by liquidity risk. Unlike risks that threaten the very solvency of an FI, liquidity risk is a normal aspect of the everyday management of an FI. Only in extreme cases do liquidity risk problems develop into solvency risk problems. This chapter identifies the causes of liquidity risk on the liability side of an FI's balance sheet as well as on the asset side. We discuss methods used to measure an FI's liquidity risk exposure and consequences of extreme liquidity risk (such as deposit or liability drains and runs) and briefly examine regulatory mechanisms put in place to ease liquidity problems and prevent runs on depository institutions. Moreover, some FIs are more exposed to liquidity risk than others. At one extreme, depository institutions are highly exposed; in the middle, life insurance companies are moderately exposed; and at the other extreme, mutual and pension funds and property–casualty insurance companies have relatively low exposure. We examine the reasons for these differences.

CAUSES OF LIQUIDITY RISK

Liquidity risk arises for two reasons: a liability-side reason and an asset-side reason. The liability-side reason occurs when an FI's liability holders, such as depositors or insurance policyholders, seek to cash in their financial claims immediately. When liability holders demand cash by withdrawing deposits, the FI needs to borrow additional funds or sell assets to meet the withdrawal. The most liquid asset is cash; FIs use this asset to pay claim holders who seek to withdraw funds. However, FIs tend to minimize their holdings of cash reserves as assets because those reserves pay no interest. To generate interest revenues, most FIs invest in less liquid and/or longer-maturity assets. While most assets can be turned into cash eventually, for some assets this can be done only at a high cost when the asset must be liquidated immediately. The price the asset holder must accept for immediate sale may be far less than it would receive with a longer horizon over which to negotiate a sale. Thus, some assets may be liquidated only at low **fire-sale prices,** thus threatening the solvency of the FI. Alternatively, rather than liquidating assets, an FI may seek to purchase or borrow additional funds.

fire-sale price
The price received for an asset that has to be liquidated (sold) immediately.

The second cause of liquidity risk is asset-side liquidity risk: supplying off-balance-sheet loan commitments. As we described in Chapter 13, a loan commitment allows a customer to borrow (take down) funds from an FI (over a commitment period) on demand. When a borrower draws on its loan commitment, the FI must fund the loan on the balance sheet immediately; this creates a demand for liquidity. As it can with liability withdrawals, an FI can meet such a liquidity need by running down its cash assets, selling off other liquid assets, or borrowing additional funds.

To analyze the differing degrees of importance of liquidity risk across FIs, we next consider liquidity risk problems faced by depository institutions, insurance companies, and mutual and pension funds.

Concept Questions

1. What are the sources of liquidity risk?
2. Why is cash more liquid than loans for an FI?

LIQUIDITY RISK AT DEPOSITORY INSTITUTIONS

Liability-Side Liquidity Risk

As discussed in Chapter 2, a depository institution's (DI's) balance sheet typically has a large amount of short-term liabilities, such as demand deposits and other transaction accounts, which fund relatively long-term assets. Demand deposit accounts and other transaction accounts are contracts that give the holders the right to put their claims back to the DI on any given day and demand immediate repayment of the face value of their deposit claims in cash.[1] Thus, an individual demand deposit account holder with a balance of $10,000 can demand cash to be repaid immediately, as can a corporation with $100 million in its demand deposit account.[2] In theory, at least, a DI that has 20 percent of its liabilities in demand deposits and other transaction accounts must stand ready to pay out that amount by liquidating an equivalent amount of assets on any banking day. Table 17–1 shows the aggregate balance sheet of the assets and liabilities of U.S. commercial banks. As seen in this table, total deposits are 70.44 percent of total liabilities (with 13.53 percent demand deposits and other transaction accounts). By comparison, cash assets are only 4.16 percent of total assets. Also note that borrowed funds are 23.31 percent of total liabilities.

In reality, a depository institution knows that normally only a small proportion of its deposits will be withdrawn on any given day. Most demand deposits act as consumer **core deposits** on a day-by-day basis, providing a relatively stable or long-term source of savings and time deposit funds for the DI. Moreover, deposit withdrawals may in part be offset by the inflow of new deposits (and income generated from the DI's on- and off-balance-sheet activities). The DI manager must

core deposits
Those deposits that provide a DI with a long-term funding source.

---

[1] Accounts with this type of put option include demand deposits, NOW accounts (interest bearing checking accounts with minimum balance requirements), and money market accounts (checking accounts with minimum balance and number-of-checks-written restrictions). We describe these accounts in more detail in Chapter 18. Depository institutions typically liquidate deposit account contracts immediately upon request of the customer. Many savings account contracts, however, give a DI some powers to delay withdrawals by requiring notification of withdrawal a certain number of days before withdrawal or by imposing penalty fees such as loss of interest.

[2] Technology is compounding the risk in these withdrawals. The Internet enables depositors to transfer money between FIs quickly to take advantage of higher rates.

TABLE 17–1
Assets and
Liabilities of U.S.
Banks, December
2003 (in billions of
dollars)

Source: Federal Reserve
Board website, January 2004.
www.federalreserve.gov

Assets			Liabilities*		
Total cash assets	$ 303.6	4.16%	Total deposits	$4,741.3	70.44%
Total securities	2,135.8	29.25	Borrowings	1,569.2	23.31
Total loans	4,300.3	58.88	Other liabilities	420.9	6.25
Other assets	563.0	7.71	Total liabilities	$6,731.4	
Total assets	$7,302.7				

* Excluding bank equity capital.

FIGURE 17–1
Distribution of Net
Deposit Drains

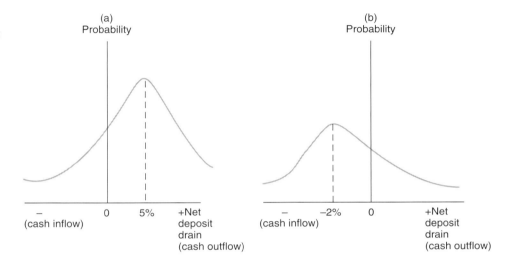

net deposit drains
The amount by which
cash withdrawals ex-
ceed additions; a net
cash outflow.

monitor the resulting net deposit withdrawals or net deposit drains.[3] Specifically, over time, a DI manager can normally predict—with a good degree of accuracy—the probability distribution of **net deposit drains** (the difference between deposit withdrawals and deposit additions) on any given normal banking day.[4]

Consider the two possible distributions shown in Figure 17–1. In panel (a) of Figure 17–1, the distribution is assumed to be strongly peaked at the 5 percent net deposit withdrawal level—this DI expects approximately 5 percent of its net deposit funds to be withdrawn on any given day with the highest probability.

---

[3] Also a part of liquidity risk (although not as likely to cause an FI to fail) is an unexpected inflow of funds. For example, in the early 2000s as stock prices fell, investors liquidated their mutual fund shares and deposited these funds in their banks and credit unions. With interest rates at historic lows, depository institutions faced a problem of finding sufficiently attractive (in a return sense) loans and securities in which to invest these funds.

[4] Apart from predictable daily seasonality to deposit flows, there are other seasonal variations, many of which are, to a greater or lesser degree, predictable. For example, many retail DIs face above-average deposit outflows around the end of the year and in the summer (due to Christmas and the vacation season). Also, many rural DIs face a deposit inflow–outflow cycle that closely matches the agricultural cycle of the local crop or crops. In the planting and growing season, deposits tend to fall, while in the harvest season, deposits tend to rise (as crops are sold). J. H. Gilkeson, J. A. List, and C.K. Ruff, in "Evidence of Early Withdrawal in Time Deposit Portfolios," *Journal of Financial Services Research* 15:2 (1999), pp. 103–22, find that early withdrawals of time deposits are also somewhat predictable in that, for all but the very short-term deposits, the size of early withdrawals is significantly related to changes in interest rates relative to the rate paid on existing time deposits. The size of the penalties for early withdrawals is also found to affect the size of these withdrawals.

In panel (a) a net deposit drain means that the DI is receiving insufficient additional deposits (and other cash inflows) to offset deposit withdrawals.

The DI in panel (a) has a mean, or expected, net positive drain on deposits, so its new deposit funds and other cash flows are expected to be insufficient to offset deposit withdrawals. The liability side of its balance sheet is contracting. Table 17–2 illustrates an actual 5 percent net drain of deposit accounts (or, in terms of dollars, a drain of $5 million).

For a DI to be growing, it must have a mean or average deposit drain such that new deposit funds more than offset deposit withdrawals. Thus, the peak of the net deposit drain probability distribution would be at a point to the left of zero. See the −2 percent in panel (b) in Figure 17–1, where the distribution of net deposit drains is peaked at −2 percent, or the FI is receiving net cash inflows with the highest probability.

A DI can manage a drain on deposits in two major ways: (1) purchased liquidity management and/or (2) stored liquidity management. Traditionally, DI managers have relied on stored liquidity management as the primary mechanism of liquidity management. Today, many DIs—especially the largest banks with access to the money market and other nondeposit markets for funds—rely on purchased liquidity (or liability) management to deal with the risk of cash shortfalls.[5] A more extensive discussion of liability management techniques is left to Chapter 18. Here we briefly discuss the alternative methods of liquidity risk management.

Purchased Liquidity Management

A DI manager who purchases liquidity turns to the markets for purchased funds, such as the federal funds market and/or the repurchase agreement markets,[6] which are interbank markets for short-term loans. Alternatively, the DI manager could issue additional fixed-maturity wholesale certificates of deposit or even sell some notes and bonds.[7] In the example above, as long as the total amount of funds raised equals $5 million, the DI in Table 17–2 could fully fund its net deposit drain. However, this can be expensive for the DI since it is paying *market rates* for funds in the wholesale money market to offset net drains on low-interest-bearing deposits.[8] Thus, the higher the cost of purchased funds relative to the rates earned on assets, the less attractive this approach to liquidity management becomes. Further, since most of these funds are not covered by deposit insurance, their availability may be limited should the depository institution incur insolvency difficulties. Table 17–3 shows the DI's balance sheet if it responds to deposit drains by using purchased liquidity management techniques.

purchased liquidity management
An adjustment to a deposit drain that occurs on the liability side of the balance sheet.

Note that **purchased liquidity management** has allowed the DI to maintain its overall balance sheet size of $100 million without disturbing the size and

[5] However, using the loan-to-deposit ratio as their main indicator of proper management strategy, J. P. Lajaunie, T. O. Stanley, and C. Roger argue that the vast majority of U.S. commercial banks should focus on nonpurchased liquidity management strategies. See "Liability Management and Commercial Banks: Fact or Fiction," *Journal of Financial and Economic Practice*, Spring 2003, pp. 53–66.

[6] Securities companies and institutional investors use the repurchase agreement market extensively for liquidity management purposes.

[7] The discount window is also a source of funds. See the section "Bank Runs, the Discount Window, and Deposit Insurance" in this chapter and Chapter 19 for more discussion of the role of the discount window.

[8] While checking accounts pay no explicit interest, other transaction accounts such as NOW and money market accounts do. However, the rates paid are normally sticky, are slow to adjust to changes in market interest rates, and lie below purchased fund rates (see Chapter 18).

TABLE 17–2
Effect of Net Deposit Drains on the Balance Sheet (in millions of dollars)

Before the Drain				After the Drain			
Assets		Liabilities		Assets		Liabilities	
Assets	100	Deposits	70	Assets	100	Deposits	65
		Borrowed funds	10			Borrowed funds	10
		Other liabilities	20			Other liabilities	20
	100		100		100		95

TABLE 17–3
Adjusting to a Deposit Drain through Liability Management (in millions of dollars)

Assets		Liabilities	
Assets	100	Deposits	65
		Borrowed funds	15
		Other liabilities	20
	100		100

composition of the asset side of its balance sheet—that is, the complete adjustment to the deposit drain occurs on the liability side of the balance sheet. In other words, purchased liquidity management can insulate the asset side of the balance sheet from normal drains on the liability side of the balance sheet. This is one of the reasons for the enormous growth in recent years of FI purchased liquidity management techniques and associated purchased fund markets such as fed funds, repurchase agreements, and wholesale CDs. (We describe and discuss these instruments in more detail in Chapter 18.) Indeed, in the early 2000s regulators expressed concerns about the increased use of these (wholesale) funding sources by DIs. Regulators noted that during the 1990s, as savers put more into investments (instead of DI deposit accounts), DIs were unable to increase deposits as fast as loans (and loan commitments) increased on the asset side of the balance sheet. In the event of a liquidity crunch (for example, because of an economic slowdown), additional (wholesale) funds could be hard to obtain.[9]

Stored Liquidity Management

stored liquidity management
An adjustment to a deposit drain that occurs on the asset side of the balance sheet.

Instead of meeting the net deposit drain by purchasing liquidity in the wholesale money markets, the DI could use **stored liquidity management.** That is, the FI could liquidate some of its assets, utilizing its stored liquidity. Traditionally, U.S. DIs have held stored cash reserves only at the Federal Reserve and in their vaults for this very purpose. The Federal Reserve sets minimum reserve requirements for the cash reserves banks must hold.[10] Even so, DIs still tend to hold cash reserves in excess of the minimum required to meet liquidity drains. As an example, the United Kingdom has no official central bank–designated cash reserve requirements; even so, banks still hold 1 percent or more of their assets in cash reserves.

[9] See "Regulators Press for Safeguards," *Financial Times*, June 4, 2001, p. 24.

[10] Currently, the Fed requires 3 percent on the first $42.1 million and 10 percent on the rest of a DI's demand deposit and transaction account holdings. The $42.1 million figure is adjusted annually along with the growth in bank deposits. The first $6.0 million of the $42.1 million is not subject to reserve requirements (the figures are as of January 2004).

TABLE 17–4
Composition of the
DI's Balance Sheet
(in millions of
dollars)

Assets		Liabilities	
Cash	9	Deposits	70
Other assets	91	Borrowed funds	10
		Other liabilities	20
	100		100

TABLE 17–5
Reserve Asset
Adjustment to
Deposit Drain (in
millions of dollars)

Assets		Liabilities	
Cash	4	Deposits	65
Other assets	91	Borrowed funds	10
		Other liabilities	20
	95		95

Suppose, in our example, that on the asset side of the balance sheet the DI normally holds $9 million of its assets in cash (of which $3 million are to meet Federal Reserve minimum reserve requirements and $6 million are in an "excess" cash reserve). We depict the situation before the net drain in liabilities in Table 17–4. As depositors withdraw $5 million in deposits, the DI can meet this directly by using the excess cash stored in its vaults or held on deposit at other DIs or at the Federal Reserve. If the reduction of $5 million in deposit liabilities is met by a $5 million reduction in cash assets held by the DI, its balance sheet will be as shown in Table 17–5.

When the DI uses its cash as the liquidity adjustment mechanism, both sides of its balance sheet contract. In this example, the DI's total assets and liabilities shrink from $100 to $95 million. The cost to the DI from using stored liquidity, apart from decreased asset size,[11] is that it must hold excess non-interest-bearing assets in the form of cash on its balance sheet.[12] Thus, the cost of using cash to meet liquidity needs is the forgone return (or opportunity cost) of being unable to invest these funds in loans and other higher-income-earning assets.

Finally, note that while stored liquidity management and purchased liquidity management are alternative strategies for meeting deposit drains, a DI can combine the two methods by using some purchased liquidity management and some stored liquidity management to meet liquidity needs.

Asset-Side Liquidity Risk

Just as deposit drains can cause a DI liquidity problems, so can the exercise by borrowers of their loan commitments and other credit lines. In recent years, DIs, especially commercial banks, have increased their loan commitments tremendously, with the belief they would not be used. A recent study by regulators found that banks' unused loan commitments to "on-hand liquidity" (such as deposit accounts and CDs) grew from a ratio of 3.5 in 1994 to 11 in the early 2000s.[13] Thus loan commitments outstanding are dangerously high for banks and other DIs. Table 17–6 shows the effect of a $5 million exercise of a loan commitment by

[11] It should be noted that there is no empirical evidence showing a significant correlation between a DI's asset size and profits.

[12] DIs could hold highly liquid interest-bearing assets such as T-bills, but these are still less liquid than cash and immediate liquidation may result in some small capital value losses.

[13] See "Years of Living Dangerously Set to Haunt Banks," *Financial Times,* June 4, 2001, p. 24.

TABLE 17–6
Effects of a Loan Commitment Exercise (in millions of dollars)

(a) Before				(b) After			
Cash	9	Deposits	70	Cash	9	Deposits	70
Other assets	91	Borrowed funds	10	Other assets	96	Borrowed funds	10
		Other liabilities	20			Other liabilities	20
	100		100		105		100

TABLE 17–7
Adjusting the Balance Sheet to a Loan Commitment Exercise (in millions of dollars)

(a) Purchased Liquidity Management				(b) Stored Liquidity Management			
Cash	9	Deposits	70	Cash	4	Deposits	70
Other assets	96	Borrowed funds	15	Other assets	96	Borrowed funds	10
		Other liabilities	20			Other liabilities	20
	105		105		100		100

TABLE 17–8
Net Liquidity Position (in millions of dollars)

Sources of Liquidity	
1. Total cash-type assets	$ 2,000
2. Maximum borrowed funds limit	12,000
3. Excess cash reserves	500
Total	$14,500
Uses of Liquidity	
1. Funds borrowed	$ 6,000
2. Federal Reserve borrowing	1,000
Total	7,000
Total net liquidity	$ 7,500

a borrower. As a result, the DI must fund $5 million in additional loans on the balance sheet.[14] Consider panel (a) in Table 17–6 (the balance sheet before the commitment exercise) and panel (b) (the balance sheet after the exercise). In particular, the exercise of the loan commitment means that the DI needs to provide $5 million in loans immediately to the borrower (other assets rise from $91 to $96 million). This can be done either by purchased liquidity management (borrowing an additional $5 million in the money market and lending these funds to the borrower) or by stored liquidity management (decreasing the DI's excess cash assets from $9 million to $4 million). We present these two policies in Table 17–7.

Measuring a DI's Liquidity Exposure

Sources and Uses of Liquidity

As discussed above, a DI's liquidity risk can arise from a drain on deposits or from new loan demand, and the subsequent need to meet those demands through liquidating assets or borrowing funds. Therefore, a DI manager must be able to measure its liquidity position on a daily basis, if possible. A useful tool is a *net liquidity statement* that lists sources and uses of liquidity and thus provides a measure of a DI's net liquidity position. Such a statement for a hypothetical U.S. money center bank is presented in Table 17–8.

---

[14] Larger DIs with more extensive commercial loan portfolios tend to be more susceptible to this type of risk than are smaller retail-oriented (or consumer-oriented) DIs.

The DI can obtain liquid funds in three ways. First, it can sell its liquid assets such as T-bills immediately with little price risk and low transaction cost.[15] Second, it can borrow funds in the money/purchased funds market up to a maximum amount (this is an *internal* guideline based on the manager's assessment of the credit limits that the purchased or borrowed funds market is likely to impose on the DI). Third, it can use any excess cash reserves over and above the amount held to meet regulatory imposed reserve requirements.[16] The DI's *sources* of liquidity total $14,500 million. Compare this with the DI's *uses* of liquidity, in particular the amount of borrowed or purchased funds it has already utilized (e.g., fed funds, RPs borrowed) and the amount of cash it has already borrowed from the Federal Reserve through discount window loans. These total $7,000 million. As a result, the DI has a positive net liquidity position of $7,500 million. These liquidity sources and uses can be easily tracked on a day-by-day basis.

The net liquidity position in Table 17–8 lists management's expected sources and uses of liquidity for a hypothetical money center bank. All FIs report their historical sources and uses of liquidity in their annual and quarterly reports. Appendix A to this chapter (located at the book's Web site, www.mhhe.com/saunders5e) presents the 2002 Sources and Uses of Liquidity Statement for Bank of America. As an FI manager deals with liquidity risk, historical sources and uses of liquidity statements can assist the manager in determining where future liquidity issues may arise.

Peer Group Ratio Comparisons

Another way to measure a DI's liquidity exposure is to compare certain key ratios and balance sheet features of the DI—such as its loans to deposits, borrowed funds to total assets, and commitments to lend to assets ratios—with those of DIs of a similar size and geographic location. A high ratio of loans to deposits and borrowed funds to total assets means that the DI relies heavily on the short-term money market rather than on core deposits to fund loans. This could mean future liquidity problems if the DI is at or near its borrowing limits in the purchased funds market. Similarly, a high ratio of loan commitments to assets indicates the need for a high degree of liquidity to fund any unexpected takedowns of these loans—high-commitment DIs often face more liquidity risk exposure than do low-commitment DIs.

Liquidity Index

liquidity index
A measure of the potential losses an FI could suffer as the result of sudden (or fire-sale) disposal of assets.

A third way to measure liquidity risk is to use a **liquidity index.** Developed by Jim Pierce at the Federal Reserve, this index measures the potential losses an FI could suffer from a sudden or fire-sale disposal of assets compared with the amount it would receive at a fair market value established under normal market (sale) conditions—which might take a lengthy period of time as a result of a careful search and bidding process. The greater the differences between immediate fire-sale asset prices (P_i) and fair market prices (P_i^*), the less liquid is the DI's portfolio of assets. Define an index I such that:

$$I = \sum_{i=1}^{N} [(w_i)(P_i/P_i^*)]$$

[15] In recent years, as the loan sales and securitization markets have grown, many banks have added to their sources statement loan assets that can be immediately sold or securitized. Chapters 27 and 28 describe the loan sales and securitization markets.

[16] Some banks add net cash inflows to their sources statement.

where w_i is the percent of each asset in the FI's portfolio:

$$\sum_{i=1}^{N} w_i = 1$$

EXAMPLE 17–1 *Calculation of the Liquidity Index*	Suppose that a DI has two assets: 50 percent in one-month Treasury bills and 50 percent in real estate loans. If the DI must liquidate its T-bills today (P_1), it receives $99 per $100 of face value; if it can wait to liquidate them on maturity (in one month's time), it will receive $100 per $100 of face value ($P_1^*$). If the DI has to liquidate its real estate loans today, it receives $85 per $100 of face value ($P_2$); liquidation at the end of one month (closer to maturity) will produce $92 per $100 of face value ($P_2^*$). Thus, the one-month liquidity index value for this DI's asset portfolio is:

$$I = (^1/_2)\,[(.99/1.00)] + {}^1/_2\,[(.85/.92)]$$
$$= 0.495 + 0.462$$
$$= 0.957$$

Suppose, alternatively, that a slow or thin real estate market caused the DI to be able to liquidate the real estate loans at only $65 per $100 of face value ($P_2$). The one-month liquidity index for the DI's asset portfolio is:

$$I = (^1/_2)(.99/1.00) + (^1/_2)(.65/.92)$$
$$= 0.495 + 0.353$$
$$= 0.848$$

The value of the one-month liquidity index decreases as a result of the larger discount on the fire-sale price—from the fair (full value) market price of real estate—over the one-month period. The larger the discount from fair value, the smaller the liquidity index or higher the liquidity risk the DI faces.

The liquidity index will always lie between 0 and 1. The liquidity index for this DI could also be compared with similar indexes calculated for a peer group of similar DIs.

Financing Gap and the Financing Requirement

A fourth way to measure liquidity risk exposure is to determine the DI's financing gap. As we discussed earlier, even though demand depositors can withdraw their funds immediately, they do not do so in normal circumstances. On average, most demand deposits stay at DIs for quite long periods—often two years or more.[17] Thus, a DI manager often thinks of the average deposit base, including demand deposits, as a core source of funds that over time can fund a DI's average amount of loans.

financing gap
The difference between a DI's average loans and average (core) deposits.

We define a **financing gap** as the difference between a DI's average loans and average (core) deposits, or:

Financing gap = Average loans − Average deposits

If this financing gap is positive, the DI must fund it by using its cash and liquid assets and/or borrowing funds in the money market. Thus:

Financing gap = −Liquid assets + Borrowed funds

[17] See Federal Reserve Board of Governors, "Risk-Based Capital and Interest Rate Risk," press release, July 30, 1992.

TABLE 17–9
Financing
Requirement
of a DI (in millions
of dollars)

Assets		Liabilities	
Loans	$25	Core deposits	$20
Liquid assets	5	Financing requirement (borrowed funds)	10
Total	$30	Total	$30
		Financing gap	5

We can write this relationship as:

Financing gap + Liquid assets = Financing requirement (borrowed funds)

financing requirement
The financing gap plus a DI's liquid assets.

As expressed in this fashion, the liquidity and managerial implications of the **financing requirement** (the financing gap plus a DI's liquid assets) are that the level of core deposits and loans as well as the amount of liquid assets determines the DI's borrowing or purchased fund needs. In particular, the larger a DI's financing gap and liquid asset holdings, the larger the amount of funds it needs to borrow in the money markets and the greater is its exposure to liquidity problems from such a reliance.

The balance sheet in Table 17–9 indicates the relationship between the financing gap, liquid assets, and the borrowed fund financing requirement. See also the following equation:

Financing gap + Liquid assets = Financing requirement

($5 million)   ($5 million)   ($10 million)

A widening financing gap can warn of future liquidity problems for a DI since it may indicate increased deposit withdrawals (core deposits falling below $20 million in Table 17–9) and increasing loans due to increased exercise of loan commitments (loans rising above $25 million). If the DI does not reduce its liquid assets—they stay at $5 million—the manager must resort to more money market borrowings. As these borrowings rise, sophisticated lenders in the money market may be concerned about the DI's creditworthiness. They may react by imposing higher risk premiums on borrowed funds or establishing stricter credit limits by not rolling over funds lent to the DI. If the DI's financing requirements exceed such limits, it may become insolvent. A good example of an excessive financing requirement resulting in bank insolvency was the failure of Continental Illinois in 1984.[18] This possibility of insolvency also highlights the need for DI managers to engage in active liquidity planning to avoid such crises.

---

[18] Continental Illinois Bank, headquartered in Chicago, had a very small core deposit base as a result of restrictions on bank branching within the state. As a result, it had to rely extensively on borrowed funds such as fed funds, RPs, and Eurodollar deposits (wholesale CDs from the offshore Euromarkets). As these borrowings grew, there were increased concerns about the bank's ability to meet its payment commitments—especially in view of a worsening loan portfolio. This resulted in the eventual refusal of a number of large money market lenders (such as Japanese banks) to renew or roll over their borrowed funds held by Continental Illinois on maturity. With the rapid withdrawal of such borrowed funds, Continental Illinois was unable to survive and was eventually taken over by the FDIC. For good detailed descriptions of the Continental Illinois failure, see I. Swary, "Stock Market Reaction to Regulatory Action in the Continental Illinois Crisis," *Journal of Business* 59 (1986), pp. 451–73; and L. Wall and D. R. Peterson, "The Effect of Continental Illinois' Failure on the Performance of Other Banks," *Journal of Monetary Economics*, 1990, pp. 77–99.

TABLE 17–10
Net Funding
Requirement Using
the BIS Maturity
Laddering Model
(in millions of
dollars)

	1 Day	1 Month	6 Months
Cash Inflows			
Maturing assets	$10	$150	$1,500
Salable nonmaturing assets	12	250	4,000
Access to deposit liabilities	15	200	2,000
Established credit lines	12	100	750
Ability to securitize	5	50	400
	$54	$750	$8,650
Cash Outflows			
Liabilities falling due	$30	$490	$4,500
Committed lines of credit that can be drawn on and other contingent liabilities	16	300	2,960
Cash outflows from unanticipated events	4	10	40
	$50	$800	$7,500
Net funding requirement	$ 4	($ 50)	$1,150
Cumulative net funding requirement	$ 4	($ 46)	$1,104

BIS Approach: Maturity Ladder/Scenario Analysis

www.bis.org   In February 2000, recognizing that liquidity is crucial to the ongoing viability of a DI, the Bank for International Settlements (BIS) outlined a Maturity Laddering method for measuring liquidity risk, and specifically, net funding (financing) requirements.[19] At a minimum, liquidity measurement involves assessing all cash inflows against its outflows, as outlined in Table 17–10. Once identified, a maturity ladder model allows a comparison of cash inflows and outflows on a day-to-day basis and/or over a series of specified time periods. Daily and cumulative net funding requirements can then be determined from the maturity ladder.

For the DI in Table 17–10, for example, excess cash of $4 million is available over the one-day time horizon. However, a cumulative net cash shortfall of $46 million is expected to exist over the next month. The DI will need to start planning immediately to obtain additional funding to fill this net funding requirement. Over the six-month period, the DI has cumulative excess cash of $1,104 million. If these expectations hold true, the DI will need to find a place to invest these excess funds until they are needed.

The relevant time frame for active liquidity management is generally quite short, including intraday liquidity. However, the appropriate time frame will depend on the nature of a DI's business. DIs that rely on short-term funding concentrate primarily on managing their liquidity in the very short term (e.g., the BIS recommends a five-day horizon for such DIs). DIs that are less dependent on short-term funding might actively manage their net funding requirements over a slightly longer period. In addition, DIs should analyze and monitor their liquidity positions over the longer term. Typically, a DI may find substantial funding gaps in distant periods and thus need to plan ways to fill these gaps by influencing the maturity of transactions to offset the future funding gap.

While liquidity is typically managed under normal conditions, the BIS cautions that DIs must also be prepared to manage liquidity under abnormal conditions.

---

[19] See "Sound Practices for Managing Liquidity in Banking Organizations," Basel Committee on Banking Supervision, BIS, Basel, Switzerland, February 2000.

FIGURE 17–2   **Cumulative Excess or Shortages of Funds for a High-Quality DI under Various Market Conditions**

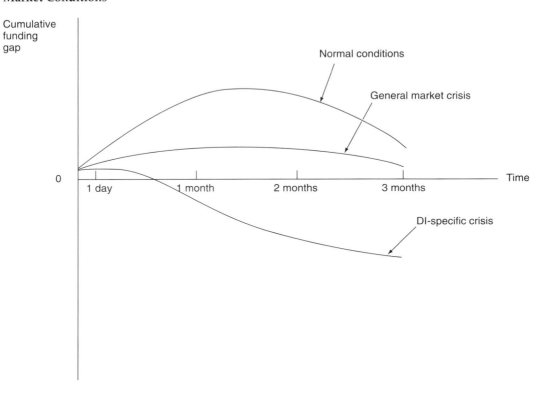

Analyzing liquidity thus entails generating and analyzing various what-if scenarios. Under each scenario, the DI should try to account for any significant positive or negative liquidity swings that could occur. These scenarios should take into account factors both internal (bank specific) and external (market related). Under the BIS Scenario Analysis, a DI needs to assign a timing of cash flows for each type of asset and liability by assessing the probability of the behavior of those cash flows under the scenario being examined. Accordingly, the timing of cash inflows and outflows on the maturity ladder can differ among scenarios, and the assumptions may differ quite sharply. For example, a DI may believe, based on its historical experience, that its ability to control the level and timing of future cash flows from a stock of salable assets in a DI-specific funding crisis would deteriorate little from normal conditions. However, in a market crisis, this capacity may fall off sharply if few institutions are willing or able to make cash purchases of less liquid assets.

The evolution of a DI's liquidity profile under each scenario can be portrayed graphically, as in Figure 17–2. A stylized liquidity graph enables the evolution of the cumulative net excess or shortages of funds to be compared under the major scenarios (e.g., normal conditions, general market crisis conditions, DI-specific crisis conditions). The DI can use this profile to provide additional insights into how consistent and realistic the assumptions are for its liquidity. For example, in Figure 17–2, a high-quality bank may look very liquid under normal circumstances and remain so in a general market crisis, but may suffer a liquidity crisis only in a DI-specific crisis. In contrast, a lower-quality DI might be equally illiquid in a general and a DI-specific crisis. Because a DI's future liquidity position can be affected by factors that cannot always be accurately predicted, it is critical that assumptions used to determine its funding requirements be reviewed and revised frequently.

Liquidity Planning

As implied by the BIS maturity ladder approach, liquidity planning is a key component in measuring (and being able to deal with) liquidity risk and its associated costs. Specifically, liquidity planning allows managers to make important borrowing priority decisions before liquidity problems arise. Such planning can lower the cost of funds (by determining an optimal funding mix) and can minimize the amount of excess reserves that a DI needs to hold.

A liquidity plan has a number of components. The first component is the delineation of managerial details and responsibilities. Responsibilities are assigned to key management personnel should a liquidity crisis occur. The plan identifies those managers responsible for interacting with various regulatory agencies such as the Federal Reserve, the FDIC, and Office of Thrift Supervision (OTS). It also specifies areas of managerial responsibility in disclosing information to the public—including depositors. The second component of a liquidity plan is a detailed list of fund providers who are most likely to withdraw, as well as the pattern of fund withdrawals. For example, in a crisis, financial institutions such as mutual funds and pension funds are more likely than correspondent banks and small business corporations to withdraw funds quickly from banks and thrifts. In turn, correspondent banks and small corporations are more likely than individual depositors to withdraw funds quickly. This makes liquidity exposure sensitive to the effects of future funding composition changes. Further, DIs face particularly heavy seasonal withdrawals of deposits in the quarter before Christmas. The third component of liquidity planning is the identification of the size of potential deposit and fund withdrawals over various time horizons in the future (one week, one month, one quarter, etc.) as well as alternative private market funding sources to meet such withdrawals (e.g., emergency loans from other FIs and the Federal Reserve). The fourth component of the plan sets internal limits on separate subsidiaries' and branches' borrowings as well as bounds for acceptable risk premiums to pay in each market (fed funds, RPs, CDs, etc.). In addition, the plan details a sequencing of assets for disposal in anticipation of various degrees or intensities of deposit/fund withdrawals. Such a plan may evolve from a DI's asset–liability management committee and may be relayed to various key departments of the DI (e.g., the money desk and the treasury department), which play vital day-to-day roles in liability funding.

Consider, for example, Table 17–11. The data are for a DI that holds $250 million in deposits from mutual funds, pension funds, correspondent banks, small businesses, and individuals. The table includes the average and maximum expected withdrawals over the next one-week, one-month, and one-quarter periods. The liquidity plan for the DI outlines how to cover expected deposit withdrawals should they materialize. In this case, the DI will seek to cover expected deposit withdrawals over the next three months, first with new deposits, then with the liquidation of marketable securities in its investment portfolio, then with borrowings from other FIs, and finally, if necessary, with borrowings from the Federal Reserve.

Liquidity Risk, Unexpected Deposit Drains, and Bank Runs

Under normal conditions and with appropriate management planning, neither net deposit withdrawals nor the exercise of loan commitments pose significant

TABLE 17–11
Deposit
Distributions and
Possible
Withdrawals
Involved in a DI's
Liquidity Plan (in
millions of dollars)

Deposits from		$250	
Mutual funds		60	
Pension funds		50	
Correspondent banks		15	
Small businesses		70	
Individuals		55	
Expected Withdrawals	**Average**	**Maximum**	
One week	$40	$105	
One month	55	140	
Three months	75	200	
Sequence of Deposit Withdrawal Funding	**One Week**	**One Month**	**Three Months**
New deposits	$10	$35	$75
Investment portfolio asset liquidation	50	60	75
Borrowings from other FIs	30	35	45
Borrowings from Fed	15	10	5

liquidity problems for DIs because borrowed funds availability or excess cash reserves are adequate to meet anticipated needs. For example, even in December and the summer vacation season, when net deposit withdrawals are high, DIs anticipate these *seasonal* effects by holding larger than normal excess cash reserves or borrowing more than normal on the wholesale money markets.

Major liquidity problems can arise, however, if deposit drains are abnormally *large* and unexpected. Abnormal deposit drains (shocks) may occur for a number of reasons, including:

1. Concerns about a DI's solvency relative to those of other DIs.
2. Failure of a related DI leading to heightened depositor concerns about the solvency of other DIs (the contagion effect).
3. Sudden changes in investor preferences regarding holding nonbank financial assets (such as T-bills or mutual fund shares) relative to deposits.

In such cases, any sudden and unexpected surges in net deposit withdrawals risk triggering a **bank run** that could eventually force a bank into insolvency.[20]

Deposit Drains and Bank Run Liquidity Risk

At the core of bank run liquidity risk is the fundamental and unique nature of the *demand deposit contract*. Specifically, demand deposit contracts are first-come, first-served contracts in the sense that a depositor's place in line determines the amount he or she will be able to withdraw from a DI. In particular, a depositor either gets

bank run
A sudden and unexpected increase in deposit withdrawals from a DI.

---

[20] For more analysis regarding the details of bank runs, see D. W. Diamond and P. H. Dybvig, "Bank Runs, Deposit Insurance, and Liquidity," *Journal of Political Economy* 91 (1983), pp. 401–19; and G. Kaufman, "Bank Contagion: Theory and Evidence," *Journal of Financial Services Research* 8 (1994), pp. 123–50. Most recently, D. R. Skeie shows that with demand deposits payable in money using modern electronic payment systems, panic runs do not occur if there is efficient lending among banks. Aggregate shocks also do not cause bank runs because nominal deposits allow consumption to adjust efficiently with prices. However, Skeie finds that if interbank lending breaks down, bank runs occur as the result of a coordination failure in which banks do not lend to a bank in need, and can lead to price deflation and contagion to other banks' being run. See "Money and Modern Bank Runs," Princeton University Working Paper, January 2004.

Industry Perspectives

PUBLIC'S CONFIDENCE IN BANK SYSTEM TESTED

The weekend run on Bank of New England (BNE) and its subsequent seizure by the government underscore the public's fragile confidence in the banking system. While the large increase in troubled loans announced last Friday apparently prompted large withdrawals, the insolvency of Rhode Island's private deposit insurance fund earlier in the week and large losses reported in the national deposit fund played a role as well. "The psychological atmosphere in New England following the Rhode Island debacle is not good," said William Isaac, head of the Secura Group, a Washington consulting firm. Bert Ely, a financial consultant based in Alexandria, VA, chalked it up to "jitteriness, uncertainty and confusion." "I think we're asking too much of people to worry about how sound their bank is," he said. Ely called the seizure a "terrible comment on the bank regulatory process."

To some extent, the run and seizure were unexpected, even though analysts noted that Bank of New England has been the nation's largest problem bank for the past year. The bank also had recently worked out a deal to swap some of its debt for equity. Yet, analysts said, failure may have been inevitable. "Failure was in the cards," said Gerard Cassidy, a banking analyst with Tucker Anthony, based in Portland, Maine. "And the FDIC played them this weekend." "They were somewhat of an aberration in their lending and the way they ran the institution," said Ely. . . . "They were not representative of the New England banks, and New England is not representative of the rest of the country." After years as the region's most aggressive real estate lender, BNE was particularly hard hit when that market headed south, analysts said. The large increase in troubled loans BNE reported Friday was mainly due to real estate and effectively wiped out its capital. . . .

All of BNE's depositors will be covered by deposit insurance, regardless of the amount. By contrast, the larger depositors at Freedom National Bank in Harlem, formerly the nation's largest minority-owned bank, got only 50 cents for each $1 above $100,000. But some of that money may be recovered after assets are sold, according to regulators.

Source: Karen Padley, *Investor's Daily*, January 8, 1991, p. 1.

---

paid in full or gets nothing.[21] Because demand deposit contracts pay in full only a certain proportion of depositors when a DI's assets are valued at less than its deposits—and because depositors realize this—any line outside a DI encourages other depositors to join the line immediately even if they do not need cash today for normal consumption purposes. Thus, even the DI's core depositors, who do not really need to withdraw deposits for consumption needs, rationally seek to withdraw their funds immediately when they observe a sudden increase in the lines at their DI. The Industry Perspectives box describes events associated with a Bank run in New England.

As a bank run develops, the demand for net deposit withdrawals grows. The DI may initially meet this by decreasing its cash reserves, selling off liquid or readily marketable assets such as T-bills and T-bonds, and seeking to borrow in the money markets. As a bank run increases in intensity, more depositors join the withdrawal line, and a liquidity crisis develops. Specifically, the DI finds it difficult, if not impossible, to borrow on the money markets at virtually any price. Also, it has sold all its liquid assets, cash, and bonds as well as any salable loans (see Chapter 27). The DI is likely to have left only relatively illiquid loans on the

---

[21] We are assuming no deposit insurance exists that guarantees payments of deposits and no discount window borrowing is available to fund a temporary liquidity need for funds. The presence of deposit insurance and the discount window alters the incentives to engage in a bank run, as we describe later in this chapter and in Chapter 19.

asset side of the balance sheet to meet depositor claims for cash. However, these loans can be sold or liquidated only at very large discounts from face value. A DI needing to liquidate long-term assets at fire-sale prices to meet continuing deposit drains faces the strong possibility that the proceeds from such asset sales are insufficient to meet depositors' cash demands. The DI's liquidity problem then turns into a solvency problem; that is, the DI must close its doors.

The incentives for depositors to run first and ask questions later creates a fundamental instability in the banking system in that an otherwise sound DI can be pushed into insolvency and failure by unexpectedly large depositor drains and liquidity demands. This is especially so in periods of contagious runs, or **bank panics,** when depositors lose faith in the banking system as a whole and engage in a run on all DIs by not materially discriminating among them according to their asset qualities.[22]

bank panic
A systemic or contagious run on the deposits of the banking industry as a whole.

Bank Runs, the Discount Window, and Deposit Insurance

Regulators have recognized the inherent instability of the banking system due to the all-or-nothing payoff features of the deposit contract. As a result, regulatory mechanisms are in place to ease DIs' liquidity problems and to deter bank runs and panics. The two major liquidity risk insulation devices are *deposit insurance* and the *discount window.* Because of the serious social welfare effects that a contagious run on DIs could have, government regulators of depository institutions have established guarantee programs offering deposit holders varying degrees of insurance protection to deter runs. Specifically, if a deposit holder believes a claim is totally secure, even if the DI is in trouble, the holder has no incentive to run. The deposit holder's place in line no longer affects his or her ability to obtain the funds. Deposit insurance deters runs as well as contagious runs and panics.

www.federalreserve. gov

In addition to deposit insurance, central banks, such as the Federal Reserve, have traditionally provided a discount window facility to meet DIs' short-term nonpermanent liquidity needs. Three lending programs are offered through the Fed's discount window. Primary credit is available to generally sound depository institutions on a very short-term basis, typically overnight, at a rate above the Federal Open Market Committee's (FOMC) target rate for federal funds. Secondary credit is available to depository institutions that are not eligible for primary credit. It is extended on a very short-term basis, typically overnight, at a rate that is above the primary credit rate. The Federal Reserve's seasonal credit program is designed to assist small depository institutions in managing significant seasonal swings in their loans and deposits. Seasonal credit is available to depository institutions that can demonstrate a clear pattern of recurring intrayearly swings in funding needs. Eligible institutions are usually located in agricultural or tourist areas. We discuss these in detail in Chapter 19. As we describe there, deposit insurance has effectively deterred bank panics since 1933, although the provision of deposit insurance has not been without other costs.

Concept Questions

1. List two benefits and two costs of using (a) purchased liquidity management and (b) stored liquidity management to meet a deposit drain.
2. What are the three major sources of DI liquidity? What are the two major uses?
3. What are the five measures of liquidity risk used by FIs?

---

[22] See Kaufman, "Bank Contagion," for an excellent review of the nature and causes of bank runs and panics. There is strong evidence of contagious bank runs or panics in 1930–32 in the United States. See A. Saunders and B. Wilson, "Informed and Uninformed Depositor Runs and Panics: Evidence from the 1929–33 Period," *Journal of Financial Intermediation* 5 (1996), pp. 409–23.

LIQUIDITY RISK AND LIFE INSURANCE COMPANIES

surrender value
The amount received by an insurance policyholder when cashing in a policy early.

Depository institutions are not the only FIs exposed to liquidity risk or run problems. Like DIs, life insurance companies hold cash reserves and other liquid assets to meet policy cancelations (surrenders) and other working capital needs that arise in the course of writing insurance. The early cancelation of an insurance policy results in the insurer's having to pay the insured the **surrender value** of that policy.[23] In the normal course of business, premium income and returns on an insurer's asset portfolio are sufficient to meet the cash outflows required when policyholders cash in or surrender their policies early. As with DIs, the distribution or pattern of premium income minus policyholder liquidations is normally predicable. When premium income is insufficient to meet surrenders, however, a life insurer can sell some of its relatively liquid assets, such as government bonds. In this case, bonds act as a buffer or reserve asset source of liquidity for the insurer.

Nevertheless, concerns about the solvency of an insurer can result in a run in which new premium income dries up and existing policyholders seek to cancel their policies by cashing them in early. To meet exceptional demands for cash, a life insurer could be forced to liquidate the other assets in its portfolio, such as commercial mortgage loans and other securities, potentially at fire-sale prices.[24] As with DIs, forced asset liquidations can push an insurer into insolvency.[25]

Concept Questions

1. What is likely to be a life insurance company's first source of liquidity when premium income is insufficient?
2. Can a life insurance company be subjected to a run? If so, why?

LIQUIDITY RISK AND PROPERTY–CASUALTY INSURERS

As discussed in Chapter 3, property–casualty (PC) insurers sell policies insuring against certain contingencies impacting either real property or individuals. Unlike those of life insurers, PC contingencies (and policy coverages) are relatively short term, often one to three years. With the help of mortality tables, claims on life insurance policies are generally predictable. PC claims (such as those associated with natural disasters), however, are virtually impossible to predict. As a result, PC insurers'

---

[23] A surrender value is usually some proportion or percent less than 100 percent of the face value of the insurance contract. The surrender value continues to grow as funds invested in the policy earn interest (returns). Earnings to the policyholder are taxed if and when the policy is actually surrendered or cashed in before the policy matures. Some insurance companies have faced run problems resulting from their sale of guaranteed investment contracts (GICs). A GIC, similar to a long-term, fixed-rate bank deposit, is a contract between an investor and an insurance company. As market interest rates rose, many investors withdrew their funds early and reinvested elsewhere in higher-return investments. This created both liquidity and refinancing problems for life insurers that supplied such contracts and eventually led to restrictions on withdrawals.

[24] Life insurers also provide a considerable amount of loan commitments, especially in the commercial property area. As a result, they face asset-side loan commitment liquidity risk in a fashion similar to that of DIs.

[25] State guaranty schemes deter policyholder runs. In general, the level of coverage and the value of the guarantees are less than deposit insurance. We discuss these guaranty schemes in Chapter 19. See also H. L. DeAngelo, L. DeAngelo, and S. Gilson, "The Collapse of First Executive Corporation: Junk Bonds, Adverse Publicity, and the 'Run on the Bank' Phenomenon," *Journal of Financial Economics* 36 (1994), pp. 287–336.

assets tend to be shorter term and more liquid than those of life insurers. PC insurers' contracts and premium-setting intervals are usually relatively short term as well, so problems caused by policy surrenders are less severe. PC insurers' greatest liquidity exposure occurs when policyholders cancel or fail to renew policies with an insurer because of insolvency risk, pricing, or competitive reasons. This may cause an insurer's premium cash inflow, when added to its investment returns, to be insufficient to meet policyholders' claims. Alternatively, large unexpected claims may materialize and exceed the flow of premium income and income returns from assets. Disasters such as Hurricane Andrew in 1991 and the East Coast "blizzard of the century" in 1996 have caused severe liquidity crises and failures among smaller PC insurers.[26]

Concept Questions

1. What is the greatest cause of liquidity exposure faced by property–casualty insurers?
2. Is the liquidity risk of property–casualty insurers in general greater or less than that of life insurers?

MUTUAL FUNDS

closed-end fund
An investment fund that sells a fixed number of shares in the fund to outside investors.

open-end fund
An investment fund that sells an elastic or nonfixed number of shares in the fund to outside investors.

net asset value
The price at which mutual funds shares are sold (or can be redeemed). It equals the total market value of the assets of the fund divided by the number of shares in the funds outstanding.

Mutual funds sell shares as liabilities to investors and invest the proceeds in assets such as bonds and equities. Mutual funds are open-end or closed-end. **Closed-end funds** issue a fixed number of shares as liabilities; unless the issuing fund chooses to repurchase them, the number of outstanding shares does not change. As discussed in Chapter 5, by far the majority of U.S. mutual funds are **open-end funds;** that is, they can issue an unlimited supply of shares to investors. Open-end funds must also stand ready to buy back previously issued shares from investors at the current market price for the fund's shares. Thus, at a given market price, P, the supply of open-end fund shares is perfectly elastic. The price at which an open-end mutual fund stands ready to sell new shares or redeem existing shares is the **net asset value** (NAV) of the fund. NAV is the current or market value of the fund's assets less any accrued liabilities divided by the number of shares in the fund. A mutual fund's willingness to provide instant liquidity to shareholders while it invests funds in equities, bonds, and other long-term instruments could expose it to liquidity problems similar to those banks, thrifts, and life insurance companies face when the number of withdrawals (or mutual fund shares cashed in) rises to abnormally and unexpectedly high levels. Indeed, mutual funds can be subject to dramatic liquidity runs if investors become nervous about the NAV of the mutual funds' assets.[27] However, the fundamental difference in the way mutual fund contracts are valued compared with the valuation of DI deposit and insurance policy contracts mitigates the incentives for mutual fund shareholders to engage in runs. Specifically, if a mutual fund were to be liquidated, its assets would be distributed to fund shareholders on a pro rata basis rather than the first-come, first-served basis employed under deposit and insurance contracts.

---

[26] Also, claims may arise in long-tail lines where a contingency takes place during the policy period but a claim is not lodged until many years later. As mentioned in Chapter 3, one example is the claims regarding damage caused by asbestos contacts.

[27] For example, this happened to the value of assets held by mutual funds specializing in equities of Asian countries such as Indonesia and Thailand as well as Russia during the emerging market crisis of 1997–98.

TABLE 17–12
Run Incentives of
DI Depositors
versus Mutual Fund
Investors

Depository Institution		Mutual Fund	
Assets	**Liabilities**	**Assets**	**Liabilities**
Assets $90	$100 Deposits (100 depositors with $1 deposits)	Assets $90	$100 Shares (100 shareholders with $1 shares)

To illustrate this difference, we can directly compare the incentives for mutual fund investors to engage in a run with those of DI depositors. Table 17–12 shows a simple balance sheet of an open-end mutual fund and a DI. When they perceive that a DI's assets are valued below its liabilities, depositors have an incentive to engage in a run on the DI to be first in line to withdraw. In the example in Table 17–12, only the first 90 bank depositors would receive $1 back for each $1 deposited. The last 10 would receive nothing at all.

Now consider the mutual fund with 100 shareholders who invested $1 each for a total of $100, but whose assets are worth $90. If these shareholders tried to cash in their shares, *none* would receive $1. Instead, a mutual fund values its balance sheet liabilities on a market value basis; the price of any share liquidated by an investor is:

$$P = \frac{\text{Value of assets}}{\text{Shares outstanding}} = \text{NAV (net asset value)}$$

Thus, unlike deposit contracts that have fixed face values of $1, the value of a mutual fund's shares reflects the changing value of its assets divided by the number of shares outstanding.

In Table 17–12, the value of each shareholder's claim is:

$$P = \frac{\$90}{100} = \$.9$$

That is, each mutual fund shareholder participates in the fund's loss of asset value on a *pro rata,* or proportional, basis. Technically, whether first or last in line, each mutual fund shareholder who cashes in shares on any given day receives the same net asset value per share of the mutual fund. In this case, it is 90 cents, representing a loss of 10 cents per share. All mutual fund shareholders realize this and know that investors share asset losses on a pro rata basis; being the first in line to withdraw has no overall advantage as it has at DIs.

This is not to say that mutual funds bear no liquidity risk, but that the incentives for mutual fund shareholders to engage in runs that produce the extreme form of liquidity problems faced by DIs and life insurance companies are generally absent.[28] This situation has led some academics to argue for deposit contracts to be

---

[28] A sudden surge of mutual fund shareholder redemptions might require a mutual fund manager to sell some of its less marketable bonds and equities at fire-sale prices. For example, in 1994, Piper Jafray—a funds adviser—injected $10 million of its own funds to defray a liquidity problem at the Institutional Government Income mutual fund. Relatedly, a number of hedge funds, such as Long-Term Capital Management, faced severe liquidity problems when trying to unwind large positions in many asset markets at the end of 1998. For example, some mortgage-backed securities markets (see Chapter 28) were insufficiently deep to be able to absorb the massive sale of hedge fund assets without major price dislocations.

restructured in a form more similar to mutual fund or equity contracts. This might also obviate the need for deposit insurance to deter bank runs.[29]

Concept Questions

1. What would be the impact on their liquidity needs if DIs offered deposit contracts of an open-end mutual fund type rather than the traditional all-or-nothing demand deposit contract?

2. How do the incentives of mutual fund investors to engage in runs compare with the incentives of DI depositors?

Summary

Liquidity risk, as a result of heavier-than-anticipated liability withdrawals or loan commitment exercise, is a common problem faced by FI managers. Well-developed policies for holding liquid assets or having access to markets for purchased funds are normally adequate to meet liability withdrawals. However, very large withdrawals can cause asset liquidity problems that can be compounded by incentives for liability claim holders to engage in runs at the first sign of a liquidity problem. These incentives for depositors and life insurance policyholders to engage in runs can push normally sound FIs into insolvency. Mutual funds are able to avoid runs because liabilities are marked to market so that losses are shared equally among liability holders. Since such insolvencies have costs to society as well as to private shareholders, regulators have developed mechanisms such as deposit insurance and the discount window to alleviate liquidity problems. We discuss these mechanisms in detail in Chapter 19.

Questions and Problems

1. How does the degree of liquidity risk differ for different types of financial institutions?

2. What are the two reasons liquidity risk arises? How does liquidity risk arising from the liability side of the balance sheet differ from liquidity risk arising from the asset side of the balance sheet? What is meant by fire-sale prices?

3. What are core deposits? What role do core deposits play in predicting the probability distribution of net deposit drains?

4. The probability distribution of the net deposit drain of a DI has been estimated to have a mean of 2 percent and a standard deviation of 1 percent. Is this DI increasing or decreasing in size? Explain.

5. How is a DI's distribution pattern of net deposit drains affected by the following?
   a. The holiday season.
   b. Summer vacations.

---

[29] See C. S. Jacklin, "Demand Deposits, Trading Restrictions, and Risk Sharing," in *Contractual Arrangements for Intertemporal Trade*, ed. E. Prescott and N. Wallace (Duluth: University of Minnesota, 1987). A common argument against this is that since deposits are money and money is the unit of account in the economy, equity-type contracts could pose a problem if the value of a deposit were to fluctuate from day to day. However, note that money market mutual funds offer depositlike contracts as well. As their NAV varies, they solve the fluctuating share value problem by setting the value of each share at $1 but allowing the number of shares an individual holds to fluctuate so that the value of the individual's overall holdings moves in line with asset values, while the price of each money market mutual fund share remains at $1. A similar policy could be adopted for deposits at DIs.

    c. A severe economic recession.

    d. Double-digit inflation.

6. What are two ways a DI can offset the liquidity effects of a net deposit drain of funds? How do the two methods differ? What are the operational benefits and costs of each method?

7. What are two ways a DI can offset the effects of asset-side liquidity risk such as the drawing down of a loan commitment?

8. A DI with the following balance sheet (in millions) expects a net deposit drain of $15 million.

Assets		Liabilities and Equity	
Cash	$10	Deposits	$68
Loans	50	Equity	7
Securities	15		
Total assets	$75	Total liabilities and equity	$75

Show the DI's balance sheet if the following conditions occur:

    a. The DI purchases liabilities to offset this expected drain.

    b. The stored liquidity management method is used to meet the expected drain.

9. AllStarBank has the following balance sheet (in millions):

Assets		Liabilities and Equity	
Cash	$ 30	Deposits	$110
Loans	90	Borrowed funds	40
Securities	50	Equity	20
Total assets	$170	Total liabilities and equity	$170

AllStarBank's largest customer decides to exercise a $15 million loan commitment. How will the new balance sheet appear if AllStar uses the following liquidity risk strategies?

    a. Asset management.

    b. Liability management.

10. A DI has assets of $10 million consisting of $1 million in cash and $9 million in loans. The DI has core deposits of $6 million, subordinated debt of $2 million, and equity of $2 million. Increases in interest rates are expected to cause a net drain of $2 million in core deposits over the year.

    a. The average cost of deposits is 6 percent, and the average yield on loans is 8 percent. The DI decides to reduce its loan portfolio to offset this expected decline in deposits. What will be the effect on net interest income and the size of the DI after the implementation of this strategy?

    b. If the interest cost of issuing new short-term debt is expected to be 7.5 percent, what would be the effect on net interest income of offsetting the expected deposit drain with an increase in interest-bearing liabilities?

    c. What will be the size of the DI after the drain if the DI uses this strategy?

    d. What dynamic aspects of DI management would further support a strategy of replacing the deposit drain with interest-bearing liabilities?

11. Define each of the following four measures of liquidity risk. Explain how each measure would be implemented and utilized by a DI.

    a. Sources and uses of liquidity.

    b. Peer group ratio comparisons.

    c. Liquidity index.

    d. Financing gap and financing requirement.

12. A DI has $10 million in T-bills, a $5 million line of credit to borrow in the repo market, and $5 million in excess cash reserves (above reserve requirements) with the Fed. The DI currently has borrowed $6 million in fed funds and $2 million from the fed discount window to meet seasonal demands.

    a. What is the DI's total available (sources of) liquidity?

    b. What is the DI's current total uses of liquidity?

    c. What is the net liquidity of the DI?

    d. What conclusions can you derive from the result?

13. A DI has the following assets in its portfolio: $20 million in cash reserves with the Fed, $20 million in T-bills, $50 million in mortgage loans, and $10 million in fixed assets. If the assets need to be liquidated at short notice, the DI will receive only 99 percent of the fair market value of the T-bills and 90 percent of the fair market value of the mortgage loans. Estimate the liquidity index using the above information.

14. Conglomerate Corporation has acquired Acme Corporation. To help finance the takeover, Conglomerate will liquidate the overfunded portion of Acme's pension fund. The face values and current and one-year future liquidation values of the assets that will be liquidated are given below.

Liquidation Values

Asset	Face Value	$t = 0$	$t = 1$
IBM stock	$10,000	$9,900	$10,500
GE bonds	5,000	4,000	4,500
Treasury securities	15,000	13,000	14,000

Calculate the one-year liquidity index for these securities.

15. Plainbank has $10 million in cash and equivalents, $30 million in loans, and $15 million in core deposits.

    a. Calculate the financing gap.

    b. What is the financing requirement?

    c. How can the financing gap be used in the day-to-day liquidity management of the bank?

16. How can an FI's liquidity plan help reduce the effects of liquidity shortages? What are the components of a liquidity plan?

17. What is a bank run? What are some possible withdrawal shocks that could initiate a bank run? What feature of the demand deposit contract provides deposit withdrawal momentum that can result in a bank run?

18. The following is the balance sheet of a DI (in millions):

Assets		Liabilities and Equity	
Cash	$ 2	Demand deposits	$50
Loans	50		
Plant and equipment	3	Equity	5
Total	$55	Total	$55

The asset–liability management committee has estimated that the loans, whose average interest rate is 6 percent and whose average life is three years, will have to be discounted at 10 percent if they are to be sold in less than two days. If they can be sold in four days, they will have to be discounted at 8 percent. If they can be sold later than a week, the DI will receive the full market value. Loans are not amortized; that is, the principal is paid at maturity.

a. What will be the price received by the DI for the loans if they have to be sold in two days? In four days?

b. In a crisis, if depositors all demand payment on the first day, what amount will they receive? What will they receive if they demand to be paid within the week? Assume no deposit insurance.

19. What government safeguards are in place to reduce liquidity risk for DIs?

20. What are the levels of defense against liquidity risk for a life insurance company? How does liquidity risk for a property–casualty insurer differ from that for a life insurance company?

21. How is the liquidity problem faced by mutual funds different from that faced by DIs and insurance companies? How does the liquidity risk of an open-end mutual fund compare with that of a closed-end fund?

22. A mutual fund has the following assets in its portfolio: $40 million in fixed-income securities and $40 million in stocks at current market values. In the event of a liquidity crisis, the fund can sell the assets at 96 percent of market value if they are disposed of in two days. The fund will receive 98 percent if the assets are disposed of in four days. Two shareholders, A and B, own 5 percent and 7 percent of equity (shares), respectively.

a. Market uncertainty has caused shareholders to sell their shares back to the fund. What will the two shareholders receive if the mutual fund must sell all the assets in two days? In four days?

b. How does this situation differ from a bank run? How have bank regulators mitigated the problem of bank runs?

23. A mutual fund has $1 million in cash and $9 million invested in securities. It currently has 1 million shares outstanding.

a. What is the net asset value (NAV) of this fund?

b. Assume that some of the shareholders decide to cash in their shares of the fund. How many shares at its current NAV can the fund take back without resorting to a sale of assets?

c. As a result of anticipated heavy withdrawals, the fund sells 10,000 shares of IBM stocks currently valued at $40. Unfortunately, it receives only $35 per share. What is the net asset value after the sale? What are the cash assets of the fund after the sale?

d. Assume that after the sale of IBM shares, 100,000 shares are sold back to the fund. What is the current NAV? Is there a need to sell more securities to meet this redemption?

Web Question

24. Go to the Federal Reserve Board's Web site (**www.federalreserve.gov**) and Click on "Economic Research and Data." Click on "Statistics: Releases and Historical Data." Click on "Assets and Liabilities of Commercial Banks in the United States. "Releases." Click on the most recent date. Using information in this file update Table 17–1. How have the assets and liabilities of U.S. banks increased since December 2003?

S&P Question

STANDARD
&POOR'S

25. Go to Standard & Poor's Market Insight Web site (**www.mhhe.com/edumarketinsight**) and Click on "Educational Version of Market Insight." Enter your Site ID and click on "Login." Click on "Company." Find the most recent balance sheets for Mellon Financial Corp. (MEL), Wachovia Corp. (WB), and Suntrust Banks Inc. (STI). Enter "MEL" in the "Ticker:" box and click on "Go!" Click on "FS Ann. Balance Sheet." This will download the Balance Sheet for Mellon Financial. From these balance sheets, calculate the following liquidity ratios: loans to deposits and borrowed funds to total assets using the balances for Total Loans, Total Deposits, Total Borrowed Funds, and Total Assets. Repeat the process by entering "WB" in the "Ticker:" box to get information on Wachovia Corp. Repeat the process by entering "STI" in the "Ticker:" box to get information on Suntrust Banks. How do these ratios differ for the three banks?

Pertinent Web Sites

Bank for International Settlements	**www.bis.org**
Board of Governors of the Federal Reserve	**www.federalreserve.gov**

Chapter Notation

View Chapter Notation at the Web site to the textbook (**www.mhhe.com/ saunders5e**).

Appendix 17A

Sources and Uses of Funds Statements, Bank of America December 2002

View Appendix 17A at the Web site for this textbook (**www.mhhe.com/saunders5e**).

Part **Three**

Managing Risk

Chapter **Eighteen**

Liability and Liquidity Management

INTRODUCTION

Depository institutions as well as life insurance companies are especially exposed to liquidity risk (see Chapter 17). The essential feature of this risk is that an FI's assets are relatively illiquid when liquid claims are suddenly withdrawn (or not renewed). The classic case is a bank run in which depositors demand cash as they withdraw their claims from a bank and the bank is unable to meet those demands because of the relatively illiquid nature of its assets. For example, the bank could have a large portfolio of nonmarketable small business or real estate loans.

To reduce the risk of a liquidity crisis, FIs can insulate their balance sheets from liquidity risk by efficiently managing their liquid asset positions or managing the liability structure of their portfolios. In reality, an FI manager can optimize over both liquid asset and liability structures to insulate the FI against liquidity risk. This chapter discusses the various liquid assets and liabilities an FI might use and the risk-return trade-off across these assets. In addition to ensuring that FIs can meet expected and unexpected liability withdrawals, two additional motives exist for holding liquid assets: monetary policy implementation and taxation reasons. The chapter concludes with a look at specific issues associated with liability and liquidity risk management in depository institutions, insurance companies, and other FIs.

LIQUID ASSET MANAGEMENT

A liquid asset can be turned into cash quickly and at a low transaction cost with little or no loss in principal value (see the discussion in Chapter 17 on the liquidity index). Specifically, a liquid asset is traded in an active market so that even large transactions in that asset do not move the market price or move it very little. Good examples of liquid assets are newly issued T-bills, T-notes, and T-bonds. The ultimate liquid asset is, of course, cash. While it is obvious that an FI's liquidity risk can be reduced by holding large amounts of assets such as cash, T-bills, and T-bonds, FIs usually face a return or interest earnings penalty from doing this. Because of their high liquidity and low default risks, such assets often bear low returns that reflect their essentially risk-free nature. By contrast, nonliquid assets often must promise additional returns or liquidity risk premiums to compensate

Handwritten margin notes:

Small amts of liquid assets
Enhance Liquidity Risk

not Enough Liquidity
Illiquidity
creates insolvency

Requirements
① Liquidity Exposure of FI
② Monetary policy implementation
③ Taxation

DI's
Increasing
credit in
the Economy

Multiplier
Affect

decrease
in money Supply

an FI for the relative lack of marketability and often greater default risk of the instrument.

Holding relatively small amounts of liquid assets exposes an FI to enhanced illiquidity and risk of a bank run. Excessive illiquidity can result in an FI's inability to meet required payments on liability claims and, at the extreme, in insolvency. It can even lead to contagious effects that negatively impact other FIs (see Chapter 17). Consequently, regulators have often imposed minimum liquid asset reserve requirements on FIs. In general, these requirements differ in nature and scope for various FIs and even according to country. The requirements depend on the liquidity risk exposure perceived for the FI's type and other regulatory objectives that relate to minimum liquid asset requirements. Further, regulators often set minimum liquid asset requirements for at least two other reasons than simply ensuring that FIs can meet expected and unexpected liability withdrawals. The other two reasons are monetary policy implementation and taxation. We discuss these two reasons next.

Monetary Policy Implementation Reasons

Many countries set minimum liquid asset reserve requirements to strengthen their monetary policy. Specifically, setting a minimum ratio of liquid reserve assets to deposits limits the ability of depository institutions (DIs) to expand lending and enhances the central bank's ability to control the money supply.[1]

A decrease in the reserve requirement ratio means that depository institutions may hold fewer reserves (vault cash plus reserve deposits at the Fed) against their transaction accounts (deposits). Consequently, they are able to lend out a greater percentage of their deposits, thus increasing credit availability in the economy. As new loans are issued and used to finance consumption and investment expenditures, some of these funds will return to depository institutions as new deposits by those receiving them, in return for supplying consumer and investment goods to bank borrowers. In turn, after deducting the appropriate reserve requirement, these new deposits can be used by DIs to create additional loans, and so on. This process continues until the DIs' deposits have grown sufficiently large that the DI willingly holds its *current* reserve balance at the new lower reserve ratio. Thus, a decrease in the reserve requirement results in a multiplier effect on the supply of DI deposits and thus the money supply.

Conversely, an increase in the reserve requirement ratio means that depository institutions must hold more reserves against the transaction accounts (deposits) on their balance sheets. Consequently, they are only able to lend out a smaller percentage of their deposits than before, thus decreasing credit availability and lending, and eventually, leading to a multiple contraction in deposits and a decrease in the money supply. In this context, requiring depository institutions to hold minimum ratios of liquid assets to deposits allows the central bank to gain greater control over deposit growth and thus over the money supply (of which bank deposits are a significant portion) as part of its overall macrocontrol objectives. Appendix 18A to the Chapter (located at the book's Web site, **www.mhhe.com/saunders5e**) describes the accounting treatment of the reserve ratio regime imposed by the U.S. Federal Reserve.

---

[1] For example, in the United States the Federal Reserve system is divided into 12 districts that are the "operating arms" of the central banking system. Each of the 12 regional banks deals specifically with the liquidity issues in its section of the country.

Taxation Reasons

reserve requirement "tax"
The cost of holding reserves that pay no interest at the central bank. This cost is increased further if inflation erodes the purchasing power value of these reserve balances.

Another reason for minimum requirements on DI liquid asset holdings is to force DIs to invest in government financial claims rather than private sector financial claims. That is, a minimum required liquid asset reserve requirement is an indirect way for governments to raise additional "taxes" from DIs. While these reserves are not official government taxes, having DIs hold cash in the vault or cash reserves at the central bank (when there is no interest rate compensation paid)[2] requires DIs to transfer a resource to the central bank.[3] In fact, the profitability of many central banks is contingent on the size of the **reserve requirement "tax,"** which can be viewed as the equivalent of a levy on DIs under their jurisdiction. The tax or cost effect of non-interest-bearing reserve requirements is increased if inflation erodes the purchasing power value of those balances.

Concept Questions

1. Why do regulators set minimum liquid asset requirements for FIs?
2. Can we view reserve requirements as a tax when the consumer price index (CPI) is falling?

THE COMPOSITION OF THE LIQUID ASSET PORTFOLIO

liquid assets ratio
A minimum ratio of liquid assets to total assets set by the central bank.

secondary or buffer reserves
Nonreserve assets that can be quickly turned into cash.

The composition of an FI's liquid asset portfolio, especially among cash and government securities, is determined partly by earnings considerations and partly by the type of minimum liquid asset reserve requirements the central bank imposes. In many countries, such as the United Kingdom, reserve ratios have historically been imposed to encompass both cash and liquid government securities such as T-bills.[4] Thus, a 20 percent **liquid assets ratio** requires a DI to hold $1 of cash plus government securities for every $5 of deposits. Many states in the United States impose liquid asset ratios on life insurance companies that require minimum cash and government securities holdings in their balance sheets. By contrast, the minimum liquid asset requirements on DIs in the United States have been cash based and have excluded government securities. As a result, government securities are less useful because they are not counted as part of reserves held by DIs and at the same time yield lower promised returns than loans. Nevertheless, many DIs view government securities holdings as performing a useful **secondary** or **buffer reserve** function. In times of a liquidity crisis, when significant drains on cash

---

[2] Regulators are currently considering legislation that would allow DIs to earn a low rate of interest on these reserve balances.

[3] To lower the cost of the reserve requirement tax, Banc Investment Group, the broker-dealer unit of Pacific Coast Bankers' Bancshares (PCBB), recently announced an innovative ATM funding program to help independent banks generate fee-based income from excess liquidity on their balance sheets. Known as ATM Cash Advantage, the program enables independent banks to advance up to $400 million in currency to more than 17,000 nonbank ATMs throughout the United States, such as those at convenience stores, airports, and casinos. In return, independent banks can generate fee income equal to the federal funds rate, plus a substantial spread. In addition to fee income, participating independent banks may also be able to reduce their own vault cash balances under Regulation D (see below), pending a review from the Federal Reserve. Such a reduction would lower the size of the reserve requirement "tax" paid to the Federal Reserve. See "Program Gives Banks Fees for Supplying ATM Cash," *The American Banker*, September 22, 2003, p. 7. In addition, a number of banks offer "sweep" programs in which funds are automatically transferred out of reserve-bearing demand deposits into non-reserve-bearing mutual funds at the end of each day. Such programs reduce bank deposits and thus bank reserve requirements and the need for vault cash.

[4] The United Kingdom no longer imposes minimum reserve requirements on banks.

reserves occur, these securities can be turned into cash quickly and with very little loss of principal value because of the deep nature of the markets in which these assets are traded.

Concept Question

1. In general, would it be better to hold three-month T-bills or 10-year T-notes as buffer assets? Explain.

RETURN-RISK TRADE-OFF FOR LIQUID ASSETS

Constrained optimization

In optimizing its holdings of liquid assets, an FI must trade the benefit of cash immediacy for lower returns. In addition, the FI manager's choice is one of *constrained optimization* in the sense that liquid asset reserve requirements imposed by regulators set a minimum bound on the level to which liquid reserve assets can fall on the balance sheet. Thus, an FI facing little risk of liquidity withdrawals and holding only a small amount of liquid assets for prudential reasons finds that it is forced to hold more than is privately optimal as a result of minimum reserve restrictions imposed by regulators.

The Liquid Asset Reserve Management Problem for U.S. Depository Institutions

This section examines the risk-return trade-off in running a liquid asset position and the constraints imposed on this position. We present a detailed example of U.S. DIs liquidity management under the current minimum reserve requirements imposed by the Federal Reserve. However, many of the issues and trade-offs are readily generalizable to any FI facing liability withdrawal risk under conditions in which regulators impose minimum liquid asset reserve ratios.

The issues involved in the optimal management of a liquid asset portfolio are illustrated by the problems faced by the money desk manager in charge of a U.S. DI's reserve position. In the context of U.S. DI regulation, we concentrate on a DI's management of its **cash reserves,** defined as vault cash (currency and coin used to meet depositor withdrawals) and cash deposits held by the DI at the Federal Reserve.[5] As of January 2004, in accordance with Regulation D of the Securities Act of 1933, depository institutions in the United States are required to hold the following "target" minimum cash reserves against net transaction accounts:[6]

cash reserves
Vault cash and cash deposits held at the Federal Reserve.

www.federalreserve. gov

< $6.0 million	0%
$6.0 million−$42.1 million	3
> $42.1 million	10

transaction accounts
Deposits that permit the account holder to make multiple withdrawals.

Transaction accounts include all deposits on which an account holder may make withdrawals by negotiable or transferable instruments and may make more than

---

[5] However, DIs that are not members of the Federal Reserve System—mostly very small banks and savings institutions—may maintain reserve balances with a Federal Reserve Bank indirectly (on a pass-through basis) with certain approved institutions, such as correspondent banks.

[6] The Garn–St. Germain Depository Institutions Act of 1982 (Public Law 97–320) requires that $2 million of reservable liabilities of each depository institution be subject to a 0 percent reserve requirement. Each year the Federal Reserve adjusts the amount subject to this 0 percent reserve requirement for the succeeding calendar year by 80 percent of the percentage increase in the total reservable liabilities of all depository institutions, measured on an annual basis as of June 30. In 2004 this figure was $6.0 million. The reserve was also reduced from 12 to 10 percent for transaction accounts in April 1992.

three monthly telephone or preauthorized fund transfers for the purpose of making payments to third parties (i.e., demand deposits, NOW accounts, and share draft accounts—offered by credit unions).[7] Transaction account balances are reduced by demand balances due from U.S. depository institutions and cash items in process of collection.

To calculate the target amount of reserves and to determine whether the DI is holding too many or too few reserves, the DI reserve manager requires two additional pieces of information to manage the position. First, over what period's deposits does the manager compute the DI's reserve requirement? Second, for which period or periods must the DI maintain the target reserve requirement just computed?

The U.S. system is complicated by the fact that the period for which the DI manager computes the required reserve target differs from the period during which the reserve target is maintained or achieved. We describe the computation and maintenance periods for DI reserves next.

reserve computation period
Period over which required reserves are calculated.

Computation Period

For the purpose of reserve management, a U.S. DI reserve manager must think of time as being divided into two-week periods. The **reserve computation period** always begins on a Tuesday and ends on a Monday 14 days later.

EXAMPLE 18–1
Computation of Daily Average Required Reserves

Consider ABC bank's reserve manager, who wants to assess the bank's minimum cash reserve requirement target. The manager knows the bank's net transaction accounts balance at the close of the banking day on each of the 14 days over the period Tuesday, June 30, to Monday, July 13. Of course, in reality, the manager knows these deposit positions with certainty only at the very end of the two-week period. Consider the realized net transaction account positions of ABC bank in Table 18–1.

The minimum daily average reserves that a bank must maintain are computed as a percentage of the daily average net transaction accounts held by the bank over the two-week reserve computation period, where Friday's balances are carried over for Saturday and Sunday. The minimum daily average for ABC Bank to hold against the daily average of $1,350.70 million in its net transaction accounts is calculated as follows (amounts in millions):

Daily average net transaction accounts × Reserve percentage = Daily average reserves required

$6.0	0%	$ 0.000
$42.1–$6.0	3	1.083
$1,350.7–$42.1	10	130.860
Minimum average reserves to be held		$131.943

Note that the daily average target in Example 18.1 is calculated by taking the 14-day average of net transaction accounts, even though the DI is closed for 4 of the 14 days (two Saturdays and two Sundays). Effectively, Friday's deposit figures count three times compared with those of other days in the business week. This means that a DI manager who can engage in a strategy whereby deposits are lower on Fridays can, on average, lower the DI's reserve requirements. This may be important if required liquid asset reserve holdings are above the optimal level from

---

[7] Historically, U.S. DIs also had to hold reserves against time deposits and personal savings deposits (including MMDAs). However, this was reduced from 3 to 0 percent at the beginning of 1991.

TABLE 18–1 Net Transaction Accounts and Vault Cash Balances of ABC Bank (in millions of dollars)

	Transaction Accounts	Less Demand Balances Due from U.S. Depository Institutions	Less Cash Items in Process of Collection	Net Transaction Accounts	Vault Cash
Tuesday, June 30	$ 1,850	$ 240	$ 140	$ 1,470	$ 30
Wednesday, July 1	1,820	235	135	1,450	28
Thursday, July 2	1,770	250	120	1,400	24
Friday, July 3	1,610	260	100	1,250	21
Saturday, July 4	1,610	260	100	1,250	21
Sunday, July 5	1,610	260	100	1,250	21
Monday, July 6	1,655	250	125	1,280	24
Tuesday, July 7	1,650	230	130	1,290	26
Wednesday, July 8	1,690	240	130	1,320	25
Thursday, July 9	1,770	275	135	1,360	25
Friday, July 10	1,820	280	140	1,400	27
Saturday, July 11	1,820	280	140	1,400	27
Sunday, July 12	1,820	280	140	1,400	27
Monday, July 13	1,785	260	135	1,390	29
Total	$24,280	$3,600	$1,770	$18,910	$355
Daily average net transaction accounts				$ 1,350.7	$ 25.357

the DI's perspective to handle liquidity drains due to expected and unexpected deposit withdrawals.

One strategy employed in the past was for a DI to send deposits out of the country (i.e., transfer them to a foreign subsidiary) on a Friday, when a reduction in deposits effectively counts for $3/14$ths of the two-week period, and to bring them back on the following Monday, when an increase counts for just $1/14$th of the two-week period. This action effectively reduced the average demand deposits in the balance sheet of the DI over the 14-day period by $2/14$ths times the amount sent out of the country and thus, reduced the amount of reserves it needed to hold. Analysts term this the **weekend game**.[8]

weekend game
Lowering deposit balances on Fridays since that day's figures count three times for reserve accounting purposes.

A second strategy is for the DI to offer its customers "sweep accounts," in which high reserve ratio demand deposits are "swept" out of customers' accounts on Friday into higher-interest-bearing savings accounts. On Monday (or in many cases when the depositor needs funds in his or her checking account) these funds are swept back. The effective result is lower average balances in a DI's demand deposit accounts and thus lower required reserve holdings at the Federal Reserve.

Note that the $131.943 million figure is a minimum reserve target. The DI manager may hold excess cash reserves above this minimum level if the privately optimal or prudential level for the DI exceeds the regulatory specified minimum level because this DI is especially exposed to deposit withdrawal risk. In addition, the DI manager may hold some buffer reserves in the form of government securities that can be turned into cash quickly if deposit withdrawals are unusually high or to preempt the early stages of a bank run.

[8] In fact, the weekend game is a special case of bank window dressing in which transactions are undertaken to reduce reported deposits below their true or actual figures. For a discussion of window dressing in banking and the incentives for bankers to window-dress, see L. Allen and A. Saunders, "Bank Window Dressing: Theory and Evidence," *Journal of Banking and Finance* 16 (1992), pp. 585–624.

Maintenance Period

We have computed a daily average minimum cash reserve requirement for ABC bank but have yet to delineate the exact period over which the bank manager has to maintain this $131.943 million daily average reserve target. Reserves may be held either as vault cash or as deposits held (by the bank) at the Federal Reserve. Under the current set of regulations, the average daily vault cash held during the reserve computation period (June 30 through July 13 in our example) is deducted from the institution's required reserves to determine the reserve balance to be maintained at the Federal Reserve. In addition, a lag of 30 days exists between the beginning of the reserve computation period and the beginning of the **reserve maintenance period** (over which deposits at the Federal Reserve Bank must meet or exceed the required reserve target). For ABC Bank, this reserve maintenance period is from July 30 through August 12 (see Figure 18–1). Thus, the bank's reserve manager knows the value of the target reserves with perfect certainty throughout the reserve maintenance period. However, the manager still has a challenge in maintaining sufficient deposits on reserve at the Fed to hit the reserve target without holding too large an excess reserve balance (since this bears a zero interest return).

reserve maintenance period
Period over which actual reserves have to meet or exceed the required reserve target.

The reserve manager knows the vault cash component of the reserve target, since this is based on the average vault cash held by the bank over the reserve computation period, as reported in Table 18–1. The daily balances in deposits at the Federal Reserve for ABC Bank for the 14-day reserve maintenance period from July 30 through August 12 are shown in Table 18–2. Since the average daily balance in vault cash is shown (in Table 18–1) at $25.357 million, the average daily target balance for deposits at the Federal Reserve is $106.586 million (i.e., $25.357 million + $106.586 million = $131.943 million). Essentially, since the vault cash component of the reserve target is based on vault cash held over the reserve computation 14-day period, the bank's active target during the maintenance period itself is its reserve position at the Fed (in this case, it seeks to hold an average deposit of $106.586 million per day at the Fed over the 14-day maintenance period).

As discussed above, currently, the reserve maintenance period for meeting the reserve target begins 30 days after the start of the reserve computation period.

FIGURE 18–1
Lagged Reserve Requirements

Reserve Computation Period

Begins													Ends

June 30	July 1	2	3	4	5	6	7	8	9	10	11	12	13

Reserve Maintenance Period

Begins													Ends

July 30	31	Aug 1	2	3	4	5	6	7	8	9	10	11	12

TABLE 18–2
ABC Bank's Daily Reserve Position over the July 30–August 12 Reserve Maintenance Period (in millions of dollars)

Date	Deposits at the Federal Reserve
Thursday, July 30	$ 98.050
Friday, July 31	100.000
Saturday, August 1	100.000
Sunday, August 2	100.000
Monday, August 3	98.004
Tuesday, August 4	91.000
Wednesday, August 5	102.050
Thursday, August 6	101.000
Friday, August 7	99.000
Saturday, August 8	99.000
Sunday, August 9	99.000
Monday, August 10	107.050
Tuesday, August 11	154.000
Wednesday, August 12	144.050
Total	$1,492.204
Daily average	106.586

lagged reserve accounting system
An accounting system in which the reserve computation and reserve maintenance periods do not overlap.

contemporaneous reserve accounting system
An accounting system in which the reserve computation and reserve maintenance periods overlap.

Given that the computation period is two weeks, the reserve maintenance period does not begin until 17 days after the *end* of the computation period. Regulators introduced this **lagged reserve accounting system** to make it easier for bank reserve managers to calculate their required reserve balances and to increase the accuracy of information on aggregate required reserve balances. Prior to July 1998, regulators used a **contemporaneous reserve accounting system,** in which the two-week reserve maintenance period for meeting the reserve target began only two days (as opposed to the current 30 days) after the start of the computation period. This contemporaneous reserve system resulted in only a two-day window during which required reserves were known with certainty.[9] In the above example, the reserve maintenance period would have been from Thursday, July 2, through Wednesday, July 15, for a reserve computation period beginning Tuesday, June 30, and ending Monday, July 13.

Undershooting/Overshooting of the Reserve Target

Undershooting

What happens if, at the end of the reserve maintenance period (on August 12 from the previous example) the DI *undershoots* the regulatory required daily minimum reserve ratio—that is, holds less than the required amount ($131.943 daily average million in our example)? The Federal Reserve allows the DI to make up to a 4 percent daily average error without penalty.[10] Thus, if the DI is 4 percent in the red on

[9] One result of this system was that DIs tended to hold more reserves during the last few days of each reserve maintenance period, when the opportunity cost of holding reserves was typically the highest. Uncertainty over reserve needs and the small cost of trading induced DIs to hold reserves when they had the most accurate information on their reserve needs—the last two days of the reserve maintenance period. See K. Bartolini, G. Bertola, and A. Prati, "Banks' Reserve Management, Transaction Costs, and the Timing of Federal Reserve Intervention," *Journal of Banking and Finance* 25 (2001), pp. 1287–1317.

[10] The carryover was changed from 2 percent to 4 percent on September 3, 1992. See Federal Reserve Board of Governors (1992). CSC no. 92–35, Attachment Docket no. R–0750, p. 5.

its reserve target to the tune of 4 percent $\times$ \$131.943 million = \$5.278 million, it must make this up in the next two-week reserve maintenance period that runs from August 13 to August 26.[11]

When a DI holds a deficit in its required reserves in a given two-week period, it *must* hold a surplus amount of reserves in the subsequent two-week period. If the reserve shortfall exceeds 4 percent, the DI is liable to explicit and implicit penalty charges from the Federal Reserve. The explicit charges include the imposition of a penalty interest rate charge equal to the central bank's discount rate plus a 2 percent markup; the implicit charges can include more frequent monitoring, examinations, and surveillance if DI regulators view the undershooting of the reserve requirements as a reflection of an unsafe and unsound practice by the DI's manager. Such a view is likely to be taken only if the DI consistently undershoots its reserve targets.

In undershooting the target, the DI manager must weigh the explicit and implicit costs of undershooting against any potential benefits. Specifically, it may be beneficial to undershoot if the privately optimal or prudential reserve position of the DI is less than the regulatory set minimum and/or there are very high opportunity costs of meeting the reserve requirement targets. There may be high opportunity costs of meeting reserve targets if interest rates and loan demands are high so that the cost of forgone loans on future profits may be significant.

A DI that undershoots the reserve target has two principal ways to build up reserves to meet the target as the reserve maintenance period comes to an end: It can (1) liquidate assets (e.g., by selling off some buffer assets such as Treasury bills) or (2) borrow in the interbank market for reserves, especially in the fed funds and repurchase agreement markets[12] described later. The DI manager is likely to choose the least costly method to meet any reserve deficiency, such as borrowing fed funds if this rate is less than the cost of selling off liquid assets. The manager may be reluctant to fund the entire reserve deficiency in this manner, however, if the costs of adjusting to a deficiency are high and the privately optimal amount of reserves is less than the regulatory required minimum amount.

www.federalreserve.
gov

Such cost considerations lead some DI managers to use the Federal Reserve's discount window to borrow the required funds to meet temporary reserve shortfalls because the cost of borrowing from the discount window is the discount rate, an administered rate set by the Federal Reserve. The discount window rate was historically set below fed funds and government security rates and offered a very attractive borrowing cost to a DI with deficient reserves as the reserve maintenance period came to an end. However, discount window loans were meant to be used by DIs on a need rather than a profit basis—that is, by DIs that were solvent but faced sudden liquidity crises due to deposit withdrawals caused by seasonality in deposit flows or some other similar lender of last resort need. In January 2003, the Fed implemented changes to its discount window lending that increased the cost of borrowing but eased the terms. Through the Fed's primary credit program, discount window loans are available to generally sound depository institutions on a very short-term basis, typically overnight, at a rate above the Federal

---

[11] This means that the allowable deficiency over the full 14 days would be:

$$\$131.943 \text{ million} \times .04 \times 14 = \$73.888 \text{ million}$$

[12] The trade-off faced by thrifts is essentially the same as that faced by banks with the exception of thrifts' access to borrowings from Federal Home Loan banks, while banks tend to have more direct access to the federal funds and repurchase agreement markets.

Open Market Committee's (FOMC) target rate for federal funds.[13] Primary credit may be used for any purpose, including financing the sale of fed funds. Primary credit may be extended for periods of up to a few weeks to depository institutions in generally sound financial condition that cannot obtain temporary funds in the financial markets at reasonable terms. We discuss the role of the discount window, and particularly the limits on its use as a source of funds during periods of economic distress, in more detail in Chapter 19.

Overshooting

The cost of *overshooting*, or holding cash reserves in excess of the minimum required level, depends on whether the DI perceives its prudent level of reserves to meet expected and unexpected deposit withdrawals to be higher or lower than the regulatory imposed minimum reserve requirement.

If its required minimum reserves are higher than the amount managers perceive to be optimal, the first 4 percent of excess reserves can be carried forward to the next reserve period. The Federal Reserve allows this amount to count toward meeting the reserve requirement in the next two-week maintenance period. After that, any reserves held above the required minimum plus 4 percent constitute a drag on DI earnings since every dollar that is held as excess reserves—either in cash or on deposit at the central bank—earns no interest[14] and could have been lent out at the DI lending rate. For example, if the DI's lending rate to its best customers is 12 percent, the DI and its shareholders have suffered an opportunity cost of 12 percent for every dollar of excess cash reserves held by the DI.

In contrast, if the DI manager perceives that the regulatory required minimum level of reserves is lower than what it needs for expected and unexpected deposit withdrawal exposure, the DI overshoots the required minimum reserve target. This policy maintains the DI's liquidity position at a prudently adequate level. In choosing to overshoot the target, the manager must consider the least-cost instrument in which to hold such reserves.

Thus, while some excess reserves might be held in highly liquid (non-interest-bearing) cash form, at least part of any excess reserve position might be held in buffer assets such as short-term securities or Treasury bills that earn interest but are not quite as liquid as cash. The proportion between cash and Treasury bills held depends in large part on yield spreads.

For example, suppose the loan rate is 12 percent, the T-bill rate is 7 percent, and the interest earned on excess cash holdings is 0 percent. The opportunity cost of a forgone return to the DI from holding excess reserves in cash form or T-bill form is:

$$\text{Opportunity cost cash} = 12\% - 0\% = 12\%$$

$$\text{Opportunity cost T-bills} = 12\% - 7\% = 5\%$$

Thus, T-bills have a significantly lower opportunity cost than cash, and the manager must weigh the 7 percent net opportunity cost savings of holding

---

[13] For more on the use of fed funds versus the discount window as a borrowing source, see T. Ho and A. Saunders, "A Micro Model of the Federal Funds Market," *Journal of Finance* 40 (1985), pp. 977–88; M. Smirlock and J. Yawitz, "Asset Returns, Discount Rate Changes, and Market Efficiency," *Journal of Finance* 40 (1985), pp. 1141–58; S. Peristiani, "An Empirical Examination of the Determinants of Discount Window Borrowing: A Dissaggregate Analysis," *Journal of Banking and Finance* (1994), pp. 183–94; and C. H. Furfine, "Banks as Monitors of Other Banks: Evidence from the Overnight Federal Funds Market," *Journal of Business* 74 (2001), pp. 33–57.

[14] As mentioned earlier, regulators are currently considering legislation that would allow DIs to earn a (low) rate of interest on their deposits at the Federal Reserve.

TABLE 18–3   Reserves and Excess Reserves of U.S. Depository Institutions (in millions of dollars)

	December 1990	December 1995	December 2000	January 2004
Total reserves	$59,120	$56,452	$38,537	$42,418
Required reserves	57,456	55,162	37,110	40,815
Excess reserves	1,664	1,290	1,427	1,603

Source: Federal Reserve Board Web site, various dates. *www.federalreserve.gov*

excess reserves in T-bill form against the ease with which such instruments can be sold and turned into cash to meet liability withdrawals or liquidity crunches. Table 18–3 shows excess cash reserves of U.S. DIs between 1990 and January 2004. Because of their opportunity cost, excess reserves are invariably kept at very low levels; this was 3.78 percent of required reserves in January 2004.

Internet Exercise	Go to the Web site of the Board of Governors of the Federal Reserve and find the latest information available for reserves and excess reserves of U.S. depository institutions. Go to the Board of Governors of the Federal Reserve website at **www.federalreserve.gov**. Click on "Economic Research and Data." Click on "Statistics: Releases and Historical Data." Click on "Aggregate Reserves of Depository Institutions and the Monetary Base: Releases." Click on the most recent date. This will download a file on to your computer that will contain the most recent information.

Liquidity Management as a Knife-Edge Management Problem

The management of a DI's liquidity position is something of a knife-edge situation because holding too many liquid assets penalizes a DI's earnings and, thus, its stockholders. A DI manager who holds excessive amounts of liquid assets is unlikely to survive long. Similarly, a manager who excessively undershoots the reserve target faces enhanced risks of liquidity crises and regulatory intervention. Again, such a manager's tenure at the DI may be relatively short.

Concept Questions

1. In addition to the target reserve ratio, what other pieces of information does the DI reserve manager require to manage the DI's reserve requirement position?
2. For a DI that undershoots its reserve target, what ways are available to a reserve manager to build up reserves to meet the target?
3. Since 1998, U.S. DIs have operated under a lagged reserve accounting system in which the reserve computation period ends 17 days before the reserve maintenance period begins. Does the reserve manager face any uncertainty at all in managing a DI's reserve position? Explain your answer.
4. What explains the decline in the level of required reserves held by DIs between 1990 and January 2004 (see Table 18–3)?

LIABILITY MANAGEMENT

Liquidity and liability management are closely related. One aspect of liquidity risk control is the buildup of a prudential level of liquid assets. Another aspect is the management of the DI's liability structure to reduce the need for large amounts of liquid assets to meet liability withdrawals. However, excessive use of purchased

FIGURE 18–2
Funding Risk versus Cost

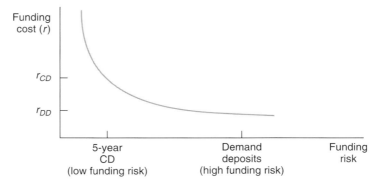

funds in the liability structure can result in a liquidity crisis if investors lose confidence in the DI and refuse to roll over such funds.

Funding Risk and Cost

Unfortunately, constructing a low-cost, low-withdrawal-risk liability portfolio is more difficult than it sounds. This is true because those liabilities, or sources of DI funds, that are the most subject to withdrawal risk are often the least costly to the DI. That is, a DI must trade off the benefits of attracting liabilities at a low funding cost with a high chance of withdrawal against liabilities with a high funding cost and low liquidity. For example, demand deposits are relatively low funding cost vehicles for DIs but can be withdrawn without notice.[15] By contrast, a five-year, fixed-term certificate of deposit may have a relatively high funding cost but can be withdrawn before the five-year maturity is up only after the deposit holder pays a substantial interest rate penalty.

Thus, in structuring the liability, or funding, side of the balance sheet, the DI manager faces a trade-off along the lines suggested in Figure 18–2. That is, funding costs are generally inversely related to the period of time the liability is likely to remain on the DI's balance sheet (i.e., to funding risk).

Although we have discussed depository institutions' funding risk, other FIs face a similar trade-off. For example, investment banks can finance through overnight funds (repurchase agreements and brokered deposits) or longer-term sources such as notes and bonds. Finance companies have a choice between commercial paper and longer-term notes and bonds.

The next section looks at the spectrum of liabilities available to a DI manager in seeking to actively impact liquidity risk exposure through the choice of liability structure.

Concept Questions

1. How are liquidity and liability management related?
2. Describe the trade-off faced by an FI manager in structuring the liability side of the balance sheet.

CHOICE OF LIABILITY STRUCTURE

This section considers in more detail the withdrawal (or funding) risk and funding cost characteristics of the major liabilities available to a modern DI manager.

[15] Depositors do not always exercise this option; therefore, some demand deposits behave like longer-term core deposits.

Demand Deposits

Withdrawal Risk

Demand deposits issued by DIs have a high degree of withdrawal risk. Withdrawals can be instantaneous and largely expected by the DI manager, such as pre-weekend cash withdrawals, or unexpected, as occur during economic crisis situations (so-called bank runs; see Chapter 17).

Costs

In the United States, demand deposits have paid zero explicit interest since the 1930s by law. This does not mean that they are a costless source of funds for DIs or that DIs have no price or interest mechanisms available to partially control the withdrawal risk associated with these contracts. Despite the zero explicit interest paid on demand deposit accounts, competition among DIs and other FIs (e.g., money market mutual funds) has resulted in the payment of implicit interest, or payments of interest in kind, on these accounts. Specifically, in providing demand deposits that are checkable accounts, a DI must provide a whole set of associated services from providing checkbooks, to clearing of checks, to sending out statements with cleared checks or check images. Because such services absorb real resources of labor and capital, they are costly for DIs to provide. DIs can recapture these costs by charging fees, such as 10 cents per check cleared. To the extent that these fees do not fully cover the DI's cost of providing such services, the depositor receives a subsidy or an implicit interest payment.

EXAMPLE 18–2
Calculation of Average Implicit Interest Rate

Suppose a DI pays 15 cents to clear a check but charges a fee of only 10 cents per check cleared. The customer receives a 5 cent subsidy per check. We can calculate implicit yields for each service, or an average implicit interest rate, for each demand deposit account. For example, an average implicit interest rate for a DI's demand deposits might be calculated as:

$$\text{Average implicit interest rate (IIR)} = \frac{\text{DI's average management costs per account per annum} - \text{Average fees earned per account per annum}}{\text{Average annual size of account}}$$

Suppose that:

$$\text{DI's average management costs per account per annum} = \$\ 150$$
$$\text{Average fees earned per account per annum} = \$\ 100$$
$$\text{Average annual size of account} = \$1,200$$

Then:

$$IIR = \frac{\$150 - \$100}{\$1,200} = 4.166\%$$

The payment of implicit interest means that the DI manager is not absolutely powerless to mitigate deposit withdrawals, especially if rates on competing instruments are rising. In particular, the DI could lower check-clearing fees, which in turn raises implicit interest payments to depositors. Such payments are *payments in kind* or *subsidies* that are not paid in actual dollars and cents as is interest earned on competing instruments. Nevertheless, implicit payments of interest are tax free to the depositor, but explicit interest payments are taxable. Finally, demand deposits have an additional cost in the form of non-interest-bearing reserve requirements the DI must hold at the Federal Reserve.

Interest-Bearing Checking (NOW) Accounts

Withdrawal Risk

NOW account
Negotiable order of withdrawal account that is like a demand deposit account but has a minimum balance requirement, and, when the minimum balance is maintained, pays interest.

Since 1980 banks in the United States have been able to offer checkable deposits that pay interest and are withdrawable on demand; they are called negotiable order of withdrawal accounts or **NOW accounts.**[16] The major distinction between these instruments and traditional demand deposits is that these instruments require the depositor to maintain a minimum account balance to earn interest. If the minimum balance falls below some level, such as $500, the account formally converts to a status equivalent to demand deposits and earns no interest. The payment of explicit interest and the existence of minimum balance requirements make NOW accounts potentially less prone to withdrawal risk than demand deposits. Nevertheless, NOW accounts are still highly liquid instruments from the depositor's perspective.

Costs

As with demand deposits, the DI can influence the potential withdrawability of NOW accounts by paying implicit interest or fee subsidies such as not charging the full cost of check clearance. However, the manager has two other ways to impact the yield paid to the depositor. The first is by varying the minimum balance requirement. If the minimum balance requirement is lowered—say, from $500 to $250—a larger portion of a NOW account becomes subject to interest payments and thus the explicit return and attractiveness of these accounts increases.[17] The second is to vary the explicit interest rate payment itself, such as increasing it from 5 to $5\frac{1}{4}$ percent. Thus, the DI manager has three pricing mechanisms to increase or decrease the attractiveness, and therefore impact the withdrawal rate, of NOW accounts: implicit interest payments, minimum balance requirements, and explicit interest payments.[18,19]

EXAMPLE 18–3 *Gross Interest Return*	Consider a depositor who holds on average $250 per month for the first three months of the year, $500 per month for the next three months, and $1,000 per month for the final six months of the year in a NOW account. The NOW account pays 5 percent per annum if the minimum balance is $500 or more, and it pays no interest if the account falls below $500. The depositor writes an average of 50 checks per month and pays a service fee of 10 cents for each check although it costs the bank 15 cents to process each check. The account

---

[16] There are also Super-NOW accounts that have very similar features to NOW accounts but require a larger minimum balance.

[17] Subject to any regulatory requirement on the minimum balance.

[18] As transactions accounts, these deposits are also subject to reserve requirements at the same rate as on demand deposits as well as deposit insurance premiums. Using a 5 percent NOW account interest rate, a 10 percent reserve ratio (R), and a 27–basis point deposit insurance premium (Premium) and ignoring implicit interest, the effective cost of the marginal dollar of NOW accounts to the issuing DI is:

$$\text{Effective cost} = [r_{NOW}/(1 - R)] + \text{Premium} = [.05/.09] + .0027 = .0583 \text{ or } 5.83\%$$

Currently, for most banks, deposit insurance premiums are zero (see Chapter 19).

[19] Recent research shows that customers are, in fact, fairly tolerant of such price changes. A 2001 market research study of more than 500 banking customers in the U.S. Southeast and Midwest suggests that few depositors actually change banks as a result of changes in the cost of the deposits. Checking account customers, for instance, were surprisingly "sticky," citing convenience, the quality of service, and their relationships with bank personnel as reasons for not switching to other banks after price increases. In selecting a bank for CDs, customers said that interest rates accounted for 45 percent of their decision. Yet at renewal time, only a third of CD customers shopped around at all for a better rate and 85 percent of them renewed at the same bank. See V. Cvsa, A. M. Degeratu, and R. L. Ott-Wadhawan, "Bank Deposits Get Interesting," *The McKinsey Quarterly,* no. 2 (2002), pp. 1–5.

holder's gross interest return, consisting of implicit plus explicit interest, is:

$$\text{Gross interest return} = \text{Explicit interest} + \text{Implicit interest} = \$500 \,(.05)(.25)$$
$$+ \$1000 \,(.05)(.5) + (\$.15 - \$.10)(50)(12)$$
$$= \$6.25 + \$25 + \$30 = \$61.25$$

Suppose the minimum balance was lowered from $500 to $250 and check service fees were lowered from 10 cents to 5 cents per check. Then:

$$\text{Gross interest return} = \$250(.05)(.25) + \$500(.05)(.25) + \$1000(.05)(.5)$$
$$+ (\$.15 - \$.05)(50)(12)$$
$$= \$3.125 + \$6.25 + \$25 + \$60$$
$$= \$94.375$$

Passbook Savings

Withdrawal Risk

Passbook savings are generally less liquid than demand deposits and NOW accounts for two reasons. First, they are noncheckable and usually involve physical presence at the institution for withdrawal. Second, the DI has the legal power to delay payment or withdrawal requests for as long as one month. This is rarely done and DIs normally meet withdrawal requests with immediate cash payment, but they have the legal right to delay, which provides important withdrawal risk control to DI managers.

Costs

Since these accounts are noncheckable, any implicit interest rate payments are likely to be small; thus, the principal costs to the DI are the explicit interest payments on these accounts. In recent years, DIs have normally paid slightly higher explicit rates on passbook savings than on NOW accounts.

Money Market Deposit Accounts (MMDAs)

Withdrawal Risk

MMDAs
Money market deposit accounts; retail savings accounts with some limited checking account features.

Under the Garn–St. Germain Act, introduced in 1982, DIs can use money market deposit accounts (MMDAs) as an additional liability instrument to control their overall withdrawal risk—in particular, the risk of funds' disintermediating from DIs and flowing to money market mutual funds (MMMFs) (see Chapter 5). If DIs are to be competitive with the money market mutual funds offered by groups such as Vanguard and Fidelity, the **MMDAs** they offer must be liquid but not as liquid as demand deposits and NOW accounts. In the United States, MMDAs are checkable but subject to restrictions on the number of checks written on each account per month, the number of preauthorized automatic transfers per month, and the minimum denomination of the amount of each check. For example, one DI may allow a customer with an MMDA to make a maximum of six preauthorized transfers, of which no more than three can be checks of at least $500 each. In addition, MMDAs impose minimum balance requirements on depositors. The Federal Reserve does not require DIs to hold reserves against MMDAs. Accordingly, DIs generally pay higher rates on MMDAs than on NOW accounts.

Costs

The explicit interest paid to depositors is the major cost of MMDAs; it is also the pricing mechanism DIs use to control withdrawal risk. Since MMDAs are in direct competition with MMMFs, the DI manager can influence their net withdrawal rate by varying the rate the DI pays on such accounts. In particular, while the rate that MMMFs pay on their shares directly reflects the rates earned on the underlying money market assets in which the portfolio manager invests, such as commercial paper, banker's acceptances, repurchase agreements, and T-bills, the rates that DI managers pay on MMDAs are not based directly on any underlying portfolio of money market assets. In general, DI managers have considerable discretion to alter the rates paid on MMDAs and thus the spread on MMMF–MMDA accounts. This can directly impact the rate of withdrawals and withdrawal risk on such accounts. Allowing MMDA rates to have a large negative spread with MMMFs increases the net withdrawal rate on such accounts.

Retail Time Deposits and CDs

Withdrawal Risk

retail CDs
Time deposits with a face value below $100,000.

By contractual design, time deposits and retail certificates of deposit (CDs) reduce the withdrawal risk to issuers. **Retail CDs** are fixed-maturity instruments with face values under $100,000. Small time deposits carry early withdrawal penalties. Although the size, maturity, and rate on these CDs are negotiable, most DIs issue standardized retail CDs. In a world of no early withdrawal requests, the DI knows the exact scheduling of interest and principal payments to depositors holding such deposit claims, since these payments are contractually specified. As such, the DI manager can directly control fund inflows and outflows by varying the maturities of the time deposits and CDs it offers to the public. In general, DIs offer time deposits and CDs with maturities varying from two weeks to eight years.

When depositors wish to withdraw before the maturity of a time deposit or CD contract, regulation empowers DIs to impose penalties on a withdrawing depositor, such as the loss of a certain number of months' interest depending on the maturity of the deposit. While this does impose a friction or transaction cost on withdrawals, it is unlikely to stop withdrawals when the depositor has exceptional liquidity needs. Also, withdrawals may increase if depositors perceive the DI to be insolvent, despite interest penalties and deposit insurance coverage up to $100,000. Nevertheless, under normal conditions, these instruments have relatively low withdrawal risk compared with transaction accounts such as demand deposits and NOW accounts and can be used as an important liability management tool to control withdrawal/liquidity risk.

Costs

Similar to those of passbook savings, the major costs of these accounts are explicit interest payments. Short-term CDs are often competitive with T-bills, and their rates are set with the T-bill rate in mind. Note that depositors who buy CDs are subject to state and local taxes on their interest payments, whereas T-bill investors do not pay state and local taxes on T-bill interest income.[20] Finally, time deposits and CDs do not at present require the bank to hold non-interest-bearing reserves at the central bank.

---

[20] Thus, the marginal investor is indifferent between Treasury bills and insured bank CDs when:

$$r_{TB} = r_{CD}(1 - T_L)$$

where r_{TB} is the rate on T-bills, r_{CD} is the CD rate, and T_L is the local income tax rate. Suppose the average local tax rate is 8 percent. Then, if the T-bill rate is 3 percent, insured CDs must pay:

$$r_{CD} = r_{TB}/(1 - T_L) = 3.00\%/(1 - .08) = 3.26\%$$

Wholesale CDs

Withdrawal Risk

wholesale CDs
Time deposits with a
face value above
$100,000.

Wholesale CDs were innovated by banks in the early 1960s as a contractual mechanism to allow depositors to liquidate their positions in these CDs by selling them in the secondary market rather than settling up with the DI. Thus, a depositor can sell a relatively liquid instrument without causing adverse liquidity risk exposure for the DI. Thus, the unique feature of these wholesale CDs is not so much their large minimum denomination size of $100,000 or more but the fact that they are **negotiable instruments.** That is, they can be resold by title assignment in a secondary market to other investors. This means, for example, that if IBM bought a $1 million three-month CD from Citibank but for unexpected liquidity reasons needs funds after only one month has passed, it could sell this CD to another outside investor in the secondary market. This does not impose any obligation on Citibank in terms of an early funds withdrawal request. Thus, a depositor can sell a relatively liquid instrument without causing adverse withdrawal risk exposure for the DI. Essentially, the only withdrawal risk (which can be substantial) is that these wholesale CDs are not rolled over and reinvested by the holder of the deposit claim on maturity.[21]

**negotiable
instrument**
An instrument whose
ownership can be
transferred in the secondary market.

Costs

The rates that DIs pay on these instruments are competitive with other wholesale money market rates, especially those on commercial paper and T-bills. This competitive rate aspect is enhanced by the highly sophisticated nature of investors in such CDs, such as money market mutual fund managers, and the fact that these deposits are not covered by explicit deposit insurance guarantees. Only the first $100,000 invested in these CDs (per investor, per institution) is covered by insurance. To the extent that these CDs are offered by large DIs perceived as being too big to fail, the required credit risk premium on CDs is less than that required for similar-quality instruments issued by the nonbank private sector (e.g., commercial paper). In addition, required interest yields on CDs reflect investors' perceptions of the depth of the secondary market for CDs. In recent years, the liquidity of the secondary market in CDs appears to have diminished as dealers have withdrawn. This has increased DIs' relative cost of issuing such instruments.[22]

---

[21] Wholesale dollar CDs are also offered in countries other than the United States, in which case they are called Eurodollar CDs. Eurodollar CDs may sell at slightly different rates from domestic CDs because of differences in demand and supply for CDs between the domestic market and the Euromarket and differences in credit risk perceptions of depositors buying a CD from a foreign branch (e.g., Citibank in London) rather than a domestic branch (Citibank in New York). To the extent that it is believed that banks are too big to fail, a guaranty that only extends to domestic branches, a higher risk premium may be required of overseas CDs. Indeed, FDICIA, passed in 1991, has severely restricted the ability of the FDIC to rescue overseas depositors of a failed U.S. bank.

[22] In addition, for all the liability instruments considered so far (with the exception of Euro CDs), the DI may have to pay an FDIC insurance premium depending on its perceived riskiness (see Chapter 19). For example, consider a bank issuing CDs at 3.26 percent, at which rate a depositor might just be indifferent to holding T-bills at 3.00 percent, given a local tax rate of 8 percent. However, the cost to the bank of the CD issue is not 3.26 percent but:

$$\text{Effective CD cost} = 3.26\% + \text{Insurance premium} = 3.26\% + .27\% = 3.53\%$$

where 27 basis points is the assumed size of the deposit insurance premium. Thus, deposit insurance premiums add to the cost of deposits as a source of funds. However, in 2004, the insurance premium was set by the FDIC at zero for most DIs, with only the very riskiest DIs having to pay 27 basis points.

Federal Funds

Withdrawal Risk

The liabilities just described are all deposit liabilities, reflecting deposit contracts issued by DIs in return for cash. However, DIs not only fund their assets by issuing deposits but also can borrow in various markets for purchased funds. Since the funds generated from these purchases are borrowed funds, not deposits, they are subject to neither reserve requirements (as with demand deposits and NOW accounts) nor deposit insurance premium payments to the FDIC (as with all the domestic deposits described earlier).[23] The largest market available for purchased funds is the federal funds market. While DIs with excess cash reserves can invest some of this excess in interest-earning liquid assets such as T-bills and short-term securities, an alternative is to lend excess reserves for short intervals to other DIs seeking increased short-term funding. The interbank market for excess cash reserves is called the federal funds (fed funds) market. In the United States, **federal funds** are short-term uncollateralized loans made by one DI to another; more than 90 percent of such transactions have maturities of one day. The DI that purchases funds shows them as a liability on its balance sheet, while the DI that sells them shows them as an asset.

For the liability-funding DIs, there is no risk that the fed funds they have borrowed can be withdrawn within the day, although there is settlement risk at the end of each day (see Chapter 14). However, there is some risk that fed funds will not be rolled over by the lending bank the next day if rollover is desired by the borrowing DI. In reality, this has occurred only in periods of extreme crisis, such as the failure of Continental Illinois in 1984. Nevertheless, since fed funds are uncollateralized loans, institutions selling fed funds normally impose maximum bilateral limits or credit caps on borrowing institutions. This may constrain the ability of a bank to expand its federal funds–borrowing position very rapidly if this is part of its overall liability management strategy.

Costs

The cost of fed funds for the purchasing institution is the federal funds rate. The federal funds rate is set by DIs (mostly banks) that trade in the fed funds market and can vary considerably both within the day and across days—although rate variability has fallen since the introduction of lagged reserve accounting in July 1998.[24]

Repurchase Agreements (RPs)

Withdrawal Risk

Repurchase agreements (RPs or repos) can be viewed as collateralized federal funds transactions. In a federal funds transaction, the DI with excess reserves sells fed funds for one day to the purchasing DI. The next day, the purchasing DI returns the fed funds plus one day's interest reflecting the fed funds rate. Since a

federal funds
Short-term uncollateralized loans made by one DI to another.

repurchase agreements
Agreements involving the sale of securities (i.e., for fed funds) by one party (i.e., a DI) to another with a promise to repurchase the securities (with fed funds) at a specified date and price in the future.

[23] Foreign deposits are not subject to deposit insurance premiums. However, in the exceptional event of a very large failure in which all deposits are protected, under the 1991 FDICIA, the FDIC is required to levy a charge on surviving large DIs proportional to their total asset size. To the extent that assets are partially funded by foreign liabilities, this is an implied premium on foreign deposits.

[24] See C. H. Furfine, "The Microstructure of the Federal Funds Market," *Financial Markets, Institutions and Instruments,* no. 5 (1999), pp. 24–44; and C. H. Furfine, "The Fed's New Discount Window and Interbank Borrowing," Federal Reserve Bank of Chicago, Working Paper, 2003.

credit risk exposure exists for the selling DI because the purchasing DI may be unable to repay the fed funds the next day, the seller may seek collateral backing for the one-day loan of fed funds. In an RP transaction, the funds-selling DI receives government securities as collateral from the funds-purchasing DI. That is, the funds-purchasing DI temporarily exchanges securities for cash.[25] The next day, this transaction is reversed. The funds-purchasing DI sends back the fed funds it borrowed plus interest (the RP rate); it receives in return (or repurchases) its securities used as collateral in the transaction.

As with the fed funds market, the RP market is a highly liquid and flexible source of funds for DIs needing to increase their liabilities and to offset deposit withdrawals. Moreover, like fed funds, these transactions can be rolled over each day. The major liability management flexibility difference between fed funds and RPs is that a fed funds transaction can be entered into at any time in the business day as long as the Fedwire is open (see Chapter 14).[26] In general, it is difficult to transact an RP borrowing late in the day since the DI sending the fed funds must be satisfied with the type and quality of the securities collateral proposed by the borrowing institution. This collateral is normally in the form of T-bills, T-notes, T-bonds, and mortgage-backed securities, but their maturities and other features, such as callability and coupons, may be unattractive to the funds seller. Negotiations over the collateral package can delay RP transactions and make them more difficult to arrange than simple uncollateralized fed fund loans.

Costs

Because of their collateralized nature, RP rates normally lie below federal funds rates. Also, RP rates generally show less interday fluctuation than do fed funds rates. This is partly due to the lesser intraday flexibility of RPs relative to fed fund transactions.

Other Borrowings

While fed funds and RPs have been the major sources of borrowed funds, DIs have utilized a host of other borrowing sources to supplement their liability management flexibility. We describe these briefly in the following sections.

Bankers Acceptances

Banks often convert off-balance-sheet letters of credit into on-balance-sheet bankers acceptances (BAs) by discounting the letter of credit the holder presents for acceptance (see Chapter 13). Further, these BAs may then be resold to money market investors. Thus, BA sales to the secondary market are an additional funding source. We describe BAs in more detail in Appendix 18B to the Chapter (located at the book's Web site (**www.mhhe.com/saunders5e**).

Commercial Paper

Although a DI subsidiary itself cannot issue commercial paper, its parent holding company can; that is, Citigroup can issue commercial paper but Citibank cannot. This provides DIs owned by holding companies—most of the largest banks in the United States—with an additional funding source. Specifically, when the DI subsidiary itself finds funding tight, it can utilize the funds downstreamed from its

---

[25] Since Treasury securities are of a book-entry form, the title to ownership is transferred along a securities Fedwire, in a manner similar to cash transfers.

[26] Normally, Fedwire closes at 6:30 PM EST.

holding company's issue of commercial paper. Indeed, Citigroup is one of the largest issuers of commercial paper in the United States. Note that funds down-streamed to an affiliated DI are subject to reserve requirements, detracting from the attractiveness of this mechanism as a regular funding source. We discuss commercial paper in more detail in Appendix 18B to the Chapter located at the book's Web site (**www.mhhe.com/saunders5e**).

Medium-Term Notes

A number of DIs in search of more stable sources of funds with low withdrawal risk have begun to issue medium-term notes, often in the five- to seven-year range. These notes are additionally attractive because they are subject to neither reserve requirements nor deposit insurance premiums.

Discount Window Loans

As discussed earlier, DIs facing temporary liquidity crunches can borrow from the central bank's discount window at the discount rate. We discuss discount window loans in detail in Chapter 19.

Concept Questions

1. Describe the withdrawal risk and funding cost characteristics of some of the major liabilities available to a modern DI manager.
2. Since transaction accounts are subject to both reserve requirements and deposit insurance premiums, whereas fed funds are not, why should a DI not fund all its assets through fed funds? Explain your answer.
3. What are the major differences between fed funds and repurchase agreements?

LIQUIDITY AND LIABILITY STRUCTURES FOR U.S. DEPOSITORY INSTITUTIONS

We summarize the preceding discussion by considering some balance sheet data for U.S. banks. Table 18–4 shows the liquid asset–nonliquid asset composition of insured U.S. banks in (January) 2004 versus 1960. We use 1960 as a benchmark year since the next year (1961) is widely viewed as the date when banks first began to actively manage their liabilities—with Citibank's innovation of wholesale CDs.

TABLE 18–4
Liquid Assets versus Nonliquid Assets for Insured Commercial Banks, 1960 and 2004* (in percentages)

Source: Federal Reserve Board Web site, *www.federalreserve.gov*

Assets	1960	2004 All Banks	2004 Large Banks**	2004 Small Banks
Cash	20%	4.2%	3.5%	4.8%
Government and agency securities	24	14.7	12.9	16.4
Other securities†	8	13.8	13.9	13.8
Loans‡	46	59.8	60.2	59.4
Other assets	2	7.5	9.5	5.6
	100%	100%	100%	100%

*As of January 2004.
† Other securities = state and local, mortgage-backed, plus others.
‡ Loans = C&I, mortgage, consumer, and others.
** Large banks are those 423 banks with total assets greater than $1 billion.
   Small banks are those 7,389 banks with total assets of $1 billion or less.

Clearly, the ratio of traditional liquid to illiquid assets has declined since 1960, with cash plus securities in 2004 constituting 32.7 percent of the asset balance sheet of insured banks versus 52 percent in 1960. However, it may be argued that such a comparison misrepresents and overstates the fall in bank asset liquidity, since bank loans themselves became significantly more liquid over this 30-year period. As we discuss in Chapters 27 and 28, DI loans are increasingly being securitized and/or sold in secondary markets. This has fundamentally altered the illiquidity of bank loan portfolios and has made them more similar to securities than in the past. The more liquid the loan portfolio, the less the need for large amounts of traditional liquid assets, such as cash and securities, to act as buffer reserves against unexpected liability withdrawals.

Notice also from Table 18–4 that in 2004 liquid asset holdings were higher at small banks, 35.0 percent, than large banks, 30.3 percent. Large banks' relatively easier access to purchased funds and capital markets compared with small banks' access is the main reason for this difference.

Table 18–5 presents the liability composition of banks in 1960 and January 2004. The most striking feature of Table 18–5 is the shift by banks from funds sources with relative high withdrawal risk—transaction accounts (demand deposits and NOW accounts) and retail savings and time deposit accounts—to accounts or instruments over which the banks have greater potential control concerning the supply—for example, liability managed accounts. Specifically, the sum of transaction and retail savings and time deposit accounts fell from 90 percent in 1960 to 51.0 percent in January 2004. By contrast, wholesale CDs and time deposits plus borrowed funds (fed funds, RPs, plus other borrowed funds) increased from 2 percent in 1960 to 41.1 percent in 2004. As discussed in Chapters 2 through 6 of this textbook, the increased competition among banks and other FIs for funds over this period certainly contributed to the change in the composition of the liabilities presented in Table 18–5. DIs have intentionally managed liabilities, however, to reduce withdrawal risk. As implied in Figure 18–2, there is often a trade-off between withdrawal risk and funding cost. DIs' attempts to reduce their withdrawal risk by relying more on borrowed and wholesale funds have added to their interest expense.

Notice too that in 2004, small banks used slightly more transaction accounts plus retail CDs and time deposits, 51.6 percent, than large banks, 50.3 percent. Similar to the case with liquid asset management, small banks' relative inability to purchase funds and access the capital markets (compared with that of large banks) means these DIs must hold more deposit liabilities on their balance sheets.

TABLE 18–5
Liability Structure of Insured Commercial Banks, 1960 and 2004* (in percentages)

Source: Federal Reserve Board Web site, *www.federalreserve.gov*

Liabilities	1960	2004		
		All Banks	Large Banks**	Small Banks
Transaction accounts	61%	8.6%	7.1%	10.1%
Retail CDs and time deposits	29	42.4	43.2	41.5
Wholesale CDs and time deposits	0	13.9	7.5	20.2
Borrowings and other liabilities	2	27.2	31.8	22.7
Bank capital	8	7.9	10.4	5.5
	100%	100%	100%	100%

* As of January 2004.
** Large banks are those with total assets greater than $1 billion.
  Small banks are those with total assets of $1 billion or less.

Finally, it should be noted that too heavy a reliance on borrowed funds can be a risky strategy in itself. Even though withdrawal risk may be reduced if lenders in the market for borrowed funds have confidence in the borrowing DI, perceptions that the DI is risky can lead to sudden nonrenewals of fed fund and RP loans and the nonrollover of wholesale CDs and other purchased funds as they mature. The best example of a DI's failure as a result of excessive reliance on large CDs and purchased funds was Continental Illinois in 1984, with more than 80 percent of its funds borrowed from wholesale lenders. Consequently, excessive reliance on borrowed funds may be as bad an overall liability management strategy as excessive reliance on transaction accounts and passbook savings. Thus, a well-diversified portfolio of liabilities may be the best strategy to balance withdrawal risk and funding cost considerations.

Concept Questions

1. Look at Table 18–4. How has the ratio of traditional liquid to illiquid assets changed over the 1960–2004 period?
2. Look at Table 18–5. How has the liability composition of banks changed over the 1960–2004 period?

LIABILITY AND LIQUIDITY RISK MANAGEMENT IN INSURANCE COMPANIES

Insurance companies use a variety of sources to meet liquidity needs. As discussed in Chapters 3 and 17, liquidity is required to meet claims on the insurance policies these FIs have written as well as unexpected surrenders of those policies. These contracts therefore represent a potential future liability to the insurance company. Ideally, liquidity management in insurance companies is conducted so that funds needed to meet claims on insurance contracts written can be met with premiums received on new and existing contracts. However, a high frequency of claims at a single point in time (e.g., an unexpectedly severe hurricane season) could force insurers to liquidate assets at something less than their fair market value.

Insurance companies can reduce their exposure to liquidity risk by diversifying the distribution of risk in the contracts they write. For example, property–casualty insurers can diversify across the types of disasters they cover (e.g., in the early 2000s the top two property–casualty insurance companies [in terms of premiums sold] held policies for 18 different lines—from medical malpractice, for which they wrote 17.9 percent of all industry premiums, to homeowners multiple peril, for which they wrote 33.9 percent of all industry premiums).[27]

Alternatively, insurance companies can meet liquidity needs by holding relatively marketable assets to cover claim payments. Assets such as government and corporate bonds and corporate stock usually can be liquidated quickly at close to their fair market values in financial markets to pay claims on insurance policies when premium income is insufficient. For example, in 2003, life and property–casualty insurance companies held approximately 80 percent of their assets in the form of government securities and corporate securities (see Chapter 3).

Concept Questions

1. Discuss two strategies insurance companies can use to reduce liquidity risk.
2. Why would property–casualty insurers hold more short-term liquid assets to manage liquidity risk than life insurers hold?

[27] See *Best's Review,* August and November 2003.

LIABILITY AND LIQUIDITY RISK MANAGEMENT IN OTHER FIs

Other FIs, such as securities firms, investment banks, and finance companies, may experience liquidity risk if they rely on short-term financing (such as commercial paper or bank loans) and investors become reluctant to roll those funds over. Remember from Chapter 4 that the main sources of funding for securities firms are repurchase agreements, bank call loans,[28] and short positions in securities. Liquidity management for these FIs requires the ability to have sufficient cash and other liquid resources at hand to underwrite (purchase) new securities from quality issuers before reselling these securities to other investors. Liability management also requires an investment bank or securities firm to be able to act as a market maker, which requires the firm to finance an inventory of securities in its portfolio. As discussed in Chapter 6, finance companies fund assets mainly with commercial paper and long-term debt. Liquidity management for these FIs requires the ability to fund loan requests and loan commitments of sufficient quality without delay.

The experience of Drexel Burnham Lambert in 1989 is a good example of a securities firm being subjected to a liquidity challenge. Throughout the 1980s, Drexel Burnham Lambert captured the bulk of the junk bond market by promising investors that it would act as a dealer for junk bonds in the secondary market. Investors were, therefore, more willing to purchase these junk securities because Drexel provided an implied guarantee that it would buy them back or find another buyer at market prices should an investor need to sell. However, the junk bond market experienced extreme difficulties in 1989 as their prices fell, reflecting the economy's move into a recession. Serious concerns about the creditworthiness of Drexel's junk bond–laden asset portfolio led creditors to deny Drexel extensions of its vital short-term commercial paper financings. As a result, Drexel declared bankruptcy. Drexel's sudden collapse makes it very clear that access to short-term purchased funds is crucial to the health of securities firms.[29]

Concept Questions

1. What is a bank call loan?
2. Give two reasons an investment bank needs liquidity.

Summary

Liquidity and liability management issues are intimately linked for the modern FI. Many factors, both cost and regulatory, impact an FI manager's choice of the amount of liquid assets to hold. An FI's choice of liquidity is something of a knife-edge situation, trading off the costs and benefits of undershooting or overshooting regulatory specified (and prudentially specified) reserve asset targets.

An FI can manage its liabilities in a fashion that affects the overall withdrawal risk of its funding portfolio and therefore the need for liquid assets to meet such withdrawals. However, reducing withdrawal risk often comes at a cost because liability sources that are easier to control from a withdrawal risk perspective are often more costly for the FI to utilize.

[28] A bank call loan means that a lending bank can call in the loan from an investment bank with very little notice.
[29] For additional discussion of the failure of Drexel Burnham Lambert, see W. S. Haraf, "The Collapse of Drexel Burnham Lambert: Lessons for Bank Regulators," *Regulation,* Winter 1991, pp. 22–25.

Questions and Problems

1. What are the benefits and costs to an FI of holding large amounts of liquid assets? Why are Treasury securities considered good examples of liquid assets?

2. How is an FI's liability and liquidity risk management problem related to the maturity of its assets relative to its liabilities?

3. Consider the assets (in millions) of two banks, A and B. Both banks are funded by $120 million in deposits and $20 million in equity. Which bank has the stronger liquidity position? Which bank probably has a higher profit?

Bank A Assets		Bank B Assets	
Cash	$ 10	Cash	$ 20
Treasury securities	40	Consumer loans	30
Commercial loans	90	Commercial loans	90
Total assets	$140	Total assets	$140

4. What concerns motivate regulators to require DIs to hold minimum amounts of liquid assets?

5. How do liquid asset reserve requirements enhance the implementation of monetary policy? How are reserve requirements a tax on DIs?

6. Rank these financial assets according to their liquidity: cash, corporate bonds, NYSE-traded stocks, and T-bills.

7. Define the reserve computation period, the reserve maintenance period, and the lagged reserve accounting system.

8. City Bank has estimated that its average daily demand deposit balance over the recent 14-day computation period was $225 million. The average daily balance with the Fed over the 14-day maintenance period was $11 million, and the average daily balance of vault cash over the two-week period prior to the computation period was $7 million.

    a. Under the rules effective in 2004, what is the amount of average daily reserves required to be held during the reserve maintenance period for these demand deposit balances?

    b. What is the average daily balance of reserves held by the bank over the maintenance period? By what amount were the average reserves held higher or lower than the required reserves?

    c. If the bank had transferred $20 million of its deposits every Friday over the two-week computation period to one of its offshore facilities, what would be the revised average daily reserve requirement?

9. Assume that the 14-day reserve computation period for problem 8 above extended from May 18 through May 31.

    a. What is the corresponding reserve maintenance period under the rules effective in 2004?

    b. Given your answers to parts (a) and (b) of problem 8, what would the average required reserves need to be for the maintenance period for the bank to be in reserve compliance?

10. The average demand deposit balance of a local bank during the most recent reserve computation period is $225 million. The amount of average daily reserves at the Fed during the reserve maintenance period is $16 million, and the average daily vault cash corresponding to the computation period is $4.3 million.

a. What is the average daily reserve balance required to be held by the bank during the maintenance period?

b. Is the bank in compliance with the reserve requirements?

c. What amount of reserves can be carried over to the next maintenance period either as excess or as shortfall?

d. If the local bank has an opportunity cost of 6 percent, what is the effect on the income statement from this reserve period?

11. The following demand deposits and cash reserves at the Fed have been documented by a bank for computation of its reserve requirements (in millions) under lagged reserve accounting.

	Monday 10th	Tuesday 11th	Wednesday 12th	Thursday 13th	Friday 14th
Demand deposits	$200	$300	$250	$280	$260
Reserves at Fed	20	22	21	18	27

	Monday 17th	Tuesday 18th	Wednesday 19th	Thursday 20th	Friday 21st
Demand deposits	$280	$300	$270	$260	$250
Reserves at Fed	20	35	21	18	28

	Monday 24th	Tuesday 25th	Wednesday 26th	Thursday 27th	Friday 28th
Demand deposits	$240	$230	$250	$260	$270
Reserves at Fed	19	19	21	19	24

	Monday 1st	Tuesday 2nd	Wednesday 3rd	Thursday 4th	Friday 5th
New Month					
Demand deposits	$200	$300	$250	$280	$260
Reserves at Fed	20	22	21	18	27

	Monday 8th	Tuesday 9th	Wednesday 10th	Thursday 11th	Friday 12th
Demand deposits	$280	$300	$270	$260	$250
Reserves at Fed	20	35	21	18	27

	Monday 15th	Tuesday 16th	Wednesday 17th	Thursday 18th	Friday 19th
Demand deposits	$240	$230	$250	$260	$270
Reserves at Fed	20	35	21	18	28

	Monday 22nd	Tuesday 23rd	Wednesday 24th	Thursday 25th	Friday 26th
Demand deposits	$200	$300	$250	$280	$260
Reserves at Fed	19	19	21	19	24

The average vault cash for the computation period has been estimated to be $2 million per day.

   a. What level of average daily reserves is required to be held by the bank during the maintenance period?

   b. Is the bank in compliance with the requirements?

   c. What amount of required reserves can be carried over to the following computation period?

   d. If the average cost of funds to the bank is 8 percent per year, what is the effect on the income statement for this bank for this reserve period?

12. In July 1998 the lagged reserve accounting (LRA) system replaced a contemporaneous reserve accounting (CRA) system as the method of reserve calculation for DIs.

   a. Contrast a contemporaneous reserve accounting (CRA) system with a lagged reserve accounting (LRA) system.

   b. Under which accounting system, CRA or LRA, are DI reserves higher? Why?

   c. Under which accounting system, CRA or LRA, is DI uncertainty higher? Why?

13. What is the "weekend game"? Contrast the DI's ability and incentive to play the weekend game under LRA as opposed to CRA.

14. Under CRA, when is the uncertainty about the reserve requirement resolved? Discuss the feasibility of making large reserve adjustments during this period of complete information.

15. What is the relationship between funding cost and funding or withdrawal risk?

16. An FI has estimated the following annual costs for its demand deposits: management cost per account = $140, average account size = $1,500, average number of checks processed per account per month = 75, cost of clearing a check = $0.10, fees charged to customer per check = $0.05, and average fee charged per customer per month = $8.

   a. What is the implicit interest cost of demand deposits for the FI?

   b. If the FI has to keep an average of 8 percent of demand deposits as required reserves with the Fed, what is the implicit interest cost of demand deposits for the FI?

   c. What should be the check-clearing fees to reduce the implicit interest cost to 3 percent? Ignore the reserve requirements.

17. A NOW account requires a minimum balance of $750 for interest to be earned at an annual rate of 4 percent. An account holder has maintained an average balance of $500 for the first six months and $1,000 for the remaining six months. She writes an average of 60 checks per month and pays $0.02 per check, although it costs the bank $0.05 to clear a check.

   a. What average return does the account holder earn on the account?

   b. What is the average return if the bank lowers the minimum balance to $400?

   c. What is the average return if the bank pays interest only on the amount in excess of $400? Assume that the minimum required balance is $400.

   d. How much should the bank increase its check-clearing fee to ensure that the average interest it pays on this account is 5 percent? Assume that the minimum required balance is $750.

18. Rank the following liabilities with respect, first, to funding risk and, second, to funding cost.
    a. Money market mutual funds.
    b. Demand deposits.
    c. Certificates of deposit.
    d. Federal funds.
    e. Bankers acceptances.
    f. Eurodollar deposits.
    g. Money market demand deposits.
    h. NOW accounts.
    i. Wholesale CDs.
    j. Passbook savings.
    k. Repos.
    l. Commercial paper.

19. How is the withdrawal risk different for federal funds and repurchase agreements?

20. How does the cash balance, or liquidity, of an FI determine the types of repurchase agreements into which it will enter?

21. How does the cost of MMMFs differ from the cost of MMDAs? How is the spread useful in managing the withdrawal risk of MMDAs?

22. Why do wholesale CDs have minimal withdrawal risk to the issuing bank?

23. What characteristics of fed funds may constrain a DI's ability to use fed funds to expand its liquidity quickly?

24. What does a low fed funds rate indicate about the level of bank reserves? Why does the fed funds rate have higher-than-normal variability around the last two days in the reserve maintenance period?

25. What trends have been observed between 1960 and 2004 in regard to liquidity and liability structures of commercial banks? What changes have occurred in the management of assets that may cause the measured trends to be overstated?

26. What are the primary methods that insurance companies can use to reduce their exposure to liquidity risk?

Web Question

27. Go to the Federal Reserve Board's Web site at **www.federalreserve.gov** and Click on "Economic Research and Data." Click on "Statistics: Releases and Historical Data." Click on "Assets and Liabilities of Commercial Banks in the United States. *Releases*." Click on the most recent date. Use the data in this file to update Tables 18–4 and 18–5. How have the assets and liabilities of commercial banks changed since January 2004?

S&P Question

STANDARD
&POOR'S

28. Go to the Standard & Poor's Market Insight Web site at **www.mhhe.com/edu-marketinsight** and find the most recent balance sheets and income statements for Bank of America (BAC), FleetBoston Financial (FBF), and Wells Fargo (WFC). Click on "Educational Version of Market Insight." Enter your Site ID and click on "Login." Click on "Company." Enter "BAC" in the "Ticker:" box and click on "Go!" Click on "Excel Analytics." Click on "FS Ann. Balance Sheet." This will download the Balance Sheet for Bank of America. This statement contains the balances for Total Deposits. Click on "FS Ann. Income Stmt." This will download the Income Statement for Bank of America which contains the Interest Expense. Using the interest expense items from the income statement and the values of the deposit accounts from the balance sheets, calculate the cost of the deposit accounts for the three banks. Repeat the process by entering "FBF" in the "Ticker:" box to get information on FleetBoston Financial. Repeat the process by entering "WFC" in the "Ticker:" box to get information on Wells Fargo. How do these ratios differ for the three banks?

Pertinent Web Site

Board of Governors of the Federal Reserve   **www.federalreserve.gov**

Appendix 18A

Federal Reserve Requirement Accounting

View Appendix 18A at the Web site for this textbook (**www.mhhe.com/saunders5e**).

Appendix 18B

Bankers Acceptances and Commercial Paper as a Source of Financing

View Appendix 18B at the Web site for this textbook (**www.mhhe.com/saunders5e**).

Chapter **Nineteen**

Deposit Insurance and Other Liability Guarantees

INTRODUCTION

Chapter 17 discussed the liquidity risks faced by FIs and Chapter 18 described ways FIs can better manage that risk. Because of concerns about the asset quality or solvency of an FI, liability holders such as depositors and life insurance policyholders (and to a lesser extent, mutual fund shareholders) have incentives to engage in runs, that is, to withdraw all their funds from an FI. As we discussed in Chapter 17, the incentive to run is accentuated in banks, thrifts, and insurance companies by the sequential servicing rule used to meet liability withdrawals. As a result, deposit and liability holders who are first in line to withdraw funds get preference over those last in line.

While a run on an unhealthy FI is not necessarily a bad thing—it can discipline the performance of managers and owners—there is a risk that runs on bad FIs can become contagious and spread to good or well-run FIs. In contagious run or panic conditions, liability holders do not bother to distinguish between good and bad FIs but instead seek to turn their liabilities into cash or safe securities as quickly as possible. Contagious runs can have a major contractionary effect on the supply of credit as well as the money supply regionally, nationally, or even internationally.[1]

Moreover, a contagious run on FIs can have serious social welfare effects. For example, a major run on banks can have an adverse effect on the level of savings in all types of FIs and therefore can inhibit the ability of individuals to transfer wealth through time to protect themselves against major risks such as future ill health and falling income in old age.

Because of such wealth, money supply, and credit supply effects, government regulators of financial service firms have introduced guaranty programs to deter runs by offering liability holders varying degrees of failure protection. Specifically, if a liability holder believes a claim is totally secure even if the FI is in trouble, there is no incentive to run. The liability holder's place in line no longer affects getting his or her funds back. Regulatory guaranty or insurance programs for liability holders deter runs and thus deter contagious runs and panics.

---

[1] For example, a run on Rhode Island state-chartered banks in 1990 had a major negative effect on the local (state) economy, but very little effect nationally.

Federally backed insurance programs include the Federal Deposit Insurance Corporation (FDIC) (created in 1933) for banks and thrifts, the Securities Investors Protection Corporation (SIPC) (created in 1970) for securities firms, and the Pension Benefit Guaranty Corporation (PBGC) (created in 1974) for private pension funds.[2] In addition, because of their state rather than federal regulation, state-organized guaranty funds back up most life and property–casualty insurance companies.

This chapter discusses federal deposit insurance funds for banks and thrifts, beginning with the history of these insurance or guaranty funds and including the problems (and in one case, failure) experienced by these funds. We then analyze methods available to reduce DI risk taking, thus reducing the probability that deposit holders must be paid off with deposit insurance. We also look at the Federal Reserve's discount window as a (limited) alternative to deposit insurance. Other guarantee programs, including those for insurance companies, securities firms, and pension funds are also analyzed. Appendix 19B to the chapter (located at the book's Web site, www.mhhe.com/saunders5e) presents a summary of deposit insurance schemes for commercial banks in the EU and G-10 countries.

BANK AND THRIFT GUARANTY FUNDS

www.fdic.gov

The FDIC was created in 1933 in the wake of the banking panics of 1930–33, when some 10,000 commercial banks failed. The original level of individual depositor insurance coverage at commercial banks was $2,500, which was increased (six times since 1934) to $100,000 in 1980.[3] Between 1945 and 1980, commercial bank deposit insurance clearly worked; there were no runs or panics, and the number of individual bank failures was very small (see Figure 19–1). Beginning in 1980, however, bank failures accelerated, with more than 1,039 failures in the decade ending in 1990, peaking at 221 in 1988. This number of failures was actually larger than that for the entire 1933–79 period. Moreover, the costs of each of these failures to the FDIC were often larger than the total costs for the mainly small bank failures in 1933–79. As the number and costs of these closures mounted in the 1980s, the FDIC fund, built up from premiums paid by banks (and the reinvestment income from those premiums), was rapidly drained. Any insurance fund becomes insolvent if the premiums collected and the reserves built up from investing premiums are insufficient to offset the cost of failure claims. The FDIC's resources were virtually depleted by early 1991, when it was given permission to borrow $30 billion from the U.S. Treasury. Even then, it ended 1991 with a deficit of $7 billion. In response to this crisis, Congress passed the FDIC Improvement Act (FDICIA) in December 1991 to restructure the bank insurance fund and prevent its potential insolvency.

Since 1991 there has been a dramatic turnaround in the fund's finances and a drop in bank failures—partially in response to record profit levels in banks. Specifically, as of January 2004, the FDIC's Bank Insurance Fund (BIF) had reserves of

---

[2] Until its insolvency in 1989, FSLIC (the Federal Savings and Loan Insurance Corporation) insured the deposits of most thrifts. Since 1989, both banks and thrifts have been insured under the umbrella of the FDIC, as we discuss later in this chapter.

[3] The FDIC is currently considering an increase in deposit insurance coverage to $130,000 and then indexing coverage to some major inflation or price index such as the CPI (see below).

FIGURE 19–1   **Number of Failed Banks by Year, 1934–2003**

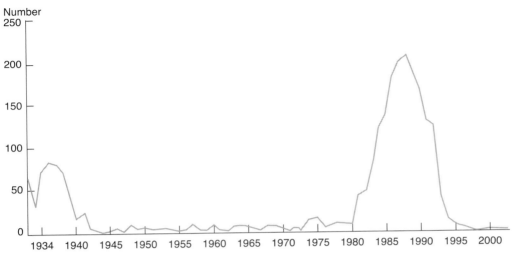

Source: FDIC annual reports and statistics on banking. *www.fdic.gov*

$33.5 billion. In 2003, the number of bank failures had fallen to two. In 2002 there were 10 failures, in 2001 there were 3 failures, and in 2000 there were 6 failures. The largest of these recent failures was that of Superior Bank of Illinois in July 2001. The original expected loss to the FDIC from this failure was $1 billion. However, in December 2001, the owners agreed to pay a fine of $460 million to the FDIC to avoid being punished for mismanagement resulting in the failure. The final cost of this failure to the FDIC was $428 million. The fund's reserves now exceed 1.31 percent of insured deposits.

The Federal Savings and Loan Insurance Corporation (FSLIC) covered savings associations (formerly called S&Ls); other thrifts, such as mutual savings banks, often chose to be insured under the FDIC rather than the FSLIC.[4] Like the FDIC, this insurance fund was in relatively good shape until the end of the 1970s. Beginning in 1980, the fund's resources were rapidly depleted as more and more thrifts failed and had to be closed or merged. In August 1989, Congress passed the Financial Institutions Reform, Recovery, and Enforcement Act (FIRREA), largely in response to the deepening crisis in the thrift industry and the growing insolvency of the FSLIC. This act completely restructured the savings association fund and transferred its management to the FDIC.[5] At the same time, the restructured savings association insurance fund became the Savings Association Insurance Fund (SAIF). Currently, the FDIC manages the SAIF separately from the commercial bank fund, which is now called the Bank Insurance Fund (BIF). (As of

[4] As we discussed in Chapter 2, credit union depositors enjoy a degree of coverage similar to that of bank, savings association, and savings bank depositors via coverage through the National Credit Union Insurance Fund (established in 1971). See E. J. Kane and R. Hendershott, "The Federal Deposit Insurance Fund That Didn't Put a Bite on U.S. Taxpayers," *Journal of Banking and Finance* 20, no. 5 (1996), pp. 1305–27. C. A. McClatchey and G. V. Karels, in "Deposit Insurance and Risk-Taking Behavior in the Credit Union Industry," University of Nebraska, Working Paper, 1996, look at whether credit unions increased their risk-taking behavior after credit union deposits became federally insured. They find that asset quality and liquidity improved over the period following the institution of deposit insurance.

[5] At that time, the FSLIC ceased to exist.

FIGURE 19–2
FDIC, BIF, and SAIF

Source: FDIC, *Quarterly Banking Profile,* September 2003. *www.fdic.gov*

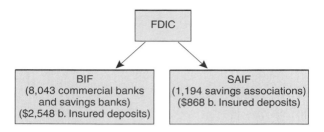

September 2003, SAIF had $12.2 billion in reserves, representing 1.40 percent of insured deposits.) In the period 1996–2003, only 5 SAIF member DIs failed. In Figure 19–2, we present the organizational structure of the FDIC and these funds (including the number of DIs insured and the dollar value of insured deposits) as of September 2003.

Internet Exercise	Go to the Federal Deposit Insurance Corporation Web site and find the latest information available for the number of depository institutions insured by the FDIC and the dollar value of insured deposits.
	Go to the Federal Deposit Insurance Corporation website at **www.fdic.gov**. Click on *"Analysts."* Click on "FDIC Quarterly Banking Profile." Click on "Quarterly Banking Profile." Click on "Deposit Insurance Fund Trends." Click on "Table III-B. Selected Indicators, By Fund Membership." This will download a file on to your computer that will contain the most recent information on the number of depository institutions insured by BIF and SAIF. Go back to Deposit Insurance Fund Trends. Click on "Table I-B. Selected Insurance Fund Indicators." This will download a file on to your computer that will contain the most recent information on the dollar value of insured deposits at depository institutions insured by BIF and SAIF.

Based on the performance of banks and thrifts in the 1990s, the FDICIA and FIRREA, along with a strong economy, appear to have been successful in helping strengthen the financial condition of DIs. Whether these regulations will continue to work (particularly in the event of a major economic downturn) remains to be seen. One argument is that the continued success of these regulations depends on the political will of bank regulators to carry out the intent of the legislation, even at the cost of reducing their own discretionary power.[6]

In April 2001, the FDIC proposed the merger of the BIF and the SAIF into one insurance fund called the Deposit Insurance Fund. The FDIC argued that the BIF and SAIF offer identical services. Yet, as long as two separate funds exist, the potential for a premium disparity and competitive inequality between banks and thrifts exists. Moreover, many institutions have both BIF-insured and SAIF-insured deposits as a result of mergers, acquisitions, and expansion of bank powers. Specifically, more than 40 percent of SAIF-insured deposits are now held by commercial banks. The costs to insured institutions associated with tracking their BIF and SAIF deposits separately could be eliminated by merging both funds. This proposal was passed by the U.S. House of Representatives in early 2003 as part of

---

[6] This argument includes a call for fully implementing market value accounting and increasing the thresholds for all capital adequacy categories (see Chapter 20) to levels more consistent with those the market imposes on uninsured competitors of banks and thrifts. See G. J. Benston and G. G. Kaufman, "FDICIA after Five Years," *Journal of Economic Perspectives,* Summer 1997, pp. 139–58.

TABLE 19–1
Merging the BIF and SAIF

Source: FDIC, Quarterly Banking Profile, September 2003. *www.fdic.gov*

Bank Data	BIF	SAIF	Merged Funds
Number of fund member banks	8,043	1,194	9,905
Insured deposits (in billions)	$2,548	$ 868	$3,416
Insurance Fund Data			
Fund balance (in billions)	$33.46	$12.19	$45.65
Reserve ratio*	1.31%	1.40%	1.34%

*Reserve ratio is the amount of reserves on hand as a percent of total insured deposits.

the Deposit Insurance Reform Act of 2003. In early 2004 the bill was awaiting action by the U.S. Senate. Table 19–1 shows the effects of a possible BIF/SAIF merger as of September 2003.

Concept Questions

1. What events led to Congress's passing of the FDIC Improvement Act (FDICIA)?
2. What events brought about the demise of the FSLIC?

THE CAUSES OF THE DEPOSITORY FUND INSOLVENCIES

There are at least two, not necessarily independent, views as to why depository institution insurance funds became economically insolvent. In addition, some factors offer better explanations of the FSLIC insolvency in the 1980s than of the FDIC's (near) insolvency, especially since the FSLIC insolvency was far worse than the financial problems of the FDIC.

The Financial Environment

One view of the cause of insolvency is that a number of external events or shocks adversely impacted U.S. banks and thrifts in the 1980s. The first was the dramatic rise in interest rates in the 1979–82 period. This rise in rates had a major negative effect on those thrifts funding long-term, fixed-rate mortgages with short-term deposits. The second event was the collapse in oil, real estate, and other commodity prices, which particularly harmed oil, gas, and agricultural loans in the southwestern United States. The third event was increased financial service firm competition at home and abroad, which eroded the value of bank and thrift charters during the 1980s (see Chapters 21 to 23).[7]

Moral Hazard

A second view is that these financial environment effects were catalysts for, rather than the causes of, the crisis. At the heart of the crisis was deposit insurance itself, especially some of its contractual features. Although deposit insurance had deterred depositors and other liability holders from engaging in runs prior to 1980, in so doing it had also removed or reduced depositor discipline. Deposit insurance allowed DIs to borrow at rates close to the risk-free rate and, if they chose, to undertake high-risk asset investments. DI owners and managers knew that insured

---

[7] The value of a bank or thrift charter is the present value of expected profits from operating in the industry. As expected profits fall, so does the value of a bank or thrift charter. See A. Saunders and B. Wilson, "An Analysis of Bank Charter Value and Its Risk-Constraining Incentives," *Journal of Financial Services Research*, April/June 2001, pp.185–96.

depositors had little incentive to restrict such behavior, either through fund withdrawals or by requiring risk premiums on deposit rates, since they were fully insured by the FDIC if a DI failed. Given this scenario, losses on oil, gas, and real estate loans in the 1980s are viewed as the outcome of bankers' exploiting underpriced or mispriced risk under the deposit insurance contract. The provision of insurance that encourages rather than discourages risk taking is called **moral hazard.**[8] This is because, with deposit insurance, a highly leveraged bank whose debt holders need not monitor the DI's (borrower's) actions has a strong incentive to undertake excessively risky investment decisions, such as in its loan-generating activities.[9]

In the absence of depositor discipline (as will be explained below), regulators could have priced risk taking by DIs either through charging explicit deposit insurance premiums linked to DI risk taking or by charging **implicit premiums** through restricting and monitoring the risky activities of DIs. This could potentially have substituted for depositor discipline; those DIs that took more risk would have paid directly or indirectly for this risk-taking behavior. However, from 1933 until January 1, 1993, regulators based deposit insurance premiums on a DI's deposit size rather than on its risk. The 1980s were also a period of deregulation and capital adequacy forbearance rather than stringent activity regulation and tough capital requirements. Moreover, for the FSLIC, the number of bank examinations and examiners actually fell between 1981 and 1984.[10] Finally, prompt corrective action and closure for severely undercapitalized banks did not begin until the end of 1992 (see Chapter 20).

moral hazard
The loss exposure faced by an insurer when the provision of insurance encourages the insured to take more risks.

implicit premiums
Deposit insurance premiums or costs imposed on a DI through activity constraints rather than direct monetary charges.

Concept Questions

1. What two basic views are offered to explain why depository institution insurance funds became insolvent during the 1980s?
2. Why was interest rate risk less of a problem for banks than for thrifts in the early 1980s?

PANIC PREVENTION VERSUS MORAL HAZARD

A great deal of attention has focused on the moral hazard reason for the collapse of the bank and thrift insurance funds in the 1980s. The less DI owners have to lose from taking risks, the greater are their incentives to take excessively risky asset positions. When asset investment risks or gambles pay off, DI owners make windfall gains in profits. If they fail, however, the FDIC, as the insurer, bears most of the costs, given that owners of DIs—like owners of regular corporations—have limited liability. It's a "heads I win, tails I don't lose (much)" situation.

Note that even without deposit insurance, the limited liability of DI owners or stockholders always creates incentives to take risk at the expense of fixed

---

[8] The precise definition of moral hazard is the loss exposure of an insurer (the FDIC) that results from the character or circumstances of the insured (here, the bank).

[9] Recent research found that explicit deposit insurance tends to be detrimental to bank stability, more so when bank interest rates have been deregulated and moral hazard opportunities are great. In countries in which moral hazard opportunities are limited, regulation and supervision are more effective at offsetting the adverse incentives created by deposit insurance. See A. Demirgüç-Kunt and E. Detragiache, "Does Deposit Insurance Increase Banking System Stability? An Empirical Investigation," *Journal of Monetary Economics,* 2002, pp. 1373–1406.

[10] L. J. White points to a general weakness of thrift supervision and examination in the 1980s. The number of examinations fell from 3,210 in 1980 to 2,347 in 1984, and examinations per billion dollars of assets fell from 5.41 in 1980 to 2.4 in 1984. See L. J. White, *The S and L Debacle* (New York: Oxford University Press, 1991), p. 89.

actuarially fairly priced insurance
Insurance pricing based on the perceived risk of the insured.

claimants such as depositors and debt holders.[11] The difference between DIs and other firms is risk-taking incentives induced by mispriced deposit insurance. That is, when risk taking is not **actuarially fairly priced** in deposit insurance premiums, this adds to the incentives of DI stockholders to take additional risks.

Nevertheless, even though mispriced deposit insurance potentially accentuates DI risk taking, deposit insurance effectively deterred DI panics and runs of the 1930–33 kind in the postwar period (see Figure 19–1). That is, deposit insurance has ensured a good deal of stability in the credit and monetary system.

This suggests that, ideally, regulators should design the deposit insurance contract with the trade-off between moral hazard risk and DI panic or run risk in mind. For example, by providing 100 percent coverage of all depositors and reducing the probability of runs to zero, the insurer may be encouraging certain DIs to take a significant degree of moral hazard risk-taking behavior.[12] On the other hand, a very limited degree of deposit insurance coverage might encourage runs and panics, although moral hazard behavior itself would be less evident.

In the 1980s, extensive insurance coverage for deposit holders and the resulting lack of incentive for deposit holders to monitor and restrict DI owners' and managers' risk taking resulted in small levels of DI run risk but high levels of moral hazard risk.[13] By restructuring the deposit insurance contract, it may be possible to reduce moral hazard risk quite a bit without a very large increase in DI run risk. To some extent, these were the objectives behind the passage of the FDIC Improvement

---

[11] Thus, one possible policy to reduce excessive bank risk taking would be to eliminate limited liability for bank stockholders. A study by L. J. White found that bank failures in private banking systems with unlimited liability, such as that which existed in 18th-century Scotland, were rare. Indeed, in the United States, double liability existed for bank stockholders prior to the introduction of deposit insurance; that is, on failure, the stockholders would lose their initial equity contribution and be assessed by the receiver an extra amount equal to the par value of their stock, which would be used to pay creditors (over and above the liquidation value of the bank's assets). See L. J. White, "Scottish Banking and Legal Restrictions Theory: A Closer Look," *Journal of Money Credit and Banking* 22 (1990), pp. 526–36. For a discussion of double liability in pre-1933 United States, see A. Saunders and B. Wilson, "If History Could Be Re-Run: The Provision and Pricing of Deposit Insurance in 1933," *Journal of Financial Intermediation* 4 (1995), pp. 396–413; and J. R. Macey and G. P. Miller, "Double Liability of Bank Shareholders: History and Implications," *Wake Forest Law Review* 27 (1992), pp. 31–62.

[12] Indeed, research on deposit insurance schemes in over 60 countries found that explicit deposit insurance tends to be detrimental to banking system stability, particularly when bank interest rates have been deregulated and where the regulatory environment is weak. In particular, deposit insurance encourages DIs to finance high-risk, high-return projects. However, when opportunities for moral hazard are more limited and more effective prudential regulation and supervision exist, the adverse incentives created by deposit insurance are limited. This, in turn, improves banking system stability. See A. Kunt and E. Detragiache, "Does Deposit Insurance Increase Banking System Stability? An Empirical Investigation," Working Paper, World Bank, June 2000.

[13] At this point, note that managers may not have the same risk-taking incentives as owners. This is especially true if managers are compensated through wage and salary contracts rather than through shares and share option programs. When managers are on fixed-wage contracts, their preferences in regard to risk lean toward being risk averse. That is, they are unlikely to exploit the same type of moral hazard incentives that stock owner–controlled banks would. This is because managers have little to gain if their banks do exceptionally well (their salaries are fixed) but probably will lose their jobs and human capital investments in a bank if they fail. A study by A. Saunders, E. Strock, and N. Travlos showed that stock owner–controlled banks tend to be more risky than manager-controlled banks. Thus, understanding the agency structure of the bank is important in identifying which banks are most likely to exploit risk-taking (moral hazard) incentives. See A. Saunders, E. Strock, and N. Travlos, "Ownership Structure, Deregulation, and Bank Risk Taking," *Journal of Finance* 45 (1989), pp. 643–54. Moreover, as pointed out by K. John, A. Saunders, and L. Senbet in "A Theory of Bank Regulation and Management Compensation," *Review of Financial Studies* (2000), pp. 95–126, deposit insurers might usefully take into account managerial compensation structures and incentives in setting deposit insurance premiums.

Act (FDICIA) of 1991 and the depositor preference legislation contained in the Omnibus Budget Reconciliation Act of 1993, discussed later in this chapter.[14]

Concept Question

1. Historically, what effect has deposit insurance had on DI panics and runs?

CONTROLLING DEPOSITORY INSTITUTION RISK TAKING

There are three ways deposit insurance could be structured to reduce moral hazard behavior:

1. Increase stockholder discipline.
2. Increase depositor discipline.
3. Increase regulator discipline.

Specifically, redesigning the features of the insurance contract can either directly or indirectly impact DI owners' and stockholders' risk-taking incentives by altering the behavior of depositors and regulators. In the wake of the solvency problems of the FDIC, in 1991 FDICIA was passed with the objective of increasing discipline in all three areas.

Stockholder Discipline

Insurance Premiums

One approach toward making stockholders' risk taking more expensive is to link FDIC insurance premiums to the risk profile of the DI. Below we look at ways this might be done, including the risk-based premium scheme adopted by the FDIC since 1993.

Theory   A major feature of the pre-1993 FDIC deposit insurance contract was the flat deposit insurance premium levied on banks and thrifts. Specifically, each year a DI paid a given sum or premium to the FDIC based on a fixed proportion of its domestic deposits.[15] Until 1989, the premium was 8.33 cents per $100 in domestic deposits.[16] As the FDIC fund became increasingly depleted, the level of the premium was raised several times, but its risk-insensitive nature was left unaltered. By 1993, the premiums DIs had to pay had risen to 23 cents per $100 of their domestic deposits, almost a tripling of their premiums since 1988.

To see why a flat or size-based premium schedule does not discipline a DI's risk taking, consider two banks of the same domestic deposit size, as shown in Table 19–2. Banks A and B have domestic deposits of $100 million and (in 1993) would pay the same premium to the FDIC (.0023 × $100 million = $230,000 per annum). However, their risk-taking behavior is completely different. Bank A is

---

[14] E. Kane, "Three Paradigms for the Role of Capitalization Requirements in Insured Financial Institutions," *Journal of Banking and Finance* 19 (June 1995), pp. 431–60, models the trade-off between the level of risk taking eventually undertaken by banks, contractual features of deposit insurance, and capital regulation as the outcome of a "bargaining game" among three different groups of agents (with different preferences regarding risk taking) and the "agency conflicts" among these groups. The groups are bank stockholders, bank managers, and the providers of insurance guarantees (the FDIC).

[15] In actual practice, premiums are levied and paid semiannually.

[16] In the pre-1980 period, the FDIC was able to rebate some of these premiums because it felt it had adequate reserves at the time. See S. A. Buser, A. H. Chen, and E. J. Kane, "Federal Deposit Insurance, Regulatory Policy, and Optimal Bank Capital," *Journal of Finance* 36 (1981), pp. 51–60.

TABLE 19–2
Flat Deposit
Insurance
Premiums and Risk
Taking

	Bank A			Bank B	
Assets		**Liabilities**	**Assets**		**Liabilities**
Real estate loans	100	Domestic deposits 100	T-bills	100	Domestic deposits 100

FIGURE 19–3
Premium Schedules
Relative to Risk

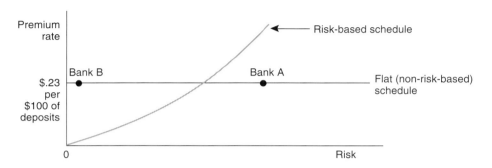

excessively risky, investing all its assets in real estate loans. Bank B is almost risk free, investing all its assets in government T-bills. We graph the insurance premium rates paid by the two banks compared with their asset risk in Figure 19–3.

In Figure 19–3, note that under the pre-1993 flat premium schedule, banks A and B would have been charged the same deposit insurance premium based on a bank's domestic deposit size. Critics of flat premiums argue that the FDIC should act more like a private property–casualty insurer. Under normal property–casualty insurance premium-setting principles, insurers charge those with higher risks higher premiums. That is, low-risk parties (such as bank B) do not generally subsidize high-risk parties (such as bank A) as they did under the pre-1993 FDIC premium-pricing scheme. If premiums increased as bank risk increased, banks would have reduced incentives to take risks. Therefore, the ultimate goal might be to price risk in an actuarially fair fashion, similar to the process used by a private property–casualty insurer, so that premiums reflect the expected private costs or losses to the insurer from the provision of deposit insurance.

Note that there are arguments against imposing an actuarially fair risk-based premium schedule. If the deposit insurer's mandate is not to act as if it were a private cost-minimizing insurer such as a PC insurance company because of social welfare considerations, some type of subsidy to banks and thrifts can be justified. Remember that the FDIC is a quasi-government agency, and broader banking market stability concerns and savers' welfare concerns might arguably override private cost-minimizing concerns and require subsidies.[17] Other authors have argued that if an actuarially fair premium is imposed on a banking system that is fully competitive, banking itself cannot be profitable. That is, some subsidy is needed for banks to exist profitably.[18] However, while U.S. banking is competitive, it probably deviates somewhat from the perfectly competitive model.

---

[17] Most of the deposit insurance literature, however, assumes that the objective of the FDIC should be to minimize cost; see S. Acharya and J. F. Dreyfus, "Optimal Bank Reorganization Policies and the Pricing of Federal Deposit Insurance," *Journal of Finance* 44 (1988), pp. 1313–34. Also, the FDIC Improvement Act generally confirms cost minimization as an important objective defining FDIC's policies.

[18] See Y. S. Chan, S. I. Greenbaum, and A. V. Thakor, "Is Fairly Priced Deposit Insurance Possible?" *Journal of Finance* 47 (1992), pp. 227–46; and Buser, Chen, and Kane, "Federal Deposit Insurance."

FIGURE 19–4
Deposit Insurance as a Put Option (0*D* = DI's deposits; 0*A* = DI's assets; 0*P* = premium paid by DI)

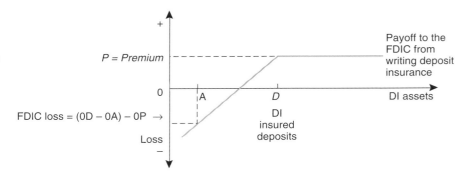

Calculating the Actuarially Fair Premium[19]   Economists have suggested a number of approaches for calculating the fair deposit insurance premium that a cost-minimizing insurer such as the FDIC should charge. One approach would be to set the premium equal to the expected severity of loss times the frequency of losses due to DI failure plus some load or markup factor.[20] This would exactly mimic the approach toward premium setting in the property–casualty industry. However, the most common approach, the **option pricing model of deposit insurance** (OPM), has been to view the FDIC's provision of deposit insurance as virtually identical to the FDIC's writing a put option on the assets of the DI that buys the deposit insurance.[21,22] We depict the conceptual idea underlying the option pricing model approach in Figure 19–4.

In this framework, the FDIC charges the DI a premium 0*P* to insure the DI's deposits (0*D*). If the DI does well and the market value of the DI's assets is greater than 0*D*, its net worth is positive and it can continue in business. The FDIC would face no charge against its resources and would keep the premium paid to it by the DI (0*P*). If the DI is insolvent, possibly because of a bad or risky asset portfolio, such that the value of the DI's assets falls below 0*D* (say to 0*A*), and its net worth is negative, the DI owners will "put the bank" back to the FDIC. If this happens, the FDIC will pay out to the insured depositors an amount 0*D* and will liquidate the DI's assets (0*A*). As a result, the FDIC bears the cost of the insolvency (or negative net worth) equal to (0*D* − 0*A*) minus the insurance premiums paid by the DI (0*P*).

option pricing model of deposit insurance
A model for calculating deposit insurance as a put option on the DI's assets.

---

[19] This section, which contains more technical topics, may be included in or dropped from the chapter reading depending on the rigor of the course.

[20] D. Duffie, R. Jarrow, A. Purnanandam, and W. Yang develop a reduced-form model in which fair market deposit insurance rates can be inferred from market pricing of the credit risk in bank debt instruments. They find fair market deposit insurance rates to be much larger than actuarially calculated mean loss rates to the insurer. The fair market insurance rate of a given bank is the risk-neutral mean loss rate to the insurer, which is the product of (a) the annualized likelihood of failure during the period covered by the current contract and (b) the expected loss to the insurer given failure, as a fraction of assessed deposits. See "Market Pricing of Deposit Insurance," *Journal of Financial Services Research,* October/December 2003, pp. 93–119.

[21] See, for example, R. C. Merton, "An Analytic Derivation of the Cost of Deposit Insurance and Loan Guarantees: An Application of Modern Option Pricing Theory," *Journal of Banking and Finance* 1 (1977), pp. 3–11; and E. Ronn and A. K. Verma, "Pricing Risk-Adjusted Deposit Insurance: An Option-Based Model," *Journal of Finance* 41 (1986), pp. 871–96.

[22] There is a third approach that views deposit insurance premiums being set as the outcome of an agency conflict among three groups of self-interested parties: bank stockholders, bank managers, and bank regulators. See Kane, "Three Paradigms."

FIGURE 19–5
Average Deposit
Insurance Liability,
OPM Estimates

Source: Federal Reserve
Bank of San Francisco,
Newsletter 95–08, 1995

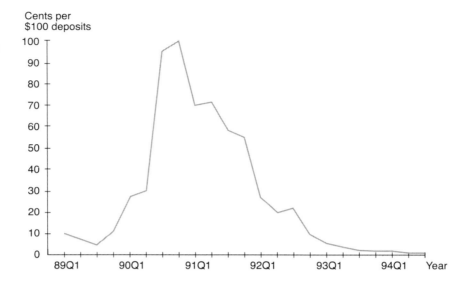

When valued in this fashion as a simple European put option, the FDIC's cost of providing deposit insurance increases with the level of asset risk (σ_A^2) and with the DI's leverage (D/A). That is, the actuarially fair premium ($0P$) is equivalent to the premium on a put option and as such should be positively related to both asset risk (σ_A^2) and leverage risk (D/A).[23] One OPM estimate of the average fair insurance premium based on the option pricing model for 300 banks is shown in Figure 19–5 for 1989–94.[24] The decline in average fair premiums after 1991 reflects a decline in bank asset volatility and improvements in bank leverage risk (D/A) since 1991.

Even though the option pricing model is a conceptually and theoretically elegant tool, it is difficult to apply in practice—especially because a DI's asset value (A) and its asset risks (σ_A^2) are not directly observable. While values of these variables can be extracted from the equity value and the volatility of equity value of the DI (see the discussion on the KMV model in Chapter 11), only 300 DIs have their stocks traded on the three major exchanges (AMEX, NASDAQ, and NYSE),

---

[23] In Merton, "An Analytic Derivation," the value of a deposit insurance guaranty is shown to be the same as the Black-Scholes model for a European put option of maturity T (where T is the time period until the next premium assessment):

$$0P(T) = De^{-rT} \phi(X_2) - A\phi(X_1)$$

where

$$X_1 = \{\log (D/A) - (r + \sigma_A^2/2)T\}/\sigma_A \sqrt{T}$$

$$X_2 = X_1 + \sigma_A \sqrt{T}$$

and ϕ is the standard normal distribution.

Other authors have relaxed many of Merton's assumptions, including (1) allowing for partial deposit insurance coverage (Ronn and Verma, "Pricing Risk-Adjusted Deposit Insurance"), (2) closure taking place when $D < A$ (i.e., forbearance) rather than $D = A$ (Ronn and Verma; and Acharya and Dreyfus, "Optimal Bank Reorganization"), (3) surveillance and monitoring involving costs (R. C. Merton, "On the Cost of Deposit Insurance When There Are Surveillance Costs," *Journal of Business* 51 (1978), pp. 439–52), and (4) the option being American rather than European, that is, closure exercisable at any time during the insurance contract period rather than at the end (Merton, "On the Cost").

[24] See M. Levonian and F. Furlong, "Reduced Deposit Insurance Risk," Federal Reserve Bank of San Francisco Weekly Letter, no. 95–08, February 24, 1995.

and there are over 9,200 DIs (8,000 BIF-insured DIs and 1,200 SAIF-insured DIs).[25] Even so, the option model framework is useful because it indicates that both leverage and asset quality (or risk) are important elements that should enter into any deposit insurance pricing model.

Next, we look at the risk-based deposit insurance premium scheme introduced by the FDIC in January 1993; it is directly linked to both bank leverage and asset quality.

Concept Questions

1. Bank A has a ratio of deposits to assets of 90 percent and a variance of asset returns of 10 percent. Bank B has a ratio of deposits to assets of 85 percent and a variance of asset returns of 5 percent. Which bank should pay the higher insurance premium?
2. If deposit insurance is similar to a put option, who exercises that option?

Implementing Risk-Based Premiums The FDICIA required the FDIC to establish risk-based premiums by January 1, 1994. The FDIC now has to base premiums on:[26]

1. Different categories and concentrations of assets.
2. Different categories and concentrations of liabilities—insured, uninsured, contingent, and noncontingent.
3. Other factors that affect the probability of loss.
4. The deposit insurer's revenue needs.[27]

FDIC risk-based deposit insurance program
A program that assesses insurance premiums on the basis of capital adequacy and supervisory judgments on DI quality.

The FDIC first introduced a **risk-based deposit insurance program** on January 1, 1993. Under this program, which applied equally to all depository-insured institutions, a bank or thrift's risk would be ranked along a capital adequacy dimension and a supervisory dimension. That is, rankings are partly based on regulators' judgments regarding asset quality, loan underwriting standards, and other operating risks. Since each dimension had three categories, a bank or thrift was placed in any one of nine cells. See Table 19–3, panel (a), for the original structure of premiums.

The best DIs, those in cell 1 that were well capitalized and healthy, paid an annual insurance premium of 23 cents per $100 of deposits, while the worst DIs paid 31 cents. Although the 8-cent differential in insurance premiums between the safest and the riskiest DIs was a first step in risk-based pricing, it was widely considered so small that it did not effectively price insurance according to DI risk exposures. At the time of the risk-based premiums' introduction, the FDIC estimated that about 75 percent of the over 12,000 insured commercial banks and savings banks (with 51 percent of the bank deposit base) and 60 percent of the 2,300 insured thrifts (with approximately 43 percent of the thrift deposit base) were in the group paying the lowest premium. Only about 220 banks (2 percent of all insured commercial and savings banks) and 160 thrifts (7 percent of all insured thrifts) were in the group paying the highest insurance premiums of 31 cents. The average assessment rate in 1993 was 23.2 cents per $100 of deposits.

---

[25] The problem of pricing deposit insurance for private (nontraded) banks has been noted by M. Falkenheim and G. Pennacchi, "The Cost of Deposit Insurance for Privately Held Banks: A Market Comparable Approach," *Journal of Financial Services Research,* October 2003, pp. 121–48.

[26] The FDIC is also allowed to reinsure up to 10 percent of an insured institution's risk and to use reinsurance prices to set the insured's premiums.

[27] In particular, it cannot cut premiums until the fund's reserves exceed 1.25 percent of insured deposits. Since 1996 this target level has been exceeded by both BIF and SAIF.

TABLE 19–3   Shifting the Deposit Insurance Burden

(a) The fee structure for deposit insurance, effective January 1, 1993.

Supervisory Groups

Capital Category	Healthy[1]	Supervisory Concern[2]	Substantial Supervisory Concern[3]
Well capitalized[4]	23 cents per $100	26 cents per $100	29 cents per $100
Adequately capitalized[5]	26 cents per $100	29 cents per $100	30 cents per $100
Undercapitalized[6]	29 cents per $100	30 cents per $100	31 cents per $100

(b) The fee structure for deposit insurance, effective January 1, 1997.

Supervisory Groups

Capital Category	Healthy[1]	Supervisory Concern[2]	Substantial Supervisory Concern[3]
Well capitalized[4]	0 cents per $100	3 cents per $100	17 cents per $100
Adequately capitalized[5]	3 cents per $100	10 cents per $100	24 cents per $100
Undercapitalized[6]	10 cents per $100	24 cents per $100	27 cents per $100

Note: Numbers in cells show premiums.
[1] Financially sound and only a few weaknesses.
[2] Weaknesses that if not corrected could result in significant risk to the fund.
[3] Substantial probability of loss to the fund unless effective corrective action is taken.
[4] Total risk based $\geq$ 10 percent, Tier 1 risk based $\geq$ 6 percent, Tier 1 leverage $\geq$ 5 percent.
[5] Total risk based $\geq$ 8 percent, Tier 1 risk based $\geq$ 4 percent, Tier 1 leverage $\geq$ 4 percent.
[6] Does not meet the capital criteria for well- or adequately capitalized depository institutions.

Source: Office of the Comptroller of the Currency, January 1993 and January 1997.

However, the improving solvency position of the FDIC (and of the banks and thrifts it insures) has resulted in a considerable reduction in insurance premiums. In 1996 (for BIF-insured DIs) and 1997 (for SAIF-insured DIs) the fee structure for deposit insurance was changed to that in panel (b) of Table 19–3. As a result, in September 2003, 91.8 percent of all BIF-insured DIs and 91.5 percent of all SAIF-insured DIs paid the statutory minimum premium (which has fallen to zero) and the average assessment rate was equal to 0.26 cents per $100 of deposits.[28]

April 2001 FDIC Proposal for Deposit Insurance Reform   In the early 2000s, the FDIC identified several weaknesses with the current system of deposit insurance that it felt needed to be corrected.[29] Among these was that the current system did not effectively price risk. At the time, regulations restricted the FDIC from charging premiums to well-capitalized and highly rated DIs as long as the insurance fund reserves were above 1.25 percent of insured deposits—this was called the designated reserve ratio (DRR). As a result, (as noted above) over 90 percent of all insured banks did not pay deposit insurance premiums in the late 1990s and early 2000s. The FDIC argued that it should charge regular premiums for risk regardless of the reserve levels of the fund.

---

[28] Beginning in January 1997, all insured banks also had to pay a charge of 1.3 cents per $100 of deposits to help pay off the bonds (so-called FICO bonds) issued to aid the FDIC's restructuring operations in the 1990s.

[29] See "Keeping the Promise: Recommendations for Deposit Insurance Reform," FDIC, April 2001; and "A Guide to Deposit Insurance Reform," *Economic Review*, Federal Reserve Bank of Kansas City, First Quarter 2003, pp. 29–54.

TABLE 19–4
Pricing Deposit Insurance with a Scoring Model

Source: FDIC Web site, April, 2001. *www.fdic.gov*

Scoring factors	Range of Scores	Maximum Score
CAMEL rating = 1	0	
CAMEL rating = 2	1	
CAMEL rating = 3	4	
CAMEL rating = 4	15	
CAMEL rating = 5	50	50
Equity to assets > 12%	0	
Equity to assets = 6% to 12%	1	
Equity to assets < 6%	14	14
Net income to total assets > 1.25%	0	
Net income to total assets = 0.65% to 1.25%	1	
Net income to total assets = 0% to 0.65%	2	
Net income to total assets < 0%	10	10
Nonperforming loans to total assets < 1%	0	
Nonperforming loans to total assets = 1% to 3%	2	
Nonperforming loans to total assets > 3%	10	10
ORE to total assets < 1%	0	
ORE to total assets = 1% to 3%	2	
ORE to total assets > 3%	6	6
Noncore funding to total assets < 15%	0	
Noncore funding to total assets = 15% to 30%	1	
Noncore funding to total assets > 30%	3	3
Liquid assets to total assets > 50%	0	
Liquid assets to total assets = 30%	1	
Liquid assets to total assets < 30%	2	2
Asset growth < 40%	0	
Asset growth > 40%	5	5
Total		100

One approach for measuring risk, suggested by the FDIC, was to use a statistical credit-scoring model that uses examination ratings, financial ratios, and for large banks, certain market signals as inputs to project failure rates. Table 19–4 presents the scoring model suggested by the FDIC. Each DI would receive a score based on such risk factors as its CAMEL rating (regulators' assessment of the DI's overall risk), capital ratios, profitability ratios, nonperforming loans, other real estate owned (ORE) to total assets, core funding ratios, liquidity ratios, and asset growth. The score could then be used to evaluate all DIs and to replace the current nine-cell matrix. For example, using the scoring model to disaggregate cell 1 DIs (under the current scheme, see Table 19–3) into three separate risk categories might be as follows:

Group 1a+: score of 3 or less

Group 1a: score of 4 or 5

Group 1a−: score of 6 through 11

By disaggregating the (best) cell 1 DIs in this manner, 92 percent of the industry would no longer pay the same (zero) assessment rate. The FDIC proposal disaggregates only the A-rated, well capitalized DIs (92 percent of all banks) into three subgroups (i.e., 1a+, 1a, 1a−). Because of the relatively small number, DIs in the other eight cells (the remaining 8 percent of all DIs) are not disaggregated.

TABLE 19–5
Assessment Rates (cents per $100 of deposits) Based on Modified 1a Category

Source: FDIC Web site, April 2001. *www.fdic.gov*

Capital group	Supervisory Subgroups				
	A*			B	C
	1a+	1a	1a−		
Well capitalized	1	3	6	12	25
Adequately capitalized	N/A	12	N/A	25	30
Undercapitalized	N/A	25	N/A	30	40

*Only A-rated, well-capitalized banks are disaggregated into three subgroups (i.e., 1a+, 1a, 1a−).

TABLE 19–6
Distribution of DIs with a Modified 1a Category

Source: FDIC Web site, April 2001. *www.fdic.gov*

Capital group	Supervisory Subgroups				
	A*			B	C
	1a+	1a	1a−		
Well capitalized	4,233 (42.7%)	2,634 (26.5%)	2,282 (23.0%)	485 (4.9%)	70 (0.7%)
Adequately capitalized	N/A	172 (1.7%)	N/A	25 (0.3%)	11 (0.1%)
Undercapitalized	N/A	4 (0.0%)	N/A	2 (0.0%)	6 (0.1%)

*Only A-rated, well-capitalized banks are disaggregated into three subgroups (i.e., 1a+, 1a, 1a−).

Table 19–5 shows a schedule of assessment rates under this scoring model scheme, and Table 19–6 shows the distribution of DIs across this assessment schedule based on year-end 2000 data. Notice under this scheme, 42.7 percent of the institutions would still find themselves in the lowest-risk, 1a+, category (paying a proposed insurance premium of 1 cent per $100 of deposits); 26.5 percent would be in the new 1a category (paying an insurance premium of 3 cents per $100 of deposits); and 23.0 percent would be in the 1a− category (paying an insurance premium of 6 cents per $100 of deposits). The riskiest DIs would incur an annual deposit insurance premium of 40 cents per $100 of deposits. As of early 2004, the proposed Deposit Insurance Reform Act has been approved by the U.S. House of Representatives and is awaiting consideration by the U.S. Senate.

Increased Capital Requirements and Stricter Closure Rules

A second way to reduce stockholders' incentives to take excessive risks is to (1) require higher capital—lower leverage—ratios (so that stockholders have more at stake in taking risky investments) and (2) impose stricter DI closure rules. The moral hazard risk-taking incentives of DI owners increase as their capital or net worth approaches zero and their leverage increases. For those thrifts allowed to operate in the 1980s with virtually no book equity capital and with negative net worth, the risk-taking incentives of their owners were enormous.

capital forbearance
Regulators' policy of allowing an FI to continue operating even when its capital funds are fully depleted.

By failing to close such DIs, regulators exhibited excessive **capital forbearance.** In the short term, forbearance may save the insurance fund some liquidation costs. In the long run, owners of bad banks or thrifts have continuing incentives to grow and take additional risks in the hope of a large payoff that could turn the institution around. This strategy potentially adds to the future liabilities of the insurance fund and to the costs of DI liquidation. We now know that huge additional costs were the actual outcome of the regulators' policy of capital forbearance in the thrift industry in the 1980s.

As we discuss in Chapter 20, a system of risk-based capital requirements mandates that those banks and thrifts taking greater on- and off-balance-sheet, market, credit, operating, and interest rate risks must hold more capital. Thus, risk-based capital supports risk-based deposit insurance premiums by increasing the cost of risk taking for DI stockholders.[30] In addition, the 1991 FDIC Improvement Act has sought to increase significantly the degree of regulatory discipline over DI stockholders by introducing a **prompt corrective action** program. This has imposed five capital zones for banks and thrifts, with progressively harsher mandatory actions being taken by regulators as capital ratios fall. Under this carrot-and-stick approach, a bank or thrift is placed into receivership within 90 days of the time when its capital falls below some positive book value level, that is, when it is critically undercapitalized (currently 2 percent of assets for DIs).

To the extent that the book value of capital approximates true net worth or the market value of capital, this enhances stockholder discipline by imposing additional costs on DI owners for risk taking. It also increases the degree of coinsurance, in regard to risks taken, between DI owners and regulators such as the FDIC.[31]

Since the mid-1980s, a growing number of observers have proposed using subordinate debt (SD) in addition to common stock to increase the degree of overall market discipline (by stockholders and uninsured debt holders) at U.S. depository institutions. In response to these concerns, the Financial Services Modernization Act of 1999 directed the Federal Reserve and the U.S. Treasury to study and report to Congress whether it would be feasible and appropriate to require all or some DIs to maintain some portion of their capital in the form of SD.

In their report,[32] these agencies concluded that an SD policy could be designed to achieve varying degrees of five objectives.[33] First, SD could improve direct market discipline if a DI's expected cost of issuing SD becomes directly related to the debtholders perceptions of the DI's risk. The anticipation of higher funding costs would provide an incentive for DI managers to refrain from taking excessive risk. Second, subordinate debt would augment indirect market discipline if secondary market prices for a DI's debt were directly related to the DI's risk. Further, DI supervisors could exert indirect discipline on a DI if they took

prompt corrective action
Mandatory actions that have to be taken by regulators as a DI's capital ratio falls.

www.federalreserve.gov

www.ustreas.gov

---

[30] On the assumption that new equity is more costly to raise than deposits for banks.

[31] Looking at the implementation of prompt corrective action between December 1992 and December 1995, the GAO found that regulators closed or merged all but 2 of 25 critically undercapitalized banks within the required 90-day time frame. See GAO, "Bank and Thrift Regulation: Implementation of FDICIA's Prompt Regulatory Action Provisions," GAO/GGO, 97–18 (November 1996).

[32] See "The Feasibility and Desirability of Mandatory Subordinated Debt," Board of Governors of the Federal Reserve and U.S. Department of the Treasury, December 2000.

[33] The academic literature has also reported on the desirability of using subordinate debt to impact risk taking by DIs. See, for example, M. M. Flannery and S. M. Sorescu, "Evidence of Bank Market Discipline in Subordinated Debenture Yields: 1983–1991,"*Journal of Finance* 51 (1996), pp. 1347–77; C. W. Calomiris, "Building an Incentive-Compatible Safety Net," *Journal of Banking and Finance* 23 (1999), pp. 1499–1519; R. R. Bliss, "Market Discipline and Subordinated Debt: A Review of Some Salient Issues," Working Paper, Federal Reserve Bank of Chicago, 2000; D. Hancock and M. L. Kwast, "Using Subordinated Debt to Monitor Bank Holding Companies: Is It Feasible?" Working Paper, Board of Governors of the Federal Reserve, 2000; and R. Fan, J. G. Haubrich, P. Ritchken, and J. B. Thomson, "Getting the Most Out of a Mandatory Subordinated Debt Requirement," *Journal of Financial Services Research* 24 (2003), pp. 149–80.

an increase in secondary market yields as a signal of increased DI risk and took actions to address such increased risk. Third, mandatory SD would stimulate transparency and disclosure at DIs, thereby encouraging both direct and indirect market discipline. Fourth, the issuance of SD might also increase the size of the DI's capital cushion, protecting the federal deposit insurer (e.g., the FDIC). When a DI failed, SD holders would receive their funds only after the deposit insurer had been fully compensated. Finally, SD would reduce the tendency for DI supervisors to forbear their resolution of troubled institutions. Because SD holders receive their funds after the deposit insurer when a DI fails, SD holders may have an incentive to encourage regulators to take prompt corrective actions against a troubled DI.

With respect to the amount of mandatory subordinate debt, the proposal falls into two groups. One group recommended that 2 percent of risk-weighted assets be funded with subordinate debt. The other group would require substantially more funding by subordinate debt, typically in the range of 4 to 6 percent of either book or risk-weighted asset values. In the early 2000s, virtually all the largest DIs issued SD in excess of 1 percent of the book value of their assets. While it was agreed that a policy of mandatory SD issuance would potentially enhance market discipline, safety, and soundness, the Fed and Treasury stated in their 2000 report that additional evidence needed to be gathered before they could support the imposition of a mandatory SD requirement for large DIs. Thus, no final mandate has been implemented.

Concept Questions

1. If you are managing a DI that is technically insolvent but has not yet been closed by the regulators, would you invest in Treasury bonds or real estate development loans? Explain your answer.
2. Do we need both risk-based capital requirements and risk-based insurance premiums to discipline shareholders?

Depositor Discipline

An alternative, more indirect route to disciplining riskier DIs is to create conditions for a greater degree of depositor discipline. Depositors could either require higher interest rates and risk premiums on deposits or ration the amount of deposits they are willing to hold in riskier DIs.

Critics argue that under the current deposit insurance regulations, neither insured depositors nor uninsured depositors have sufficient incentives to discipline riskier DIs. To understand these arguments, we consider the risk exposure of both insured and uninsured depositors under the current deposit insurance contract.

Insured Depositors

When the deposit insurance contract was introduced in 1933, the level of coverage per depositor was $2,500. This coverage cap has gradually risen through the years, reaching $100,000 in 1980. The $100,000 cap concerns a depositor's beneficial interest and ownership of deposited funds. In actuality, by structuring deposit funds in a bank or thrift in a particular fashion, a depositor can achieve many times the $100,000 coverage cap on deposits. To see this, consider the different categories of deposit fund ownership available to an individual, shown in Table 19–7. Each of these categories represents a distinct accumulation of funds toward the $100,000 deposit insurance cap, the coverage ceiling per bank. We give an example of how depositors can raise the coverage level by adopting certain strategies.

TABLE 19–7
Deposit Ownership Categories

Source: U.S. Department of the Treasury, "Modernizing the Financial System; Recommendations for Safer More Competitive Banks," Washington, DC, February 1991.

IRAs and Keogh accounts
Private pension plans held by individuals with banks or other FIs.

Individual ownership, such as a simple checking account.
Joint ownership, such as the savings account of a husband and wife.
Revocable trusts, in which the beneficiary is a qualified relative of the settlor, and the settlor has the ability to alter or eliminate the trust.
Irrevocable trusts, where the beneficial interest is not subject to being altered or eliminated.
Interests in employee benefit plans where the interests are vested and thus are not subject to being altered or eliminated.
Public units, that is, accounts of federal, state, and municipal governments.
Corporations and partnerships.
Unincorporated businesses and associations.
Individual retirement accounts (IRAs).
Keogh accounts.
Executor or administrator accounts.
Accounts held by banks in an agency or fiduciary capacity.

EXAMPLE 19–1
Calculation of Insured Deposits

A married couple with one daughter, where both husband and wife had **individual retirement accounts (IRAs)** and **Keogh** private pension plans at the bank, could accrue a total coverage cap of $800,000 as a family: his individual deposit account, her individual deposit account, their joint deposit account, their daughter's deposit account held in trust, his IRA account, his Keogh account, her IRA account, and her Keogh account. When the range of ownership is expanded in this fashion, the coverage cap for a family can rapidly approach $1 million or more.

deposit brokers
Brokers who break up large deposits into smaller units at different banks to ensure full coverage by deposit insurance.

Note that this coverage ceiling is *per bank or thrift;* wealthy and institutional investors can employ **deposit brokers** to spread their funds over many DIs up to the permitted cap. In this way, all their deposits become explicitly insured. For example, a wealthy individual with $1 million in deposits could hire a deposit broker such as Merrill Lynch to split the $1 million into 10 parcels of $100,000 and deposit those funds at 10 different banks. During the 1980s, the greatest purchasers of brokered deposits were the most risky banks that had no, or limited, access to the borrowed funds market. These risky banks attracted brokered deposits by offering higher interest rates than did relatively healthy banks. In fact, a high proportion of brokered deposits held by a bank became an early warning signal of its future failure risk. Neither the depositors nor the fund brokers were concerned about the risk of these funds because every parcel of $100,000 was fully insured, including interest accrued up until time of failure.[34]

In 1984, the FDIC and FSLIC introduced a joint resolution intending to deny insurance coverage to funds invested by deposit brokers. After extensive congressional hearings, this resolution was ultimately rejected; however, in 1989 Congress passed the Financial Institutions Reform, Recovery, and Enforcement Act (FIRREA). It specified that insured depository institutions that failed to meet capital standards would be prohibited from accepting brokered deposits as well as from soliciting deposits by offering interest rates significantly higher than prevailing rates. The FDIC Improvement Act (FDICIA) of 1991 formalized these restrictions by allowing access to brokered deposits only to banks and thrifts in Zone 1 capital

[34] Technically, principal on deposits plus accrued interest up to $100,000 is covered.

range. Under the prompt corrective action plan, this means DIs with total risk-based capital ratios exceeding 10 percent. DIs outside this range are generally precluded from accepting brokered deposits unless they receive specific approval from the FDIC. These restrictions became effective in June 1992.

The FDIC Improvement Act left the insured depositor coverage cap unchanged at $100,000. While lowering the coverage cap would increase the incentives of depositors to monitor and run from more risky DIs, it would also increase the number of DI failures and the probability of panics. Thus, the gains to the FDIC from covering a smaller dollar amount of deposits per head would have to be weighed against the possibility of more failures, with their attendant liquidation costs. This suggests that setting the optimal level of the insurance cap per depositor per DI is a far from easy problem.[35]

In April 2001, the FDIC proposed that the deposit insurance coverage level should be indexed to maintain its real value. Between 1980 (when the coverage cap was increased to $100,000) and 2001, the real value of deposit insurance coverage had fallen by half. Rather than advocating ad hoc increases in deposit insurance coverage levels, as had occurred since 1934, the FDIC proposed a more systematic method of maintaining the real monetary value of coverage through an indexing system. Indexing (for example, based on the consumer price index, or CPI) would increase predictability and lessen the potential of large sudden increases in insurance premiums and payouts. Both DI owners and depositors would be able to predict the timing and implications of coverage level increases with more accuracy, which would in turn lower the risks of financial planning associated with coverage changes. The FDIC recommended that coverage be adjusted at a maximum interval of every five years (and never be allowed to decrease) and then only if the real value of coverage dropped below 80 percent of the existing coverage level. While an initial increase in coverage to $130,000 was mentioned, the FDIC, in its 2001 report, stated that the appropriate level of coverage was open to debate and for Congress to ultimately determine. As of 2004, the U.S. House of Representatives, as part of the Deposit Insurance Reform Act of 2003, had approved the increase in deposit insurance coverage to $130,000, as well as the adjustment to the maximum coverage every five years to reflect changes in the consumer price index. The U.S. Senate had yet to vote on the bill but was considering a bill that did not include an immediate increase in coverage beyond $100,000.

Uninsured Depositors

The primary intention of deposit insurance is to deter DI runs and panics. A secondary and related objective has been to protect the smaller, less informed saver against the reduction in wealth that would occur if that person were last in line when a DI fails. Under the current deposit insurance contract, the small, less informed depositor is defined by the $100,000 ceiling. Theoretically at least, larger, more informed depositors with more than $100,000 on deposit are at risk if a DI fails. As a result, these large uninsured depositors should be sensitive to DI risk and seek to discipline more risky DIs by demanding higher interest rates on their deposits or withdrawing their deposits completely.[36] Until recently, the manner in

---

[35] For a modeling of this problem, see J. F. Dreyfus, A. Saunders, and L. Allen, "Deposit Insurance and Regulatory Forbearance: Are Caps on Insured Deposits Optimal?" *Journal of Money, Credit and Banking* 26 (August 1994), part 1, pp. 412–38.

[36] L. G. Goldberg and S. C. Hudgins, in "Depositor Discipline and the Behavior of Uninsured Deposits: FSLIC vs. SAIF," *Journal of Financial Economics* 63 (2002), pp. 263–74, examine the behavior of uninsured deposits at S&Ls from 1984–1995. They find that failed institutions exhibit declining levels of uninsured deposits prior to failure, that failing institutions attract fewer uninsured deposits prior to failure

too-big-to-fail banks

Banks that are viewed by regulators as being too big to be closed and liquidated without imposing a systemic risk to the banking and financial system.

which DI failures have been resolved meant that both large and small depositors were often fully protected against losses. This was especially so where large banks got into trouble and were viewed as **too big to fail.** That is, they were too big to be liquidated by regulators either because of the draining effects on the resources of the insurance fund or for fear of contagious or systemic runs spreading to other major banks. Thus, although uninsured depositors tended to lose in thrift and small-bank failures, in large-bank failures the failure resolution methods employed by regulators usually resulted in implicit 100 percent deposit insurance. As a result, for large banks in particular, neither small nor large depositors had sufficient incentives to impose market discipline on riskier banks.

To understand these arguments, we look at the major ways DI failures were resolved before the passage of the FDIC Improvement Act in 1991. We also look at the post-1992 procedures required under the FDICIA and the depositor preference legislation under the Omnibus Budget Reconciliation Act of 1993 to create greater exposure for uninsured depositors and creditors and to reduce the FDIC's failure resolution costs.

Failure Resolution Procedures Pre-FDICIA   Pre-FDICIA, the three failure resolution methods were the payoff method, the purchase and assumption method, and the open assistance method. Before the passage of the FDICIA in 1991, the FDIC had to liquidate the DI (the **payoff method**) unless an alternative method was judged by the FDIC to cost less. This method of choosing the closure policy is a less than liquidation cost requirement and contrasts with a true least-cost resolution policy, in which the lowest-cost method of all closure methods available would be selected. Not until the passage of the FDICIA was the least-cost resolution required of the FDIC. In addition, prior to 1991, the less than liquidation cost requirement could be overridden and the DI kept open in a restructured form if its continued operation was deemed essential for the local community. The FDICIA also repealed this essentiality provision.

Next, we look in more detail at the three principal methods of failure resolution employed by the FDIC. We also discuss how the FDICIA and the depositor preference legislation of 1993 have changed the FDIC's strategy and, most importantly, the potential effects of these changes on increasing depositor discipline.

payoff method of closure

Failure resolution method in which the FDIC liquidates the DI and pays off the DI's depositors.

- *The payoff method (liquidation).* Historically, the payoff method has resolved most small DI failures when a merger was unavailable or too costly or when the DI's loss to the community would impose few local social costs. Under a payoff closure, regulators liquidate the assets of the DI and pay off the insured depositors in full (insured deposit payoff). They could also transfer these deposits in full to another local DI (insured deposit transfer). In Table 19–8, compare the relative sizes of these two payoff methods over the 1986–2003 period.[37] On liquidation, uninsured depositors and the FDIC, which assumes the claims of the

---

than do solvent institutions, and that factors indicating the well-being and aggressiveness of institutions affect the level of uninsured deposits. Further, M. S. M. Peria and S. L. Schmukler, in "Do Depositors Punish Banks for Bad Behavior? Market Discipline, Deposit Insurance, and Banking Crises," *Journal of Finance* 56 (2001), pp. 1029–52, find that (insured as well as uninsured) depositors in Argentina, Chile, and Mexico punish banks for risky behavior, both by withdrawing their deposits and by requiring higher interest rates. Market discipline is more significant after banking crises, suggesting that following bank interventions and failures, depositors become more aware of the risk of losing deposits; thus, they start exercising a stricter market discipline.

[37] There were five payoffs in 1993, zero in 1994–2000, and five in 2001–2003. The remaining resolutions were all purchase and assumptions (P&As).

TABLE 19–8   Summary Statistics for DIs Resolved by the Federal Deposit Insurance Corporation by Type of Resolution, 1986–2003

Type of Resolution	Bank Resolved 1986–2003		Estimated Losses to the Bank Insurance Fund		Assets Recorded at Time of Resolution		Losses as a Percentage of Assets*	Average Asset Size of Resolved Bank (millions of dollars)*
	Number of Banks	(percentage of total)	(millions of dollars)	(percentage of total)	(millions of dollars)	(percentage of total)		
Payoffs and transfers								
Deposit payoff	80	6%	$ 1,653	5%	$ 4,887	2%	34%	$ 52.9
Deposit transfer	154	12	3,036	9	11,134	5	27	72.3
Subtotal	234	18	4,689	14	16,021	7	29	68.5
Purchases and assumption								
Total bank	291	23	9,802	31	72,120	31	14	247.8
Insured deposits only	100	8	3,478	11	24,283	10	14	242.8
Clean and other	613	47	12,259	38	105,664	45	12	172.4
Subtotal	1,004	78	25,539	80	202,067	86	13	201.3
Assistance transactions	54	4	1,860	6	16,914	7	11	313.2
Total	1,292	100%	$32,008	100%	$235,002	100%	14%	$181.9

Notes: Sample includes commercial and savings banks insured by the Bank Insurance Fund that were resolved between 1986 and 2003. Assets are those recorded at time of resolution.
*Figures represent averages for each type of resolution.

Source: Congressional Budget Office analysis based on Federal Deposit Insurance Corporation, *Failed Bank Cost Analysis,* 1985–1995; and FDIC Historical Statistics, 1996–2003. *www.fdic.gov*

insured depositors, had pro rata claims to the remaining value of the failed DI's assets up until 1993. However, with the passage of the 1993 depositor protection legislation, the FDIC and *domestic* uninsured depositors have been given priority over *foreign* uninsured depositors (e.g., in overseas branches of a failed DI) as well as over creditors supplying federal funds on the interbank market. This reduces the FDIC's potential liability.[38]

EXAMPLE 19–2
Liquidation and Payoff of a Failed Bank Using the Payoff Method

To understand who gains and who potentially loses under the payoff (liquidation) method, consider the simple example of a failed bank in Table 19–9. The failed bank's liquidation value of assets is only $80 million. It has $50 million in outstanding claims held by small insured depositors whose claims individually are $100,000 or less and $50 million in uninsured domestic depositor claims that individually exceed $100,000. The net worth of the failed bank is negative $20 million.

On closure, the insured depositors receive a $50 million payoff in full.[39] The FDIC liquidates the $80 million in assets and shares it on an equal, or pro rata, basis with the uninsured domestic depositors. Since the FDIC owns 50 percent of deposit claims and the uninsured domestic depositors own the other 50 percent, each gets $40 million on the liquidation of the bank's assets.

[38] The FDIC has estimated savings of up to $1 billion since 1993. However, this ignores the greater incentives of uninsured foreign depositors and bank creditors to engage in runs.

[39] Instead of a payoff in full, in an insured deposit transfer their deposits are transferred in full to another local bank.

TABLE 19–9
Failed Bank Balance Sheet (in millions of dollars)

Assets		Liabilities	
Asset (liquidation value)	$80	Insured deposits	$ 50
		Uninsured domestic deposits	50
	$80		$100

The allocation of the $20 million net worth loss of the bank among the three parties or claimants follows:[40]

	Loss (in millions of dollars)
Insured depositors	$ 0
FDIC	10
Uninsured domestic depositors	10
	$20

The negative $20 million net worth loss of the bank is shared pro rata by the FDIC and the uninsured domestic depositors.[41]

From this example, it is clear that if the payoff method were always used to resolve DI failures, uninsured depositors would have very strong incentives to monitor DI risk taking. They would also discipline owners by requiring higher risk premiums on their deposits and/or withdrawing their deposits from riskier banks.

While regulators have frequently used the payoff method, this has been mostly for thrifts and small failing banks (see the relatively small average asset size of these DIs in Table 19–8). The FDIC press release announcing the payoff of insured deposits of the failed Bank of Alamo in November 2002 is presented in Appendix 19A to the chapter (located at the book's Web site, www.mhhe.com/saunders5e). Regulators have used the second and third closure methods, described next, most often for large failing banks. As will become clear, these methods impose much less discipline on uninsured depositors.

purchase and assumption (P&A)
Merger of a failed DI with a healthy DI.

• *Purchase and assumption.* As shown in Table 19–8, there are three types of **purchase and assumption (P&A)** resolutions. That most commonly used prior to the FDIC Improvement Act was the traditional "clean" P&A method; beginning in 1987, regulators tried total bank P&As. Since 1992 (and post-FDICIA), the FDIC has used insured deposit P&As in an increasing number of cases. Under a traditional clean purchase and assumption, a stronger, healthy DI purchases and assumes both the insured and uninsured deposits of the failed DI as well as its remaining good assets, mostly securities. The difference between the total deposits

[40] We do not show the value of the equity holders' claims or those of foreign uninsured depositors and creditors in this example. Since they have junior claims to these three parties (the FDIC, the insured depositors, and uninsured domestic depositors), their claims are reduced to zero on failure.

[41] In insured deposit transfers, when the insured deposits of the failed bank are transferred to another bank and its assets are liquidated, the acquirer of the insured deposits sometimes pays a premium to the FDIC reflecting the value of picking up new deposit customers. Any such premium would lower the costs of liquidation to the FDIC.

TABLE 19–10
Traditional Clean
P&A Transaction (in
millions of dollars)

Assets		Liabilities		
Good assets	$ 80	Insured depositors	$ 50	
			→	Good bank (acquirer)
FDIC cash infusion	20	Uninsured depositors	50	
	$ 100		$100	

of the failed DI and the market value of the failed DI's good assets is met by a cash infusion from the FDIC minus any takeover premium the acquiring DI is willing to pay. For large-bank failures, total or whole bank P&As transferred all assets, good and bad, with a lower initial FDIC cash infusion but with an option for the acquiring bank to put back uncollectible bad assets (up to some limit) to the FDIC at a later date. Insured deposit P&As will be discussed later in this chapter, as they have significantly altered the degree of risk borne by uninsured depositors post-FDICIA. The FDIC press release announcing the purchase and assumption of insured deposits of the failed Farmers Bank and Trust of Cheneyville in December 2002 is presented in Appendix 19A to the chapter (located at the book's Web site, **www.mhhe.com/saunders5e**).

EXAMPLE 19–3
*Liquidation and
Payoff of a Failed
Bank Using the
P&A Method*

To understand the mechanics of a traditional clean P&A and who bears the losses, we look at a P&A of the same bank discussed in the *payoff* (liquidation) example earlier (see Table 19–10). The clean P&A transfers all depositors, insured and uninsured (both domestic and foreign), as well as other liabilities to the acquiring bank. Thus, neither the insured nor the uninsured depositors lose. The full $20 million loss is borne by the FDIC through its cash injection to clean up the failed bank's bad assets prior to the merger with the acquiring bank minus any premium it can obtain from the acquiring bank.[42] For example, a bank in New York may pay a premium to acquire a failing bank in Florida because Florida is a high-growth market and it is often cheaper to acquire a bank and its existing branches than to establish completely new branches.

To summarize the losses of the three parties in a traditional clean P&A:

	Loss (in millions of dollars)	
Insured depositors	0	
Uninsured depositors	0	
FDIC	$20	(minus any merger premium)
	Total $20	

Clearly, with a clean P&A, large uninsured depositors are de facto insured depositors.

---

[42] In recent years, regulators have held auctions to select the acquiring bank. However, the bank that bids the highest premium does not always win; the FDIC takes into account the quality of the bidder as well. For example, a low-quality bank that acquires a failed bank in an auction might become a bigger problem bank in the future.

open assistance
Provision of FDIC loans or capital funds to keep a large failing DI open as part of a restructuring plan.

• *Open assistance.* The third main method of closure regulators used is **open assistance** (see Table 19–8). When very large DIs fail, such as Continental Illinois in 1984 with $36 billion in assets and First City Bancorporation of Texas in 1987 with $11 billion in assets, it is often difficult, if not impossible, to find a DI sound and big enough to engage in a P&A. Moreover, regulators fear that smaller correspondent DIs will be hurt by a large DI's closure and that big depositors and investors might lose confidence in all large U.S. DIs if they used payoff and liquidation. Open assistance can take the form of promissory notes, net worth certificates, cash, infusions of equity, and so on. An example of open assistance was the commitment of $870 million by the FDIC to an investor group headed by Robert Abboud to take over control of First City Bancorporation of Texas in September 1987. However, failure to close and liquidate a bad DI sends a strong and undesirable signal to large uninsured depositors at other big DIs that their deposits are safe and that regulators will not permit big DIs to fail. That is, all large uninsured depositors with big DIs are really implicitly 100 percent insured, thereby alleviating depositors from any monitoring/market discipline responsibilities.[43] Such an implicit guaranty to uninsured depositors at large DIs is often called the too-big-to-fail guaranty.[44]

In 1987, the Competitive Equality Banking Act allowed a new form of open assistance called the bridge bank. Two examples of bridge banks were First Republic Bancorp ($33.7 billion) and MCorp ($15.4 billion). In these cases, the FDIC took over the bank and managed its operations prior to sale. A bridge bank can last as long as five years. Technically, bridge banks are government-run banks.

Failure Resolution Policies Post-FDICIA   In the wake of the FDIC's growing deficit, the 1991 FDICIA sought to pass more of the costs of insured DI failures on to uninsured depositors, thereby enhancing their incentives to monitor DIs and to control risk through requiring higher deposit rates and/or through their deposit placement decisions. The FDICIA required that a **least-cost resolution** (LCR) strategy be put in place by the FDIC. In applying the LCR strategy, the FDIC evaluates failure resolution alternatives on a present value basis and documents their assumptions in deciding which method to use (see Table 19–11). These decisions can be audited by the General Accounting Office, the government's audit watchdog.

least-cost resolution
Policy requiring that the lowest-cost method of closure be used for failing DIs.

However, there was a very important and controversial exemption to using least-cost resolution in all cases. Specifically, a *systemic risk* exemption applies where a large DI failure could cause a threat to the whole financial system. Then methods that could involve the full protection of uninsured depositors as well as insured depositors could be used. This appears to allow the too-big-to-fail guaranty to large DI uninsured depositors prevalent in the pre-1991 system to carry over after the passage of the FDICIA. However, the act has restricted the circumstances when this

---

[43] For example, in the final restructuring arrangement for Continental Illinois, all depositors were protected; the FDIC assumed a large amount of problem loans and infused $1 billion new capital into the bank with a part convertible into a direct ownership interest. By taking an equity stake in the failed bank, the FDIC stood to gain, with outside equity owners, from any improvement in the performance of the bank as well. Indeed, in a number of open assistance programs, the FDIC held (holds) long-term options or warrants that allow it to share in the upside of improved bank performance (if any). Nevertheless, the incentive to impose market discipline has still been eliminated for large uninsured depositors.

[44] O'Hara and Shaw and Mei and Saunders seek to calculate the value of such a too-big-to-fail guarantee. O'Hara and Shaw find significant value, while Mei and Saunders find little value from such guarantees. See M. O'Hara and W. Shaw, "Deposit Insurance and Wealth Effects: The Value of Being Too Big to Fail," *Journal of Finance* 45 (1990), pp. 1587–1600; and J. P. Mei and A. Saunders, "Bank Risk and Too Big to Fail Guarantees: An Asset Pricing Perspective," *Journal of Real Estate Finance and Economics* 10 (1995), pp. 199–224.

TABLE 19–11
Least-Cost Resolutions (LCR) Requirements under FDICIA

Source: GAO, 1992 Bank Resolutions, GAO/GGD-94–197, p. 14.

The FDIC must:
- Consider and evaluate all possible resolution alternatives by computing and comparing their costs on a present value basis, using realistic discount rates.
- Select the least costly alternative based on the evaluation.
- Document the evaluation and the assumption on which it is based, including any assumptions with regard to interest rates, asset recovery rates, asset holding costs, and contingent liabilities.
- Retain documentation for at least five years.

systemic risk exemption can be used. Such an exemption is allowed only if a two-thirds majority of the boards of the Federal Reserve and the FDIC recommend it to the secretary of the Treasury, and if the secretary of the Treasury, in consultation with the president of the United States, agrees. Further, any cost of such a bailout of a big DI would have to be shared among all other DIs by charging them an additional deposit insurance premium based on their size as measured by their domestic and foreign deposits as well as their borrowed funds, excluding subordinated debt. Because large DIs have more foreign deposits and borrowed funds, they will have to make bigger contributions (per dollar of assets) than smaller DIs to any future bailout of a large DI.

Nevertheless, some concern has been raised about the continuance of the too-big-to-fail (TBTF) guarantee even in its more restricted form. With the growing wave of bank and financial service firm mergers, it is argued that more and more FIs are likely to be covered by TBTF guarantees.[45] If we use the same asset-size cutoff (adjusted for inflation) that the comptroller of the currency used in specifying the 11 banks that were to be protected as being TBTF after the Continental Illinois failure in 1984, we find that today this amounts to an asset size of around $42 billion. As of 2004, 31 banking organizations had assets exceeding this figure.

With the exception of the systemic risk exemption, the least-cost resolution strategy requires the FDIC to employ the method that imposes most failure costs on the uninsured depositors. To this end, the FDIC has been increasingly using an **insured depositor transfer** (IDT), or "haircut," method to resolve a number of post-1991 failures. Under the IDT method of resolution, the insured deposits of a closed DI are usually transferred in full to another local DI in the community to conduct a direct payoff of the depositors for the FDIC. By contrast, uninsured depositors must file a claim against the receiver of the failed DI and share with the FDIC in any receivership distributions from the liquidation of the closed DI's assets. This usually results in a loss for uninsured depositors (a so-called haircut). For example, in 60 out of 122 failures in 1992, the FDIC imposed initial losses, or haircuts, on uninsured depositors, ranging from 13 to 69 percent. The size of the haircut depends mostly on the FDIC-estimated value of the failed DI's assets. The total dollar size of 1992 haircuts

insured depositor transfer
Method of resolution in which uninsured depositors take a loss, or haircut, on failure equal to the difference between their deposit claims and the estimated value of the failed DI's assets minus insured deposits.

[45] Indeed, the Federal Reserve–organized $3.5 billion bank bailout of the Long-Term Capital Management (LTCM) hedge fund has been described by some as a TBTF bailout because the fund was allowed to continue operations largely on the basis of the size of its exposure both in capital market instruments and in derivatives of over $1.25 trillion in nominal value. The fear here was that allowing LTCM to liquidate its positions at a massive loss could cause a number of banks that had lent money to the fund to fail or be significantly undercapitalized once losses were written off. Others have argued that this was not really a TBTF bailout in the conventional sense since no government money was directly involved.

FIGURE 19–6   Failed DIs by Uninsured Depositor Treatment, 1986–2003

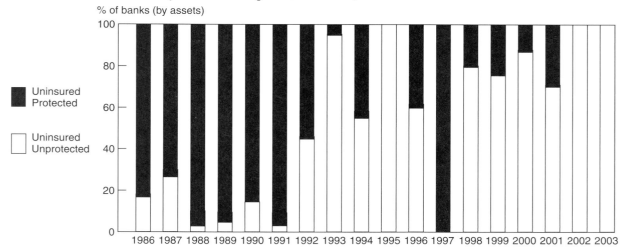

Source: Federal Deposit Insurance Corporation website, Historical Statistics, various dates. *www.fdic.gov*

taken by uninsured depositors was $80 million. Figure 19–6 shows the increased propensity of uninsured depositors to be left unprotected (and thus subject to haircuts) since 1986. We describe a simplified form of the IDT, or haircut, method next. This allows us to compare the cost of this new approach to that of previous methods, such as the traditional P&A and payoff methods.

EXAMPLE 19–4

Liquidation and Payoff of a Failed Bank Using the Insured Deposit Transfer (IDT) Method

In Table 19–12, the failed bank in panel (a) has only $80 million in good assets to meet the $50 million in deposit claims of insured depositors and the $50 million in claims of the uninsured depositors.[46] Under an IDT, in panel (b), the FDIC would transfer the $80 million in assets to an acquiring bank along with the full $50 million in small insured deposits but only $30 million of the $50 million in uninsured deposits.[47] Notice that the uninsured depositors get protection against losses only up to the difference between the estimated value of the failed bank's assets and its insured deposits. In effect, the uninsured depositors are subject to a haircut to their original deposit claims of $20 million (or, as a percentage, 40 percent of the value of their deposit claims on the failed bank). After the IDT, the uninsured depositors own $30 million in deposits in the acquiring bank and $20 million in receivership claims on the bad assets of the failed bank. Only if the FDIC as a receiver can recover some value from the $20 million in bad assets will the loss to the uninsured be less than $20 million.

To summarize the losses of the three parties under the IDT:

Loss (in millions of dollars)		
Insured depositors	=	0
FDIC	=	0
Uninsured depositors	=	$20

[46] That is, it has $20 million negative net worth.

[47] Unlike in a P&A, it would not inject cash into the failed bank prior to a merger with the acquiring bank.

TABLE 19–12   Insured Depositor Transfer Resolution (in millions of dollars)

(a) Failed				(b) Insured Depositor Transfer				
Assets		**Liabilities**		**Assets**		**Liabilities**		
Good assets	$80	Insured deposits	$ 50	Good assets	$80	Insured deposits	$50	Merger with good bank
		Uninsured deposits	50			Uninsured deposits	30	$\rightarrow$
	$80		$100		$80		$80	

As you can see from this simple example, the uninsured depositors bear all the losses and now have a much stronger incentive than before to monitor and control the actions of DI owners through imposing market discipline via interest rates and the amount of funds deposited.

Concept Questions

1. In Table 19–9, how would the losses of the DI be shared if insured deposits were $30m and uninsured deposits were $70m?
2. List four factors that might influence an acquirer to offer a large premium when bidding for a failed DI.
3. Make up a simple balance sheet example to show a case where the FDIC can lose even when it uses an IDT to resolve a failed DI.

Regulatory Discipline

In the event that stockholder and deposit holder discipline does not reduce moral hazard–induced risk taking by banks and thrifts, regulations can require regulators to act promptly and in a more consistent and predictable fashion to restrain DI risk-taking behavior. To bolster increased stockholder and depositor discipline, the FDICIA perceived two areas of regulatory weakness: (1) the frequency and thoroughness of examinations and (2) the forbearance shown to weakly capitalized banks in the pre-1991 period. The FDICIA included key provisions to address these weaknesses.

Examinations

First, the FDICIA required improved accounting standards for DIs, including working toward the market valuation of balance sheet assets and liabilities. This improves the ability of examiners to monitor DIs' net worth positions off-site and is consistent with monitoring the true net worth of the DI (see Chapters 8 and 9). Second, beginning in December 1992, FDICIA required an annual on-site examination of every DI.[48] Third, private accountants were given a greater role in monitoring a DI's performance, with independent audits being mandated. This is similar to the situation in the United Kingdom, where the 1987 Bank Act

---

[48] Although the timing of examinations is secret, M. Flannery and J. Houston, in "The Value of a Government Monitor for U.S. Banking Firms," *Journal of Money, Credit, and Banking,* February 1999, pp. 14–34, find that examinations have a positive effect on bank equity values since an examination is seen as certifying (or reducing uncertainty surrounding) reported accounting values of banks, for example, the size of nonperforming loans. See also R. DeYoung et al., "Could Publication of Bank CAMEL Ratings Improve Market Discipline?" Comptroller of the Currency, 1998, *Proceedings,* Federal Reserve Bank of Chicago, May 1998, pp. 402–21.

required an enhanced role for private auditors as a backup for regulatory examiners.

Capital Forbearance

The introduction of prompt corrective action capital zones (see Chapter 20), along with the mandatory actions required of regulators in each of those zones (including closure), is symptomatic of a movement toward a regulatory policy based on rules rather than discretion. Such rules clearly direct regulators to act in a certain manner even if they are reluctant to do so out of self-interest or for other reasons. The weakness of such rules is that if a policy is bad, then bad policy becomes more effective.[49]

Concept Question

1. What additional measures were mandated by the FDICIA to bolster stockholder and depositor discipline?

NON-U.S. DEPOSIT INSURANCE SYSTEMS

Deposit insurance systems are increasingly being adopted worldwide. See Appendix 19B (located at the book's Web site, www.mhhe.com/saunders5e) for a description of systems in various countries. Many of these systems offer quite different degrees of protection to depositors compared with systems in the United States.[50] In response to the single banking and capital market in Europe, the EC established (at the end of 1999) a single deposit insurance system covering all European Community–located banks. This directive requires the insurance of deposit accounts in EC countries up to 20,000 ECUs. However, depositors are subject to a 10 percent deductible in order to create incentives for them to monitor banks. The idea underlying the EC plan is to create a level playing field for banks across all European Community countries.

Japan also has a deposit insurance system that was established in 1971. In the late 1990s and early 2000s, the Japanese banking system was going through an experience similar to that of U.S. banks and thrifts in the 1930s and 1980s, with record bad debts and bank failures. Over the decade 1992–2002, Japanese banks had written off over $650 billion in nonperforming loans. As of 2003, these banks still had over $400 billion in bad loans on their balance sheets. The effect on Japan's deposit insurance fund has also been similar to that of the United States in the 1980s, with a rapidly declining reserve fund that has limited its ability to deal with the crisis. These problems have led to a government "bailout" to the tune of over $500 billion and blanket, until April 2005, protection of all bank deposits.[51] Japanese regulators

---

[49] Similar arguments have been made in the area of monetary policy, where proponents (such as monetarist Milton Friedman) have argued for a rules-based policy built around a constant growth rate of the money supply. However, most central bankers prefer discretion in deciding on the timing and size of monetary policy actions such as their open market operations.

[50] A. Demirgüç and E. J. Kane conclude that in institutionally weak environments, it is hard to design deposit insurance arrangements that will not increase the probability and depth of future banking crises. For countries with weak institutions, adopting explicit deposit insurance promises to spur financial development only in the very short run, if at all. Over longer periods, it is more likely to undermine market discipline in ways that reduce bank solvency, destroy real economic capital, increase financial fragility, and deter financial development. See "Deposit Insurance around the Globe: Where Does It Work?" *Journal of Economic Perspectives* 16 (2002), pp. 175–95.

[51] See "Net Effect," *The Economist,* November 10, 2001, pp. 68–69.

have stated that as of April 2005, only the first 10 million yen ($91,000) in each savings account will be insured.

THE DISCOUNT WINDOW

Deposit Insurance versus the Discount Window

The previous sections have described how a well-designed deposit insurance system might impose stockholder, depositor, and regulator discipline. Such a system can potentially stop runs on DIs and extreme liquidity problems arising in the banking system without introducing significant amounts of moral hazard risk-taking behavior among insured institutions. Whether the FDICIA (and the depositor preference legislation) has priced risk accurately enough to stop all but the most egregious cases of moral hazard, only time will tell. However, the fact that only 13 of almost 8,000 banks failed in 2001 and 2002, during and after a recession of the U.S. economy, is a first indication that the regulations work. The FDICIA has certainly increased the incentives of DI owners, uninsured depositors, and regulators to monitor and control DI risk. As such, changes made under the FDICIA are considerable improvements over the old deposit insurance contract. However, deposit insurance is not the only mechanism by which regulators mitigate bank liquidity risk. A second mechanism has been the central banks' provision of a lender of last resort facility through the discount window.

The Discount Window

discount window
Central bank lender of last resort facility.

www.federalreserve. gov

Traditionally, central banks such as the Federal Reserve have provided a **discount window** facility to meet the short-term, nonpermanent liquidity needs of DIs.[52] For example, suppose a DI has an unexpected deposit drain close to the end of a reserve requirement period and cannot meet its reserve target. It can seek to borrow from the central bank's discount window facility. Alternatively, short-term seasonal liquidity needs due to crop planting cycles can also be met through discount window loans.[53] Normally, such loans are obtained by a DI's discounting short-term high-quality paper such as Treasury bills and bankers acceptances with the central bank. The interest rate at which such securities are discounted is called the *discount rate* and is set by the central bank.

In the wake of the terrorist attacks of September 11, 2001, the Federal Reserve's discount window supplied funds to the banking system in unprecedented amounts. The magnitude of destruction resulting from the attacks caused severe disruptions to the U.S. banking system, particularly in DIs' abilities to send payments. The physical disruptions caused by the attacks included outages of telephone switching equipment in Lower Manhattan's financial district, impaired records processing and communications systems at individual banks, the evacuation of buildings that were the sites for the payment operations of several large DIs, and the suspended delivery of checks by air couriers. These disruptions left some

---

[52] In times of extreme crisis, the discount window can meet the liquidity needs of securities firms as well (as was the case during the stock market crash of October 19, 1987, and the terrorist attacks on the United States on September 11, 2001).

[53] It has also been shown that, in normal economic conditions, the availability of the discount window induces banks to lend more than they would without the discount window. See S. Shaffer, "The Discount Window and Credit Availability," *Journal of Banking and Finance* 23 (1999), pp. 1383–1406.

TABLE 19–13
Spread between the
Discount Rate and
the Fed Funds Rate

Source: Federal Reserve
Board Web site, various
dates. *www.federalreserve.gov*

	1990	1994	2000	2004 (Jan.)
Federal funds	8.10%	4.21%	6.40%	0.98
Discount window	6.98	3.60	5.73	2.00

DIs unable to execute payments to other DIs through the Fed's Fedwire system (see Chapter 14), which in turn resulted in an unexpected shortfall for other DIs. The Federal Reserve took several steps to address the problems in the payments system on and after September 11, 2001. Around noon on the 11th, the Board of Governors of the Fed released a statement saying that the Fed was open and operating, and that the discount window was available to meet liquidity needs of all DIs. The Fed staff also contacted DIs often during the next few days, encouraging them to make payments and to consider the use of the discount window to cover unexpected shortfalls that the DIs might encounter. Thus, the Fed's discount window was a primary tool used to restore payments coordination during this period.[54]

In the United States the central bank has traditionally set the discount rate below market rates, such as the overnight federal funds rates (see Table 19–13). The volume of outstanding discount loans was ordinarily small, however, because the Fed prohibited DIs from using discount window loans to finance sales of fed funds or to finance asset expansion. However, in January 2003, the Fed implemented changes to its discount window lending that increased the cost of borrowing but eased the terms. Specifically, three lending programs are now offered through the Fed's discount window. *Primary credit* is available to generally sound depository institutions on a very short-term basis, typically overnight, at a rate above the Federal Open Market Committee's (FOMC) target rate for federal funds. Primary credit may be used for any purpose, including financing the sale of fed funds. Primary credit may be extended for periods of up to a few weeks to depository institutions in generally sound financial condition. *Secondary credit* is available to depository institutions that are not eligible for primary credit. It is extended on a very short-term basis, typically overnight, at a rate that is above the primary credit rate. Secondary credit is available to meet backup liquidity needs when its use is consistent with a timely return to a reliance on market sources of funding or the orderly resolution of a troubled institution. Secondary credit may not be used to fund an expansion of the borrower's assets. The Federal Reserve's seasonal credit program is designed to assist small depository institutions in managing significant seasonal swings in their loans and deposits. *Seasonal credit* is available to depository institutions that can demonstrate a clear pattern of recurring intrayearly swings in funding needs. Eligible institutions are usually located in agricultural or tourist areas. Under the seasonal program, borrowers may obtain longer-term funds from the discount window during periods of seasonal need so that they can carry fewer liquid assets during the rest of the year and make more funds available for local lending.

[54] See J. J. McAndrews and S. M. Potter, "Liquidity Effect of the Events of September 11, 2001," *Economic Policy Review*, Federal Reserve Bank of New York, November 2002, pp. 59–79.

With the changes, discount window loans to healthy banks would be priced at 1 percent above (rather than below) the fed funds rate. Loans to troubled banks would cost 1.5 percent above the fed funds rate. The changes were not intended to change the Fed's use of the discount window to implement monetary policy, but to significantly increase the discount rate while making it easier to get a discount window loan. By increasing banks' use of the discount window as a source of funding, the Fed hopes to reduce volatility in the fed funds market as well. The changes also allow healthy banks to borrow from the Fed regardless of the availability of private funds. Previously, the Fed required borrowers to prove they could not get funds from the private sector, which put a stigma on discount window borrowing. With the changes, the Fed will lend to all banks, but the subsidy will be gone.

Despite the recent changes in the Fed's policy regarding discount window lending, there are a number of reasons why DI access to the discount window is unlikely to deter DI runs and panics to the extent deposit insurance does. The first reason is that to borrow from the discount window, a DI needs high-quality liquid assets to pledge as collateral. Failing, highly illiquid DIs are unlikely to have such assets available to discount. The second reason is that discount window borrowing, unlike deposit insurance coverage, is not automatic. That is, discount window loans are made at the discretion of the central bank. Third, discount window loans are meant to provide temporary liquidity for inherently solvent DIs, not permanent long-term support for otherwise insolvent DIs.[55] Specifically, discount window loans are limited to no more than 60 days in any 120-day period unless both the FDIC and the institution's primary regulator certify that the DI is viable. Additional extensions of up to 60 days are allowed subject to regulator certification. Finally, any discount window advances to undercapitalized DIs that eventually fail would require the Federal Reserve to compensate the FDIC for incremental losses caused by the delay in keeping the troubled DI open longer than necessary.[56] Consequently, the discount window is a partial but not a full substitute for deposit insurance as a liquidity stabilizing mechanism.

Concept Question

1. Is a DI's access to the discount window as effective as deposit insurance in deterring bank runs and panics? Why or why not?

OTHER GUARANTY PROGRAMS

As discussed in Chapter 17, other FIs are also subject to liquidity crises and liability holder runs. To deter such runs and protect small claim holders, guaranty programs have appeared in other sectors of the financial services industry. We describe these programs and their similarities to and differences from deposit insurance next.

---

[55] Note that all three of these reasons are the result of regulations set by U.S. regulators. If regulators and politicians want to use the discount window as a substitute for deposit insurance, it is within their jurisdiction to alleviate these barriers.

[56] In practice, the Fed would be penalized by a loss in the interest income on discount window loans made to banks that eventually fail.

National Credit Union Administration

www.ncua.org

The National Credit Union Administration (NCUA) is an independent federal agency that charters, supervises, examines, and insures the nation's 10,000 credit unions (see Chapter 2). Through its insurance fund, the National Credit Union Insurance Fund (NCUIF), the NCUA provides deposit insurance guarantees of up to $100,000 for insured credit unions. The fund's reserves come entirely from premiums paid by member credit unions. Insurance coverage and premiums are generally identical to those assessed by the FDIC. Indeed, changes to insurance coverage and premiums listed in the Deposit Insurance Reform Act of 2003 will apply to NCUIF-insured credit unions as well.

Because credit unions hold almost 30 percent of their assets in government securities and hold relatively small amounts of residential mortgages, they have been less affected by the crises experienced by other thrifts such as savings associations. In addition, more than 40 percent of credit union assets are in small consumer loans, often for amounts less than $10,000. Thus, credit unions have a significant degree of credit risk diversification, which also lowers their risk of insolvency.

Property–Casualty and Life Insurance Companies

Both life insurance companies and property–casualty (PC) insurance companies are regulated at the state level (see Chapter 3). Unlike banks and thrifts, no federal guaranty fund exists for either life or PC insurers. Beginning in the 1960s, most states began to sponsor state guaranty funds for firms selling insurance in that state. By 1991 all states had established such funds. These state guaranty funds have a number of important differences from deposit insurance. First, while these programs are sponsored by state insurance regulators, they are actually run and administered by the private insurance companies themselves.

Second, unlike the SAIF or BIF, in which the FDIC established a permanent reserve fund by requiring DIs to pay annual premiums in excess of payouts to resolve failures, no such permanent guaranty fund exists for the insurance industry, with the sole exception of the PC and life guaranty funds for the state of New York. This means that contributions are paid into the guaranty fund by surviving firms only after an insurance company has failed.

Third, the size of the required contributions that surviving insurers make to protect policyholders in failed insurance companies differs widely across states. In those states that have no permanent guaranty fund, each surviving insurer is normally levied a pro rata amount, according to the size of its statewide premium income. This amount either helps pay off small policyholders after the assets of the failed insurer have been liquidated or acts as a cash injection to make the acquisition of a failed insurer attractive. The definition of small policyholders generally varies across states from $100,000 to $500,000.[57]

---

[57] Since insurance industry guaranty fund premiums are size based, they are similar to the pre-1993 flat insurance premiums under deposit insurance. Indeed, similar types of moral hazard behavior (related to fixed-premium, risk-insensitive insurance) have been found for property–casualty companies. See, for example, S. J. Lee, D. Mayers, and C. W. Smith, Jr., "Guaranty Funds and Risk-Taking Behavior: Evidence from the Insurance Industry," *Journal of Financial Economics* 44 (1997), pp. 3–24.

Finally, because no permanent fund exists and the annual pro rata contributions are often legally capped (often at 2 percent of premium income), there is usually a delay before small policyholders get the cash surrender values of their policies, or other payment obligations are met from the guaranty fund. This contrasts with deposit insurance, where insured depositors normally receive immediate coverage of their claims. For example, the failure in 1991 of Executive Life Insurance in Hawaii left approximately $117.3 million in outstanding claims. But the Hawaii life insurance guaranty fund could raise only $13.1 million a year because of legal caps on surviving firms' contributions. This means that it took nine years for surviving firms to meet the claims of Executive Life policyholders in Hawaii. In the failure of Baldwin United in 1983, the insurers themselves raised additional funds, over and above the guaranty fund, to satisfy policyholders' claims. In May 1999, Martin Frankel fled to Italy after he allegedly stole $215 million from seven insurance companies he controlled. While Frankel was eventually found and extradited to the United States for trial, at year-end 2003 insurance commissioners in the five states involved were still trying to compensate policyholders, stating that some policyholders would not receive their full payment.[58] For example, in June 2003 in Williamson County (Tennessee) Circuit Court, Gary Atnip, a former accountant of Frankel's, was found guilty of funneling more than $18 million in funds from an insurance company to Frankel. Atnip was sentenced to 10 years in jail and to pay $208 million in restitution.

Thus, the private nature of insurance industry guaranty funds, their lack of permanent reserves, and low caps on annual contributions mean that they provide less credible protection to claimants than do the bank and thrift insurance funds.[59] As a result, the incentives for insurance policyholders to engage in a run if they perceive that an insurer has asset quality problems or insurance underwriting problems is quite strong even in the presence of such guaranty funds.

The Securities Investor Protection Corporation

www.sipc.org

Since the passage of the Securities Investor Protection Act in 1970 and the creation of the Securities Investor Protection Corporation (SIPC), securities firm customers have been given specific, but limited, protection against insolvencies. Basically, customers receive pro rata shares of a liquidated securities firm's assets, with SIPC satisfying remaining claims up to a maximum of $500,000 per individual. Since its inception, the SIPC has had to intervene in approximately 1 percent of the 20,000 security dealers–brokers that have failed or ceased operations. Through 2003, the SIPC has advanced $531 million in order to make possible the recovery of $13.9 billion in assets for some 622,000 investors. Most of these firms had fewer than 1,000 customers, with the biggest loss involving 6,500 customers (and a payout of $31.7 million) following the failure of Bell and Beckwith. Thus, compared with those of banking and insurance funds, SIPC losses have been very small. Criminal action has been initiated in 120 of the 304 SIPC proceedings commenced since 1970. A total of 273 indictments have been returned in federal or state courts, resulting in 242 convictions to date. At year-end 2002, the fund's reserves stood at $1.26 billion and the premium rate was a flat assessment of $150 per member.

---

[58] See "States Scramble after Millions in Frankel Case," *The Wall Street Journal*, July 23, 2001, p. C1.

[59] It has been found that the creation of PC insurance guarantee funds in the United States has been associated with a decrease in insurers' loss ratios. See S. Lee and M. L. Smith, "Property-Casualty Insurance Guaranty Funds and Insurer Vulnerability to Misfortune," *Journal of Banking and Finance* 23 (1999), pp. 1437–56.

However, some concerns have been raised regarding the adequacy of this fund in the wake of increased stock and bond market volatility and the growth of highly complex derivative instruments.[60]

The Pension Benefit Guaranty Corporation

www.pbgc.gov

In 1974, the Employee Retirement Income Security Act (ERISA) established the Pension Benefit Guaranty Corporation (PBGC). Currently, the PBGC protects the retirement benefits of more than 44.3 million workers and has 31,000 insured pension plan sponsors. Prior to 1974, an employee's pension benefits with a private corporation had very limited backing from that firm's assets. The establishment of the PBGC insured pension benefits against the underfunding of plans by corporations.

When the PBGC was created in 1974, the single-employer premium was a flat-rate $1 per plan participant. Congress raised the premium to $2.60 in 1979 and to $8.50 in 1986. In 1987, the basic premium was raised to $16 and an additional variable-rate premium was imposed on underfunded plans up to a maximum of $50. In 1991, Congress set the maximum at $72 per participant for underfunded plans and $19 per participant for fully funded plans.

However, despite these premiums, the PBGC entered into a deficit of $2.7 billion at the end of 1992. This reflects the fact that unlike the FDIC, the PBGC has little regulatory power over the pension plans it insures. Thus, it cannot use portfolio restrictions or on-site supervision to restrict the risk taking of plan managers.[61] Partly in response to the growing PBGC deficit, the 1994 Retirement Protection Act was passed. Under the act (in 1997), the $72 premium cap was phased out (80 percent of underfunded plans were at the cap in 1997). Thus, underfunded programs are now subjected to even higher premiums (some as high as several hundred dollars per participant).[62] As a result of these changes (as of 1999), the PBGC's insurance fund operated at a record surplus of $5 billion. Thus, like the FDIC in 1993, the PBGC has changed to a more overtly risk-based premium plan.

Despite risk-based premiums, however, in the early 2000s, falling stock market values, low interest rates, and rising employer bankruptcies (particularly in the steel and airline industries) forced the PBGC to assume billions of dollars worth of pension fund debt. As a result, the PBGC suffered a net loss of $7.6 billion in 2003. At year-end 2003 the long-term deficit of the insurance fund rose to $11.2 billion, three times larger than any previously recorded deficit. This compares with a surplus of $5 billion in 1999. In late 2003, the PBGC warned the U.S. Congress against passing proposals to give airlines and other struggling companies a temporary, but significant, break in pension funding requirements. The PBGC was concerned that this type of relief would increase its overall unfunded pension liability by $40 billion over the next three years. The fear was that this would raise the risk of an eventual taxpayer-funded bailout of the PBGC. Disregarding this warning, in January 2004, the U.S. Senate approved a pension bailout bill that would save U.S. corporations at least $80 billion in pension guarantees over a two-year period.[63]

---

[60] See U.S. General Accounting Office, *Securities Investor Protection,* GAO/GGD-92-109, September 1992.

[61] To the extent that regulation restricts the asset and liability activities of a firm or FI, it is similar to imposing an implicit premium or tax on the activities of the firm.

[62] Underfunded plans pay a surcharge of $9 per participant per $1,000 of underfunding.

[63] See "Pension Agency Warns against Corporate Relief, "*The Wall Street Journal,* November 12, 2003, p. A3; and "Senate Passes Pension Bailout, Pleasing Both Business, Labor, "*The Wall Street Journal,* January 29, 2004, p. A2.

Concept Questions

1. How do state-sponsored guaranty funds for insurance companies differ from deposit insurance?
2. What specific protection against insolvencies does the Securities Investor Protection Corporation provide to securities firm customers?

Summary

A contagious run on FIs can have serious social welfare effects. Because of adverse wealth, money supply, and credit supply effects, regulators of FIs have introduced guaranty programs to deter runs by offering liability holders varying degrees of failure protection. Mispriced insurance or guarantee programs, however, can lead to moral hazard behavior by FI owners. That is, since insurance guarantees result in little risk to FI owners with limited liability, they have an incentive to take excessively risky asset positions.

In recent years, DI and other financial industry guaranty programs have weakened and in some cases have been rendered insolvent. This chapter looked at the causes of the deposit insurance fund insolvencies in the late 1980s, including external economic events and moral hazard behavior induced by the structure of the insurance plan itself. The failure of the FSLIC led to a major restructuring of the FDIC and deposit guarantees in general. We discussed the post-1991 restructuring of deposit insurance, including the introduction of risk-related premiums, risk-based capital, and increased market and regulatory discipline on DI owners and liability holders. As a result, the provision and cost of deposit insurance is currently more sensitive to a DI's risk exposure than prior to 1991. This chapter also examined liability guaranty programs for other FIs, including the credit unions, securities firms, and pension plans, as well as life and PC insurance firms.

Questions and Problems

1. What is a contagious run? What are some of the potentially serious adverse social welfare effects of a contagious run? Do all types of FIs face the same risk of contagious runs?

2. How does federal deposit insurance help mitigate the problem of bank runs? What other elements of the safety net are available to DIs in the United States?

3. What major changes did the Financial Institutions Reform, Recovery, and Enforcement Act of 1989 make to the FDIC and the FSLIC?

4. Contrast the two views on, or reasons why, depository institution insurance funds became insolvent in the 1980s.

5. What is moral hazard? How did the fixed-rate deposit insurance program of the FDIC contribute to the moral hazard problem of the savings association industry? What other changes in the savings association environment during the 1980s encouraged the developing instability of that industry?

6. How does a risk-based insurance program solve the moral hazard problem of excessive risk taking by FIs? Is an actuarially fair premium for deposit insurance always consistent with a competitive banking system?

7. What are three suggested ways a deposit insurance contract could be structured to reduce moral hazard behavior?

8. What are some ways of imposing stockholder discipline to prevent stockholders from engaging in excessive risk taking?

9. How is the provision of deposit insurance by the FDIC similar to the FDIC's writing a put option on the assets of a DI that buys the insurance? What two factors drive the premium of the option?

10. What is capital forbearance? How does a policy of forbearance potentially increase the costs of financial distress to the insurance fund as well as the stockholders?

11. Under what conditions may the implementation of minimum capital guidelines, either risk-based or non-risk-based, fail to impose stockholder discipline as desired by regulators?

12. What four factors were provided by FDICIA as guidelines to assist the FDIC in the establishment of risk-based deposit insurance premiums? What has happened to the level of deposit insurance premiums since the risk-based program was implemented in 1993? Why?

13. Why did the fixed-rate deposit insurance system fail to induce insured and uninsured depositors to impose discipline on risky banks in the United States in the 1980s?

    a. How is it possible to structure deposits in a DI to reduce the effects of the insured ceiling?

    b. What are brokered deposits? Why are brokered deposits considered more risky than nonbrokered deposits by DI regulators?

    c. How did FIRREA and FDICIA change the treatment of brokered deposits from an insurance perspective?

    d. What trade-offs were weighed in the decision to leave the deposit insurance ceiling at $100,000?

14. What is the too-big-to-fail doctrine? What factors caused regulators to act in a way that caused this doctrine to evolve?

15. What failure resolution methods were available to regulators before the passage of FDICIA in 1991? What was the "essentiality" provision?

16. What procedural steps are involved under the payoff method of failure resolution?

17. How was the FDIC's potential liability reduced by the 1993 depositor protection legislation? How does this method of failure resolution encourage uninsured depositors to monitor more closely a DI's risk taking?

18. What are the three types of purchase and assumption failure resolution?

    a. How does the "clean" P&A differ from the "total bank" P&A?

    b. How are the uninsured depositors treated differently in a clean P&A as opposed to a payoff method of failure resolution?

    c. How does the open assistance process solidify the too-big-to-fail guaranty?

19. What are some of the essential features of the FDICIA of 1991 with regard to the resolution of failing DIs?

    a. What is the least-cost resolution (LCR) strategy?

    b. When can the systemic risk exemption be used as an exception to the LCR policy of DI closure methods?

    c. What procedural steps must be taken to gain approval for using the systemic risk exemption?

d. What are the implications to the other DIs in the economy of the implementation of this exemption?

20. What is the primary goal of the FDIC in employing the LCR strategy?

   a. How is the insured depositor transfer method implemented in the process of failure resolution?

   b. Why does this method of failure resolution encourage uninsured depositors to more closely monitor the strategies of DI managers?

21. The following is a balance sheet of a commercial bank (in millions of dollars):

Assets		Liabilities and Equity	
Cash	$ 5	Insured deposits	$30
Loans	40	Uninsured deposits	10
		Equity	5
Total assets	$45	Total liabilities and equity	$45

The bank experiences a run on its deposits after it declares that it will write off $10 million of its loans as a result of nonpayment. The bank has the option of meeting the withdrawals by first drawing down its cash and then selling off its loans. A fire sale of loans in one day can be accomplished at a 10 percent discount. They can be sold at a 5 percent discount if they are sold in two days. The full market value will be obtained if they are sold after two days.

   a. What is the amount of loss to the insured depositors if a run on the bank occurs on the first day? On the second day?

   b. What amount do the uninsured depositors lose if the FDIC uses the insured depositor transfer method to close the bank immediately? The assets will be sold after the two-day period.

22. A bank with insured deposits of $55 million and uninsured deposits of $45 million has assets valued at only $75 million. What is the cost of failure resolution to insured depositors, uninsured depositors, and the FDIC if the following occur?

   a. The payoff method is used.

   b. A purchase and assumption is arranged with no purchase premium.

   c. A purchase and assumption is arranged with a $5 million purchase premium.

   d. A purchase and assumption is arranged with a $25 million purchase premium.

   e. An insured depositor transfer method is used.

23. A commercial bank has $150 million in assets at book value. The insured and uninsured deposits are valued at $75 and $50 million, respectively, and the book value of equity is $25 million. As a result of loan defaults, the market value of the assets has decreased to $120 million. What is the cost of failure resolution to insured depositors, uninsured depositors, shareholders, and the FDIC if the following occur?

    a. A payoff method is used to close the bank.

    b. A purchase and assumption method with no purchase premium paid is used.

    c. A purchase and assumption method is used with $10 million paid as a purchase premium.

    d. An insured depositor transfer method is used.

24. In what ways did FDICIA enhance the regulatory discipline to help reduce moral hazard behavior? What has the operational impact of these directives been?

25. Match the following policies with their intended consequences:

    Policies:

    a. Lower FDIC insurance levels

    b. Stricter reporting standards

    c. Risk-based deposit insurance

    Consequences:

    1. Increased stockholder discipline

    2. Increased depositor discipline

    3. Increased regulator discipline

26. Why is access to the discount window of the Fed less of a deterrent to bank runs than deposit insurance?

27. How do insurance guaranty funds differ from deposit insurance? What impact do these differences have on the incentive for insurance policyholders to engage in a contagious run on an insurance company?

28. What was the purpose of the establishment of the Pension Benefit Guaranty Corporation (PBGC)?

    a. How does the PBGC differ from the FDIC in its ability to control risk?

    b. How is the 1994 Retirement Protection Act expected to reduce the deficits currently experienced by the PBGC?

Web Questions

29. Go to the FDIC Web site at **www.fdic.gov.** Click on "Statistics on Banking." Click on "Historical Statistics on Banking." Click on "Bank & Thrift Failures." Select a time period and click on "Produce Report." In this file find the most recent information on failed banks and thrifts. How has the number of depository institution failures changed since 2003?

30. Go to the Federal Reserve Board's Web site at **www.federalreserve.gov** and click on "Economic Research and Data." Click on "Statistics: Releases and Historical Data." Under Weekly Releases, click on "Selected Interest Rates, *Releases*." Click on the most recent date. In this file find the most recent values for the fed funds rate and the discount window rate. What is the percentage increase or decrease in these rates since 2003?

www.mhhe.com/saunders5e

Pertinent Web Sites

Board of Governors of the Federal Reserve	www.federalreserve.gov
Federal Deposit Insurance Corporation	www.fdic.gov
National Credit Union Administration	www.ncua.org
Pension Benefit Guaranty Corporation	www.pbgc.gov
Securities Investor Protection Corporation	www.sipc.org
U.S. Treasury	www.ustreas.gov

Appendix 19A

FDIC Press Releases of Bank Failures

View Appendix 19A at the Web site for this textbook (**www.mhhe.com/saunders5e**).

Appendix 19B

Deposit Insurance Schemes for Commercial Banks in Various Countries

View Appendix 19B at the Web site for this textbook (**www.mhhe.com/saunders5e**).

Chapter Twenty

Capital Adequacy

INTRODUCTION

Chapters 7 to 17 examined the major areas of risk exposure facing a modern FI manager. These risks can emanate from both on- and off-balance-sheet (OBS) activities and can be either domestic or international in source. To ensure survival, an FI manager needs to protect the institution against the risk of insolvency, that is, shield it from risks sufficiently large to cause the institution to fail. The primary means of protection against the risk of insolvency and failure is an FI's capital. This leads to the first function of capital, namely:

1. To absorb unanticipated losses with enough margin to inspire confidence and enable the FI to continue as a going concern.

In addition, capital protects nonequity liability holders—especially those uninsured by an external guarantor such as the FDIC—against losses. This leads to the second function of capital:

2. To protect uninsured depositors, bondholders, and creditors in the event of insolvency, and liquidation.

When FIs fail, regulators such as the FDIC have to intervene to protect insured claimants (see Chapter 19). The capital of an FI offers protection to insurance funds and ultimately the taxpayers who bear the cost of insurance fund insolvency. This leads to the third function of capital:

3. To protect FI insurance funds and the taxpayers.

At this time, each of the government deposit insurance funds is fully funded. By holding capital and reducing the risk of insolvency, an FI protects the industry from larger insurance premiums. Such premiums are paid out of the net profits of the FI. Thus, a fourth function of capital is as follows:

4. To protect the FI owners against increases in insurance premiums.

Finally, just as for any other firm, equity or capital is an important source of financing for an FI. In particular, subject to regulatory constraints, FIs have a choice between debt and equity to finance new projects and business expansion. Thus, the traditional factors that affect a business firm's choice of a capital structure—for instance, the tax deductibility of the interest on debt or the private costs of failure or insolvency—also interpose on the FI's capital decision.[1] This leads to a fifth function of capital:

5. To fund the branch and other real investments necessary to provide financial services.[2]

In the following sections, we focus on the first four functions concerning the role of capital in reducing insolvency risk and in particular the adequacy of capital in attaining these functional objectives. Specifically, we examine the different measures of capital adequacy used by FI owners, managers, and regulators, and the argument for and against each. We then look at current and proposed capital adequacy requirements for depository institutions, securities firms, and insurance companies set by U.S. (and in some cases, international) regulators such as the Bank for International Settlements (BIS). Appendix 20A to the chapter describes the foundations and advanced approaches used to calculate adequate capital according to internal ratings–based models of measuring credit risk that are currently being proposed by the BIS for banks (to be introduced in 2006).

www.bis.org

CAPITAL AND INSOLVENCY RISK

Capital

To see how capital protects an FI against insolvency risk, we must define *capital* more precisely. The problem is that there are many definitions of capital: an economist's definition of capital may differ from an accountant's definition, which, in turn, may differ from the definition used by regulators. Specifically, the economist's definition of an FI's capital or owners' equity stake in an FI is the difference between the market values of its assets and its liabilities. This is also called the **net worth** of an FI. While this is the *economic* meaning of capital, regulators have found it necessary to adopt definitions of capital that depart by a greater or lesser degree from economic net worth. The concept of an FI's economic net worth is really a *market value accounting concept*. With the exception of the investment banking industry, regulatory-defined capital and required leverage ratios are based in whole or in part on historical or **book value** accounting concepts.

We begin by looking at the role of economic capital or net worth as an insulation device against two major types of risk: credit risk and interest rate risk. We then compare this market value concept with the book value concept of capital. Because it can actually distort the true solvency position of an FI, the book value of capital concept can be misleading to managers, owners, liability holders, and regulators. We also examine some possible reasons why FI regulators continue to rely on book value concepts in the light of such economic value transparency problems and rulings by the Financial Accounting Standards Board (such as *FASB Statement No. 115*).

net worth
A measure of an FI's capital that is equal to the difference between the market value of its assets and the market value of its liabilities.

book value
Historical cost basis for asset and liability values.

The Market Value of Capital

To see how economic net worth or equity insulates an FI against risk, consider the following example. Table 20–1 presents a simple balance sheet where all the assets and liabilities of an FI are valued in **market value** terms at current prices on a **mark-to-market basis** (see Chapter 8). On a mark-to-market or market value basis,

market value or mark-to-market basis
Allowing balance sheet values to reflect current rather than historical prices.

---

[1] See S. A. Ross, R. W. Westerfield, and B. D. Jordan, *Fundamentals of Corporate Finance* (Chicago: Irwin/ McGraw-Hill, 1998).

[2] A sixth function might be added. This would focus on the role of capital regulation in restraining the rate of asset growth.

TABLE 20–1
An FI's Market Value Balance Sheet (in millions of dollars)

Assets		Liabilities	
Long-term securities	$ 80	Liabilities (short-term, floating-rate deposits)	$ 90
Long-term loans	20	Net worth	10
	$100		$100

TABLE 20–2
An FI's Market Value Balance Sheet after a Decline in the Value of Loans (in millions of dollars)

Assets		Liabilities	
Long-term securities	$80	Liabilities	$90
Long-term loans	12	Net worth	2
	$92		$92

TABLE 20–3
An FI's Balance Sheet after a Major Decline in the Value of the Loan Portfolio (in millions of dollars)

Assets		Liabilities	
Long-term securities	$80	Liabilities	$90
Long-term loans	8	Net worth	−2
	$88		$88

the economic value of the FI's equity is $10 million, which is the difference between the market value of its assets and liabilities. On a market value basis, the FI is economically solvent and imposes no failure costs on depositors or regulators if it were liquidated today. Let's consider the impact of two classic types of FI risk on this FI's net worth: credit risk and interest rate risk.

Market Value of Capital and Credit Risk

In Table 20–1, an FI has $20 million in long-term loans. (For simplicity, we drop the $ sign and "million" notation in the rest of the example.) Suppose that, because of a recession, a number of these borrowers get into cash flow problems and are unable to keep up their promised loan repayment schedules. A decline in the current and expected future cash flows on loans lowers the market value of the loan portfolio held by the FI below 20. Suppose that loans are really worth only 12 (the price the FI would receive if it could sell these loans in a secondary market at today's prices). This means the market value of the loan portfolio has fallen from 20 to 12. Look at the revised market value balance sheet in Table 20–2.

The loss of 8 in the market value of loans appears on the liability side of the balance sheet as a loss of 8 to the FI's net worth. That is, the loss of asset value is charged against the equity owners' capital or net worth. As you can see, the liability holders (depositors) are fully protected in that the total market value of their claims is still 90. This is the case because debt holders legally are senior claimants and equity holders are junior claimants to an FI's assets. Consequently, equity holders bear losses on the asset portfolio first. In fact, in our example, liability holders are hurt only when losses on the loan portfolio exceed 10, the original net worth of the FI. Let's consider a larger credit risk shock such that the market value of the loan portfolio plummets from 20 to 8, a loss of 12 (see Table 20–3).

This larger loss renders the FI insolvent; the market value of its assets (88) is now less than the value of its liabilities (90). The owners' net worth stake has been

TABLE 20–4
An FI's Market Value Balance Sheet after a Rise in Interest Rates (in millions of dollars)

Assets		Liabilities	
Long-term securities	$75	Liabilities	$90
Long-term loans	17	Net worth	2
	$92		$92

completely wiped out (reduced from 10 to −2), making net worth negative. As a result, liability holders are hurt, but only a bit. Specifically, the first 10 of the 12 loss in value of the loan portfolio is borne by the equity holders. Only after the equity holders are wiped out do the liability holders begin to lose. In this example, the economic value of their claims on the FI has fallen from 90 to 88, or a loss of 2 (a percentage loss of 2.22 percent). After insolvency and the liquidation of the remaining 88 in assets, the depositors would get only 88/90 on the dollar, or 97.77 cents per $1 of deposits. Note here that we are ignoring deposit insurance.[3]

If the FI's net worth had been larger—say 15 rather than 10 in the previous example—the liability holders would have been fully protected against the loss of 12.[4] This example clearly demonstrates the concept of net worth or capital as an insurance fund protecting liability holders, such as depositors, against insolvency risk. The larger the FI's net worth relative to the size of its assets, the more insolvency protection or insurance there is for liability holders and liability guarantors such as the FDIC. This is why regulators focus on capital requirements such as the ratio of net worth to assets in assessing the insolvency risk exposure of an FI and in setting risk–based deposit insurance premiums (see Chapter 19).

Market Value of Capital and Interest Rate Risk

Consider the market value balance sheet in Table 20–1 after a rise in interest rates. As we discuss in Chapter 8, rising interest rates reduce the market value of the FI's long-term fixed-income securities and loans while floating-rate instruments, if instantaneously repriced, find their market values largely unaffected. Suppose a rise in interest rates reduces the market value of the FI's long-term securities investments from 80 to 75 and the market value of its long-term loans from 20 to 17. Because all deposit liabilities are assumed to be short-term floating-rate deposits, their market values are unchanged at 90.

After the shock to interest rates, the market value balance sheet is represented in Table 20–4. The loss of 8 in the market value of the FI's assets is once again reflected on the liability side of the balance sheet by a fall in FI net worth from 10 to 2. Thus, as for increased credit risk, losses in asset values due to adverse interest rate changes are borne first by the equity holders. Only if the fall in the market value of assets exceeds 10 are the liability holders, as senior claimants to the FI's assets, adversely affected.

These examples show that market valuation of the balance sheet produces an economically accurate picture of the net worth, and thus, the solvency position of an FI. Credit risk and interest rate risk shocks that result in losses in the market value of assets are borne directly by the equity holders in the sense that such losses

---

[3] In the presence of deposit insurance, the insurer, such as the FDIC, would bear some of the depositors' losses; for details, see Chapter 19.

[4] In this case, the 12 loss reduces net worth to +3.

TABLE 20–5
Book Value of an
FI's Assets and
Liabilities (in
millions of dollars)

Assets		Liabilities	
Long-term securities	$ 80	Short-term liabilities	$ 90
Long-term loans	20	Net worth	10
	$100		$100

are charges against the value of their ownership claims in the FI. As long as the owners' capital or equity stake is adequate, or sufficiently large, liability holders (and, implicitly, regulators that back the claims of liability holders) are protected against insolvency risk. That is, if an FI were closed by regulators before its economic net worth became zero, neither liability holders nor those regulators guaranteeing the claims of liability holders would stand to lose. Thus, many academics and analysts have advocated the use of market value accounting and market value of capital closure rules for all FIs, especially in the light of the book value of capital rules associated with the savings association disaster in the 1980s (see Chapter 19).[5]

For example, the Financial Accounting Standards Board (*FASB*) *Statement No. 115* technically requires securities classified as "available for sale" to be marked to market.[6] By comparison, no similar marked-to-market requirement exists on the liabilities side. In the absence of any contrary ruling by regulators, this would require FI capital (net worth) positions to be adjusted downward if interest rates rose. However, as discussed later in this chapter, DI regulators, in December 1994, exempted banks from the need to adjust their net worth positions for capital losses on securities, thereby reconfirming their preference for book value–based capital rules. The rationale is that regulators might be forced to close too many DIs in the event of temporary spikes in interest rates.

The Book Value of Capital

We contrast market value or economic net worth with book value of capital or net worth. As we discuss in later sections, book value capital and capital rules based on book values are most commonly used by FI regulators. In Table 20–5, we use the same initial balance sheet we used in Table 20–1 but assume that assets and liabilities are now valued at their historical book values.

In Table 20–5, the 80 in long-term securities and the 20 in long-term loans reflect the historic or original book values of those assets. That is, they reflect the values when the loans were made and the bonds were purchased, which may have been many years ago. Similarly, on the liability side, the 90 in liabilities reflects their historical cost, and net worth or equity is now the book value of the stockholders' claims rather than the market value of those claims. For example, the book value of

---

[5] See, for example, G. J. Benston and G. C. Kaufman, "Risk and Solvency Regulation of Depository Institutions: Past Policies and Current Options," Monograph Series in Finance and Economics, 1988–1 (New York University, Salomon Brothers Center, 1988); and L. J. White, *The S and L Debacle* (New York: Oxford University Press, 1991).

[6] M. M. Cornett, Z. Rezaee, and H. Tehranian, in "An Investigation of Capital Market Reactions to Pronouncements on Fair Value Accounting," *Journal of Accounting and Economics* 22 (1996), pp. 119–54, find that announcements that signaled an increased (decreased) probability of issuance of fair value accounting standards produced negative (positive) abnormal stock price reactions for sample banks. Further, the magnitude of the stock price reactions was negatively related to a bank's leverage ratio and positively related to the ratio of the book value of the investment portfolio to total assets and the ratio of the difference between the market and book value of the investment portfolio to total assets.

capital—the difference between the book values of assets and liabilities—usually comprises the following four components for an FI:

1. *Par value of shares.* The face value of the common stock shares issued by the FI (the par value is usually $1 per share) times the number of shares outstanding.
2. *Surplus value of shares.* The difference between the price the public paid for common stock or shares when originally offered (e.g., $5 share) and their par values (e.g., $1) times the number of shares outstanding.
3. *Retained earnings.* The accumulated value of past profits not yet paid out in dividends to shareholders. Since these earnings could be paid out in dividends, they are part of the equity owners' stake in the FI.
4. *Loan loss reserve.* A special reserve set aside out of retained earnings to meet expected and actual losses on the portfolio. Loan loss reserves reflect an estimate by the FI's management of the losses in the loan portfolio. While tax laws influence the reserve's size, FI managers actually set the level.

Consequently, book value of capital equals the par value plus surplus plus retained earnings plus loan loss reserves. As the example in Table 20–5 is constructed, the book value of capital equals 10. However, invariably, the *book value of equity does not equal the market value of equity* (the difference between the market value of assets and that of liabilities). This inequality in book and market value of equity can be understood by examining the effects of the same credit and interest rate shocks on the FI's capital position, but assuming book value accounting methods.

Book Value of Capital and Credit Risk

Suppose that some of the 20 in loans are in difficulty regarding repayment schedules. We assumed in Table 20–2 that the revaluation of cash flows leads to an immediate downward adjustment of the loan portfolio's market value from 20 to 12, a market value loss of 8. By contrast, under historic book value accounting methods such as generally accepted accounting principles (GAAP), FIs have greater discretion in reflecting or timing problem loan loss recognition on their balance sheets and thus in the impact of such losses on capital. Indeed, FIs may well resist writing down the values of bad assets as long as possible to try to present a more favorable picture to depositors and regulators. Such resistance may be expected if managers believe their jobs could be threatened when they recognize such losses. Only pressure from regulators such as bank, thrift, or insurance examiners may force loss recognition and write-downs in the values of problem assets. For example, in recent years, on-site examinations of property insurance companies have taken place as infrequently as once every three years and off-site analysis of balance sheet information as infrequently as once every 18 months. While on-site examinations are *more frequent* for depositor institutions, there is still a tendency to delay writing down the book values of loans. A good international example is the delay shown by Japanese banks in recognizing loan losses incurred over the 1996–2000 period, as a result of the Asian crisis and an economic recession domestically. As of year-end 2000 the collective bad debts of Japanese banks were conservatively estimated to exceed 32 trillion yen, most of which remained on their balance sheets at original book values. Moreover, even when loans are declared substandard by examiners, they usually remain on the balance sheet at book value. A problem loan may require a write-down of only 50 percent, while only an outright loss requires a full 100 percent charge-off against the FI's equity position.

TABLE 20–6
Effect of a Loan Loss Charge-Off against the Book Value of an FI's Equity (in millions of dollars)

Assets		Liabilities	
Long-term securities	$80	Liabilities	$90
Long-term loans	17	Equity (loss of 3 on loan loss reserve)	7
	$97		$97

Suppose that in our example of historical book value accounting, the FI is forced to recognize a loss of 3 rather than 8 on its loan portfolio. The 3 is a charge against the 10 of stockholders' book equity value. Technically, the 3 loss on assets would be charged off against the loan loss reserve component of equity.[7] The new book value balance sheet is shown in Table 20–6.

Book Value of Capital and Interest Rate Risk

Although book value accounting systems do recognize credit risk problems, albeit only partially and usually with a long and discretionary time lag, their failure to recognize the impact of interest rate risk is more extreme.

In our market value accounting example in Table 20–4, a rise in interest rates lowered the market values of long-term securities and loans by 8 and led to a fall in the market value of net worth from 10 to 2. In a book value accounting world, when all assets and liabilities reflect their original cost of purchase, the rise in interest rates has no effect on the value of assets, liabilities, or the book value of equity. That is, the balance sheet remains unchanged; Table 20–5 reflects the position both before and after the interest rate rise. Consider those thrifts that, even though interest rates rose dramatically in the early 1980s, continued to report long-term fixed-rate mortgages at historical book values and, therefore, a positive book capital position. Yet, on a market value net worth basis, their mortgages were worth far less than the book values shown on their balance sheets. Indeed, more than half of the firms in the industry were economically insolvent—many massively so.[8]

The Discrepancy between the Market and Book Values of Equity

The degree to which the book value of an FI's capital deviates from its true economic market value depends on a number of factors, especially:

1. *Interest rate volatility.* The higher the interest rate volatility, the greater the discrepancy.

2. *Examination and enforcement.* The more frequent the on-site and off-site examinations and the stiffer the examiner/regulator standards regarding charging off problem loans, the smaller the discrepancy.

In actual practice, for large publicly traded FIs, we can get a good idea of the discrepancy between book values (*BV*) and market values (*MV*) of equity even when the FI itself does not mark its balance sheet to market. Specifically, in an

---

[7] Banks normally get a tax shelter against the cost of the write-off, thus reducing its cost. If losses exceed the bank's loan loss reserves, the bank is likely to use its retained earnings as its next line of defense.

[8] See White, *The S and L Debacle*, p. 89.

efficient capital market, investors can value the shares of an FI by doing an as-if market value calculation of the assets and liabilities of the FI. This valuation is based on the FI's current and expected future net earnings or dividend flows. The stock price of the FI reflects this valuation and thus the market value of its shares outstanding. The market value of equity per share is therefore:

$$MV = \frac{\text{Market value of equity ownership shares outstanding}}{\text{Number of shares}}$$

By contrast, the historical or book value of the FI's equity per share (*BV*) is equal to:

$$BV = \frac{\begin{array}{c}\text{Par value}\\\text{of equity}\end{array} + \begin{array}{c}\text{Surplus}\\\text{value}\end{array} + \begin{array}{c}\text{Retained}\\\text{earnings}\end{array} + \begin{array}{c}\text{Loan loss}\\\text{reserves}\end{array}}{\text{Number of shares}}$$

market to book ratio
Ratio showing the discrepancy between the stock market value of an FI's equity and the book value of its equity.

The ratio *MV/BV* is often called the **market to book ratio** and shows the degree of discrepancy between the market value of an FI's equity capital as perceived by investors in the stock market and the book value of capital on its balance sheet. The lower this ratio, the more the book value of capital *overstates* the true equity or economic net worth position of an FI as perceived by investors in the capital market.

Given such discrepancies, why do regulators and FIs continue to oppose the implementation of market value accounting? As noted above, the foremost accounting standards body, the Financial Accounting Standards Board, has recommended such a move, as has the Securities and Exchange Commission.

Arguments against Market Value Accounting

The first argument against market value (*MV*) accounting is that it is difficult to implement. This may be especially true for small commercial banks and thrifts with large amounts of nontraded assets such as small loans on their balance sheets. When it is impossible to determine accurate market prices or values for assets, marking to market may be done only with error. A counterargument to this is that the error resulting from the use of market valuation of nontraded assets is still likely to be less than that resulting from the use of original book or historical valuation since the market value approach does not require all assets and liabilities to be traded. As long as current and expected cash flows on an asset or liability and an appropriate discount rate can be specified, approximate market values can always be imputed (see CreditMetrics, described in Appendix 11A). Further, with the growth of loan sales and asset securitization (see Chapters 27 and 28), indicative market prices are available on an increasing variety of loans.[9]

The second argument against market value accounting is that it introduces an unnecessary degree of variability into an FI's earnings—and thus net worth—because paper capital gains and losses on assets are passed through the FI's income statement. Critics argue that reporting unrealized capital gains and losses is distortionary if the FI actually plans to hold these assets to maturity. Insurers and FI managers argue that in many cases they do hold loans and other assets to maturity and,

---

[9] Recently, Congress also proposed a number of initiatives to securitize small business loans using a public agency similar to the Government National Mortgage Association (GNMA), the public agency that facilitates residential mortgage securitizations. Additionally, Angbazo, Mei, and Saunders (1998) analyze the pricing of loans in the secondary market by looking at highly leveraged transaction loans; see "Credit Spreads in the Market for Highly Leveraged Transaction Loans," *Journal of Banking and Finance* 22 (1998), pp. 1249–82.

therefore, never actually realize capital gains or losses. Further, regulators have argued that they may be forced to close banks too early under the prompt corrective action requirements imposed by the FDICIA (discussed later in this chapter)—especially if an interest rate spike is only temporary and capital losses on securities can be quickly turned into capital gains as rates fall again (e.g., if interest rates are mean reverting, as much empirical evidence shows). The counterargument is that FIs are increasingly trading, selling, and securitizing assets rather than holding them to maturity. Further, the failure to reflect capital gains and losses from interest rate changes means that the FI's equity position fails to reflect its true interest rate risk exposure.

The third argument against market value accounting is that FIs are less willing to accept longer-term asset exposures, such as mortgage loans and C&I loans, if these assets have to be continuously marked to market to reflect changing credit quality and interest rates. For example, as shown in Chapter 8, long-term assets are more interest rate sensitive than are short-term assets. The concern is that market value accounting may interfere with FIs' special functions as lenders and monitors (see Chapter 1) and may even result in (or accentuate) a major credit crunch. Of the three arguments against market value accounting, this one is probably the most persuasive to regulators concerned about small business finance and economic growth.[10]

www.sec.gov

Having discussed the advantages and disadvantages of book- and market-based measures of an FI's capital, we should note that most FI regulators have chosen some form of book value accounting standard to measure an FI's capital adequacy. The major exception is the Securities and Exchange Commission (SEC). Along with the NYSE and other major stock exchanges, the SEC imposes on securities firms, retail brokers, and specialists a capital or net worth rule that is, for all intents and purposes, a market value accounting rule.

Next, we examine the capital adequacy rules imposed in key FI sectors: (1) commercial banks and thrifts, (2) securities firms, (3) life insurers, and (4) PC insurers. Because many of the capital adequacy rules currently differ considerably across these sectors, the current wave of consolidation in the U.S. financial industry into financial conglomerates (or universal banks) is likely to be more difficult than it would be if market value accounting rules were adopted across all sectors. Nevertheless, there is a clear trend toward similar risk-based capital rules in the banking, thrift, and insurance (both PC and life) industries. We discuss this trend in more detail in the remainder of the chapter.

Concept Questions

1. Why is an FI economically insolvent when its net worth is negative?
2. What are the four major components of an FI's book equity?
3. Is book value accounting for loan losses backward looking or forward looking?
4. What does a market to book ratio that is less than 1 imply about an FI's performance?

CAPITAL ADEQUACY IN THE COMMERCIAL BANKING AND THRIFT INDUSTRY

Actual Capital Rules

The FDIC Improvement Act of 1991 requires that banks and thrifts adopt essentially the same capital requirements. While there are some minor differences, the

---

[10] This was a particularly sensitive issue in the early 1990s, when a credit crunch was already perceived to exist and the proportion of C&I loans in bank portfolios was falling (also see Chapter 2).

two industries have converged toward a level playing field as far as capital requirements are concerned. Given this, we concentrate on describing the recent evolution of capital requirements in commercial banking.

Since 1988, U.S. commercial banks have faced two different capital requirements: a capital-assets (leverage) ratio and a risk-based capital ratio that is in turn subdivided into a Tier I capital risk-based ratio and a total capital (Tier I plus Tier II capital) risk-based ratio. We describe these in more detail next.

The Capital–Assets Ratio (or Leverage Ratio)

leverage ratio
Ratio of an FI's core capital to its assets.

The capital–assets ratio, or **leverage ratio,** measures the ratio of a bank's book value of primary or core capital to the book value of its assets. The lower this ratio is, the more highly leveraged the bank is. Primary or core capital is a bank's common equity (book value) plus qualifying cumulative perpetual preferred stock plus minority interests in equity accounts of consolidated subsidiaries.

With the passage of the FDIC Improvement Act in 1991, a bank's capital adequacy is assessed according to where its leverage ratio (L) places in one of the five target zones listed in the Leverage Ratio column (3) of Table 20–7. The leverage ratio is:

$$L = \frac{\text{Core capital}}{\text{Assets}}$$

If a bank's leverage ratio is 5 percent or more, it is well capitalized. If it is 4 percent or more, it is adequately capitalized; if it is less than 4 percent, it is undercapitalized; if it is less than 3 percent, it is significantly undercapitalized; and if it is 2 percent or less, it is critically undercapitalized. Since 1995, less than 0.5 percent of banking industry assets have been classified as undercapitalized. This compares with 31.3 percent undercapitalized in the fourth quarter of 1990 (i.e., during the 1989–91 recession). As discussed in the Industry Perspectives box, despite a downturn in the U.S. economy and an increase in problem loans at U.S. commercial banks, banks had built up record capital levels in the early 2000s. Indeed, the industry's ratio of equity capital to total assets was 9.12 percent in the third quarter of 2003.

TABLE 20–7   Specifications of Capital Categories for Prompt Corrective Action

Zone	(1) Total Risk-Based Ratio		(2) Tier I Risk-Based Ratio		(3) Leverage Ratio		Capital Directive/Other
1. Well capitalized	10% or above	and	6% or above	and	5% or above	and	Not subject to a capital directive to meet a specific level for any capital measure
2. Adequately capitalized	8% or above	and	4% or above	and	4% or above	and	Does not meet the definition of well capitalized
3. Undercapitalized	Under 8%	or	Under 4%	or	Under 4%		
4. Significantly undercapitalized	Under 6%	or	Under 3%	or	Under 3%		
5. Critically undercapitalized	2% or under	or	2% or under	or	2% or under		

Source: Federal Reserve Board of Governors, September 10, 1993.

Associated with each zone is a mandatory set of actions as well as a set of discretionary actions for regulators to take. The idea here is to enforce minimum capital requirements and limit the ability of regulators to show forbearance to the worst capitalized banks. Analysts blame such forbearance and regulator discretion for the size of the losses borne by taxpayers due to the widespread collapse of thrifts and the Federal Saving's and Loan Insurance Corporation (FSLIC) in the 1980s and the technical insolvency of the FDIC in 1991.

prompt corrective action
Mandatory actions that have to be taken by regulators as a bank's capital ratio falls.

Since December 18, 1992, under the FDICIA legislation, regulators must take specific actions—**prompt corrective action** (PCA)—when a bank falls outside the zone 1,[11] or the well-capitalized, category. Most important, a receiver must be appointed when a bank's book value of capital to assets (leverage) ratio falls to 2 percent or less.[12] That is, receivership is mandatory even before the book value ratio falls to 0 percent.

Unfortunately, the leverage ratio has three problems as a measure of capital adequacy:

1. *Market value.* Even if a bank is closed when its leverage ratio falls below 2 percent, a 2 percent book capital–asset ratio could be consistent with a massive *negative* market value net worth. That is, there is no assurance that depositors and regulators (including taxpayers) are adequately protected against losses. Many thrifts that were closed with low book capital values in the 1980s had negative net worths on a market value basis exceeding 30 percent.

2. *Asset risk.* By taking the denominator of the leverage ratio as total assets, the leverage ratio fails to take into account, even partially, the different credit, interest rate, and other risks of the assets that constitute total assets.

3. *Off-balance-sheet activities.* Despite the massive growth in banks' off-balance-sheet activities, no capital is required to be held to meet the potential insolvency risks involved with such contingent assets and liabilities.

Risk–Based Capital Ratios

www.bis.org

Basel Agreement
The requirement to impose risk-based capital ratios on banks in major industrialized countries.

In light of the weaknesses of the simple capital–assets ratio just described, U.S. bank regulators formally agreed with other member countries of the Bank for International Settlements (BIS) to implement two new risk-based capital ratios for all commercial banks under their jurisdiction. The BIS phased in and fully implemented these risk-based capital ratios on January 1, 1993, under what has become known as the **Basel** (or Basle) **Agreement** (now called Basel I). The 1993 Basel Agreement explicitly incorporated the different credit risks of assets (both on and off the balance sheet) into capital adequacy measures. This was followed with a revision in 1998 in which market risk was incorporated into risk-based capital in the form of an add-on to the 8 percent ratio for credit risk exposure (see Chapter 11). In 2001, the BIS issued a Consultative Document, "The New Basel Capital Accord," that proposed the incorporation (effective by year-end 2006) of operational risk into

---

[11] M. J. Flannery and J. F. Houston, in "The Value of a Government Monitor for U.S. Banking Firms," *Journal of Money, Credit, and Banking* 31 (1999), pp. 14–34, find that the market is aware of bank examinations and takes them into account when valuing bank stocks.

[12] Admittedly, there are a number of loopholes and delaying tactics managers and stockholders might exploit, especially through the courts. This loss of discretion in closure is also one reason bank regulators have resisted *FASB Statement 115,* as described earlier.

Industry Perspectives

DEPOSITORY INSTITUTIONS: THIRD QUARTER 2003 PERFORMANCE

Net Income Sets a Record for Third Consecutive Quarter

Commercial banks and savings institutions insured by the FDIC reported record-high earnings in the third quarter of 2003, the third consecutive quarter that industry earnings have set a record. Net income totaled $30.4 billion, an increase of $147 million (0.5 percent) from the second quarter, and $3.1 billion (11.3 percent) more than the industry earned in the third quarter of 2002. The average return on assets was 1.36 percent, compared to 1.38 percent in the second quarter, and 1.34 percent a year earlier. More than half of all institutions (55.3 percent) reported an ROA of 1 percent or higher for the quarter. Slightly more than half reported increased net income compared to the second quarter (50.8 percent), and a similar proportion (50.7 percent) reported higher net income than in the third quarter of 2002.

C&I Loans Remain at Forefront of Asset Quality Improvement

The improving trend in asset quality that began late last year continued through the third quarter, as both noncurrent loans and net charge-offs declined. Net charge-offs were $684 million (6.7 percent) lower than in the second quarter, and were $2.4 billion (20.3 percent) below the level of a year ago. Charge-offs of commercial and industrial (C&I) loans fell by $423 million (13.4 percent) from the second quarter, accounting for 62 percent of the improvement in total net charge-offs. Compared to the third quarter of 2002, C&I charge-offs were down by $2.2 billion (44.2 percent), representing 88.6 percent of the improvement in all net charge-offs. Net charge-offs on credit-card loans declined by $363 million (9.0 percent) from the second quarter, and were $306 million (7.7 percent) lower than a year earlier. The only loan category that had a significant increase in charge-offs was loans to foreign governments, where net charge-offs rose by $133 million.

Noncurrent Rate Falls to Two-Year Low

Noncurrent loans declined for the fourth quarter in a row, falling by $2.6 billion (4.0 percent). Compared to the level of a year ago, noncurrent loans are down by $6.7 billion (9.7 percent). Noncurrent C&I loans fell by $1.4 billion (5.7 percent) during the quarter, and have fallen by $5.3 billion (18.5 percent) in the past 12 months. As with net charge-offs, improvements in C&I loans have accounted for the majority of the improvement in total noncurrent loans. At the end of September, the percent of total loans that were noncurrent stood at 1.17 percent, the lowest level since midyear 2001.

Coverage Ratio Improves Despite Decline in Loss Reserves

Total loan-loss provisions fell short of total net charge-offs for the third quarter in a row, contributing to a $991 million (1.2 percent) decline in the industry's loss reserves. This ratio of reserves to total loans declined from 1.64 percent to 1.59 percent during the quarter. This is the lowest level for this ratio in more than 2 years (it was 1.55 percent at the end of the second quarter of 2001). In contrast, the industry's "coverage ratio" increased to $1.36 in reserves for every $1.00 of noncurrent loans, from $1.33 at midyear, thanks to the decline in noncurrent loans.

Regulatory Capital Ratios Hit New Highs

Total equity capital increased by only $5.0 billion (0.6 percent) during the quarter, the smallest quarterly increase since the third quarter of 1999. The main reason that equity growth slowed was depreciation in the market values of institutions' available-for-sale securities, caused by rising interest rates. Under Generally Accepted Accounting Principles (GAAP), changes in the values of these securities are reflected in equity capital. At midyear, commercial banks' available-for-sale securities contained about $26 billion in unrealized gains; at the end of the third quarter, this figure had declined to $14 billion. Even with the small increase in equity capital, the industry's equity-to-assets ratio registered a modest improvement, from 9.10 percent to 9.13 percent. Because regulatory capital definitions do not include adjustments for unrealized gains in securities portfolios, two of the industry's three regulatory capital ratios—Tier 1 risk-based capital and total risk-based capital—rose to record-high levels during the quarter.

Source: *Quarterly Banking Profile,* FDIC, Third Quarter 2003. *www.fdic.gov*

FIGURE 20–1
Basel II Pillars of
Capital Regulation

Pillar 1	Pillar 2	Pillar 3
Calculation of regulatory minimum capital requirements	Regulatory supervisory review so as to complement and enforce minimum capital requirements calculated under Pillar 1	Requirements on rules for disclosure of capital structure, risk exposures, and capital adequacy so as to increase FI transparency and enhance market/investor discipline
1. Credit risk: on-balance-sheet and off-balance-sheet (Standardized vs. Internal Ratings–Based Approach)		
2. Market risk (Standardized vs. Internal Ratings–Based Approach)		
3. Operational risk (Basic Indicator vs. Standardized vs. Advanced Measurement Approach)		

capital requirements (see Chapter 14 and below) and updated the credit risk assessments in the 1993 agreement.[13]

The proposed new Basel Accord or Agreement (called Basel II) consists of three mutually reinforcing pillars (illustrated in Figure 20–1), which together contribute to the safety and soundness of the financial system. Pillar 1 covers regulatory minimum capital requirements for credit, market, and operational risk. The measurement of market risk did not change from that adopted in 1998 and is presented in Chapter 10. In the 2001 consultative document, the BIS proposed a range of options for addressing both credit and operational risk. Two options were proposed for the measurement of credit risk. The first is the Standardized Approach, discussed below, and the second is an Internal Ratings–Based (IRB) approach—see Appendix 20A. The Standardized Approach is similar to that of the 1993 agreement, but is more risk sensitive. Under the IRB approach, banks are allowed to use their internal estimates of borrower creditworthiness to assess credit risk in their portfolios (using their own internal rating systems and credit scoring models) subject to strict methodological and disclosure standards.[14] Three different

[13] See Basel Committee on Banking Supervision, "The New Basel Capital Accord," January 2001; "Potential Modifications to the Committee's Proposals," November 2001; "The New Basel Capital Accord," April 2003; and "International Convergence of Capital Measurement and Capital Standards, June 2004. **www.bis.org**

[14] Several papers have debated the ability and practicalities of implementing internal bank models. See, for example, B. J. Hirtle, M. Levonian, M. Saidenberg, S. Walter, and D. Wright, "Using Credit Risk Models for Regulatory Capital: Issues and Options," *FRBNY Economic Policy Review,* March 2001, pp. 19–36; M. Carey, "Dimensions of Credit Risk and Their Relationship to Economic Capital Requirements," NBER Working Paper 7629, March 2000; A. Garrett, "Insight on Basel II Loan Pricing," *International Treasurer,* July 2, 2001, pp. 10–11; and "Basel Gives Banks the Whip Hand," *Euromoney,* March 2001, pp. 48–53. See also A. Saunders and L. Allen, *Credit Risk Measurement: Value at Risk and Other New Paradigms,* 2nd ed. (New York: John Wiley and Sons, 2002).

approaches are available to measure operational risk: the Basic Indicator, Standardized, and Advanced Measurement approaches. We discussed these briefly in Chapter 14 and will do so in more detail below.

In Pillar 2, the BIS stressed the importance of the regulatory supervisory review process as a critical complement to minimum capital requirements. Specifically, the BIS proposed procedures through which regulators ensure that each bank has sound internal processes in place to assess the adequacy of its capital and set targets for capital that are commensurate with the bank's specific risk profile and control environment. In Pillar 3, the BIS sought to encourage market discipline by developing a set of requirements on the disclosure of capital structure, risk exposures, and capital adequacy. Such disclosure requirements allow market participants to assess critical information describing the risk profile and capital adequacy of banks.

U.S. regulators currently enforce the Basel I risk-based capital ratios as well as the traditional leverage ratio. Unlike the simple capital– assets (leverage) ratio, the calculation of these risk-based capital adequacy measures is quite complex. Their major innovation is to distinguish among the different credit risks of assets on the balance sheet and to identify the credit risk inherent in instruments off the balance sheet by using a risk-adjusted assets denominator in these capital adequacy ratios. In a very rough fashion, these capital ratios mark to market a bank's on- and off-balance-sheet positions to reflect its credit risk. Further, additional capital charges must be held against market risk and operational risk.

In the measurement of a bank's risk-based capital adequacy, its capital is the standard by which each of these risks is measured.

Capital

A bank's capital is divided into Tier I and Tier II. Tier I capital is primary or core capital; Tier II capital is supplementary capital. The total capital that the bank holds is defined as the sum of Tier I and Tier II capitals. The definitions of Tier I core capital and Tier II supplementary capital are listed in Table 20–8.

Tier I Capital   Tier I capital is closely linked to a bank's book value of equity, reflecting the concept of the core capital contribution of a bank's owners.[15] Basically, it includes the book value of common equity plus an amount of perpetual (nonmaturing) preferred stock plus minority equity interests held by the bank in subsidiaries minus goodwill. Goodwill is an accounting item that reflects the amount a bank pays above market value when it purchases or acquires other banks or subsidiaries.

Tier II Capital   Tier II capital is a broad array of secondary capital resources. It includes a bank's loan loss reserves up to a maximum of 1.25 percent of risk-adjusted assets plus various convertible and subordinated debt instruments with maximum caps.

We first look at how this capital is used as a cushion against credit risk using the BIS approach currently in operation (Basel I). We then examine its use as a cushion against credit risk using the BIS Standardized Approach described in Basel II and proposed to be effective in 2006. We also examine the required

---

[15] However, loan loss reserves are assigned to Tier II capital because they often reflect losses that have already occurred rather than losses or insolvency risks that may occur in the future.

TABLE 20–8   Summary Definition of Qualifying Capital for Bank Holding Companies

Components	Minimum Requirements
Core capital (Tier I)	
Common stockholders' equity	Must equal or exceed 4 percent of weighted-risk assets
Qualifying cumulative and noncumulative perpetual preferred stock	No limit
Minority interest in equity accounts of consolidated subsidiaries	Limited to 25 percent of the sum of common stock, minority interests, and qualifying perpetual preferred stock
Less: Goodwill*	Organizations should avoid using minority interests to introduce elements not otherwise qualifying for Tier I capital
Supplementary capital (Tier II)	Total of Tier II is limited to 100 percent of Tier I†
Allowance for loan and lease losses	Limited to 1.25 percent of weighted-risk assets
Perpetual preferred stock	No limit within Tier II
Hybrid capital instruments, perpetual debt, and mandatory convertible securities	No limit within Tier II
Subordinated debt and intermediate-term preferred stock (original weighted-average maturity of five years or more)	Subordinated debt and intermediate-term preferred stock are limited to 50 percent of Tier I; amortized for capital purposes as they approach maturity†
Revaluation reserves (equity and buildings)	Not included; organizations encouraged to disclose; may be evaluated on a case-by-case basis for international comparisons and taken into account in making an overall assessment of capital
Deductions (from sum of Tier I and Tier II)	
Investments in unconsolidated subsidiaries	
Reciprocal holdings of banking organizations' capital securities	As a general rule, one-half of the aggregate investments would be deducted from Tier I capital and one-half from Tier II capital‡
Other deductions (such as other subsidiaries or joint ventures) as determined by supervisory authority	On a case-by-case basis or as a matter of policy after formal rule making
Total capital (Tier I + Tier II − Deductions)	Must equal or exceed 8 percent of weighted-risk assets

*Goodwill on the books of bank holding companies before March 12, 1988, would be grandfathered.
†Amounts in excess of limitations are permitted but do not qualify as capital.
‡A proportionately greater amount may be deducted from Tier I capital if the risks associated with the subsidiary so warrant.

Source: Federal Reserve Board of Governors press release, January 1989, Attachment II.

add-ons to capital under Basel II that cushion a bank against market and operational risk.

Credit Risk–Adjusted Assets

credit risk–adjusted assets
On- and off-balance-sheet assets whose values are adjusted for approximate credit risk.

Under both the current (Basel I) and proposed (Basel II) capital adequacy rules, risk-adjusted assets represent the denominator of the risk-based capital ratio. Two components make up **credit risk–adjusted assets:** (1) credit risk–adjusted on-balance-sheet assets, and (2) credit risk–adjusted off-balance-sheet assets.

total risk–based capital ratio
The ratio of the total capital to the risk-adjusted assets of an FI.

To be adequately capitalized, a bank must hold a minimum ratio of total capital (Tier I core capital plus Tier II supplementary capital) to credit risk–adjusted assets of 8 percent; that is, its **total risk–based capital ratio** is calculated as:

$$\text{Total risk–based capital ratio} = \frac{\text{Total capital (Tier I + Tier II)}}{\text{Credit risk–adjusted assets}} \geq 8\%$$

Tier I (core) capital ratio
The ratio of core capital to the risk-adjusted assets of an FI.

In addition, the Tier I core capital component of total capital has its own minimum guideline. The **Tier I (core) capital ratio** is calculated as:

$$\text{Tier I (core) capital ratio} = \frac{\text{Core capital (Tier I)}}{\text{Credit risk–adjusted assets}} \geq 4\%$$

That is, of the 8 percent total risk–based capital ratio, a minimum of 4 percent has to be held in core or primary capital.[16] Thrifts must also operate according to these ratios. Minimum capital ratios for credit unions vary by state.

In addition to their use to define adequately capitalized banks, risk-based capital ratios—along with the traditional leverage ratio—also define well-capitalized, undercapitalized, significantly undercapitalized, and critically undercapitalized banks as part of the prompt corrective action program under the FDICIA. As with the simple leverage ratio, for both the total risk–based capital ratio and the Tier I risk–based capital ratios, these five zones—specified in columns (1) and (2) of Table 20–7—assess capital adequacy and the actions regulators are mandated to take and those they have the discretion to take.[17] Table 20–9 summarizes these regulatory actions.

Calculating Risk-Based Capital Ratios

Credit Risk–Adjusted On-Balance-Sheet Assets under Basel I

Under the current BIS risk-based capital plan (Basel I), each bank assigns its assets to one of four categories of credit risk exposure: 0 percent, 20 percent, 50 percent, or 100 percent. In Table 20–10 we list the key categories and assets in these categories. The main features are that cash assets; U.S. T-bills, notes, and bonds of all maturities; and GNMA (Ginnie Mae) mortgage-backed securities (mortgage securitization packages backed by a government agency) are all zero risk based. In the 20 percent class are U.S. agency–backed securities, municipal-issued general obligation bonds, FHLMC and FNMA mortgage-backed securities, and interbank deposits.[18] In the 50 percent class are regular residential mortgage loans and other municipal (revenue) bonds. Finally, all other on-balance-sheet assets, such as C&I, consumer, and credit card loans; premises; and other assets are in the 100 percent risk category. To figure the credit risk–adjusted assets of the bank, we multiply the dollar amount of assets it has in each category by the appropriate risk weight.

---

[16] The difference between the 8 percent and the 4 percent can be made up with noncore or other capital sources; see the description in Table 20–8.

[17] It has been argued that capital adequacy rules may induce a DI to make portfolio choices that actually increase the risk of the DI. The intuition behind the result is that under binding capital requirements, an additional unit of equity tomorrow is more valuable to a DI. If issuing new equity is excessively costly, the only possibility to increase equity tomorrow is to increase risk today in the hope that high-risk investments produce higher returns and thus boost the retained earnings component of equity tomorrow. Thus, some view higher minimum capital requirements as inducing a greater, not lesser, risk of DI insolvency (e.g., if the high-risk investments result in significant losses rather than profits). See J. Blum, "Do Capital Adequacy Requirements Reduce Risks in Banking?" *Journal of Banking and Finance* 23 (1999), pp. 755–71.

[18] The Federal Home Loan Mortgage Corporation (FHLMC) and the Federal National Mortgage Association (FNMA) are quasi-government or government-backed mortgage securitization agencies. (See Chapter 28 for more details on these agencies.)

TABLE 20–9 **Summary of Prompt Corrective Action Provisions of the Federal Deposit Insurance Corporation Improvement Act of 1991**

Zone	Mandatory Provisions	Discretionary Provisions
1. Well capitalized		
2. Adequately capitalized	1. No brokered deposits except with FDIC approval	
3. Undercapitalized	1. Suspend dividends and management fees 2. Require capital restoration plan 3. Restrict asset growth 4. Approval required for acquisitions, branching, and new activities 5. No brokered deposits	1. Order recapitalization 2. Restrict interaffiliate transactions 3. Restrict deposit interest rates 4. Restrict certain other activities 5. Any other action that would better carry out prompt corrective action
4. Significantly undercapitalized	1. Same as for Zone 3 2. Order recapitalization* 3. Restrict interaffiliate transactions* 4. Restrict deposit interest rates* 5. Pay of officers restricted	1. Any Zone 3 discretionary actions 2. Conservatorship or receivership if fails to submit or implement plan or recapitalize pursuant to order 3. Any other Zone 5 provisions if such action is necessary to carry out prompt corrective action
5. Critically undercapitalized	1. Same as for Zone 4 2. Receiver/conservator within 90 days* 3. Receiver if still in Zone 5 four quarters after becoming critically undercapitalized 4. Suspend payments on subordinated debt* 5. Restrict certain other activities	

*Not required if primary supervisor determines action would not serve purpose of prompt corrective action or if certain other conditions are met.

Source: Federal Reserve Board of Governors, September 10, 1993.

EXAMPLE 20–1

Calculation of On-Balance-Sheet Credit Risk–Adjusted Assets under Basel I

Consider the balance sheet in Table 20–11 as an example. The risk-adjusted value of the bank's on-balance-sheet assets (under Basel I) would be:

$$\sum_{i=1}^{n} w_i a_i$$

where

w_i = Risk weight of the ith asset

a_i = Dollar (book) value of the ith asset on the balance sheet

Thus,

Credit risk–adjusted on-balance-sheet assets = 0(8 m + 13 m + 60 m + 50 m + 42 m)
+ .2(10 m + 10 m + 20 m) + .5(34 m + 308 m) + 1(10 m + 55m + 75 m + 390 m
+ 10 m + 108 m + 22m) = \$849 million

While the simple book value of on-balance-sheet assets is \$1,215 million, its credit risk–adjusted value is \$849 million.

TABLE 20–10
Summary of the Risk-Based Capital Standards for On-Balance-Sheet Items under Basel I

Source: Federal Reserve Board of Governors press release, January 1989, Attachment III.

Risk Categories
Category 1 (0% weight)
Cash, Federal Reserve Bank balances, securities of the U.S. Treasury, OECD governments, and some U.S. agencies.
Category 2 (20% weight)
Cash items in the process of collection. U.S. and OECD interbank deposits and guaranteed claims.
Some non-OECD bank and government deposits and securities. General obligation municipal bonds.
Some mortgage-backed securities. Claims collateralized by the U.S. Treasury and some other government securities.
Category 3 (50% weight)
Loans fully secured by first liens on the one- to four-family residential properties. Other (revenue) municipal bonds.
Category 4 (100% weight)
All other on-balance-sheet assets not listed above, including loans to private entities and individuals, some claims on non-OECD governments and banks, real assets, and investments in subsidiaries.

Credit Risk–Adjusted On-Balance-Sheet Assets under Basel II

A major criticism of the original Basel Agreement is that individual risk weights depend on the broad categories of borrowers (i.e., sovereigns, banks, or corporates). For example, under Basel I all corporate loans have a risk weight of 100 percent regardless of the borrowing firm's credit risk. The Basel II Standardized Approach aligns regulatory capital requirements more closely with the key elements of banking risk by introducing a wider differentiation of credit risk weights. Specifically, the risk weights are refined by reference to a rating provided by an external credit rating agency (such as Standard & Poor's).[19] Accordingly, compared with the current accord (Basel I), the Standardized Approach of Basel II should produce capital ratios more in line with the actual economic risks that DIs are facing.

Under the Basel II risk-based capital plan proposed for implementation in 2006, each bank assigns its assets to one of five categories of credit risk exposure: 0 percent, 20 percent, 50 percent, 100 percent, or 150 percent. Table 20–12 lists the key categories and assets in these categories. The main features are that in addition to those assets listed as Category 1 under Basel I, loans to sovereigns with an S&P

---

[19] Several recent papers have analyzed and critiqued the use of rating agency credit ratings in assigning risk weights. These include E. I. Altman and A. Saunders, "An Analysis and Critique of the BIS Proposal on Capital Adequacy and Ratings," *Journal of Banking and Finance* 25 (2001), pp. 25–46; G. Ferri, L. Liu, and D. Majnoni, "The Role of Rating Agency Assessments in Less Developed Countries: Impact of the Proposed Basel Guidelines," *Journal of Banking and Finance* 25 (2001), pp. 115–48; I. Linnell, "A Critical Review of the New Capital Adequacy Framework Paper Issued by the Basle Committee on Banking Supervision and Its Implications for the Rating Agency Industry," *Journal of Banking and Finance* 25 (2001), pp. 187–96; M. Carey and M. Hrycay, "Parameterizing Credit Risk Models with Rating Data," *Journal of Banking and Finance* 25 (2001), pp. 197–270; and E. Altman, S. Bharath, and A. Saunders, "Credit Ratings and the BIS Capital Adequacy Reform Agenda," *Journal of Banking and Finance*, 2002, pp. 909–22.

TABLE 20–11   Bank's Balance Sheet under Basel I (in millions of dollars)

Weight	Assets		Liabilities/Equity		Capital Class
0%	Cash	$ 8	Demand deposits	$ 150	
	Balances due from Fed	13	Time deposits	500	
	Treasury bills	60	CDs	400	
	Long-term Treasury securities	50	Fed funds purchased	80	
	Long-term government agencies (GNMAs)	42			
20	Items in process of collection	10	Convertible bonds	15	Tier II
	Long-term government agencies (FNMAs)	10	Subordinated bonds	15	Tier II
	Munis (general obligation)	20			
50	University dorm bonds (revenue)	34	Perpetual preferred	5	Tier II
	Residential one- to four-family mortgages	308	stock (Nonqualifying)		
100	AA+-rated loan to Bank of America	10			
	Commercial loans, AAA− rated	55	Retained earnings	10	Tier I
	Commercial loans, A rated	75	Common stock	30	Tier I
	Commercial loans, BB+ rated	390	Perpetual preferred	10	Tier I
	Commercial loans, CCC+ rated	10	stock (Qualifying)		
	Third World loans, B+ rated	108		$1,215	
	Premises, equipment	22			
N/A	Reserve for loan losses	(10)			Tier II
	Total assets	$1,215			

Off-Balance-Sheet Items:

	$80 m in two-year loan commitments to a large BB+-rated U.S. corporation
100%	$10 m direct credit substitute standby letters of credit issued to a BBB-rated U.S. corporation
	$50 m in commercial letters of credit issued to a BBB−-rated U.S. corporation
50%	One fixed–floating interest rate swap for 4 years with notional dollar value of $100m and replacement cost of $3 m
	One two-year Euro$ contract for $40 m with a replacement cost of −$1 m

credit rating of AA− or better are zero risk based. The 20 percent class now includes loans to sovereigns with an S&P credit rating of A+ to A− and loans to banks and corporates with a credit rating of AA− or better. The 50 percent class now includes loans to sovereigns with an S&P credit rating of BBB+ to BBB− and loans to banks and corporates with a credit rating of A+ to A−. Loans to sovereigns with an S&P credit rating of BB+ to B−, loans to banks with a credit rating of BBB+ to B−, and loans to corporates with a credit rating of BBB+ to BB− are now the only loans included in the 100 percent class. Finally, loans to sovereigns and banks with a credit rating below B− and loans to corporates with a credit rating below BB− are in the 150 percent risk category.[20]

To figure the credit risk–adjusted assets of the bank, we again multiply the dollar amount of assets it has in each category by the appropriate risk weight.

[20] Using a sample of loans made by Spanish banks, J. Saurina and C. Trucharte find that changes in the weight on loans would detrimentally affect banks' patterns of financing to small and medium-sized firms; see "The Impact of Basel II on Lending to Small and Medium-Sized Firms," *Journal of Financial Services Research*, forthcoming. Lending for project financing is also likely to be reduced as a result of Basel II credit risk weighting. See "React or Die," *Project Finance*, February 2002, pp. 40–43; and "Basel II Discontent the Theme," *Project Finance*, June 2002, pp. 46–48.

TABLE 20–12
Summary of the Risk-Based Capital Standards for On-Balance-Sheet Items under Basel II

Source: Federal Reserve Board of Governors press release, January 1989, Attachment III; and Bank for International Settlements, "The New Basel Capital Accord," January 2001. *www.federalreserve.gov* *www.bis.org*

Risk Categories

Category 1 (0% weight)
Cash, Federal Reserve Bank balances, securities of the U.S. Treasury, OECD governments, some U.S. agencies, and loans to sovereigns with an S&P credit rating of AA− or better.

Category 2 (20% weight)
Cash items in the process of collection. U.S. and OECD interbank deposits and guaranteed claims.
Some non-OECD bank and government deposits and securities. General obligation municipal bonds.
Some mortgage-backed securities. Claims collateralized by the U.S. Treasury and some other government securities.
Loans to sovereigns with an S&P credit rating of A+ to A−. Loans to banks and corporates with an S&P credit rating of AA− or better.

Category 3 (50% weight)
Loans fully secured by first liens on one- to four-family residential properties. Other (revenue) municipal bonds. Loans to sovereigns with an S&P credit rating of BBB+ to BBB−. Loans to banks and corporates with an S&P credit rating of A+ to A−.

Category 4 (100% weight)
Loans to sovereigns with an S&P credit rating of BB+ to B−. Loans to banks with a credit rating of BBB+ to B−. Loans to corporates with a credit rating of BBB+ to BB−.
All other on-balance-sheet assets not listed above, including loans to private entities and individuals, some claims on non-OECD governments and banks, real assets, and investments in subsidiaries.

Category 5 (150% weight)
Loans to sovereigns, banks, and securities firms with an S&P credit rating below B−. Loans to corporates with a credit rating below BB−.

EXAMPLE 20–2
Calculation of On-Balance-Sheet Credit Risk–Adjusted Assets under Basel II

Consider our bank's balance sheet in Table 20–13, categorized according to the risk weights of Basel II. Under Basel II, the credit risk–adjusted value of the bank's on-balance-sheet assets would be:

Credit risk–adjusted on-balance-sheet assets = 0(8 m + 13 m + 60 m + 50 m + 42 m)
+ .2(10 m + 10 m + 20 m + 10 m + 55 m) + .5(34 m + 308 m + 75 m)
+ 1(390 m + 108 m + 22 m) + 1.5(10 m) = $764.5 million

The simple book value of on-balance-sheet assets is $1,215 million, its credit risk–adjusted value under Basel I is $849 million and under Basel II is $764.5 million. Basel II modifies the treatment of sovereign, bank, and corporate loans by using credit agency ratings of borrowers to improve the risk sensitivity of the Standardized Approach. The result, in our examples, is a decrease in the credit risk–weighted value of the bank's on-balance-sheet assets.

Credit Risk–Adjusted Off-Balance-Sheet Activities

The credit risk–adjusted value of on-balance-sheet assets is only one component of the capital ratio denominator; the other is the credit risk–adjusted value of the bank's off-balance-sheet (OBS) activities. These OBS activities represent contingent rather than actual claims against depository institutions (see Chapter 14). Thus, regulations require that capital be held not against the full face value of these items, but against an amount equivalent to any eventual on-balance-sheet credit risk these securities might create for a depository institution. Therefore, in calculating the

TABLE 20–13 Bank's Balance Sheet under Basel II (in millions of dollars)

Weight	Assets		Liabilities/Equity		Capital Class
0%	Cash	$ 8	Demand deposits	$ 150	
	Balances due from Fed	13	Time deposits	500	
	Treasury bills	60	CDs	400	
	Long-term Treasury securities	50	Fed funds purchased	80	
	Long-term government agencies (GNMAs)	42			
20	Items in process of collection	10	Convertible bonds	15	Tier II
	Long-term government agencies (FNMAs)	10	Subordinated bonds	15	Tier II
	Munis (general obligation)	20			
	AA+-rated loans to Bank of America	10			
	Commercial loans, AAA− rated	55	Perpetual preferred stock		
50	University dorm bonds (revenue)	34	(Nonqualifying)	5	Tier II
	Residential 1–4 family mortgages	308	Retained earnings	10	Tier I
	Commercial loans, A rated	75	Common stock	30	Tier I
100	Commercial loans, BB+ rated	390	Perpetual preferred stock		
	Third world loans, B+ rated	108	(Qualifying)	10	Tier I
	Premises, equipment	22		$1,215	
150	Commercial loans, CCC+ rated	10			
N/A	Reserve for loan losses	(10)			Tier II
	Total assets	$1,215			

Off-Balance-Sheet Items:

	$80 m in two-year loan commitments to a large BB+-rated U.S. corporation
100%	$10 m direct credit substitute standby letters of credit issued to a BBB-rated U.S. corporation
	$50 m in commercial letters of credit issued to a BBB-rated U.S. corporation
50%	One fixed–floating interest rate swap for four years with notional dollar value of $100 m and replacement cost of $3 m
	One two-year Euro$ contract for $40 m with a replacement cost of −$1 m

credit equivalent amount
The on-balance-sheet equivalent credit risk exposure of an off-balance-sheet item.

credit risk–adjusted asset values of these OBS items we must first convert them into **credit equivalent amounts**—amounts equivalent to an on-balance-sheet item. Further the calculation of the credit risk–adjusted values of the off-balance-sheet activities involves some initial segregation of these activities. In particular, the calculation of the credit risk exposure or the credit risk–adjusted asset amounts of contingent or guaranty contracts such as letters of credit differs from the calculation of the credit risk–adjusted asset amounts for foreign exchange and interest rate forward, option, and swap contracts. We consider the credit risk–adjusted asset value of OBS guaranty-type contracts and contingent contracts and then derivative or market contracts.

The Credit Risk–Adjusted Asset Value of Off-Balance-Sheet Contingent Guaranty Contracts

Basel I. Consider the appropriate conversion factors in Table 20–14.[21] Note that under Basel I, direct credit substitute standby letter of credit guarantees issued by banks have a 100 percent conversion factor rating. Similarly, sale and repurchase

[21] Appropriate here means those factors used by the regulators and required to be used by banks rather than being equal to conversion factors that might be calculated from a contingent asset valuation (option) model. Indeed, regulators used no such valuation model in deriving the conversion factors in Table 20–14.

TABLE 20–14
Conversion Factors for Off-Balance-Sheet Contingent or Guaranty Contracts, Basel I and Basel II

Source: Federal Reserve Board of Governors press release, January 1989, Attachment IV.

Sale and repurchase agreements and assets sold with recourse that are not included on the balance sheet (100%)
Direct-credit substitute standby letters of credit (100%)
Performance-related standby letters of credit (50%)
Unused portion of loan commitments with original maturity of *more than one year* (50%)*
Commercial letters of credit (20%)
Bankers acceptances conveyed (20%)
Other loan commitments (10%)

*Proposed for 2006, the unused portion of loan commitments with an original maturity of one year or less will be 20 percent. Under Basel I such commitments have a 0 percent risk weight.

agreements and assets sold with recourse are also given a 100 percent conversion factor rating. Future performance-related SLCs and unused loan commitments of more that one year have a 50 percent conversion factor. Other loan commitments, those with one year or less to maturity, impose no credit risk on the bank and have a 0 percent credit conversion factor. However, under Base1 II, it is proposed that in 2006, this conversion factor will increase to 20 percent. Standard trade-related commercial letters of credit and bankers acceptances sold have a 20 percent conversion factor.

EXAMPLE 20–3
Calculating Off-Balance-Sheet Contingent or Guaranty Contracts' Credit Risk–Adjusted Assets

To see how OBS activities are incorporated into the risk-based ratio, we can extend Example 20–1 for the bank in Table 20–11. Assume that in addition to having $849 million in credit risk–adjusted assets on its balance sheet, the bank also has the following off-balance-sheet contingencies or guarantees:

1. $80 million two-year loan commitments to large BB+-rated U.S. corporations.
2. $10 million direct credit substitute standby letters of credit issued to a BBB-rated U.S. corporation.
3. $50 million commercial letters of credit issued to a BBB−-rated U.S. corporation.

To find the risk-adjusted asset value for these OBS items, we follow a two-step process.

Step 1. Convert OBS Values into On-Balance-Sheet Credit Equivalent Amounts
In the first step we multiply the dollar amount outstanding of these items to derive the credit equivalent amounts using the conversion factors (CF) listed in Table 20–14.

OBS Item	Face Value		Conversion Factor		Credit Equivalent Amount
Two-year loan commitment	$80 m	×	.5	=	$40 m
Standby letter of credit	10 m	×	1.0	=	10 m
Commercial letter of credit	50 m	×	.2	=	10 m

Thus, the credit equivalent amounts of loan commitments, standby letters of credit, and commercial letters of credit are, respectively, $40, $10, and $10 million. These conversion factors convert an OBS item into an equivalent credit or on-balance-sheet item.

Step 2. Assign the OBS Credit Equivalent Amount to a Risk Category
In the second step we multiply these credit equivalent amounts by their appropriate risk weights. Under Basel I, the appropriate risk weight in each case depends on the underlying

counterparty to the OBS activity, such as a municipality, a government, or a corporation. For example, if the underlying party being guaranteed is a municipality issuing general obligation (GO) bonds, and a bank issued an OBS standby letter of credit backing the credit risk of the municipal GO issue, then the risk weight is 0.2. However if, as in our example, the counterparty being guaranteed is a *private agent,* the appropriate risk weight in each case is 1. Note that if the counterparty had been the central government, the risk weight would have been zero. The appropriate risk weights for our example are:

OBS Item	Credit Equivalent Amount		Risk Weight (w_i)		Risk-Adjusted Asset Amount
Two-year loan commitment	$40 m	×	1.0	=	$40 m
Standby letter of credit	10 m	×	1.0	=	10 m
Commercial letter of credit	10 m	×	1.0	=	10 m
					$60 m

The bank's credit risk–adjusted asset value of its OBS contingencies and guarantees is $60 million.

Basel II. Under Basel II, except for loan commitments with an original maturity of one year or less (which will have a conversion factor of 20 percent), the conversion of OBS values to on-balance-sheet credit equivalent amounts is the same as under Basel I. However, risk weights assigned to OBS contingent guaranty contracts are the same as if the bank had entered into the transactions as a principal. Thus, the credit ratings used to assign a credit risk weight for on-balance-sheet assets (listed in Table 20–12) are also used to assign credit risk weights on these OBS activities (e.g., issuing a commercial letter of credit to a CCC-rated counterparty would result in a risk weight of 150 percent). In our example, because each of the contingent guarantee contracts involves a U.S. corporation with a credit rating between BBB+ and BB–, each is assigned a risk weight of 100 percent (the same weight as under Basel I). Thus, the bank's credit risk–adjusted value of its OBS contingencies and guarantees is again $60 million.

The Credit Risk–Adjusted Asset Value of Off-Balance-Sheet Market Contracts or Derivative Instruments   In addition to having OBS contingencies and guarantees, modern FIs engage heavily in buying and selling OBS futures, options, forwards, swaps, caps, and other derivative securities contracts for interest rate and foreign exchange management and hedging reasons, as well as buying and selling such products on behalf of their customers (see Chapter 13). Each of these positions potentially exposes FIs to **counterparty credit risk,** that is, the risk that the counterparty (or other side of a contract) will default when suffering large actual or potential losses on its position. Such defaults mean that an FI would have to go back to the market to replace such contracts at (potentially) less favorable terms.

Under the risk-based capital ratio rules, a major distinction is made between exchange-traded derivative security contracts (e.g., Chicago Board of Trade's exchange-traded options) and over-the-counter–traded instruments (e.g., forwards, swaps, caps, and floors). The credit or default risk of exchange-traded derivatives is approximately zero because when a counterparty defaults on its obligations, the exchange itself adopts the counterparty's obligations in full. However, no such guarantees exist for bilaterally agreed, over-the-counter contracts originated and

counterparty credit risk
The risk that the other side of a contract will default on payment obligations.

TABLE 20–15
Credit Conversion Factors for Interest Rate and Foreign Exchange Contracts in Calculating Potential Exposure

Remaining Maturity	(1) Interest Rate Contracts	(2) Exchange Rate Contracts
1. Less than one year	0	1.0%
2. One to five years	0.5%	5.0%
3. Over five years	1.5%	7.5%

Source: Federal Reserve Board of Governors press release, August 1995, Section II.

traded outside organized exchanges. Hence, most OBS futures and options positions have no capital requirements for a bank while most forwards, swaps, caps, and floors do.[22]

As with contingent or guaranty contracts, the calculation of the risk-adjusted asset values of OBS market contracts requires a two-step approach (under both Basel I and Basel II). First, we calculate a conversion factor to create credit equivalent amounts. Second, we multiply the credit equivalent amounts by the appropriate risk weights.

Step 1. Convert OBS Values into On-Balance-Sheet Credit Equivalent Amounts. We first convert the notional or face values of all non-exchange-traded swap, forward, and other derivative contracts into credit equivalent amounts. The credit equivalent amount itself is divided into a *potential exposure* element and a *current exposure* element. That is:

$$\begin{array}{l}\text{Credit equivalent amount} \\ \quad \text{of OBS derivative} \\ \quad \text{security items (\$)} \end{array} = \text{Potential exposure (\$)} + \text{Current exposure (\$)}$$

potential exposure
The risk that a counterparty to a derivative securities contract will default in the future.

The **potential exposure** component reflects the credit risk if the counterparty to the contract defaults in the *future.* The probability of such an occurrence depends on the future volatility of either interest rates for an interest rate contract or exchange rates for an exchange rate contract. The Bank of England and the Federal Reserve carried out an enormous number of simulations and found that FX rates were far more volatile than interest rates.[23] Thus, the potential exposure conversion factors in Table 20–15 are larger for foreign exchange contracts than for interest rate contracts. Also, note the larger potential exposure credit risk for longer-term contracts of both types.

current exposure
The cost of replacing a derivative securities contract at today's prices.

In addition to calculating the potential exposure of an OBS market instrument, a bank must calculate its **current exposure** with the instrument. This reflects the cost of replacing a contract if a counterparty defaults *today.* The bank calculates this *replacement cost* or *current exposure* by replacing the rate or price initially in the contract with the current rate or price for a similar contract and recalculates all the current and future cash flows that would have been generated under current rate

[22] This may create some degree of preference among banks for using exchange-traded hedging instruments rather than over-the-counter instruments, because using the former may save a bank costly capital resources.

[23] The Bank of England and the Federal Reserve employed a Monte Carlo simulation approach in deciding on the size of the appropriate conversion factors. See C. W. Smith, C. W. Smithson, and D. S. Wilford, *Managing Financial Risk* (New York: Ballinger, 1990), pp. 225–56.

or price terms.[24] The bank discounts any future cash flows to give a current present value measure of the contract's replacement cost. If the contract's replacement cost is negative (i.e., the bank profits on the replacement of the contract if the counterparty defaults), regulations require the replacement cost (current exposure) to be set to zero. If the replacement cost is positive (i.e., the bank loses on the replacement of the contract if the counterparty defaults), this value is used as the measure of current exposure. Since each swap or forward is in some sense unique, calculating current exposure involves a considerable computer processing task for the bank's management information systems. Indeed, specialized service firms are likely to perform this task for smaller banks.[25]

Step 2. Assign the OBS Credit Equivalent Amount to a Risk Category.   Once the current and potential exposure amounts are summed to produce the credit equivalent amount for each contract, we multiply this dollar number by a risk weight to produce the final credit risk–adjusted asset amount for OBS market contracts.

Basel I.   Under Basel I, the appropriate risk weight is generally .5, or 50 percent. That is:

$$\begin{array}{l}\text{Credit risk–adjusted} \\ \quad \text{value of OBS} \\ \quad \text{market contracts} \end{array} = \text{Total credit equivalent amount} \times .5 \text{ (risk weight)}$$

EXAMPLE 20–4
Calculating Off-Balance-Sheet Market Contract Credit Risk–Adjusted Assets

Suppose the bank in Examples 20–1 and 20–3 had taken one interest rate hedging position in the fixed–floating interest rate swap market for four years with a notional dollar amount of $100 million and one two-year forward foreign exchange contract for $40 million (see Table 20–11).

Step 1
We calculate the credit equivalent amount for each item or contract as:

Type of Contract (remaining maturity)	Notional Principal	×	Potential Exposure Conversion Factor	=	Potential Exposure	Replacement Cost	Current Exposure	=	Credit Equivalent Amount
			Potential Exposure + Current Exposure						
Four-year fixed–floating interest rate swap	$100 m	×	.005	=	**$0.5 m**	$3 m	**$3 m**		**$3.5 m**
Two-year forward foreign exchange contract	$ 40 m	×	.050	=	**$2 m**	$−1 m	**$0**		**$2 m**

(continued)

---

[24] For example, suppose a two-year forward foreign exchange contract was entered into in January 2006 at $1.55/£. In January 2007, the bank has to evaluate the credit risk of the contract, which now has one year remaining. To do this, it replaces the agreed forward rate $1.55/£ with the forward rate on current one-year forward contracts, $1.65/£. It then recalculates its net gain or loss on the contract if it had to be replaced at this price. This is the contract's replacement cost.

[25] One large New York money center bank has to calculate, on average, the replacement cost of more than 6,000 different forward contracts alone.

For the four-year fixed–floating interest rate swap, the notional value (contract face value) of the swap is $100 million. Since this is a long-term (one to five years to maturity) interest rate market contract, its face value is multiplied by .005 to get a potential exposure or credit risk equivalent value of $0.5 million (see row 2 of Table 20–15). We add this potential exposure to the replacement cost (current exposure) of this contract to the bank. The replacement cost reflects the cost of having to enter into a new four-year fixed–floating swap agreement at today's interest rates for the remaining life of the swap should the counterparty default. Assuming that interest rates today are less favorable, on a present value basis, the cost of replacing the existing contract for its remaining life would be $3 million. Thus, the total credit equivalent amount—current plus potential exposures—for the interest rate swap is $3.5 million.

Next, look at the foreign exchange two-year forward contract of $40 million face value. Since this is a foreign exchange contract with a maturity of one to five years, the potential (future) credit risk is $40 million × .05, or $2 million (see row 2 in Table 20–15). However, its replacement cost is *minus* $1 million. That is, in this example our bank actually stands to gain if the counterparty defaults. Exactly why the counterparty would do this when it is in the money is unclear. However, regulators cannot permit a bank to gain from a default by a counterparty since this might produce all types of perverse risk-taking incentives. Consequently, as in our example, current exposure has to be set equal to zero (as shown). Thus, the sum of potential exposure ($2 million) and current exposure ($0) produces a total credit equivalent amount of $2 million for this contract. Since the bank has just two OBS derivative contracts, summing the two credit equivalent amounts produces a total credit equivalent amount of $3.5 m + $2 m = $5.5 million for the bank's OBS market contracts.

Step 2
The next step is to multiply this credit equivalent amount by the appropriate risk weight. Specifically, to calculate the risk-adjusted asset value for the bank's OBS derivative or market contracts, we multiply the credit equivalent amount by the appropriate risk weight, which under Basel I is generally .5, or 50 percent:

$$\begin{matrix} \text{Credit risk–adjusted} \\ \text{asset value of} \\ \text{OBS derivatives} \end{matrix} = \begin{matrix} \$5.5 \text{ million} \\ \text{(credit equivalent} \\ \text{amount)} \end{matrix} \times \begin{matrix} 0.5 \\ \text{(risk weight)} \end{matrix} = \$2.75 \text{ million}$$

Basel II.   As stated above, Basel I assigns a 50 percent weight to the total credit equivalent amount of these contracts. Basel II assigns these contracts a risk weight of 100 percent, assuming the OBS activities are more risky to the FI than assumed under Basel I. Under Basel II the risk weight assigned to the credit equivalent amount, $5.5 million, is 100 percent. Thus, the credit risk–adjusted value of the OBS derivatives is $5.5 million.

Total Credit Risk–Adjusted Assets under Basel I
From Examples 20–1 through 20–4, under the current Basel Agreement, Basel I, the total risk-adjusted assets for the bank are the sum of the credit risk–adjusted assets on the balance sheet ($849 million), the risk-adjusted value of OBS contingencies and guarantees ($60 million), and the risk-adjusted value of OBS derivatives ($2.75 million), or $911.75 million.

Total Credit Risk–Adjusted Assets under Basel II
Under Basel II, effective year-end 2006, the total credit risk–adjusted assets are $830 million ($764.5 million from on-balance-sheet activities, plus $60 million for the risk-adjusted value of OBS contingencies and guarantees, plus $5.5 million for the risk-adjusted value of OBS derivatives).

The Credit Risk–Adjusted Asset Value of Off-Balance-Sheet Derivative Instruments with Netting under Basel I[26,27]

One criticism of the above method is that it ignores the netting of exposures. In response, the Fed has adopted a proposal put forward by the BIS that allows netting of off-balance-sheet derivative contracts as long as the bank has a bilateral netting contract that clearly establishes a legal obligation by the counterparty to pay or receive a single net amount on the different contracts. This rule has been in effect since October 1, 1995.[28] Provided that such written contracts are clearly documented by the bank, the new rules require the estimation of *net current exposure* and *net potential exposure* of those positions included in the bilateral netting contract. The sum of the net current exposure and the net potential exposure equals the total credit equivalent amount.

The rules define net current exposure as the net sum of all positive and negative replacement costs (or mark-to-market values of the individual derivative contracts). If the sum of the replacement costs is positive, then the net current exposure equals the sum. If it is negative, the net current exposure is zero. The net potential exposure is defined by a formula that adjusts the gross potential exposure estimated earlier:

$$A_{\text{net}} = (0.4 \times A_{\text{gross}}) + (0.6 \times \text{NGR} \times A_{\text{gross}})$$

where A_{net} is the net potential exposure (or adjusted sum of potential future credit exposures), A_{gross} is the sum of the potential exposures of each contract, and NGR is the ratio of net current exposure to gross current exposure. The 0.6 is the amount of potential exposure that is reduced as a result of netting.[29]

The same example used in the previous section (without netting) will be used to show the effect of netting on the total credit equivalent amount. *Here we assume that both contracts are with the same counterparty.*

Type of Contract (remaining maturity)	Potential Exposure	Replacement Cost	Current Exposure
Four-year fixed–floating interest rate swap	$0.5 m	$ 3 m	$3 m
Two-year forward foreign exchange contract	$2 m	$−1 m	$0

$A_{\text{gross}} = \$2.5 \text{ m}$ Net current exposure = \$2 m   Current exposure = \$3 m

The net current exposure is the sum of the positive and negative replacement costs—that is, $+3 m and $−1 m = $2 m. The gross potential exposure (A_{gross}) is the sum of the individual potential exposures = $2.5 m. To determine the net potential exposure, the following formula is used:

$$A_{\text{net}} = (0.4 \times A_{\text{gross}}) + (0.6 \times \text{NGR} \times A_{\text{gross}})$$

$$\text{NGR} = \text{Net current exposure/Current exposure} = 2/3$$

---

[26] This section, which involves more technical material, may be included in or dropped from the chapter reading depending on the rigor of the course without harming the continuity of the chapter.

[27] Under Basel II, off-balance-sheet netting of credit derivatives will be left to Pillar II (i.e., to the discretion of regulators). Originally, a specific netting formula had been proposed (the "w" factor).

[28] See Federal Reserve Board of Governors press release, August 29, 1995, p. 17.

[29] The original Fed proposal had ratios of 50/50, but these were reduced to 40/60 after public comments were received.

$$A_{net} = (0.4 \times 2.5 \text{ m}) + (0.6 \times 2/3 \times 2.5 \text{ m})$$
$$= \$2 \text{ million}$$

$$\text{Total credit equivalent} = \text{Net potential exposure} + \text{Net current exposure}$$
$$= 2 \text{ m} + 2 \text{ m} = \$4 \text{ million}$$

$$\frac{\text{Risk-adjusted asset value}}{\text{of OBS market contracts}} = \text{Total credit equivalent amount} \times 0.5 \text{ (risk weight)}$$
$$= 4 \text{ m} \times 0.5 = \$2 \text{ million}$$

As can be seen, netting reduces the credit risk–adjusted asset value from \$2.75 million to \$2 million.

Calculating the Overall Risk-Based Capital Position

After calculating the risk-weighted assets for a depository institution, the final step is to calculate the Tier I and total risk–based capital ratios.

EXAMPLE 20–5

Calculating the Overall Risk-Based Capital Position of a Bank

From Tables 20–11 and 20–13, the bank's Tier I capital (retained earnings, common stock, and qualifying perpetual preferred stock) totals \$50 million; Tier II capital (convertible bonds, subordinate bonds, nonqualifying perpetual preferred stock, and reserve for loan losses) totals \$45 million. The resulting total Tier I and Tier II capital is, therefore, \$95 million.

We can now calculate our bank's overall capital adequacy in light of the current (Basel I) and proposed (Basel II) risk-based capital requirements as:

	Basel I	Basel II
Tier I (core) capital =	$\dfrac{\$50 \text{ m}}{\$911.75 \text{ m}} = 5.48\%$	$\dfrac{\$50 \text{ m}}{\$830.0 \text{ m}} = 6.02\%$

and

	Basel I	Basel II
Total risk–based capital ratio =	$\dfrac{\$95 \text{ m}}{\$911.75 \text{ m}} = 10.42\%$	$\dfrac{\$95 \text{ m}}{\$830.0 \text{ m}} = 11.45\%$

The difference in these ratios under the two capital adequacy formulas is due to the modified treatment of sovereign, bank, and corporate loans under Basel II. Specifically, Basel II aligns regulatory capital requirements more closely with the key elements of banking risk by introducing a wider differentiation of credit risk weights. The risk weights are refined by reference to a rating provided by an external credit rating agency. The bank in our example held many low-risk, highly rated loans in its portfolio. Under Basel I these loans are all assigned a credit risk weight of 100 percent. Under Basel II, however, low-risk, highly rated loans are assigned a lower risk weight (20 and 50 percent) reflecting their decreased risk to the bank. Thus, the credit risk–adjusted assets for our bank are smaller under the proposed Basel II than under the currently used Basel I. Note that for a bank with a higher proportion of lower-quality loans, Basel II would likely result in higher credit risk–adjusted assets than under Basel I. Such a bank would be required to hold more capital to meet the required minimum risk-based ratios.

Since the minimum Tier I capital ratio required (see Table 20–7) is 4 percent and the minimum risk-based capital ratio required is 8 percent, the bank in our example has more than adequate capital under both capital requirement formulas.[30]

Interest Rate Risk, Market Risk, and Risk-Based Capital

From a regulatory perspective, a credit risk–based capital ratio is adequate only as long as a depository institution is not exposed to undue interest rate or market risk. The reason is that the risk-based capital ratio takes into account only the

---

[30] With netting, the total credit risk–adjusted assets ratio would have been \$95 m/\$911 m, or 10.43 percent, under Basel I and \$95 m/\$829.25 m, or 11.46 percent, under Basel II.

adequacy of a bank's capital to meet both its on- and off-balance-sheet credit risks. Not explicitly accounted for is the insolvency risk emanating from interest rate risk (duration mismatches) and market (trading) risk.

To meet these criticisms, in 1993 the Federal Reserve (along with the Bank for International Settlements) developed additional capital requirement proposals for interest rate risk (see Chapter 9) and market risk (see Chapter 10). As is discussed in Chapter 10, since 1998 DIs have had to calculate an add-on to the 8 percent risk-based capital ratio to reflect their exposure to market risk. There are two approaches available to DIs to calculate the size of this add-on: (1) the standardized model proposed by regulators and (2) the DI's own internal market risk model. To date, no formal add-on has been required for interest rate risk, although in 2001 the BIS suggested a framework for a future capital ratio for interest rate risk similar to the original 1993 proposal.[31]

Operational Risk and Risk-Based Capital

In its 2001 proposed amendments to capital adequacy rules, the BIS proposed an additional add-on to capital for operational risk. Prior to this proposal, the BIS had argued that the operational risk exposures of banks were adequately taken care of by the 8 percent credit risk–adjusted ratio. But increased visibility of operational risks in recent years (see Chapter 14) has induced regulators to propose a separate capital requirement for credit and operational risks. As noted above, the BIS now believes that operational risks are sufficiently important for DIs to devote resources to quantify such risks and to incorporate them separately into their assessment of their overall capital adequacy. In the 2001 and 2003 Consultative Documents the Basel Committee proposed three specific methods (proposed for 2006) by which depository institutions would calculate capital to protect against operational risk: the Basic Indicator Approach, the Standardized Approach, and the Advanced Measurement Approach.[32]

The Basic Indicator approach is structured so that banks, on average, will hold 12 percent of their total regulatory capital for operational risk. This 12 percent target was based on a widespread survey conducted internationally of current practices by large banks. To achieve this target, the Basic Indicator Approach focuses on the gross income of the bank, that is, its net profits, or what Europeans called value added. This equals a bank's net interest income plus net noninterest income:

$$\text{Gross income} = \text{Net interest income} + \text{Net noninterest income}$$

According to BIS calculations, a bank that holds a fraction (alpha) of its gross income for operational risk capital, where alpha (α) is set between 17 and 20 percent, will generate enough capital for operational risk such that this amount will be 12 percent of its total regulatory capital holdings against all risks (i.e., credit, market, and operational risks). For example, under the Basic Indicator Approach:

$$\text{Operational capital} = \alpha \times \text{Gross income}$$

or

$$= .2 \times \text{Gross income}$$

---

[31] Specifically, the proposal states that banks should have interest rate risk measurement systems that assess the effects of interest rate changes on both earnings and economic value. These systems should provide meaningful measures of a bank's current levels of interest rate risk exposure, and should be capable of identifying any excessive exposures that might arise. See Basel Committee on Banking Supervision, "Principles for the Management and Supervision of Interest Rate Risk," January 2001. **www.bis.org**

[32] See Basel Committee on Banking Supervision, "Working Paper on Regulatory Treatment of Operational Risk," September 2001. **www.bis.org**

TABLE 20–16
BIS Standardized Approach Business Units and Lines

Source: Bank for International Settlements, "Working Paper on the Regulatory Treatment of Operational Risk," September 2001. *www.bis.org*

Business Line	Indicator	Capital Factors
Corporate finance	Gross income*	$\beta_1 = 18\%$
Trading and sales	Gross income	$\beta_2 = 18\%$
Retail banking	Gross income	$\beta_3 = 12\%$
Commercial banking	Gross income	$\beta_4 = 15\%$
Payment and settlement	Gross income	$\beta_5 = 18\%$
Agency services and custody	Gross income	$\beta_6 = 15\%$
Retail brokerage	Gross income	$\beta_7 = 12\%$
Asset management	Gross income	$\beta_8 = 12\%$

*The indicator relates to gross income reported for the particular line of business.

The problem with the Basic Indicator Approach is that it is too aggressive, or "top-down," and does not differentiate at all among different areas in which operational risks may differ (e.g., Payment and Settlement may have a very different operational risk profile from Retail Brokerage).[33]

In an attempt to provide a finer differentiation of operational risks in a bank across different activity lines while still retaining a basically top-down approach, the BIS proposed a second method for operational capital calculation. The second method, the Standardized Approach, divides activities into eight major business units and lines (shown in Table 20–16). Within each business line, there is a specified broad indicator (defined as beta, β) that reflects the scale or volume of a DI's activities in that area. The indicator relates to the gross income reported for a particular line of business. It serves as a rough proxy for the amount of operational risk within each of these lines. A capital charge is calculated by multiplying the β for each line by the indicator assigned to the line and then summing these components. The βs reflect the importance of each activity in the average bank. The βs are set by regulators and are calculated from average industry figures from a selected sample of banks.

Suppose the industry β for Corporate Finance is 18% and gross income from the Corporate Finance line of business (the activity indicator) is $30 million for the bank. Then, the regulatory capital charge for this line for this year is:

$$\text{Capital}_{\text{Corporate Finance}} = \beta \times \text{Gross income from the Corporate Finance line of}$$
$$\text{business for the bank}$$
$$= 18\% \times \$30 \text{ million}$$
$$= \$5,400,000$$

The total capital charge is calculated as the three-year average of the simple summation of the regulatory capital charge across each of the eight business lines.[34]

The third method, the Advanced Measurement Approach, allows individual banks to rely on internal data for regulatory capital purposes. There are three broadly categorized methods currently under development: the Internal Measurement Approach (IMA), the Loss Distribution Approach (LDA), and the Scorecard Approach (SA).

[33] A second issue is that the α term implies operational risk that is proportional to gross income. This ignores possible economies-of-scale effects that would make this relationship nonlinear (nonproportional); that is, α might fall as bank profits and/or size grows.

[34] The Basel Committee's Loss Data Collection Exercise for Operational Risk (March 2003), based on data provided by 89 banks from 19 countries, revealed that about 61 percent of operational loss events occurred in the retail area, with an average loss of $79,300. Also, only 0.9 percent of operational loss events occurred in the corporate finance area, but with an average loss of $646,600.

FIGURE 20–2
Internal
Measurement
Approach for
Operational Risk as
an Example of the
Advanced
Measurement
Approach

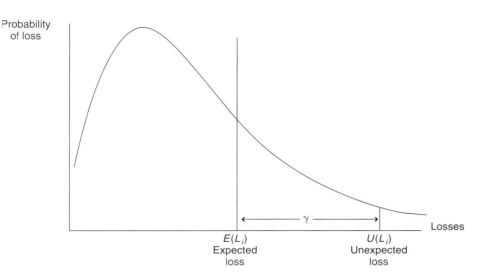

The IMA calculations are based on a framework that separates a bank's operational risk exposures into lines of business and operational risk event types. As an encouragement for banks to move toward the adoption of more advanced measures of operational risk, the target for operational risk capital is set at 75 percent of the level of that for the Basic Indicator and Standardized Models. That is, $.75 \times 12\% = 9\%$ of a bank's total regulatory capital. Banks will need three sets of data for a specified set of business lines and risk types: an operational risk exposure indicator (EI)—supplied by the regulator—plus data representing the probability that a loss event occurs (PE) and the losses given such events (LGE). The product of the three produces the expected loss, E(L), in an operational risk area (say, Corporate Finance). See Figure 20–2. That is:

$$E(L_i) = EI_i \times PE_i \times LGE_i$$

where

$$i = \text{business activity area}$$

Since capital is meant to protect the bank against the risk of insolvency due to extreme or unexpected losses, $U(L_i)$, the $E(L_i)$ amount is multiplied by a factor defined as gamma (γ_i) that translates the estimate of expected losses for a business line into a capital charge (K_i) that covers losses at least up to the 99.9 percentile of likely losses based on average industry experience. Thus:

$$K_i = E(L_i) \times \gamma_i$$

To get the total operational risk capital requirement, the risks of the different activity areas are added using the same methodology. Unfortunately, doing this is difficult for the less quantitative areas of operational risk, such as fraud.[35]

The LDA method differs from the IMA method in one aspect: The LDA method assess unexpected losses at the 99.9 percentile directly rather than via an

---

[35] For a discussion of some of these models, see M. Cruz, R. Coleman, and G. Salkin, "Modeling and Measuring Operational Risk," *The Journal of Risk* 1 (1998), pp. 63–72; R. Ceski and J. Hernandez, "Where Theory Meets Practice," *Risk: Operational Risk Special Report,* November 1999, pp. 17–20; and L. Allen, J. Boudoukh, and A. Saunders, *Understanding Market, Credit, and Operational Risk: The Value at Risk Approach* (Malden, MA: Blackwell, 2004).

assumption about the relationship between expected loss and unexpected loss. Thus, there is no need for the determination of a gamma factor (γ_i) with the LDA method.

With the SA method, banks determine an initial level of operational risk capital at the firm or business line level and then modify these amounts over time on the basis of "scorecards" that attempt to capture the underlying risk profile and risk control environment of the various lines of business. The scorecards bring a forward-looking component to the capital calculations. That is, they reflect improvements in the risk control environment that will reduce both the frequency and severity of future operational risk losses.

The three methods involved are increasingly sophisticated in the measurement of operational risks. As the new standards are implemented (in 2006) DIs would start out using the Basic Indicator Approach and would be encouraged to move along the spectrum of approaches as they develop more sophisticated operational risk measurement systems because of the lower operational risk capital requirement (8 percent) associated with the Advanced Measurement Approach compared with the requirement of the Standardized or Basic Indicator Approach (12 percent).

Criticisms of the Risk–Based Capital Ratio

The risk-based capital requirement seeks to improve on the simple leverage ratio by (1) incorporating credit, market, and operational risks into the determination of capital adequacy; (2) more systematically accounting for credit risk differences among assets; (3) incorporating off-balance-sheet risk exposures; and (4) applying a similar capital requirement across all the major DIs (and banking centers) in the world. Unfortunately, the requirements have a number of conceptual and applicability weaknesses in achieving these objectives:

1. *Risk weights.* It is unclear how closely the four (five) risk weight categories in Basel I (Basel II) reflect true credit risk. For example, commercial loans have risk weights between 20 and 150 percent under Basel II. Taken literally, these relative weights imply that some commercial loans are exactly four and a half times as risky as other loans.[36]

2. *Risk weights based on external credit rating agencies.* While Basel II proposed reforms to improve on Basel I in measuring credit risk, that is, by replacing the current single 100 percent risk weight for sovereign, bank, and commercial loans with five different risk weights, depending on the loan's credit rating, it is unclear whether the risk weights accurately measure the relative (or absolute) risk exposures of individual borrowers. Moreover, Standard & Poor's and Moody's ratings are often accused of lagging behind rather than leading the business cycle. As a

---

[36] R. B. Avery and A. Berger show evidence that these risk weights do a good job of distinguishing between failing and nonfailing banks. See "Risk–Based Capital and Deposit Insurance Reform," *Journal of Banking and Finance* 15 (1991), pp. 847–74. However, D. S. Jones and K. K. King, in "The Implementation of Prompt Corrective Action: An Assessment," *Journal of Banking and Finance,* 1995, pp. 491–510, find that risk–based capital would have done a poor job in identifying failing banks over the 1981–89 period if it had been used for prompt corrective action purposes. P. S. Calem and M. LaCour-Little, in "Risk–Based Capital Requirements for Mortgage Loans, "*Journal of Banking and Finance*, 2004, pp. 647–72, find that risk–based capital requirements for mortgage loans offer little risk differentiation and result in significant divergence between regulatory and economic capital. L. Allen, "The Basel Capital Accords and International Mortgage Markets: A Survey of the Literature," Baruch College, CUNY Working Paper, 2003, surveys the literature to date on the impact of the Basel Accords on bank profitability, competitiveness, structure, and risk taking.

result required capital may peak during a recession, when banks are least able to meet the requirements.[37]

3. *Portfolio aspects.* The BIS plans largely ignore credit risk portfolio diversification opportunities. As we discuss in Chapter 12, when returns on assets have negative or less than perfectly positive correlations, an FI may lower its portfolio risk through diversification. As constructed, both Basel I and Basel II (standardized model) capital adequacy plans are essentially linear risk measures that ignore correlations or covariances among assets and asset group credit risks—such as between residential mortgages and commercial loans.[38] That is, the DI manager weights each asset separately by the appropriate risk weight and then sums those numbers to get an overall measure of credit risk. No account is taken of the covariances among asset risks between different counterparties (or risk weights).[39]

4. *DI specialness.* Giving private sector moderate- and high-risk commercial loans the highest credit risk weighting may reduce the incentive for DIs to make such loans relative to holding other assets. This may reduce the amount of DI loans to these businesses, as well as the degree of DI monitoring, and may have associated negative externality effects on the economy. That is, one aspect of banks' special functions—bank lending—may be muted.[40] This effect has been of great concern and controversy. Indeed, the high-risk weight given to commercial loans relative to securities has been blamed in part for inducing a credit crunch and a reorientation of bank portfolios away from commercial loans toward securities in the early 1990s.

5. *Excessive complexity.* Basel II will greatly raise the cost of regulation by adding new levels of complexity. The cost of developing and implementing new risk management systems will clearly be significant, and the benefits may turn out to be small. Initial calculations suggest that most banks using the IRB Approach for operational risk will end up with a higher capital charge than those using the Standardized Approach. In other words, not only is the most advanced approach extremely complex, it may also not deliver all the benefits that are generally expected. The U.S. Comptroller of the Currency said the "mind-numbing" complexity of the

---

[37] E. I. Altman, S. T. Bharath, and A. Saunders, in "Credit Ratings and the BIS Reform Agenda," *Journal of Banking and Finance*, 2002, pp. 909–22, find that although the new BIS guidelines are an improvement over the original ones, several of the rating categories carry underweighted capital requirements, and that banks will continue to be motivated to skew their portfolios toward lower-rated loans. Moreover, relying on rating agencies to determine a borrower's credit risk questions the specialness of banks as monitors—see Chapter 1.

[38] In a portfolio context, it assumes that asset and OBS risks are independent of each other.

[39] However, the more advanced internal ratings–based approach (IRB—see Appendix 20A to this chapter) assumes a correlation among all loans of either 10 or 20 percent. Currently, it is estimated that only approximately 15 (the biggest) U.S. banks will use the IRB approach. Moreover, private sector models, such as KMV and CreditMetrics (see Chapters 11 and 12), generally find correlations of less than 10 percent. Most commonly, they find correlations in the 0 to 5 percent range—indicating a greater degree of diversification potential than implied by the IRB.

[40] In addition, since many emerging-market countries have low credit ratings, under the Basel II plan, banks may have to hold considerably more capital against such loans than under Basel I. This may adversely affect the flow of bank financing to these less-developed countries—with major adverse effects on their economies. See C. Jacklin, "Bank Capital Requirements and Incentives for Lending," Working Paper, Stanford University, February 1993; and J. Haubich and P. Wachtel, "Capital Requirements and Shifts in Commercial Bank Portfolios," Federal Reserve Bank of Cleveland, *Economic Review* 29 (3rd quarter, 1994), pp. 2–15. However, A. Berger and G. Udell, "Did Risk–Based Capital Allocate Bank Credit and Cause a Credit Crunch in the U.S.?" *Journal of Money, Credit and Banking* 26 (August 1994), pp. 585–628, dispute these findings.

proposed accords underscores a number of voices in the United States that are uncomfortable with Basel II.[41]

6. *Other risks.* While market risk exposure was integrated into the risk-based capital requirements in 1998 and operational risk is proposed for 2006, the BIS plan does not yet account for other risks, such as interest rate and liquidity risk in the banking book, although these risks are accounted for in the market or trading book. A more complete risk-based capital requirement would include these risks.[42]

7. *Impact on capital requirements.* In December 2003, the FDIC issued a study making the case that the new rules would water down capital in place for U.S. banks, instead of providing more protection against losses. The study found that Tier 1 capital requirements would plunge form the pre–Basel II levels of approximately 5 percent to between 2.5 and 4 percent, generally below levels U.S. regulators consider sound. Further, smaller U.S. banks complain that the proposed bank standards are unfair. Smaller banks that do not have risk evaluation systems required by Basel II must comply with the existing standardized formulas, which likely would mean they would have higher capital charges.[43]

8. *Competition.* The Federal Reserve has stated that Basel II would be initially applied to internationally active banks. Thus, U.S. regulators will initially apply the new rules to fewer than a dozen U.S. banks. Further, in the United States, Basel II will not apply to securities firms or investment banks. In Europe, Basel II is to be incorporated into European Union law and applied to all banks and investment firms, not just internationally active banks. Thus, different standards will apply to American and European banks, giving the American banks a theoretically lower (regulatory) cost of making loans. In addition, as a result of tax and accounting differences across banking systems and in safety net coverages, the 8 percent risk-based capital requirement has not created a level competitive playing field across banks. This is different from what proponents of the scheme claim. In particular, Japan and the United States have very different accounting, tax, and safety net rules that significantly affect the comparability of U.S. and Japanese bank risk-based capital ratios.[44]

9. *Pillar 2 may ask too much of regulators.* Pillar 2 of Basel II will require lots of very sensitive judgment calls from regulators who may be ill-equipped to make them. This will particularly be a problem for developing-country regulators. If Pillar 2 is taken seriously, supervisors may be exposed to a lot of criticism that most would rather avoid.

Concept Questions

1. What are the major strengths of the risk-based capital ratios?
2. You are a DI manager with a total risk-based capital ratio of 6 percent. Discuss four strategies to meet the required 8 percent ratio in a short period of time without raising new capital.
3. Why isn't a capital ratio levied on exchange-traded derivative contracts?
4. What are three problems with the simple leverage ratio measure of capital adequacy?

[41] See "Banking Talks Face Criticism," *The Wall Street Journal*, December 16, 2003, p. C15.

[42] Interestingly, the risk-based capital schemes for property–casualty and life insurers (discussed later in this chapter) have more complete coverage of risks than does the bank scheme.

[43] See "Rules on Bank Capital Draw Fire," *The Wall Street Journal*, December 8, 2003, p. B8.

[44] H. S. Scott and S. Iwahara, "In Search of a Level Playing Field," Group of Thirty, Washington, D.C., 1994, argue that these distortions are so large that they render meaningful comparisons impossible. Indeed, many analysts have argued that a majority of the largest Japanese banks would have violated the 8 percent rule in 1998 under U.S. accounting and regulatory practices. This is one of the major reasons for the bailout plan announced by the Japanese government in October 1998. See "The Timid Japanese Bailout Just Might Do the Job," *New York Times,* October 22, 1998, p. C2.

5. What is the difference between Tier I capital and Tier II capital?
6. Identify one asset in each of the four (five) credit risk weight categories.

CAPITAL REQUIREMENTS FOR OTHER FIS

Securities Firms

Unlike the book value capital rules employed by bank and thrift regulators, the capital requirements for broker–dealers set by the SEC's Rule 15C 3–1 in 1975 are close to a market value accounting rule. Essentially, broker–dealers must calculate a market value for their net worth on a day-to-day basis and ensure that their net worth–assets ratio exceeds 2 percent:

$$\frac{\text{Net worth}}{\text{Assets}} \geq 2\%$$

The essential idea is that if a broker–dealer has to liquidate all assets at near market values, a capital cushion of 2 percent should be sufficient to satisfy all customer liabilities, such as brokerage accounts held with the firm.[45]

Specifically, to compute net capital, the broker–dealer calculates book capital or net worth—the difference between the book values of assets and liabilities—and then makes a number of adjustments: subtracting (1) all assets such as fixed assets not readily convertible into cash and (2) securities that cannot be publicly offered or sold. Moreover, the dealer must make other deductions, or haircuts, reflecting potential market value fluctuations in assets. For example, the net capital rule requires haircuts on illiquid equities of up to 40 percent and on debt securities generally between 0 and 9 percent. Finally, other adjustments must reflect unrealized profits and losses, subordinated liabilities, contractual commitments, deferred taxes, options, commodities and commodity futures, and certain collateralized liabilities.

Thus, broker–dealers must make significant adjustments to the book value of net worth to reach an approximate market value net worth figure. This figure must exceed 2 percent of assets.

Life Insurance

In 1993 the life insurance industry adopted a model risk-based capital scheme. Although similar in nature to that adopted by banks and thrifts, it is more extensive in that it also covers other types of risk (discussed later in this chapter). Although capital requirements are imposed at the state level, they are heavily influenced by recommendations from the National Association of Insurance Commissioners (NAIC). We describe the NAIC model next.

www.naic.org

The model begins by identifying four risks faced by the life insurer:

$C1$ = Asset risk
$C2$ = Insurance risk
$C3$ = Interest rate risk
$C4$ = Business risk

C1: Asset Risk

Asset risk reflects the riskiness of the asset portfolio of the life insurer. It is similar in spirit to the credit risk–adjusted asset calculations for DIs in that a credit risk

---

[45] If a broker–dealer fails with negative net worth, the SIPC provides guarantees of up to $500,000 per customer (see Chapter 19).

TABLE 20–17
Risk-Based Capital (RBC) Factors for Selected Assets

Source: Salomon Brothers, *Insurance Strategies,* August 2, 1993.

Asset	Insurer	
	Life	Property–Casualty
Bonds		
U.S. government	0.0%	0.0%
NAIC 1: AAA–A*	0.3	0.3
NAIC 2: BBB	1.0	1.0
NAIC 3: BB	4.0	2.0
NAIC 4: B	9.0	4.5
NAIC 5: CCC	20.0	10.0
NAIC 6: In or near default	30.0	30.0
Residential mortgages (whole loans)	0.5†	5.0
Commercial mortgages	3.0†	5.0
Common stock	30.0	15.0
Preferred stock—bond factor for same NAIC category plus:	2.0	2.0

*Includes agencies and most collateralized mortgage obligations.
†Mortgage factors are for loans in good standing. These factors will be adjusted for a company's default experience relative to the industry.

weight is multiplied by the dollar or face value of the assets on the balance sheet. Table 20–17 shows the relative asset risk weights for life and PC insurers. Thus, an insurer with $100 million in common stocks would have a risk-based capital requirement of $30 million, while for one with $100 million in BBB corporate bonds, only $1 million would be required.

C2: Insurance Risk

mortality risk
The risk of death.

morbidity risk
The risk of ill health.

Insurance risk captures the risk of adverse changes in **mortality risk** and **morbidity risk.** As we discuss in Chapter 3, mortality tables give life insurers an extremely accurate idea of the probability that an insured will die in any given year. However, epidemics such as AIDS can upset these predictions drastically. As a result, insurers adjust insurance in force for the current level of reserves and multiply the resulting number by an insurance risk factor. Similar calculations are carried out for accident and health insurance, which covers morbidity (ill health) risk.

C3: Interest Rate Risk

Interest rate risk in part reflects the liquidity of liabilities and their probability or ease of withdrawal as interest rates change. For example, insurance company–issued guaranteed investment contracts (GICs) have characteristics similar to those of long-term, fixed-rate bank deposits and are often highly sensitive to interest rate movements. As we also discuss in Chapter 17, illiquidity problems have led to a number of insurer insolvencies in past years. With respect to interest rate risk, insurers must divide liabilities into three risk classes: low risk (0.5 percent risk-based capital requirement), medium risk (1 percent capital requirement), and high risk (2 percent capital requirement).

C4: Business Risk

As we discuss in Chapter 19, states have organized guaranty funds that partially pay for insurer insolvencies by levying a charge on surviving firms. Thus, the capital requirement for business risk is set to equal the maximum potential assessment by state guaranty funds (2 percent for life and annuity premiums and 0.5 percent

TABLE 20–18
Calculation of Total
Risk–Based Capital
(*RBC*)

Source: Salomon Brothers,
Insurance Strategies,
August 2, 1993.

Risk	Type	Description
R0	Asset	*RBC* for investments (common and preferred) in property–casualty affiliates
R1	Asset	*RBC* for fixed income
R2	Asset	*RBC* for equity—includes common and preferred stocks (other than in property–casualty affiliates) and real estate
R3	Credit	*RBC* for reinsurance recoverables and other receivables
R4	Underwriting	*RBC* for loss and loss adjustment expense (LAE) reserves plus growth surcharges
R5	Underwriting	*RBC* for written premiums plus growth surcharges

$$RBC = R0 + \sqrt{R1^2 + R2^2 + R3^2 + R4^2 + R5^2}$$

for health premiums for each surviving insurer). Also, company-specific fraud and litigation risks may require an additional capital charge.

After calculating $C1$, $C2$, $C3$ and $C4$, the life insurance manager computes a risk-based capital measure (*RBC*) based on the following equation:

$$RBC = \sqrt{(C1 + C3)^2 + C2^2} + C4$$

As calculated, the *RBC* is the minimum required capital for the life insurer. The insurer compares this risk-based capital measure to the actual capital and surplus (total capital) held:

$$\frac{\text{Total surplus and capital}}{\text{Risk-based capital } (RBC)}$$

If this ratio is greater than 1, the life insurance manager is meeting or is above the minimum capital requirements. If the ratio falls below 1, the manager will be subject to regulatory scrutiny.[46]

Property–Casualty Insurance

Capital requirements for property–casualty (PC) insurers are quite similar to the life insurance industry's *RBC*—introduced by the NAIC in 1993—except that there are six (instead of four) risk categories, including three separate asset risk categories. The risk weights for these different types of assets are shown in Table 20–18. The risk weights in some areas—especially common stock—are lower than those for life insurers because of the relatively smaller exposures of PC companies to this type of asset risk. The six different types of risk and the calculation of *RBC* (to be compared with a PC insurer's total capital and surplus) are shown in Table 20–18.

The calculation of *RBC* assumes that risks $R1$ to $R5$ are independent of each other—that is, have a zero correlation coefficient, whereas investments in PC affiliates

[46] NAIC testing found that 87 percent of the industry had a total surplus and capital–*RBC* ratio above 1 at the time of the RBC ratio's introduction. This description of the life insurance risk–based capital ratio is based on L. S. Goodman, P. Fischer, and C. Anderson, "The Impact of Risk-Based Capital Requirements on Asset Allocation for Life Insurance Companies," *Insurance Executive Review,* Fall 1992, pp. 14–21; and P. J. Bouyoucos, M. H. Siegel, and E. B. Raisel, "Risk-Based Capital for Insurers: A Strategic Opportunity to Enhance Franchise Value," Goldman Sachs, Industry Resource Group, September 1992.

TABLE 20–19
Risk-Based Capital (*RBC*) Charges for Typical Company

Risk	Description	RBC Charge (millions)
R0	Affiliated property–casualty	$ 10
R1	Fixed income	5
R2	Common stock	10
R3	Credit	10
R4	Reserve	40
R5	Premium	25
	Total charges before covariance	$100

$$RBC = 10 + \sqrt{5^2 + 10^2 + 10^2 + 40^2 + 25^2} = \$59.50$$

(risk *R0*) are assumed to be perfectly correlated with the net risk of the *R1* to *R5* components.[47] If the total capital and surplus of a PC insurer exceed the calculated *RBC*, the insurer is viewed as being adequately capitalized. For example, suppose a PC insurer had total capital and surplus of $60 million and its *RBC* charge is calculated as $59.5 million (as shown in Table 20–19); it has a capital–*RBC* ratio exceeding 1 (i.e., $60/59.5 = 1.008$) and is adequately capitalized.[48]

Concept Questions

1. How do the capital requirements for securities firms differ from the book value capital rules employed by DI regulators?
2. What types of risks are included by the NAIC in estimating the *RBC* of life insurance firms?
3. How do the NAIC's model risk-based capital requirements for PC insurers differ from the life insurance industry's *RBC*?

Summary

This chapter reviewed the role of an FI's capital in insulating it against credit, interest rate, and other risks. According to economic theory, capital or net worth should be measured on a market value basis as the difference between the market values of assets and liabilities. In actuality, regulators use book value accounting rules. While a book value capital adequacy rule accounts for credit risk exposure in a rough fashion, it overlooks the effects of interest rate changes and interest rate exposure on net worth. We analyzed the specific and proposed capital rules adopted by the regulators of banks and thrifts, insurance companies, and securities firms and discussed their problems and weaknesses. In particular, we looked at how bank, thrift, PC, and life insurance regulators are now adjusting book value–based capital rules to account for different types of risk as part of their imposition of risk-based capital adequacy ratios. As a result, actual capital requirements in banks, life insurance companies, PC insurance companies, and thrifts are moving closer to the market value–based net worth requirements of broker–dealers.

[47] See Alfred Weinberger, *Insurance Strategies*, Salomon Brothers, August 2, 1993.

[48] For a critical evaluation of the NAIC's *RBC* plan, see J. Commins, S. E. Harrington, and R. Klein, "Insolvency Exercise, Risk-Based Capital and Prompt Corrective Action in Property–Liability Insurance," *Journal of Banking and Finance*, 1995, pp. 511–27.

Questions and Problems

1. Identify and briefly discuss the importance of the five functions of an FI's capital.

2. Why are regulators concerned with the levels of capital held by an FI compared with those held by a nonfinancial institution?

3. What are the differences between the economic definition of capital and the book value definition of capital?

   a. How does economic value accounting recognize the adverse effects of credit and interest rate risk?

   b. How does book value accounting recognize the adverse effects of credit and interest rate risk?

4. A financial intermediary has the following balance sheet (in millions) with all assets and liabilities in market values.

Assets		Liabilities and Equity	
6 percent semiannual four-year Treasury notes (par value $12)	$10	5 percent two-year subordinated debt (par value $25)	$20
7 percent annual three-year AA-rated bonds (par-$15)	15		
9 percent annual five-year BBB-rated bonds (par-$15)	15	Equity capital	20
Total assets	$40	Total liabilities and equity	$40

   a. Under *FASB Statement No. 115*, what would be the effect on equity capital (net worth) if interest rates increased by 30 basis points? The T-notes are held for trading purposes; the rest are all classified as held to maturity.

   b. Under *FASB Statement No. 115*, how are the changes in the market value of assets adjusted in the income statements and balance sheets of FIs?

5. Why is the market value of equity a better measure of an FI's ability to absorb losses than book value of equity?

6. State Bank has the following year-end balance sheet (in millions).

Assets		Liabilities and Equity	
Cash	$ 10	Deposits	$ 90
Loans	90	Equity	10
Total assets	$100	Total liabilities and equity	$100

The loans primarily are fixed-rate, medium-term loans, while the deposits are either short-term or variable-rate deposits. Rising interest rates have caused the failure of a key industrial company, and as a result, 3 percent of the loans are considered uncollectable and thus have no economic value. One-third of these uncollectable loans will be charged off. Further, the increase in interest rates has caused a 5 percent decrease in the market value of the remaining loans.

   a. What is the impact on the balance sheet after the necessary adjustments are made according to book value accounting? According to market value accounting?

   b. What is the new market to book value ratio if State Bank has 1 million shares outstanding?

7. What are the arguments for and against the use of market value accounting for FIs?

8. How is the leverage ratio for an FI defined?

9. What is the significance of prompt corrective action as specified by the FDICIA legislation?

10. Identify and discuss the weaknesses of the leverage ratio as a measure of capital adequacy.

11. What is the Basel Agreement?

12. What is the major feature in the estimation of credit risk under Basel I capital requirements?

13. What is the total risk–based capital ratio?

14. Identify the five zones of capital adequacy and explain the mandatory regulatory actions corresponding to each zone.

15. What are the definitional differences between Tier I and Tier II capital?

16. What components are used in the calculation of risk-adjusted assets?

17. Explain the process of calculating risk-adjusted on-balance-sheet assets.

   a. What assets are included in the four (five) categories of credit risk exposure under Basel I (Basel II)?

   b. What are the appropriate risk weights for each category?

18. National Bank has the following balance sheet (in millions) and has no off-balance-sheet activities.

Assets		Liabilities and Equity	
Cash	$ 20	Deposits	$ 980
Treasury bills	40	Subordinated debentures	40
Residential mortgages	600	Common stock	40
Other loans	430	Retained earnings	30
Total assets	$1,090	Total liabilities and equity	$1,090

   a. What is the leverage ratio?

   b. What is the Tier I capital ratio?

   c. What is the total risk–based capital ratio?

   d. In what capital category would the bank be placed?

19. Onshore Bank has $20 million in assets, with risk-adjusted assets of $10 million. Tier I capital is $500,000, and Tier II capital is $400,000. How will each of the following transactions affect the value of the Tier I and total capital ratios? What will the new values of each ratio be?

    a. The bank repurchases $100,000 of common stock.

    b. The bank issues $2,000,000 of CDs and uses the proceeds for loans to homeowners.

    c. The bank receives $500,000 in deposits and invests them in T-bills.

    d. The bank issues $800,000 in common stock and lends it to help finance a new shopping mall.

    e. The bank issues $1,000,000 in nonqualifying perpetual preferred stock and purchases general obligation municipal bonds.

    f. Homeowners pay back $4,000,000 of mortgages, and the bank uses the proceeds to build new ATMs.

20. Explain the process of calculating risk-adjusted off-balance-sheet contingent guaranty contracts.

    a. What is the basis for differentiating the credit equivalent amounts of contingent guaranty contracts?

    b. On what basis are the risk weights for the credit equivalent amounts differentiated?

21. Explain how off-balance-sheet market contracts, or derivative instruments, differ from contingent guaranty contracts.

    a. What is counterparty credit risk?

    b. Why do exchange-traded derivative security contracts have no capital requirements?

    c. What is the difference between the potential exposure and the current exposure of over-the-counter derivative contracts?

    d. Why are the credit conversion factors for the potential exposure of foreign exchange contracts greater than they are for interest rate contracts?

    e. Why do regulators not allow banks to benefit from positive current exposure values?

22. What is the process of netting off-balance-sheet derivative contracts under Basel I? What requirement is necessary to allow a bank to calculate this exposure? How is net current exposure defined? How does net potential exposure differ from net current exposure?

23. How does the risk-based capital measure attempt to compensate for the limitations of the static leverage ratio?

24. Identify and discuss the problems in the risk-based capital approach to measuring capital adequacy.

25. What is the contribution to the credit risk–adjusted asset base of the following items under the Basel I requirements? Under Basel II requirements? Under the U.S. capital–assets ratio?

    a. $10 million cash reserves.

    b. $50 million 91-day U.S. Treasury bills.

    c. $25 million cash items in the process of collection.

    d. $5 million U.K. government bonds, AAA rated.

    e. $5 million Australian short-term government bonds, A−rated.

    f. $1 million general obligation municipal bonds.

    g. $40 million repurchase agreements (against U.S. Treasuries).

h. $500 million one- to-four family home mortgages.

i. $500 million commercial and industrial loans, BBB− rated.

j. $100,000 performance-related standby letters of credit to a blue-chip corporation.

k. $100,000 performance-related standby letters of credit to a municipality issuing general obligation bonds.

l. $7 million commercial letter of credit to a foreign, A-rated corporation.

m. $3 million five-year loan commitment to an OECD government.

n. $8 million bankers acceptance conveyed to a U.S., AA-rated corporation.

o. $17 million three-year loan commitment to a private agent.

p. $17 million three-month loan commitment to a private agent.

q. $30 million standby letter of credit to back a corporate issue of commercial paper.

r. $4 million five-year interest rate swap with no current exposure (the counterparty is a private agent).

s. $4 million five-year interest rate swap with no current exposure (the counterparty is a municipality).

t. $6 million two-year currency swap with $500,000 current exposure (the counterparty is a low credit-risk entity).

The bank balance sheet information below is for questions 26 through 29.

26. What is the bank's risk-adjusted asset base under Basel I? Under Basel II?

27. What are the bank's Tier I and total risk–based capital requirements under Basel I? Under Basel II?

28. Using the leverage ratio requirement, what is the minimum regulatory capital required to keep the bank in the well-capitalized zone?

29. What is the bank's capital adequacy level (under Basel I and Basel II) if the par value of its equity is $150,000, the surplus value of equity is $200,000, and the qualifying perpetual preferred stock is $50,000? Does the bank meet Basel (Tier I) capital standards? Does the bank comply with the well-capitalized leverage ratio requirement?

On-Balance-Sheet Items	Category	Face Value
Cash	1	$ 121,600
Short-term government securities (<92 days)	1	5,400
Long-term government securities (>92 days)	1	414,400
Federal Reserve stock	1	9,800
Repos secured by federal agencies	2	159,000
Claims on U.S. depository institutions	2	937,900
Short-term (<1 year) claims on foreign banks	2	1,640,000
General obligation municipals	2	170,000
Claims on or guaranteed by federal agencies	2	26,500
Municipal revenue bonds	3	112,900
Commercial loans, BB+ rated	4	6,645,700
Claims on foreign banks (>1 year)	4	5,800

Off-Balance-Sheet Items	Conversion Factor	Face Value
U.S. government counterparty		
Loan commitments, AAA rated:		
<1 year	0%	$ 300
1–5 years	50%	1,140
Standby letters of credit, AA rated:		
Performance-related	50%	200
Direct credit substitute	100%	100
U.S. depository institution counterparty		
(risk weight category 2)		
Loan commitments, BBB+ rated:		
<1 year	0%	1,000
>1 year	50%	3,000
Standby letters of credit, AA− rated:		
Performance-related	50%	200
Direct credit substitute	100%	56,400
Commercial letters of credit, BBB+ rated	20%	400
State and local government counterparty		
(risk weight category 3)		
Loan commitments, BBB− rated:		
>1 year	50%	100
Standby letters of credit, AAA rated:		
Performance-related	50%	135,400
Corporate customer counterparty		
Loan Commitments, CCC rated:		
<1 year	0%	2,980,000
>1 year	50%	3,046,278
Standby letters of credit, BBB rated:		
Performance-related	50%	101,543
Direct credit substitute	100%	485,000
Commercial letters of credit, AA− rated	20%	78,978
Note issuance facilities	50%	20,154
Forward agreements	100%	5,900
Interest rate market contracts		
(Current exposure assumed to be zero)		
<1 year (notional amount)	0%	2,000
>1–5 years (notional amount)	.5%	5,000

30. How does the leverage ratio test impact the stringency of regulatory monitoring of bank capital positions?

31. Third Bank has the following balance sheet (in millions) with the risk weights in parentheses.

Assets		Liabilities and Equity	
Cash (0%)	$ 20	Deposits	$175
OECD interbank deposits (20%)	25	Subordinated debt (5 years)	3
Mortgage loans (50%)	70	Cumulative preferred stock	5
Consumer loans (100%)	70	Equity	2
Total assets	$185	Total liabilities and equity	$185

The cumulative preferred stock is qualifying and perpetual. In addition, the bank has $30 million in performance-related standby letters of credit (SLCs), $40 million in two-year forward FX contracts that are currently in the money by $1 million, and $300 million in six-year interest rate swaps that are currently out of the money by $2 million. Credit conversion factors follow:

Performance-related standby LCs	50%
1- to 5-year foreign exchange contracts	5%
1- to 5-year interest rate swaps	0.5%
5- to 10-year interest rate swaps	1.5%

a. What are the risk-adjusted on-balance-sheet assets of the bank as defined under the Basel Accord?

b. What is the total capital required for both off- and on-balance-sheet assets?

c. Does the bank have enough capital to meet the Basel requirements? If not, what minimum Tier I or total capital does it need to meet the requirement?

32. Third Fifth Bank has the following balance sheet (in millions) with the risk weights in parentheses.

Assets		Liabilities and Equity	
Cash (0%)	$ 20	Deposits	$130
Mortgage loans (50%)	50	Subordinated debt (>5 years)	5
Consumer loans (100%)	70	Equity	5
Total assets	$140	Total liabilities and equity	$140

In addition, the bank has $20 million in commercial standby letters of credit and $40 million in 10-year FX forward contracts that are in the money by $1 million.

a. What are the risk-adjusted on-balance-sheet assets of the bank as defined under the Basel Accord?

b. What is the total capital required for both off- and on-balance-sheet assets?

c. Does the bank have sufficient capital to meet the Basel requirements? How much in excess? How much short?

33. According to SEC Rule 15C 3–1, what adjustments must securities firms make in the calculation of the book value of net worth?

34. A securities firm has the following balance sheet (in millions):

Assets		Liabilities and Equity	
Cash	$ 40	Five-day commercial paper	$ 20
Debt securities	300	Bonds	550
Equity securities	500	Debentures	300
Other assets	60	Equity	30
Total assets	$900	Total liabilities and equity	$900

The debt securities have a coupon rate of 6 percent, 20 years remaining until maturity, and trade at a yield of 8 percent. The equity securities have a market value equal to book value, and the other assets represent building and equipment that was recently appraised at $80 million. The company has 1 million shares of stock outstanding and its price is $35 per share. Is this company in compliance with SEC Rule 15C 3–1?

35. An investment bank specializing in fixed-income assets has the following balance sheet (in millions). Amounts are in market values, and all interest rates are annual unless indicated otherwise.

Assets		Liabilities and Equity	
Cash	$0.50	5% 1-year Eurodollar deposits	$ 5.0
8% 10-year Treasury notes		6% 2-year subordinated debt	
semiannual (par value $16.0)	15.0	(par = $10.0)	10.0
		Equity	0.5
Total assets	$15.5	Total liabilities and equity	$15.5

Assume that the haircut for all assets is 15 basis points and for all liabilities, 25 basis points (per annum).

a. Does the investment bank have sufficient liquid capital to cushion any unexpected losses per the net capital rule?

b. What should the FI do to maintain the net minimum required liquidity?

c. How does the net capital rule for investment banks differ from the capital requirements imposed on commercial banks and other depository institutions?

36. Identify and define the four risk categories incorporated into the life insurance risk-based capital model.

37. A life insurance company has estimated the following capital requirements for each of the risk classes: asset risk (*C1*) = $5 million, insurance risk (*C2*) = $4 million, interest rate risk (*C3*) = $1 million, and business risk (*C4*) = $3 million.

a. What is the required risk-based capital for the life insurance company?

b. If the total surplus and capital held by the company is $9 million, does it meet the minimum requirements?

c. How much capital must be raised to meet the minimum requirements?

38. How do the risk categories in the risk-based capital model for property–casualty insurance companies differ from those for life insurance companies? What are the assumed relationships between the risk categories in the model?

39. A property–casualty insurance company has estimated the following required charges for its various risk classes (in millions):

Risk	Description	RBC Charge
R0	Affiliated P/C	$ 2
R1	Fixed income	3
R2	Common stock	4
R3	Reinsurance	3
R4	Loss adjustment expense	2
R5	Written premiums	3
Total		$17

a. What is the *RBC* charge per the model recommended by the NAIC?

b. If the firm currently has $7 million in capital, what should be its surplus to meet the minimum capital requirement?

Web Question

40. Go to the Web site of the Bank for International Settlements at **www.bis.org.** Click on "Basel Committee." Click on "Basel II." This will bring the file onto your computer that contains information on the most recent set of capital requirements for depository institutions. How have these changed since 2003?

S&P Question

STANDARD &POOR'S

41. Go to the Standard & Poor's Market Insight Web site at **www.mhhe.com/edu-marketinsight.** Click on "Educational Version of Market Insight." Enter your Site ID and click on "Login." Click on "Company." Find the most recent balance sheets for Bank of New York (BK), Citigroup (C), Merrill Lynch (MER), and Allstate (ALL) using the following steps. Enter "BK" in the "Ticker:" box and click on "Go!" Click on "Excel Analytics." Click on "FS Ann. Balance Sheet." This will download the Balance Sheet for Bank of New York which contains the balances for Total Equity and Total Assets. Repeat the process by entering "C" in the "Ticker:" box to get information on Citigroup. Repeat the process by entering "MER" in the "Ticker:" box to get information on Merrill Lynch. Repeat the process by entering "ALL" in the "Ticker:" box to get information on Allstate. Calculate the equity ratios for these four financial institutions. How do these ratios differ for the FIs?

Pertinent Web Sites

Bank for International Settlements	**www.bis.org**
Board of Governors of the Federal Reserve	**www.federalreserve.gov**
Federal Deposit Insurance Corporation	**www.fdic.gov**
National Association of Insurance Commissioners	**www.naic.org**
Securities and Exchange Commission	**www.sec.gov**

Chapter Notation

View Chapter Notation at the Web site to the textbook (**www.mhhe.com/saunders5e**).

www.mhhe.com/saunders5e

Appendix 20A

Internal Ratings–Based Approach to Measuring Credit Risk–Adjusted Assets

The main body of this chapter described the Standardized Approach to measuring credit risk–adjusted asset values for DIs under Basel II. Rather than using the Standardized Approach, banks with a sufficient number of internal credit risk rating grades for loans and whose borrowers are largely unrated by the major credit rating agencies may (with regulatory approval) adopt one of two Internal Ratings–Based (IRB) approaches to calculating credit risk–adjusted assets for capital requirements: the *Foundations Approach* and the *Advanced Approach*.[1] The IRB results in an individualized capital requirement for each asset depending on five key variables. That is, in general, for asset *i*:

$$\text{Capital requirement}_i = f(PD_i, LGD_i, R_i, EAD_i, M_i)$$

where

> PD_i = One-year probability of default of the *i*th borrower
>
> LGD_i = Loss given default of the *i*th borrower
>
> R_i = Correlation of the *i*th borrower with the rest of the portfolio
>
> EAD_i = Amount (in dollars) of exposure at default
>
> M_i = Maturity of the loan

Under the Foundations Approach to corporate, bank, and sovereign exposures, a bank internally estimates the one-year probability of default (*PD*) associated with a borrower class, while relying on supervisory rules for the estimation of other risk components. With regulatory approval, a bank may use the Advanced Approach, in which banks use internal estimates of three additional risk

components: loss given default (*LGD*), exposure at default (*EAD*), and maturity (*M*). For both models, R is set by the regulator.

Under both approaches of IRB capital requirement calculations, benchmark risk weights (BRWs) are calculated for different loans. Under the Foundations Approach, the bank calculates the expected (mean) probability of default (*PD*) for each of its rating classes based on historical experience to generate the BRW. Then, given an *LGD* for the loan (assumed by the BIS to be 50 percent for unsecured loans, 45 percent for loans secured by physical non–real estate collateral, and 40 percent if secured by receivables), an effective maturity (M), and correlation (R) of between 10 and 20 percent, it calculates an individualized BRW and RW (risk weight) for each of its corporate loans. The BRW for each loan under the Foundations Approach is calculated using a formula that calibrates the default risk at the 99.9 percent level using the following formula:

$$BRW = 12.5 \times LGD \times M \times N[(1 - R)^{-0.5} \times G(PD) + (R/(1 - R))^{0.5} \times G(0.999)] \quad \textbf{(A1)}$$

where

$$M = 1 + 0.047 \times ((1 - PD)/PD^{0.44}) \quad \textbf{(A2)}$$

$$R = 0.10 \times [(1 - \exp^{-50PD})/(1 - \exp^{-50})] + 0.20 \times [1 - (1 - \exp^{-50PD})/(1 - \exp^{-50})] \quad \textbf{(A3)}$$

and the risk weight (RW) for a loan is:

$$RW = (LGD/50) \times BRW \quad \textbf{(A4)}$$

Note that in the Foundations Approach model, if the loan is not secured, LGD equals 50 percent (so that the ratio LGD/50 = 1). If, however, the loan is secured by collateral such as non–real estate collateral or receivables, the LGD/50 ratio is less than 1 (e.g., (45/50) or (40/50)), thus reducing the overall risk weight on the loan. The term "exp" in equation A3 stands for the natural exponential function; N(x) is the cumulative distribution function for a standard normal cumulative distribution

---

[1] For a more detailed analysis of these two approaches, see Basel Committee on Banking Supervision, "The New Basel Capital Accord," January 2001; "Potential Modifications to the Committee's Proposals," November 2001; and "International Convergence of Capital Measurement and Capital Standards," June 2004; www.bis.org. See also E. Altman, S. T. Bharath, and A. Saunders, "Credit Ratings and the BIS Reform Agenda," *Journal of Banking and Finance,* 2002, pp. 909–21.

function (i.e., the probability that a normal random variable with mean zero and variance of one is less than or equal to x), and G(z) is the inverse standard normal cumulative distribution function for a standard normal random variable (i.e., the value x such that N(x) = z).[2] Equation A2 denotes the maturity factor M given by the regulator. The correlation coefficient R is computed in equation A3. The correlation ranges from 0.20 for the lowest PD value to 0.10 for the highest PD value.

The LGD shows the severity of loss as a percent of original loan value, and RW shows the overall risk weight or the capital requirement on the loan.[3] Note that the 8 percent capital requirement on all loans under Basel I translates into a (one-year) probability of default (PD) of 1 percent. Thus, under Basel I, loans with PDs less than 1 percent generally "charged" too much capital and loans with PDs greater than 1 percent

"charged" too little capital. Table 20A–1 shows the impact of the probability of default (PD) on capital requirements under the IRB Foundations Approach assuming LGD equals 50 percent.

Under the Advanced Approach, the bank inputs (using its own data) the values of four variables: PD_i, EAD_i, M_i, and LGD_i for each borrower. The fifth variable is set by the regulators using the formula in equation A3.

TABLE 20A–1 Capital Requirements under IRB Foundations Approach

Probability of Default (PD)	Capital Requirement
0.03%	1.4%
0.10	2.7
0.25	4.3
0.50	5.9
0.75	7.1
1.00 (Basel I)	8.0
1.25	8.7
1.50	9.3
2.00	10.3
2.50	11.1
3.00	11.9
4.00	13.4
5.00	14.8
10.00	21.0
20.00	30.0

---

[2] According to the BIS, the functions N and G are generally available in spreadsheet and statistical packages. For both functions, the mean should be set equal to zero and the standard deviation should be set equal to 1. See BIS Consultative Document, "New Basel Capital Accord," January 2001, p. 36, footnote 28.

[3] For example, a PD of 1 percent translates to a capital requirement of 8 percent and to a risk weight of 100 percent [(100%/8%) × 8% = 100%]. Similarly, a PD of 20 percent translates to a capital requirement of 30 percent and to a risk weight of 375 percent [(100%/8%) × 30%].

Chapter **Twenty-One**

Product Diversification

INTRODUCTION

universal FI
An FI that can engage in a broad range of financial service activities.

The U.S. financial system has traditionally been structured along separatist or segmented product lines. Regulatory barriers and restrictions have often inhibited the ability of an FI operating in one area of the financial services industry to expand its product set into other areas. This might be compared with FIs operating in Germany, Switzerland, and the United Kingdom, where a more **universal FI** structure allows individual financial services organizations to offer a far broader range of banking, insurance, securities, and other financial services products.[1] However, the merger between Citicorp and Travelers to create Citigroup, the then third largest universal bank or financial conglomerate in the world, was a sign that the importance of regulatory barriers in the United States is receding. Moreover, the passage of the Financial Services Modernization Act of 1999 (discussed below) has accelerated the reduction in the barriers among financial service firms. Indeed, as consolidation in the U.S. and global financial services industry proceeds apace, we are likely to see an acceleration in the creation of very large, globally oriented, multiproduct financial service firms that will operate with a new set of risks and management strategies to handle these risks. Table 21–1 shows the largest financial service firms in the world (measured by assets) as of 2003.

This chapter first analyzes the problems and risks that can arise, and have arisen historically, for U.S. FIs constrained to limited financial service sectors or franchises as well as the potential benefits from greater product expansion of the Citigroup kind. Second, the chapter analyzes the laws and regulations that have restricted product expansions for banks, insurance companies, and securities firms in the United States and elsewhere, as well as the recent modifications of many of these laws and regulations. In addition, it looks at barriers to product expansion between the financial sector and the real or commercial sector of the economy. Third, it evaluates the advantages and disadvantages of allowing U.S. FIs to adopt more universal franchises, as appears to be the current trend.

RISKS OF PRODUCT SEGMENTATION

Historically, many U.S. financial service firms have faced return and risk problems due to constraints on product diversification. Arguably, product expansion

[1] For a thorough analysis of universal banking systems overseas, see A. Saunders and I. Walter, *Universal Banking in the U.S.?* (New York: Oxford University Press, 1994); and A. Saunders and I. Walter, eds., *Financial System Design: Universal Banking Considered* (Burr Ridge, IL: McGraw-Hill/Irwin, 1996).

TABLE 21–1
The 10 Largest
Banks in the World
(in billions of
dollars)

Source: *The Banker,* July 2003.
www.thebanker.com

	Total Assets
Citigroup (United States)	$1,097.2
Mizuho Financial Group (Japan)	1,080.8
UBS (Switzerland)	851.7
Sumitomo Mitsui Banking Corp. (Japan)	844.8
Deutsche Bank (Germany)	795.3
Bank of Tokyo-Mitsubishi (Japan)	781.1
HSBC Holdings (United Kingdom)	759.2
J. P. Morgan Chase (United States)*	758.8
BNP Paribas (France)	744.9
HVB Group (Germany)	724.8

*J. P. Morgan Chase's merger with Bank One, announced in early 2004, will move it up to the number three spot among the world's largest banks.

**money market
mutual funds
(MMMFs)**

Mutual funds that
offer high liquidity,
check-writing ability,
and a money market
return to smaller indi-
vidual investors.

restrictions have affected commercial banks the most. For example, to the extent that regulations have limited the franchise of banks to traditional areas such as deposit taking and commercial lending, banks have been increasingly susceptible to nonbank competition on both the liability and asset sides of their balance sheets. Specifically, the growth of **money market mutual funds (MMMFs)** that offer checking account–like deposit services with high liquidity, stability of value, and an attractive return has proven to be very strong competition for bank deposit and transaction account products.[2] From virtually no assets in 1972, MMMFs had grown to more than $2,072 billion by year-end 2003, compared to small time deposits and money market accounts of approximately $2,291 billion in commercial banks. In addition, until recently banks have been threatened by the growth of annuities offered by the life insurance industry. Annuities are a savings product that have many of the same features as bank CDs. In the early 2000s, fixed and variable annuities were selling at the rate of about $250 billion a year.[3]

On the asset side of the balance sheet, the commercial and industrial (C&I) loans of banks have faced increased competition from the dynamic growth of the commercial paper market as an alternative source of short-term financing for large- and middle-sized corporations. For example, in January 1988, C&I loans outstanding were $565 billion versus $380 billion of commercial paper; in December 2003, C&I loans were $879 billion versus $1,265.4 billion of commercial paper outstanding. In addition, relatively unregulated finance companies are taking an increasing share of the business credit market. In December 2003, the ratio of finance company business credit to bank C&I loans was approximately 35 percent.

These trends mean that the economic value of narrowly defined bank franchises has declined. In particular, product line restrictions inhibit the ability of an FI to optimize the set of financial services it can offer, potentially forcing it to adopt a more risky set of activities than it would adopt if it could fully diversify.[4]

[2] As we discuss in Chapter 5, MMMFs collect small savers' funds and invest in a diversified portfolio of short-term money market instruments. This allows the small saver indirect access to the wholesale money market and to the relatively more attractive rates in those markets.

[3] An annuity is a contract where the purchaser makes one or more payments up front to receive a fixed or variable flow of payments over time. These instruments are normally tax sheltered. As will be discussed below, the Supreme Court upheld the legality of banks' selling these instruments in 1996.

[4] While it is true that banks earned very high profits in the 1993–2000 period, this was in large part due to relatively low interest rates for deposits and relatively high interest rates for loans. The increased profitability of banks in the 1990s and early 2000s may well be more cyclical than secular.

Product restrictions also limit the ability of FI managers to adjust flexibly to shifts in the demand for financial products by consumers and to shifts in costs due to technology and related innovations. We analyze the advantages and disadvantages of increased product line diversification in more detail after we look more closely at the major laws and regulations segmenting the U.S. financial services industry and ways in which U.S. FIs have tried to overcome the effects of such regulations, culminating in the passage of the Financial Services Modernization Act of 1999.

Concept Questions

1. Offer support for the claim that product expansion restrictions have affected commercial banks more than any other type of financial services firm.
2. What sources of competition have had an impact on the asset side of banks' balance sheets?

SEGMENTATION IN THE U.S. FINANCIAL SERVICES INDUSTRY

Commercial and Investment Banking Activities

commercial banking
Banking activity of deposit taking and lending.

investment banking
Banking activity of underwriting, issuing, and distributing securities.

Since 1863 the United States has experienced several phases in regulating the links between the commercial and investment banking industries. Simply defined, **commercial banking** is the activity of deposit taking and commercial lending; **investment banking** is the activity of underwriting, issuing, and distributing securities. Early legislation such as the 1863 National Bank Act prohibited nationally chartered commercial banks from engaging in corporate securities activities such as underwriting and the distribution of corporate bonds and equities. However, as the United States industrialized and the demand for corporate finance grew, the largest banks, such as National City Bank (today's Citigroup), found ways around this restriction by establishing state-chartered affiliates to do the underwriting. By 1927 these bank affiliates were underwriting approximately 30 percent of the corporate securities being issued. In that year the Comptroller of the Currency, the regulator of national banks, relaxed the controls on national banks underwriting securities, thereby allowing them to pursue an even greater market share of securities underwritings.

After the 1929 stock market crash, the United States entered a major recession and some 10,000 banks failed between 1930 and 1933. A commission of inquiry (the Pecora Commission), established in 1932, began looking into the causes of the crash. The commission pointed to banks' securities activities and the inherent abuses and conflicts of interest that arise when commercial and investment banking activities were mixed as major causes.[5] The findings resulted in new legislation, the 1933 Banking Act, or the Glass-Steagall Act.

The Glass-Steagall Act sought to impose a rigid separation between commercial banking—taking deposits and making commercial loans—and investment

---

[5] Today, many question the Pecora Commission's findings, believing that the slow growth in bank reserves and the money supply by the Federal Reserve lay at the heart of the post-crash recession. For a major critique of the facts underlying the Pecora Commission's findings and the Glass-Steagall Act, see G. J. Benston, *The Separation of Commercial and Investment Banking: The Glass-Steagall Act Revisited and Reconsidered* (New York: St. Martins Press, 1989); and G. J. Benston, "Universal Banking," *Journal of Economic Perspectives* 8 (1994), pp. 121–43. For a monetary explanation of the 1930–33 contraction, see M. Freidman and A. J. Schwartz, *A Monetary History of the United States, 1867–1960* (Princeton, NJ: Princeton University Press, 1963).

banking—underwriting, issuing, and distributing stocks, bonds, and other securities. Sections 16 and 21 of the act limited the ability of banks and securities firms to engage directly in each other's activities, while Sections 20 and 32 limited the ability of banks and securities firms to engage indirectly in such activities through separately established affiliates. Nevertheless, the act defined three major securities underwriting exemptions. First, commercial banks were to continue to underwrite new issues of Treasury bills, notes, and bonds. Thus, the largest commercial banks today, such as J. P. Morgan Chase, actively compete with securities firms such as Goldman Sachs in government bond auctions. Second, commercial banks were allowed to continue underwriting municipal general obligation (GO) bonds.[6] Third, commercial banks were allowed to continue engaging in private placements of all types of bonds and equities, corporate and otherwise. In a **private placement,** a bank seeks to find a large institutional buyer or investor such as another FI for a new securities issue. As such, the bank acts as an agent for a fee. By comparison, in a public offering of securities, a bank normally acts as a direct principal and has an underwriting stake in the issue. This principal position, such as in **firm commitment underwriting,** involves buying securities from the issuer at one price and seeking to resell them to the public at a slightly higher price. Failure to sell these securities can result in a major loss to the underwriter of publicly issued securities. Thus, the act distinguished between the private placement of securities, which was allowed, and public placement, which was not.

For most of the 1933–63 period, commercial banks and investment banks generally appeared to be willing to abide by the letter and spirit of the Glass-Steagall Act. However, between 1963 and 1987, banks challenged restrictions on municipal revenue bond underwriting, commercial paper underwriting, discount brokerage, managing and advising of open- and closed-end mutual funds, underwriting of mortgage-backed securities, and selling annuities.[7] In most cases, the courts have eventually upheld these activities.[8]

With this onslaught and de facto erosion of the Glass-Steagall Act by legal interpretation, in April 1987 the Federal Reserve Board allowed commercial bank holding companies—such as Citigroup, the parent of Citibank—to establish separate **Section 20 affiliates** as investment banks. Through these Section 20 affiliates, bank holding companies began to conduct all their ineligible or gray area securities activities, such as commercial paper underwriting, mortgage-backed securities underwriting, and municipal revenue bond underwriting.[9] Note the organizational

---

private placement
The placement of a whole issue of securities with a single or a few large investors by a bank acting as a placing agent.

firm commitment underwriting
An underwriter buys securities from an issuer and reoffers them to the public at a slightly higher price.

Section 20 affiliate
A securities subsidiary of a bank holding company through which a banking organization can engage in investment banking activities.

---

[6] A municipal general obligation bond is a bond issued by a state, city, or local government whose interest and principal payments are backed by the full faith and credit of that local government, that is, its full tax and revenue base.

[7] Municipal revenue bonds are more risky than municipal GO bonds, since their interest and principal are guaranteed only by the revenue from the projects they finance. One example would be the revenue from road tolls if the bond funded the building of a new section of highway.

[8] To see the type of issues involved, discount brokerage was held to be legal since it was not viewed as being the same as full-service brokerage supplied by securities firms. In particular, a full-service brokerage combines both the agency function of securities purchase along with investment advice (e.g., hot tips). By contrast, discount brokers only carry out the agency function of buying and selling securities for clients; they do not give investment advice. For further discussion of these issues, see M. Clark and A. Saunders, "Judicial Interpretation of Glass-Steagall: The Need for Legislative Action," *The Banking Law Journal* 97 (1980), pp. 721–40; and "Glass-Steagall Revisited: The Impact on Banks, Capital Markets, and the Small Investor," *The Banking Law Journal* 97 (1980), pp. 811–40.

[9] In 1989 corporate bond and in 1990 corporate equities underwriting were added to the permitted list.

FIGURE 21–1
A Bank Holding
Company and Its
Bank and Section 20
Subsidiary

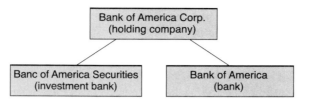

structure of Bank of America Corp., its bank, and the Section 20 subsidiary (or investment bank) in Figure 21–1.

Legally, these Section 20 subsidiaries did not violate Section 20 of the Glass-Steagall Act, which restricts bank–securities firm affiliations as long as the revenue generated from the securities underwriting activities restricted under the act amounted to less than 50 percent of the total revenues they generated; that is, a majority of a Section 20 subsidiary's revenue does *not* come from ineligible security activities. To avoid legal challenges, the Federal Reserve initially set the revenue limit at a very conservative 5 percent of total revenue (increased later to 10 percent, and then to 25 percent).

Significant changes occurred in 1997 as the Federal Reserve and the Office of the Comptroller of the Currency (OCC) took actions to expand bank holding companies' permitted activities. In particular, the Federal Reserve allowed commercial banks to acquire directly existing investment banks rather than establish completely new Section 20 investment banking subsidiaries.

The result was a number of mergers and acquisitions between commercial and investment banks in 1997 through 2000. Some of the largest mergers included UBS's $12.0 billion purchase of Paine Webber in 2000, Credit Suisse First Boston's purchase of Donaldson Lufkin Jenrette for $11.5 billion in 2000, Deutsche Bank's $9.7 billion purchase of Banker's Trust in 1999, Citicorp's $83 billion merger with Travelers Group in April 1998, Banker's Trust's April 1997 acquisition of Alex Brown for $1.7 billion, NationsBank's 1997 purchase of Montgomery Securities for more than $1 billion, U.S. Bancorp's December 1997 acquisition of Piper Jaffray for $730 million, and Bank of America's June 1997 purchase of Robertson Stephens for $540 million (resold to Bank of Boston for $800 million in April 1998). In each case the banks stated that one motivation for the acquisition was the desire to establish a presence in the securities business as laws separating investment banking and commercial banking were changing. Also noted as a motivation in these aquisitions was the opportunity to expand business lines, taking advantage of economies of scale and scope to reduce overall costs and merge the customer bases of the respective commercial and investment banks involved in the acquisitions. The slumping stock market and U.S. economy in 2001–2003 resulted in a reduction in these acquisitions.[10]

Not all of these acquisitions were successful, however. For example, in July 2002 FleetBoston (the merged Fleet Financial and Bank of Boston) shut down its Robertson Stephens investment banking unit to refocus on its core commercial and retail banking operation. Problems between the two units began in 2001 when

[10] K. P. Coyne, L. T. Mendonca, and G. Wilson, in "Can Banks Grow Beyond M&A?" *The McKinsey Quarterly* (2004), conclude that for most large banks, further expansion will not necessarily yield dramatic scale-based savings in technology and production development costs.

FleetBoston asked for and received the resignations of both Robertson's CEO and CFO following a high-profile pay flap where FleetBoston accused senior Robertson management of paying themselves over $70 million more than had been agreed upon. Then amid the 2001 hi-tech meltdown, Robertson's revenue plunged 71 percent and it lost $61 million.

The erosion of the product barriers between the commercial and investment banking industries was not one way.[11] Large investment banks such as Merrill Lynch increasingly sought to offer banking products. For example, in the late 1970s, Merrill Lynch introduced the cash management account (CMA), which allowed investors to own a money market mutual fund with checkwriting privileges into which bond and stock sale proceeds could be swept on a daily basis. This account allowed the investor to earn interest on cash held in a brokerage account. In addition, many investment banks acted as deposit brokers. As we discussed in Chapter 19, deposit brokers charge a fee to break large deposits into $100,000 deposit units and place them in banks across the country. Further, investment banks have been major participants as traders and investors in the secondary market for LDC and other loans (see Chapters 16 and 27). In 2000, Merrill Lynch introduced the CMA 2.0, a federally insured, interest-bearing account tied to its customers' investment accounts.

Finally, in recognition of the years of "homemade" deregulation by banks and securities firms described above, the U.S. Congress passed the Financial Services Modernization Act, which repealed the Glass-Steagall barriers between commercial banking and investment banking.[12] The bill, promoted as the biggest change in the regulation of financial institutions in nearly 70 years, allowed for the creation of "financial services holding companies" that could engage in banking activities *and* securities activities through a Section 4(k)(4)(E) securities subsidiary (replacing the Section 20 subsidiary). The bill also allowed large national banks to place certain activities, including some securities underwritings, in direct bank subsidiaries regulated by the Office of the Comptroller of the Currency. Thus, after nearly 70 years of partial or complete separation between investment banking and commercial banking, the Financial Services Modernization Act of 1999 opened the door for the creation of full-service financial institutions in the United States similar to those that existed before 1933 and that exist in many other countries today.

Banking and Insurance

Prior to the passage of the Financial Services Modernization Act of 1999, very strong barriers restricted the entry of banks into insurance and vice versa. One notable exception was Travelers Corp.'s merger with Citicorp to form Citigroup in 1998, which to some extent proved to be a catalyst for the eventual passage of the 1999 act. Insurance activities can be either of the property-casualty kind (homeowners insurance, auto insurance) or of the life/health kind (term life insurance). Moreover, we must make a distinction between a bank selling insurance as an agent by selling

---

[11] J. P. Choi and C. Stefanadis, in "Financial Conglomerates, Informational Leverage, and Innovation: The Investment Banking Connection," Michigan State University Working Paper, 2003, develop a model that shows that by expanding into commercial banking and building lending relationships, an investment bank (IB) may erode the informational advantage of rival IBs. In equilibrium, these financial conglomerates earn higher expected profits than pure investment banks.

[12] The Financial Services Modernization Act also reduced the barriers between commercial banking, investment banking, and insurance (see below).

other FIs' policies for a fee and a bank acting as an insurance underwriter and bearing the direct risk of underwriting losses. In general, the risks of insurance agency activities are quite low in loss potential compared to insurance underwriting. Certain types of insurance—for example, credit life insurance, mortgage insurance, and auto insurance—tend to have natural synergistic links to bank lending products.[13]

Prior to the Financial Services Modernization Act of 1999, banks were under very stringent restrictions when selling and underwriting almost every type of insurance. For example, national banks were restricted to offering credit-related life, accident, health, or unemployment insurance. Moreover, they could act as insurance agents only in small towns of less than 5,000 people (although they could sell insurance from these offices anywhere in the United States). Further, the Bank Holding Company Act of 1956 (and its 1970 amendments) and the Garn-St Germain Depository Institutions Act of 1982 placed severe restrictions on bank holding companies establishing separately capitalized insurance affiliates and on insurance companies acquiring banks. Most states also took quite restrictive actions regarding the insurance activities of state-chartered banks. A few states—most notably Delaware—passed liberal laws allowing state-chartered banks to underwrite and broker various types of property-casualty and life insurance. This encouraged large bank holding companies such as Chase to enter Delaware and establish state-chartered banking subsidiaries with their own insurance affiliates.

One area where banks successfully survived legal challenges was in the area of annuities. In 1986, Nationsbank (which merged with Bank of America in 1997) started selling annuities and was aggressively challenged in court by the insurance industry. In the meantime, a large number of other banks began offering annuities as well. In 1995, the Supreme Court upheld the legality of banks' selling annuities, arguing they should be viewed more as investment products rather than as insurance products.[14] It is estimated that such sales add close to $1 billion a year to bank profits.

nonbank bank
A bank divested of its commercial loans and/or demand deposits.

Beginning in the early 1980s, several insurance companies and commercial firms found indirect ways to engage in banking activities. This was through the organizational mechanism of establishing **nonbank bank** subsidiaries. The 1956 Bank Holding Company Act legally defined a bank as an organization that both accepts demand deposits and makes commercial and industrial loans and severely limited the ability of an insurance company or commercial firm to acquire such a bank. An insurance company could get around this restrictive provision by buying a full-service bank and then divesting its demand deposits or commercial loans.

[13] See Saunders and Walter, *Universal Banking,* for an elaboration of these arguments. Further, D. Rule points out that bank/insurance company mergers produce portfolios that carry a mixture of insurance and banking exposure, which is likely to alter the diversification characteristics of the merged institutions; see "Risk Transfer Between Banks, Insurance Companies and Capital Markets," *Financial Stability Review,* December 2001.

[14] K. A. Carow, in "The Wealth Effects of Allowing Bank Entry into the Insurance Industry," Indiana University Working Paper, 1999, found that bank stock prices did not, on average, change significantly at the announcement of this act. However, life insurance companies' stock prices fell significantly. PC insurer stock prices dropped as well, but less significantly than life insurers. Around the Citicorp-Travelers Group merger, he found that life insurance companies and large banks had significant stock price increases, while small banks, health insurers, and PC insurers' stock price changes were not significantly affected. See "Citicorp-Travelers Group Merger: Challenging Barriers between Banking and Insurance," *Journal of Banking and Finance* 25 (2001), pp. 1553–71.

This converted the bank into a nonbank bank. In 1987, Congress passed the Competitive Equality Banking Act (CEBA), blocking the nonbank bank loophole. This essentially prevented the creation of any new nonbank banks by redefining a bank as any institution that accepts and is accepted for deposit insurance coverage. This meant that any new nonbank bank established after 1987 would have to forgo deposit insurance coverage, making it very difficult to raise deposits. Although nonbank banks established prior to 1987 were grandfathered by CEBA, their growth rates were capped.[15] Insurance companies found a way around this legislation as well by opening federally chartered thrifts. Indeed, under the Savings and Loan Holding Company Act of 1968 (and in direct contrast to the Bank Holding Company Act), any corporation or insurance firm can acquire one savings institution.

A great challenge to the Bank Holding Company Act's restrictions on bank–insurance company affiliations came from the 1998 merger between Citicorp and Travelers to create the largest financial services conglomerate in the United States. The primary activity of Travelers was insurance (life and property-casualty), while the primary activity of Citicorp was banking (both also were engaged in securities activities: Citicorp through its Section 20 subsidiary and Travelers through its earlier acquisition of Smith–Barney and Salomon Brothers). Under the Bank Holding Company Act, the Federal Reserve had up to five years to formally approve the merger. The Federal Reserve gave initial approval in September 1998. (In a turnaround in strategy, Citigroup sold most of the Travelers Property/Casualty Insurance unit in 2002.)

The Financial Services Modernization Act of 1999 completely changed the landscape for insurance activities (and implicitly ratified the Citicorp-Travelers merger) as it allowed bank holding companies to open insurance underwriting affiliates and insurance companies to open commercial bank as well as securities firm affiliates through the creation of financial service holding companies (FSHC). With the passage of this act, banks no longer have to fight legal battles in states such as Texas and Rhode Island to overcome restrictions on their ability to sell insurance in these states. Indeed, by 2002 more than 50 percent of all U.S. banks sold insurance products, totalling a record $3.49 billion in insurance commissions and premium income. The insurance industry applauded the act, as it forced banks that underwrite and sell insurance to operate under the same set of state regulations (pertaining to their insurance lines) as insurance companies. Under the new act, a financial services holding company that engages in commercial banking, investment banking, and insurance activities will be functionally regulated. This means that the holding company's banking activities will be regulated by bank regulators (such as the Federal Reserve, FDIC, OCC), its securities activities will be regulated by the SEC, and its insurance activities will be regulated by up to 50 state insurance regulators (since insurance is not regulated at the federal level—see Chapter 3).

Commercial Banking and Commerce

The 1863 National Bank Act severely limited the ability of nationally chartered banks, which were the nation's largest, to expand into commercial activities by

---

[15] Specifically, nonbank banks established before March 5, 1987, were allowed to continue in business but were limited to a maximum growth in assets of 7 percent during any 12-month period beginning one year after the act's passage. It also permitted those nonbank banks that were allowed to remain in business to engage only in the activities in which they were engaged as of March 1987 and limited the cross-marketing of products and services by nonbank banks and affiliated companies.

taking direct equity stakes in firms. Provisions of the National Bank Act limit participation by national banks in nonbank subsidiaries to those activities permitted by statute or regulation. Banks could engage only in commercial sector activities "incidental to banking" and even then, only through service or subsidiary corporations. However, broader powers to take equity stakes exist when a borrower is in distress. In this case, national banks have unlimited powers to acquire corporate stock and hold it for up to 10 years.

While the direct holding of equity by national banks has been constrained since 1863, restrictions on the commercial activities of bank holding companies are more recent phenomena. In particular, the 1970 amendments to the 1956 Bank Holding Company Act required bank holding companies to divest themselves of nonbank-related subsidiaries over a 10-year period following the amendment. When Congress passed the amendments, bank holding companies owned some 3,500 commercial sector subsidiaries ranging from public utilities to transportation and manufacturing firms. Nevertheless, prior to late 1999 bank holding companies could hold up to 4.9 percent of the voting shares in any commercial firm without regulatory approval.[16]

The Financial Services Modernization Act of 1999 changed restrictions on ownership limits imposed on financial services holding companies. Commercial banks belonging to a financial service holding company can now take a controlling interest in a nonfinancial enterprise provided that two conditions are met. First, the investment cannot be made for an indefinite period of time. The act did not provide an explicit time limit and simply states that the investment can be "held for a period of time to enable the sale or disposition thereof on a reasonable basis consistent with the financial viability of the [investment]." Second, the bank cannot become actively involved in the management of the corporation in which it invests. Nevertheless, corporate stocks or equities are still conspicuously absent from most bank balance sheets (see Chapter 2).[17]

Nonbank Financial Service Firms and Commerce

In comparison with the barriers separating banking and either securities, insurance, or commercial sector activities, the barriers among nonbank financial service firms and commercial firms are generally much weaker. Indeed, in recent years, nonbank financial service firms and commercial firms have faced few barriers to entering into and exiting from various areas of nonbank financial service activity. For example, Travelers Group acquired Salomon Brothers in 1997, one year after acquiring Smith Barney. Various other major nonbank financial service acquisitions and divestitures have occurred, many involving commercial firms such as Sears Roebuck, Xerox, and Gulf and Western.

Importantly, however, the passage of the Financial Services Modernization Act of 1999 standardized the relationship among financial service sectors (commercial

[16] Under the Bank Holding Company Act, *control* is defined as when a holding company has an equity stake exceeding 25 percent in a subsidiary bank or affiliate.

[17] S. Park, in "Effects of the Affiliation of Banking and Commerce on the Firm's Investment and the Bank's Risk," *Journal of Banking and Finance* 24 (2000), pp. 1629–50, finds that a bank's holding of a borrowing firm's equity reduces the agency conflict between the firm and the bank, but increases the monitoring need of uninformed debtholders. The bank's risk exposure can increase in one of two ways. With a large equity share, the bank has more incentive to allow the firm to undertake risky projects. Further, when it has control over the bank, the firm may force the bank to finance its risky projects.

banking, insurance, investment banking) and commerce. Specifically, a financial services holding company is now defined as holding a minimum of 85 percent of its assets in financial assets (i.e., a maximum of 15 percent in commercial sector or real assets). Any nonfinancial assets (activities) exceeding the maximum are grandfathered for at least 10 years (with a possible additional 5-year extension). Nevertheless, eventually, many financial service firms may well have to sell off (divest) some of their real sector assets and activities.

Concept Questions

1. What was the rationale for the passage of the Glass-Steagall Act in 1933? What permissible underwriting activities did it identify for commercial banks?

2. Why do you think that there was a 25 percent rather than a 50 percent maximum ceiling on the revenues earned from the ineligible underwriting activities of a Section 20 subsidiary?

3. Does a bank that currently specializes in making consumer loans but makes no commercial loans qualify as a nonbank bank?

4. How did the provisions of the National Bank Act of 1863 affect the participation of national banks in establishing nonbank subsidiaries?

5. How has the Financial Services Modernization Act of 1999 opened the doors for the establishment of full-service financial institutions in the United States?

ACTIVITY RESTRICTIONS IN THE UNITED STATES VERSUS OTHER COUNTRIES

We have just described the barriers to product expansion and financial conglomeration in the United States. Although many of the barriers have been eroded, those that remain fall most heavily on this nation's commercial banks. This is shown in Appendix 21A located at the book's Web site (www.mhhe.com/saunders5e), which compares the range of activities permitted to U.S. commercial banks with the range of product activities permitted to banks in other major industrialized countries and financial centers.[18] Figure 21–2 shows the highly diversified product structure of the Swiss universal bank Credit Suisse First Boston. Universal banks offer not just investment banking services, but also commercial lending, foreign exchange, and custody and cash management services. Universal banks include Citigroup, J. P. Morgan Chase, UBS, Deutsche Bank, Credit Suisse First Boston, and to a lesser extent Bank of America. However, with the possible exception of Japan, U.S. banks are still among the most constrained of all the major industrialized countries in terms of the range of nonbank product activities permitted.[19] This has created continuing pressure on Congress to bring U.S. banks' activity powers in line

---

[18] See also J. R. Barth, R. D. Brumbaugh Jr., and J. A. Wilcox, "The Repeal of Glass-Steagall and the Advent of Broad Banking," Office of the Comptroller of the Currency, Economic and Policy Analysis Working Paper 2000–5, April 2000.

[19] Many of Japan's postwar regulations were modeled on those of the United States. Thus, Article 65 in Japan separates commercial banking from investment banking in a similar fashion to the Glass-Steagall Act. However, Japan has recently passed a major deregulation law that will considerably weaken the historic barriers between commercial and investment banking in that country. See T. Ito, T. Kiso, and H. Uchibori, "The Impact of the Big Bang on the Japanese Financial System," Fuji Research Paper No. 9, Fuji Research Institute Corporation, Tokyo, Japan, May 1998.

FIGURE 21–2   The Structure of a Universal Bank: CS Holding Group

CREDIT SUISSE GROUP

Credit Suisse Financial Services
is a leading provider of comprehensive financial services in Europe and other selected markets. Under the brands Credit Suisse and Winterthur, it offers investment products, private banking, and financial advisory services, including insurance and pension solutions, for private and corporate clients.

| Private Banking | Life & Pensions |
| Corporate & Retail Banking | Insurance |

Credit Suisse First Boston
is a leading global investment bank serving institutional, corporate, government, and high-net-worth clients. Its businesses include securities underwriting, sales and trading, investment banking, private equity, financial advisory services, investment research, venture capital, and asset management.

| Institutional Securities | CSFB Financial Services |

Credit Suisse
Legal entity

Subsidiaries

Bank Leu AG*

Clariden Bank*

Bank Hofmann*

Neue Aargauer Bank*
(98.6%)

BGP Banca di Gestione
Patrimoniale*

JO Hambro Investment
Management Limited

Frye-Louis Capital
Management, Inc.

Credit Suisse Trust*

Credit Suisse Fides*

Winterthur
Legal entity

Subsidiaries

Winterthur Life

DBV-Winterthur
Versicherung AG,
Germany

Winterthur
Assicurazioni S. p. A.,
Italy

Credit Suisse First Boston
Legal entity

Subsidiaries

Credit Suisse First
Boston (USA), Inc.

Credit Suisse First
Boston International

Credit Suisse First
Boston, LLC

Credit Suisse First
Boston (Europe)
Limited

Subsidiaries

Credit Suisse Asset
Management, LLC

Credit Suisse Trust &
Banking Co Ltd.

Credit Suisse Asset
Management
(Australia) Limited

Credit Suisse Asset
Management, Limited

* Direct holding of Credit Suisse Group.

Source: Credit Suisse Group Web site, *www.credit-suisse.com.*

with those of their global competitors and counterparts such as those in the EU and Switzerland.

In the next section, we look at the issues that have been raised and will continue to be raised whenever the question of expanded product (or more universal) powers for banks and other FIs arise.

Concept Questions

1. How does the range of product activities permitted for U.S. commercial banks compare to that of banks in other major industrialized countries?
2. How are the product activities of U.S. commercial banks likely to change in the future?

ISSUES INVOLVED IN THE DIVERSIFICATION OF PRODUCT OFFERINGS

Whether the debate concerns existing or expanded bank expansion into securities activities, insurance, or commerce, similar issues arise. These include

1. Safety and soundness issues.
2. Economy of scale and scope issues.
3. Conflict of interest issues.
4. Deposit insurance issues.
5. Regulatory oversight issues.
6. Competition issues.

This section evaluates these issues in the context of banks entering into securities activities.

Consider the three alternative organizational structures for linking banking and securities activities in Figure 21–3. The financial services holding company structure in panel (c) of the figure is the organizational form within which we will evaluate the six issues just identified. This is the form adopted under the Financial Services Modernization Act to accommodate most bank organization expansions into nonbank activities.

In Figure 21–3, panel (a) shows the fully integrated universal bank, where banking and securities activities are conducted in different departments of a single organization. This is typical of the way in which large banks in Germany, such as Deutsche Bank, engage in securities activities. Panel (b) shows the universal subsidiary model where a bank engages in securities activities through a separately owned securities affiliate. This is typical of the way in which commercial banks such as Barclay's in the United Kingdom and Toronto Dominion in Canada conduct their securities activities. This is also the model adopted in 1997 by the OCC to allow U.S. nationally chartered banks to expand their nonbank activities.

FIGURE 21–3
Alternative Organizational Forms for Nonbank Product Expansions of Banking Organizations

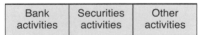

(a) Full Universal

Bank activities	Securities activities	Other activities

(b) Universal-Subsidiary

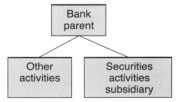

(c) Financial Services Holding Company (FSHC)

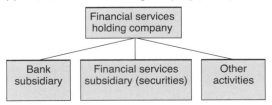

Note that the degree of bank-nonbank integration is much less with the financial services holding company model [panel (c)] than with either the full or subsidiary universal banking model.[20] For example, in the universal subsidiary model, the bank holds a direct ownership stake in the securities subsidiary. By comparison, in the financial services holding company model, the bank and securities subsidiary are separate companies with their own equity capital; the link is that their equity is held by the same parent company, the financial services holding company (such as Bank of America Corp.).[21]

Safety and Soundness Concerns

With respect to the securities activities of commercial banks and the possible effects on their safety and soundness, two key questions arise: How risky is securities underwriting? And if losses occur for a securities subsidiary, can this cause the affiliated bank to fail?

The Risk of Securities Underwriting

firm commitment offering
Securities offered from the issuing firm, purchased by an underwriter.

To understand the risk of securities underwriting, you must understand the mechanics of firm commitment securities offerings. In a **firm commitment offering,** the underwriter purchases securities directly from the issuing firm (say, at $99 per share) and then reoffers them to the public or the market at large at a slightly higher price, say, $99.50. The difference between the underwriter's buy price ($99) and the public offer price ($99.50) is the spread that compensates the underwriter for accepting the principal risk of placing the securities with outside investors as well as any administrative and distribution costs associated with the underwriting. In our simple example of a $0.50 spread, the maximum revenue the underwriter can gain from underwriting the issue is $0.50 times the number of shares issued. Thus, if 1 million shares were offered, the maximum gross revenue for the underwriting would be $0.50 times 1,000,000, or $500,000. Note that once the public offering has been made and the price specified in the prospectus, the underwriter cannot raise the price over the offering period. In this example, the underwriter could not raise the price above $99.50 even after determining that the market valued the shares more highly.[22]

The upside return from underwriting is normally capped, but the downside risk is not, and can be very large. The downside risk arises if the underwriter overprices the public offering, setting the public offer price higher than outside investors' valuations. As a result, the underwriter will be unable to sell the shares during the public offering period and will have to lower the price to get rid of the inventory of unsold shares, especially because this inventory is often financed through issuing commercial paper or repurchase agreements. In our example, if the underwriter has to lower the offering price to $99, the gross revenue from the underwriting will be zero, since this is the price paid to the issuing firm. Any price less than $99 generates a loss. For example, suppose that the issue can be placed only at $97; the underwriter's losses will be $2 times 1,000,000 shares, or $2 million.

There are a number of possible reasons why an underwriter may take a big loss or big hit on an underwriting. The first is simply overestimating the market's

---

[20] For a comparative analysis of these three models, see Saunders and Walter, *Universal Banking.*

[21] In general, the advantages of the full universal model is greater resource flexibility and integration of commercial bank and investment bank product lines. Its perceived disadvantages include greater monopoly power and greater potential conflicts of interest.

[22] The offering period is usually a maximum of 10 business days.

FIGURE 21–4
The Role of Firewalls in Protecting Banks

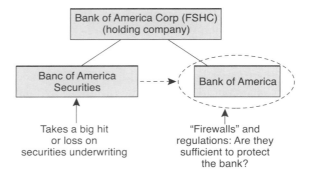

demand for the shares. The second is that in the short period between setting the public offering price and seeking to sell the securities to the public, there may be a major drop in security values in general.

If Underwriting Losses Occur for the Securities Affiliate, Can This Cause a Bank to Fail?

Proponents of allowing banking organizations to expand their securities activities argue that the answer to this question is no, as long as the bank subsidiary is sufficiently insulated from the risk problems of the securities affiliate. As noted earlier, in a financial services holding company structure, the bank is legally a separate corporation from the securities affiliate. As shown in Figure 21–4, its only link to its securities affiliate is indirect, through the holding company that owns a controlling equity stake in both the bank and securities affiliate. However, even this indirect link raises the concern that the effects of losses by the securities affiliate could threaten the safety of the bank unless firewalls or regulatory barriers are introduced to insulate the bank against such losses (see Figure 21–4).

There are at least three ways a bank could be harmed by losses of a securities affiliate in a holding company structure. First, a holding company might be tempted to drain capital and funds from the bank by requiring excessive dividends and fees from the bank (this is called *upstreaming*). The holding company could then *downstream* these funds to protect the failing securities affiliate from insolvency. As a result, the bank would be weakened at the expense (or because) of the securities affiliate. Currently, the Federal Reserve closely monitors bank dividend payments to holding company owners and must restrict dividend payments of the bank if it is undercapitalized under the prompt corrective action plan (see Chapter 20). Also, Section 23B of the 1982 Federal Reserve Act limits the size of management and other fees banks can pay for services provided by the holding company to the fee normally established by the market for such services.

www.federalreserve. gov

A second way in which a bank could be harmed is through interaffiliate loans. For example, the holding company may induce the bank to extend loans to the securities affiliate to keep it afloat even though such loans are excessively risky. To prevent this, the Federal Reserve Act limits bank loans to any single nonbank affiliate to 10 percent of a bank's capital. If bank capital is approximately 5 percent of bank assets, this limits loans to an affiliate to $.05 \times .1$ of bank assets, or 0.5 percent of bank assets. Prior to 1997, firewalls prohibited a bank from lending anything at all to its securities affiliates.[23]

---

[23] This also holds for the sale of assets by the affiliate to the bank.

The third way in which a bank may be affected is through a contagious confidence problem. Specifically, difficulty of a securities firm subsidiary may result in a negative information signal to financial service consumers and investors regarding the quality of the management of the holding company and its bank affiliate. Such negative information can create incentives for large depositors and investors to withdraw their money from the bank in the manner described in Chapter 19. This bank run possibility seems more likely to occur if the bank and its securities affiliate share similar names and logos, which in general they do.[24]

Obviously, a big hit taken by the securities subsidiary can potentially threaten the safety and solvency of the affiliated bank, especially through the confidence effect. However, at least two countervailing risk-reducing effects may enhance the safety and soundness of a bank indirectly linked to a securities subsidiary in a holding company framework. The first effect is a **product diversification benefit.** A well-diversified financial services firm (financial services holding company) potentially enjoys a far more stable earnings and profit stream over time than does a product-specialized bank. As demand and cost shifts reduce earnings in one activity area, such as banking, offsetting demand and cost shifts may take place in other activity areas, such as securities or insurance, increasing the holding company's earnings. Advocates argue that a more stable and diversified earnings stream for the holding company enables it to act as a source of strength in keeping the affiliated bank well capitalized.

In the academic literature, a number of empirical studies have evaluated the gains from bank activity diversification by looking at the correlations of accounting earnings for segmented financial firms or industries and analyzing correlations between firms' stock market returns. Essentially, the lower these correlations, the greater the potential gains from activity diversification and the lower the coefficient of variation (COV)—the standard deviation divided by the mean—of a banking organization's earnings flows. Other studies have sought to evaluate the potential effects of activity diversification on the risk of failure (ROF) of banks and simulate the effects of bank–nonbank mergers (MS) on bank risk. We summarize the findings of a number of these COV, ROF, and MS studies in Table 21–2.

As you can see from Table 21–2, the majority of the studies find that a financial services holding company's risk could be reduced by diversification. However, the optimal proportion of investment in individual nonbank product lines often falls in the 5 to 25 percent range. This suggests that excessive product expansion in some nonbank lines could actually increase the total risk exposure of a banking organization.

In addition to the potential risk-reducing gains of product diversification, by diversifying its earnings stream geographically, a holding company can generate

product diversification benefit
Stabilization of earnings and profits resulting from a well-diversified financial services holding company.

[24] Recognizing that allowing banking organizations to expand their securities activities may lead to more risk in the banking system, the Financial Services Modernization Act of 1999 explicitly incorporated provisions regarding the way the new financial services holding companies would be regulated. For example, the act streamlines bank holding company supervision by clarifying the regulatory roles of the Federal Reserve as the umbrella holding company supervisor, and the state and federal financial regulators that "functionally" regulate various affiliates. It provides for federal bank regulators to prescribe prudential safeguards for bank organizations engaging in new financial activities. It provides for state regulation of insurance, subject to a standard that no state may discriminate against persons affiliated with a bank. Finally, the act prohibits FDIC assistance to affiliates and subsidiaries of banks and savings institutions.

TABLE 21–2   Review of Selected Studies of the Risk of Nonbank Activities*

Study	Time Period	Methodology[†]	Nonbank Activities Reduce BHC Risk
Johnson and Meinster (1974)	1954–69 (annual data)	COV	Yes. Impermissible activities: insurance agents and brokers, portfolio holding and investment companies, and real estate agents, analysis brokers and managers. Studies 13 activities. Portfolio analysis based on earnings and cash flow concludes there are diversification benefits into nonbank activities but that the benefits are sensitive to the percentage of assets in each activity.
Heggestad (1975)	1953–67	COV	Yes. Impermissible activities: insurance agents and brokers, and real estate agents, brokers, managers, holding, and investment companies, and lessors of R.R., oil, and mining properties. Banking is among the riskiest activities based on the coefficient of variation in profits. [Studies activities of one bank holding company (BHC) prior to 1970 BHC Act amendments.]
Eiseman (1976)	1961–68 (monthly data)	Industry (portfolio) selection model (COV)	Yes. Banking is minimum-risk activity. Lowest-risk BHC includes permissible activity of sales finance and impermissible activities of insurance and investment banking. Highest-risk BHC includes permissible activity of data processing. Studies 20 activities.
Jessee and Seelig (1977)		COV	No. Risk reduction is not related to share of nonbank investment.
Meinster and Johnson (1979)	1973–77	ROF	Yes. BHCs effectively diversified but slightly increased probability of capital impairment with debt financing. (Sample of only two BHCs in seven permissible activities of leasing, consumer finance, mortgage banking, bank management consulting, financial services, and foreign bank services.)
Boyd, Hanweek, and Pithyachanyakul (1980)	1971–77	COV/ROF	Yes, but limited. Permissible activities: mortgage banking, factoring, consumer finance, credit card, loan servicing, investment advisers, leasing (except auto), community welfare, data processing, credit life, accident and health insurance agents, and underwriters and management consulting.

No (any investment increases probability of bankruptcy). Permissible activities: commercial and sales finance, industrial banks, trust services, auto leasing. (Study covered only permissible activities.) |
| Stover (1982) | 1959–68 | Wealth-maximization debt capacity | Yes. Impermissible activities: S&Ls, investment banking, land development, fire and casualty insurance. Measures equity returns and diversification benefits of 14 permissible and impermissible activities in wealth-maximization model. |

TABLE 21–2   (*continued*)

Study	Time Period	Methodology[†]	Nonbank Activities Reduce BHC Risk
Wall and Eisenbeis (1984)	1970–80	COV	Yes. Impermissible activities: S&Ls, security brokers and dealers, life insurance, general merchandise stores, lessor of R.R. property. Permissible activities personal and business credit agency. Banking neither highest nor lowest risk based on coefficient of variation. Results are sensitive to time period.
Wall (1984)	Select dates	Bond returns	No significant effect.
Wall and Eisenbeis (1984)	Select dates (monthly data)	Bond returns	No. (Study covered only permissible activity of discount brokerage.)
Litan (1985)	1978–83	COV	As likely to reduce volatility of BHC income as to increase it. (Sample of 31 large BHCs.)
Boyd and Graham (1986)	1971–83 (1971–77 and 1978–83)	ROF	Entire period: no significant relationship between nonbank activity and any risk or return measures. Less stringent policy period (1971–77): no nonbank activity is positively related to risk. More stringent policy period (1978–83): weak negative relationship between nonbank activity and risk.
Wall (1986)	1976–84	ROF	Nonbank activity either decreases BHC risk slightly or has no impact. The positive relationship between nonbank risk and BHC risk, BHC leverage, and bank risk is consistent with the possibility that management preferences influence the riskiness of the BHC's subsidiaries and determine the use of leverage to influence overall risk.
Boyd and Graham (1988)	1971–84 (annual data)	COV/ROF/MS	Study covers six impermissible activities. Yes for life insurance. The standard deviation and bankruptcy risk measures indicate risk is likely to increase for real estate development, securities firms, and property-casualty insurance activities and increase slightly for other real estate and insurance agency and brokerage activities. BHC is lowest-risk activity.
Brewer (1988)	1979–85	COV	Yes. One standard deviation increase in investment in nonbank subsidiaries leads to 6-basis-point drop in BHC risk (approximately 7 percent).
Brewer (1988)	1979–83 (daily data)	COV	Yes. One standard deviation increase in investment in nonbank subsidiaries leads to an 8 to 11 percent basis point drop in BHC risk. Results are sensitive to the time period studied.
Brewer, Fortier, and Pavel (1988)	1980, 1982 and 1986 and 1979–83	COV/MS	Yes. Impermissible activities of insurance agents and brokers, property and casualty and life insurance underwriting. Investment of 5 percent or less for any of the tested activities would not increase the variance of the BHC significantly;

(*continued*)

TABLE 21–2 Review of Selected Studies of the Risk of Nonbank Activities* (*concluded*)

Study	Time Period	Methodology[†]	Nonbank Activities Reduce BHC Risk
			the investment of 25 percent or more for all but the above-listed activities would increase the riskiness of the BHC significantly. Examination of the impact of total investment in nonbank activities regardless of the specific activities finds increases in nonbank activity tend to lower BHC risk significantly.
Wall, Reichart, and Mohanty (1993)	1981–89	COV	Yes, for insurance and real estate. The securities brokerage industry does not enter the efficient portfolio.
Saunders and Walter(1994)	1984–88	COV/MS	Yes. Looks at 250,000 possible merger combinations among the largest FIs in the United States. Finds that a full multiple activity universal bank with optimal investments in different financial service activities can lower risk by as much as one-third compared to specialized banks.
Berger, Demsetz, and Strahan (1999)	1985–97	MS	Yes. Looks at ability to diversify bank risk after a merger or acquisition.
Fields and Fraser (1999)	1992	ROF	Yes. Looks at moral hazard risk reduction as banks enter securities underwriting.
Cornett, Ors, and Tehranian (2002)	1987–97	COV	No significant effect. Looks at commercial bank entry into underwriting.
Roten and Mullineaux (2002)	1995–1998	MS	No. Finds only limited evidence that commercial bank Section 20 subsidiaries perform differently from investment banks.

*Permissible activities refer to those nonbank activities currently permissible, whether or not they were permissible at the time of the study. Impermissible activities also include activities not yet ruled upon by the Board at the time of the study.
[†]COV—analysis of coefficient of variation of rates of return of banking and nonbanking activities.
ROF—risk of failure (bankruptcy analysis).
MS—simulated merger analysis.

Source: From "Bank Risk from Nonbank Activities," by E. Brewer, D. Fortier, and C. Pavel, in *Economic Perspective*, July–August 1988, pp. 14–26; A. Saunders and I. Walter, *Universal Banking in the U.S.?* (New York: Oxford University Press, 1994), chapter 6; and author's research.

additional risk reduction gains when there are regional imperfections in the costs of raising debt and equity (see Chapter 22).

Economies of Scale and Scope

A second issue concerning the expansion of banks into securities and other nonbank activities is the potential for additional economies of scale and scope. As we discuss in Chapter 14, there appear to be economy of scale opportunities for financial firms up to $25 billion in asset size. However, most studies find cost-based economies of scope are negligible, although revenue-based economies of scope may arise for the largest FIs. Arguably, the pre-1997 restrictions between banks and their Section 20 investment banking affiliates covering finance, management and cross marketing severely limited economies of scope and related revenue and cost synergies. Post-1997, and more so, post-1999 U.S. financial service firms may realize greater economies of scope as restrictions are removed and the FSHCs become more universal in product scope.[25]

Conflicts of Interest

A third issue—the potential for conflicts of interest—lies at the very heart of opposition to an expansion of banking powers into other financial service areas. Indeed, concerns regarding conflicts of interest provided the main foundation for the passage of the Glass-Steagall Act in 1933.[26] The two principal questions that arise are (1) the potential conflicts of interest arising from the expansion of banks' securities activities and (2) the type of incentive structures that change *potential* conflicts into *actual* conflicts.

Six Potential Conflicts of Interest

Conflicts of interest that arise when commercial banks, investment banks, and insurance companies combine operations have been prominent in U.S. financial markets throughout the early 2000s. Several high-profile legal violations as well as a loss of investor confidence rocked Wall Street and the financial services industry. In this section, we discuss the six most common potential conflicts of interest identified by regulators and academics.[27]

Salesperson's Stake   Critics argue that when banks have the power to sell non-bank products, bank employees no longer dispense dispassionate advice to their customers about which product to buy. Instead, they have a salesperson's stake in pushing the bank's own products, often to the disadvantage of the customer. For example, in 2002, Citigroup was under investigation from securities regulators, who were investigating whether Citigroup's stock research was tainted and whether its transactions with corporations and top corporate executives illegally helped the firm win lucrative underwriting contracts. Similarly, Goldman Sachs was under investigation as a result of e-mails written by two of its telecom-sector analysts in which they candidly discuss how investment-banking considerations influenced how many telecom stocks they were recommending in mid-2000 even as the stocks' prices were plummeting. Finally, several commercial/investment banks (such as Credit Suisse First Boston) were charged with "spinning" initial public offerings of stock to executives and directors of companies to induce them to provide corporate business to the commercial bank arm of the financial institution.

Stuffing Fiduciary Accounts   Suppose a bank is acting as a securities underwriter and is unable to place these securities in a public offering. To avoid being exposed

---

[25] See T. F. Huertas, "Redesigning Regulation: The Future of Finance in the United States," Jackson Hole, Wyoming, August 22, 1987, mimeographed; and J. R. Barth, R. D. Brumbaugh Jr., and J. A. Wilcox, "The Repeal of Glass-Steagall and the Advent of Broad Banking," Office of the Comptroller of the Currency, Economic and Policy Analysis Working Paper 2000–5, April 2000. Nevertheless, Saunders and Walter, *Universal Banking,* could find no evidence of cost economies of scope for the world's 100 largest banks, many of which are universal banks.

[26] See Benson, *The Separation of Commercial and Investment Banking.*

[27] See A. Saunders, "Conflicts of Interest: An Economic View," in *Deregulating Wall Street,* ed. I. Walter (New York: John Wiley & Sons, 1985), pp. 207–30; M. Puri, "Commercial Banks in Investment Banking: Conflict of Interest or Certification Role?" *Journal of Financial Economics* 40 (1996), pp. 373–401; I. Walter, "Conflicts of Interest in Merger Advisory Services," Working Paper, New York University, January 2004; L. Allen, J. Jagtiani, S. Peristiani, and A. Saunders, "The Role of Commercial Bank Advisors in Mergers and Acquisitions," *Journal of Money, Credit, and Banking,* forthcoming; S. Baharath, S. Dahiya, A. Saunders, and A. Srinivasan, "So What Do I Get? The Bank's View of Lending Relationships," Working Paper, New York University, 2004; and L. Allen and S. Peristiani, "Conflicts of Interest in Merger Advisory Services," Working Paper, Baruch College, CUNY, January 2004.

to potential losses, the bank may "stuff" these unwanted securities in accounts managed by its own trust department and over which it has discretionary investment powers. For example, a federal judge threw money manager Alan Bond, CIO of Albriond Capital, in jail after he was convicted on charges of allocating winning trades to his own brokerage account and saddling his clients' accounts with losers.

Bankruptcy Risk Transference   Assume that a bank has a loan outstanding to a firm whose credit or bankruptcy risk has increased to the private knowledge of the banker. With this private knowledge, the banker may have an incentive to induce the firm to issue bonds underwritten by the bank's securities affiliate to an unsuspecting public. The proceeds of this bond issue could then be used to pay down the bank loan. As a result, the bank would have transferred the borrowing firm's credit risk from itself to less-informed outside investors, while the securities affiliate also earned an underwriting fee. For example, in 2002 J. P. Morgan Chase and Citigroup faced several investor lawsuits over funding deals for high-profile bankruptcies such as Enron and WorldCom. Investors say that because of their lending relationships, the banks knew or should have known of the problems at these companies when they sold the firms' bonds to the public.

Third-Party Loans   To ensure that an underwriting goes well, a bank may make cheap loans to third-party investors on the implicit condition that this loan is used to purchase securities underwritten by its securities affiliate.

Tie-Ins   A bank may use its lending powers to coerce or "tie in" a customer to the products sold by its securities affiliate. For example, the bank may threaten to credit ration unless the customer agrees to let the bank's securities affiliate do its securities underwritings. In the early 2000s, J. P. Morgan Chase poured money into the telecommunications and cable businesses, not expecting to make much money on the loans themselves. Rather, it anticipated a huge payback from investment banking business these firms would send its way.

Information Transfer   In acting as a lender, the bank may become privy to certain inside information about its customers or rivals that it can use to set the prices, or help the distribution of securities offerings by its affiliate. This information could also flow from the securities affiliate to the bank. Such conflicts are potentially present when M&A activity is involved along with new security issues and loan originations.[28] Such was the case with J. P. Morgan Chase and Citigroup, FIs involved as lead advisors *and* lead bankers in Enron's failed merger attempt with Dynegy in 2001. The two FIs had large balance sheets and boasted of their ability to provide both loans and advice in the merger. However, the FIs lost their bragging rights for pulling off a difficult deal as Dynegy pulled out of the merger stating they were deprived of enough information on the deal and then learning that Enron had been hiding billions of dollars in debt and had been reporting exaggerated profits for years. Enron ended up declaring bankruptcy in December 2001 and J. P. Morgan Chase and Citigroup ended up losing between $800 and $900 million each on loans to Enron.

Potential Conflicts of Interest and Their Actual Exploitation

On their own, and unquestionably accepted, these conflicts appear to be extremely troublesome. Remember, however, that specific and general checks and balances limit their exploitation. Many of these conflicts are likely to remain potential rather

---

[28] L. Allen, J. Jagtiani, and A. Saunders, in "The Role of Bank Advisors in Mergers and Acquisitions," *Journal of Money, Credit, and Banking*, forthcoming, find that, in their merger and acquisition advisory function the certification effect of commercial banks dominates the conflict-of-interest effect. See also L. Allen and S. Peristiani, "Conflicts of Interest in Merger Advisory Services," 2004 Working Paper, for evidence on this type of conflict of interest.

Chinese wall
An internally imposed barrier within an organization that limits the flow of confidential client information among departments or areas.

than become actual conflicts of interest. Specifically, many of these conflicts, such as tie-ins and third-party loans, breach existing bank regulations and laws.[29] Also, internal barriers or **Chinese walls** in most banks prohibit internal information transfers when they potentially conflict with the best interests of the customer. Further, sales of debt issues to a less-informed public to pay down bank loans may result in future lawsuits against the underwriter once investors discover their losses.[30]

More generally, conflicts of interest are exploitable only under three conditions. First, markets for bank services are uncompetitive so that banks have monopoly power over their customers, for example, in making loans. Second, information flows between the customer and the bank are imperfect or asymmetric so that the bank possesses an information advantage over its customers. Third, the bank places a relatively low value on its reputation. The discovery of having exploited a conflict can result in considerable market and regulatory penalties.[31] Nevertheless, as noted above, in recent years some banks, such as the former Nationsbank, have been subject to a number of lawsuits alleging overzealous selling tactics and incomplete information disclosure that amount to conflicts of interest.

Deposit Insurance

A traditional argument against expanded powers is that the explicit and implicit protection given to banks by deposit insurance coverage give banks a competitive advantage over other financial service firms (see Chapter 19). For example, because bank deposits up to $100,000 are covered by explicit deposit insurance, banks are able to raise funds at subsidized, lower-cost rates than are available to traditional securities firms. This may allow them to pass on these lower costs in cheaper loans to their affiliates. However, since the Financial Service Modernization Act allowed other financial service firms such as Merrill Lynch to establish banks that offer deposit insurance coverage, this explicit subsidy advantage has largely been removed. Nevertheless, there still may be an *indirect* deposit insurance–related advantage to banking organizations undertaking securities activities compared to traditional securities firms. This advantage may result if bank regulators regard certain large banking organizations as being too-big-to-fail (TBTF), thereby encouraging these institutions to take excessive risks such as placing aggressive underwriting bids for new issues. This situation would limit the underwriting shares of traditional investment banks, especially as TBTF guarantees do not appear to exist for them—as shown by the failure of Drexel Burnham Lambert in February 1990. Consequently, TBTF guarantees tend to give banks some unfair competitive advantages as long as TBTF bailouts are potentially possible.[32]

---

[29] Involuntary tie-ins are illegal under various sections of the Clayton Act, the Sherman Antitrust Act, and the Bank Holding Company Act.

[30] In particular, the underwriter may be accused of lack of due diligence in not disclosing information in the new issue's prospectus.

[31] R. G. Rajan models these incentives in "A Theory of the Costs and Benefits of Universal Banking," C. R. S. P. Working Paper no. 346, University of Chicago, 1992. See also G. Kanatas and J. Qi, "Underwriting by Commercial Banks: Conflicts of Interest vs. Scope Economics," *Journal of Money, Credit, and Banking,* February 1998, pp. 119–133. For an assessment of the reputational costs of exploiting conflicts of interest, see R. Smith and I. Walter, *Street Smarts: Leadership, Conduct and Shareholder Value in the Securities Industry* (Boston: Harvard Business School Press, 1997).

[32] This point has also been made with respect to bank sales of mutual funds. See E. J. Kane, "What Is the Value-Added Large U.S. Banks Find in Offering Mutual Funds?" Working Paper, Boston College, November 1994. One way to reduce this problem would be to subject uninsured depositors in a TBTF bailout to a loss (or haircut). This would create incentives for them to impose market discipline on even the biggest banks (see Federal Reserve Bank of Minneapolis, Annual Report 1997, "Fixing FDICIA: A Plan to Address the Too-Big-To-Fail Problem"). Nevertheless, as described in Chapters 19 and 20, the ability of regulators to pursue TBTF bailouts has been severely restricted by the provisions of the FDICIA of 1991.

Regulatory Oversight

www.federalreserve.
gov
www.occ.treas.gov
www.fdic.gov
www.sec.gov

Currently, most bank holding companies with extensive nonbank subsidiaries face a diffuse and multilayered regulatory structure that would potentially hinder the monitoring and control of conflicts of interest abuses and excessive risk taking as banks are allowed to expand their securities activities further. Specifically, for a financial services holding company such as J. P. Morgan Chase, the Federal Reserve is the primary regulator. For its bank subsidiary, the Office of the Comptroller of the Currency, which is the charterer of national banks, shares regulatory oversight with the Federal Reserve and the FDIC. For its securities subsidiary, the primary regulator is the SEC, although the Federal Reserve also has some oversight powers. It is far from clear that such a complex and overlapping regulatory structure is efficient from a public policy perspective.[33] This is the case because it can lead to waste of monitoring and surveillance resources as well as unnecessary fights over bureaucratic turf. Furthermore, coordination problems can weaken monitoring and surveillance efficiency, especially in an economic downturn. Thus, a case can be made for subsuming all regulatory power in a single regulatory body as banks' securities powers are extended further.[34]

To make matters even murkier, in early 2004 Eliot Spitzer, the attorney general of the state of New York, filed a lawsuit challenging the federal regulation of national banks as they interact with consumers. The suit, filed in New York State Supreme Court, was submitted on behalf of a consumer who alleged wrongdoing by a subsidiary of First Tennessee National Corp., a nationally chartered bank. The case is destined to attract attention because it is aimed squarely at challenging assertions made by the Office of the Comptroller of the Currency in late 2003 that it alone has the right to regulate nationally chartered banks. Rules enacted at the beginning of 2004 gave the OCC sole right to regulate national banks and excluded states from any oversight powers. Consumer groups allege that a complaint to the OCC's consumer division in some states typically takes 60 days to be processed. Foreclosure proceedings often occur as quickly as 30 days. The case is likely to be headed to the U.S. Supreme Court.

Competition

The final issue concerns the effects of bank activity expansions on competition in investment banking product lines. In securities underwriting, there are three primary factors for believing that bank expansions would enhance competition. One factor is cited as a reason that it would do the reverse; that is, bank expansion would increase both market concentration and the monopoly power of commercial banks over customers.

---

[33] In the context of allowing banks to expand into insurance activities (as in the Citigroup case), the problem of aligning the differences between (largely) federal bank regulations and state-based insurance regulations would have to be faced as well.

[34] Despite numerous attempts in recent years to reform and rationalize the regulatory structure through Congress, none has been successful. For a criticism of the structure of U.S. regulation, see General Accounting Office, "Bank Oversight Structure," GAO/GGO–97–23, November 1997. J. R. Barth, D. E. Nolle, T. Phumiwasana, and G. Yago find little support, at best, to the belief that any particular bank supervisory structure will greatly affect bank performance. They suggest that the ongoing debate might more broadly focus on the impact of the supervisory structure on other aspects of the health of the banking system, including individual bank safety and soundness, systemic stability, and the development of the banking system. See "A Cross-Country Analysis of the Bank Supervisory Framework and Bank Performance," *Financial Markets, Institutions & Instruments*, May 2003, pp. 67–120.

Procompetitive Effects

The three factors supporting a procompetitive effect of banks' expansion of their securities activities are in the following sections.

Increased Capital Market Access for Small Firms   Most large investment banks are headquartered in New York and the Northeast. As a result, small U.S. firms based in the Midwest and Southwest have often had a more difficult time accessing national capital markets than have firms of a similar size in the Northeast. Consequently, the entry of regional and superregional banks into securities underwriting through securities affiliates could potentially expand the national capital market access of smaller firms.[35]

Lower Commissions and Fees   Increased competition for securities underwritings should reduce the underwriter's spread. That is, it should reduce the spread between the new issue bid price paid to the issuing firm and the offer price at which those securities are resold to the market. This potentially raises the amount of new issue proceeds for the issuing firm by raising the underwriter's bid price. (Such an effect was claimed when banks expanded their municipal bond underwritings, although this has been disputed.)[36] In recent years, the spreads on investment-grade debt underwritings fell from approximately 78 basis points in 1986 to 36 basis points in 2000. Similarly, the spread on equity underwritings fell from 334 basis points in 1986 to 224 basis points in 1996. However, as the stock market declined in the early 2000s, this spread increased again to 395 basis points.[37] In the early 2000s, banks' securities subsidiaries had almost a 60 percent share of new issue underwritings of debt and equity. Indeed, in 2003 Citigroup's securities subsidiary Salomon Smith Barney led the industry in investment grade debt underwriting, with $148 billion more underwritten than its closest competitior Morgan Stanley and far exceeding Merrill Lynch (an investment bank), which had been the top securities underwriter for most of the 1990s. There is some empirical evidence to support the view that part of the reason for the decline in debt underwriting spreads is due to enhanced competition to underwrite securities issues emanating from the entry of banks' securities subsidiaries into this market.[38]

---

[35] Some support for this can be found in A. Gande, M. Puri, A. Saunders, and I. Walter, "Bank Underwriting of Debt Securities: Modern Evidence," *Review of Financial Studies* 10, no. 4 (1997), pp. 1175–1201. They found that the size of debt issues underwritten by Section 20 subsidiaries was significantly smaller than those underwritten by investment banks in the early years of Section 20 subsidiary underwriting. More recent studies, e.g., I. C. Roten and D. J. Mullineaux, question the persistence of such benefits over the more recent 1995–1998 period ("Debt Underwriting by Commercial Bank-Affiliated Firms and Investment Banks: More Evidence," *Journal of Banking and Finance*, 2002, pp. 689–718). For Canadian evidence, see G. M. Hebb and D. R. Fraser, "Conflict of Interest in Commercial Bank Security Underwriting: Canadian Evidence," *Journal of Banking and Finance*, 2002, pp. 1935–49.

[36] For a review of this debate and the evidence, see W. L. Silber, "Municipal Revenue Bond Costs and Bank Underwriting: A Survey of the Evidence," Monograph Series in Finance and Economics, Salomon Center for the Study of Financial Institutions, New York University, 1979. For recent evidence, see A. Saunders and R. Stover, "Commercial Bank Underwriting of Credit-Enhanced Banks: Are There Certification Benefits to the Issuer?" *Journal of International Money and Finance*, forthcoming.

[37] See A. Gande, M. Puri, and A. Saunders, "Bank Entry, Competition and the Market for Corporate Securities Underwriting," *Journal of Financial Economics* 54 (1999), pp. 165–95. See also "Banks Push into Securities Squeezes Fees," *The Wall Street Journal*, December 16, 1997.

[38] See "Into the Crucible," *Investment Dealers Digest,* June 11, 2001.

Reduce the Degree of Underpricing of New Issues   The greatest risk to the underwriter is to price a new issue too high relative to the market's valuation of that security. That is, underwriters stand to lose when they overprice new issues. Given this, underwriters have an incentive to underprice new issues by setting the public offer price (OP) below the price established for the security in the secondary market once trading begins (P). The investment banker stands to gain by underpricing as it increases the probability of selling out the issue without affecting the fixed underwriting spread. That is, a spread of $.50 at a bid-offer price spread of $93 and $93.50 produces the same gross revenue (spread) of $.50 per share to the underwriter as a bid-offer price spread of $97 and $97.50. The major difference is that a lower offer price (i.e., $93 rather than $97) increases the demand for the shares by investors and the probability of selling the whole issue to the public very quickly. Both the underwriter and the outside investor may benefit from underpricing; the loser is the firm issuing the securities because it obtains lower proceeds than if the offer price had been set at a higher price reflecting a more accurate market valuation. In this example, the issuer receives only $93 per share rather than $97. Consequently, underpricing new issues is an additional cost of securities issuance borne by issuing firms. Most empirical research on the underpricing of U.S. new issues, or **initial public offerings (IPOs),** has found that they are underpriced in the range of 8 to 48 percent depending on the sample and time period chosen.[39] In contrast, **secondary issues** tend to be underpriced by less than 3 percent.[40]

If a major cause of IPO underpricing is a lack of competition among existing investment banks, then bank entry and competition should lower the degree of underpricing and increase the new issue proceeds for firms. Nevertheless, many economists argue that monopoly power is not the primary reason for the underpricing of new issues; in their view, underpricing reflects a risk premium that must be paid to investors and investment bankers for information imperfections. That is, underpricing is a risk premium for the information advantage possessed by issuers who better know the true quality of their firm's securities and its assets.[41] If this is so, bank entry into securities underwriting may only reduce the degree of underpricing to the extent that it reduces the degree of information imperfection among issuers and investors. This might reasonably be expected given the specialized role of banks as delegated monitors (see Chapter 1).[42]

Anticompetitive Effects

While bank entry may be procompetitive in the short term, there still exists considerable concern about potential anticompetitive behavior in the long term. The biggest banking organizations, measured by either capital or assets, are many times larger than the biggest securities firms—or insurance firms, for that matter (see Table 21–1). The largest bank organizations may aggressively compete for

IPO (initial public offering)
A corporate equity or debt security offered to the public for the first time through an underwriter.

secondary issues
A new issue of equity or debt of firms whose securities are already traded in the market.

---

[39] See the review of some 20 studies of underpricing by A. Saunders, "Why Are So Many Stock Issues Underpriced?" Federal Reserve Bank of Philadelphia, *Business Review,* March–April 1990, pp. 3–12.

[40] See C. F. Loderer, D. P. Sheehan, and G. B. Kadler, "The Pricing of Equity Offerings," *Journal of Financial Economics,* 1991, pp. 35–37.

[41] See F. Beatty and J. Ritter, "Investment Banking, Reputation, and the Underpricing of Initial Public Offerings," *Journal of Financial Economics* 15 (1986), pp. 213–32; and K. Rock, "Why New Issues Are Underpriced," *Journal of Financial Economics* 15 (1986), pp. 187–212.

[42] However, firewalls limited the efficiency with which the delegated monitor can transfer information to its affiliate. See M. Puri, "Conflicts of Interest, Intermediation and the Pricing of Underwritten Securities," *Journal of Financial Economics,* October 1999, pp. 133–64.

business in the short run, trying to force traditional investment banks out of business. If successful, they would assume quasi-oligopoly positions, market concentration may rise, and in the long run prices for investment banking services would rise rather than fall. Such a long-run outcome would outweigh any short-term procompetitive benefits.[43]

Concept Questions

1. What are some of the issues that tend to arise in response to bank expansion into securities, insurance, and commercial activities?
2. Explain how firm commitment underwriting of securities is similar to writing put options on assets.
3. Describe three ways in which the losses of a securities affiliate in a holding company structure could be transmitted to a bank.
4. In addition to the six potential conflicts of interest discussed in this section, can you think of any additional possible conflicts that might arise if commercial banks were allowed to expand their investment banking activities?
5. What are three potential procompetitive effects cited in support of banks' expansion into securities activities? What reason is given to support the opposite claim (i.e., that bank expansion would not enhance competition)?

Summary

Traditionally, the U.S. financial system has been structured on segmented product lines. Unlike most other countries, until 1999 commercial banking, investment banking, and insurance activities have been separated by several legislative acts, including the Glass-Steagall Act of 1933 and the Bank Holding Company Act of 1956. These restrictions on product or activity expansion have had some significant costs. Most important has been the loss of potential risk-reducing gains that arise from both regional and product diversification, as well as gains from the potential generation of cost and revenue synergies. However, a set of important public policy or social welfare concerns relate to conflicts of interest, safety and soundness, competition, and regulation. Nevertheless, in recent years, there has been a dramatic breakdown in many of the regulatory barriers to financial service conglomeration culminating with the Financial Services Modernization Act of 1999. The act allowed the creation of a financial service holding company that could engage in banking activities *and* securities underwriting and insurance. As a result, the U.S. financial system is rapidly converging toward a "universal banking"–type system. In such a system, bank, insurance, and securities products are increasingly cross-sold by large conglomerate (universal) financial service firms with the objective of maximizing revenue and cost synergies and reducing risk through diversification.

Questions and Problems

1. How does product segmentation reduce the risks of FIs? How does it increase the risks of FIs?
2. In what ways have other FIs taken advantage of the restrictions on product diversification imposed on commercial banks?

---

[43] One possible reason for slow development of the German corporate bond market is that German universal banks wish to preserve their monopoly power over corporate debt. This may best be done by encouraging corporate loans rather than bond issues.

3. How does product segmentation reduce the profitability of FIs? How does product segmentation increase the profitability of FIs?

4. What general prohibition regarding the activities of commercial banking and investment banking did the Glass-Steagall Act impose? What investment banking activities have been permitted for U.S. commercial banks?

5. What restrictions were placed on Section 20 subsidiaries of U.S. commercial banks that made investment banking activities other than those permitted by the Glass-Steagall Act less attractive? How does this differ from banking activities in other countries?

6. A Section 20 subsidiary of a major U.S. bank is planning to underwrite corporate securities and expects to generate $5 million in revenues. It currently underwrites U.S. Treasury securities and general obligation municipal bonds, earning annual fees of $40 million.

    a. Is the bank in compliance with the current laws regulating the revenue generation of Section 20 subsidiaries? With the laws in place prior to 1999?

    b. The bank plans to increase its private placement activities and expects to generate $11 million in revenue. Is it in compliance with the revenue generation requirements?

    c. If it plans to increase underwriting of corporate securities and generate $11 million in revenues, is it in compliance? If not, what should it do to ensure that it is in compliance?

7. Explain in general terms what impact the Financial Services Modernization Act of 1999 should have on the strategic implementation of Section 20 activities.

8. The Garn-St Germain Act of 1982 and several subsequent banking laws clearly established the separation of banking and insurance firms. What were the likely reasons for this separation?

9. What types of insurance products were commercial banks permitted to offer before 1997? How did the Financial Services Modernization Act of 1999 change this?

10. How have nonbanks managed to exploit the loophole in the Bank Holding Company Act of 1956 and engage in banking activities? What law closed this loophole? How did insurance companies circumvent this law?

11. The Financial Services Modernization Act of 1999 allows banks to own controlling interests in nonfinancial companies. What are the two restrictions on such ownership?

12. What are the restrictions on the structure of a financial services holding company as specified by the Financial Services Modernization Act of 1999?

13. What are the differences in the risk implications of a firm commitment securities offering versus a best-efforts offering?

14. An FI is underwriting the sales of 1 million shares of Ultrasonics, Inc., and is quoting a bid–ask price of $6.00–6.50.

    a. What are the fees earned by the FI if a firm commitment method is used to underwrite the securities?

    b. What are the fees if it uses the best-efforts method and a commission of 50 basis points is charged?

    c. How would your answer be affected if it manages to sell the shares only at $5.50 using the firm commitment method? The commission for best efforts is still 50 basis points.

15. What is the maximum possible underwriter's fee on both the best-efforts and firm commitment underwriting contracts on an issue of 12 million shares at a bid price of $12.45 and an offer price of $12.60? What is the maximum possible loss? The best-efforts underwriting commission is 75 basis points.

16. A Section 20 affiliate agrees to underwrite a debt issue for one of its clients. It has suggested a firm commitment offering for issuing 100,000 shares of stock. The bank quotes a bid–ask spread of $97–$97.50 to its customers on the issue date.

    a. What are the total underwriting fees generated if all the issue is sold? If only 60 percent is sold?

    b. Instead of taking a chance that only 60 percent of the shares will be sold on the issue date, a bank suggests a price of $95 to the issuing firm. It expects to quote a bid–ask spread of $95–$95.40 and sell 100 percent of the issue. From the FI's perspective, which price is better if it expects to sell the remaining 40 percent at the bid price of $97 under the first quote?

17. What are the reasons why the upside returns from firm commitment securities offerings are not symmetrical in regard to the downside risk? How is underwriting on a firm commitment basis similar to writing a put option on a firm's assets?

18. What are three ways that the failure of a securities affiliate in a holding company organizational form could negatively affect a bank? How has the Fed attempted to prevent a breakdown of the firewalls between banks and affiliates in these situations?

19. What are two operational strategies to reduce the risk to the safety and soundness of a bank resulting from the failure of a securities affiliate or many other types of financial distress?

20. What do empirical studies reveal about the effect of activity diversification on the risk of failure of banks?

21. What role does bank activity diversification play in the ability of a bank to exploit economies of scale and scope? What remains as the limitation to creating potentially greater benefits?

22. What six conflicts of interest have been identified as potential roadblocks to the expansion of banking powers into the financial services area?

23. What are some of the legal, institutional, and market conditions that lessen the likelihood that an FI can exploit conflicts of interest from the expansion of commercial banks into other financial service areas?

24. Under what circumstances could the existence of deposit insurance provide an advantage to banks in competing with other traditional securities firms?

25. In what ways does the current regulatory structure argue against providing additional securities powers to the banking industry? Does this issue just concern banks?

26. What are the potential procompetitive effects of allowing banks to enter more fully into securities underwriting? What is the anticompetitive argument or position?

Web Question

27. Go to the Board of Governors of the Federal Reserve Web site at **www.federalreserve.gov**. Locate the organizational structure of the two largest U.S. commercial bank holding companies using the following steps. Click on "Banking Information and Regulation." Click on "National Information Center." Click on "Top 50 BHCs/Banks." Click on the top listed (largest) bank holding company. Click on "Institution Organization Hierarchy." Click on "Submit." Click on "Display *Complete Summary Hierarchy Report* for the selected institution." This will download a file onto your computer that will contain the most recent information on the organizational structure of the largest bank. Repeat these steps for the second listed (largest) bank holding company. Compare the organizational structure of the two institutions.

Pertinent Web Sites

Board of Governors of the Federal Reserve	**www.federalreserve.gov**
Credit Suisse Group	**www.credit-suisse.com**
Federal Deposit Insurance Corporation	**www.fdic.gov**
Office of the Comptroller of the Currency	**www.occ.treas.gov**
Securities and Exchange Commission	**www.sec.gov**

Appendix 21A

EU and G-10 Countries: Regulatory Treatment of the Mixing of Banking, Securities, and Insurance Activities and the Mixing of Banking and Commerce

View Appendix 21A at the Web site for this textbook (**www.mhhe.com/saunders5e**).

Chapter **Twenty-Two**

Geographic Diversification: Domestic

INTRODUCTION

Just as product expansion (see Chapter 21) may enable an FI to reduce risk and increase returns, so may geographic expansion. Geographic expansions can have a number of dimensions. In particular, they can be either domestic within a state or region or international by participating in a foreign market. Expansions can also be effected through opening a new office or branch or by acquiring another FI. This chapter traces the potential benefits and costs to the risk management strategies considered by FI managers from domestic geographic expansion—especially through mergers and acquisitions. Chapter 23 then considers international or cross-border expansions. In particular, we look at the reasons underlying the current merger wave among U.S. financial service firms that is dramatically changing and consolidating the structure of the U.S. financial system. In addition, we present some evidence on the cost and revenue synergies as well as other market and firm-specific factors impacting geographic expansion.

DOMESTIC EXPANSIONS

de novo office
A newly established office.

In the United States, the ability of FIs to expand domestically has historically been constrained by regulation. By comparison, no special regulations have inhibited the ability of commercial firms such as General Motors, IBM, and Sears from establishing new or **de novo offices,** factories, or branches anywhere in the country. Nor have commercial firms been prohibited from acquiring other firms—as long as they are not banks. While securities firms and insurance companies have faced relatively few restrictions in expanding their business domestically, other FIs, especially banks, have faced a complex and changing network of rules and regulations. While such regulations may inhibit expansions, they also create potential opportunities to increase an FI's returns. In particular, regulations may create locally uncompetitive markets with monopoly economic rents that new entrants can potentially exploit. Thus, for the most innovative FIs, regulation can provide profit opportunities as well as costs. As a result, regulation both inhibits and creates incentives to engage in geographic expansions.[1]

In addition, the economic factors that impact commercial firm expansion and acquisition decisions are likely to impact the decisions of FIs as well. Two major groups of factors are cost and revenue synergies and firm/market-specific attractions, such as the specialized skills of an acquired firm's employees and the markets of the firm to be acquired. Thus, the attractiveness of a geographic expansion, whether through acquisition, branching, or opening a new office, depends on a broad set of factors encompassing

1. Regulation and the regulatory framework.
2. Cost and revenue synergies.
3. Firm- or market-specific factors.

We start by considering how the first factor—regulation—impacts a U.S.-based FI's geographic expansion decision. Specifically, we briefly discuss the restrictions applying to insurance companies and thrifts; then we look in more detail at regulations affecting commercial banks.

Concept Questions

1. Explain why regulation both inhibits and provides incentives to an FI to engage in geographic expansion.
2. What three basic factors influence the attractiveness of geographic expansion to an FI?

REGULATORY FACTORS IMPACTING GEOGRAPHIC EXPANSION

Insurance Companies

As discussed in Chapter 3, insurance companies are state-regulated firms. By establishing a subsidiary in one state, an insurance company normally has the opportunity to sell insurance anywhere in that state and often to market the product nationally by telemarketing and direct sales. To deliver a financial service effectively, however, it is often necessary to establish a physical presence in a local market. To do this, insurance companies establish subsidiaries and offices in other states. This is usually easy since the initial capital requirement for establishing a new subsidiary is set at a relatively low level by state regulators. Thus, most large insurance companies have a physical presence in virtually every state in the union.

Thrifts

www.ots.treas.gov

The ability of thrifts to branch or expand geographically—whether intrastate (within a state) or interstate (between states)—was under the power of the Federal Home Loan Bank Board until 1989. Since 1989, the ability to branch has been under the power of the Office of Thrift Supervision (OTS) as part of the 1989 FIRREA legislation (see Chapter 19). Historically, the policy was that a federally chartered thrift could not branch across state lines. In the 1980s, a considerable loosening of these restrictions occurred. Both the Garn-St Germain Act of 1982 and the Financial Institutions Reform, Recovery, and Enforcement Act (FIRREA) of 1989 allowed sound banks and thrifts to acquire failing thrifts across state lines and to run

---

[1] E. Kane has called this interaction between regulation and incentives the regulatory dialectic. See "Accelerating Inflation, Technological Innovation, and the Decreasing Effectiveness of Banking Regulation," *Journal of Finance* 36 (1981), pp. 335–67. Expansions that are geographic market extensions involving firms in the same product areas are part of a broader set of horizontal mergers.

TABLE 22–1
Relaxation of Geographic Expansion Restrictions for Savings Institutions

Source: S. Cebonoyan et al., unpublished Working Paper, University of Maryland, School of Business, Baltimore, 1998.

1982	The *Garn-St Germain Act* allows interstate branching with the acquisition of failed savings institutions by out-of-state savings institutions.
1989	The Office of Thrift Supervision (OTS) assumes power to regulate interstate branching for federally chartered thrifts as part of the *Financial Institutions Reform, Recovery, and Enforcement Act of 1989,* allowing healthy thrifts to be acquired across state lines by holding companies. The Resolution Trust Company is placed in charge of resolving failed thrifts, at times overriding state branching laws.
1992	OTS allows interstate branching for all federally chartered thrifts.

them either as separate subsidiaries or convert them into branches. Finally, in 1992 the OTS announced that it was willing to allow interstate branching for all federally chartered savings institutions. By 1993 interstate savings institutions controlled 25 percent of all savings institutions' assets and had established over 1,200 branches across state lines. Table 22–1 summarizes the loosening of interstate branching and acquisition activity regulation for thrifts.

Commercial Banks

Restrictions on Intrastate Banking

unit bank
A bank with a single office.

At the beginning of the century most U.S. banks were **unit banks** with a single office. Improving communications and customer needs resulted in a rush to branching in the first two decades of the 20th century. Increasingly, this movement ran into opposition from the smallest unit banks and the largest money center banks. The smallest unit banks perceived a competitive threat to their retail business from the larger branching banks; money center banks feared a loss of valuable correspondent business such as check clearing and other payment services. As a result, several states restricted the ability of banks to branch within the state. Indeed, some states prohibited intrastate branching per se, effectively constraining a bank to unit status. Over the years and in a very piecemeal fashion, states have liberalized their restrictions on within-state branching.[2] As we show in Table 22–2 column (1), by 1994 (prior to the passage of the Riegle-Neal Act) only one state (Iowa) had not deregulated intrastate banking.

Restrictions on Interstate Banking

The defining piece of legislation affecting interstate branching until 1997 was the McFadden Act, passed in 1927 and amended in 1933. The McFadden Act and its amendments restricted nationally chartered banks' branching abilities to the same extent allowed to state-chartered banks. Because states prohibit interstate banking

---

[2] R. B. Avery, R. W. Bostic, and P. S. Calem, in "Consolidation and Bank Branching Patterns," *Journal of Banking and Finance* 23 (1999), pp. 497–532, find that (contrary to the fears of small unit banks) consolidation allowed by changes in geographic expansion regulations did not, in general, change the number of banking offices per capita within a local market area. Only when two banks located in the same ZIP code merged did the number of bank offices per capita fall. J. McAndrews and P. E. Strahan find that (as feared by money center banks) the regulatory changes did result in the entry of new correspondent banks who provided new competition for the incumbent banks (see "Deregulation and Correspondent Banking," FRBN, Working Paper, September 2000).

TABLE 22–2
The States Remove
Restrictions on
Geographic
Expansion Pre-1994

Source: J. Jayaratne and P. E. Strahan, "The Benefits of Branching Deregulation," *Economic Policy Review,* Federal Reserve Bank of New York, December 1997, pp. 13–29.

State	Intrastate Branching Deregulated	Interstate Banking Deregulated
Alabama	1981	1987
Alaska	Before 1970	1982
Arizona	Before 1970	1986
Arkansas	1994	1989
California	Before 1970	1987
Colorado	1991	1988
Connecticut	1980	1983
Delaware	Before 1970	1988
District of Columbia	Before 1970	1985
Florida	1988	1985
Georgia	1983	1985
Hawaii	1986	—
Idaho	Before 1970	1985
Illinois	1988	1986
Indiana	1989	1986
Iowa	—	1991
Kansas	1987	1992
Kentucky	1990	1984
Louisiana	1988	1987
Maine	1975	1978
Maryland	Before 1970	1985
Massachusetts	1984	1983
Michigan	1987	1986
Minnesota	1993	1986
Mississippi	1986	1988
Missouri	1990	1986
Montana	1990	1993
Nebraska	1985	1990
Nevada	Before 1970	1985
New Hampshire	1987	1987
New Jersey	1977	1986
New Mexico	1991	1989
New York	1976	1982
North Carolina	Before 1970	1985
North Dakota	1987	1991
Ohio	1979	1985
Oklahoma	1988	1987
Oregon	1985	1986
Pennsylvania	1982	1986
Rhode Island	Before 1970	1984
South Carolina	Before 1970	1986
South Dakota	Before 1970	1983
Tennessee	1985	1985
Texas	1988	1987
Utah	1981	1984
Vermont	1970	1988
Virginia	1978	1985
Washington	1985	1987
West Virginia	1987	1988
Wisconsin	1990	1987
Wyoming	1988	1987

Note: Before the passage of the 1994 Riegle-Neal Act, Iowa had not deregulated intrastate branching and Hawaii had not deregulated interstate banking.

multibank holding company (MBHC)
A parent banking organization that owns a number of individual bank subsidiaries.

for state-chartered banks in general, nationally chartered banks were similarly prohibited.[3]

Between 1927 and 1997 (see later), given the McFadden prohibition on interstate branching, bank organizations expanding across state lines largely relied on establishing subsidiaries rather than branches. Some of the biggest banking organizations established **multibank holding companies** for that purpose. A multibank holding company (MBHC) is a parent company that acquires more than one bank as a direct subsidiary. While MBHCs had been around in the early part of the 20th century, the 1927 restrictions on interstate branching gave the bank acquisition movement an added impetus. By 1956, some 47 multibank holding companies were established, many owning banks in two or more states.[4]

In 1956, Congress recognized the potential loophole to interstate banking posed by the MBHC movement and passed the Douglas Amendment to the Bank Holding Company Act. This act permitted MBHCs to acquire bank subsidiaries only to the extent allowed by the laws of the state in which the proposed bank target resided. Because states prohibited out-of-state bank acquisitions, this essentially curtailed the growth of the MBHC movement until the emergence and expansion of regional banking pacts (see later). Any MBHCs with out-of-state subsidiaries established prior to 1956 were **grandfathered;** that is, MBHCs were allowed to keep them. (One such example was First Interstate.)

grandfathered subsidiary
A subsidiary established prior to the passage of a restrictive law and not subject to that law.

one-bank holding company
A parent banking organization that owns one bank subsidiary and nonbank subsidiaries.

The passage of the 1956 Douglas Amendment did not close all potential interstate banking loopholes. Since the amendment pertained to MBHC acquisitions, it still left open the potential for **one-bank holding company** (OBHC) geographic extensions. An OBHC is a parent bank holding company that has a single bank subsidiary and a number of other nonbank subsidiaries. By creating an OBHC and establishing across state lines various nonbank subsidiaries that sell financial services such as consumer finance, leasing, and data processing, a bank could almost replicate an out-of-state banking presence. However, doing interstate banking in this fashion is far more expensive than establishing either direct branches or full-service subsidiaries. Nevertheless, one-bank holding expansions are excellent examples of Kane's regulatory dialectic—blocking one path to geographic expansion simply resulted in banks exploiting a loophole elsewhere if they believed it was net profitable to do so.[5] The OBHC movement grew tremendously from 117 banking organizations in 1956 to 1,318 in 1970, with all manner of financial and nonfinancial subsidiaries established both within the home state of the affiliated bank and across state lines. For example, some OBHCs even had ownership stakes in supermarket chains and railroads.

In 1970 Congress again acted, recognizing that bankers had creatively innovated yet another loophole to interstate banking restrictions. The 1970 Bank Holding Company Act Amendments effectively restricted the nonbank activities an OBHC could engage in to those "closely related to banking," as defined by the Federal Reserve under Section 4(c)(8) of the act. Further, acquisitions of nonbank subsidiaries after 1970 were subject to the approval of the Federal Reserve. Initially, the

---

[3] It is arguable, contrary to conventional wisdom, that the McFadden Act actually enlarged the geographic expansion powers of nationally chartered banks since the prime regulator of nationally chartered banks had restricted national bank branching even within a state until the act's passage.

[4] By 1990, there were 157 interstate multibank holding companies with the growth reflecting the presence of regional banking pacts.

[5] See E. Kane, "Accelerating Inflation, Technological Innovation and the Decreasing Effectiveness of Banking Regulation," *Journal of Finance* 36 (1981), pp. 335–67.

act permitted only six nonbank activities, including consumer finance and credit cards. Moreover, subsidiaries engaged in activities not closely related to banking had to be divested by 1980. Thus, the year 1970 and the passage of the Bank Holding Company Act amendments are probably the low point of interstate banking in the United States. Since that time, five developments have resulted in the virtual erosion of interstate banking restrictions. We describe these developments next.

Regional and National Banking Pacts Maine took the first step in eroding interstate banking restrictions in 1978 by passing a law that exploited a loophole in the Douglas Amendments of 1956. This loophole occurred because the law prohibited the acquisition of a bank across state lines unless directly permitted by the state in which the proposed target bank resided. To increase employment in and growth of its financial services industry, Maine passed a law allowing banks from any other state to enter and acquire local banks even if the banks in Maine could not engage in such acquisitions in other states. This nationwide nonreciprocal bank acquisition law led to a rapid acquisition of Maine's banking assets by out-of-state bank holding companies. Indeed, by 1988, some 85 percent of bank assets in Maine were held by out-of-state banking organizations such as Citicorp (now Citigroup).

regional or interstate banking pact
An agreement among states describing the conditions for entrance of out-of-state banks by acquisition.

In the early 1980s other states in New England sought to follow Maine's example by enacting their own **interstate banking pacts.** However, these laws were often more restrictive in that they allowed banks from only a certain geographic region—in one case, New England—to enter their banking markets by acquisition. In particular, acquisitions by out-of-state banks from New York and California were generally prohibited. This created some concern about the legality of these more restrictive regional pacts until Connecticut's restrictive law was upheld by the U.S. Supreme Court in the face of a challenge to its legality by New York–based Citicorp in 1984.

By 1994, all states but Hawaii had passed some form of interstate banking law or pact. There were three general types of interstate banking laws:

Nationwide (N). Nationwide laws allowed an out-of-state bank to acquire an in-state target bank even if the acquirer's home state did not give banks from the target's state similar acquisition powers.

Nationwide reciprocal (NR). An out-of-state acquirer could purchase a target bank as long as the acquirer's state allowed other banks from the target's state to enter by acquisition as well. States with a large concentration of bank assets such as New York and California had such laws.

Regional reciprocal (RR). These regional banking pacts allowed banks from a regional group of states to acquire a target bank in a given state as long as there was reciprocity, that is, as long as home state banks could acquire targets in other regional pact states and vice versa. For example, Wisconsin's regional reciprocal law allowed entry by acquisition for banks from Iowa, Illinois, Indiana, Kentucky, Michigan, Minnesota, Missouri, and Ohio as long as those states reciprocated by allowing acquisitions by Wisconsin banks in their markets.

In Table 22–2, column (2) shows the condition of interstate banking laws before passage of the Riegle-Neal Act of 1994 (see later).

Purchase of Troubled Banks The acquisition of failing or troubled banks across state lines has been a second way that interstate banking barriers have been eroded. Following the passage of the Garn-St Germain Act in 1982, the bankruptcy of the FSLIC, and the depletion of the FDIC's reserves, regulators increasingly turned to out-of-state acquisitions to resolve bank failures. Thus, for example, in 1987, Chemical Bank (which has itself been acquired by J. P. Morgan Chase) acquired Texas

Commerce and gained a foothold in the Texas banking market. Through its Texas Commerce unit, Chemical Bank acquired most of the banks of the failed First City Bancorporation of Texas in January 1993. In addition, the 1982 Garn-St Germain Act allowed banks to acquire failing thrifts as well as banks. Through this mechanism, Citicorp acquired thrifts in growing banking markets such as California and Florida. Finally, the passage of FIRREA in August 1989 extended the interstate acquisition powers of banks to encompass healthy thrifts as well.

Nonbank Banks A third way interstate banking barriers were eroded came through the establishment of nonbank banks (described in Chapter 21). Until 1987, a large U.S. bank could acquire a full-service out-of-state bank, divest it of its commercial loans, and legally operate it as a nonbank bank specializing in consumer finance.[6] However, the Competitive Equality Banking Act (CEBA) effectively put an end to this loophole in 1987, although it grandfathered existing nonbank banks.

Also exempted from the CEBA legislation were industrial loan corporations (ILCs) located in the state of Utah. ILCs, owned by nonbanking companies such as General Electric, Merrill Lynch, and Pitney Bowes, provide loans to low-quality, high-interest-rate corporations that banks avoid. While headquartered in Utah, ILCs can operate in nearly all 50 states by direct mail and other electronic means. ILCs are regulated by the state of Utah and deposits of ILCs are insured by the Federal Deposit Insurance Corporation. Yet ILCs are regulated by neither the Federal Reserve nor the Office of the Comptroller of the Currency. By operating in Utah, nonbank companies can behave like commercial banks without being regulated like them. As a result, assets under management in ILCs grew from $2.9 billion at the end of 1995 to $115 billion in 2003 (held by 51 ILCs). This compares to total commercial and industrial loans at commercial banks of $871 billion. In March 2004, the U.S. House of Representatives tightened the ability of new (as of October 1, 2003) nonbank banks to open and operate by overwhelmingly passing a bill that required any banking company to earn at least 85 percent of its revenue from financial services. The bill effectively prohibited a firm such as Wal-Mart from operating its own bank in any meaningful way.

Expansion in OBHC Activities Increasingly, after 1970, banks could virtually replicate a full interstate banking presence by establishing out-of-state nonbank subsidiaries. For example, in 1994 Norwest Corporation, a bank holding company from Minneapolis, had mortgage subsidiaries in 49 states and more than 770 consumer lending subsidiaries in 46 states. Moreover, while the 1970, Section 4(c)(8) of the Bank Holding Company Act amendments specified that permitted nonbank activities of bank holding companies had to be "closely related to banking" (as defined by the Federal Reserve), the permitted list had grown close to 60 by 1998 compared to only 6 in 1970.[7]

Riegle-Neal Interstate Banking and Branching Efficiency Act of 1994 It had long been recognized that nationwide banking expansion through multibank

---

[6] For the purposes of the 1956 Bank Holding Company Act's restrictions on MBHC acquisitions, the definition of a bank was an institution that accepted demand deposits and made commercial and industrial loans. By stripping a bank of its commercial loans, it turned into a nonbank bank that was not subject to restrictions on interstate banking.

[7] K. J. Stiroh and P. E. Strahan find that, after states passed interstate banking laws, the profitability of banks that expanded across state lines increased. Further, the link between performance and market share increased significantly. The results lead the authors to conclude that the opening up of the banking markets resulted in a reallocation of market power in the banking industry toward the better-run banks. See "U.S. Banking Deregulation: Competitive Forces Unleashed," FRBNY Working Paper, July 2000.

TABLE 22–3 Key Dates for the Riegle-Neal Interstate Banking and Branching Efficiency Act of 1994

Date	Event	Summary
September 24, 1994, to May 31, 1997	Interstate bank merger and branch acquisition early opt-in	A state may "opt in early" to allow interstate merger transactions, including branch acquisitions, to occur prior to June 1, 1997.
	Interstate bank merger opt-out	A state may "opt out" to prohibit interstate merger transactions entirely.
Any time after date of enactment	Interstate de novo branching opt-in	A state may expressly permit out-of-state banks to establish de novo branches within its limits.
One year after date of enactment and thereafter	Interstate banking	A bank holding company may acquire banks located in any state. States do not have the ability to opt out. However, the acquiring institution is not permitted to control more than 10 percent of nationwide deposits or 30 percent of deposits in the state entered.
June 1, 1997, and thereafter	Interstate bank mergers	Banks in different states may merge unless one of the states has opted out of interstate merger transactions by June 1, 1997.
	Interstate branching acquisitions	Banks may acquire an existing branch in another state if the law of that state permits it.

Source: Office of the Comptroller of the Currency. *www.occ.treas.gov*

holding companies was potentially far more expensive than through branching. Separate corporations and boards of directors must be established for each bank in an MBHC, and it is hard to achieve the same level of economic and financial integration as with branches. Moreover, most of the major banking competitor countries, such as Japan, Germany, France, and the United Kingdom, have nationwide branching.

In the fall of 1994, the U.S. Congress passed an interstate banking law that allows U.S. and nondomestic banks to branch interstate by consolidating out-of-state bank subsidiaries into a branch network and/or acquiring banks or individual branches of banks by merger and acquisition. (The effective date for these new branching powers was June 1, 1997.) While the act is silent on the ability of banks to establish de novo (new) branches in other states—essentially leaving it to individual states to pass laws allowing de novo branching—it became possible under the new law for a New York bank such as Citibank to purchase a single branch of a California bank such as a branch of Bank of America in San Francisco.

The implication of the Riegle-Neal Act is that full interstate banking—with the exception of de novo branching—became a reality in the United States in 1997. Further details of the Riegle-Neal Act are provided in Table 22–3.[8] The relaxation of the branching restrictions, along with recognition of the potential cost, revenue, and risk benefits from geographic expansions (discussed next), set off a wave of consolidation in the U.S. banking system. This consolidation trend has been particularly evident among the largest U.S. banks in a wave of "megamergers." Table 22–4 shows some of the biggest mergers between 1995 and 2004 that are reshaping the U.S. banking industry into a nationwide banking system along European and Canadian lines. Many of these mergers are discussed below.

[8] The reason for the restriction on de novo branching is to protect smaller community banks' franchise values. If you can branch only by acquisition, the franchise values of small banks will be greater than when larger banks have the alternative of branching de novo.

TABLE 22–4   The New Shape of U.S. Banking Major Mergers, 1995–2004

	1995–1996		1996–1997		1997–1998		1998–1999	
	Capital, $million	Assets, $million	Capital, $million	Assets, $million	Capital, $million	Assets, $million	Capital, $million	Assets, $million
Chemical	$11,436	$ 82,296⎤	(Chase Manhattan Corp.)					
Chase	8,444	121,173⎦	$21,095	$336,099	$22,594	$365,521	$23,617	$406,105⎤
J. P. Morgan	11,432	222,026	11,404	262,159	11,261	261,067	11,439	260,898⎦
Banc One	7,824	90,176	8,107	102,034	8,701	115,901⎤	(Bank One)	
First Chicago NBD	7,890	122,002	9,318	104,619	8,541	114,096⎦	19,900	269,425
Citicorp	19,239	256,853	20,109	281,018	21,096	310,897⎤	(Citigroup)	
Travelers	15,853	302,344	17,942	345,948	20,893	386,555⎦	58,290	795,584
BankAmerica	14,820	232,446	17,181	250,753	17,200	260,159⎤		
NationsBank	11,074	187,298	12,662	185,794⎤				
Boatmen's	2,666	33,704⎤						
Fourth Financial	592	7,456⎦	3,359	41,200			(Bank of America)	
Barnett Banks	2,491	41,631	3,289	41,456⎦	13,593	310,602⎦	44,432	632,574
FleetFinancial	7,415	85,518	8,452	91,047	9,409	104,382⎤	(Fleet Boston)	
Bank Boston	4,934	62,306	4,610	69,268	4,817	73,513⎦	18,074	226,817
First Union	4,479	96,740⎤						
First Fidelity	2,301	35,366⎦	7,790	140,127	10,215	157,274⎤		
CoreStates	2,165	29,729⎤						
Meridian	1,191	14,740⎦	3,725	45,651⎤			(First Union)	
Signet	779	11,100	857	11,751⎦	3,756	48,461⎦	15,347	253,024
Wachovia	3,625	44,964	3,963	46,886⎤	(Wachovia)			
Central Fidelity	739	10,822	778	10,556⎦	5,465	65,397	5,658	67,352
Wells Fargo	3,505	50,316⎤	(Wells Fargo)					
First Interstate	3,431	58,071⎦	6,572	108,888⎤	20,759	202,475	23,871	241,053⎤
Norwest	5,875	80,175	6,834	88,540⎦				
First Security	1,217	15,457	1,400	18,152	1,595	21,689	1,770	22,993⎦

Source: *The Banker*, May 1998, p. 5, and authors' research.

Concept Questions	1. What was the difference between the interstate banking restrictions imposed under the 1956 Bank Holding Company Act and those passed under the 1970 amendments to the Bank Holding Company Act?
	2. What are some of the ways in which interstate banking barriers have been eroded?
	3. What were the main features of the Riegle-Neal Interstate Banking and Branching Efficiency Act of 1994?

COST AND REVENUE SYNERGIES IMPACTING GEOGRAPHIC EXPANSION BY MERGER AND ACQUISITION

One reason for an FI deciding to expand (or not to expand) geographically by acquisition relates to the regulations defining its merger opportunities.[9] Other

---

[9] It should be noted that expansion via de novo entry is a possible method of geographic expansion as well as M&A. However, de novo entry generally involves small banks that can be financially fragile and the degree to which they are reliable long-run sources of expansion depends on whether they can survive to financial maturity. See R. DeYoung, "De Novo Bank Exit," *Journal of Money, Credit, and Banking*, October 2003, pp. 711–28.

	1999–2000		2000–2001		2001–2002		2002–2003		2003–2004	
	Capital, $million	Assets, $million	Capital, $million	Assets, $million	Capital, $million	Assets, $million	Capital, $million	Assets, $million	Capital, $million	Assets, $million
(J. P. Morgan Chase)	$ 42,338	$715,348	$41,099	$693,575	$42,306	$758,800	$46,154	$770,912	(J. P. Morgan Chase)	
	18,635	269,300	20,226	268,954	22,440	277,985	23,419	326,563		
	66,206	902,210	81,247	1,051,450	86,718	1,097,190	98,014	1,264,032		
	47,628	642,191	48,520	621,764	47,980	660,951	50,319	736,445	(Bank of America)	
	19,361	219,095	17,608	203,744	16,833	190,453	18,280	200,235		
(Wachovia)										
	16,709	254,170	28,455	330,452	32,078	341,834	32,428	401,032		
	6,285	74,032								
(Wells Fargo)										
	26,488	272,426	27,214	307,569	30,358	349,259	32,372	390,813		

reasons relate to the exploitation of potential cost and revenue synergies from merging (as well as the associated diversification of risk benefits). We look at these potential gains next.

Cost Synergies

X efficiency
Cost savings due to the greater managerial efficiency of the acquiring bank.

A common reason given for bank mergers is the potential cost synergies that may result from economies of scale, economies of scope, or managerial efficiency sources (often called **X efficiencies**[10] because they are difficult to pin down in a quantitative fashion). For example, in 1996, Chase Manhattan and Chemical Bank merged, creating the (then) largest banking organization in the United States, with assets of $300 billion. It was estimated that annual cost savings from the merger would be $1.5 billion, to be achieved by consolidating certain operations and eliminating redundant costs, including the elimination of some 12,000 positions from a combined staff of

---

[10] X efficiencies are those cost savings not directly due to economies of scope or economies of scale. As such, they are usually attributed to superior management skills and other difficult-to-measure managerial factors. To date, the explicit identification of what composes these efficiencies remains to be established in the empirical banking literature.

75,000 in 39 states and 51 countries. Similarly, Milwaukee-based Firstar's $18.7 billion acquisition of Minneapolis-based U.S. Bancorp in late 2000 was expected to reduce combined expenses by $206 million per year (an amount equivalent to 5 percent of the combined bank's expenses prior to the acquisition). Savings were estimated to come through the closing of overlapping branches and laying off of personnel. Finally, in 2001 First Union acquired Wachovia for $14.6 billion. The merger of these two North Carolina banks was expected to reduce annual expenses by $890 million through the consolidation of 250 to 300 branches and cutting of some 7,000 jobs.

megamerger
The merger of two large banks.

While the mergers discussed above are interesting examples of **megamergers,** they are still essentially mergers in the same or closely related banking markets.[11] By comparison, the two largest pure bank mergers in 1998—those between BancOne (now Bank One) and First Chicago and between NationsBank and Bank of America—were clearly geographic extension mergers with little or no geographic overlap. For example, a major aim of the BancOne and First Chicago merger was to generate an enhanced national presence and economies of scale in the credit card business. Before the merger, BancOne and First Chicago were the third and fifth largest credit card companies. Their merger created the then second largest credit card bank (behind Citigroup), with 40 million accounts and over $56 billion in loans outstanding. It is also perceived that the enhanced scale of the new bank's credit card business allows it to invest in even more innovative computer technology.

Another example of a market extension megamerger that has both geographic and cost synergy dimensions was North Carolina–based NationsBank's acquisition of Boatmen's Bancshares of St. Louis, Missouri, in 1997. The acquisition gave NationsBank entry into markets in Missouri, Arkansas, Kansas, Oklahoma, and New Mexico. The shift to statewide banking groups and the use of combined technology as a result of the acquisition were expected to produce cost savings of $335 million. Bank of America and NationsBank became the first truly nationwide bank when they merged in 1998, a transaction valued at $60 billion. The banks estimated the merger would cut their combined expenses by $1.3 billion and would eliminate between 5,000 and 8,000 jobs (3 to 4 percent of their workforce).

Finally, the most recent examples of these types of mergers are those by Bank of America and J. P. Morgan Chase. By acquiring FleetBoston for $43 billion, Bank of America added nearly 1,500 branches and 3,400 ATM machines in the New England area. The combined banks projected annual cost savings to be $1.1 billion, including consolidation of redundant technology systems. This was followed in 2004 by J. P. Morgan Chase's $60 billion merger with Bank One to form the second largest bank in the United States. With this merger J. P. Morgan Chase (which had been operating in only four states) acquired Bank One's First USA credit card operations and a massive retail network of about 1,800 branches concentrated in the Midwest. Together the merged bank would hold about $125 billion in credit card balances, giving the combined company an almost 20 percent share of the credit card market. Further, the combined bank was projecting before-tax savings of $2.2 billion in the three years after the merger with job cuts estimated to total 10,000 of a combined 140,000 workers.

---

[11] Indeed, it is worth noting that in merging, Chase–Chemical chose a New York State bank charter rather than a national bank charter (see Chapter 2 for a discussion of state versus national charters).

In a comprehensive study, Berger and Humphrey used data from 1981 to 1989 to analyze the cost savings from megamergers, which they defined as a merger in which the acquirer's and the target bank's assets combined exceeded $1 billion. They could find very little evidence of potential gains from economies of scale and scope. Indeed, the cost savings they could find were related to improved managerial efficiency (X efficiency). Their study had three major findings. First, the managerial efficiency of the acquirer tended to be superior to that of the acquired bank. Second, the 57 megamergers analyzed produced small but significant X efficiency gains. Third (and perhaps surprisingly), the degree of cost savings in market overlap mergers (e.g., as in the Chase/Chemical case) was apparently no greater than for geographic extension mergers (as in the Bank of America/NationsBank case). Overall, they could not find the sizable cost synergies of 30 percent or so that are often given as the motivational forces behind such mergers.[12]

In a more recent study of nine megamergers by Rhoades (seven of the nine occurring since 1990), large cost savings were found. Specifically, four of the nine mergers showed significant cost efficiency gains relative to a peer group of nonmerged banks and seven of the nine showed a significant improvement in their return on assets. Interestingly, where cost efficiency gains were *not* realized, the major problems came from integrating data processing and operating systems. Houston, James, and Ryngaert examined large bank mergers over the period 1985 through 1996. They found that cost savings represented the primary source of gains in the large majority of recent mergers and that managerial cost savings projections have significant capital market credibility.[13]

Berger and DeYoung examined the effects of geographic expansion on bank efficiency using cost and profit efficiencies estimates for over 7,000 U.S. banks from 1993 to 1998. They found both positive and negative links between geographic scope and bank efficiency. Parent organizations exercised some control over the efficiency of their affiliates, although the control dissipated with physical distance to the affiliate. On average, the distance-related effect was small, and thus results suggested that the more efficient banks could export efficient practices to their affiliates and overwhelm any effects of distance. The results suggested that some banks may operate efficiently only within a single region, while others may operate efficiently on a nationwide or even international basis.[14]

Finally, G. DeLong and M. M. Cornett et al. find that mergers of banks that are activity or geographically focusing earn significantly higher ARs than those that are activity or geographically diversifying. The conclusion from these result is that focusing mergers involve banks engaged in similar types of business (either activity or geographically). Thus, they increase opportunities for greater cost efficiency or for concentrating the bidder's existing market power and brand recognition . In contrast, diversifying mergers are those in which the bidder bank has lines of business that are not common to those of the target bank. These mergers required the

---

[12] A. Berger and D. B. Humphrey, "Megamergers in Banking and the Use of Cost Efficiency as an Antitrust Defense," *The Antitrust Bulletin* 37 (1992), pp. 541–600.

[13] S. A. Rhoades, "The Efficiency Effects of Bank Mergers: An Overview of Case Studies of Nine Mergers," *Journal of Banking and Finance* 22, no. 3 (1998), pp. 273–92; and J. F. Houston, C. M. James, and M. D. Ryngaert, "Where Do Merger Gains Come From? Bank Mergers from the Perspective of Insiders and Outsiders," *Journal of Financial Economics* 60 (2001), pp. 285–331.

[14] A. N. Berger and R. DeYoung, "The Effects of Geographic Expansion on Bank Efficiency," *Journal of Financial Services Research* 19 (2001), pp. 163–84.

bidder bank to extend operations into new areas and devote additional resources beyond the current operations.[15]

Revenue Synergies

The revenue synergies argument has three dimensions. First, revenues may be enhanced by acquiring a bank in a growing market. For example, while the 2000 merger of J. P. Morgan and Chase Manhattan to form J. P. Morgan Chase was estimated to produce a cost savings of $1.5 billion, the CEOs of both companies stated that the success of the merger was pinned on revenue growth. The merger combined J. P. Morgan's greater array of products with Chase's broad client base. The merger added substantially to many businesses (such as equity underwriting, equity derivatives, and asset management) that Chase had been trying to build on its own through smaller deals and gave it a bigger presence in Europe where investment and corporate banking were fast-growing businesses. When J. P. Morgan Chase then acquired Bank One, analysts praised the combination as one that offered revenue growth potential, the result of the combination of two different business models as well as expense reduction.

Similarly, in 2001 Washington Mutual, a Seattle-based thrift, purchased New York–based Dime Bancorp for $5.2 billion. The purchase provided Washington Mutual with an entry into the Northeast mortgage market. Washington Mutual and Dime had a combined mortgage production of $59 billion in the second quarter of 2001, surpassing J. P. Morgan Chase's offerings of $54 billion. Washington Mutual estimated it could generate $1 trillion in mortgage originations in the first 10 years of operations in New York, stating that steady customer growth and high satisfaction ratings would lead to increased revenues and long-term shareholder value.

Second, the acquiring bank's revenue stream may become more stable if the asset and liability portfolio of the target institution exhibits different credit, interest rate, and liquidity risk characteristics from the acquirer.[16] For example, real estate loan portfolios showed very strong regional cycles in the 1980s. Specifically, U.S. real estate declined in value in the Southwest, then in the Northeast, and then in California with a long and variable lag. Thus, a geographically diversified real estate portfolio may be far less risky than one in which both acquirer and target specialize in a single region.[17] Studies confirm risk diversification gains from geographic expansions.[18]

Third, there is an opportunity for revenue enhancement by expanding into markets that are less than fully competitive. That is, banks may be able to identify and expand geographically into those markets where *economic rents* potentially exist, but where such entry will not be viewed as being potentially anticompetitive by

---

[15] G. L. DeLong, "Gains from Focusing versus Diversifying Bank Mergers," *Journal of Financial Economics* 59 (2001), pp. 221–52; G. L. DeLong, "Does Long-Term Performance of Mergers Match Market Expectations? Evidence from the U. S. Banking Industry," Working Paper, City University of New York, 2002; and M. M. Cornett, G. Hovakimian, D. Palia, and H. Tehranian, "The Impact of the Manager-Shareholder Conflict on Acquiring Bank Returns," *Journal of Banking and Finance* 27 (2003), pp. 103–31.

[16] See B. Esty et al., "Interest Rate Exposure and Bank Mergers," *Journal of Banking and Finance* 23 (February 1999), pp. 255–85, for evidence on the opposing interest rate risk exposures of acquirers and targets.

[17] As a result, the potential revenue diversification gains for more geographically concentrated mergers are likely to be relatively low.

[18] M. Levonian, "Interstate Banking and Risk," Federal Reserve Bank of San Francisco, *Weekly Letter* 94–26 (1994); W. Lee, "The Value of Risk Reduction to Investors," unpublished Research Paper 9312, Federal Reserve Bank of New York, 1993; and P. S. Rose, "The Diversification and Cost Effects of Interstate Banking," *The Financial Review* 13 (May 1996), pp. 431–51.

FIGURE 22–1

The Branching
Presence of J. P.
Morgan Chase as a
Result of Its Merger
with Bank One

Source: Federal Deposit
Insurance Corporation.
www.fdic.gov

regulators. Arguably, one of the great potential benefits of the J. P. Morgan Chase
and Bank One merger was the potential for enhanced revenue diversification due
to the lack of overlap of the branch networks of the two systems due to the merger.
The new bank had a branching presence in 17 states and an 8.3 percent share of
federally insured banking deposits (see Figure 22–1).

Merger Guidelines for Acceptability

To the extent that geographic expansions of the J. P. Morgan Chase–Bank One kind
are viewed as enhancing the monopoly power of an FI, regulators may act to prevent a merger unless the merger produces potential efficiency gains that cannot be
reasonably achieved by other means.[19] In recent years, the ultimate enforcement of
antimonopoly laws and guidelines has fallen to the U.S. Department of Justice. In
particular, the Department of Justice has laid down guidelines regarding the acceptability or unacceptability of acquisitions based on the potential increase in
concentration in the market in which an acquisition takes place, with the cost-
efficiency exception just noted.[20]

www.usdoj.gov

[19] U.S. Department of Justice, "Horizontal Merger Guidelines," April 2, 1982. It should also be added
that the Riegle-Neal Act of 1994 placed a maximum 10 percent cap on the market share of the national
(insured) deposit base held by any bank. As of 2004, the date of the merger, the national insured deposit
base was $4.3 trillion. This suggests that the new J. P. Morgan Chase may be limited by this cap if it seeks
further acquisitions beyond its current 8.3 percent national market share.

[20] The Federal Reserve also has the power to approve or disapprove mergers among state member banks
and bank holding companies. The Comptroller of the Currency has similar powers over nationally chartered banks. The Federal Reserve's criteria are similar to those of the Department of Justice in that they
take into account the HHI (market concentration index). However, it also evaluates the risk effects of the
merger. The Department of Justice has powers to review the decisions made by the bank regulatory agencies. For example, in 1990 and 1991, the Department of Justice successfully challenged two mergers approved by the Federal Reserve Board. These two mergers eventually went ahead only after the acquiring
bank had divested some branches and offices. The two mergers were First Hawaiian's acquisition of First
Interstate of Hawaii and the Society–Ameritrust merger. See D. Palia, "Recent Evidence of Bank Mergers,"
Financial Markets, Instruments, and Institutions 3, no. 5 (1994), pp. 36–59, for further details.

HHI
An index or measure of market concentration based on the squared market shares of market participants.

These merger guidelines are based on a measure of market concentration called the Herfindahl-Hirschman Index **(HHI)**. This index is created by taking the percentage market shares of each firm in a market, squaring them, and then adding these squared shares. Thus, in a market where a single firm had a 100 percent market share, the HHI would be

$$\text{HHI} = (100)^2 = 10,000$$

Alternatively, in a market in which there were an infinitely large number of firms of equal size, then

$$\text{HHI} = 0$$

Thus, the HHI must lie between 0 and 10,000.

Whether a merger will be challenged under the Department of Justice guidelines depends on the postmerger HHI level. As you can see in Table 22–5, the Department of Justice defines a *concentrated* market as having a postmerger HHI ratio of 1,800, a moderately concentrated market as having a ratio of 1,000 to 1,800, and an unconcentrated market as having a ratio of less than 1,000. In either a concentrated or a moderately concentrated market, postmerger HHI increases of 100 or more may be challenged.[21]

EXAMPLE 22–1

Calculation of Change in the HHI Associated with a Merger

Consider a market that has three banks with the following market shares:

Bank A = 50%
Bank B = 46%
Bank C = 4%

The premerger HHI for the market is

$$\text{HHI} = (50)^2 + (46)^2 + (4)^2 = 2,500 + 2,116 + 16 = 4,632$$

Thus, the market is highly concentrated according to the Department of Justice guidelines.
   Suppose Bank A wants to acquire Bank C so that the postacquisition market would exhibit the following shares:[22]

$$A + C = 54\%$$
$$B = 46\%$$

The postmerger HHI would be

$$\text{HHI} = (54)^2 + (46)^2 = 2,916 + 2,116 = 5,032$$

Thus, the increase or change in the HHI (ΔHHI) postmerger is

$$\Delta\text{HHI} = 5,032 - 4,632 = 400$$

Since the increase is 400, which is more than the 100 benchmark defined in the Department of Justice guidelines, the market is heavily concentrated and the merger could be challenged.

---

[21] In practice, it is only when the change exceeds 200 in banking that a challenge may occur. This is the case because banking is generally viewed as being more competitive than most industries. See Department of Justice, "Horizontal Merger Guidelines."

[22] Here we consider the effect on the HHI of a within-market acquisition; similar calculations can be carried out for between-market acquisitions.

TABLE 22–5
1982 Department of Justice Horizontal Merger Guidelines

Source: Department of Justice, Merger Guidelines, 1982.

Postmerger Market Concentration	Level of Herfindahl-Hirschman Index	Percentage Change in Herfindahl-Hirschman Index and Likelihood of a Challenged Merger
Highly concentrated	Greater than 1,800	Greater than 100—likely to be challenged 50 to 100—depends on other factors* Less than 50—unlikely to be challenged
Moderately concentrated	1,000–1,800	Greater than 100—likely to be challenged; other factors considered* Less than or equal to 100—unlikely to be challenged
Unconcentrated	Less than 1,000	Any increase—unlikely to be challenged

*In addition to the postmerger concentration of the market and the size of the resulting increase in concentration, the department will consider the presence of the following factors in deciding whether to challenge a merger: ease of entry; the nature of the product and its terms of sale; market information about specific transactions; buyer market characteristics; conduct of firms in the market; and market performance. [For a detailed explanation of these factors see Sections III(B) and III(C) of the 1982 Department of Justice Merger Guidelines.]

There are two problems of interpretation of the HHI in the context of banking and financial services. First, what is the relevant geographic scope of the market for financial services—national, regional, or city?[23] Second, once that market is defined, do we view banks, thrifts, and insurance companies as separate or unique lines of business, or are they competing in the same financial market? That is, what defines the institutional scope of the market? In the case of financial services, it has been traditional to define markets on functional, or line of business, criteria, so that commercial banking is a separate market from savings (thrift) banking and other financial services. Further, the relevant market area has usually been defined as highly localized: the standard metropolitan statistical areas (SMSAs) or rural areas (non-SMSAs). Unfortunately, such definitions become increasingly irrelevant in a world of greater geographic and product expansions. Indeed, the use of HHIs should increasingly be based on regional or national market lines and include a broad financial service firm definition of the marketplace. Consequently, in recent years the Federal Reserve has often included one-half of thrift deposits in calculating bank market HHIs.

Interestingly, comparing asset concentrations by bank size, the merger wave in banking appears to have decreased the national asset share of the very smallest banks (under $100 million) from 16.1 percent in 1984 to 2.6 percent in 2003 while the relative size of the very biggest banks (over $10 billion) has increased from 34.5 percent in 1984 to 72.9 percent in 2003. The relative market shares of intermediate-sized banks ($100 million to $10 billion) have decreased as well, falling from 49.4 percent in 1984 to 24.5 percent in 2003 (see Table 22–6). However, even though the degree of concentration of assets among the largest banks has increased, the percentage share exhibited by the largest U.S. banks is still well below the shares attained by the largest Canadian and European banks in their domestic markets. Thus, mergers involving the largest U.S. banks will likely continue to be approved by the Department of Justice as well as other regulatory bodies.

[23] K. A. Gilbert and A. M. Zaretsky, in "Banking Antitrust: Are the Assumptions Still Valid?" *Review,* The Federal Reserve Bank of St. Louis, November/December 2003, pp. 29–52, review the literature on antitrust analysis of bank M&As and conclude that the evidence is consistent with the view that the relevant market areas for banking antitrust actions are local communities.

TABLE 22–6   U.S. Bank Asset Concentration, 1984 versus 2003

	2003				1984			
	Number	Percent of Total	Assets (in billions)	Percent of Total	Number	Percent of Total	Assets (in billions)	Percent of Total
All FDIC-insured commercial banks	7,769		$7,602.5		14,483		$2,508.9	
1. Under $100 million	3,911	50.3%	200.7	2.6%	12,044	83.2%	404.2	16.1%
2. $100 million–$1 billion	3,434	44.2	910.0	12.0	2,161	14.9	513.9	20.5
3. $1–$10 billion	341	4.4	947.3	12.5	254	1.7	725.9	28.9
4. $10 billion or more	83	1.1	5,544.5	72.9	24	0.2	864.8	34.5

Source: General Accounting Office, *Interstate Banking,* GAO/GGD, 95–35, December 1994, p. 101; and *FDIC Quarterly Banking Profile,* December 2003.

Concept Questions

1. What recent bank mergers have been motivated by cost synergies?
2. What are the three dimensions of revenue synergy gains?
3. Suppose each of five firms in a banking market has a 20 percent share. What is the HHI?

OTHER MARKET- AND FIRM-SPECIFIC FACTORS IMPACTING GEOGRAPHIC EXPANSION DECISIONS

In addition to regulation and cost and revenue synergies, other factors may impact an acquisition decision. For example, an acquiring FI may be concerned about the solvency and asset quality of a potential target FI in another region. Thus, important factors influencing the acquisition decision may include the target FI's leverage or capital ratio, its loss reserves, and the amount of nonperforming loans in its portfolio.

An early study by Beatty, Santomero, and Smirlock is indicative of the type of tests conducted. They analyzed the factors potentially impacting the attractiveness of bank mergers and identified some 13 factors or variables, many of them bank specific. In particular, they analyzed 149 bank acquisitions over the period 1984–85; they measured the attraction of the merger by the size of the **merger premium** the acquiring bank was willing to pay for a target bank. Analytically, we measure this premium by the ratio of the purchase price of the target bank's equity to its book price or the market to book ratio (see Chapter 20).

merger premium
The ratio of the purchase price of a target bank's equity to its book value.

The variables analyzed, their average values, and the expected direction of their effect on the merger premium appear in Table 22–7, panel (a), with the regression results in panel (b). As you can see, 6 of the 13 variables are bank-specific variables measuring the quality of the bank and 3 variables are regulatory variables reflecting the degree of barriers to entry into the market of the target bank. Two variables are market structure variables reflecting the possibilities of revenue synergies and rents from entry as measured by the market HHI and the deposit share of the target bank. Panel (b) indicates that the highest merger premiums are paid for well-managed banks in relatively uncompetitive environments.[24]

---

[24] R. P. Beatty, A. M. Santomero, and M. L. Smirlock, "Bank Merger Premiums: Analysis and Evidence," *The Salomon Center Monograph Series on Economics and Finance,* New York University, 1987.

TABLE 22–7   **Determinants of Bank Merger Premiums**

(a) Variable Definitions and Expected Coefficient Signs

	Variable	Definition	Average	Expected Sign
Bank Variables	TREAS	Ratio of U.S. Treasury investments to total assets	.203	−
	LNTOAST	Ratio of net loans to total assets	.482	?
	PROV	Ratio of loan loss provision to net loans	.007	+
	CHARGOFF	Ratio of loan write-offs to net loans	.008	−
	ROEQ	Ratio of net income to equity capital	.091	+
	CAPDEV	(Ratio of loan loss allowance plus equity capital to assets) − .06	.030	−
Regulatory Variables	UNIT	Equals 1 if acquired bank located in unit bank state and zero otherwise	.276	+
	MULTI	Equals 1 if state law permits multibank holding companies and zero otherwise	.002	?
	ELECT	Equals 1 if state law permits statewide electronic banking and zero otherwise	.397	−
Market Structure Variables	MS	Ratio of bank's total deposits to those of the market; its market share	.179	+
	HERF	The Herfindahl index of the target bank's market	.253	+
Other Variables	PURCH	Equals 1 if the acquisition was a purchase of the acquired bank	.609	?
	COMB	Equals 1 if the acquisition involved a combination of cash and equity shares	.166	?

(b) Bank Merger Premium Regression Equation Results*

$$
\begin{aligned}
\text{Premium} = \ & 1.927^{\dagger} & - & \ .771\,\text{TREAS}^{\dagger} & - & \ .574\,\text{LNTOAST}^{\dagger} & + & \ 10.438\,\text{PROV} \\
& (9.27) & & (-2.76) & & (-1.96) & & (1.41) \\
& - \ 6.684\,\text{CHARGOFF} & - & \ 1.786\,\text{CAPDEV}^{\dagger} & + & \ .510\,\text{ROEQ}^{\dagger} & + & \ .096\,\text{UNIT}^{\dagger} \\
& (-1.08) & & (-1.76) & & (2.10) & & (1.66) \\
& - \ .506\,\text{MULTI} & - & \ .061\,\text{ELECT} & - & \ .306\,\text{MS}^{\dagger} & + & \ .392\,\text{HERF}^{\dagger} \\
& (-1.26) & & (-1.19) & & (-1.66) & & (1.70) \\
& - \ .176\,\text{PURCH}^{\dagger} & - & \ .171\,\text{COMB}^{\dagger} & & & & \\
& (-2.85) & & (-2.2) & & & &
\end{aligned}
$$

R^2 = .121   Number of observations = 264   F-statistic = 2.68*†

*T-statistics in parentheses below estimated coefficients.
†Coefficient on variable or test statistic significant at the 10 percent level.

Source: R. P. Beatty, A. M. Santomero, and M. L. Smirlock, "Bank Merger Premiums: Analysis and Evidence," *The Salomon Center Monograph Series on Economics and Finance*, New York University, 1987. Reprinted by permission.

In a review of a number of studies that analyzed the determinants of merger bid premiums (the ratio of the purchase price of a target bank's equity to its book value), Darius Palia found some support for the Beatty, Santomero, and Smirlock findings.[25] Specifically, other empirical studies appear to confirm that premiums are higher (1) in states with the most restrictive regulations and (2) for target banks with high-quality loan portfolios. Palia also concludes that the growth rate of the

[25] D. Palia, "Recent Evidence of Bank Mergers," *Financial Markets, Instruments, and Institutions* 3, no. 5 (1994), pp. 36–59; and E. Brewer II, W. E. Jackson III, J. A. Jagtiani, and T. Nguyen, "The Price of Bank Mergers in the 1990s," Federal Reserve Bank of Chicago, *Economic Perspectives* 24, no. 1 (2000), pp. 2–24.

target bank has little effect on bid premiums, while the results for the effects on bid premiums of target bank profitability and capital adequacy are rather mixed. More recently, Brewer, Jackson, Jagtiani, and Nguyen find that, in the 1990s, higher-performing targets (as measured by both return on equity and return on assets) receive higher bids; the lower the capital-to-deposit ratio, the larger the bid the acquiring bank is willing to offer; larger targets' loan-to-assets ratios and bank size are positively related to bid premiums; and higher prices occurred in the post-Riegle-Neal environment.

Concept Questions

1. Suppose you are a manager of an FI looking at another FI as a target for acquisition. What three characteristics of the target FI would most attract you?
2. Given the same scenario as in question (1), what three characteristics would most discourage you?

THE SUCCESS OF GEOGRAPHIC EXPANSIONS

A variety of regulatory and economic factors impact the attractiveness of geographic expansions to an FI manager. This section evaluates some of the empirical evidence on the success of market extension mergers. There are at least two levels at which such an evaluation can be done: First, how do investors react when an interstate bank merger is announced? Second, once interstate bank mergers have taken place, do they produce, in aggregate, the expected gains in efficiency and profitability? Both the announcement effect studies and the postmerger performance studies generally support the existence of gains from domestic geographic expansions by U.S. commercial banks.

Investor Reaction

Investors do not necessarily react positively to the news of an acquisition or merger between financial institutions. For example, at the announcement of the merger of J. P. Morgan and Chase, shares of J. P. Morgan Chase fell from $3.46 in 1999 to $1.67 per share in 2002. Researchers have conducted a number of studies on both nonbank and bank mergers, looking at the announcement effects of mergers on both bidding and target firms' share values. The studies measure the announcement effect by the reaction of investors in the stock market to the news of a merger event. In particular, economists have been interested in whether a merger announcement generates positive **abnormal returns**—risk-adjusted stock returns above normal levels—for the bidding and/or target firms. Unlike the situation with commercial firms, where the typical study finds that only target firms' shareholders gain from merger announcements through significantly positive abnormal returns, studies in banking find that occasionally both the acquiring bank and the target bank gain.[26] For example, Cornett and De studied interstate merger proposals during the period 1982–86. They found that on the day of the merger announcement, bidding bank stockholders enjoyed positive abnormal returns of 0.65 percent while target bank shareholders enjoyed 6.08 percent abnormal returns. They also found that bidding bank returns were higher for those banks seeking to acquire targets in states with more restrictive banking pact laws that prohibited

abnormal returns
Risk-adjusted stock returns above expected levels.

---

[26] See, for example, N. Travlos, "Corporate Takeover Bids, Methods of Payment, and Bidding Firm Stock Returns," *Journal of Finance* 42 (1987), pp. 943–63.

nationwide entry and where the target bank was not a failed bank. Studies by Desai and Stover and James and Weir also report significant abnormal returns for bidding bank stockholders even for intrastate mergers. More recently, Becher finds that bank mergers from 1990 through 1997 produce positive abnormal returns for targets and bidders. Kane examines bank megamergers in the mid-1990s. He finds that large bank bidders gain value when a target is large and when the large target is headquartered in the same state as the bidder. The gain is likely due to the fact that megamergers are more likely to create a bank that regulators would find too big to fail. Nevertheless, other studies—for example, by Hawawini and Swary—find negative returns for bidding banks.[27] Table 22–8 summarizes these and other findings.

Postmerger Performance

Even though the expectation, on announcement, might be favorable for enhanced profitability and performance as a result of an interstate geographic expansion, are such mergers actually proving successful in the postmerger period? For example, after its acquisition of First Chicago, profits of Bank One fell from $3.45 per share in 1999 to $2.77 in 2002. Cornett and Tehranian studied the postacquisition performance of large bank mergers between 1982 and 1987 and again from 1990 through 2000. Using operating cash flows (defined as earnings before depreciation, goodwill, interest on long-term debt, and taxes) divided by assets as a performance measure, they found that merged banks tended to outperform the banking industry. They found that superior performance resulted from improvements in these banks' ability to (1) attract loans and deposits, (2) increase employee productivity, and (3) enhance asset growth. Further, for 1990 through 2000, they found that large bank mergers produced greater performance gains than small bank mergers, activity-focusing mergers produced greater performance gains than diversifying mergers, geographically focusing mergers produced greater performance gains than geographically diversifying mergers, and performance gains were larger after the implementation of nationwide banking in 1997. Finally, they found improved performance of a merged bank is the result of both revenue enhancements and cost-reduction activities. However, revenue enhancements are most significant in those mergers that also experience reduced costs. Both studies find that the announcement period abnormal stock returns are significantly related to the changes in operating performance after the merger. Stiroh and Strahan studied the performance of banks that merged as their home state passed regulations allowing intrastate and interstate banking. They show that after deregulation, poor-performing banks come under increased pressure as well-run banks entered their previously shielded markets. They found a large and significant change in the control of bank assets (from poor- to high-performing banks) after deregulation. They

[27] M. M. Cornett and S. De, "Common Stock Returns in Corporate Takeover Bids: Evidence of Interstate Bank Mergers," *Journal of Banking and Finance* 15 (1991), pp. 273–95; A. Desai and R. Stover, "Bank Holding Company Acquisitions, Stockholders Returns, and Regulatory Uncertainty," *Journal of Financial Research* 8 (1985), pp. 145–56; C. James and P. Weir, "Returns to Acquirers and Competition in the Acquisition Market: The Case of Banking," *Journal of Political Economy* 95 (1983), pp. 355–70; G. Hawawini and I. Swary, *Mergers and Acquisitions in the U.S. Banking Industry* (Amsterdam: North Holland, 1990), p. 211; D. A. Becher, "The Valuation Effects of Bank Mergers," *Journal of Corporate Finance,* 2000, pp. 189–214; and E. J. Kane, "Incentives for Banking Megamergers: What Motives Might Regulators Infer from Event-Study Evidence?" *Journal of Money, Credit, and Banking,* 2000, pp. 671–701.

TABLE 22–8   Summary of Event Studies

Study	Sample	Definition of Event*	Definition of Market[†]	Target's Excess Returns[‡]	Acquirer's Excess Returns
Baradwaj, Dubofsky, and Fraser, 1991	108 interstate (July 1981–87)	1	Nasdaq value weighted	N/A	Negative
Baradwaj, Fraser, and Furtado, 1990	23 hostile 30 nonhostile (1980–87)	1	OTC equally weighted	Positive	Negative
Becher, 2000	558 mergers (1960–97)	1, 2	Value weighted	Positive	Positive
Cornett and De, 1991a	152 interstate 152 acquirers 37 targets (1982–86)	1, 4 5	Equally weighted, value weighted	Positive	Positive
Cornett and De, 1991b	132 interstate 132 acquirers 36 targets (1982–86)	1, 4 5	Equally weighted, value weighted	Positive	Positive
Cornett and Tehranian, 1992	30 mergers (1982–87)	7	Equally weighted	Positive	Negative
Cornett, Hovakimian, Palia, and Tehranian, 2001	423 acquirers (1988–95)	1, 8	Equally weighted	N/A	Focusing, no change Diversifying, negative
Cornett, McNutt, and Tehranian, 2004	193 mergers (1990–2000)	1, 2, 9	Value weighted	Positive	Negative
DeLong, 2001	280 mergers (1988–1995)	1, 9	Value weighted	Positive	Focusing, negative Diversifying, more negative
Desai and Stover, 1985	18 BHCs (1976–82)	1,2 3	Equally weighted	N/A	Positive
Dubofsky and Fraser, 1989	101 mergers (1973–83)	1	Equally weighted, value weighted	N/A	Positive (before June 1981), negative (after June 1981)
Hannan and Wolken, 1989	43 acquirers 69 targets (1982–87)	1	Wilshire Index	Positive	Negative
Hawawini and Swary 1990	78 acquirers 123 targets (1971–86)	1, 2	Nasdaq value weighted	Positive	Negative
James and Weir, 1987a	60 mergers (1972–83)	1	Equally weighted	N/A	Positive
Kane and Tehranian, 1989	33 New Hampshire mergers (June 1979–87)	1, 6 9	Nasdaq equally weighted bank index	N/A	Zero
Kane, 2000	110 megamergers (1991–98)	9	Value weighted	Positive	Giant banks, positive
Lobue, 1984	37 BHCs (N/A)	3	OTC general market index and OTC banking index	N/A	Positive
Neely, 1987	26 mergers (1979–85)	1, 5	Creates bank index from S&P	Positive	Negative
Palia, 1994	48 mergers (1984–87)	1	Nasdaq value weighted	N/A	Negative
Sushka and Bendeck, 1988	41 mergers (1972–85)	2	Uses mean adjusted returns model	N/A	Negative

TABLE 22–8   (*concluded*)

Study	Sample	Definition of Event*	Definition of Market†	Target's Excess Returns‡	Acquirer's Excess Returns
Trifts and Scanlon, 1987	21 interstate 14 acquirers 17 targets (1982–85)	1	S&P 500 index	Positive	Negative
Wall and Gup, 1989	23 mergers (June 1981–83)	1	Value weighted	N/A	Negative

*The event dates among the various studies are coded (for easy presentation) as follows: 1 = *Wall Street Journal* announcement date; 2 = Federal Reserve Board approval date; 3 = acquisition completion date; 4 = Dow Jones News Wire announcement date; 5 = *New York Times* announcement date; 6 = Cates MergerWatch announcement date; 7 = Shearson Lehman Brothers' Bank Merger and Acquisition study announcement date; 8 = LEXIS/NEXIS; 9 = Securities Data Company.
†Whenever the study specifies that Nasdaq stocks have been included in the market portfolio, we explicitly specify so. Otherwise, we present the market portfolio as an equally weighted and/or value weighted portfolio. Other market portfolios (such as the Standard & Poor's 500 Index) are also presented.
‡We do not present the actual excess returns earned because many studies provide results for a larger number of differing event windows (which are not comparable). Accordingly, we present whether the excess returns were positive or negative. N/A stands for not available or not examined.

Source: D. Palia, "Recent Evidence of Bank Mergers," *Financial Markets, Instruments, and Institutions* 3, no. 5 (1994), pp. 36–59, and author's research.

concluded that the transfer of assets to better banks represents a clear benefit from the deregulation.[28]

Boyd and Graham studied small bank mergers (with combined total deposits less than $400 million) from 1989 through 1991. Comparing industry-adjusted return on assets (ROA) before versus after a merger, they found that 1989 mergers saw large ROA increases, 1991 mergers resulted in decreases, and 1990 mergers had results somewhere in the middle. However, for all years the merged banks outperformed the banking industry. DeLong found that mergers that "focused" activities over the 1988–95 period improved the performance of the merging firms while those that diversified activities did not.[29] Finally, using 1994 data, Hughes et al. found that banks that engage in interstate expansion outperform banks that do not. Not only do these banks experience gains in financial performance, but society also benefits from enhanced bank safety that follows from improved performance.[30]

[28] M. M. Cornett and H. Tehranian, "Changes in Corporate Performance Associated with Bank Acquisitions," *Journal of Financial Economics* 31 (1992), pp. 211–34; K. J. Stiroh and P. E. Strahan, "Competitive Dynamics of Deregulation: Evidence from U. S. Banking, "*Journal of Money, Credit, and Banking* 35, no. 5 (2003), pp. 801–28; and M. M. Cornett, J. J. McNutt, and H. Tehranian, "Performance Changes Around Bank Mergers: Revenue Enhancements versus Cost Reductions," Working Paper, 2004.

[29] While most research has found bank acquisitions improve financial performance of the combined bank, results to the contrary have been found in some papers. See B. G. Baradwaj, D. A. Dubofsky, and D. R. Fraser, "Bidder Returns in Interstate and Intrastate Bank Acquisitions," *Journal of Financial Services Research* 5 (1992), pp. 261–73; D. Palia, "Recent Evidence of Bank Mergers," *Financial Markets, Instruments, and Institutions* 3, no. 5 (1994), pp. 36–59; Hawawini and I. Swary, *Mergers and Acquisitions in the U.S. Banking Industry* (New York: Elsevier Science, 1990); and M. F. Toyne and J. D. Tripp, "Interstate Bank Mergers and Their Impact on Shareholder Return: Evidence from the 1990's," *Quarterly Journal of Business and Economics* 37, no. 4 (1998), pp. 48–58.

[30] J. D. Boyd and S. L. Graham, "Consolidation in U.S. Banking: Implications for Efficiency and Competitive Risk, "*Bank Mergers and Acquisitions,* eds. T. Amihud and G. Miller (Amsterdam: Kluwer, 1998); G. DeLong, "Domestic and International Bank Mergers: The Gains from Focusing versus Diversifying," *Journal of Financial Economics* 59 (2001), pp. 221–52; G. DeLong, "Does Long-Term Performance of Mergers Match Market Expectations? Evidence from the U. S. Banking Industry," *Financial Management,* 2003, pp. 5–25; and J. P. Hughes, W. W. Lang, L. J. Mester, and C. Moon, "The Dollars and Sense of Bank Consolidation," *Journal of Banking and Finance* 23 (1999), pp. 291–324.

Concept Questions

1. If the abnormal returns for target banks are usually positive, does this mean that managers of acquiring banks tend to overpay the shareholders of the target bank?
2. In general, what do studies of the announcement effect and postmerger performance conclude?

Summary

Domestic geographic expansions are one way in which an FI can improve its return-risk performance. This chapter reviewed the various restrictions existing in the United States that inhibit geographic expansions for different types of FIs. While, traditionally, commercial banks have faced the most restrictions on their geographic expansions (especially in their branching activities), these restrictions have recently been removed. Partly as a result of this and other factors relating to cost and revenue synergies, the U.S. financial system is now in a dramatic period of consolidation. This consolidation has resulted in a number of megamergers among large FIs and the movement of the United States toward a nationwide banking system similar to those that exist in Canada and major European countries.

Questions and Problems

1. How do limitations on geographic diversification affect an FI's profitability?
2. How are insurance companies able to offer services in states beyond their state of incorporation?
3. In what way did the Garn-St Germain Act and FIRREA provide incentives for the expansion of interstate branching?
4. Why were unit and money center banks opposed to bank branching in the early 1900s?
5. In what ways did the banking industry continuously succeed in maintaining interstate banking activities during the 50-year period beginning in the early 1930s? What legislative efforts did regulators use to respond to each foray by banks into previously prohibited banking and commercial activities?
6. What is the difference between an MBHC and an OBHC?
7. What is an interstate banking pact? How did the three general types of interstate banking pacts differ in their encouragement of interstate banking?
8. What significant economic events during the 1980s provided the incentive for the Garn-St Germain Act and FIRREA to allow further expansion of interstate banking?
9. What is a nonbank bank? What legislation allowed the creation of nonbank banks? What role did nonbank banks play in the further development of interstate banking activities?
10. How did the development of the nonbank bank competitive strategy further clarify the meaning of the term *activities closely related to banking?* In a more general sense, how has this strategy assisted the banking industry in its attempts to provide services and products outside the strictly banking environment?
11. How did the provisions of the Riegle-Neal Interstate Banking and Branching Efficiency Act of 1994 allow for full interstate banking? What are the expected

profit performance effects of interstate banking? What has been the impact on the structure of the banking and financial services industry?

12. Bank mergers often produce hard-to-quantify benefits called X efficiencies and costs called X inefficiencies. Give an example of each.

13. What does the Berger and Humphrey study reveal about the cost savings from bank mergers? What differing results are revealed by the Rhoades study?

14. What are the three revenue synergies that may be obtained by an FI from expanding geographically?

15. What is the Herfindahl-Hirschman Index? How is it calculated and interpreted?

16. City Bank currently has a 60 percent market share in banking services, followed by NationsBank with 20 percent and State Bank with 20 percent.

    a. What is the concentration ratio as measured by the Herfindahl-Hirschman Index (HHI)?

    b. If City Bank acquires State Bank, what will be the new HHI?

    c. Assume that the Justice Department will allow mergers as long as the changes in HHI do not exceed 1,400. What is the minimum amount of assets that City Bank will have to divest after it merges with State Bank?

17. The Justice Department has been asked to review a merger request for a market with the following four FIs:

Bank	Assets
A	$ 12 million
B	25 million
C	102 million
D	3 million

    a. What is the HHI for the existing market?

    b. If bank A acquires bank D, what will be the impact on the market's level of concentration?

    c. If bank C acquires bank D, what will be the impact on the market's level of concentration?

    d. What is likely to be the Justice Department's response to the two merger applications?

18. The Justice Department measures market concentration using the HHI of market share. What problems does this measure have for (a) multiproduct FIs and (b) FIs with global operations?

19. What factors other than market concentration does the Justice Department consider in determining the acceptability of a merger?

20. What are some plausible reasons for the percentage of assets of small banks decreasing and the percentage of assets of large banks increasing while the percentage of assets of intermediate banks has stayed constant since 1984?

21. According to empirical studies, what factors have the highest impact on merger premiums as defined by the ratio of a target bank's purchase price to book value?

22. What are the results of studies that have examined the mergers of banks, including postmerger performance? How do they differ from the studies examining mergers of nonbanks?
23. What are some of the important firm-specific financial factors that influence the acquisition of an FI?
24. How has the performance of merged banks compared to that of bank industry averages?
25. What are some of the benefits for banks engaging in geographic expansion?

S&P Question

STANDARD &POOR'S

26. Go to the Standard & Poor's Market Insight Web site at **www.mhhe.com/edu-marketinsight.** Click on "Educational Version of Market Insight." Enter your Site ID and click on "Login." Click on "Company." Find the most recent data for Deposits, Equity, and Assets held by the Bank of New York (BK), Citigroup (C), J. P. Morgan Chase (JPM), and Bank of America (BAC) using the following steps. Enter "BK" in the "Ticker:" box and click on "Go!" Click on "Excel Analytics." Click on "FS Ann. Balance Sheet." This will download the Balance Sheet for Bank of New York, which contains the balances for Total Equity and Total Assets. Repeat the process by entering "C" in the "Ticker:" box to get information on Citigroup. Repeat the process by entering "JPM" in the "Ticker:" box to get information on J. P. Morgan Chase. Repeat the process by entering "BAC" in the "Ticker:" box to get information on Bank of America. Calculate the deposits to assets and equity to assets ratios for these four financial institutions. How do these ratios differ for the FIs?

Web Questions

27. Go to the FDIC Web site at **www.fdic.gov**. Find the most recent breakdown of bank holding company deposit share for the State of New York using the following steps. Click on "Analysts." From there click on "Summary of Deposits" and then click on "Market Share and Bank Holding Co." Click on "State->County->City->Zip." Under "State," select "New York," and then click on "Continue." Click on "Continue." Click on "Run Report." This will bring the files up on your computer that contain the relevant data. What banks are the top deposit holders in the state?
28. Go to the FDIC Web site at **www.fdic.gov.** Find the most recent data on bank asset concentration by size using the following steps. Click on "Analysts." From there click on "FDIC Quarterly Banking Profile" and then click on "Quarterly Banking Profile." Click on "Commercial Bank Section." Click on "*Table III-A.* First Quarter XXXX, FDIC-Insured Commercial Banks." This will bring the file up on your computer that contains the relevant data. How have these data changed from those reported in Table 22–6?

Pertinent Web Sites

Department of Justice	www.usdoj.gov
Federal Deposit Insurance Corporation	www.fdic.gov
Office of the Comptroller of the Currency	www.occ.treas.gov
Office of Thrift Supervision	www.ots.treas.gov

Chapter Twenty-Three

Geographic Diversification: International

INTRODUCTION

Many FIs can diversify domestically, but only the very largest can aspire to diversify beyond national frontiers. This chapter analyzes recent trends toward the globalization of FI franchises and examines the potential return-risk advantages and disadvantages of such expansions. While FIs from some countries, such as the United States, are currently seeking to expand internationally as fast as possible, others, most notably those from Japan, are contracting their international operations. The extent to which an FI expands internationally is thus part of the overall risk management of the FI.

GLOBAL AND INTERNATIONAL EXPANSIONS

There are at least three ways an FI can establish a global or international presence: (1) selling financial services from its domestic offices to foreign customers, such as a loan originated in the New York office of J. P. Morgan Chase made to a Brazilian manufacturer; (2) selling financial services through a branch, agency, or representative office established in the foreign customer's country, such as making a loan to the Brazilian customer through J. P. Morgan Chase's branch in Brazil; and (3) selling financial services to a foreign customer through subsidiary companies in the foreign customer's country, such as J. P. Morgan Chase buying a Brazilian bank and using that wholly owned bank to make loans to the Brazilian customer. Note that these three methods of global activity expansion are not mutually exclusive; an FI could use all three simultaneously to expand the scale and scope of its operations.

U.S. banks, insurance companies, and securities firms have all expanded abroad in recent years, often through branches and subsidiaries; this has been reciprocated by the entrance and growth until recently of foreign FIs in U.S. financial service markets. At the end of 2002, 15 banks in the world had more than 50 percent of their bank assets held in foreign countries. Table 23–1 lists the top six banks in terms of global activity. Of the top 30 global banks, no single country dominated the list. Canada had five banks in the top 30; Ireland, the Netherlands, and the United States all had three banks, while Austria, Germany, Spain, Switzerland, and

TABLE 23–1
Top Global Banks

Source: "Top 50 Global Banks," *The Banker,* February 2003. *www.thebanker.com*

Banks	Home Country	Percentage of Overseas Business*
1. American Express Bank	United States	80.9%
2. Standard Chartered	United Kingdom	79.2
3. UBS	Switzerland	76.8
4. Investec	South Africa	74.2
5. Credit Suisse Group	Switzerland	72.9
6. Deutsche Bank	Germany	64.4

*Overseas business refers to the percentage of assets banks hold outside their home country.

the United Kingdom each had two banks. A severe economic recession and burgeoning bad debts in their loan portfolios have left Japanese banks noticeably absent even though, based on size of assets, they are among the largest in the world.

The next section concentrates on the growth of global banking. It begins with U.S. bank expansions into foreign countries and the factors motivating these expansions and then discusses foreign bank expansions into the United States.

U.S. Banks Abroad

While some U.S. banks, such as J. P. Morgan Chase, have had offices abroad since the beginning of the twentieth century, the major phase of growth began in the early 1960s after the passage of the Overseas Direct Investment Control Act of 1964. This law restricted domestic U.S. banks' ability to lend to U.S. corporations that wanted to make foreign investments. The law was eventually repealed, but it created incentives for U.S. banks to establish foreign offices to service the funding and other business needs of their U.S. clients in other countries. This offshore funding and lending in dollars created the beginning of a market we now call the *Eurodollar market*. The term **Eurodollar transaction** denotes any transaction involving dollars that takes place outside the United States. For example, a banking transaction booked externally to the boundaries of the United States, often through an overseas branch or subsidiary, qualifies as a Eurodollar transaction.[1]

Eurodollar transaction
Any transaction involving dollars that takes place outside the United States.

Table 23–2 shows the aggregate size of U.S. bank activities abroad between 1980 and 2003 as well as the different types of loan activities those subsidiaries engage in. As reported in Table 23–2, assets in U.S. bank foreign offices increased from $353.8 billion in 1980 to $804.4 billion in 2003. However, as a percent of these banks' total assets, assets in foreign offices fell from 32.4 percent in 1980 to 16.2 percent in 2003. The same trend is found for much of the loan portfolio. The majority of loans (in dollar terms) in foreign offices of U.S. banks are commercial and industrial (C&I) loans, $127.6 billion in 2003. In 1980, 38.6 percent of these banks' C&I loans were in foreign offices, compared to 19.9 percent in 2003. In 1980, 5.8 percent of these banks' real estate loans were in foreign offices compared to 2.7 percent in 2003. In contrast to C&I and mortgage loans, in 1980 8.7 percent of the loans to individuals in these banks were in foreign offices compared to 16.3 percent in 2003.

Factors Encouraging U.S. Bank Expansions Abroad

While regulation of foreign lending was the original impetus for the early growth of the Eurodollar market and the associated establishment of U.S. branches and

---

[1] That is, the definition of a Eurodollar transaction is more general than "a transaction booked in Europe." In fact, any deposit in dollars taken externally to the United States normally qualifies that transaction as a Eurodollar transaction.

TABLE 23–2
Assets of U.S. Banks with Foreign Offices, 1980–2003 (in billions of dollars)

Source: *Federal Reserve Bulletin,* various issues, Table 4–20.

	1980	1990	1995	2000	2003
Total assets	$1,091.4	$1,901.5	$2,530.1	$4,311.4	$4,961.7
Domestic assets	768.7	1,559.3	1,962.8	3,576.3	4,157.3
Foreign assets	353.8	410.7	666.3	735.1	804.4
C&I loans (domestic)*	173.8	326.1	356.8	647.2	514.3
C&I loans (foreign)	109.4	103.6	125.5	189.8	127.6
Real estate loans (domestic)	108.9	387.2	486.1	955.5	1,211.2
Real estate loans (foreign)	6.7	26.6	27.2	32.0	33.4
Individual loans (domestic)	67.1	151.9	207.0	302.1	329.1
Individual loans (foreign)	6.4	17.2	30.6	44.3	64.1

*Commercial and Industrial loans.

subsidiaries outside the United States, other regulatory and economic factors also have impacted the growth of U.S. offshore banking. These factors are discussed next.

The Dollar as an International Medium of Exchange   The growth of international trade after World War II and the use of the dollar as an international medium of exchange encouraged foreign corporations and investors to demand dollars. A convenient way to do this was by using U.S. banks' foreign offices to intermediate such fund flows between the United States and foreigners wishing to hold dollars. Today, trade-related transactions underlie much of the activity in the Eurodollar market.[2] However, with the creation of the new euro currency in January 2002, the importance of the dollar as the "international medium of exchange" may well decline, especially among major European corporations.

Political Risk Concerns   Political risk concerns among savers in emerging market countries have led to enormous outflows of dollars from those countries, often to U.S. branches and subsidiaries in the Cayman Islands and the Bahamas, where there are very stringent bank secrecy rules. Because of the secrecy rules in some foreign countries and the possibility that these rules may result in money laundering and the financing of terrorist activities, the U.S. government enacted the USA Patriot Act of 2001. The act prohibits U.S. banks from providing banking services to foreign banks that have no physical presence in any country (so-called shell banks). The bill also added foreign corruption offenses to the list of crimes that can trigger a U.S. money-laundering prosecution. Also, federal authorities have the power to subpoena the records of a foreign bank's U.S. correspondent account. Further, the bill makes a depositor's funds in a foreign bank's U.S. correspondent account subject to the same civil forfeiture rules that apply to depositors' funds in other U.S. accounts. Finally, the act requires U.S. banks to improve their due diligence reviews in order to guard against money laundering.

Violations of the USA Patriot Act have resulted in large fines and actions taken against violating banks. For example, in 2004 Hudson United Bank agreed to pay $5 million to settle a probe into whether a branch failed to monitor accounts in its correspondent banking business. Investigators discovered that more than $1 billion flowed through suspicious accounts used by customers from South America and the Caribbean at a Hudson United Bank branch over a 16-month period ending in November 2003, when the bank shut down the correspondent business dealing with international customers. The branch was not following required "know

---

[2] The decline in the dollar relative to the yen and mark in recent years has weakened the role of the dollar as the international medium of exchange.

your customer" rules set out in the Patriot Act. More recently, in April 2004, federal officials intensified their inquiry into Riggs Bank's handling of large amounts of cash for foreign accounts, and a central focus was on the bank's failure to report properly dozens of substantial withdrawals from the personal accounts of Saudi Arabia's longtime ambassador to Washington. The Saudi accounts and other international transactions at Riggs were being investigated by the Federal Bureau of Investigation and two Treasury Department agencies, the Office of the Comptroller of the Currency and the Financial Crimes Enforcement Network. Further, regulators threatened to impose new requirements and other penalties on Riggs.

Domestic Regulatory Restrictions/Foreign Regulatory Relaxations   As discussed in Chapter 21, prior to the 1999 Financial Services Modernization Act, U.S. banks faced considerable activity restrictions at home regarding their securities, insurance, and commercial activities. However, with certain exceptions, Federal Reserve regulations have allowed U.S. banking offices in other countries to engage in the permitted banking activities of the foreign country even if such activities were not permitted in the United States. For example, U.S. banks setting up foreign subsidiaries can lease real property, act as general insurance agents, and underwrite and deal in foreign corporate securities (up to a maximum commitment of $2 million). Foreign activity regulations also encourage U. S. bank expansion abroad. For example, in late 2003 the Chinese Banking Regulatory Commission signaled a shift in policy away from restricting overseas competition to one of cautiously embracing it when it announced a comprehensive plan to overhaul the country's shaky banking system. The plan gave foreign banks greater scope to operate in China, including increasing the ceiling on foreign ownership in Chinese financial institutions from 15 percent to 20 percent for a single investor, expanding the number of cities where foreign branches could do local currency business, and easing capital requirements for foreign branches.[3] In a recent study Whalen[4] has shown that many of these nonbanking activities produce revenue flows that have a low or negative correlation with the revenues from domestic (U.S.) banking. That is, international expansions appear to produce important revenue-risk diversification benefits for U.S. banks.

Technology and Communications Improvements   The improvements in telecommunications and other communications technologies such as CHIPS (the international payment system, see Chapter 14) and the development of proprietary communication networks by large FIs have allowed U.S. parent FIs to extend and maintain real-time control over their foreign operations at a decreasing cost. The decreasing operating costs of such expansions have made it feasible to locate offices in an even wider array of international locations.[5]

---

[3] C. M. Buch and G. DeLong find that as countries increase regulatory transparency, their banks become more attractive targets of international bank mergers. At the same time, they find some evidence that increased supervisory power reduces the incentives of banks to engage as acquirers in international mergers. In addition, banks from more developed countries tend to take over banks in less developed countries. See "Cross-Border Bank Mergers: What Lures the Rare Animal?" Working Paper, Baruch College, CUNY, 2003.

[4] See G. Whalen, "The Securities Activities of the Foreign Subsidiaries of U.S. Banks: Evidence of Risk and Returns," White Paper 98–2, OCC, Washington, D.C., February 1998.

[5] M. E. Chaffai, M. Dietsch, and A. Lozano-Vivas, in "Technological and Environmental Differences in the European Banking Industries," *Journal of Financial Studies Research* 19 (2001), pp. 147–62, break bank productivity into technological differences and environmental differences. They find that while technology improves bank productivity, differences due to environmental conditions are larger than those due to technology. Even if the banking industry in a country uses better technology, it could be less productive in a hostile environment.

Factors Deterring U.S. Expansions Abroad

A number of potential factors deter international expansion, as discussed next.

Capital Constraints   The proposed (2006) reforms of the Bank for International Settlements (BIS) capital requirements will raise the required capital needed to back loans to sovereign countries outside of the OECD rated below B− as well as any loans to OECD countries who are rated below AA− (i.e., it is only the OECD countries rated above AA− that will have zero risk weight as under the current BIS risk-based capital system—see Chapter 20).

Emerging Market Problems

NAFTA
The North American
Free Trade Agreement.

The problems of other emerging market countries such as Korea, Thailand, and Indonesia in 1997 and 1998 and more recently (in the early 2000s) in Argentina have made many U.S. banks more cautious in expanding outside traditional foreign markets.[6] This is despite the existence of increasingly favorable regulatory environments. For example, the 1994 **NAFTA** agreement has given U.S. (and Canadian) banks greater powers to expand into Mexico. See Table 23–3 for details on the NAFTA agreement.[7] The December 1997 agreement by 100 countries, reached under the auspices of the World Trade Organization (WTO), is also an important step toward dismantling the regulatory barriers inhibiting the entry of U.S. FIs into emerging market countries.[8]

Competition   During the 1990s, U.S. banks faced extensive competition from Japanese banks for overseas business. Aiding the Japanese banks was their access to a large domestic savings base at a relatively low funding cost, the relatively slow pace of deregulation in the Japanese domestic financial markets, and their size. For example, for most of the 1990s, Japan had 9 of the 10 largest banks, measured by asset size, in the world. While large size does not necessarily mean high profits,[9] it gives a bank a greater ability to diversify across borders (and products) and to attract business by aggressively cutting fees and spreads in selected areas. However, in the late 1990s and early 2000s, as the Japanese economy moved into recession and the bad debts of Japanese banks mounted, the main competitive threat to U.S. banks has come from European banks.

Aiding the competitive position of European banks has been the passage of the European Community (EC) Second Banking Directive, which has created a single banking market in Europe as well as the introduction of a single currency for much of Europe (the euro). Under the Directive, European banks are allowed to branch and acquire banks throughout the European Community—that is, they have a

---

[6] One notable exception is Citigroup's $12.5 billion purchase of Mexico's second largest bank, Grupo Financiero Banamex-Accival in 2000. Citing Citigroup's faith in the recovery of Mexico's economy and banking system, the company hoped to use the Banamex brand name to serve the fast-growing Hispanic population in the United States as well.

[7] For an excellent discussion of the effects of NAFTA on U.S. banks, securities firms, and insurance companies, see R. S. Sczudio, "NAFTA: Opportunities Abound for U.S. and Canadian Financial Institutions," *Bankers Magazine*, July–August 1993, pp. 28–32.

[8] See "Accord Is Reached to Lower Barriers in Global Finance," *New York Times*, December 12, 1997, p. A1.

[9] In fact, Credit Lyonnais is a good example of why large size does not necessarily correlate with high profitability. In spring 1995, the French government had to bail out the bank by shifting its bad loans into a newly created entity. In addition, most Japanese banks have had severe problems with bad loans in recent years, which has meant a reduced tendency to expand abroad further.

TABLE 23–3
The NAFTA Agreement and U.S. Banks

Source: Institute of International Bankers, *1994 Global Survey of Regulatory and Market Developments in Banking, Securities and Insurance,* September 1994, p. 17.

- Any bank chartered in Canada or the United States, including Canadian or U.S. banks owned by nondomestic banks, may establish a bank subsidiary in Mexico that may expand in Mexico without geographic restriction. Canadian and U.S. banks, however, may not branch directly into Mexico.
- Banks from Mexico and Canada may establish direct branches and subsidiaries in the United States subject to the same geographic restrictions imposed on direct branches of other nondomestic banks and on other U.S. chartered banks, respectively.
- Banks from the United States and Mexico that are not controlled by investors from other countries may establish Schedule II bank subsidiaries in Canada, which subsidiaries enjoy nationwide branching powers. Mexican and U.S. banks may not branch directly into Canada.

Notes:
1. Nondomestic banks cannot open branches but are allowed to establish Schedule II subsidiary banks in Canada. Schedule II subsidiary banks owned by banks from the United States or Mexico have the same nationwide branching privileges as domestic Canadian banks. Schedule II banks owned by banks from other countries must seek government approval to open additional branches. This geographic restriction on Schedule II subsidiaries will be eliminated when the latest round of GATT comes into effect.
2. Mexico does not permit nondomestic banks to establish domestic branches. However, nondomestic banks can establish representative offices and offshore branches and take minority interests in local banking institutions. In addition, under NAFTA, banks from the United States and Canada, including U.S. and Canadian banks owned by banks from other countries, are allowed to establish bank subsidiaries with the same nationwide branching privileges as Mexican banks.

single EC passport.[10] While the Second Banking Directive did not come fully into effect until the end of 1992, it had been announced as early as 1988. As a result, there has been a cross-border merger wave among European banks that has paralleled the U.S. domestic merger and acquisition wave that followed the dismantling of interstate branching restrictions after the passage and implementation of the Reigle-Neal Act in 1994 (see Chapter 22).[11] In addition, a number of European banks have formed strategic alliances that will enable retail bank customers to open new accounts, access account information, and make payments to third parties through any of the branches of the member banks in the alliance. This greater consolidation in European banking has created more intense competition for U.S. and other foreign banks in European wholesale markets and has made it more difficult for them to penetrate European retail markets.

Foreign Banks in the United States

Just as U.S. banks can profitably expand into foreign markets, foreign banks have historically viewed the United States as an attractive market for entry. The following sections discuss foreign banks in the United States.

Organizational Form

Foreign banks use five primary forms of entry into the U.S. market. The choice of which organizational form to use is a function of regulations in the bank's home country as well as the risk management strategies followed by the bank.

---

[10] Direct branching by non-EC banks into member states was not governed by the Second Banking Directive but the laws of each member state. Currently, all EC countries allow foreign banks to branch.

[11] See A. Cybo-Ottone and M. Murgia, "Mergers and Acquisitions in the European Banking Markets," *Journal of Banking and Finance* 24 (2000), pp. 831–59; A. W. A. Boot, "European Lessons on Consolidation in Banking," *Journal of Banking and Finance* 23 (1999), pp. 609–13; C. M. Buch, "Why Do Banks Go Abroad? Evidence from German Data," *Financial Markets, Institutions, and Instruments* 9 (2000), pp. 33–67; C. M. Buch and G. DeLong, "Determinants of Cross-Border Bank Mergers: Is Europe Different?" in *Foreign Direct Investment in the Real and Financial Sector of Industrial Countries*, ed. H. Herrmann and R. Lipsey (Berlin: Springer, 2003); and P. Angelini and N. Citorellis. "The Effects of Regulatory Reform on Competition in the Banking Industry," *Journal of Money, Credit, and Banking*, October 2003, pp. 663–84.

TABLE 23–4
U.S. and Foreign
Bank Assets,
1980– 2003

Source: *Federal Reserve
Bulletin,* various issues,
Tables 1.26 and 4.30.

	Bank Assets Held in United States (billions of dollars)	
	U.S.-Owned	**Foreign-Owned**
1980	$1,537.0	$ 166.7
1985	2,284.8	175.5
1990	3,010.3	389.6
1992	3,138.4	514.3
1994	3,409.9	471.1
1995	3,660.6	530.1
2000	6,088.2	984.3
2003	7,385.4	1,069.6

Subsidiary   A foreign bank subsidiary has its own capital and charter; it operates in the same way as any U.S. domestic bank, with access to both retail and wholesale markets.

Branch   A branch bank is a direct expansion of the parent bank into a foreign or U.S. banking market. As such, it is reliant on its parent bank, such as Sumitomo Mitsui Banking Corporation in Japan, for capital support; normally, it has access to both wholesale and retail deposit and funding markets in the United States.

Agency   An agency is a restricted form of entry; this organizational form restricts access of funds to those funds borrowed on the wholesale and money markets (i.e., an agency cannot accept deposits). A special case of an agency is a New York Agreement Company that has both agency functions and limited investment banking functions.

**Edge Act
Corporation**
Specialized organiza-
tional form open to
U.S. domestic banks
that specialize in
international trade-
related banking
transactions or
investments.

Edge Act Corporation   An **Edge Act Corporation** is a specialized organizational form open to U.S. domestic banks since 1919 and to foreign banks since 1978. These banks specialize in international trade-related banking transactions or investments.

Representative Office   Even though a representative office books neither loans nor deposits in the United States, it acts as a loan production office, generating loan business for its parent bank at home. This is the most limited organizational form for a foreign bank entering the United States.[12]

Trends and Growth

Table 23–4 shows the expansion of foreign banks in the United States between 1980 and 2003. In 1980 foreign banks had $166.7 billion in assets (10.8 percent of the size of total U.S. bank assets). This activity grew through 1992, when foreign banks had $514.3 billion in assets (16.4 percent of the size of U.S. assets). In the mid-1990s, there was a modest retrenchment in the asset share of foreign banks in the United States. In 1994, their U.S. assets totaled $471.1 billion (13.8 percent of the size of U.S. assets). This retrenchment reflected a number of factors, including the highly competitive market for wholesale banking in the United States, a decline in average U.S. loan quality, capital constraints on Japanese banks at home,

---

[12] Also note the existence of International Banking Facilities (IBF) in the United States since 1981. These are specialized vehicles that are allowed to take deposits from and make loans to foreign (non-U.S.) customers only. As such, they are essentially offshore banking units that operate onshore. Most are located in New York, Illinois, and California and are generally free of U.S. bank regulation and taxes.

and their poor lending performance at home, and the introduction of the Foreign Bank Supervision and Enhancement Act (FBSEA) of 1991, which tightened regulations on foreign banks in the United States (discussed below).[13] However, as foreign banks adjusted to these developments and because of the strong U.S. economy in the late 1990s, activity of foreign banks in the United States has grown again, reaching 16.1 percent in 2000. The worldwide economic recession in the early 2000s again depressed the level of international activity in the United States. For example, in 2003 the percent of foreign bank assets in the United States dipped to 14.5 percent.

Regulation of Foreign Banks in the United States

Before 1978, foreign branches and agencies entering the United States were licensed mostly at the state level. As such, their entry, regulation, and oversight were almost totally confined to the state level. Beginning in 1978 with the passage of the International Banking Act (IBA) and the more recent passage of the Foreign Bank Supervision Enhancement Act (FBSEA), Title II of the FDICIA of December 1991, federal regulators have exerted increasing control over foreign banks operating in the United States.

The International Banking Act of 1978

Pre-IBA.   Before the passage in 1978 of the IBA, foreign agencies and branches entering the United States with state licenses had some competitive advantages and disadvantages relative to most domestic banks. On the one hand, as state-licensed organizations, they were not subject to the Federal Reserve's reserve requirements, audits, and exams; interstate branching restrictions (the McFadden Act); or restrictions on corporate securities underwriting activities (the Glass-Steagall Act). However, they had no access to the Federal Reserve's discount window (i.e., lender of last resort); no direct access to Fedwire, and, thus, the fed funds market; and no access to FDIC deposit insurance.

www.federalreserve.gov

Their inability to gain access to deposit insurance effectively precluded them from the U.S. retail banking market and its deposit base. As a result, prior to 1978, foreign banks in the United States largely concentrated on wholesale banking.

Post-IBA.   The unequal treatment of domestic and foreign banks regarding federal regulation and lobbying by domestic banks regarding the unfairness of this situation provided the impetus for Congress to pass the International Banking Act in 1978. The fundamental regulatory philosophy underlying the IBA was one of **national treatment**, a philosophy that attempted to create a level playing field for both domestic and foreign banks in U.S. banking markets. As a result of this act, foreign banks were required to hold Federal Reserve–specified reserve requirements if their worldwide assets exceeded $1 billion, were subjected to Federal Reserve examinations, and were subjected to both the McFadden and Glass-Steagall Acts. With respect to the latter, an important grandfather provision in the act allowed

national treatment
Regulating foreign banks in the same fashion as domestic banks or creating a level playing field.

---

[13] J. Peek, E. Rosengren, and F. Kasirye, "The Poor Performance of Foreign Subsidiaries: Were the Problems Acquired or Created?" *Journal of Banking and Finance* 23 (2000), pp. 579–604, find that many foreign banks acquiring U.S. banks have been hurt by the fact that the target banks already had problems at the time of acquisition. Moreover, they find that the changes in strategy introduced by foreign owners were generally insufficient in raising the performance of foreign banks relative to U.S. domestically owned peer banks.

foreign banks established in the United States prior to 1978 to keep their "illegal" interstate branches and securities-activity operations. That is, interstate and security-activity restrictions were applied only to new foreign banks entering the United States after 1978.14

If anything, the passage of the IBA accelerated the expansion of foreign bank activities in the United States. A major reason for this was that for the first time, the IBA gave foreign banks access to the Federal Reserve's discount window, Fedwire, and FDIC insurance. In particular, access to FDIC insurance allowed entry into retail banking. For example, in 1979 alone foreign banks acquired four large U.S. banks (Crocker, National Bank of North America, Union Planters, and Marine Midland). In addition, in the early 1980s the Bank of Tokyo, Mitsubishi Bank, and Sanwa Bank invested $1.3 billion in California bank acquisitions. Overall, Japanese banks owned over 25 percent of California bank assets at the end of the 1980s. (By the end of the 1990s, many of these Japanese-owned California bank assets were up for sale.)

The Foreign Bank Supervision Enhancement Act (FBSEA) of 1991   Along with the growth of foreign bank assets in the United States came concerns about foreign banks' rapidly increasing share of U.S. banking markets as well as about the weakness of regulatory oversight of many of these institutions. Three events focused attention on the weaknesses of foreign bank regulation. The first event was the collapse of the Bank of Credit and Commerce International (BCCI), which had a highly complex international organizational structure based in the Middle East, the Cayman Islands, and Luxembourg and had undisclosed ownership stakes in two large U.S. banks (see Figure 23–1). BCCI was not subject to any consolidated supervision by a home country regulator; this quickly became apparent after its collapse, when massive fraud, insider lending abuses, and money-laundering operations were discovered. The second event was the issuance of more than $1 billion in unauthorized letters of credit to Saddam Hussein's Iraq by the Atlanta agency of the Italian Banca Nazionale del Lavoro. The third event was the unauthorized taking of deposit funds by the U.S. representative office of the Greek National Mortgage Bank of New York.

These events and related concerns led to the passage of the FBSEA of 1991. The objective of this act was to extend federal regulatory authority over foreign banking organizations in the United States, especially where these organizations have entered using state licenses. The act's five main features have significantly enhanced the powers of federal bank regulators over foreign banks in the United States.[15]

1. *Entry.* Under FBSEA, a foreign banking organization must now have the Fed's approval to establish a subsidiary, branch, agency, or representative office in the United States. The approval applies to both a new entry and an entry by acquisition. To get Fed approval, the organization must meet a number of standards, two of which are mandatory. First, the foreign bank must be subject to comprehensive supervision on a consolidated basis by a home country regulator.[16]

---

[14] For example, in 1978, some 60 foreign banks had branches in at least three states. As noted earlier, the McFadden Act prevented domestic banks from engaging in interstate branching.

[15] See S. Bellanger, "Stormy Weather: The FBSEA's Impact on Foreign Banks," *Bankers Magazine,* November–December 1992, pp. 25–31; and GAO, "Foreign Banks: Implementation of the Foreign Bank Supervision and Enhancement Act of 1991," GAO/GGD–96–187, September 1996, Washington, D.C.

[16] A requirement for consolidated supervision also has been proposed by the Bank for International Settlements in its "Minimum Standards for the Supervision of International Banking Groups and Their Cross Border Establishments," Basel, Switzerland, June 1992.

FIGURE 23–1
The Bank of Credit and Commerce International's Organizational Structure

Source: U.S. General Accounting Office, *International Banking,* GAO/GGD–94–68 (1994), p. 17.

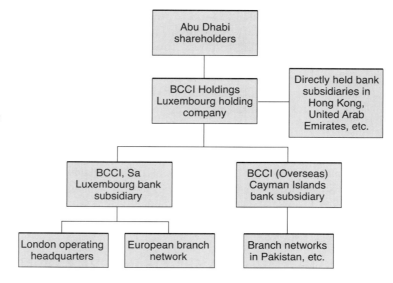

Second, that regulator must furnish all the information needed by the Federal Reserve to evaluate the application. Both standards are aimed at avoiding the lack of disclosure and lack of centralized supervision associated with BCCI's failure.

2. *Closure.* The act also gives the Federal Reserve authority to close a foreign bank if its home country supervision is inadequate, if it has violated U.S. laws, or if it is engaged in unsound and unsafe banking practices.

3. *Examination.* The Federal Reserve has the authority to examine each office of a foreign bank, including its representative offices. Further, each branch or agency must be examined at least once a year.

4. *Deposit taking.* Only foreign subsidiaries with access to FDIC insurance can take retail deposits under $100,000. This effectively rolls back the provision of the IBA that gave foreign branches and agencies access to FDIC insurance.

5. *Activity powers.* Beginning on December 19, 1992, state-licensed branches and agencies of foreign banks could not engage in any activity that was not permitted to a federal branch.[17]

Overall, the FBSEA considerably increased the Federal Reserve's authority over foreign banks and added to the regulatory burden or costs of entry into the United States. Indeed, in the two years after the passage of the FBSEA, federal bank supervisors issued 40 formal enforcement actions against foreign banks operating in the United States. In the most serious case, the Japanese Daiwa bank was ordered to cease its U.S. banking operations. Underlying its forced closure were losses by a single bond trader that had been concealed by Daiwa's management from U.S. regulators for over six weeks, and that amounted to over $1 billion. In January 1996 Daiwa's U.S. bank assets were sold to Sumitomo Bank of Japan, and in

---

[17] See M. Gruson, "Non-Banking Investments and Activities of Foreign Banks in the United States," paper presented at the Salomon Center, New York University, Conference on Universal Banking, February 23–24, 1995.

February 1996 Daiwa paid a fine of $340 million to the U.S. authorities for settlement of charges against the bank. This sent a strong signal regarding the willingness of the authorities to take a tough stand against errant foreign banks. More recently, in November 2001, the State Bank of India was ordered by U.S. federal and state banking regulators to pay $7.5 million in fines resulting from the bank's apparent engagement in unsafe and unsound practices in its branches in New York, Chicago, and Los Angeles.

Concept Questions	1. What regulatory and economic factors have encouraged the growth of U.S. offshore banking? What factors have deterred U.S. offshore banking?
	2. What were the major policy changes pertaining to bank expansion introduced by NAFTA?
	3. What are the primary forms of entry by foreign banks into the U.S. market?
	4. What impact did the passage of the International Banking Act of 1978 have on foreign bank activities in the United States?

ADVANTAGES AND DISADVANTAGES OF INTERNATIONAL EXPANSION

Historical and recent trends affecting the geographic expansion of FIs both into and outside the United States have been discussed above. Here we summarize the advantages and disadvantages of international expansions to the individual FI seeking to generate additional returns or better diversify its risk.

Advantages

These are the six major advantages of international expansion:[18]

Revenue and Risk Diversification

As with domestic geographic expansions, an FI's international activities potentially enhance its opportunity to diversify the risk of its revenue flows. Often, domestic revenue flows from financial services are strongly linked to the state of that economy. Therefore, the less integrated the economies of the world are, the greater is the potential for revenue diversification through international expansions.[19] For example, operating in Malaysia with just three branches but a strong marketing program, Citigroup became one of the country's largest mortgage lenders in the

---

[18] See, for example, L. Goldberg and A. Saunders, "The Determinants of Foreign Banking Activity in the United States," *Journal of Banking and Finance* 5 (1981), pp. 17–32; and C. W. Hultman and L. R. McGee, "Factors Affecting the Foreign Banking Presence in the United States," *Journal of Banking and Finance* 13 (1989), pp. 383–96.

[19] G. Whalen, in "The Securities Activities," provides empirical evidence on the benefits of international expansions as a mechanism of reducing risk. For example, he finds that for 1987–96 domestic bank and foreign insurance underwriting had a return correlation that was highly negative: −0.56. S. Claessens, A. Demirguc-Kunt, and H. Hisizinga, in "How Does Foreign Entry Affect Domestic Banking Markets?" *Journal of Banking and Finance* 25 (2001), pp. 891–911, find that foreign banks have higher profits than domestic banks in developing countries. However, they also show that domestic banks have higher profits than foreign banks in developed countries. Finally, Y. Amihud, G. DeLong, and A. Saunders, in "The Effects of Cross-Border Mergers on Bank Risk and Values," *Journal of International Money and Finance* 21, (2002), pp. 857–77, find that overall, in cross-border bank mergers, the acquirers' risk neither increases nor decreases.

early 2000s. Despite protectionist laws that bar foreign banks from opening new branches, Citigroup countered with aggressive marketing, strong customer service, and an assertive sales force that made house calls. The result was that, as the U.S. economy experienced a recession, Citigroup grew to hold 8 percent of Malaysia's fast-growing mortgage market. Indeed, in the early 2000s, while its biggest U.S. rivals, J. P. Morgan and Bank of America, grabbed headlines with megamergers, Citigroup undertook a strategy of projecting products and services globally. Citigroup's goal during the early 2000s was to aggressively expand its consumer banking presence outside the United States to boost profits and to leave behind rival U.S. banks who were just starting to take steps to combine corporate and consumer banking as a strategy.[20] International expansions also can reduce risk if the FI can undertake activities that are not permitted domestically but that have a low, or negative, correlation with domestic activities.

Economies of Scale

To the extent that economies of scale exist, an FI can potentially lower its average operating costs by expanding its activities beyond domestic boundaries.

Innovations

An FI can generate extra returns from new product innovations if it can sell such services internationally rather than just domestically. For example, consider complex financial innovations, such as securitization, caps, floors, and options, that FIs have innovated in the United States and sold to new foreign markets with few domestic competitors. It has been argued that the increasing dominance of U.S. securities firms in Japan is attributable to their comparative advantage and knowledge of risk management techniques and the use of derivatives compared to domestic Japanese securities firms.[21] However, the large losses incurred by many of these U.S. securities firms from trading in Asian and Russian markets in the late 1990s raise doubts about the size of any such comparative advantage.

Funds Source

International expansion allows an FI to search for the cheapest and most available sources of funds. This is extremely important given the very thin profit margins in domestic and international wholesale banking. Also, it reduces the risk of fund shortages (credit rationing) in any one market.

Customer Relationships

International expansions also allow an FI to maintain contact with and service the needs of domestic multinational corporations. Indeed, one of the fundamental factors determining the growth of FIs in foreign countries has been the parallel

---

[20] See "In Malaysia, Citibank Shows the Difference Marketing Makes," *The Wall Street Journal,* December 12, 2002, p. A20, and "Citigroup Looks Abroad for Its Future Growth," *The Wall Street Journal*, March 15, 2004, p. C1.

[21] In 1998, Merrill Lynch absorbed 30 branches and 2,000 employees of the defunct Yamaichi Securities (traditionally the fourth largest domestic securities firm in Japan). In the same year Travelers (and its Salomon Securities subsidiary) bought a 25 percent share in Nikko Securities (traditionally the third largest securities firm in Japan). The comparative advantage of U.S. FIs over Japanese FIs in risk management is discussed in "Rich Pickings for the Gaijin," *The Economist,* May 16, 1998, p. 83.

growth of foreign direct investment and foreign trade by globally oriented multinational corporations from the FI's home country.[22]

Regulatory Avoidance

To the extent that domestic regulations such as activity restrictions and reserve requirements impose constraints or taxes on the operations of an FI, seeking out low regulatory tax countries can allow an FI to lower its net regulatory burden and to increase its potential net profitability.

Disadvantages

These are the three major disadvantages of international expansion:

Information/Monitoring Costs

While global expansions give an FI the potential to better diversify its geographic risk, the absolute level of exposure in certain areas such as lending can be high, especially if the FI fails to diversify in an optimal fashion. For example, the FI may fail to choose a loan portfolio combination on the efficient lending frontier (see Chapter 12). Foreign activities may also be riskier for the simple reason that monitoring and information collection costs are often higher in foreign markets. For example, Japanese and German accounting standards differ significantly from the generally accepted accounting principles (GAAP) used by U.S. firms. In addition, language, legal, and cultural issues can impose additional transaction costs on international activities. Finally, because the regulatory environment is controlled locally and regulation imposes a different array of net costs in each market, a truly global FI must master the various rules and regulations in each market.[23]

Nationalization/Expropriation

To the extent that an FI expands by establishing a local presence through investing in fixed assets such as branches or subsidiaries, it faces the political risk that a change in government may lead to the nationalization of those fixed assets.[24] Further, if foreign FI depositors take losses following a nationalization, they may seek legal recourse from the FI in U.S. courts rather than from the nationalizing government. For example it took many years to resolve the outstanding claims of depositors in Citicorp's branches in Vietnam following the Communist takeover and expropriation of those branches.[25]

---

[22] R. Seth et al., "Do Banks Follow Their Customers Abroad?" *Financial Markets, Institutions, and Instruments* no. 4 (1998), find that the customer relationships are getting weaker as banks and firms become more global. For example, they find that foreign banks in the United States from Japan, Canada, the Netherlands, and the United Kingdom allocated a majority of their loans to non–home country borrowers over the 1981–92 period. Further, B. Williams, in "The Defensive Expansion Approach to Multinational Banking: Evidence to Date," *Financial Markets, Institutions, and Instruments*, May 2002, pp. 127–203, concludes that defensive expansion (in which banks follow their customers abroad) increases multinational bank size but has little impact upon these banks' profit.

[23] C. M. Buch and G. DeLong find that high information costs, as proxied by distance and common cultural factors (measured by geographic distance and language differences), tend to hold back merger activity. Moreover, information costs have larger effects on the number of bank mergers than regulatory variables. See "Cross-Border Bank Mergers: What Lures the Rare Animal?" Working Paper, Baruch College, CUNY, 2003.

[24] Such nationalizations have occurred with some frequency in African countries.

[25] See G. Dufey and I. Giddy, "Eurocurrency Deposit Risk," *Journal of Banking and Finance* 8 (1984), pp. 567–89.

Fixed Costs

The fixed costs of establishing foreign organizations may be extremely high. For example, a U.S. FI seeking an organizational presence in the Tokyo banking market faces real estate prices significantly higher than those in New York. Such relative costs can be even higher if an FI chooses to enter by buying an existing Japanese bank rather than establishing a new operation because of the considerable cost of acquiring Japanese equities measured by price-earnings ratios (despite significant loan problems in Japanese banks and recent falls in the Nikkei Index). These relative cost considerations become even more important if there is uncertainty about the expected volume of business to be generated and thus revenue flows from foreign entry. The failure of U.S. acquisitions to realize expected profits following the 1986 "big bang" deregulation in the United Kingdom is a good example of unrealized revenue expectations vis-à-vis the high fixed costs of entry and the costs of maintaining a competitive position.[26]

Concept Questions

1. What are the major advantages of international expansion to an FI?
2. What are the major disadvantages of international expansion to an FI?
3. Comparing the advantages and disadvantages discussed above, why do you think so few U.S. banks have established branches in the Ukraine?

Summary

In this chapter, we examined the potential return-risk advantages and disadvantages to FIs from international geographic expansions. While regulatory considerations and costs are fundamental to such decisions, several other economic factors play an important role in the net return or benefit-cost calculus for any given FI. For example, considerations such as earnings diversification, economies of scale and scope, extension of customer relationships, and better exploiting of financial service innovations add to the potential benefits from international geographic expansions. However, there are also costs or risks of such expansions such as monitoring costs, expropriation of assets, and the fixed costs of market entry. Managers need to carefully weigh each of these factors before making a geographic expansion decision, whether international or domestic.

Questions and Problems

1. What are three ways in which an FI can establish a global or international presence?
2. How did the Overseas Direct Investment Control Act of 1964 assist in the growth of global banking activities? How much growth in foreign assets occurred from 1980 to 2003? Which types of foreign assets saw the largest amount of growth?
3. What is a Eurodollar transaction? What are Eurodollars?

[26] For example, the return on US. banks' foreign subsidiaries securities activities (assets) in 1987 were −0.96 percent. However, U.S. banks and securities firms have fared better in the Canadian "big bang" deregulation of securities business (see "Canada's Borrowing with Its Fat Fees Lures Wall Street," *New York Times,* April 15, 1995, p. D1).

4. Identify and explain the impact of at least four factors that have encouraged global U.S. bank expansion.

5. What is the expected impact of the implementation of the revised BIS risk-based capital requirements on the international activities of some major U.S. banks?

6. What effect have the problems of emerging-market economies in the late 1990s had on the global expansion of traditional banking activities by U.S. banks?

7. What factors gave Japanese banks significant advantages in competing for international business for an extended period through the mid-1990s? What are the advantages of size in a competitive market? Does size necessarily imply high profitability?

8. What is the European Community (EC) Second Banking Directive? What impact has the Second Banking Directive had on the competitive banking environment in Europe?

9. Identify and discuss the various ways in which foreign banks can enter the U.S. market. What are international banking facilities?

10. What factors affected the relative growth of the proportion of U.S. banking assets that are controlled by foreign banks during the 1990s into 2003?

11. What was the fundamental philosophical focus of the International Banking Act (IBA) of 1978?

    a. What advantages and disadvantages did foreign banks have relative to domestic banks before the passage of this legislation?

    b. What requirements were placed on foreign banks by the IBA?

    c. What was the likely effect of the IBA on the growth of foreign bank activities in the United States? Why?

12. What events led to the passage of the Foreign Bank Supervision Enhancement Act (FBSEA) of 1991? What was the main objective of this legislation?

13. What were the main features of FBSEA? How did FBSEA encourage cooperation with the home country regulator? What was the effect of the FBSEA on the Federal Reserve and on foreign banks?

14. What are the major advantages of international expansion to FIs? Explain how each advantage can affect the operating performance of FIs.

15. What are the difficulties of expanding globally? How can each of these difficulties create negative effects on the operating performance of FIs?

Web Question

16. Go to the Federal Reserve Board's Web site at **www.federalreserve.gov**. Find the latest data on domestic bank assets held in foreign countries using the following steps. Click on "Economic Research and Data." From there click on "Statistics: Releases and Historical Data" and then click on "Assets and Liabilities of Commercial Banks in the United States *Releases*." Click on the most recent date. This will bring the files up on your computer that contain the relevant data. How have these numbers changed since those for 2003 reported in Table 23–4?

Pertinent Web Sites

Board of Governors of the Federal Reserve	www.federalreserve.gov
Federal Deposit Insurance Corporation	www.fdic.gov
The Banker	www.thebanker.com

Chapter **Twenty-Four**

Futures and Forwards

INTRODUCTION

Chapter 13 describes the growth in FIs' off-balance-sheet activities. A major component of this growth has been in derivative contracts such as futures and forwards. While a significant amount of derivatives reflect the trading activity of large banks and other FIs, FIs of all sizes have used these instruments to hedge their asset-liability risk exposures and thus reduce the value of their net worth at risk due to adverse events. As will be discussed in this chapter, derivative contracts—such as futures and forwards—potentially allow an FI to manage (or hedge) its interest rate, foreign exchange (FX), and credit risk exposures and even its exposure to catastrophes such as hurricanes.[1] Indeed, in late 2002, Federal Reserve Board Chair Alan Greenspan praised the growth of the derivative markets, stating this growth was one of the major reasons the U.S. economy was able to fend off extraordinary shocks in the early 2000s.

Table 24–1 lists the derivative contract holdings of all commercial banks, and specifically, the 25 largest U.S. banks, as of September 2003. The table shows notional (dollar) contract volumes for these 25 banks exceeding $67 trillion, while the other 547 bank and trust companies with derivatives activity report notional contract volumes of $340 billion. Table 24–1 shows the breakdown of those positions into futures and forwards, swaps, options, and credit derivatives. As can be seen, swaps ($41.2 trillion) are the largest group of derivatives, followed by options ($14.2 trillion), futures and forwards ($10.9 trillion) and credit derivatives ($869 billion). The replacement cost of these derivative contracts (bilaterally netted current exposure) for the top 25 derivative users is reported at $202 billion, while credit exposure is $710 billion (or 92.6 percent of the capital of these banks).[2] Not only do FIs hold these contracts to hedge their own risk (interest rate, credit, etc.), but FIs also serve as the counterparty (for a fee) in these contracts for other (financial and nonfinancial) firms wanting to hedge risks on their balance sheets.

---

[1] In fact, a survey of financial institutions, foundations, and university endowments conducted by New York University's Stern School of Business, CIBC World Markets, and KPMG Investment Consulting Group found that the most commonly cited reason for using derivatives was risk reduction and hedging. Among large institutions, 41 percent had a designated risk manager or risk management committee and, among derivatives users, 68 percent had a written policy on risk management. See 1998 Survey of Derivative and Risk Management Practices by U.S. Institutional Investors, 1999, NYU Stern School of Business, CIBC World Markets, and KPMG.

[2] See Chapter 20 for a discussion of how the credit exposure of derivatives is calculated for regulatory reporting.

TABLE 24–1 Derivative Contracts: Notional Amount and Credit Equivalent Exposure of the 25 Commercial Banks and Trust Companies with the Most Derivative Contracts, September 2003 (in millions of dollars)

| Rank | Bank Name | Total Assets | Derivative Contracts | | | | | | Replacement Cost of All Contracts | Future Exposure RBC* Add-On | Credit Exposure from All Contracts | Credit Exposure to Capital Ratio |
			Futures & Forwards	Total Swaps	Total Options	Credit Derivatives	Spot FX	Total Derivatives				
1.	J. P. Morgan Chase Bank	$638,120	$4,228,366	$22,459,088	$6,967,128	$496,561	$193,596	$34,151,143	$66,134	$288,707	$354,841	783.0
2.	Bank of America NA	624,723	2,638,710	8,654,660	2,385,906	123,939	95,294	13,803,216	35,184	90,335	125,518	237.1
3.	Citibank NA	554,540	2,022,072	6,731,694	1,912,884	145,976	214,854	10,812,626	42,388	84,711	127,340	240.8
4.	Wachovia Bank NA	344,056	337,622	865,446	1,117,400	30,236	32,544	2,350,704	16,946	11,356	28,302	91.5
5.	Bank One National Assn.	216,452	265,042	730,626	196,972	16,645	16,598	1,209,285	5,913	7,180	13,093	57.5
6.	HSBC Bank USA	90,157	255,176	540,347	378,434	25,678	27,995	1,199,636	6,207	9,448	15,655	219.9
7.	Wells Fargo Bank NA	224,376	302,367	86,933	341,368	2,889	8,027	733,557	6,683	1,225	7,908	37.9
8.	Bank of New York	92,203	124,129	181,121	224,829	1,659	10,662	531,738	3,800	2,615	6,414	77.8
9.	Fleet National Bank	188,775	41,511	115,660	305,223	11,739	4,561	474,133	2,783	1,591	4,374	22.0
10.	State Street Bank & TC	74,100	290,254	37,243	3,529	0	30,283	331,026	3,692	2,279	5,972	140.7
11.	National City Bank	45,799	41,041	92,037	124,059	0	499	257,137	2,210	860	3,071	65.2
12.	National City Bank of IN	50,104	59,152	32,860	75,478	0	0	167,489	1,112	1,252	2,364	74.1
13.	Mellon Bank NA	20,830	56,314	15,274	29,820	410	7,377	101,818	1,072	761	1,833	67.8
14.	Standard Federal Bank NA	50,489	23,944	55,985	11,751	4,207	0	95,887	59	558	617	10.9
15.	Keybank National Assn.	73,939	20,308	68,054	1,930	0	842	90,292	2,105	471	2,575	30.8
16.	LaSalle Bank NA	62,830	8,230	70,031	2,944	0	0	81,206	174	716	890	16.8
17.	SunTrust Bank	125,027	16,502	47,440	13,030	398	805	77,370	1,928	522	2,450	20.6
18.	Merrill Lynch Bank NA	66,735	20,100	35,640	320	2,608	0	58,667	148	166	314	6.7
19.	PNC Bank NA	65,167	3,557	40,045	5,266	225	711	49,092	1,100	327	1,427	20.5
20.	Deutsche Bank Tr. Co. American	35,838	662	37,987	7,711	3,140	43	49,500	868	1,938	2,806	40.3
21.	U.S. Bank National Assn.	186,464	6,257	36,474	2,280	2	189	45,014	764	210	974	5.4
22.	First Tennessee Bank NA	24,984	13,290	6,028	14,811	0	1	34,129	393	55	449	19.8
23.	Capital One Bank	22,510	804	24,224	0	0	0	25,027	0	172	172	4.3
24.	Northern Trust Co.	33,026	22,621	1,086	34	99	4,706	23,840	427	203	631	23.5
25.	Irwin Union B&T Co.	4,727	13,847	25	6,477	0	0	20,350	1	2	3	0.5
	Total 25 commercial banks	**$3,915,971**	**$10,811,876**	**$40,966,009**	**$14,179,676**	**$866,411**	**$649,587**	**$66,773,883**	**$202,091**	**$507,660**	**$709,851**	**92.6†**
	Other 547 commercial banks	**$2,110,959**	**$47,436**	**$239,442**	**$50,089**	**$2,362**	**$2,888**	**$339,514**	**$5,397**	**$2,481**	**$7,878**	**N/A**
	Total for all banks	**$6,026,930**	**$10,859,331**	**$41,205,451**	**$14,229,765**	**$868,773**	**$652,475**	**$67,113,397**	**$207,488**	**$510,141**	**$717,629**	**5.6**

* Risk-based capital
† Average

Source: Office of the Comptroller of the Currency Web site, September 2003. *www.occ.treas.gov*

The rapid growth of derivatives use by both FIs and nonfinancial firms has been controversial. Critics charge that derivatives contracts contain potential losses that can materialize to haunt their holders, particularly banks and insurance companies that deal heavily in these instruments. As will be discussed in this chapter and the following two chapters, when employed appropriately, derivatives can be used to hedge (or reduce an FI's risk).[3] However, when misused, derivatives can increase the risk of an FI's insolvency. A number of recent scandals involving FIs, firms, and municipalities (such as Bankers Trust and the Allied Irish Bank) have led to a tightening of the accounting (reporting) requirements for derivative contracts.[4] Specifically, beginning in 2000, the Financial Accounting Standards Board (FASB) required all derivatives to be marked to market and mandated that losses and gains be immediately transparent on FIs' and other firms' financial statements. Further, as discussed in the Industry Perspectives box, uncertainty about the direction of interest rates in 2003–2004 caused banks to be more cautious about their use of derivatives.

www.fasb.org

In this chapter, we look at the role futures and forward contracts play in managing an FI's interest rate, FX, and credit risk exposures as well as their role in hedging natural catastrophes. We start with a comparison of forward and futures contracts to spot contracts. We then examine how forwards and futures can be used to hedge interest rate risk, FX risk, credit risk, and catastrophe risk. We look at option-type derivatives and swaps in Chapters 25 and 26.

FORWARD AND FUTURES CONTRACTS

To understand the essential nature and characteristics of forward and futures contracts, we can compare them with spot contracts. We show appropriate time lines for each of the three contracts using a bond as the underlying financial security to the derivative contract in Figure 24–1.

Spot Contracts

spot contract
An agreement involving the immediate exchange of an asset for cash.

A **spot contract** is an agreement between a buyer and a seller at time 0, when the seller of the asset agrees to deliver it immediately and the buyer of the asset agrees to pay for that asset immediately.[5] Thus, the unique feature of a spot market contract is the immediate and simultaneous exchange of cash for securities, or what is often called *delivery versus payment*. A spot bond quote of $97 for a 20-year maturity

---

[3] E. Brewer III, B. A. Minton, and J. T. Moser, in "Interest-Rate Derivatives and Bank Lending," *Journal of Banking and Finance* 24 (2000), pp. 353–79, find that banks using interest rate derivatives experience greater growth in their commercial and industrial loan portfolios than banks that do not use these financial instruments. Their results suggest that FIs' use of derivatives enables increased reliance on their comparative advantage as delegated monitors (see Chapter 1).

[4] From March through May 1994, several large nonfinancial firms announced millions of dollars in losses from derivatives deals, especially those arranged by Bankers Trust. Accompanying these announcements and related new stories were allegations that Bankers Trust had either misrepresented, lied, or deceived its clients. J. F. Sinkey Jr. and D. A. Carter, in "The Reaction of Bank Stock Prices to News of Derivatives Losses by Corporate Clients," *Journal of Banking and Finance* 23 (1999), pp. 1725–43, investigated how these announcements affected Bankers Trust and three portfolios of banks' stock returns: dealers, non-dealers, and nonusers. They report significant negative cumulative abnormal returns of −12.14 percent for Bankers Trust, −5.56 percent for dealer banks, and −2.45 percent for nondealer, user banks, indicating that banks were adversely affected by these news stories.

[5] Technically, physical settlement and delivery may take place one or two days after the contractual spot agreement in bond markets. In equity markets, delivery and cash settlement normally occur three business days after the spot contract agreement.

Industry Perspectives

RATES TEMPER USE OF DERIVATIVES

Uncertainty about the direction of interest rates made commercial banks more cautious in their use of derivatives contracts in the third quarter, the Office of the Comptroller of the Currency said Friday. Derivatives held by banks increased $1.3 trillion, to a record $67.1 trillion. However, the OCC emphasized that was only a 1.9 percent increase in notional value, the smallest percentage growth since a decline in the fourth quarter of 2001.

"Uncertainty and volatility are driving those numbers," Kathryn E. Dick, the deputy comptroller for risk evaluation, said at a briefing in the agency's Quarterly Bank Derivatives Report. "We're really coming off of three years of rates steadily declining. Now we're in what we refer to as the 'freezer' where it's a little bit harder to tell if rates are staying steady" or "if rates are going up," she said. "What we're finding with respect to the notional volume is you're not going to see a lot of activity in the third quarter because

you have some risk managers that are waiting for a little bit more of an indication."

Despite the slower pace of growth of contracts, the number of commercial banks that use derivatives to manage their balance sheets increased by 35 in the third quarter, to 534. Ms. Dick said the increase could be explained by the large volume of mortgage products, which institutions must hedge against, and smaller institutions becoming more comfortable with new accounting rules for derivatives. "Of course we like to see banks manage their risk. At the same time, we watch that number carefully because derivatives are a complicated product," Ms. Dick said.

The report also said that total credit exposure, which reflects both current exposure and potential future exposure, fell for the first time in six quarters. It declined $6 billion, to $718 billion.

Source: *The American Banker*, December 15, 2003, p. 9, by Michele Heller. *www.americanbanker.com*

FIGURE 24–1
Contract Time Lines

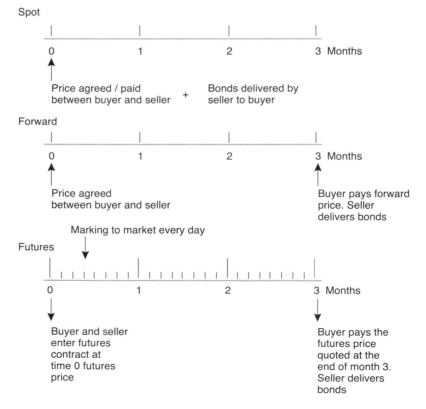

bond is the price the buyer must pay the seller, per $100 of face value, for immediate (time 0) delivery of the 20-year bond.

Forward Contracts

forward contract
An agreement involving the exchange of an asset for cash at a fixed price in the future.

A **forward contract** is a contractual agreement between a buyer and a seller at time 0 to exchange a prespecified asset for cash at a later date. For example, in a three-month forward contract to deliver 20-year bonds, the buyer and seller agree on a price and quantity today (time 0) but the delivery (or exchange) of the 20-year bond for cash does not occur until three months hence. If the forward price agreed to at time 0 was $97 per $100 of face value, in three months' time the seller delivers $100 of 20-year bonds and receives $97 from the buyer. This is the price the buyer must pay and the seller must accept no matter what happened to the spot price of 20-year bonds during the three months between the time the contract was entered into and the time the bonds are delivered for payment.

Futures Contracts

futures contract
An agreement involving the future exchange of an asset for cash at a price that is determined daily.

marking to market
The process by which the prices on outstanding futures contracts are adjusted each day to reflect current futures market conditions.

A **futures contract** is normally arranged through an organized exchange. It is an agreement between a buyer and a seller at time 0 to exchange a standardized, prespecified asset for cash at a later date. As such, a futures contract is very similar to a forward contract. The difference relates to the price, which in a forward contract is fixed over the life of the contract ($97 per $100 of face value for three months), but in a futures contract is **marked to market** daily. This means the contract's price is adjusted each day as the futures price for the contract changes. Therefore, actual daily cash settlements occur between the buyer and seller in response to this marking-to-market process. This can be compared to a forward contract, where the whole cash payment from buyer to seller occurs at the end of the contract period.[6]

Concept Questions

1. What is the difference between a futures contract and a forward contract?
2. What are the major differences between a spot contract and a forward contract?

FORWARD CONTRACTS AND HEDGING INTEREST RATE RISK

naive hedge
When a cash asset is hedged on a direct dollar-for-dollar basis with a forward or futures contract.

To see the usefulness of forward contracts in hedging the interest rate risk of an FI, consider a simple example of a **naive hedge** (the hedge of a cash asset on a direct dollar-for-dollar basis with a forward or futures contract). Suppose an FI portfolio manager holds a 20-year, $1 million face value bond on the balance sheet. At time 0, these bonds are valued by the market at $97 per $100 face value, or $970,000 in total. Assume the manager receives a forecast that interest rates are expected to rise by 2 percent from their current level of 8 to 10 percent over the next three months. Knowing that rising interest rates mean that bond prices will fall, the manager stands to make a capital loss on the bond portfolio. Having read Chapters 8 and 9, the manager is an expert in duration and has calculated the

---

[6] Aside from the marking-to-market process, the two major differences between forwards and futures are that (1) forwards are tailor-made contracts while futures are standardized contracts and (2) forward contracts are bilateral contracts subject to counterparty default risk, while the default risk on futures is significantly reduced by the futures exchange guaranteeing to indemnify counterparties against credit or default risk.

20-year maturity bonds' duration to be exactly 9 years. Thus, the manager can predict a capital loss, or change in bond values (ΔP) from the duration equation of Chapter 9:[7]

$$\frac{\Delta P}{P} = -D \times \frac{\Delta R}{1 + R}$$

where

ΔP = Capital loss on bonds = ?

P = Initial value of bond position = $970,000

D = Duration of the bonds = 9 years

ΔR = Change in forecast yield = .02

$1 + R$ = 1 plus the current yield on 20-year bonds = 1.08

$$\frac{\Delta P}{\$970,000} = -9 \times \left[\frac{.02}{1.08}\right]$$

$$\Delta P = -9 \times \$970,000 \times \left[\frac{.02}{1.08}\right] = -\$161,666.67$$

As a result, the FI portfolio manager expects to incur a capital loss on the bond portfolio of $161,666.67 (as a percentage loss ($\Delta P/P$) = 16.67%) or as a drop in price from $97 per $100 face value to $80.833 per $100 face value. To offset this loss—in fact, to reduce the risk of capital loss to zero—the manager may hedge this position by taking an off-balance-sheet hedge, such as selling $1 million face value of 20-year bonds for forward delivery in three months' time.[8] Suppose at time 0 the portfolio manager can find a buyer willing to pay $97 for every $100 of 20-year bonds delivered in three months' time.

Now consider what happens to the FI portfolio manager if the gloomy forecast of a 2 percent rise in interest rates proves to be true. The portfolio manager's bond position has fallen in value by 16.67 percent, equal to a capital loss of $161,667. After the rise in interest rates, the manager can buy $1 million face value of 20-year bonds in the spot market at $80.833 per $100 of face value, a total cost of $808,333, and deliver these bonds to the forward contract buyer. Remember that the forward contract buyer agreed to pay $97 per $100 of face value for the $1 million of face value bonds delivered, or $970,000. As a result, the portfolio manager makes a profit on the forward transaction of:

$970,000	−	$808,333	=	$161,667
(price paid by forward buyer to forward seller)		(cost of purchasing bonds in the spot market at t = month 3 for delivery to the forward buyer)		

As you can see, the on-balance-sheet loss of $161,667 is exactly offset by the off-balance-sheet gain of $161,667 from selling the forward contract. In fact, for any

---

[7] For simplicity, we ignore issues relating to convexity here.

[8] Since a forward contract involves delivery of bonds in a future time period, it does not appear on the balance sheet, which records only current and past transactions. Thus, forwards are one example of off-balance-sheet items (see Chapter 13).

immunized
Describes an FI that is fully hedged or protected against adverse movements in interest rates (or other asset prices).

change in interest rates, a loss (gain) on the balance sheet is offset by a gain (loss) on the forward contract. Indeed, the success of a hedge does not hinge on the manager's ability to accurately forecast interest rates. Rather, the reason for the hedge is the lack of ability to perfectly predict interest rate changes. The hedge allows the FI manager to protect against interest rate changes even if they are unpredictable. Thus, the FI's net interest rate exposure is zero; in the parlance of finance, it has **immunized** its assets against interest rate risk.

Concept Questions

1. Explain how a naive hedge works.
2. What does it mean to say that an FI has immunized its portfolio against a particular risk?

HEDGING INTEREST RATE RISK WITH FUTURES CONTRACTS

Even though some hedging of interest rate risk does take place using forward contracts—such as forward rate agreements commonly used by insurance companies and banks prior to mortgage loan originations—most FIs hedge interest rate risk either at the micro level (called *microhedging*) or at the macro level (called *macrohedging*) using futures contracts. Before looking at futures contracts, we explain the difference between microhedging and macrohedging and between routine hedging and selective hedging.

Microhedging

microhedging
Using a futures (forward) contract to hedge a specific asset or liability.

An FI is **microhedging** when it employs a futures or a forward contract to hedge a particular asset or liability risk. For example, earlier we considered a simple example of microhedging asset-side portfolio risk, where an FI manager wanted to insulate the value of the institution's bond portfolio fully against a rise in interest rates. An example of microhedging on the liability side of the balance sheet occurs when an FI, attempting to lock in a cost of funds to protect itself against a possible rise in short-term interest rates, takes a short (sell) position in futures contracts on CDs or T-bills. In microhedging, the FI manager often tries to pick a futures or forward contract whose underlying deliverable asset is closely matched to the asset (or liability) position being hedged. The earlier example, where we had an exact matching of the asset in the portfolio with the deliverable security underlying the forward contract (20-year bonds) was unrealistic. Such exact matching cannot be achieved often, and this produces a residual unhedgable risk termed **basis risk.** We discuss basis risk in detail later in this chapter; it arises mainly because the prices of the assets or liabilities that an FI wishes to hedge are imperfectly correlated over time with the prices on the futures or forward contract used to hedge risk.

basis risk
A residual risk that arises because the movement in a spot (cash) asset's price is not perfectly correlated with the movement in the price of the asset delivered under a futures or forward contract.

Macrohedging

macrohedging
Hedging the entire duration gap of an FI.

Macrohedging occurs when an FI manager wishes to use futures or other derivative securities to hedge the entire balance sheet duration gap. This contrasts to microhedging, where an FI manager identifies specific assets and liabilities and seeks individual futures and other derivative contracts to hedge those individual risks. Note that macrohedging and microhedging can lead to quite different hedging strategies and results. In particular, a macrohedge takes a whole portfolio view and allows for individual asset and liability interest sensitivities or durations to net each other out. This can result in a very different aggregate futures position than

FIGURE 24–2
The Effects of
Hedging on Risk
and Expected
Return

when an FI manager disregards this netting or portfolio effect and hedges individual asset and liability positions on a one-to-one basis.[9]

Routine Hedging versus Selective Hedging

routine hedging
Seeking to hedge all interest rate risk exposure.

Routine hedging occurs when an FI reduces its interest rate or other risk exposure to the lowest possible level by selling sufficient futures to offset the interest rate risk exposure of its whole balance sheet or cash positions in each asset and liability. For example, this might be achieved by macrohedging the duration gap, as described next. However, since reducing risk also reduces expected return and thus shareholder wealth, not all FI managers seek to do this. Indeed, a manager would follow this strategy only if the direction and size of interest rate changes are extremely unpredictable to the extent that the manager is willing to forgo return to hedge this risk. Figure 24–2 shows the trade-off between expected return and risk and the minimum-risk fully hedged portfolio.[10]

hedging selectively
Only partially hedging the gap or individual assets and liabilities.

Rather than a fully hedged position, most FIs choose to bear some interest rate risk as well as credit and FX risks because of their comparative advantage as FIs (see Chapter 1). One possibility is that an FI may choose to **hedge selectively** its portfolio. For example, an FI manager may generate expectations regarding future interest rates before deciding on a futures position. As a result, the manager may selectively hedge only a proportion of its balance sheet position. Alternatively, the FI manager may decide to remain unhedged or even to overhedge by selling more futures than required by the cash position, although regulators may view this as speculative. Thus, the fully hedged position—and the minimum risk portfolio—becomes one of several choices depending, in part, on managerial interest rate expectations, managerial objectives, and the nature of the return-risk trade-off from hedging. Finally, an FI may selectively hedge in an attempt to arbitrage profits between a spot asset's price movements and movements in a futures price.

[9] P. H. Munter, D. K. Clancy, and C. T. Moores found that macrohedges provided better hedge performance than microhedges in a number of different interest rate environments. See "Accounting for Financial Futures: A Question of Risk Reduction," *Advances in Accounting* 3 (1986), pp. 51–70. See also R. Stoebe, "Macrohedging Bank Investment Portfolios," *Bankers Magazine,* November–December 1994, pp. 45–48.

[10] The minimum-risk portfolio is not shown as zero here because of basis risk that prevents perfect hedging. In the absence of basis risk, a zero-risk position becomes possible.

Macrohedging with Futures

The number of futures contracts that an FI should buy or sell in a macrohedge depends on the size and direction of its interest rate risk exposure and the return-risk trade-off from fully or selectively hedging that risk. Chapter 9 showed that an FI's net worth exposure to interest rate shocks was directly related to its leverage-adjusted duration gap as well as its asset size. Again, this is

$$\Delta E = -[D_A - kD_L] \times A \times \frac{\Delta R}{1 + R}$$

where

ΔE = Change in an FI's net worth

D_A = Duration of its asset portfolio

D_L = Duration of its liability portfolio

k = Ratio of an FI's liabilities to assets (L/A)

A = Size of an FI's asset portfolio

$\dfrac{\Delta R}{1 + R}$ = Shock to interest rates

EXAMPLE 24–1 *Calculation of Change in FI Net Worth as Interest Rates Rise*	To see how futures might fully hedge a positive or negative portfolio duration gap, consider the following FI where

$$D_A = 5 \text{ years}$$
$$D_L = 3 \text{ years}$$

Suppose the FI manager receives information from an economic forecasting unit that interest rates are expected to rise from 10 to 11 percent over the next year. That is:

$$\Delta R = 1\% = .01$$
$$1 + R = 1.10$$

The FI's initial balance sheet is

Assets (in millions)	Liabilities (in millions)
$A = \$100$	$L = \$\ 90$
	$E = \ \ \ 10$
$\overline{\$100}$	$\overline{\$100}$

so that k equals L/A equals 90/100 equals 0.9.

The FI manager wants to calculate the potential loss to the FI's net worth (E) if the forecast of rising rates proves to be true. As we showed in Chapter 9:

$$\Delta E = -(D_A - kD_L) \times A \times \frac{\Delta R}{1 + R}$$

so that

$$\Delta E = -(5 - (.9)(3)) \times \$100 \times \frac{.01}{1.1} = -\$2.091 \text{ million}$$

The FI could expect to lose $2.091 million in net worth if the interest rate forecast turns out to be correct. Since the FI started with a net worth of $10 million, the loss of $2.091 million is almost 21 percent of its initial net worth position. Clearly, as this example illustrates, the impact of the rise in interest rates could be quite threatening to the FI and its insolvency risk exposure.

The Risk-Minimizing Futures Position

The FI manager's objective to fully hedge the balance sheet exposure would be fulfilled by constructing a futures position such that if interest rates do rise by 1 percent to 11 percent, as in the prior example, the FI will make a gain on the futures position that just offsets the loss of balance sheet net worth of $2.091 million.

When interest rates rise, the price of a futures contract falls since its price reflects the value of the underlying bond that is deliverable against the contract. The amount by which a bond price falls when interest rates rise depends on its duration. Thus, we expect the price of the 20-year T-bond futures contract to be more sensitive to interest rate changes than the price of the 3-month T-bill futures contract since the former futures price reflects the price of the 20-year T-bond deliverable on contract maturity. Thus, the sensitivity of the price of a futures contract depends on the duration of the deliverable bond underlying the contract, or

$$\frac{\Delta F}{F} = -D_F \frac{\Delta R}{1 + R}$$

where

ΔF = Change in dollar value of futures contracts

F = Dollar value of the initial futures contracts

D_F = Duration of the bond to be delivered against the futures contracts such as a 20-year, 8 percent coupon T-bond

ΔR = Expected shock to interest rates

$1 + R$ = 1 plus the current level of interest rates

This can be rewritten as

$$\Delta F = -D_F \times F \times \frac{\Delta R}{1 + R}$$

The left side of this expression (ΔF) shows the dollar gain or loss on a futures position when interest rates change.

To see this dollar gain or loss more clearly, we can decompose the initial dollar value position in futures contracts, F, into its two component parts:

$$F = N_F \times P_F$$

The dollar value of the outstanding futures position depends on the number of contracts bought or sold (N_F) and the price of each contract (P_F). N_F is positive when the futures contracts are bought and is assigned a negative value when contracts are sold.

Futures contracts are homogeneous in size. Thus, futures exchanges sell T-bond futures in minimum units of $100,000 of face value; that is, one T-bond future ($N_F = 1$) equals $100,000. T-bill futures are sold in larger minimum units: one T-bill future ($N_F = 1$) equals $1,000,000. The price of each contract quoted in the newspaper is the price per $100 of face value for delivering the underlying bond. Looking at Figure 24–3, a price quote of $115^{10}/_{32}$ on March 18, 2004, for the T-bond futures contract maturing in June 2004 means that the buyer is required to pay $115,312.50 for

FIGURE 24–3
**Futures Contracts
on Interest Rates**

Source: *The Wall Street Journal*, March 18, 2004, p. B6. Reprinted by permission of The Wall Street Journal, © 2004 Dow Jones & Company, Inc. All Rights Reserved Worldwide.

Interest Rate Futures

	OPEN	HIGH	LOW	SETTLE	CHG	LIFETIME HIGH	LIFETIME LOW	OPEN INT
Treasury Bonds (CBT)-$100,000; pts 32nds of 100%								
Mar	117-04	117-10	116-15	116-25	-21	117-26	101-00	28,546
June	115-23	115-31	114-31	115-10	-21	116-15	104-00	522,017
Sept	113-28	114-15	113-19	113-29	-21	114-30	101-25	11,850
Est vol 216,969; vol Wed 258,838; open int 562,788, -2,710.								
Treasury Notes (CBT)-$100,000; pts 32nds of 100%								
Mar	117-18	117-22	117-05	117-08	-15.5	117-31	106-29	47,574
June	16-045	116-09	115-20	15-255	-16.0	16-185	107-13	1,257,280
Est vol 680,136; vol Wed 732,007; open int 1,318,731, +13,896.								
5 Yr. Treasury Notes (CBT)-$100,000; pts 32nds of 100%								
Mar	115-02	15-035	114-25	114-27	-10.5	19-215	09-145	45,394
Est vol 254,899; vol Wed 286,275; open int 1,005,955, +13,094.								
2 Yr. Treasury Notes (CBT)-$200,000; pts 32nds of 100%								
Mar	08-022	08-022	08-005	08-012	-2.0	08-045	106-02	25,304
Est vol 20,836; vol Wed 25,977; open int 176,294, -1,371.								
30 Day Federal Funds (CBT)-$5,000,000; 100 - daily avg.								
Mar	...	...	...	98.995	...	99.160	98-47	46,584
Apr	99.00	99.00	99.00	99.00	...	99.17	89.96	95,607
May	99.00	99.00	99.00	99.00	...	99.79	98.40	58,336
July	98.98	98.98	98.97	98.98	...	98.98	98.20	64,430
Aug	98.94	98.95	98.94	98.95	...	98.95	98.24	15,103
Sept	98.90	98.92	98.90	98.92	...	98.93	98.22	19,557
Oct	98.88	98.88	98.86	98.88	...	98.88	98.58	12,092
Nov	98.79	98.82	98.79	98.81	...	98.83	98.37	8,552
Dec	98.73	98.75	98.73	98.73	-.01	98.75	98.63	201
Est vol 15,968; vol Wed 16,471; open int 367,835, +494.								
10 Yr. Interest Rate Swaps (CBT)-$100,000; pts 32nds of 100								
June	114-13	114-22	114-03	114-06	-19	115-04	109-06	38,871
Est vol 833; vol Wed 835; open int 38,872, +543.								
10 Yr. Muni Note Index (CBT)-$1,000 x index								
Mar	107-07	107-11	107-04	107-05	-13	107-24	99-21	1,162
Est vol 124; vol Wed 163; open int 3,004, -15.								
Index: Close 107-05; Yield 4.118.								

	OPEN	HIGH	LOW	SETTLE	CHG	YIELD	CHG	OPEN INT
1 Month Libor (CME)-$3,000,000; pts of 100%								
Apr	98.90	98.90	98.90	98.90	...	1.10	...	21,868
May	98.90	98.90	98.90	98.90	...	1.10	...	11,457
June	98.88	98.88	98.88	98.88	...	1.12	...	23,235
July	98.86	98.87	98.86	98.86	...	1.14	...	31,776
Aug	98.82	98.82	98.82	98.82	-.01	1.18	.01	87,903
Est vol 4,093; vol Wed 4,541; open int 349,461, +664.								
Eurodollar (CME)-$1,000,000; pts of 100%								
Apr	98.87	98.88	98.87	98.88	...	1.12	...	85,224
May	98.86	98.87	98.86	98.86	...	1.14	...	35,817
June	98.83	98.85	98.83	98.84	...	1.16	...	876,378
July	98.80	98.80	98.80	98.80	-.01	1.20	.01	14,001
Sept	98.70	98.74	98.68	98.70	-.01	1.30	.01	881,589
Dec	98.46	98.49	98.44	98.46	-.03	1.54	.03	738,811
Mr05	98.19	98.21	98.13	98.16	-.04	1.84	.04	541,141
June	97.86	97.87	97.80	97.82	-.05	2.18	.05	398,581
Sept	97.54	97.55	97.47	97.49	-.05	2.51	.05	337,331
Dec	97.26	97.25	97.19	97.20	-.06	2.80	.06	241,323
Mr06	97.04	97.04	96.95	96.96	-.07	3.04	.07	211,567
June	96.78	96.79	96.72	96.74	-.07	3.26	.07	147,497
Sept	96.57	96.58	96.51	96.53	-.07	3.47	.07	154,596
Dec	96.37	96.38	96.31	96.32	-.08	3.68	.08	123,503
Mr07	96.20	96.21	96.14	96.15	-.08	3.85	.08	103,626
June	96.03	96.05	95.97	95.99	-.08	4.01	.08	79,357
Sept	95.88	95.90	95.81	95.83	-.08	4.17	.08	73,086
Dec	95.69	95.74	95.65	95.67	-.08	4.33	.08	60,833
Mr08	95.54	95.61	95.52	95.54	-.07	4.46	.07	45,208
June	95.41	95.47	95.38	95.41	-.08	4.59	.08	50,190
Sept	95.29	95.34	95.26	95.28	-.08	4.72	.08	35,215
Dec	95.17	95.22	95.13	95.15	-.08	4.85	.08	34,646
Mr09	95.08	95.08	95.02	95.04	-.08	4.96	.08	15,403
Dec	94.72	94.73	94.70	94.73	-.07	5.27	.07	5,844
Dc10	94.39	94.42	94.35	94.39	-.07	5.61	.07	3,852
Est vol 793,815; vol Wed 944,786; open int 5,347,589, +49,467.								

one contract.[11] The subsequent profit or loss from a position in the June 2004 T-bond taken on March 18, 2004, is graphically described in Figure 24–4. A short position in the futures contract will produce a profit when interest rates rise (meaning that the value of the underlying T-bond decreases). Therefore, a short position in the futures market is the appropriate hedge when the FI stands to lose on the balance sheet if interest rates are expected to rise (e.g., the FI has a positive duration gap). A long position in the futures market produces a profit when interest rates fall (meaning that the value of the underlying T-bond increases).[12] Therefore, a long position is the appropriate hedge when the FI stands to lose on the balance sheet if interest rates are expected to fall (e.g., has a negative duration gap).

If, at maturity (in June 2004), the price quote on the T-bond futures contract was $115^{10}/_{32}$, the buyer would pay $115,312.50 to the seller and the futures seller would deliver one $100,000, 20-year, 8 percent T-bond to the futures buyer. In actuality, the seller of the futures contract has a number of alternatives other than an 8 percent coupon 20-year bond that can be delivered against the T-bond futures contract. If only one type of bond could be delivered, a shortage or squeeze might develop, making it very hard for the short side or seller to deliver. In fact, the seller

[11] In practice, the futures price changes day to day and gains or losses would be generated for the seller/buyer over the period between when the contract is entered into and when it matures. See our later discussion of this unique marking-to-market feature. Note that the FI could sell contracts in T-bonds maturing at later dates. However, while contracts exist for up to two years into the future, longer-term contracts tend to be infrequently traded and therefore relatively illiquid.

[12] Notice that if rates move in an opposite direction from that expected, losses are incurred on the futures position. That is, if rates rise and futures prices drop, the long hedger loses. Similarly, if rates fall and futures prices rise, the short hedger loses. However, such losses are offset by gains on their cash market positions. Thus, the hedger is still protected.

FIGURE 24–4
Profit or Loss on a Futures Position in Treasury Bonds Taken on March 18, 2004

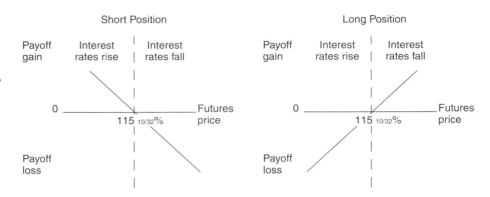

has quite flexible delivery options; apart from delivering the 20-year, 8 percent coupon bond, the seller can deliver bonds that range in maturity from 15 years upward. Often, up to 25 different bonds may qualify for delivery. When a bond other than the 20-year benchmark bond is delivered, the buyer pays a different invoice price for the futures contract based on a **conversion factor** that calculates the price of the deliverable bond if it were to yield 8 percent divided by face value. Suppose $100,000 worth of 18-year, 6 percent semiannual coupon Treasury bonds were valued at a yield of 5.5 percent. This would produce a fair present value of the bond of approximately $105,667. The conversion factor for the bond would be 1.057 (or $105,667/$100,000). This means the buyer would have to pay the seller the conversion factor of 1.057 times the published futures price of $115,312.50. That is, the futures price would be $121,885.31.[13]

We can now solve for the number of futures contracts to buy or sell to fully macro-hedge an FI's on-balance-sheet interest rate risk exposure. We have shown that:

1. *Loss on balance sheet.* The loss of net worth for an FI when rates rise is equal to:

$$\Delta E = -(D_A - kD_L)A \frac{\Delta R}{1 + R}$$

2. *Gain off balance sheet on futures.* The gain off balance sheet from selling futures is equal to[14]

$$\Delta F = -D_F(N_F \times P_F)\frac{\Delta R}{1 + R}$$

Fully hedging can be defined as buying or selling a sufficient number of futures contracts (N_F) so that the loss of net worth on the balance sheet (ΔE) when interest rates change is just offset by the gain from off-balance-sheet buying or selling of futures (ΔF), or

$$\Delta F = \Delta E$$

Substituting in the appropriate expressions for each:

$$-D_F(N_F \times P_F)\frac{\Delta R}{1 + R} = -(D_A - kD_L)A\frac{\Delta R}{1 + R}$$

conversion factor
A factor used to figure the invoice price on a futures contract when a bond other than the benchmark bond is delivered to the buyer.

[13] In practice, the seller exploits the delivery option by choosing the cheapest bond to deliver, that is, bonds whose conversion factor is most favorable (being based on an 8 percent yield) relative to the true price of the bond to be delivered (which reflects the actual level of yields). See S. Figlewski, *Hedging with Financial Futures for Institutional Investors: From Theory to Practice* (Cambridge, MA: Ballinger, 1986).

[14] When futures prices fall, the buyer of the contract compensates the seller, here the FI. Thus, the FI gains when the prices of futures fall.

Canceling $\Delta R/(1 + R)$ on both sides:[15]

$$D_F (N_F \times P_F) = (D_A - kD_L) A$$

Solving for N_F (the number of futures to sell):

$$N_F = \frac{(D_A - kD_L)A}{D_F \times P_F}$$

Appendix 24A (located at the book's Web site, **www.mhhe.com/saunders5e**) derives the equation for the number of futures contracts to buy or sell for a microhedge.[16]

Short Hedge

An FI takes a short position in a futures contract when rates are expected to rise; that is, the FI loses net worth on its balance sheet if rates rise, so it seeks to hedge the value of its net worth by selling an appropriate number of futures contracts.

EXAMPLE 24–2

Macrohedge of Interest Rate Risk Using a Short Hedge

From the equation for N_F, we can now solve for the correct number of futures positions to sell (N_F) in the context of Example 24–1 where the FI was exposed to a balance sheet loss of net worth (ΔE) amounting to $2.091 million when interest rates rose. In that example:

D_A = 5 years
D_L = 3 years
k = .9
A = $100 million

Suppose the current futures price quote is $97 per $100 of face value for the benchmark 20-year, 8 percent coupon bond underlying the nearby futures contract, the minimum contract size is $100,000, and the duration of the deliverable bond is 9.5 years. That is:

$$D_F = 9.5 \text{ years}$$

$$P_F = \$97,000$$

Inserting these numbers into the expression for N_F, we can now solve for the number of futures to sell:[17]

$$N_F = \frac{(5 - (.9)(3)) \times \$100 \text{ million}}{9.5 \times \$97,000}$$

$$= \frac{\$230,000,000}{\$921,500}$$

$$= 249.59 \text{ contracts to be sold}$$

---

[15] This amounts to assuming that the interest changes of the cash asset position match those of the futures position; that is, there is no basis risk. This assumption is relaxed later.

[16] For a microhedge, this equation becomes

$$N_F = \frac{D \times P}{D_F \times P_F}$$

where P is the price of the asset or liability being hedged and D is its duration.

[17] For further discussions of this formula, see Figlewski, *Hedging with Financial Futures,* and E. Brewer, "Bank Gap Management and the Use of Financial Futures," Federal Reserve Bank of Chicago, *Economic Perspectives,* March–April 1985. Also note that if the FI intends to deliver any bond other than the 20-year benchmark bond, the P_F has to be multiplied by the appropriate conversion factor (c). If $c = 1.19$, then $P_F = 97 \times 1.19 = \$115.43$ per $100 of face value and the invoice price per contract would be $115,430.

Since the FI cannot sell a part of a contract, the number of contracts should be rounded down to the nearest whole number, or 249 contracts.[18]

Next, we verify that selling 249 T-bond futures contracts will indeed hedge the FI against a sudden increase in interest rates from 10 to 11 percent, or a 1 percent interest rate shock.

On Balance Sheet

As shown above, when interest rates rise by 1 percent, the FI loses $2.091 million in net worth (ΔE) on the balance sheet:

$$\Delta E = -(D_A - kD_L) A \frac{\Delta R}{1 + R}$$

$$-\$2.091 \text{ million} = -(5 - (.9)(3)) \times \$100 \text{ million} \times \left(\frac{.01}{1.1}\right)$$

Off Balance Sheet

When interest rates rise by 1 percent, the change in the value of the futures position is:

$$\Delta F = -D_F (N_F \times P_F) \frac{\Delta R}{1 + R}$$

$$= -9.5 (-249 \times \$97,000) \left(\frac{.01}{1.1}\right)$$

$$= \$2.086 \text{ million}$$

The value of the off-balance-sheet futures position (ΔF) falls by $2.086 million when the FI sells 249 futures contracts in the T-bond futures market. Such a fall in value of the futures contracts means a positive cash flow to the futures seller as the buyer compensates the seller for a lower futures price through the marking-to-market process. This requires a cash flow from the buyer's margin account to the seller's margin account as the price of a futures contract falls.[19] Thus, as the seller of the futures, the FI makes a gain of $2.086 million. As a result, the net gain/loss on and off the balance sheet is

$$\Delta E + \Delta F = -\$2.091 \text{ m} + \$2.086 \text{ m} = -\$0.005 \text{ million}$$

This small remaining net loss of $.005 million to equity or net worth reflects the fact that the FI could not achieve the perfect hedge—even in the absence of basis risk—as it needed to round down the number of futures to the nearest whole contract from 249.59 to 249

(continued)

[18] The reason for rounding down rather than rounding up is technical. The target number of contracts to sell is that which minimizes interest rate risk exposure. By slightly underhedging rather than overhedging, the FI can generate the same risk exposure level but the underhedging policy produces a slightly higher return (see Figure 24–2).

[19] An example of marking to market might clarify how the seller gains when the price of the futures contract falls. Suppose on day 1 the seller entered into a 90-day contract to deliver 20-year T-bonds at $P = \$97$. The next day, because of a rise in interest rates, the futures contract, which now has 89 days to maturity, is trading at $96 when the market closes. Marking to market requires the prices on all contracts entered into on the previous day(s) to be marked to market at each night's closing (settlement) price. As a result, the price of the contract is lowered to $96 per $100 of face value, but in return for this lowering of the price from $97 to $96, the buyer has to compensate the seller to the tune of $1 per $100 of face value. Thus, given a $100,000 contract, there is a cash flow payment of $1,000 on that day from the buyer to the seller. Note that if the price had risen to $98, the seller would have had to compensate the buyer $1,000. The marking-to-market process goes on until the futures contract matures. If, over the period, futures prices have mostly fallen, then the seller accumulates positive cash flows on the futures position. It is this accumulation of cash flows that can be set off against losses in net worth on the balance sheet.

contracts. Table 24–2 summarizes the key features of the hedge (assuming no rounding of futures contracts).

Suppose instead of using the 20-year T-bond futures to hedge, it had used the three-month Eurodollar futures.[20] We can use the same formula to solve for N_F in the case of Eurodollar futures:

$$N_F = \frac{(D_A - kD_L)A}{D_F \times P_F}$$

$$= \frac{(5 - (.9)(3))\ \$100\ \text{million}}{D_F \times P_F}$$

Assume that $P_F = \$97$ per $100 of face value or $970,000 per contract (the minimum contract size of a Eurodollar future is $1,000,000) and $D_F = .25$ (the duration of a three-month Eurodollar deposit that is the discount instrument deliverable under the contract).[21] Then:

$$N_F = \frac{(5 - (.9)(3))\$100\ \text{million}}{.25 \times \$970,000} = \frac{\$230,000,000}{\$242,500}$$

$$N_F = 948.45 \text{ contracts to be sold}$$

Rounding down to the nearest whole contract, $N_F = 948$.

TABLE 24–2   On- and Off-Balance-Sheet Effects of a Macrohedge Hedge

	On Balance Sheet	Off Balance Sheet
Begin hedge $t = 0$	Equity value of $10 million exposed to impact of rise in interest rates.	Sell 249.59 T-bond futures contracts at $97,000. Underlying T-bond coupon rate is 8%.
End hedge $t = 1$ day	Interest rates rise on assets and liabilities by 1%. Opportunity loss on-balance-sheet: $$\Delta E = -[5 - .9(3)] \times \$100m \times \frac{.01}{1.1}$$ $$= -\$2.091 \text{ million}$$	Buy 249.59 T-bond futures (closes out futures position). Real gain on futures hedge: $$\Delta F = -9.5 \times (-249.59 \times \$97,000) \times \frac{.01}{1.1}^{*}$$ $$= \$2.091 \text{ million}$$

*Assuming no basis risk and no contract "rounding."

As this example illustrates, we can hedge an FI's on-balance-sheet interest rate risk when its $D_A > kD_L$ by shorting or selling either T-bond or Eurodollar futures. In general, fewer T-bond than Eurodollar contracts need to be sold—in our case, 948 Eurodollar versus 249 T-bond contracts. This suggests that on a simple transaction cost basis, the FI might normally prefer to use T-bond futures. However, other considerations can be important, especially if the FI holds the futures contracts until the delivery date. The FI needs to be concerned about the availability of

[20] As Figure 24–3 shows, three-month Eurodollar futures are an alternative interest rate futures contract to the long-term bond futures contract.

[21] We assume the same futures price ($97) here for purposes of comparison. Of course, the actual prices of the two futures contracts are very different (see Figure 24–3).

the deliverable set of securities and any possible supply shortages or squeezes. Such liquidity concerns may favor Eurodollars.[22]

The Problem of Basis Risk

Because spot bonds and futures on bonds are traded in different markets, the shift in yields, $\Delta R/(1 + R)$, affecting the values of the on-balance-sheet cash portfolio may differ from the shift in yields, $\Delta R_F/(1 + R_F)$, affecting the value of the underlying bond in the futures contract; that is, changes in spot and futures prices or values are not perfectly correlated. This lack of perfect correlation is called *basis risk*. In the previous section, we assumed a simple world of no basis risk in which $\Delta R/(1 + R) = \Delta R_F/(1 + R_F)$.

Basis risk occurs for two reasons. First, the balance sheet asset or liability being hedged is not the same as the underlying security on the futures contract. For instance, in Example 24–2 we hedged interest rate changes on the FI's entire balance sheet with T-bond futures contracts written on 20-year maturity bonds with a duration of 9.5 years. The interest rates on the various assets and liabilities on the FI's balance sheet and the interest rates on 20-year T-bonds do not move in a perfectly correlated (or one-to-one) manner. The second source of basis risk comes from the difference in movements in spot rates versus futures rates. Because spot securities (e.g., government bonds) and futures contracts (e.g., on the same bonds) are traded in different markets, the shift in spot rates may differ from the shift in futures rates (i.e., they are not perfectly correlated).

To solve for the risk-minimizing number of futures contracts to buy or sell, N_F, while accounting for greater or less rate volatility and hence price volatility in the futures market relative to the spot or cash market, we look again at the FI's on-balance-sheet interest rate exposure:

$$\Delta E = -(D_A - kD_L) \times A \times \Delta R/(1 + R)$$

and its off-balance-sheet futures position:

$$\Delta F = -D_F(N_F \times P_F) \times \Delta R_F/(1 + R_F)$$

Setting:

$$\Delta E = \Delta F$$

and solving for N_F, we have

$$N_F = \frac{(D_A - kD_L) \times A \times \Delta R/(1 + R)}{D_F \times P_F \times \Delta R_F/(1 + R_F)}$$

Let *br* reflect the relative sensitivity of rates underlying the bond in the futures market relative to interest rates on assets and liabilities in the spot market, that is, $br = (\Delta R_F/(1 + R_F))/(\Delta R/(1 + R))$. Then the number of futures contracts to buy or sell is

$$N_F = \frac{(D_A - kD_L)A}{D_F \times P_F \times br}$$

---

[22] However, when rates change, the loss of net worth on the balance sheet and the gain on selling the futures are instantaneous; therefore, delivery need not be a concern. Indeed, because of the daily marking-to-market process, an FI manager can close out a futures position by taking an exactly offsetting position. That is, a manager who had originally sold 100 futures contracts could close out a position on any day by buying 100 contracts. Because of the unique marking-to-market feature, the marked-to-market price of the contracts sold equals the price of any new contracts bought on that day.

The only difference between this and the previous formula is an adjustment for basis risk (*br*), which measures the degree to which the futures price (yield) moves more or less than spot bond price (yield).

| **EXAMPLE 24–3**

Macrohedging
Interest Rate
Risk When Basis
Risk Exists | From Example 24–2, let $br = 1.1$. This means that for every 1 percent change in discounted spot rates ($\Delta R/(1 + R)$), the implied rate on the deliverable bond in the futures market moves by 1.1 percent. That is, futures prices are more sensitive to interest rate shocks than are spot market prices. Solving for N_F we have

$$N_F = \frac{(5 - (.9)(3))\$100 \text{ million}}{9.5 \times \$97,000 \times 1.1}$$

$$= 226.9 \text{ contracts}$$

or 226 contracts, rounding down. This compares to 249 when we assumed equal rate shocks in both the cash and futures markets ($\Delta R/(1 + R) = \Delta R_F/(1 + R_F)$). Here we need fewer futures contracts than was the case when we ignored basis risk because futures rates and prices are more volatile, so that selling fewer futures would be sufficient to provide the same change in ΔF (the value of the futures position) than before when we implicitly assumed $br = 1$. Note that if futures rates or prices had been less volatile than spot rates or prices, we would have had to sell more than 249 contracts to get the same dollar gain in the futures position as was lost in net worth on the balance sheet so that $\Delta E = \Delta F$. |

An important issue FIs must deal with in hedging interest rate and other risks is how to estimate the basis risk adjustment in the preceding formula. One method is to look at the ratio between $\Delta R/(1 + R)$ and $\Delta R_F/(1 + R_F)$ today. Since this is only one observation, the FI might better analyze the relationship between the two interest rates by investigating their relative behavior in the recent past. We can do this by running an ordinary least squares linear regression of implied futures rate changes on spot rate changes with the slope coefficient of this regression giving an estimate of the degree of comovement of the two rates over time. We discuss this regression procedure in greater detail next in connection with calculating basis risk when hedging with FX futures.[23]

Concept Questions

1. What is the difference between microhedging and macrohedging and between routine hedging and selective hedging?
2. In Example 24–2, suppose the FI had the reverse duration gap; that is, the duration of its assets was shorter ($D_A = 3$) than the duration of its liabilities ($D_A = 5$). (This might be the case of a bank that borrows with long-term notes or time deposits to finance floating-rate loans.) How should it hedge using futures?
3. In Example 24–3, how many futures contracts should have been sold using the 20-year bond and 3-month Eurodollar contracts, if the basis risk measure $br = .8$?

HEDGING FOREIGN EXCHANGE RISK

Just as forwards and futures can hedge an FI against losses due to interest rate changes, they also can hedge against foreign exchange risk.

[23] Another problem with the simple duration gap approach to determining N_F is that it is assumed that yield curves are flat. This could be relaxed by using duration measures that allow for nonflat yield curves (see Chapter 9).

Forwards

Chapter 15 analyzed how an FI uses forward contracts to reduce the risks due to FX fluctuations when it mismatches the sizes of its foreign asset and liability portfolios. That chapter considered the simple case of an FI that raised all its liabilities in dollars while investing half of its assets in British pound sterling–denominated loans and the other half in dollar-denominated loans. Its balance sheet looks as follows:

Assets	Liabilities
U.S. loans ($) $100 million	U.S. CDs $200 million
U.K. loans (£) $100 million	

All assets and liabilities are of a one-year maturity and duration. Because the FI is net long in pound sterling assets, it faces the risk that over the period of the loan, the pound will depreciate against the dollar so that the proceeds of the pound loan (along with the dollar loan) will be insufficient to meet the required payments on the maturing dollar CDs. Then the FI will have to meet such losses out of its net worth; that is, its insolvency risk will increase.

Chapter 15 showed that by selling both the pound loan principal and interest forward one year at the known forward exchange rate at the beginning of the year, the FI could hedge itself against losses on its pound loan position due to changes in the dollar/pound exchange rate over the succeeding year. Note the strategy for hedging (£100 million) of British pound sterling loans with forwards in Figure 24–5.

Futures

Instead of using FX forward contracts to hedge foreign exchange risk, the FI could use FX futures contracts. Consider a U.S.-based FI wishing to hedge a one-year British pound loan of £100 million principal plus £15 million interest (or £115 million) against the risk of the pound falling in value against the dollar over the succeeding year. Suppose the FI wished to hedge this loan position on March 18, 2004. On that day, there were two British pound futures contracts outstanding: a contract expiring in June 2004 (the "nearby" contract) and a contract expiring in December 2004. Thus, the futures market did not allow the FI to institute a long-term one-year hedge that day. The longest maturity contract available matured in just over five months (December 2004). Thus, the FI could use futures only by rolling over the hedge into a new futures contract on maturity. Considerations such as the transactions costs from having to roll over the hedge and uncertainty regarding the prices of new futures contracts may make hedging through forwards or swaps relatively more attractive to those FIs that want to lock in a longer-term hedge (see Chapter 26).

FIGURE 24–5

Hedging a Long Position in Pound Assets through Sale of Pound Forwards

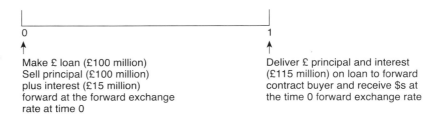

0

Make £ loan (£100 million)
Sell principal (£100 million)
plus interest (£15 million)
forward at the forward exchange
rate at time 0

1

Deliver £ principal and interest
(£115 million) on loan to forward
contract buyer and receive $s at
the time 0 forward exchange rate

However, suppose the FI still wants to hedge fully via the futures markets. How many futures should it sell? The answer to this question is that it should sell the amount that produces a sufficient profit on the pound futures contracts to just off-set any exchange rate losses on the pound loan portfolio should the pound fall in value relative to the dollar. There are two cases to consider:

1. The futures dollar/pound price is expected to change in exactly the same fashion as the spot dollar/pound price over the course of the year. That is, futures and spot price changes are perfectly correlated; there is no basis risk.
2. Futures and spot prices, while expected to change in the same direction, are not perfectly correlated (there is basis risk).

EXAMPLE 24–4

Hedging Foreign Exchange Risk Assuming Perfect Correlation between Spot and Futures Prices

On March 18, 2004, *The Wall Street Journal* reported:

$$S_t = \text{Spot exchange rate (\$/£): \$1.8057 per £1}$$

$$f_t = \text{Futures price (\$/£) for the nearby contract}$$
$$\text{(June 2004): \$1.7916 per £1}$$

Suppose the FI made a £100 million loan at 15 percent interest and wished to hedge fully the risk that the dollar value of the proceeds would be eroded by a declining British pound sterling over the year. Also suppose that the FI manager receives a forecast that in one year's time the spot and futures will be

$$S_{t+1} = \text{\$1.7557 per £1}$$

$$f_{t+1} = \text{\$1.7416 per £1}$$

so that over the year,

$$\Delta S_t = -5 \text{ cents}$$

$$\Delta f_t = -5 \text{ cents}$$

For a manager who believes this forecast of a depreciating pound against the dollar, the correct full-hedge strategy is to cover the £115 million of expected earnings on the British loan by selling, or shorting, £115 million of British pound futures contracts on March 18, 2004. We assume here that the FI manager continuously rolls over the futures position into new futures contracts and will get out of futures on March 18, 2005.

The size of each British pound futures contract is £62,500. Therefore, the number (N_F) of futures to be sold is

$$N_F = \frac{£115,000,000}{£62,500} = \frac{\text{Size of long position}}{\text{Size of a pound futures contract}}$$

$$= 1,840 \text{ contracts to be sold}$$

Next, we consider whether losses on the long asset position (the British loan) would just offset gains on the futures should the FI sell 1,840 British pound futures contracts should spot and futures prices change in the direction and amount expected.

Loss on British Pound Loan
The loss on the British pound loan in dollars would be

$$[£ \text{ Principal} + \text{Interest}] \times \Delta S_t$$

$$[£115 \text{ million}] \times [\$1.8057/£ - \$1.7557/£] = \$5.75 \text{ million}$$

That is, the dollar value of the British pound loan proceeds would be $5.75 million less should the pound depreciate from $1.8057/£ to $1.7557/£ in the spot market over the year.

Gain on Futures Contracts

The gain on the futures contracts would be

$$[N_F \times £62,500] \times \Delta f_t$$

$$[1,840 \times £62,500] \times [\$1.7916/£ - \$1.7416/£] = \$5.75 \text{ million}$$

By selling 1,840 futures contracts of 62,500 each, the seller makes $5.75 million as the futures price falls from $1.7916/£ at the contract initiation on March 18, 2004, to $1.7416/£ at the futures position termination on March 18, 2005. This cash flow of $5.75 million results from the marking to market of the futures contract. As the futures price falls, due to the daily marking to market, the pound futures contract buyer has the contract repriced to a lower level in dollars to be paid per pound. But the seller must be compensated from the buyer's margin account for the difference between the original contract price and the new lower marked-to-market contract price. Thus, over the one year, the buyer compensates the seller by a net of 5 cents per £1 of futures purchased: that is, $1.7916/£1 minus $1.7416/£1 as the futures price falls, or a total of 5 cents × the number of contracts (1,840) × the pound size of each contract (62,500). Note that on March 18, 2005, when the principal and interest on the pound loan are paid by the borrower, the FI seller of the pound futures terminates its position in 1,840 short contracts by taking an opposing position of 1,840 long in the same contract. This effectively ends any net cash flow implications from futures positions beyond this date.

tail the hedge
Reducing the number of futures contracts that are needed to hedge a cash position because of the interest income that is generated from reinvesting the marked-to-market cash flows generated by the futures contract.

Finally, in this example we have ignored the interest income effects of marking to market. In reality, the $5.75 million from the futures position would be received by the FI seller over the course of the year. As a result, this cash flow can be reinvested at the current short-term dollar interest rate to generate a cash flow of more than $5.75 million. Given this, an FI hedger can sell slightly fewer contracts in anticipation of this interest income. The number of futures that could be sold, below the 1,840 suggested, would depend on the level and pattern of short-term rates over the hedging horizon as well as the precise expected pattern of cash flows from marking to market. In general, the higher the level of short-term interest, the more an FI manager could **tail the hedge** in this fashion.[24]

EXAMPLE 24–5
Hedging Foreign Exchange Risk Assuming Imperfect Correlation between Spot and Futures Prices (Basis Risk)

Suppose, instead, the FI manager did not believe that the spot exchange rate and futures price on the dollar/pound contract would fall by exactly the same amount. Instead, let the forecast for one year's time be:

$$S_{t+1} = 1.7557/£1$$

$$f_{t+1} = \$1.7616/£1$$

Thus, in expectation, over the succeeding year:

$$\Delta S_t = -5 \text{ cents}$$

$$\Delta f_t = -3 \text{ cents}$$

(continued)

[24] See Figlewski, *Hedging with Financial Futures*, for further discussion. One way to do this is to discount the calculated hedge ratio (the optimal number of futures to sell per $1 of cash position) by a short-term interest rate such as the federal funds rate.

This means that the dollar/pound futures price is expected to depreciate less than the spot dollar/pound. This basis risk arises because spot and futures contracts are traded in different markets with different demand and supply functions. Given this, even though futures and spot prices are normally highly correlated, this correlation is often less than 1.

Because futures prices and spot prices do not always move exactly together, this can create a problem for an FI manager seeking to hedge the long position of £115 million with pound futures. Suppose the FI manager ignored the fact that the spot pound is expected to depreciate faster against the dollar than the futures price for pounds and continued to believe that selling 1,840 contracts would be the best hedge. That manager could be in for a big (and nasty) surprise in one year's time. To see this, consider the loss on the cash asset position and the gain on the futures position under a new scenario where the dollar/pound spot rate falls by 2 cents more than dollar/pound futures over the year.

Loss on British Pound Loan
The expected fall in the spot value of the pound by 5 cents over the year results in a loss of

$$[£115 \text{ million}] \times [\$1.8057/£ - \$1.7557/£] = \$5.75 \text{ million}$$

Gain on Futures Position
The expected gain on the futures position is

$$[1,840 \times £62,500] \times [\$1.7916/£ - \$1.7616/£] = \$3.45 \text{ million}$$

Thus, the net loss to the FI is

Net loss = Loss on British pound loan − Gain on British pound futures

Net loss = \$5.75 − \$3.45

Net loss = \$2.3 million

Such a loss would have to be charged against the FI's profits and implicitly its net worth or equity. As a result, the FI manager needs to take into account the lower sensitivity of futures prices relative to spot exchange rate changes by selling more than 1,840 futures contracts to hedge fully the British pound loan risk.

To see how many more contracts are required, we need to know how much more sensitive spot exchange rates are relative to futures prices. Let h be the ratio of ΔS_t to Δf_t:

$$h = \frac{\Delta S_t}{\Delta f_t}$$

Then, in our example:

$$h = \frac{\$.05}{\$.03} = 1.66$$

That is, spot rates are 66 percent more sensitive than futures prices, or—put slightly differently—for every 1 percent change in futures prices, spot rates change by 1.66 percent.[25]

hedge ratio
The dollar value of futures contracts that should be sold per $ of cash position exposure.

An FI manager could use this ratio, h, as a **hedge ratio** to solve the question of how many futures should be sold to hedge the long position in the British pound when the spot and futures prices are imperfectly correlated. Specifically, the value of h means that for every £1 in the long asset position, £1.66 futures contracts should be sold. To see this, look at the FI's losses on its long asset position in pound loans relative to the gains on its selling pound futures.

Loss on British Pound Loans
As before, its losses are

$$[£115 \text{ million}] \times [\$1.8057/£ - \$1.7557/£] = \$5.75 \text{ million}$$

(continued)

---

[25] Of course, this can always be expressed the other way around: a 1 percent change in spot prices leads, on average, to only a 0.6 percent change in futures prices.

Gains on British Pound Futures Position

Taking into account the degree to which spot exchange rates are more sensitive than futures prices—the hedge ratio (h)— we can solve for the number of futures (N_F) to sell as

$$N_F = \frac{\text{Long asset position} \times h}{\text{Size of one futures contract}}$$

$$N_F = \frac{\text{£115 million} \times 1.66}{\text{£62,500}} = 3,054.4 \text{ contracts}$$

or, rounding down to the nearest whole contract, 3,054 contracts. Selling 3,054 British pound futures results in expected profits of

$$[3,054 \times \text{£62,500}] \times [\$1.7916/\text{£} - \$1.7616/\text{£}] = \$5.73 \text{ million}$$

The difference of \$0.02 million between the loss on British pound loans and the gain on the pound futures is due to rounding.

Estimating the Hedge Ratio[26]

The previous example showed that the number of FX futures that should be sold to hedge fully foreign exchange rate risk exposure depends crucially on expectations regarding the correlation between the change in the dollar/pound spot rate (ΔS_t) and the change in its futures price (Δf_t). When:

$$h = \frac{\Delta S_t}{\Delta f_t} = \frac{\$.05}{\$.05} = 1$$

there is no basis risk. Both the spot and futures are expected to change together by the same absolute amount, and the FX risk of the cash position should be hedged dollar for dollar by selling FX futures. When basis risk is present, the spot and future exchange rates are expected to move imperfectly together:

$$h = \frac{\Delta S_t}{\Delta f_t} = \frac{\$.05}{\$.03} = 1.66$$

The FI must sell a greater number of futures than it has to when basis risk is absent.

Unfortunately, without perfect foresight, we cannot know exactly how exchange rates and futures prices will change over some future time period. If we did, we would have no need to hedge in the first place! Thus, a common method to calculate h is to look at the behavior of ΔS_t relative to Δf_t over the *recent past* and to use this past behavior as a prediction of the appropriate value of h in the future. One way to estimate this past relationship is to run an ordinary least squares regression of recent changes in spot prices on recent changes in futures prices.[27]

Consider Figure 24–6, where we plot hypothetical monthly changes in the spot pound/dollar exchange rate (ΔS_t) against monthly changes in the futures pound/dollar price (Δf_t) for the year 200X. Thus, we have 12 observations from January through December. For information purposes, the first observation (January) is

---

[26] The material in this section is more technical in nature. It may be included or dropped from the chapter reading depending on the rigor of the course without harming the continuity of the chapter.

[27] When we calculate h (the hedge ratio), we could use the ratio of the most recent spot and futures price changes. However, this would amount to basing our hedge ratio estimate on *one* observation of the change in S_t and f_t. This is why the regression model, which uses many past observations, is usually preferred by market participants.

FIGURE 24–6
Monthly Changes in ΔS_t and Δf_t in 200X

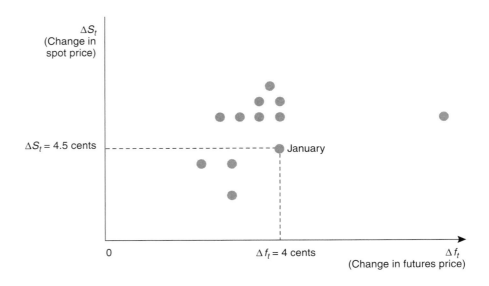

labeled in Figure 24–6. In January, the dollar/pound spot rate rose by 4.5 cents and the dollar/pound futures price rose by 4 cents. Thus, the pound appreciated in value over the month of January but the spot exchange rate rose by more than the futures price did. In some other months, as implied by the scatter of points in Figure 24–6, the futures price rose by more than the spot rate did.

An ordinary least squares (OLS) regression fits a line of best fit to these monthly observations such that the sum of the squared deviations between the observed values of ΔS_t and its predicted values (as given by the line of best fit) is minimized. This line of best fit reflects an intercept term α and a slope coefficient β. That is:

$$\Delta S_t = \alpha + \beta \, \Delta f_t + u_t$$

where the u_t are the regression's residuals (the differences between actual values of ΔS_t and its predicted values based on the line of best fit).

Definitionally, β, or the slope coefficient, of the regression equation is equal to

$$\beta = \frac{\mathrm{Cov}\,(\Delta S_t,\, \Delta f_t)}{\mathrm{Var}\,(\Delta f_t)}$$

that is, the covariance between the change in spot rates and change in futures prices divided by the variance of the change in futures prices. Suppose ΔS_t and Δf_t moved perfectly together over time. Then:

$$\mathrm{Cov}\,(\Delta S_t,\, \Delta f_t) = \mathrm{Var}\,(\Delta f_t)$$

$$\text{and } \beta = 1$$

If spot rate changes are greater than futures price changes, then $\mathrm{Cov}\,(\Delta S_t,\, \Delta f_t) > \mathrm{Var}\,(\Delta f_t)$ and $\beta > 1$. Conversely, if spot rate changes are less sensitive than futures price changes over time, then $\mathrm{Cov}\,(\Delta S_t,\, \Delta f_t) < \mathrm{Var}\,(\Delta f_t)$ and $\beta < 1$.

Moreover, the value of β, or the estimated slope of the regression line, has theoretical meaning as the hedge ratio (h) that minimizes the risk of a portfolio of spot assets and futures contracts.[28] Put more simply, we can use the estimate of β from

---

[28] For proof of this, see L. H. Ederington, "The Hedging Performance of the New Futures Markets," *Journal of Finance* 34 (1979), pp. 157–70.

the regression model as the appropriate measure of h (the hedge ratio) to be used by the FI manager. For example, suppose we used the 12 observations on ΔS_t and Δf_t in 200X to estimate an OLS regression equation (the equation of the line of best fit in Figure 24–6). This regression equation takes the form:

$$\Delta S_t = 0.15 + 1.2\,\Delta f_t$$

Thus:

$$\alpha = 0.15$$

$$\beta = 1.2$$

Using $\beta = 1.2$ as the appropriate risk minimizing hedge ratio h for the portfolio manager, we can solve our earlier problem of determining the number of futures contracts to sell to protect the FI from FX losses on its £115 million loan:

$$N_F = \frac{\text{Long position in £ assets} \times \beta \text{ (the estimated value of the hedge ratio } h \text{ using past data)}}{\text{Size of one £ futures contract}}$$

$$N_F = \frac{£115 \text{ million} \times 1.2}{£62,500} = 2,208 \text{ contracts}$$

Thus, using the past relationship between ΔS_t and Δf_t as the best predictor of their future relationship over the succeeding year dictates that the FI manager sell 2,208 contracts.

The degree of confidence the FI manager may have in using such a method to determine the appropriate hedge ratio depends on how well the regression line fits the scatter of observations. The standard measure of the goodness of fit of a regression line is the R^2 of the equation, where the R^2 is the square of the correlation coefficient between ΔS_t and Δf_t:

$$R^2 = \rho^2 = \left[\frac{(\text{Cov}\,(\Delta S_t, \Delta f_t))}{\sigma_{\Delta S_t} \times \sigma_{\Delta f_t}}\right]^2$$

The term in brackets is the statistical definition of a correlation coefficient. If changes in the spot rate (ΔS_t) and changes in the futures price (Δf_t) are perfectly correlated, then:

$$R^2 = \rho^2 = (1)^2 = 1$$

and all observations between ΔS_t and Δf_t lie on a straight line. By comparison, an $R^2 = 0$ indicates that there is no statistical association at all between ΔS_t and Δf_t.

hedging effectiveness
The (squared) correlation between past changes in spot asset prices and futures prices.

Since we are using futures contracts to hedge the risk of loss on spot asset positions, the R^2 of the regression measures the degree of **hedging effectiveness** of the futures contract. A low R^2 means that we might have little confidence that the slope coefficient β from the regression is actually the true hedge ratio. As the R^2 approaches 1, the degree of confidence increases in the use of futures contracts, with a given hedge ratio (h) estimate, to hedge our cash asset-risk position.

Concept Questions

1. Circle an observation in Figure 24–6 that shows futures price changes exceeding spot price changes.
2. Suppose that $R^2 = 0$ in a regression of ΔS_t on Δf_t. Would you still use futures contracts to hedge? Explain your answer.
3. In running a regression of ΔS_t on Δf_t, the regression equation is $\Delta S_t = .51 + .95\Delta f_t$ and $R^2 = .72$. What is the hedge ratio? What is the measure of hedging effectiveness?

HEDGING CREDIT RISK WITH FUTURES AND FORWARDS

Chapter 12 demonstrated that by diversifying their loan portfolios across different borrowers, sectors, and regions, FIs can diversify away much of the borrower-specific or unsystematic risk of the loan portfolio. Of course, the ability of an FI manager to diversify sufficiently depends in part on the size of the loan portfolio under management. Thus, the potential ability to diversify away borrower-specific risk increases with the size of the FI.

In recent years, however, new types of derivative instruments have been developed (including forwards, options, and swaps) to better allow FIs to hedge their credit risk. Credit derivatives can be used to hedge the credit risk on individual loans or bonds or on portfolios of loans and bonds. The credit derivative market, while still relatively young, has already gained a reputation as an early warning signal for spotting corporate debt problems. As shown in Table 24–1, commercial banks had over $866 million of notional value in credit derivatives outstanding in September 2003, and there were an estimated $2 trillion outstanding worldwide. The emergence of these new derivatives is important since more FIs fail due to credit risk exposures than to either interest rate or FX risk exposures. We discuss credit forward contracts below. In Chapter 25 we discuss credit options, and in Chapter 26 we discuss credit swaps.

Credit Forward Contracts and Credit Risk Hedging

credit forward
An agreement that hedges against an increase in default risk on a loan after the loan terms have been determined and the loan has been issued.

A **credit forward** is a forward agreement that hedges against an increase in default risk on a loan (a decline in the credit quality of a borrower) after the loan rate is determined and the loan is issued. Common buyers of credit forwards are insurance companies and common sellers are banks. The credit forward agreement specifies a credit spread (a risk premium above the risk-free rate to compensate for default risk) on a benchmark bond issued by an FI borrower. For example, suppose the benchmark bond of a bank borrower was rated BBB at the time a loan was originated. Further, at the time the loan was issued, the benchmark bonds had a 2 percent interest rate or credit spread (representing default risk on the BBB bonds) over a U.S. Treasury bond of the same maturity. To hedge against an increase in the credit risk of the borrower, the bank enters into (sells) a credit forward contract when the loan is issued. We define CS_F as the credit spread over the U.S. Treasury rate on which the credit forward contract is written (equals 2 percent in this example). Table 24–3 illustrates the payment pattern resulting from this credit forward. In Table 24–3, CS_T is the actual credit spread on the bond when the credit forward matures, for example, one year after the loan was originated and the credit forward contract was entered into, MD is the modified duration on the benchmark BBB bond, and A is the principal amount of the forward agreement.

From the payment pattern established in the credit forward agreement, Table 24–3 shows that the credit forward buyer (an insurance company) bears the

TABLE 24–3
Payment Pattern on a Credit Forward

Credit Spread at End of Forward Agreement	Credit Spread Seller (Bank)	Credit Spread Buyer (Counterparty)
$CS_T > CS_F$	Receives $(CS_T - CS_F) \times MD \times A$	Pays $(CS_T - CS_F) \times MD \times A$
$CS_F > CS_T$	Pays $(CS_F - CS_T) \times MD \times A$	Receives $(CS_F - CS_T) \times MD \times A$

FIGURE 24–7
Impact on a Bank of Hedging a Loan with a Credit Forward Contract

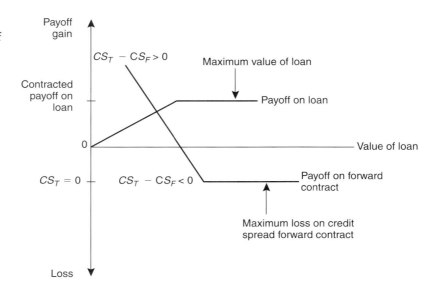

risk of an increase in default risk on the benchmark bond of the borrowing firm, while the credit forward seller (the bank lender) hedges itself against an increase in the borrower's default risk. That is, if the borrower's default risk increases so that when the forward agreement matures the market requires a higher credit spread on the borrower's benchmark bond, CS_T, than that originally agreed to in the forward contract, CS_F, (i.e., $CS_T > CS_F$), the credit forward buyer pays the credit forward seller, which is the bank, $(CS_T - CS_F) \times MD \times A$. For example, suppose the credit spread between BBB bonds and U.S. Treasury bonds widened to 3 percent from 2 percent over the year, the modified duration (MD) of the benchmark BBB bond was five years, and the size of the forward contract A was \$10,000,000. Then the gain on the credit forward contract to the seller (the bank) would be \$500,000 [(3% $-$ 2%) $\times$ 5 $\times$ \$10,000,000]. This amount could be used to offset the loss in market value of the loan due to the rise in the borrower's default risk. However, if the borrower's default risk and credit spread decrease over the year, the credit forward seller pays the credit forward buyer $(CS_F - CS_T) \times MD \times A$. [However, the maximum loss on the forward contract (to the bank seller) is limited, as will be explained below.]

Figure 24–7 illustrates the impact on the bank from hedging the loan.[29] If the default risk on the loan increases, the market or present value of the loan falls below its value at the beginning of the hedge period. However, the bank hedged the change in default risk by selling a credit forward contract. Assuming the credit spread on the borrower's benchmark bond also increases (so that $CS_T > CS_F$), the bank receives $(CS_T - CS_F) \times MD \times A$ on the forward contract. If the characteristics of the benchmark bond (i.e., change in credit spread, modified duration, and principal value) are the same as those of the bank's loan to the borrower, the loss on the balance sheet is offset completely by the gain (off the balance sheet) from the credit forward (i.e., in our example a \$500,000 market value loss in the loan would be offset by a \$500,000 gain from selling the credit forward contract).

[29] For additional discussion, see J. D. Finnerty, "Credit Derivatives, Infrastructure Finance, and Emerging Market Risk," *The Financier*, ACMT, February 1996, pp. 64–75.

If the default risk does not increase or decreases (so that $CS_T < CS_F$), the bank selling the forward contract will pay $(CS_F - CS_T) \times MD \times A$ to the credit forward buyer (the insurance company). However, importantly, this payout by the bank is limited to a maximum. This is when CS_T falls to zero, that is, the default spread on BBB bonds falls to zero or the original BBB bonds of the borrower are viewed as having the same default risk as Treasury bonds (in other words, the credit spread or rate on the benchmark bond cannot fall below the risk-free rate). In this case the maximum loss on the credit forward $[CS_F - (0)] \times MD \times A$ mirrors (offsets) the maximum and limited upside gain (return) on the loan. Anyone familiar with options will recognize that (as was discussed in Chapter 11) when the bank makes a loan, it is similar to writing a put option. In selling a credit forward, the payoff is similar to buying a put option (see Chapter 25 as well).

Futures Contracts and Catastrophe Risk

www.cbot.com

In recent years, the Chicago Board of Trade (CBOT) has introduced futures and options for catastrophe insurance. This chapter discusses catastrophe insurance futures, and the next chapter discusses catastrophe insurance options. The essential idea of catastrophe futures is to allow property-casualty insurers to hedge the extreme losses that occur after major hurricanes, such as the series of hurricanes that hit Florida in September 2004, which resulted in damage of over $25 billion on the properties directly affected. Since in a catastrophe the ratio of insured losses to premiums rises (i.e., the so-called loss ratio increases), the payoff on a catastrophe futures contract is directly linked to the loss ratio. Specifically, on settlement, the payoff to the buyer of the futures is equal to the nominal value of the futures contract (which is $25,000) times the actual loss ratio incurred by insurers. Suppose that on maturity of the futures contract the loss ratio was 1.5. This means that the payoff to the insurance company futures hedger would be $1.5 \times \$25,000 = \$37,500$. Also suppose that three months earlier (before the catastrophe occurred) the market expected the loss ratio to be only 0.8. Thus, the insurer would have been able to pay $0.8 \times \$25,000 = \$20,000$ to buy the futures contract. Because actual losses exceeded expected losses, the insurer makes a profit of $\$37,500 - \$20,000 = \$17,500$ on each contract. These profits on futures contracts can be used to help offset the huge payouts on hurricane insurance contracts.[30]

Futures and Forward Policies of Regulators

www.sec.gov

www.cftc.gov

Derivatives are subject to three levels of institutional regulation. First, regulators of derivatives specify "permissible activities" that institutions may engage in. Second, once permissible activities have been specified, institutions engaging in those activities are subjected to supervisory oversight. Third, regulators attempt to judge the overall integrity of each institution engaging in derivative activities by assessing the capital adequacy of the institutions and by enforcing regulations to ensure compliance with those capital requirements. The Securities and Exchange Commission (SEC) and the Commodities Futures Trading Commission (CFTC) are often

---

[30] For more details on catastrophe insurance, see J. D. Cummins and H. Geman, "Pricing Catastrophe Insurance Futures and Call Spreads: An Arbitrage Model," *Journal of Fixed Income,* March 1995, pp. 46–57; K. K. Aase, "A Markov Model for the Pricing of Catastrophe Insurance Futures and Spreads," *Journal of Risk and Insurance,* March 2001, pp. 25–49; and G. Zanjani, "Pricing and Capital Allocation in Catastrophe Insurance," *Journal of Financial Economics,* August 2002, pp. 283–305.

viewed as "functional" regulators. The SEC regulates all securities traded on national securities exchanges, including several exchange-traded derivatives. The SEC's regulation of derivatives includes price reporting requirements, antimanipulation regulations, position limits, audit trail requirements, and margin requirements. The CFTC has exclusive jurisdiction over all exchange-traded derivative securities. It therefore regulates all national futures exchanges, as well as all futures and options on futures. The CFTC's regulations include minimum capital requirements for traders, reporting and transparency requirements, antifraud and antimanipulation regulations, and minimum standards for clearinghouse organizations.

www.federalreserve.gov

www.fdic.gov

www.occ.treas.gov

The main bank regulators—the Federal Reserve, the FDIC, and the Comptroller of the Currency—also have issued uniform guidelines for banks that trade in futures and forwards.[31] These guidelines require a bank to (1) establish internal guidelines regarding its hedging activity, (2) establish trading limits, and (3) disclose large contract positions that materially affect bank risk to shareholders and outside investors. Overall, the policy of regulators is to encourage the use of futures for hedging and discourage their use for speculation, although on a practical basis it is often difficult to distinguish between the two.

www.fasb.org

As of January 1, 2000, the main regulator of accounting standards (the FASB) required all FIs (and nonfinancial firms) to reflect the mark-to-market value of their derivative positions in their financial statements. This means that FIs must immediately recognize all gains and losses on such contracts and disclose those gains and losses to shareholders and regulators. Further, firms must show whether they are using derivatives to hedge risks connected to their business or whether they are just taking an open (risky) position.

Finally, as noted in Chapter 20, exchange-traded futures contracts are not subject to risk-based capital requirements; by contrast, OTC forward contracts are potentially subject to capital requirements. Other things being equal, the risk-based capital requirements favor the use of futures over forwards.

Concept Questions

1. Why are credit forwards useful for hedging the credit risk of an FI's portfolio?
2. What are some of the practical problems an FI manager may face when using catastrophe futures to hedge losses on insurance lines?

Summary

This chapter analyzed the risk-management role of futures and forwards. We saw that while they are close substitutes, they are not perfect substitutes. A number of characteristics, such as maturity, liquidity, flexibility, marking to market, and capital requirements, differentiate these products and make one or the other more attractive to any given FI manager. These products might be used to partially or fully hedge at least four types of risk commonly faced by an FI: interest rate risk, foreign exchange risk, credit risk, and catastrophe risk. An FI can engage in microhedging or macrohedging as well as engage in selective or routine hedging. In all cases, perfect hedging is shown to be difficult because of basis risk. Finally, accounting rules require FIs to disclose the market values of their (off-balance-sheet) derivatives positions.

[31] See B. C. Gendreau, "The Regulation of Bank Trading in Futures and Forward Markets," in *Below the Bottom Line: The Use of Contingencies and Commitments by Commercial Banks* (Washington, DC: Federal Reserve Board of Governors, 1982).

Questions and Problems

1. What are derivative contracts? What is the value of derivative contracts to the managers of FIs? Which type of derivative contracts had the highest volume among all U.S. banks as of September 2003?

2. What has been the regulatory result of some of the misuses by FIs of derivative products?

3. What are some of the major differences between futures and forward contracts? How do these contracts differ from spot contracts?

4. What is a naive hedge? How does a naive hedge protect an FI from risk?

5. An FI holds a 15-year, par value, $10,000,000 bond that is priced at 104 with a yield to maturity of 7 percent. The bond has a duration of eight years, and the FI plans to sell it after two months. The FI's market analyst predicts that interest rates will be 8 percent at the time of the desired sale. Because most other analysts are predicting no change in rates, two-month forward contracts for 15-year bonds are available at 104. The FI would like to hedge against the expected change in interest rates with an appropriate position in a forward contract. What will this position be? Show that if rates rise 1 percent as forecast, the hedge will protect the FI from loss.

6. Contrast the position of being short with that of being long in futures contracts.

7. Suppose an FI purchases a Treasury bond futures contract at 95.
   a. What is the FI's obligation at the time the futures contract is purchased?
   b. If an FI purchases this contract, in what kind of hedge is it engaged?
   c. Assume that the Treasury bond futures price falls to 94. What is the loss or gain?
   d. Assume that the Treasury bond futures price rises to 97. Mark to market the position.

8. Long Bank has assets that consist mostly of 30-year mortgages and liabilities that are short-term time and demand deposits. Will an interest rate futures contract the bank buys add to or subtract from the bank's risk?

9. In each of the following cases, indicate whether it would be appropriate for an FI to buy or sell a forward contract to hedge the appropriate risk.
   a. A commercial bank plans to issue CDs in three months.
   b. An insurance company plans to buy bonds in two months.
   c. A thrift is going to sell Treasury securities next month.
   d. A U.S. bank lends to a French company: the loan is payable in euros.
   e. A finance company has assets with a duration of six years and liabilities with a duration of 13 years.

10. The duration of a 20-year, 8 percent coupon Treasury bond selling at par is 10.292 years. The bond's interest is paid semiannually, and the bond qualifies for delivery against the Treasury bond futures contract.
   a. What is the modified duration of this bond?
   b. What is the impact on the Treasury bond price if market interest rates increase 50 basis points?
   c. If you sold a Treasury bond futures contract at 95 and interest rates rose 50 basis points, what would be the change in the value of your futures position?

d. If you purchased the bond at par and sold the futures contract, what would be the net value of your hedge after the increase in interest rates?

11. What are the differences between a microhedge and a macrohedge for an FI? Why is it generally more efficient for FIs to employ a macrohedge than a series of microhedges?

12. What are the reasons why an FI may choose to hedge selectively its portfolio?

13. Hedge Row Bank has the following balance sheet (in millions):

Assets	$150	Liabilities	$135
		Equity	$ 15
Total	$150	Total	$150

The duration of the assets is six years, and the duration of the liabilities is four years. The bank is expecting interest rates to fall from 10 percent to 9 percent over the next year.

a. What is the duration gap for Hedge Row Bank?

b. What is the expected change in net worth for Hedge Row Bank if the forecast is accurate?

c. What will be the effect on net worth if interest rates increase 100 basis points?

d. If the existing interest rate on the liabilities is 6 percent, what will be the effect on net worth of a 1 percent increase in interest rates?

14. For a given change in interest rates, why is the sensitivity of the price of a Treasury bond futures contract greater than the sensitivity of the price of a Treasury bill futures contract?

15. What is the meaning of the Treasury bond futures price quote 101–13?

16. What is meant by fully hedging the balance sheet of an FI?

17. Tree Row Bank has assets of $150 million, liabilities of $135 million, and equity of $15 million. The asset duration is six years, and the duration of the liabilities is four years. Market interest rates are 10 percent. Tree Row Bank wishes to hedge the balance sheet with Treasury bond futures contracts, which currently have a price quote of $95 per $100 face value for the benchmark 20-year, 8 percent coupon bond underlying the contract.

a. Should the bank go short or long on the futures contracts to establish the correct macrohedge?

b. How many contracts are necessary to fully hedge the bank?

c. Verify that the change in the futures position will offset the change in the cash balance sheet position for a change in market interest rates of plus 100 basis points and minus 50 basis points.

d. If the bank had hedged with Treasury bill futures contracts that had a market value of $98 per $100 of face value, how many futures contracts would have been necessary to fully hedge the balance sheet?

e. What additional issues should be considered by the bank in choosing between T-bond and T-bill futures contracts?

18. Reconsider Tree Row Bank in problem 17 but assume that the cost rate on the liabilities is 6 percent.

    a. How many contracts are necessary to fully hedge the bank?

    b. Verify that the change in the futures position will offset the change in the cash balance sheet position for a change in market interest rates of plus 100 basis points and minus 50 basis points.

    c. If the bank had hedged with Treasury bill futures contracts that had a market value of $98 per $100 of face value, how many futures contracts would have been necessary to fully hedge the balance sheet?

19. What is basis risk? What are the sources of basis risk?

20. How would your answers for part (b) in problem 17 change if the relationship of the price sensitivity of futures contracts to the price sensitivity of underlying bonds were $br = 0.92$?

21. A mutual fund plans to purchase $500,000 of 30-year Treasury bonds in four months. These bonds have a duration of 12 years and are priced at 96–08 (32nds). The mutual fund is concerned about interest rates changing over the next four months and is considering a hedge with T-bond futures contracts that mature in six months. The T-bond futures contracts are selling for 98–24 (32nds) and have a duration of 8.5 years.

    a. If interest rate changes in the spot market exactly match those in the futures market, what type of futures position should the mutual fund create?

    b. How many contracts should be used?

    c. If the implied rate on the deliverable bond in the futures market moves 12 percent more than the change in the discounted spot rate, how many futures contracts should be used to hedge the portfolio?

    d. What causes futures contracts to have a different price sensitivity than assets in the spot markets?

22. Consider the following balance sheet (in millions) for an FI:

Assets		Liabilities	
Duration = 10 years	$950	Duration = 2 years	$860
		Equity	90

    a. What is the FI's duration gap?

    b. What is the FI's interest rate risk exposure?

    c. How can the FI use futures and forward contracts to put on a macrohedge?

    d. What is the impact on the FI's equity value if the relative change in interest rates is an increase of 1 percent? That is $\Delta R/(1 + R) = 0.01$.

    e. Suppose that the FI in part (c) macrohedges using Treasury bond futures that are currently priced at 96. What is the impact on the FI's futures position if the relative change in all interest rates is an increase of 1 percent? That is, $\Delta R/(1 + R) = 0.01$. Assume that the deliverable Treasury bond has a duration of nine years.

f. If the FI wants a perfect macrohedge, how many Treasury bond futures contracts does it need?

23. Refer again to problem 22. How does consideration of basis risk change your answers to problem 22?

a. Compute the number of futures contracts required to construct a perfect macrohedge if

$$[\Delta R_f/(1 + R_f)/\Delta R/(1 + R)] = br = 0.90$$

b. Explain what is meant by $br = 0.90$.

c. If $br = 0.90$, what information does this provide on the number of futures contracts needed to construct a perfect macrohedge?

24. An FI is planning to hedge its $100 million bond instruments with a cross hedge using Eurodollar interest rate futures. How would the FI estimate

$$br = [\Delta R_f/(1 + R_f)/\Delta R/(1 + R)]$$

to determine the exact number of Eurodollar futures contracts to hedge?

25. Village Bank has $240 million worth of assets with a duration of 14 years and liabilities worth $210 million with a duration of 4 years. In the interest of hedging interest rate risk, Village Bank is contemplating a macrohedge with interest rate futures contracts now selling for 102–21 (32nds). If the spot and futures interest rates move together, how many futures contracts must Village Bank sell to fully hedge the balance sheet?

26. Assume that an FI has assets of $250 million and liabilities of $200 million. The duration of the assets is six years, and the duration of the liabilities is three years. The price of the futures contract is $115,000, and its duration is 5.5 years.

a. What number of futures contracts is needed to construct a perfect hedge if $br = 1.10$?

b. If $\Delta R_f/(1 + R_f) = 0.0990$, what is the expected $\Delta R/(1 + R)$?

27. Suppose an FI purchases a $1 million 91-day Eurodollar futures contract trading at 98.50.

a. If the contract is reversed two days later by purchasing the contract at 98.60, what is the net profit?

b. What is the loss or gain if the price at reversal is 98.40?

28. What factors may make the use of swaps or forward contracts preferable to the use of futures contracts for the purpose of hedging long-term foreign exchange positions?

29. An FI has an asset investment in euros. The FI expects the exchange rate of $/€ to increase by the maturity of the asset.

a. Is the dollar appreciating or depreciating against the euro?

b. To fully hedge the investment, should the FI buy or sell euro futures contracts?

c. If there is perfect correlation between changes in the spot and futures contracts, how should the FI determine the number of contracts necessary to hedge the investment fully?

30. What is meant by tailing the hedge? What factors allow an FI manager to tail the hedge effectively?

31. What does the hedge ratio measure? Under what conditions is this ratio valuable in determining the number of futures contracts necessary to hedge fully an investment in another currency? How is the hedge ratio related to basis risk?

32. What technique is commonly used to estimate the hedge ratio? What statistical measure is an indicator of the confidence that should be placed in the estimated hedge ratio? What is the interpretation if the estimated hedge ratio is greater than one? Less than one?

33. An FI has assets denominated in British pounds sterling of $125 million and sterling liabilities of $100 million.

    a. What is the FI's net exposure?

    b. Is the FI exposed to a dollar appreciation or depreciation?

    c. How can the FI use futures or forward contracts to hedge its FX rate risk?

    d. What is the number of futures contracts that must be utilized to fully hedge the FI's currency risk exposure?

    e. If the British pound falls from $1.60/£ to $1.50/£, what will be the impact on the FI's cash position?

    f. If the British pound futures price falls from $1.55/£ to $1.45/£, what will be the impact on the FI's futures position?

    g. Using the information in parts (e) and (f), what can you conclude about basis risk?

34. Refer to problem 33, part (f).

    a. If the British pound futures price fell from $1.55/£ to $1.43/£, what would be the impact on the FI's futures position?

    b. Does your answer to part (a) differ from your answer to part (f) in problem 33? Why or why not?

    c. How would you fully hedge the FX risk exposure in problem 33 using the new futures price change?

35. An FI is planning to hedge its one-year $100 million Swiss francs (Sf)–denominated loan against exchange rate risk. The current spot rate is $0.60/Sf. A 1-year Sf futures contract is currently trading at $0.58/Sf. Sf futures are sold in standardized units of Sf125,000.

    a. Should the FI be worried about the Sf appreciating or depreciating?

    b. Should it buy or sell futures to hedge against exchange rate exposure?

    c. How many futures contracts should it buy or sell if a regression of past changes in spot prices on changes in future prices generates an estimated slope of 1.4?

    d. Show exactly how the FI is hedged if it repatriates its principal of Sf100 million at year end, the spot price of Sf at year end is $0.55/Sf, and the forward price is $0.5443/Sf.

36. An FI has made a loan commitment of Sf10 million that is likely to be taken down in six months. The current spot rate is $0.60/Sf.

    a. Is the FI exposed to the dollar's depreciating or appreciating? Why?

    b. If the spot rate six months from today is $0.64/Sf, what amount of dollars is needed if the loan is taken down and the FI is unhedged?

    c. If it decides to hedge using Sf futures, should the FI buy or sell Sf futures?

    d. A six-month Sf futures contract is available for $0.61/Sf. What net amount would be needed to fund the loan at the end of six months if the FI had hedged using the Sf10 million futures contract? Assume that futures prices are equal to spot prices at the time of payment (i.e., at maturity).

37. A U.S. FI has assets denominated in Swiss francs (Sf) of 75 million and liabilities of 125 million. The spot rate is $0.6667/Sf, and one-year futures are available for $0.6579/Sf.

    a. What is the FI's net exposure?

    b. Is the FI exposed to dollar appreciation or depreciation?

    c. If the Sf spot rate changes from $0.6667/Sf to $0.6897/Sf, how will this impact the FI's currency exposure? Assume no hedging.

    d. What is the number of futures contracts necessary to fully hedge the currency risk exposure of the FI? The contract size is Sf125,000 per contract.

    e. If the Sf futures price falls from $0.6579/Sf to $0.6349/Sf, what will be the impact on the FI's futures position?

38. What is a credit forward? How is it structured?

39. What is the gain on the purchase of a $20,000,000 credit forward contract with a modified duration of seven years if the credit spread between a benchmark Treasury bond and a borrowing firm's debt decreases 50 basis points?

40. How is selling a credit forward similar to buying a put option?

41. A property-casualty (PC) insurance company purchased catastrophe futures contracts to hedge against loss during the hurricane season. At the time of purchase, the market expected a loss ratio of 0.75. After processing claims from a severe hurricane, the PC actually incurred a loss ratio of 1.35. What amount of profit did the PC make on each $25,000 futures contract?

42. What is the primary goal of regulators in regard to the use of futures by FIs? What guidelines have regulators given to banks for trading in futures and forwards?

Web Question

43. Go to the Office of the Comptroller of the Currency Web site at **www.occ.treas.gov.** Find the most recent levels of futures, forwards, options, swaps, and credit derivatives using the following steps. Click on "Publications." From there click on "Qrtrly. Derivative Fact Sheet." Click on the most recent date. This will bring the files up on your computer that contain the relevant data. The tables containing the data are at the bottom of this document. How have these values increased since September 2003 (as reported in Table 24–1)?

Pertinent Web Sites

American Banker	www.americanbanker.com
Board of Governors of the Federal Reserve	www.federalreserve.gov
Chicago Board of Trade	www.cbot.com
Commodity Futures Trading Commission	www.cftc.gov
Federal Deposit Insurance Corporation	www.fdic.gov
Financial Accounting Standards Board	www.fasb.org
Office of the Comptroller of the Currency	www.occ.treas.gov
Securities and Exchange Commission	www.sec.gov

Chapter Notation

View Chapter Notation at the Web site to the textbook (**www.mhhe.com/ saunders5e**).

Appendix 24A

Microhedging with Futures

View Appendix 24A at the Web site for this textbook (**www.mhhe.com/saunders5e**).

Chapter **Twenty-Five**

Options, Caps, Floors, and Collars

INTRODUCTION

Just as there is a wide variety of forward and futures contracts available for an FI to use in hedging, there is an even wider array of option products, including exchange-traded options, over-the-counter options, options embedded in securities, and caps, collars, and floors. As we saw with futures contracts (in Chapter 24), the use of options can protect an FI against a loss of net worth due to unexpected changes in interest rates, credit risk, foreign exchange risk, and so forth. Not only have the range of option products increased in recent years, but the use of options has increased as well. However, options can also lead to huge losses for FIs (see the Ethical Dilemmas box).

This chapter starts with a review of the four basic options strategies: buying a call, writing a call, buying a put, and writing a put.[1] We then look at economic and regulatory reasons FIs choose to buy versus write (sell) options. The chapter then concentrates on the use of fixed-income or interest rate options to hedge interest rate risk. We also discuss the role of options in hedging foreign exchange and credit risks as well as catastrophe risk. The chapter concludes with an examination of caps, floors, and collars. As with futures and forwards, discussed in Chapter 24, options, caps, floors, and collars are held by FIs not only to hedge their own risk, but also to serve as counterparties (for a fee) for other (financial and nonfinancial) firms wanting to hedge risk on their own balance sheets.

BASIC FEATURES OF OPTIONS

call option
Gives a purchaser the right (but not the obligation) to buy the underlying security from the writer of the option at a prespecified exercise price on a prespecified date.

In describing the features of the four basic option strategies FIs might employ to hedge interest rate risk, we discuss their return payoffs in terms of interest rate movements. Specifically, we consider bond options whose payoff values are inversely linked to interest rate movements in a manner similar to bond prices and interest rates in general (see Chapter 8).

Buying a Call Option on a Bond

The first strategy of buying (or taking a long position in) a call option on a bond is shown in Figure 25–1. A **call option** gives the purchaser the right (but not the obligation) to buy the underlying security—a bond—at a prespecified *exercise* or *strike*

---

[1] There are two basic option contracts: puts and calls. However, an FI could potentially be a buyer or seller (writer) of each.

Ethical **Dilemmas**

price (X). In return, the buyer of the call option must pay the writer or seller an upfront fee known as a *call premium* (C). This premium is an immediate negative cash flow for the buyer of the call, who potentially stands to make a profit if the underlying bond's price rises above the exercise price by an amount exceeding the premium. If the price of the bond never rises above X, the buyer of the call never exercises the option (i.e., buying the bond at X when its market value is less than X). In this case, the option matures unexercised. The call buyer incurs a cost, C, for the option, and no other cash flows result.

As shown in Figure 25–1, if the price of the bond underlying the option rises to price B, the buyer makes a profit of π, which is the difference between the bond price (B) and the exercise price of the option (X) minus the call premium (C). If the bond price rises to A, the buyer of the call has broken even in that the profit from exercising the call ($A - X$) just equals the premium payment for the call (C).

Notice two important things about bond call options in Figure 25–1:

1. As interest rates fall, bond prices rise and the call option buyer has large profit potential; the more that rates fall, the higher bond prices rise and the larger the profit on the exercise of the option.

FIGURE 25–1
Payoff Function for the Buyer of a Call Option on a Bond

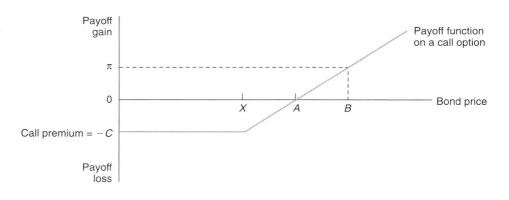

FIGURE 25–2
Payoff Function for the Writer of a Call Option on a Bond

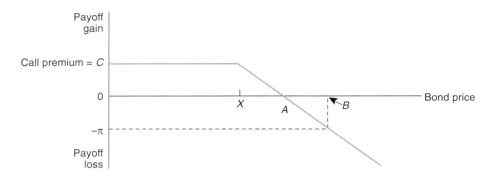

2. As interest rates rise, bond prices fall and the potential for a negative payoff (loss) for the buyer of the call option increases. If rates rise so that bond prices fall below the exercise price X, the call buyer is not obliged to exercise the option. Thus, the losses of the buyer are truncated by the amount of the up-front premium payment (C) made to purchase the call option.

Thus, buying a call option is a strategy to take when interest rates are expected to fall. Notice that unlike interest rate futures, whose prices and payoffs move symmetrically with changes in the level of rates, the payoffs on bond call options move asymmetrically with interest rates (see Chapter 24).

Writing a Call Option on a Bond

The second strategy is writing (or taking a short position in) a call option on a bond. In writing a call option on a bond, the writer or seller receives an up-front fee or premium (C) and must stand ready to sell the underlying bond to the purchaser of the option at the exercise price, X. Note the payoff from writing a call option on a bond in Figure 25–2.

There are two important things to notice about this payoff function:

1. When interest rates rise and bond prices fall, there is an increased potential for the writer of the call to receive a positive payoff or profit. The call buyer is less likely to exercise the option, which would force the option writer to sell the underlying bond at the exercise price. However, this profit has a maximum equal to the call premium (C) charged up front to the buyer of the option.

2. When interest rates fall and bond prices rise, the writer has an increased potential to take a loss. The call buyer will exercise the option, forcing the option writer to sell the underlying bonds. Since bond prices are theoretically unbounded in the upward direction, although they must return to par at maturity, these losses could be very large.

Thus, writing a call option is a strategy to take when interest rates are expected to rise. Caution is warranted, however, because profits are limited but losses are potentially large if rates fall. In Figure 25–2, a fall in interest rates and a rise in bond prices to B results in the writer of the option losing π.

put option
Gives a purchaser the right (but not the obligation) to sell the underlying security to the writer of the option at a prespecified exercise price on a prespecified date.

Buying a Put Option on a Bond

The third strategy is buying (or taking a long position in) a put option on a bond. The buyer of a **put option** on a bond has the right (but not the obligation) to sell the underlying bond to the writer of the option at the agreed exercise price (X). In return for this option, the buyer of the put option pays a premium to the writer (P).

FIGURE 25–3
Payoff Function for
the Buyer of a Put
Option on a Bond

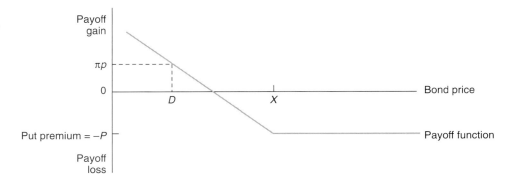

We show the potential payoffs to the buyer of the put option in Figure 25–3. Note that

1. When interest rates rise and bond prices fall, the buyer of the put has an increased probability of making a profit from exercising the option. Thus, if bond prices fall to D, the buyer of the put option can purchase bonds in the bond market at that price and put them (sell them) back to the writer of the put at the higher exercise price (X). As a result, the buyer makes a profit, after deducting the cost of the put premium (P), of πp in Figure 25–3.

2. When interest rates fall and bond prices rise, the probability that the buyer of a put will lose increases. If rates fall so that bond prices rise above the exercise price X, the put buyer does not have to exercise the option. Thus, the maximum loss is limited to the size of the up-front put premium (P).

Thus, buying a put option is a strategy to take when interest rates are expected to rise.

Writing a Put Option on a Bond

The fourth strategy is writing (or taking a short position in) a put option on a bond. In writing a put option on a bond, the writer or seller receives a fee or premium (P) in return for standing ready to buy bonds at the exercise price (X) if the buyer of the put chooses to exercise the option to sell. See the payoff function for writing a put option on a bond in Figure 25–4. Note that

1. If interest rates fall and bond prices rise, the writer has an enhanced probability of making a profit. The put buyer is less likely to exercise the option, which would force the option writer to buy the underlying bond. However, the writer's maximum profit is constrained to be equal to the put premium (P).

2. If interest rates rise and bond prices fall, the writer of the put is exposed to potentially large losses (e.g., $-\pi p$, if bond prices fall to D in Figure 25–4).

Thus, writing a put option is a strategy to take when interest rates are expected to fall. However, profits are limited and losses are potentially unlimited.

**Concept
Questions**

1. How do interest rate increases affect the payoff from buying a call option on a bond? How do they affect the payoff from writing a call option on a bond?
2. How do interest rate increases affect the payoff from buying a put option on a bond? How do they affect the payoff from writing a put option on a bond?

FIGURE 25–4
Payoff Function for the Writer of a Put Option on a Bond

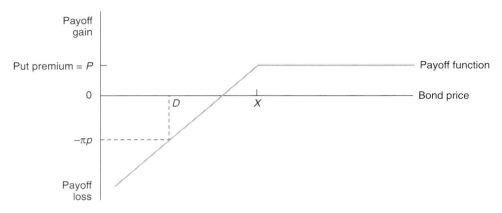

FIGURE 25–5
Writing a Call Option to Hedge the Interest Rate Risk on a Bond

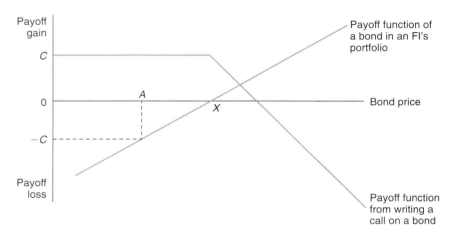

WRITING VERSUS BUYING OPTIONS

Many small FIs are restricted to buying rather than writing options. There are two reasons for this, one economic and the other regulatory. However, as we note later, large FIs such as money center banks often both write and buy options including caps, floors, and collars, which are complex forms of interest rate options.

Economic Reasons for Not Writing Options

In writing an option, the upside profit potential is truncated, but the downside losses are not. While such risks may be offset by writing a large number of options at different exercise prices and/or hedging an underlying portfolio of bonds, the downside risk exposure of the writer may still be significant. To see this, look at Figure 25–5, where an FI is long in a bond in its portfolio and seeks to hedge the interest rate risk on that bond by writing a bond call option.

Note that writing the call may hedge the FI when rates fall and bond prices rise; that is, the increase in the value of the bond is offset by losses on the written call. When the reverse occurs and interest rates rise, the FI's profits from writing the

FIGURE 25–6
Buying a Put Option to Hedge the Interest Rate Risk on a Bond

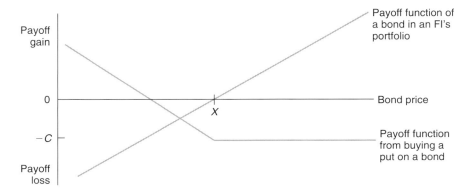

FIGURE 25–7
Net Payoff of Buying a Bond Put and Investing in a Bond

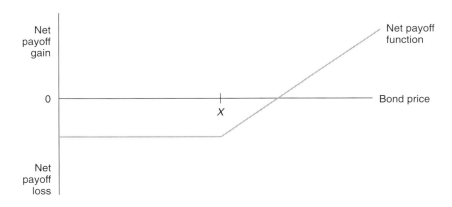

call may be insufficient to offset the loss on its bonds. This occurs because the upside profit (per call written) is truncated and is equal to the premium income (C). If the decrease in the bond value is larger than the premium income (to the left of point A in Figure 25–5), the FI is unable to offset the associated capital value loss on the bond with profits from writing options.

By contrast, hedging the FI's risk by buying a put option on a bond offers the manager a much more attractive alternative. Figure 25–6 shows the gross payoff of the bond and the payoff from buying a put option on a bond. In this case, any losses on the bond (as rates rise and bond values fall) are offset with profits from the put option that was bought (points to the left of point X in Figure 25–6). If rates fall, the bond value increases, yet the accompanying losses on the purchased put option positions are limited to the option premiums paid (points to the right of point X). Figure 25–7 shows the net payoff or the difference between the bond and option payoff.

Note that

1. Buying a put option truncates the downside losses on the bond following interest rate rises to some maximum amount and scales down the upside profits by the cost of bond price risk insurance—the put premium—leaving some positive upside profit potential.

FIGURE 25–8
**Buying a Futures
Contract to Hedge
the Interest Rate
Risk on a Bond**

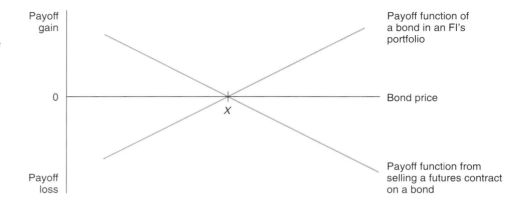

2. The combination of being long in the bond and buying a put option on a bond mimics the payoff function of buying a call option (compare Figures 25–1 and 25–7).

Regulatory Reasons

naked options
Option positions that do not identifiably hedge an underlying asset or liability.

There are also regulatory reasons why FIs buy options rather than write options. Regulators view writing options, especially **naked options** that do not identifiably hedge an underlying asset or liability position, to be risky because of the large loss potential. Indeed, bank regulators prohibit banks from writing puts or calls in certain areas of risk management.

Futures versus Options Hedging

To understand the differences between using futures versus options contracts to hedge interest rate risk, compare the payoff gains illustrated in Figure 25–8 (for futures contracts) with those in Figure 25–6 (for buying put option contracts). A hedge with futures contracts reduces volatility in payoff gains on both the upside and downside of interest rate movements. That is, if the FI in Figure 25–8 loses value on the bond resulting from an interest rate increase (to the left of point X), a gain on the futures contract offsets the loss. If the FI gains value on the bond due to an interest rate decrease (to the right of point X), however, a loss on the futures contract offsets the gain.

In comparison, the hedge with the put option contract completely offsets losses but only partly offsets gains. That is, in Figure 25–6, if the FI loses value on the bond due to an interest rate increase (to the left of point X), a gain on the put option contract offsets the loss. However, if the FI gains value on the bond due to an interest rate decrease (to the right of point X), the gain is offset only to the extent that the FI loses the put option premium (because it never exercises the option). Thus, the put option hedge protects the FI against value losses when interest rates move against the on-balance-sheet securities but, unlike futures hedging, does not reduce value when interest rates move in favor of on-balance-sheet securities.

**Concept
Questions**

1. What are some of the economic reasons for an FI not to write options?
2. What are some regulatory reasons why an FI might choose to buy options rather than write options?

THE MECHANICS OF HEDGING A BOND OR BOND PORTFOLIO[2]

You have seen how buying a put option on a bond can potentially hedge the interest rate risk exposure of an FI that holds bonds as part of its investment portfolio. In this section, we use a simple example to demonstrate the mechanics of buying a put option as a hedging device and how an FI manager can calculate the fair premium value for a put option on a bond.

In calculating the fair value of an option, two alternative models can be used: the binomial model and the Black-Scholes model. The Black-Scholes model produces a closed-form solution to the valuation of call and put options. Appendix 25A to this chapter (located at the book's Web site, www.mhhe.com/saunders5e) shows how to calculate the value of an option using the Black-Scholes model. Although it works well for stocks, the Black-Scholes model has two major problems when employed to value bond options. First, it assumes that short-term interest rates are constant, which they generally are not. Second, it assumes a constant variance of returns on the underlying asset.[3] The application of the Black-Scholes formula to bonds is problematic because of the way bond prices behave between issuance and maturity.[4] This is shown in Figure 25–9, where a bond is issued at par, that is, the price of the bond is 100 percent times its face value at time of issue. If interest rates fall, its price may rise above 100 percent, and if interest rates rise, its price may fall below 100 percent. However, as the bond approaches maturity, all price paths must lead to 100 percent of the face value of the bond or principal paid by the issuer on maturity. Because of this **pull-to-par,** the variance of bond prices is nonconstant over time, rising at first and then falling as the bond approaches maturity. We evaluate the mechanics of hedging using bond put options in a simple binomial framework next.

pull-to-par
The tendency of the variance of a bond's price or return to decrease as maturity approaches.

---

[2] The material in this section is more technical in nature. It may be included or dropped from the chapter reading depending on the rigor of the course without harming the continuity of the chapter.

[3] The Black-Scholes formulas for a put and a call are

$$P = Xe^{-rT}N[-D + \sigma\sqrt{T}] - SN[-D]$$

$$C = SN[D] - Xe^{-rT}N[D - \sigma\sqrt{T}]$$

where

S = Price of the underlying asset

X = Exercise price

T = Time to option expiration

r = Instantaneous riskless interest rate

$$D = \frac{\ln(S/X) + (r + \sigma^2/2)T}{\sigma\sqrt{T}}$$

$\ln[\ .\ ]$ = Natural logarithm

σ = Volatility of the underlying asset

$N[\ .\ ]$ = Cumulative normal distribution function, that is, the probability of observing a value less than the value in brackets when drawing randomly from a standardized normal distribution

[4] There are models that modify Black-Scholes to allow for nonconstant variance. These include Merton, who allows variance to be time dependent; Ball and Tourous, who allow bond prices to change as a stochastic process with a variance that first increases and then decreases (the Brownian bridge process); and the Schaefer-Schwartz model, which assumes that the standard deviation of returns is proportional to a bond's duration. See R. C. Merton, "On the Pricing of Corporate Debt: The Risk Structure of Interest Rates," *Journal of Finance* 29 (1974), pp. 449–70; C. Ball and W. N. Tourous, "Bond Price Dynamics and Options," *Journal of Financial and Quantitative Analysis* 18 (1983), pp. 517–31; and S. Schaefer and E. S. Schwartz, "Time Dependent Variance and the Pricing of Bond Options," *Journal of Finance* 42 (1987), pp. 1113–28.

FIGURE 25–9
The Variance of a Bond's Price

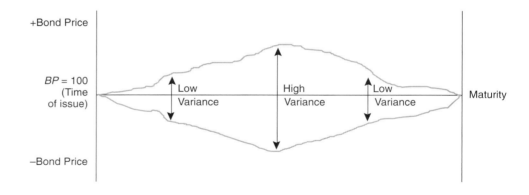

Hedging with Bond Options Using the Binomial Model

Suppose that an FI manager has purchased a $100 zero-coupon bond with exactly two years to maturity. A zero-coupon bond, if held to maturity, pays its face value of $100 on maturity in two years. Assume that the FI manager pays $80.45 per $100 of face value for this zero-coupon bond. This means that if held to maturity, the FI's annual yield to maturity (R_2) from this investment would be

$$BP_2 = \frac{100}{(1 + R_2)^2}$$

$$80.45 = \frac{100}{(1 + R_2)^2}$$

$$(1 + R_2)^2 = \frac{100}{80.45}$$

$$1 + R_2 = \sqrt{\frac{100}{80.45}}$$

$$R_2 = \sqrt{\frac{100}{80.45}} - 1 = .115 = 11.5\%$$

Suppose also that, at the end of the first year, interest rates rise unexpectedly. As a result, depositors, seeking higher returns on their funds, withdraw deposits. To meet these unexpected deposit withdrawals, the FI manager is forced to liquidate (sell) the two-year bond before maturity, at the end of year one. As we discuss in Chapter 17, Treasury securities are important liquidity sources for an FI. Because of the unexpected rise in interest rates at the end of year one, the FI manager must sell the bond at a low price.

Assume when the bond is purchased, the current yield on one-year discount bonds (R_1) is $R_1 = 10$ percent. Also, assume that at the end of year one, the one-year interest rate (r_1) is forecasted to rise to either 13.82 percent or 12.18 percent. If one-year interest rates rise from $R_1 = 10$ percent when the bond is purchased to $r_1 = 13.82$ percent at the end of year one, the FI manager will be able to sell the zero-coupon bond with one year remaining to maturity for a bond price, BP, of

$$BP_1 = \frac{100}{(1 + r_1)} = \frac{100}{(1.1382)} = \$87.86$$

If, on the other hand, one-year interest rates rise to 12.18 percent, the manager can sell the bond with one year remaining to maturity for

$$BP_1 = \frac{100}{(1 + r_1)} = \frac{100}{(1.1218)} = \$89.14$$

In these equations, r_1 stands for the two possible one-year rates that might arise one year into the future.[5] That is,

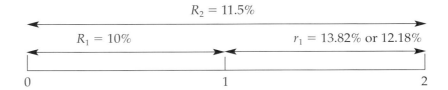

Assume the manager believes that one-year rates (r_1) one year from today will be 13.82 percent or 12.18 percent with an equal probability. This means that the expected one-year rate one year from today would be

$$[E(r_1)] = .5(.1382) + .5(.1218) = .13 = 13\%$$

Thus, the expected price if the bond has to be sold at the end of the first year is[6]

$$E(P_1) = \frac{100}{(1.13)} = \$88.5$$

Assume that the FI manager wants to ensure that the bond sale produces at least $88.5 per $100; otherwise the FI has to find alternative and very costly sources of liquidity (for example, the FI might have to borrow from the central bank's discount window and incur the direct and indirect penalty costs involved, see Chapter 19). One way for the FI to ensure that it receives at least $88.5 on selling the bond at the end of the year is to buy a put option on the bond at time 0 with an exercise price of $88.5 at time (year) 1. If the bond is trading below $88.5 at the end of the year—say, at $87.86—the FI can exercise its option and put the bond back to the writer of the option, who will have to pay the FI $88.5. If, however, the bond is trading above $88.5—say, at $89.14—the FI does not have to exercise its option and instead can sell the bond in the open market for $89.14.

The FI manager will want to recalculate the fair premium to pay for buying this put option or bond insurance at time 0. Figure 25–10 shows the possible paths (i.e., the binomial tree or lattice) of the zero-coupon bond's price from purchase to

---

[5] If one-year bond rates next year equaled the one-year bond rate this year, $R_1 = r_1 = 10$ percent, then the bond could be sold for $BP_1 = \$90.91$.

[6] The interest rates assumed in this example are consistent with arbitrage-free pricing under current term structure conditions. [See T. S. Y. Ho and S. B. Lee, "Term Structure Movements and Pricing Interest Rate Contingent Claims," *Journal of Finance* 61 (1986), pp. 1001–29.] That is, the expectations theory of interest rates implies that the following relationship must hold:

$$(1 + R_2)^2 = (1 + R_1) \times (1 + E(r_1))$$

As you can easily see, when the interest rates from our example are inserted, $R_1 = 10\%$, $R_2 = 11.5\%$, $E(r_1) = 13\%$, this equation holds. Also, the two interest rates (prices) imply that the current volatility of one-year interest rates is 6.3 percent. That is, from the binomial model, $\sigma = 1/2ln[r_u/r_d]$, such that $\sigma = 1/2ln[13.82/12.18] = .063$ or 6.3%.

FIGURE 25–10
**Binomial Model of
Bond Prices: Two-
Year Zero-Coupon
Bond**

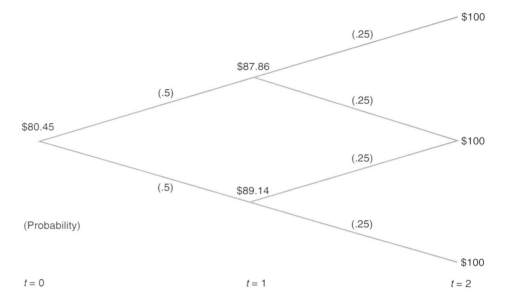

FIGURE 25–11
**The Value of a Put
Option on the Two-
Year Zero-Coupon
Bond**

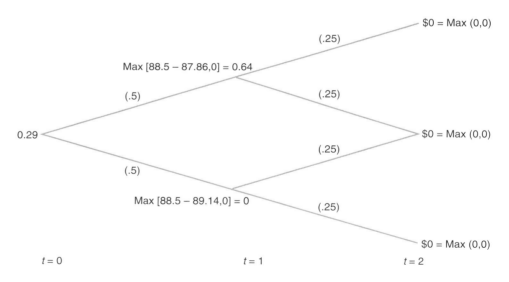

maturity over the two-year period.[7] The FI manager purchased the bond at $80.45
with two years to maturity. Given expectations of rising rates, there is a 50 percent
probability that the bond with one year left to maturity will trade at $87.86 and a
50 percent probability that it will trade at $89.14. Note that between $t = 1$, or one
year left to maturity, and maturity ($t = 2$), there must be a pull to par on the bond;
that is, all paths must lead to a price of $100 on maturity.

The value of the option is shown in Figure 25–11. The option in Figure 25–11 can
be exercised only at the end of year 1 ($t = 1$). If the zero-coupon bond with one
year left to maturity trades at $87.86, the option is worth $88.5 − $87.86 in time 1
dollars, or $0.64. If the bond trades at $89.14, the option has no value since the

[7] This example is based on R. Litterman and T. Iben, "Corporate Bond Valuation and the Term Structure
of Credit Spreads," *Journal of Portfolio Management,* 1989, pp. 52–64.

bond could be sold at a higher value than the exercise price of $88.5 on the open market. This suggests that in time 1 dollars, the option is worth

$$.5(0.64) + .5(0) = \$0.32$$

However, the FI is evaluating the option and paying the put premium at time $t = 0$, that is, one year before the date when the option might be exercised. Thus, the fair value of the put premium (P) the FI manager should be willing to pay is the discounted present value of the expected payoff from buying the option. Since one-year interest rates (R_1) are currently 10 percent, this implies

$$P = \frac{\$0.32}{1 + R_1} = \frac{\$0.32}{(1.1)} = \$0.29$$

or a premium, P, of approximately 29 cents per $100 bond option purchased.

Further, as you can easily see, the option becomes increasingly valuable as the variability of interest rates increases. Conceptually, the branches of the binomial tree diagram become more widely dispersed as variability increases. For example, suppose one-year interest rates on the upper branch were expected to be 14.82 percent instead of 13.82 percent. Then, the price on a one-year, zero-coupon bond associated with a one-year yield of 14.82 percent is $87.09 and the option is worth $88.5 − $87.09 in time 1 dollars, or $1.41. Thus, the value of the put option (P) with the same exercise price of $88.5 is

$$P = \frac{.5(1.41) + .5(0)}{1.1}$$

$$= 64 \text{ cents}$$

Notice the familiar result from option pricing theory holds

$$\frac{\delta P}{\delta \sigma} > 0$$

That is, the value of the put option increases with an increase in underlying variance of asset returns.

Concept Questions	1. What are two common models used to calculate the fair value of a bond option? Which is preferable, and why?
	2. In the example above, calculate the value of the option if the exercise price (X) = $88. ($P = \$0.064$)

ACTUAL BOND OPTIONS

www.cboe.com

open interest
The outstanding stock of put or call contracts.

futures option
An option contract that, when exercised, results in the delivery of a futures contract as the underlying asset.

We have presented a simple example of how FIs may use bond options to hedge exposure to liability withdrawal and forced liquidation of assets in a world of interest rate variability. In actuality, FIs have a wide variety of over-the-counter (OTC) and exchange-traded options available. Interest rate options are listed on the Chicago Board Options Exchange (CBOE). However, these contracts are rarely traded. For example, on March 18, 2004, **open interest** (the outstanding stock of put or call contracts) in short-term interest rate options was 217 contracts. In actual practice, most pure bond options trade over-the-counter. This is not because interest rate or bond options are not used, although the open interest is relatively small, but because the preferred method of hedging is an option on an interest rate futures contract. See these **futures options** (i.e., an option contract that, when exercised, results in the delivery of a futures contract as the underlying asset) on bonds in Figure 25–12 for trading on Thursday, March 18, 2004. Bond or interest rate

FIGURE 25–12

Futures Options on Interest Rates, March 18, 2004

Interest Rate

STRIKE	CALLS-SETTLE			PUTS-SETTLE		

T-Bonds (CBT)
$100,000; points and 64ths of 100%

Price	Apr	May	Jun	Apr	May	Jun
115	0-54	1-46	2-13	0-34	1-26	1-57
116	0-24	1-14	1-45	1-04	1-58	2-25
117	0-09	0-53	1-18	1-53	2-33	2-62
118	0-03	0-35	0-61	2-47	3-14	3-40
119	0-01	0-22	0-44	...	...	...
120	0-01	0-13	0-31	...	...	5-10

Est vol 43,594;
Wd vol 42,376 calls 21,923 puts
Op int Wed 357,398 calls 413,632 puts

T-Notes (CBT)
$100,000; points and 64ths of 100%

Price	Apr	May	Jun	Apr	May	Jun
115	1-00	1-34	1-54	0-13	0-47	1-03
116	0-24	0-61	1-17	0-37	1-09	1-30
117	0-06	0-34	0-53	1-19	1-47	2-02
118	0-01	0-17	0-32	2-14	...	2-45
119	0-01	0-08	0-18	...	...	3-30
120	...	0-04	0-10	...	...	...

Est vol 158,759 Wd 158,543 calls 120,182 puts
Op int Wed 1,166,258 calls 1,222,764 puts

5 Yr Treas Notes (CBT)
$100,000; points and 64ths of 100%

Price	Apr	May	Jun	Apr	May	Jun
11400	0-09	0-31	0-46	0-31	0-54	1-04
11450	0-02	0-20	0-33	...	...	...
11500	0-01	0-11	0-23	...	...	...
11550	0-01	0-06	0-15	...	...	.
11600	...	0-03	0-09	...	...	...
11650	...	0-02	0-06	...	...	...

Est vol 34,573 Wd 10,626 calls 19,813 puts
Op int Wed 172,925 calls 518,654 puts

30 Day Federal Funds (CBT)
$5,000,000; 100 minus daily average

Price	Mar	Apr	May	Mar	Apr	May
988750	.122	.127	.122	.002	.002	.002
989375	.062	.065	.065	.002	.002	.005
990000	.002	.007	.010	.007	.007	.015
990625	.002	.002	...	...	...	...
991250	.002	...	.002	...	...	.132
991875	...	...	...	...	...	...

Est vol 410 Wd 11,175 calls 300 puts
Op int Wed 163,010 calls 161,971 puts

Eurodollar (CME)
$ million; pts. of 100%

Price	Apr	May	Jun	Apr	May	Jun
9850	3.40	...	3.47	0.00	0.05	0.07
9875	1.00	1.10	1.17	0.10	0.20	0.27
9900	0.02	0.07	0.10	...	...	1.70
9925	...	...	0.02	...	...	4.12
9950	...	...	0.00	...	...	...
9975	...	...	0.00	...	...	...

Est vol 276,654;
Wd vol 134,553 calls 520,901 puts
Op int Wed 3,568,321 calls 3,950,481 puts

1 Yr. Mid-Curve Eurodlr (CME)
$1,000,000 contract units; pts. of 100%

Price	Apr	May	Jun	Apr	May	Jun
9725	5.85	...	6.52	0.15	0.47	0.85
9750	3.60	4.15	4.60	0.40	0.95	1.40
9775	1.80	2.40	2.92	1.10	1.70	2.22
9800	0.62	1.17	1.62	2.42	...	3.42
9825	0.17	...	0.72	...	...	...
9850	0.05	...	0.27	...	...	7.05

Est vol 71,710 Wd 28,000 calls 37,835 puts
Op int Wed 730,247 calls 727,189 puts

2 Yr. Mid-Curve Eurodlr (CME)
$1,000,000 contract units; pts. of 100%

Price	Jun	Sep	Dec	Jun	Sep	Dec
9625	6.05	5.72	5.50	1.15	2.95	4.75
9650	4.20	4.20	4.15	1.80	3.90	5.90
9675	2.65	2.90	...	2.75	5.10	...
9700	1.52	...	2.20	...	...	...
9725	...	1.20	...	...	...	...
9750	...	...	0.92	...	...	...

Est vol 2,350 Wd 6,530 calls 3,080 puts
Op int Wed 60,547 calls 20,705 puts

Euribor (LIFFE)
Euro 1,000,000

Price	Apr	May	Jun	Apr	May	Jun
97750	0.32	0.32	0.32	...	...	0.00
97875	0.19	0.20	0.20	...	0.00	0.01
98000	0.08	0.09	0.11	0.01	0.02	0.04
98125	0.02	0.04	0.05	0.07	0.09	0.10
98250	0.00	0.02	0.02	0.18	0.20	0.20
98375	...	0.00	0.01	0.30	0.31	0.31

Vol Th 270,614 calls 46,921 puts
Op int Wed 5,303,386 calls 1,809,827 puts

Euro-BUND (EUREX)
100,000; pts. In 100%

Price	Apr	May	Jun	Apr	May	Jun
11500	1.26	1.52	1.75	0.02	0.28	0.51
11550	0.81	1.16	1.40	0.07	0.42	0.66
11600	0.43	0.85	1.10	0.19	0.61	0.86
11650	0.18	0.59	0.84	0.44	0.85	1.10
11700	0.06	0.38	0.62	0.82	1.14	1.38
11750	0.01	0.24	0.45	1.27	1.50	1.71

Vol Th 48,047 calls 34,758 puts
Op int Wed 505,506 calls 589,281 puts

Currency

Japanese Yen (CME)
12,500,000 yen; cents per 100 yen

Price	Apr	May	Jun	Apr	May	Jun
9300	1.51	1.94	2.24	0.59	1.02	1.32
9350	1.23	1.68	1.97	0.81	1.26	1.55
9400	1.00	1.44	1.72	1.08	1.52	1.80
9450	0.79	...	1.52	1.37	...	2.10
9500	0.61	...	1.34	1.69	...	2.42
9550	0.48	0.90	1.18	2.06	...	2.75

Est vol 1,940 Wd 1,596 calls 1,006 puts
Op int Wed 21,813 calls 17,559 puts

Canadian Dollar (CME)
100,000 Can.$, cents per Can.$

Price	Apr	May	Jun	Apr	May	Jun
7400	...	...	1.84	0.30	...	0.81
7450	0.98	...	1.53	0.45	...	1.00
7500	0.69	1.01	1.25	0.66	0.98	1.22
7550	0.48	0.80	1.03	0.95	1.27	1.50
7600	0.34	...	0.85	1.31	...	1.82
7650	0.24	...	0.69	...	...	2.15

Est vol 188 Wd 127 calls 175 puts
Op int Wed 9,077 calls 4,985 puts

British Pound (CME)
62,500 pounds; cents per pound

Price	Apr	May	Jun	Apr	May	Jun
1800	3.08	4.09	4.63	1.16	2.17	2.72
1810	2.50	...	1.58	...	...	...
1820	2.00	3.00	3.56	2.08	3.08	3.64
1830	1.64	2.55	3.10	2.72	...	4.18
1840	1.28	2.17	2.69	3.36	4.25	4.76
1850	1.00	1.83	2.31	4.08	...	5.38

Est vol 1,559 Wd 377 calls 53 puts
Op int Wed 9,050 calls 3,590 puts

Swiss Franc (CME)
125,000 francs; cents per franc

Price	Apr	May	Jun	Apr	May	Jun
7850	1.57	...	2.29	0.47	...	1.19
7900	1.25	1.69	2.00	0.65	1.09	1.40
7950	0.96	1.42	...	0.86	1.32	...
8000	0.73	1.19	1.50	1.13	1.59	1.90
8050	0.55	...	...	1.45	...	...
8100	0.40	...	1.10	1.80	...	2.49

Est vol 145 Wd 9 calls 7 puts
Op int Wed 1,010 calls 2,094 puts

Euro Fx (CME)
125,000 euros; cents per euro

Price	Apr	May	Jun	Apr	May	Jun
12250	1.92	...	3.10	0.96	...	2.14
12300	1.63	2.31	2.83	1.17	1.85	2.37
12350	1.37	...	...	1.41	...	...
12400	1.14	1.83	2.35	1.68	2.37	2.89
12450	0.94	...	2.13	1.98	...	3.17
12500	0.76	1.42	1.92	2.30	2.96	3.45

Est vol 7,717 Wd 1,551 calls 2,278 puts
Op int Wed 28,166 calls 28,727 puts

futures options are generally preferred to options on the underlying bond because they combine the favorable liquidity, credit risk, homogeneity, and marking-to-market features of futures with the same asymmetric payoff functions as regular puts and calls (see Chapter 24).

Specifically, when the FI hedges by buying put options on bond futures, if interest rates rise and bond prices fall, the exercise of the put causes the FI to deliver a bond futures contract to the writer at an exercise price higher than the cost of the bond future currently trading on the futures exchange. The futures price itself reflects the price of the underlying deliverable bond such as a 20-year, 8 percent coupon T-bond; see Figure 25–12. As a result, a profit on futures options may be made to offset the loss on the market value of bonds held directly in the FI's portfolio. If interest rates fall and bond and futures prices rise, the buyer of the futures option will not exercise the put, and the losses on the futures put option are limited to the put premium. Thus, if on March 18, 2004, the FI had bought one $100,000 June 2004 T-bond futures put option at a strike price of $117 but did not exercise the option, the FI's loss equals the put premium of $2^{62}/_{64}$ per $100, or $2,968.75 per $100,000 contract. Offsetting these losses, however, would be an increase in the market value of the FI's underlying bond portfolio. Unlike futures positions in Chapter 24, an upside profit potential remains when interest rates fall and FIs use put options on futures to hedge interest rate risk. We show this in the next section.

Concept Questions

1. Why are bond or interest rate futures options generally preferred to options on the underlying bond?
2. If an FI hedges by buying put options on futures and interest rates rise (i.e., bond prices fall), what is the outcome?

USING OPTIONS TO HEDGE INTEREST RATE RISK ON THE BALANCE SHEET

Our previous simple example showed how a bond option could hedge the interest rate risk on an underlying bond position in the asset portfolio. Next, we determine the put option position that can hedge the interest rate risk of the overall balance sheet; that is, we analyze macrohedging rather than microhedging.

Chapter 8 showed that an FI's net worth exposure to an interest rate shock could be represented as

$$\Delta E = -(D_A - kD_L) \times A \times \frac{\Delta R}{1 + R}$$

where

$$\Delta E = \text{Change in the FI's net worth}$$

$$(D_A - kD_L) = \text{FI's duration gap}$$

$$A = \text{Size of the FI's assets}$$

$$\frac{\Delta R}{1 + R} = \text{Size of the interest rate shock}$$

$$k = \text{FI's leverage ratio } (L/A)$$

Suppose the FI manager wishes to determine the optimal number of put options to buy to insulate the FI against rising rates. An FI with a positive duration gap (see Figure 25–13) would lose on-balance-sheet net worth when interest rates

FIGURE 25–13
Buying Put Options to Hedge the Interest Rate Risk Exposure of the FI

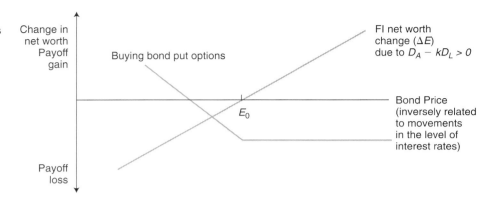

rise. In this case, the FI manager would buy put options.[8] That is, the FI manager wants to adopt a put option position to generate profits that just offset the loss in net worth due to an interest rate shock (where E_0 is the FI's initial equity (net worth) position in Figure 25–13).

Let ΔP be the total change in the value of the put option position in T-bonds. This can be decomposed into

$$\Delta P = (N_p \times \Delta p) \qquad \textbf{(1)}$$

where N_p is the number of \$100,000 put options on T-bond contracts to be purchased (the number for which we are solving) and Δp is the change in the dollar value for each \$100,000 face value T-bond put option contract.

The change in the dollar value of each contract (Δp) can be further decomposed into

$$\Delta p = \frac{dp}{dB} \times \frac{dB}{dR} \times \Delta R \qquad \textbf{(2)}$$

This decomposition needs some explanation. The first term (dp/dB) shows the change in the value of a put option for each \$1 change in the underlying bond. This is called the *delta of an option* (δ) and lies between 0 and 1. For put options, the delta has a negative sign since the value of the put option falls when bond prices rise.[9] The second term (dB/dR) shows how the market value of a bond changes if interest rates rise by one basis point. This value of one basis point term can be linked to duration. Specifically, we know from Chapter 9 that

$$\frac{dB}{B} = -MD \times dR \qquad \textbf{(3)}$$

That is, the percentage change in the bond's price for a small change in interest rates is proportional to the bond's modified duration (MD). Equation (3) can be rearranged by cross multiplying as

$$\frac{dB}{dR} = -MD \times B \qquad \textbf{(4)}$$

[8] Conversely, an FI with a negative duration gap would lose on-balance-sheet net worth when interest rates fall. In this case, the FI manager wants to buy call options to generate profits to offset the loss in net worth due to an interest rate shock.

[9] For call options, the delta has a positive sign since the value of the call rises when bond prices rise. As we proceed with the derivation, we examine only the case of a hedge using a put option contract (i.e., the FI has a positive duration gap and expects interest rates to rise). For a hedge with a call option contract (i.e., the FI has a negative duration gap), the derivation below changes only in that the sign on the delta is reversed (from negative to positive).

Thus, the term dB/dR is equal to minus the modified duration on the bond (MD) times the current market value of the T-bond (B) underlying the put option contract. As a result, we can rewrite equation (2) as

$$\Delta p = [(-\delta) \times (-MD) \times B \times \Delta R] \tag{5}$$

where ΔR is the shock to interest rates (i.e., the number of basis points by which rates change). Since from Chapter 9 we know that $MD = D/(1 + R)$, we can rewrite equation (5) as

$$\Delta p = \left[(-\delta) \times (-D) \times B \times \frac{\Delta R}{1 + R} \right] \tag{6}$$

Thus, the change in the total value of a put position[10] (ΔP) is

$$\Delta P = N_p \times \left[\delta \times D \times B \times \frac{\Delta R}{1 + R} \right] \tag{7}$$

The term in brackets is the change in the value of one \$100,000 face-value T-bond put option as rates change, and N_p is the number of put option contracts.

To hedge net worth exposure, we require the profit on the off-balance-sheet put options (ΔP) to just offset the loss of on-balance-sheet net worth ($-\Delta E$) when interest rates rise (and thus, bond prices fall). That is,[11]

$$\Delta P = -\Delta E$$

$$N_p \times \left[\delta \times D \times B \times \frac{\Delta R}{1 + R} \right] = [D_A - kD_L] \times A \times \frac{\Delta R}{1 + R}$$

Canceling $\Delta R/(1 + R)$ on both sides, we get

$$N_p \times [\delta \times D \times B] = [D_A - kD_L] \times A$$

Solving for N_p—the number of put options to buy—we have[12]

$$N_P = \frac{[D_A - kD_L] \times A}{[\delta \times D \times B]} \tag{8}$$

Appendix 25B (located at the book's Web site, www.mhhe.com/saunders5e) derives the equation for the number of option contracts to buy or sell for a microhedge.[13]

---

[10] Note that since both the delta and D of the put option and bond have negative signs, their product will be positive. Thus, these negative signs are not shown in the equation to calculate N_p.

[11] Note that $\quad \Delta E = -(D_A - kD_L) \times A \times \dfrac{\Delta R}{1 + R}$

Thus: $\quad -\Delta E = +(D_A - kD_L) \times A \times \dfrac{\Delta R}{1 + R}$

[12] For a hedge involving a call option, the formula is

$$N_C = \frac{[D_A - kD_L] \times A}{-[\delta \times D \times B]}$$

[13] For a microhedge, this equation becomes

$$N_o = \frac{D \times P}{\delta \times D \times B}$$

where P is the price of the asset or liability being hedged and D is its duration.

EXAMPLE 25–1

Macrohedge of Interest Rate Risk Using a Put Option

Suppose, as in Chapter 24, an FI's balance sheet is such that $D_A = 5$, $D_L = 3$, $k = .9$, and $A = \$100$ million. Rates are expected to rise from 10 to 11 percent over the next six months, which would result in a $2.09 million loss in net worth to the FI. Suppose also that δ of the put option is .5, which indicates that the option is close to being in the money, $D = 8.82$ for the bond underlying the put option contract, and the current market value of $100,000 face value of long-term Treasury bonds underlying the option contract, B, equals $97,000. Solving for N_p, the number of put option contracts to buy:

$$N_p = \frac{\$230,000,000}{[.5 \times 8.82 \times \$97,000]} = \frac{\$230,000,000}{\$427,770}$$

$$= 537.672 \text{ contracts}$$

If the FI slightly underhedges, this will be rounded down to 537 contracts. If rates increase from 10 to 11 percent, the value of the FI's put options will change by

$$\Delta P = 537 \times \left[.5 \times 8.82 \times \$97,000 \times \frac{.01}{1.1} \right] = \$2.09 \text{ million}$$

just offsetting the loss in net worth on the balance sheet.

The total premium cost to the FI of buying these puts is the price (premium) of each put times the number of puts:

$$\text{Cost} = N_p \times \text{Put premium per contract}$$

Suppose that T-bond put option premiums are quoted at $2\frac{1}{2}$ per $100 of face value for the nearby contract or $2,500 per $100,000 put contract; then the cost of macrohedging the gap with put options will be

$$\text{Cost} = 537 \times \$2,500 = \$1,342,500$$

or just over $1.3 million. Remember, the total assets of the FI were assumed to be $100 million.

Figure 25–14 summarizes the change in the FI's overall value from a one percent increase in interest rates and the offsetting change in value from the hedge in the put option market. If rates increase as predicted, the FI's gap exposure results in a decrease in net worth of $2.09 million. This decrease is offset with a $2.09 million gain on the put option position held by the FI. Should rates decrease, however, the resulting increase in net worth is not offset by a decrease in an out-of-the-money put option.

FIGURE 25–14   **Buying Put Options to Hedge an FI's Interest Rate Gap Risk Exposure**

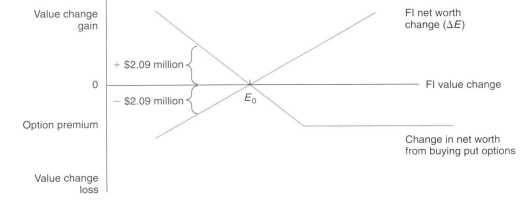

Appendix 25B to this chapter (located at the book's Web site, www.mhhe.com/saunders5e) illustrates how these options can be used to microhedge a specific asset or liability on an FI's balance sheet against interest rate risk.

Basis Risk

It is again important to recognize that in the previous examples, the FI hedged interest rate risk exposure perfectly because basis risk was assumed to be zero. That is, we assumed the change in interest rates on the balance sheet is equal to the change in the interest rate on the bond underlying the option contract (i.e., $\Delta R/(1 + R) = \Delta R_b/(1 + R_b)$). As discussed in Chapter 24, the introduction of basis risk means that the FI must adjust the number of option contracts it holds to account for the degree to which the rate on the option's underlying security (i.e., T-bond) moves relative to the spot rate on the asset or liability the FI is hedging.

Allowing basis risk to exist, the equation used to determine the number of put options to buy to hedge interest rate risk becomes

$$N_p = \frac{(D_A - kD_L) \times A}{\delta \times D \times B \times br}$$

where br is a measure of the volatility of interest rates (R_b) on the bond underlying the options contract relative to the interest rate that impacts the bond on the FI's balance sheet (R). That is,

$$br = \frac{\dfrac{\Delta R_b}{1 + R_b}}{\dfrac{\Delta R}{1 + R}}$$

EXAMPLE 25–2 *Put Option Macrohedge with Basis Risk*	Refer to Example 25–1. Suppose that basis risk, *br*, is 0.92 (i.e., the rate on the option's underlying bond changes by 92 percent of the spot rate change on the balance sheet being hedged). In Example 25–1, with no basis risk, the number of options needed to hedge interest rate risk on the bond position is 537.672 put option contracts. Introducing basis risk, *br* = 0.92:

$$N_p = \frac{\$230{,}000{,}000}{.5 \times 8.82 \text{ years} \times \$97{,}000 \times 0.92} = 584.4262 \text{ put option contracts}$$

Additional put option contracts are needed to hedge interest rate risk because interest rates on the bond underlying the option contract do not move as much as interest rates on the bond held as an asset on the balance sheet.

Concept Questions

1. If interest rates fall, are you better off purchasing call or put options on T-bonds, and why?
2. In the example above, what number of put options should you purchase if $\delta = .25$ and $D = 6$? ($N_p = 1{,}718.213$)

USING OPTIONS TO HEDGE FOREIGN EXCHANGE RISK

Just as an FI can hedge a long position in bonds against interest rate risk through bond options or futures options on bonds, a similar opportunity is available to microhedge long or short positions in a foreign currency asset against foreign exchange rate risk. To see this, suppose that an FI bought, or is long in, a Canadian dollar (C$) asset in March 2004. This C$ asset is a one-month T-bill paying C$100 million in April 2004. Since the FI's liabilities are in U.S. dollars, it may wish to hedge the FX risk that the Canadian dollar will depreciate over the forthcoming month. Suppose that if the C$ were to fall from the current exchange rate of $0.7531/C$1, the FI would make a loss on its Canadian T-bill investment when measured in U.S. dollar terms. For example, if the C$ depreciated from $0.7531/C$ in March 2004 to $0.7350/C$1 in April 2004, the C$100 million asset would be worth only $73.50 million on maturity instead of the expected $75.31 million when it was purchased in March. If the foreign exchange rate depreciation is sufficiently severe, the FI might be unable to meet its dollar liability commitments used to fund the T-bill purchase. To offset this exposure, the FI may buy one-month put options on Canadian dollars at an exercise price of $0.740/C1$. Thus, if the exchange rate does fall to $0.7350/C$1 at the end of the month, the FI manager can put the C$100 million proceeds from the T-bill on maturity to the writer of the option. Then the FI receives $74 million instead of the $73.50 million if the Canadian dollars were sold at the open market spot exchange rate at the end of the month. If the C$ actually appreciates in value, or does not depreciate below $0.74/C$1, the option expires unexercised and the proceeds of the C$100 million asset will be realized by the FI manager by a sale of Canadian dollars for U.S. dollars in the spot foreign exchange market one month into the future (see Figure 25–15).

As with bonds, the FI can buy put options on foreign currency futures contracts to hedge this currency risk. The futures option contracts for foreign currencies traded on the Chicago Mercantile Exchange (CME) are shown in Figure 25–12. A put position in one foreign currency futures contract with expiration in April 2004 and exercise price of $0.74/C$1 would have cost the FI a premium of $.0030 per C$1 on March 18, 2004. Since each Canadian dollar futures option contract is C$100,000 in size, the cost would have been $300 per contract. If we ignore the question of basis risk—that is, the imperfect correlation between the U.S.$/C$ exchange rate on the spot and futures in options markets—the optimal number of futures options purchased would be

www.cme.com

$$\frac{C\$100,000,000}{C\$100,000} = 1,000 \text{ contracts}$$

with a total premium cost of $300,000.

FIGURE 25–15
Hedging FX Risk by Buying a Put Option on Canadian Dollars

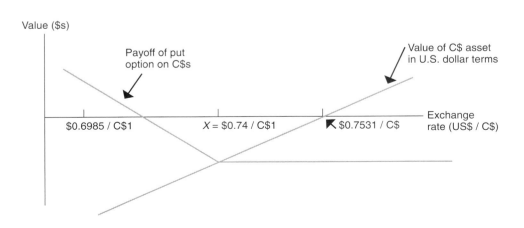

Concept Questions

1. What is the difference between options on foreign currency and options on foreign currency futures?
2. If an FI has to hedge a $5,000,000 liability exposure in Swiss francs (SF), what options should it purchase to hedge this position? Using Figure 25–12, how many contracts of Swiss franc futures options should it purchase (assuming no basis risk) if it wants to hedge against the SF falling in value against the dollar given a current exchange rate of $0.7957/SF1 (or 1.2568 SF/$1). (Buy 50.272 call options on SF futures)

HEDGING CREDIT RISK WITH OPTIONS

Options also have a potential use in hedging the credit risk of an FI. Relative to their use in hedging interest rate risk, option use to hedge credit risk is a relatively new phenomenon. Although FIs are always likely to be willing to bear some credit risk as part of the intermediation process (i.e., exploit their comparative advantage to bear such risk), options may allow them to modify that level of exposure selectively. In Chapter 24 we stated that an FI could seek an appropriate credit risk hedge by selling credit forward contracts. Rather than using credit forwards to hedge, an FI has at least two alternative credit option derivatives with which it can hedge its on-balance-sheet credit risk.

credit spread call option
A call option whose payoff increases as a yield spread increases above some stated exercise spread.

A **credit spread call option** is a call option whose payoff increases as the (default) risk premium or yield spread on a specified benchmark bond of the borrower increases above some exercise spread, S. An FI concerned that the risk on a loan to that borrower will increase can purchase a credit spread call option to hedge the increased credit risk.

Figure 25–16 illustrates the change in the FI's capital value and its payoffs from the credit spread call option as a function of the credit spread. As the credit spread increases on an FI's loan to a borrower, the value of the loan, and consequently the FI's net worth, decreases. However, if the credit risk characteristics of the benchmark bond (i.e., change in credit spread) are the same as those on the FI's loan, the loss of net worth on the balance sheet is offset with a gain from the credit spread call option. If the required credit spread on the FI's loan decreases (perhaps because the credit quality of the borrower improves over the loan period), the value of the FI's loan and net worth increases (up to some maximum value), but the credit spread call option will expire out of the money. As a result, the FI will suffer a maximum loss equal to the required (call) premium on the credit option, which will be offset by the market value gain of the

FIGURE 25–16
Buying Credit Spread Call Options to Hedge Credit Risk

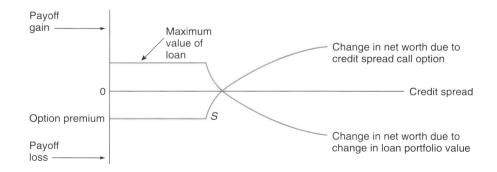

FIGURE 25–17
Buying a Digital Default Option to Hedge Credit Risk

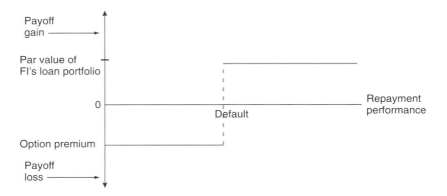

FIGURE 25–18
Catastrophe Call Spread Options

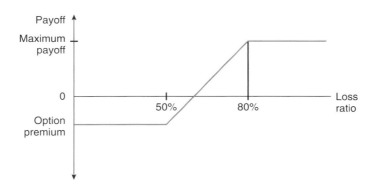

loan in the portfolio (which is reflected in a positive increase in the FI's net worth).[14]

digital default option
An option that pays the par value of a loan in the event of default.

A **digital default option** is an option that pays a stated amount in the event of a loan default (the extreme case of increased credit risk). As shown in Figure 25–17, the FI can purchase a default option covering the par value of a loan (or loans) in its portfolio. In the event of a loan default, the option writer pays the FI the par value of the defaulted loans. If the loans are paid off in accordance with the loan agreement, however, the default option expires unexercised. As a result, the FI will suffer a maximum loss on the option equal to the premium (cost) of buying the default option from the writer (seller).

HEDGING CATASTROPHE RISK WITH CALL SPREAD OPTIONS

www.cbot.com

catastrophe (CAT) call spread
A call option on the loss ratio incurred in writing catastrophe insurance with a capped (or maximum) payout.

In 1993 the Chicago Board of Trade (CBOT) introduced **catastrophe (CAT) call spread** options to hedge the risk of unexpectedly high losses being incurred by property-casualty insurers as a result of catastrophes such as hurricanes. The basic idea can be seen in Figure 25–18. For an option premium, the insurer can hedge a range of loss ratios that may occur (remember that the loss ratio is the ratio of losses incurred divided by premiums written). In Figure 25–18, the insurer buys a call spread to hedge the risk that the loss ratio on its catastrophe insurance may be

---

[14] For additional discussion, see J. D. Finnerty, "Credit Derivatives, Infrastructure Finance, and Emerging Market Risk," *The Financier, ACMT,* February 1996, pp. 64–75.

anywhere between 50 percent and 80 percent. If the loss ratio ends up below 50 percent (perhaps because of a mild hurricane season), the insurance company loses the option premium. For loss ratios between 50 percent and 80 percent, it receives an increasingly positive payoff. For loss ratios above 80 percent, the amount paid by the writers of the option to the buyer (the insurer) is capped at the 80 percent level. Cummins, Lalonde, and Phillips examined catastrophe loss index options in hedging hurricane losses in Florida. Using data from 255 of 264 property insurers operating in Florida in 1998, they found that these options can be used effectively by insurers to hedge catastrophe risk.[15]

Concept Questions

1. What is the difference between a credit spread call option and a digital default option?
2. What is the difference between the payoff on the catastrophe call spread option in Figure 25–18 and the payoff of a standard call option on a stock?

CAPS, FLOORS, AND COLLARS

cap

A call option on interest rates, often with multiple exercise dates.

Caps, floors, and collars are derivative securities that have many uses, especially in helping an FI hedge interest rate risk exposure as well as risk unique to its individual customers. Buying a **cap** means buying a call option or a succession of call options on interest rates. Specifically, if interest rates rise above the cap rate, the seller of the cap—usually a bank—compensates the buyer—for example, another FI—in return for an up-front premium. As a result, buying an interest rate cap is like buying insurance against an (excessive) increase in interest rates. A cap agreement can have one or many exercise dates.

floor

A put option on interest rates, often with multiple exercise dates.

Buying a **floor** means buying a put option on interest rates. If interest rates fall below the floor rate, the seller of the floor compensates the buyer in return for an up-front premium. As with caps, floor agreements can have one or many exercise dates.

collar

A position taken simultaneously in a cap and a floor.

A **collar** occurs when an FI takes a simultaneous position in a cap and a floor, such as buying a cap and selling a floor. The idea here is that the FI wants to hedge itself against rising rates but wants to finance the cost of the cap. One way to do this is to sell a floor and use the premiums on the floor to pay the premium on the purchase of the cap. Thus, these three over-the-counter instruments are special cases of options; FI managers use them like bond options and bond futures options to hedge the interest rate risk of an FI's portfolios.

In general, FIs purchase interest rate caps if they are exposed to losses when interest rates rise. Usually, this happens if they are funding assets with floating-rate liabilities such as notes indexed to LIBOR (or some other cost of funds) and they have fixed-rate assets or they are net long in bonds, or—in a macrohedging context—their duration gap is $D_A - kD_L > 0$. By contrast, FIs purchase floors when they have fixed costs of debt and have variable rates (returns) on assets, are net short in bonds, or $D_A - kD_L < 0$. Finally, FIs purchase collars when they are concerned about excessive volatility of interest rates and to finance cap or floor positions.

Caps

For simplicity, assume that an FI buys a 9 percent cap at time 0 from another FI with a notional face value of $100 million. In return for paying an up-front premium, the

[15] For more information, see J. D. Cummins and H. Geman, "Pricing Catastrophe Insurance Futures and Call Spreads: An Arbitrage Approach," ibid.; and J. D. Cummins, D. Lalonde, and R. D. Phillips, "The Basis Risk of Catastrophe-Loss Index Securities," *Journal of Financial Economics*, January 2004, pp. 77–111.

FIGURE 25–19
Hypothetical Path
of Interest Rates

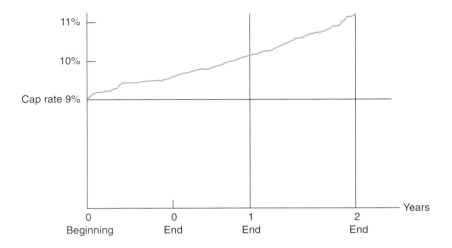

TABLE 25–1
Payments under
the Cap

End of Year	Cap Rate	Actual Interest Rate	Interest Differential	Payment by Seller to Buyer
1	9%	10%	1%	$1 million
2	9	11	2	$2 million
Total				$3 million

seller of the cap stands ready to compensate the buying FI whenever the interest rate index defined under the agreement is above the 9 percent cap rate on the dates specified under the cap agreement. This effectively converts the cost of the FI's floating-rate liabilities into fixed-rate liabilities. In this example, we assume that the purchasing FI buys a cap at time 0 with cap exercise dates at the end of the first year and the end of the second year. That is, the cap has a three-year maturity from initiation until the final exercise dates, with exercise dates at the end of year 1 and year 2.[16]

Thus, the buyer of the cap would demand two cash payments from the seller of the cap if rates lie above 9 percent at the end of the first year and at the end of the second year on the cap exercise dates. In practice, cap exercise dates usually closely correspond to payment dates on liabilities, for example, coupon dates on floating-rate notes. Consider one possible scenario in Figure 25–19.

In Figure 25–19, the seller of the cap has to pay the buyer of the cap the amount shown in Table 25–1. In this scenario, the cap-buying FI would receive $3 million (undiscounted) over the life of the cap to offset any rise in the cost of liability funding or market value losses on its bond/asset portfolio. However, the interest rates in Figure 25–19 are only one possible scenario. Consider the possible path to interest rates in Figure 25–20. In this interest scenario, rates fall below 9 percent at the end of the first year to 8 percent and at the end of the second year to 7 percent on the cap exercise dates. Thus, the cap seller makes no payments. This example makes it clear that

---

[16] There is no point exercising the option at the end of year 0 (i.e., having three exercise dates) since interest rates for year 0 are set at the beginning of that year and are contractually set throughout. As a result, the FI does not bear interest rate uncertainty until the end of year 0 (i.e., interest uncertainty exists only in years 1 and 2).

FIGURE 25–20
Hypothetical Path of Interest Rates

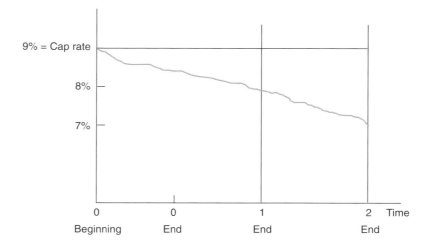

FIGURE 25–21
Interest Rate Cap with a 9 Percent Cap Rate

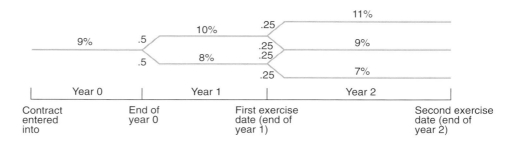

buying a cap is similar to buying a call option on interest rates in that when the option expires out of the money, because the interest rate is below the cap level, the cap seller makes no payments to the buyer. Conceptually, buying this cap is like buying a complex call option on an interest rate or a put option on a bond price with a single exercise price or interest rate and two exercise dates: the end of year 1 and the end of year 2.

The problem for the FI manager is to calculate the fair value of this 9 percent cap in the face of interest rate uncertainty. In particular, the FI manager does not know whether interest rates will be 10 percent at the end of year 1 or 8 percent. Similarly, the manager does not know whether interest rates will be 11 percent or 7 percent at the end of year 2. Nevertheless, to buy interest rate risk insurance in the form of a cap, the manager has to pay an up-front fee or premium to the seller of the cap. Next, we solve for the fair value of the cap premium in the framework of the binomial model introduced earlier to calculate the premium on a bond option.[17]

Consider Figure 25–21, the binomial tree for the cap contract entered into at the beginning of year 0. The cap can be exercised at the end of the first year and the end of the second year.[18] The current (time 0) value of the cap or the fair cap premium is

---

[17] For more details and examples, see R. C. Stapleton and M. Subrahmanyam, "Interest Rate Caps and Floors," in *Financial Options: From Theory to Practice,* ed. S. Figlewski (Homewood, IL: Business One-Irwin, 1990), pp. 220–80.

[18] Interest rates are normally set at the *beginning* of each period and paid at the *end* of each period.

the sum of the present value of the cap option exercised at the end of year 1 plus the present value of the cap option exercised at the end of year 2:

$$\text{Fair premium} = P = PV \text{ of year 1 option} + PV \text{ of year 2 option}$$

EXAMPLE 25–3 *Calculating the Premium on an Interest Rate Cap*	**PV of Year 2 Option** At the end of year 2, there are three possible interest rate scenarios: 11 percent, 9 percent, and 7 percent. With a cap exercise price of 9 percent and the 9 percent or 7 percent scenarios realized, the cap would have no value to the buyer. In other words, it would expire out of the money. The only interest rate scenario where the cap has exercise value to the buyer at the end of the second year is if rates rise to 11 percent. With rates at 11 percent, the interest differential would be 11 percent minus 9 percent, or 2 percent. But since there is only a 25 percent probability that interest rates will rise to 11 percent at the end of the second year, the expected value of this interest differential is

$$.25 \times 2\% = 0.5\%$$

With a $100 million cap, therefore, the expected cash payment at the end of year 2 would be $0.5 million. However, to calculate the fair value of the cap premium in current dollars, the expected cash flow at the end of year 2 has to be discounted back to the present (time 0):

$$PV_2 = \frac{0.5}{(1.09)(1.1)(1.11)} = .3757$$

where 9 percent, 10 percent, and 11 percent are the appropriate one-year discount rates for payments in years 0, 1, and 2. Thus, the fair present value of the option at the end of year 2 is .3757, or $375,700, given the $100 million face value of the cap.

PV of Year 1 Option

At the end of year 1, there are two interest rate scenarios: Interest rates could rise to 10 percent or fall to 8 percent. If rates fall to 8 percent, the 9 percent cap has no value to the buyer. However, if rates rise to 10 percent, this results in a positive interest differential of 1 percent at the end of year 1. However, the expected interest differential is only .5 of 1 percent since this is the probability that rates will rise from 9 percent to 10 percent between the beginning of year 0 and end of year 1:

$$.5 \times 1\% = 0.5\%$$

In dollar terms, with a $100 million cap, the expected value of the cap at the end of year 1 is $0.5 million. To evaluate the time 0 or present value of a cap exercised at the end of time period 1, this expected cash flow has to be discounted back to the beginning of time 0 using the appropriate one-year discount rates. That is:

$$PV_1 = \frac{0.5}{(1.09)(1.1)} = .417$$

or $417,000, given the $100 million face value of the cap. As a result, the fair value of the premium the FI should be willing to pay for this cap is:

$$\text{Cap premium} = PV_1 + PV_2$$
$$= \$417,000 + \$375,700$$
$$= \$792,700$$

That is, under the interest rate scenarios implied by this simple binomial model, the FI should pay no more than $792,700, or 0.7927 percent of notional face value, in buying the cap from the seller.

FIGURE 25–22
Interest Rate Floor with a 4 Percent Floor

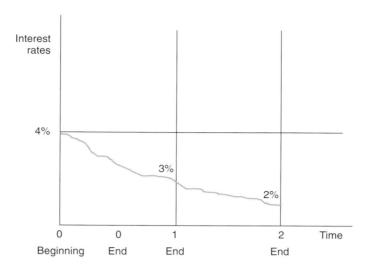

TABLE 25–2
Hypothetical Floor Payments

End of Year	Cap Rate	Actual Interest Rate	Interest Differential	Payment by Seller to Buyer
1	4%	3%	1%	$1 million
2	4	2	2	$2 million
Total				$3 million

Floors

A floor is a put option or a collection of put options on interest rates. Here the FI manager who buys a floor is concerned about falling interest rates. Perhaps the FI is funding liabilities at fixed rates and has floating-rate assets, or maybe it is short in some bond position and will lose if it has to cover the position with higher-priced bonds after interest rates fall. In a macrohedging sense, the FI could face a duration gap where the duration of assets is less than the leverage-adjusted duration of liabilities $(D_A - kD_L < 0)$. For an example of the payoff from buying a floor, see Figure 25–22.

In this simple example, the floor is set at 4 percent and the buyer pays an up-front premium to the seller of the floor. While caps can be viewed as buying a complex call option on interest rates, a floor can be viewed as buying a complex put option on interest rates. In our example, the floor has two exercise dates: the end of year 1 and the end of year 2.

If the interest scenario in Figure 25–22 is the actual interest rate path, the payments from the seller to the buyer would be as shown in Table 25–2. However, since the buyer of the cap is uncertain about the actual path of interest rates—rates could rise and not fall—such profits are only probabilistic. That is, the buyer would have to use a model similar to the binomial model for caps to calculate the fair up-front premium to be paid for the floor at time 0.

Collars

FI managers who are very risk averse and overly concerned about the exposure of their portfolios to increased interest rate volatility may seek to protect the FI

FIGURE 25–23
Payoffs from a
Collar

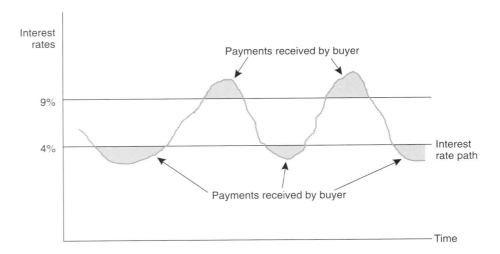

against such increases. One method of hedging this risk is through buying a cap and a floor together. This is usually called a collar. Figure 25–23 illustrates the essential risk-protection features of a collar when an FI buys a 9 percent cap and a 4 percent floor.

The shaded areas in Figure 25–23 show the interest rate payment regions (>9 percent or < 4 percent) where the cap or floor is in the money and the buyer potentially receives either a cap or a floor payment from the seller. If interest rates stay in the 4 through 9 percent range, the buyer of the collar receives no compensation from the seller. In addition, the buyer has to pay two up-front premiums: one for the cap and one for the floor to the cap and floor sellers. As is clear, buying a collar is similar to simultaneously buying a complex put and call bond option, or straddle.

An alternative and more common use of a collar is to finance the cost of purchasing a cap. In our earlier example of the $100 million cap, the fair cap premium (pc) was $792,700, or 0.7927 percent of the notional face value (NV_c) of the cap. That is, the cost (C) of the cap is

$$C = NV_c \times pc$$
$$= \$100 \text{ million} \times .007927$$
$$= \$792,700$$

To purchase the cap, the FI must pay this premium to the cap seller in up-front dollars.

Many large FIs, more exposed to rising interest rates than falling interest rates—perhaps because they are heavily reliant on interest-sensitive sources of liabilities—seek to finance a cap by selling a floor at the same time.[19] In so doing, they generate up-front revenues; this floor premium can finance the cost of the cap purchase or the cap premium. Nevertheless, they give up potential profits if rates fall rather than rise. Indeed, when rates fall, the floor is more likely to be triggered and the FI must compensate the buyer of the floor.

---

[19] In this context, the sale of the floor is like the sale of any revenue-generating product.

FIGURE 25–24
In-the-Money Floor and Out-of-the-Money Cap

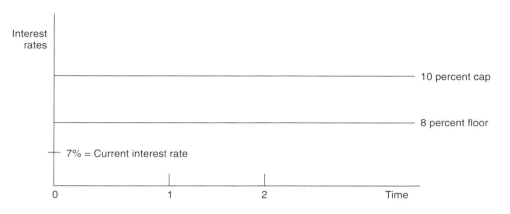

After an FI buys a cap and sells a floor, its net cost of the cap is[20]

$$C = (NV_c \times pc) - (NV_f \times pf)$$

$$C = \text{Cost of cap} - \text{Revenue on floor}$$

where

NV_f = Notional principal of the floor

pf = Premium rate on the floor

Calculating the Cost of a Collar

Suppose that, in the example above, while buying the cap the FI sold a two-year $100 million notional face value floor at a premium of .75 percent. The net up-front cost of purchasing the cap is reduced to

$$C = (\$100 \text{ million} \times .007927) - (\$100 \text{ million} \times .0075) = \$42,700$$

Note that if the FI is willing to raise the floor exercise interest rate, thereby exposing itself to increasing losses if rates fall, it can generate higher premiums on the floor it sells. Like any option, as the exercise price or rate moves from being out of the money, when current rates are above the floor, to being in the money, when current rates are below the floor, the floor buyer would be willing to pay a higher premium to the writer (the FI). Given this, the buyer of the cap could set the floor rate with notional face values of $100 million each so that the floor premium earned by the FI just equals the cap premium paid:

$$C = (\$100 \text{ million} \times .007927) - (\$100 \text{ million} \times .007927)$$

$$C = 0$$

When $pc = pf$, the cap buyer–floor seller can reduce the cap's net cost of purchase to zero.

Indeed, if the cap buyer bought a very out-of-the-money cap and sold a very in-the-money floor, as shown in Figure 25–24, the net cost of the cap purchase could actually be negative. In Figure 25–24, the current interest rate is 7 percent while the cap rate is 10 percent. Thus, rates would have to rise at least 3 percent for the cap buyer to receive a payment at the end of year 1. By contrast, the 8 percent floor is

[20] See K. C. Brown and D. J. Smith, "Recent Innovations in Interest Rate Risk Management and the Reintermediation of Commercial Banking," *Financial Management* 17 (1988), pp. 45–58.

already 1 percent above the current 7 percent rate. If rates stay at 7 percent until the end of year 1, the FI seller of the floor is already exposed to a 1 percent notional face value loss in writing the floor.

If the out-of-the-money cap can be bought at a premium of .7927 percent, but the in-the-money floor is sold at a premium of .95 percent, the (net) cost of the cap purchase is

$$C = (NV_c \times pc) - (NV_f \times pf)$$

$$= \$792,700 - \$950,000$$

$$= -\$157,300$$

Raising the floor exercise rate and thus the floor premium also can be combined with mismatching the notional principal amounts of the cap and the floor to produce a zero net cost financing for the cap. That is, there is no reason why both the floor and cap agreements have to be written against the same notional face values ($NV_c = NV_f = \$100$ million).

Suppose the out-of-the-money cap can be bought at a premium of .7927 percent and the in-the-money floor can be sold at a .95 percent premium. An FI manager might want to know what notional principal on the floor (or contract size) is necessary to finance a $100 million cap purchase at zero net up-front cost. That is,

$$C = (NV_c \times pc) - (NV_f \times pf) = 0$$

$$= (\$100 \text{ million} \times .007927) - (NV_f \times .0095) = 0$$

Solving for NV_f:

$$NV_f = \frac{(\$100 \text{ million} \times .007927)}{.0095} = \frac{(NV_c \times pc)}{pf}$$

$$= \$83.44 \text{ million}$$

Clearly, the higher premium rate on the floor requires a lower notional face value floor amount to generate sufficient premium income up front to finance the cap's purchase. In general, to fund fully the cap purchase ($C = 0$), the relationship between premium rates and notional value should be:[21]

$$\frac{NV_f}{NV_c} = \frac{pc}{pf}$$

[21] As shown earlier in this chapter, it is possible to macrohedge a gap position of an FI using put options. A cap is economically equivalent to a call option on an interest rate or a put option on a bond. However, the major difference is that the cap is a complex option in that there are multiple exercise dates. For example, in our simple model of the determination of the fair cap premium, there were two exercise dates: the end of year 1 and the end of year 2. However, we showed that we could decompose the value of the cap as a whole into the value of the (end of) year 1 option and the value of the (end of) year 2 option. Both of these options would have their own deltas (δ) because of the different maturity of these options. Thus, the change in the total value of the cap (ΔC) position would equal

$$\Delta C = N_c \times \{[\delta_1 \times (D_1 \times B)] + [\delta_2 \times (D_2 \times B)]\} \times \Delta R/(1 + R)$$

where N_c—the number of $100,000 cap contracts—is calculated by solving

$$N_c = \frac{[D_A - kD_L] \times S}{\{[\delta_1 \times (D_1 \times B)] + [\delta_2 \times (D_2 \times B)]\}}$$

Caps, Floors, Collars, and Credit Risk

One important feature of buying caps, collars, and floors for hedging purposes is the implied credit risk exposure involved that is absent for exchange-traded futures and options. Since these are multiple exercise over-the-counter contracts, the buyer of these instruments faces a degree of counterparty credit risk. To see this, consider the cap example just discussed. Suppose the writer of the cap defaulted on the $1 million due at the end of the first year if interest rates rose to 10 percent. The buyer not only would fail to collect on this in-the-money option but also would lose a potential payment at the end of year 2. In general, a default in year 1 would mean that the cap buyer would have to find a replacement contract for year 2 (and any succeeding years thereafter) at the cap rate terms or premiums prevailing at the end of year 1 rather than at the beginning of year 0. These cap rates may be far less favorable than those under the original cap contract (reflecting the higher interest rate levels of time 1). In addition, the buyer could incur further transaction and contracting costs in replacing the original contract. Because of the often long-term nature of cap agreements, occasionally extending up to 10 years, only FIs that are the most creditworthy are likely to be able to write and run a large cap/floor book without the backing of external guarantees such as standby letters of credit. As we discuss in the next chapter, swaps have similar credit risk exposures due to their long-run contractual nature and their OTC origination.

Concept Questions

1. In Example 25–3 suppose that in year 2 the highest and lowest rates were 12 percent and 6 percent instead of 11 percent and 7 percent. Calculate the fair premium on the cap. ($980,500)

2. Assume two exercise dates at the end of year 1 and the end of year 2. Suppose the FI buys a floor of 4 percent at time 0. The binomial tree suggests that rates at the end of year 1 could be 3 percent ($p = .5$) or 5 percent ($p = .5$) and at the end of year 2 rates could be 2 percent ($p = .25$), 4 percent ($p = .5$), or 6 percent ($p = .25$). Calculate the fair value of the floor premium. Assume the one-year discount rates for payments in years 0, 1, and 2 are 9 percent, 10 percent, and 11 percent, respectively. ($792,700)

3. An FI buys a $100 million cap at a premium of .75 percent and sells a floor at a .85 percent premium. What size floor should be sold so that the net cost of the cap purchase is zero? ($88,235,394)

4. Why are only the most creditworthy FIs able to write a large cap/floor book without external guarantees?

Summary

In this chapter we evaluated a wide range of option-type contracts that are available to FI managers to hedge the risk exposures of individual assets, portfolios of assets, and the balance sheet gap itself. We illustrated how these options—some of which are exchange traded and some of which are sold OTC—can hedge the interest rate, credit, FX, and catastrophe risks of FIs. In particular, we described how the unique nature of the asymmetric payoff function of option-type contracts often makes them more attractive to FIs than other hedging instruments, such as forwards and futures.

Questions and Problems

1. How does using options differ from using forward or futures contracts?

2. What is a call option?

3. What must happen to interest rates for the purchaser of a call option on a bond to make money? How does the writer of the call option make money?

4. What is a put option?

5. What must happen to interest rates for the purchaser of a put option on a bond to make money? How does the writer of the put option make money?

6. Consider the following:

   a. What are the two ways to use call and put options on T-bonds to generate positive cash flows when interest rates decline? Verify your answer with a diagram.

   b. Under what balance sheet conditions can an FI use options on T-bonds to hedge its assets and/or liabilities against interest rate declines?

   c. Is it more appropriate for FIs to hedge against a decline in interest rates with long calls or short puts?

7. In each of the following cases, identify what risk the manager of an FI faces and whether that risk should be hedged by buying a put or a call option.

   a. A commercial bank plans to issue CDs in three months.

   b. An insurance company plans to buy bonds in two months.

   c. A thrift plans to sell Treasury securities next month.

   d. A U.S. bank lends to a French company with a loan payable in euros.

   e. A mutual fund plans to sell its holding of stock in a British company.

   f. A finance company has assets with a duration of six years and liabilities with a duration of 13 years.

8. Consider an FI that wishes to use bond options to hedge the interest rate risk in the bond portfolio.

   a. How does writing call options hedge the risk when interest rates decrease?

   b. Will writing call options fully hedge the risk when interest rates increase? Explain.

   c. How does buying a put option reduce the losses on the bond portfolio when interest rates rise?

   d. Diagram the purchase of a bond call option against the combination of a bond investment and the purchase of a bond put option.

9. What are the regulatory reasons why FIs seldom write options?

10. What are the problems of using the Black-Scholes option pricing model to value bond options? What is meant by the term *pull-to-par*?

11. An FI has purchased a two-year, $1,000 par value zero-coupon bond for $867.43. The FI will hold the bond to maturity unless it needs to sell the bond at the end of one year for liquidity purposes. The current one-year interest rate is 7 percent, and the one-year rate in one year is forecast to be either 8.04 percent or 7.44 percent with equal likelihood. The FI wishes to buy a put option to protect itself against a capital loss if the bond needs to be sold in one year.

    a. What was the yield on the bond at the time of purchase?

    b. What is the market-determined, implied one-year rate one year before maturity?

    c. What is the expected sale price if the bond has to be sold at the end of one year?

    d. Diagram the bond prices over the two-year horizon.

    e. If the FI buys a put option with an exercise price equal to your answer in part (c), what will be its value at the end of one year?

    f. What should be the premium on the put option today?

    g. Diagram the values of the put option on the two-year, zero-coupon bond.

    h. What would have been the premium on the option if the one-year interest rates at the end of one year were expected to be 8.14 percent and 7.34 percent?

12. A pension fund manager anticipates the purchase of a 20-year, 8 percent coupon Treasury bond at the end of two years. Interest rates are assumed to change only once every year at year-end, with an equal probability of a 1 percent increase or a 1 percent decrease. The Treasury bond, when purchased in two years, will pay interest semiannually. Currently the Treasury bond is selling at par.

    a. What is the pension fund manager's interest rate risk exposure?

    b. How can the pension fund manager use options to hedge that interest rate risk exposure?

    c. What prices are possible on the 20-year T-bonds at the end of year 1 and year 2?

    d. Diagram the prices over the two-year period.

    e. If options on $100,000, 20-year, 8 percent coupon Treasury bonds (both puts and calls) have a strike price of 101, what are the possible (intrinsic) values of the option position at the end of year 1 and year 2?

    f. Diagram the possible option values.

    g. What is the option premium? (Use an 8 percent discount factor.)

13. Why are options on interest rate futures contracts preferred to options on cash instruments in hedging interest rate risk?

14. Consider Figure 25–12. What are the prices paid for the following futures option?

    a. June T-bond calls at 116.

    b. June five-year T-note puts at 116.

    c. June Eurodollar calls at 9900 (99.00).

15. Consider Figure 25–12 again. What happens to the price of the following?

    a. A call when the exercise price increases.

    b. A call when the time until expiration increases.

    c. A put when the exercise price increases.

    d. A put when the time to expiration increases.

16. An FI manager writes a call option on a T-bond futures contract with an exercise price of 114 at a quoted price of 0–55.

    a. What type of opportunities or obligations does the manager have?

    b. In what direction must interest rates move to encourage the call buyer to exercise the option?

17. What is the delta of an option (δ)?

18. An FI has a $100 million portfolio of six-year Eurodollar bonds that have an 8 percent coupon. The bonds are trading at par and have a duration of five years. The FI wishes to hedge the portfolio with T-bond options that have a delta of −0.625. The underlying long-term Treasury bonds for the option have a duration of 10.1 years and trade at a market value of $96,157 per $100,000 of par value. Each put option has a premium of $3.25.

a. How many bond put options are necessary to hedge the bond portfolio?

b. If interest rates increase 100 basis points, what is the expected gain or loss on the put option hedge?

c. What is the expected change in market value on the bond portfolio?

d. What is the total cost of placing the hedge?

e. Diagram the payoff possibilities.

f. How far must interest rates move before the payoff on the hedge will exactly offset the cost of placing the hedge?

g. How far must interest rates move before the gain on the bond portfolio will exactly offset the cost of placing the hedge?

h. Summarize the gain, loss, and cost conditions of the hedge on the bond portfolio in terms of changes in interest rates.

19. Corporate Bank has $840 million of assets with a duration of 12 years and liabilities worth $720 million with a duration of 7 years. The bank is concerned about preserving the value of its equity in the event of an increase in interest rates and is contemplating a macrohedge with interest rate options. The call and put options have a delta (δ) of 0.4 and -0.4, respectively. The price of an underlying T-bond is 104–34, and its modified duration is 7.6 years.

a. What type of option should Corporate Bank use for the macrohedge?

b. How many options should be purchased?

c. What is the effect on the economic value of the equity if interest rates rise 50 basis points?

d. What will be the effect on the hedge if interest rates rise 50 basis points?

e. What will be the cost of the hedge if each option has a premium of $0.875?

f. Diagram the economic conditions of the hedge.

g. How much must interest rates move against the hedge for the increased value of the bank to offset the cost of the hedge?

h. How much must interest rates move in favor of the hedge, or against the balance sheet, before the payoff from the hedge will exactly cover the cost of the hedge?

i. Formulate a management decision rule regarding the implementation of the hedge.

20. An FI has a $200 million asset portfolio that has an average duration of 6.5 years. The average duration of its $160 million in liabilities is 4.5 years. The FI uses put options on T-bonds to hedge against unexpected interest rate increases. The average delta (δ) of the put options has been estimated at -0.3, and the average duration of the T-bonds is 7 years. The current market value of the T-bonds is $96,000.

a. What is the modified duration of the T-bonds if the current level of interest rates is 10 percent?

b. How many put option contracts should it purchase to hedge its exposure against rising interest rates? The face value of the T-bonds is $100,000.

c. If interest rates increase 50 basis points, what will be the change in value of the equity of the FI?

d. What will be the change in value of the T-bond option hedge position?

e. If put options on T-bonds are selling at a premium of $1.25 per face value of $100, what is the total cost of hedging using options on T-bonds?

f. Diagram the spot market conditions of the equity and the option hedge.

g. What must be the change in interest rates before the change in value of the balance sheet (equity) will offset the cost of placing the hedge?

h. How much must interest rates change before the payoff of the hedge will exactly cover the cost of placing the hedge?

i. Given your answer in part (g), what will be the net gain or loss to the FI?

21. A mutual fund plans to purchase $10,000,000 of 20-year T-bonds in two months. These bonds have a duration of 11 years. The mutual fund is concerned about interest rates changing over the next four months and is considering a hedge with a two-month option on a T-bond futures contract. Two-month calls with a strike price of 105 are priced at 1–25, and puts of the same maturity and exercise price are quoted at 2–09. The delta of the call is .5 and the delta of the put is −.7. The current price of a deliverable T-bond is $103−08 per $100 of face value, and its modified duration is nine years.

a. What type of option should the mutual fund purchase?

b. How many options should it purchase?

c. What is the cost of those options?

d. If rates change +/− 50 basis points, what will be the impact on the price of the desired T-bonds?

e. What will be the effect on the value of the hedge if rates change +/− 50 basis points?

f. Diagram the effects of the hedge and the spot market value of the desired T-bonds.

g. What must be the change in interest rates to cause the change in value of the hedge to exactly offset the change in value of the T-bonds?

22. An FI must make a single payment of 500,000 Swiss francs in six months at the maturity of a CD. The FI's in-house analyst expects the spot price of the franc to remain stable at the current $0.80/Sf. But as a precaution, the analyst is concerned that it could rise as high as $0.85/Sf or fall as low as $0.75/Sf. Because of this uncertainty, the analyst recommends that the FI hedge the CD payment using either options or futures. Six-month call and put options on the Swiss franc with an exercise price of $0.80/Sf are trading at 4 cents and 2 cents, respectively. A six-month futures contract on the Swiss franc is trading at $0.80/Sf.

a. Should the analysts be worried about the dollar depreciating or appreciating?

b. If the FI decides to hedge using options, should the FI buy put or call options to hedge the CD payment? Why?

c. If futures are used to hedge, should the FI buy or sell Swiss franc futures to hedge the payment? Why?

d. What will be the net payment on the CD if the selected call or put options are used to hedge the payment? Assume the following three scenarios: the spot price in six months will be $0.75, $0.80, or $0.85/Sf. Also assume that the options will be exercised.

e. What will be the net payment if futures had been used to hedge the CD payment? Use the same three scenarios as in part (a).

f. Which method of hedging is preferable after the fact?

23. An American insurance company issued $10 million of one-year, zero-coupon GICs (guaranteed investment contracts) denominated in Swiss francs at a rate of 5 percent. The insurance company holds no Sf-denominated assets and has neither bought nor sold francs in the foreign exchange market.

a. What is the insurance company's net exposure in Swiss francs?

b. What is the insurance company's risk exposure to foreign exchange rate fluctuations?

c. How can the insurance company use futures to hedge the risk exposure in part (b)? How can it use options to hedge?

d. If the strike price is $0.6667/Sf and the spot price is $0.6452/Sf, what is the intrinsic value (on expiration) of a call option on Swiss francs? What is the intrinsic value (on expiration) of a Swiss franc put option? (*Note:* Swiss franc futures options traded on the Chicago Mercantile Exchange are set at Sf125,000 per contract.)

e. If the June delivery call option premium is 0.32 cent per franc and the June delivery put option is 10.7 cents per franc, what is the dollar premium cost per contract? Assume that today's date is April 15.

f. Why is the call option premium lower than the put option premium?

24. An FI has made a loan commitment of Sf10 million that is likely to be taken down in six months. The current spot rate is $0.60/Sf.

a. Is the FI exposed to the dollar depreciating or the dollar appreciating? Why?

b. If it decides to hedge using Sf futures, should it buy or sell Sf futures?

c. If the spot rate six months from today is $0.64/Sf, what dollar amount is needed in six months if the loan is drawn?

d. A six-month Sf futures contract is available for $0.61/Sf. What is the net amount needed at the end of six months if the FI has hedged using the Sf10 million of futures contracts? Assume that futures prices are equal to spot prices at the time of payment, that is, at maturity.

e. If it decides to use options to hedge, should it purchase call or put options?

f. Call and put options with an exercise price of $0.61/Sf are selling for $0.02 and $0.03, respectively. What would be the net amount needed by the FI at the end of six months if it had used options instead of futures to hedge this exposure?

25. What is a credit spread call option?

26. What is a digital default option?

27. How do the cash flows to the lender differ for a credit spread call option hedge from the cash flows for a digital default option?

28. What is a catastrophe call option? How do the cash flows of this option affect the buyer of the option?

29. What are caps? Under what circumstances would the buyer of a cap receive a payoff?

30. What are floors? Under what circumstances would the buyer of a floor receive a payoff?

31. What are collars? Under what circumstances would an FI use a collar?

32. How is buying a cap similar to buying a call option on interest rates?

33. Under what balance sheet circumstances would it be desirable to sell a floor to help finance a cap? When would it be desirable to sell a cap to help finance a floor?

34. Use the following information to price a three-year collar by purchasing an in-the-money cap and writing an out-of-the-money floor. Assume a binomial options pricing model with an equal probability of interest rates increasing 2 percent or decreasing 2 percent per annum. Current rates are 7 percent, the cap rate is 7 percent, and the floor rate is 4 percent. The notional value is $1 million. All interest payments are annual payments as a percent of notional value, and all payments are made at the end of year 1 and the end of year 2.

35. Use the following information to price a three-year collar by purchasing an out-of-the-money cap and writing an in-the-money floor. Assume a binomial options pricing model with an equal probability of interest rates increasing 2 percent or decreasing 2 percent per annum. Current rates are 4 percent, the cap rate is 7 percent, and the floor rate is 4 percent. The notional value is $1 million. All interest payments are annual payments as a percent of notional value, and all payments are made at the end of year 1 and the end of year 2.

36. Contrast the total cash flows associated with the collar position in question 34 against the collar in question 35. Do the goals of FIs that utilize the collar in question 34 differ from those that put on the collar in question 35? If so, how?

37. An FI has purchased a $200 million cap (i.e., call options on interest rates) of 9 percent at a premium of 0.65 percent of face value. A $200 million floor (i.e., put options on interest rates) of 4 percent is also available at a premium of 0.69 percent of face value.

    a. If interest rates rise to 10 percent, what is the amount received by the FI? What are the net savings after deducting the premium?

    b. If the FI also purchases a floor, what are the net savings if interest rates rise to 11 percent? What are the net savings if interest rates fall to 3 percent?

    c. If, instead, the FI sells (writes) the floor, what are the net savings if interest rates rise to 11 percent? What if they fall to 3 percent?

    d. What amount of floors should it sell to compensate for its purchase of caps, given the above premiums?

38. What credit risk exposure is involved in buying caps, floors, and collars for hedging purposes?

Web Question

39. Go to the Chicago Board Options Exchange Web site at **www.cboe.com**. Find the most recent data on 10-Year Treasury Yield Options (TNX) by clicking on "CBOE Daily Market Statistics" under "Data." Clicking on the current date on

the calendar at the top of the page will allow the user to retrieve data on any particular day. What is the reported Volume, Open Interest, and Level of trading for calls and puts on these options? What is the percent change in the most recent data from that of one year earlier?

Pertinent Web Sites

Chicago Board of Trade	**www.cbot.com**
Chicago Board Options Exchange	**www.cboe.com**
Chicago Mercantile Exchange	**www.cme.com**
The Wall Street Journal	**www.wsj.com**

Chapter Notation

View Chapter Notation at the Web site to the textbook (**www.mhhe.com/ saunders5e**).

Appendix 25A

Black-Scholes Option Pricing Model

View Appendix 25A at the Web site for this textbook (**www.mhhe.com/saunders5e**).

Appendix 25B

Microhedging with Options

View Appendix 25B at the Web site for this textbook (**www.mhhe.com/saunders5e**).

Chapter **Twenty-Six**

Swaps

INTRODUCTION

The market for swaps has grown enormously in recent years; the notional value of swap contracts outstanding of U.S. commercial banks was $41.2 trillion in 2003 (see Chapter 24). Commercial banks and investment banks are major participants in the market as dealers, traders, and users for proprietary hedging purposes. Insurance companies have only recently adopted hedging strategies using swaps, but their interest in this market is growing quickly. A swap dealer can act as an intermediary or third party by putting a swap together and/or creating an over-the-counter (OTC) secondary market for swaps for a fee. The massive growth of the swap market has raised regulatory concerns regarding the credit risk exposures of banks engaging in this market. This growth was one of the motivations behind the introduction of the Bank for International Settlements (BIS)–sponsored risk-based capital adequacy reforms described in Chapter 20. In addition, in recent years there has been a growth in exotic swap products such as "inverse floater" swaps that have raised considerable controversy—especially since the bankruptcy of Orange County and the legal suits filed against swap-selling banks and investment banks. Indeed, the legal costs and reputational damage emanating from the Orange County bankruptcy have been huge.

The five generic types of swaps, in order of their quantitative importance, are interest rate swaps, currency swaps, credit swaps, commodity swaps, and equity swaps.[1] While the instrument underlying the swap may change, the basic principle of a swap agreement is the same in that there is a restructuring of asset or liability cash flows in a preferred direction by the transacting parties. Next, we consider the role of the two major generic types of swaps—interest rate and currency—in hedging FI risk. We then go on to examine the newest and fastest growing type of swap: the credit swap.

INTEREST RATE SWAPS

interest rate swap
An exchange of fixed interest payments for floating interest payments by two counterparties.

By far the largest segment of the global swap market is comprised of **interest rate swaps.** Conceptually, an interest rate swap is a succession of forward contracts on interest rates arranged by two parties.[2] As such, it allows an FI to put in place a

---

[1] There are also *swaptions,* which are options to enter into a swap agreement at some preagreed contract terms (e.g., a fixed rate of 10 percent) at some time in the future in return for the payment of an up-front premium.

[2] See C. W. Smith, C. W. Smithson, and D. S. Wilford, *Managing Financial Risk* (Cambridge, MA: Ballinger Publishing, 1990). For example, a four-year swap with annual swap dates involves four net cash flows between the parties to a swap. This is essentially similar to arranging four forward contracts: a one-year, a two-year, a three-year, and a four-year contract.

TABLE 26-1
Money Center Bank
Balance Sheet

Assets		Liabilities	
C&I loans (rate indexed to LIBOR) =	$100 million	Medium-term notes (coupons fixed) =	$100 million

long-term hedge sometimes for as long as 15 years. This hedge reduces the need to roll over contracts if reliance had been placed on futures or forward contracts to achieve such long-term hedges.

swap buyer
By convention, makes the fixed-rate payments in an interest rate swap transaction.

swap seller
By convention, makes the floating-rate payments in an interest rate swap.

In a swap, the **swap buyer** agrees to make a number of fixed interest rate payments on periodic settlement dates to the **swap seller.** The seller of the swap in turn agrees to make floating-rate payments to the swap buyer on the same periodic settlement dates. The fixed-rate side—by convention, the swap buyer—generally has a comparative advantage in making fixed-rate payments, while the floating-rate side—by convention, the swap seller—generally has a comparative advantage in making variable or floating-rate payments. In undertaking this transaction, the FI that is the fixed-rate payer is seeking to transform the variable-rate nature of its liabilities into fixed-rate liabilities to better match the fixed returns earned on its assets. Meanwhile, the FI that is the variable-rate payer seeks to turn its fixed-rate liabilities into variable-rate liabilities to better match the variable returns on its assets.[3]

To explain the role of a swap transaction in hedging FI interest rate risk, we use a simple example. Consider two FIs: The first is a money center bank that has raised $100 million of its funds by issuing four-year, medium-term notes with 10 percent annual fixed coupons rather than relying on short-term deposits to raise funds (see Table 26–1). On the asset side of its portfolio, the bank makes commercial and industrial (C&I) loans whose rates are indexed to annual changes in the London Interbank Offered Rate (LIBOR). As we discussed in Chapter 11, banks currently index most large commercial and industrial loans to either LIBOR or the federal funds rate in the money market.

As a result of having floating-rate loans and fixed-rate liabilities in its asset-liability structure, the money center bank has a negative duration gap: the duration of its assets is shorter than that of its liabilities.

$$D_A - kD_L < 0$$

One way for the bank to hedge this exposure is to shorten the duration or interest rate sensitivity of its liabilities by transforming them into short-term floating-rate liabilities that better match the duration characteristics of its asset portfolio. The bank can make changes either on or off the balance sheet. On the balance sheet, the bank could attract an additional $100 million in short-term deposits that are indexed to the LIBOR rate (say, LIBOR plus 2.5 percent) in a manner similar to its loans. The proceeds of these deposits can be used to pay off the medium-term notes. This reduces the duration gap between the bank's assets and liabilities. Alternatively, the bank could go off the balance sheet and sell an interest rate swap—that is, enter into a swap agreement to make the floating-rate payment side of a swap agreement.

---

[3] In the early 2000s, record low interest rates and depressed equity values reduced the value of many defined benefit pension plan surpluses. To protect their surplus values from declining further, many pension plans entered into interest rate swaps that protected them from further falls in interest rates. See "Solving the Pension Puzzle," *Risk*, March 2002, pp. 23–25.

TABLE 26–2
The Savings Bank Balance Sheet

Assets	Liabilities
Fixed-rate mortgages = $100 million	Short-term CDs (one year) = $100 million

The second party in the swap is a thrift institution (savings bank) that has invested $100 million in fixed-rate residential mortgages of long duration. To finance this residential mortgage portfolio, the savings bank has had to rely on short-term certificates of deposit with an average duration of one year (see Table 26–2). On maturity, these CDs have to be rolled over at the current market rate.

Consequently, the savings bank's asset-liability balance sheet structure is the reverse of the money center bank's; that is,

$$D_A - kD_L > 0$$

The savings bank could hedge its interest rate risk exposure by transforming the short-term floating-rate nature of its liabilities into fixed-rate liabilities that better match the long-term maturity/duration structure of its assets. On the balance sheet, the thrift could issue long-term notes with a maturity equal or close to that on the mortgages (at, say, 12 percent). The proceeds of the sale of the notes can be used to pay off the CDs and reduce the duration gap. Alternatively, the thrift can buy a swap—take the fixed payment side of a swap agreement.

The opposing balance sheet and interest rate risk exposures of the money center bank and the savings bank provide the necessary conditions for an interest rate swap agreement between the two parties. This swap agreement can be arranged directly between the parties. However, it is likely that an FI—another bank or an investment bank—would act as either a broker or an agent, receiving a fee for bringing the two parties together or intermediating fully by accepting the credit risk exposure and guaranteeing the cash flows underlying the swap contract. By acting as a principal as well as an agent, the FI can add a credit risk premium to the fee. However, the credit risk exposure of a swap to an FI is somewhat less than that on a loan (this is discussed later in this chapter). Conceptually, when a third-party FI fully intermediates the swap, that FI is really entering into two separate swap agreements: one with the money center bank and one with the savings banks.

plain vanilla
Standard agreement without any special features.

For simplicity, we consider a **plain vanilla** fixed–floating rate swap where a third-party intermediary acts as a simple broker or agent by bringing together two FIs with opposing interest rate risk exposures to enter into a swap agreement or contract.

EXAMPLE 26–1

Expected Cash Flows on an Interest Rate Swap

Suppose the notional value of a swap is $100 million—equal to the assumed size of the money center bank's medium-term note issue—and the maturity of four years is equal to the maturity of the bank's note liabilities. The annual coupon cost of these note liabilities is 10 percent, and the money center bank's problem is that the variable return on its assets may be insufficient to cover the cost of meeting these coupon payments if market interest rates, and therefore asset returns, *fall*. By comparison, the fixed returns on the thrift's mortgage asset portfolio may be insufficient to cover the interest cost of its CDs if market rates *rise*. As a result, a feasible swap agreement might dictate that the thrift send fixed payments of 10 percent per annum of the notional $100 million value of the swap to the money center bank to allow the bank to cover fully the coupon interest payments on its note issue. In return, the money center bank sends annual payments indexed to one-year LIBOR to help the thrift cover

(continued)

FIGURE 26–1
Fixed–Floating
Rate Swap

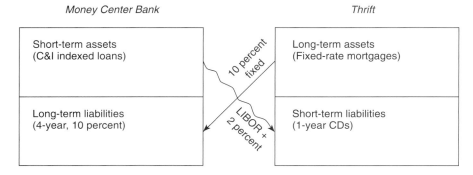

TABLE 26–3
Financing Cost
Resulting from
Interest Rate Swap
(in millions of
dollars)

	Money Center Bank	**Thrift**
Cash outflows from balance sheet financing	$-10\% \times \$100$	$-(CD) \times \$100$
Cash inflows from swap	$10\% \times \$100$	$(LIBOR + 2\%) \times \$100$
Cash outflows from swap	$-(LIBOR + 2\%) \times \$100$	$-10\% \times \$100$
Net cash flows	$-(LIBOR + 2\%) \times \$100$	$-(8\% + CD\ Rate - LIBOR) \times \$100$
Rate available on:		
Variable-rate debt	$LIBOR + 2\frac{1}{2}\%$	
Fixed-rate debt		12%

the cost of refinancing its one-year renewable CDs. Suppose that one-year LIBOR is currently 8 percent and the money center bank agrees to send annual payments at the end of each year equal to one-year LIBOR plus 2 percent to the thrift[4] We depict this fixed–floating rate swap transaction in Figure 26–1; the expected net financing costs for the FIs are listed in Table 26–3.

As a result of the swap, the money center bank has transformed its four-year, fixed-rate interest payments into variable-rate payments, matching the variability of returns on its assets. Further, through the interest rate swap, the money center bank effectively pays LIBOR plus 2 percent for its financing. Had it gone to the debt market, we assumed (on page 762) that the money center bank would pay LIBOR plus 2.5 percent (a savings of 0.5 percent with the swap). Further, the thrift has transformed its variable-rate interest payments into fixed-rate payments, plus a "small" variable component (CD rate − LIBOR), similar to those received on its assets. Had it gone to the debt market, we assumed (on page 763) that the savings bank would pay 12 percent (a savings of 4 percent + CD rate − LIBOR with the swap).

Note in Example 26–1 that in the absence of default/credit risk, only the money center bank is really fully hedged. This happens because the annual 10 percent payments it receives from the savings bank at the end of each year allow it to meet the promised 10 percent coupon rate payments to its note holders regardless of the return it receives on its variable-rate assets. By contrast, the savings bank receives variable-rate payments based on LIBOR plus 2 percent. However, it is quite possible that the CD rate the savings bank has to pay on its deposit liabilities does not exactly track the LIBOR-indexed payments sent by the money center bank. That is, the

[4] These rates implicitly assume that this is the cheapest way each party can hedge its interest rate exposure. For example, LIBOR + 2 percent is the lowest-cost way in which the money center bank can transform its fixed-rate liabilities into floating-rate liabilities.

savings bank is subject to basis risk exposure on the swap contract. There are two possible sources of this basis risk. First, CD rates do not exactly match the movements of LIBOR rates over time since the former are determined in the domestic money market and the latter in the Eurodollar market. Second, the credit/default risk premium on the savings bank's CDs may increase over time; thus, the +2 percent add-on to LIBOR may be insufficient to hedge the savings bank's cost of funds. The savings bank might be better hedged by requiring the money center bank to send it floating payments based on U.S. domestic CD rates rather than LIBOR. To do this, the money center bank would probably require additional compensation since it would then be bearing basis risk. Its asset returns would be sensitive to LIBOR movements while its swap payments were indexed to U.S. CD rates.

In analyzing this swap, one has to distinguish between how it should be priced at time 0 (now); that is, how the exchange rate of fixed (10 percent) for floating (LIBOR + 2 percent) is set when the swap agreement is initiated and the actual realized cash flows on the swap. As we discuss in Appendix 26A to this chapter, *fair pricing* on initiation of the swap depends on the market's expectations of future short-term rates, while realized cash flows on the swap depend on the actual market rates (here, LIBOR) that materialized over the life of the swap contract.

Realized Cash Flows on an Interest Rate Swap

EXAMPLE 26–2
Calculation of Realized Cash Flows

We assume that the realized or actual path of interest rates (LIBOR) over the four-year life of the contract would be

End of Year	LIBOR
1	9%
2	9
3	7
4	6

The money center bank's variable payments to the thrift were indexed to these rates by the formula

(LIBOR + 2%) × $100 million

By contrast, the fixed annual payments the thrift made to the money center bank were the same each year: 10% × $100 million. We summarize the actual or realized cash flows among the two parties over the four years in Table 26–4. The savings bank's net gains from the swap in years 1 and 2 are $1 million per year. The enhanced cash flow offsets the increased cost of refinancing its CDs in a higher interest rate environment—that is, the savings bank is hedged against rising rates. By contrast, the money center bank makes net gains on the swap in years 3 and 4 when rates fall; thus, it is hedged against falling rates. The positive cash flow from the swap offsets the decline in the variable returns on the money center bank's asset portfolio. Overall, the money center bank made a net dollar gain of $1 million in nominal dollars; its true realized gain would be the present value of this amount.

Swaps can always be molded or tailored to the needs of the transacting parties as long as one party is willing to compensate the other party for accepting nonstandard

TABLE 26–4
Realized Cash
Flows on the Swap
Agreement
(in millions of
dollars)

End of Year	One-Year LIBOR	One-Year LIBOR +2 percent	Cash Payment by MCB	Cash Payment by Savings Bank	Net Payment Made by MCB
1	9%	11%	$11	$10	$+1
2	9	11	11	10	+1
3	7	9	9	10	−1
4	6	8	8	10	−2
Total			$39	$40	$−1

FIGURE 26–2
Inverse Floater
Swap–Structured
Note

off-market swaps
Swaps that have non-standard terms that require one party to compensate another.

terms or **off-market swap** arrangements, usually in the form of an up-front fee or payments. Relaxing a standardized swap can include special interest rate terms and indexes as well as allowing for varying notional values underlying the swap.

For example, in the case we just considered, the notional value of the swap was fixed at $100 million for each of the four annual swap dates. However, swap notional values can be allowed either to decrease or to increase over a swap contract's life. This flexibility is useful when one of the parties has heavy investments in mortgages (in our example, the savings bank) and the mortgages are **fully amortized,** meaning that the annual and monthly cash flows on the mortgage portfolio reflect repayments of both principal and interest such that the periodic payment is kept constant (see Chapter 28). Fixed-rate mortgages normally have larger payments of interest than principal in the early years, with the interest component falling as mortgages approach maturity. One possibility is for the savings bank to enter into a mortgage swap to hedge the amortizing nature of the mortgage portfolio or alternatively to allow the notional value of the swap to decline at a rate similar to the decline in the principal component of the mortgage portfolio.[5]

fully amortized mortgages
Mortgage portfolio cash flows that have a constant payment.

Another example of a special type of interest rate swap is the inverse floater swap, which was engineered by major FIs as part of structured note financing deals to lower the cost of financing to various government agencies. Such arrangements have resulted in enormous problems for investor groups such as municipal authorities and corporations that are part of the overall swap deal.

A structured note–inverse floater swap arrangement is shown in Figure 26–2. In this arrangement, a government agency issues notes (say, $100 million) to investors with a coupon that is equal to 7 percent minus LIBOR—that is, an (inverse) floating coupon. The novel feature of this coupon is that when market rates fall (and thus LIBOR is low), the coupon received by the investor is large. The government agency then converts this spread liability (7 percent − LIBOR) into a LIBOR liability by entering into a swap with an FI dealer (e.g., a bank such as J. P. Morgan Chase). In effect, the cost of the $100 million note issue is LIBOR to the agency plus any fees relating to the swap.

---

[5] For further details of nonstandard swaps, see P. A. Abken, "Beyond Plain Vanilla: A Taxonomy of Swaps," Federal Reserve Bank of Atlanta, *Economic Review*, March–April 1991, pp. 21–29; and C. James and C. Smith, "The Use of Index Amortizing Swaps by Banc One," *Journal of Applied Corporate Finance* 7, no. 5 (Fall 1994), pp. 54–59.

The risk of these notes to the investor is very clear. If LIBOR is 2 percent, then the investor will receive coupons of 7 percent − 2 percent = 5 percent, which is an excellent spread return if the investor can borrow at close to LIBOR (or 2 percent in this case). However, consider what happens if interest rates rise. If LIBOR rises from 2 to 8 percent, the promised coupon becomes 7 percent − 8 percent = −1 percent. Since negative coupons cannot be paid, the actual coupon paid to the investor is 0 percent. However, if the investor borrowed funds to buy the notes at LIBOR, the cost of funds is 8 percent in this case. Thus, the investor is facing an extremely large negative spread and loss.

Macrohedging with Swaps

The duration model shown in Chapters 24 and 25 to estimate the optimal number of futures and options contracts to hedge an FI's duration gap also can be applied to estimate the optimal number of swap contracts. For example, an FI manager might wish to know how many 10-year (or 5-year) swap contracts are needed to hedge its overall risk exposure. The optimal notional value of swap contracts should be set so that the gain on swap contracts entered into off the balance sheet just offsets any loss in net worth on the balance sheet when interest rates change.

Assume that an FI (such as a thrift) has a positive duration gap so that it has positive net worth exposure to rising interest rates:

$$\Delta E = -(D_A - kD_L)A \frac{\Delta R}{1 + R} > 0$$

As discussed above, the thrift can seek to hedge by paying fixed and receiving floating payments through an interest rate swap. However, many different maturity swaps are available. As will be shown below, the size of the notional value of the interest rate swaps entered into will depend on the maturity (duration) of the swap contract. Suppose the FI manager chooses to hedge with 10-year swaps.

In terms of valuation, a 10-year swap arrangement can be considered in terms of bond equivalent valuation. That is, the fixed-rate payments on a 10-year swap are formally equivalent to the fixed payments on a 10-year T-bond. Similarly, the floating-rate payments on a 10-year swap with *annual* payments can be viewed as equivalent to floating coupons on a bond where coupons are repriced (to LIBOR) every year. That is, the change in the value of the swap (ΔS) when interest rates ($\Delta R/(1 + R)$) rise will depend on the relative interest sensitivity of 10-year bonds to 1-year bonds, or in duration terms, $(D_{10} - D_1)$.[6] In general,

$$\Delta S = -(D_{fixed} - D_{float}) \times N_S \times \frac{\Delta R}{1 + R}$$

where

$$\Delta S = \text{Change in the market value of the swap contract}$$

$(D_{fixed} - D_{float}) = $ Difference in durations between a government bond that has the same maturity and coupon as the fixed-payment side of the swap and a government bond that has the same duration as the swap-payment interval (e.g., annual floating payments)

$$N_S = \text{Notional value of swap contracts}$$

$$\frac{\Delta R}{1 + R} = \text{Shock to interest rates}$$

---

[6] Although principal payments on bonds are not swapped on maturity, this does not matter since the theoretical payment and receipt of principal values cancel each other out.

Note that as long as $D_{fixed} > D_{float}$, when interest rates rise, the market (present) value of fixed-rate payments will fall by more than the market (present) value of floating-rate payments; in market (or present) value terms, the fixed-rate payers gain when rates rise and lose when rates fall.

To solve for the optimal notional value of swap contracts,[7] we set

$$\Delta S = \Delta E$$

The gain on swap contracts entered into off the balance sheet just offsets the loss in net worth on the balance sheet when rates rise. Substituting values for ΔS and ΔE

$$-(D_{fixed} - D_{float}) \times N_S \times \frac{\Delta R}{1+R} = -(D_A - kD_L) \times A \times \frac{\Delta R}{1+R}$$

Canceling out the common terms

$$(D_{fixed} - D_{float}) \times N_S = (D_A - kD_L) \times A$$

Solving for N_S

$$N_S = \frac{(D_A - kD_L) \times A}{D_{fixed} - D_{float}}$$

EXAMPLE 26–3

Calculating the Notional Value of Swaps in a Macrohedge

Suppose $D_A = 5$, $D_L = 3$, $k = .9$, and $A = \$100,000,000$. Also, assume the duration of a current 10-year, fixed-rate T-bond with the same coupon as the fixed rate on the swap is seven years, while the duration of a floating-rate bond that reprices annually is one year:[8]

$$D_{fixed} = 7 \quad \text{and} \quad D_{float} = 1$$

Then:

$$N_S = \frac{(D_A - kD_L) \times A}{D_{fixed} - D_{float}} = \frac{\$230,000,000}{(7-1)} = \$38,333,333$$

If each swap contract is \$100,000 in size,[9] the number of swap contracts into which the FI should enter will be \$38,333,333/\$100,000 = 383.33, or 383 contracts, rounding down. Table 26–5 summarizes the key features of the hedge assuming that the initial rate on the T-bond is 10 percent and is expected to rise by 1 percent. As shown in Table 26–5, the loss of \$2.09 million in net worth on the balance sheet is exactly offset by a gain off the balance sheet on the swap hedge.

If the FI engaged in a longer-term swap—for example, 15 years—such that $D_{fixed} = 9$ and $D_{float} = 1$, then the notional value of swap contracts would fall to \$230,000,000/(9 − 1) = \$28,750,000. If each swap contract is \$100,000 in size, the FI should enter into 287 swap contracts.

While it may seem logical that fewer contracts are preferable in the sense of saving on fees and other related costs of hedging, this advantage is offset by the fact

---

[7] Note that the FI wants to enter swaps to protect itself against rising rates. Thus, it will pay fixed and receive floating. In the context of swap transactions, when an FI pays fixed, it is said to be "buying swaps." Thus, we are solving for the optimal number of swaps contracts the FI should buy in this example.

[8] See Chapter 8 for a discussion of the duration on floating-rate bonds.

[9] The notional value of swap contracts can take virtually any size since they are individually tailored OTC contracts.

TABLE 26–5
On- and Off-
Balance Sheet
Effects of a Swap
Hedge

	On Balance Sheet	Off Balance Sheet
Begin hedge, $t = 0$	Equity exposed to impact of rise in interest rates	Sell interest rate swap
End hedge, $t = 1$	Interest rates rise on assets and liabilities by 1%	Buy interest rate swap

Opportunity loss on balance sheet:
$\Delta E = -[5 - .9(3)] \times \$100m \times (.01/(1.1))]$
$\qquad = -\$2.09$ million

Gain on interest rate swap:
$\Delta S = [(7-1) \times \$38,333,333 \times (.01/(1.1))]$
$\qquad = \$2.09$ million

that longer-term swaps have greater counterparty default or credit risk (discussed later in this chapter).

Concept Questions

1. In Example 26–2, which of the two FIs has its liability costs fully hedged and which is only partially hedged? Explain your answer.
2. What are some nonstandard terms that might be encountered in an off-market swap?
3. In Example 26–3, what is the notional size of swap contracts if $D_{fixed} = 5$ and swap contracts require payment every six months? ($N_s = \$51,111,111$)

CURRENCY SWAPS

currency swap
A swap used to hedge against exchange rate risk from mismatched currencies on assets and liabilities.

Just as swaps are long-term contracts that can hedge interest rate risk exposure, they can also be used to hedge currency risk exposures of FIs. The following section considers a simple plain vanilla example of how **currency swaps** can immunize FIs against exchange rate risk when they mismatch the currencies of their assets and liabilities.

Fixed-Fixed Currency Swaps

Consider a U.S. FI with all of its fixed-rate assets denominated in dollars. It is financing part of its asset portfolio with a £50 million issue of four-year, medium-term British pound sterling notes that have a fixed annual coupon of 10 percent. By comparison, there is a U.K. FI that has all its assets denominated in sterling; it is partly funding those assets with a $100 million issue of four-year, medium-term dollar notes with a fixed annual coupon of 10 percent.

These two FIs are exposed to opposing currency risks. The U.S. FI is exposed to the risk that the dollar will depreciate against the pound over the next four years, making it more costly to cover the annual coupon interest payments and the principal repayment on its pound-denominated notes. On the other hand, the U.K. FI is exposed to the dollar appreciating against the pound, making it more difficult to cover the dollar coupon and principal payments on its four-year $100 million note issue out of the sterling cash flows on its assets.

The FIs can hedge the exposures either on or off the balance sheet. Assume that the dollar/pound exchange rate is fixed at $2/£1. On the balance sheet, the U.S. FI can issue $100 million in four-year, medium-term dollar notes (at, say, 10.5 percent). The proceeds of the sale can be used to pay off the £50 million of four-year, medium-term sterling notes. Similarly, the U.K. FI can issue £50 million in four-year, medium-term sterling notes (at, say, 10.5 percent), using the proceeds to pay off the $100 million of four-year, medium-term dollar notes. Both FIs have taken actions on the balance sheet so that they are no longer exposed to movements in the exchange rate between the two currencies.

FIGURE 26–3
Fixed-Fixed
Pound/Dollar
Currency Swap

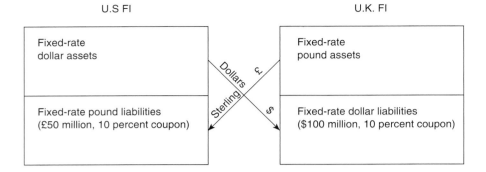

TABLE 26–6
Financing Costs
Resulting from the
Fixed-Fixed
Currency Swap
Agreement
(in millions of
dollars)

	U.S. FI	**U.K. FI**
Cash outflows from balance sheet financing	$-10\% \times$ £50	$-10\% \times$ \$100
Cash inflows from swap	$10\% \times$ £50	$10\% \times$ \$100
Cash outflows from swap	$-10\% \times$ \$100	$-10\% \times$ £50
Net cash flows	$-10\% \times$ \$100	$-10\% \times$ £50
Rate available on		
Dollar-denominated notes	10.5%	
Pound-denominated notes		10.5%

EXAMPLE 26–4
*Expected Cash
Flows on Fixed-
Fixed Currency
Swap.*

Rather than make changes on the balance sheet, a feasible currency swap in which the U.K. and U.S. FIs can enter is one under which the U.K. FI sends annual payments in pounds to cover the coupon and principal repayments of the U.S. FI's pound sterling note issue, and the U.S. FI sends annual dollar payments to the U.K. FI to cover the interest and principal payments on its dollar note issue.[10] We summarize the currency swap in Figure 26–3 and Table 26–6. As a result of the swap, the U.K. FI transforms fixed-rate dollar payments into fixed-rate sterling payments that better match the sterling fixed-rate cash flows from its asset portfolio. Similarly, the U.S. FI transforms fixed-rate sterling payments into fixed-rate dollar payments that better match the fixed-rate dollar cash flows from its asset portfolio. Further, both FIs transform the pattern of their payments at a lower rate than if they had made changes on the balance sheet. Both FIs effectively obtain financing at 10 percent while hedging against exchange rate risk. Had they gone to the market, we assumed above that they would have paid 10.5 percent to do this. In undertaking this exchange of cash flows, the two parties normally agree on a fixed exchange rate for the cash flows at the beginning of the period.[11] In this example, the fixed exchange rate would be \$2/£1.

In this example, both liabilities bear a fixed 10 percent interest rate. This is not a necessary requirement for the fixed-fixed currency swap agreement. For example, suppose that the U.S. FI's note coupons were 5 percent per annum, while the U.K. FI's note coupons were 10 percent. The swap dollar payments of the U.S. FI would remain unchanged, but the U.K. FI's sterling payments would be reduced by

---

[10] In a currency swap, it is usual to include both principal and interest payments as part of the swap agreement. For interest rate swaps, it is usual to include just interest rate payments. The reason for this is that both principal and interest are exposed to FX risk.

[11] As with interest rate swaps, this exchange rate reflects the contracting parties' expectations in regard to future exchange rate movements.

£2.5 million (or $5 million) in each of the four years. This difference could be met either by some up-front payment by the U.K. FI to the U.S. FI, reflecting the difference in the present value of the two fixed cash flows, or by annual payments that result in zero net present value differences among the fixed-fixed currency swap participants' payments. Also note that if the exchange rate changed from the rate agreed in the swap ($2/£1), either one or the other side would be losing in the sense that a new swap might be entered into at an exchange rate more favorable to one party. Specifically, if the dollar were to appreciate (rise in value) against the pound over the life of the swap, the agreement would become more costly for the U.S. FI. If, however, the dollar were to depreciate (fall in value), the U.K. FI would find the agreement increasingly costly over the swap's life.

By combining an interest rate swap of the fixed-floating type described earlier with a currency swap, we can also produce a fixed-floating currency swap that is a hybrid of the two plain vanilla swaps we have considered so far.

Fixed-Floating Currency Swaps

EXAMPLE 26–5

Financing Costs Associated with a Fixed-Floating Currency Swap

Consider a U.S. FI that primarily holds floating-rate, short-term U.S. dollar–denominated assets. It has partly financed this asset portfolio with a £50 million, four-year note issue with fixed 10 percent annual coupons denominated in sterling. By comparison, a U.K. FI that primarily holds long-term, fixed-rate assets denominated in sterling has partly financed this portfolio with $100 million short-term dollar-denominated Euro CDs whose rates reflect changes in one-year LIBOR plus a 2 percent premium. As a result, the U.S. FI is faced with both an interest rate risk and a foreign exchange risk. Specifically, if dollar short-term rates fall and the dollar depreciates against the pound, the FI may face a problem in covering its promised fixed-coupon and principal payments on the pound-denominated note. Consequently, it may wish to transform its fixed-rate, pound-denominated liabilities into variable-rate, dollar-denominated liabilities. The U.K. FI also faces interest rate and foreign exchange rate risk exposures. If U.S. interest rates rise and the dollar appreciates against the pound, the U.K. FI will find it more difficult to cover its promised coupon and principal payments on its dollar-denominated CDs out of the cash flows from its fixed-rate pound asset portfolio. Consequently, it may wish to transform its floating-rate, short-term, dollar-denominated liabilities into fixed-rate pound liabilities.

Both FIs can make changes on the balance sheet to hedge the interest rate and foreign exchange rate risk exposure. The U.S. FI can issue $100 million U.S. dollar-dominated, floating-rate, short-term debt (at, say, LIBOR plus 2.5 percent), the proceeds of which can be used to pay off the existing £50 million four-year note. The U.K. FI can issue £50 million in four-year notes (at, say, 11 percent) and use the proceeds to pay off the $100 million in short-term Euro CDs. Both FIs, by changing the financing used on the balance sheet, hedge both the interest rate and foreign exchange rate risk. We again assume that the dollar/pound exchange rate is $2/£1.

Alternatively, each FI can achieve its objective of liability transformation by engaging in a fixed-floating currency swap. A feasible swap would be one in which each year, the two FIs swap payments at some prearranged dollar/pound exchange rate, assumed to be $2/£1. The U.K. FI sends fixed payments in pounds to cover the cost of the U.S. FI's pound-denominated note issue, while the U.S. FI sends floating payments in dollars to cover the U.K. FI's floating-rate dollar CD costs. The resulting expected financing costs are calculated in Table 26–7. As a result of the fixed-floating currency swap, both FIs have hedged interest rate and foreign exchange rate risk and have done so at a rate below what they could have achieved by making on-balance-sheet changes. The U.S. FI's net financing cost is LIBOR plus 2 percent with the swap, compared to LIBOR plus 2.5 percent in the debt market. The U.K. FI's financing cost is 10 percent with the swap, compared to 11 percent had it refinanced on the balance sheet.

Given the realized LIBOR rates in column (2), we show the relevant payments among the contracting parties in Table 26–8. The realized cash flows from the swap result in a net nominal payment of $2 million by the U.S. FI to the U.K. FI over the life of the swap.

TABLE 26–7   Financing Costs Resulting from the Fixed-Floating Currency Swap (in millions of dollars)

	U.S. FI	U.K. FI
Cash outflows from balance sheet financing	−10% × £50	−(LIBOR + 2%) × $100
Cash inflows from swap	10% × £50	(LIBOR + 2%) × $100
Cash outflows from swap	−(LIBOR + 2%) × $100	−10% × £50
Net cash outflows	−(LIBOR + 2%) × $100	−10% × £50
Rate available on		
Dollar-denominated variable-rate debt	LIBOR + 2½%	
Pound-denominated fixed-rate debt		11%

TABLE 26–8
Realized Cash Flows on a Fixed-Floating Currency Swap (in millions of dollars)

Year	LIBOR	LIBOR +2 percent	Floating Rate Payment by U.S. Bank ($s)	Fixed Rate Payment by U.K. FI (£s)	($ at $2/£1)	Net Payment by U.S. FI ($s)
1	9%	11%	$ 11	£5	$ 10	$+1
2	7	9	9	5	10	−1
3	8	10	10	5	10	0
4	10	12	112	55	110	+2
Total net payment						$+2

Concept Questions

1. Referrring to the fixed-fixed currency swap in Table 26–6, if the net cash flows on the swap are zero, why does either FI enter into the swap agreement?
2. Referring to Table 26–8, suppose that the U.S. FI had agreed to make floating payments of LIBOR + 1 percent instead of LIBOR + 2 percent. What would its net payment have been to the U.K. FI over the four-year swap agreement?

CREDIT SWAPS

In recent years the fastest growing types of swaps have been those developed to better allow FIs to hedge their credit risk. This is important for two reasons. First, credit risk is still more likely to cause an FI to fail than is either interest rate risk or FX risk. Second, credit swaps allow FIs to maintain long-term customer lending relationships without bearing the full credit risk exposure from those relationships. Indeed, Federal Reserve Board Chairman Alan Greenspan has credited this market with helping the banking system maintain its strength through an economic recession in the early 2000s. He argued that credit swaps were effectively used to shift a significant part of banks' risk from their corporate loan portfolios.[12] For example, significant exposures to telecommunication firms were hedged by banks through credit swaps. However, the Fed chairman also commented that these derivative securities are prone to induce speculative excesses that need to be contained through regulation, supervision, and private sector action.[13]

---

[12] Much of this risk exposure was absorbed by domestic and foreign insurance and reinsurance companies.
[13] See "Derivatives Growth Has Helped Banks, Greenspan Says," *The Wall Street Journal*, October 8, 2002, p. A2.

FIGURE 26–4
Cash Flows on a
Total Return Swap

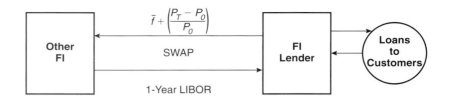

TABLE 26–9   Cash Flows on a Total Return Swap

	Annual Cash Flow for Year 1 through Final Year	Additional Payment by FI	Total Return
Cash inflow on swap to FI lender	1-year LIBOR (11%)	—	1-year LIBOR (11%)
Cash outflow on swap to other FI	Fixed rate ($\bar{f}$) (12%)	$P_T - P_0$ (90 2 100)	$\left[\bar{f} + \dfrac{P_T - P_0}{P_0}\right]$
			$(12\% + \dfrac{90 - 100}{100} = 12\% - 10\% = 2\%)$
		Net profit	9%

Below we look at two types of credit swaps: (1) the total return swap and (2) the pure credit swap. We then look at credit risk concerns with the swaps themselves.

Total Return Swaps

total return swap
A swap involving an obligation to pay interest at a specified fixed or floating rate for payments representing the total return on a specified amount.

Although FIs spend significant resources attempting to evaluate and price expected changes in a borrower's credit risk over the life of a loan, a borrower's credit situation (credit quality) sometimes deteriorates unexpectedly after the loan terms are determined and the loan is issued. A lender can use a total return swap to hedge this possible change in credit risk exposure. A **total return swap** involves swapping an obligation to pay interest at a specified fixed or floating rate for payments representing the total return on a loan or a bond (interest and principal value changes) of a specified amount.

EXAMPLE 26–6
Calculation of Cash Flows on a Total Return Swap

Suppose that an FI lends $100 million to a Brazilian manufacturing firm at a fixed rate of 10 percent. If the firm's credit risk increases unexpectedly over the life of the loan, the market value of the loan and consequently the FI's net worth will fall. The FI can hedge an unexpected increase in the borrower's credit risk by entering into a total return swap in which it agrees to pay a total return based on an annual fixed rate (f) plus changes in the market value of Brazilian (U.S. dollar–denominated) government debt (changes in the value of these bonds reflect the political and economic events in the firm's home country and thus will be correlated with the credit risk of the Brazilian borrowing firm). Also, the bonds are in the same currency (U.S. dollars) as the loans. In return, the FI receives a variable market rate payment of interest annually (e.g., one-year LIBOR rate). Figure 26–4 and Table 26–9 illustrate the cash flows associated with the typical total return swap for the FI.

(continued)

Using the total return swap, the FI agrees to pay a fixed rate of interest annually and the capital gain or loss on the market value of the Brazilian (U.S. dollar) bond over the period of the hedge. In Figure 26–4, P_0 denotes the market value of the bond at the beginning of the swap period and P_T represents the market value of the bond at the end of the swap period. If the Brazilian bond decreases in value over the period of the hedge ($P_0 > P_T$), the FI pays a relatively small (possibly negative) amount to the counterparty equal to the fixed payment on the swap minus the capital loss[14] on the bond. For example, suppose the Brazilian (U.S. dollar) bond was priced at par ($P_0 = 100$) at the beginning of the swap period. At the end of the swap period or the payment date, the Brazilian bond had a secondary market value of 90 ($P_T = 90$) due to an increase in Brazilian country risk. Suppose that the fixed-rate payment ($\bar{f}$) as part of the total return swap was 12 percent; then the FI would send to the swap counterparty the fixed rate of 12 percent minus 10 percent (the capital loss on the Brazilian bond), or a total of 2 percent, and would receive in return a floating payment (e.g., LIBOR = 11 percent) from the counterparty to the swap. Thus, the net profit on the swap to the FI lender is 9 percent (11 percent minus 2 percent) times the notional amount of the swap contract. This gain can be used to offset the loss of market value on the loan to the Brazilian firm. This example is illustrated in Table 26–9.[15]

Thus, the FI benefits from the total return swap if the Brazilian bond value deteriorates as a result of a political or economic shock. Assuming that the Brazilian firm's credit risk deteriorates along with the local economy, the FI will offset some of this loss of the Brazilian loan on its balance sheet with a gain from the total return swap.

Note that hedging credit risk in this fashion allows the FI to maintain its customer relationship with the Brazilian firm (and perhaps earn fees from selling other financial services to that firm) without bearing a large amount of credit risk exposure. Moreover, since the Brazilian loan remains on the FI's balance sheet, the Brazilian firm may not even know its loan is being hedged. This would not be the case if the FI sought to reduce its risk by selling all or part of the loan (see Chapter 27). Finally, the swap does not completely hedge credit risk in this case. Specifically, basis risk is present to the extent that the credit risk of the Brazilian firm's US. dollar loan is imperfectly correlated with Brazilian country risk reflected in the price of the Brazilian (U.S. dollar) bonds.[16]

Pure Credit Swaps

While total return swaps can be used to hedge credit risk exposure, they contain an element of interest rate risk as well as credit risk. For example, in Table 26–9, if the LIBOR rate changes due to Federal Reserve monetary policy, the *net* cash flows on the total return swap also will change—even though the credit risks of the underlying loans (and bonds) have not changed.

To strip out the "interest rate" sensitive element of total return swaps, an alternative swap has been developed called a **"pure" credit swap.** In this case, as shown in Figure 26–5, the FI lender will send (each swap period) a fixed fee or

pure credit swap
A swap by which an FI receives the par value of the loan on default in return for paying a periodic swap fee.

[14] Total return swaps are typically structured so that the capital gain or loss is paid at the end of the swap. However, an alternative structure does exist in which the capital gain or loss is paid at the end of each interest period during the swap.

[15] For additional discussion, see J. D. Finnerty, "Credit Derivatives, Infrastructure Finance, and Emerging Market Risk," *The Financier, ACMT,* February 1996, pp. 64–75.

[16] In many swaps, the total return on a loan (rather than a bond as in this example) is swapped for a floating payment such as LIBOR. In this case, $\bar{f}$ would equal any fees paid for loan origination and $((P_T - P_0)/P_0)$ would reflect the estimated change in market value of the loan as perceived by brokers/traders in the secondary market for loan sales. The secondary market for loans is described in Chapter 27.

FIGURE 26–5
A Pure Credit Swap

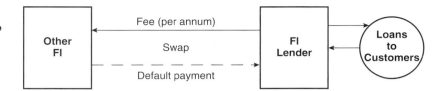

payment (like an insurance premium) to the FI counterparty. If the FI lender's loan or loans do not default, it will receive nothing back from the FI counterparty. However, if the loan or loans default, the FI counterparty will cover the default loss by making a default payment that is often equal to the par value of the original loan (e.g., $P_0 = \$100$) minus the secondary market value of the defaulted loan (e.g., $P_T = \$40$); that is, the FI counterparty will pay $P_0 - P_T$ (or $60, in this example).[17] Thus, a pure credit swap is like buying credit insurance and/or a multiperiod credit option.

SWAPS AND CREDIT RISK CONCERNS

www.bis.org

The growth of the over-the-counter (OTC) swap market was one of the major motivating factors underlying the imposition of the BIS risk-based capital requirements in January 1993 (see Chapter 20). The fear was that in a long-term OTC swap-type contract, the out-of-the-money counterparty would have incentives to default to deter future and current losses. Consequently, the BIS requirements imposed a required capital ratio for depository institutions against their holdings of both interest rate and currency swaps (and, more recently, other types of swaps, including credit swaps). Many analysts have argued that these capital requirements work against the growth of the swap market since they can be viewed as a cost or tax on market participants.

Both regulators and market participants have a heightened awareness of credit risks. If the transaction is not structured carefully, it may pass along unintended risks to participants, exposing them to higher frequency and severity of losses than if they had held an equivalent cash position.[18] As defined by Moody's Investor Service, default risk on swaps comes from three sources: (1) any missed or delayed payment of interest and/or principal; (2) bankruptcy or receivership; and (3) distressed exchange, where the borrower offers debtholders a new security that amounts to a diminished financial obligation, or the swap dealer has the apparent purpose of helping the borrower avoid default. Both Merrill Lynch and J. P. Morgan Chase are heavy participants as intermediaries in the swap market; for example, they act as counterparty guarantors to both the fixed and floating sides in swaps. To do this successfully and to maintain market share, a high if not the highest credit rating is increasingly required.

This raises a question: Is credit or default risk on swaps the same as or different from the credit or default risk on loans? In fact, there are three major differences between the credit risk on swaps and the credit risk on loans. As a result, the credit

www.moodys.com

---

[17] While a pure credit swap is like a default option (e.g., the digital default option in Chapter 25), a key difference is that the fee (or premium) payments on the swap are paid over the life of the swap, whereas for a default option the whole fee (premium) is paid up front.

[18] See J. S. Tolk, "Understanding the Risks in Credit Default Swaps," *The Financier,* Spring 2002, pp. 87–100.

risk on a swap is generally much less than that on a loan.[19] We discuss these differences next.[20]

Netting and Swaps

One factor that mitigates the credit risk on swaps is the netting of swap payments. On each swap payment date, a fixed payment is made by one party and a floating payment is made by the other. However, in general, each party calculates the net difference between the two payments, and a single payment for the net difference is made by one party to the other. This netting of payments implies that the default exposure of the in-the-money party is limited to the net payment rather than either the total fixed or floating payment. Further, when two parties have large numbers of contracts outstanding against each other, they tend to net across contracts. This process, called *netting by novation*—often formalized through a master netting agreement in the United States—further reduces the potential risk of loss if some contracts are in the money and other are out of the money to the same counterparty.[21] However, note that netting by novation has not been fully tested in all international courts of law. For example, in the 1990s a number of U.K. municipal authorities engaged in swaps with U.S. and U.K. banks and investment banks. These municipal authorities, after taking major losses on some swap contracts, defaulted on further payments. The U.K. High Court supported the municipal authorities' right to default by stating that their entering into such swaps had been outside their powers of authority in the first place. This still did not stop these municipal authorities from seeking to collect on in-the-money swaps.

Payment Flows Are Interest and Not Principal

While currency swaps involve swaps of interest and principal, interest rate swaps involve swaps of interest payments only measured against some notional principal value. This suggests that the default risk on such swaps is less than that on a regular loan, where both interest and principal are exposed to credit risk.

Standby Letters of Credit

In cases where swaps are made between parties of different credit standing, such that one party perceives a significant risk of default by the other party, the poor-quality credit risk party may be required to buy a standby letter of credit (or another form of performance guaranty) from a third-party high-quality (AA) FI such that if default occurs, the standby letter of credit will provide the swap payments in lieu of the defaulting party. Further, low-quality counterparties are increasingly

---

[19] As with loans, swap participants deal with the credit risk of counterparties by setting bilateral limits on the notional amount of swaps entered into (similar to credit rationing on loans) as well as adjusting the fixed and/or floating rates by including credit risk premiums. For example, a low-credit-quality fixed-rate payer may have to pay an additional spread to a high-credit-quality floating-rate payer. For a discussion on pricing swap default risk, see E. H. Sorensen and T. F. Bollier, "Pricing Swap Default Risk," *Financial Analyst's Journal,* May–June 1994, pp. 23–33.

[20] See also A. Saunders and L. Allen, *Credit Risk Measurement, New Approaches to Value at Risk and Other Paradigms,* 2nd ed. (New York: John Wiley & Sons, 2002), chapters 14 and 15; and C. Finger, "Credit Derivatives in Credit Metrics," *The Financier,* Winter 1999, pp. 18–27.

[21] In January 1995, FASB Interpretation No. 39 (FIN 39) established the right of setoff under a master netting agreement. Also, since 1995, the BIS has allowed banks to use bilateral netting of swap contracts in calculating their risk-based capital requirements (see Chapter 20). It is estimated that this reduces banks' capital requirements against swaps by up to 40 percent. See also D. Hendricks, "Netting Agreements and the Credit Exposures of OTC Derivatives Portfolios," Federal Reserve Bank of New York, *Quarterly Review,* Spring 1994.

required to post collateral in lieu of default. This collateral is an incentive mechanism working to deter swap defaults.[22]

Concept Questions

1. What is the link between preserving "customer relationships" and credit derivatives such as total return swaps?
2. Is there any difference between a digital default option (see Chapter 25) and a pure credit swap?
3. Are swaps as risky as equivalent-sized loans?

Summary

This chapter evaluated the role of swaps as risk-management vehicles for FIs. We analyzed the major types of swaps: interest rate and currency swaps as well as credit swaps. Swaps have special features of long maturity, flexibility, and liquidity that make them attractive alternatives relative to shorter-term hedging vehicles such as the futures, forwards, options, and caps discussed in Chapters 24 and 25. However, even though the credit risk of swaps is less than that of loans, because of their OTC nature and long maturities, their credit risk is still generally greater than that for other OTC derivative instruments such as floors and caps. Also, the credit risk on swaps compares unfavorably with that on exchange-traded futures and options, whose credit risk is approximately zero.

Questions and Problems

1. Explain the similarity between a swap and a forward contract.
2. Forwards, futures, and options contracts had been used by FIs to hedge risk for many years before swaps were invented. If FIs already had these hedging instruments, why did they need swaps?
3. Distinguish between a swap buyer and a swap seller. In which markets does each have the comparative advantage?
4. An insurance company owns $50 million of floating-rate bonds yielding LIBOR plus 1 percent. These loans are financed by $50 million of fixed-rate guaranteed investment contracts (GICs) costing 10 percent. A finance company has $50 million of auto loans with a fixed rate of 14 percent. The loans are financed by $50 million in CDs at a variable rate of LIBOR plus 4 percent.
   a. What is the risk exposure of the insurance company?
   b. What is the risk exposure of the finance company?
   c. What would be the cash flow goals of each company if they were to enter into a swap arrangement?

www.mhhe.com/saunders5e

---

[22] One solution being considered by market participants (such as the International Association of Swap Dealers) is to use collateral to mark to market a swap contract in a way similar to that in which futures are marked to market to prevent credit risk building up over time. Remember, a swap contract is like a succession of forwards. A survey by Arthur Andersen showed that approximately $6.9 billion was posted as collateral against a net replacement value of $77.9 billion of swaps. (See "A Question of Collateral," *Euromoney*, November 1995, pp. 46–49.)

d. Which company would be the buyer and which company would be the seller in the swap?

e. Diagram the direction of the relevant cash flows for the swap arrangement.

f. What are reasonable cash flow amounts, or relative interest rates, for each of the payment streams?

5. In a swap arrangement, the variable-rate swap cash flow streams often do not fully hedge the variable-rate cash flow streams from the balance sheet due to basis risk.

a. What are the possible sources of basis risk in an interest rate swap?

b. How could the failure to achieve a perfect hedge be realized by the swap buyer?

c. How could the failure to achieve a perfect hedge be realized by the swap seller?

6. A commercial bank has $200 million of floating-rate loans yielding the T-bill rate plus 2 percent. These loans are financed by $200 million of fixed-rate deposits costing 9 percent. A savings bank has $200 million of mortgages with a fixed rate of 13 percent. They are financed by $200 million in CDs with a variable rate of the T-bill rate plus 3 percent.

a. Discuss the type of interest rate risk each FI faces.

b. Propose a swap that would result in each FI having the same type of asset and liability cash flows.

c. Show that this swap would be acceptable to both parties.

d. What are some of the practical difficulties in arranging this swap?

7. Bank 1 can issue five-year CDs at an annual rate of 11 percent fixed or at a variable rate of LIBOR plus 2 percent. Bank 2 can issue five-year CDs at an annual rate of 13 percent fixed or at a variable rate of LIBOR plus 3 percent.

a. Is a mutually beneficial swap possible between the two banks?

b. Where is the comparative advantage of the two banks?

c. What is the net quality spread?

d. What is an example of a feasible swap?

8. First Bank can issue one-year floating-rate CDs at prime plus 1 percent or fixed-rate CDs at 12.5 percent. Second Bank can issue one-year floating-rate CDs at prime plus 0.5 percent or fixed-rate CDs at 11 percent.

a. What is a feasible swap with all the benefits going to First Bank?

b. What is a feasible swap with all the benefits going to Second Bank?

c. Diagram each situation.

d. What factors will determine the final swap arrangement?

9. Two multinational corporations enter their respective debt markets to issue $100 million of two-year notes. Firm A can borrow at a fixed annual rate of 11 percent or a floating rate of LIBOR plus 50 basis points, repriced at the end of the year. Firm B can borrow at a fixed annual rate of 10 percent or a floating rate of LIBOR, repriced at the end of the year.

a. If firm A is a positive duration gap insurance company and firm B is a money market mutual fund, in what market(s) should each firm borrow to reduce its interest rate risk exposure?

b. In which debt market does firm A have a comparative advantage over firm B?

c. Although firm A is riskier than firm B and therefore must pay a higher rate in both the fixed-rate and floating-rate markets, there are possible gains to trade. Set up a swap to exploit firm A's comparative advantage over firm B. What are the total gains from the swap trade? Assume a swap intermediary fee of 10 basis points.

d. The gains from the swap trade can be apportioned between firm A and firm B through negotiation. What terms of trade would give all the gains to firm A? What terms of trade would give all the gains to firm B?

e. Assume swap pricing that allocates all the gains from the swap to firm A. If A buys the swap from B and pays the swap intermediary's fee, what are the end-of-year net cash flows if LIBOR is 8.25 percent?

f. If A buys the swap in part (e) from B and pays the swap intermediary's fee, what are the end-of-year net cash flows if LIBOR is 11 percent? Be sure to net swap payments against cash market payments for both firms.

g. If all barriers to entry and pricing inefficiencies between firm A's debt markets and firm B's debt markets were eliminated, how would that affect the swap transaction?

10. What are off-market swap arrangements? How are these arrangements negotiated?

11. Describe how an inverse floater works to the advantage of an investor who receives coupon payments of 10 percent minus LIBOR if LIBOR is currently at 4 percent. When is it a disadvantage to the investor? Does the issuing party bear any risk?

12. An FI has $500 million of assets with a duration of nine years and $450 million of liabilities with a duration of three years. The FI wants to hedge its duration gap with a swap that has fixed-rate payments with a duration of six years and floating-rate payments with a duration of two years. What is the optimal amount of the swap to effectively macrohedge against the adverse effect of a change in interest rates on the value of the FI's equity?

13. A Swiss bank issues a $100 million, three-year Eurodollar CD at a fixed annual rate of 7 percent. The proceeds of the CD are lent to a Swiss company for three years at a fixed rate of 9 percent. The spot exchange rate is Sf1.50/$.

a. Is this expected to be a profitable transaction?

b. What are the cash flows if exchange rates are unchanged over the next three years?

c. What is the risk exposure of the bank's underlying cash position?

d. How can the Swiss bank reduce that risk exposure?

e. If the U.S. dollar is expected to appreciate against the Sf to Sf1.65/$, Sf1.815/$, and Sf2.00/$ over the next three years, what will be the cash flows on this transaction?

f. If the Swiss bank swaps U.S.$ payments for Sf payments at the current spot exchange rate, what are the cash flows on the swap? What are the cash flows on the entire hedged position? Assume that the U.S.$ appreciates at the rates in part (e).

g. What are the cash flows on the swap and the hedged position if actual spot exchange rates are as follows:

End of year 1: Sf1.55/US$

End of year 2: Sf1.47/US$

End of year 3: Sf1.48/US$

h. What would be the bank's risk exposure if the fixed-rate Swiss loan was financed with a floating-rate U.S. $100 million, three-year Eurodollar CD?

i. What type(s) of hedge is appropriate if the Swiss bank in part (h) wants to reduce its risk exposure?

j. If the annual Eurodollar CD rate is set at LIBOR and LIBOR at the end of years 1, 2, and 3 is expected to be 7 percent, 8 percent, and 9 percent, respectively, what will be the cash flows on the bank's unhedged cash position? Assume no change in exchange rates.

k. What are the cash flows on the bank's unhedged cash position if exchange rates are as follows:

End of year 1: Sf1.55/US$

End of year 2: Sf1.47/US$

End of year 3: Sf1.48/US$

l. What are both the swap and the total hedged position cash flows if the bank swaps out its floating rate U.S.$ CD payments in exchange for 7.75 percent fixed-rate Sf payments at the current spot exchange rate of Sf1.50/$?

m. Use the following spot rates for par value coupon bonds to forecast expected future spot rates. (*Hint:* Forecast expected future spot rates using implied forward rates.)

One-year 7.0 percent

Two-year 8.5 percent

Three-year 9.2 percent

n. Use the rate forecasts in part (m) to calculate the cash flows on an 8.75 percent fixed-floating rate swap of U.S. dollars to Swiss francs at Sf1.50/$.

14. Use the following balance sheet information (in millions) to construct a swap hedge against interest rate risk exposure.

Assets		Liabilities and Equity	
Rate-sensitive assets	$ 50	Rate-sensitive liabilities	$ 75
Fixed-rate assets	150	Fixed-rate liabilities	100
		Net worth	25
Total assets	$200	Total liabilities and equity	$200

Rate-sensitive assets are repriced quarterly at the 91-day Treasury bill rate plus 150 basis points. Fixed-rate assets have five years until maturity and are paying 9 percent annually. Rate-sensitive liabilities are repriced quarterly at the 91-day Treasury bill rate plus 100 basis points. Fixed-rate liabilities have two years until maturity and are paying 7 percent annually. Currently, the 91-day Treasury bill rate is 6.25 percent.

a. What is the bank's current net interest income? If Treasury bill rates increase 150 basis points, what will be the change in the bank's net interest income?

b. What is the bank's repricing or funding gap? Use the repricing model to calculate the change in the bank's net interest income if interest rates increase 150 basis points.

c. How can swaps be used as an interest rate hedge in this example?

15. Use the following information to construct a swap of asset cash flows for the bank in problem 14. The bank is a price taker in both the fixed-rate market at 9 percent and the rate-sensitive market at the T-bill rate plus 1.5 percent. A securities dealer has a large portfolio of rate sensitive assets funded with fixed rate liabilities. The dealer is a price taker in a fixed-rate asset market paying 8.5 percent and a floating-rate asset market paying the 91-day T-bill rate plus 1.25 percent. All interest is paid annually.

a. What is the interest rate risk exposure to the securities dealer?

b. How can the bank and the securities dealer use a swap to hedge their respective interest rate risk exposures?

c. What are the total potential gains to the swap trade?

d. Consider the following two-year swap of asset cash flows: An annual fixed-rate asset cash flow of 8.6 percent in exchange for a floating-rate asset cash flow of T-bill plus 125 basis points. The total swap intermediary fee is 5 basis points. How are the swap gains apportioned between the bank and the securities dealer if they each hedge their interest rate risk exposures using this swap?

e. What are the swap net cash flows if T-bill rates at the end of the first year are 7.75 percent and at the end of the second year 5.5 percent? Assume that the notional value is $107.14 million.

f. What are the sources of the swap gains to trade?

g. What are the implications for the efficiency of cash markets?

16. Consider the following currency swap of coupon interest on the following assets:

5 percent (annual coupon) fixed-rate U.S. $1 million bond

5 percent (annual coupon) fixed-rate bond denominated in Swiss francs (Sf)

Spot exchange rates: Sf1.5/$

a. What is the face value of the Sf bond if the investments are equivalent at spot rates?

b. What are the end-of-year cash flows, assuming no change in spot exchange rates? What are the net cash flows on the swap?

c. What are the cash flows if spot exchange rates fall to Sf0.50/$? What are the net cash flows on the swap?

d. What are the cash flows if spot exchange rates rise to Sf 2.25/$? What are the net cash flows on the swap?

e. Describe the underlying cash position that would prompt the FI to hedge by swapping dollars for Swiss Francs.

17. Consider the following fixed–floating rate currency swap of assets: 5 percent (annual coupon) fixed-rate U.S. $1 million bond and floating-rate Sf1.5 million

bond set at LIBOR annually. Currently LIBOR is 4 percent. Face value of swap is Sf1.5 million. Spot exchange rate: Sf1.5/$.

   a. What are the end-of-year cash flows assuming no change in the spot exchange rate? What are the net cash flows on the swap at the spot exchange rate?

   b. If the 1-year forward rate is Sf1.538 per U.S.$, what are the end-of-year net cash flows on the swap? Assume LIBOR is unchanged.

   c. If LIBOR increases to 6 percent, what are the end-of-year net cash flows on the swap? Evaluate at the forward rate.

18. What is a total return swap?

19. Give two reasons why credit swaps have been the fastest growing form of swaps in recent years.

20. How does a pure credit swap differ from a total return swap? How does it differ from a digital default option?

21. Why is the credit risk on a swap lower than the credit risk on a loan?

22. What is netting by novation?

23. A U.S. thrift has most of its assets in the form of Swiss franc–denominated floating-rate loans. Its liabilities consist mostly of fixed-rate dollar-denominated CDs. What type of currency risk and interest rate risk does this FI face? How might it use a swap to eliminate some of those risks?

The following, problem refers to material in Appendix 26A.

24. The following information is available on a three-year swap contract. One-year maturity notes are currently priced at par and pay a coupon rate of 5 percent annually. Two-year maturity notes are currently priced at par and pay a coupon rate of 5.5 percent annually. Three-year maturity notes are currently priced at par and pay a coupon rate of 5.75 percent annually. The terms of a three-year swap of $100 million notional value are 5.45 percent annual fixed-rate payments in exchange for floating-rate payments tied to the annual discount yield.

   a. If an insurance company buys this swap, what can you conclude about the interest rate risk exposure of the company's underlying cash position?

   b. What are the end-of-year cash flows expected over the three-year life of the swap? (*Hint*: Be sure to convert par value coupon yields to discount yields and then solve for the implied forward rates.)

   c. What are end-of-year actual cash flows that occur over the three-year life of the swap if $d_2 = 4.95$ percent and $d_3 = 6.1$ percent (where d_i are discount yields)?

Pertinent Web Sites

Chapter Notation

View Chapter Notation at the Web site to the textbook (**www.mhhe.com/ saunders5e**).

Appendix 26A

Pricing an Interest Rate Swap

In this appendix, we discuss fair pricing of the swap at the time the parties enter into the swap agreement. As with much of financial theory, there are important no-arbitrage conditions that should hold in setting rates in a fixed-floating rate swap agreement. The most important no-arbitrage condition is that the expected present value of the cash flow payments made by the fixed-rate payer, the buyer, should equal the expected present value of the cash flow payments made by the floating-rate payer, the seller:

$$\text{Expected fixed-payment } PV$$
$$= \text{Expected floating-payment } PV$$

If this no-arbitrage condition does not hold, one party usually has to compensate the other with an up-front payment equal to the difference between the two expected present values of the cash flows.

The fixed-rate payment of the swap is usually priced off the newly issued or *on-the-run* yield curve of U.S. Treasury notes and bonds. Thus, if four-year Treasuries are currently yielding 10 percent, a quote of 10.25 percent (bid) and 10.35 percent (offer) would mean that the commercial or investment bank acting as a swap dealer is willing to buy or become the fixed-rate payer in a swap agreement at a contractual swap rate of 10.25 percent. It is also willing to take the other side of the swap (become the fixed-rate receiver) if the swap fixed rate is set higher at 10.35 percent. The 10-basis-point spread is the dealer's spread or the return for intermediating the swap. As discussed earlier, in intermediating, the FI has to cover the credit risk assumed in the swap transaction and cover its costs of search and intermediation as well. In the next subsection of this appendix, we develop a detailed example of how a swap might be priced.

PRICING A SWAP: AN EXAMPLE

We develop an example of swap pricing under simplified assumptions by applying the no-arbitrage condition and pricing swaps off the Treasury yield curve. This provides an understanding of why expected cash flows from the swap agreement can differ from actual or realized cash flows. It also explains why, when yield curves slope upward, the fixed-rate payer (swap buyer) faces an inherent credit risk in any swap contract.

Assume that in a four-year swap agreement, the fixed-rate payer makes fixed-rate payments at the end of each year. Also assume that while these payments are made at the end of each year, interest rates are determined at the beginning of each year.[1] That is,

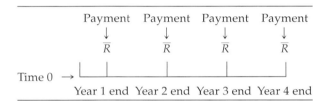

Since this is a four-year swap agreement, the fixed-rate payer knows in advance the annual interest rate to pay each year:

$$\overline{R}_1 = \overline{R}_2 = \overline{R}_3 = \overline{R}_4 = Fixed$$

Let R be priced off the current *Treasury bond par yield curve* for four-year, on-the-run Treasury note issues. The assumed current par yield curve is represented in Figure 26A–1. Suppose that newly issued four-year Treasury bonds are currently yielding 10 percent and that the fixed-rate payments on the swap are set at 10 percent for each of the four years

$$R_i = 10\% \qquad i = 1, \dots, 4$$

Here we ignore the usual markup in the swap market over Treasuries for simplicity. For the no-arbitrage condition to hold, the present value of these fixed payments made must equal the expected stream of variable one-year payments received from the floating-rate payer. If we assume that the expectations theory of interest rates holds, we can extract the expected one-year rates

---

[1] This is not always the case. Further, in practice many swaps are now priced off the LIBOR yield curve (reflecting some credit risk premium over Treasuries).

FIGURE 26A–1
T-bond Par Yield
Curve

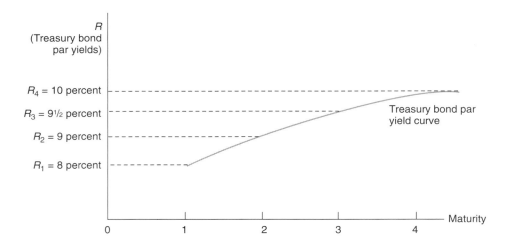

(payments) from the Treasury yield curve. Specifically, we wish to determine

where $E(\tilde{r}_i)$ are the expected one-year (forward) interest payments to be made at the end of years 1, 2, 3, and 4, respectively.

Extracting these expected one-year forward rates is a little awkward. We begin by extracting the spot or zero-coupon discount bond yield curve from the coupon par yield curve on Treasury bonds; then we derive expected one-year forward rates from this zero-coupon yield curve. The reason we need to extract the zero-coupon discount yield curve is that this yield curve reflects the time value of money for single payments (bonds) at 1 year's, 2 years', 3 years', and 4 years' time. Unfortunately, the yield to maturity on a coupon bond is a complex weighted average of the time value of money discount yields on zero-coupon bonds. Specifically, a yield to maturity on a coupon bond is the internal rate of return on that bond or the single interest rate (yield) that equates the promised cash flows on the bond to its price. Such a yield is not the same as the time value of money. For example, assuming annual coupon payments, the 10 percent yield to maturity on the four-year T-bond is a complex average of the yields to maturity on a one-year, two-year, three-year, and four-year zero-coupon discount bond.

To see this, consider the cash flows on the four-year coupon par value Treasury bond

$$100 = P_4 = \frac{10}{(1 + R_4)} + \frac{10}{(1 + R_4)^2}$$
$$+ \frac{10}{(1 + R_4)^3} + \frac{110}{(1 + R_4)^4}$$

and the yield to maturity on this par bond, $R_4 = 10$ percent. Thus,

$$P_4 = \frac{10}{(1.1)} + \frac{10}{(1.1)^2} + \frac{10}{(1.1)^3} + \frac{110}{(1.1)^4} = 100$$

Conceptually, this coupon bond could be broken down and sold as four separate zero-coupon bonds with one year, two years, three years, and four years to maturity. This is similar to how the U.S. Treasury currently creates zero-coupon bonds through its *Treasury Strips* program.[2] That is,

$$P_4 = \underbrace{\frac{10}{(1 + R_4)} + \frac{10}{(1 + R_4)^2} + \frac{10}{(1 + R_4)^3} + \frac{110}{(1 + R_4)^4}}_{\text{Coupon bond value}}$$

$$= \underbrace{\frac{10}{(1 + d_1)} + \frac{10}{(1 + d_2)^2} + \frac{10}{(1 + d_3)^3} + \frac{110}{(1 + d_4)^4}}_{\text{Sum of separate zero-coupon bond values}}$$

The first relationship is the value of the coupon bond as a whole, while the second is the

---

[2] Apart from semiannual rather than annual coupon stripping, the other major difference in practice is that the final coupon payment of 10 is separated and sold independently from the 100 face value, even though both are paid at the same time and have the same time value of money.

value of four stripped coupon and principal discount bonds of 10, 10, 10, and 110, each sold separately to different investors. The time value of money for the single payments in each of the four years, or required discount yields, is d_1, d_2, d_3, and d_4. Further, this equation confirms that the yield to maturity on the four-year coupon bond, when sold as a whole bond (R_4), is a complex average of the discount rates on four different zero-coupon bonds—d_1, d_2, d_3, and d_4—where the d_i are discount yields on single-payment bonds of i year to maturity, $i = 1, 2, 3$, and 4

$$P_1^D = \frac{10}{(1 + d_1)}$$

$$P_2^D = \frac{10}{(1 + d_2)^2}$$

$$P_3^D = \frac{10}{(1 + d_3)^3}$$

$$P_4^D = \frac{10}{(1 + d_4)^4}$$

$$\text{and } P_4 = \sum_{i=1}^{4} P_i^D$$

P_i^D represent the market values of the four different stripped or zero-coupon bonds. The no-arbitrage condition requires that the values of the four zero-coupon bonds sum to the price of the four-year Treasury coupon bond (P_4) when sold as a whole.

To derive the expected one-year forward rates implied by the yield curve, we need to calculate the discount yields themselves: d_1, d_2, d_3, and d_4.

Solving the Discount Yield Curve

To calculate the discount yields, we use a process of forward iteration. From Figure 26A–1, which shows the T-bond yield curve, we note that one-year par value coupon Treasury bonds are currently yielding 8 percent

$$P_1 = \frac{108}{(1 + R_1)} = \frac{108}{1.08} = 100$$
$$R_1 = 8\%$$

Because the one-year coupon bond has exactly one year left to maturity, and thus only one final payment of interest (8) and principal (100), its valuation is exactly the same as a one-year zero-coupon

bond with one payment at the end of the year. Thus, by definition, under no arbitrage,

$$R_1 = d_1 = 8\%$$

Once we have solved for d_1, we can go on to solve for d_2 by forward iteration. Specifically, from the par coupon yield curve we can see that two-year coupon-bearing bonds are yielding 9 percent

$$P_2 = \frac{9}{(1 + R_2)} + \frac{109}{(1 + R_2)^2}$$

$$= \frac{9}{(1.09)} + \frac{109}{(1.09)^2} = 100$$

$$R_1 = 9\%$$

The no-arbitrage condition between coupon bonds and zero-coupon bonds implies that

$$P_2 = \frac{9}{(1.09)} + \frac{109}{(1.09)^2}$$

$$= \frac{9}{(1 + d_1)} + \frac{109}{(1 + d_2)^2} = 100$$

Since we have solved for $d_1 = 8$ percent, we can directly solve for d_2

$$100 = \frac{9}{(1.08)} + \frac{109}{(1 + d_2)^2}$$

$$d_2 = 9.045\%$$

Similarly, we know from the current par T-bond yield curve that three-year coupon-bearing bonds are yielding $9\frac{1}{2}$ percent. The no arbitrage requires

$$P_3 = \frac{9\frac{1}{2}}{(1 + R_3)} + \frac{9\frac{1}{2}}{(1 + R_3)^2} + \frac{109\frac{1}{2}}{(1 + R_3)^3}$$

$$= \frac{9\frac{1}{2}}{(1 + d_1)} + \frac{9\frac{1}{2}}{(1 + d_2)^2} + \frac{109\frac{1}{2}}{(1 + d_3)^3} = 100$$

$$R_3 = 9\frac{1}{2}\%$$

To solve for d_3, the yield on a three-year zero-coupon bond, we have

$$100 = \frac{9\frac{1}{2}}{(1.08)} + \frac{9\frac{1}{2}}{(1.09045)^2} + \frac{109\frac{1}{2}}{(1 + d_3)^3}$$

Thus, since d_1 and d_2 have already been determined, $d_3 = 9.58$ percent.

FIGURE 26A–2
Discount Yield Curve versus Par Yield Curve

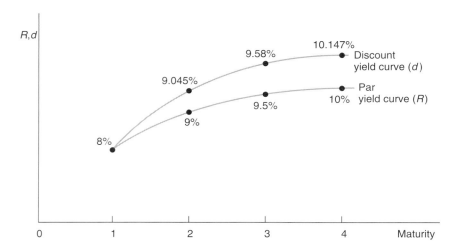

Finally, to solve for the discount rate on a four-year zero-coupon bond (d_4), we know that

$$P_4 = 100 = \frac{10}{(1 + R_4)} + \frac{10}{(1 + R_4)^2}$$
$$+ \frac{10}{(1 + R_4)^3} + \frac{110}{(1 + R_4)^4}$$
$$= \frac{10}{(1 + d_1)} + \frac{10}{(1 + d_2)^2}$$
$$+ \frac{10}{(1 + d_3)^3} + \frac{110}{(1 + d_4)^4}$$

$$R_4 = 10\%$$

To solve for d_4, we have

$$100 = \frac{10}{(1.08)} + \frac{10}{(1.09045)^2}$$
$$+ \frac{10}{(1.0958)^3} + \frac{110}{(1 + d_4)^4}$$

As a result, since d_1, d_2, and d_3 were solved, $d_4 =$ 10.147 percent.

In Figure 26A–2 we plot the derived zero-coupon discount bond yield curve alongside the coupon par yield curve. As you can see, the derived zero-coupon yield curve slopes upward faster than does the coupon bond yield curve. This result is a mathematical relationship and comes from the no-arbitrage derivation of the zero-coupon curve from the T-bond par yield curve. There is an intuitive explanation for this result as well. Remember that R_4 (= 10 percent, the yield to maturity or internal rate of return on a

four-year coupon bond) can conceptually be viewed as a complex weighted average of the discount rates on four successive one-year zero-coupon bonds (d_1, d_2, d_3, and d_4). Since R_4 at 10 percent is higher than d_1 = 8 percent, d_2 = 9.045 percent, and d_3 = 9.58 percent, then d_4 (10.147 percent) must be above R_4 (10 percent) if R_4 is to be a weighted average of the individual zero-coupon discount rates. This same reasoning explains why $R_3 < d_3$ and $R_2 < d_2$.

Note, however, that if the coupon yield curve was flat, then $R_i = d_i$ for every maturity. If the coupon yield curve were downward sloping, the discount or zero-coupon yield curve would lie below the coupon yield curve (for the converse reason used to explain why it must be above when the coupon yield curve is rising). We can now solve for the expected one-year floating rates implied by the zero-coupon yield curve.

We are assuming that floating interest rate payments are made at the end of each year and are based on the one-year interest rates that are set at the beginning of each year. We can use the zero-coupon bond yield curve to derive the expected one-year forward rates that reflect the expected floating swap payments at the end of each year.

Solving for the Implied Forward Rates/Floating Payments on a Swap Agreement

End of Year 1 Payment

The expected end of year 1 payment $E(\tilde{r}_1)$ must be equal to the current one-year rate set for one-year

FIGURE 26A–3
Fixed and Expected
Floating Swap
Payments

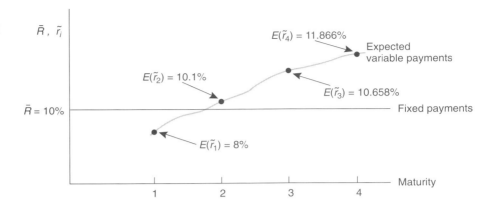

discount bonds at time 0 since floating rates paid at the end of a period are assumed to depend on rates set or expected at the beginning of that period. That is, the expected first-year floating payment equals the current one-year discount rate

$$E(\tilde{r}_1) = d_1 = 8 \text{ percent}$$

End of Year 2 Payment

To determine the end of year 2 payment, we need to solve the expected one-year interest rate or forward rate in year 2. This is the rate that reflects expected payments at the end of year 2. We know that no arbitrage requires[3]

$$(1 + d_2)^2 = (1 + d_1)(1 + E(\tilde{r}_1))$$

That is, the yield from holding a two-year zero-coupon bond to maturity must equal the expected yield from holding the current one-year, zero-coupon bond to maturity times the expected yield from investing in a new one-year, zero-coupon bond in year 2. Rearranging this equation, we have

$$(1 + E(\tilde{r}_2)) = \frac{(1 + d_2)^2}{(1 + d_1)}$$

Since we have already solved for $d_2 = 9.045$ percent and $d_1 = 8$ percent, we can solve for $E(\tilde{r}_2)$

$$1 + E(\tilde{r}_2) = \frac{(1.09045)^2}{(1.08)}$$

$$E(\tilde{r}_2) = 10.1\%$$

End of Year 3 Payment

In a similar fashion

$$(1 + E(\tilde{r}_3)) = \frac{(1 + d_3)^3}{(1 + d_2)^2}$$

[3] Under the pure expectations theory of interest rates.

Substituting in the d_2 and d_3 values from the zero-coupon bond yield curve

$$1 + E(\tilde{r}_3) = \frac{(1.0958)^3}{(1.09045)^2}$$

$$E(\tilde{r}_3) = 10.658\%$$

End of Year 4 Payment

Using the same procedure

$$1 + E(\tilde{r}_4) = \frac{(1 + d_4)^4}{(1 + d_3)^3} = \frac{(1.10147)^4}{(1.0958)^3}$$

$$E(\tilde{r}_4) = 11.866\%$$

These four expected one-year payments by the floating-rate payer are plotted against the fixed-rate payments by the buyer of the swap in Figure 26A–3. Although expecting to pay a net payment $[\overline{R} - E(\tilde{r}_2)]$ of 2 percent to the floating-rate payer in the first year, the fixed-rate payer expects to receive net payments of 0.1 percent, 0.658 percent, and 1.866 percent from the floating-rate seller in years 2, 3, and 4. This has important credit risk implications. It implies that when the yield curve is upward sloping, the fixed-rate payer can expect not only to pay more than the floating-rate payer in the early years of a swap agreement but also to receive higher cash flows from the seller or floating-rate payer in the later years of the swap agreement. Thus, the fixed-rate payer faces the risk that if expected rates are actually realized, the floating-rate payer may have an incentive to default toward the end of the swap agreement as a net payer. In this case the swap buyer might have to replace the swap at less favorable market conditions in the future.[4]

Finally, note that in this appendix we have been comparing expected cash flows in the swap agreement under no-arbitrage conditions. If the term structure shifts after the swap has been entered into, realized one-year rates (and payments) will not equal expected rates for the floating-rate payer. In our example, if the term structure shifts,

$$r_2 \neq E(\tilde{r}_2)$$
$$r_3 \neq E(\tilde{r}_3)$$
$$r_4 \neq E(\tilde{r}_4)$$

where r_2, r_3, and r_4 are realized or actual one-year rates on new one-year discount bonds issued in years 2, 3, and 4, respectively. Of course, the floating-rate payer has to make payments on actual or realized rates rather than expected rates, as we discussed in the first section of this chapter.

---

[4] This example is based on the discussion in C. W. Smith, C. W. Smithson, and L. M. Wakeman, "The Market for Interest Rate Swaps," *Financial Management* 17 (1988), pp. 34–44.

Chapter Twenty-Seven

Loan Sales and Other Credit Risk Management Techniques

INTRODUCTION

Traditionally, banks and other FIs have relied on a number of contractual mechanisms to control the credit risks of lending. These have included (1) requiring higher interest rate spreads and fees on loans to more risky borrowers, (2) restricting or rationing loans to more risky borrowers, (3) requiring enhanced seniority (collateral) for the bank over the assets of risky borrowers, (4) diversifying across different types of risky borrowers, and (5) placing more restrictive covenants on risky borrowers' actions, such as restrictions on the use of proceeds from asset sales, new debt issues, and dividend payments. These traditional mechanisms for controlling or managing credit risk were described in Chapters 11 and 12.

Additionally, in Chapters 24 through 26 we discussed the increasing use of credit derivatives in the forward, options, and swaps markets to manage credit risk—for example, the use of digital put options to control the credit risk of an individual loan or portfolio of loans. In addition, FIs are increasingly requiring borrowers to hedge their own risks, especially when the FI makes floating-rate loans to borrowers. When interest rates rise, the borrower of a floating-rate loan may have greater difficulty meeting interest rate payments. However, if the borrower has hedged the risk of rising rates in the derivatives market (e.g., by selling interest rate futures or receiving floating payments–paying fixed payments in an interest rate swap), the borrower is in a far better position to meet its contractual payments to the FI. As a result, the credit risk exposure of the FI is reduced.[1]

This and the following chapter on securitization describe the growing role of loan sales and other newer types of techniques (such as the good bank–bad bank structure) increasingly used by FI managers to control credit risk. While loan sales have been in existence for many years, the use of loan sales (by removing existing

---

[1] In addition, the floating-rate loans may enable the FI to better hedge its own duration gap exposure.

Industry Perspectives

SUDDENLY, BANKS ARE ACTING A LOT LIKE BOND MARKETS

When numerous companies suddenly found investors unwilling to buy their debt this year, amid a rocky economy and accounting scandals, many turned to their lenders of last resort, their banks. They discovered banking has changed a lot. And some discovered that loans cost them a good deal more. Banks traditionally have been the institutions that take a long-term view of a company's prospects, management and ability to repay a debt. By contrast, the fast-paced, fickle bond market can change its mind in an instant about a company's creditworthiness and how much to charge. But many borrowers are finding that banks' loan business had come to look a lot like the markets. . . .

Scarred by their early-1990s experience, they often don't hold onto loans, especially those to lower quality companies. Increasingly, banks sell pieces of their loans to other banks, to specialized investment funds, insurance companies or to other institutional investors. As a result, the loans are subject to all the pricing and other tactics of the markets. And the banks are acting less like lenders and more like middlemen between borrowers and investors.

Although this shift means painfully high interest rates for some, it has benefits to the overall economy in making credit available. Even if a bank considers a particular borrower too risky, it can usually find someone willing to share the risk. And the capital markets help it find out what interest rate is needed to compensate for the risk. "The actual creditworthiness of borrowers had come down," Fed Chairman Alan Greenspan observed earlier this year. "There has, however, been no evidence of anything remotely resembling the credit crunch that we had a decade ago, where you just could not get a loan out of a commercial bank no matter what your creditworthiness was, at least in some cases." . . .

Bank loans and pieces of them now change hands in an increasingly active secondary market. Its daily turnover of about $500 million is puny next to the stock and bond markets but up 15-fold from a decade earlier, according to Credit Suisse First Boston. When a company sets out to borrow now, its lenders can see how this secondary market is valuing its old loans, and adjust terms of this new borrowing accordingly. Initially, many companies weren't happy that banks were selling off their loans. "Today everyone accepts that if you want a noninvestment-grade loan, it's very similar to a bond deal," says Scott Page, co-manager of senior debt portfolios at Eaton Vance Management in Boston. "You're not doing a handshake deal on the golf course with a handful of banks. But ultimately you have a more reliable source of capital." . . .

Source: Greg Ip, *The Wall Street Journal*, September 17, 2002, p. A1. *www.wsj.com*

loans from the balance sheet) is increasingly being recognized as a valuable additional tool in an FI manager's portfolio of credit risk management techniques (see the Industry Perspectives box). The chapter begins with an overview of the loan sales market. We define and look at the types of loan sales and summarize who are the buyers and sellers of loans. We then discuss why banks and other FIs would sell loans, as well as the factors that deter and encourage loan sales. The chapter concludes with a review of the purchase and sale of foreign loans.

LOAN SALES

correspondent banking
A relationship entered into between a small bank and a big bank in which the big bank provides a number of deposit, lending, and other services.

Banks and other FIs have sold loans among themselves for over 100 years. In fact, a large part of **correspondent banking** involves small banks making loans that are too big for them to hold on their balance sheets—for lending concentration, risk, or capital adequacy reasons—and selling parts of these loans to large banks with whom they have a long-term deposit-lending correspondent relationship. In turn, the large banks often sell parts of their loans called *participations* to smaller banks. Even though this market has existed for many years, it grew slowly until the early 1980s, when it entered a period of spectacular growth, largely due to expansion in

highly leveraged transaction (HLT) loan
A loan made to finance a merger and acquisition: a leveraged buyout results in a high leverage ratio for the borrower.

highly leveraged transaction (HLT) loans to finance leveraged buyouts (LBOs) and mergers and acquisitions (M&As). Specifically, the volume of loans sold by U.S. banks grew from less than $20 billion in 1980 to $285 billion in 1989. Between 1990 and 1994 the volume of loan sales fell almost equally dramatically, along with the decline in LBOs and M&As as a result of the credit crunch associated with the 1990–91 recession. In 1994, the volume of loan sales had fallen to approximately $20 billion.

In the late 1990s, the volume of loan sales expanded again, partly due to an expanding economy and a resurgence in M&As. For example, the loan market research firm, Loan Pricing Corporation, reported secondary trading volume in 1999 was more than $79 billion. Loan sales continued to grow to almost $120 billion in the early 2000s as FIs sold distressed loans (loans trading below 90 cents on the dollar). Triggered by an economic slowdown, distressed loan sales jumped from 11 percent of total loan sales in 1999 to 35 percent in 2001, and 42 percent in 2002. As the U.S. economy improved in 2003, the percent of distressed loan sales fell to 40 percent. Figure 27–1 shows the growth in loan sales over the 1994–2003 (third quarter) period.

Many of these loans are syndicated, involving many sponsoring banks. For example, in 2003 the Loan Pricing Corporation reported that J. P. Morgan Chase was

FIGURE 27–1
Recent Trends in the Loan Sales Market, Secondary loan volume, (1994–3Q2003)

Source: Loan Pricing Corporation Web site, April 2004. *www.loanpricing.com*

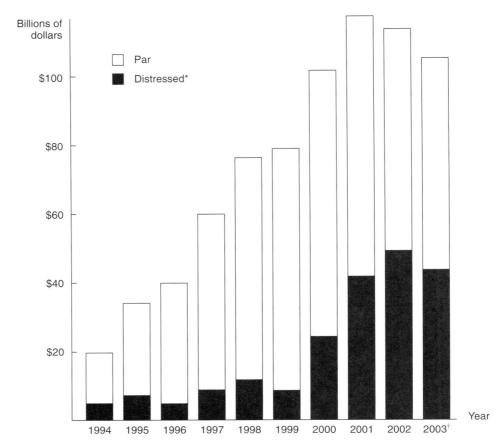

*Trading at less than 90 cents on the dollar.
†As of September.

the leading loan syndicator in the worldwide secondary loan market sponsoring 620 deals worth $567 billion. Yet J. P. Morgan Chase retained risk for only $283 billion of these loans. Along with J. P. Morgan Chase, Citigroup ($496 billion), Bank of America ($292 billion), Barclays Bank ($263 billion), and HSBC ($242 billion) were the top five secondary-market loan syndicators in 2003.

Concept Question

1. Explain the main reason behind the explosion in loan sales in the 1980s.

THE BANK LOAN SALES MARKET

Definition of a Loan Sale

bank loan sale
Sale of a loan originated by an FI with or without recourse to an outside buyer.

A **bank loan sale** occurs when an FI originates a loan and sells it either with or without recourse to an outside buyer. As an extreme example, GreenPoint Financial Corp. issued in excess of $33.9 billion in mortgage loans in 2003. By year-end, GreenPoint had sold over $33.3 billion of these loans to secondary market investors .

If a loan is sold without recourse, not only is it removed from the FI's balance sheet but the FI has no explicit liability if the loan eventually goes bad. Panel A of Table 27–1 shows an FI's balance sheet before and after a $20 million loan sale. The buyer (and not the FI that originated the loan) bears all the credit risk. If, however, the loan is sold with **recourse,** under certain conditions the buyer can put the loan back to the selling FI; therefore, the FI retains a contingent credit risk liability. Panel B of Table 27–1 shows the FI's balance sheet, including the contingent liability from the loan sale held off the balance sheet. In practice, most loans are sold without recourse because a loan sale is technically removed from the balance sheet only when the buyer has no future credit risk claim on the FI. Importantly, loan sales involve no creation of new types of securities such as the pass-throughs, CMOs, and MBBs described in Chapter 28. As such, loan sales are a primitive form

recourse
The ability of a loan buyer to sell the loan back to the originator if it goes bad.

TABLE 27–1   **FI Balance Sheet before and after a $20 Million Loan Sale (in millions)**

Panel A Loan Sale without Recourse

Before Loan Sale				After Loan Sale			
Assets		**Liabilities/Equity**		**Assets**		**Liabilities/Equity**	
Cash assets	$ 10	Deposit	$ 90	Cash assets	$ 10	Deposits	$ 90
				Loans	70		
Loans	90	Equity	10	New investments	20	Equity	10
	$100		$100		$100		$100

Panel B Loan Sale with Recourse

Before Loan Sale				After Loan Sale			
Assets		**Liabilities/Equity**		**Assets**		**Liabilities/Equity**	
Cash assets	$ 10	Deposit	$ 90	Cash assets	$ 10	Deposits	$ 90
				Loans	70		
Loans	90	Equity	10	New investments	20	Equity	10
	$100		$100		$100		$100
				Off balance sheet: Loan sale (contingent liability)			$20

of securitization in that loan selling creates a secondary market for loans in which ownership of the loan is simply transferred to the loan buyer.

Types of Loan Sales

The U.S. loan sales market has three segments: two involve the sale and trading of domestic loans, while the third involves emerging-market loan sales and trading. Since we fully described emerging-market loan sales in Chapter 16 on sovereign risk, we concentrate on the domestic loan sales market here.

Traditional Short Term

In the traditional short-term segment of the market, FIs sell loans with short maturities, often one to three months. This market has characteristics similar to those of the market for commercial paper issued by corporations in that loan sales have similar maturities and issue size. Loan sales, however, usually have yields that are 1 to 10 basis points above those of commercial paper of a similar rating. In particular, the loan sales market in which an FI originates and sells a short-term loan of a corporation is a close substitute for the issuance of commercial paper—either directly or through dealers—for the 1,000 or so largest U.S. corporations. The key characteristics of the short-term loan sales market are

Secured by assets of the borrowing firm.

Made to investment grade borrowers or better.

Issued for a short term (90 days or less).

Has yields closely tied to the commercial paper rate.

Sold in units of $1 million and up.

Until 1984 and the emergence of the HLT and emerging market loan markets, traditional short-term loan sales dominated the loan sales market. The growth of the commercial paper market (and its accessibility by over 20,000 corporations), as well as the increased ability of banks (through their Section 20 securities affiliates) to underwrite commercial paper (see Chapter 21), also has reduced the importance of this market segment.

HLT Loan Sales

**www.loanpricing.
com**

With the growth in M&As and LBOs via highly leveraged transactions (HLTs), especially during the period 1985–89, a new segment in the loan sales market appeared. One measure of the increase in HLTs is that between January 1987 and September 1994, the Loan Pricing Corporation reported 4,122 M&A deals with a combined dollar amount of new-issue HLT loans estimated at $593.5 billion.

What constitutes an HLT loan has often caused dispute. However, in October 1989 the three U.S. federal bank regulators adopted a definition of an HLT loan as one that (1) involves a buyout, acquisition, or recapitalization and (2) doubles the company's liabilities and results in a leverage ratio higher than 50 percent, results in a leverage ratio higher than 75 percent, or is designated as an HLT by a syndication agent. HLT loans mainly differ according to whether they are nondistressed (bid price exceeds 90 cents per $1 of loans) or distressed (bid price is less than 90 cents per $1 of loans or the borrower is in default).[2]

---

[2] See Walter J. Blumenthal, "Loan Trading: A New Business Opportunity for Your Bank," *Commercial Lending Review*, Winter 1997–1998, pp. 26–31.

Virtually all HLT loans have the following characteristics:

They are term loans (TLs).

They are secured by assets of the borrowing firm (usually given senior secured status).

They have a long maturity (often three- to six-year maturities).

They have floating rates tied to LIBOR, the prime rate, or a CD rate (normally 200 to 275 basis points above these rates).

They have strong covenant protection.

financial distress
A period when a borrower is unable to either meet a payment obligation to lenders and other creditors.

Nevertheless, HLTs tend to be quite heterogeneous with respect to the size of the issue, the interest payment date, interest indexing, and prepayment features. After origination, some HLT borrowers, such as Macy's and El Paso Electric, suffered periods of **financial distress.** As a result, a distinction is usually made between the markets for distressed and nondistressed HLTs.

Approximately 100 banks and securities firms make a market in this debt either as brokers or (less commonly) as broker-dealers, including Bear Stearns, CIBC, Prudential Securities, and Goldman Sachs. Most of these FIs view trading in this debt as similar to trading in junk bonds.[3]

Types of Loan Sales Contracts

There are two basic types of loan sale contracts or mechanisms by which loans can be transferred between seller and buyer: participations and assignments. Currently, assignments comprise the bulk of loan sales trading.

Participations

participation in a loan
Buying a share in a loan syndication with limited, contractual control and rights over the borrower.

The unique features of **participations in loans** are

- The holder (buyer) is not a party to the underlying credit agreement so that the initial contract between loan seller and borrower remains in place after the sale.
- The loan buyer can exercise only partial control over changes in the loan contract's terms. The holder can only vote on material changes to the loan contract, such as the interest rate or collateral backing.

The economic implication of these features is that the buyer of the loan participation has a double risk exposure: a risk exposure to the borrower and a risk exposure to the loan selling FI. Specifically, if the selling FI fails, the loan participation bought by an outside party may be characterized as an unsecured obligation of the FI rather than as a true sale if there are grounds for believing that some explicit or implicit recourse existed between the loan seller and the loan buyer. Alternatively, the borrower's claims against a failed selling FI may be set off against its loans from that FI, reducing the amount of loans outstanding and

---

[3] In a study comparing the determinants of the yield spreads on HLT loans versus those on high-yield (junk) bonds, it was found that the spreads on HLT loans behaved more like investment grade bonds than like high-yield bonds. A possible reason for this is that HLT loans tend to be more senior in bankruptcy and to have greater collateral backing than do high-yield bonds. See L. Angbazo, Jianping Mei, and Anthony Saunders, "Credit Spreads in the Market for Highly Leveraged Transaction Loans," *Journal of Banking and Finance* 22 (1998), pp. 1249–82. Also, E. Altman, A. Gande, and A. Saunders, in "Informational Efficiency of Loans versus Bonds: Evidence from Secondary Market Prices," Working Paper, Department of Finance, New York University, 2004, find that the correlations among loan and bond prices of the same company are generally quite low, except in periods approaching distress.

adversely impacting the buyer of a participation in those loans. As a result of these exposures, the buyer bears a double monitoring cost as well.

Assignments

assignment
Buying a share in a loan syndication with some contractual control and rights over the borrower.

Because of the monitoring costs and risks involved in participations, loans are sold on an assignment basis in more than 90 percent of the cases on the U.S. domestic market. The key features of an **assignment** are

- All rights are transferred on sale, meaning the loan buyer now holds a direct claim on the borrower.
- Transfer of U.S. domestic loans is normally associated with a Uniform Commercial Code filing (as proof that a change of ownership has been perfected).

While ownership rights are generally much clearer in a loan sale by assignment, frequently contractual terms limit the seller's scope regarding to whom the loan can be sold. In particular, the loan contract may require either the FI agent or the borrower to agree to the sale. The loan contract may also restrict the sale to a certain class of institutions, such as those that meet certain net worth/net asset size conditions. (An *FI agent* is an FI that distributes interest and principal payments to lenders in loan syndications with multiple lenders.)

accrued interest
The loan seller's claim to part of the next interest payment on the loan.

Currently, the trend appears to be toward loan contracts being originated with very limited assignment restrictions. This is true in both the U.S. domestic and the emerging-market loan sales markets. The most tradable loans are those that can be assigned without buyer restrictions. Even so, one has to distinguish between floating-rate and fixed-rate assignment loans. For floating-rate loans, most loan sales by assignment occur on the loan's repricing date (which may be two or four times a year), due to complexities for the agent FI in calculating and transferring accrued interest—especially given the heterogeneous nature of floating-rate loan indexes such as fed funds plus, T-bond plus, and LIBOR plus. In addition, the nonstandardization of **accrued interest** payments in fixed-rate loan assignments (trade date, assignment date, coupon payment date) adds complexity and friction to this market. Moreover, while the FI agent may have a full record of the initial owners of the loans, it does not always have an up-to-date record of loan ownership changes and related transfers following trades. This means that great difficulties often occur for the borrower, FI agent, and loan buyer in ensuring that the current holder of the loan receives the interest and principal payments due. Finally, the buyer of the loan often needs to verify the original loan contract and establish the full implications of the purchase regarding the buyer's rights to collateral if the borrower defaults.

Because of these contractual problems, trading frictions, and costs, some loan sales take as long as three months to complete; reportedly, up to 50 percent eventually fail to be completed at all. In many cases, the incentive to renege on a contract arises because market prices move away from those originally agreed so that the counterparty finds reasons to delay the completion of a loan sale and/or eventually refuses to complete the transaction.[4]

The Buyers and the Sellers

The Buyers

Of the wide array of potential buyers, some are concerned with only a certain segment of the market for regulatory and strategic reasons. In particular, an

---

[4] See "In Distress but Booming," *The Independent,* February 19, 1993. However, in recent years, completion of a trade within 10 days (or $T + 10$) has become an increasing convention.

vulture fund
A specialized fund that invests in distressed loans.

increasingly specialized group of buyers of distressed HLT loans includes investment banks, hedge funds, and **vulture funds.**

Investment Banks   Investment banks are predominantly buyers of HLT loans because (1) analysis of these loans utilizes investment skills similar to those used in junk bond trading and (2) investment banks were often closely associated with the HLT distressed borrower in underwriting the original junk bond/HLT deals. As such, large investment banks—for example, CSFB, Merrill Lynch, and Goldman Sachs—are relatively more informed agents in this market, either by acting as market makers or in taking short-term positions on movements in the discount from par.

Vulture Funds   Vulture funds are specialized hedge funds established to invest in distressed loans, often with an agenda that may not include helping the distressed firm to survive (see Appendix 5A located at the book's Web site (www.mhhe.com/saunders5e) for a discussion of hedge funds). They include funds run by entrepreneurs such as George Soros and Sam Zell. These investments can be active, especially for those seeking to use the loans purchased for bargaining in a restructuring deal; this generates restructuring returns that strongly favor the loan purchaser. Alternatively, such loans may be held as passive investments, such as high-yield securities in a well-diversified portfolio of distressed securities. Many vulture funds are in fact managed by investment banks.

The common perception of vulture funds is that after picking up distressed loans at a discount, they force firms to restructure or are quick to realize the breakup value of the firm: turning their 50-cent-on-the-dollar investment to a fast 70-cent-on-the-dollar profit. Thus, a vulture fund's reputation is often not a congenial one. A possible reason for this adverse reputation is that while banks are looking for a return of loan principal in a restructuring, vulture funds are looking for a return on capital invested. That is, vulture funds are transaction driven, not relationship based. Unlike banks, vulture funds are far less interested in making decisions based on developing and maintaining long-term relationships with the corporation in question. Nevertheless, they provide an exit strategy for investors and creditors, and enable assets to be liquidated in an orderly manner.

For the nondistressed HLT market and the traditional U.S. domestic loan sales market, the five major buyers are other domestic banks, foreign banks, insurance companies and pension funds, closed-end bank loan mutual funds, and nonfinancial corporations.

Other Domestic Banks   Interbank loan sales are at the core of the traditional market and have historically revolved around correspondent banking relationships and regional banking/branching restrictions (such as the McFadden Act of 1927 and the Bank Holding Company Act of 1956 and its 1970 Amendments). Restrictions on nationwide banking have often led banks to originate regionally undiversified and borrower-undiversified loan portfolios. Small banks often sell loan participations to their large correspondents to improve regional/borrower diversification and to avoid regulatory-imposed single-borrower loan concentration ceilings. (Credit exposure to a single borrower should not exceed 10 percent of a bank's capital.) This arrangement also can work in the other direction, with the larger banks selling participations to smaller banks.

The traditional interbank market, however, has been shrinking. This is due to at least three factors. First, the traditional correspondent banking relationship is breaking down in a more competitive and increasingly consolidated banking market. Second, concerns about counterparty risk and moral hazard have increased (e.g., Penn Square, a small bank, made bad loan sales to its larger correspondent bank, Continental Illinois, in the early 1980s). Third, the barriers to nationwide banking were largely eroded with the passage of the Riegle-Neal Interstate Branching and Efficiency Act of 1994. Nevertheless, some small banks find the loan sales market enormously useful as a way to regionally diversify their loan portfolios.

Foreign Banks   Foreign banks remain an important buyer of domestic U.S. loans. In recent years they have purchased over 40 percent of loans sold. Because of the high cost of branching, the loan sales market allows foreign banks to achieve a well-diversified domestic U.S. loan portfolio without developing a costly nationwide banking network. However, renewed interest in asset **downsizing,** especially among Japanese banks (see Chapter 23), has caused this source of demand to contract.

downsizing
Shrinking the asset size of an FI.

Insurance Companies and Pension Funds   Subject to meeting liquidity and quality or investment grade regulatory restrictions, insurance companies (such as Aetna) and pension funds are important buyers of long-term maturity loans.

Closed- and Open-End Bank Loan Mutual Funds   First established in 1988, these leveraged mutual funds, such as Merrill Lynch Prime Fund, invest in domestic U.S. bank loans. While they purchase loans on the secondary market, such as loan resales, the largest funds also have moved into primary loan syndications because of the attractive fee income available. That is, these mutual funds participate in funding loans originated by commercial banks. The mutual fund, in turn, receives a fee or part of the interest payment. Indeed, some money center banks, such as J. P. Morgan Chase, have actively encouraged closed-end fund participation in primary loan syndications.

Nonfinancial Corporations   There are some corporations that buy loans, but this activity is limited mostly to the financial services arms of the very largest U.S. and European companies (e.g., GE Capital and ITT Finance) and amounts to no more than 5 percent of total U.S. domestic loan sales.[5]

The Sellers

The sellers of domestic loans and HLT loans are major money center banks, foreign banks, investment banks, and the U.S. government and its agencies.

Major Money Center Banks   Loan selling has been dominated by the largest money center banks. In recent years, market concentration on the loan-selling side has been accentuated by the growth of HLTs (and the important role major money center banks have played in originating loans in HLT deals) as well as the growth in real estate loan sales. In recent years, large money center banks have engaged in large (real estate) loan sales directly or have formalized such sales through the mechanism of a "good bank–bad bank" structure.

Good Bank–Bad Bank   Bad banks are special-purpose vehicles organized to liquidate portfolios of nonperforming loans. The principal objective in their creation is to maximize asset values by separating good loans (in the "good bank") from bad loans (in the "bad bank"). Past examples of bad banks include Grant Street National Bank (established by Mellon bank), National Loan Bank (established by Chemical), and National Asset Bank (established by First Interstate).[6] For example,

---

[5] Nonfinancial corporations are bigger buyers in the emerging-market loan sales market as part of debt-equity swaps (see Chapter 16).

[6] This technique also has been used outside the United States. For example, in 1998 the good bank–bad bank structure was adopted by the Indonesian government as a way of resolving the bad debt crisis in the domestic banking industry. In the early 2000s, this format was adopted in Japan as a way to separate nonperforming loans from other bank assets.

TABLE 27–2   Good Bank–Bad Bank Balance Sheets before and after a Loan Sale (in millions)

Panel A: Good Bank

	Before Loan Sale				After Loan Sale		
Assets		**Liabilities/Equity**		**Assets**		**Liabilities/Equity**	
Cash assets	$ 500	Deposits	$2,500	Cash assets	$ 500	Deposits	$2,500
Loans		Purchased		Loans		Purchased	
Performing	2,500	funds	750	Performing	2,500	funds	170
Nonperforming	950	Equity	700	Nonperforming	0	Equity	330
	$3,950		$3,950		$3,000		$3,000

Panel B: Bad Bank

	Before Loan Sale				After Loan Sale		
Assets		**Liabilities/Equity**		**Assets**		**Liabilities/Equity**	
Cash assets	$ 600	Bonds	$300	Cash assets	$ 20	Bonds	$300
Loans	0	Preferred		Loans	580	Preferred	
		stock	100			stock	100
		Common				Common	
		stock	200			stock	200
	$ 600		$600		$600		$600

Mellon Bank wrote down the face value of $941 million in real estate loans and sold them to a specially created bad bank subsidiary—Grant Street National Bank—for $577 million. This special-purpose bad bank was funded by bond issues and common and preferred stock. Managers of the bad bank were given equity (junior preferred stock) as an incentive mechanism to generate maximum values in liquidating the loans purchased from Mellon (i.e., achieving a market resale value greater than $577 million).

Table 27–2 illustrates the sale of nonperforming loans from a good bank to a subsidiary bad bank. In panel A of Table 27–2, the good bank has $950 million of nonperforming loans along with $2,500 million in performing loans and $500 million in cash assets on its balance sheet before the loan sale. The assets are financed with $2,500 million in deposits, $750 million in purchased funds, and $700 million in equity. If the bad bank, in panel B, buys the nonperforming loans (with the proceeds of a bond, preferred stock, and common stock financing) for $580 million, the good bank gets these loans off of its balance sheet, incurring a $370 million loss in equity (i.e., $950 million face value of loans minus $580 million received in their purchase). The proceeds of the loan sale are then used to pay off purchased funds, bringing their balance down to $170 million, or $750 million minus $580 million. The bad bank now has the $950 million face value loans (for which it paid $580 million) on its balance sheet. These loans can be restructured or disposed of. If the loans realize more than $580 million, additional returns can be passed through to the bad bank common stockholders in dividends or used to repurchase bonds or preferred stock.

There are at least five reasons for believing that loan sales through a bad bank vehicle will be value enhancing compared to the originating bank itself retaining (and eventually selling) these loans:

1. The bad bank enables bad assets to be managed by loan workout specialists.

2. The good bank's reputation and access to deposit and funding markets tend to be improved once bad loans are removed from the balance sheet.

3. Because the bad bank does not have any short-term deposits (i.e., is a self-liquidating entity), it can follow an optimal disposition strategy for bad assets, as it is not overly concerned with liquidity needs.

4. As in the case of Mellon's bad bank, contracts for managers can be created to maximize their incentives to generate enhanced values from loan sales.

5. The good bank–bad bank structure reduces information asymmetries about the value of the good bank's assets (the so-called lemons problem), thus potentially increasing its attractiveness to risk-averse investors.

Foreign Banks   To the extent that foreign banks are sellers rather than buyers of loans, these loans come out of branch networks such as Japanese-owned banks in California or through their market-making activities selling loans originated in their home country in U.S. loan sales markets. One of the major market makers in the U.S. loan sales market (especially the HLT market) is the Dutch FI, ING Bank.

Investment Banks   Investment banks, such as Bear Stearns, act as loan sellers either as part of their market-making function (selling loans they have originated) or as active traders. Again, these loan sales are generally confined to large HLT transactions.

The U.S. Government and Its Agencies.   In recent years the U.S. government and its agencies have shown an increased willingness to engage in loan sales. This has been aided by the passage of the 1996 Federal Debt Collection Improvements Act, which authorizes federal agencies to sell delinquent and defaulted loan assets. Figure 27–2 shows an advertisement by the FDIC of a sale of assets in November 2001. The Department of Housing and Urban Development also has been an increasingly large seller of mortgage loans on multifamily apartment properties. However, the largest loan sales by a government agency to date were made by the Resolution Trust Corporation (RTC). Established in 1989, and disbanded at the end of 1995, the RTC had to resolve more than 700 problem savings institutions through merger, closure, or conservatorship. With respect to the U.S. commercial and industrial loan sale market, RTC dispositions had a relatively moderate supply-side effect largely because the bulk of RTC's asset sales were real estate assets (such as multifamily mortgages). The tendency of the RTC was to combine good and bad loans into loan packages and sell them at auction to bidders. For example, in an April 21, 1995, auction, it offered the highest bidder a package of 29 different commercial assets for sale—located in New Jersey, New York, and Pennsylvania—with aggregate estimated market values of $7.5 million. Bidders had only four days to enter bids on this asset package.

www.fdic.gov

www.hud.gov

Concept Questions

1. Which loans should have the highest yields: (*a*) loans sold with recourse or (*b*) loans sold without recourse?

2. Which have higher yields, junk bonds or HLT loans? Explain your answer.

3. Describe the two basic types of loan sale contracts by which loans can be transferred between seller and buyer.

4. What institutions are the major buyers in the traditional U.S. domestic loan sales market? What institutions are the major sellers in this market?

FIGURE 27–2
Loan Sale
Announcement by
the FDIC

FDIC

Special Sales Announcement - 4th Quarter Performing/Non-Performing
Loan Sale

The Dallas Field Operations Branch of the FDIC is offering for sale the following Loan Sale Pools. Loans in these packages are stratified as listed below.

Pool Number	Description	# of Loans	Book Value
1152MC	Primarily Performing SFR's	88	3,138,914
1180DJ	Non-Performing Chapter 11 Bankruptcy	1	748,556
1185CF	Performing Auto / SFR / Manufactured Housing	10	171,984
1191CW	Non-Performing / Performing Autos / Real Estate / Unsecured	10	90,774
1195RK	Charge-offs	64	177,392
SNB175RK	Non-Performing Automobile Retail Installment Contracts	35	140,798
SNB200RK	Non-Performing Manufactured Housing Contracts	14	604,788
SNB250RK	Non-Performing Real Estate Mortgages	18	1,129,402
SNB275RK	Non-Performing Consumer Loans	17	559,293
SNB415RK	Performing Automobile Retail Installment Contracts	791	2,622,463
SNB425RK	Performing Manufactured Housing Contracts	130	6,078,566

The size of these packages may change without notice

Bid Package information and package updates will be available via a secured Internet site at IntraLinks.com. If you would like access to the secured website, please fax a signed Confidentiality Agreement to 972-761-8241.
Confidentiality Agreement for 4th Quarter Loan Sale

Please make sure to include your phone number and e-mail address on the Confidentiality Agreement. This information will be required to give you access to the secured website and bid package. Hard copy Bid Packages will be available by contacting Twila Tedder (ttedder@fdic.gov) at 1-800-568-9161, Ext. 8232 or Beatrice Culley (bculley@fdic.gov) at Ext. 8228.

Interested bidders may schedule on-site due diligence, which will commence on Monday, October 22, 2001 through Friday, November 9, 2001. Due diligence will be held at the FDIC - Dallas Field Operations Branch, Pacific Place, 1910 Pacific Avenue, Dallas, Texas 75201 from 7:30 a.m. to 5:00 p.m. Monday through Friday. Access to the files will be granted by appointment only. A Confidentiality Agreement is required prior to viewing.

To schedule an appointment for due diligence please e-mail or call 1-800-568-9161 and ask for one of the following individuals: Edith Allen, ext. 2326 (eallen@fdic.gov), or Beatrice Culley, ext. 8228 (bculley@fdic.gov).

BID DEADLINE: 1:00 P.M. (CST) WEDNESDAY, NOVEMBER 14, 2001

WHY BANKS AND OTHER FIs SELL LOANS

The introduction to this chapter stated that one reason that FIs sell loans is to manage their credit risk better. Loan sales remove assets (and credit risk) from the balance sheet and allow an FI to achieve better asset diversification. However, other than credit risk management, there are a number of economic and regulatory reasons that encourage FIs to sell loans. These are discussed below.

Reserve Requirements

Regulatory requirements, such as noninterest-bearing reserve requirements that a bank has to hold at the central bank, are a form of tax that adds to the cost of funding the loan portfolio. Regulatory taxes such as reserve requirements create an incentive for banks to remove loans from the balance sheet by selling them without recourse to outside parties.[7] Such removal allows banks to shrink both their assets and deposits and, thus, the amount of reserves they have to hold against their deposits.

Fee Income

An FI can often report any fee income earned from originating (and then selling) loans as current income, whereas interest earned on direct lending can be accrued (as income) only over time. As a result, originating and quickly selling loans can boost an FI's reported income under current accounting rules.

Capital Costs

Like reserve requirements, the capital adequacy requirements imposed on FIs are a burden as long as required capital exceeds the amount the FI believes to be privately beneficial. For tax reasons, debt is a cheaper source of funds than equity capital. Thus, FIs struggling to meet a required capital (K) to assets (A) ratio can boost this ratio by reducing assets (A) rather than boosting capital (K) (see Chapter 20). One way to downsize or reduce A and boost the K/A ratio is through loan sales.

Liquidity Risk

In addition to credit risk and interest rate risk, holding loans on the balance sheet can increase the overall illiquidity of an FI's assets. This illiquidity is a problem because FI liabilities tend to be highly liquid. Asset illiquidity can expose an FI to harmful liquidity squeezes whenever liability holders unexpectedly liquidate their claims. To mitigate a liquidity problem, an FI's management can sell some of its loans to outside investors. Thus, the loan sales market has created a secondary market in loans that has significantly reduced the illiquidity of FI loans held as assets on the balance sheet.

Concept Questions

1. What are some of the economic and regulatory reasons why FIs choose to sell loans?
2. How can an FI use its loans to mitigate a liquidity problem?

FACTORS DETERRING LOAN SALES GROWTH IN THE FUTURE

The loan sales market has gone through a number of up and down phases in recent years (as discussed above). However, notwithstanding the value of loan sales as a credit risk management tool, there remain a number of factors that will both spur and deter the market's growth and development in future years. We first discuss factors that may deter the market's growth.

---

[7] Under current reserve requirement regulations (Regulation D, amended May 1986), bank loan sales with recourse are regarded as a liability and hence are subject to reserve requirements. The reservability of loan sales extends to when a bank issues a credit guaranty as well as a recourse provision. Loans sold without recourse (or credit guarantees by the selling bank) are free of reserve requirements. With the elimination of reserve requirements on nontransaction accounts, the lowering of reserve requirements on transaction accounts in 1991, and the innovation of deposit sweep accounts (see Chapter 18), the reserve tax effect is likely to become a less important feature driving bank loan sales (as well as the recourse/nonrecourse mix) in the future.

Access to the Commercial Paper Market

Beginning with the advent of Section 20 subsidiaries in 1987, large banks have enjoyed much greater powers to underwrite commercial paper (and other securities) directly without legal challenges by the securities industry that underwriting by banks is contrary to the Glass-Steagall Act. With the passage of the Financial Services Modernization Act of 1999 and the abolition of the Glass-Steagall Act, the need to underwrite or sell short-term bank loans as an imperfect substitute for commercial paper underwriting is even less important. In addition, more and more smaller middle market firms are gaining direct access to the commercial paper market. As a result, they have less need to rely on bank loans to finance their short-term expenditures.

Customer Relationship Effects

As the financial institutions industry consolidates and expands the range of financial services sold, customer relationships are likely to become even more important than they are today. To the extent that a loan customer (borrower) views the sale of its loan by its FI as an adverse statement about the customer's value to the FI,[8] loan sales can harm revenues generated by the FI as current and potential future customers take their business elsewhere.

Legal Concerns

fraudulent conveyance
When a transaction such as a sale of securities or transference of assets to a particular party is ruled illegal.

A number of legal concerns hamper the loan sale market's growth, especially for distressed HLT loans. In particular, while banks are normally secured creditors, this status may be attacked by other creditors if the firm enters bankruptcy. For example, **fraudulent conveyance** proceedings have been brought against the secured lenders to Revco, Circle K, Allied Stores, and RJR Nabisco. If such legal moves are upheld, then the sale of loans to a particular party may be found to be illegal. Such legal suits represent one of the factors that have slowed the growth of the distressed loan market. Indeed, in many of the most recent HLT sales, loan buyers have demanded a put option feature that allows them to put the loan back to the seller at the purchase price if a transaction is proved to be fraudulent under the Uniform Fraudulent Conveyance Act. Further, a second type of distressed-firm risk may result if, in the process of a loan workout, the FI lender acts more like an equity owner than an outside debtor. For example, the FI may get involved in the day-to-day running of the firm and make strategic investment and asset sales decisions. This could open up claims that the FI's loans should be treated like equity rather than secured debt. That is, the FI's loans may be subordinated in the claims priority ranking.[9]

Concept Questions

1. What are some of the factors that are likely to deter the growth of the loan sales market in the future?
2. What are some specific legal concerns that have hampered the growth of the loan sales market?

---

[8] S. Dahiya, M. Puri, and A. Saunders, in "Bank Borrowers and Loan Sales: New Evidence on the Uniqueness of Bank Loans," *Journal of Business,* 2003, pp. 563–82, find that stock returns of borrowers are significantly negatively impacted in the period surrounding the announcement of a loan sale. Further, the post-loan sale period is also marked by a large incidence of bankruptcy filings by those borrowers whose loans are sold. The results support the hypothesis that news of a bank loan sale has a negative certification impact.

[9] See C. James, "When Do Banks Take Equity in Debt Restructurings," *Review of Financial Studies,* 1995, pp. 1209–34.

FACTORS ENCOURAGING LOAN SALES GROWTH IN THE FUTURE

There are at least six factors that point to an increasing volume of loan sales in the future. These are in addition to the credit risk "hedging" value of loan sales.

BIS Capital Requirements

www.bis.org

The Bank for International Settlements (BIS) risk-based capital rules and the proposed reforms to those rules (see Chapter 20) mean that bankers will continue to have strong incentives to sell commercial loans to other FIs and investors to downsize their balance sheets and boost bank capital ratios.

Market Value Accounting

www.sec.gov

www.fasb.org

The Securities and Exchange Commission and the Financial Accounting Standards Board (FASB) have advocated the replacement of book value accounting with market value accounting for financial services firms (see Chapter 20). In addition, capital requirements for interest rate risk and market risk have moved banks toward a market value accounting framework (see Chapter 10). The trend towards the marking to market of assets will make bank loans look more like securities and thus make them easier to sell and/or trade.

Asset Brokerage and Loan Trading

The increased emphasis of large money center banks as well as investment banks on trading and trading income suggests that significant attention will still be paid to those segments of the loan sales market where price volatility is high and thus potential trading profits can be made. Most HLT loans have floating rates so that their underlying values are in large part insulated from swings in the level of interest rates (unlike fixed-income securities such as Treasury bonds). Nevertheless, the low credit quality of many of these loans and their long maturities create an enhanced potential for credit risk volatility. As a result, a short-term, three-month secured loan to a AAA-rated company is unlikely to show significant future credit risk volatility compared to an eight-year HLT loan to a distressed company. This suggests that trading in loans to below-investment-grade companies will always be attractive for FIs that use their specialized credit monitoring skills as asset traders rather than as asset transformers in participating in the market.

Government Loan Sales

With the passage of the 1996 Federal Debt Collection Improvements Act and the continued downsizing of federal government departments, there is a strong likelihood that the sale of loans by the government and its agencies will increase in the future.

Credit Ratings

There is a growing trend toward the "credit rating" of loans offered for sale. Unlike bonds, a loan credit rating reflects more than the financial soundness of the underlying borrowing corporation. In particular, the value of the underlying collateral can change a loan's credit rating up to one full category above a standard bond rating.[10] As more loans are rated, their attractiveness to secondary market buyers is likely to increase.

---

[10] See L. S. Alex, "How S and P Rates Commercial Loans: Implications for Bank Portfolios," *Commercial Lending Review,* Winter 1997–1998, pp. 32–37.

Purchase and Sale of Foreign Bank Loans

With over $1,200 billion in doubtful and troubled loans on their books in the early 2000s, Japanese banks present a huge potential market for the sale of distressed loans. Indeed, a number of commercial banks and investment banks have established funds to buy up some of these bad loans. For example, in 2003 Goldman Sachs announced a $9.3 billion fund to buy troubled loans from Japan's second largest bank, SMFG. This fund represented the first transfer of a bad loan package of this size to a non-government-affiliated entity in Japan. This deal was watched closely as it provided banks with a way of removing bad loans from their balance sheets while still retaining control over the corporate restructuring process.[11]

Concept Questions

1. What are some of the factors that are likely to encourage loan sales growth in the future?
2. Why have the FASB and the SEC advocated that financial services firms replace book value accounting with market value accounting?

Summary

Loan sales provide a primitive alternative to the full securitization of loans through bond packages. In particular, they provide a valuable off-balance-sheet tool to an FI that wishes to manage its credit risk exposure better. The new loan sales market grew rapidly in the 1980s and allowed FIs to sell off short-term and long-term loans of both high and low credit quality. There are a number of important factors that suggest that the loan sales market will continue to grow.

Questions and Problems

1. What is the difference between loans sold with recourse and loans sold without recourse from the perspective of both sellers and buyers?
2. A bank has made a three-year $10 million loan that pays annual interest of 8 percent. The principal is due at the end of the third year.
   a. The bank is willing to sell this loan with recourse at an interest rate of 8.5 percent. What price should it receive for this loan?
   b. The bank has the option to sell this loan without recourse at a discount rate of 8.75 percent. What price should it receive for this loan?
   c. If the bank expects a 0.5 percent probability of default on this loan, is it better to sell this loan with or without recourse? It expects to receive no interest payments or principal if the loan is defaulted.
3. What are some of the key features of short-term loan sales?
4. Why are yields higher on loan sales than on commercial paper issues with similar maturity and issue size?
5. What are highly leveraged transactions? What constitutes the federal regulatory definition of an HLT?
6. How do the characteristics of an HLT loan differ from those of a short-term loan that is sold?
7. What is a possible reason why the spreads on HLT loans perform differently than do the spreads on junk bonds?

[11] See "SMFG Links with Goldman to Tackle Bad Loans," *Financial Times,* October 9, 2003, p. 32.

8. City Bank has made a 10-year, $2 million HLT loan that pays an annual interest of 10 percent. The principal is expected at maturity.

   a. What should City Bank expect to receive from the sale of this loan if the current market interest rate on loans of this risk is 12 percent?

   b. The price of loans of this risk is currently being quoted in the secondary market at bid-offer prices of 88–89 cents (on each dollar). Translate these quotes into actual prices for the above loan.

   c. Do these prices reflect a distressed or nondistressed loan? Explain.

9. What is the difference between loan participations and loan assignments?

10. What are the difficulties in completing a loan assignment?

11. Who are the buyers of U.S. loans, and why do they participate in this activity?

    a. What are vulture funds?

    b. What are three reasons why the interbank market has been shrinking?

    c. What are reasons why a small bank would be interested in participating in a loan syndication?

12. Who are the sellers of U.S. loans, and why do they participate in this activity?

    a. What is the purpose of a bad bank?

    b. What are the reasons why loan sales through a bad bank will be value enhancing?

    c. What impact has the 1996 Federal Debt Collection Improvements Act had on the loan sale market?

13. In addition to managing credit risk, what are some other reasons for the sale of loans by FIs?

14. What are factors that may deter the growth of the loan sales market in the future? Discuss.

15. An FI is planning the purchase of a $5 million loan to raise the existing average duration of its assets from 3.5 years to 5 years. It currently has total assets worth $20 million, $5 million in cash (0 duration) and $15 million in loans. All the loans are fairly priced.

    a. Assuming it uses the cash to purchase the loan, should it purchase the loan if its duration is seven years?

    b. What asset duration loans should it purchase to raise its average duration to five years?

16. In addition to hedging credit risk, what are five factors that are expected to encourage loan sales in the future? Discuss the impact of each factor.

Web Question

17. Go to the FDIC Web site at **www.fdic.gov**. From there, click on "Investors," then click on "Closed Real Estate Sales," and then click on "Find" to get information on recent real estate loan sales by banks. Repeat the process clicking on "Closed Loan Sales." What percentage of these loan sales consisted of performing versus nonperforming loans? Calculate the average percentage loss on these sales.

www.mhhe.com/saunders5e

Pertinent Web Sites

Bank for International Settlements	www.bis.org
Department of Housing and Urban Development	www.hud.gov
Federal Deposit Insurance Corporation	www.fdic.gov
Financial Accounting Standards Board	www.fasb.org
Loan Pricing Corporation	www.loanpricing.com
Securities and Exchange Commission	www.sec.gov
The Wall Street Journal	www.wsj.com

Chapter **Twenty-Eight**

Securitization

INTRODUCTION

asset securitization
The packaging and selling of loans and other assets backed by securities.

Along with futures, forwards, options, swaps, and loan sales, **asset securitization**—the packaging and selling of loans and other assets backed by securities—is a mechanism that FIs use to hedge their interest rate exposure gaps. In addition, the process of securitization allows FI asset portfolios to become more liquid, provides an important source of fee income (with FIs acting as servicing agents for the assets sold), and helps reduce the effects of regulatory taxes such as capital requirements, reserve requirements, and deposit insurance premiums. Thus, as of year-end 2003, over 63 percent of all residential mortgages were securitized, compared with less than 15 percent in 1980.

This chapter investigates the role of securitization in improving the return-risk trade-off for FIs. We describe the three major forms, or vehicles, of asset securitization and analyze their unique characteristics. The major forms of asset securitization are the pass-through security, the collateralized mortgage obligation (CMO), and the mortgage-backed bond. Chapter 27 dealt with a more primitive form of asset securitization—loan sales—whereby loans are sold or traded to other investors and no new securities are created. In addition, although all three forms of securitization originated in the real estate lending market, these techniques are currently being applied to loans other than mortgages—for example, credit card loans, auto loans, student loans, and commercial and industrial (C&I) loans.

THE PASS-THROUGH SECURITY

FIs frequently pool mortgages and other assets they originate and offer investors an interest in the pool in the form of *pass-through securities*. While many different types of loans and assets on FIs' balance sheets are currently being securitized, the original use of securitization is a result of government-sponsored programs to enhance the liquidity of the residential mortgage market. These programs indirectly subsidize the growth of home ownership in the United States.

Given this, we begin by analyzing the government-sponsored securitization of residential mortgage loans. Three government agencies or government-sponsored enterprises are directly involved in the creation of mortgage-backed, pass-through securities. Informally, they are known as Ginnie Mae (GNMA), Fannie Mae (FNMA), and Freddie Mac (FHLMC).

GNMA

www.ginniemae.gov

The Government National Mortgage Association (GNMA), or "Ginnie Mae," began in 1968 when it split off from the FNMA. GNMA is a government-owned agency with two major functions. The first is sponsoring mortgage-backed securities programs by FIs such as banks, thrifts, and mortgage bankers. The second is acting as a guarantor to investors in mortgage-backed securities regarding the timely pass-through of principal and interest payments on their sponsored bonds. In other words, GNMA provides **timing insurance.** We describe this more fully later in the chapter. In acting as a sponsor and payment-timing guarantor, GNMA supports only those pools of mortgage loans whose default or credit risk is insured by one of three government agencies: the Federal Housing Administration (FHA), the Veterans Administration (VA), and the Farmers Home Administration (FMHA). Mortgage loans insured by these agencies target groups that might otherwise be disadvantaged in the housing market, such as low-income families, young families, and veterans. As such, the maximum mortgage under the FHA/VA/FMHA–GNMA securitization program is capped.

timing insurance
A service provided by a sponsor of pass-through securities (such as GNMA) guaranteeing the bondholder interest and principal payments at the calendar date promised.

FNMA

www.fanniemae.com

Originally created in 1938, the Federal National Mortgage Association (FNMA), or "Fannie Mae," is the oldest of the three mortgage-backed security sponsoring agencies. While it is now a private corporation owned by shareholders with stock traded on major exchanges, in the minds of many investors it still has implicit government backing that makes it equivalent to a government-sponsored agency.[1] Indeed, supporting this view is the fact that FNMA has a secured line of credit available from the U.S. Treasury should it need funds in an emergency. FNMA is a more active agency than GNMA in creating pass-through securities. GNMA merely sponsors such programs. FNMA actually helps create pass-throughs by buying and holding mortgages on its balance sheet; it also issues bonds directly to finance those purchases.

Specifically, FNMA creates mortgage-backed securities (MBSs) by purchasing packages of mortgage loans from banks and thrifts; it finances such purchases by selling MBSs to outside investors such as life insurers and pension funds. In addition, FNMA engages in swap transactions whereby it swaps MBSs with an FI for original mortgages. Since FNMA guarantees securities as to the full and timely payment of interest and principal, the FI receiving the MBSs can then resell them on the capital market or hold them in its portfolio. Unlike GNMA, FNMA securitizes conventional mortgage loans as well as FHA/VA insured loans, as long as the conventional loans have acceptable loan-to-value or collateral ratios normally not exceeding 80 percent. Conventional loans with high loan-to-value ratios usually require additional private sector credit insurance before they are accepted into FNMA securitization pools.

FHLMC

www.freddiemac.com

The Federal Home Loan Mortgage Corporation (FHLMC), or "Freddie Mac," performs a function similar to that of FNMA except that its major securitization role has historically involved savings institutions. Like FNMA, FHLMC is a stockholder-owned corporation with a line of credit from the U.S. Treasury. Further, like FNMA, it buys mortgage loan pools from FIs and swaps MBSs for loans. FHLMC also sponsors conventional loan pools as well as FHA/VA mortgage pools and guarantees timely payment of interest and ultimate payment of principal on the securities it issues.

Together FNMA and FHLMC represent a huge presence in the financial system as they have over 63 percent of the single-family mortgage pools in the United States.

---

[1] See R. W. Spahr and M. A. Sunderman, "The Effect of Prepayment Modeling in Pricing Mortgage-Backed Securities," *Journal of Housing Research* 3 (1992), pp. 381–400.

Some regulators and politicians have argued that these two government-sponsored agencies have gained too much of a market share. In the early 2000s, their credit losses increased as did their debt-to-equity ratios. Debt to equity for these two agencies ranged from 30 to 97 percent depending on the assumptions made about off-balance-sheet exposures. Recent balance sheets for the two agencies are reported in Appendix 28A, located at the book's Web site (**www.mhhe.com/saunders5e**).

Also, in the early 2000s, these two agencies came under fire for several reasons. First, in September 2002 Fannie Mae was criticized for allowing a sharp increase in interest rate risk to exist on its balance sheet. The Office of Federal Housing Enterprise Oversight (OFHEO), a main regulator of Fannie Mae, required Fannie Mae to submit weekly reports to the OFHEO on the company's exposure to interest rate risk. The OFHEO also instructed Fannie Mae to keep regulators apprised of any challenges associated with returning its interest rate risk measure to more acceptable levels, and warned that the office may take additional action if there were adverse developments with Fannie Mae's management's effectiveness in lowering interest rate risk. In October 2003, Fannie Mae and Freddie Mac came under new criticism for allegedly overcharging lenders for services they provide. The overcharges came in the fees that the companies collect from banks, thrifts, and other lenders for guaranteeing repayment of their mortgages. If true, the overcharges hurt mortgage lenders, squeezing their profit margins and perhaps home buyers, too, as lenders increased mortgage interest rates to recover the increased fees. Later that same month, Fannie Mae announced that it miscalculated the value of its mortgages, forcing it to make a $1.1 billion restatement of its stockholders' equity. Earlier in the year, Freddie Mac announced a $4.5 billion misstatement of its earnings. While both were claimed to be computational errors, the episodes reinforced fears that Fannie Mae and Freddie Mac lack the necessary skills to operate their massive and complex businesses, which some investors and political critics worry could pose risk to the nation's financial system if not properly managed. Finally, in February 2004, Federal Reserve Chairman Alan Greenspan stated that Fannie Mae and Freddie Mac pose very serious risks to the U.S. financial system and urged Congress to curb their growth sooner rather than later.

Underlying the concerns about the actions of these two government-sponsored agencies is the widespread perception among investors that neither would be allowed to fail if they got into trouble. This perception creates a subsidy for the agencies and allows them to borrow more cheaply than other firms with similar balance sheets. The fear is that the two agencies use their implicit federal backing to assume more risk and finance expansion through increased debt. Such actions create a source of systematic risk for the U.S. financial system.

As a result of these problems and the potential risk to the financial system, in 2004 the U.S. Senate proposed a bill that would create a new independent regulator of Fannie Mae and Freddie Mac with broad authority to determine the companies' safety and soundness, capital standards, and new lines of business, and even to decide the companies' ultimate fate in the event of insolvency. The OFHEO followed up the Senate's actions with the drafting of a rule that would spell out how it could take over and wind down Fannie Mae and Freddie Mac's operations if they ever get into financial trouble. Adoption of that rule would send a strong signal to investors that the two agencies are not fully guaranteed by the U.S. government and not immune from market forces.[2]

---

[2] See "Fannie, Freddie Face a Tough Plan," *The Wall Street Journal*, March 29, 2004, p. A2; and "Regulators Hit Fannie, Freddie with New Assault," *The Wall Street Journal*, April 28, 2004, p. A1.

The Incentives and Mechanics of Pass-Through Security Creation

In order to analyze the securitization process, we trace through the mechanics of a mortgage pool securitization to provide insights into the return-risk benefits of this process to the mortgage-originating FI as well as the attractiveness of these securities to investors. Given that more than $3 trillion of mortgage-backed securities are outstanding—a large proportion sponsored by GNMA—we analyze an example of the creation of a GNMA pass-through security next.[3]

Suppose a bank has just originated 1,000 new residential mortgages in its local area. The average size of each mortgage is $100,000. Thus, the total size of the new mortgage pool is

$$1,000 \times \$100,000 = \$100 \text{ million}$$

Each mortgage, because of its small size, will receive credit risk insurance protection from the FHA. This insurance costs a small fee to the originating bank. In addition, each of these new mortgages has an initial stated maturity of 30 years and a mortgage rate—often called the mortgage coupon—of 12 percent per annum. Suppose the bank originating these loans relies mostly on liabilities such as demand deposits as well as its own capital or equity to finance its assets. Under current capital adequacy requirements, each $1 of new residential mortgage loans has to be backed by some capital. Since residential mortgages fall into Category 3 [50 percent risk weight in the risk-based capital standards (see Chapter 20)], and the risk-based capital requirement is 8 percent, the bank capital needed to back the $100 million mortgage portfolio would be

$$\text{Capital requirement} = \$100 \text{ million} \times .5 \times .08 = \$4 \text{ million}$$

We assume that the remaining $96 million needed to fund the mortgages come from the issuance of demand deposits. Current regulations require that for every dollar of demand deposits held by the bank, however, $0.10 in cash reserves be held at the Federal Reserve Bank (see Chapter 19). Assuming that the bank funds the cash reserves with demand deposits, the bank must issue $106.67m. ($96m./ [1−.1]) in demand deposits (i.e., $96m. to fund mortgages and $10.67m. to fund the required cash reserves on the demand deposits). The reserve requirement on demand deposits is essentially an additional "regulatory" tax, over and above the capital requirement, on funding the bank's residential mortgage portfolio.[4] Note that since a 0 percent reserve requirement currently exists on CDs and time deposits, the FI needs no extra funds to pay reserve requirements if it uses CDs to fund the mortgage portfolio.

Given these considerations, the bank's initial postmortgage balance sheet may look like that in Table 28–1. In addition to the capital and reserve requirement taxes, the bank has to pay an annual insurance premium to the FDIC based on the risk of the bank. Assuming a deposit insurance premium of 27 basis points (for the lowest-quality banks), the fee would be[5]

$$\$106.67 \text{ million} \times .0027 = \$288,000$$

---

[3] In 2003, outstanding mortgage pools were $4.3 trillion, with GNMA pools amounting to $516 billion; FNMA, $1,637 billion; and FHLMC, $1,073 billion.

[4] Implicitly viewing the capital requirement as a tax assumes that regulators set the minimum level above the level that would be privately optimal.

[5] In 2004 the deposit insurance premium was zero for the highest-quality banks (see Chapter 19).

TABLE 28–1
Bank Balance Sheet (in millions of dollars)

Assets		Liabilities	
Cash reserves	$10.67	Demand deposits	$106.67
Long-term mortgages	100.00	Capital	4.00
	$110.67		$110.67

Although the bank is earning a 12 percent mortgage coupon on its mortgage portfolio, it is facing three levels of regulatory taxes:

1. Capital requirements.
2. Reserve requirements.
3. FDIC insurance premiums.

Thus, one incentive to securitize is to reduce the regulatory tax burden on the FI to increase its after-tax return.[6] In addition to facing regulatory taxes on its residential mortgage portfolio earnings, the bank in Table 28–1 has two risk exposure problems.

Gap Exposure or $D_A > kD_L$

The FI funds the 30-year mortgage portfolio with short-term demand deposits; thus, it has a duration mismatch.[7] This is true even if the mortgage assets have been funded with short-term CDs, time deposits, or other purchased funds.

Illiquidity Exposure

The bank is holding a very illiquid asset portfolio of long-term mortgages and no excess reserves; as a result, it is exposed to the potential liquidity shortages discussed in Chapter 17, including the risk of having to conduct mortgage asset fire sales to meet large unexpected demand deposit withdrawals.

One possible solution to these duration mismatch and illiquidity risk problems is to lengthen the bank's on-balance-sheet liabilities by issuing longer-term deposits or other liability claims, such as medium-term notes. Another solution is to engage in interest rate swaps to transform the bank's liabilities into those of a long-term, fixed-rate nature (see Chapter 26). These techniques do not resolve the problem of regulatory taxes and the burden they impose on the FI's returns.

By contrast, creating GNMA pass-through securities can largely resolve the duration and illiquidity risk problems on the one hand and reduce the burden of regulatory taxes on the other. This requires the bank to securitize the $100 million in residential mortgages by issuing GNMA pass-through securities. In our example, the bank can do this since the 1,000 underlying mortgages each has FHA/VA mortgage insurance, the same stated mortgage maturity of 30 years, and coupons of 12 percent. Therefore, they are eligible for securitization under the GNMA program if the bank is an approved lender (which we assume it is).

The bank begins the securitization process by packaging the $100 million in mortgage loans and removing them from the balance sheet by placing them with a third-party trustee, in a special-purpose vehicle (SPV) off the balance sheet. This third-party trustee may be another bank of high creditworthiness or a legal trustee.

[6] Other reasons for securitization include greater geographic diversification of the loan portfolio. Specifically, many FIs originate mortgages from the local community; the ability to securitize facilitates replacing them with MBSs based on mortgages from other cities and regions.

[7] As we discuss in Chapters 8 and 9, core demand deposits usually have a duration of less than three years. Depending on prepayment assumptions, mortgages normally have durations of at least 4.5 years.

Next, the bank determines that (1) GNMA will guarantee, for a fee, the timing of interest and principal payments on the bonds issued to back the mortgage pool and (2) the bank itself will continue to service the pool of mortgages for a fee, even after they are placed in trust. Then GNMA issues pass-through securities backed by the underlying $100 million pool of mortgages. These GNMA securities or pass-through bonds are sold to outside investors in the capital market and the proceeds (net of any underwriting fees) go to the originating bank. Large purchasers of these securities include insurance companies and pension funds.

Before we examine the mechanics of the repayment on a pass-through security, we consider the attractiveness of these bonds to investors. In particular, investors in these bonds are protected against two levels or types of default risk.

Default Risk by the Mortgagees

Suppose that because of rapidly falling house prices, a homeowner walked away from a mortgage, leaving behind a low-valued house to be foreclosed at a price below the outstanding mortgage. This might expose the mortgage bondholders to losses unless there are external guarantors. Through FHA/VA housing insurance, government agencies bear the risk of default, thereby protecting bondholders against such losses.

Default Risk by Bank/Trustee

Suppose the bank that had originated the mortgages went bankrupt or the trustee absconded with the mortgage interest and principal due to bondholders. Because it guaranteed the prompt timing of interest and principal payments on GNMA securities, GNMA would bear the cost of making the promised payments in full and on time to GNMA bondholders.

Given this default protection, GNMA bondholders' (or investors') returns from holding these bonds would be the monthly repayments of interest and principal on the 1,000 mortgages in the pool, after the deduction of a mortgage-servicing fee by the mortgage-originating bank and a monthly timing insurance fee to be paid to GNMA. The total sum of these fees is around 50 basis points, or $\frac{1}{2}$ percent, with approximately 6 basis points going as a fee to GNMA for timing insurance and the remaining 44 basis points going to the mortgage originator as a servicing fee. As a result, the stated coupons on the GNMA bonds would be set at approximately $\frac{1}{2}$ percent below the coupon rate on the underlying mortgages. In our example:

Mortgage coupon rate	=	12.00%
minus		
Servicing fee	=	0.44
minus		
GNMA insurance fee	=	0.06
GNMA pass-through bond coupon	=	11.50%

Suppose that GNMA issues $100 million face value bonds at par to back the pool of mortgage loans. The minimum size of a single bond is $25,000; each bondholder gets a pro rata monthly share of all the interest and principal received by the bank minus servicing costs and insurance fees. Thus, if a life insurance company bought 25 percent of the GNMA bond issue (or 1,000 bonds × $25,000 each = $25 million), it would get a 25 percent share of the 360 promised monthly payments from the mortgages comprising the mortgage pool.

fully amortized
An equal periodic repayment on a loan that reflects part interest and part principal over the life of the loan.

Every month, each mortgagee makes a payment to the bank. The bank aggregates these payments and passes the funds through to GNMA bond investors via the trustee net of servicing fee and insurance fee deductions. To make things easy, most fixed-rate mortgages are **fully amortized** over the mortgage's life. This means that as long as the mortgagee does not seek to prepay the mortgage early within the 30-year period, either to buy a new house or to refinance the mortgage should interest rates fall, bondholders can expect to receive a constant stream of payments each month analogous to the stream of income on other fixed-coupon, fixed-income bonds. In reality, however, mortgagees do not act in such a predictable fashion. For a variety of reasons, they relocate (sell their house) or refinance their mortgages (especially when current mortgage rates are below mortgage coupon rates). This propensity to **prepay** early, before a mortgage matures, and then refinance with a new mortgage means that *realized* coupons/cash flows on pass-through securities can often deviate substantially from the stated or expected coupon flows in a no-prepayment world. This unique prepayment risk provides the attraction of pass-throughs to some investors but leads other, more risk-averse, investors to avoid these instruments. Before we analyze in greater detail the unique nature of prepayment risk, we summarize the steps followed in the creation of a pass-through in Figure 28–1. Then we analyze how this securitization has helped solve the duration, illiquidity, and regulatory tax problems of the FI manager.

prepay
A borrower pays back a loan before maturity to the FI that originated the loan.

In the previous discussion we traced the GNMA securitization process, the origination of mortgages on the balance sheet (Figure 28–1, Box 1) through to the sale of GNMA bonds to outside investors (Box 4). To close the securitization process, the cash proceeds of the sale of GNMA bonds (Box 5) net of any underwriting fees go to the originating bank. As a result, the bank has substituted long-term mortgages for cash by using the GNMA securitization mechanism. Abstracting from the various fees and underwriting costs in the securitization process, the balance

FIGURE 28–1
Summary of a GNMA Pass-Through

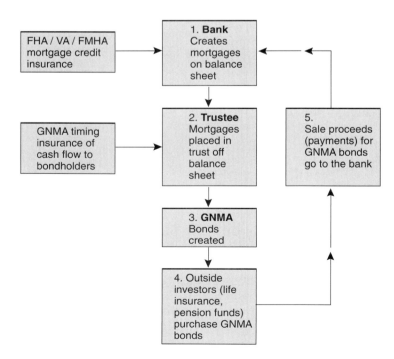

TABLE 28–2
The Bank's Balance Sheet after Securitization (in millions of dollars)

Assets		Liabilities	
Cash reserves	$10.67	Demand deposits	$106.67
Cash proceeds from mortgage securitization	100.00	Capital	4.00
	$110.67		$110.67

sheet of the bank might look like the one in Table 28–2 immediately after the securitization has taken place.

There has been a dramatic change in the balance sheet exposure of the bank. First, $100 million illiquid mortgage loans have been replaced by $100 million cash. Second, the duration mismatch has been reduced since both D_A and D_L are now low. Third, the bank has an enhanced ability to deal with and reduce its regulatory taxes. Specifically, it can reduce its capital since capital standards require none be held against cash on the balance sheet compared to residential mortgages that require a 4 percent capital ratio. Reserve requirements and deposit insurance premiums are also reduced if the bank uses part of the cash proceeds from the GNMA sale to pay off or retire demand deposits and downsize its balance sheet.

Of course, keeping an all or highly liquid asset portfolio and/or downsizing is a way to reduce regulatory taxes, but these strategies are hardly likely to enhance an FI's profits. The real logic of securitization is that the cash proceeds from the mortgage/GNMA sale can be reused to create or originate new mortgages, which in turn can be securitized. In so doing, the FI is acting more like an asset (mortgage) broker than a traditional asset transformer, as we discussed in Chapter 1. The advantage of being an asset broker is that the FI profits from mortgage pool servicing fees plus up-front points and fees from mortgage origination. At the same time, the FI no longer has to bear the illiquidity and duration mismatch risks and regulatory taxes that arise when it acts as an asset transformer and holds mortgages to maturity on its balance sheet. Put more simply, the FI's profitability becomes more fee dependent than interest rate spread dependent.

The limits of this securitization process clearly depend on the supply of mortgages (and other assets) that can be securitized and the demand by investors for pass-through securities. As was noted earlier, the unique feature of pass-through securities from the demand-side perspective of investors is prepayment risk. To understand the unique nature of this risk and why it might deter or limit investments by other FIs and investors, we next analyze the characteristics of pass-through securities more formally.

Concept Questions

1. What is a pass-through security?
2. Why did Fannie Mae and Freddie Mac come under fire from regulators in the early 2000s?
3. Should an FI with $D_A > kD_L$ seek to securitize its assets? Why or why not?

Prepayment Risk on Pass-Through Securities

To understand the effects of prepayments on pass-through security returns, it is necessary to understand the nature of the cash flows received by investors from the underlying portfolio of mortgages. In the United States, most conventional mortgages are fully amortized. This means that the mortgagee pays back to the mortgage lender (mortgagor) a constant amount each month that contains some principal and some interest. While the total monthly promised payment remains unchanged, the interest component declines throughout the life of the mortgage contract and the principal component increases.

The problem for the FI is to figure a constant monthly payment that exactly pays off the mortgage loan at maturity. This constant payment is formally equivalent to a monthly "annuity" paid by the mortgagee. Consider our example of 1,000 mortgages comprising a $100 million mortgage pool that is to be paid off monthly over 360 months at an annual mortgage coupon rate of 12 percent.

$$\text{Size of pool} = \$100,000,000$$

$$\text{Maturity} = 30 \text{ years } (n = 30)$$

$$\text{Number of monthly payments} = 12 \ (m = 12)$$

$$r = \text{Annual mortgage coupon rate} = 12 \text{ percent}$$

$$PMT = \text{Constant monthly payment to pay off the mortgage over its life}$$

Thus, we solve for *PMT* from the following equation:

$$\$100,000,000 = \left[PMT \left(1 + \frac{r}{m} \right)^{-1} + PMT \left(1 + \frac{r}{m} \right)^{-2} \right.$$

$$\left. + \ \cdots \ + PMT \left(1 + \frac{r}{m} \right)^{-360} \right]$$

$$= PMT \left[\left(1 + \frac{r}{m} \right)^{-1} + \left(1 + \frac{r}{m} \right)^{-2} + \ \cdots \ + \left(1 + \frac{r}{m} \right)^{-360} \right]$$

The term in square brackets is a geometric expansion that in the limit equals

$$100,000,000 = \left[\frac{1 - \dfrac{1}{\left(1 + \dfrac{r}{m} \right)^{mn}}}{\dfrac{r}{m}} \right] \times PMT$$

The new term in brackets is the present value of the annuity factor, *PVAF*, or $100,000,000 = PMT[PVAF]$. Rearranging to solve for *PMT*, the required equal monthly payment on the mortgages, we have

$$PMT = \frac{100,000,000}{PVAF}$$

$$PMT = \frac{100,000,000}{\left[\dfrac{1 - \dfrac{1}{\left(1 + \dfrac{r}{m} \right)^{mn}}}{\dfrac{r}{m}} \right]}$$

$$PMT = \frac{100,000,000}{\left[\dfrac{1 - \dfrac{1}{\left(1 + \dfrac{.12}{12} \right)^{360}}}{\dfrac{.12}{12}} \right]} = \$1,028,613$$

TABLE 28–3
Fully Amortized
Mortgages

Month	Outstanding Balance Payment	Fixed Monthly (*PMT*)	Interest Component	Principal Component	Principal Remaining
1	$100,000,000	$1,028,610	$1,000,000	$28,610	$99,971,390
2	99,971,390	1,028,610	999,714	28,896	99,942,494
.	.	.	.	.	.
.	.	.	.	.	.
.	.	.	.	.	.
360					

As a result, $PMT = \$1,028,613$, or, given 1,000 individual mortgages, $1,028.61 per mortgage rounding to the nearest cent. Thus, payments by the 1,000 mortgagees of an average monthly mortgage payment of $1,028.61 will pay off the mortgages outstanding over 30 years, assuming no prepayments.

The aggregate monthly payments of $1,028,610 comprise different amounts of principal and interest each month.[8] Table 28–3 breaks down the aggregate monthly amortized mortgage payments of $PMT = \$1,028,610$ into their interest and principal components. In month 1, the interest component is 12 percent divided by 12 (or 1 percent) times the outstanding balance on the mortgage pool ($100 million). This comes to $1,000,000, meaning that the remainder of the aggregate monthly payment, or $28,610, can be used to pay off outstanding principal on the pool. At the end of month 1, the outstanding principal balance on the mortgages has been reduced by $28,610 to $99,971,390. In month 2 and thereafter, the interest component declines and the principal component increases, but the two still sum to $1,028,610. Thus, in month 2, the interest component has declined to $999,714 (or 1 percent of the outstanding principal at the beginning of month 2) and the principal component of the payment has increased to $28,896.

While 12 percent is the coupon or interest rate the housebuyers pay on the mortgages, the rate passed through to GNMA investors is $11\frac{1}{2}$ percent, reflecting an average 6-basis-point insurance fee paid to GNMA and a 44-basis-point servicing fee paid to the originating bank. The servicing fees are normally paid monthly rather than as lump-sum single payments up front to create the appropriate collection/servicing incentives over the life of the mortgage for the originating bank. For example, the bank's incentive to act as an efficient collection/servicing agent over 360 months would probably decline if it received a single large up-front fee in month 1 and nothing thereafter.

The effect of the $\frac{1}{2}$ percent fee is to reduce the cash flows passed through to the bondholders. As can be checked, using a *PVAF* that reflects an 11.5 percent annual rate rather than a 12 percent annual rate, GNMA bondholders would collectively receive $990,291 per month over the 30 years instead of $1,028,610 under conditions of no prepayments.

As we have shown so far, the cash flows on the pass-through directly reflect the interest and principal cash flows on the underlying mortgages minus service and insurance fees. However, over time, mortgage rates change. Let Y be the current annual mortgage coupon rate, which could be higher or lower than 12 percent, and let y be the yield on newly issued par value GNMA pass-through bonds. With

[8] Because of the rounding of each monthly payment to the nearest cent, we assume that aggregate monthly cash flows are 1,000 × $1,028.61 cents = $1,028,610.

no prepayments, the market value of the 12 percent mortgage coupon pool ($11\frac{1}{2}$ percent actual coupons) could be calculated as

$$V = \frac{\$990{,}291}{\left(1 + \dfrac{y}{12}\right)^1} + \frac{\$990{,}291}{\left(1 + \dfrac{y}{12}\right)^2} + \cdots + \frac{\$990{,}291}{\left(1 + \dfrac{y}{12}\right)^{360}}$$

If y is less than $11\frac{1}{2}$ percent, the market value of the pool will be greater than its original value; if y is greater than $11\frac{1}{2}$ percent, the pool will decrease in value. However, valuation is more complex than this since we have ignored the prepayment behavior of the 1,000 mortgages. In effect, prepayment risk has two principal sources: refinancing and housing turnover.

Refinancing

As coupon rates on new mortgages fall, there is an increased incentive for individuals in the pool to pay off old, high-cost mortgages and refinance at lower rates. However, refinancing involves transaction costs and recontracting costs. Many banks and thrifts have sought to charge prepayment penalty fees on the outstanding mortgage balance prepaid.[9] In addition, there are often origination costs or points for new mortgages to consider along with the cost of appraisals and credit checks. As a result, mortgage rates may have to fall by some amount below the current coupon rate before there is a significant increase in prepayments in the pool.[10]

Housing Turnover

The other factor that affects prepayments is the propensity of the mortgagees in the pool to move before their mortgages reach maturity. The decision to move or turn over a house may be due to a complex set of factors, such as the level of house prices, the size of the underlying mortgage, the general health of the economy, and even the season (e.g., spring is a good time to move). In addition, if the existing mortgage is an **assumable mortgage,** the buyer of the house takes over the outstanding mortgage's payments. Thus, the sale of a house in a pool does not necessarily imply that the mortgage has to be prepaid. By contrast, nonassumability means a one-to-one correspondence between sale of a house and mortgage prepayment. Most GNMA pools allow mortgages to be assumable; the reverse holds true for pass-throughs sponsored by FNMA and FHLMC.

Figure 28–2 plots the prepayment frequency of a pool of mortgages in relation to the spread between the current mortgage coupon rate (Y) and the mortgage coupon rate (r) in the existing pool (12 percent in our example). Notice when the current mortgage rate (Y) is above the rate in the pool ($Y > r$), mortgage prepayments are small, reflecting monthly forced turnover as people have to relocate because of jobs, divorces, marriages, and other considerations. Even when the current mortgage rate falls below r, those remaining in the mortgage pool do not rush to prepay because up-front refinancing, contracting, and penalty costs are likely to outweigh any present value savings from lower mortgage rates. However, as current mortgage rates continue to fall, the propensity for mortgage holders to

assumable mortgage
The mortgage contract is transferred from the seller to the buyer of a house.

---

[9] However, federal regulations typically forbid prepayment penalties on residential first mortgages.

[10] J. R. Follian and D. Tzang, in "The Interest Rate Differential and Refinancing a Home Mortgage," *Appraisal Journal* 56, no. 2 (1988), pp. 243–51, found that only when the mortgage rate fell below the coupon rate by 60 basis points was there an incentive to refinance a mortgage with an average of 10 years left to maturity. As might be expected, this required differential declined as the holding period increased.

FIGURE 28–2
The Prepayment
Relationship

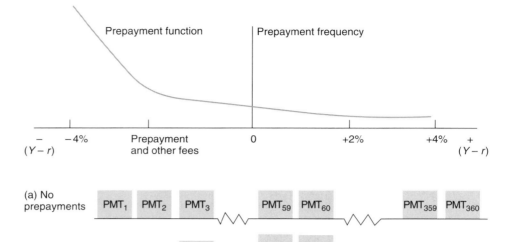

FIGURE 28–3
The Effects of
Prepayments on
Pass-Through
Bondholders' Cash
Flows

prepay increases significantly. Conceptually, mortgage holders have a very valuable call option on the mortgage when this option is in the money.[11] That is, when current mortgage rates fall sufficiently low so that the present value savings of refinancing outweigh the exercise price (the cost of prepayment penalties and other fees and costs), the mortgage will be called.

Since the bank has sold the mortgage cash flows to GNMA investors and must by law pass through all payments received (minus servicing and guaranty fees), investors' cash flows directly reflect the rate of prepayment. As a result, instead of receiving an equal monthly cash flow, *PMT*, as is done under a no-prepayment scenario, the actual cash flows (*CF*) received on these securities by investors fluctuate monthly with the rate of prepayments (see Figure 28–3).

In a no-prepayment world, each month's cash flows are the same: $PMT_1 = PMT_2 = \cdots = PMT_{360}$. However, in a world with prepayments, each month's realized cash flows from the mortgage pool can differ. In Figure 28–3 we show a rising level of cash flows from month 2 onward peaking in month 60, reflecting the effects of early prepayments by some of the 1,000 mortgagees in the pool. This leaves less outstanding principal and interest to be paid in later years. For example, if 300 mortgagees fully prepay by month 60, only 700 mortgagees will remain in the pool at that date. The effect of prepayments is to lower dramatically the principal and interest cash flows received in the later months of the pool's life. For instance, in Figure 28–3, the cash flow received by GNMA bondholders in month 360 is very small relative to month 60 and even months 1 and 2. This reflects the decline in the pool's outstanding principal.

The lowering of current mortgage interest rates and faster prepayments have some good news and bad news effects on the current market valuation of the 12 percent mortgage pool, that is, the $11\frac{1}{2}$ percent GNMA bond.

---

[11] The option is a call option on the value of the mortgage since falling rates increase the value of calling the old mortgage and refinancing a new mortgage at lower rates for the owner of the call option, who is the mortgagee. See M. J. Brennan and E. S. Schwartz, "Savings Bonds, Retractable Bonds, and Callable Bonds," *Journal of Financial Economics* 5 (1977), pp. 67–88. This option also can be viewed as a put option on interest rates.

Good News Effects First, lower market yields reduce the discount rate on any mortgage cash flow and increase the present value of any given stream of cash flows. This would also happen for any fixed-income security. Second, lower yields lead to faster prepayment of the mortgage pool's principal. As a result, instead of principal payments being skewed toward the end of the pool's life, the principal is received (paid back) much faster.

Bad News Effects First, with early prepayment comes fewer interest payments in absolute terms. Thus, instead of receiving scheduled interest payments over 360 months, some of these payments are irrevocably lost as principal outstanding is paid early; that is, mortgage holders are not going to pay interest on mortgage loans they no longer have outstanding. Second, faster cash flow due to prepayments induced by interest rate falls can only be reinvested at lower interest rates when they are received. That is, instead of reinvesting monthly cash flows at 12 percent, investors may reinvest only at lower rates such as 8 percent.

Concept Questions

1. What are the two sources of cash flows on a pass-through security?
2. What two factors can cause prepayments on the mortgages underlying pass-through securities?

Prepayment Models

Clearly, managers running FI investment portfolios need to factor in assumptions about the prepayment behavior of mortgages before they can assess the fair value and risk of their GNMA and FNMA/FHLMC bond portfolios. Next, we consider three alternative ways to model prepayment effects using the Public Securities Association (PSA) prepayment model, other empirical models, and option valuation models.

www.psa.com

To begin, we look carefully at the results of one prepayment model. Look at the reported prices and yields on pass-through securities in Figure 28–4. The first columns in the figure show the sponsor of the issue (GNMA/FNMA/FMAC), the stated maturity of the issue (30 years or 15 years), the mortgage coupons on the mortgages in each pool (e.g., 6 percent), and information about the maximum delay between the receipt of interest by the servicer/sponsor and the actual payment of interest to bondholders. The Gold next to FMAC indicates a maximum stated delay of 55 days; this is the same as FNMA and FHLMC and 10 days more than GNMA.[12] The current market price is shown in column (2), with the daily price change in column (3) (in 32nds).

Column (4) shows the weighted-average life of the bond reflecting an assumed prepayment schedule. This weighted-average life is not the same as duration, which measures the weighted-average time to maturity based on the relative present values of cash flows as weights. Instead, it is a significant simplification of the duration measure seeking to concentrate on the expected timing of payments of principal. Technically, **weighted-average life (WAL)** is measured by

weighted-average life (WAL)
The sum of the products of the time when principal payments are received and the amount of principal received all divided by total principal outstanding.

$$WAL = \frac{\Sigma \, (\text{Time} \times \text{Expected principal received})}{\text{Total principal outstanding}}$$

[12] FMAC (or Farmer MAC) stands for the Federal Agricultural Mortgage Corporation. FMAC is smaller than the three main mortgage sponsoring agencies (GNMA, FNMA, and FHLMC) and specializes in agricultural mortgages.

FIGURE 28–4

Pass-Through Securities, April 23, 2004

Source: *The Wall Street Journal*, April 23, 2004 p. C13. Reprinted by permission of The Wall Street Journal, © 2004. Dow Jones & Company, Inc. All Rights Reserved Worldwide.

	(1)	(2)	(3)	(4)	(5)	(6)	(7)	(8)

MORTGAGE-BACKED SECURITIES

Indicative, not guaranteed; from Bear Stearns Cos./Street Pricing Service

		PRICE Nov (Pts-32ds)	PRICE CHANGE (32ds)	AVG LIFE (years)	SPRD TO AVG LIFE (8ps)	SPREAD CHANGE	PSA (Prepay Speed)	YIELD TO MAT.*
30-YEAR								
FMAC GOLD	5.5%	100-18	– 13	6.2	169	– 7	239	5.46
FMAC GOLD	6.0%	102-20	– 10	3.7	210	– 8	394	5.16
FMAC GOLD	6.5%	104-14	– 04	2.3	189	+ 7	582	4.31
FNMA	5.5%	100-06	– 13	6.2	166	– 5	237	5.44
FNMA	6.0%	102-23	– 11	3.5	206	– 4	427	5.02
FNMA	6.5%	104-12	– 05	2.3	182	+ 7	597	4.22
GNMA**	5.5%	100-15	– 13	6.2	164	– 3	232	5.41
GNMA**	6.0%	102-31	– 10	4.2	190	– 8	338	5.14
GNMA**	6.5%	104-24	– 05	2.8	186	– 1	492	4.53
15-YEAR								
FMAC GOLD	5.0%	100-31	– 09	4.4	141	–14	250	4.74
FNMA	5.0%	100-29	– 10	4.4	138	–13	246	4.72
GNMA**	5.0%	101-10	– 11	4.5	129	– 5	234	4.65

*Extrapolated from benchmarks based on projections from Bear Stearns prepayment model, assuming interest rates remain unchanged. **Government guaranteed.

COLLATERALIZED MORTGAGE OBLIGATIONS

Spread of CMO yields above U.S. Treasury securities of comparable maturity, in basis points (100 basis points = 1 percentage point of interest)

MAT	SPREAD	CHG FROM PREV DAY
SEQUENTIALS		
2-year	210	unch
5-year	215	unch
7-year	175	unch
10-year	165	unch
20-year	90	unch
PACS		
2-year	110	unch
5-year	130	unch
7-year	130	unch
10-year	115	unch
20-year	55	unch

For example, consider a loan with two years to maturity and $100 million in principal. Investors expect $40 million of the principal to be repaid at the end of year 1 and the remaining $60 million to be repaid at maturity.

Time	Expected Principal Payments	Time × Principal
1	$40	$40
2	60	120
	$100	$160

$$WAL = \frac{160}{100} = 1.6 \text{ years}$$

Notice in Figure 28–4, the *WAL*s of these pools are all 6.2 years or less.

The fifth and sixth columns show the yield spread of mortgage-backed securities over Treasuries and its daily change. The yield spread shown here is the spread to average life, while the more complicated (and most used) is the option-adjusted spread (OAS), which is explained in detail later.

www.bearstearns. com

The OAS can be calculated by using the yield to maturity in the final column [column (8)] and deducting from this the yield on a matched maturity Treasury bond. The yield to maturity in the final column is calculated according to prepayment behavior estimated and valued by Bear Stearns, the investment bank. As will be discussed later, allowing for prepayment behavior, the bond is valued and its yield calculated using an explicit prepayment "option" model. This is only one way to calculate the prepayment behavior of mortgagees and the effects of their behavior on yields. Two alternative ways of modeling prepayment behavior are (1) the Public Securities Association (PSA) model approach and (2) the empirical model approach. These two approaches are discussed in the next section, along with the option-based approach. Note that the PSA prepayment speed (see below) of the various securities is shown in Column 7 of Figure 28–4. These speeds vary from 232 to 597 "percent" of the PSA benchmark prepayment speed.

FIGURE 28–5
PSA Prepayment
Model

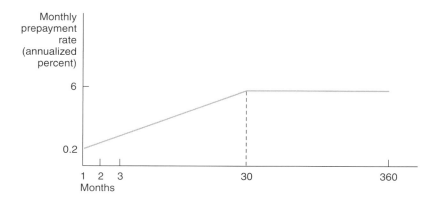

PSA Model

www.psa.com The prepayment model developed by the Public Securities Association is an empirically based model that reflects an average rate of prepayment based on the past experience of pools of FHA-insured mortgages. Essentially, the PSA model assumes that the prepayment rate starts at 0.2 percent (per annum) in the first month, increasing by 0.2 percent per month for the first 30 months, until the annualized prepayment rate reaches 6 percent. This model assumes that the prepayment rate then levels off at a 6 percent annualized rate for the remaining life of the pool[13] (see Figure 28–5). Issuers or investors who assume that their mortgage pool prepayments exactly match this pattern are said to assume 100 percent PSA behavior. Realistically, the actual prepayment rate on any specific mortgage pool backing a specific pass-through security may differ from PSA's assumed pattern for general and economic reasons, including

1. The level of the pool's coupon relative to the current mortgage coupon rate (the weighted-average coupon).
2. The age of the mortgage pool.
3. Whether the payments are fully amortized.
4. Assumability of mortgages in the pool.
5. Size of the pool.
6. Conventional or nonconventional mortgages (FHA/VA).
7. Geographic location.
8. Age and job status of mortgagees in the pool.

One approach would be to approximately control for these factors by assuming some fixed deviation of any specific pool from PSA's assumed average or benchmark pattern. For example, one pool may be assumed to be 75 percent PSA, and another 125 percent PSA. The former has a slower prepayment rate than historically experienced; the latter, a faster rate. Note these values in Figure 28–6 relative to 100 percent PSA. In column (7) of Figure 28–4 it can be seen that FMAC gold, 5.5 percent 30-year bonds have a PSA of 239. That is, they are expected to prepay at a rate much *faster* than that normally experienced for 30-year mortgage-backed securities. This is because interest rates on new mortgages in April 2004 were well below historic levels.

---

[13] Or, after month 30, prepayments are made at approximately ½ percent per *month*.

FIGURE 28–6
**Deviations from
100 Percent PSA**

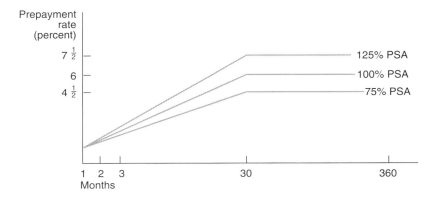

Other Empirical Models

FIs that are trading, dealing, and issuing pass-throughs have also developed their own proprietary empirical models of prepayment behavior to get a pricing edge on other issuers/investors. Clearly, the FI that can develop the best, most accurate, prepayment model stands to make large profits either in originating and issuing such bonds or in trading such instruments in the secondary market. As a wide variety of empirical models have been developed, we briefly look at the types of methodology followed.

Specifically, most empirical models are proprietary versions of the PSA model in which FIs make their own estimates of the pattern of monthly prepayments. From this modeling exercise, an FI can estimate either the fair price or the fair yield on the pass-through. Of course, those FIs that make the most profits from buying and selling pass-throughs over time are the ones that have most accurately predicted actual prepayment behavior.

In constructing an empirical valuation model, FIs begin by estimating a prepayment function from observing the experience of mortgage holders prepaying during any particular period on mortgage pools similar to the one to be valued. This is conditional, of course, on the mortgages not having been prepaid prior to that period. These conditional prepayment rates in month i (p_i) for similar pools would be modeled as functions of the important economic variables driving prepayment—for example, $p_i = f$ (mortgage rate spread, age, collateral, geographic factors, **burn-out factor**).[14] This modeling should take into account the idiosyncratic factors affecting this specific pool, such as its age and burn-out factor, as well as market factors affecting prepayments in general, such as the mortgage rate spread. Once the frequency distribution of the p_i's is estimated, as shown in Figure 28–7, the FI can calculate the expected cash flows on the mortgage pool under consideration and estimate its fair yield given the current market price of the pool.[15]

burn-out factor
The aggregate percent of the mortgage pool that has been prepaid prior to the month under consideration.

---

[14] A burn-out factor is a summary measure of a pool's prepayments in total prior to month i. As such, it is meant to capture heterogeneity of prepayment behavior within any given pool rather than between pools. See E. S. Schwartz and W. N. Tourous, "Prepayment and the Valuation of Mortgage-Backed Securities," *Journal of Finance* 44 (1989), pp. 375–92.

[15] A commonly used empirical model is the proportional hazards model. This model produces a prepayment function similar to that in Figure 28–7 where, other things being equal, conditional prepayment rates are typically low in the early years of a mortgage, increase as the age of the mortgage increases, and then diminish with further seasoning (see Schwartz and Tourous, "Prepayment").

FIGURE 28–7
Estimated
Prepayment
Function for
a Given Pool

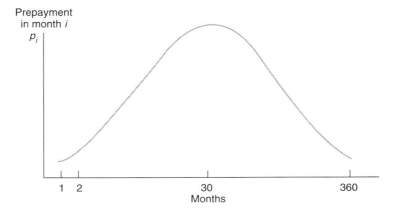

Option Models[16]

The third class of models uses option pricing theory to figure the fair yield on pass-throughs [see column (8) in Figure 28–4] and, in particular, the fair yield spread of pass-throughs over Treasuries. These so-called option-adjusted spread (OAS) models focus on the prepayment risk of pass-throughs as the essential determinant of the required yield spread of pass-through bonds over Treasuries. As such, they are open to the criticism that they fail to properly include nonrefinancing incentives to prepay and the variety of transaction costs and recontracting costs involved in refinancing. Recent research has tried to integrate the option model approach with the empirical model approach.[17]

Stripped to its basics, the option model views the fair price on a pass-through such as a GNMA as being decomposable into two parts:[18]

$$P_{GNMA} = P_{TBOND} - P_{PREPAYMENT\ OPTION}$$

That is, the value of a GNMA bond to an investor (P_{GNMA}) is equal to the value of a standard noncallable Treasury bond of the same duration (P_{TBOND}) minus the value of the mortgage holder's prepayment call option ($P_{PREPAYMENT\ OPTION}$). Specifically, the ability of the mortgage holder to prepay is equivalent to the bond investor writing a call option on the bond and the mortgagee owning or buying the option. If interest rates fall, the option becomes more valuable as it moves into the money and more mortgages are prepaid early by having the bond called or the prepayment option exercised. This relationship can also be thought of in the yield dimension:

$$Y_{GNMA} = Y_{TBOND} + Y_{OPTION}$$

[16] This section contains material that is relatively technical. It may be included or dropped from the chapter reading depending on the rigor of the course without harming the continuity of the chapter.

[17] See J. P. Kau et al., "A Generalized Valuation Model for Fixed-Rate Residential Mortgages," *Journal of Money, Credit and Banking* 24 (1992); W. Archer and D. C. Ling, "Pricing Mortgage-Backed Securities: Should Contingent-Claim Models Be Abandoned for Empirical Models of Prepayments?" paper presented at the AFA Conference, Anaheim, California, January 1993; and M. LaCour-Little, "Another Look at the Role of Borrower Characteristics in Predicting Mortgage Prepayments," *Journal of Housing Research* 10 (1999), pp. 45–60.

[18] For an excellent review of these option models, see Spahr and Sunderman, "The Effect of Prepayment Modeling."

option-adjusted spread (OAS)
The required interest spread of a pass-through security over a Treasury when prepayment risk is taken into account.

The investors' required yield on a GNMA should equal the yield on a similar duration T-bond plus an additional yield for writing the valuable call option. That is, the fair yield spread or **option-adjusted spread (OAS)** between GNMAs and T-bonds should reflect the value of this option.

To gain further insights into the option model approach and the OAS, we can develop an example along the lines of S. D. Smith showing how to calculate the value of the option-adjusted spread on GNMAs.[19] To do this, we make a number of simplifying assumptions indicative of the restrictive nature of many of these models:

1. The only reasons for prepayment are due to refinancing mortgages at lower rates; there is no prepayment for turnover reasons.

2. The current discount (zero-coupon) yield curve for T-bonds is flat (this could be relaxed).

3. The mortgage coupon rate is 10 percent on an outstanding pool of mortgages with an outstanding principal balance of $1,000,000.

4. The mortgages have a three-year maturity and pay principal and interest only once at the end of each year. Of course, real-world models would have 15- or 30-year maturities and pay interest and principal monthly. These assumptions are made for simplification purposes only.

5. Mortgage loans are fully amortized, and there is no servicing fee (again, this could be relaxed). Thus, the annual fully amortized payment under no prepayment conditions is

$$PMT = \frac{1,000,000}{\left[\dfrac{1 - \dfrac{1}{(1 + .10)^3}}{.1}\right]} = \frac{1,000,000}{2.48685} = \$402,114$$

In a world without prepayments, no default risk, and current mortgage rates (y) of 9 percent, we would have the GNMA bond selling at a premium over par:

$$P_{GNMA} = \frac{PMT}{(1 + y)} + \frac{PMT}{(1 + y)^2} + \frac{PMT}{(1 + y)^3}$$

$$P_{GNMA} = \frac{\$402,114}{(1.09)} + \frac{\$402,114}{(1.09)^2} + \frac{\$402,114}{(1.09)^3}$$

$$P_{GNMA} = \$1,017,869$$

6. Because of prepayment penalties and other refinancing costs, mortgagees do not begin to prepay until mortgage rates, in any year, fall 3 percent or more below the mortgage coupon rate for the pool (the mortgage coupon rate is 10 percent in this example).

7. Interest rate movements over time change a maximum of 1 percent up or down each year. The time path of interest rates follows a binomial process.

8. With prepayments present, cash flows in any year can be the promised payment $PMT = \$402,114$, the promised payment ($PMT$) plus repayment of any outstanding principal, or zero if all mortgages have been prepaid or paid off in the previous year.

---

[19] S. D. Smith, "Analyzing Risk and Return for Mortgage-Backed Securities," Federal Reserve Bank of Atlanta, *Economic Review*, January–February 1991, pp. 2–11.

FIGURE 28–8
Mortgage Rate Changes: Assumed Time Path

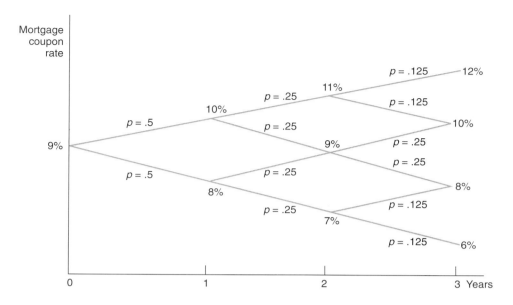

In Figure 28–8 we show the assumed time path of interest rates over the three years with associated probabilities (p).

End of Year 1   Since rates can change up or down by only 1 percent per annum, the farthest they can be expected to fall in the first year is to 8 percent. At this level, no mortgage holder would prepay since any mortgage rate savings would be off-set by the penalty costs of prepayment, that is, by the assumption it is worth pre-paying only when the mortgage rate falls at least 3 percent below its 10 percent coupon rate. As a result, the GNMA pass-through investor could expect to receive $PMT = \$402,114$ with certainty. Thus, $CF_1 = \$402,114$.

End of Year 2   In year 2, there are three possible mortgage interest rate scenarios. However, the only one that triggers prepayment is when mortgage rates fall to 7 percent (3 percent below the 10 percent mortgage coupon rate of the pool). According to Figure 28–8, this occurs with only a 25 percent probability. If prepay-ment does not occur with 75 percent probability, the investor receives $PMT = \$402,114$. If prepayment occurs with 25 percent probability, the investor receives

$$PMT + \text{Principal balance remaining at end of year 2}$$

We can calculate the principal balance remaining at the end of year 2 as follows. At the end of the first year, we divide the amortized payment, $PMT = \$402,114$, into a payment of interest and a payment of principal. With a 10 percent mortgage coupon rate, the payment of interest component would be $.10 \times \$1,000,000 = \$100,000$, and the repayment of principal component $= \$402,114 - \$100,000 = \$302,114$. Thus, at the beginning of the second year, there would be $\$1,000,000 - \$302,114 = \$697,886$ principal outstanding. At the end of the second year, the promised amortized payment of $PMT = \$402,114$ can be broken down to an inter-est component of 10 percent $\times \$697,886 = \$69,788.6$, and a principal component amount of $\$402,114 - \$69,788.6 = \$332,325.4$, leaving a principal balance at the end of year 2 of $\$1,000,000 - \$302,114 - \$332,325.4 = \$365,560.6$.

Consequently, if yields fall to 7 percent, the cash flow received by the investor in year 2 would be

$$PMT + \text{Principal balance outstanding at end of year 2}$$
$$= \$402,114 + \$365,560.6 = \$767,674.6$$

Thus, expected cash flows at the end of year 2 would be

$$CF_2 = .25(\$767,674.6) + .75(\$402,114)$$
$$= \$191,918.64 + \$301,585.5$$
$$= \$493,504.15$$

End of Year 3　Since there is a 25 percent probability that mortgages will be pre-paid in year 2, there must be a 25 percent probability that the investor will receive no cash flows at the end of year 3 since mortgage holders owe nothing in this year if all mortgages have already been paid off early in year 2. However, there is also a 75 percent probability that mortgages will not be prepaid at the end of year 2. Thus, at the end of year 3 (maturity), the investor has a 75 percent probability of receiving the promised amortized payment $PMT = \$402,114$. The expected cash flow in year 3 is

$$CF_3 = .25(0) + .75(\$402,114) = \$301,585.5$$

Derivation of the Option-Adjusted Spread　As just discussed, we conceptually divide the required yield on a GNMA, or other pass-throughs, with prepayment risk, into the required yield on T-bonds plus a required spread for the prepayment call option given to the mortgage holders:

$$P = \frac{E(CF_1)}{(1 + d_1 + O_S)} + \frac{E(CF_2)}{(1 + d_2 + O_S)^2} + \frac{E(CF_3)}{(1 + d_3 + O_S)^3}$$

where

P = Price of GNMA

d_1 = Discount rate on one-year, zero-coupon Treasury bonds

d_2 = Discount rate on two-year, zero-coupon Treasury bonds

d_3 = Discount rate on three-year, zero-coupon Treasury bonds

O_S = Option-adjusted spread on GNMA

Assume that the T-bond yield curve is flat, so that

$$d_1 = d_2 = d_3 = 8\%$$

We can now solve for O_S:

$$1,017,869 = \frac{\$402,114}{(1+.08+O_S)} + \frac{\$493,504.15}{(1+.08+O_S)^2} + \frac{\$301,185.5}{(1+.08+O_S)^3}$$

Solving for O_S, we find that

$$O_S = 0.96\% \text{ (to two decimal places)}$$
$$Y_{GNMA} = Y_{TBOND} + O_S$$
$$= 8\% + 0.96\%$$
$$= 8.96\%$$

Notice that when prepayment risk is present, the expected cash flow yield at 8.96 percent is 4 basis points less than the required 9 percent yield on the GNMA when no prepayment occurs. The slightly lower yield results because the positive effects of early prepayment (such as earlier payment of principal) dominate the negative effects (such as loss of interest payments). Note, however, that this result might well be reversed if we altered our assumptions by allowing a wider dispersion of possible interest rate changes and having heavier penalties for prepayment.

Nevertheless, the option-adjusted spread approach is useful for FI managers in that they can place lower bounds on the yields they are willing to accept on GNMA and other pass-through securities before they place them in their portfolios. Realistically, some account has to be taken of nonrefinancing prepayment behavior and patterns; otherwise significant mispricing may occur.

Concept Questions

1. Should an FI with $D_A < kD_L$ seek to securitize its assets? Why or why not?
2. In general terms, discuss the three approaches developed by analysts to model prepayment behavior.
3. In the context of the option model approach, list three ways in which transaction and other contracting costs are likely to interfere with the accuracy of its predictions regarding the fair price or interest spread on a pass-through security.

THE COLLATERALIZED MORTGAGE OBLIGATION (CMO)

While pass-throughs are still the primary mechanism for securitization, the CMO is a second and growing vehicle for securitizing FI assets. Innovated in 1983 by the FHLMC and First Boston, the CMO is a device for making mortgage-backed securities more attractive to investors. The CMO does this by repackaging the cash flows from mortgages and pass-through securities in a different fashion to attract different types of investors. While a pass-through security gives each investor a pro rata share of any promised and prepaid cash flows on a mortgage pool, the CMO is a multiclass pass-through with a number of different bondholder classes or tranches. Unlike a pass-through, each bondholder class has a different guaranteed coupon just like a regular T-bond; but more importantly, the allocation of early cash flows due to mortgage prepayments is such that at any one time, all prepayments go to retiring the principal outstanding of only one class of bondholders at a time, leaving the other classes' prepayment protected for a period of time. Thus, a CMO serves as a way to mitigate or reduce prepayment risk.

Creation of CMOs

CMO
Collateralized mortgage obligation is a mortgage-backed bond issued in multiple classes or tranches.

CMOs can be created either by packaging and securitizing whole mortgage loans or, more usually, by placing existing pass-throughs in a trust off the balance sheet. The trust or third-party FI holds the GNMA pass-through as collateral against issues of new CMO securities. The trust issues these CMOs in three or more different classes. For example, the first CMO that Freddie Mac issued in 1983, secured by 20,000 conventional home mortgages worth $1 billion, had three classes: A, $215 million; B, $350 million; and C, $435 million. We show a three-class or tranche CMO in Figure 28–9.

Issuing CMOs is often equivalent to double securitization. Mortgages are packaged, and a GNMA pass-through is issued. An investment bank such as Goldman Sachs or another CMO issuer such as FHLMC, a commercial bank, or a savings

FIGURE 28–9
The Creation of a
CMO

institution may buy this whole issue or a large part of the issue. Goldman Sachs would then place these GNMA securities as collateral with a trust and issue three new classes of bonds backed by the GNMA securities as collateral.[20] As a result, the investors in each CMO class have a sole claim to the GNMA collateral if the issuer fails. The investment bank or other issuer creates the CMO to make a profit by repackaging the cash flows from the single-class GNMA pass-through into cash flows more attractive to different groups of investors. The sum of the prices at which the three CMO bond classes can be sold normally exceeds that of the original pass-through:

$$\sum_{i=1}^{3} P_{i,CMO} > P_{GNMA}$$

To understand the gains from repackaging, it is necessary to understand how CMOs restructure prepayment risk to make it more attractive to different classes of investors. We explain this in the following simple example.

EXAMPLE 28–1

*The Value
Additivity of
CMOs*

Suppose an investment bank buys a $150 million issue of GNMAs and places them in trust as collateral. It then issues a CMO with these three classes:

> Class A: Annual fixed coupon 7 percent, class size $50 million
> Class B: Annual fixed coupon 8 percent, class size $50 million
> Class C: Annual fixed coupon 9 percent, class size $50 million

Under the CMO, each class has a guaranteed or fixed coupon.[21] By restructuring the GNMA as a CMO, the investment bank can offer investors who buy bond class C a higher degree of mortgage prepayment protection compared to a pass-through. Those who buy bond class B receive an average degree of prepayment protection, and those who take class A receive virtually no prepayment protection.

Each month, mortgagees in the GNMA pool pay principal and interest on their mortgages; each payment includes the promised amortized amount (*PMT*) plus any additional payments as some of the mortgage holders prepay principal to refinance their mortgages or because they have sold their houses and are relocating. These cash flows are passed through to the owner of the GNMA bonds, in our example Goldman Sachs. The CMO issuer uses the cash flows to pay promised coupon interest to the three classes of CMO bondholders. Suppose that in month 1 the promised amortized cash flows (PMT) on the mortgages underlying the GNMA pass-through collateral are $1 million, but an additional $1.5 million cash flow results from early mortgage prepayments. Thus, the cash flows in the first month available to pay promised coupons to the three classes of bondholders would be

> *PMT* + Prepayments = $1 million + $1.5 million = $2.5 million

---

[20] These trusts are sometimes called REMICs, or real estate mortgage investment conduits.

[21] In some cases, coupons are paid monthly, in others quarterly, and in still others semiannually.

This cash flow is available to the trustee, who uses it in the following fashion.

1. *Coupon payments.* Each month (or more commonly, each quarter or half year), the trustee pays out the guaranteed coupons to the three classes of bondholders at annualized coupon rates of 7 percent, 8 percent, and 9 percent, respectively. Given the stated principal of $50 million for each class, the class A (7 percent coupon) bondholders receive approximately $291,667 in coupon payments in month 1, the class B (8 percent coupon) receive approximately $333,333 in month 1, and the class C (9 percent coupon) receive approximately $375,000 in month 1. Thus, the total promised coupon payments to the three classes amount to $1,000,000 (equal to *PMT*, the no-prepayment cash flows in the GNMA pool).

2. *Principal payments.* The trustee has $2.5 million available to pay out as a result of promised mortgage payments plus early prepayments, but the total payment of coupon interest amounts to $1 million. For legal and tax reasons, the remaining $1.5 million has to be paid out to the CMO bondholders. The unique feature of the CMO is that the trustee would pay this remaining $1.5 million only to class A bondholders to retire these bondholders' principal. This retires early some of these bondholders' principal outstanding. At the end of month 1, only $48.5 million ($50 million − $1.5 million) of class A bonds remains outstanding, compared to $50 million class B and $50 million class C. These payment flows are shown graphically in Figure 28–10.

Let's suppose that in month 2 the same thing happens. The cash flows from the mortgage/GNMA pool exceed the promised coupon payments to the three classes of bondholders. Again, the trustee uses any excess cash flows to pay off or retire the principal of class A bondholders. If the excess cash flows again amount to $1.5 million, at the end of month 2 there will be only $47 million ($48.5 million—$1.5 million) of class A bonds outstanding.

Given any positive flow of prepayments, it is clear that within a few years the class A bonds will be fully retired. In practice, this often occurs between 1.5 and 3 years after issue. After the trustee retires class A, only classes B and C remain.

As before, out of any cash flows received from the mortgage/GNMA pool, the trustee pays the bondholders their guaranteed coupons, C_B = $333,333 and C_C = $375,000 for a total of $708,333. Suppose that total cash flows received by the trustee are $1,208,333 in the first month after the total retirement of class A bonds, reflecting amortized mortgage payments by the remaining mortgagees in the pool plus any new prepayments. The excess cash flows of $500,000 ($1,208,333 − $708,333) then go to retire the principal outstanding of CMO bond class B. At the end of that month, there are only $49.5 million class B bonds outstanding. This is shown graphically in Figure 28–11.

As the months pass, the trustee will use any excess cash flows over and above the promised coupons to class B and C bondholders to retire bond class B's principal. Eventually, all of the $50 million principal on class B bonds will be retired—in practice, five to seven years after the CMO issue. After class B bonds are retired, all remaining cash flows will be dedicated to paying the promised coupon of class C bondholders and retiring the $50 million principal on class C bonds. In practice, class C bonds can have an average life as long as 20 years.

Class A, B, and C Bond Buyers

Class A

These bonds have the shortest average life with a minimum of prepayment protection. They are, therefore, of great interest to investors seeking short-duration mortgage-backed assets to reduce the duration of their mortgage-related asset portfolios. In recent years depository institutions have been large buyers of CMO class A securities.

Figure 28–10
Allocation of Cash Flows to Owners of CMO Tranches

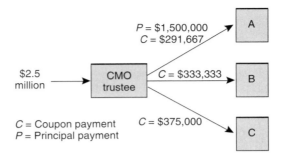

FIGURE 28–11
Allocation of Cash Flows to Remaining Tranches of CMO Bonds

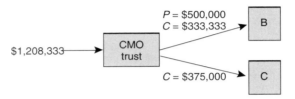

Class B

These bonds have some prepayment protection and expected durations of five to seven years depending on the level of interest rates. Pension funds and life insurance companies primarily purchase these bonds, although some depository institutions buy this bond class as well.

Class C

Because of their long expected duration, Class C bonds are highly attractive to insurance companies and pension funds seeking long-term duration assets to match their long-term duration liabilities. Indeed, because of their failures to offer prepayment protection, regular GNMA pass-throughs may not be very attractive to these institutions. Class C CMOs, with their high but imperfect degree of prepayment protection, may be of greater interest to the FI managers of these institutions.

In summary, by splitting bondholders into different classes and by restructuring cash flows into forms more valued by different investor clienteles, the CMO issuer stands to make a profit.

Other CMO Classes

CMOs can always have more than the three classes described in the previous example. Indeed, issues of up to 17 different classes have been made. Clearly, the 17th-class bondholders would have an enormous degree of prepayment protection since the first 16 classes would have had their bonds retired before the principal outstanding on this bond class would be affected by early prepayments. In addition, trustees have created other special types of classes as products to attract investor interest; we discuss these classes next.

Z class
An accrual class of a CMO that makes a payment to bondholders only when preceding CMO classes have been retired.

Class Z

Frequently, CMO issues contain a **Z class** as the last regular class. The Z implicitly stands for zero, but these are not really zero-coupon bonds. This class has a stated coupon such as 10 percent and accrues interest for the bondholder on a monthly

TABLE 28–4 CMO with Five Bond Classes (in millions of dollars)

Fannie Mae REMIC Trust 1987-1					
Collateral					
Type	**Coupon**	**Amount**	**Original Term**	**Average Remaining Term**	**Assumed Prepayment Rate**
FNMA	9.99%	$500	360 months	349 months	200% PSA
Bonds					
Class	**A**	**B**	**C**	**Z**	**R**
Amount	$150.9	$238.6	$85.5	$24.0	$1.0
Bond type	Fixed	Fixed	Fixed	Accrual	Residual
Coupon (percent)	7.95	9.35	9.60	9.99	503.88
Price (percent)	99.8099	99.3083	N/A	89.4978	1445.1121
Yield (bond equivalent)	7.85	9.55	N/A	10.86	10.30
Weighted-average life (years)	1.6	5.9	11.2	18.4	3.6
Benchmark Treasury (years)	2	5	N/A	20	N/A
Spread over Treasury (basis points)	15	125	N/A	180	N/A

Note: All data in this table are as of the pricing date (FNMA has retained Class C).
Pricing date: 8/18/87.
Accural date: 9/01/87.
First payment: 10/25/87.
Payment frequency/Delay: Monthly pay, 25-day delay.

Source: GAO/GGD-88-111 (1988).

basis at this rate. The trustee does not pay this interest, however, until all other classes of bonds are fully retired. When the other classes have been retired, the Z-class bondholder receives the promised coupon and principal payments plus accrued interest payments. Thus, the Z class has characteristics of both a zero-coupon bond (no coupon payments for a long period) and a regular bond.

Class R

In placing the GNMA collateral with the trustee, the CMO issuer normally uses very conservative prepayment assumptions. If prepayments are slower than expected, there is often excess collateral left over in the pool when all regular classes have been retired. Further, trustees often reinvest funds or cash flows received from the underlying instrument (GNMA) in the period prior to paying interest on the CMOs. In general, the size of any excess collateral and interest on interest gets bigger when rates are high and the timing of coupon intervals is semiannual rather than monthly. This residual **R class** or "garbage class" is a high-risk investment class that gives the investor the rights to the overcollateralization and reinvestment income on the cash flows in the CMO trust. Because the value of the returns in this bond class increases when interest rates increase, while normal bond values fall with interest rate increases, class R often has a negative duration. Thus, it is potentially attractive to depository institutions seeking to hedge their regular bond and fixed-income portfolios.[22]

Consider the example of a CMO with classes A, B, C, Z, and R in Table 28–4. From Table 28–4, you can see that the underlying pass-through bond held as

R class
The residual class of a CMO giving the owner the right to any remaining collateral in the trust after all other bond classes have been retired plus any reinvestment income earned by the trust.

---

[22] Negative duration implies that bond prices increase with interest rates; that is, the price–yield curve is positively sloped.

collateral is a FNMA 9.99 percent coupon bond with an original maturity of 30 years, an issue size of $500 million, and a prepayment rate assumed to be twice the size assumed by the PSA model (200 percent PSA). The five CMO bond classes are issued in different amounts, with the largest class being B. Note that the principal amounts of the five classes sum to $500 million.

Concept Questions

1. Would thrifts or insurance companies prefer Z-class CMOs? Explain your answer.
2. Are Z-class CMOs exactly the same as T-bond strips? If not, why not?
3. In our example, the coupon on the class C bonds was assumed to be higher than that on the class B bonds and the coupon on class B bonds was assumed to be higher than that on class A bonds. Under what term structure conditions might this not be the case?

THE MORTGAGE-BACKED BOND (MBB)

mortgage (asset)-backed bonds
Bonds collateralized by a pool of assets.

Mortgage (asset)-backed bonds (MBBs) are the third asset-securitization vehicle. These bonds differ from pass-throughs and CMOs in two key dimensions. First, while pass-throughs and CMOs help depository institutions remove mortgages from their balance sheets as forms of off-balance-sheet securitization, MBBs normally remain on the balance sheet. Second, pass-throughs and CMOs have a direct link between the cash flows on the underlying mortgages and the cash flows on the bond vehicles. By contrast, the relationship for MBBs is one of collateralization— there is no direct link between the cash flow on the mortgages backing the bond and the interest and principal payments on the MBB.

An FI issues an MBB to reduce risk to the MBB bondholders, who have a first claim to a segment of the FI's mortgage assets. Practically speaking, the FI segregates a group of mortgage assets on its balance sheet and pledges this group as collateral against the MBB issue. A trustee normally monitors the segregation of assets and makes sure that the market value of the collateral exceeds the principal owed to MBB holders. That is, FIs back most MBB issues by excess collateral. This excess collateral backing of the bond, in addition to the priority rights of the bondholders, generally ensures that these bonds can be sold with a high credit rating such as AAA. In contrast, the FI, when evaluated as a whole, could be rated BBB or even lower. A high credit rating results in lower coupon payments than would be required if significant default risk had lowered the credit rating (see Chapter 11). To explain the potential benefits and the sources of any gains to an FI from issuing MBBs, we examine the following simple example.

EXAMPLE 28–2
Gains to an FI from Issuing MBBs

Consider an FI with $20 million in long-term mortgages as assets. It is financing these mortgages with $10 million in short-term uninsured deposits (e.g., wholesale deposits over $100,000) and $10 million in insured deposits (e.g., retail deposits of $100,000 or less). In this example, we ignore the issues of capital and reserve requirements. Look at the balance sheet structure in Table 28–5.

This balance sheet poses problems for the FI manager. First, the FI has a positive duration gap ($D_A > kD_L$). Second, because of this interest rate risk and the potential default and prepayment risk on the FI's mortgage assets, uninsured depositors are likely to require a positive and potentially significant risk premium to be paid on their deposits. By contrast, the insured depositors may require approximately the risk-free rate on their deposits as they are fully insured by the FDIC (see Chapter 19).

TABLE 28–5
Balance Sheet of
Potential MBB
Issuer (in millions
of dollars)

Assets		Liabilities	
Long-term mortgages	$20	Insured deposits	$10
		Uninsured deposits	10
	$20		$20

TABLE 28–6
FI's Balance Sheet
after MBB Issue
(in millions of
dollars)

Assets		Liabilities	
Collateral = (market value of segregated mortgages)	$12	MBB issue	$10
Other mortgages	8	Insured deposits	10
	$20		$20

To reduce its duration gap exposure and lower its funding costs, the FI can segregate $12 million of the mortgages on the asset side of its balance sheet and pledge them as collateral backing a $10 million long-term MBB issue. Because of this overcollateralization, the mortgage-backed bond issued by the FI may cost less to issue, in terms of required yield, than uninsured deposits; that is, it may well be rated AAA while uninsured deposits might be rated BBB. The FI can therefore use the proceeds of the $10 million bond issue to retire the $10 million of uninsured deposits.

Consider the FI's balance sheet after the issue of the MBBs in Table 28–6. It might seem that the FI has miraculously engineered a restructuring of its balance sheet that has resulted in a better matching of D_A to D_L and a lowering of funding costs. The bond issue has lengthened the average duration of liabilities by replacing short-term deposits with long-term MBBs and lowered funding costs because AAA-rated bond coupon rates are below BBB-rated uninsured deposit rates. However, this outcome occurs only because the insured depositors do not worry about risk exposure since they are 100 percent insured by the FDIC. The result of the MBB issue and the segregation of $12 million of assets as collateral backing the $10 million bond issue is that the $10 million insured deposits are now backed only by $8 million in free or unpledged assets. If smaller depositors were not insured by the FDIC, they would surely demand very high risk premiums to hold these risky deposits. The implication of this is that the FI gains only because the FDIC is willing to bear enhanced credit risk through its insurance guarantees to depositors.[23] As a result, the FI is actually gaining at the expense of the FDIC. Consequently, it is not surprising that the FDIC is concerned about the growing use of this form of securitization by risky depository institutions.

Other than regulatory discouragement and the risk of regulatory intervention, there are private return reasons why an FI might prefer the pass-through/CMO forms of securitization to issuing MBBs. First MBBs tie up mortgages on the FI's balance sheet for a long time. This increases the illiquidity of the asset portfolio. Second, the amount of mortgages tied up is enhanced by the need to overcollateralize to ensure a high-quality credit risk rating for the bond issue; in our example, the overcollateralization was $2 million. Third, by keeping mortgages on the balance sheet, the FI continues to be liable for capital adequacy and reserve

[23] And does not make the risk-based deposit insurance premium to banks and thrifts sufficiently large to reflect this risk.

FIGURE 28–12
IO/PO Strips

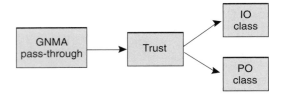

requirement taxes. Because of these problems, MBBs are the least used of the three basic vehicles of securitization.

Concept Question

1. Would a AAA FI ever issue mortgage-backed bonds? Explain your answer.

INNOVATIONS IN SECURITIZATION

We now turn our attention to the growing innovations in FIs' asset securitization. We discuss two major innovations and their use in return-risk management by FIs: mortgage pass-through strips and the extension of the securitization concept to other assets.

Mortgage Pass-Through Strips

The mortgage pass-through strip is a special type of a CMO with only two classes. The fully amortized nature of mortgages means that any given monthly payment, *PMT*, contains an interest component and a principal component. Beginning in 1987, investment banks and other FI issuers stripped out the interest component from the principal component and sold each payment stream separately to different bond class investors. They sold an interest only (IO) class and a principal only (PO) class; these two bond classes have very special cash flow characteristics, especially regarding the interest rate sensitivity of these bonds. We show this stripping of the cash flows in Figure 28–12 and consider the effects of interest rate changes on the value of each of these stripped instruments below.

IO Strips

IO strip
A bond sold to investors whose cash flows reflect the monthly interest payments received from a pool of mortgages.

The owner of an **IO strip** has a claim to the present value of interest payments made by the mortgageholders in the GNMA pool—that is, to the IO segments of each month's cash flow received from the underlying mortgage pool:

$$P_{IO} = \frac{IO_1}{\left(1 + \dfrac{y}{12}\right)} + \frac{IO_2}{\left(1 + \dfrac{y}{12}\right)^2} + \frac{IO_3}{\left(1 + \dfrac{y}{12}\right)^3} + \cdots + \frac{IO_{360}}{\left(1 + \dfrac{y}{12}\right)^{360}}$$

When interest rates change, they affect the cash flows received on mortgages. We concentrate on two effects: the discount effect and the prepayment effect on the price or value of IOs, denoted by P_{IO}.

Discount Effect   As interest rates (y) fall, the present value of any cash flows received on the strip—the IO payments—rises, increasing the value (P_{IO}) of the bond.

Prepayment Effect   As interest rates fall, mortgagees prepay their mortgages. In absolute terms, the number of IO payments the investor receives is likely to shrink. For example, the investor might receive only 100 monthly IO payments instead of the expected 360 in a no-prepayment world. The shrinkage in the size and value of IO payments reduces the value (P_{IO}) of the bond.

FIGURE 28–13
Price-Yield Curve of
an IO Percent Strip

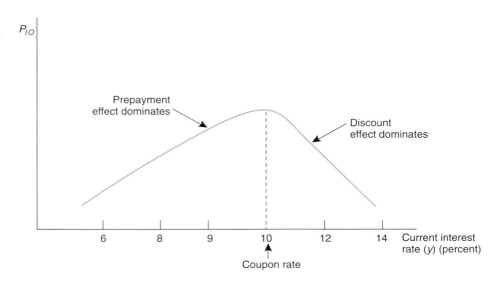

Specifically, one can expect that as interest rates continue to fall below the mortgage coupon rate of the bonds in the pool, the prepayment effect gradually dominates the discount effect, so that over some range the price or value of the IO bond falls as interest rates fall. Note the price-yield curve in Figure 28–13 for an IO strip on a pass-through bond with 10 percent mortgage coupon rates. The price-yield curve slopes upward in the interest rate range below 10 percent. This means that as current interest rates rise or fall, IO values or prices rise or fall. As a result, the IO is a rare example of a **negative duration** asset that is very valuable as a portfolio-hedging device for an FI manager when included with regular bonds whose price-yield curves show the normal inverse relationship. That is, while as interest rates rise the value of the regular bond portfolio falls, the value of an IO portfolio may rise. Note in Figure 28–13 that at rates above the pool's mortgage coupon of 10 percent, the price-yield curve changes shape and tends to perform like any regular bond. In recent years, thrifts have been major purchasers of IOs to hedge the interest rate risk on the mortgages and other bonds held as assets in their portfolios. We depict the hedging power of IOs in Figure 28–14.

negative duration
When the price of a bond increases or decreases as yields increase or decrease.

PO Strips

PO strip
A bond sold to investors whose cash flows reflect the monthly principal payments received from a pool of mortgages.

The value of the **PO strip** (P_{PO}) is defined by

$$P_{PO} = \frac{PO_1}{\left(1 + \frac{y}{12}\right)} + \frac{PO_2}{\left(1 + \frac{y}{12}\right)^2} + \frac{PO_3}{\left(1 + \frac{y}{12}\right)^3} + \cdots + \frac{PO_{360}}{\left(1 + \frac{y}{12}\right)^{360}}$$

where the PO_i represents the mortgage principal components of each monthly payment by the mortgage holders. This includes both the monthly amortized payment component of *PMT* that is principal and any early prepayments of principal by the mortgagees. Again, we consider the effects on a PO's value (P_{PO}) of a change in interest rates.

Discount Effect As yields (y) fall, the present value of any principal payments must increase and the value of the PO strip rises.

Prepayment Effect As yields fall, the mortgage holders pay off principal early. Consequently, the PO bondholder receives the fixed principal balance outstanding

FIGURE 28–14
Hedging with IOs

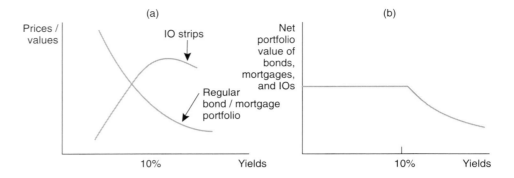

FIGURE 28–15
Price-Yield Curve of
a PO Strip

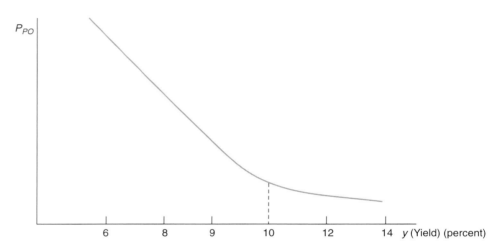

on the pool of mortgages earlier than stated. Thus, this prepayment effect must also work to increase the value of the PO strip.

As interest rates fall, both the discount and prepayment effects point to a rise in the value of the PO strip. The price-yield curve reflects an inverse relationship, but with a steeper slope than for normal bonds; that is, PO strip bond values are very interest rate sensitive, especially for yields below the stated mortgage coupon rate. We show this in Figure 28–15 for a 10 percent PO strip. (Note that a regular coupon bond is affected only by the discount effect.) As you can see, when yields fall below 10 percent, the market value or price of the PO strip can increase very fast. At rates above 10 percent, it tends to behave like a regular bond (as the incentive to prepay disappears).

The IO–PO strip is a classic example of financial engineering. From a given GNMA pass-through bond, two new bonds have been created: the first with an upward-sloping price-yield curve over some range and the second with a steeply downward-sloping price-yield curve over some range. Each class is attractive to different investors and investor segments. The IO is attractive to depository institutions as an on-balance-sheet hedging vehicle. The PO is attractive to FIs that wish to increase the interest rate sensitivity of their portfolios and to investors or traders who wish to take a naked or speculative position regarding the future course of interest rates. This high and complex interest sensitivity has resulted in major traders such as J. P. Morgan Chase and Merrill Lynch, as well as many investors such as hedge funds, suffering considerable losses on their investments in these instruments when interest rates have moved unexpectedly against them.

Securitization of Other Assets

While the major use of the three securitization vehicles—pass-throughs, CMOs, and mortgage-backed bonds—has been in packaging fixed-rate mortgage assets, these techniques can and have been used for other assets, including

Automobile loans.

Credit card receivables (certificates of amortizing revolving debts).

Small business loans guaranteed by the Small Business Administration.

Junk bonds.

Adjustable rate mortgages.

Commercial and industrial loans [collateralized loan obligations (CLOs)].

To examine the securitization of other assets, we use the example of certificates of amortizing revolving debts.

Certificates of Amortizing Revolving Debts (CARDs)

CARDs
Asset-backed securities backed by credit card receivables.

Rather than holding all credit card receivables until they pay off, an FI can segregate a set of receivables and sell them to an off-balance-sheet trust. A good example is J. P. Morgan Chase, which is a major sponsor of credit cards. (J. P. Morgan Chase retains the role of servicing the credit card pool, including collection, administration, and bookkeeping of the underlying credit card accounts.) J. P. Morgan Chase recently sold $280 million of receivables to a trust. The trust in turn issued asset-backed securities (**CARDs**) in which investors had a pro rata claim on the cash flows from the credit card receivables. As the trust received payments on the credit card receivables each month, they were passed through to the bondholders. In practice, bonds of a lesser principal amount than the $280 million credit card pool are issued. In this example, $250 million in bonds were issued, with the difference—$30 million—being a claim retained by J. P. Morgan Chase. The reason for this is that credit card holders can either increase or repay their credit card balances at any time. The risk of variations in principal outstanding and thus collateral for the bonds is borne solely by the FI (i.e., the $30 million component), while the investors' collateral claim remains at $250 million until maturity unless a truly exceptional rate of debt repayment occurs. Indeed, J. P. Morgan Chase's segment is structured to bear even the most extreme cases of early repayment of credit card debts. We show this credit card example in Figure 28–16. Notice from the figure that this securitization of credit card assets is very similar in technology to the pass-through mortgage bond.

Concept Questions

1. Would an FI with $D_A < kD_L$ be interested in buying an IO strip for hedging purposes?
2. To which investors or investor segments is the IO attractive? To which investors or investor segments is the PO attractive? Explain your answer.

CAN ALL ASSETS BE SECURITIZED?

The extension of securitization technology to other assets raises questions about the limits of securitization and whether all assets and loans can be securitized. Conceptually the answer is that they can, so long as it is profitable to do so or the

FIGURE 28–16
The Structure of
a Credit Card
Securitization

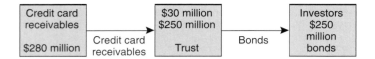

TABLE 28–7
Benefits versus
Costs of
Securitization

Benefits	Costs
1. New funding source (bonds versus deposits)	1. Cost of public/private credit risk insurance and guarantees
2. Increased liquidity of FI loans	2. Cost of overcollateralization
3. Enhanced ability to manage the duration gap of $(D_A - kD_L)$	3. Valuation and packaging costs (the cost of asset heterogeneity)
4. If off balance sheet, the issuer saves on reserve requirements, deposit insurance premiums, and capital adequacy requirements	

benefits to the FI from securitization outweigh the costs of securitization.[24] In Table 28–7, we summarize the benefits versus the costs of securitization.

From Table 28–7, given any set of benefits, the more costly and difficult it is to find asset packages of sufficient size and homogeneity, the more difficult and expensive it is to securitize. For example, commercial and industrial (C&I) loans have maturities running from a few months up to eight years; further, they have varying interest rate terms (fixed, LIBOR floating, federal funds–rate floating) and fees. In addition, they contain differing covenants and are made to firms in a wide variety of industries. Despite this, FIs have still been able to issue securitization packages called CLOs (collateralized loan obligations) containing high-quality low–default risk loans and CDOs (collateralized debt obligations) containing a diversified collection of junk bonds or risky bank loans. The interest and principal payments on a CDO are linked to the timing of default losses and repayments on a pool of underlying loans or bonds. The riskiest of the CDOs, sometimes called toxic waste, pay out only if everything goes right. The best CDOs will pay out unless the entire portfolio defaults. The volume of CDO issues has grown from $10 billion in 1995 to over $523 billion in 2003.[25] Generally, it has been much harder to securitize low-quality loans into CDOs. Specifically, the harder it is to value a loan or asset pool, the greater the costs of securitization due to the need for overcollateralization or credit risk insurance. Further, given the economic recession of the early 2000s and some large defaults and frauds at once highly rated companies (such as Enron and Worldcom), many CDOs debt pools have suffered large value losses. For example, American Express discovered the risk of CDOs in the early 2000s. In 1997 and 1998, American Express took a $3.5 billion position in CDOs based on an assumed default rate of 2 percent on the underlying assets. In early 2001, the actual default rate was 8 percent and

---

[24] See C. Pavel, "Securitization," Federal Reserve Bank of Chicago, *Economic Perspectives,* 1985, pp. 16–31.

[25] See, "Irresistible Reasons for Better Models of Credit Risk," *Financial Times*, April 16, 2004, p. 17.

American Express was forced to take an $830 million charge for losses on their CDOs. Similarly, Barclay's issued over $3.5 billion of CDO bonds between 1999 and 2001, of which $2.9 billion were rated AAA by Fitch Investors Services. By March 2003 only $128 million of the bonds were still AAA rated and the underlying debtors had defaulted on over $120 million face value of bonds. [26]

The potential boundary to securitization may well be defined by the relative degree of heterogeneity and credit quality of an asset type or group. It is not surprising that 30-year fixed-rate residential mortgages were the first assets to be securitized since they are the most homogeneous of all assets in FI balance sheets. For example, the existence of secondary markets for houses provides price information that allows reasonably accurate market valuations of the underlying asset to be made, and extensive data are available on mortgage default rates by locality.

Concept Question

1. Can all assets and loans be securitized? Explain your answer.

Summary

In Chapter 1 we distinguished between FIs that are asset transformers and those that are asset brokers. By becoming increasingly reliant on securitization, banks and thrifts are moving away from being asset transformers that originate and hold assets to maturity; they are becoming asset brokers more reliant on servicing and other fees. This makes banks and thrifts look more similar to securities firms. Thus, over time, we can expect the traditional financial technology differences between commercial (and savings) banking and investment banking to diminish as more loans and assets are securitized. Three major forms of securitization—pass-through securities, collateralized mortgage obligations (CMOs), and mortgage-backed bonds—were discussed. Also, the impact of prepayment behavior on MBS valuation was discussed. Finally, recent innovations in securitization were described.

Questions and Problems

1. What has been the effect of securitization on the asset portfolios of financial institutions?
2. What are the primary functions of GNMA? What is timing insurance?
3. How does FNMA differ from GNMA?
4. How does FHLMC differ from FNMA? How are they the same?
5. What three levels of regulatory taxes do FIs face when making loans? How does securitization reduce the levels of taxation?
6. An FI is planning to issue $100 million in commercial loans. The FI will finance the loans by issuing demand deposits.
    a. What is the minimum amount of capital required by the Basel accord?
    b. What is the minimum amount of demand deposits needed to fund this loan assuming there is a 10 percent average reserve requirement on demand deposits?

www.mhhe.com/saunders5e

[26] See "CDO—Not Cash on Delivery," *The Economist,* July 28, 2001, p. 68.

   c. Show a simple balance sheet with total assets, total liabilities, and equity if this is the only project funded by the bank.

   d. How does this balance sheet differ from Table 28–1? Why?

7. Consider the FI in problem 6.

   a. What additional risk exposure problems does the FI face?

   b. What is the duration of a 30-year, 12 percent annual $100,000 monthly amortizing mortgage loan if the yield to maturity is 12 percent? *Hint:* Use a spreadsheet for calculations.

   c. What are some possible solutions to the duration mismatch and the illiquidity problems?

   d. What advantages does securitization have in dealing with the FI's risk exposure problems?

8. How are investors in pass-through bonds protected against default risk emanating from the mortgagees and the FI/trustee?

9. What specific changes occur on the balance sheet at the completion of the securitization process? What adjustments occur to the risk profile of the FI?

10. Consider the mortgage pass-through example presented in Table 28–3. The total monthly payment by the borrowers reflecting a 12 percent mortgage rate is $1,028,610. The payment passed through to the ultimate investors reflecting an 11.5 percent return is $990,291. Who receives the difference between these two payments? How are the shares determined?

11. Consider a GNMA mortgage pool with principal of $20 million. The maturity is 30 years with a monthly mortgage payment of 10 percent per annum. Assume no prepayments.

   a. What is the monthly mortgage payment (100 percent amortizing) on the pool of mortgages?

   b. If the GNMA insurance fee is 6 basis points and the servicing fee is 44 basis points, what is the yield on the GNMA pass-through?

   c. What is the monthly payment on the GNMA in part (b)?

   d. Calculate the first monthly servicing fee paid to the originating FIs.

   e. Calculate the first monthly insurance fee paid to GNMA.

12. Calculate the value of (a) the mortgage pool and (b) the GNMA pass-through in question 11 if market interest rates increase 50 basis points. Assume no prepayments.

13. What would be the impact on GNMA pricing if the pass-through was not fully amortized? What is the present value of a $10 million pool of 15-year mortgages with an 8.5 percent per annum monthly mortgage coupon if market rates are 5 percent? The GNMA guarantee fee is assumed to be 6 basis points, and the FI servicing fee is 44 basis points.

   a. Assume that the GNMA is fully amortized.

   b. Assume that the GNMA is only half amortized. There is a lump-sum payment at the maturity of the GNMA that equals 50 percent of the mortgage pool's face value.

14. What is prepayment risk? How does prepayment risk affect the cash flow stream on a fully amortized mortgage loan? What are the two primary factors that cause early payment?

15. Under what conditions do mortgage holders have a call option on their mortgages? When is the call option in the money?

16. What are the benefits of market yields that are less than the average rate in the GNMA mortgage pool? What are the disadvantages of this rate inversion? To whom do the good news and the bad news accrue?

17. What is the weighted-average life (WAL) of a mortgage pool supporting pass-through securities? How does WAL differ from duration?

18. If 150 $200,000 mortgages are expected to be prepaid in three years and the remaining 150 $200,000 mortgages in a $60 million 15-year mortgage pool are to be prepaid in four years, what is the weighted-average life of the mortgage pool? Mortgages are fully amortized, with mortgage coupon rates set at 10 percent to be paid annually.

19. A FI originates a pool of 500 30-year mortgages, each averaging $150,000 with an annual mortgage coupon rate of 8 percent. Assume that the GNMA credit risk insurance fee is 6 basis points and that the FI's servicing fee is 19 basis points.

    a. What is the present value of the mortgage pool?

    b. What is the monthly mortgage payment?

    c. For the first two payments, what portion is interest and what portion is principal repayment?

    d. What are the expected monthly cash flows to GNMA bondholders?

    e. What is the present value of the GNMA pass-through bonds? Assume that the risk-adjusted market annual rate of return is 8 percent compounded monthly.

    f. Would actual cash flows to GNMA bondholders deviate from expected cash flows as in part (d)? Why or why not?

    g. What are the expected monthly cash flows for the FI and GNMA?

    h. If all the mortgages in the pool are completely prepaid at the end of the second month, what is the pool's weighted-average life? *Hint:* Use your answer to part (c).

    i. What is the price of the GNMA pass-through security if its weighted-average life is equal to your solution for part (h)? Assume no change in market interest rates.

    j. What is the price of the GNMA pass-through with a weighted-average life equal to your solution for part (h) if market yields decline 50 basis points?

20. What is the difference between the yield spread to average life and the option-adjusted spread on mortgage-backed securities?

21. Explain precisely the prepayment assumptions of the Public Securities Association prepayment model.

22. What does an FI mean when it states that its mortgage pool prepayments are assumed to be 100 percent PSA equivalent?

23. What factors may cause the actual prepayment pattern to differ from the assumed PSA pattern? How would an FI adjust for the presumed occurrence of some of these factors?

24. What is the burnout factor? How is it used in modeling prepayment behavior? What other factors may be helpful in modeling the prepayment behavior of a given mortgage pool?

25. What is the goal of prepayment models that use option pricing theory? How do these models differ from the PSA or empirical models? What criticisms often are directed toward these models?

26. How does the price on a GNMA bond relate to the yield on a GNMA option from the perspective of the investor? What is the option-adjusted spread (OAS)?

27. Use the options prepayment model to calculate the yield on a $30 million three-year fully amortized mortgage pass-through where the mortgage coupon rate is 6 percent paid annually. Market yields are 6.4 percent paid annually. Assume that there is no servicing or GNMA guarantee fee.

    a. What is the annual payment on the GNMA pass-through?

    b. What is the present value of the GNMA pass-through?

    c. Interest rate movements over time are assumed to change a maximum of 0.5 percent per year. Both an increase of 0.5 percent and a decrease of 0.5 percent in interest rates are equally probable. If interest rates fall 1.0 percent below the current mortgage coupon rates, all of the mortgages in the pool will be completely prepaid. Diagram the interest-rate tree and indicate the probabilities of each node in the tree.

    d. What are the expected annual cash flows for each possible situation over the three-year period?

    e. The Treasury bond yield curve is flat at a discount yield of 6 percent. What is the option-adjusted spread on the GNMA pass-through?

28. Use the options prepayment model to calculate the yield on a $12 million, five-year, fully amortized mortgage pass-through where the mortgage coupon rate is 7 percent paid annually. Market yields are 8 percent paid annually. Assume that there is no servicing or GNMA guarantee fee.

    a. What is the annual payment on the GNMA pass-through?

    b. What is the present value of the GNMA pass-through?

    c. Interest rate movements over time are assumed to change a maximum of 1 percent per year. Both an increase of 1 percent and a decrease of 1 percent in interest rates are equally probable. If interest rates fall 3 percent below the current mortgage coupon rates, all mortgages in the pool will be completely prepaid. Diagram the interest rate tree and indicate the probabilities of each node in the tree.

    d. What are the expected annual cash flows for each possible situation over the five-year period?

    e. The Treasury bond yield curve is flat at a discount yield of 6 percent. What is the option-adjusted spread on the GNMA pass-through?

29. What conditions would cause the yield on pass-through securities with prepayment risk to be less than the yield on pass-through securities without prepayment risk?

30. What is a collateralized mortgage obligation (CMO)? How is it similar to a pass-through security? How does it differ? In what way does the creation of a CMO use market segmentation to redistribute prepayment risk?

31. Consider $200 million of 30-year mortgages with a coupon of 10 percent per annum paid quarterly.

    a. What is the quarterly mortgage payment?

b. What are the interest repayments over the first year of life of the mortgages? What are the principal repayments?

c. Construct a 30-year CMO using this mortgage pool as collateral. The pool has three tranches, where tranche A offers the least protection against prepayment and tranche C offers the most protection against prepayment. Tranche A of $50 million receives quarterly payments at 9 percent per annum, tranche B of $100 million receives quarterly payments at 10 percent per annum, and tranche C of $50 million receives quarterly payments at 11 percent per annum. Diagram the CMO structure.

d. Assume nonamortization of principal and no prepayments. What are the total promised coupon payments to the three classes? What are the principal payments to each of the three classes for the first year?

e. If, over the first year, the trustee receives quarterly prepayments of $10 million on the mortgage pool, how are these funds distributed?

f. How are the cash flows distributed if prepayments in the first half of the second year are $20 million quarterly?

g. How can the CMO issuer earn a positive spread on the CMO?

32. How does a class Z tranche of a CMO differ from a class R tranche? What causes a Z class to have characteristics of both a zero-coupon bond and a regular bond? What factors can cause an R class to have a negative duration?

33. Why would buyers of class C tranches of collateralized mortgage obligations (CMOs) be willing to accept a lower return than purchasers of Class A tranches?

34. What are mortgage-backed bonds (MBBs)? How do MBBs differ from pass-through securities and CMOs?

35. From the perspective of risk management, how does the use of MBBs by an FI assist the FI in managing credit and interest rate risk?

36. What are four reasons why an FI may prefer the use of either pass-through securities or CMOs to the use of MBBs?

37. What is an interest-only (IO) strip? How do the discount effect and the prepayment effect of an IO create a negative duration asset? What macroeconomic effect is required for this negative duration effect to be possible?

38. What is a principal-only (PO) strip? What causes the price-yield profile of a PO strip to have a steeper slope than a normal bond?

39. An FI originates a pool of short-term real estate loans worth $20 million with maturities of five years and paying interest rates of 9 percent per annum.

a. What is the average payment received by the FI, including both principal and interest, if no prepayment is expected over the life of the loan?

b. If the loans are converted into pass-through certificates and the FI charges a servicing fee of 50 basis points, including insurance, what is the payment amount expected by the holders of the pass-through securities if no prepayment is expected?

c. Assume that the payments are separated into interest-only (IO) and principal-only (PO) payments, that prepayments of 5 percent occur at the end of years 3 and 4, and that the payment of the remaining principal occurs at the end of year 5. What are the expected annual payments for each instrument? Assume discount rates of 9 percent.

    d. What is the market value of IOs and POs if the market interest rates for instruments of similar risk decline to 8 percent?

40. What are the factors that, in general, allow assets to be securitized? What are the costs involved in the securitization process?

41. How does an FI use loan sales and securitization to manage interest rate, credit, and liquidity risks? Summarize how each of the possible methods of securitization products affects the balance sheet and profitability of an FI in the management of these risks.

Web Question

42. Go to the Federal Reserve Board's Web site at **www.federalreserve.gov**. From there, click on "Economic Research and Data," then click on "Statistics: Releases and Historical Data." Click on "Flow of Funds Accounts of the United States *Releases*," then click on the most recent date. Click on "Level tables." Go to the Table titled "Total Mortgages" to get the most recent data on total mortgages held by government-sponsored and federally related mortgage pools. How have these values changed over the years reported in this table?

Pertinent Web Sites

Bear Stearns	**www.bearstearns.com**
Board of Governors of the Federal Reserve	**www.federalreserve.gov**
Federal Home Loan Mortgage Corporation	**www.freddiemac.com**
Federal National Mortgage Association	**www.fanniemae.com**
Government National Mortgage Association	**www.ginniemae.gov**
Public Securities Association	**www.psa.com**
The Bond Market Association	**www.bondmarkets.com**

Appendix 28A

Fannie Mae and Freddie Mac Balance Sheets

View Appendix 28A at the Web site for this textbook (**www.mhhe.com/saunders5e**).

Index